Football
Yearbook
1999–2000

Acknowledgements

Written, devised and compiled by Rob Bateman,
Dominic Sutton, Gary Taphouse and Tim Wheal.
With contributions from Simon Head,
Debbie Levy and David Riley.

Thanks are due to: Richard Couchman, Nicky
Evans, Maree Lovell and Suzie Russell at Carling
Opta; Graham Cull, Kevin Glumart, Adam Hirst
and Mike Murphy for the unenviable task of
checking much of the data; Sian Russell for
researching information on the clubs; Philip Don
for his assistance regarding referees; the Premier
League for their support, in particular Sarah
Smith for her assistance with regard to
disciplinary data; all the clubs for their help in
verifying information and responding so quickly;
and the team at Carlton Books for their patience
and hard work.

THIS IS A CARLTON BOOK

Text © Opta Index Limted, 1999
Design © Carlton Books Limited, 1999

First published in 1999 by Carlton Books

10 9 8 7 6 5 4 3 2 1

A CIP catalogue record for this book is available
from the British Library

ISBN 1 85868 739 X

Project editor: Martin Corteel
Project art direction: Trevor Newman
Design and editorial team: Matt Ross, Fehmi
Comert, Dave Sutton, Roland Hall, Phil Wisdom
and David Ballheimer
Picture research: Lorna Ainger
Production: Sarah Schuman

Printed and bound in Italy

Carlton Books Limited
20 St Anne's Court, Wardour Street
London W1V 3AW

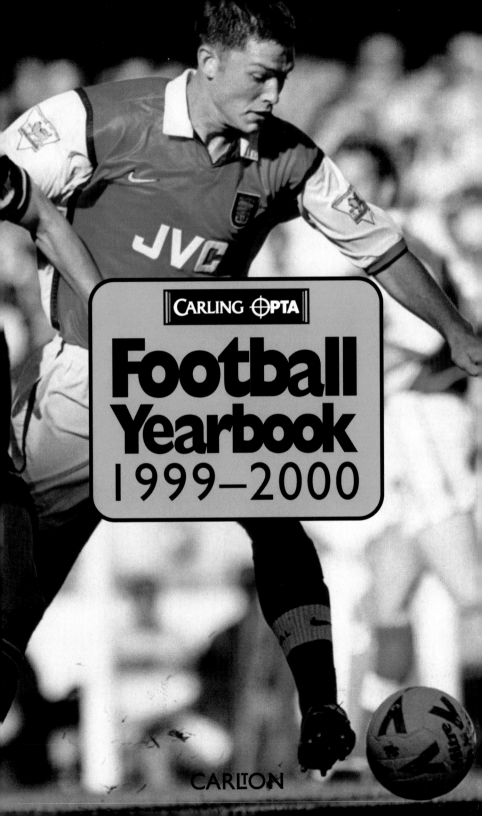

CARLING OPTA

Football Yearbook
1999–2000

CARLTON

CONTENTS

Foreword by Angus Loughran 6

1 INTRODUCTION 9

2 THE TEAMS 20

Introduction	20	Manchester United	198
Arsenal	22	Middlesbrough	214
Aston Villa	38	Newcastle United	230
Blackburn Rovers	54	Nottingham Forest	246
Charlton Athletic	70	Sheffield Wednesday	262
Chelsea	86	Southampton	278
Coventry City	102	Tottenham Hotspur	294
Derby County	118	West Ham United	310
Everton	134	Wimbledon	326
Leeds United	150	Bradford City	342
Leicester City	166	Sunderland	348
Liverpool	182	Watford	354

3 THE PLAYERS 360

Pen portraits and Carling Opta statistics for every player who took to the pitch in a Premiership match in 1998–99, and profiles of players to watch in the coming season.

4 COMPARATIVE TABLES 614

The Teams	616	Teams of the Season	658
The Players	638	Referees	670
The Index	652		

FA Premier League Fixture List 1999–2000 674

FOREWORD BY
ANGUS LOUGHRAN, AKA 'STATTO'

Remember the first FA Cup final to be shown in colour? It was West Brom v Everton, 1968. The BBC would cover the match with just three or four cameras, a far cry from the 25 used by Sky to cover a Carling Premiership match these days. Replays were far from instant and statistics from the match just didn't exist. In fact, detailed sports stats were compiled only in the cricketing world.

The relaxed pace of a test match made live scoring and analysis simple – but compiling stats for any other sport simply wasn't cricket.

These days, of course, the thirst for player performance statistics within the ever-expanding media and the opulent professional sporting world itself is seemingly unquenchable – and barely a single sport has been left untouched by the sprawling stat attack. Lee Westwood's season-to-date and save percentage or average drive length; Paul Grayson's kicking success rate; Jockey Wilson's three-dart average – they're all available and all in demand.

Similar in-depth analysis of football is a relatively new concept – even newer than the FA Carling Premiership itself, in fact. With the English league so notoriously fast-paced, and with so many positions and actions to measure, fully analysing a player's performance live is impossible, unless you are merely recording action-stopping events such as goals, shots on target, fouls, yellow cards etc.

That's where Carling Opta come in. The history of the company is well-documented in this book but, basically speaking, they have exclusive access to video footage of every Carling Premiership fixture, which is analysed in painstaking detail to record every single touch of the ball from a completed short pass to an unsuccessful dribble.

Analysing one game can take as long as nine hours, but accuracy is the watchword. A close call – did the goalkeeper just get his fingertips to that one? – will be watched numerous times by several Opta analysts before the tick goes on the sheet.

Those ticks are fed into a huge database, from which Carling Opta's unique player performance information is extracted. The database provides stats which are not based on opinion or bias, but cold, hard facts.

For stattos like me, the wealth of information Carling Opta can produce is a dream come true, but the stats have become so much a part of Premiership football as we enter the new Millennium that they are now quintessential reading for supporters, journalists and indeed managers alike.

As you will see in this inaugural football yearbook, performance statistics this detailed can be used by coaches to enhance training. They can be used by reporters to back up an argument about a player or team. Even managers can point to the statistics to back up their opinions. Arsenal boss Arsene Wenger leapt on the opportunity to defend his side's much-criticized disciplinary record after looking at Carling Opta data.

Former England boss Glenn Hoddle was entering a minefield when he said it took striker Andy Cole "four or five" chances to score one goal. That was his opinion, but Carling Opta had the facts at hand to prove Hoddle was far more accurate than he could ever have realized.

Some of the data reassuringly confirms what we already believe. But much of it provides supporters with talking points, the media with stories and players with much to ponder. Which Chelsea player committed the most fouls in 1998–99? Who was caught offside the most? Which team were the least accurate

Six-gun salute: Nwankwo Kanu and Nigel Winterburn, Middlesbrough 1 Arsenal 6

passers? And which referees were the most whistle-happy?

You'll find the answers to all these questions – and plenty more besides – in this book, which I believe provides the most comprehensive retrospective guide to a football season available – anywhere in the world.

Of course, what you won't find is the identity of the 1999–2000 season's champions – but for the gamblers among you, maybe I can be of some help in this department. Last year's top three will certainly be favourites once again, but why not consider an each-way flutter on David O'Leary's young Leeds United side? If it weren't for some silly dropped points in 1998–99, they could well be challenging in the revamped UEFA Champions League.

Some people believe statistics are turning football into a contrived number-crunching exercise rather than a flowing sport. But my own view is that analysis and controversy are every bit as important to the game as the numbers on shirts, the physio's magic sponge and the half-time hot dog.

No one can pretend that statistics hold the answers to the endless debates over who should play for England or which striker performs best under pressure. The atmosphere of a big local derby can turn the form book upside-down and bring the best out of under-performing players, posing question marks over retrospective performance analysis.

What Carling Opta provide is a starting-point. They are the provocative opening question in a heated debate, the first sentence in a long drawn-out game of Chinese whispers.

If you think of them in these terms, Carling Opta provide categorically the most fascinating insights available into the national game we all adore.

INTRODUCTION

This book is the definitive review of the 1998–99 FA Carling Premiership season. In it you will discover the reasons why Manchester United became champions, what factors consigned Nottingham Forest, Charlton Athletic and Blackburn Rovers to relegation and who are the top-rated players in the English top flight.

Every touch of the ball has been recorded, every foul registered and each goal analysed to provide a compelling insight into the performances of each team in the Premiership and every player who appeared during the nine months of passion and excitement that characterize the most exciting league in the world.

The first section covers the teams. You will find everything you need to know about each club which featured in the 1998–99 Premiership, plus the three teams which were promoted from Nationwide Division One, aiming to pit their wits against the elite in the 1999–2000 season.

This is followed by a profile of every player who kicked a ball in anger, whether they were ever-present or made just one appearance as a substitute. There is also a team consisting of players who did not feature in 1998–99, but who are ones to watch for the future.

Finally, the section that is sure to cause debate and controversy in every bar, school and household in the country — the Comparative Tables. Here you will see how each team compares to the rest and how the top players compare with each other across various categories. And there are the teams of the season; plus you will be able to see how the men in black have performed this season in our unique and exclusive insight into the referees.

WHO ARE CARLING OPTA?

Carling Opta are the official player performance statisticians to the Premier League. The company is little more than three years old, but it has already had a major impact on the way that clubs are able to monitor player performance and how the media have been able to offer their customers a revealing insight into the game.

The company's origins lie in a management consultancy group formed by ex-directors of Coopers Lybrand, called Opta Consulting.

In 1996, Opta recruited Suzie Russell as a sales and marketing executive and set her the task of branding the group.

The idea that Suzie developed was to follow the path of her employer's previous company and create a sports ranking system. Whereas Coopers Lybrand had developed the cricket ratings, Opta would concentrate on football.

Suzie contacted the Premier League and the Premiership clubs to elicit their support and arrange access to television footage of all the Premiership matches. Once that was agreed, her next task was to encourage media interest, so her first stop was Vic Wakeling – the head of Sky Sports.

When that interest was in place, Suzie turned her attention to developing the system of analysis. After due deliberation, Don Howe was asked to bring his experience to the project and help create a system for analysing the game and then develop a ranking system to compare players' performances. He worked with a software developer to create a unique database system that would fulfil all of his specifications.

Little more than two months later, the Opta Index was launched live on Sky Sports' *Monday Night Football* and shortly afterwards in *The Observer*. Other national newspapers picked up on the coverage and before long, other parties had developed an interest in the information that was being collected.

Paul Austin of City Index was the first to realize that the data being collected would lend itself perfectly to spread betting – and soon Opta were providing information during live matches to several betting companies.

After three months, it was decided to set up a new company within the auspices of the group with David Honey as chairman and Suzie Russell as managing director. The new company was called Opta Index Ltd.

At the end of the first year, Opta Index Ltd were given the title of Official Player Performance Statisticians to the Premier League and a sponsorship deal with the Premier League sponsors Carling was brokered. The company became known to everyone as Carling Opta.

The firm has roughly doubled in size each year since it was formed and now comprises a team of 12 full-time staff, with as many part-time analysts providing a crucial supporting role.

At the end of the first season, Carling Opta recruited its first journalist as the media began to demand an element of interpretation as well as the raw data. That demand has increased dramatically as the media seek to satisfy its customers' need for information and there are currently four journalists supplying statistics, stories and copy to a wide range of media.

In future, Carling Opta will begin monitoring football in countries such as Italy, France and Holland and have already begun working with Austria. And with Trans-World International's (TWI) worldwide broadcasts bringing Carling Opta's statistics to a wider audience, there has been demand from countries as varied as Australia, Singapore and Estonia.

With advances in technology and demand, Carling Opta will be analysing games in even more detail, providing an ever-greater understanding of the most popular sport in the world.

> **"The FA Premier League is pleased to be associated with Carling Opta, whose performance ratings and statistical analysis have done much to stimulate debate on and increase awareness of FA Premier League players, systems and styles of play."**
>
> *Mike Foster,*
> **The FA Premier League**

HOW IS PLAYER PERFORMANCE MEASURED?

The system of analysis was developed by Carling Opta, in conjunction with former England coach Don Howe. A specially-trained analyst watches a match on video and notes down each action performed by every single player on the ball, their fouls and discipline, and key decisions made by the officials.

There are currently 92 distinct actions and outcomes for players that range from different kinds of shots and passes to tackles and blocks, and from different kinds of fouls and yellow cards to saves made by the goalkeeper. Every close season, the list of actions is discussed to determine the value of each element and new categories may be added.

Carling Opta receive the referee's copy of the video the morning after a game and then begin the analysis. An analyst can take up to nine hours to complete a full match, depending on the flow of the game and the number of contentious decisions.

Once the game is analysed, the data is manually input into a database from which Carling Opta are able to provide information in a number of different ways.

Managers' Reports are created for each match and sent to a number of key personnel at the Premiership clubs involved, including managers, directors and coaching staff.

In addition, some clubs request further details on player positions at set-pieces, moves leading to goalscoring opportunities or where free kicks are conceded or won, for both their own teams and forthcoming opposition.

Referees' Reports are produced identifying key decisions (including commendable and controversial ones) made in each match, details of goals and disciplinary issues. These are sent to referees' officer Philip Don.

And the data that is collected is then downloaded from the database into a spreadsheet, from which all of the media requirements for player profiles, match reports and key data about the Premiership can be provided.

The analysis is checked by the operations director and key information such as cards issued and disputed goals are checked with the official referees' reports and the FA's goal committee respectively as and when those organisations have the information available. Any discrepancies or differences are checked and the database is updated if necessary.

Two new systems are currently being developed for analysis purposes. The first will use voice recognition to replace the manual collection and input of data. In addition to the current information being collected, the database will be able to calculate distances, pinpoint key action areas, identify who passes to whom or who tackles whom and show the direction of the action in any given match.

The other system has more of a coaching application. It involves setting up a series of cameras at each stadium, covering every angle of the pitch. This allows all players to be tracked at all times. The video footage is then digitized for the computerized tracking system which will monitor positional play.

The system will be able to show whether players are in the correct positions at key moments, whether they are marking correctly, how far and how fast players run and the velocity of their shooting. It will also show how far the referee is from the action when making key decisions.

This means that in future the Carling Opta database, which is the most comprehensive record of Premiership player performance in existence, will be able to offer an even greater insight into the game for managers, media and fans alike into the new Millennium.

> **"Carling Opta's unique analysis of Premiership matches and players has provided something which had never been available before; detailed statistics to back up arguments."**
>
> **Mick Dennis,**
> **London Evening Standard**

THE CARLING OPTA INDEX

The Carling Opta Index is basically a form guide. When a match is analysed, each player's actions are recorded. For each of these actions, a player earns or loses points – for example, a goal is worth up to 500 points, whereas a short pass in a player's own half only earns five points and a foul costs a player 50 points.

Over the course of a game, a player will accumulate a total number of points to give him a Game Score. This can be used to compare his performance with other players and the player with the most points is nominated as Carling Opta's man of the match.

The Index, which has featured in many newspapers and on television, uses these Game Scores to provide a form guide which is calculated over a period encompassing the previous six Carling Premiership matches. You can see an example in the table below.

Each player's points from the last six games are added to give him a total, which is then divided by the number of minutes played and then multiplied by 90 (minutes), to give him an average score per game played. This is his Index Score.

These Index Scores can then be used to compare players' performances over those six games, the player who has the highest average being the most in-form.

The players are then split up by the position that they play – goalkeepers, defenders, midfielders, attacking midfielders and attackers – to create a series of tables providing an at-a-glance guide to current Premiership player form.

The following week, when Arsenal play again, Bergkamp's score will change as the Sheffield Wednesday match drops out of the last six and is replaced with his latest score.

Carling Opta also produce a Season Index. This shows each player's average score across every game they have played during the 1998–99 season and this is the figure which is featured in tables throughout this book.

DENNIS BERGKAMP

OPPOSITION	MINS PLAYED	OPTA GAME SCORE
vs Sheffield Wednesday	90	1,112
vs Everton	90	1,313
vs Coventry City	90	1,413
vs Southampton	0	0
vs Blackburn Rovers	90	1,515
vs Wimbledon	71	1,616
TOTAL	431	6,969

Carling Opta Index Score	6,969/431 x 90(mins) = 1,455

WHO USES THIS INFORMATION?

The data gathered by Carling Opta's team of highly-trained analysts is extremely valuable to a range of different audiences.

● **THE PROFESSIONALS**

A report on each match is sent to the participating teams 48 hours after the game, usually to the manager or coach, but also to a range of other personnel within the club.

Some use the data to identify weaknesses in aspects of particular players' performances; others use it to set targets. Carling Opta have also supplied data to certain Premiership clubs relating to set-pieces, goals scored and off-the-ball runs of their forthcoming opponents.

● **THE BETTING INDUSTRY**

Carling Opta monitor the performances of players in live televized matches for a selection of spread betting companies and supply ongoing information so that bookies can adjust the spread if necessary during the course of the event.

Carling Opta also conduct post-match measurement and adjudication for several members of the betting industry. Analysts can also be called upon to settle any disputes between the betting industry and its customers.

● **THE MEDIA**

The demand for information on and analysis of football has increased dramatically over the last few years. Not only are there supplements in nearly all national newspapers after the weekend's games, but also the first national Sunday newspaper devoted to serious analysis of sport has been launched.

There are also pages to fill in matchday programmes; regional newspapers look to provide in-depth information to readers on their local clubs; and Internet sites meet the demand for Carling Premiership football from a worldwide audience.

Carling Opta offer the media information to satisfy the demand from their customers – from previews of forthcoming matches, where the key strengths of opponents can be identified, to match reviews where it is possible to see just how and where a game was won or lost.

● **GAMES**

Carling Opta's statistics are used by many clients to run interactive fantasy games in their publication.

A set of actions are agreed with points scores allocated and customers are invited to use their knowledge to earn as many points as they can across the course of a season. The contestant with the most points is then the winner.

● **THE LAW**

Carling Opta's data and expertise have been used in several cases where a dispute between players and associations or other organizations exists.

CARLING OPTA CLIENTS 1998–99

NATIONAL NEWSPAPERS
The Guardian, The Express, The Mirror, Sport First, The Observer, The Sunday Times, The Sunday Express, News of the World, The Sunday Mirror, The Star

REGIONAL NEWSPAPERS
Evening Standard, Newcastle Evening Chronicle, North Eastern Evening Gazette, Coventry Evening Telegraph, Sheffield Star, Leicester Evening Mercury

MATCHDAY PROGRAMMES

TV STATIONS
Sky Sports, ITV, TWI, MUTV

MISCELLANEOUS
Football 365, ITV Teletext, Topps UK (Merlin Stickers), Sports Interactive, AOL, Hasbro

MAGAZINES
Four Four Two, MOTD, Man Utd, Leeds, Chelsea

THE BETTING INDUSTRY

NEIL REDFEARN vs. PATRICK VIEIRA

On December 28, 1998, Charlton Athletic entertained Arsenal at the Valley and lost narrowly 1–0 to a penalty by Marc Overmars.

The game, though, was over-shadowed by an incident involving Arsenal's Patrick Vieira and Charlton's Neil Redfearn, after which the Frenchman was sent off by match referee Uriah Rennie for elbowing the Charlton midfielder.

Video evidence suggested that Redfearn had exaggerated the impact of the offence by clutching his face when the elbow appeared to have struck him on the shoulder, and claims of gamesmanship were levelled at the Charlton midfield player.

Charlton boss Alan Curbishley responded by accusing Arsenal of being "dirty" and needing to put their own house in order instead of looking to put the blame on opponents. He also claimed that the intent of using the elbow justified the red card in itself.

Arsenal's sense of injustice and the animosity between the two sides was increased when they highlighted an incident in the same match, when Eddie Youds had brought down Dennis Bergkamp from behind with the type of tackle that has been outlawed in the game. The Charlton defender escaped with a yellow card despite this offence being deemed worthy of a red card by the Football Association and FIFA. To add insult to injury the Dutch forward was forced to limp out of the game and missed the next two matches.

A few days later, Alex Ferguson was quoted in a Sunday newspaper, accusing Arsenal of "liking a scrap" and turning games into battles if events were not going their way. This caused a huge furore over Arsenal's disciplinary record and brought Arsene Wenger's defence of his players into question given the large numbers of red cards his side had earned during his two-year tenure at the north London club.

Ferguson claimed the comments had been off the record and that he would send a letter of apology to Wenger, but the damage had been done.

The row rumbled on and many newspapers and TV stations approached Carling Opta to shed some light on the various disciplinary issues.

The *Evening Standard* published a table on January 6, 1999, showing "The Dirty Dozen" – the Premiership's top 12 dirty players. Featuring in the list were Patrick Vieira in 12th position, Eddie

Flash point: Patrick Vieira is shown the red card by referee Uriah Rennie

Youds in 10th but, most intriguingly, Neil Redfearn top of the lot. Arsenal had always insisted that Redfearn should have been penalized for the shirt-pulling and fouling long before Vieira had felt the need to retaliate, and Arsene Wenger used these statistics to blast Redfearn once more for committing "more fouls than anybody else in the Premiership".

The London Evening Standard
January 6, 1999

Another table showed team discipline, and Wenger took the opportunity to point out that Charlton were a far "dirtier" side – and would have taken great satisfaction that Manchester United were also "dirtier" than the Gunners, despite Alex Ferguson's observations.

Arsenal received a large number of red cards in 1998–99 and a good deal of criticism over their discipline, but in overall terms their record was not as bad as it seemed – they are only 13th in the discipline table (see page 626).

The fact is that high-profile disciplinary incidents tend to grab the headlines. Players such as Emmanuel Petit and clubs such as Arsenal have been pilloried in the past, when their overall record shows that they are not as bad as the media suggest and that perhaps they suffer as a result of their reputations.

Above: *The Express*
April 8, 1999

Left: *The Mirror*
January 7, 1999

PETER SCHMEICHEL

The Observer
November, 1999

Some high-profile mistakes in crucial games started to bring into question the form of Manchester United's Peter Schmeichel in 1998–99.

The Great Dane has been arguably the finest goalkeeper in the world over the past five or six seasons, with his unorthodox style of shot-stopping and his ability to out-psyche strikers in one-on-one situations now legendary in the English game.

Much of his style is attributed to the fact that he used to play handball back in Denmark which enables him to claw shots out of the air that are seemingly destined to find the back of the net.

United's inability to keep their opponents at bay cost them several points in the Champions League and Schmeichel seemed to shoulder much of the blame.

Carling Opta looked back at Schmeichel's performances over the last three seasons and noted that there was in fact a decline in the high standards that he had set himself.

There was a year-on-year decline in his ability to stop shots from his 1997–98 ratio of 85%, to the current campaign where his saves to shots ratio was as low as 79%. In the Champions League it was even lower at just 57% and for the first time questions were being asked about one of United's all-time greats.

Schmeichel was conceding a goal on average every 90 minutes as opposed to roughly every 140 minutes in 1997–98.

His catching was also poor and the only two 'keepers with worse catching success rates were the Liverpool duo of David James and Brad Friedel, consistently blamed for Liverpool's poor performances.

Schmeichel's distribution – so often a strong point of his game in launching swift counter-attacks – was declining, with only 26% of his long kicks/throws finding a team-mate – again a record where only Brad Friedel was poorer.

These statistics were highlighted in several newspapers such as The Observer, and little more than two weeks later Peter Schmeichel announced his decision to retire from English Football at the end of the season.

There is no doubt that after his decision Schmeichel's form returned, and some excellent displays helped United end the season with an historic treble. But perhaps his best days are behind him and he clearly wanted to finish his United career at the top.

What is certain is that his replacement Mark Bosnich has a very tough act to follow.

PAUL GASCOIGNE

The Mirror
December 8, 1998

Irrepressible Geordie Paul Gascoigne is arguably the most talented, but certainly the most high-profile English player over the course of the last decade.

After several years in Italy and Scotland, Gazza had returned to England to help Middlesbrough gain promotion and earn himself a swansong in the top flight.

After his exclusion from Glenn Hoddle's World Cup squad, the football-watching public were keen to see whether those dazzling skills would still light up league matches or whether his injuries and excessive lifestyle would affect Gascoigne's ability to compete at the top level.

Then, in October, Middlesbrough announced that Gazza had admitted himself to a clinic for treatment for stress and other problems.

Less than a month later, Gazza was back on the pitch, claiming to have given up the booze, the junk food and the bright lights in an attempt to salvage his career. After the high-profile cases involving Paul Merson and Tony Adams, it was hoped that yet another of the Premiership's sporting heroes could successfully deal with his problems and come back to form on the pitch.

Several games into his comeback, there was a feeling that he was getting his game together and there were even claims that he should be given a recall to the England squad. Several publications including *The Mirror* wrote features about the maverick midfielder's return to form and wanted to illustrate just how his performances had improved.

Carling Opta used its unique system of measurement to analyse Gazza's performances pre and post-treatment and the results showed a definite improvement in pass and cross completion, dribble completion and tackle success rate, plus an improvement in his shooting accuracy.

He was looking slimmer and fitter, plus he was learning to pace himself for 90 minutes. He had also realized that while some assets such as his pacy dribbling that enabled him to get away from defenders had diminished, his vision and passing ability could be used in other ways to benefit the team.

At one point he was rated as the top midfield player in the country in the Carling Opta Index. But as Boro's season fell away so did Gazza's. His problems resurfaced once more and these, combined with niggling injuries, restricted him to only a handful of appearances in the last stages of the season.

THE CARLING OPTA PORTFOLIO

Carling Opta's unique raw data can be presented in a variety of innovative, media-friendly ways thanks to the statistical database's inherent versatility.

By manipulating individual match performance data, monthly statistics or season-to-date figures, Carling Opta are able to produce numerous regular features for their diverse media clients.

For example, Carling Opta have the clear edge when it comes to supplying a Team of the Week. Whereas most teams featured in the newspapers are merely the opinions of journalists, however sage, the Carling Opta team is based on hard facts, showing which players outscored their peers by position in terms of touches of the ball.

The Carling Opta Team of the Week is sent to a host of newspapers and TV stations and is a regular feature in such respected regionals as the *Newcastle Evening Chronicle*, the *Leicester Mercury* and the *Coventry Evening Telegraph*.

Also compiled on a weekly basis is the Carling Opta Index, the quintessential Premiership form guide based on every player's performances over the last six league games. The Index, which includes the league's top 50 players with their average points scores, has been featured in many sections of the national and regional press, as well as in magazines, on Sky Sports and on the Internet.

Some media clients, such as the *Sunday Mirror* and *Football 365* prefer to have an Index based on the whole season rather than the last six games, so this is regularly updated too.

With every touch of the ball analysed, Carling Opta can provide the most in-depth previews and reports of individual matches available. Regional newspapers will feature their local team every week, showing which players to look out for in the forthcoming fixture or comparing two key men in the match.

Afterwards, Carling Opta supply the full match statistics showing who did what in the weekend's all-important Premiership game.

Meanwhile, national newspapers will use Carling Opta's analysis of England matches and English teams in the Champions League. No other company provides such an in-depth post-match service for these games.

Carling Opta carefully monitor attacking, defending and discipline statistics, and team tables are compiled on a regular basis. The team attacking table shows which sides are hitting the back of the net the most frequently via their goals-to-shots ratio and which teams are testing the goalkeeper the most via their shooting accuracy.

Each teams' tackling success rates are displayed in the defending table, along with how many goals they concede per game and how many defensive blocks, clearances and interceptions they have made throughout the season.

Many agencies calculate the number of bookings and sendings-off amassed by teams in the Premiership, but Carling Opta are the only company which can accurately record the exact numbers of free kicks conceded by each team, broken down into fouls, handballs, penalties and offsides. These are all displayed in the Carling Opta discipline table.

A regular table is produced by Carling Opta showing how many fouls, yellow and red cards and penalties have been awarded by each Premiership referee.

Thanks to Carling Opta's reputation for accuracy, many clients approach the company for information they may well be able to get elsewhere. But they choose Carling Opta because they are the official supplier of player performance statistics to the Premier League. Many official club magazines ask Carling Opta to provide match statistics, from full team details to the number of corners won by each side.

Carling Opta statistics are also featured on Teletext, with season-to-date team stats and post-match player analysis displayed weekly in the Premiership section on page 170 on Channel 4. These stats are updated on a regular basis as soon as the week's games have been analysed.

And if there is a big football story breaking, telephones in the Carling Opta press office begin ringing frantically with newspapers asking the Opta journalists for help in the great debate.

Man United are always ( p171)
on the telly
...but so are:

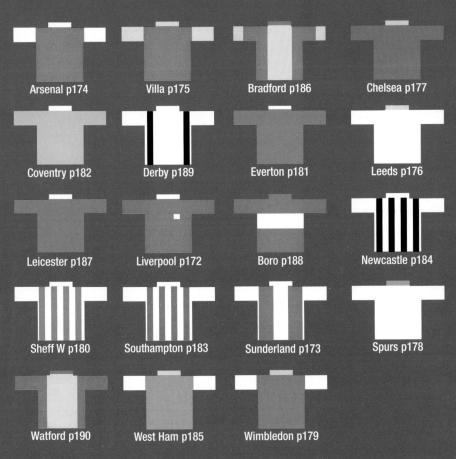

Arsenal p174

Villa p175

Bradford p186

Chelsea p177

Coventry p182

Derby p189

Everton p181

Leeds p176

Leicester p187

Liverpool p172

Boro p188

Newcastle p184

Sheff W p180

Southampton p183

Sunderland p173

Spurs p178

Watford p190

West Ham p185

Wimbledon p179

Teletext Premiership pages: **Channel 4**, all day, every day.
If you want to know the score, turn to

Teletext

ITV / Ch4, Web, Digital

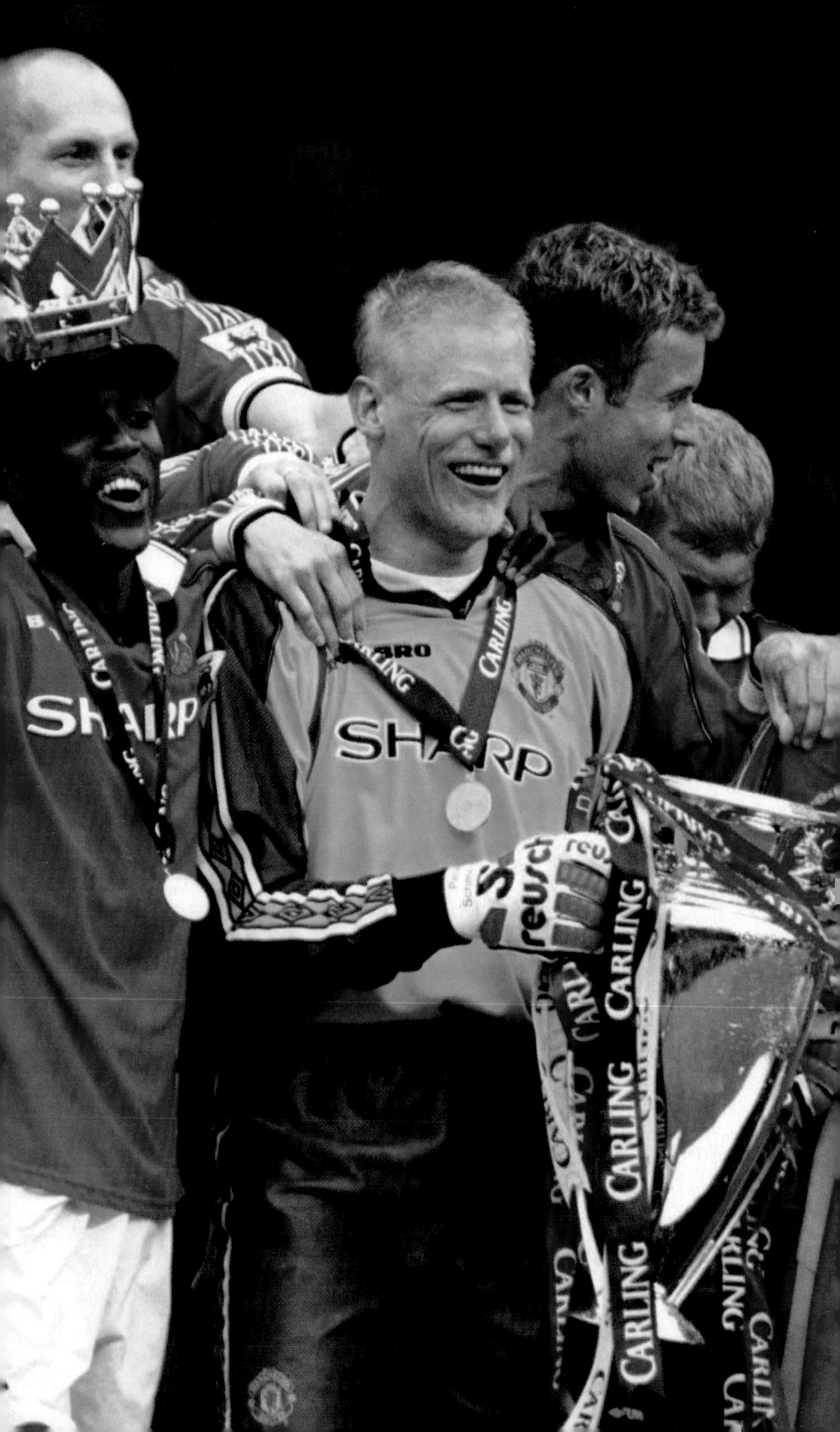
SHARP
SHARP
CARLING
reusch

THE TEAMS

Each club that participated in the 1998–99 Carling Premiership season has its own section within this part of the book. The sections are in alphabetical order with Arsenal at the beginning and Wimbledon at the end.

You will find:

- important details about each club;
- 20 interesting facts about the history of each club and their performance over the 1998–99 season;
- a review of the season;
- a full breakdown of league appearances, goalscorers and discipline;
- a profile of the manager;
- a graph charting the league position across the season;
- charts that show how, when and where each team scored or conceded their goals;
- a full breakdown of each player's performance;
- Carling Opta's nomination for their player of the season;
- the top performers at each club across key categories;
- match reports on two of each club's best performances.

For Bradford City, Watford and Sunderland

You will find:

- important details about each club, highlighting key personnel and contact details;
- 20 interesting facts about the history of each club and their performance in all competitions over the 1998–99 season;
- a review of the season;
- a full breakdown of league appearances and goalscorers;
- a profile of the manager.

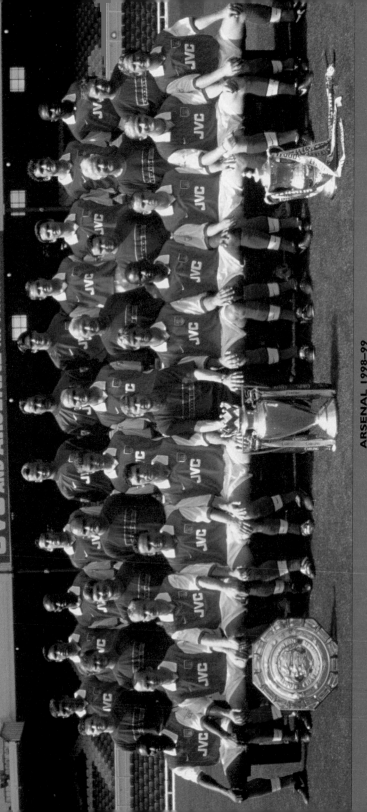

ARSENAL 1998–99

Back row (left to right): Nelson Vivas, Alberto Mendez, Luis Boa Morte, David Grondin, Alex Manninger, David Seaman, Stuart Taylor, Matthew Upson, Remi Garde, Gilles Grimandi, Christopher Wreh.

Middle row: Colin Lewin (Assistant Physiotherapist), Gary Lewin (Physiotherapist), Pat Rice (Assistant Manager), Boro Primorac (First Team Coach), Stephen Hughes, Steve Bould, Bob Wilson (Goalkeeping Coach), Mark James (Masseur), George Armstrong (Reserve Team Manager), Vic Akers (Kit Manager).

Front row: Nicolas Anelka, Lee Dixon, Dennis Bergkamp, Marc Overmars, Martin Keown, Arsene Wenger (Manager), Tony Adams, Patrick Vieira, Nigel Winterburn, Emmanuel Petit, Ray Parlour.

ARSENAL

ADDRESS

Avenell Rd, Highbury, London N5 1BU

CONTACT NUMBERS

Telephone: 0171 704 4000
Fax: 0171 704 4001
Ticket Office: 0171 704 4040
24hr Information: 09068 202020
The Gunners Shop: 0171 704 4120
e-mail: enquiries@arsenal.co.uk
Website: www.arsenal.co.uk

SPONSORS

SEGA

FANZINES

The Gooner
Up The Arse
Highbury High

KEY PERSONNEL

Chairman: P D Hill-Wood
Vice Chairman: D B Dein
Directors: Sir Roger Gibbs,
C E B L Carr, D D Fiszman,
K J Friar, R Carr
Club Secretary: D Miles
Manager: Arsene Wenger

COLOURS

Home: Red shirts with
white sleeves, white shorts
and red stockings
Away: Yellow shirts with
blue shorts and stockings

NICKNAME

The Gunners

20 FACTS

1 Arsenal were founded in 1886 by workers at the Royal Arsenal in Woolwich and were originally called Dial Square. The club then changed its name to Royal Arsenal and then Woolwich Reds, although their official title soon became Woolwich Arsenal.

2 Arsenal have been league champions on 11 occasions – in 1930–31, 1932–33, 1933–34, 1934–35, 1937–38, 1947–48, 1952–53, 1970–71, 1988–89, 1990–91 and 1997–98 – and they are one of only three clubs to have completed a hat-trick of league titles.

3 Arsenal have the longest unbroken run in the top division. The last time they were relegated was in 1913. Their current run in the top flight stretches back to 1919.

4 They have played in the FA Cup final on 13 occasions, winning the trophy seven times – in 1930, 1936, 1950, 1971, 1979, 1993 and 1998.

5 In 1998 they completed the famed Double for the second time – the first being in 1971.

6 They have also won the Football League Cup twice – in 1987 and 1993 – having reached the final five times.

7 Arsenal have triumphed in Europe on just two occasions. In 1970, they won the Fairs Cup and they brought home the European Cup Winners Cup in 1994. They have also reached two other finals – in 1980 and 1995, both in the Cup Winners Cup – in their 14 seasons of European football.

8 Arsenal Underground station is the only station in Britain to be named after a football team. It was originally called Gillespie Road, but Herbert Chapman had it renamed Arsenal Highbury Hill in October 1932. By February 1934 the suffix had been dropped.

9 Arsenal's record win was a 12–0 triumph over Loughborough in January 1900 and their record 8–0 defeat was against the same side in December 1896.

10 Their all-time record goalscorer is Ian Wright, who found the net 185 times in an Arsenal shirt over the course of seven seasons.

11 The player with the record number of league appearances for Arsenal is David O'Leary who played in 558 matches between 1975 and 1993.

12 The club's record attendance of 73,707 saw Arsenal lose 1–0 to Lens in the 1998–99 Champions League tie at Wembley. The record attendance at Highbury of 73,295 was in 1935.

13 During the 1990–91 season, Arsenal were only defeated in one game out of 38, which is a top-flight record this century.

14 The club's motto is Victoria Concordia Crescit, which means Victory Through Harmony.

15 Arsene Wenger's side finished second in the Premiership. Their league record was:

Pld	W	D	L	F	A	Pts
38	22	12	4	59	17	78

16 The Gunners reached the semi-final of the AXA-sponsored FA Cup, where they lost 2–1 after extra time in a replay against Manchester United following a 0–0 draw in the first encounter. On the way they defeated Preston North End, Wolves, Sheffield United and Derby County.

17 Arsenal fielded under-strength line-ups in the Worthington Cup, and after defeating Derby County 2–1 at Pride Park they were knocked out 5–0 by Chelsea at Highbury in the fourth round.

18 Wembley was used by Arsenal as their home ground in the Champions League. They began well, drawing 1–1 away at Lens, winning 2–1 at home against Panathinaikos and drawing 1–1 at home against Dynamo Kiev. They finished third in their group after losing to Kiev and Lens, before winning 3–1 in Athens against Panathinaikos.

19 The top goalscorer in all competitions for Arsenal was Nicolas Anelka with 18 goals.

20 Despite much high-profile coverage, Arsenal's disciplinary record was not as bad as many others. The Gunners were only 13th in the discipline stakes, committing 470 fouls, earning 62 yellow cards and seven reds.

SEASON REVIEW

So near and yet so far. After winning the double in 1997–98, Arsenal found themselves the nearly men of 1998–99.

Their season started off slowly, as a 2–1 win over newly-promoted Nottingham Forest was followed by a series of four straight draws. Title rivals Manchester United were beaten 3–0 in September, but the Gunners did not hit top spot in the Premiership until the end of April.

A failure to convert possession into goals was to blame for their sluggish start to the season. The team carved out more scoring chances than any other Premiership side and their final tally of 524 shots was the highest in the division, yet they scored 21 fewer goals than Manchester United.

Part of the reason for this lay with Dennis Bergkamp. The Dutchman struggled for form after the rigours of Holland's World Cup campaign and the team became over-reliant on Nicolas Anelka. The young Frenchman had knocked in seven league goals by the end of November, but it took Bergkamp until February to do the same.

Fortunately for Arsene Wenger, his defence was performing as well as ever. Only Aston Villa managed to score more than one goal against them in a match, and they finished the season with 23 clean sheets and just 17 goals conceded – the best defensive record in Europe.

They received less credit for their disciplinary record. Wenger claimed that his side were harshly treated and more sinned against than sinners (see page 627). Carling Opta statistics, which showed that only two teams committed fewer fouls, would seem to back up the Arsenal manager's claims; but the fact remains that a total of 10 Arsenal players were sent off in all competitions.

Suspensions for the likes of Patrick Vieira, Martin Keown and Emmanuel Petit – who almost quit the club over his three dismissals – disrupted the shape of the side and underlined Arsenal's lack of strength in depth compared to Manchester United.

There were also persistent and unsettling rumours surrounding the future of Anelka. The club's leading scorer was constantly linked with a string of top European sides, and did little to allay fears that he was unhappy with life in England with some of his comments to the French press and his failure to collect his PFA Young Player of the Year Award in person.

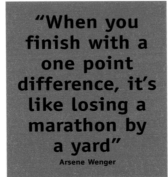

> **"When you finish with a one point difference, it's like losing a marathon by a yard"**
>
> **Arsene Wenger**

In spite of these problems, the team managed an unbeaten run of 19 league games between December 20 and May 11. They reached their peak after an agonisingly close defeat in the semi-final of the FA Cup by Manchester United, a result which seemed to spur the players to new heights in the Premiership.

Inspired by a resurgent Dennis Bergkamp and the signing of Nwankwo Kanu, the Gunners touched the heights of the previous season with 11 goals in two games against Wimbledon and Middlesbrough. But it was all to no avail, as Manchester United pipped them to the top spot by one point.

A 1–0 defeat by Leeds United was widely seen as the moment the title was lost. But the real damage to their challenge came not with Jimmy Floyd Hasselbaink's match-winning header at Elland Road, but with the slow start to the season that left them playing catch-up with Alex Ferguson's side.

Arsene Wenger was left with the consolation of a Champions League place and the knowledge that his team were still way ahead of most of the chasing pack. But United's triumph clearly hurt the Gunners' manager and he will be desperate to put the record straight in the 1999–2000 campaign.

ARSENAL

DATE	OPPONENT	SCORE	ATT.	ADAMS	ANELKA	BERGKAMP	BOA MORTE	BOULD	CABALLERO	DIAWARA	DIXON	GARDE	GRIMANDI
17.8.98	Nott'm For H	2–1	38,064	90	90	90	–	–	–	–	90	–	–
22.8.98	Liverpool A	0–0	44,429	–	84	90	–	90	–	–	90□	–	–
29.8.98	Charlton H	0–0	38,014	90	70	90	–	–	–	–	67	–	–
9.9.98	Chelsea A	0–0	34,647	90	75	85	–	–	–	–	60■	s30	–
12.9.98	Leicester A	1–1	21,628	–	s30	90	–	90	–	–	74	s19	–
20.9.98	Man Utd H	3–0	38,142	90^1	79^1	90	–	–	–	–	90	–	–
26.9.98	Sheff Wed A	0–1	27,949	90	90	90	–	s45	–	–	–	–	–
4.10.98	Newcastle H	3–0	38,102	90	90^1	90^2	–	s7	–	–	90	–	–
17.10.98	Southampton H	1–1	38,027	90	90^1	90	–	–	–	–	90	–	–
25.10.98	Blackburn A	2–1	27,012	–	90^1	90	–	90	–	–	90	–	–
31.10.98	Coventry A	1–0	23,039	–	90^1	–	s45	90	–	–	90	–	–
8.11.98	Everton H	1–0	38,088	–	90^1	–	–	–	–	–	90	–	90□
14.11.98	Tottenham H	0–0	38,278	90	80	–	s10	–	–	–	90	–	–
21.11.98	Wimbledon A	0–1	26,003	90□	90	37	–	–	–	–	90	–	–
29.11.98	Middlesbro H	1–1	38,075	–	90^1	–	s27	90□	s15	–	90	90□	–
5.12.98	Derby Co A	0–0	29,018	–	90	–	s13	90	–	–	90	67	90
13.12.98	Aston Villa A	2–3	39,217	–	90	90^2□	s1	90	–	–	90□	–	s22
20.12.98	Leeds Utd H	3–1	38,025	–	90	90^1□	–	90	–	–	90	–	s16■
26.12.98	West Ham H	1–0	38,098	–	30	90	–	90	–	–	90	–	s13
28.12.98	Charlton A	1–0	20,043	–	–	40□	62	90	–	–	90	–	s28
9.1.99	Liverpool H	0–0	38,107	–	88	–	90	32□	–	–	90	s5	–
16.1.99	Nott'm For A	1–0	26,021	90	86□	–	–	–	–	–	90	90□	–
31.1.99	Chelsea H	1–0	38,121	90	68	89^1□	–	–	–	s15	90	90	–
6.2.99	West Ham A	4–0	26,042	90	90^1	90^1	–	–	–	–	90	–	–
17.2.99	Man Utd A	1–1	55,171	90	90^1	–	–	90□	–	s2	90	s30	–
20.2.99	Leicester H	5–0	38,069	90	68^3	90	–	–	–	s22	90	90	90
28.2.99	Newcastle A	1–1	36,708	90	90^1	90□	–	–	–	–	90	4	–
9.3.99	Sheff Wed H	3–0	37,792	90	61	90^2	–	–	–	s45	90	–	–
13.3.99	Everton A	2–0	38,049	90□	62	90^1	–	–	–	–	90	–	–
20.3.99	Coventry H	2–0	38,074	90	77	90	–	–	–	s5	30	–	–
3.4.99	Southampton A	0–0	15,255	90	90	–	s23	s2	–	79	90	–	–
6.4.99	Blackburn H	1–0	37,762	90	–	90^1	–	s18	–	62	90□	–	–
19.4.99	Wimbledon H	5–1*	37,982	90	–	70^1	–	s1	–	s20	–	–	–
24.4.99	Middlesbro A	6–1	34,630	90	90^1	–	–	90	–	s20	90	–	–
2.5.99	Derby Co H	1–0	37,323	90	78^1	s28	–	90	–	s12	90	–	–
5.5.99	Tottenham A	3–1	36,019	90	90^1	75	–	–	–	–	90□	–	s2
11.5.99	Leeds Utd A	0–1	40,124	90□	90	90	–	–	–	s19	90□	–	–
16.5.99	Aston Villa H	1–0	38,308	90□	61	90	–	–	–	s9	90	–	–

□ Yellow card, ■ Red card, s Substitute, 90^2 Goals scored
*including one own goal

1998–99 PREMIERSHIP APPEARANCES

GRONDIN	HUGHES	KANU	KEOWN	LJUNGBERG	MANNINGER	MENDEZ	OVERMARS	PARLOUR	PETIT	SEAMAN	UPSON	VIEIRA	VIVAS	WINTERBURN	WREH	TOTAL
–	–	–	90	–	–	–	90¹	90	90¹	90	–	90	–	90	–	990
–	–	–	90	–	–	–	90	90□	90□	90	–	90	s6	90	–	990
–	s14	–	90□	–	–	–	90	90	56■	90	–	76	s23□	90□	s20	956
–	s15	–	90	–	–	–	60	90	90	90	–	90	–	90	s5	960
–	90¹□	–	90	–	–	–	90	90	–	90	–	71□	s16	90□	60	990
–	90□	–	90	s11¹□	–	–	90	90	–	90	–	90	–	90	–	990
–	s12	–	44■	s12	90	–	45	78	78	–	–	90□	90□	90□	–	944
–	s23	–	83	75	–	s15	90	–	67	90	–	90	–	90	–	990
–	90	–	90	–	–	–	90□	81	–	90	–	90	–	90	s9	990
–	–	–	90	90□	–	–	90	–	90¹	90	–	90□	–	90	–	990
–	s10	–	90	45□	–	–	80	90	90	90	–	90	–	90	–	990
–	–	–	90□	90	–	–	90	90	90□	90	–	90	–	90	–	990
–	–	–	90	63	–	–	90	90	90	90	–	90	–	90□	s27	990
–	s70	–	90	s18	–	–	72	90	90	90	–	20	–	90□	s53	990
–	–	–	90	75	–	–	90	90	–	90	–	–	s62	28	63	990
–	–	–	90	s23	–	–	90	90	–	90	–	–	90□	–	77	990
–	–	–	90	68□	–	–	90	89	–	90	–	90	90	–	–	990
–	–	–	90	70	90	–	87	–	90¹	–	–	90¹□	90	–	s3	986
–	–	–	90	–	90	–	90¹	90	90	–	–	90	90□	–	s47	990
–	–	–	90□	–	90	–	90¹	90	90	–	–	51■	s61	29	s50	951
90	–	–	90□	–	90	–	85	90	90	–	s58	90	–	–	s2	990
–	–	–	90¹	–	90	–	66	90	90	–	s4	–	s24	90□	–	990
–	–	–	90□	–	–	–	75	90	90	90	s1	–	s22	90	–	990
–	–	–	90	–	–	–	90¹	90¹	90	90	–	90	–	90□	–	990
–	90	60	–	–	–	–	88	90□	–	90	–	90□	s12	78	–	990
–	s18	s22	–	–	–	–	68	90²	–	90	–	72	90	–	–	990
–	s86	–	90	–	–	–	85□	90	–	90	s5	90	–	90	–	990
–	–	s29¹	90	45	–	–	90	70	s20	90	–	90	90	–	–	990
–	–	–	90	–	–	–	87	90¹	61■	90	s3	90	s28	90	–	961
–	–	s13	90	s60	–	–	85¹	90¹	90	90	–	90	–	90□	–	990
–	–	90	88	67	–	–	–	90	–	90	–	90□	s11	90	–	990
–	–	s28	70■	–	–	–	72	90	–	90	–	90	90□	90	–	970
–	–	90¹	89	–	–	–	90	90¹	90	90	–	90¹	90	90	–	990
–	s4	79²	–	–	–	–	70¹	90	86	90	–	90¹	s11	90	–	990
–	s14	62	–	–	–	–	76	90	90	90	–	90	–	90	–	990
–	–	s15¹	90	–	–	–	88	57□	90¹□	90	–	90	s33	90	–	990
–	–	s25	90	–	–	–	65	71□	90□	90	–	90□	s9	81	–	990
–	–	s29¹	90	s75	–	–	81	90	90	90	–	90	15	–	–	990

THE MANAGER

ARSENE WENGER

Arsenal's remarkable achievements over the last three years can be credited almost entirely to the work of shrewd Frenchman Arsene Wenger.

The bespectacled tactician transformed Arsenal from Premiership also-rans into league and cup Double winners in two seasons, after joining from Japanese club Grampus Eight in September 1996.

Wenger began his playing career with Mutzig in 1969, moving to Strasbourg in 1978. Three years later, he was made youth team coach at the French club before becoming assistant manager at Cannes in 1983. Within a year he was in the hot seat at Nancy and in 1987 he took the vacant job at AS Monaco.

Under his tutelage, Monaco won the French Championship in 1988 and the French Cup three years later. He moved to Japan in 1995, but the lure of managing a top Carling Premiership club proved too much to resist.

With Wenger in charge, Arsenal have developed a thrilling attacking streak while losing none of their legendary meanness in defence, resulting in a truly potent force.

Surrendering the Double to Manchester United is certain to make the media-friendly Frenchman all the more determined to see his side scale new heights in 1999–2000.

LEAGUE POSITION

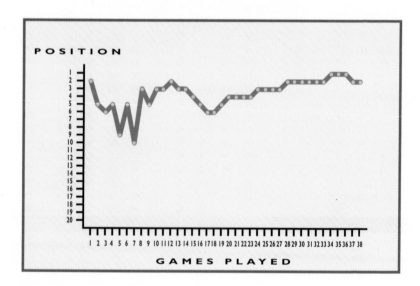

POSITION

GAMES PLAYED

THE GOALS

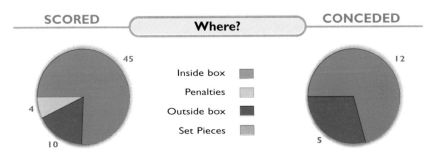

SCORED — Where? — CONCEDED

Inside box	
Penalties	
Outside box	
Set Pieces	

Scored: 45, 4, 10

Conceded: 12, 5

Arsenal attempted more shots at goal than any other side in the Premiership and were the league's fourth-highest scorers. More than three-quarters of their strikes came from inside 18 yards, with the front two of Nicolas Anelka

and Dennis Bergkamp bagging nearly half the goals. The meanest defence in the country held firm in their own area, conceding just 70.6% of all goals from inside the penalty box, by far the smallest proportion in the league.

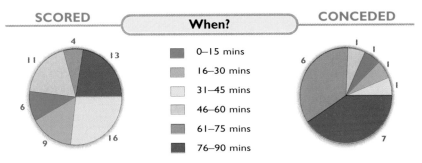

SCORED — When? — CONCEDED

0–15 mins	
16–30 mins	
31–45 mins	
46–60 mins	
61–75 mins	
76–90 mins	

Scored: 4, 13, 11, 6, 9, 16

Conceded: 1, 1, 1, 6, 1, 7

Arsenal were at their best in the opening half of Premiership matches. The Gunners managed 52.5% of all goals before the half-time whistle, a higher proportion than any other club. David Seaman conceded just three first-half goals all

season, the best record in the league, and overall, 13 out of the 17 goals Arsenal conceded were scored in the last half-hour, possibly as a result of their experienced defence beginning to tire as the game went on.

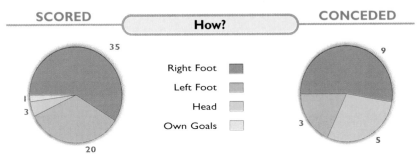

SCORED — How? — CONCEDED

Right Foot	
Left Foot	
Head	
Own Goals	

Scored: 35, 1, 3, 20

Conceded: 9, 3, 5

The Premiership runners-up scored a higher proportion of goals with their feet than any other side, and only Liverpool players registered from more left-footed efforts. Surprisingly, despite the presence of Tony Adams and Martin

Keown in the side, the Gunners managed just three headed goals, or 5.1% of all their strikes, the lowest in the league. Paradoxically, Arsenal conceded the highest proportion of headed goals in the Premiership.

ARSENAL

	ADAMS	ANELKA	BERGKAMP	BOA MORTE	BOULD	CABALLERO	DIAWARA	DIXON	GARDE	GRIMANDI
APPEARANCES										
Start	26	34	28	2	14	0	2	36	6	3
Sub	0	1	1	6	5	1	10	0	4	5
Minutes on pitch	2340	2807	2404	271	1275	15	310	3111	515	351
GOAL ATTEMPTS										
Goals	1	17	12	0	0	0	0	0	0	0
Shots on target	4	51	47	1	0	0	5	8	2	0
Shots off target	12	44	34	6	1	0	13	18	5	2
Shooting accuracy	25%	54%	58%	14%	0%	0%	28%	31%	29%	0%
PASSING										
Goal assists	0	5	12	0	1	0	0	1	0	0
Long passes	172	23	102	1	60	0	7	252	31	27
Short passes	892	804	939	79	437	8	116	1358	207	138
PASS COMPLETION										
Own half %	94%	78%	88%	67%	95%	100%	78%	91%	93%	97%
Opposition half %	71%	68%	66%	60%	69%	83%	65%	73%	75%	66%
CROSSING										
Total crosses	3	28	52	12	0	0	9	43	27	3
Cross completion %	67%	14%	35%	25%	0%	0%	0%	19%	19%	67%
DRIBBLING										
Dribbles & runs	37	149	102	10	8	0	19	52	5	3
Dribble completion %	92%	63%	63%	80%	88%	0%	63%	71%	100%	100%
DEFENDING										
Tackles made	98	57	42	12	30	0	9	90	23	19
Tackles won %	68%	42%	55%	50%	70%	0%	67%	61%	48%	79%
Blocks	27	2	0	1	23	0	0	21	1	2
Clearances	388	2	3	0	236	0	1	155	15	32
Interceptions	57	6	10	3	24	0	0	24	8	12
DISCIPLINE										
Fouls	28	27	36	6	26	1	5	29	3	11
Offside	0	58	22	0	1	0	2	1	0	1
Yellow cards	4	1	5	0	3	0	0	5	2	1
Red cards	0	0	0	0	0	0	0	1	0	1

GOALKEEPER NAME	START/ (SUB)	TIME ON PITCH	GOALS CONCEDED	MINS/GOALS CONCEDED	SAVES MADE	SAVES/ SHOTS
MANNINGER	6	540	2	270	18	90%
SEAMAN	32	2880	15	192	75	83%

PLAYERS' STATISTICS

GRONDIN	HUGHES	KANU	KEOWN	LJUNGBERG	MENDEZ	OVERMARS	PARLOUR	PETIT	UPSON	VIEIRA	VIVAS	WINTERBURN	WREH	TOTAL	RANK
1	4	5	34	10	0	37	35	26	0	34	10	30	3		
0	10	7	0	6	1	0	0	1	5	0	13	0	9		
90	626	542	2984	887	15	3055	3056	2258	71	2900	1143	2556	416		
0	1	6	1	1	0	6	6	4	0	3	0	0	0	59*	4th
0	1	9	1	10	0	45	27	13	1	10	1	8	3	247	1st
0	5	6	6	9	1	35	31	19	0	20	2	6	2	277	1st
0%	17%	60%	14%	53%	0%	56%	47%	41%	100%	33%	33%	57%	60%	47%	4th
0	2	2	1	0	0	7	3	3	0	3	0	2	0	42	4th
9	36	13	216	23	2	97	142	222	9	145	63	157	6	1815	=12th
40	313	229	905	310	6	965	1360	1183	36	1614	491	1152	178	13761	4th
100%	95%	88%	93%	83%	50%	87%	88%	89%	100%	89%	85%	92%	91%	91%	4th
86%	79%	77%	67%	73%	83%	75%	77%	72%	56%	79%	76%	79%	73%	73%	4th
1	27	5	5	25	2	113	86	124	0	8	39	25	8	645	15th
0%	30%	0%	20%	12%	0%	17%	29%	27%	0%	25%	23%	16%	63%	24%	20th
3	16	35	24	68	1	236	183	51	2	94	35	55	11	1199	1st
100%	75%	69%	100%	60%	100%	64%	74%	76%	100%	80%	86%	87%	27%	71%	11th
3	29	23	105	41	0	61	130	122	2	209	69	147	11	1333	3rd
67%	72%	57%	70%	61%	0%	51%	58%	66%	100%	70%	54%	61%	64%	62%	5th
0	1	0	31	2	1	2	4	9	0	14	4	26	0	171	17th
9	19	0	476	8	0	6	47	93	13	97	61	161	0	1857	19th
2	8	2	48	2	0	15	23	41	3	48	12	36	0	384	1st
0	13	6	35	13	0	12	63	19	0	85	20	24	8	470	18th
0	0	10	2	0	0	23	11	0	0	2	0	1	4	138	8th
0	2	0	5	4	0	2	4	4	0	7	5	8	0	62	15th
0	0	0	2	0	0	0	0	2	0	1	0	0	0	7	2nd

*Including one own goal

CROSSES CAUGHT	CROSSES PUNCHED	CROSSES NOT CLAIMED	CATCH SUCCESS	THROWS/SHORT KICKS	% COMPLETION	LONG KICKS	% COMPLETION
10	4	7	77%	43	95%	114	18%
69	17	7	93%	358	97%	574	25%

PLAYER OF THE SEASON

PLAYER	INDEX SCORE
EMMANUEL PETIT	1084
Dennis Bergkamp	1079
Tony Adams	1063
Patrick Vieira	1029
Nigel Winterburn	983
Nicolas Anelka	964
Marc Overmars	921
Ray Parlour	907
Martin Keown	868
David Seaman	763

The 1998–99 season was not without its troubles for Emmanuel Petit, but there was nothing "petit" about his contribution to Arsenal's Premiership campaign.

Many pundits' pick for the league's Player of the Year, Petit was just as influential in the Gunners' midfield alongside countryman Patrick Vieira as he had been in 1997–98.

The sticking point was discipline, thanks to the two red cards he picked up in the Premiership (and one more in the FA Cup). An exasperated Petit felt he was being victimized by referees, bearing in mind he conceded just 19 fouls all season – and even threatened to quit the Premiership.

But despite losing points for his disciplinary misdemeanours, he still ended up as the highest-scoring Gunner in the Carling Opta Season Index, with an average points score of 1,084. He built up that average thanks to his eye-catching attacking flair coupled with the almost instinctive desire to protect the back four – not surprising, considering he was a defender himself at Monaco.

And he ended the season on the front cover of *Hello!* magazine, an indication of the celebrity status the skilful midfield man has attained.

Close behind in the top 10 for Arsenal was Dennis Bergkamp, who finished the season as the top-rated player in the overall strikers' Index for 1998–99.

Despite a poor start to the campaign, Bergkamp's breathtaking vision and awesome striking ability shone through in the second half of the season as the Gunners came so close to defending their title successfully.

Skipper Tony Adams finished in third, just ahead of Vieira and veteran left-back Nigel Winterburn. These three showed great consistency throughout 1998–99, which is why they appear above the likes of Nicolas Anelka and wingers Marc Overmars and Ray Parlour. They enjoyed brilliant spells, but struggled to maintain their form over the whole season.

FIVE OF THE BEST

Despite winning 13 of their last 17 Premiership matches, the Gunners lost their title to Manchester United on the last day of the 1998–99 season. The veteran defence continued to defy the ageing process and no other top-flight team in the twentieth century has conceded so few goals without winning the title.

TOP GOALSCORERS

	GOALS	GOALS/SHOTS
NICOLAS ANELKA	17	18%
Dennis Bergkamp	12	15%
Nwankwo Kanu	6	40%
Ray Parlour	6	10%
Marc Overmars	6	8%

Nicolas Anelka finished top scorer with 17 goals, hitting the back of the net with 18% of his shots. Deadly Dutchman Dennis Bergkamp, so often the Gunners' goal provider, weighed in with a dozen Premiership strikes of his own, four fewer than in 1997–98. Fellow-Dutchman Marc Overmars and England wide man Ray Parlour scored six apiece, but the real star of the run-in was Nigerian Nwankwo Kanu. With 40% of his shots resulting in a goal, he might well have propelled Arsenal to the title had he arrived at Highbury a little sooner.

Arsenal's slick passing style has smashed the "boring, boring" stereotype of recent years and transformed the Gunners into one of the most attractive and deadliest teams in the Premiership.

The midfield engine-room of Parlour, Vieira and Petit play past opponents with their quick one-twos and are as happy receiving the ball off the back four as they are trying to create chances at the other end. Petit has a slightly lower completion rate because he frequently looks for the more difficult "killer" pass.

TOP PASSERS

	SUCC PASSES	COMPLETION
PATRICK VIEIRA	1,464	83%
Lee Dixon	1,291	80%
Ray Parlour	1,188	79%
Nigel Winterburn	1,109	85%
Emmanuel Petit	1,101	78%

TOP TACKLERS

	WON	SUCCESS
PATRICK VIEIRA	146	70%
Nigel Winterburn	89	61%
Emmanuel Petit	81	66%
Ray Parlour	75	58%
Martin Keown	73	70%

Arsenal enjoyed harrying opponents out of their stride with their uncompromising style, both in defence and midfield. Patrick Vieira was destroyer-in-chief in 1998–99, breaking down opposition attacks and protecting the defence. His telescopic legs robbed opponents when they seemed to have escaped.

Petit, too, won his fair share of challenges and of course defensive stalwarts like Martin Keown and Nigel Winterburn are renowned for their never-say-die attitude.

Arsenal's poor disciplinary record was well-documented and is undoubtedly something the club needs to work on. Ten dismissals in 1998–99, including seven in the Premiership, saw them branded as "dirty" by the media.

Patrick Vieira was the Gunners' worst offender, but he is by no means the only player who needs to improve his record. It is interesting to note that Emmanuel Petit, sent off three times in all competitions in 1998–99, does not figure in the top five. He conceded only 19 fouls all season.

DISCIPLINE

	POINTS	FOULS & CARDS
PATRICK VIEIRA	112	85F, 7Y, 1R
Ray Parlour	75	63F, 4Y, 0R
Martin Keown	62	35F, 5Y, 2R
Dennis Bergkamp	51	36F, 5Y, 0R
Lee Dixon	50	29F, 5Y, 1R

ACTION	ADAMS	ANELKA	BERGKAMP	DIXON	HUGHES	KEOWN	LJUNGBERG	OVERMARS	PARLOUR	SEAMAN	VIEIRA	WINTERBURN	TOTAL	MANCHESTER UNITED
Time on pitch	90	79	90	90	90	90	11	90	90	90	90	90	990	950
GOALS														
Goal	–	1	–	–	–	–	–	–	–	–	–	–	3	–
Shot on target	–	2	–	1	–	–	–	3	–	–	–	–	7	4
Shot off target	–	1	3	–	1	–	–	–	1	–	–	–	7	4
Blocked shot	–	–	–	–	–	–	–	–	–	–	–	–	4	1
Own goal	–	–	–	–	–	–	–	–	–	–	–	–	–	–
PASSES														
Pass to own player	29	23	25	34	53	18	3	30	36	–	56	29	336	298
Pass to opposition	6	9	13	10	4	5	1	3	6	–	6	5	68	74
Cross to own player	–	–	2	–	1	1	–	–	–	–	–	–	2	–
Cross to opposition player	–	–	2	–	2	–	–	1	3	–	1	–	9	11
Goal assist	–	–	–	–	2	–	–	1	–	–	–	–	3	–
Pass completion %	83%	72%	63%	77%	90%	79%	75%	89%	80%	0%	89%	85%	82%	78%
TACKLES & CLEARANCES														
Tackle	1	1	2	7	1	5	–	1	4	1	12	7	41	41
Clearances, blocks and interceptions	30	–	–	11	3	22	–	–	2	–	7	11	87	53
DRIBBLES & RUNS														
Dribble ball retained	2	3	3	2	2	–	–	9	3	–	5	2	31	14
Dribbles ball lost	1	1	4	–	–	–	1	3	2	–	3	–	15	9
Dribble success %	67%	75%	43%	100%	100%	0%	0%	75%	60%	0%	63%	100%	67%	61%
DISCIPLINE														
Fouls	2	2	2	1	1	–	1	–	2	–	4	1	16	12
Penalty conceded	–	–	–	–	–	–	–	–	–	–	–	–	–	–
Free kick - offside	–	2	–	–	–	–	–	1	1	–	–	–	5	3
Yellow cards	–	–	–	–	1	–	–	–	–	–	–	–	2	3
Red cards	–	–	–	–	–	–	–	–	–	–	–	–	–	1
GOALKEEPERS														
Distribution to own player	–	–	–	–	–	–	–	–	–	14	–	–	14	19
Distribution to opposition player	–	–	–	–	–	–	–	–	–	20	–	–	20	28
Goalkeeper distribution%	0%	0%	0%	0%	0%	0%	0%	0%	0%	41%	0%	0%	41%	40%
Save	–	–	–	–	–	–	–	–	–	4	–	–	4	6
Ball caught	–	–	–	–	–	–	–	–	–	3	–	–	3	2
Ball dropped	–	–	–	–	–	–	–	–	–	–	–	–	–	–
Goal conceded	–	–	–	–	–	–	–	–	–	–	–	–	–	3

After just one win in their first five Premiership matches, Arsenal's home game against Manchester United took on greater significance in the defence of their title. Already a point behind the Red Devils having played one less game, it was vital Arsenal did not lose any more ground.

September 20, 1998

3 – 0

ARSENAL
MANCHESTER UNITED

The game started at a brisk tempo and Arsenal were rewarded for their endeavours with a goal on 14 minutes.

The Gunners won a free kick on the right of United's penalty area which was taken by Stephen Hughes, standing in for the injured Emmanuel Petit. The youngster's curling cross was met by skipper Tony Adams, rising above Jaap Stam and the flailing arms of Peter Schmeichel to bury a header into the unguarded net.

The game opened up, and end-to-end forays created several chances. Nicolas Anelka was denied by a brilliant save from Schmeichel and David Beckham saw a long-range effort hit the post.

Just before half-time, a superb tackle by Martin Keown on Ryan Giggs saw the ball break to Patrick Vieira, who in turn found Marc Overmars. The Dutchman played an inch-perfect pass over the top of the defence for Anelka to chase. The Frenchman beat the offside trap, leaving Stam in his wake, and although his first shot was saved, Anelka slotted the rebound into the net with his left foot.

The second half started with some unsavoury challenges when both Roy Keane and Beckham appeared to stamp on Hughes; and moments later, there was a controversial incident that in reality brought an early end to the game as a contest.

A break by Vieira from midfield was halted by a late challenge from Nicky Butt, when the Frenchman appeared to be through on goal. The result was a red card for Butt, despite vociferous protests that saw Keane booked.

Arsenal had to wait until the 83rd minute before adding to their tally. A misplaced pass by Hughes wrong-footed the United defence and saw new signing Fredrik Ljungberg beat the offside trap to lob Peter Schmeichel and claim a goal on his Arsenal debut.

The Gunners' fourth straight win over their closest rivals saw them leapfrog United into fifth place. The win was thoroughly deserved, with Arsenal scoring three times from ten shots on target and making a further 11 efforts at goal that did not trouble the keeper. United had just nine efforts, eight of which came from Beckham, but none really tested David Seaman.

Arsenal dominated possession, completing 82% of their passes to United's 78%, though the sending-off of Nicky Butt gave Arsenal an advantage. Three other players were booked: Hughes, Ljungberg and Keane.

Man of the match was Patrick Vieira with a score of 1,755 points. He earned that total by completing 56 passes, making 12 tackles and embarking on five successful dribbles out of eight attempts.

The match proved to be a significant win in an inconsistent run, showing Arsenal were still likely to be the team who would run Manchester United closest for the League title.

ACTION	ADAMS	ANELKA	BOULD	DIAWARA	DIXON	HUGHES	KANU	OVERMARS	PARLOUR	PETIT	SEAMAN	VIEIRA	VIVAS	WINTERBURN	TOTAL	MIDDLESBROUGH
Time on pitch	90	90	90	20	90	4	79	70	90	86	90	90	11	90	990	990
GOALS																
Goal	–	2	–	–	–	–	2	–	–	–	–	–	–	–	6	1
Shot on target	–	2	–	–	–	–	2	–	–	–	–	–	–	–	4	4
Shot off target	1	–	–	1	1	–	–	–	–	–	–	–	–	1	6	6
Blocked shot	–	1	–	–	–	–	–	1	1	–	–	–	–	–	3	4
Own goal	–	–	–	–	–	–	–	–	–	–	–	–	–	–	–	–
PASSES																
Pass to own player	51	19	43	6	52	2	25	22	39	58	–	57	8	58	440	236
Pass to opposition	2	13	–	1	6	–	10	10	8	12	–	3	2	7	74	102
Cross to own player	–	3	–	–	2	–	–	2	–	–	–	–	–	–	7	6
Cross to opposition player	–	–	–	–	–	–	–	3	7	–	–	1	–	1	12	12
Goal assist	–	1	–	1	1	–	1	–	–	–	–	1	–	–	5	1
Pass completion %	96%	62%	100%	86%	90%	67%	72%	66%	72%	83%	0%	95%	80%	89%	84%	68%
TACKLES & CLEARANCES																
Tackle	1	2	2	–	–	–	4	–	5	3	1	6	1	–	25	28
Clearances, blocks and interceptions	18	–	16	–	2	–	–	–	2	3	–	2	1	2	46	33
DRIBBLES & RUNS																
Dribble ball retained	1	5	1	–	1	–	5	4	3	–	–	1	–	3	24	12
Dribbles ball lost	–	1	–	–	–	–	3	1	2	–	–	–	–	–	7	4
Dribble success %	100%	83%	100%	0%	100%	0%	63%	80%	60%	0%	0%	100%	0%	100%	77%	75%
DISCIPLINE																
Fouls	1	–	1	–	2	–	–	–	2	–	–	4	1	–	12	14
Penalty conceded	–	1	–	–	–	–	–	–	–	–	–	–	–	–	1	1
Free kick - offside	–	1	–	–	–	–	–	–	–	–	–	–	–	–	2	3
Yellow cards	–	–	–	–	–	–	–	–	–	–	–	–	–	–	2	2
Red cards	–	–	–	–	–	–	–	–	–	–	–	–	–	–	–	–
GOALKEEPERS																
Distribution to own player	–	–	–	–	–	–	–	–	–	–	17	–	–	–	17	12
Distribution to opposition player	–	–	–	–	–	–	–	–	–	–	17	–	–	–	17	15
Goalkeeper distribution%	0%	0%	0%	0%	0%	0%	0%	0%	0%	0%	50%	0%	0%	0%	50%	44%
Save	–	–	–	–	–	–	–	–	–	–	4	–	–	–	4	4
Ball caught	–	–	–	–	–	–	–	–	–	–	4	–	–	–	4	1
Ball dropped	–	–	–	–	–	–	–	–	–	–	1	–	–	–	1	–
Goal conceded	–	–	–	–	–	–	–	–	–	–	–	–	–	–	–	6

Arsenal made a brave attempt to retain their title in the final few months of the season, putting in some amazing performances along the way. Nowhere did they demonstrate their desire and ability better than in the 6–1 hammering of Middlesbrough at the Riverside. The Gunners were under pressure in a must-win situation.

April 24, 1999

1–6

MIDDLESBROUGH ARSENAL

Any early nerves were calmed in the third minute when Nicolas Anelka accelerated into the penalty area and was brought down by Steve Vickers. Marc Overmars placed his penalty in the centre of the goal: 1–0 to the Arsenal.

There followed a period of sustained Arsenal pressure that was to set the pattern of the match but Arsene Wenger's side were given a sharp warning in the 35th minute when David Seaman was forced into a good save from Brian Deane's fierce volley.

This spurred Arsenal on, and a neat piece of play from Patrick Vieira in the 38th minute released Anelka to score Arsenal's second, the French star making no mistake from the edge of the area.

Although Dean Gordon came close to pulling a goal back for the home side, Arsenal went further ahead on the stroke of half-time. Kanu turned Gordon and released Anelka with an angled pass. Continuing his run into the penalty area, Kanu received Anelka's cross, sidestepped Gordon and placed the ball beyond the reach of Schwarzer.

The Gunners increased their lead after 58 minutes. Another lightning break involving Anelka and Vieira saw the pair play a brilliant one-two just inside the Boro half. Anelka surged down the line and when his cross was dinked on by Overmars, Vieira was on hand to finish off.

With Arsenal rampant, Kanu scored one of the goals of the season. Dixon crossed from the right and the Nigerian international beat Schwarzer with a brilliant mid-air, back-heeled volley which was greeted with applause by Boro as well as Arsenal fans.

Hamilton Ricard hit the post with a free kick, but it was no surprise when Anelka grabbed Arsenal's sixth goal with a cracking drive in the 78th minute.

Substitute Alun Armstrong scored a late consolation for Middlesbrough with a header from an Andy Townsend cross, but there was no denying Arsenal their glory or the three points that took them to the top of the League for the first time in the race for the Championship.

The statistics prove how superior Arsenal were on the day. They completed almost twice as many passes as the home side, ending the match with an excellent pass completion rate of 84%; and although Middlesbrough attempted almost as many shots, they could not match the visitors' clinical finishing.

Man of the match for Arsenal was Kanu with 2,374 points. He scored two goals and laid on one more for Anelka. The Frenchman scored 2,342 points and also bagged two goals and an assist.

Arsenal were unable to hold on to top spot, but the quality of some of their play – particularly in the second half of the season – was irresistible. The performance against Middlesbrough was probably their best of the campaign.

Livewire striker: Julian Joachim finished as Villa top scorer with 14 goals

ASTON VILLA

ADDRESS

Villa Park, Birmingham B6 6HE

CONTACT NUMBERS

Telephone: 0121 327 2299
Fax: 0121 322 2107
Commercial: 0121 327 5399
Ticket Office: 0121 327 5353
24hr Information: 09068 121148
Villa Village Superstore:
0121 327 2800
e-mail: postmaster@astonvilla-fc.co.uk
Website: www.astonvilla-fc.co.uk

SPONSORS

LDV

FANZINES

Heroes and Villans
The Holy Trinity

KEY PERSONNEL

Club President: Tony Alderson
Chairman: H D Ellis
Directors: H D Ellis
S M Stride, M J Ansell
PLC Non-Executive Directors: D M Owen
A J Hales
Club Secretary: S M Stride
Manager: John Gregory

COLOURS

Home: Claret shirts with light blue
sleeves, white shorts and light blue
stockings
Away: Turquoise shirts, black shorts
and turquoise stockings

NICKNAME

The Villans

20 FACTS

1 Aston Villa were founded during the winter of 1874–75 by a group of cricket fans.

2 In 1876 George Ramsay joined Aston Villa and went on to become their club captain. Ramsay was to lead Villa from a non-league club to one of the country's top sides in less than 10 years.

3 Aston Villa moved to Villa Park in 1897.

4 Aston Villa have been league champions on seven occasions, in 1893–94, 1895–96, 1896–97, 1898–99, 1899–1900, 1909–1910 and 1980–81.

5 They have won the FA Cup seven times and have been runners-up on two occasions. Their victories came in 1887, 1895, 1897, 1905, 1913, 1920 and 1957.

6 They are one of only six clubs to complete the league and FA Cup Double, which they achieved in the 1896–97 season.

7 Villa have also won the Football League Cup five times, a joint record number matched by Liverpool. Their triumphs came in 1961, 1975, 1977, 1994 and 1996.

8 Aston Villa have competed in European competition on 11 occasions. They won the European Cup in 1981–82, but failed in their defence of the trophy the following season. Their other eight European campaigns were in the UEFA Cup in 1975–76, 1977–78, 1983–84, 1990–91, 1993–94, 1994–95, 1996–97, 1997–98 and 1998–99.

9 Villa's 1961 League Cup win made them the first English club to have won all three major domestic trophies.

10 Their record league victory is a 12–2 win over Accrington Stanley on March 12, 1892, but that did not surpass their record FA Cup win of 13–0 against Wednesday Old Athletic on October 30, 1886.

11 Villa's record defeat was against Blackburn Rovers in 1889 when they lost 8–1.

12 Aston Villa hold the record for the most goals scored in the top flight in a single season. The club scored 128 goals in 42 games during the 1930–31 season, of which 49 were scored by "Pongo" Waring. That is a Villa record for the most league goals scored in a season by a single player.

13 Their record attendance is 76,588 against Derby County during an FA Cup sixth-round tie in March 1946.

14 Charlie Aitkin holds Villa's record for the most league appearances. He played 561 games for Villa between 1961 and 1976.

15 After setting the pace for the first half of the season, Aston Villa finished sixth in the 1998–99 Premiership. Their league record was:

Pld	W	D	L	F	A	Pts
38	15	10	13	51	46	55

16 Aston Villa reached the fourth round of the AXA-sponsored FA Cup where they surprisingly lost to Kevin Keegan's Fulham. The Second Division leaders won 2–0 at Villa Park after John Gregory's side had seen off Hull City 3–0 in the third round.

17 Villa's Worthington Cup campaign ended in the third round when they were defeated 4–1 by the holders Chelsea, when both sides fielded under-strength line-ups.

18 Aston Villa reached the second round of the UEFA Cup. They survived an early scare against Stromsgodset of Norway to win their first-round tie 6–2 on aggregate. They secured an excellent 1–0 away victory in the first leg of their second-round tie with Spanish side Celta Vigo, but lost the home leg 3–1.

19 The top goalscorer in all competitions for Aston Villa was Julian Joachim with 16 goals.

20 Villa's disciplinary record was the seventh-best. They committed 485 fouls, earned 63 yellow cards and just three red, with one of those – for Michael Oakes – being expunged on appeal.

SEASON REVIEW

It was a season of two halves for Aston Villa supporters. A stunning start to the campaign put the club in pole position in the title race – but the Midlanders ran out of fuel once 1999 had begun and in the end did not even qualify for Europe.

A goalless draw at Everton on the opening day of the season was to be no indication of the drama about to unfold at Villa Park. First Dwight Yorke confirmed what every Villa fan had feared when he quit the club in favour of Manchester United, despite having recently signed a seven-year contract in 1997–98. He left saying he wanted to play in the Champions League, a comment which incensed Doug Ellis. The Villa chairman said the club had every intention of winning the title and playing in that very competition themselves.

For a long time it looked as if that might actually happen. After conceding just one goal in their first seven games, Villa had 17 points and topped the table by five; and despite crashing out of the UEFA Cup and the Worthington Cup in the early stages, the club were still unbeaten in the Premiership at the beginning of November.

John Gregory, in his first full season of Premiership management, then went straight for the jugular by signing striker Dion Dublin from local rivals Coventry City. Dublin made an immediate impact, scoring five goals in his first two games and finding the net twice more against Liverpool on November 21, as Villa surrendered their unbeaten start to the season in a thrilling match, losing 4–2.

A draw at struggling Forest suggested the cracks were starting to appear and the next three games would be crucial with Manchester United, Chelsea and Arsenal on the agenda. They lost to Chelsea, drew with United, then came from two goals down to beat the Gunners in an extraordinary contest, Dublin again bagging a brace.

But a Boxing Day defeat at Blackburn Rovers lost Villa top spot in the Premiership for the first time. Meanwhile, centre-back Ugo Ehiogu suffered an eye injury at Newcastle which ended his season and Fulham stunned Villa Park by winning 2–0 in the FA Cup. Gregory's men embarked on a disastrous run, losing seven of the next eight Premiership matches and scoring just five goals in the process.

Any hope of winning the title, or even securing a top three place, evaporated – but the side then won three-in-a-row to keep in the hunt for a UEFA Cup spot. Defeat in the last two matches (against Charlton and Arsenal) left Villa in sixth place, wondering what might have been.

Off the field, troubled stars Stan Collymore and Paul Merson gave great cause for concern. Collymore was admitted into a clinic, suffering from stress, while reformed alcoholic Merson admitted publicly that he had started drinking again. These two vastly expensive signings were simply not pulling their weight on the pitch.

That meant some of the younger players were given their chance and the likes of Gareth Barry and Julian Joachim revelled in the chance to shine, Joachim ending up as the club's top scorer.

Villa saw plenty of the ball in 1998–99 and they were not afraid to adopt a direct approach, attempting the second-highest number of long passes in the Premiership. But they made the fewest tackles in the league and the third fewest clearances, which may account for their tendency to leak goals in the second half of the season.

With the likes of England under-21 star Darius Vassell waiting in the wings, though, Villa fans will hope that the club can achieve greater things in 1999–2000.

> ## "We were top for 14 weeks... we are going to have to cope with that kind of pressure better"
>
> John Gregory

ASTON VILLA

DATE	OPPONENT	SCORE	ATT.	BARRY	BOSNICH	CALDERWOOD	CHARLES	COLLYMORE	DELANEY	DRAPER	DUBLIN	EHIOGU	GRAYSON
15.8.98	Everton A	0–0	40,112	90	90	–	90	–	–	s16	–	–	–
23.8.98	Middlesbro H	3–1	29,559	90	90	–	90¹	–	–	s6	–	90	s22
29.8.98	Sheff Wed A	1–0	25,989	90	90	–	90	90	–	77	–	90	s13
9.9.98	Newcastle H	1–0	39,241	90	90	–	90	–	–	68	–	90	s7
12.9.98	Wimbledon H	2–0	32,959	90	90	–	90	–	–	s2	–	90	s16
19.9.98	Leeds Utd A	0–0	33,162	90	90	–	82	–	–	s29	–	90	s8
26.9.98	Derby Co H	1–0	38,007	65	90	–	90□	s2	–	s17	–	90	s25
3.10.98	Coventry A	2–1	22,650	90	90	–	69□	90□	–	–	–	90	s21
17.10.98	West Ham A	0–0	26,002	90	–	–	90	90□	–	–	–	90	–
24.10.98	Leicester H	1–1	39,241	90	–	–	60	90	–	–	–	90¹□	–
7.11.98	Tottenham H	3–2	39,241	90	–	–	–	90¹	–	s8	82²□	90□	–
14.11.98	Southampton A	4–1	15,242	90	–	–	–	78□	–	s12	90³	90	–
21.11.98	Liverpool H	2–4	39,241	90	–	–	s4	68■	–	52	90²	90	–
28.11.98	Nott'm For A	2–2	25,753	90	–	–	–	–	–	–	90	90	–
5.12.98	Man Utd H	1–1	39,241	90	–	–	–	–	–	–	90	90□	–
9.12.98	Chelsea A	1–2	34,765	90□	–	–	–	s8□	–	–	90□	90	–
13.12.98	Arsenal H	3–2	39,217	54	–	–	–	s36	–	–	90²	90	s3
21.12.98	Charlton A	1–0*	20,043	–	–	–	–	55	–	–	90	90	–
26.12.98	Blackburn A	1–2	27,536	–	–	–	–	s21	–	–	90	90	s8
28.12.98	Sheff Wed H	2–1	39,217	90	–	–	–	s37	–	s37	90	90¹	–
9.1.99	Middlesbro A	0–0	34,643	90□	–	–	–	–	–	–	90	90	s20
18.1.99	Everton H	3–0	32,488	90	–	–	–	s44	–	s8	46□	90	–
30.1.99	Newcastle A	1–2	36,766	90	–	–	–	–	–	–	–	40	s50
6.2.99	Blackburn H	1–3	37,404	79	–	–	–	–	–	–	90	–	90
17.2.99	Leeds Utd H	1–2	37,510	66	–	–	–	s19	–	–	71	–	–
21.2.99	Wimbledon A	0–0	15,582	–	–	–	–	s13	–	–	90	–	90□
27.2.99	Coventry H	1–4	38,799	s46	–	–	–	s35	–	s26	90¹	–	90□
10.3.99	Derby Co A	1–2	26,836	90	90	–	–	90□	–	90	90	–	–
13.3.99	Tottenham A	0–1	35,963	90□	90	–	–	90	–	90□	–	–	–
21.3.99	Chelsea H	0–3	39,217	90	90	–	–	74	–	–	74	–	–
2.4.99	West Ham H	0–0	36,813		90	90	–	–	–	90□	90	–	–
6.4.99	Leicester A	2–2	20,652	s14	90	90□	–	–	–	90□	90	–	–
10.4.99	Southampton H	3–0	32,203	s2	90	90	–	–	–	57¹	88¹	–	–
17.4.99	Liverpool A	1–0	44,306	s1	90□	90	–	–	–	90	90	–	–
24.4.99	Nott'm For H	2–0	34,492	s45¹	–	90	–	–	s7	90¹	45	s18	–
1.5.99	Man Utd A	1–2	55,189	–	–	90	–	–	–	68	76	–	–
8.5.99	Charlton H	3–4	37,705	90¹	–	62	–	–	–	62	–	s28	–
16.5.99	Arsenal A	0–1	38,308	–	–	80	–	–	s17	90□	–	90	73

□ Yellow card, ■ Red card, s Substitute, 90³ Goals scored, + Red card later rescinded
*including own goal

1998–99 PREMIERSHIP APPEARANCES

HENDRIE	JOACHIM	MERSON	OAKES	RACHEL	SCIMECA	SOUTHGATE	STONE	TAYLOR	THOMPSON	VASSELL	WATSON	WRIGHT	YORKE	TOTAL
90□	90□	–	–	–	90□	90	–	90	74	–	–	90	90	990
84	82¹	–	–	–	68	90	–	90	90¹	s8	–	90□	–	990
90	90¹	–	–	–	–	90	–	–	90	–	–	90	–	990
90¹□	90	–	–	–	89	90	–	s22□	83	s1	–	90	–	990
90	90	89¹	–	–	s1	90	–	88¹	74	–	–	90	–	990
90	90	90	–	–	–	90	–	90□	61	–	–	90□	–	990
90	88	90¹	–	–	–	90	–	90	73	–	–	90	–	990
90	s21	69	–	–	–	90	–	90²□	90□	–	–	90	–	990
90	–	90	90	–	–	90	–	90	90□	–	–	90	–	990
90	s30	82	90	–	–	90	–	90	90	–	s8	90	–	990
90	–	90	90	–	–	90	–	90□	–	–	–	90	90	990
90	s7	83¹	90	–	–	90	–	90	–	–	–	90	90	990
90	s15	90	90	–	–	90	–	–	s38	–	86	75	–	968
90□	90²	46	90	–	–	90□	–	90	s44	–	–	90	90	990
90	90¹	–	90	–	–	90	–	90	90	–	90	90	90	990
90¹□	82	–	90	–	–	90	–	90	90□	–	90	90	–	990
90	87¹	–	90	–	–	90	–	90	90□	–	90	90□	–	990
90	90	–	90	–	–	90□	–	90□	90□	–	90□	90	–	990
55	82	–	55■+	s35	90¹□	90	–	69	90	–	90	90	–	955
90	90	–	90	–	53	90¹	–	53	–	–	90	90	–	990
90	90	–	90	–	70	90	–	90	–	–	90	90	–	990
82	90²	s31¹	90	–	90	90	–	59	–	–	90	90	–	990
90□	90	90¹□	90	–	90	90	–	90	–	s6	84	90	–	990
–	90¹	90	90	–	90	90	–	90	s11	–	90	90	–	990
90	90	90	90	–	90¹	90	–	90	s24	–	90	90	–	990
90	77	90	90	–	90	90	–	90	–	–	90	90	–	990
90□	90	90	90	–	90	90□	–	29	–	–	44	90	–	990
90□	s14	90□	–	–	76	90□	–	–	90¹	–	–	90	–	990
90□	s22	68	–	–	90	90	90□	–	90	–	–	90	–	990
83	s16	s16	–	–	90	90	90	s7	90□	–	90	90	–	990
–	90	s3	–	–	–	90	90	90	87	–	90	90	–	990
90¹	90¹	–	–	–	–	90	90	90	–	–	76	90	–	990
s85	90¹	s33	–	–	–	90	90	90	5	–	90	90	–	990
70	89	s20	–	–	–	90	90	90¹	–	–	90	90	–	990
–	90	90	90	–	–	90	83	90	–	–	72	90	–	990
–	90¹	90	90	–	–	90	90	90□	s22	s14	90	90	–	990
–	90²	90	90	–	–	90	90	90□	–	s28	89■	90	–	989
–	90	90	90	–	90□	90□	s10	–	–	s17	73□	90	–	990

THE MANAGER

JOHN GREGORY

When Brian Little parted company with the club in February 1998 after four years, Aston Villa fans hoped the club would replace him with a big-name to bring back the good times.

In truth, Wycombe Wanderers boss John Gregory, who was appointed 20 years after quitting Villa Park as a player, was hardly the man most supporters would have gone for. But few are questioning the decision now.

Gregory won six England caps in a distinguished playing career as a central midfielder, enjoying spells with Northampton Town, Brighton and Hove Albion, QPR, Derby County – and, of course, Aston Villa.

At just 45, he is one of the Carling Premiership's youngest managers and for a long time, in 1998–99, it looked as if he might lead the Villans to the title in his first full season. In the end, though, a miserable run of 12 games without a win from January to April put paid to any such thoughts and the side didn't even automatically qualify for a place in the UEFA Cup.

Thanks to Gregory's efforts, Villa could well be challenging for honours again in 1999–2000 after several seasons in footballing limbo.

LEAGUE POSITION

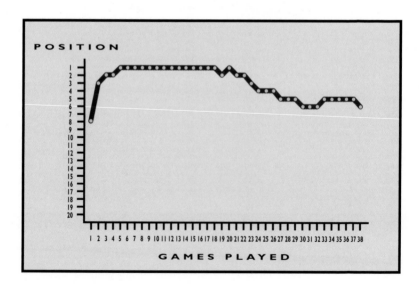

THE GOALS

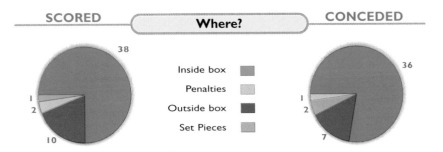

SCORED — Where? — CONCEDED

Inside box
Penalties
Outside box
Set Pieces

Aston Villa were one of only five teams to register double figures for goals scored from outside the box, thanks to the long-range accuracy of players such as Paul Merson and Julian Joachim. But although the side boasts talented free kick-takers, Villa scored via set-pieces just once. John Gregory's men conceded 80.4% of goals from inside the area, slightly below the Premiership average for goals scored within the 18-yard box.

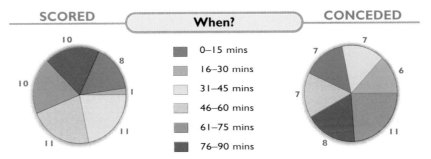

SCORED — When? — CONCEDED

0–15 mins
16–30 mins
31–45 mins
46–60 mins
61–75 mins
76–90 mins

Villa were deadliest either side of half-time, scoring 44% of all their goals in the 15 minutes preceding and following the break. They were also extremely quick out of the blocks, scoring eight goals in the first quarter of an hour, which no other team bettered. Villa conceded slightly more goals in the second halves of their matches, but were strong in the final 15 minutes, letting only eight goals in across the whole of the 1998–99 Premiership season.

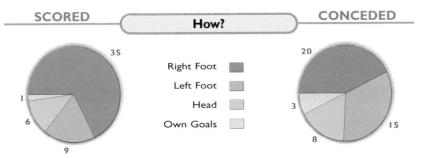

SCORED — How? — CONCEDED

Right Foot
Left Foot
Head
Own Goals

John Gregory's strikers scored 68.6% of their goals with the right foot, a higher proportion than any other Premiership side. Despite the presence of Dion Dublin in attack, Villa scored with only six headers from their total of 51 league goals.

The Villa defence dealt efficiently with high balls, though, restricting the opposition to eight headed goals. But the defence also gifted three own-goals to their opponents, a total matched only by Wimbledon and Southampton.

ASTON VILLA

	BARRY	CALDERWOOD	CHARLES	COLLYMORE	DELANEY	DRAPER	DUBLIN	EHIOGU	GRAYSON	HENDRIE
APPEARANCES										
Start	27	8	10	11	0	13	24	23	4	31
Sub	5	0	1	9	1	10	0	2	11	1
Minutes on pitch	2442	682	845	1120	24	1175	2012	2066	536	2799
GOAL ATTEMPTS										
Goals	2	0	1	1	0	2	11	2	0	3
Shots on target	5	0	2	12	0	7	33	6	2	14
Shots off target	5	0	1	13	0	7	46	12	1	20
Shooting accuracy %	50%	0%	67%	48%	0%	50%	42%	33%	67%	41%
PASSING										
Goal assists	1	0	0	3	0	0	2	1	0	6
Long passes	212	31	103	50	3	62	46	115	21	130
Short passes	871	121	269	403	13	562	783	579	178	1168
PASS COMPLETION										
Own half %	91%	94%	87%	86%	100%	91%	88%	92%	89%	89%
Opposition half %	67%	47%	60%	65%	60%	74%	67%	69%	73%	72%
CROSSING										
Total crosses	15	0	31	20	0	35	8	2	6	102
Cross completion %	47%	0%	10%	30%	0%	29%	0%	0%	33%	32%
DRIBBLING										
Dribbles & runs	46	0	41	37	0	40	9	14	9	113
Dribble completion %	78%	0%	71%	76%	0%	75%	33%	64%	67%	74%
DEFENDING										
Tackles made	74	17	18	16	2	39	54	85	14	102
Tackles won %	68%	82%	72%	38%	100%	64%	59%	61%	57%	50%
Blocks	22	7	3	2	0	1	4	20	5	12
Clearances	224	79	36	12	1	19	45	320	38	37
Interceptions	30	9	7	4	0	17	6	29	2	23
DISCIPLINE										
Fouls	17	15	7	26	0	27	53	30	13	37
Offside	0	0	1	27	0	2	15	1	1	11
Yellow cards	3	1	2	5	0	4	4	3	2	8
Red cards	0	0	0	1	0	0	0	0	0	0

GOALKEEPER NAME	START/ (SUB)	TIME ON PITCH	GOALS CONCEDED	MINS/GOALS CONCEDED	SAVES MADE	SAVES/ SHOTS
BOSNICH	15	1350	10	135	55	85%
OAKES	23	2035	35	58.1	75	68%
RACHEL	0 (1)	35	1	35	0	0%

PLAYERS' STATISTICS

	JOACHIM	MERSON	SCIMECA	SOUTHGATE	STONE	TAYLOR	THOMPSON	VASSELL	WATSON	WRIGHT	YORKE	TOTAL	RANK
	29	21	16	38	9	31	20	0	26	38	1		
	7	5	2	0	1	2	5	6	1	0	0		
	2692	1890	1382	3420	813	2667	1766	74	2242	3405	90		
	14	5	2	1	0	4	2	0	0	0	0	51*	6th
	26	21	3	3	3	9	11	1	5	3	1	167	=15th
	25	18	5	9	5	17	23	2	6	7	0	222	13th
	51%	54%	38%	25%	38%	35%	32%	33%	45%	30%	100%	43%	17th
	4	2	0	0	3	5	3	1	3	2	0	36	7th
	19	127	58	381	35	45	165	2	222	277	1	2105	2nd
	624	757	419	838	292	889	734	30	730	1398	22	11680	8th
	82%	86%	89%	89%	85%	89%	91%	100%	86%	90%	88%	89%	8th
	73%	76%	75%	59%	71%	79%	74%	60%	66%	74%	86%	71%	8th
	40	54	5	1	48	9	91	0	74	129	0	670	14th
	33%	37%	0%	0%	25%	11%	30%	0%	34%	29%	0%	29%	8th
	115	57	20	41	35	19	46	6	101	35	8	792	16th
	65%	77%	75%	78%	69%	58%	61%	50%	75%	94%	13%	72%	9th
	54	27	37	131	29	134	60	2	82	77	2	1056	20th
	48%	41%	59%	62%	52%	62%	60%	100%	63%	52%	50%	59%	17th
	2	1	9	39	4	12	4	0	17	23	0	188	13th
	8	4	94	537	13	72	26	0	142	178	0	1902	17th
	9	10	22	72	6	27	9	1	18	41	2	345	8th
	44	14	24	40	19	48	31	6	12	19	2	485	14th
	34	11	8	0	5	9	0	3	1	2	1	132	12th
	1	2	3	5	1	7	6	0	2	3	0	63	=13th
	0	0	0	0	0	0	0	0	1	0	0	2	=14th

*Including one own goal

CROSSES CAUGHT	CROSSES PUNCHED	CROSSES NOT CLAIMED	CATCH SUCCESS	THROWS/ SHORT KICKS	% COMPLETION	LONG KICKS	% COMPLETION
43	11	5	96%	91	97%	332	33%
69	11	4	99%	99	99%	507	29%
1	1	0	100%	1	0%	10	30%

PLAYER OF THE SEASON

PLAYER	INDEX SCORE
UGO EHIOGU	939
Gareth Southgate	897
Dion Dublin	882
Steve Watson	809
Gareth Barry	754
Paul Merson	749
Alan Thompson	747
Alan Wright	712
Lee Hendrie	711
Julian Joachim	708

It would be unfair to attribute Aston Villa's retreat from the title race in the second half of the 1998–99 Carling Premiership season to any one factor.

But there is little doubt that the long-term loss of Ugo Ehiogu from the defence was instrumental in the side's dramatic dip in form in the second half of the campaign.

His importance to the club could not be more graphically illustrated than in the Carling Opta Season Index, in which Ehiogu is Villa's top-rated player.

It is unlikely anyone at the club could have realized he would have been so conspicuous by his absence, after his accidental collision with Alan Shearer at Newcastle left his season in tatters. Pundits waiting for Villa to fall had often remarked on the club's lack of strength in depth – and the hole in the back-line left by Ehiogu's enforced absence proved too big to fill.

Villa skipper Gareth Southgate was the second-highest rated player after a consistent campaign alongside Ehiogu. The fact that the team conceded only one goal in their first seven league games is testament to the effectiveness of their defensive partnership.

Goal machine Dion Dublin amassed some mammoth scores when he first arrived at Villa Park, thanks to nine goals in his first seven games, helping him to third place in the Villa top 10. New signing Steve Watson and teenage defender Gareth Barry impressed greatly and performed as well as John Gregory could have hoped for.

Paul Merson's problems were well-documented throughout the season but his performances when he did play thrilled the supporters. Top scorer Julian Joachim featured only in 10th place. He tended to be Villa's outlet on the break, meaning he spent long periods of matches not involved in the play, restricting his opportunities to pick up Opta points.

FIVE OF THE BEST

After a sensational first half of the 1998–99 season, Villa eventually fell away from the Championship picture and had to settle for a top six place. But manager John Gregory has given his side a taste for the big time and the Villa players have shown they are close to having what it takes to compete with the very best in England.

TOP GOALSCORERS

	GOALS	GOALS/SHOTS
JULIAN JOACHIM	14	27%
Dion Dublin	11	14%
Paul Merson	5	13%
Ian Taylor	4	15%
Lee Hendrie	3	9%

Livewire striker Julian Joachim finished as Villa top scorer with 14 goals, hitting the back of the net with more than a quarter of all his shots – an incredible effort. Joachim has had to bide his time at Villa, but he emerged in 1998–99 as one of the league's deadliest front men. Dion Dublin, arguably Gregory's best signing, scored 11 times, including seven in his first three games. No one else reached double figures, with mercurial Paul Merson third after bagging five league strikes.

Villa, with their direct, pacy wing-backs, played fewer passes than many of the sides in the Premiership. Their three central midfielders saw most of the ball. Alan Wright, Lee Hendrie and Ian Taylor all figure in the top five, with ever-present Wright having made more passes than anyone else. Defenders Gareth Southgate and Gareth Barry both had impressive seasons, with Barry completing almost eight out of 10 passes in 1998–99. Southgate's lower pass completion rate can be attributed to his willingness to look for the strikers with the long ball.

TOP PASSERS

	SUCC PASSES	COMPLETION
ALAN WRIGHT	1,334	80%
Lee Hendrie	999	77%
Gareth Southgate	918	75%
Gareth Barry	860	79%
Ian Taylor	764	82%

TOP TACKLERS

	WON	SUCCESS
IAN TAYLOR	83	62%
Gareth Southgate	81	62%
Steve Watson	52	63%
Ugo Ehiogu	52	61%
Lee Hendrie	51	50%

Hardly renowned for their physical approach to the game, Villa won fewer tackles than any Premiership team in the 1998–99 season. Most top defenders will look to win two-thirds of their challenges, but Southgate, Watson and Ehiogu were all below this figure. Nonetheless, Southgate made three last man saving tackles and cleared four shots off the line in a fine personal season for the Villa skipper. Top tackler was experienced midfield man Ian Taylor, who won 62% of his 83 challenges.

Villa can be proud of their disciplinary record in 1998–99, which saw just three players sent off all season – and Michael Oakes's red card was expunged. Suspensions were a minor problem for John Gregory, with only Lee Hendrie collecting eight league bookings. Ian Taylor was the Villa villain, conceding 48 fouls and collecting seven yellow cards. Despite his red card in the home defeat by Liverpool, there is no place in the top five for perennial media "bad boy" Stan Collymore, who conceded only 26 fouls in the 1998–99 Premiership.

DISCIPLINE

	POINTS	FOULS & CARDS
IAN TAYLOR	69	48F, 7Y, 0R
Dion Dublin	65	53F, 4Y, 0R
Lee Hendrie	61	37F, 8Y, 0R
Gareth Southgate	55	40F, 5Y, 0R
Alan Thompson	49	31F, 6Y, 0R

ACTION	BARRY	COLLYMORE	DRAPER	DUBLIN	EHIOGU	HENDRIE	MERSON	OAKES	SOUTHGATE	TAYLOR	WATSON	WRIGHT	TOTAL	TOTTENHAM
Time on pitch	90	90	8	82	90	90	90	90	90	90	90	90	990	990
GOALS														
Goal	–	1	–	2	–	–	–	–	–	–	–	–	3	2
Shot on target	–	–	–	–	1	–	1	–	–	–	–	1	3	3
Shot off target	–	3	–	3	–	–	1	–	–	–	–	–	7	7
Blocked shot	–	–	–	–	–	1	1	–	–	–	–	–	2	–
Own goal	–	–	–	–	–	–	–	–	–	–	–	–	–	–
PASSES														
Pass to own player	29	20	1	20	22	35	21	–	25	27	16	31	247	299
Pass to opposition	15	14	1	8	7	7	9	–	15	5	9	11	101	102
Cross to own player	–	2	–	–	–	–	1	–	1	–	1	2	7	7
Cross to opposition player	–	3	–	–	–	4	–	–	–	–	2	6	15	24
Goal assist	–	–	–	–	–	1	–	–	–	–	–	–	1	1
Pass completion %	66%	56%	50%	71%	76%	77%	71%	0%	63%	84%	61%	66%	69%	71%
TACKLES & CLEARANCES														
Tackle	2	–	1	4	1	9	3	–	3	8	2	2	35	34
Clearances, blocks and interceptions	5	1	3	3	14	2	–	–	11	3	5	3	48	46
DRIBBLES & RUNS														
Dribble ball retained	1	–	–	–	1	1	1	–	1	–	3	–	8	23
Dribbles ball lost	–	–	–	–	–	–	–	–	–	–	–	1	1	7
Dribble success %	100%	0%	0%	0%	100%	100%	100%	0%	100%	0%	100%	0%	89%	77%
DISCIPLINE														
Fouls	–	1	1	1	–	–	–	–	1	2	–	1	7	13
Penalty conceded	–	–	–	–	–	–	–	–	–	–	–	–	–	–
Free kick - offside	–	5	–	2	–	–	2	–	–	–	–	1	10	2
Yellow cards	–	–	–	1	–	–	–	–	1	–	–	1	3	1
Red cards	–	–	–	–	–	–	–	–	–	–	–	–	–	–
GOALKEEPERS														
Distribution to own player	–	–	–	–	–	–	–	12	–	–	–	–	12	17
Distribution to opposition player	–	–	–	–	–	–	–	19	–	–	–	–	19	14
Goalkeeper distribution%	0%	0%	0%	0%	0%	0%	0%	39%	0%	0%	0%	0%	39%	55%
Save	–	–	–	–	–	–	–	3	–	–	–	–	3	3
Ball caught	–	–	–	–	–	–	–	2	–	–	–	–	2	7
Ball dropped	–	–	–	–	–	–	–	–	–	–	–	–	–	–
Goal conceded	–	–	–	–	–	–	–	2	–	–	–	–	2	3

Aston Villa sat proudly at the top of the Carling Premiership table when Tottenham arrived at Villa Park. The team were playing well and manager John Gregory had just added a new attacking threat in Dion Dublin, who was making his debut. Spurs were showing signs of recovery after a nightmare start to the 1998–99 season.

November 7, 1998

3–2

ASTON VILLA
TOTTENHAM HOTSPUR

Dublin took just half an hour to notch his first goal in a Villa shirt. Alan Wright's corner was miscontrolled by John Scales, and the ball went straight to the former Coventry City striker, who could not miss from four yards out.

Five minutes later, Dublin scored again. Tottenham suffered an horrendous defensive mix-up when Scales and Darren Anderton left the ball to one another and Dublin stole in to roll the ball under Espen Baardsen, making it 2–0 to the home side.

Just two minutes of the second half had elapsed before Villa further extended their lead. Another defensive blunder presented the ball to Lee Hendrie. He fed Stan Collymore, who held off Sol Campbell and rifled a shot into the top right-hand corner, leaving Baardsen helpless.

Tottenham rallied, and in the 57th minute Anderton's 30-yard blockbuster came back off the underside of the crossbar, on to the goal line and out, with Michael Oakes just a spectator. It was a close shave for Villa, who had taken their feet off the gas somewhat after scoring their third goal.

On the hour mark, David Ginola's dribble into the box was abruptly halted when Ugo Ehiogu bundled him over. It looked more like obstruction than a foul, but referee Rob Harris pointed to the spot. Anderton took the responsibility and the plaudits as he smashed his penalty past Oakes to make it 3–1.

The home fans were starting to get jittery with 15 minutes to go. Spurs were on top and piling the pressure on. An Anderton corner from the left was flicked on by Allan Nielsen for Ramon Vega to stab a volley home from close range. Tottenham were back in it at 3–2, with a quarter of an hour remaining.

Virtually straight after Vega's goal, Villa sprang into action and hit the back of the net again. Merson hooked a cross into the box, Collymore flicked on and the ball found its way to Dublin, who buried the shot from inside the six-yard box. The big striker thought he had sealed a hat-trick on his debut, but the assistant referee's flag ruled the goal out for a marginal offside decision against the big striker.

Dublin departed with eight minutes to go to a standing ovation from the Villa crowd. His goals had earned Villa the three points – and kept the club at the top of the table.

The momentum swung back and forth in an exciting, end-to-end match. Villa dominated for the first 60 minutes, and Spurs were on top for the last half-hour. The Carling Opta stats show Spurs actually had more possession and out-passed Villa 299 to 247, but Villa had the better of the chances, scoring three and hitting the target three more times. Tottenham scored twice and troubled Oakes on three more occasions, but it was not enough to cap what would have been a memorable comeback.

ACTION	BARRY	COLLYMORE	DUBLIN	EHIOGU	GRAYSON	HENDRIE	JOACHIM	OAKES	SOUTHGATE	TAYLOR	THOMPSON	WATSON	WRIGHT	TOTAL	ARSENAL
Time on pitch	54	36	90	90	3	90	87	90	90	90	90	90	90	990	990
GOALS															
Goal	–	–	2	–	–	–	1	–	–	–	–	–	–	3	2
Shot on target	–	–	–	1	–	2	–	–	–	–	–	–	–	3	2
Shot off target	–	3	5	–	–	–	2	–	–	–	1	–	–	12	4
Blocked shot	–	–	–	–	–	1	–	–	–	–	–	–	–	2	1
Own goal	–	–	–	–	–	–	–	–	–	–	–	–	–	–	–
PASSES															
Pass to own player	14	12	33	15	1	23	9	–	15	25	35	20	24	226	232
Pass to opposition	3	6	6	8	–	8	4	–	5	5	7	12	10	75	78
Cross to own player	–	–	–	–	–	1	–	–	–	1	2	2	–	6	6
Cross to opposition player	–	–	–	–	–	–	–	–	1	–	5	1	2	10	11
Goal assist	–	–	–	–	–	–	–	–	–	–	2	–	–	3	2
Pass completion %	82%	67%	85%	65%	50%	74%	71%	0%	75%	81%	76%	63%	67%	73%	73%
TACKLES & CLEARANCES															
Tackle	2	2	1	–	–	1	2	–	4	7	5	6	3	34	26
Clearances, blocks and interceptions	10	–	2	18	1	4	–	1	17	3	3	9	9	77	88
DRIBBLES & RUNS															
Dribble ball retained	1	1	–	–	–	2	3	–	2	–	–	–	1	11	14
Dribbles ball lost	1	–	1	1	–	3	1	–	–	–	2	3	–	11	13
Dribble success %	50%	100%	0%	50%	0%	40%	75%	0%	100%	0%	0%	0%	100%	50%	52%
DISCIPLINE															
Fouls	1	–	1	3	–	2	2	–	2	4	1	–	1	18	10
Penalty conceded	–	–	1	–	–	–	–	–	–	–	–	–	–	–	–
Free kick - offside	–	–	–	–	–	–	2	–	–	–	–	–	–	3	4
Yellow cards	–	–	–	–	–	–	–	–	–	–	–	–	1	3	3
Red cards	–	–	–	–	–	–	–	–	–	–	–	–	–	–	–
GOALKEEPERS															
Distribution to own player	–	–	–	–	–	–	–	7	–	–	–	–	–	7	12
Distribution to opposition player	–	–	–	–	–	–	–	14	–	–	–	–	–	14	17
Goalkeeper distribution%	–	–	–	–	–	–	–	33%	–	–	–	–	–	33%	41%
Save	–	–	–	–	–	–	–	2	–	–	–	–	–	2	3
Ball caught	–	–	–	–	–	–	–	3	–	–	–	–	–	3	3
Ball dropped	–	–	–	–	–	–	–	–	–	–	–	–	–	–	1
Goal conceded	–	–	–	–	–	–	–	2	–	–	–	–	–	2	3

The league leaders had just suffered their second defeat of the season against title rivals Chelsea — and had failed to beat Manchester United at home the previous weekend — when they entertained Arsenal at Villa Park. Pundits were questioning Villa's ability to mix it with the Premiership elite.

December 13, 1998

3–2

ASTON VILLA

ARSENAL

Despite being without four key players and not having won any of their four previous League matches, Arsenal started the game brightly and were rewarded with a goal in the 14th minute.

A long kick by Dave Seaman was flicked on by Fredrik Ljungberg and then by Nicolas Anelka into the path of Dennis Bergkamp. The Dutchman surprised Michael Oakes with a brilliant shot from the edge of the area that found the bottom corner of the net.

Villa struggled to get back into the game and on the stroke of half-time Arsenal doubled their lead. A goal-kick by Seaman was controlled by Bergkamp, who played a succession of one-twos with Anelka to cut a swathe through the Villa defence before neatly slotting the ball home.

Aston Villa exerted more pressure at the start of the second half, particularly after John Gregory brought on Stan Collymore for Gareth Barry and changed formation from 5–3–2 to 4–3–3. Within 10 minutes, Villa were level.

A long ball by Gareth Southgate was flicked on by Collymore to Lee Hendrie, bursting into the penalty area. A lucky break of the ball helped the youngster find Julian Joachim, who in turn had the simple task of finding the net.

Just three minutes later, the ball broke to Joachim on the right flank. The Villa striker crossed to Dion Dublin whose shot deflected off Steve Bould to Alan Thompson. The Villa midfielder's mis-hit volley ran directly back into the path of Dublin, who finished from close range.

Villa had the bit between their teeth now and in the 83rd minute a corner by Alan Thompson was misjudged by Keown, leaving Dublin with time to bring the ball down and fire it into the net to send the Villa faithful into raptures.

It was the proverbial game of two halves, though both sides had chances to add to their tally. Villa scored three times from six shots on target and 20 in total. The Gunners had nine efforts with four of those on target.

Possession was fairly even with both sides completing 73% of around 300 passes each, but Villa's crossing caused problems to an Arsenal defence missing Tony Adams. They connected with six out of 16 crosses, including the corner that led directly to the third goal.

Man of the match was Dion Dublin, whose performance proved crucial in securing all three points. His Carling Opta points score of 1,654 was earned through scoring two goals, attempting five other shots that were all off target and completing 33 out of 39 passes during the match.

At this stage of the season, no one would have predicted that Arsenal would be the team which was to go on to mount a Championship challenge, while Villa's title chances fell by the wayside.

BLACKBURN ROVERS 1998–99

Back row (from left to right): David Worrell, Jeff Kenna, James Thomas, Tore Pedersen, John Filan, Tim Flowers, Alan Fettis, Darren Peacock, Stephane Henchoz, Jason Wilcox, Gary Croft.

Middle row: Alan Whitehead (Kit Manager), Terry Darracott (Reserve Team Manager), David Dunn, Marlon Broomes, Martin Dahlin, Chris Sutton, Martin Taylor, Tim Sherwood (now Tottenham Hotspur), Garry Flitcroft, Kevin Davies, Jimmy Corbett, Sebastien Perez (no longer at club), Arnoldo Longaretti (Fitness Coach), Colin Lancaster (Masseur).

Front row: Roy Tunks (Goalkeeping Coach), Derek Fazackerley (First Team Coach), Billy McKinlay, Anders Andersson, Callum Davidson, Roy Hodgson (Manager – no longer at club), Tony Parkes (Assistant Manager), Damien Duff, Damien Johnson, Kevin Gallacher, Mark Taylor, Alan Smith (both Physiotherapists).

BLACKBURN ROVERS

ADDRESS

Ewood Park, Blackburn,
Lancashire BB2 4JF

CONTACT NUMBERS

Telephone: 01254 698888
Fax: 01254 671042
Ticket Office: 01254 671666
(Freephone 08080 101010)
24hr Information: 09068 121179
The Roverstore: 01254 672333
(Freephone 08080 202020)
e-mail: enquiries@rovers.co.uk
Website: www.rovers.co.uk

SPONSORS

CIS

FANZINES

Loadsamoney

KEY PERSONNEL

Club President: W H Bancroft
Senior Vice-President: J Walker
Chairman: R D Coar BSc
Chief Executive: J O Williams
Vice Chairman: R L Matthewman
Directors: R D Coar
R L Matthewman, K C Lee
G R Root FCMA, I R Stanners
J O Williams, T M Finn
Club Secretary: T M Finn
Manager: Brian Kidd

COLOURS

Home: Blue and white
halved shirts, white shorts
and blue stockings
Away: Yellow shirts, blue
shorts and yellow stockings

NICKNAME

Rovers

20 FACTS

1 Blackburn Rovers were originally founded in 1875 by a group of public school old boys.

2 Blackburn Rovers have been league champions on three different occasions, most recently winning the FA Carling Premiership in the 1994–95 season. Previously, they won the title in 1911–12 and 1913–14.

3 They have won the FA Cup six times – in 1884, 1885, 1886, 1890, 1891 and 1928 – and have played in a total of eight finals, the last occasion being in 1960.

4 The club still holds the record for the longest unbeaten run in the FA Cup, going unbeaten for 24 matches between December 1883 and November 1886.

5 Blackburn Rovers have never won the Football League Cup. The closest they have come to reaching the final was in 1962 and 1993, when they were eliminated at the semi-final stage on each occasion.

6 Rovers have entered European competition just three times. They played in the UEFA Cup in the 1994–95 and 1998–99 seasons and in the Champions League in 1995–96, winning just one match in 10 ties.

7 Their record league victory was a 9–0 win over Middlesbrough in November 1954, but that did not quite match their overall record where they beat Rossendale 11–0 in the 1884 FA Cup.

8 Blackburn's record defeat was an 8–0 loss to Arsenal in Division One in 1933.

9 Chris Sutton became the UK's first ever £5 million player when he joined Blackburn Rovers from Norwich City in July 1994.

10 Rovers' record transfer fee received was £15 million from Newcastle United for Alan Shearer in July 1996. This fee is also a British record (correct to 16 June 1999).

11 Simon Garner holds Blackburn's record for the most league goals. He scored 168 times between 1978 and 1992, though none of them were scored in the top flight.

12 Bob Crompton holds the record as Blackburn's most capped player. During his time with the club he gained 41 caps for England between 1902 and 1914.

13 The 1994–95 season saw Alan Shearer equal the Premiership record by scoring 34 league goals in a single season.

14 Blackburn Rovers' record attendance was in 1929 when they played Bolton Wanderers in an FA Cup sixth-round tie. They packed 62,522 fans into Ewood Park.

15 Blackburn Rovers finished 19th in the 1998–99 Premiership and were relegated to Division One. Their league record was:

Pld	W	D	L	F	A	Pts
38	7	14	17	38	52	35

16 Brian Kidd's side reached the fifth round of the 1998–99 AXA-sponsored FA Cup where they lost to Newcastle United 1–0 in a replay after drawing 0–0 at St James's Park. In previous rounds they had defeated Charlton Athletic 2–0 and Sunderland 1–0 at Ewood Park.

17 Blackburn were knocked out of the Worthington Cup by finalists Leicester City at the quarter-final stage, losing 1–0 at Filbert Street. Rovers reached that stage with consecutive away victories at Crewe Alexandra (1–0) and then at Newcastle United (4–2 on penalties after a 1–1 draw).

18 Blackburn's European adventure ended at the first hurdle. A 1–0 home defeat in the UEFA Cup first round first leg against Olympique Lyonnais was followed by a 2–2 draw in France, thus eliminating Roy Hodgson's side from the competition.

19 The top goalscorers for Blackburn were Kevin Gallacher and, despite only joining in February, Ashley Ward, with five Premiership goals each.

20 Blackburn will be keen to improve their disciplinary record which saw them commit 530 fouls, earn 80 yellow cards and see red on eight occasions, which was the fifth-worst record in the league.

SEASON REVIEW

On May 12, 1999, Blackburn Rovers drew 0–0 with Manchester United and were relegated. It completed one of the most remarkable falls from grace in the history of the Carling Premiership.

Having pumped an estimated £100 million into the club he grew up supporting, Benefactor Jack Walker is now faced with the knowledge that he is back where he started.

The prospect of relegation seemed impossible at the start of the season – but the signs were there for all to see. Under the management of Roy Hodgson, Rovers had qualified for Europe in 1997–98 but had taken just 18 points from their final 20 games.

Losing inspirational captain Colin Hendry to Glasgow Rangers did not bode well for the new season, but there was hope that new signing Kevin Davies would score enough goals at the other end of the pitch to cover for any defensive shortcomings.

The season started with a 0–0 draw at home to Derby and was followed by a 1–0 defeat at Leeds. The first win came against Leicester City, but that was followed by three straight losses.

The strain was beginning to tell on Roy Hodgson. A 4–3 reverse by Chelsea was the first time that the cracks began to show – but with injuries piling up and Davies yet to score, the pressure was really mounting.

With just nine points on the board by the time Southampton made the visit to Ewood Park in late November, Hodgson's reign was almost at an end. Two goals from two shots on target gave Saints a 2–0 victory and left Rovers rooted to the bottom of the table. Hodgson parted company with the club immediately after the match.

Tony Parkes stepped into the breach for the 2–0 defeat at Liverpool but Jack Walker was determined to get a big name in to save the club he loved. Enter the highly respected Brian Kidd.

The former Manchester United man's impact was immediate. Relegation rivals Charlton were beaten 1–0 and, much to the relief of everyone at the club, the goal was scored by Kevin Davies.

Kidd realised that a combination of injuries and high-profile departures had left the team in a weak position, and he turned to Jack Walker for the funds needed to keep the club afloat. In all, Walker opened his wallet to the tune of almost £19 million, but the men Kidd brought in were simply not good enough to replace those who had either left the club or were consigned to the treatment table.

The departure of club captain Tim Sherwood to Tottenham in January was a fatal blow. Blackburn's midfield, already weakened by the loss of Garry Flitcroft and Billy McKinlay, was reduced to rubble and opponents found they were able to take advantage.

The team won just five out of 23 games under Kidd, and that was never going to be enough to stay up. Kevin Davies, Matt Jansen, Nathan Blake and Ashley Ward were all willing competitors, but none carried the same threat as a fit Chris Sutton. Rovers finished with just 38 goals, the third-worst figure in the 1998–99 Carling Premiership.

Despite coming under intense pressure at the back, the defence completed only 1,860 clearances – the third fewest in the Premiership – and made far fewer interceptions than any other team. Had it not been for the acrobatics of goalkeeper and Player of the Season John Filan, the club would have conceded even more goals and been relegated to Division One even earlier.

Keeping key players like Chris Sutton and Stephane Henchoz at Ewood Park will prove a real test this summer. But getting back into the Premiership will be Brian Kidd's toughest task.

> **"The Premiership is the only place to be. It is history now and we have to get on with it"**
>
> **Brian Kidd**

BLACKBURN ROVERS

DATE	OPPONENT	SCORE	ATT.	BLAKE	BROOMES	CARSLEY	CROFT	DAHLIN	DAILLY	DAVIDSON	DAVIES	DUFF	DUNN	FETTIS	FILAN
15.8.98	Derby Co H	0–0	24,235	–	–	–	–	s12	–	90	78	s32	–	–	90
24.8.98	Leeds Utd A	0–1	30,541	–	–	–	–	s12	–	90	78	–	–	–	90
29.8.98	Leicester H	1–0	22,544	–	–	–	–	–	s19	90	s6	71	–	–	–
9.9.98	Tottenham A	1–2	28,338	–	–	–	–	–	–	90	90	–	s21	–	–
12.9.98	Sheff Wed A	0–3	20,846	–	–	–	90□	–	90	–	90□	61	–	–	–
21.9.98	Chelsea H	3–4	23,113	–	–	–	–	90	90	90	–	–	–	–	–
26.9.98	Everton A	0–0	36,404	–	–	–	–	78▪	90	90	–	70	s10	–	–
3.10.98	West Ham H	3–0	25,213	–	–	–	–	s25	90	90¹	–	77	–	–	–
17.10.98	Middlesbro A	1–2	34,413	–	–	–	–	–	–	90□	73	90	s17	–	–
25.10.98	Arsenal H	1–2	27,012	–	–	–	–	–	–	90	s44	90	–	–	–
31.10.98	Wimbledon A	1–1	12,526	s13	–	–	–	–	s24	90	77	90	–	–	–
7.11.98	Coventry H	1–2	23,779	90	–	–	–	–	90	90	s45	90	–	–	–
14.11.98	Man Utd A	2–3	55,198	90¹	–	–	s35	–	90	55	77□	51	–	–	90
21.11.98	Southampton H	0–2	22,812	90	–	–	53	–	90	–	s17	90	–	–	90
29.11.98	Liverpool A	0–2	41,753	90	–	–	–	–	90	90□	s3	90	90	–	90
5.12.98	Charlton H	1–0	22,568	90	s6	–	90	–	90	90	s48¹	90	84□	90	–
12.12.98	Newcastle H	0–0	27,569	90	–	–	–	–	90	90	90□	–	–	90	–
19.12.98	Nott'm For A	2–2	22,013	90²	–	–	–	–	90	90	–	s1	–	–	90
26.12.98	Aston Villa H	2–1	27,536	–	s45□	–	–	–	90	90□	s24□	s16	–	–	90
28.12.98	Leicester A	1–1	21,083	–	s70	–	–	–	20	90	90	–	–	–	90
9.1.99	Leeds Utd H	1–0	27,620	–	90	–	–	–	–	90	–	26	s64	–	90□
16.1.99	Derby Co A	0–1	27,386	90	90□	–	–	–	–	90	–	–	–	–	90
30.1.99	Tottenham H	1–1	29,643	–	90	–	–	–	–	90	s27□	62	85□	–	90□
6.2.99	Aston Villa A	3–1*	37,404	–	90	–	–	–	–	90	–	s10	90¹	–	90
17.2.99	Chelsea A	1–1	34,822	–	85▪	90	–	–	–	–	–	5	90	–	90
20.2.99	Sheff Wed H	1–4	24,643	s45	90	–	–	–	–	90	–	90	90	–	90
27.2.99	West Ham A	0–2	25,529	90	90	–	s26	–	–	90	s39	s35	64	–	90
10.3.99	Everton H	1–2	27,219	–	–	–	50	–	–	90	80	90	–	–	90
13.3.99	Coventry A	1–1	19,694	–	–	–	–	–	–	90	–	s38	59	–	90
20.3.99	Wimbledon H	3–1*	21,754	–	–	–	–	–	–	90□	–	s33	–	–	90
3.4.99	Middlesbro H	0–0	27,482	–	–	s29	–	–	–	90	s3	–	–	–	90
6.4.99	Arsenal A	0–1	37,762	–	s23□	67	–	–	–	90□	–	–	–	–	90□
17.4.99	Southampton A	3–3	15,209	–	s45	90	–	–	s11	90	s20	–	–	–	90
24.4.99	Liverpool H	1–3	29,944	–	–	90	90	–	–	–	–	90¹	s38	–	90
1.5.99	Charlton A	0–0	20,043	–	–	90□	90	–	–	90□	–	s16	–	–	90
8.5.99	Nott'm For H	1–2	24,565	–	–	90	61	–	–	90	s31	68	s22	–	90
12.5.99	Man Utd H	0–0	30,436	–	–	90	90	–	–	90□	–	–	90	–	90
16.5.99	Newcastle A	1–1	36,623	–	90	90	90	–	–	90	–	–	45	–	45

□ Yellow card, ▪ Red card, s Substitute, 90³ Goals scored
*including own goal

1998–99 PREMIERSHIP APPEARANCES

FLITCROFT	FLOWERS	GALLACHER	GILLESPIE	HENCHOZ	JANSEN	JOHNSON	KENNA	MARCOLIN	MCATEER	MCKINLAY	PEACOCK	PEREZ	SHERWOOD	SUTTON	TAYLOR	WARD	WILCOX	TOTAL	
90	–	s20	–	90	–	–	90	–	–	–	90	70	90	90	–	–	58	990	
90	–	s12	–	90□	–	–	90	–	–	–	90	90	90	90	–	–	78	990	
90□	90□	84[1]	–	90	–	–	90	–	–	–	90□	71□	90	90□	–	–	s19	990	
90	90	90[1]	–	90	–	–	69	–	–	90	90	s21□	–	90□	–	–	69	990	
–	90	–	–	90	–	–	90	–	–	90	90	–	90□	90□	–	–	s29	990	
90□	90	–	–	90	–	–	–	–	–	s12	90	67[1]□	90	90[2]□	–	–	78	967	
90	90	–	–	90□	–	–	90	–	–	s10□	90□	–	90□	–	–	–	90□	978	
90[2]□	90	65	–	45	–	s13	s45	–	–	90	90	–	90	–	–	–	90	990	
90	90	–	–	90	–	90	90	–	–	–	90□	–	90[1]	–	–	–	90	990	
–	90	–	–	90	–	90[1]	90	–	–	90	90	–	90□	89□■	–	–	46	989	
–	90	–	–	90	–	90	90	–	–	66□	90	–	90	90[1]	–	–	–	990	
–	90	–	–	90	–	90□	90	s45	–	–	45□	–	90[1]	45□	–	–	–	900	
–	–	s13	–	90□	–	90□	90	s39[1]	–	–	90	–	48■	–	–	–	–	948	
–	–	90	–	90	–	90	90	s37□	–	–	73	–	90	–	–	–	–	990	
–	–	90	–	90	–	87	90	90	–	–	–	–	–	–	–	–	–	990	
–	–	42	–	90	–	90	–	–	–	90	–	–	–	–	–	–	–	990	
–	–	–	–	90	–	90	90	–	–	90	–	–	90	–	–	–	90	990	
–	–	–	78□	90□	–	s12	90	–	–	90□	–	–	90	90□	–	–	89	990	
–	–	74[1]	90	45	–	–	90	–	–	90	–	–	90[1]	66	–	–	90□	990	
–	–	90[1]	90	–	–	–	90	–	–	90	90□	–	90	–	–	–	90	990	
–	–	–	90[1]	90	–	–	90	–	–	90	–	–	25■	–	–	90	90□	925	
–	–	–	90	90	–	–	90□	–	–	90□	–	–	90	–	–	90	90	990	
–	–	–	90	63[1]	–	90	s28	90	–	s5	–	–	–	–	90□	61■		961	
–	–	–	–	–	80	–	90	90	90	90	–	–	90[1]	–	90	90	–	990	
–	–	–	s45	90	82	–	90	45□	90	–	s3□	–	–	90□	–	90[1]	–	985	
–	–	–	90	s49	45	–	90	–	90[1]	–	s41	–	–	–	–	90	–	990	
–	–	–	90	–	51	–	–	–	90□	–	90□	–	–	–	–	90	55	990	
–	–	–	–	90	s10	90□	–	s40	90	–	90	–	–	–	–	90[1]	90	990	
–	–	–	–	90□	52	s31	–	90□	90□	–	–	–	–	90□	90	90	90[1]	990	
–	–	–	s9	90	57[1]	89	–	90	90	–	90	–	–	90	s1	90[1]	81	990	
–	–	–	s29	90	87	61	–	61□	90□	–	90	–	–	90	–	90	90	990	
–	–	–	83■	90	–	s45	–	–	90	45	90	–	–	90	–	90□	90	983	
–	–	70	90□	45	–	79	–	–	90□	–	90[1]	–	–	–	–	90[1]	90[1]	990	
–	–	90	–	90□	–	52	–	–	90	–	90	–	–	–	–	90	90	990	
–	–	74	90	90	–	–	–	–	90	–	90	–	–	–	90□	90□		990	
–	–	90[1]	90	90	59	s29	–	–	–	–	90	–	–	–	–	–	90□	990	
–	–	–	81	90	90	s9	–	–	–	–	90	–	–	–	–	90	90	990	
–	s45	54	90	–	–	s45	–	–	–	–	90	–	–	–	s36	90	90[1]□	990	

THE MANAGER

BRIAN KIDD

Blackburn boss Brian Kidd has been left with much to prove after failing to save big-spending Rovers from the drop in 1998–99.

Kidd's first game in charge was a 1–0 home win over Charlton on December 5, 1999. He took over from former Switzerland manager Roy Hodgson, who was sacked after 14 games of the season. The final straw for chairman Jack Walker was a 2–0 home defeat by bottom club Southampton and Hodgson left the club "by mutual consent".

Kidd enjoyed a fine career as a striker, playing six seasons at Manchester United before moving to Arsenal, Manchester City, Everton and Bolton. He also won two England caps.

He had enjoyed much success as Alex Ferguson's assistant at Manchester United but the lure of managing a big Premiership club made it an easy decision to leave Old Trafford.

Kidd was left devastated by his side's relegation and was at times highly critical of his players' attitudes on the pitch. Now he must use all his coaching experience as Blackburn bid for a swift return to the top flight.

LEAGUE POSITION

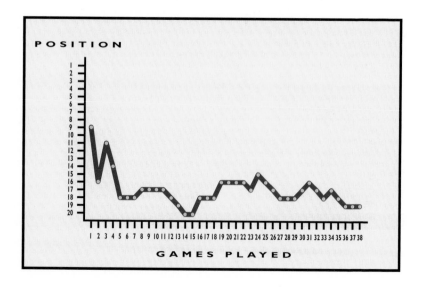

THE GOALS

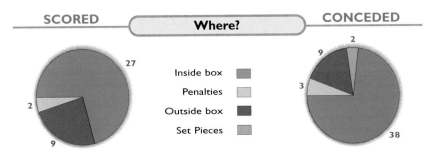

SCORED | Where? | CONCEDED

Inside box
Penalties
Outside box
Set Pieces

Blackburn may have shelled out more than £20 million for strikers during the 1998–99 campaign but they still struggled to find the net from close range. Rovers scored just 27 goals while inside their opponent's box, the fewest in

the Premiership. More than one in five of all goals conceded by Blackburn were from distance and only West Ham and Charlton fared worse with efforts attempted from 18 yards and over by their various opponents.

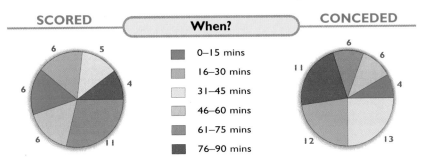

SCORED | When? | CONCEDED

0–15 mins
16–30 mins
31–45 mins
46–60 mins
61–75 mins
76–90 mins

Carling Opta's statistics suggest that, had Blackburn generally shown more discipline during the first 45 minutes of their Premiership contests, they may well have survived the drop. Rovers' opponents scored 55.8% of their goals

against the Lancashire side during the first half and only Sheffield Wednesday leaked a higher percentage of goals in this period. Blackburn peaked between the 60th and 75th minute, scoring nearly a third of all their goals then.

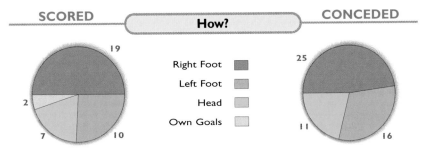

SCORED | How? | CONCEDED

Right Foot
Left Foot
Head
Own Goals

The manner in which Blackburn scored their goals during the 1998–99 Carling Premiership was typical of the average top-flight side. Seven of Blackburn's goals were headers, equating to 18.4% of all goals, and these were shared out

between six different players. But the relegated side were troubled by high balls into their own area, conceding the fourth-highest proportion of goals via the heads of their opponents in the Premiership.

BLACKBURN ROVERS

	BLAKE	BROOMES	CARSLEY	CROFT	DAHLIN	DAILLY	DAVIDSON	DAVIES	DUFF	DUNN	FLITCROFT	GALLACHER
APPEARANCES												
Start	9	8	7	10	2	14	34	9	19	10	8	13
Sub	2	5	1	2	3	3	0	12	9	5	0	3
Minutes on pitch	868	904	636	855	217	1244	3025	1040	1593	938	720	1048
GOAL ATTEMPTS												
Goals	3	0	0	0	0	0	1	1	1	1	2	5
Shots on target	9	0	3	1	1	7	2	13	7	5	6	19
Shots off target	20	3	1	0	3	3	7	26	11	3	5	15
Shooting accuracy %	31%	0%	75%	100%	25%	70%	22%	33%	39%	63%	55%	56%
PASSING												
Goal assists	0	0	0	0	1	0	1	2	2	0	3	1
Long passes	6	47	36	67	1	91	255	12	30	27	25	12
Short passes	282	142	242	282	50	357	894	390	461	295	285	307
PASS COMPLETION												
Own half %	83%	92%	88%	85%	67%	92%	86%	78%	87%	86%	85%	86%
Opposition half %	75%	59%	66%	70%	69%	67%	68%	62%	75%	71%	78%	76%
CROSSING												
Total crosses	10	0	6	21	3	17	44	9	101	7	7	13
Cross completion %	30%	0%	0%	38%	33%	41%	27%	0%	32%	0%	43%	23%
DRIBBLING												
Dribbles & runs	17	2	3	20	6	12	59	59	90	20	7	23
Dribble completion %	65%	100%	100%	75%	67%	50%	85%	59%	77%	70%	57%	65%
DEFENDING												
Tackles made	12	24	43	29	6	26	100	42	48	34	35	16
Tackles won %	58%	54%	63%	59%	50%	54%	63%	40%	46%	59%	71%	75%
Blocks	1	20	8	8	1	8	24	4	7	3	2	4
Clearances	6	110	29	61	2	111	256	8	16	35	32	10
Interceptions	1	12	7	5	1	5	23	2	9	7	3	1
DISCIPLINE												
Fouls	22	14	11	12	5	14	28	30	17	14	11	15
Offside	14	0	0	1	7	0	0	12	7	0	4	8
Yellow cards	0	3	1	1	0	0	7	5	0	2	3	0
Red cards	0	1	0	0	1	0	0	0	0	0	0	0

GOALKEEPER NAME	START/ (SUB)	TIME ON PITCH	GOALS CONCEDED	MINS/GOALS CONCEDED	SAVES MADE	SAVES/ SHOTS
FETTIS	2	180	0	N/a	10	100%
FILAN	26	2295	35	65.6	96	73%
FLOWERS	10 (1)	945	17	55.6	34	67%

PLAYERS' STATISTICS

	GILLESPIE	HENCHOZ	JANSEN	JOHNSON	KENNA	MARCOLIN	MCATEER	MCKINLAY	PEACOCK	PEREZ	SHERWOOD	SUTTON	TAYLOR	WARD	WILCOX	TOTAL	RANK
	13	33	10	14	22	5	13	14	27	4	19	17	1	17	28		
	3	1	1	7	1	5	0	2	3	1	0	0	2	0	2		
	1225	2884	676	1362	2004	565	1170	1213	2417	319	1603	1460	127	1530	2373		
	1	0	2	1	0	1	1	0	1	1	3	3	0	5	3	38*	18th
	3	0	9	3	0	3	2	0	5	5	13	18	0	15	22	171	13th
	8	2	11	11	3	5	3	2	2	3	14	14	0	23	9	207	=14th
	27%	0%	45%	21%	0%	38%	40%	0%	71%	63%	48%	56%	0%	39%	71%	45%	12th
	2	0	1	1	1	0	1	0	1	0	0	1	0	1	3	22	19th
	38	327	13	32	221	38	142	89	129	10	122	13	5	12	113	1913	8th
	366	712	188	456	566	221	406	538	623	110	707	577	27	582	924	10990	12th
	83%	92%	78%	89%	88%	89%	95%	89%	90%	72%	93%	84%	58%	91%	87%	89%	10th
	69%	58%	71%	75%	66%	75%	64%	71%	61%	73%	74%	70%	63%	73%	73%	69%	10th
	84	2	13	84	48	14	43	11	1	15	13	13	0	4	200	783	9th
	35%	0%	15%	30%	31%	36%	30%	27%	0%	20%	38%	15%	0%	100%	32%	31%	4th
	85	18	65	84	28	2	39	10	2	14	18	16	5	47	62	813	14th
	74%	94%	66%	71%	75%	100%	82%	100%	50%	71%	83%	69%	40%	64%	82%	73%	5th
	33	124	17	51	64	19	53	52	80	13	61	35	5	31	76	1132	14th
	67%	63%	65%	67%	66%	79%	57%	65%	63%	69%	64%	49%	80%	42%	54%	60%	14th
	5	35	2	8	16	2	4	4	33	1	3	1	0	3	5	212	7th
	16	387	5	22	116	14	55	42	330	5	50	14	23	19	56	1860	18th
	8	34	2	8	12	8	17	5	20	3	14	2	0	6	25	244	20th
	9	40	7	17	14	8	24	19	30	10	24	60	2	49	22	530	8th
	2	0	6	4	0	0	0	0	0	1	2	26	0	24	11	129	13th
	2	6	0	3	1	4	4	4	7	2	3	9	0	3	6	80	7th
	1	0	0	0	0	0	0	0	0	0	1	2	1	0	1	8	1st

*Including two own goals

CROSSES CAUGHT	CROSSES PUNCHED	CROSSES NOT CLAIMED	CATCH SUCCESS	THROWS/ SHORT KICKS	% COMPLETION	LONG KICKS	% COMPLETION
1	1	1	50%	16	100%	36	47%
72	26	9	94%	146	97%	613	36%
16	6	4	94%	116	97%	221	33%

PLAYER OF THE SEASON

PLAYER	INDEX SCORE
JASON WILCOX	868
Tim Sherwood	767
Stephane Henchoz	758
Darren Peacock	728
Callum Davidson	709
Damien Johnson	699
Damien Duff	675
Jeff Kenna	655
Ashley Ward	654
John Filan	630

In the match against Manchester United which confirmed Rovers' relegation to Division One, winger Jason Wilcox was the only player in the Blackburn team who had been part of the 1994–95 Championship-winning side.

His experience and commitment to the club were vital to Rovers as they battled to beat the drop, and the cultured left-sided midfielder ended the campaign as the highest-rated Rovers player in the Carling Opta Season Index, averaging 868 points a match in 1998–99.

Blackburn struggled to score goals in a miserable campaign, but the forwards could have no complaints about a lack of service, with Wilcox completing 32% of his 200 crosses and corners – well above the average for an attacking midfielder.

The fact that former captain Tim Sherwood was second in the Blackburn top 10 emphasizes his importance to the club. His sale to Tottenham in the wake of Roy Hodgson's departure hardly helped the club escape relegation, with several other key midfielders suffering from long-term injuries.

Swiss defender Stephane Henchoz, one of Hodgson's best buys at Rovers, was third in the top 10 and the side's highest-ranked defender. He and fellow-centre-back Darren Peacock were higher in the chart than the likes of Johnson, Duff and Kenna who did not figure in the starting XI on a consistent basis.

Of the front players, only £4.5 million man Ashley Ward made the top 10, an indication of how much the side struggled in front of goal in 1998–99.

Goalkeeper John Filan, who successfully displaced former England 'keeper Tim Flowers in the first team, finished 10th. The Carling Opta Index gave him plenty of credit for his superb performances, such as away at Chelsea, but penalized him for conceding so many goals.

FIVE OF THE BEST

Despite benefactor Jack Walker's £100 million outlay and a mid-season shift in the managerial hot-seat, Rovers succumbed to the dreaded drop just four years after storming to the FA Carling Premiership title. Horrific injury problems undoubtedly played their part in the relegation debacle, but the Carling Opta statistics show exactly what went wrong.

TOP GOALSCORERS

	GOALS	GOALS/SHOTS
KEVIN GALLACHER	5	15%
Ashley Ward	5	13%
Tim Sherwood	3	11%
Nathan Blake	3	10%
Jason Wilcox	3	10%

Finding the net proved a major problem for Rovers, with the top scorers managing just five League strikes each. Kevin Gallacher would surely have added to his tally without his injury problems, as would multi-million pound stars Nathan Blake and Chris Sutton. But the contributions from elsewhere simply did not amount to enough under either Roy Hodgson or Brian Kidd, with only the departed Tim Sherwood and left-winger Jason Wilcox contributing more than two goals from midfield.

Rovers were rarely in command in their 1998–99 Premiership matches, with no player completing more than 1,000 passes all season. Most prolific was Scottish under-21 full-back Callum Davidson, with Swiss defender Stephane Henchoz not too far behind. The amount of pressure Blackburn were under in the season is highlighted by the inclusion of three defenders in the top five. Even Tim Sherwood makes the chart despite leaving the club midway through the season, showing what a pivotal figure he was to the Blackburn team.

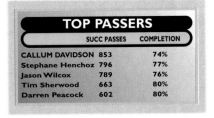

TOP PASSERS

	SUCC PASSES	COMPLETION
CALLUM DAVIDSON	853	74%
Stephane Henchoz	796	77%
Jason Wilcox	789	76%
Tim Sherwood	663	80%
Darren Peacock	602	80%

TOP TACKLERS

	WON	SUCCESS
STEPHANE HENCHOZ	78	63%
Callum Davidson	63	63%
Darren Peacock	50	63%
Jeff Kenna	42	66%
Jason Wilcox	41	54%

Despite their willingness to adopt a physical approach when needed, only Nottingham Forest, West Ham and Aston Villa won fewer tackles than Rovers in 1998–99. Most defenders would expect to win two-thirds of their challenges, but only Jeff Kenna achieved this ratio. Top tackler was Stephane Henchoz, who enjoyed a fine season in the centre of defence. Callum Davidson and Darren Peacock are also present in the chart, with Jason Wilcox completing the top five.

One foul every 24 minutes: that is the sorry tale of Chris Sutton's injury-wrecked 1998–99 season. Sutton was easily the Rovers' most spoken to player, picking up nine yellow cards and one red in just 1,460 minutes of Premiership football. He also conceded more fouls than any of his team-mates, even the ones who played for the whole season. Rovers picked up more red cards than any other team in the league, which can hardly have helped in their battle to avoid relegation to Division One.

DISCIPLINE

	POINTS	FOULS & CARDS
CHRIS SUTTON	93	60F, 9Y, 1R
Ashley Ward	58	49F, 3Y, 0R
Stephane Henchoz	58	40F, 6Y, 0R
Darren Peacock	51	30F, 7Y, 0R
Callum Davidson	49	28F, 7Y, 0R

ACTION	DAHLIN	DAILLY	DAVIDSON	DUFF	FLITCROFT	FLOWERS	GALLACHER	HENCHOZ	JOHNSON	KENNA	MCKINLAY	PEACOCK	SHERWOOD	WILLCOX	TOTAL	WEST HAM
Time on pitch	25	90	90	77	90	90	65	45	13	45	90	90	90	90	990	990
GOALS																
Goal	-	-	1	-	-	-	1	-	-	-	-	-	1	-	3	-
Shot on target	1	-	-	-	2	-	1	-	-	-	-	-	1	2	7	3
Shot off target	-	-	2	-	1	-	2	-	-	-	-	-	1	2	8	8
Blocked shot	-	-	-	-	-	-	1	2	-	-	-	-	-	-	3	3
Own goal	-	-	-	-	-	-	-	-	-	-	-	-	-	-	-	-
PASSES																
Pass to own player	3	44	47	19	42	-	20	24	4	23	64	56	64	41	451	245
Pass to opposition	2	5	8	4	11	-	4	5	-	4	5	4	2	9	63	64
Cross to own player	-	-	1	3	2	-	1	-	-	-	-	-	-	2	9	9
Cross to opposition player	-	1	-	4	-	-	-	-	-	2	2	-	-	4	13	3
Goal assist	-	-	-	-	-	-	-	-	-	-	-	-	-	-	-	7
Pass completion %	60%	88%	86%	73%	79%	0%	81%	83%	100%	85%	90%	93%	97%	77%	86%	78%
TACKLES & CLEARANCES																
Tackle	1	-	4	3	6	-	2	-	1	2	3	3	3	2	30	26
Clearances, blocks and interceptions	-	3	9	1	3	-	-	8	1	2	13	1	3	-	44	56
DRIBBLES & RUNS																
Dribble ball retained	-	-	4	4	-	-	2	2	2	-	1	-	2	1	18	-
Dribbles ball lost	-	-	-	1	-	-	-	1	1	-	-	-	1	-	4	-
Dribble success %	0%	0%	100%	80%	0%	0%	100%	67%	67%	0%	100%	0%	67%	100%	82%	52%
DISCIPLINE																
Fouls	1	1	1	-	2	-	1	-	-	1	2	-	-	2	11	10
Penalty conceded	-	-	-	-	-	-	-	-	-	-	-	-	-	-	-	-
Free kick - offside	1	-	-	-	-	-	-	-	-	-	1	-	-	3	5	9
Yellow cards	-	-	-	-	1	-	-	-	-	-	-	-	-	-	1	3
Red cards	-	-	-	-	-	-	-	-	-	-	-	-	-	-	-	-
GOALKEEPERS																
Distribution to own player	-	-	-	-	-	21	-	-	-	-	-	-	-	-	21	20
Distribution to opposition player	-	-	-	-	-	13	-	-	-	-	-	-	-	-	13	14
Goalkeeper distribution%	0%	0%	0%	0%	0%	62%	0%	0%	0%	0%	0%	0%	0%	0%	62%	59%
Save	-	-	-	-	-	3	-	-	-	-	-	-	-	-	3	7
Ball caught	-	-	-	-	-	-	-	-	-	-	-	-	-	-	-	3
Ball dropped	-	-	-	-	-	-	-	-	-	-	-	-	-	-	-	-
Goal conceded	-	-	-	-	-	-	-	-	-	-	-	-	-	-	-	3

Blackburn Rovers took on West Ham looking for their second win at home to push them away from the relegation zone early in the season. West Ham had started the season somewhat better, and Harry Redknapp was looking to move into the top six. But by October they had already been beaten twice away from home.

October 3, 1998

3–0

BLACKBURN ROVERS
WEST HAM UNITED

A good opening 10 minutes resulted in an early goal for the home side. Jason Wilcox's knock-down fell kindly for Garry Flitcroft, whose shot took an early deflection off Steve Lomas to wrong-foot Shaka Hislop and put Blackburn 1–0 up.

Five minutes later, Blackburn nearly scored a spectacular second when Kevin Gallacher's 25-yard shot dipped just over the bar.

The tight first half was a tough midfield battle, with the home side coming out on top. Chances were at a premium and Flitcroft's strike separated the sides at half-time. The second half saw Blackburn start to take control of the game. In the 46th minute, Rio Ferdinand drilled a backpass at Hislop, whose chest control gave Wilcox a chance to close him down. The goalkeeper stretched out a boot to clear but the ball went straight to Flitcroft who produced a superb first-time strike, in off the post from 25 yards.

Despite dominating the possession, Rovers still found it difficult to create genuine chances. Both teams were defending deep and stifling the game but Blackburn looked the more likely to score.

On 68 minutes, Callum Davidson brought the Ewood Park crowd to their feet with a brilliant individual goal. The young Scot picked up the ball in his own half and ran down the left channel, cut across the edge of the penalty area and unleashed a brilliant 25-yard curling shot which gave Hislop no chance.

Blackburn nearly made it four when a Wilcox corner from the left was played out to Davidson on the edge of the area. He laid the ball off to Billy McKinlay, whose screamer fizzed two yards wide of the post.

With ten minutes remaining, substitute Damien Johnson was left to run through the middle of the West Ham defence and pick his spot – but the young striker's shot went agonizingly wide.

The final chance of the match came in stoppage time. Andy Impey was dispossessed by McKinlay and Wilcox crossed for the other substitute Martin Dahlin, who rose well at the back post but could not keep his header down.

The Carling Opta statistics illustrate the difference between the two sides. Blackburn totally dominated possession, comprehensively out-passing West Ham. The Lancashire team also completed a higher percentage of their balls (86% compared to West Ham's 78%) and out-shot their London opponents 21 to 5.

Tim Flowers in the Blackburn goal had an easy time, being called upon to make just three routine saves, while Hislop made seven stops and conceded three goals. The home side were far more composed on the ball, completing 82% of their dribbles and runs compared with West Ham's 52%.

A gruelling midfield tussle was won by the Blackburn trio of Flitcroft, McKinlay and Tim Sherwood who together laid the foundations of what was a comfortable, if unspectacular, 3–0 win for the home side.

ACTION	BROOMES	DAVIDSON	DUFF	DUNN	FILAN	JANSEN	McATEER	McKINLAY	PEACOCK	SUTTON	WARD	WILCOX	TOTAL	ASTON VILLA
Time on pitch	90	90	10	90	90	80	90	90	90	90	90	90	990	990
GOALS														
Goal	-	-	-	1	-	-	-	-	-	-	1	-	2	1
Shot on target	-	-	-	-	-	2	-	-	-	-	-	1	3	6
Shot off target	-	-	-	-	-	2	-	-	-	-	-	1	3	14
Blocked shot	-	-	-	-	-	-	-	1	-	1	-	-	-	2
Own goal	-	-	-	-	-	-	1	-	-	-	-	-	-	-
PASSES														
Pass to own player	19	20	4	28	-	24	27	33	17	29	29	28	258	324
Pass to opposition	4	7	4	11	-	5	11	12	3	8	18	12	95	99
Cross to own player	-	1	-	1	-	-	-	-	-	-	-	-	2	8
Cross to opposition player	-	-	-	-	-	2	3	-	-	-	-	2	9	18
Goal assist	-	-	-	-	-	-	-	-	-	1	-	-	-	-
Pass completion %	83%	71%	50%	70%	0%	77%	66%	73%	85%	79%	62%	68%	72%	74%
TACKLES & CLEARANCES														
Tackle	2	3	-	-	-	-	2	3	2	-	-	-	12	15
Clearances, blocks and interceptions	11	4	2	2	-	-	2	2	9	-	-	-	32	25
DRIBBLES & RUNS														
Dribble ball retained	-	2	2	2	-	6	3	-	-	2	2	1	20	16
Dribbles ball lost	-	-	-	-	-	2	-	-	-	-	2	-	6	3
Dribble success %	0%	100%	100%	100%	0%	75%	75%	0%	0%	100%	50%	50%	77%	84%
DISCIPLINE														
Fouls	1	-	-	1	-	-	-	-	-	2	3	-	7	14
Penalty conceded	-	-	-	-	-	-	-	-	-	-	-	-	-	-
Free kick - offside	-	-	-	-	-	1	-	-	-	3	5	-	9	4
Yellow cards	-	-	-	-	-	-	-	-	-	-	-	-	-	-
Red cards	-	-	-	-	-	-	-	-	-	-	-	-	-	-
GOALKEEPERS														
Distribution to own player	-	-	-	-	20	-	-	-	-	-	-	-	20	14
Distribution to opposition player	-	-	-	-	17	-	-	-	-	-	-	-	17	9
Goalkeeper distribution%	0%	0%	0%	0%	54%	0%	0%	0%	0%	0%	0%	0%	54%	61%
Save	-	-	-	-	6	-	-	-	-	-	-	-	6	3
Ball caught	-	-	-	-	6	-	-	-	-	-	-	-	6	2
Ball dropped	-	-	-	-	-	-	-	-	-	-	-	-	-	-
Goal conceded	-	-	-	-	1	-	-	-	-	-	-	-	1	3

Blackburn Rovers' run of fine form under new boss Brian Kidd had faltered in the games leading up to their visit to Villa Park and they were still sitting just two points above the relegation zone. They had also just seen skipper Tim Sherwood leave for Tottenham Hotspur and Tim Flowers put in a transfer request, prompted by his frustration at not being first-choice goalkeeper.

February 6, 1999

1-3

ASTON VILLA
BLACKBURN ROVERS

Aston Villa were looking to bounce back from their FA Cup exit at the hands of Fulham and a Premiership defeat away at Newcastle when they entertained Blackburn – but it was to be Rovers' day.

Villa started enthusiastically, but Rovers took the lead against the run of play when a cross from youngster David Dunn was headed into his own net by defender Gareth Southgate in the 32nd minute.

Rovers visibly grew in confidence and on 62 minutes Chris Sutton, who had just returned from injury, beat Riccardo Scimeca and crossed for Ashley Ward to slide in and score his first goal since his £4.5 million move from Barnsley.

Just two minutes later another new signing, Matt Jansen, crossed the ball into the Villa penalty area. Gareth Barry headed the ball away, but only as far as Dunn who was on hand to volley the ball into the back of the net.

Julian Joachim grabbed a late consolation goal for Aston Villa when he latched on to a flick-on by Dion Dublin from a long pass by Gareth Barry; but Villa could not find a way back and slipped to another defeat in a poor run that eventually saw them take just one point from a possible 24.

Villa edged the possession and had far more chances, firing in 23 shots at goal to Rovers' nine. The difference on the day was the quality of the finishing, with Villa only finding the target with 30% of their shots compared to Blackburn's 56%, in addition to the gift of an own goal.

Matt Jansen was particularly impressive, firing in four shots for Rovers in total with 50% on target, whereas Dion Dublin showed just why he had not scored a Premiership goal since December 13, missing the target with six out of seven attempts he made in the match.

Referee Keith Burge did not have to show the yellow card at all in a match that produced just 21 fouls, with only seven of those being committed by Rovers – a figure at odds with their poor disciplinary record in the 1998–99 Premiership season.

Man of the match was John Filan with a points score of 1,157. The Australian 'keeper showed just why Tim Flowers was sitting on the bench by making six saves, half of which came from shots inside the box. He also made six catches and completed 54% of his distribution during the match. He claimed after the game that he was "in the best form of my career".

Blackburn failed to build on this result and embarked on a run which saw them win just one of their last 14 games and suffer relegation to Nationwide Division One.

CHARLTON ATHLETIC 1998–99

Back row (left to right): Anthony Allman, Kevin Lisbie (now Gillingham), Scott Parker, Frazer Toms, Michael Beale, Mike Salmon, Danny Mills (now Leeds United), Andy Petterson, Kevin Nicholls, Matt Lee, Paul Konchesky, Anthony Barness, Kevin James.
Middle row: Keith Peacock (Assistant Manager), Shaun Newton, Paul Emblem (now Wycombe Wanderers), Steve Jones, Jon Fortune, Eddie Youds, Simon Royce, Sasa Ilic, Paul Smith, Richard Rufus, Andy Hunt, Emeka Ifejiagwa, Gary Poole, Chris Powell, Jimmy Hendrie (Physiotherapist).

Front row: John Robinson, Paul Mortimer, Bradley Allen, Keith Jones, Mark Bright, Mark Kinsella, Alan Curbishley (Manager), Mervyn Day (First Team Coach), Clive Mendonca, Mark Bowen, Carl Tiler, Steve Brown, Neil Redfearn, Matt Holmes.

CHARLTON ATHLETIC

20 FACTS

1 Charlton Athletic were founded in 1905 and turned professional in 1920, when they joined the Southern League. They were elected to Division Three South a year later.

2 Although Charlton are known as the Addicks, they have had other nicknames including the Robins and the Valiants.

3 Charlton's highest-ever league finish was second in Division One in the 1936–37 season. It capped a meteoric rise that saw them finish second in Division Two the previous year after winning Division Three South the year before that.

4 The Addicks have won the FA Cup once, in 1947, when they beat Burnley 1–0. They were runners-up a year earlier when Bert Turner, aged 36 years and 312 days, became the oldest player to score a goal in a Wembley final. Unfortunately, he also scored an own-goal in the same game!

5 Charlton's best performance in the Football League Cup has been reaching the fourth round, which they have achieved on just three occasions.

6 Charlton Athletic participated in the first-ever play-offs in 1987, when they finished 19th in Division One. They defeated Leeds United in the final to retain their top-flight status. Although both sides won their respective home legs 1–0, the Addicks triumphed 2–1 in a replay at St Andrews.

7 Charlton's record attendance came against Aston Villa on February 12, 1938. A total of 75,031 fans crammed into the Valley.

8 The Addicks' record victory came in 1953 when they comprehensively beat Middlesbrough 8–1 in Division One.

9 Their record defeat came six years later in Division Two. They lost 11–1 to Aston Villa.

10 The Valley has been Charlton's home since 1920, but in 1985 the Greater London Council ordered the massive East Terrace to be closed for safety reasons. The Addicks had to ground-share, firstly with Crystal Palace and then with West Ham, before moving back to the revamped Valley in 1992.

11 Charlton Athletic were the winners of the only league match ever to finish with a 7–6 scoreline, beating Huddersfield Town in December 1957. The achievement was all the more notable because Charlton were 5–1 down and reduced to 10 men!

12 Charlton's record league goalscorer in a single season was Ralph Allen, who scored 32 goals in their 1934–35 Division Three South Championship-winning side.

13 In October 1972, Peter Hunt was credited with his first goal for Charlton, even though the ball actually hit the side netting.

14 Charlton equalled a record in 1998–99 by losing eight consecutive matches in the Premiership to match Manchester City in 1995, Middlesbrough in 1996 and Crystal Palace in 1997.

15 The current assistant manager, Keith Peacock, was the first substitute to be used in a Football League match when Charlton met Bolton in August 1965.

16 Charlton finished 18th in the 1998–99 Premiership and were relegated. Their league record was:

Pld	W	D	L	F	A	Pts
38	8	12	18	41	56	36

17 Alan Curbishley's side were knocked out of the AXA-sponsored FA Cup in the third round when they lost 2–0 to Blackburn Rovers.

18 Charlton were knocked out of the Worthington Cup by Leicester City in the third round, losing 2–1 at home. The Addicks had already beaten QPR in both legs of the second round, 2–0 at Loftus Road and 1–0 at the Valley.

19 The top goalscorer in all competitions for Charlton was Clive Mendonca with eight goals.

20 Charlton's disciplinary record was the eighth-worst in the Premiership. They committed 574 fouls, earned 63 yellow cards and suffered four red cards, though one for Richard Rufus was expunged.

SEASON REVIEW

Top of the table after two games, Charlton seemed determined to defy the critics and survive in the Premiership. Unfortunately their 5–0 hammering of Southampton on August 22 proved to be a false dawn. For all the optimism that surrounded the Valley that day, it was the Saints who had the last laugh in the battle for survival.

In their defence, the Addicks were arguably the unluckiest team ever to grace the Premiership. They missed penalties, scored own-goals at crucial moments and conceded a total of 12 times in the last 15 minutes of matches.

The fact that they also managed a run of 13 Premiership games without a win cannot be ignored, though. Setting records like that makes survival very difficult.

The season started well enough. The win against Southampton – in which striker Clive Mendonca scored a hat-trick – was sandwiched between excellent 0–0 draws at both Newcastle and Arsenal. Even a 4–1 thrashing at the hands of eventual champions Manchester United did little to dampen spirits.

It was after an excellent 4–2 victory over West Ham on October 24 that things began to go wrong. After that victory, Charlton were ninth in the Premiership. By the time they won their next game against Wimbledon on February 8 they were 18th.

In that period they lost striker Clive Mendonca to injury, saw the confidence of goalkeeper Sasa Ilic evaporate in the face of concerted pressure and picked up just four points.

The signing of Swedish striker Martin Pringle temporarily lifted the gloom around the club in much the same way that the introduction of Graham Stuart did in the final month of the season. But although both players scored some vital goals, they were unable to provide the long-term

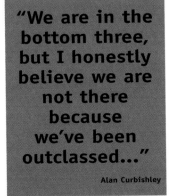

"We are in the bottom three, but I honestly believe we are not there because we've been outclassed..."

Alan Curbishley

solutions that the club required.

To their credit Charlton's players won 64% of their tackles – the most in the Premiership. But they also ended the season with the second-highest number of clearances in the division, a fact that highlights the pressure that their defence came under.

As hard as they fought, they were unable to convert their effort into results consistently enough to pull clear of the relegation zone. By the time they made the long journey to Villa Park on the penultimate weekend of the season they were in dire straits.

The 4–3 victory which they earned that day was made all the more important by the news that Southampton had won at Wimbledon. Alan Curbishley had always said he would be happy if the club went into the last day of the season with a chance of survival, and although Southampton held the advantage going into their game with Everton, Charlton still had a chance.

The Addicks lost their game against Sheffield Wednesday – but the result was academic anyway. Southampton beat Everton to stay up and complete yet another amazing escape from relegation.

It was hard luck on a Charlton team that never stopped believing it could stay up, even in the midst of that dreadful losing streak. Roared on by full houses for the entire season and managed by one of the brightest young bosses in the game, the club were a credit to the Premiership.

Curbishley's assertion that they were not outclassed is supported by the fact that they lost only five matches by more than two goals and were beaten by more than one clear goal in only one meeting with any of the top three sides.

They return to the Nationwide league disappointed at the brief nature of their stay in the big time, but stronger for the experience.

CHARLTON ATHLETIC

DATE	OPPONENT	SCORE	ATT.	BARNES	BARNESS	BOWEN	BRIGHT	BROWN	HUNT	ILIC	K JONES	S JONES	KINSELLA
15.8.98	Newcastle A	0–0	36,719	–	–	–	–	s62	28	90	–	s30	90
22.8.98	Southampton H	5–0	16,488	–	–	–	–	–	90	90	s5	–	85
29.8.98	Arsenal A	0–0	38,014	–	–	–	–	90□	65□	90	–	s25□	90
9.9.98	Man Utd A	1–4	55,147	–	–	–	–	90	90	90	s15	s19	75^1
12.9.98	Derby Co H	1–2	19,516	–	–	–	–	90	90	90	–	s18	45
19.9.98	Liverpool A	3–3	44,526	–	–	–	–	–	77	90	s17	$s13^1$	73
26.9.98	Coventry H	1–1	20,048	–	–	–	–	–	90^1	90	s41	s5	90
3.10.98	Nott'm For A	1–0	22,661	–	–	–	–	s1	79	90	s18	s11	90
17.10.98	Chelsea A	1–2	34,642	–	–	–	–	–	90	44□	s6	–	84
25.10.98	West Ham H	4–2	20,043	–	–	–	–	–	90^1	–	–	s5	90
2.11.98	Tottenham A	2–2	32,202	–	–	–	–	s7	90^2	90	–	s28	90□
7.11.98	Leicester H	0–0	20,021	–	–	–	–	–	90	90	90	s59	90
14.11.98	Middlesbro H	1–1	19,906	–	–	–	–	–	90	90	90	s17□	90
21.11.98	Leeds Utd A	1–4	32,487	–	–	–	–	–	69	90	s13	s21	77
28.11.98	Everton H	1–2	20,043	–	–	–	–	–	90	90	–	s45	90^1
5.12.98	Blackburn A	0–1	22,568	–	–	–	–	–	90	90	–	s23	90□
12.12.98	Sheff Wed A	0–3	26,010	–	s18	–	–	–	80	90	s18	90	90
21.12.98	Aston Villa H	0–1	20,043	–	–	–	–	–	90	90	–	90□	90
26.12.98	Wimbledon A	1–2	19,106	–	–	–	–	90	–	90	–	90	90
28.12.98	Arsenal H	0–1	20,043	–	–	–	–	–	90	68□	–	90	90□
9.1.99	Southampton A	1–3	15,222	–	–	–	–	–	90^1□	90	–	71	90
17.1.99	Newcastle H	2–2	20,043	–	–	–	$s28^1$	–	62	–	80	–	90□
31.1.99	Man Utd H	0–1	20,043	–	–	–	s12	90	78	–	90	–	90
8.2.99	Wimbledon H	2–0*	20,002	–	–	–	–	90	90	–	–	–	90
13.2.99	Liverpool H	1–0	20,043	s23	–	–	s7	90	90	–	90^1	–	90
20.2.99	Derby Co A	2–0	27,853	s71	s25	–	–	90	90^1	–	65	–	19
27.2.99	Nott'm For H	0–0	20,007	–	–	–	–	90	72	–	90	–	90
6.3.99	Coventry A	1–2	20,255	s27	s21	–	–	90	79	–	90	–	90
13.3.99	Leicester A	1–1	20,220	s16	–	–	–	90	74	90	78■	s16	90
3.4.99	Chelsea H	0–1	20,046	s35	–	–	–	90	s12	90	–	s7	90
5.4.99	West Ham A	1–0	26,041	90	–	s50	–	–	83□	45	s7	–	90
10.4.99	Middlesbro A	0–2	34,529	90	–	66	–	s24	66	–	s8	s24	82
17.4.99	Leeds Utd H	1–1	20,043	–	–	s21	s9	–	90	–	90	–	90
20.4.99	Tottenham H	1–4	20,043	s25	–	90	–	–	90	–	90	–	90^1
24.4.99	Everton A	1–4	40,089	s21	–	s2	69	–	s21	–	90	–	90
1.5.99	Blackburn H	0–0	20,043	s16	–	–	–	–	69	–	–	s21	90
8.5.99	Aston Villa A	4–3*	37,705	s7	–	–	–	s11	–	–	–	90□	90
16.5.99	Sheff Wed H	0–1	20,043	s29	–	s27	–	63	–	–	–	90□	90

□ Yellow card, ■ Red card, s Substitute, 90^3 Goals scored, +Red card later rescinded
*including own goal

1998–99 PREMIERSHIP APPEARANCES

KONCHESKY	LISBIE	MENDONCA	MILLS	MORTIMER	NEWTON	PARKER	PETTERSON	POWELL	PRINGLE	REDFEARN	ROBINSON	ROYCE	RUFUS	STUART	TILER	YOUDS	TOTAL
–	–	60	90	s9	90□	–	–	90	–	90□	81□	–	25▪	–	–	90	925
–	–	90[3]	90	s12	78□	–	–	90	–	90[1]	90[1]□	–	90	–	–	90	990
–	–	90	90	s17	90	–	–	90	–	90	73	–	–	–	–	90□	990
–	–	71	90	s35	55	–	–	90	–	90	90	–	–	–	–	90	990
–	–	90[1]	90	s45	72	–	–	90□	–	90	90	–	–	–	–	90□	990
–	–	90[1]	90□	–	90	–	–	90	–	90□	90	–	90[1]	–	–	90	990
–	–	85	90	90	49	–	–	90	–	90	–	–	90	–	–	90	990
–	–	90	90□	72	–	–	–	90□	–	89	–	–	90	–	90□	90[1]	990
–	–	90	90	76	–	–	s46	90	–	90	s14	–	90□	–	90□	90[1]	990
–	–	85	90[1]	90	–	–	90	90	–	90[1]	s25	–	90	–	65[1]	90	990
–	–	90	90	62□	–	–	–	90	–	83	s48	–	42	–	90□	90	990
–	–	90	90	31	–	–	–	90	–	–	90□	–	–	–	–	90	990
–	–	73[1]	61	–	–	–	–	90	–	s29	90□	–	90	–	90	90	990
–	–	90	59□	s31[1]	–	–	–	90	–	90	90	–	90	–	90	90□	990
–	–	90	90	67	s23	–	–	90	–	90	–	–	90	–	45	90	990
–	–	67	90	52	s38	–	–	90	–	90□	90	–	90	–	–	90□	990
–	–	s10	90	–	72	–	–	90	–	72	90	–	90	–	–	90	990
–	–	s20	90□	–	70	–	–	90	–	90	90	–	90	–	90□	–	990
–	–	–	83	–	73	s7	–	90	–	90[1]□	90	–	90	–	90	s17	990
–	s22	–	90	–	90	s10	–	90	–	80□	90□	–	90	–	–	90□	990
–	–	–	90□	–	90	–	–	90	s19	90	90	–	90	–	–	90□	990
s28	–	–	90	–	62	s10	–	90	90[1]	–	90	90	–	–	90	90	990
–	–	–	–	–	–	s7	–	90	83	90	90	90	90	–	90	–	990
90	–	–	90	–	s19	–	–	90	90[1]	90□	71	90	–	–	90	–	990
–	–	–	90□	–	–	–	–	90	83	67	90	90	–	–	90	–	990
–	–	s16	90	–	–	–	–	90	90[1]	90	74□	90	–	–	90	–	990
–	–	s18	90	–	–	–	–	90	90	90	90□	90	–	–	90□	–	990
–	–	–	90	s11	–	–	–	90	90	63□	69[1]	90	–	–	90	–	990
–	–	s16[1]	90□	–	–	–	–	90	74	74	–	–	90	–	90	–	978
–	–	78	55	–	–	–	–	83	90	–	90	–	90	90□	90	–	990
–	–	–	90□	–	–	–	s45	90	90	–	40	–	90	90[1]	90	–	990
–	–	–	90□	–	–	–	–	90	90	90	–	–	–	90	90	90	990
–	–	–	90	69	–	–	–	90	90	81	–	–	64▪*	90[1]	90	–	964
–	–	s15	–	65	–	–	–	90	90	75	–	–	90	90	90	–	990
–	–	–	90	–	–	–	–	90	88	90	–	–	69	90□[1]	90	90	990
–	–	–	90□	–	–	–	s45	90	90□	90□	74	45	90	90	90□	–	990
–	–	83[1]	90[1]	–	–	–	79▪	90	s7	83□	79[1]	–	90	90	90	–	979
–	–	90	90	–	–	–	–	90	90	s21	61	69□	–	90	90	–	990

THE MANAGER

ALAN CURBISHLEY

Charlton stalwart Alan Curbishley was a midfielder with the Addicks when the club reached the top flight in 1986.

But despite his titanic effort to keep Charlton in the Premiership in 1998–99, the club were relegated on the final day of the season.

Curbishley's playing career began at West Ham in 1975 and he went on to play for Birmingham City and Aston Villa before moving back to London with Charlton in 1984. After two years there, he switched to the south coast with Brighton and Hove Albion before returning to the Valley to end his playing days.

He was coach under Lennie Lawrence until summer 1991 when he took over as joint manager with fellow-midfielder Steve Gritt. But after a disappointing 1994–95 campaign, he assumed sole control and guided the club to the First Division play-offs in his first year.

They were beaten by local rivals Crystal Palace, but two years later they achieved their Premiership dreams with a stunning penalty shoot-out win over Sunderland at Wembley.

Curbishley now faces a difficult task to lift the club as he tries to launch yet another promotion bid.

LEAGUE POSITION

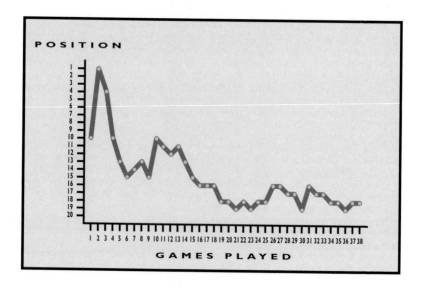

THE GOALS

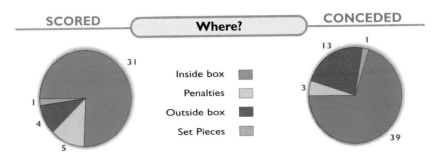

SCORED — Where? — CONCEDED

Inside box
Penalties
Outside box
Set Pieces

In their opponents' 18-yard box, Charlton were one of the most successful teams in the Carling Premiership, whereas in their own half they had difficulty dealing with long-range efforts. The

Addicks scored a healthy 36 goals from close range, but exactly a quarter of all goals scored against them were from outside the area, the second-highest ratio in the league.

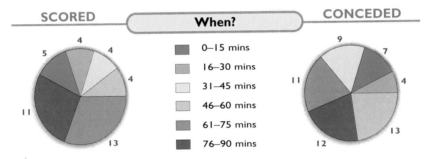

SCORED — When? — CONCEDED

0–15 mins
16–30 mins
31–45 mins
46–60 mins
61–75 mins
76–90 mins

With only 13 goals scored in the first half throughout the 1998–99 Premiership campaign, Charlton clearly did not put enough early pressure on their opponents. They scored more than two-thirds of all goals in the second

period, with a massive 59% coming in the final 30 minutes – easily the highest quota in the league. Unfortunately for Charlton, they were also at their most vulnerable in the second half, leaking 64.3% of all goals after the break.

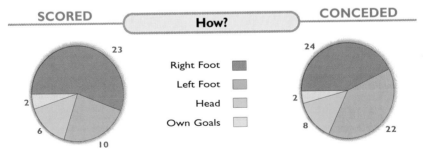

SCORED — How? — CONCEDED

Right Foot
Left Foot
Head
Own Goals

A very low proportion of goals both scored and conceded by Alan Curbishley's side were from headers. Overall, the south London side headed just six goals, the third-fewest in the league, and conceded eight. Of the 48 other strikes

registered in their "goals against" column, nearly half were from left-footed efforts. No other Premiership side had such a poor record against left-footers, Charlton having conceded 22 goals in this way.

CHARLTON ATHLETIC

	BARNES	BARNESS	BOWEN	BRIGHT	BROWN	HUNT	K JONES	S JONES	KINSELLA	KONCHESKY	LISBIE
APPEARANCES											
Start	2	0	2	1	13	32	13	7	38	1	0
Sub	10	3	4	4	5	2	10	18	0	1	1
Minutes on pitch	450	64	256	125	1248	2634	1249	998	3240	118	22
GOAL ATTEMPTS											
Goals	0	0	0	1	0	7	1	1	3	0	0
Shots on target	1	0	1	1	3	31	3	7	20	0	0
Shots off target	1	3	0	1	3	24	9	8	36	0	0
Shooting accuracy %	50%	0%	100%	50%	50%	56%	25%	47%	36%	0%	0%
PASSING											
Goal assists	0	0	0	0	1	2	0	2	2	0	0
Long passes	21	1	19	0	72	14	44	8	212	22	0
Short passes	248	11	80	48	247	1081	449	230	1243	25	7
PASS COMPLETION											
Own half %	86%	100%	73%	73%	92%	89%	91%	77%	90%	87%	100%
Opposition half %	84%	70%	59%	86%	59%	73%	77%	64%	76%	47%	67%
CROSSING											
Total crosses	20	0	3	0	3	20	9	21	240	0	1
Cross completion %	25%	0%	33%	0%	0%	20%	56%	24%	34%	0%	100%
DRIBBLING											
Dribbles & runs	8	0	5	1	2	53	10	17	45	1	1
Dribble completion %	88%	0%	80%	0%	100%	66%	80%	71%	89%	100%	100%
DEFENDING											
Tackles made	19	5	14	1	39	49	44	17	163	4	0
Tackles won %	58%	80%	57%	0%	62%	55%	66%	47%	67%	100%	0%
Blocks	2	0	1	0	14	2	4	3	18	1	0
Clearances	14	5	8	1	151	22	39	1	130	24	0
Interceptions	13	0	5	0	29	10	14	4	46	1	0
DISCIPLINE											
Fouls	3	0	2	4	11	64	20	29	47	0	0
Offside	0	0	0	1	0	29	0	24	3	0	2
Yellow cards	0	0	0	0	1	3	1	5	4	0	0
Red cards	0	0	0	0	0	0	1	0	0	0	0

GOALKEEPER NAME	START/ (SUB)	TIME ON PITCH	GOALS CONCEDED	MINS/GOALS CONCEDED	SAVES MADE	SAVES/ SHOTS
ILIC	23	1979	33	60	78	70%
PETTERSON	7 (3)	755	18	41.9	21	54%
ROYCE	8	675	5	135	16	76%

PLAYERS' STATISTICS

	MENDONCA	MILLS	MORTIMER	NEWTON	PARKER	POWELL	PRINGLE	REDFEARN	ROBINSON	RUFUS	STUART	TILER	YOUDS	TOTAL	RANK
	19	36	10	13	0	38	15	29	27	27	9	27	21		
	6	0	7	3	4	0	3	1	3	0	0	0	1		
	1687	3138	834	1061	34	3411	1343	2501	2337	2270	810	2360	1907		
	8	2	1	0	0	0	3	3	2	1	3	1	2	41*	=12th
	20	11	6	4	0	3	21	27	15	5	5	8	3	195	7th
	10	19	4	5	0	3	5	46	12	5	9	13	4	220	=11th
	67%	37%	60%	44%	0%	50%	81%	37%	56%	50%	36%	38%	43%	47%	5th
	2	2	1	2	1	0	0	1	1	1	0		2	21	20th
	12	359	43	35	1	278	8	127	93	116	21	150	110	1766	15th
	485	740	265	362	7	819	447	829	604	448	294	466	410	9845	19th
	87%	85%	89%	89%	100%	87%	80%	87%	88%	90%	83%	83%	89%	87%	14th
	75%	59%	65%	66%	60%	70%	69%	67%	67%	66%	75%	67%	66%	69%	13th
	6	87	35	37	2	106	11	20	143	6	38	8	1	817	5th
	0%	16%	31%	27%	0%	24%	27%	20%	25%	17%	16%	25%	0%	26%	17th
	14	101	43	53	0	111	52	38	120	15	27	4	7	728	19th
	79%	71%	53%	75%	0%	70%	58%	76%	56%	87%	70%	100%	86%	69%	13th
	18	133	37	39	2	100	32	83	85	71	25	63	61	1106	17th
	28%	62%	68%	56%	50%	75%	41%	66%	61%	68%	56%	71%	79%	64%	1st
	1	22	3	4	0	29	1	10	10	27	3	26	23	204	10th
	4	318	23	34	0	231	11	72	56	323	2	391	278	2171	2nd
	2	38	3	4	0	38	14	10	14	29	3	24	17	322	13th
	28	46	12	7	1	26	18	83	40	25	11	42	53	574	4th
	34	0	5	2	0	4	22	5	16	1	1	1	1	151	5th
	0	10	1	2	0	2	1	9	8	1	2	6	6	63	=13th
	0	0	0	0	0	0	0	0	0	2†	0	0	0	4†	=7th

†one red card vs Leeds United expunged   *including two own goals

CROSSES CAUGHT	CROSSES PUNCHED	CROSSES NOT CLAIMED	CATCH SUCCESS	THROWS/ SHORT KICKS	% COMPLETION	LONG KICKS	% COMPLETION
69	9	10	95%	89	83%	613	37%
16	4	1	100%	28	86%	231	38%
23	12	3	96%	45	96%	207	41%

PLAYER OF THE SEASON

PLAYER	INDEX SCORE
MARK KINSELLA	1023
Danny Mills	889
Carl Tiler	838
Chris Powell	774
Richard Rufus	774
Eddie Youds	727
John Robinson	726
Andy Hunt	709
Neil Redfearn	627
Sasa Ilic	518

A key figure in Charlton's promotion-winning side of 1997–98, Mark Kinsella was subsequently voted the club's Player of the Season.

After a barnstorming 1998–99, toiling as hard as anyone to try and keep the Addicks in the Premiership, he was honoured with the same accolade. And his performances also resulted in the Eire international becoming the highest-rated Charlton player in the Carling Opta Season Index.

He was the club's top passer and tackler, and the most accurate corner-taker in the Premiership among those players who took 100 corners or more – not bad for a player who only arrived at Charlton from lowly Colchester in September 1996. That £150,000 price tag looks like a real snip these days.

Another bargain-basement buy, Danny Mills, finished second in the top 10. Mills had made just 10 appearances for Charlton before this season, having cost £350,000 from Norwich. But he was thrust straight into the thick of the Premiership campaign and his mature performances were enough to earn call-ups to the England under-21 side.

Central defender Carl Tiler was bought from Everton and immediately made an impression with a goal on his debut. Alan Curbishley clearly hoped Tiler's top-flight experience would be an important factor in his back-line. He joined Kinsella and Mills as probably the most consistent performers in the squad.

The other players in the top 10 all showed flashes of Premiership class without being able to maintain that form throughout the season. Players such as Neil Redfearn, Eddie Youds and Sasa Ilic all enjoyed superb 1997–98 campaigns but, for various reasons, struggled to reach their peak in Charlton's first Premiership season.

There is no place in the top 10 for top scorer Clive Mendonca, who did not play enough games to qualify after suffering with injury.

FIVE OF THE BEST

Charlton Athletic began the 1998–99 season as hot favourites to be relegated, with some sections of the media cheekily suggesting they might be the first side ever to be down by Bonfire Night. But Charlton's fight to beat the drop lasted until the final day of a dramatic season, when Alan Curbishley and his battling troops finally bade farewell to the Carling Premiership.

TOP GOALSCORERS	GOALS	GOALS/SHOTS
CLIVE MENDONCA	8	27%
Andy Hunt	7	13%
Graham Stuart	3	21%
Martin Pringle	3	12%
Mark Kinsella	3	5%

Scoring goals did not prove as much of a problem for Charlton as it did for some of the other Premiership strugglers, but there is no doubt that their lack of firepower told in the end. Clive Mendonca finished once again as the club's top scorer, scoring with more than a quarter of his shots, but he had six goals by Christmas and added only two more before the end of the campaign. New signings Graham Stuart and Martin Pringle weighed in to ensure Charlton fought to the very death.

Player of the Season for the second year running was skipper Mark Kinsella, who epitomised Charlton's marvellous spirit with his energetic performances in midfield. He was the only Addick to complete more than 1,000 passes, finding a team-mate with more than four out of every five balls. Chris Powell enjoyed a good season after his switch from Derby, while Andy Hunt saw plenty of the ball for a striker. Danny Mills and the experienced Neil Redfearn complete the top five passers.

TOP PASSERS	SUCC PASSES	COMPLETION
MARK KINSELLA	1,174	81%
Chris Powell	822	75%
Andy Hunt	772	71%
Danny Mills	710	65%
Neil Redfearn	697	73%

TOP TACKLERS	WON	SUCCESS
MARK KINSELLA	110	67%
Danny Mills	83	62%
Chris Powell	75	75%
Neil Redfearn	55	66%
John Robinson	52	61%

Charlton might have had a miserable run of eight straight defeats during the course of the season – but they were rarely a pushover, even for the top teams. They played a crisp, attractive passing game, but were not afraid to adopt a physical approach to stifle the opposition and only three teams scored more than three goals against them. Mark Kinsella was the side's best tackler, winning more than 100 challenges over the course of the season, with promising full-back Danny Mills second.

Veteran of the lower leagues and the focal point of Barnsley's battle to avoid the drop in 1997–98, Neil Redfearn curried no favour with referees at Charlton. He and Danny Mills picked up 19 league bookings between them, with Redfearn committing 83 fouls, the fourth most in the Premiership. Richard Rufus, who picked up two red cards during the season, is only 10th in the Charlton discipline charts, having committed just 25 fouls, so Andy Hunt, Eddie Youds and John Robinson complete the top five.

DISCIPLINE	POINTS	FOULS & CARDS
NEIL REDFEARN	110	83F, 9Y, 0R
Danny Mills	76	46F, 10Y, 0R
Andy Hunt	73	64F, 3Y, 0R
Eddie Youds	71	53F, 6Y, 0R
John Robinson	64	40F, 8Y, 0R

ACTION	HUNT	S JONES	KINSELLA	MENDONCA	MILLS	MORTIMER	PETTERSON	POWELL	REDEARN	ROBINSON	RUFUS	TILER	YOUDS	TOTAL	WEST HAM
Time on pitch	90	5	90	85	90	90	90	90	90	25	90	65	90	990	990
GOALS															
Goal	–	–	–	–	1	–	–	–	–	–	–	–	–	4	–
Shot on target	2	–	–	–	–	–	–	–	–	–	–	–	–	9	2
Shot off target	–	–	–	1	2	–	–	–	5	–	–	–	–	11	4
Blocked shot	–	–	–	–	2	–	–	–	–	–	–	–	–	5	1
Own goal	–	–	–	–	–	–	–	–	–	–	–	–	–	–	–
PASSES															
Pass to own player	28	1	41	19	28	29	–	21	26	12	25	15	23	268	203
Pass to opposition	11	2	5	5	9	7	–	–	8	–	4	4	7	63	51
Cross to own player	1	–	8	–	–	–	–	–	–	–	–	–	–	10	2
Cross to opposition player	2	–	8	–	6	5	6	–	2	2	–	–	1	30	16
Goal assist	–	–	–	–	–	1	–	–	–	–	–	–	–	2	2
Pass completion %	69%	25%	79%	79%	65%	72%	0%	75%	76%	86%	86%	79%	77%	75%	76%
TACKLES & CLEARANCES															
Tackle	2	–	8	–	2	11	–	5	5	1	5	2	2	43	38
Clearances, blocks and interceptions	–	–	–	–	1	5	–	6	2	–	15	17	11	57	104
DRIBBLES & RUNS															
Dribble ball retained	1	–	2	–	6	2	–	4	1	3	3	–	–	22	16
Dribble ball lost	–	–	–	–	4	1	–	1	2	3	–	–	–	11	10
Dribble success %	100%	0%	100%	0%	60%	67%	0%	80%	33%	50%	100%	0%	0%	67%	62%
DISCIPLINE															
Fouls	2	–	–	–	–	2	–	–	5	–	–	–	2	11	15
Penalty conceded	–	–	–	–	–	–	–	–	–	–	–	–	–	1	1
Free kick - offside	–	–	2	–	–	–	–	–	–	–	–	–	–	2	10
Yellow cards	–	–	–	–	–	–	–	–	–	–	–	–	–	–	3
Red cards	–	–	–	–	–	–	–	–	–	–	–	–	–	–	–
GOALKEEPERS															
Distribution to own player	–	–	–	–	–	–	4	–	–	–	–	–	–	4	19
Distribution to opposition player	–	–	–	–	–	–	18	–	–	–	–	–	–	18	12
Goalkeeper distribution %	–	–	–	–	–	–	18%	–	–	–	–	–	–	18%	61%
Save	–	–	–	–	–	–	2	–	–	–	–	–	–	2	2
Ball caught	–	–	–	–	–	–	3	–	–	–	–	–	–	3	9
Ball dropped	–	–	–	–	–	–	–	–	–	–	–	–	–	–	11
Goal conceded	–	–	–	–	–	–	2	–	–	–	–	–	–	2	4

Charlton went into the second of three consecutive London derbies on the back of a 2–1 defeat by Chelsea. Their opponents West Ham had just fought out a goalless draw with early season pace-setters Aston Villa and were looking to consolidate with a win at the Valley.

October 24, 1998

4–2

CHARLTON ATHLETIC
WEST HAM UNITED

The match itself was played in dreadful conditions, with driving rain and a strong wind making it a difficult day for defenders. Charlton made their intentions clear as early as the seventh minute when Danny Mills embarked on the first of six successful runs past Julian Dicks to drive in a left-footed shot that was well saved by Shaka Hislop.

However, West Ham survived this early Charlton pressure to take the lead in the 17th minute, when the unfortunate Richard Rufus, under pressure from an onrushing Ian Wright, headed into his own net.

The visitors then squandered the chance to go further ahead when an unmarked John Hartson blasted over the bar from eight yards out. This spurred Charlton into action and, when Mark Kinsella swung in a corner in the 29th minute, Carl Tiler scrambled the ball into the net for his first goal in a Charlton shirt.

The Addicks pressed forward after that, but it was West Ham who went into the break with the advantage. Berkovic fed the ball to Lomas and the Northern Ireland international played a slide-rule pass to Wright on the flank. Charlton appealed in vain for offside as Wright centred the ball for a grateful Berkovic to stab home from six yards.

The pattern of the game changed in the 65th minute when Alan Curbishley brought on John Robinson for Tiler and switched to a 4–4–2 formation. The move paid dividends after 73 minutes when the already beleaguered Dicks was forced to concede a corner under pressure from Robinson and Mills headed home from Paul Mortimer's centre.

With their tails up, Charlton went further ahead in the 87th minute. Trevor Sinclair was judged to be offside and from the free kick Eddie Youds launched a rocket into the West Ham box. Andy Hunt was alive to the opportunity, slipping in between two defenders to smash the ball home with his left foot.

Then, with the game already won, Charlton added a final flourish when Robinson was checked in the box by Rio Ferdinand and Neil Redfearn lashed in the resulting penalty.

Man of the match with 1,590 points was Danny Mills, who tormented Julian Dicks with his pace down the right. He scored one and came close with a further five efforts. Mark Kinsella came second with 1,535 and John Robinson scored a creditable 645 points in his 25 minutes as a substitute.

In a frantic and often entertaining match, Charlton made the most of West Ham's uncertainty in defence with three goals from set-pieces. The never-say-die attitude which got them back into the match was to be a hallmark of their season – but could not save them from the drop.

ACTION	BARNES	BROWN	S. JONES	KINSELLA	MENDONCA	MILLS	PETTERSON	POWELL	PRINGLE	REDFEARN	ROBINSON	RUFUS	STUART	TILER	TOTAL	ASTON VILLA
Time on pitch	7	11	90	90	83	90	79	90	7	83	79	90	90	90	979	989
GOALS																
Goal	–	–	–	–	1	1	–	–	–	1	–	–	–	–	3	3
Shot on target	–	–	–	–	1	–	–	–	–	–	1	–	–	–	2	6
Shot off target	–	–	–	–	–	–	–	–	–	3	–	–	2	–	5	2
Blocked shot	–	–	1	–	–	–	–	–	–	–	–	–	–	–	1	6
Own goal	–	–	–	–	–	–	–	–	–	–	–	–	–	–	–	1
PASSES																
Pass to own player	3	–	18	24	17	25	–	12	1	24	16	10	30	13	193	329
Pass to opposition	2	–	17	5	9	10	–	8	1	7	7	6	7	9	88	99
Cross to own player	–	–	–	–	–	–	–	–	–	–	–	–	–	–	1	3
Cross to opposition player	–	–	1	5	1	2	–	1	–	–	2	–	1	–	13	19
Goal assist	–	–	–	1	–	–	–	–	–	–	–	–	–	–	2	2
Pass completion %	60%	0%	53%	71%	63%	68%	0%	57%	50%	77%	64%	63%	79%	59%	66%	74%
TACKLES & CLEARANCES																
Tackle	1	–	5	3	–	8	–	–	–	2	3	4	6	4	36	37
Clearances, blocks and interceptions	–	–	2	13	1	13	–	6	2	3	3	20	2	25	90	70
DRIBBLES & RUNS																
Dribble ball retained	1	–	3	3	1	3	–	–	–	2	–	1	2	–	16	17
Dribble ball lost	–	–	–	–	1	3	–	1	–	–	2	–	1	–	8	7
Dribble success %	100%	0%	100%	100%	50%	50%	0%	0%	0%	100%	0%	100%	67%	0%	67%	71%
DISCIPLINE																
Fouls	–	–	3	1	4	2	1	1	–	3	3	1	–	1	20	10
Penalty conceded	–	–	–	–	–	–	–	–	–	–	–	–	–	–	–	–
Free kick - offside	–	–	2	1	–	–	–	–	–	1	–	–	–	–	3	–
Yellow cards	–	–	1	–	–	–	–	–	–	1	–	–	–	–	2	1
Red cards	–	–	–	–	–	–	1	–	–	–	–	–	–	–	1	1
GOALKEEPERS																
Distribution to own player	–	1	–	–	–	–	16	–	–	–	–	–	–	1	17	10
Distribution to opposition player	–	3	–	–	–	–	11	–	–	–	–	–	–	–	14	18
Goalkeeper distribution%	0%	25%	0%	0%	0%	0%	59%	0%	0%	0%	0%	0%	0%	0%	55%	36%
Save	3	1	–	–	–	–	3	–	–	–	–	–	–	–	6	2
Ball caught	–	1	–	–	–	–	3	–	–	–	–	–	–	–	4	2
Ball dropped	–	–	–	–	–	–	–	–	–	–	–	–	–	–	–	–
Goal conceded	–	–	–	–	–	–	3	–	–	–	–	–	–	–	3	4

Charlton travelled to Villa Park with their whole season hanging in the balance. The match was a must-win. Should they lose, and results go against them, the men from the Valley would be relegated from the Carling Premiership. The match caught fire straight away, and the first goal came after just four minutes had elapsed.

May 8, 1999

3–4

ASTON VILLA
CHARLTON ATHLETIC

John Robinson crossed from the left and Villa defender Gareth Barry beat Graham Stuart to the ball but headed it into his own net. Villa drew level three minutes later, and it was Barry who atoned for his earlier error by scoring the equalizer. A breakdown in communication between Richard Rufus and keeper Andy Petterson caused Rufus to clear across the face of the penalty area – straight to Barry, who side-footed first-time into the empty net for 1–1.

The second-half scoring began in the 57th minute. Clive Mendonca took a Steve Jones flick-on, held off the challenge from Gareth Southgate and slammed the ball past Oakes.

Eleven minutes later Villa equalized again, when substitute Darius Vassell's flick-on was pounced on by Julian Joachim. He sped away down the left channel and planted a left-footed angled drive into the far corner. It took Charlton just two minutes to retake the lead. Mendonca's close-range shot was parried into the air by Oakes and Robinson rose to head the ball just over the line before Southgate could clear.

The Charlton fans' ecstasy turned to despair when, with 12 minutes to go, a goalmouth scramble led to Joachim side-footing into the roof of the net from close range. With results going against them, things looked bad for the Addicks – but they were to get worse a minute later.

Joachim flew through the middle but was pole-axed 20 yards from goal by the onrushing Petterson, who was sent off for a professional foul. With no replacement goalkeeper on the bench, substitute full-back Steve Brown pulled on the gloves. He lined up his wall for the free kick, then dived spectacularly to his left to palm away Steve Stone's curling shot.

With just one minute of normal time remaining, Jones's flick-on put substitute Martin Pringle through the middle, but he was pulled down just outside the area by Steve Watson, who was dismissed.

From the free kick, Charlton's captain Mark Kinsella rolled the ball into the path of Danny Mills, and he rifled a deflected shot into the top left-hand corner of the Villa goal. It was Mills's goal, and the strike that gave Charlton hope going into their last game of the season at Sheffield Wednesday.

Charlton were comprehensively out-passed and out-shot by Villa, but were far more efficient in front of goal. The Carling Opta stats confirm that Charlton scored with three of their five efforts on target (Villa also scored an own goal), while Villa made nine attempts but scored with only three.

The tackle count was 37 to 36 in favour of the Birmingham club, but Charlton made a superb 90 defensive clearances, blocks and interceptions to Villa's 70. Despite being dominated in the middle of the field, Charlton fought for their chances, and were clinical enough to win a superbly entertaining match.

CHELSEA 1998–99

Back row (left to right): John Kelly (Masseur), Jon Harley, Andy Myers, Steve Hampshire, Paul Hughes, Neil Clement, Joe Sheerin, Kevin Hitchcock, David Lee, Stephen Broad, John Terry, Robert Wolleaston, Nick Crittenden, Luca Percasi, Aaron Lincoln (Kit Manager).

Middle row: Eddie Niedzwiecki (Goalkeeping Coach), Mick McGiven (Reserve Team Coach), Celestine Babayaro, Mark Nicholls, Bernard Lambourde, Marcel Desailly, Tore Andre Flo, Ed De Goey, Steve Clarke (Coach, now Newcastle United), Dmitri Kharine, Michael Duberry, Gustavo Poyet, Brian Laudrup (now Ajax), Jay Richardson, Albert Ferrer, Mike Banks (Physiotherapist), Terry Byrne (Assistant Physiotherapist).

Front row: Antonio Pintus (Fitness Coach), Graeme Le Saux, Dan Petrescu, Eddie Newton, Frank Leboeuf, Dennis Wise, Graham Rix (First Team Coach), Gianluca Vialli (Manager), Gwyn Williams (Assistant Manager), Roberto Di Matteo, Pierluigi Casiraghi, Frank Sinclair (now Leicester City), Gianfranco Zola, Jody Morris, Ade Mafe (Fitness Coach).

CHELSEA

20 FACTS

1 Chelsea owe their existence to Fulham. The Cottagers rejected an offer to rent Stamford Bridge from the owner Mr H A Mears in 1905. Mears was determined to develop the ground as a football stadium and Chelsea were formed in the same year.

2 Chelsea have been league champions just once – in 1954–55.

3 The Blues have played in the FA Cup final on five occasions, winning the trophy in 1970 and 1997.

4 The club have also played in three Football League Cup finals, winning the trophy in 1965 and 1998.

5 Chelsea have played in European competitions on eight occasions and won the European Cup Winners Cup twice in 1970–71 and 1997–98. They have never appeared in the European Cup but will feature in 1999–2000 Champions League competition.

6 Chelsea's Championship-winning points total of 52 in the 1954–55 season is the lowest title-winning total in the post-war period.

7 Chelsea's record league victory was a 9–2 win against Glossop in September 1906. Their record win in cup competition came in September 1971, in the second round of the European Cup Winners Cup, when they beat Jeunesse Hautcharage 8–0 and 13–0. The 21–0 aggregate is the joint highest in the history of European club competition.

8 The club's record defeat came in September 1953 when they were beaten 8–1 by Wolverhampton Wanderers.

9 George Hilsdon holds the English record for the most goals scored on a league debut. He scored five in the Blues' record league win against Glossop.

10 Hilsdon also holds Chelsea's record for the most goals scored in one match – six in the club's 9–1 FA Cup victory over Worksop in January 1908.

11 The player with the record number of league appearances for Chelsea is Ron Harris who played 655 league matches in a total of 803 appearances in all competitions from 1962 to 1980.

12 Ex-Chelsea player Vinnie Jones holds the record for the fastest-ever booking. He was shown the yellow card after only three seconds in an FA Cup fifth-round match between Chelsea and Sheffield United in 1992.

13 The club's record attendance came in 1935 when 82,905 people watched a Division One match between Chelsea and Arsenal.

14 Chelsea's Jimmy Greaves became the youngest player to reach 100 league goals when he scored against Manchester City in November 1960 at the age of 20 years and 261 days.

15 Chelsea finished third in the 1998–99 Carling Premiership, qualifying for the Champions League. Their league record was:

Pld	W	D	L	F	A	Pts
38	20	15	3	57	30	75

16 Chelsea reached the quarter-finals of the AXA-sponsored FA Cup. The Blues defeated Oldham 2–0, Oxford 4–1 after a 1–1 draw, and Sheffield Wednesday 1–0 to reach the sixth round. They drew with Manchester United 0–0 at Old Trafford before being eliminated 2–0 in the replay.

17 The Blues also reached the last eight in the Worthington Cup. After beating Aston Villa 4–1 and Arsenal 5–0, Gianluca Vialli's team were beaten 2–1 by Wimbledon at Selhurst Park.

18 Chelsea failed in their bid to become the only team to retain the European Cup Winners Cup. They beat Helsingborg of Sweden 1–0 on aggregate in the first round and FC Copenhagen 2–1 on aggregate in the second round. Valerenga of Norway were beaten 6–2 over two legs in the quarter-finals. But after a 1–1 home draw in the semi-final first leg against Real Mallorca of Spain, Chelsea lost the away game 1–0 and were went out of the competition.

19 The top goalscorer in 1998–99 in all competitions for Chelsea was Gianfranco Zola with 15 goals.

20 Chelsea's disciplinary record was the second-worst in the Premiership. They committed 548 fouls, earned 85 yellow cards and received four red cards.

SEASON REVIEW

Chelsea set a host of club records in 1998–99, yet the major trophies eluded them. On their day the team were world-beaters, but the lack of a real killer instinct in front of goal cost them dearly in the Championship run-in. Despite losing just three games, the fewest in the club's history, they had to settle for third place in the Premiership.

The opening day loss at Coventry seemed to delight those who were critical of the club's foreign policy. Chelsea fielded just two English players in their first starting line-up and the sight of Dion Dublin getting the better of World Cup-winning duo Frank Leboeuf and compatriot Marcel Desailly was almost welcomed by those who disapproved of the "foreign invasion".

That defeat was to be the last in the league for nearly six months. The first league victory of the season came with a 2–1 result against Nottingham Forest at Stamford Bridge. Gustavo Poyet – who had hit the winner in the European Super Cup game with Real Madrid two weeks earlier – scored the second goal.

The Uruguayan's form in the opening months of the season was a major factor in the club's rise up the table, and he was badly missed after his injury in the Boxing Day game with Southampton.

Of more concern in these early months was the form of Pierluigi Casiraghi. The former Lazio player had arrived for a club record £5.4 million in July, but did not find the net until October. Many fans had grown impatient with the Italian. Their belief that Norwegian Tore Andre Flo should be in the side instead was given weight by his two-goal performance as a substitute at Blackburn, but Gianluca Vialli was determined to keep faith with his fellow-Italian.

Casiraghi's season ended with a serious injury at West Ham – and Brian Laudrup's departure from the club three days earlier left Chelsea short of options up front.

Despite the best efforts of the player-manager Vialli, Gianfranco Zola, Flo and the Finnish youngster Mikael Forssell, the club's lack of a prolific goalscorer arguably cost them the title.

They had no problem imposing their slick passing style on opponents. Neither did they shirk the more physical side of the game, committing the fifth-highest number of fouls in the Premiership and picking up the second-highest amount of bookings.

It was the fact that they finished the season with the second largest number of shots off target and the third-worst shooting accuracy which cost them top spot. In home games against Arsenal, Manchester United, Blackburn Rovers, West Ham and Leicester City they completely dominated the play but failed to come away with maximum points.

Off-the-field problems involving coach Graham Rix did not help matters and encouraged the previously media-friendly Vialli to retreat from the public eye. By the time his team had surrendered a two-goal lead against Leicester City on April 18, their Championship challenge was all but over.

Chelsea fans contented themselves with Champions League qualification, Vialli pointed to the fact that his side conceded fewer goals and kept more clean sheets in all competitions than any other Chelsea side before them and chairman Ken Bates afforded himself a smile at the fact that every home game had been a sell-out. But in truth everyone connected with Chelsea knew that the team could, and perhaps should, have won the Championship.

The season was barely over before rumours linking Chelsea with strikers of the calibre of Marco Delvecchio and Chris Sutton began to appear on the back pages. With a 20-goal-a-season man up front the Blues would undoubtedly be a force to be reckoned with both at home and abroad.

> **"The Championship was within our grasp but in the end we threw it away"**
>
> **Ken Bates**

CHELSEA

DATE	OPPONENT	SCORE	ATT.	BABAYARO	CASIRAGHI	DE GOEY	DESAILLY	DI MATTEO	DUBERRY	FERRER	FLO	FORSSELL	GOLDBAEK
15.8.98	Coventry A	1–2	23,042	90	90	90	90	76	–	90□	s22	–	–
22.8.98	Newcastle H	1–1	34,795	90[1]	90□	90	90	90	90□	90	s17	–	–
9.9.98	Arsenal H	0–0	34,647	90	90□	90	90	90	90□	–	s7	–	–
12.9.98	Nott'm For H	2–1	34,809	90	89	90	90	–	90	–	–	–	–
21.9.98	Blackburn A	4–3	23,113	90	78	90	90	s36	90□	90	s12[2]	–	–
26.9.98	Middlesbro A	2–0*	34,814	90□	45	90	90	90□	s6	90□	s45	–	–
4.10.98	Liverpool A	1–1	44,404	–	70[1]	90	90	90	90□	90	s20	–	–
17.10.98	Charlton H	2–1	34,642	90	73	90	54	90□	90	90□	s17	–	–
25.10.98	Leeds Utd A	0–0	35,833	90□	75	90□	90	90□	90□	90	s15	–	–
8.11.98	West Ham A	1–1	26,023	90[1]	24	90	90	45	–	90	s66	–	–
14.11.98	Wimbledon H	3–0	34,800	90	–	90	90	85	s10	–	90	–	–
21.11.98	Leicester A	4–2	21,401	90	–	90□	90	90	s25	90	90[1]	–	65
28.11.98	Sheff Wed H	1–1	34,451	90	–	90	90□	77	–	90	90	–	77
5.12.98	Everton A	0–0	36,430	90	–	90	90	90	s57	90	90□	–	s27
9.12.98	Aston Villa H	2–1	34,765	80	–	90	90	90□	90	90	s25[1]	–	–
12.12.98	Derby Co A	2–2	29,056	s1	–	90	–	–	90	–	90[1]□	–	45
16.12.98	Man Utd A	1–1	55,159	90	–	90	–	90□	90	90□	90	–	–
19.12.98	Tottenham H	2–0	34,881	90□	–	90	–	–	90□	90	s19[1]	–	s1
26.12.98	Southampton A	2–0	15,253	90□	–	90	–	–	90	90	83[1]	–	90
29.12.98	Man Utd H	0–0	34,741	90	–	90	s17	90□	90	90	90	–	s2
9.1.99	Newcastle A	1–0	36,711	–	–	90	90□	90	90	90□	–	–	–
16.1.99	Coventry H	2–1	34,869	90	–	90	–	90[1]	–	85	–	–	s5
31.1.99	Arsenal A	0–1	38,121	90	–	90	90	90	39	–	–	s16	s51□
6.2.99	Southampton H	1–0	34,920	78	–	90	90	90□	–	–	62	–	s12
17.2.99	Blackburn H	1–1	34,822	90□	–	90	90	90	–	–	–	s1	s8
20.2.99	Nott'm For A	3–1	26,351	90	–	90	90	–	–	90	s29	86[1]	90[2]
27.2.99	Liverpool H	2–1	34,822	–	–	90	90	90	–	90[1]	87	s3	90[1]
13.3.99	West Ham H	0–1	34,765	90	–	90	60	90	s30□	90	90	s7	90
21.3.99	Aston Villa A	3–0	39,217	–	–	90	90□	–	–	90□	89[2]	–	90[1]
3.4.99	Charlton H	1–0	20,046	–	–	45	90	86[1]	s4	90	90	–	90
11.4.99	Wimbledon A	2–1	21,577	–	–	90	–	45	90□	–	90[1]	–	90
14.4.99	Middlesbro A	0–0	34,406	–	–	90	90□	s44	90	90□	90	–	90□
18.4.99	Leicester H	2–2*	34,535	–	–	90	90	90	s15	75	90	–	45
25.4.99	Sheff Wed A	0–0	21,652	90□	–	–	90	–	–	90□	–	45	90
1.5.99	Everton H	3–1	34,909	s8	–	90	90	–	–	90	–	90	s30
5.5.99	Leeds Utd H	1–0	34,762	–	–	90	90	s8	–	90	82	s1	s23
10.5.99	Tottenham A	2–2	35,878	–	–	–	90□	s25□	–	90□	90	s35	s25[1]
16.5.99	Derby Co H	2–1	35,016	45[1]	–	–	–	76	57	90	90	–	–

□ Yellow card, ■ Red card, s Substitute, 90[3] Goals scored
*including own goal

1998–99 PREMIERSHIP APPEARANCES

HITCHCOCK	KHARINE	LAMBOURDE	LAUDRUP	LE SAUX	LEBOEUF	MORRIS	MYERS	NEWTON	NICHOLLS	PETRESCU	POYET	TERRY	VIALLI	WISE	ZOLA	TOTAL
–	–	–	–	90	90	–	–	–	–	–	90¹	–	68□	90□	s14	990
–	–	–	–	57	90□	–	–	–	–	s33	73	–	–	–	90	990
–	–	70	58	90□	90	–	–	–	–	s20	s32	–	–	–	83	990
–	–	s7	s1	90	90	–	90	–	–	90□	83¹	–	–	–	90¹	990
–	–	–	s20	67□	90¹□	–	–	–	–	–	90	–	–	54	70¹	967
–	–	–	75	90	84	–	–	–	–	s15	90	–	–	–	90¹	990
–	–	s1	89	90	90	–	–	–	–	90□	s29	–	–	–	61	990
–	–	–	90	–	90¹□	–	–	–	–	s17	90¹	–	–	s36□	73	990
–	–	–	90	–	61□	–	–	–	–	–	s24	–	–	90□	66□	961
–	–	90	–	90	–	–	–	–	s24	s45	90□	–	–	90	66	990
–	–	90	–	90□	90	s5	–	–	s10	90¹	80¹	–	–	–	80¹	990
–	–	–	–	90	90	–	–	–	–	–	90¹	–	–	–	90²	990
–	–	–	–	90	90□	s13	–	–	–	s13	90	–	–	–	90¹	990
–	–	–	–	–	90	–	–	–	–	90□	33□	–	–	37□	63	937
–	–	–	–	90	90	–	–	–	–	90	s10	–	90□	–	65¹	990
–	–	90	–	90	90	89	–	–	s1	s45	90¹	–	–	90	89	990
–	–	90□	–	44	–	–	–	–	–	90□	s46	–	–	90□	90¹	990
–	–	89	–	–	90	90	–	–	–	90	90¹	–	90□	–	71	990
–	–	–	–	90	90□	73	–	–	s7	90	73¹	s17	–	–	90	990
–	–	–	–	88	90□	73	–	–	–	90	–	–	–	–	90	990
–	–	–	–	90□	90	–	–	–	s1	90¹	–	–	90	90	89	990
–	–	90	–	90	90¹	–	–	–	–	90	–	–	90	90	90	990
–	–	–	–	90	90□	–	–	–	–	90□	–	–	90	90	74	990
–	–	–	–	90	90	90	–	–	s28	90	–	–	–	90	90¹	990
–	–	90□	–	26	90□	89¹□	s64	–	–	82	–	–	85□	–	90	985
–	–	90	–	–	90	90□	–	s45	s4	45	–	–	–	–	61	990
–	–	s55	–	84□	35¹	90	–	s6	–	90	–	–	–	–	90	990
–	–	–	–	60	–	–	83	–	–	s30□	–	–	–	90	90	990
–	–	s12	–	90	90	90	–	–	s1	78	–	–	–	90□	90	990
s45	–	–	–	90	90	71	–	–	–	–	s19□	–	–	90□	90	990
–	–	90	–	90	90	s45	–	s3	s1	87	90¹	–	–	–	89	990
–	–	–	–	90	–	s22	–	–	–	46	68	–	–	90	90	990
–	–	–	–	s45	90	70	–	–	–	90□	s20	–	–	90	90¹	990
90	–	90	–	–	90	–	–	s30	–	–	60	–	90	90	s45	990
–	–	s19	–	90	71	82	–	–	–	60¹	90	–	–	90	90²	990
–	–	–	–	90	90	67□	–	–	–	90□	90¹	–	–	90□	89	990
90	–	–	–	90	90	65	–	–	–	65	90¹□	–	–	90	55	990
–	90	90□	–	90	–	–	–	s14	–	s45	90	s33	90¹	90	–	990

THE MANAGER

GIANLUCA VIALLI

Young, rich and gifted Chelsea manager Gianluca Vialli enjoyed a hugely impressive, if ultimately unfruitful, first full season as leader of the Blues brigade.

Vialli was thrust into the hot seat after Ruud Gullit's sharp exit and Chelsea's new player-boss responded perfectly, bagging a League Cup and European Cup Winners' Cup double in the club's most successful season ever. The Super Cup followed, and the Stamford Bridge outfit were installed as many people's favourites for the Carling Premiership.

Vialli drafted in compatriot Pierluigi Casiraghi for £5.4 million and Denmark's Brian Laudrup on a free, while Marcel Desailly and Albert Ferrer arrived to shore up the defence. But the early losses of Casiraghi and Laudrup interrupted Chelsea's title surge, and the Blues had to settle for third place.

Vialli's glittering playing career took him to Stamford Bridge via Cremonese, Sampdoria and Juventus. Luca was capped 59 times for Italy and played for his country when they hosted the 1990 World Cup.

Back in 1995 Vialli lifted the Champions League trophy in his last game for Juventus. He leads Chelsea into their first-ever European Cup campaign hoping that history will repeat itself come May 2000.

LEAGUE POSITION

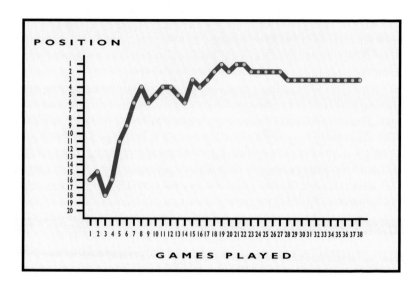

THE GOALS

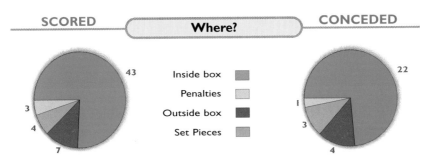

SCORED — Where? — CONCEDED

Inside box
Penalties
Outside box
Set Pieces

Chelsea's Gianfranco Zola scored more set-piece goals during the 1998–99 season than any of his rivals. The Blues registered four goals direct from free kicks – all courtesy of the cultured boot of Zola – and no other Premiership side could match this total. Ed De Goey showed excellent close-range reflexes as Chelsea conceded just 22 goals from inside the area, fewer than all other teams in the Premiership except Arsenal.

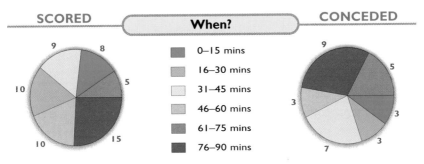

SCORED — When? — CONCEDED

0–15 mins
16–30 mins
31–45 mins
46–60 mins
61–75 mins
76–90 mins

The intensive fitness regime imposed on his players by Gianluca Vialli conditioned the team to keep concentrating right to the final whistle. On the whole, Chelsea managed to fulfil their manager's wishes and were particularly strong with two-thirds of the match gone, conceding just five goals in the last half-hour of matches. But Steve Guppy's late goal at Stamford Bridge highlighted Chelsea's tendency, like most sides, to lose concentration in the final 15 minutes.

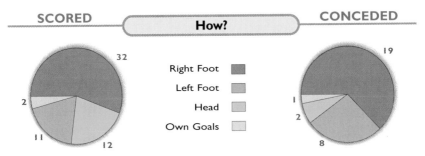

SCORED — How? — CONCEDED

Right Foot
Left Foot
Head
Own Goals

Arguably Chelsea's most influential campaigner of the 1998–99 season, Gustavo Poyet scored more headers than any other player in the Premiership. Chelsea posted the fourth-highest total of headed goals in the league with 12 and Poyet got half of them. The Blues were also the most adept side at dealing with high balls, as the opposition managed to sneak just two goals past them from headers. Left-footers had little success either.

CHELSEA

	BABAYARO	CASIRAGHI	DESAILLY	DI MATTEO	DUBERRY	FERRER	FLO	FORSSELL	GOLDBAEK	LAMBOURDE
APPEARANCES										
Start	26	10	30	26	18	30	18	4	13	12
Sub	2	0	1	4	7	0	12	6	10	5
Minutes on pitch	2282	724	2651	2313	1683	2680	1895	346	1226	1153
GOAL ATTEMPTS										
Goals	3	1	0	2	0	0	10	1	5	0
Shots on target	8	11	2	17	1	3	33	2	13	1
Shots off target	5	11	12	32	5	6	35	6	16	3
Shooting accuracy %	62%	50%	14%	35%	17%	33%	49%	25%	45%	25%
PASSING										
Goal assists	1	0	1	4	0	2	4	0	2	0
Long passes	66	3	171	96	84	213	13	2	52	56
Short passes	907	230	952	1220	315	1023	689	117	481	467
PASS COMPLETION										
Own half %	90%	98%	92%	94%	91%	91%	84%	65%	91%	88%
Opposition half %	81%	65%	79%	82%	42%	71%	75%	71%	77%	77%
CROSSING										
Total crosses	57	2	2	52	1	63	38	3	51	8
Cross completion %	23%	0%	0%	40%	100%	11%	16%	0%	25%	25%
DRIBBLING										
Dribbles & runs	50	14	11	63	8	66	103	20	48	34
Dribble completion %	60%	43%	73%	81%	75%	83%	62%	60%	73%	82%
DEFENDING										
Tackles made	82	15	124	118	55	131	33	10	37	54
Tackles won %	63%	60%	76%	59%	69%	63%	30%	50%	59%	70%
Blocks	9	0	27	7	17	14	0	0	3	10
Clearances	98	12	252	48	284	226	16	0	26	85
Interceptions	12	1	48	27	19	39	9	0	8	26
DISCIPLINE										
Fouls	54	23	29	49	43	43	50	5	11	22
Offside	5	11	0	4	2	0	39	1	5	0
Yellow cards	6	2	5	8	8	9	2	0	2	3
Red cards	0	0	0	0	0	0	0	0	0	0

GOALKEEPER NAME	START/ (SUB)	TIME ON PITCH	GOALS CONCEDED	MINS/GOALS CONCEDED	SAVES MADE	SAVES/ SHOTS
DE GOEY	35	3105	27	115	95	78%
HITCHCOCK	2 (1)	225	2	112.5	4	67%
KHARINE	1	90	1	90	4	80%

PLAYERS' STATISTICS

	LAUDRUP	LE SAUX	LEBOEUF	MORRIS	MYERS	NEWTON	NICHOLLS	PETRESCU	POYET	TERRY	VIALLI	WISE	ZOLA	TOTAL	RANK
	5	30	33	14	1	1	0	23	21	0	9	21	35		
	2	1	0	4	0	6	9	9	7	2	0	1	2		
	423	2541	2861	1231	83	252	77	2166	1910	50	783	1837	2923		
	0	0	4	1	0	0	0	3	11	0	1	0	13	57*	5th
	4	1	8	7	0	0	0	8	28	0	5	7	46	205	5th
	4	16	15	7	0	0	1	12	36	0	11	16	27	276	=2nd
	50%	6%	35%	50%	0%	0%	0%	40%	44%	0%	31%	30%	63%	43%	18th
	1	2	1	2	0	0	0	4	3	0	2	5	3	38	5th
	11	288	557	44	10	8	1	90	79	1	17	153	80	2095	3rd
	164	973	892	510	31	116	45	936	846	22	330	884	1183	13333	5th
	97%	93%	91%	90%	100%	96%	50%	90%	89%	77%	92%	92%	92%	91%	2nd
	77%	70%	62%	80%	63%	89%	84%	78%	75%	80%	70%	78%	75%	75%	3rd
	24	132	9	12	0	0	4	73	21	0	26	153	216	947	2nd
	42%	26%	33%	33%	0%	0%	50%	29%	38%	0%	15%	31%	30%	28%	11th
	49	114	57	25	0	3	2	34	29	0	31	27	145	933	8th
	67%	74%	98%	76%	0%	67%	50%	76%	72%	0%	61%	81%	71%	73%	6th
	7	101	139	35	2	9	3	76	60	1	14	89	42	1238	6th
	86%	65%	70%	51%	100%	78%	33%	57%	60%	100%	71%	57%	50%	63%	3rd
	0	5	37	7	1	0	0	8	5	1	1	10	4	169	18th
	2	175	427	26	10	14	0	74	68	5	6	30	6	1931	15th
	2	31	67	7	0	1	0	29	11	2	5	16	11	373	3rd
	1	21	37	31	2	2	2	17	30	1	19	38	17	548	5th
	11	2	0	0	0	0	5	6	3	0	23	4	36	157	4th
	0	4	7	4	0	0	0	8	4	0	3	7	1	85	=2nd
	0	1	1	0	0	0	0	0	0	0	1	1	0	4	=7th

*Including two own goals

CROSSES CAUGHT	CROSSES PUNCHED	CROSSES NOT CLAIMED	CATCH SUCCESS	THROWS/ SHORT KICKS	% COMPLETION	LONG KICKS	% COMPLETION
76	36	4	99%	292	96%	602	36%
5	3	1	100%	17	100%	55	25%
3	0	0	100%	11	82%	16	38%

PLAYER OF THE SEASON

PLAYER	INDEX SCORE
GUSTAVO POYET	1103
Frank Leboeuf	1102
Gianfranco Zola	1013
Roberto Di Matteo	965
Tore Andre Flo	910
Graeme Le Saux	905
Marcel Desailly	900
Dennis Wise	860
Albert Ferrer	856
Dan Petrescu	829

Gustavo Poyet had scored four goals in his first nine matches for Chelsea in 1997–98 before injury cut a swathe through his season. A sustained bid for Championship glory relied heavily on the former Real Zaragoza midfielder staying fit in 1998–99.

Sadly for Chelsea, history was to repeat itself. Having scored a goal at Southampton on Boxing Day to help the Blues climb to the top of the table, a tackle by Saints left-back Patrick Colleter left Poyet's season in tatters – and Chelsea faltered without him.

His importance to the side was reflected in the Carling Opta Season Index. He was Chelsea's highest-scoring player over the season, thanks to his delightful playmaking skills and surging runs into the penalty box. No one in the league scored more headed Premiership goals than him in 1998–99.

Second by just one point was World Cup-winning centre-back Frank Leboeuf.

His elegant performances in defence alongside ice-cool compatriot Marcel Desailly earned him a lucrative new contract. He earned extra Opta points for his four goals, but his week-on-week consistency held the key to his high average score across the season.

Sparkling striker Gianfranco Zola completed the international flavour of the top three, the Chelsea top scorer regularly dazzling the Stamford Bridge faithful with his mesmeric trickery. He was one of the Premiership's sharpest shooters in 1998–99, hitting the target with 63% of his shots.

Roberto Di Matteo may not have reached the form of previous seasons but the Italian was still the club's best passer, completing more than eight out of every 10 balls in the Premiership. He finished above striker Tore Andre Flo in the top 10. Flo shed his "super sub" tag after forcing his way into the first team in the second half of the season.

FIVE OF THE BEST

Chelsea surged to the top of the table for the first time in 10 years after 19 weeks of the 1998–99 season. Their squad of talented stars looked capable of securing the title — but in the end they could not keep pace with Manchester United and Arsenal and had to beat off a resurgent Leeds United side to secure third place and a Champions League spot.

TOP GOALSCORERS	GOALS	GOALS/SHOTS
GIANFRANCO ZOLA	13	18%
Gustavo Poyet	11	17%
Tore Andre Flo	10	15%
Bjarne Goldbaek	5	17%
Frank Leboeuf	4	17%

Gianluca Vialli began the 1998–99 season with a glittering portfolio of top international strikers. But with homesick Brian Laudrup leaving for Copenhagen, Gigi Casiraghi suffering an horrific knee injury and Vialli himself preferring to play mainly in the cup competitions, the Chelsea boss was not nearly so spoilt for choice as he must have hoped. Top scorer was Gianfranco Zola, with 13 Premiership goals. Midfielder Gustavo Poyet was second, despite missing a large part of the season through injury.

Chelsea's flowing European style makes them an instant hit with the football purist - and Gianluca Vialli's side is crammed full of players with slick passing skills. Italian midfielder Roberto Di Matteo heads the Chelsea passing chart with more than 1,100 completed passes and a superb success rate of 86%. French stopper Frank Leboeuf also had an impressive season, with Spanish full-back Albert Ferrer in third place after a fine first campaign in the Premiership.

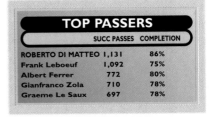

TOP PASSERS	SUCC PASSES	COMPLETION
ROBERTO DI MATTEO	1,131	86%
Frank Leboeuf	1,092	75%
Albert Ferrer	772	80%
Gianfranco Zola	710	78%
Graeme Le Saux	697	78%

TOP TACKLERS	WON	SUCCESS
FRANK LEBOEUF	97	70%
Marcel Desailly	94	76%
Albert Ferrer	83	63%
Roberto Di Matteo	70	59%
Graeme Le Saux	66	65%

World Cup-winning defensive duo Frank Leboeuf and Marcel Desailly enjoyed a terrific partnership for the Blues, winning almost 200 tackles between them. Leboeuf pipped his classy compatriot with 97 successful challenges, but Desailly had a better tackle success rate, with more than three quarters of all challenges won. Albert Ferrer and Roberto Di Matteo again appear, with England left-back Graeme Le Saux in fifth after winning 65% of his tackles.

Chelsea's cosmopolitan class of 1999 were generally pinpoint in the pass and clean in the tackle – but they ended the season with the second worst disciplinary record. Four red cards were accrued by The Blues but only Dennis Wise of those four makes the top five. Roberto Di Matteo heads the list, with full-backs Celestine Babayaro and Albert Ferrer close behind after a glut of bookings. Many of Wise's disciplinary faux pas were in cup competitions and so do not count in this list.

DISCIPLINE	POINTS	FOULS & CARDS
ROBERTO DI MATTEO	73	49F, 8Y, 0R
Celestine Babayaro	72	54F, 6Y, 0R
Albert Ferrer	70	43F, 9Y, 0R
Michael Duberry	67	43F, 8Y, 0R
Dennis Wise	65	38F, 7Y, 1R

ACTION	BABAYARO	CASIRAGHI	DE GOEY	DESAILLY	DI MATTEO	DUBERRY	FERRER	FLO	LAUDRUP	LE SAUX	LEBOEUF	POYET	WISE	ZOLA	TOTAL	BLACKBURN
Time on pitch	90	78	90	90	36	90	90	12	20	67	90	90	54	70	967	967
GOALS																
Goal	–	–	–	–	–	–	–	2	–	–	–	–	–	1	4	3
Shot on target	–	–	–	–	–	–	–	2	–	–	–	–	1	–	2	4
Shot off target	–	–	–	2	–	1	–	–	1	–	–	–	1	1	7	9
Blocked shot	–	–	–	1	1	1	–	1	–	1	–	1	–	2	3	5
Own goal	–	–	–	–	–	–	–	–	–	–	–	–	–	–	–	–
PASSES																
Pass to own player	36	23	–	42	15	13	41	5	10	23	32	35	24	21	320	273
Pass to opposition	5	7	–	3	1	3	9	1	–	5	19	6	10	8	77	70
Cross to own player	1	–	–	–	–	–	–	–	4	–	–	–	–	2	8	5
Cross to opposition player	2	–	–	–	–	–	–	–	–	–	–	–	1	–	7	20
Goal assist	–	–	–	–	–	–	1	–	–	–	–	–	–	1	2	2
Pass completion %	84%	77%	0%	93%	94%	81%	81%	83%	94%	82%	63%	83%	69%	72%	80%	76%
TACKLES & CLEARANCES																
Tackle	3	–	–	6	1	3	1	–	–	3	4	1	–	1	23	17
Clearances, blocks and interceptions	4	2	1	2	–	22	7	–	1	8	18	2	2	–	69	58
DRIBBLES & RUNS																
Dribble ball retained	2	–	–	–	1	–	2	1	5	–	–	–	3	3	20	15
Dribble ball lost	–	2	–	–	–	–	–	–	2	–	–	–	–	–	5	2
Dribble success %	100%	0%	0%	0%	100%	0%	100%	100%	71%	0%	0%	0%	100%	100%	80%	88%
DISCIPLINE																
Fouls	–	1	–	1	–	4	–	–	–	–	–	2	–	–	10	16
Penalty conceded	–	–	–	–	–	–	–	–	–	–	–	–	–	–	–	–
Free kick – offside	1	2	–	–	–	1	–	–	–	1	–	1	–	1	5	4
Yellow cards	–	–	–	–	–	1	–	–	–	–	–	–	–	–	2	2
Red cards	–	–	–	–	–	–	–	–	–	–	–	–	–	–	1	–
GOALKEEPERS																
Distribution to own player	–	–	11	–	–	–	–	–	–	–	–	–	–	–	11	30
Distribution to opposition player	–	–	12	–	–	–	–	–	–	–	–	–	–	–	12	7
Goalkeeper distribution%	0%	–	48%	0%	0%	0%	0%	0%	0%	0%	0%	0%	0%	0%	48%	81%
Save	–	–	4	–	–	–	–	–	–	–	–	–	–	–	4	2
Ball caught	–	1	3	–	–	–	–	–	–	–	–	–	–	–	3	1
Ball dropped	–	–	–	–	–	–	–	–	–	–	–	–	–	–	–	–
Goal conceded	–	–	3	–	–	–	–	–	–	–	–	–	–	–	3	4

Both sides entered this match languishing in the bottom five of the Premiership table. Blackburn were in poor form, having lost three of their first five Premiership matches, and the Blues were having difficulty integrating all their new players into a cohesive unit.

September 21, 1998

3–4

BLACKBURN ROVERS
CHELSEA

The game opened with some half-chances for both sides, but on 15 minutes the deadlock was broken. Christian Dailly barged into Pierluigi Casiraghi outside the Blackburn area and Gianfranco Zola took full advantage by blasting the resulting free kick past the despairing dive of Tim Flowers.

Zola was denied a second when Davidson cleared off the line, and barely a minute later the young full-back chipped the ball forward, only for Frank Leboeuf to misdirect a header into the penalty area to the feet of Martin Dahlin. The Swedish striker found Chris Sutton who side-stepped Graeme Le Saux and drilled the ball past Ed de Goey.

In the 51st minute, Flowers brought down Zola in the box and Frank Leboeuf stepped up to drive home the penalty.

Rovers drew level just seven minutes later. A long throw by Davidson saw Garry Flitcroft eventually find Sebastien Perez who prodded home from close range.

In the 64th minute, a bad foul by Perez on Le Saux saw the Frenchman booked. Just a few minutes later both players appeared to be pulling each other's shirts, and the tussle ended with the fiery Channel Islander lashing out at Perez and being shown the red card. Perez was shown a second yellow card and also dismissed. The normally mild-mannered Roy Hodgson was seen protesting vigorously to the officials, all to no avail.

Gianluca Vialli then made two substitutions that sparked a grand finale, bringing on Brian Laudrup in the 71st minute and Tore Andre Flo in the 79th.

Almost immediately Dahlin beat Michael Duberry, only for the Chelsea defender to foul him inside the penalty area. Sutton blasted the penalty straight down the middle to score his 100th club career goal.

But the lead lasted barely a couple of minutes, with Laudrup playing a neat one-two before swinging over a cross for Flo to divert the ball home.

Just three minutes later, Flo latched on to a long ball from Ferrer, beating the offside trap to run clear and side-foot the ball past Flowers.

Man of the match was Tore Andre Flo, who in just 12 minutes scored twice, forced two more saves with efforts on target and had one other shot blocked. Zola came closest to the Norwegian's points total of 1,573.

The game was quite even, with Chelsea firing in 16 shots to Rovers' 21 but making more than 50 extra passes in the match. Both sides earned two yellow cards and one red, and this was the only match in the entire Premiership season where both sides won a penalty.

Blackburn continued to struggle and parted company with Roy Hodgson soon afterwards, while the Blues went on to mount a serious challenge, finishing third and giving themselves a shot at qualifying for the Champions League.

ACTION	DE GOEY	DESAILLY	FERRER	FLO	GOLDBAEK	LAMBOURDE	LE SAUX	LEBOEUF	MORRIS	NICHOLLS	PETRESCU	WISE	ZOLA	TOTAL	ASTON VILLA
Time on pitch	90	90	90	89	90	12	90	90	90	1	78	90	90	990	990
GOALS															
Goal	-	-	-	2	1	-	-	-	-	-	-	-	-	3	1
Shot on target	-	-	-	1	-	-	-	-	-	-	-	1	4	6	2
Shot off target	-	-	-	1	-	1	1	-	-	-	-	-	1	3	5
Blocked shot	-	-	-	-	-	-	-	-	-	-	-	1	-	2	-
Own goal	-	-	-	-	-	-	-	-	-	-	-	-	-	-	-
PASSES															
Pass to own player	16	40	39	31	7	33	26	32	1	26	45	31	327	200	
Pass to opposition	3	3	7	6	2	2	10	7	1	1	4	5	10	61	53
Cross to own player	-	-	-	-	-	-	-	-	-	-	-	-	-	2	2
Cross to opposition player	1	1	2	1	-	-	3	-	-	-	5	3	-	17	9
Goal assist	-	1	-	1	-	-	-	-	-	-	-	-	1	3	-
Pass completion %	0%	84%	82%	85%	82%	78%	72%	79%	94%	100%	74%	85%	74%	81%	77%
TACKLES & CLEARANCES															
Tackle	-	2	2	-	5	2	2	1	4	-	1	2	5	26	29
Clearances, blocks and interceptions	3	11	8	-	3	1	11	11	3	-	-	-	-	53	65
DRIBBLES & RUNS															
Dribble ball retained	-	-	3	2	4	-	2	-	2	-	-	1	1	15	5
Dribbles ball lost	-	-	-	-	-	-	-	-	-	-	-	-	1	1	2
Dribble success %	0%	0%	100%	100%	100%	0%	100%	0%	100%	0%	0%	100%	50%	94%	71%
DISCIPLINE															
Fouls	-	1	1	2	1	-	1	-	1	-	-	1	-	10	16
Penalty conceded	-	-	-	-	-	-	-	-	-	-	-	-	-	-	-
Free kick - offside	-	-	-	1	-	-	-	-	-	-	-	-	1	2	2
Yellow cards	1	-	1	-	-	-	-	-	-	-	1	-	-	3	1
Red cards	-	-	-	-	-	-	-	-	-	-	-	-	-	-	-
GOALKEEPERS															
Distribution to own player	13	-	-	-	-	-	-	-	-	-	-	-	-	13	12
Distribution to opposition player	10	-	-	-	-	-	-	-	-	-	-	-	-	10	10
Goalkeeper distribution%	57%	0%	0%	0%	0%	-	0%	0%	-	0%	0%	0%	0%	57%	55%
Save	2	-	-	-	-	-	-	-	-	-	-	-	-	2	6
Ball caught	3	-	-	-	-	-	-	-	-	-	-	-	-	3	4
Ball dropped	-	-	-	-	-	-	-	-	-	-	-	-	-	-	1
Goal conceded	-	-	-	-	-	-	-	-	-	-	-	-	-	-	3

Fans of Aston Villa and Chelsea had an early start, as the match was put forward to the morning to accommodate Sky's television coverage of the Worthington Cup final. Unfortunately for Villa fans, the change of kick-off time seemed to have an adverse effect on their team as they crashed to a 3–0 defeat.

March 21, 1999

0–3

ASTON VILLA
CHELSEA

Chelsea took control of the match virtually from the start and completely dominated the first 30 minutes with their slick passing and possession football. Tore Andre Flo was involved in the action, firing an early shot against Mark Bosnich's legs, and later was unlucky when the diving duo of Bjarne Goldbaek and Dennis Wise both narrowly failed to get a head to his superb cross.

It took Villa 42 minutes to create a decent opportunity. Gareth Barry's excellent cross was met at the back post by Dion Dublin, but his downward header was smartly saved by Ed de Goey in the Chelsea goal.

Villa started the second half with greater purpose, but were still second best to Chelsea's immaculate passing game.

On 57 minutes, Albert Ferrer played a long ball down the right channel to Flo, who with a quick change of feet cut inside the England defender and put the ball beyond Bosnich into the far corner. It was a top-class goal from a player who was at the peak of his game.

Seven minutes later it was nearly 2–0. A mistake from Barry was seized upon by Gianfranco Zola, who found himself one-on-one with Bosnich. The big Australian 'keeper got down well to his left to save the Italian's shot.

With 15 minutes remaining, a poor back-pass from Marcel Desailly let in substitute Julian Joachim, whose lob went the wrong side of the post.

With five minutes left on the clock, Chelsea upped the pressure and went looking for more goals. Bosnich spectacularly saved Zola's 25-yard screamer. Then, a minute later, Flo cut into the penalty area and flicked a ball wide into the path of the Dane Goldbaek, who fired high into the net at the near post for Chelsea's second.

Flo made it three in stoppage time. The big Norwegian made a brilliant run into the penalty area and Jody Morris found him with an exquisite pass. Flo's first touch took him past Bosnich and his second put the ball into the back of the net for another well-worked Chelsea goal.

It was one of the most one-sided games in the Carling Premiership during 1998–99. Chelsea kept the ball and controlled the play. The London side completed 127 more passes than Aston Villa, and had a higher pass completion percentage (81% compared to Villa's below average 77%).

De Goey was called upon just twice during the match, while Bosnich pulled off six very good saves. Villa hit the target twice from their seven attempts, whereas Chelsea had 14 shots, scoring with three and hitting the target with six others.

The final result mirrored the fortunes of the two teams in the final months of the season. Villa suffered a dreadful run of form, while Chelsea hung on to the coat-tails of Arsenal and Manchester United at the top.

COVENTRY CITY 1998–99

Back row (from left to right): Liam Daish, Gary Breen, Steve Ogrizovic, Magnus Hedman, Philippe Clement, Paul Williams.
Middle row: Garry Pendrey (Coach), Jim Blythe (Goalkeeping Coach), Willie Boland, Roland Nilsson (no longer at club), Marcus Hall, Jean-Guy Wallemme (no longer at the club), Simon Haworth (now Wigan Athletic), Richard Shaw, Trevor Peake (Coach), Stuart Collie (Physiotherapist).
Front row: Ian Brightwell, Paul Telfer, Gavin Strachan, Trond Soltvedt, Gary McAllister, Gordon Strachan (Manager), Dion Dublin (now Aston Villa), George Boateng, David Burrows, Noel Whelan, Darren Huckerby.

COVENTRY CITY

20 FACTS

1 Coventry City were founded by workers at the Singer's cycle factory in 1883. They were known as Singers FC until 1898, when they changed their name to Coventry City.

2 The start of the 1999–2000 season marks 100 years since Coventry City first played at Highfield Road. In 1981, the ground became the first all-seater stadium in English football.

3 Their highest-ever league placing was sixth in Division One in 1969–70. They have survived in the top flight since being promoted to Division One in 1967 – a record only surpassed by three other clubs: Arsenal, Everton and Liverpool.

4 Coventry's only major trophy is the FA Cup, which they won in 1987 by beating Tottenham Hotspur 3–2 at Wembley in one of the most thrilling finals of recent years.

5 Coventry have twice played in the Football League Cup semi-finals – in 1981 and 1990 – but have never reached the final.

6 The Fairs Cup of 1970–71 is the only time Coventry have participated in European competition. After beating Trakia Plovdiv 6–1 on aggregate they were heavily defeated 7–3 by Bayern Munich in the second round, though they did beat the famous German side 2–1 in the return at Highfield Road.

7 Coventry City have played in more divisions than any other League side. They have featured in the Premier League and in Divisions One, Two, Three, Four, Three South and Three North.

8 Steve Ogrizovic is one of the few goalkeepers to have scored a goal. He did so with a clearance from hand for Coventry in a match against Sheffield Wednesday in 1986.

9 The record attendance at Highfield Road was 51,455 for a Division Two match against Wolverhampton Wanderers on April 29, 1967.

10 Coventry's record transfer fee paid was for Romanian international Viorel Moldovan who joined in January 1998 from Grasshoppers of Zurich for £3.5 million. He was sold in July 1998 for £4 million to Turkish side Fenerbahce.

11 Their record sale was in 1998–99 when Dion Dublin joined Aston Villa for £5.75 million.

12 Coventry City's record victory was a 9–0 triumph against Bristol City in Division Three South in April 1934.

13 Their record defeat came at the hands of Norwich City, where they lost 10–2 in Division Three South in March 1930.

14 One unwanted record held by Coventry is the longest sequence of matches without scoring a goal. They failed to find the net in 11 consecutive matches in 1919–20 in Division Two.

15 Clarrie Bourton holds the record for the most league goals scored in a season for Coventry. He bagged 49 goals for the Sky Blues in Division Three South in 1931–32.

16 Coventry secured their place in the Premiership with one game to go and finished 15th in 1998–99. Their league record was:

Pld	W	D	L	F	A	Pts
38	11	9	18	39	51	42

17 Coventry's AXA-sponsored FA Cup run came to an end at Goodison Park when they lost 2–1 to Everton in the fifth round. Earlier they had equalled their best-ever FA Cup victory by beating Macclesfield 7–0 at Highfield Road, before going on to beat Leicester City 3–0 in the fourth round.

18 Gordon Strachan's side were knocked out of the Worthington Cup by Luton Town at Kenilworth Road. They lost 2–0, having negotiated the second round with a 5–0 aggregate victory over Southend.

19 The top goalscorer in all competitions for Coventry City was Noel Whelan with 13 goals, including 10 in the Carling Premiership.

20 The Sky Blues' disciplinary record was the ninth-best in the Premiership. They committed 497 fouls, earned 76 yellow cards and suffered just one dismissal – John Aloisi in the match against Charlton Athletic, on March 6, at Highfield Road.

SEASON REVIEW

Having started the season with a top 10 finish on their minds, Coventry City were relieved rather than elated by their eventual escape from relegation. After finishing in the relative comfort of mid-table the previous season, 15th place in 1998–99 represented a considerable disappointment.

The Sky Blues started the season with a fine 2–1 win over Chelsea but did not win for another seven games in the Premiership. That start set the tone for the season. As Gordon Strachan said at the end of the campaign: "Once you are down near the bottom of the table, it is very hard to lift yourself up and forget the pressures."

Their real problems began in November though, when their talismanic striker Dion Dublin was sold to fierce rivals Aston Villa for £5.75 million. A clause in his contract meant that there was little anyone at Coventry could do about the move, but there is no doubt that the club sorely missed their big striker. Although the Sky Blues had other good front men in Darren Huckerby and Noel Whelan, the squad was not strong enough to fill the hole left by the departure of such an important player.

The rancour surrounding Dublin's exit did not help. Withdrawn from the squad before a disastrous Worthington Cup exit at the hands of Luton Town, the constant speculation about his future clearly angered the fans and unsettled his team-mates. Although they dug out two good results against struggling Blackburn Rovers and Everton in early November, City did not win again until the New Year.

Efforts were made to sign a replacement for Dublin. Unfortunately, deals for two Scandinavian players fell through and loan signing Darren Jackson failed to impress. John Aloisi arrived from crisis-hit Portsmouth in December to score some important goals, but it was Noel Whelan

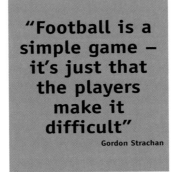

"Football is a simple game – it's just that the players make it difficult"

Gordon Strachan

and Darren Huckerby who kept the club up with 19 league goals between them.

The rest of the side scored just 17 times (discounting Dublin's three goals) and it is hardly surprising that only three sides – Blackburn, Southampton and Nottingham Forest – managed fewer goals. The team's overall shooting accuracy rating of 42% was the second-worst figure in the entire Premiership.

Results picked up in January with impressive wins over Nottingham Forest and Liverpool, and although February was less fruitful a first-ever league victory at Aston Villa provided fans with their most memorable moment of the season.

Victory over Charlton Athletic lifted the club to 15th place in the table and the players did themselves another big favour with a 1–0 victory over relegation rivals Southampton in early April, the impressive George Boateng grabbing the crucial goal.

Safety was finally secured in the club's penultimate game of the season against Derby at Pride Park. The 0–0 draw saw Strachan's side match their hosts stride-for-stride and left him wondering how two teams with similar resources could be separated by some seven positions at the end of the season.

The statistics suggest that the shock of losing Dublin had much to do with it. So accustomed to seeking out their big target man with long balls, City found it hard to vary the pattern of their play after his departure and continued to try and hit their front players with balls over the top. They finished with a total of 1,207 attempted long passes – the most in the Premiership – but completed just 44%.

Players like George Boateng, Darren Huckerby and Noel Whelan provide the club with hope for the future - but Strachan will realize that his squad needs significant strengthening to reach the security of mid-table.

COVENTRY CITY

DATE	OPPONENT	SCORE	ATT.	ALOISI	BOATENG	BREEN	BURROWS	CLEMENT	DUBLIN	EDWORTHY	FROGGATT	GIOACCHINI	M HALL	P HALL
15.8.98	Chelsea H	2–1	23,042	–	88	–	90□	–	90¹	–	–	–	s21	s2
22.8.98	Nott'm For A	0–1	22,546	–	90□	90	90	–	90	–	–	–	–	s13
29.8.98	West Ham H	0–0	20,818	–	90□	90	90	–	90	s10	–	–	–	s25
9.9.98	Liverpool A	0–2	41,771	–	90	90	90	–	90	s26	–	–	–	75
12.9.98	Man Utd A	0–2	55,193	–	90	90	90□	–	90	90	–	–	–	s18
19.9.98	Newcastle H	1–5	22,639	–	90	90	90	–	90□	90	–	–	–	62
26.9.98	Charlton A	1–1	20,048	–	90	90□	16	–	90	s74	–	–	–	s35
3.10.98	Aston Villa H	1–2	22,650	–	90	76	–	–	90	90	90	–	–	–
18.10.98	Sheff Wed A	1–0	16,003	–	90	90	–	–	90¹	90	90	–	–	–
24.10.98	Southampton A	1–2	15,152	–	80□	90	45	–	90¹	s45	90	–	–	–
31.10.98	Arsenal H	0–1	23,039	–	70	90	–	s20	–	–	90	–	90□	s12
7.11.98	Blackburn A	2–1	23,779	–	s1	53	–	90□	–	90	90	–	–	–
15.11.98	Everton H	3–0	19,279	–	–	–	–	90	–	90	90¹	–	–	–
21.11.98	Middlesbro A	0–2	34,287	–	s6	–	–	90	–	90	90	–	–	–
28.11.98	Leicester H	1–1	19,887	–	s58	–	–	32	–	90	90□	–	–	–
5.12.98	Wimbledon A	1–2	11,717	–	90□	s1	–	–	–	90□	90	–	–	–
14.12.98	Leeds Utd A	0–2	31,799	–	77	–	–	53	–	90	90	–	–	s13
19.12.98	Derby Co H	1–1	16,602	s2	s5	s17	–	–	–	73	90□	–	–	–
26.12.98	Tottenham H	1–1	23,091	s26¹	90□	s29	–	–	–	64	90□	–	–	–
28.12.98	West Ham A	0–2	25,662	58	90	90	–	–	–	79	90	–	–	–
9.1.99	Nott'm For H	4–0	17,158	68	–	–	73	–	–	–	–	–	–	–
16.1.99	Chelsea A	1–2	34,869	s1	90□	–	90□	–	–	–	90	–	–	–
30.1.99	Liverpool H	2–1	23,057	–	90¹	s45	90	–	–	–	90	–	–	–
6.2.99	Tottenham A	0–0	34,376	s1	–	89□	–	s19	–	–	90	–	–	–
17.2.99	Newcastle A	1–4	36,352	s15	90□	–	90□	s25	–	–	90	–	–	–
20.2.99	Man Utd H	0–1	22,594	s26	90□	–	87□	–	–	–	90	–	–	–
27.2.99	Aston Villa A	4–1	38,799	90²	90²	–	90	–	–	–	90	–	–	–
6.3.99	Charlton H	2–1	20,255	56■	–	–	90	–	–	–	90	–	–	–
13.3.99	Blackburn H	1–1	19,694	90¹	90	–	90□	s21	–	–	90	–	–	–
20.3.99	Arsenal A	0–2	38,074	–	–	–	90	–	–	s20	90	s13	–	–
3.4.99	Sheff Wed A	2–1	28,136	–	90	90	–	s1	–	90	90	–	–	–
5.4.99	Southampton H	1–0	21,404	–	90¹□	90	90	–	–	–	–	s2	–	–
11.4.99	Everton A	0–2	32,341	s75	90□	90	90	–	–	–	–	–	–	–
17.4.99	Middlesbro H	1–2	19,228	90	90	87□	90	s3	–	–	–	–	–	–
24.4.99	Leicester A	0–1	20,224	60	90	90	90□	71	–	–	–	s30	s45	–
1.5.99	Wimbledon H	2–1	21,198	–	90	90	45	–	–	90	–	–	s45	–
8.5.99	Derby Co A	0–0	32,450	s3	90	90	–	–	–	90□	–	–	90	–
16.5.99	Leeds Utd H	2–2	23,049	s32¹	90	45	38	–	–	s52□	–	–	–	–

□ Yellow card, ■ Red card, s Substitute, 90³ Goals scored

1998–99 PREMIERSHIP APPEARANCES

HAWORTH	HEDMAN	HUCKERBY	JACKSON	KONJIC	McALLISTER	McSHEFFREY	NILSSON	OGRIZOVIC	QUINN	SHAW	SHILTON	SOLTVEDT	TELFER	WALLEMME	WHELAN	WILLIAMS	TOTAL
–	90	90¹□	–	–	–	–	90	–	–	90	–	90□	90□	–	69	90	990
–	90	90	–	–	–	–	44	–	–	90	–	77	90	s46	90	–	990
–	90	90□	–	–	–	–	–	–	–	90	–	65	90	80	90	–	990
–	90	90	–	–	–	–	69	–	–	s21	s15	64	90	90□	–	–	990
–	90	72	–	–	–	–	–	90	90	–	s28	–	90	90	–	–	990
90	90	–	–	–	–	–	–	–	90	–	s28	–	–	90□	90¹	–	990
–	90	–	–	–	–	–	90	–	90	90	55	–	90□	–	90¹	–	990
–	90	–	–	–	–	–	90	–	59	90	–	s31¹	90	s14	90□	–	990
–	90	s26	–	–	90	–	90	–	–	90	–	–	64□	–	90	–	990
–	90	90	–	–	90	–	71	–	–	90	–	s10	s19	–	90□	–	990
–	90	78	–	–	78	–	90	–	–	90	–	s12	90□	–	90	–	990
–	90	90¹	–	–	89□	–	90	–	–	90	–	–	90	–	90¹	s37	990
–	90	90¹□	–	–	90	–	90	–	–	90	–	–	90	–	90¹	90	990
–	90	69□	s21	–	84□	–	90	–	–	90	–	–	90	–	90□	90□	990
–	90	90¹□	–	–	90	–	90	–	–	90	–	90	90□	–	–	90	990
–	90	90	–	–	90¹	–	89	–	–	90	–	–	90	–	90	90	990
–	90	–	s37	–	90	–	90	–	–	90□	–	90□	–	–	90	90	990
–	90	90	–	–	88	–	90	–	–	90	–	90	85□	–	90¹	90	990
–	–	77	–	–	90	–	90	90	–	90	s13	90	–	–	90	61	990
–	–	s32	–	–	90	–	90	90	–	90	–	90	s11	–	90	–	990
–	90	90³	s22	–	87□	–	90	–	s3	90	s17	90	90¹□	–	90□	90	990
–	90□	90¹	–	–	89	–	90	–	–	90	–	90	90□	–	–	90	990
–	90	90	–	–	90	–	45	–	–	90	–	90	–	–	90¹	90	990
–	90	90	–	s37	90□	–	90	–	–	90	–	71	90□	–	90□	53	990
–	90	75	–	90□	90	–	90	–	–	90	–	65	–	–	90¹	–	990
–	90	90	–	–	90	–	90	–	–	90	–	s3	90	–	64	90	990
–	90	89	–	–	90	s1	90	–	–	90	–	–	90	–	–	90□	990
–	90□	75	–	–	90	–	90	–	–	90	–	s15¹	90	–	90¹□	90	956
–	90	s20	–	69	70	–	90	–	–	90	–	–	90	–	90	–	990
–	90	90	–	90□	70	–	90	–	90	90	–	77	90□	–	–	–	990
–	90	90	–	–	89¹	–	–	–	–	90	–	–	90□	–	90¹□	90	990
–	90	88	–	–	90□	–	–	–	–	90	–	90	90	–	90□	90□	990
–	90	90□	–	–	90	–	–	–	–	90	–	90	15	–	90	90	990
–	90	90	–	–	90¹	–	–	–	–	90	–	90	–	–	90	90	990
–	90	90□	–	–	–	–	–	–	90□	90□	–	s19	45	–	–	90	990
–	90	90¹	–	–	90	–	–	–	–	90	–	90	90	–	90¹□	–	990
–	90	87	–	–	90	–	–	–	–	90	–	90	90	–	90	–	990
–	90	58	–	–	90	–	90	–	–	90	–	90	90¹	–	90	s45	990

THE MANAGER

GORDON STRACHAN

At just 42, Coventry boss Gordon Strachan is one of the most respected young managers in the Carling Premiership. He joined Coventry three seasons ago as Ron Atkinson's assistant, but took over the hot seat in November 1996.

As a player, Strachan will probably be best remembered for his time at Manchester United, having spent four years at Old Trafford before winning the title with Leeds United and then ending up at Highfield Road. A much-respected right-sided midfielder with an array of tricks, Strachan also played 50 times for Scotland.

Strachan reluctantly parted with City's prize asset Dion Dublin for £5.75 million early in the season, though few supporters would have expected the club to sell him to arch-rivals Aston Villa. Strachan shrewdly replaced him with cut-price Australian John Aloisi from Portsmouth for just £650,000.

So after another escape act, Strachan has once again guaranteed that there will be Premiership football at Highfield Road this year. But there is always a fear among City fans that Strachan will soon be snapped up by a bigger club, after he was linked with the vacant Leeds post last season.

LEAGUE POSITION

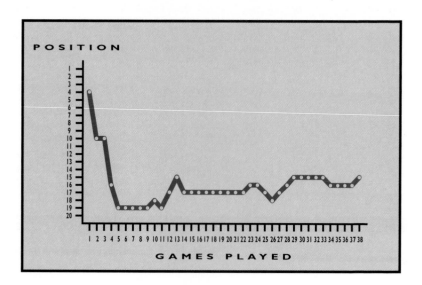

THE GOALS

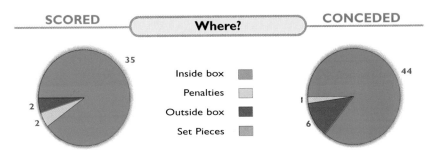

SCORED — Where? — CONCEDED

Inside box
Penalties
Outside box
Set Pieces

The loss of Dion Dublin to Aston Villa made a noticeable difference to Coventry's goal output over the course of the 1998–99 Carling Premiership. Their total of 39 goals was seven fewer than last season and 94.9% of these were scored inside the opposition box, the highest ratio in the league. Similarly, a high proportion of goals against Coventry were scored inside the Sky Blues' 18-yard zone, perhaps indicating that the defence backed off too far on occasion.

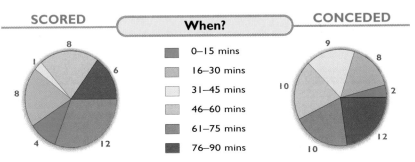

SCORED — When? — CONCEDED

0–15 mins
16–30 mins
31–45 mins
46–60 mins
61–75 mins
76–90 mins

Coventry scored exactly one-third of their goals in the first half of Premiership matches. In the moments leading up to half-time they were the least successful team in the league, scoring just once all season between 30 and 45 minutes.

With just six goals netted in the final quarter of an hour, City apparently laboured in front of goal when approaching both the half and full-time whistles. Only in the first 15 minutes of the first half did City outscore opponents.

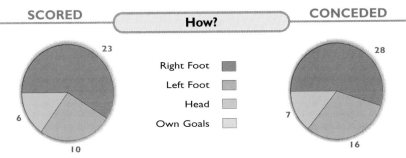

SCORED — How? — CONCEDED

Right Foot
Left Foot
Head
Own Goals

Teams playing against Gordon Strachan's side were restricted to just seven goals by way of headers, and only four sides in the Premiership conceded fewer in this fashion than Coventry. Those seven strikes represented just 13.7% of the total finishes applied by City's Premiership adversaries, a record bettered only by Chelsea and Newcastle. The Sky Blues were a rarity in that they neither conceded nor profited from any own-goals.

COVENTRY CITY

	ALOISI	BOATENG	BREEN	BURROWS	CLEMENT	DUBLIN	EDWORTHY	FROGGATT	GIOACCHINI	M HALL	P HALL	HAWORTH
APPEARANCES												
Start	7	29	21	23	6	10	16	23	0	2	2	1
Sub	9	4	4	0	6	0	6	0	3	3	7	0
Minutes on pitch	693	2635	1882	1834	515	900	1613	2070	45	291	255	90
GOAL ATTEMPTS												
Goals	5	4	0	0	0	3	0	1	0	0	0	0
Shots on target	10	15	3	1	1	12	1	12	2	0	0	0
Shots off target	9	16	4	2	7	21	6	13	1	0	3	1
Shooting accuracy %	53%	48%	43%	33%	13%	36%	14%	48%	67%	0%	0%	0%
PASSING												
Goal assists	3	6	1	1	1	3	0	5	0	0	0	0
Long passes	3	163	158	259	34	27	103	72	0	18	5	0
Short passes	220	1004	479	629	199	358	504	487	14	92	81	23
PASS COMPLETION												
Own half %	83%	83%	86%	91%	85%	86%	86%	87%	0%	83%	78%	100%
Opposition half %	69%	67%	60%	61%	65%	69%	70%	65%	69%	73%	66%	69%
CROSSING												
Total crosses	2	71	8	35	2	5	18	131	0	5	4	0
Cross completion %	50%	34%	38%	37%	50%	60%	22%	22%	0%	20%	50%	0%
DRIBBLING												
Dribbles & runs	27	108	22	57	1	3	48	130	1	5	17	0
Dribble completion %	52%	69%	86%	88%	100%	67%	79%	65%	0%	60%	65%	0%
DEFENDING												
Tackles made	11	148	37	74	21	17	48	78	2	11	8	0
Tackles won %	55%	61%	68%	62%	57%	53%	54%	55%	100%	55%	75%	0%
Blocks	0	9	26	21	3	0	12	3	0	5	2	0
Clearances	2	55	268	123	36	25	142	27	0	27	3	0
Interceptions	5	29	18	9	7	3	21	6	0	0	1	0
DISCIPLINE												
Fouls	13	51	30	30	16	24	17	25	1	3	10	0
Offside	6	4	0	0	0	5	0	4	1	0	1	0
Yellow cards	1	10	3	7	1	1	3	3	0	1	0	0
Red cards	1	0	0	0	0	0	0	0	0	0	0	0

GOALKEEPER NAME	START/ (SUB)	TIME ON PITCH	GOALS CONCEDED	MINS/GOALS CONCEDED	SAVES MADE	SAVES/ SHOTS
HEDMAN	36	3240	48	67.5	139	74%
OGRIZOVIC	2	180	3	60	7	70%

PLAYERS' STATISTICS

	HUCKERBY	JACKSON	KONJIC	McALLISTER	McSHEFFREY	NILSSON	QUINN	SHAW	SHILTON	SOLTVEDT	TELFER	WALLEMME	WHELAN	WILLIAMS	TOTAL	RANK
	31	0	3	29	0	28	6	36	1	21	30	4	31	20		
	3	3	1	0	1	0	1	1	4	6	2	2	0	2		
	2736	80	286	2564	1	2368	512	3261	128	1859	2579	410	2743	1816		
	9	0	0	3	0	0	0	0	0	2	2	0	10	0	39	17th
	28	0	0	13	0	0	1	1	0	9	13	1	35	6	164	17th
	36	0	0	17	0	13	5	0	0	14	29	0	34	0	231	7th
	44%	0%	0%	43%	0%	0%	17%	100%	0%	39%	31%	100%	51%	100%	42%	19th
	3	0	0	2	0	1	0	0	0	2	2	0	2	1	33	9th
	25	3	10	194	0	327	33	146	1	48	176	36	59	245	2145	1st
	516	35	68	1164	1	864	219	639	40	585	1019	129	917	344	10630	15th
	79%	89%	81%	86%	100%	83%	90%	90%	80%	81%	89%	91%	84%	84%	86%	16th
	64%	79%	75%	68%	0%	64%	74%	62%	77%	69%	67%	73%	69%	48%	66%	18th
	71	2	1	192	0	35	19	5	3	11	106	1	35	0	762	10th
	18%	50%	0%	26%	0%	26%	21%	0%	33%	18%	34%	0%	26%	0%	27%	16th
	245	1	1	49	0	37	2	9	3	36	56	3	108	16	987	6th
	54%	100%	100%	76%	0%	89%	100%	89%	100%	69%	84%	100%	68%	88%	69%	14th
	42	3	20	74	0	100	13	89	9	68	87	19	84	87	1151	11th
	45%	33%	90%	62%	0%	77%	62%	72%	22%	60%	61%	47%	50%	67%	62%	8th
	1	0	6	11	0	11	5	32	0	8	9	6	2	28	201	=11th
	2	2	50	64	0	216	8	448	3	63	98	57	26	340	2130	6th
	5	2	11	40	0	43	8	52	2	24	19	12	15	21	356	5th
	57	3	3	31	0	10	5	33	1	18	38	5	51	22	497	11th
	98	0	0	1	0	0	0	0	0	3	3	0	46	0	172	2nd
	7	0	2	5	0	0	1	2	0	2	11	2	9	3	76	10th
	0	0	0	0	0	0	0	0	0	0	0	0	0	0	1	=17th

CROSSES CAUGHT	CROSSES PUNCHED	CROSSES NOT CLAIMED	CATCH SUCCESS	THROWS/ SHORT KICKS	% COMPLETION	LONG KICKS	% COMPLETION
97	14	14	95%	221	94%	834	33%
7	0	0	100%	16	88%	47	32%

PLAYER OF THE SEASON

PLAYER	INDEX SCORE
PAUL WILLIAMS	1,001
Roland Nilsson	944
George Boateng	842
Noel Whelan	778
Gary McAllister	745
Steve Froggatt	696
Gary Breen	694
Paul Telfer	672
Trond-Egil Soltvedt	659
Magnus Hedman	657

It looked like being another frustrating season for big-hearted centre-back Paul Williams. After helping City to an opening-day victory over Chelsea in 1998–99, Williams was dropped from the Premiership first team until November.

But after suffering with a hernia injury in 1997–98, he was not going to waste his opportunity of regular action and impressed Gordon Strachan so much that he missed just six further Premiership games all season.

He ended the campaign as the highest-scoring player in the Carling Opta Season Index, with an average score of 1,001 points. Consistency is the key to picking up high scores – and Williams was as reliable as any of his defensive team-mates in the Sky Blues' back-line.

Roland Nilsson's City swansong season was a memorable one. He was the second-highest scorer after a series of super displays at right-back, and will depart Highfield Road leaving a gaping hole

Gordon Strachan will find it difficult to fill.

Dutchman George Boateng was another star of the 1998–99 season. His goals from midfield were vital in ensuring Coventry did not get sucked into another relegation battle and he netted in important victories over Aston Villa, Southampton and Liverpool.

Behind Boateng was top scorer Noel Whelan, who filled the departed Dion Dublin's boots with aplomb netting 10 league goals. Meanwhile Gary McAllister's brave return from injury in October thrilled many neutrals as much as it did the Coventry supporters. He ended the season as the side's most prolific passer and averaged 745 Carling Opta points a match in 1998–99.

The steady, season-long displays of Steve Froggatt, Paul Telfer and David Burrows earned them places in Coventry's top 10 players of the season list. But there was no place for the erratic Darren Huckerby, despite his nine league goals.

FIVE OF THE BEST

For the second successive season, there was no need for last-day heroics from Coventry to avoid relegation – but there was little cause for celebration. A final placing of 15th represented a step backwards for Gordon Strachan's men after the side finished 11th in 1997–98, and the much-respected Scot has much work to do to if his side are to achieve greater consistency.

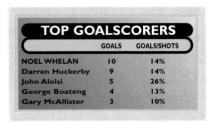

TOP GOALSCORERS		
	GOALS	GOALS/SHOTS
NOEL WHELAN	10	14%
Darren Huckerby	9	14%
John Aloisi	5	26%
George Boateng	4	13%
Gary McAllister	3	10%

The departure of fans' favourite Dion Dublin left a huge hole in the City front line and much rested on the shoulders of young duo Noel Whelan and Darren Huckerby. Former Leeds prodigy Whelan finished as the club's Premiership top scorer with 10 goals, and both strikers achieved a 14% goals-to-shots ratio. New signing John Aloisi achieved a superb strike rate, with more than a quarter of his shots hitting the back of the net, while the classy George Boateng and Scottish skipper Gary McAllister made valuable contributions from midfield.

Gary McAllister chose the 1998–99 season to announce his retirement from international football after criticism from Scottish supporters, but he showed City fans that he still has plenty to offer in the Premiership. He made precisely 1,000 successful passes, with almost three-quarters finding a team-mate. Right-sided midfielder Paul Telfer and playmaker George Boateng also saw plenty of the ball, while Roland Nilsson enjoyed a superb last season in the Premiership, completing 840 passes.

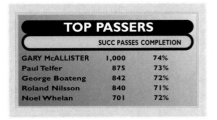

TOP PASSERS		
	SUCC PASSES	COMPLETION
GARY McALLISTER	1,000	74%
Paul Telfer	875	73%
George Boateng	842	72%
Roland Nilsson	840	71%
Noel Whelan	701	72%

TOP TACKLERS		
	WON	SUCCESS
GEORGE BOATENG	90	61%
Roland Nilsson	77	77%
Richard Shaw	64	72%
Paul Williams	58	67%
Paul Telfer	53	61%

Dutch under-21 international captain George Boateng earned much acclaim with his pinpoint passes to the front players – but he showed he had an equally-important physical side to his game by winning more tackles than any other City player. The man most likely to win possession was super Swede Roland Nilsson, who won more than three-quarters of his challenges, while fellow-defenders Richard Shaw and Paul Williams also figure in the top five.

Half the teams in the Premiership committed more than 500 fouls, but City just avoided a place among the top 10 sinners with 497. Worst offender was George Boateng, one of three players to concede more than 50 fouls. He also picked up 10 yellow cards in the league, topped in the Coventry squad only by Paul Telfer with 11. Both the main strikers feature here, illustrating their willingness to fight for the ball up front, while Paul Telfer and left-back David Burrows complete the top five.

DISCIPLINE		
	POINTS	FOULS & CARDS
GEORGE BOATENG	81	51F, 10Y, 0R
Darren Huckerby	78	57F, 7Y, 0R
Noel Whelan	78	51F, 9Y, 0R
Paul Telfer	71	38F, 11Y, 0R
David Burrows	51	30F, 7Y, 0R

ACTION

ACTION	ALOISI	BURROWS	HEDMAN	HUCKERBY	JACKSON	MCALLISTER	NILSSON	QUINN	SHAW	SHILTON	SOLTVEDT	TELFER	WHELAN	WILLIAMS	TOTAL	NOTTINGHAM FOREST
Time on pitch	68	73	90	90	22	87	90	3	90	17	90	90	90	90	990	990
GOALS																
Goal	–	–	–	–	–	–	–	–	–	–	–	–	–	–	–	–
Shot on target	1	–	–	3	–	–	–	–	–	–	–	–	–	–	4	3
Shot off target	–	–	–	–	–	1	–	–	–	–	–	2	–	–	3	3
Blocked shot	–	–	–	1	–	–	–	–	–	–	–	–	–	–	4	2
Own goal	–	–	–	–	–	–	–	–	–	–	–	–	–	–	–	–
PASSES																
Pass to own player	16	38	13	13	12	40	42	4	17	5	34	24	28	24	297	259
Pass to opposition	6	14	12	12	3	11	15	1	2	–	10	14	12	8	108	115
Cross to own player	–	3	–	–	5	5	–	–	–	–	1	–	–	–	14	3
Cross to opposition player	–	2	–	–	5	2	2	–	1	–	2	2	2	2	9	9
Goal assist	2	1	–	–	–	–	–	–	–	–	–	–	1	–	4	–
Pass completion %	75%	72%	50%	80%	80%	74%	71%	80%	89%	100%	78%	60%	67%	76%	72%	68%
TACKLES & CLEARANCES																
Tackle	–	–	–	–	1	4	4	–	2	1	4	5	2	2	23	16
Clearances, blocks and interceptions	–	7	1	–	3	6	6	–	18	2	11	6	4	12	70	91
DRIBBLES & RUNS																
Dribble ball retained	2	1	–	11	–	2	1	–	–	–	1	–	6	2	26	10
Dribbles ball lost	2	–	–	6	1	1	–	–	–	–	1	–	1	–	11	8
Dribble success %	0%	100%	0%	65%	100%	67%	100%	0%	0%	100%	50%	100%	86%	70%	70%	56%
DISCIPLINE																
Fouls	1	1	–	2	2	2	–	–	–	–	–	2	2	–	12	17
Penalty conceded	–	–	–	–	–	–	–	–	–	–	–	–	–	–	–	–
Free kick – offside	–	–	–	10	–	–	–	–	–	–	–	–	–	–	10	6
Yellow cards	–	–	–	–	–	–	–	–	–	–	–	–	–	–	3	2
Red cards	–	–	–	–	–	–	–	–	–	–	–	–	–	–	–	–
GOALKEEPERS																
Distribution to own player	–	–	19	–	–	–	–	–	–	–	–	–	–	–	19	14
Distribution to opposition player	–	–	13	–	–	–	–	–	–	–	–	–	–	–	13	13
Goalkeeper distribution %	–	–	59%	–	–	–	–	–	–	–	–	–	–	–	59%	52%
Save	–	–	3	–	–	–	–	–	–	–	–	–	–	–	3	3
Ball caught	–	–	3	–	–	–	–	–	–	–	–	–	–	–	3	–
Ball dropped	–	–	–	–	–	–	–	–	–	–	–	–	–	–	–	–
Goal conceded	–	–	–	–	–	–	–	–	–	–	–	–	–	–	–	4

With just over half the season gone, Coventry found themselves fourth from the foot of the Carling Premiership. Four points above bottom-of-the-table Nottingham Forest, Gordon Strachan's side went into the game against their relegation rivals knowing that a win was imperative.

January 9, 1999

4–0

COVENTRY CITY
NOTTINGHAM FOREST

Forest arrived at Highfield Road on the back of a record-breaking run of 17 games without a win, and minus Dave Bassett who had just been sacked – but caretaker manager Mickey Adams must have hoped for a better response from his players than the one he got.

After a nervous opening Coventry began to take control of the game, but found it hard to break down a defensive-looking Forest side. Indeed, they almost fell behind after 22 minutes, when Pierre van Hooijdonk's cross-cum-shot nearly caught out Hedman.

The want-away Dutch star was proving Forest's one threat, but even he could only watch in admiration as Darren Huckerby took control. In the 32nd minute the England under-21 star shrugged off Chris Bart-Williams deep in Coventry's half, surged forward and, shaking off the attentions of Craig Armstrong, slammed a shot against the post.

Forest's soft underbelly had been exposed and in the 45th minute Huckerby cut it wide open. Trond-Egil Soltvedt knocked a hopeful ball into the box, John Aloisi headed it on and the unmarked Huckerby arrowed the ball into the net before strolling nonchalantly into the arms of his jubilant team-mates.

Huckerby claimed his second goal within a minute of the restart. Picking up Burrows's long pass, he burst into the Forest area and chipped Dave Beasant from an acute angle.

Paul Telfer added a third goal after 54 minutes, beating Beasant with a brilliant volley, but it was left to Huckerby to have the final word. Picking up a ball in the centre circle, he turned Christopher Doig, then drifted past Steve Chettle and Jon-Olav Hjelde before slotting the ball calmly under Beasant and into the back of the net.

It was Huckerby's second hat-trick in the space of eight days, the first coming against Macclesfield in the FA Cup, and it confirmed his status as Coventry's most explosive player and one of the Premiership's brightest young stars.

He took the Carling Opta man of the match award easily, earning the bulk of his 1,849 points for his hat-trick and his 17 dribbles and runs. His score would have been even higher but for the fact that he was caught offside 10 times.

More importantly, the match emphasized the gulf in class between Coventry and the sides at the foot of the table. They outpassed and outran Forest, completing 72% of all attempted passes and 70% of their attempted dribbles on the way to a comfortable victory.

City only found themselves in the bottom three once more after their meeting with Forest and, despite flirting with the possibility of relegation, made themselves mathematically safe with one game of the season remaining.

ACTION	ALOISI	BOATENG	BURROWS	FROGGATT	HEDMAN	HUCKERBY	McALLISTER	McSHEFFREY	NILSSON	SHAW	TELFER	WILLIAMS	TOTAL	ASTON VILLA
Time on pitch	90	90	90	90	90	89	90	1	90	90	90	90	990	990
GOALS														
Goal	2	2	–	–	–	–	–	–	–	–	–	–	4	1
Shot on target	2	1	–	–	–	1	–	–	–	–	–	–	4	3
Shot off target	–	1	–	–	–	2	–	–	–	–	2	–	5	7
Blocked shot	–	–	–	–	–	–	–	–	–	–	–	–	3	3
Own goal	–	–	–	–	–	–	–	–	–	–	–	–	–	–
PASSES														
Pass to own player	16	16	29	16	–	9	34	1	24	14	25	9	193	264
Pass to opposition	7	12	4	8	–	5	11	–	13	4	7	10	81	94
Cross to own player	–	–	–	2	–	2	3	–	1	–	–	–	8	6
Cross to opposition player	–	3	–	4	–	2	8	–	–	–	–	–	17	6
Goal assist	–	–	–	2	–	1	1	–	–	–	–	–	4	4
Pass completion %	70%	52%	88%	63%	0%	67%	67%	100%	64%	78%	78%	47%	68%	73%
TACKLES & CLEARANCES														
Tackle	3	3	7	4	–	3	3	–	2	1	3	3	32	31
Clearances, blocks and interceptions	1	7	5	–	2	–	4	–	14	18	6	23	80	71
DRIBBLES & RUNS														
Dribble ball retained	4	5	1	4	–	7	1	–	–	–	–	1	23	18
Dribbles ball lost	1	–	1	–	–	5	–	–	–	–	–	1	8	3
Dribble success %	80%	83%	50%	100%	0%	58%	100%	–	0%	0%	0%	100%	74%	86%
DISCIPLINE														
Fouls	–	–	–	1	–	2	1	–	–	2	3	1	10	16
Penalty conceded	–	–	–	–	–	–	–	–	–	–	–	–	–	–
Free kick – offside	–	–	–	–	–	2	–	–	–	–	–	–	2	3
Yellow cards	1	–	–	–	–	–	–	–	–	–	–	1	2	2
Red cards	–	–	–	–	–	–	–	–	–	–	–	–	–	–
GOALKEEPERS														
Distribution to own player	–	–	–	–	11	–	–	–	–	–	–	–	11	7
Distribution to opposition player	–	–	–	–	21	–	–	–	–	–	–	–	21	25
Goalkeeper distribution%	–	–	–	–	34%	–	–	–	–	–	–	–	34%	22%
Save	–	–	–	–	3	–	–	–	–	–	–	–	3	3
Ball caught	–	–	–	–	2	–	–	–	–	–	–	–	2	6
Ball dropped	–	–	–	–	–	–	–	–	–	–	–	–	–	2
Goal conceded	–	–	–	–	1	–	–	–	–	–	–	–	1	4

The Sky Blues must have ventured into Villa Park with the sense of trepidation that their visits normally conjure up. Coventry had never won at their rivals' home in the League and Aston Villa, looking to halt a run of five successive defeats, must have been delighted to see their traditional three-point "banker" arrive.

February 27, 1999

1–4

ASTON VILLA
COVENTRY CITY

But Coventry rewrote the history books in style as they thumped four goals past a demoralized and shell-shocked Villa side whose title aspirations were to become mere memories.

The game began evenly, with neither side creating any clear-cut chances, until Coventry broke the deadlock on 25 minutes. John Aloisi fed the ball out to Steve Froggatt on the wing. The youngster played the ball back into the penalty area, where Aloisi's neat touch took him past Riccardo Scimeca and gave him the opportunity to finish smartly.

The first half continued in torrential rain, but Coventry had to wait until six minutes after the break to extend their lead. A penetrating run from Darren Huckerby carried him into the penalty area. He crossed to the near post where George Boateng was able to control the ball, turn and fire home from inside the six-yard box.

Villa got back into the game just four minutes later, when Joachim was bundled over by Richard Shaw inside the penalty area. Dion Dublin stepped up to smash the spot-kick into the top right-hand corner.

After several nervous moments, Coventry regained their two-goal lead in the 73rd minute. The ever-dangerous Huckerby won a free kick to the left of Villa's penalty area. Froggatt curled the ball into the danger area and Aloisi escaped the attentions of Gareth Southgate to shoot in from just outside the six-yard box.

Villa went close when Magnus Hedman saved from Dublin and substitute Stan Collymore hit the post from the rebound – but that only served to convince the Sky Blues' supporters that it was their day.

Coventry made it four when Gary McAllister found Boateng charging through from midfield and the Dutchman lobbed the onrushing Michael Oakes to send the Coventry fans into delirious celebrations.

It was a thoroughly deserved victory. Coventry fired in 16 shots to Villa's 14, with half on target compared with their rivals' 29% shooting accuracy. Villa dominated possession, but were unable to make it count against Strachan's determined and hard-working side. Coventry won 75% of their tackles compared to Villa's 61% and the home side's frustration resulted in four yellow cards to the Sky Blues' one.

Man of the match was George Boateng whose all-action style was attracting the attentions of the big clubs, including Villa who shortly after this game were reported to the FA for making an illegal approach to the player. Boateng earned 2,199 points by scoring twice from five attempts, completing five out of six dribbles and winning all three challenges he contested.

Coventry had finally laid their Villa Park hoodoo and walked away with three vital – and probably unexpected – points that proved crucial in their struggle to avoid the drop into the Nationwide League.

DERBY COUNTY 1998–99

Back row (from left to right): Dane Farrell (Fitness Coach), Neil Sillett (Assistant Physiotherapist), Lars Bohinen,
Horacio Carbonari, Rory Delap, Darryl Powell, Steve Elliott, Eric Steele (Goalkeeping Coach), Steve Rand (Youth Team Coach).
Middle row: Gordon Guthrie (Kit Manager), Marc Bridge-Wilkinson, Danny Porter, Paulo Wanchope, Russell Hoult, Richard Knight,
Mart Poom, Jacob Laursen, Robert Kozluk (now Sheffield United), Stefan Schnoor, Peter Melville (Physiotherapist).
Front row: John Davidson (Assistant Kit Manager), Steve McClaren (First Team Coach – no longer at club), Stefano Eranio,
Francesco Baiano, Igor Stimac, Jim Smith (Manager), Lee Carsley (now Blackburn Rovers), Deon Burton, Dean Sturridge,
Billy McEwan (Reserve Team Coach), Helen Brentnall (Masseuse).

DERBY COUNTY

20 FACTS

1 Derby County were formed by members of the Derbyshire County Cricket Club in 1884. In 1888, they became founder members of the Football League and 1998–99 marked their 100th season in the league.

2 After playing at the Racecourse Ground for 11 years, they moved to the Baseball Ground in 1895. In 1997 they moved to Pride Park.

3 Derby have been league champions on two occasions. Their first triumph, in 1971–72, was followed by another title in 1974–75.

4 They have won the FA Cup once and have been runners-up on three occasions. In 1945–46 they beat Charlton 4–1 at Wembley, but their 6–0 defeat by Bury in 1903 remains a record scoreline for a final.

5 Derby's best performance in the Football League Cup was a semi-final appearance in 1968 when they were knocked out by eventual winners Leeds.

6 The Rams have played in European competition on four occasions. They played in the European Cup in 1972–73, when they lost in the semi-final to Juventus, and again in 1975–76, and in the UEFA Cup in 1974–75 and 1976–77.

7 Derby were on the wrong end of a goalscoring record in 1964, when Kevin Smith of Crystal Palace equalled a league record by netting after just six seconds.

8 The record attendance at the Baseball Ground was 41,826 against Tottenham Hotspur in Division One in 1969. The record at Pride Park was set in 1998–99 against Liverpool, when 32,913 fans watched the Rams win 3–2.

9 Holder of the club appearance record is Kevin Hector, who played 589 times.

10 The Rams' other honours include the Texaco Cup (1972), the Watney Cup (1970) and the Charity Shield (1975).

11 The league scoring record for Derby is held jointly by Jack Bowers and Ray Straw who scored 37 league goals in the 1930–31 and 1956–57 seasons respectively.

12 Derby's record victory came in a UEFA Cup match in 1976 when they beat Finn Harps 12–0 in the first round first leg. Their record league victory is 9–0, which they have achieved twice – first against Wolverhampton Wanderers in 1891 and then against Sheffield Wednesday in 1899.

13 Derby's record defeat came in the FA Cup against Everton in 1889–90. They were beaten 11–2 by the rampant Merseysiders.

14 Midfielder Seth Johnson is the Rams' record signing. He joined from Crewe in May 1999 for a fee of £2.5 million, rising to £3 million based on appearances.

15 Their record sale was the £5.35 million Blackburn Rovers paid for Christian Dailly in August 1998.

16 Derby enjoyed another solid season, finishing eighth in the 1998–99 Premiership table. Their league record was:

Pld	W	D	L	F	A	Pts
38	13	13	12	40	45	52

17 In the AXA-sponsored FA Cup, Derby beat both Plymouth Argyle (3–0) and Swansea (1–0) away, before eliminating Huddersfield Town 3–1 in a Pride Park replay after drawing 2–2. Their dreams of a Wembley appearance were shattered by Arsenal in the quarter-final, when the Gunners won 1–0.

18 Arsenal also ended Derby's hopes in the Worthington Cup. After Derby defeated Manchester City 1–0 away in the second leg to record a 2–1 aggregate victory, the Gunners came to Pride Park and won 2–1 in the third round.

19 The top goalscorer in all competitions for Derby was Deon Burton with 11 goals – eight of which he scored in the Carling Premiership for the Rams.

20 Derby County's disciplinary record was the sixth-worst in the Premiership. They committed 540 fouls, earned 84 yellow cards and suffered two dismissals.

SEASON REVIEW

The three draws with which Derby County opened their Carling Premiership campaign were to sum up their entire season. Jim Smith's side had progressively improved in the top flight since winning promotion in 1996 and were looking to build on their ninth-placed finish of 1997–98, when they lost just eight league matches all season.

They were once again a difficult side to beat in 1998–99 but lacked the sparkling forward play that had seen them score 52 goals the previous year – and those opening three games, which included two goalless draws against sides destined to finish in the bottom five, were to epitomize the Rams' impending frustrations.

September went well, though, and after a six-match unbeaten start to the campaign the side sat in second place in the table, with UEFA Cup qualification at the very least in their sights.

But, typically of the Rams' season, three defeats followed, all of them by a single goal. Unpredictable front man Paulo Wanchope had mislaid his shooting boots, playmaker Francesco Baiano was clearly struggling to find the form that had thrilled the County faithful throughout 1997–98, and teams like West Ham United and Charlton Athletic were leaving Pride Park with three points – not at all what the expectant supporters had in mind.

Conversely, the team were doing well against the top sides, achieving creditable draws against Manchester United, Arsenal and Chelsea – and pulling off a long-overdue win at Anfield over Liverpool, their first since 1970.

But the lack of real excitement in Derby's season is best summarized by the fact that they neither scored nor conceded more than two goals in any one league game until March 13, when they did the double over Liverpool by winning 3–2 at Anfield.

Even so, there were brief glimpses of what the side were capable of. The FA Cup wins over Plymouth Argyle and Huddersfield Town reminded the supporters of the talent inside the squad, with Baiano's two-goal display over Town in the fifth-round replay mesmerising the 28,704 inside Pride Park. Sadly, high-flying Arsenal were to dump the club out of both cup competitions.

So for every encouraging step forward, such as the 2–1 win over Middlesbrough, there would be a frustrating slip-up the following week, such as the 2–1 defeat at Wimbledon. Jamaican front man Deon Burton had scored 10 goals in 15 games in all competitions to ensure the side stayed in the top 10, but the completion of that double over the Merseysiders turned out to be something of a false dawn. The next four matches saw 13 goals shipped in the side's worst run of the season. Leeds and Newcastle both bagged four against them while West Ham won 5–1 at Upton Park.

> "Given our resources, we finished higher than last term and it has been an excellent campaign with the youngsters starting to blossom"
>
> **Jim Smith**

The form of the other forwards was again cause for concern. Derby ended the season with the fewest shots on target in the Premiership. Their wide-play was not up to scratch either, as can be seen by the fact that they put in the second-fewest crosses. Jim Smith was highly critical of some of his players' attitudes off the pitch and, after the final match of the season, a 2-0 defeat at Chelsea, he transfer-listed Dean Sturridge, Wanchope and captain Igor Stimac, while completing the £3 million signing of highly-rated Crewe midfielder Seth Johnson.

Expectations at Pride Park are high, and with the club now seemingly able to comfortably reach mid-table safety, Derby fans will be hoping that these dramatic moves signal the start of a genuine push for the top six after a season of few thrills and much frustration.

DERBY COUNTY

DATE	OPPONENT	SCORE	ATT.	BAIANO	BECK	BOERTIEN	BOHINEN	BORBOKIS	BRIDGE-WILKINSON	BURTON	CARBONARI	CARSLEY	CHRISTIE	DAILLY	DELAP
15.8.98	Blackburn A	0–0	24,235	75	–	–	s15	–	–	s5	90	90□	–	90	90
22.8.98	Wimbledon H	0–0	25,710	s25	–	–	65	–	–	–	–	90	–	–	90
29.8.98	Middlesbro A	1–1	34,087	s5	–	–	90□	–	–	–	–	90	–	–	s30
9.9.98	Sheff Wed H	1–0	26,209	70	–	–	70	–	–	–	–	90	–	–	89
12.9.98	Charlton A	2–1	19,516	67¹	–	–	90	–	–	–	–	90	–	–	90
19.9.98	Leicester H	2–0	26,738	–	–	–	90	–	–	–	–	90□	–	–	90
26.9.98	Aston Villa A	0–1	38,007	s17	–	–	90	–	–	–	84	90	–	–	90
3.10.98	Tottenham H	0–1	30,083	90	–	–	72	–	–	s2	88	90	–	–	90
17.10.98	Newcastle A	1–2*	36,750	65	–	–	–	–	–	s25	90	90□	–	–	90
24.10.98	Man Utd H	1–1	30,867	–	–	–	–	–	–	90¹	–	90	–	–	90□
31.10.98	Leeds Utd H	2–2	27,034	s12	–	–	90	–	–	s21	–	–	–	–	–
7.11.98	Liverpool A	2–1	44,020	–	–	–	90□	–	s1	90	90	–	–	–	73
16.11.98	Nott'm For A	2–2	24,014	–	–	–	90	–	–	90	90¹	–	–	–	–
22.11.98	West Ham H	0–2	31,366	12	–	–	90	–	–	–	63	s78□	–	–	90
28.11.98	Southampton A	1–0	14,762	–	–	–	67□	–	–	s5	90¹□	90	–	–	90
5.12.98	Arsenal H	0–0	29,018	–	–	–	90□	–	–	–	90	–	–	–	90
12.12.98	Chelsea H	2–2	29,056	79	–	–	79	–	–	–	79¹□	–	–	–	90
19.12.98	Coventry A	1–1	16,602	–	–	–	90	–	–	–	90	s45¹	–	–	90□
26.12.98	Everton A	0–0	39,206	–	–	–	–	–	–	–	90	90□	–	–	45
28.12.98	Middlesbro H	2–1	32,726	–	–	–	83	–	–	–	90	90	–	–	–
9.1.99	Wimbledon A	1–2	12,732	–	–	–	s22	–	–	s4	90	90	–	–	–
16.1.99	Blackburn H	1–0	27,386	84□	–	–	75	–	–	90¹	90	90	–	–	–
30.1.99	Sheff Wed A	1–0	24,440	77	–	–	85	–	–	–	90	90	s44	–	–
3.2.99	Man Utd A	0–1	55,174	–	–	–	90	–	–	s20	90	90	–	–	–
7.2.99	Everton H	2–1	27,603	76	–	–	–	–	–	90²	90	90	–	–	–
20.2.99	Charlton H	0–2	27,853	–	–	–	s28	–	–	90	–	90	–	–	62
27.2.99	Tottenham A	1–1	35,392	73	–	–	90	–	–	90¹□	90	90	–	–	–
10.3.99	Aston Villa A	2–1	26,836	90¹	–	–	90□	–	–	90¹	–	–	–	–	–
13.3.99	Liverpool H	3–2	32,913	65	–	–	90	s25	–	90¹	s25	–	–	–	–
20.3.99	Leeds Utd A	1–4	38,992	45¹□	–	–	78	90	–	90	90	–	s45	–	–
3.4.99	Newcastle H	3–4	32,039	90¹	90	–	90	90	–	90¹□	65	–	–	–	–
10.4.99	Nott'm For H	1–0	32,217	45	–	–	90	16	–	60	90¹	–	–	–	–
17.4.99	West Ham A	1–5	25,485	–	57	–	90	–	–	–	90	–	–	–	–
24.4.99	Southampton H	0–0	26,557	–	45	–	90	–	–	83□	90	–	–	–	s45□
2.5.99	Arsenal A	0–1	37,323	–	90	–	68	–	–	13	90□	–	–	–	90□
5.5.99	Leicester A	2–1	20,535	–	90¹	–	89	–	–	–	90□	–	–	–	90□
8.5.99	Coventry H	0–0	32,450	s32	58	–	–	–	–	–	90	–	–	–	78
16.5.99	Chelsea A	1–2	35,016	59	s31	s9	–	–	–	–	90¹	–	–	–	90

□ Yellow card, ■ Red card, s Substitute, 90³ Goals scored

* including own goal

1998–99 PREMIERSHIP APPEARANCES

DORIGO	ELLIOTT	ERANIO	HARPER	HOULT	HUNT	KOZLUK	LAUNDERS	LAURSEN	MURRAY	POOM	POWELL	PRIOR	ROBINSON	SCHNOOR	STIMAC	STURRIDGE	WANCHOPE	TOTAL
–	s35	–	–	90	–	–	–	55	–	90	–	–	90	–	90	85	–	990
–	–	s20	–	90	–	–	–	90	–	90	70	–	90	90□	90□	90	–	990
–	90	90□	–	90	–	–	–	90	–	90	–	–	60	90□	85	90¹□	–	990
–	–	s20	–	90	–	–	s1	90	–	s20	90	–	90	90□	90¹	90	–	990
–	–	s23□	–	90	–	–	–	90	–	s45	90	–	45□	90□	90□	90¹□	–	990
–	s42□	–	s9	90□	–	–	–	90	–	90	90	–	90¹□	48	81	90¹	–	990
–	–	s6	–	90	–	73	–	90□	–	90	90	–	–	–	90	90	–	990
–	–	s11	–	90	–	–	–	90□	–	90	90	–	79□	–	s18	90	90	990
–	–	45	–	90	–	–	–	90	–	90	90	–	s45□	–	90	90	–	990
s45	–	–	–	90	–	–	–	45	–	90□	90	–	90□	90	90	90	–	990
90	78□	–	s12	90	–	78	–	90	–	90	–	–	90¹	90□	69¹	90□	–	990
90	90	–	89¹	90□	–	s17□	–	90	–	90	–	–	–	–	–	90¹	–	990
90¹	90	–	40	69	–	–	–	90	s21	90	90	–	–	–	s50	90	–	990
90	–	s3	s27	–	–	–	–	90□	–	90	87	90	–	–	–	90	90	990
90	–	–	s23	–	–	–	–	90□	–	90	90	90	–	–	–	85	–	990
90□	–	72	s18	–	–	–	–	90	–	90	90□	90	–	–	–	90	–	990
90	–	90	s11	–	–	–	–	90	–	90	90□	90	–	s11	–	s11¹	90□	990
67□	s45	–	45	–	s23	–	–	90	–	90	90□	90	–	–	–	45	90□	990
–	90□	90	s45	–	s13	90	–	77	–	90	90	90	–	–	–	–	90	990
–	90	72	s4	–	s7¹	s18	–	90	–	90	90	90	–	–	–	86¹	44■	944
90□	90	68	s4□	–	–	–	–	86	–	90	86	90	–	–	–	90	90¹	990
90	–	90	s15	–	–	s6	–	–	–	90	–	90	–	90□	–	90	–	990
90	–	s13□	90	90	–	–	–	90	–	–	–	90¹	–	s5	90	46	–	990
90	–	–	70	90	s10	–	–	90	–	–	80	90	–	–	90	–	90	990
90	–	90	s14	90	s1	–	–	76□	–	–	s14□	90	–	–	90	–	89	990
90	–	90	s12	90	–	–	–	78	–	–	90	90	–	–	90	62	s28	990
73	–	40	s17	90	s17	–	–	90□	–	–	–	s50	90	–	–	90□	–	990
–	–	90	s1	90	–	–	–	90	–	–	90□	90□	–	90	90	–	89■	990
–	–	82	s8	90	–	–	–	90	–	–	90□	90	–	65	90□	–	90²	990
–	s50	–	90	–	–	–	s12	90	–	90	90	90□	–	–	40	–	–	990
90	–	–	–	90	–	–	–	90	–	–	–	90□	–	82	–	s8	s25¹	990
–	–	–	s45	60■	–	–	–	90	–	s30	90	90	–	90	–	s74	90	960
32	–	–	s58	90	–	–	–	90	s33	–	90	90	–	90	–	90□	90¹	990
–	–	90	s7	–	–	–	–	90	–	90	90	90□	–	70	–	s20	90	990
–	–	90	s65	–	–	–	–	90	s22□	90	90	90	s12	–	–	–	90□	990
–	–	90□	–	–	–	–	–	90□	s1	90	–	90	–	90	–	90¹	90□	990
–	–	45	s12	–	–	–	–	90	s45	90	90□	90	–	90	–	90	90	990
–	–	90	s31	–	–	–	–	90	–	90	90	90	–	59	–	81	90	990

THE MANAGER

JIM SMITH

Jim Smith has now been manager of Derby County for four full seasons, overseeing their promotion to the Premiership and keeping them in the top flight ever since.

Smith began his playing career as a wing-half with his hometown club Sheffield United but was never given a chance in the first team and switched to Aldershot before spells with Halifax Town, Lincoln City and Colchester United.

In the last three years, shrewd Smith has imported a dazzling array of cosmopolitan stars, from the Costa Rican striker Paulo Wanchope and Italian stars Francesco Baiano and Stefano Eranio to £2.7 million record signing Horacio Carbonari, the Argentinean defender from Rosario Central.

In 1998–99, Smith lost his first team coach Steve McLaren, who switched to Manchester United when the Red Devils' assistant manager Brian Kidd left for Blackburn. But McLaren was swiftly replaced by former QPR manager Ray Harford, though at the end of the season he was himself replaced by former Sunderland manager Malcolm Crosby.

After two consecutive top 10 finishes, the Rams will undoubtedly be looking for a top six place in 1999–2000 and with the much-respected Smith at the helm, it would be foolish to back against them.

LEAGUE POSITION

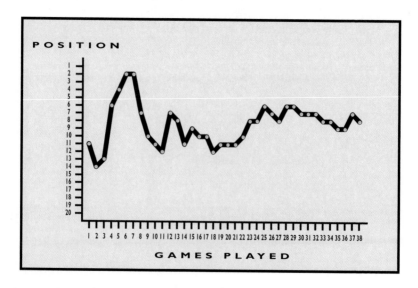

THE GOALS

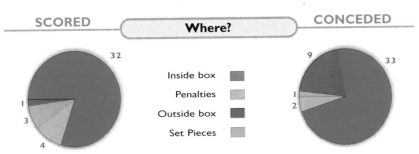

SCORED — Where? — CONCEDED

Inside box
Penalties
Outside box
Set Pieces

Only Chelsea scored more goals from direct free kicks than Derby did in the 1998–99 Premiership, but County added only one goal from open play to their total of strikes from long range. Efforts from more than 18 yards out accounted for just 10% of all Derby's league goals, the fourth-lowest percentage in the league. Their rivals, though, showed County how it should be done with a healthy nine goals scored against Derby from distance.

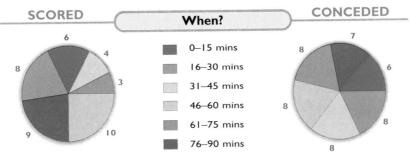

SCORED — When? — CONCEDED

0–15 mins
16–30 mins
31–45 mins
46–60 mins
61–75 mins
76–90 mins

County's resilient defence held out well under second-half pressure, conceding 23 out of 45 goals after the break – better, on average, than most top-flight clubs during the 1998–99 season. Derby's back-line were unique in that the goals they conceded were very evenly spread across the 90 minutes. Jim Smith's half-time team talks appeared to have the desired effect, prompting his team to grab 25% of their goals in the 15 minutes following the re-start.

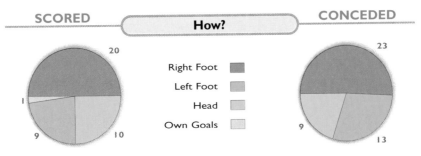

SCORED — How? — CONCEDED

Right Foot
Left Foot
Head
Own Goals

Jim Smith's side relied on the aerial prowess of Paulo Wanchope and Deon Burton in particular for a significant proportion of their league goals. The two Rams forwards butted in seven headers between them in County's total of 10, and strikes via the head accounted for a quarter of all Derby's goals. The Premiership's sixth-meanest defence allowed nine headed goals against them, representing one-fifth of all strikes conceded.

DERBY COUNTY

	BAIANO	BECK	BOERTIEN	BOHINEN	BORBOKIS	BRIDGE-WILKINSON	BURTON	CARBONARI	CARSLEY	CHRISTIE	DAILLY	DELAP	DORIGO
APPEARANCES													
Start	17	6	0	29	3	0	14	28	20	0	1	21	17
Sub	5	1	1	3	1	1	7	1	2	2	0	2	1
Minutes on pitch	1253	461	9	2516	221	1	1228	2474	1923	89	90	1862	1477
GOAL ATTEMPTS													
Goals	4	1	0	0	0	0	8	5	1	0	0	0	1
Shots on target	7	5	0	11	0	0	11	12	8	0	0	6	1
Shots off target	14	2	0	18	0	0	21	10	6	0	0	10	2
Shooting accuracy %	33%	71%	0%	38%	0%	0%	34%	55%	57%	0%	0%	38%	33%
PASSING													
Goal assists	1	0	0	4	0	0	0	0	1	0	0	1	2
Long passes	55	1	1	184	8	0	11	315	127	0	5	102	101
Short passes	548	146	2	1064	64	0	436	510	647	28	23	477	444
PASS COMPLETION													
Own half %	85%	68%	0%	85%	77%	0%	89%	83%	88%	100%	61%	80%	86%
Opposition half %	73%	75%	100%	71%	59%	0%	72%	56%	73%	61%	70%	63%	68%
CROSSING													
Total crosses	38	3	0	84	12	0	9	4	29	1	0	34	95
Cross completion %	18%	0%	0%	30%	17%	0%	11%	25%	48%	0%	0%	24%	41%
DRIBBLING													
Dribbles & runs	53	9	0	101	9	0	27	27	11	0	0	55	27
Dribble completion %	72%	78%	0%	75%	78%	0%	59%	81%	82%	0%	0%	75%	81%
DEFENDING													
Tackles made	30	7	0	115	5	0	20	82	105	1	2	65	64
Tackles won %	53%	43%	0%	63%	60%	0%	60%	62%	67%	100%	50%	55%	67%
Blocks	1	0	0	17	0	0	1	35	12	0	1	12	5
Clearances	2	2	1	43	5	0	10	331	81	0	10	96	87
Interceptions	3	3	1	32	2	0	2	22	18	0	0	32	33
DISCIPLINE													
Fouls	20	5	0	34	1	1	41	22	29	0	0	18	17
Offside	12	1	0	2	0	0	22	0	0	0	0	3	1
Yellow cards	2	0	0	6	0	0	3	4	5	0	0	6	3
Red cards	0	0	0	0	0	0	0	0	0	0	0	0	0

GOALKEEPER NAME	START/ (SUB)	TIME ON PITCH	GOALS CONCEDED	MINS/GOALS CONCEDED	SAVES MADE	SAVES/ SHOTS
HOULT	23	2019	29	69.6	77	73%
POOM	15 (2)	1401	16	87.6	54	77%

PLAYERS' STATISTICS

	ELLIOTT	ERANIO	HARPER	HUNT	KOZLUK	LAUNDERS	LAURSEN	MURRAY	POWELL	PRIOR	ROBINSON	SCHNOOR	STIMAC	STURRIDGE	WANCHOPE	TOTAL	RANK
	7	18	6	0	3	0	37	0	30	33	0	20	15	22	33		
	4	7	21	6	4	1	0	4	3	1	1	3	0	6	2		
	790	1510	862	71	283	12	3207	101	2762	3000	12	1691	1168	2081	2970		
	0	0	1	1	0	0	0	0	0	1	0	2	0	5	9	40*	=14th
	1	5	2	1	1	0	3	1	8	6	0	4	0	26	37	156	20th
	4	6	6	0	0	0	3	0	17	2	1	8	2	24	32	188	19th
	20%	45%	25%	100%	100%	0%	50%	100%	32%	75%	0%	33%	0%	52%	54%	45%	9th
	0	1	1	0	0	0	0	0	2	0	0	1	2	4	6	26	=16th
	44	37	15	5	9	1	285	10	78	102	0	83	181	17	41	1818	11th
	125	757	269	30	88	1	605	53	912	602	4	452	298	562	1069	10216	18th
	82%	89%	82%	83%	89%	0%	87%	79%	90%	87%	100%	88%	90%	83%	82%	86%	19th
	60%	80%	70%	65%	78%	0%	62%	56%	77%	65%	50%	69%	56%	72%	70%	69%	12th
	2	44	31	1	2	0	24	0	27	1	0	64	4	41	39	589	19th
	0%	20%	19%	0%	0%	0%	21%	0%	44%	0%	0%	33%	25%	39%	26%	30%	5th
	2	40	83	3	2	0	7	3	43	29	0	13	22	122	178	867	12th
	100%	55%	58%	33%	100%	0%	71%	100%	84%	97%	0%	92%	86%	66%	54%	68%	15th
	37	53	18	5	8	0	86	4	109	99	2	74	38	35	71	1135	13th
	59%	57%	72%	100%	50%	0%	59%	25%	66%	72%	50%	41%	74%	54%	63%	62%	7th
	9	7	7	1	4	0	41	2	17	41	0	15	10	3	10	252	1st
	114	14	14	3	14	0	279	1	96	472	0	88	153	3	27	1969	14th
	15	17	6	0	6	0	32	2	27	37	0	11	21	7	10	341	10th
	9	21	9	3	1	0	31	5	62	29	0	28	15	54	84	540	6th
	1	3	5	0	0	0	0	0	1	1	0	4	0	24	57	137	9th
	3	4	1	0	1	0	7	1	8	4	0	6	6	3	9	84	4th
	0	0	0	0	0	0	0	0	0	0	0	0	0	0	1	2	=14th

* including one own goal

CROSSES CAUGHT	CROSSES PUNCHED	CROSSES NOT CLAIMED	CATCH SUCCESS	THROWS/SHORT KICKS	% COMPLETION	LONG KICKS	% COMPLETION
89	11	9	95%	165	96%	492	31%
78	13	3	99%	125	95%	306	37%

PLAYER OF THE SEASON

PLAYER	INDEX SCORE
HORACIO CARBONARI	858
Tony Dorigo	857
Spencer Prior	843
Paulo Wanchope	772
Rory Delap	689
Dean Sturridge	680
Stefano Eranio	678
Russell Hoult	632
Stefan Schnoor	597
Jacob Laursen	569

"**H**oracio Who?" was the response of many Rams fans when Derby splashed out a club record £2.7 million on Horacio Carbonari from Rosario Central.

It is not a question they are asking any more. The accomplished centre-back had an extremely impressive debut season in the Carling Premiership and capped his solid defensive displays with several stunning goals, netting five times in all.

He finished the 1998–99 campaign as the highest-scoring Derby player in the Carling Opta Season Index, with an average score of 858 points per match across the season.

Veteran left-back Tony Dorigo proved to be an extremely valuable member of Jim Smith's squad in 1998–99. The experienced former Leeds United Championship winner finished in second place, just a point behind Carbonari.

It was another defender, former Leicester City centre-back Spencer Prior, who finished third, underlining the problems Derby had in front of goal compared to 1997–98.

The club's top scorer, unorthodox Costa Rican Paulo Wanchope, was the highest-placed striker, averaging 772 Opta points across the campaign. But his frustrating season was summed up by Jim Smith, who transfer-listed Wanchope, saying he should have found the net many more times than the 10 he managed.

And looking at the club's Carling Opta statistics, County's disappointing points scores simply reflect their fundamental lack of progress as a club after a sizzling 1997–98.

The club's official Player of the Year, Danish international defender Jacob Laursen, just made the top 10. He scored fewer points than other defenders because of his lack of forward play – he registered just six shots at goal all season, with only three on target. But his consistent displays, coupled with outstanding man-marking abilities, earned him an average of 569 points per Premiership match. Newcomers Stefan Schnoor and Rory Delap also featured in the top 10

FIVE OF THE BEST

Derby secured a second successive top 10 Premiership finish in 1998–99, but the general feeling around Pride Park was that the club had made little progress on the previous season. Jim Smith has drafted in Crewe midfielder Seth Johnson to add steel to the midfield and, with a few more goals, County should be eyeing a top six placing.

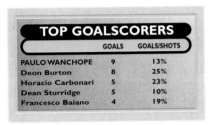

TOP GOALSCORERS

	GOALS	GOALS/SHOTS
PAULO WANCHOPE	9	13%
Deon Burton	8	25%
Horacio Carbonari	5	23%
Dean Sturridge	5	10%
Francesco Baiano	4	19%

The unpredictable Paulo Wanchope was the club's top scorer for the second year running, but only nine league goals as opposed to 13 in 1997–98 represented a disappointing return from 33 games played. Jamaican star Deon Burton scored eight, including six in seven games in February and March, underlining his potential. Defender Horacio Carbonari bagged five in a terrific season, along with speedy striker Dean Sturridge, but no player reached double figures as Derby struggled up front, scoring just 40 goals.

Scintillating one-touch football characterized Derby's 1997–98 season and the Rams' fans enjoyed plenty of repeat performances in 1998–99. But with Baiano failing to make the same impression in the first team, the onus was on the likes of Lars Bohinen and Stefano Eranio to take control and Bohinen was the club's most prolific passer. Paulo Wanchope, who loves to drop deep and take players on, is third in the table – unusual for a striker – but his completion rate suffers because he operates mainly in the opposition final third, where it is harder to retain possession.

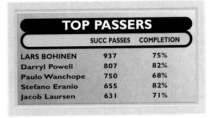

TOP PASSERS

	SUCC PASSES	COMPLETION
LARS BOHINEN	937	75%
Darryl Powell	807	82%
Paulo Wanchope	750	68%
Stefano Eranio	655	82%
Jacob Laursen	631	71%

TOP TACKLERS

	WON	SUCCESS
LARS BOHINEN	73	63%
Darryl Powell	72	66%
Spencer Prior	71	72%
Lee Carsley	70	67%
Horacio Carbonari	51	62%

Former Nottingham Forest star Lars Bohinen again tops this chart, winning one more tackle than Darryl Powell in 1998–99. The most effective in terms of tackle success rate was Spencer Prior, who enjoyed a terrific first season at Pride Park after his switch from Leicester City. Lee Carsley would doubtless have topped the list had he not moved to Blackburn Rovers, being just three successful tackles short of Bohinen.

Derby suffered just two Premiership red cards in 1998–99, one brandished at goalkeeper Russell Hoult for a professional foul in the home win over Nottingham Forest and the other shown to Paulo Wanchope for an unsightly clash with Middlesbrough's Andy Townsend. But that is not the only reason he ended up as Derby's bad boy. He conceded 84 fouls, the third most of any player in the Premiership, racking up nine yellow cards in the process. Darryl Powell and Jacob Laursen picked up a further 15 bookings between them.

DISCIPLINE

	POINTS	FOULS & CARDS
PAULO WANCHOPE	117	84F, 9Y, 1R
Darryl Powell	86	62F, 8Y, 0R
Dean Sturridge	63	54F, 3Y, 0R
Lars Bohinen	52	34F, 6Y, 0R
Jacob Laursen	52	31F, 7Y, 0R

ACTION	BOHINEN	BRIDGE-WILKINSON	BURTON	CARBONARI	DELAP	DORIGO	ELLIOTT	HARPER	HUTH	KOZLUK	LAURSEN	POWELL	MANCHOPE	TOTAL	LIVERPOOL
Time on pitch	90	1	90	90	73	90	90	89	90	17	90	90	90	990	990
GOALS															
Goal	-	-	-	-	-	-	-	-	-	-	-	-	2	2	1
Shot on target	-	-	-	-	-	-	-	-	-	-	-	-	1	1	4
Shot off target	-	-	-	-	-	1	1	1	-	-	-	1	-	4	11
Blocked shot	-	-	-	-	-	-	-	-	-	-	-	-	-	2	12
Own goal	-	-	-	-	-	-	-	-	-	-	-	-	-	-	-
PASSES															
Pass to own player	22	-	33	10	13	18	10	17	-	5	13	23	26	190	380
Pass to opposition	9	-	8	6	10	7	7	9	-	-	5	8	8	77	114
Cross to own player	-	-	-	-	1	2	-	-	-	-	-	-	-	3	7
Cross to opposition player	-	-	-	-	-	-	-	-	-	-	-	-	-	2	25
Goal assist	-	-	-	-	-	-	-	-	-	-	-	-	-	2	1
Pass completion %	71%	0%	79%	63%	71%	75%	59%	65%	0%	100%	72%	74%	76%	72%	74%
TACKLES & CLEARANCES															
Tackle	12	-	1	3	3	4	9	2	-	-	5	5	1	40	31
Clearances, blocks and interceptions	8	-	4	24	15	7	27	3	1	5	9	5	5	125	55
DRIBBLES & RUNS															
Dribble ball retained	3	-	-	-	1	3	-	4	-	-	-	-	4	15	28
Dribbles ball lost	2	-	-	-	-	-	-	3	-	-	-	-	4	9	17
Dribble success %	60%	0%	0%	0%	100%	100%	0%	57%	0%	-	0%	0%	50%	63%	62%
DISCIPLINE															
Fouls	2	-	-	1	-	1	1	2	-	1	-	5	5	18	10
Penalty conceded	-	-	-	-	-	-	-	-	-	-	-	-	-	-	-
Free kick - offside	-	-	-	-	-	-	-	-	-	-	-	-	2	2	-
Yellow cards	1	-	-	-	-	-	-	-	-	-	-	2	-	3	2
Red cards	-	-	-	-	-	-	-	-	-	-	-	-	-	-	-
GOALKEEPERS															
Distribution to own player	-	-	-	-	-	-	-	-	18	-	-	-	-	18	18
Distribution to opposition player	-	-	-	-	-	-	-	-	25	-	-	-	-	25	14
Goalkeeper distribution%	-	-	-	-	-	-	-	-	42%	-	-	-	-	42%	56%
Save	-	-	-	-	-	-	-	-	4	-	-	-	-	4	4
Ball caught	-	-	-	-	-	-	-	-	8	-	-	-	-	8	2
Ball dropped	-	-	-	-	-	-	-	-	-	-	-	-	-	-	-
Goal conceded	-	-	-	-	-	-	-	-	1	-	-	-	-	1	2

Derby County made the trip to Anfield having scored only once in their previous 10 visits, without a win in their last five Premiership matches and missing many of their first team players. Liverpool, however, were having their own problems under the joint stewardship of Roy Evans and Gerard Houllier, with the Reds winning just one of their previous seven games — and that against struggling Nottingham Forest.

November 7, 1998

1-2

LIVERPOOL
DERBY COUNTY

Liverpool were quick off the blocks with their passing game putting the Rams under early pressure, but the home side were stung in the sixth minute by a well-worked goal.

A poor clearance by David James was intercepted in midfield and the ball was eventually worked out wide to Tony Dorigo. The left-back's in-swinging cross was met by Kevin Harper at the far post, who rose unchallenged to head back across the goal into the far corner.

In the 27th minute Derby broke up another Liverpool move, switching from defence to attack in an instant. Again the ball was worked into a wide position, this time on the right flank where Rory Delap crossed for Paulo Wanchope to bury a firm header beyond James.

Liverpool dominated possession, but were unable to make an impact on the scoresheet until the 84th minute when Steve McManaman beat two defenders and set up Jamie Redknapp with a cross for the simplest of tap-ins from close range.

Redknapp had a chance to equalize late in the game and Wanchope could have eased Derby's fears, but the England midfield player failed to find the target and the Costa Rican forward missed narrowly with a left-foot shot from the edge of the box.

This was a superb victory for the Rams. In the aftermath of the game, Lars Bohinen explained: "We worked all week on crosses and tried to make them count because we knew Liverpool were weak in that department."

Derby made the best of the few chances they had in this game, scoring with their only two efforts on target from eight attempts. Liverpool could not make possession or chances count. They hit the net just once from five attempts on target and fired in 23 more efforts that didn't trouble Russell Hoult. The Derby 'keeper's handling was excellent all day and he also caught all eight crosses that he came off his line to collect.

The Reds made nearly twice as many passes as Derby during the match and the Rams had to make more than twice as many defensive blocks, clearances and interceptions.

Referee Uriah Rennie brandished the yellow card on five occasions, although the most common offender, Paulo Wanchope, was not censured despite committing five fouls.

This was another body blow for the Evans-Houllier partnership. Less than a week later, following a home defeat by Tottenham in the Worthington Cup, Evans and Liverpool parted company, leaving Frenchman Houllier in sole charge.

For Jim Smith's side, it was a superb victory that provided the springboard for a second successive challenge for a place in Europe, although once more his side fell just short of achieving their target.

ACTION	BAIANO	BOHINEN	BORROWS	BURTON	CARBONARI	ERANIO	HARPER	HOULT	LAURSEN	POWELL	PRIOR	SCHNOOR	STIMAC	WANCHOPE	TOTAL	LIVERPOOL
Time on pitch	65	90	25	90	25	82	8	90	90	90	90	65	90	90	990	990
GOALS																
Goal	–	–	–	–	–	–	–	–	–	–	–	–	–	–	3	2
Shot on target	–	–	–	1	–	–	1	–	1	–	–	–	–	2	5	4
Shot off target	3	–	–	2	–	1	–	–	–	–	–	–	–	–	5	7
Blocked shot	–	–	–	1	–	1	–	–	–	–	–	–	–	1	3	5
Own goal	–	–	–	–	–	–	–	–	–	–	–	–	–	–	–	–
PASSES																
Pass to own player	35	34	1	27	3	31	–	–	14	28	14	24	23	17	251	318
Pass to opposition	4	5	–	5	–	3	–	–	2	2	–	4	14	3	43	63
Cross to own player	–	2	–	–	–	–	–	–	–	–	–	2	–	–	5	9
Cross to opposition player	–	2	1	3	–	–	–	–	–	–	–	2	2	2	10	21
Goal assist	–	1	–	–	–	–	–	–	–	–	–	–	2	–	3	1
Pass completion %	90%	84%	0%	77%	100%	91%	0%	0%	88%	93%	100%	81%	65%	77%	83%	80%
TACKLES & CLEARANCES																
Tackle	1	4	–	3	2	1	–	–	–	–	3	4	2	–	21	33
Clearances, blocks and interceptions	1	11	–	2	3	3	2	2	18	6	19	6	25	–	98	84
DRIBBLES & RUNS																
Dribbles ball retained	3	1	–	1	–	–	1	–	–	1	–	1	–	–	8	22
Dribbles ball lost	–	–	–	–	–	–	–	–	–	–	–	–	1	–	3	1
Dribble success %	100%	100%	0%	100%	0%	0%	100%	0%	0%	100%	0%	0%	50%	0%	73%	96%
DISCIPLINE																
Fouls	1	–	1	2	1	–	–	–	–	–	–	1	1	4	12	17
Penalty conceded	–	–	–	–	–	–	–	–	–	–	–	–	–	–	–	–
Free kick - offside	–	–	–	3	–	–	–	–	–	–	–	2	–	3	8	3
Yellow cards	–	–	–	1	–	–	–	–	–	–	–	–	–	–	2	3
Red cards	–	–	–	–	–	–	–	–	–	–	–	–	–	–	–	–
GOALKEEPERS																
Distribution to own player	–	–	–	–	–	–	11	–	–	–	–	–	–	–	11	18
Distribution to opposition player	–	–	–	–	–	–	17	–	–	–	–	–	–	–	17	12
Goalkeeper distribution%	–	–	–	–	–	–	39%	–	–	–	–	–	–	–	39%	60%
Save	–	–	–	–	–	–	4	–	–	–	–	–	–	–	4	5
Ball caught	–	–	–	–	–	–	3	–	–	–	–	–	–	–	3	3
Ball dropped	–	–	–	–	–	–	1	–	–	–	–	–	–	–	1	–
Goal conceded	–	–	–	–	–	–	2	–	–	–	–	–	–	–	2	3

With the chase for European places well and truly on, Derby entertained Liverpool at Pride Park knowing a win would put them in with a real chance of qualification. Liverpool also had European ambitions, but a disappointing season left them needing three points to have any chance of making the top six.

The match began at a frenetic pace and Derby almost took the lead after just four minutes. Deon Burton controlled a long ball forward by Igor Stimac and fired a 20-yard shot, which went just the wrong side of the post.

Burton and Derby were celebrating eight minutes later when Lars Bohinen swung a corner in from the left. Burton jumped in front of David James and headed into the Liverpool net to put Derby in front.

It should have been 1–1 on 25 minutes when Michael Owen's mazy run ended with a stinging drive which was well parried by Derby 'keeper Russell Hoult. The rebound fell kindly for Robbie Fowler, but he completely missed his kick and Pride Park breathed a collective sigh of relief.

Nine minutes before half-time, Owen picked up a loose ball in midfield and ran 45 yards before he was brought down in the penalty area by Spencer Prior. Fowler stepped up and blasted the resulting penalty past Hoult into the top left corner.

Burton missed a golden one-on-one chance three minutes later when his lob over James went agonizingly wide. Burton was playing well, but it was his strike partner who produced the goods a minute before half-time. Stimac chipped a deep free kick into the box and Paulo Wanchope rose above Dominic Matteo to put his header past James for 2–1.

Liverpool tried to hit back straight after the interval. In the 48th minute, Jamie Redknapp's screamer from the edge of the area was brilliantly turned over the bar by the flying Hoult.

A minute later Derby struck the hammer-blow. Stimac's long pass picked out Wanchope, who had sprung the Liverpool offside trap and was clean through. The Costa Rican steadied himself before firing an unstoppable shot past James for 3–1.

Liverpool pressed forward and got their reward on 57 minutes when Matteo crossed from wide on the left and Fowler was free to side-foot into the roof of the net from close range.

They then went forward looking for an equalizer but were open to the counter-attack – and James had to save well from Burton's angled volley. At the other end, Redknapp's shot flew fractionally wide of the post. That was the end of Liverpool's threat, and Derby finished as 3–2 winners.

The Carling Opta statistics show that, despite the fact that Derby made fewer successful passes, they did have a higher completion percentage (83% to Liverpool's 80%). They also hit more shots on target than the Merseyside club and conceded fewer free kicks.

The season ended in disappointment for both clubs, as each missed out on European qualification. Had Liverpool won at Pride Park, they would have qualified for the InterToto Cup at the expense of West Ham. Instead, Liverpool finished in a disappointing seventh position and Derby in eighth place.

Piggy-back ride: Scot Gemmill and Kevin Campbell in celebratory mood during the 4–1 defeat of Charlton Athletic in April 1999

EVERTON

ADDRESS

Goodison Park, Liverpool L4 4EL

CONTACT NUMBERS

Telephone: 0151 330 2200
Fax: 0151 286 9112
Ticket Office: 0151 330 2300
Ticket Line: 09068 121599
24hr Information: 09068 121199
Everton FC Megastore: 0151 330 2030
e-mail: everton@evertonfc.com
Website: www.evertonfc.com

SPONSORS

One-2-One

FANZINES

When Skies Are Grey
Speke From The Harbour

KEY PERSONNEL

Chairman: Sir Phillip Carter CBE
Deputy Chairman: B Kenwright
Directors: P R Johnson,
K M Tamlin, M J L Abercromby,
Lord Grantchester
Club Secretary: M J Dunford
Manager: Walter Smith

COLOURS

Home: Blue shirts with
white shorts and stockings
Away: White shirts,
blue shorts and stockings

NICKNAME

The Toffees

20 FACTS

1 After being formed in 1878 as St Domingo FC by a Sunday School, the club changed their name to Everton just over a year later.

2 Everton were founder members of the Football League in 1888.

3 Everton have won the league title on nine occasions spread over almost 100 years. Their championships came in 1890–91, 1914–15, 1927–28, 1931–32, 1938–39, 1962–63, 1969–70, 1984–85 and 1986–87.

4 They have won the FA Cup on five occasions, in 1906, 1933, 1966, 1984 and 1995. They also hold the record for the most semi-final appearances in the competition (23).

5 The Toffees have never won the Football League Cup but have been runners-up twice – in 1977 and 1984.

6 In 11 seasons of European competition, Everton have won one trophy – the European Cup Winners Cup in 1985. They also participated in that competition in 1966–67 and 1995–96. They played in the Fairs Cup in 1962–63, 1964–65 and 1965–66, the UEFA Cup in 1975–76, 1978–79 and 1979–80 and the European Cup in 1963–64 and 1970–71.

7 William Ralph "Dixie" Dean set a league record in the 1927–28 season, when he scored 60 league goals in Division One. He holds the record for the most league goals for one club, with 349 for the Toffees.

8 The prolific striker also holds the record for the most career hat-tricks. He took home 37 match balls in his career at Tranmere Rovers and Everton.

9 Everton have boasted the outright top scorer in the top flight in 11 different seasons – more than any other club.

10 Everton have been in the top flight ever since being promoted in 1954 – the second-longest period of any club currently in the Premiership.

11 Since the introduction of three points for a win, Everton hold the record for the biggest winning margin in the league – they finished 13 points clear in 1984–85.

12 In 1924 Everton's Sam Chedgzoy took a corner to himself and dribbled past the Spurs defence before scoring. The law was subsequently changed to force players to pass to a team-mate from a corner.

13 Everton's record victory came in the FA Cup against Derby County in the 1889–90 season, when the Rams were beaten 11–2. Everton's record league victory was a 9–1 win over Manchester City in 1906.

14 Everton's record defeat was 10–4 by Tottenham Hotspur in a Division One match in October 1958.

15 The record attendance at Goodison Park was for the Merseyside Derby on September 18, 1948, when 78,299 saw Everton draw 1–1 with Liverpool.

16 Everton moved clear of the relegation dogfight after being inspired by on-loan striker Kevin Campbell, finishing 14th with a league record of:

Pld	W	D	L	F	A	Pts
38	11	10	17	42	47	43

17 Walter Smith's side were knocked out of the AXA-sponsored FA Cup for the second year running by eventual finalists Newcastle United in the sixth round. They beat Bristol City 2–0 at Ashton Gate, then won ties against Ipswich Town 1–0 and Coventry City 2–1, both at Goodison Park, before their 4–1 defeat by the Magpies at St James's Park.

18 In the Worthington Cup third round, they beat Huddersfield 2–1 at Goodison Park after drawing 1–1 away. They then defeated Middlesbrough at the Riverside Stadium 3–2 but lost 6–5 on penalties to Sunderland at the Stadium of Light after a 1–1 home draw.

19 The top goalscorer in all competitions for Everton in season 1998–99 was Kevin Campbell with nine goals.

20 The Toffees' disciplinary record was the worst in the 1998–99 Premiership season. They committed 587 fouls, earned 91 yellow cards and suffered five dismissals.

SEASON REVIEW

Everton secured Premiership survival in their penultimate match with a six-goal thrashing of West Ham. Such a feast of goals had seemed an impossibility at the start of the season.

It took Walter Smith's team until October 31 to score a Premiership goal at Goodison Park — and that came in a 4–1 defeat at the hands of Manchester United. By the time they won their first home game, they were languishing in 16th place with just 15 points from 14 games.

Fans' favourite Duncan Ferguson, who had scored four of his side's eight goals in that time, was sold to Newcastle United soon afterwards in a move that almost led to Walter Smith's resignation and spelt the end of Peter Johnson's controversial reign as chairman. In addition, summer signing and midfield playmaker John Collins had his season ended by injury in December. The club were simply in a mess.

To the players' great credit, their commitment on the pitch rarely wavered. The team were terrible to watch but could not be criticized for lack of effort. No other side made more tackles than Everton in the 1998–99 season and only three clubs won a greater percentage of their challenges.

Unfortunately, this desire to compete also manifested itself in the club's poor disciplinary record. They finished the season top of Carling Opta's sinners table (see page 626), picking up more yellow cards than any other team and committing 587 fouls. Interestingly, they were also the second most fouled team, finishing third in the most sinned-against table (see page 627), a fact that suggests the majority of their games turned into pitched battles.

There was certainly very little finesse about their play, and until the final months of the season they had competed in very few memorable matches. No team completed a lower percentage of dribbles and runs and only Wimbledon made fewer successful passes in the opposition half.

The 5–0 victory against Middlesbrough in February saw Everton fans rubbing their eyes in disbelief. But the fact that the team ended the season as the 11th highest scorers and with a respectable shooting accuracy rating of 45% is almost entirely due to one man: Kevin Campbell.

Campbell was signed on transfer deadline day in a loan deal from Turkish club Trabzonspor and made his debut in the 3–2 defeat against Liverpool. It took him three games to score, but once he hit the back of the net against Coventry he never looked back, taking his tally to nine goals in just eight games — 21% of Everton's final total in just under a quarter of the season.

Young Francis Jeffers responded superbly to the arrival of his new strike partner, playing well enough to win a place in Kevin Keegan's second England squad. Between them, Campbell and Jeffers scored more goals in their games together than Ibrahima Bakayoko, Danny Cadamarteri and Nick Barmby had managed all season in the Premiership!

The fight to stay up also featured eye-catching performances from Don Hutchison and Olivier Dacourt in midfield and some resolute work from the defence. But the feeling remained that the side lacked imagination and the ability to compete with the top teams.

This is something that Walter Smith will attempt to address in the summer. Without the financial backing he needs, though, his task will be very difficult. He did an excellent job in keeping Everton up in 1998–99 — but the club faces a hard enough task raising the money to make Kevin Campbell's transfer permanent before bringing in other new players.

> "It goes without saying that we will need to improve our playing squad throughout summer, but the financial problems which exist at present mean we will have to very carefully assess who we bring in"
>
> **Walter Smith**

EVERTON

DATE	OPPONENT	SCORE	ATT.	BAKAYOKO	BALL	BARMBY	BILIC	BRANCH	CADAMARTERI	CAMPBELL	CLELAND	COLLINS	DACOURT	DEGN	DUNNE	FARLEY
15.8.98	Aston Villa H	0–0	40,112	–	90□	90	–	–	s26	–	90	90	76□	–	–	–
22.8.98	Leicester A	0–2	21,037	–	90	62	–	–	s45	–	90	90□	90□	–	–	–
29.8.98	Tottenham H	0–1	39,378	–	90□	75	–	–	90	–	75□	90	90	–	–	–
8.9.98	Nott'm For A	2–0	25,610	–	90	66	–	–	s24	–	90	90	90	–	–	–
12.9.98	Leeds Utd H	0–0	36,687	–	90	66	–	–	s24	–	90	90	55■	–	–	–
19.9.98	Middlesbro A	2–2	34,563	–	90[1]□	90	–	–	s45	–	90	90[1]	90□	–	–	–
26.9.98	Blackburn H	0–0	36,404	–	90	46	–	–	s44	–	75	90	–	–	–	–
3.10.98	Wimbledon A	2–1	16,054	–	90	–	–	–	90[1]	–	–	90	90□	–	–	–
17.10.98	Liverpool H	0–0	40,185	68	90	–	–	–	s33	–	90□	90	–	–	–	–
24.10.98	Sheff Wed A	0–0	26,592	70	90	–	–	–	s20□	–	90	90□	90□	–	–	–
31.10.98	Man Utd H	1–4	40,087	90□	90□	–	–	–	90	–	–	90	90	–	s25	–
8.11.98	Arsenal A	0–1	38,088	90	90	–	–	–	s44□	–	78	90□	90	–	90□	–
15.11.98	Coventry A	0–3	19,279	57□	90	–	–	–	s33	–	78	90	–	–	–	–
23.11.98	Newcastle H	1–0	30,357	88[1]	90	–	–	–	89□	–	–	90	–	–	90□	–
28.11.98	Charlton A	2–1	20,043	89	90	–	–	–	90[2]	–	s1	90	–	–	90	–
5.12.98	Chelsea H	0–0	36,430	90□	90□	–	–	–	90	–	90	90	–	–	76■	–
12.12.98	Southampton H	1–0	32,073	90[1]	90□	s4	90	–	–	–	90	90	s16	–	90	–
19.12.98	West Ham A	1–2	25,998	–	–	s25	90□	s25	90[1]□	–	90	s15	90□	–	–	–
26.12.98	Derby Co H	0–0	39,206	90	90	s20	90	s5	70	–	–	85	90	–	90	–
28.12.98	Tottenham A	1–4	36,053	34[1]	90	90	90	–	s56□	–	s84	76	90	–	90	–
9.1.99	Leicester H	0–0	32,792	90	90	s15	–	–	75	–	90	–	90□	–	90	–
18.1.99	Aston Villa A	0–3	32,488	83	90	90	–	s7	s7	–	12■	–	90	–	–	–
30.1.99	Nott'm For H	0–1	34,175	s44	90	90□	–	s28	46	–	–	s28	–	90	–	–
7.2.99	Derby Co A	1–2	27,603	90	90	90[1]	–	–	–	–	–	90□	–	90□	90	s45
17.2.99	Middlesbro H	5–0	31,606	s14	90□	90[2]	–	–	–	–	–	90[1]□	–	90	–	–
20.2.99	Leeds Utd A	0–1	36,344	s29	90	90□	–	–	s29	–	–	90	–	90□	–	–
27.2.99	Wimbledon H	1–1	32,574	–	90	90	–	s7	90	–	–	90	–	–	–	–
10.3.99	Blackburn A	2–1	27,219	86[2]	90	38	–	s19	–	–	–	–	–	90□	–	–
13.3.99	Arsenal H	0–2	38,049	73	90	73	–	–	s17	–	–	90□	–	24	–	–
20.3.99	Man Utd A	1–3	55,182	5	90	–	–	–	s85	–	–	90□	s22	–	–	–
3.4.99	Liverpool A	2–3	44,852	–	90	76□	–	64	s26	90□	–	90[1]	–	–	–	–
5.4.99	Sheff Wed H	1–2	35,270	s13	s15	77	–	–	–	90	–	90	s15	–	–	–
11.4.99	Coventry H	2–0	32,341	–	90	90□	–	–	–	90[2]	–	90□	–	–	–	–
17.4.99	Newcastle A	3–1	36,775	s28	90	–	–	–	s8	62[2]	–	90	–	–	–	–
24.4.99	Charlton H	4–1	40,089	–	90□	–	–	–	–	90[2]	–	90□	–	–	–	–
1.5.99	Chelsea A	1–3	34,909	–	90	90	–	–	s19	90	–	–	–	s45	45	–
8.5.99	West Ham H	6–0	40,029	–	90[1]	–	–	–	–	90[3]	–	–	90	–	–	–
16.5.99	Southampton A	0–2	15,254	s27	90	–	–	–	s27	90	–	–	90	s16	–	–

□ Yellow card, ■ Red card, s Substitute, 90³ Goals scored

1998–99 PREMIERSHIP APPEARANCES

FARRELLY	FERGUSON	GEMMILL	GRANT	HUTCHISON	JEFFERS	JEVONS	MADAR	MATERAZZI	MILLIGAN	MYHRE	O'KANE	OSTER	SHORT	SPENCER	THOMAS	TILER	UNSWORTH	WARD	WATSON	WEIR	TOTAL
–	90	–	–	s14□	–	–	–	90	–	90	–	–	90□	64	–	90	–	–	–	–	990
–	90□	–	–	s28	–	–	–	45□	–	90	–	–	90	45	–	90□	s45	–	–	–	990
–	90	–	–	s15	–	–	–	90	–	90	–	–	90	s15	–	–	90	–	–	–	990
–	89²	–	–	90□	–	–	–	90	–	90	–	–	–	–	s1	–	90	–	90	–	990
s12	90	–	–	78	–	–	–	90	–	90	–	–	–	–	–	–	90	–	90	–	955
–	90	–	–	45□	–	–	–	90	–	90	–	–	–	–	–	–	90	–	90	–	990
–	90	–	–	90	–	–	–	90□	–	90	–	s15	90□	–	–	–	90□	–	90	–	990
–	90¹	–	–	90	–	–	–	90	–	90	–	–	90	–	–	–	90	–	90	–	990
–	90	–	57	90□	–	–	–	–	–	90	–	–	90	–	–	–	90□	s22	90	–	990
–	90	–	–	90	–	–	–	90□	–	90	–	–	–	–	–	–	90□	–	90	–	990
–	90¹	–	–	–	–	–	–	90	–	90	–	65□	–	–	–	–	90□	–	90	–	990
–	90□	–	–	s12	–	–	–	84□	s6	90	–	–	–	–	–	–	90	46	–	–	990
–	90	–	90	90	–	–	–	90□	s12	90	–	–	90	–	–	–	90□	–	–	–	990
–	–	–	90	90	s1	–	–	–	s2	90	–	–	90	–	–	–	90	–	90	–	990
–	–	–	83	90	–	–	–	s45	–	90	–	s7□	90	–	–	–	90	–	45	–	990
–	–	–	90	90	–	–	–	90	–	90	–	–	90	–	–	–	–	–	–	–	976
–	–	–	86	90	–	74	–	–	–	90	–	–	–	–	–	–	90□	–	–	–	990
–	–	–	65	90□	–	65	–	90	–	90	–	–	–	–	–	–	90	75	–	–	990
–	–	–	–	90	–	–	–	90□	–	90□	–	–	–	–	–	–	90□	–	–	–	990
–	–	–	–	90□	–	–	–	–	–	90	–	s14	6	–	–	–	90	–	–	–	990
–	–	–	–	90	–	–	–	–	–	90	90	–	–	–	–	–	90	–	90	–	990
–	–	–	69	90	–	–	–	90	–	90□	83	–	–	–	–	–	–	s21	90	–	912
–	–	–	62	90	–	–	–	90	–	90	90	–	–	–	–	–	90	62	–	–	990
–	–	–	–	90	90	–	–	–	–	90	–	–	–	–	–	–	45	90□	90	–	990
–	–	–	90	90	76	–	–	90¹	–	90	73	–	–	–	–	–	90¹	–	–	s17	990
–	–	–	61	90	61	–	–	90□	–	90	75	–	–	–	–	–	90	–	–	s15	990
–	–	–	–	–	90¹	–	–	90	–	90	83	–	–	–	–	–	90	–	90	90	990
–	–	–	s4	90	–	s52	–	90	–	90	71	–	90	–	–	–	90	–	–	90	990
–	–	–	s66	17■	s17	–	–	90	–	90	–	–	–	–	–	–	90□	–	90	90	917
–	–	–	68	90¹	s29	–	–	90	–	90	61	–	90	–	–	–	90	–	90□	–	990
–	–	90□	–	–	s14¹	–	–	45	–	90	–	–	90	–	–	–	90	–	90	s45	990
–	–	90	75	–	90¹	–	–	75	–	90	–	–	90	–	–	–	90	–	–	90	990
–	–	90□	s4	–	86	–	–	85■	–	90□	–	–	90	–	–	–	–	–	90	90	985
–	–	90¹□	–	90	82	–	–	–	–	90	–	90□	–	–	–	–	90	–	90	90	990
–	–	90	–	90¹	90¹	–	–	–	–	90	–	–	90	–	–	–	90	–	90	90□	990
–	–	–	–	90□	90¹	–	–	–	–	90	–	–	90□	–	–	–	90	71□	–	90	990
–	–	90	–	90¹	90¹	–	–	–	–	90	–	–	90	–	–	–	90	–	90	90	990
–	–	74	–	90□	63	–	–	–	–	90	–	–	63	–	–	–	90	–	90	90	990

THE MANAGER

WALTER SMITH

After 12 impossibly successful seasons at Ibrox with Glasgow Rangers, including seven as manager, Walter Smith was given the task of steering Everton back to the glory days of the 1980s following the dismissal of Howard Kendall.

During Smith's time in Scotland as manager, Rangers won seven successive Premier Division titles and six domestic cups. He retired from Rangers midway through the 1997–98 season and looked set for a peaceful semi-retirement, but after an initial approach from Sheffield Wednesday, the lure of management was too great and he eventually took charge at Goodison Park.

A lack of funds available for players has not made Smith's task at all easy, and the club was in the thick of the relegation scrap until the final three weeks of the 1998–99 season, but the shrewd deadline day signings of Kevin Campbell from Trabzonspor and Scot Gemmill from Nottingham Forest by the softly-spoken Scot wrenched Everton clear of the drop zone, the high point of which was a 6–0 demolition of West Ham United.

Hopes will be high in the blue half of Liverpool that the club has now turned the corner under Smith.

LEAGUE POSITION

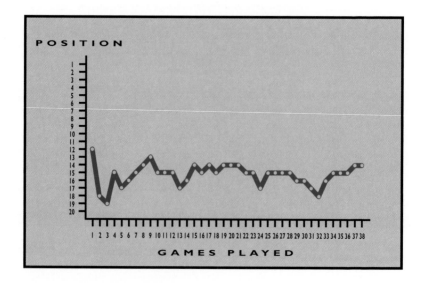

THE GOALS

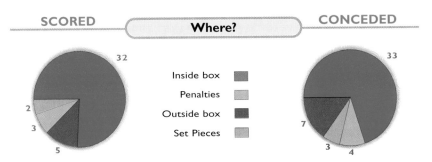

SCORED — Where? — CONCEDED

Inside box
Penalties
Outside box
Set Pieces

On average six out of seven goals scored by Everton originated from efforts inside the box, and no player was deadlier in the area than Kevin Campbell who grabbed all nine of his strikes from close in. The Toffeemen conceded the joint-highest total of goals direct from free-kicks in the league. Their opponents hit the back of the net on 47 occasions, with more than one in five of these efforts being struck from distance.

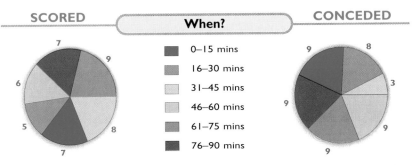

SCORED — When? — CONCEDED

0–15 mins
16–30 mins
31–45 mins
46–60 mins
61–75 mins
76–90 mins

Everton were at their most competent in the first 45 minutes of matches. They scored nearly half of all their goals before the break and conceded a smaller proportion of opposition strikes in the opening period than the typical Premiership side. In particular, the Goodison Park outfit thrived in the 15 minutes leading up to the break, scoring eight goals during this period and allowing just three in reply.

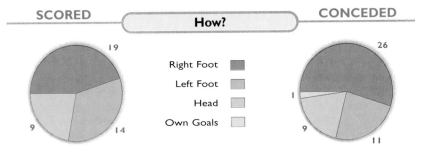

SCORED — How? — CONCEDED

Right Foot
Left Foot
Head
Own Goals

Only Southampton and Nottingham Forest scored fewer goals with the right foot than Everton during the 1998–99 season. Walter Smith's team scored just 45.2% of all goals via the right boot, the lowest proportion in the league. More than a fifth of the team's strikes were via an Everton head, a higher ratio than the average Premiership side. At the other end, the defence conceded a similar proportion of goals from opposition headers.

EVERTON

	BAKAYOKO	BALL	BARMBY	BILIC	BRANCH	CADAMARTERI	CAMPBELL	CLELAND	COLLINS	DACOURT	DEGN	DUNNE	FARLEY	FARRELLY	FERGUSON	GEMMILL
APPEARANCES																
Start	17	36	20	4	1	11	8	16	19	28	0	15	0	0	13	7
Sub	6	1	4	0	6	19	0	2	1	2	4	1	1	1	0	0
Minutes on pitch	1438	3255	1633	360	155	1522	692	1393	1706	2515	98	1250	45	12	1169	614
GOAL ATTEMPTS																
Goals	4	3	3	0	0	4	9	0	1	2	0	0	0	0	4	1
Shots on target	20	6	17	0	1	14	13	2	7	18	0	0	0	0	23	1
Shots off target	21	6	11	0	0	13	6	4	8	28	0	3	0	1	22	2
Shooting accuracy %	49%	50%	61%	0%	100%	52%	68%	33%	47%	39%	0%	0%	0%	0%	51%	33%
PASSING																
Goal assists	0	4	3	0	0	1	2	1	0	0	0	0	0	0	0	0
Long passes	10	202	37	21	3	11	9	80	57	98	4	90	2	3	13	33
Short passes	354	635	544	94	60	433	277	439	768	1015	35	290	12	7	547	231
PASS COMPLETION																
Own half %	79%	81%	89%	87%	88%	86%	86%	88%	94%	88%	100%	88%	75%	100%	92%	84%
Opposition half %	70%	57%	71%	64%	56%	67%	69%	69%	79%	72%	50%	58%	56%	33%	70%	70%
CROSSING																
Total crosses	10	84	40	2	1	29	5	46	33	16	7	15	0	0	7	27
Cross completion %	10%	21%	28%	50%	0%	31%	0%	22%	33%	31%	14%	20%	0%	0%	43%	22%
DRIBBLING																
Dribbles & runs	111	62	55	3	10	105	13	36	68	118	6	16	1	0	18	9
Dribble completion %	45%	65%	67%	100%	60%	57%	77%	86%	62%	75%	83%	69%	100%	0%	83%	78%
DEFENDING																
Tackles made	36	150	63	15	2	32	11	27	108	216	2	55	0	0	24	22
Tackles won %	50%	57%	44%	80%	50%	44%	82%	59%	64%	66%	100%	73%	0%	0%	54%	82%
Blocks	1	36	1	0	0	0	1	9	12	16	0	14	0	0	4	8
Clearances	4	186	32	57	1	3	7	69	16	44	3	150	5	0	23	16
Interceptions	2	29	4	3	0	1	1	12	19	16	1	7	1	0	1	7
DISCIPLINE																
Fouls	21	46	18	4	1	45	10	18	21	66	2	24	0	0	35	9
Offside	20	1	12	0	1	36	3	1	1	2	0	0	0	0	10	0
Yellow cards	3	8	4	1	0	6	1	2	4	13	0	5	0	0	3	3
Red cards	0	0	0	0	0	0	0	1	0	1	0	1	0	0	0	0

GOALKEEPER NAME	START/ (SUB)	TIME ON PITCH	GOALS CONCEDED	MINS/GOALS CONCEDED	SAVES MADE	SAVES/ SHOTS
MYHRE	38	3420	47	72.8	129	73%

PLAYERS' STATISTICS

	GRANT	HUTCHISON	JEFFERS	JEVONS	MADAR	MATERAZZI	MILLIGAN	O'KANE	OSTER	SHORT	SPENCER	THOMAS	TILER	UNSWORTH	WARD	WATSON	WEIR	TOTAL	RANK
	13	29	11	0	2	26	0	2	6	22	2	0	2	33	4	22	11		
	3	4	4	1	0	1	3	0	3	0	1	1	0	1	2	0	3		
	1060	2549	969	52	139	2269	20	132	530	1844	124	1	180	2970	341	1891	1067		
	0	3	6	0	0	1	0	0	0	0	0	0	0	1	0	0	0	42	11th
	3	13	12	0	1	6	0	0	3	0	0	0	1	4	0	0	3	168	14th
	8	15	17	0	1	10	0	0	4	5	1	0	0	10	1	1	9	207	=14th
	27%	46%	41%	0%	50%	38%	0%	0%	43%	0%	0%		100%	29%	0%	0%	25%	45%	13th
	0	7	5	0	0	0	0	0	0	0	0	0	0	1	1	0	2	27	=14th
	51	177	9	1	2	257	0	4	15	75	0	1	9	361	22	107	58	1822	10th
	488	1209	255	16	62	535	14	37	240	434	33	0	33	736	124	340	293	10591	16th
	90%	88%	86%	100%	100%	85%	100%	87%	83%	90%	69%	0%	83%	88%	82%	92%	86%	88%	12th
	67%	69%	65%	62%	55%	49%	90%	69%	65%	68%	63%	0%	61%	51%	61%	55%	60%	65%	19th
	14	160	15	0	0	8	3	6	31	12	0	0	0	38	9	3	15	636	16th
	21%	34%	20%	0%	0%	25%	33%	17%	32%	25%	0%	0%	0%	24%	11%	33%	33%	27%	13th
	18	71	31	0	3	10	3	2	30	24	0	0	0	27	1	2	16	869	11th
	72%	65%	68%	0%	0%	90%	33%	50%	70%	83%	0%	0%	0%	85%	0%	100%	81%	66%	20th
	45	154	10	2	1	116	3	2	9	62	5	0	9	125	8	41	40	1395	1st
	58%	62%	60%	50%	0%	73%	33%	100%	78%	69%	20%	0%	44%	65%	63%	68%	65%	63%	4th
	1	16	0	0	1	29	0	1	0	20	0	0	3	20	2	22	4	222	6th
	19	64	4	2	1	299	1	2	1	268	1	0	35	392	17	319	91	2158	5th
	14	17	2	3	0	56	1	2	2	23	0	0	3	36	2	23	10	299	17th
	14	56	10	0	1	46	0	3	4	27	2	0	2	65	4	17	16	587	2nd
	0	4	15	0	0	4	0	0	3	0	2	0	0	1	0	0	3	119	16th
	0	9	0	0	0	7	0	0	1	5	0	0	1	8	2	0	2	91	1st
	0	1	0	0	0	1	0	0	0	0	0	0	0	0	0	0	0	5	=4th

CROSSES CAUGHT	CROSSES PUNCHED	CROSSES NOT CLAIMED	CATCH SUCCESS	THROWS/ SHORT KICKS	% COMPLETION	LONG KICKS	% COMPLETION
84	29	12	94%	257	95%	918	37%

PLAYER OF THE SEASON

PLAYER	INDEX SCORE
OLIVIER DACOURT	979
Don Hutchison	962
Marco Materazzi	901
John Collins	901
Craig Short	756
David Unsworth	725
Thomas Myhre	669
Richard Dunne	666
Michael Ball	650
Danny Cadamarteri	552

Footballing frustration is rife among supporters across both halves of Merseyside, with Everton having been in limbo for far too long for the fans' liking.

But Walter Smith's dynamic midfield duo of Frenchman Olivier Dacourt and former Liverpool man Don Hutchison rightly earned acclaim for their hard-working displays – and Smith will surely look to build a successful side around the pair.

Dacourt had his fair share of disciplinary problems in 1998–99 but won the Everton supporters over with his tenacious, big-hearted displays – and his penchant for the spectacular strike, such as the first-minute stunner at Anfield.

He was the top-scoring Toffee in the Carling Opta Season Index, with an average score of 979 points over the campaign. Dacourt was an unfamiliar name to most Everton supporters before 1998–99, but he has attracted the attention of numerous top clubs across Europe with his gutsy displays for the Merseysiders.

In second place was Hutchison, who earned his first full cap for Scotland in 1998–99, scoring the winner in a fabulous friendly victory over Germany. He showed great versatility for Everton, playing in midfield and as an emergency striker, and his steady displays earned him an average points score of 962.

Other players in the top 10 struggled to achieve this level of consistency. Marco Materazzi showed he can be deadly from free kicks with his superb left foot – but was prone to the odd defensive blunder. Much was expected of Scottish star John Collins after his multi-million pound move from Monaco – but injury blighted his first season in English football.

With 14 clean sheets to his credit, goalkeeper Thomas Myhre enjoyed a fine season, but he lost points when Everton suffered heavy defeats, such as against Manchester United (1–4 and 1–3), Tottenham (1–4) and Aston Villa (0–3).

Youngsters Richard Dunne and Michael Ball look to have a bright future. Kevin Campbell and Francis Jeffers were the two top goalscorers, but both played in too few games to qualify for the season Index.

FIVE OF THE BEST

Everton sidestepped the yawning chasm of relegation on goal difference in 1997–98, but the arrival of Walter Smith gave the success-starved Toffees' supporters fresh hope that the 1980s heydays could be about to return. However, in the end a chronic lack of goals almost cost Everton their cherished pace in the top flight and Smith has been left with a lot of ground to cover.

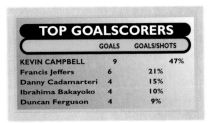

TOP GOALSCORERS

	GOALS	GOALS/SHOTS
KEVIN CAMPBELL	9	47%
Francis Jeffers	6	21%
Danny Cadamarteri	4	15%
Ibrahima Bakayoko	4	10%
Duncan Ferguson	4	9%

The inspired loan signing of Kevin Campbell played a leading role in halting Everton's slump. His nine goals from just 19 shots dragged the Toffees clear of the drop zone, helped by teenager Francis Jeffers. England boss Kevin Keegan was so impressed by Jeffers's six goals that he was called up for the friendly in Hungary. But it says a lot for goal-shy Everton that Duncan Ferguson appears in the top five, despite the fact he left the club in November.

The midfield engine-room of Don Hutchison and Olivier Dacourt was the core of Everton's season. The experienced Hutchison was the club's top passer and versatile enough to play up front when required, while Dacourt played the holding role, helping to protect the back four. He completed the second-largest number of passes, but the best marksman was former Monaco man John Collins, who makes the top five despite missing nearly half the season through injury.

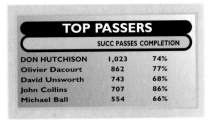

TOP PASSERS

	SUCC PASSES	COMPLETION
DON HUTCHISON	1,023	74%
Olivier Dacourt	862	77%
David Unsworth	743	68%
John Collins	707	86%
Michael Ball	554	66%

TOP TACKLERS

	WON	SUCCESS
OLIVIER DACOURT	142	66%
Don Hutchison	95	62%
Marco Materazzi	85	73%
Michael Ball	85	57%
David Unsworth	81	65%

Feisty Frenchman Olivier Dacourt was the only Toffee to get stuck in and win more than 100 challenges, though the fact that he failed to win a third of his total helps account for his poor disciplinary record. He and Hutchison played a key role in Everton's fine defensive statistics. The club conceded the ninth-fewest goals in the league, a record which undoubtedly helped save them from the drop in the final reckoning.

Ball-winning midfielders are inevitably the most likely to pick up bookings, but Olivier Dacourt will be disappointed to have collected 13 yellow cards and one red in the league. He also conceded the most fouls of anyone in the squad, suggesting he may have experienced problems in adjusting to the Premiership. Don Hutchison and David Unsworth will look at their records with some dismay too, having each picked up 89 disciplinary points, while Marco Materazzi is the third player in the top five to have been sent off in the 1998–99 Carling Premiership.

DISCIPLINE

	POINTS	FOULS & CARDS
OLIVIER DACOURT	111	66F, 13Y, 1R
Don Hutchison	89	56F, 9Y, 1R
David Unsworth	89	65F, 8Y, 0R
Marco Materazzi	73	46F, 7Y, 1R
Michael Ball	70	46F, 8Y, 0R

ACTION	BAKAYOKO	BALL	BARMBY	DACOURT	DUNNE	GRANT	HUTCHISON	JEFFERS	MATERAZZI	MYHRE	OSTER	UNSWORTH	WEIR	TOTAL	MIDDLESBROUGH
Time on pitch	14	90	90	90	90	90	90	76	90	90	73	90	17	990	990
GOALS															
Goal	–	–	2	–	–	–	–	1	1	–	–	1	–	5	–
Shot on target	–	–	1	1	–	–	1	1	–	–	–	–	–	4	2
Shot off target	–	1	1	1	–	1	2	1	–	–	–	–	–	7	4
Blocked shot	–	–	1	1	1	1	1	1	–	–	–	–	–	6	2
Own goal	–	–	–	–	–	–	–	–	–	–	–	–	–	–	–
PASSES															
Pass to own player	3	13	28	31	9	36	46	20	18	–	23	14	11	252	258
Pass to opposition	3	9	10	5	8	11	19	3	10	–	11	2	1	92	109
Cross to own player	–	–	–	–	1	–	–	–	–	–	2	–	–	5	4
Cross to opposition player	–	–	4	–	–	3	5	–	–	–	2	1	–	18	17
Goal assist	–	–	–	–	–	–	2	1	–	–	–	–	–	3	–
Pass completion %	50%	59%	67%	84%	53%	72%	67%	84%	64%	0%	66%	82%	92%	70%	68%
TACKLES & CLEARANCES															
Tackle	–	1	4	7	1	3	2	3	1	–	2	–	–	25	21
Clearances, blocks and interceptions	3	3	–	2	11	2	3	–	15	–	1	15	–	51	62
DRIBBLES & RUNS															
Dribble ball retained	–	–	3	–	2	–	3	1	–	–	2	–	–	12	17
Dribbles ball lost	–	1	1	1	–	–	–	–	–	–	–	–	–	4	9
Dribble success %	0%	0%	75%	50%	100%	0%	100%	100%	0%	0%	67%	0%	0%	75%	65%
DISCIPLINE															
Fouls	–	2	1	1	3	3	4	–	–	–	–	2	–	16	17
Penalty conceded	–	–	–	–	–	–	–	–	–	–	–	–	–	–	–
Free kick - offside	–	–	2	–	–	–	–	3	–	–	–	–	–	5	5
Yellow cards	–	1	–	1	–	–	–	–	–	–	–	–	–	2	3
Red cards	–	–	–	–	–	–	–	–	–	–	–	–	–	–	–
GOALKEEPERS															
Distribution to own player	–	–	–	–	–	–	–	–	–	7	–	–	–	7	15
Distribution to opposition player	–	–	–	–	–	–	–	–	–	17	–	–	–	17	18
Goalkeeper distribution%	–	–	–	–	–	–	–	–	–	29%	–	–	–	29%	45%
Save	–	–	–	–	–	–	–	–	–	2	–	–	–	2	4
Ball caught	–	–	–	–	–	–	–	–	–	4	–	–	–	4	2
Ball dropped	–	–	–	–	–	–	–	–	–	–	–	–	–	–	1
Goal conceded	–	–	–	–	–	–	–	–	–	–	–	–	–	–	5

In the first 12 Premiership matches at Goodison Park, the Everton faithful had had just three goals to cheer. But after such a famine, the Toffeemen gorged themselves with a feast of goals in their demolition of a Middlesbrough side who were themselves in the middle of a worrying slump and suffering a crisis of confidence.

February 17, 1999

5–0

EVERTON
MIDDLESBROUGH

The game was less than a minute old when Francis Jeffers escaped down the right flank and played a pinpoint ball across the face of goal for Nick Barmby to stab home from close range.

The diminutive forward then grabbed his second goal against his old club after 16 minutes, sending the Everton crowd into raptures as he latched on to a defence-splitting pass from Don Hutchison and lifted the ball over the onrushing Mark Schwarzer.

The fans had to wait until the 62nd minute for Everton to add to their tally, but for the Gwladys Street End it had been an even longer wait. Hutchison played a neat one-two with Jeffers but then saw his weak shot palmed out by Schwarzer. Unfortunately for the Australian, Olivier Dacourt was on hand to tap home the rebound and score the first Premiership goal at that end of the ground all season.

Having waited so long for the first, just like buses, two more came along in quick succession. Dean Gordon barged into Richard Dunne on the edge of the penalty area and Marco Materazzi stepped forward to rifle home the free kick.

Then a quickly-taken corner by Hutchison saw the Scottish Geordie pick out David Unsworth with a cross for the defender to bury his header past the hapless Schwarzer.

The only downside of the game for Everton was another yellow card for Dacourt which meant the Frenchman would have to serve a fourth ban, but manager Walter Smith was delighted with the victory. "Scoring so early was the most important factor for us," he said. "It gave us the confidence we needed."

Everton fully deserved the three points, firing in 22 attempts at goal, of which nine were on target and five found the net. Middlesbrough had managed just eight attempts and, though they briefly threatened to get back into the game early in the second half, with Bryan Robson's side managing just two attempts on target Everton were rarely in danger of conceding a goal. Possession was very even, as were tackling success rates, despite the one-sided scoreline.

Man of the match was Olivier Dacourt, who scored his goal from one of four shots during the contest. He completed 31 passes, won three out of seven tackles and would have scored more than his total of 1,547 points but for the yellow card he earned for a foul on Boro's Andy Townsend, which ruled him out of Everton's FA Cup quarter-final tie against Newcastle United.

This victory was completely out of character compared with Everton's performances up to that point, and things did not get much better until the arrival of Kevin Campbell. Thereafter the Toffees scored 13 times in their last four home games to stave off the threat of relegation.

ACTION	BALL	CAMPBELL	DACOURT	GEMMILL	HUTCHISON	JEFFERS	MAYHIRE	SHORT	UNSWORTH	WATSON	WEIR	TOTAL	WEST HAM
Time on pitch	90	90	90	90	90	90	90	90	90	90	90	990	990
GOALS													
Goal	–	3	–	–	1	1	–	–	–	–	–	6	–
Shot on target	–	–	2	–	–	–	–	–	–	–	–	4	–
Shot off target	–	2	2	–	–	5	–	–	–	–	–	10	5
Blocked shot	–	–	–	1	–	2	–	–	–	–	2	8	4
Own goal	–	–	–	–	–	–	–	–	–	–	–	–	–
PASSES													
Pass to own player	19	29	45	48	64	14	–	32	28	27	26	332	323
Pass to opposition	7	8	8	12	15	15	–	4	11	4	20	104	100
Cross to own player	–	–	1	1	2	–	–	1	–	–	–	4	1
Cross to opposition player	–	–	–	3	3	3	–	–	–	–	–	9	8
Goal assist	–	–	–	–	–	–	–	–	–	–	2	4	–
Pass completion %	70%	78%	85%	79%	79%	45%	0%	86%	72%	87%	58%	75%	75%
TACKLES & CLEARANCES													
Tackle	3	–	10	3	3	–	–	2	–	–	1	23	19
Clearances, blocks and interceptions	4	1	–	3	–	–	–	6	14	11	4	44	53
DRIBBLES & RUNS													
Dribble ball retained	1	1	4	3	–	1	–	2	–	–	–	15	32
Dribbles ball lost	2	1	–	–	–	–	–	2	–	–	–	6	16
Dribble success %	33%	50%	80%	100%	100%	100%	0%	50%	100%	0%	100%	71%	67%
DISCIPLINE													
Fouls	–	–	1	–	–	–	–	–	–	–	3	3	11
Penalty conceded	–	–	–	–	–	–	–	–	–	–	–	–	1
Free kick - offside	–	2	–	–	–	–	–	–	–	–	2	2	8
Yellow cards	–	–	–	–	–	–	–	–	–	–	–	–	4
Red cards	–	–	–	–	–	–	–	–	–	–	–	–	–
GOALKEEPERS													
Distribution to own player	–	–	–	–	–	–	14	–	–	–	–	14	20
Distribution to opposition player	–	–	–	–	–	–	15	–	–	–	–	15	17
Goalkeeper distribution%	–	–	–	–	–	–	48%	–	–	–	–	48%	54%
Save	–	–	–	–	–	–	2	–	–	–	–	–	4
Ball caught	–	–	–	–	–	–	–	–	–	–	–	2	–
Ball dropped	–	–	–	–	–	–	–	–	–	–	–	–	–
Goal conceded	–	–	–	–	–	–	–	–	–	–	–	–	6

Walter Smith's Everton went into their last home match of the season needing a point to be mathematically sure of staying up for another season. West Ham still had the carrot of a European place to reach for, with the InterToto Cup spot going to the fifth-placed team in the Premiership.

May 8, 1999
6–0
EVERTON
WEST HAM UNITED

The Hammers started the match brightly, passing well and looking to score early through Ian Wright or Paolo Di Canio. But it was Everton who struck first.

A corner from the left from Don Hutchison was met on the volley by David Unsworth, but his shot was well saved by Shaka Hislop. The ball ran loose in the goalmouth, causing a scramble, before in-form Kevin Campbell popped up to stab it into the net from close range. One-nil up after 14 minutes – and much more was to come from Everton before the day was out.

Nine minutes later Scot Gemmill's run was halted in the penalty area by Steve Lomas. Referee Alan Wilkie awarded a penalty to Everton despite the protestations of the West Ham players, who felt Gemmill had dived. England under-21 left-back Michael Ball stepped up confidently to plant the ball beyond Hislop and into the top right-hand corner of the net.

With seven first-half minutes remaining Everton struck again, and it was Hutchison who followed up after Francis Jeffers totally mis-hit his volley from Campbell's cross. The ball fell to Hutchison who drove the ball powerfully into the net from 12 yards.

The second half saw total domination by the Toffeemen, who were able to pass the ball around in midfield virtually unchallenged. On 52 minutes Campbell scored his second: David Weir pushed forward, took a quick pass from Gemmill and poked a ball through to the former Arsenal and Forest striker, who lifted the ball over the diving Hislop for 4–0.

Campbell's hat-trick was completed on 77 minutes when Hutchison played a perfectly-weighted through-ball to Campbell, who slammed a left-foot shot past Hislop from 12 yards. The hat-trick took his tally to nine goals in just five Premiership matches – a major factor in Everton's last-gasp turnaround at the end of the season.

It was party time at Goodison Park, and there was still time for one more goal. Hutchison's corner from the left was flicked on by Weir for Jeffers to stoop and head home for an extraordinary 6–0 scoreline.

The difference between the two sides on the day can be clearly seen in Carling Opta's statistics. While the two teams were evenly matched in terms of passing and tackling, the Merseyside club had the edge where it matters most – in front of goal.

Everton fired in a total of 28 shots, hitting the target with 10 and scoring with six. West Ham, on the other hand, failed to register a shot on target during the whole match.

The match demonstrated the topsy-turvy season of both clubs. West Ham found themselves in a healthy position, while Everton were struggling against relegation In 1999–2000, the roles could easily be reversed, such is the competitiveness of the Carling Premiership.

LEEDS UNITED 1998–99

Back row (from left to right): Derek Lilley, Jonathon Woodgate, Lee Matthews, David Wetherall, Mark Beeney, Nigel Martyn, Robert Molenaar, Gunnar Halle, David Hopkin, Andy Gray.

Middle row: Eddie Gray (Coach), Ian McNeill (Chief Scout), Alan Maybury, David Robertson, Clyde Wijnhard, Lee Sharpe, Jimmy Floyd Hasselbaink, Danny Granville, Mark Jackson, Stephen McPhail, David Swift (Physiotherapist), David O'Leary (Assistant Manager – now Manager).

Front row: Paul Shepherd, Harry Kewell, Ian Harte, Bruno Ribeiro, Lucas Radebe, George Graham (Manager – no longer at the club), Peter Ridsdale (Chairman), Lee Bowyer, Alfie Haaland, Martin Hiden, Gary Kelly, Tommy Knarvik.

LEEDS UNITED

ADDRESS

Elland Road, Leeds,
West Yorkshire LS11 0ES

CONTACT NUMBERS

Telephone: 0113 226 1000
Fax: 0113 226 6050
Ticket Office: 0113 292 0011
24hr Information: 09068 121180
Superstore: 0113 225 1144
Website: www.lufc.co.uk

SPONSORS

Packard Bell

FANZINES

Marching Altogether
The Hanging Sheep
The Square Ball
Till the World Stops
We Are Leeds

KEY PERSONNEL

Chairman: P Ridsdale
Directors: P Ridsdale,
J Fenn, A Pearson,
D Spencer, A Hudson
Club Secretary: I Silvester
Manager: David O'Leary

COLOURS

Home: White shirts,
shorts and stockings
Away: Yellow and blue
halved shirts with blue
shorts and stockings

NICKNAME

United
The Peacocks

20 FACTS

1 Leeds United were founded in 1919 when Leeds City were wound up following allegations of illegal payments. The new club entered the football league in 1920.

2 The club have been league champions on three occasions – 1968–69, 1973–74 and 1991–92.

3 They have won the FA Cup once – in the competition's centenary year – beating Arsenal 1–0 in the 1972 final with an Allan Clarke header. They were runners-up in 1965, 1970 and 1973.

4 Leeds have also won the Football League Cup once (1968). They were runners-up in 1996.

5 United have won two European Fairs Cup finals – in 1967–68 and 1970–71. They have competed in European competition 14 times.

6 Legendary manager Don Revie changed the club colours to the all-white of Real Madrid in a move designed to have a psychological effect on the opposition.

7 Leeds' record league victory is 8–0 against Leicester City in April 1934. Their record cup victory came in September 1969 when they beat Lyn Oslo of Norway 10–0 in the European Cup first round first leg.

8 The Peacocks hold the record for the fewest goals scored during a Carling Premiership season – 28 from 38 games in 1996–97.

9 Leeds went 29 league matches from the start of the season without defeat in 1973–74, a record equalled by Liverpool in 1988.

10 Peter Lorimer became the youngest player to appear for Leeds when he played against Southampton in September 1962 aged 15 years 289 days. Twenty-three years later, he became the oldest player to appear for the club when he took to the field against Barnsley for the Whites aged 38 years and 17 days.

11 The player with the record number of appearances for Leeds is "Big" Jack Charlton, who played in 772 matches in all competitions between 1952 and 1973.

12 Leeds hold the record for the fewest league defeats in a 42-match season – they lost two matches in 1968–69.

13 The club's record attendance came in 1967 when 57,892 people watched an FA Cup fifth round replay against Sunderland.

14 John Charles holds the club record for the most league goals scored in one season: he found the net 42 times in the 1953–54 season.

15 Leeds finished fourth in the 1998–99 Carling Premiership, qualifying for the UEFA Cup. Their league record was:

Pld	W	D	L	F	A	Pts
38	18	13	7	62	34	67

16 Leeds were knocked out of the AXA-sponsored FA Cup by Tottenham in a fifth round replay. The Peacocks defeated non-league side Rushden and Diamonds 3–1 in a third round replay after drawing the first game 0–0. They then blitzed Portsmouth 5–1 at Fratton Park in the fourth round but were eliminated 2–0 at White Hart Lane in a replay after drawing 1–1 at Elland Road.

17 The club suffered a fourth-round exit in the Worthington Cup. After beating Bradford City 1–0 in the third round, they were beaten 2–1 by Leicester City at Filbert Street.

18 Leeds beat Maritimo of Portugal on penalties in the first round of the UEFA Cup after drawing 1–1 on aggregate. They lost 1–0 in the away leg of their second-round tie with Roma but went out of the competition when they drew the second leg 0–0.

19 The top goalscorer in all competitions for Leeds was Dutchman Jimmy Floyd Hasselbaink with 20 goals.

20 Leeds' disciplinary record was the third-worst in the Premiership. They committed 590 fouls – more than any other side – and earned 77 yellow cards, but suffered just one red card all season.

SEASON REVIEW

Unthinkable as it may have been at the start of the season, Leeds United ended the 1998–99 campaign with a good deal of support among neutrals. Even Manchester United fans were forced to take their hats off to David O'Leary's talented young side after they gained a hard-fought 1–0 victory over Arsenal to tilt the title balance in United's favour.

O'Leary took over the Elland Road hot seat in the wake of George Graham's move to Tottenham. The position was originally accepted on a caretaker basis, with the most likely successor to Graham thought to be Gordon Strachan or Martin O'Neill.

The job seemed to be O'Neill's for the taking after his Leicester City side beat O'Leary's Leeds 1–0 at Elland Road. Whether it was the display of affection by Leicester fans for their manager or the rumoured £1 million in compensation it would have taken to buy him out of his contract at Filbert Street, the move never materialized and, after lengthy talks with chairman Peter Ridsdale, O'Leary agreed to take the job on a permanent basis.

One of his first moves was to bring youngsters Jonathon Woodgate and Stephen McPhail into the side. Alan Smith followed shortly afterwards, scoring on his debut against Liverpool.

Perhaps it was his own experience as a youngster under Bertie Mee and Terry Neill at Arsenal that prompted O'Leary to pitch these players in at the deep end. Maybe he was merely putting into practice what Graham had been planning. Whatever the motive, the move worked wonders and the new boys gelled superbly with more experienced members of the side like Lucas Radebe and David Hopkin.

The 3–1 win over Liverpool in November was quickly followed by a 4–1 drubbing of Charlton Athletic. The team lost 3–2 at Old Trafford but followed that with a 4–0 demolition of West Ham and a comfortable 2–0 victory against Coventry City.

They were playing the kind of free-flowing attacking football that had rarely been seen in George Graham's time at the club and O'Leary's stock was rising. He further endeared himself to the Leeds fans by re-signing David Batty from Newcastle United in a £4.4 million move.

Although the team suffered a blip in the New Year with successive defeats at the hands of Southampton and Newcastle, they were quickly back on track with victory over John Gregory's faltering Aston Villa side. That game marked the start of a seven-game winning streak which was to take them to fourth place in the league – a position which they never looked like relinquishing.

> ## "We've done brilliantly by winning the other league outside the top three"
>
> **David O'Leary**

The team retained the gritty edge instilled by Graham, committing more fouls than any of their rivals and conceding the third fewest goals in the Premiership behind Arsenal and Chelsea.

But with Jimmy Floyd Hasselbaink finding his best form since his move to the club, Lee Bowyer proving irrepressible in the midfield and Australian international Harry Kewell growing in stature with every match, Leeds were one of the most potent attacking teams in the Premiership in 1998–99. Only Manchester United and Liverpool scored more goals and no other team managed a higher percentage of their shots on target.

Champions League qualification proved beyond them, but a UEFA Cup spot was secured with a fourth place finish and the club looks in excellent shape for the new Millennium. O'Leary has been promised money to strengthen his hand for the next phase of his plan to bring silverware back to Elland Road. Plotting his side's progress in season 1999–2000 promises to be an exciting task.

LEEDS UNITED

DATE	OPPONENT	SCORE	ATT.	BATTY	BOWYER	GRANVILLE	HAALAND	HALLE	HARTE	HASSELBAINK	HIDEN	HOPKIN	JONES
15.8.98	Middlesbro A	0–0	34,160	–	90□	–	90	–	90	–	90	90	–
24.8.98	Blackburn H	1–0	30,541	–	90	–	90	–	90□	90¹	90□	90	–
29.8.98	Wimbledon A	1–1	16,473	–	90¹	–	90	–	90	90	90	90	–
8.9.98	Southampton H	3–0*	30,637	–	90	–	90	–	90¹	90	90	90	–
12.9.98	Everton A	0–0	36,687	–	90	–	90□	–	90	90	90	90	–
19.9.99	Aston Villa H	0–0	33,162	–	90	–	s15	90	90	90	90	90	–
26.9.98	Tottenham A	3–3	35,535	–	90	–	–	90¹	90	90¹	90	90	–
3.10.98	Leicester H	0–1	32,120	–	86	s44	90□	90	46	90□	90	–	–
17.10.98	Nott'm For A	1–1	23,911	–	90	32■	–	s45¹	–	80	90	90	–
25.10.98	Chelsea H	0–0	35,833	–	90□	90	s18	–	–	81□	90	72	–
31.10.98	Derby Co A	2–2	27,034	–	90	–	–	90	90□	76	–	90□	–
8.11.98	Sheff Wed H	2–1	30,012	–	90□	–	s15	–	90□	90¹	90	90	–
14.11.98	Liverpool A	3–1	44,305	–	90□	–	–	90	90	90²	90□	90	–
21.11.98	Charlton H	4–1	32,487	–	90¹□	–	–	90	90	90¹	90□	90	–
29.11.98	Man Utd A	2–3	55,172	–	–	–	90□	90	90	90¹	25	90	–
5.12.98	West Ham H	4–0	36,315	–	90²	–	90□	–	90	90¹□	–	90□	–
14.12.98	Coventry H	2–0	31,799	73□	90¹	–	–	s29	90	90□	–	90¹□	–
20.12.98	Arsenal A	1–3	38,025	–	90	81	90	90	90□	90¹	–	90□	–
26.12.98	Newcastle A	3–0	36,759	–	90¹	–	90	90	90	90¹	–	90	–
29.12.98	Wimbledon H	2–2	39,901	–	90	–	90	90	90	90	–	90¹	–
9.1.99	Blackburn A	0–1	27,620	–	90□	90	90□	90	–	90	–	90	–
16.1.99	Middlesbro H	2–0	37,394	–	90¹	90	s13	–	90□	90	–	90	–
30.1.99	Southampton A	0–3	15,236	–	90□	–	90□	–	90	90	–	90	–
6.2.99	Newcastle H	0–1	40,202	–	90	66	90	s24	90	–	–	90	–
17.2.99	Aston Villa A	2–1	37,510	–	–	s9	90	90	90	90²□	–	90	81
20.2.99	Everton H	1–0	36,344	–	84	–	90□	90	90	90□	–	90	s6
1.3.99	Leicester A	2–1	18,101	–	90	–	–	90	90□	89	–	90	–
10.3.99	Tottenham A	2–0	34,561	90□	90	–	90□	–	90	90	–	–	–
13.3.99	Sheff Wed A	2–0	28,142	90	90	–	90	–	90	90¹	–	90¹	–
20.3.99	Derby Co H	4–1	38,992	–	90¹	–	90□	–	90¹	90¹	–	90□	s1
3.4.99	Nott'm For H	3–1	39,645	–	90	–	–	–	90¹	90¹	–	90	s1
12.4.99	Liverpool H	0–0	39,372	90□	90	–	–	22	90	90	–	90□	s68
17.4.99	Charlton A	1–1	20,043	90□	90□	–	s74	–	90	32	–	16	s58
25.4.99	Man Utd H	1–1	40,255	90	90	–	–	–	90	87¹□	–	–	90
1.5.99	West Ham A	5–1	25,997	90□	90¹	–	90¹	–	90¹	83¹	–	–	–
5.5.99	Chelsea A	0–1	34,762	90	90	–	90	–	90	90	–	s2	–
11.5.99	Arsenal H	1–0	40,124	90□	90	–	90	–	90□	90¹□	–	90	–
16.5.99	Coventry A	2–2	23,049	90	–	73	45□	–	s17	90	–	s45¹	90

□ Yellow card, ■ Red card, s Substitute, 90³ Goals scored
*including own goal

1998–99 PREMIERSHIP APPEARANCES

KEWELL	KORSTEN	LILLEY	MARTYN	McPHAIL	MOLENAAR	RADEBE	RIBEIRO	ROBINSON	SHARPE	SMITH	WETHERALL	WIJNHARD	WOODGATE	TOTAL
90	–	s20	90	–	90□	90	–	–	70	–	–	90	–	990
90	–	–	90	–	90	90	–	–	s7	–	–	83	–	990
90	–	–	90	–	90	90	–	–	–	–	–	90□	–	990
90	–	–	90	–	75	90	s1	–	–	–	s15	89[1]□	–	990
69	–	s5	90	–	90□	90	s21	–	–	–	–	85	–	990
75	–	–	90	–	90	90	75	–	s15	–	–	–	–	990
90	–	–	90	–	90□	–	–	–	–	–	s18□	72[1]	–	990
s8	–	–	90	s4	90	–	–	–	90	–	90	82	–	990
89□	–	–	90	45	90	90	s10	–	–	–	–	s1	90	932
90	–	–	–	90	90□	90□	–	90	–	–	–	s9□	90	990
90[1]	–	–	–	90	90[1]	50	–	90	–	–	s40	s14	90	990
90	–	–	90	75	90	–	–	–	–	–	45	s45	90[1]	990
90	–	–	90	–	90	–	–	–	–	s14[1]□	–	76	90	990
90[1]	–	–	90	–	90	–	–	–	–	s30[1]	–	60□	90	990
90[1]	–	–	46	90	–	–	85□	s44	–	s5	s65	–	90	990
82	–	–	–	s3	90[1]	90	–	90	–	87	–	s8	90	990
90	–	–	90	s17	90	61	–	–	–	90	–	–	90	990
90	–	–	90	–	45	–	–	–	–	s9	s45	–	90□	990
89[1]	–	–	90	s32	–	–	58	–	–	s1	90	–	90	990
90	–	–	90	s9	–	–	81[1]	–	–	–	90	–	90	990
90	–	–	90	s16	–	–	74	–	–	s44	90□	–	46	990
90	s8	–	90	77	–	90	–	–	–	82[1]	90	–	–	990
90	–	–	90	–	–	90	–	–	–	90□	90	–	90□	990
90□	s24	–	90	–	–	90	–	–	–	90	–	66	90□	990
90	90	–	90	–	–	90	–	–	–	–	90	–	–	990
69	90[1]	–	90	–	–	90	–	–	–	s21	90	–	–	990
90[1]	90	–	90	–	–	90	s1	–	–	90[1]□	90	–	–	990
90[1]	–	–	90	–	–	90	–	–	–	90[1]	90	–	90	990
88	s2	–	90	–	–	87	–	–	–	90	s3	–	90	990
90	89[1]	–	90	90	–	90	–	–	–	–	–	–	90	990
89	–	–	90	–	–	90	90	–	–	90[1]	90	–	90	990
89	–	–	90	–	–	90	s1	–	–	90	–	–	90	990
90□	–	–	90	–	–	90	–	–	–	90□	90	–	90[1]□	990
90	–	–	90	90	–	90	–	–	–	90	s32	s3	58	990
90	–	–	90	90	–	90	s3	–	–	87[1]□	–	s7□	90	990
90	–	–	90	88	–	90□	–	–	–	90	–	–	90□	990
90	–	–	90	–	–	90	–	–	–	90□	–	–	90	990
s20	–	–	–	90	–	90	70	90	–	–	90□	90[1]	–	990

THE MANAGER

DAVID O'LEARY

David O'Leary began the 1998–99 season as assistant manager to George Graham – but ended it as the man seemingly capable of bringing the glory days back to Leeds United.

After two years at Elland Road, Graham quit the Yorkshire club for Tottenham at the end of September. Leeds chairman Peter Ridsdale appointed O'Leary as caretaker manager and after Leicester boss Martin O'Neill turned the job down, O'Leary's position was made permanent.

The softly-spoken 41-year-old quickly blooded a number of the club's young players, including prodigious teenage striker Alan Smith and impressive centre-back Jonathon Woodgate. He also brought back former Leeds hero David Batty from Newcastle and the side soared up the Carling Premiership table.

O'Leary enjoyed a hugely successful playing career, earning 66 caps for the Republic of Ireland in central defence. But he will be forever worshipped by Arsenal fans after his record 523 league appearances for the Gunners over a 17-year period.

Leeds went close to grabbing a surprise top-three place last season and the expectant United supporters will be looking for their side to be challenging for the title in 1999–2000.

LEAGUE POSITION

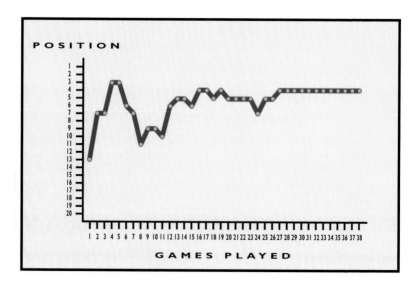

THE GOALS

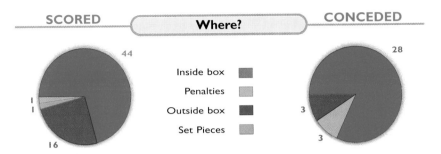

SCORED — Where? — CONCEDED

- Inside box
- Penalties
- Outside box
- Set Pieces

Leeds United were easily the most prolific long-range goalscorers in the 1998–99 Carling Premiership. They registered 17 strikes from more than 18 yards and Jimmy Hasselbaink netted seven times from distance, eclipsing all Premiership rivals. This equated to more than a quarter of all their goals coming from outside the area, the highest ratio in the league. They conceded just three strikes from distance, fewer than any other Premiership side.

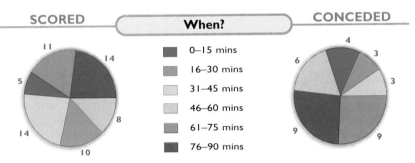

SCORED — When? — CONCEDED

- 0–15 mins
- 16–30 mins
- 31–45 mins
- 46–60 mins
- 61–75 mins
- 76–90 mins

Leeds struggled to contain opposition strikers the longer their matches wore on. More than 70% of all goals conceded by the Yorkshire side came after the re-start, the second-highest ratio in the league and over half in the last 30 minutes. Leeds were at their strongest in the half-hour preceding the break. During this period, the UEFA Cup qualifiers scored 24 times and allowed only six goals in reply, boosting their admirable goal difference.

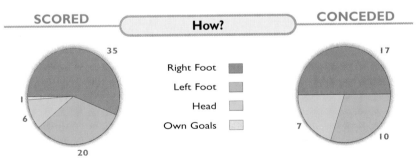

SCORED — How? — CONCEDED

- Right Foot
- Left Foot
- Head
- Own Goals

With the devastating shooting abilities of Hasselbaink, ably supported by Lee Bowyer and Alan Smith, the Elland Road outfit had little need for headed efforts, scoring more than 90% of all goals with the right or left boot. Only Arsenal relied less on headers and David O'Leary's team out-scored all Premiership teams bar Liverpool and Manchester United with their feet. In contrast, Leeds' opponents scored 20.6% of their goals against them with headers.

LEEDS UNITED

	BATTY	BOWYER	GRANVILLE	HAALAND	HALLE	HARTE	HASSELBAINK	HIDEN	HOPKIN	JONES
APPEARANCES										
Start	10	35	7	24	14	34	36	14	32	3
Sub	0	0	2	5	3	1	0	0	2	5
Minutes on pitch	883	3140	575	2250	1290	3033	3138	1195	2835	395
GOAL ATTEMPTS										
Goals	0	9	0	1	2	4	18	0	4	0
Shots on target	0	31	0	5	5	16	56	0	13	0
Shots off target	2	34	2	10	0	19	50	1	15	3
Shooting accuracy %	0%	48%	0%	33%	100%	46%	53%	0%	46%	0%
PASSING										
Goal assists	0	2	0	2	0	5	12	1	5	0
Long passes	73	181	50	61	43	361	33	82	138	25
Short passes	521	1193	187	632	335	1019	885	286	1098	142
PASS COMPLETION										
Own half %	93%	86%	88%	91%	82%	83%	78%	87%	89%	80%
Opposition half %	81%	69%	64%	68%	68%	65%	69%	59%	75%	65%
CROSSING										
Total crosses	4	47	16	23	13	179	38	26	75	9
Cross completion %	25%	17%	25%	22%	38%	35%	24%	19%	36%	44%
DRIBBLING										
Dribbles & runs	13	64	19	29	7	63	160	7	62	11
Dribble completion %	85%	72%	95%	86%	86%	90%	65%	86%	76%	73%
DEFENDING										
Tackles made	45	141	19	99	29	95	38	34	111	22
Tackles won %	76%	60%	47%	60%	55%	57%	37%	74%	67%	59%
Blocks	3	14	3	7	10	30	3	10	8	3
Clearances	31	75	45	100	62	269	5	113	60	29
Interceptions	16	29	7	30	11	29	5	23	27	9
DISCIPLINE										
Fouls	19	66	11	54	14	43	73	11	40	5
Offside	1	5	2	4	3	1	50	0	6	0
Yellow cards	6	8	0	10	0	7	8	3	6	0
Red cards	0	0	1	0	0	0	0	0	0	0

GOALKEEPER NAME	START/ (SUB)	TIME ON PITCH	GOALS CONCEDED	MINS/GOALS CONCEDED	SAVES MADE	SAVES/ SHOTS
MARTYN	34	3016	28	107.7	134	83%
ROBINSON	4 (1)	404	6	67.3	14	70%

PLAYERS' STATISTICS

	KEWELL	KORSTEN	LILLEY	McPHAIL	MOLENAAR	RADEBE	RIBEIRO	SHARPE	SMITH	WETHERALL	WIJNHARD	WOODGATE	TOTAL	RANK
	36	4	0	11	17	29	7	2	15	14	11	25		
	2	3	2	6	0	0	6	2	7	7	7	0		
	3197	393	25	996	1470	2538	570	182	1460	1433	970	2174		
	6	2	0	0	2	0	1	0	7	0	3	2	62*	3rd
	35	5	1	4	5	0	4	0	18	5	11	2	216	4th
	38	6	1	3	7	1	4	1	12	5	6	2	222	=9th
	48%	45%	50%	57%	42%	0%	50%	0%	60%	50%	65%	50%	49%	1st
	10	0	0	2	0	0	0	0	3	1	3	1	47	2nd
	88	9	1	29	140	171	16	5	18	58	9	106	1697	17th
	1200	112	3	370	317	712	179	56	397	323	272	518	10757	14th
	83%	76%	0%	85%	91%	89%	80%	75%	78%	88%	80%	89%	87%	15th
	66%	63%	75%	78%	67%	69%	73%	77%	71%	59%	68%	66%	69%	14th
	91	2	0	18	0	0	17	18	13	4	6	12	611	18th
	24%	0%	0%	28%	0%	0%	35%	39%	0%	0%	33%	25%	29%	10th
	285	21	0	12	0	9	10	16	41	2	11	35	878	10th
	63%	48%	0%	75%	0%	89%	60%	69%	63%	50%	73%	83%	70%	12th
	70	13	0	31	54	151	24	9	37	39	20	105	1186	8th
	69%	54%	0%	58%	65%	62%	67%	44%	57%	72%	60%	63%	62%	9th
	5	0	0	4	16	39	2	1	0	18	1	29	207	9th
	46	7	0	11	214	379	12	3	6	274	0	290	2077	9th
	16	3	0	9	28	62	3	1	4	13	7	27	360	4th
	46	5	1	8	28	19	6	2	42	34	30	31	590	1st
	21	1	0	2	0	0	0	0	17	0	22	1	136	10th
	3	0	0	0	4	2	1	0	6	3	5	5	77	=8th
	0	0	0	0	0	0	0	0	0	0	0	0	1	=17th

*including one own goal

CROSSES CAUGHT	CROSSES PUNCHED	CROSSES NOT CLAIMED	CATCH SUCCESS	THROWS/ SHORT KICKS	% COMPLETION	LONG KICKS	% COMPLETION
85	26	8	97%	192	94%	880	35%
11	2	1	100%	17	94%	97	34%

PLAYER OF THE SEASON

PLAYER	INDEX SCORE
LUCAS RADEBE	1,033
Ian Harte	947
Nigel Martyn	902
Jimmy F Hasselbaink	902
Harry Kewell	886
Lee Bowyer	885
Jonathon Woodgate	858
David Wetherall	825
David Hopkin	759
Alan Smith	670

The age-old blend of youth and experience catapulted Leeds to fourth place in the Premiership under the ambitious David O'Leary.

And while the young players rightly earned acclaim for their efforts throughout the season, it was South African international Lucas Radebe who finished as Leeds' highest-ranked player in the Carling Opta Index.

Radebe was tipped to follow George Graham out of Elland Road, but instead galvanized his position as the club's defensive linchpin with some stirring displays, doubtless encouraging the development of young Jonathon Woodgate in the process. Radebe conceded just 19 fouls all season.

His average score of 1,033 points put him above arguably the club's most improved player, Ian Harte. He looks like scaling the heights of another Irish left-back who played for Leeds, Denis Irwin. His constant desire to get forward and whip in dangerous crosses, plus his ability to score frequent spectacular goals, helped him achieve an average score of 947 points in 1998–99.

In joint third place were goalkeeper Nigel Martyn and Leeds' top scorer Jimmy Floyd Hasselbaink. Both on the fringes of their national sides, these two players are pivotal members of the Leeds "spine". Martyn kept 13 Premiership clean sheets while Hasselbaink finished as the league's joint hotshot with 18 league goals.

The list of stylish stars goes on, with Australian Harry Kewell and the club's official Player of the Year Lee Bowyer in fifth and sixth places respectively. Kewell would have been higher had his strike rate been better, while Bowyer lost points for his 66 fouls and eight yellow cards.

Young striker Alan Smith also had disciplinary problems, picking up six yellow cards. They certainly hampered his progress up the top 10, but that aggressive streak will be important if his expected meteoric rise up the footballing echelons is to materialize.

FIVE OF THE BEST

The mid-term departure of George Graham to Tottenham Hotspur could have had a devastating impact on Leeds United, but assistant boss David O'Leary instead inspired his players to a fabulous fourth-placed finish by giving the club's talented youngsters the same first-team opportunities he himself had been afforded at Arsenal.

TOP GOALSCORERS

	GOALS	GOALS/SHOTS
J F HASSELBAINK	18	17%
Lee Bowyer	9	14%
Alan Smith	7	23%
Harry Kewell	6	8%
David Hopkin	4	14%

Powerhouse Dutchman Jimmy Floyd Hasselbaink finished as the club's top scorer and also joint-top hotshot in the Premiership with 18 league goals. The club's Player of the Year Lee Bowyer weighed in with nine strikes, while the deadliest finisher was teenage sensation Alan Smith, who scored with 23% of his shots. Harry Kewell will be looking to improve on his disappointing goals-to-shots ratio of just 8% in 1999–2000.

The 1998–99 season was when midfield stars Lee Bowyer and David Hopkin really blossomed in the Carling Premiership. Bowyer was a commanding figure in the heart of the park, while Hopkin had easily his best year since transferring from Crystal Palace. He was the club's most accurate midfield passer, while Bowyer saw more of the ball than anyone else in the squad. The ever-improving Ian Harte finished third in the table after a terrific season at left-back.

TOP PASSERS

	SUCC PASSES	COMPLETION
LEE BOWYER	1,029	75%
David Hopkin	975	79%
Ian Harte	973	71%
Harry Kewell	866	67%
Lucas Radebe	721	82%

TOP TACKLERS

	WON	SUCCESS
LUCAS RADEBE	93	62%
Lee Bowyer	85	60%
David Hopkin	74	67%
Jonathon Woodgate	66	63%
Alfie Haaland	59	60%

Top Leeds player in the Carling Opta Index was Leeds' South African centre-back Lucas Radebe. His dominant displays in the heart of the United defence were instrumental in Leeds' success in 1998-99 and he made almost 100 successful challenges. Cleanest tackler was David Hopkin, who won two-thirds of his tackles, while Lee Bowyer and young defender Jonathon Woodgate were never afraid to help out with the ball-winning.

He may have been the darling of the East Stand with his terrific goalscoring exploits, but Jimmy Floyd Hasselbaink's strength and determination inevitably land him in trouble with the Men in Black. He committed more fouls than any other Leeds player and also picked up eight bookings to earn 97 disciplinary points. Alfie Haaland accrued 10 yellow cards and only played 2,250 minutes of football, but the only red card collected by a Leeds player in the league was shown to Danny Granville at Nottingham Forest.

DISCIPLINE

	POINTS	FOULS & CARDS
J F HASSELBAINK	97	73F, 8Y, 0R
Lee Bowyer	90	66F, 8Y, 0R
Alfie Haaland	84	54F, 10Y, 0R
Ian Harte	64	43F, 7Y, 0R
Alan Smith	60	42F, 6Y, 0R

ACTION	BOWYER	HALLE	HARTE	HASSELBAINK	HIDEN	HOPKIN	KEWELL	MARTYN	MOLENAAR	SMITH	WIJNHARD	WOODGATE	TOTAL	LIVERPOOL
Time on pitch	90	90	90	90	90	90	90	90	90	14	76	90	990	990
GOALS														
Goal	–	–	–	2	–	–	–	–	–	1	–	–	3	1
Shot on target	–	–	1	–	–	–	1	–	–	–	–	–	3	3
Shot off target	2	–	1	–	–	1	–	–	–	–	–	–	4	11
Blocked shot	–	–	–	1	–	2	–	–	–	–	–	–	2	6
Own goal	–	–	–	–	–	–	–	–	–	–	–	–	–	–
PASSES														
Pass to own player	22	15	17	20	19	26	25	–	22	4	12	21	203	271
Pass to opposition	8	5	9	7	8	11	14	–	11	–	3	8	84	84
Cross to own player	–	–	–	1	–	–	–	–	–	–	–	–	1	6
Cross to opposition player	–	–	3	–	–	–	1	–	–	–	–	–	5	15
Goal assist	–	–	–	–	–	–	2	–	–	–	–	–	2	–
Pass completion %	73%	75%	59%	72%	70%	70%	64%	0%	67%	100%	80%	72%	70%	74%
TACKLES & CLEARANCES														
Tackle	2	1	–	1	2	9	3	–	2	–	2	8	30	24
Clearances, blocks and interceptions	7	9	4	–	18	8	3	3	11	–	–	22	85	73
DRIBBLES & RUNS														
Dribble ball retained	1	1	2	6	–	–	5	–	–	–	1	–	16	20
Dribbles ball lost	–	–	–	–	–	3	3	–	–	–	–	–	6	7
Dribble success %	100%	100%	100%	100%	0%	0%	63%	0%	0%	0%	100%	0%	73%	74%
DISCIPLINE														
Fouls	3	–	–	–	1	1	1	–	2	1	3	–	12	16
Penalty conceded	–	–	–	–	–	–	–	–	–	–	–	–	1	–
Free kick - offside	–	–	–	–	–	–	–	1	–	–	–	–	1	2
Yellow cards	1	–	–	1	1	–	–	–	–	–	–	–	3	2
Red cards	–	–	–	1	–	–	–	–	–	–	–	–	1	–
GOALKEEPERS														
Distribution to own player	–	–	–	–	–	–	–	22	–	–	–	–	22	15
Distribution to opposition player	–	–	–	–	–	–	–	25	–	–	–	–	25	17
Goalkeeper distribution%	–	–	–	–	–	–	–	47%	–	–	–	–	47%	47%
Save	–	–	–	–	–	–	–	3	–	–	–	–	3	3
Ball caught	–	–	–	–	–	–	–	5	–	–	–	–	5	1
Ball dropped	–	–	–	–	–	–	–	1	–	–	–	–	1	–
Goal conceded	–	–	–	–	–	–	–	–	–	–	–	–	–	3

Leeds United arrived at Anfield to face a Liverpool team in turmoil. Defeat at the hands of Tottenham in the Worthington Cup had spelt the end for Roy Evans, and Gerard Houllier was now in sole charge of the team. Leeds had drawn their first six away games in the Premiership but were keen to chalk up a victory to consolidate their place in the top six.

November 14, 1998

1–3

LIVERPOOL
LEEDS UNITED

A nervous first half was notable only for the number of misplaced passes and aimless long balls played by both teams. Leeds' game plan involved sitting back and pressurizing a fragile Liverpool defence with balls played over the top. Their best chance fell to Harry Kewell who was unlucky to miss the target with a left-foot shot from 20 yards after a typically driving run.

Liverpool came closest to a breakthrough when Paul Ince's high ball was fumbled by Nigel Martyn under pressure from Karl-Heinz Riedle. Fortunately for Leeds, Robbie Fowler placed his resulting header over the bar from only a yard out.

Houllier's half-time team talk seemed to lift the home side and they started the second half brightly. Redknapp, Staunton, Fowler and Riedle all came close to a breakthrough before Liverpool finally broke the deadlock in the 68th minute.

Riedle chased a header by David Thompson and was taken out at shoulder height by Martyn in the area. Referee Dermot Gallagher had no hesitation in pointing to the spot and Fowler stepped up to score against Leeds for the fifth consecutive time at Anfield.

Far from capitulating, Leeds held firm and clawed their way back into the game after 79 minutes. Alan Smith, on for his Premiership debut in place of the ineffective Clyde Wijnhard, latched on to a blocked shot by David Hopkin and smashed the ball into the net from the edge of the area.

Soon afterwards Jimmy Floyd Hasselbaink, who had been having a quiet game, waltzed through the Liverpool defence to slot in Leeds' second.

In the 86th minute, with Liverpool frantically pressing for an equalizer, Leeds broke again. Kewell picked up a clearance just outside his own penalty area and flicked a good ball into the path of Hasselbaink. He ran 50 yards before turning Vegard Heggem and lashing the ball past David James in front of a stunned Kop.

Leeds deserved the victory for their brilliance on the counter-attack and refusal to collapse in the face of intense Liverpool pressure. They had fewer goal attempts than the home side, but looked more comfortable at the back, blocking six Liverpool shots and winning 80% of their attempted tackles compared to Liverpool's figure of 67%.

Man of the match with 1,715 points was Jimmy Floyd Hasselbaink. His two late goals won the game and he also made six successful dribbles and runs. Young defender Jonathon Woodgate came second with an excellent points total of 1,687.

The game was only Leeds' second league victory under David O'Leary, but it provided the launchpad for an excellent season that was eventually to bring a fourth-placed finish for the club. It also marked the emergence of Alan Smith, who ended the season with seven Premiership goals.

ACTION	BATTY	BOWYER	HAALAND	HARTE	HASSELBAINK	KEWELL	MARTYN	McPHAIL	RADEBE	RIBEIRO	SMITH	WIJNHARD	WOODGATE	TOTAL	WEST HAM
Time on pitch	90	90	90	90	83	90	90	90	90	3	87	7	90	990	882
GOALS															
Goal	–	–	–	–	1	–	–	–	–	–	–	–	–	5	1
Shot on target	–	–	–	–	–	–	–	–	–	–	2	–	2	2	6
Shot off target	–	–	–	–	–	–	–	1	–	–	2	–	1	4	8
Blocked shot	–	2	–	–	–	–	–	–	–	–	2	–	–	6	3
Own goal	–	–	–	–	–	–	–	–	–	–	–	–	–	–	–
PASSES															
Pass to own player	73	26	39	44	13	26	–	26	27	4	23	–	18	319	289
Pass to opposition	7	8	7	11	5	9	–	4	6	–	5	2	1	65	67
Cross to own player	1	–	–	4	–	2	–	1	–	–	–	–	–	8	6
Cross to opposition player	–	–	1	3	–	2	–	–	–	–	2	–	–	11	8
Goal assist	–	–	–	3	2	2	–	–	–	–	–	–	4	4	1
Pass completion %	90%	75%	83%	77%	71%	73%	0%	87%	82%	100%	77%	0%	95%	81%	80%
TACKLES & CLEARANCES															
Tackle	8	5	2	4	1	2	–	–	7	–	–	–	8	37	32
Clearances, blocks and interceptions	4	3	9	8	1	3	–	1	13	–	1	–	13	57	62
DRIBBLES & RUNS															
Dribble ball retained	1	1	2	6	–	8	–	–	–	–	2	–	22	22	24
Dribbles ball lost	–	–	–	–	–	3	–	–	–	–	–	–	3	3	7
Dribble success %	100%	100%	100%	100%	0%	73%	0%	0%	100%	0%	100%	0%	100%	88%	77%
DISCIPLINE															
Fouls	2	4	2	1	1	1	–	–	–	–	2	2	2	16	19
Penalty conceded	–	–	–	–	–	–	–	–	–	–	–	–	–	–	–
Free kick - offside	–	–	–	–	–	–	–	–	–	–	1	–	1	1	2
Yellow cards	1	–	–	–	–	–	–	–	–	–	1	1	–	3	5
Red cards	–	–	–	–	–	–	–	–	–	–	–	–	–	1	3
GOALKEEPERS															
Distribution to own player	–	–	–	–	–	–	22	–	–	–	–	–	–	22	10
Distribution to opposition player	–	–	–	–	–	–	9	–	–	–	–	–	–	9	10
Goalkeeper distribution%	–	–	–	–	–	–	71%	–	–	–	–	–	–	71%	50%
Save	–	–	–	–	–	–	6	–	–	–	–	–	–	6	2
Ball caught	–	–	–	–	–	–	3	–	–	–	–	–	–	3	1
Ball dropped	–	–	–	–	–	–	–	–	–	–	–	–	–	–	–
Goal conceded	–	–	–	–	–	–	1	–	–	–	–	–	–	1	5

Leeds United travelled to Upton Park to take on West Ham knowing their European place had already been secured. West Ham were looking to finish on a high by qualifying for Europe via the InterToto Cup.

May 1, 1999

1 – 5

WEST HAM UNITED
LEEDS UNITED

The visitors took charge of the match straight from the kick-off, when Lee Bowyer threaded the ball through to Jimmy Floyd Hasselbaink. He took it across the edge of the penalty area and shot low into the corner of the net to put Leeds in front after just 20 seconds.

West Ham were stunned, and Ian Wright was booked after going up for a header with Alf Inge Haaland. Leeds took control and after 16 minutes were handed a numerical advantage when referee Rob Harris sent Wright from the field for a second bookable offence, after he had lashed out at Ian Harte.

Trevor Sinclair, Eyal Berkovic and Frank Lampard all had chances for West Ham before Leeds extended their lead. Deep into stoppage time, Lomas was dispossessed in midfield and Kewell's left wing cross was stabbed home from close range by Alan Smith.

Ten-man West Ham started the second half well and reduced the arrears after 48 minutes. Paolo Di Canio sent Berkovic down the left wing. The little Israeli rolled the ball into the path of Di Canio, whose sliding finish from 12 yards wrong-footed goalkeeper Nigel Martyn to make it 2–1.

The Hammers piled on the pressure, but Leeds always had a spare man in defence. On the hour mark, Hasselbaink went down in the penalty area after a challenge by goalkeeper Shaka Hislop, who was instantly sent off.

The West Ham fans and players pointed accusing fingers at Hasselbaink, claiming he had dived. Harte stepped up and side-footed the penalty into the top corner, sending substitute 'keeper Craig Forrest the wrong way.

With 12 minutes to go, Leeds were finding the gaps in the West Ham defence, and Haaland fed Hasselbaink, whose back-flick was hammered into the bottom corner from 20 yards by Bowyer, giving Forrest no chance.

A minute later, Hasselbaink spotted Haaland's unmarked run down the right channel and his pass left the Norwegian with time and space to fire a low angled drive past Forrest for Leeds' fifth goal of the game.

With just two minutes to go, and 5–1 down, West Ham skipper Lomas became the game's third Hammers dismissal when he lunged at Harte's shins with his studs showing.

Leeds went on and finished the game emphatic victors, underlining the fact that they will be a major threat to the big three in 1999-2000.

Their efficiency in front of goal is illustrated in the Carling Opta stats. The Yorkshire club scored from five of their seven shots on target and kept the ball better. The Hammers were not afforded time to settle into a pattern of play and Leeds dominated proceedings over the course of the match, completing 319 passes to West Ham's 289.

In an ill-tempered match, West Ham had three players sent off and five others booked. Leeds kept their composure better and finished the match with three players booked and, more importantly, none sent off.

LEICESTER CITY 1998–99

Back row (left to right): David Nish (Academy Manager), Steve Sims (Youth Development Officer), Jon Rudkin (Academy Assistant Manager 8–16 years), Emile Heskey, Garry Parker, Gerry Taggart, Pegguy Arphexad, Kasey Keller, John Hodges, Spencer Prior (now Derby County), Matt Elliott, Steve Walsh, Gary Neil, Alan Smith (Physiotherapist) Mick Yeoman (Physiotherapist), Ian Andrews (Academy Physiotherapist).

Middle row: Seamus McDonagh (Goalkeeping Coach), Neville Hamilton (Academy Assistant Manager 16–19 years), Paul McAndrew (Kit Manager), Bob Walls (Assistant Kit Manager), Lee Allen, Pontus Kaamark (now AIK Stockholm), Lawrie Dudfield, Paul Emerson, Tommy Goodwin, Scott Taylor, Steve Guppy, Graham Fenton, Ross Mitchell, John Robertson (Assistant Manager), Steve Walford (First Team Coach), Paul Franklin (Reserve Team Coach), Jim Melrose (Chief Scout).

Front row: Tony Cottee, Tim McCann, Stephen Wenlock, Sam McMahon (now Cambridge United), Stuart Wilson, Muzzy Izzet, Robbie Savage, John Elsom (Chairman), Martin O'Neill (Manager), Stuart Campbell, Neil Lennon, Theo Zagorakis, Ian Marshall, Martin Fox, Stefan Oakes, Robert Ullathorne.

LEICESTER CITY

ADDRESS

City Stadium, Filbert Street,
Leicester LE2 7FL

CONTACT NUMBERS

Telephone: 0116 291 5000
Fax: 0116 247 0585
Ticket Office: 0116 291 5232
24hr Information: 09068 121185
Superstore: 0116 291 5253
Website: www.lcfc.co.uk

SPONSORS

Walkers Crisps

FANZINES

When You're Smiling
The Fox
Where's the Money Gone
O'Neill and Pray

KEY PERSONNEL

Chairman: J M Elsom
Directors: J M Elsom,
P H Smith, B J Pierpoint,
S A Kind
Club Secretary: A R W Neville
Manager: Martin O'Neill

COLOURS

Home: Blue shirts,
white shorts and
blue stockings
Away: White shirts,
blue shorts and
white stockings

NICKNAME

The Foxes

20 FACTS

1 Leicester City were originally founded as Leicester Fosse in 1884, but became Leicester City in 1919.

2 After two brief stints at Victoria Park and one apiece at Belgrave Road, Mill Lane and Aylestone Road, Leicester took up residence at Filbert Street in 1891 and they have been there ever since.

3 Leicester's highest placing in the league was second in 1928–29.

4 The Foxes have reached four FA Cup finals, losing on each occasion. They featured in the finals of 1949, 1961, 1963 and 1969.

5 The only major competition Leicester have won is the Football League Cup, in 1964 and 1997.

6 The Leicester faithful have seen European competition in just two seasons. After defeat in the 1961 FA Cup final, Leicester took up the European Cup Winners Cup spot vacated by Spurs, who had won the Double, and in 1997–98 their Coca-Cola Cup victory saw the Foxes compete in the UEFA Cup.

7 Leicester fought out the highest-ever score draw in top-flight Football League history. They drew 6–6 with Arsenal at Filbert Street in Division One in April 1930.

8 The Foxes' record league victory was a 10–0 thrashing of Portsmouth in 1928.

9 Leicester's record 12–0 league defeat in April 1909 by Nottingham Forest is also a joint record for the top flight.

10 Arthur Rowley holds the Leicester record for the most league goals in a single season. He scored 44 in 1956–57.

11 Peter Shilton has made the most career league appearances in English football with a total of 1,309. The total of 286 he made for Leicester was the most for any of his eight clubs.

12 Gary Lineker is the only Leicester player to be the top flight's leading goalscorer. He shared the honour in 1984–85 with Chelsea's Kerry Dixon, both players scoring 24 league goals. Lineker went on to win it outright the following season with Everton.

13 Tony Cottee scored his 200th career league goal when he netted against Tottenham Hotspur in the 2–0 win at White Hart Lane on April 3, 1999.

14 The record attendance at Filbert Street was for an FA Cup fifth-round tie against Tottenham Hotspur in February 1928, seen by 47,298.

15 David Nish was the youngest FA Cup captain when he led Leicester City in the 1969 final aged just 21 years and seven months. Peter Shilton also set a record as the youngest goalkeeper to play in an FA Cup final at 19 years and seven months.

16 Leicester spent most of the 1998–99 Carling Premiership season in mid-table and eventually finished in 10th position. Their league record was:

Pld	W	D	L	F	A	Pts
38	12	13	13	40	46	49

17 The Foxes reached the fourth round of the AXA-sponsored FA Cup, where they were beaten 3–0 at home by Coventry City. They had earlier defeated Birmingham City 4–2 at Filbert Street in the third round.

18 Martin O'Neill's side reached the League Cup final for the second time in three years, losing 1–0 at Wembley to Tottenham Hotspur. After defeating Chesterfield 6–1 on aggregate in the second round, the Foxes beat Charlton 2–1 away, Leeds 2–1 at home and Blackburn 1–0 at home, before eliminating Sunderland 3–2 on aggregate in the semi-final.

19 The top goalscorer in all competitions for Leicester City was Tony Cottee with 16 goals.

20 The Foxes' disciplinary record was the second-best in the Premiership. They committed 494 fouls, earned 51 yellow cards and suffered just one dismissal.

SEASON REVIEW

It was a massive relief to Foxes fans everywhere that Martin O'Neill decided to stay at Filbert Street after the 1997–98 season. The worry for supporters was that if O'Neill quit then key players would follow, prompting a massive re-building exercise.

The season began with a daunting trip to Old Trafford, but goals from Emile Heskey and veteran Tony Cottee should have won all three points for City. They were only denied in the last minute by a David Beckham free kick special.

Unruffled, the side shot into second place with victory over Everton, but then two very disappointing 1–0 defeats followed. In fact, City did not win again in the Premiership until October.

By this time, rumours about O'Neill's future were again surfacing. George Graham was set to switch from Leeds United to Spurs and Leeds chairman Peter Ridsdale made it plain that O'Neill was his target to replace Graham. The players responded by beating Leeds at Elland Road on October 3; then a week later, in a televized match against Tottenham, the fans showed overwhelming support by holding up "Stay Martin Stay" signs in an initiative masterminded by the Leicester Evening Mercury newspaper.

O'Neill pledged his future to City once again after the thrilling 2–1 win, and victories over Liverpool in the league and Charlton and Leeds again in the Worthington Cup followed.

Andy Impey was plucked from West Ham and Arnar Gunnlaugsson arrived from Bolton to bolster the squad and, after defeats against West Ham and Chelsea, the side won three matches in a row, including victory over Blackburn Rovers in the fifth round of the Worthington Cup.

The New Year brought little cheer, with Coventry beating the Foxes in the FA Cup and Manchester United hitting City for six at Filbert Street – but the side ignored the form book to beat Sunderland in the Worthington Cup semi-final and advance on Wembley yet again.

However, league form was slipping drastically. Leicester were given a footballing lesson at Highbury as Arsenal whipped them 5–0, while Sheffield Wednesday and Leeds also put the boot in. By the time Wembley approached, City were 13th and still far from safe from the drop.

Losing in the final minute in the Worthington Cup final, though, brought the lack of league progress firmly into focus, and the side then launched into a fine six-match unbeaten run to eliminate the threat of relegation. A revenge victory at Tottenham and a second successful win at Anfield were highlights of the sequence and a 1–0 win over Coventry City lifted the side into 11th position.

> "The $64,000 question is how we can make progress at Leicester. The only way is to improve the squad with extra quality"
>
> **Martin O'Neill**

A bonus of this run was the form of unconventional veteran striker Ian Marshall, who scored three in three games to confound the footballing purists.

A final placing of 10th equalled the achievements of 1997–98, but in truth it seems progress was rather limited. City certainly kept the goalkeepers busy, finishing as the third-sharpest shooters in the league with a shooting accuracy of 47%. With Steve Guppy impressing at left wing-back, the side also put in the fourth-highest number of crosses in the Premiership.

Thanks to the busy Neil Lennon and Muzzy Izzet in midfield, the team made the second-highest number of challenges in the league and were also the most successful dribblers, completing 75% of all dribbles and runs.

The problem facing all Foxes fans has not gone away. Speculation over O'Neill's future at the club continues to be rife in the media, particularly when a high-profile managerial vacancy arises. He is going to need to be given plenty of cash for new signings if he is to be tempted to stay at Filbert Street long-term.

LEICESTER CITY

DATE	OPPONENT	SCORE	ATT.	ARPHEXAD	CAMPBELL	COTTEE	ELLIOTT	FENTON	GUNNLAUGSSON	GUPPY	HESKEY	IMPEY	IZZET
15.8.98	Man Utd A	2–2	55,052	s29	–	84¹	88	–	–	90□	90¹	–	90
22.8.98	Everton H	2–0	21,037	–	–	90¹	90	–	–	90	90	–	90¹
29.8.98	Blackburn A	0–1	22,544	–	s35	90	67	–	–	90	90□	–	90
9.9.98	Middlesbro H	0–1	20,635	–	s24	66	90	–	–	90	90	–	90
12.9.98	Arsenal H	1–1	21,628	–	s45	90	90	–	–	90	90¹	–	90
19.9.99	Derby Co A	0–2	26,738	–	54	70	90	–	–	90	90	–	90
27.9.98	Wimbledon H	1–1	17,725	–	–	77	90¹	–	–	90	90	–	90
3.10.98	Leeds Utd A	1–0	32,120	–	s34□	90¹	90□	–	–	90	90	–	90
19.10.98	Tottenham H	2–1	20,787	–	s43	90	90	–	–	90	90¹	–	90¹
24.10.98	Aston Villa A	1–1	39,241	–	–	90¹	90	–	–	90	90	–	90
31.10.98	Liverpool H	1–0	21,837	–	–	90¹	90□	–	–	90	90	–	90
7.11.98	Charlton A	0–0	20,021	–	–	–	90	–	–	90	90□	–	90□
14.11.98	West Ham A	2–3*	25,642	–	s28	s23	90	70	–	90	–	–	67¹
21.11.98	Chelsea H	2–4	21,401	–	s35	–	90	68	–	90¹	–	–	90¹
28.11.98	Coventry A	1–1	19,887	–	–	–	90	73	–	90	90¹	90	90□
5.12.98	Southampton H	2–0	18,423	–	–	–	90	–	–	90	90¹	90	90
12.12.98	Nott'm For H	3–1	20,891	–	–	–	90¹	s14	–	90¹	87¹	90	90
19.12.98	Newcastle A	0–1	36,718	–	–	65	90□	s25	–	90	90	90	48
26.12.98	Sheff Wed A	1–0	33,513	–	–	90¹□	90	–	–	90	90	81	89
28.12.98	Blackburn H	1–1	21,083	–	–	90	90□	–	–	90	90	–	90
9.1.99	Everton A	0–0	32,792	–	–	90	90	–	–	90	90	90	90
16.1.99	Man Utd H	2–6	22,091	–	s16	89	–	s1	–	90	–	–	90
30.1.99	Middlesbro A	0–0	34,631	–	s38	90	90	s1	–	90	–	90	–
6.2.99	Sheff Wed H	0–2	20,113	–	–	90	90	–	s34	90	90	77	90
20.2.99	Arsenal A	0–5	38,069	–	–	–	90	s5	85	90	–	s45	90
1.3.99	Leeds Utd H	1–2	18,101	–	–	90¹	90	–	s24□	90	45	66	90
6.3.99	Wimbledon A	1–0	11,801	s45	–	90	90	–	–	90¹	–	–	90
13.3.99	Charlton H	1–1	20,220	–	–	–	90	–	s12	90	78	–	90
3.4.99	Tottenham A	2–0	35,415	–	–	90¹	90¹	–	–	90□	90□	90	54
6.4.99	Aston Villa H	2–2	20,652	–	–	90¹	90□	–	59	90□	90	90	–
10.4.99	West Ham H	0–0	20,402	–	–	90	90	–	64	90	90	64	–
18.4.99	Chelsea A	2–2*	34,535	–	–	90	90	–	70	90¹	90	90	–
21.4.99	Liverpool A	1–0	36,019	–	s35	90	90	–	55	90	–	90	–
24.4.99	Coventry H	1–0	20,224	–	s23	67	90□	s9	s4	90	90	90	–
1.5.99	Southampton A	1–2	15,228	–	–	65	90□	–	–	90	90	90	–
5.5.99	Derby Co H	1–2	20,535	–	–	s23	90	–	–	90	90	90	90
8.5.99	Newcastle H	2–0	21,125	90	–	90¹	90	–	–	90	–	–	90¹
16.5.99	Nott'm For A	0–1	25,353	90	–	90	90	–	–	90	s37	–	90

□ Yellow card, ■ Red card, s Substitute, 90³ Goals scored
*including own goal

1998–99 PREMIERSHIP APPEARANCES

KAAMARK	KELLER	LENNON	MARSHALL	MILLER	OAKES	PARKER	SAVAGE	SINCLAIR	TAGGART	ULLATHORNE	WALSH	WILSON	ZAGORAKIS	TOTAL
–	61	90□	–	–	–	–	90	90	s2	–	90	s6	90□	990
–	90	90□	–	–	–	–	90□	90□	–	–	90	–	90□	990
–	90	55	–	–	–	s32	90	90□	s23	–	90	–	58	990
90	90	90	–	–	–	–	74	90	s24	–	–	s16	66	990
90	90	90	–	–	–	–	90	90□	–	–	–	–	45	990
90	90	90	–	–	–	s36	54	90□	s36□	–	–	s20	–	990
s19	90	90	–	–	–	–	90	90	90	71	–	s13	–	990
–	90	90	–	–	–	–	90	–	90	90	–	56□	–	990
–	90	90	–	–	–	s2	90	90□	45	90	–	–	–	990
–	90	90□	–	–	–	–	90	90	–	90□	–	s8	82	990
–	90	90	–	–	–	–	76	90	–	90	s35	s14	55	990
–	90	90□	–	–	–	–	90	90	–	90	90	s24	66	990
–	90	90	–	–	–	62	90□	90	–	90	90	s20	–	990
–	90	90	–	–	s22	–	55	90□	–	90	90	–	90	990
–	90	90	–	–	–	–	s17	47■	–	90	90	–	–	947
–	90	90	–	–	–	–	s10	90	s6	90	84[1]	–	80	990
90	90	90	–	–	–	s3	s21	–	–	90	76	–	69	990
s29	90	90	–	–	–	–	s42	61	90	90	–	–	–	990
–	90	90	–	–	–	–	s9	90	s1	90□	90	–	–	990
–	90	90	s16	–	–	–	7	90	–	90	90[1]	–	s67□	990
–	90	90	–	–	–	–	–	90y	–	90	90	–	–	990
74	90	90□	–	–	–	s16	–	–	90	90	90[1]	74	90[1]	990
90	90	–	–	–	–	52	–	–	90□	90□	89□	–	90	990
–	90	90	–	–	–	–	–	s34	56□	90	56	–	s13	990
45	90	90	–	–	–	–	90	90	–	90	s45	–	45	990
90	90	90	s45	–	–	–	90□	–	–	90□	–	–	–	990
90	45	90	90	–	–	–	90	–	90	–	90	–	–	990
–	90	90[1]	90	–	–	–	90	–	90	90	90	–	–	990
s36	90	90	–	–	–	–	90	90□	–	90	–	–	–	990
–	90	90	–	s31	–	–	90[1]	90□	–	90	–	–	–	990
–	90	90	s26	s26	–	–	90	90	–	90	–	–	–	990
s57	90□	90	s20	–	–	–	90	90	–	33	–	–	–	990
90	90	90	90[1]	–	–	–	90	90	–	–	–	–	–	990
90	90	86	81[1]	–	–	–	90	90	–	–	–	–	–	990
82	90	90□	90[1]	s25	–	–	90	90	–	–	s8	–	–	990
90	90□	90	80	–	–	–	67	90[1]	–	–	s10	–	–	990
90	–	90	–	30	90	–	90	90	–	–	–	–	s60	990
90	–	90	–	–	53	–	90	70	–	–	s20	–	90	990

THE MANAGER

MARTIN O'NEILL

Martin O'Neill joined Leicester from Wycombe Wanderers in December 1995, got his side promoted to the Carling Premiership via the play-offs and hasn't looked back since.

City spent much of the 1998–99 season in the bottom half of the league, but their experienced players rarely looked like being sucked into a relegation battle.

For a time, in October, it looked like O'Neill's stint at Filbert Street was about to come to an end after Leeds approached him to replace George Graham. But during a televized clash with Graham's new club Tottenham, tens of thousands of Leicester supporters held up signs begging him to stay and an overwhelmed O'Neill pledged his future to the club.

Leicester celebrated by making it all the way to the Worthington Cup Final at Wembley for the second time in three years. But they were beaten by a last-gasp Allan Nielsen strike as Spurs walked off with the trophy.

Nonetheless, with limited resources former Northern Irish international midfielder O'Neill has built a resilient team at Leicester, and City fans have every reason to feel confident of future successes with the Millennium approaching.

LEAGUE POSITION

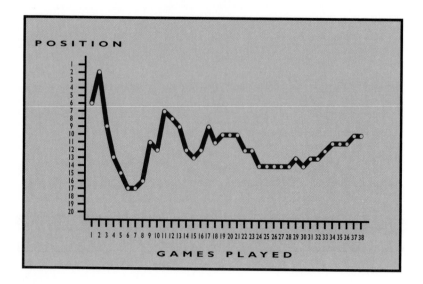

THE GOALS

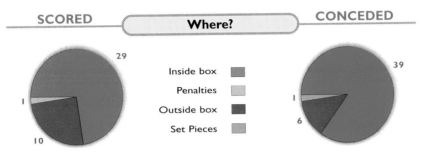

SCORED — **Where?** — **CONCEDED**

Inside box
Penalties
Outside box
Set Pieces

29
1
10

39
1
6

Martin O'Neill's Leicester fancied their luck from long range and managed 10 goals from outside the box, a quarter of all their Premiership goals. City were not involved in many penalty incidents throughout the 1998–99 season, scoring just one themselves and not conceding a single spot-kick goal in all 38 games. The Foxes failed to convert opportunities direct from free kicks but they defended very well on set-pieces, conceding just a solitary strike.

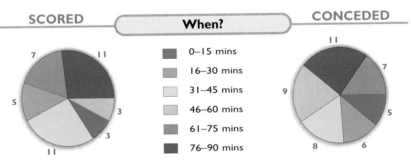

SCORED — **When?** — **CONCEDED**

0–15 mins
16–30 mins
31–45 mins
46–60 mins
61–75 mins
76–90 mins

7   11
5
3
11   3

11
9   7
8   6   5

The Foxes were slow starters on the whole, scoring only three goals within the first 15 minutes of matches. They were equally lethargic at the beginning of the second half, again managing just three strikes in the first quarter of an hour, meaning that they netted just 15% of all league goals in the 30 minutes combined. Between 60 and 75 minutes Leicester conceded just seven goals, one of the lowest totals in the league for that period.

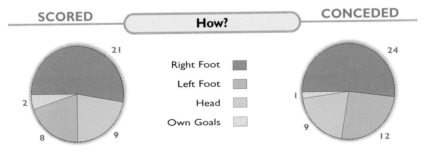

SCORED — **How?** — **CONCEDED**

Right Foot
Left Foot
Head
Own Goals

21
2
8   9

24
1
9   12

With Matt Elliott and Steve Walsh pushing forward for free kicks and corners Leicester were able to use their added height to great advantage, netting 22.5% of all league goals from headers. Despite the presence of Steve Guppy, City scored just eight goals from left-foot strikes and only Southampton registered fewer in this way. City profited from two own-goals, accounting for 5% of all goals during the season.

LEICESTER CITY

	CAMPBELL	COTTEE	ELLIOTT	FENTON	GUNNLAUGSSON	GUPPY	HESKEY	IMPEY	IZZET	KAAMARK
APPEARANCES										
Start	1	29	37	3	5	38	29	17	31	15
Sub	11	2	0	6	4	0	1	1	0	4
Minutes on pitch	410	2519	3305	266	407	3420	2587	1503	2688	1422
GOAL ATTEMPTS										
Goals	0	10	3	0	0	4	6	0	5	0
Shots on target	3	25	17	2	7	17	32	3	19	2
Shots off target	5	14	24	4	1	16	43	7	20	2
Shooting accuracy %	38%	64%	41%	33%	88%	52%	43%	30%	49%	50%
PASSING										
Goal assists	0	1	2	0	0	11	3	1	0	0
Long passes	12	22	274	0	12	240	24	39	76	145
Short passes	90	650	1000	77	121	1020	865	457	969	368
PASS COMPLETION										
Own half %	67%	93%	93%	95%	83%	88%	90%	90%	92%	92%
Opposition half %	73%	77%	71%	92%	71%	67%	69%	78%	77%	61%
CROSSING										
Total crosses	6	13	7	4	5	415	43	60	58	7
Cross completion %	17%	31%	43%	25%	0%	28%	33%	23%	14%	29%
DRIBBLING										
Dribbles & runs	14	58	30	6	24	153	119	73	97	27
Dribble completion %	64%	62%	87%	83%	75%	82%	69%	74%	76%	89%
DEFENDING										
Tackles made	16	39	122	8	27	83	58	53	141	57
Tackles won %	44%	56%	67%	75%	26%	49%	43%	55%	56%	68%
Blocks	4	2	35	1	0	13	6	9	9	11
Clearances	10	7	502	1	3	134	33	75	48	150
Interceptions	0	4	48	1	3	29	4	15	25	22
DISCIPLINE										
Fouls	7	34	68	5	3	24	76	12	32	13
Offside	0	25	4	5	0	4	40	3	14	0
Yellow cards	1	1	7	0	1	3	3	0	2	0
Red cards	0	0	0	0	0	0	0	0	0	0

GOALKEEPER NAME	START/ (SUB)	TIME ON PITCH	GOALS CONCEDED	MINS/GOALS CONCEDED	SAVES MADE	SAVES/ SHOTS
ARPHEXAD	2 (2)	254	3	84.7	10	77%
KELLER	36	3166	43	73.6	133	76%

PLAYERS' STATISTICS

	LENNON	MARSHALL	MILLER	OAKES	PARKER	SAVAGE	SINCLAIR	TAGGART	ULLATHORNE	WALSH	WILSON	ZAGORAKIS	TOTAL	RANK
	37	6	1	2	2	29	30	9	25	17	1	16		
	0	4	3	1	5	5	1	6	0	5	8	3		
	3291	628	112	165	203	2502	2642	823	2174	1593	195	1302		
	1	3	0	0	0	1	1	0	0	3	0	1	40*	=14th
	12	5	0	0	1	7	6	1	0	7	2	7	175	=10th
	14	11	0	2	1	11	4	2	0	11	1	3	196	18th
	46%	31%	0%	0%	50%	39%	60%	33%	0%	39%	67%	70%	47%	3rd
	3	0	0	0	0	2	0	2	1	0	0	2	28	=12th
	196	9	3	14	31	137	242	59	127	214	1	47	1924	7th
	1898	242	37	90	93	692	663	202	538	336	47	357	10812	13th
	93%	87%	79%	100%	87%	83%	92%	91%	91%	89%	88%	91%	91%	3rd
	81%	73%	69%	85%	74%	69%	62%	59%	72%	51%	78%	74%	72%	6th
	46	5	0	3	10	73	24	4	13	6	1	57	860	4th
	20%	0%	0%	33%	30%	18%	29%	50%	15%	0%	0%	25%	25%	19th
	85	3	3	2	2	50	43	12	21	15	16	50	904	9th
	81%	100%	0%	50%	100%	64%	95%	100%	76%	100%	56%	56%	75%	1st
	193	14	5	10	8	125	109	44	84	54	17	65	1334	2nd
	60%	57%	20%	50%	63%	54%	62%	75%	61%	67%	18%	55%	58%	19th
	18	0	2	2	1	9	21	5	25	18	0	9	201	=11th
	82	5	1	8	1	149	346	175	158	234	0	20	2165	3rd
	47	0	1	2	1	20	31	10	35	14	0	8	321	14th
	38	20	3	0	1	27	45	17	26	16	3	21	494	12th
	1	4	0	0	0	2	0	2	0	0	2	4	110	=18th
	6	0	0	0	0	3	9	3	4	2	0	4	51	=18th
	0	0	0	0	0	0	1	0	0	0	0	0	1	=17th

*including two own goals

CROSSES CAUGHT	CROSSES PUNCHED	CROSSES NOT CLAIMED	CATCH SUCCESS	THROWS/ SHORT KICKS	% COMPLETION	LONG KICKS	% COMPLETION
7	0	1	100%	19	95%	66	33%
89	15	6	97%	221	94%	802	39%

PLAYER OF THE SEASON

PLAYER	INDEX SCORE
NEIL LENNON	980
Matt Elliott	969
Steve Walsh	957
Muzzy Izzet	866
Steve Guppy	863
Frank Sinclair	796
Emile Heskey	752
Robbie Savage	738
Kasey Keller	700
Robert Ullathorne	686

Most Crewe Alexandra fans would tell you that tenacious midfielder Neil Lennon was always a certain candidate to negotiate the step up from the Nationwide League to the Premiership successfully.

But his £750,000 price tag in February 1996 hardly reflected that, and looked something of a snip even then. Now it looks like one of Leicester's biggest-ever bargains.

The midfield partnership between Lennon and Muzzy Izzet had been one of the features of City's 1997–98 campaign. Their willingness to receive the ball, protect the back three and create goalscoring opportunities, while always willing to strike at goal themselves, made them the inspirations of the side.

Lennon scaled new heights in 1998–99, being one of only three players to have made more than 2,000 passes in the Premiership. The Northern Ireland international ended the season as the club's highest-scoring player in the Carling Opta Season Index, averaging 980 points a match over the campaign.

Typically consistent form from towering centre-back Matt Elliott ensured his inclusion at second spot in the top 10. He made a huge number of headed clearances while showing a cool head when bringing the ball out of defence. A regular for City and Scotland, Elliott always picks up plenty of points for his threat at set-pieces. He fired in a total of 41 shots at goal and was always available as an emergency striker.

The same can be said of fellow-stopper Steve Walsh who, though his Premiership career is most definitely approaching the twilight stage, still turned in plenty of steady displays for City in 1998–99.

Consistent performers Izzet and Steve Guppy figure high up the top 10. But the likes of Emile Heskey and Kasey Keller, who enjoyed fine individual displays in certain games, struggled to maintain their form over the whole season.

FIVE OF THE BEST

City finished in the Premiership's top 10 for the third consecutive season, though they lost seven more games than in 1997–98. Under Martin O'Neill, the Foxes have become cunning enough to stay well clear of the relegation zone – but more investment is likely to be needed if City are to make a serious challenge for the top six.

TOP GOALSCORERS

	GOALS	GOALS/SHOTS
TONY COTTEE	10	26%
Emile Heskey	6	8%
Muzzy Izzet	5	13%
Steve Guppy	4	12%
Ian Marshall	3	19%

What a season it turned out to be for veteran front man Tony Cottee. In his 16th straight campaign in league football, he scored his 200th career league goal and fired his side to Wembley in the Worthington Cup with five goals from just seven shots. He also finished as City's top scorer in the Premiership, netting with more than a quarter of his shots. His strike rate eclipsed that of highly-rated England under-21 striker Emile Heskey, who scored with fewer than one in 10 attempts in 1998–99.

Midfielder Neil Lennon was undoubtedly the driving force behind Leicester's season, being one of only three Premiership players to make more than 2,000 passes in 1998–99. Defender Matt Elliott also enjoyed a fine campaign in the heart of the Foxes' defence, completing almost four out of every five passes and always ready to act as an emergency striker when required. Steve Guppy and Muzzy Izzet can both be pleased with their fine personal seasons, while former Chelsea man Frank Sinclair proved himself to be a fine addition to the squad.

TOP PASSERS

	SUCC PASSES	COMPLETION
NEIL LENNON	1,786	85%
Matt Elliott	1,011	79%
Steve Guppy	925	73%
Muzzy Izzet	846	81%
Frank Sinclair	687	76%

TOP TACKLERS

	WON	SUCCESS
NEIL LENNON	116	60%
Matt Elliott	82	67%
Muzzy Izzet	79	56%
Frank Sinclair	68	62%
Robbie Savage	68	54%

Neil Lennon epitomizes the strength of character in the Leicester squad under Martin O'Neill and he can be a fearsome tackler in the heart of the midfield. This natural ability to win the ball coupled with his superb distribution skills make Lennon the consummate midfield general, alongside his friend and room-mate Muzzy Izzet. The man most likely to win possession was Matt Elliott, while the inclusion of Robbie Savage is no surprise given his tenacious display in the Worthington Cup final.

Natural-born leader Matt Elliott won more than his fair share of tackles in 1998–99 but still conceded a high number of fouls, including 13 in the 30 yards-from-goal "danger area" – more than any other Fox. But Emile Heskey conceded more fouls and Frank Sinclair found himself in more trouble with referees. In fact, Sinclair was the only City player to get sent off and City finished as the second-cleanest team in the Premiership, behind Sheffield Wednesday.

DISCIPLINE

	POINTS	FOULS & CARDS
MATT ELLIOTT	89	68F, 7Y, 0R
Emile Heskey	85	76F, 3Y, 0R
Frank Sinclair	78	45F, 9Y, 1R
Neil Lennon	56	38F, 6Y, 0R
Robert Ullathorne	38	26F, 4Y, 0R

ACTION	CAMPBELL	COTTEE	ELLIOTT	GUPPY	HESKEY	IZZET	KELLER	LENNON	PARKER	SAVAGE	SINCLAIR	TAGGART	ULLATHORNE	TOTAL	TOTTENHAM
Time on pitch	43	90	90	90	90	90	90	90	2	90	90	45	90	990	990
GOALS															
Goal	–	–	–	–	1	1	–	–	–	–	–	–	–	2	1
Shot on target	–	–	–	–	–	–	–	–	–	–	–	–	–	–	5
Shot off target	–	–	1	–	3	1	–	–	–	1	2	–	–	7	5
Blocked shot	2	–	–	–	1	1	–	–	–	–	–	–	–	6	2
Own goal	–	–	–	–	–	–	–	–	–	–	–	–	–	–	–
PASSES															
Pass to own player	6	15	36	26	20	27	–	39	2	26	30	11	19	257	233
Pass to opposition	2	8	11	7	10	11	–	9	–	7	5	6	4	80	74
Cross to own player	–	1	–	3	–	–	–	–	–	–	–	–	–	6	6
Cross to opposition player	–	–	–	10	–	2	–	1	–	–	–	–	–	13	20
Goal assist	–	–	–	–	–	–	–	1	–	–	–	–	–	–	1
Pass completion %	75%	67%	77%	63%	68%	68%	0%	82%	100%	76%	86%	65%	83%	74%	72%
TACKLES & CLEARANCES															
Tackle	1	1	5	5	2	5	–	5	–	–	7	2	9	42	34
Clearances, blocks and interceptions	–	–	27	10	3	3	–	6	–	10	15	13	8	92	92
DRIBBLES & RUNS															
Dribble ball retained	–	–	5	1	2	2	–	2	–	2	–	–	–	16	17
Dribble ball lost	–	–	–	–	4	2	1	1	–	–	–	–	1	8	10
Dribble success %	100%	0%	100%	100%	33%	50%	0%	67%	0%	100%	100%	0%	0%	67%	63%
DISCIPLINE															
Fouls	–	–	–	–	5	1	–	1	–	–	2	–	2	11	15
Penalty conceded	–	–	–	–	–	–	–	–	–	–	–	–	–	–	–
Free kick - offside	–	2	–	–	4	1	–	–	–	–	–	–	–	7	3
Yellow cards	–	–	–	–	–	–	–	–	–	–	–	–	–	–	4
Red cards	–	–	–	–	–	–	–	–	–	–	–	–	–	–	–
GOALKEEPERS															
Distribution to own player	–	–	–	–	–	–	17	–	–	–	–	–	–	17	9
Distribution to opposition player	–	–	–	–	–	–	13	–	–	–	–	–	–	13	11
Goalkeeper distribution%	–	–	–	–	–	–	57%	–	–	–	–	–	–	57%	45%
Save	–	–	–	–	–	–	5	–	–	–	–	–	–	5	2
Ball caught	–	–	–	–	–	–	–	–	–	–	–	–	–	–	–
Ball dropped	–	–	–	–	–	–	–	–	–	–	–	–	–	–	–
Goal conceded	–	–	–	–	–	–	1	–	–	–	–	–	–	1	2

Both managers were in the headlines when Leicester met Spurs in the early months of the season. Rumours were circulating that Martin O'Neill was due to leave Filbert Street to take the vacant Leeds job, and meanwhile George Graham was taking charge of Tottenham for the first time since leaving Elland Road.

October 19, 1998

2 – 1

LEICESTER CITY
TOTTENHAM HOTSPUR

The first half epitomized the whole match, with both teams struggling to achieve long periods of possession. Leicester looked more likely to break through with Emile Heskey, but it was Tottenham who drew first blood on 13 minutes.

Ruel Fox sent Darren Anderton away down the right wing and his cross found Les Ferdinand in space to turn the ball past Kasey Keller from six yards.

Leicester tried to hit back through Heskey, but the big striker was suffering at the hands of the Tottenham offside trap. George Graham had made an instant impact on the Spurs defence, and it appeared to be working.

The Foxes took control and equalized on 37 minutes. Neil Lennon played a good ball in to Heskey, who had his back to goal. The England under-21 striker brilliantly spun away from Ramon Vega and fired a left-foot bullet into the top right-hand corner, giving Keller no chance.

The first half ended at 1–1 and the second looked to be a similar proposition, with both teams scrapping in midfield and finding it difficult to create chances. On 53 minutes Robbie Savage's shot was well blocked by the outstretched boot of Vega when a goal looked on the cards.

With 15 minutes to go, Tottenham had a great chance to seal victory when Lennon's back-pass went straight into the path of substitute Chris Armstrong. The striker ran through on goal, but his finish was disappointing and was easily dealt with by Keller in the Leicester goal.

In the last 10 minutes, with the score finely poised at 1–1, Leicester pushed forward in an attempt to take all three points. Matt Elliott somehow poked the ball over the bar following a Muzzy Izzet corner. But three minutes later Leicester scored a breathtaking winner. Steve Guppy sent a free kick curling into the area and Ferdinand hooked the ball clear. The ball fell to Izzet, who smashed in a spectacular volley from 25 yards. It was an incredible strike and a goal fit to win any game.

In the final moments Spurs forced the best from Keller, first from an Armstrong header, then from an Anderton free kick. But the American 'keeper stood firm, and Leicester took all three points.

A game fought largely in the midfield was settled by two outstanding Leicester goals. The Carling Opta statistics show just how important those two strikes were for Martin O'Neill's side. They had the better of the possession, making 257 successful passes to Tottenham's 233, but Spurs had the chances. Their goals apart, Leicester failed to register a shot on target for the whole 90 minutes.

The emotional fans who held up their "Stay Martin Stay" banners and chanted Martin O'Neill's name inspired their team to victory on the pitch – and persuaded their manger to stay at Filbert Street.

ACTION	COTTEE	ELLIOTT	GUPPY	HESKEY	IMPEY	IZZET	KAAMARK	KELLER	LENNON	SAVAGE	SINCLAIR	ULLATHORNE	TOTAL	TOTTENHAM
Time on pitch	90	90	90	90	90	54	36	90	90	90	90	90	990	990
GOALS														
Goal	1	1	-	-	-	-	-	-	-	-	-	-	2	1
Shot on target	-	-	-	-	-	-	-	-	-	-	-	2	2	3
Shot off target	-	-	-	-	-	-	1	-	-	-	-	-	1	12
Blocked shot	-	-	-	2	-	-	-	-	-	-	-	-	2	4
Own goal	-	-	-	-	-	-	-	-	-	-	-	-	-	-
PASSES														
Pass to own player	15	16	18	20	14	12	2	-	38	18	24	9	186	227
Pass to opposition	8	6	11	16	4	8	1	-	11	8	5	6	84	104
Cross to own player	-	-	2	1	-	-	-	-	-	1	-	-	5	5
Cross to opposition player	-	-	6	-	-	3	-	-	2	-	-	2	13	14
Goal assist	-	-	-	1	-	-	-	-	-	-	-	1	2	10
Pass completion %	65%	73%	55%	58%	78%	52%	67%	0%	75%	70%	83%	53%	67%	68%
TACKLES & CLEARANCES														
Tackle	2	5	1	8	3	7	2	-	9	10	3	3	53	35
Clearances, blocks and interceptions	-	17	4	1	2	3	3	-	4	4	10	9	57	59
DRIBBLES & RUNS														
Dribble ball retained	-	1	2	2	-	-	-	-	5	1	-	-	11	24
Dribbles ball lost	2	-	-	1	2	-	-	-	-	-	-	-	5	14
Dribble success %	0%	100%	100%	67%	33%	0%	0%	0%	100%	100%	0%	0%	69%	63%
DISCIPLINE														
Fouls	1	2	-	6	-	3	1	-	4	3	5	1	26	14
Penalty conceded	-	-	-	-	-	-	-	-	-	-	-	-	-	-
Free kick - offside	2	-	-	-	-	-	-	-	-	-	-	-	3	-
Yellow cards	-	-	-	-	-	-	-	-	-	-	1	-	3	3
Red cards	-	-	-	-	-	-	-	-	-	-	-	-	-	-
GOALKEEPERS														
Distribution to own player	-	-	-	-	-	-	-	11	-	-	-	-	11	16
Distribution to opposition player	-	-	-	-	-	-	-	29	-	-	-	-	29	3
Goalkeeper distribution%	-	-	-	-	-	-	-	28%	-	-	-	-	28%	84%
Save	-	-	-	-	-	-	-	3	-	-	-	-	3	3
Ball caught	-	-	-	-	-	-	-	-	-	-	-	-	-	-
Ball dropped	-	-	-	-	-	-	-	-	-	-	-	-	-	-
Goal conceded	-	-	-	-	-	-	-	1	-	-	-	-	1	2

When Leicester met Spurs at White Hart Lane, it was an early opportunity to gain revenge for that heartbreaking Wembley loss in the Worthington Cup final. It turned out to be a niggly affair, with issues from the Wembley final still to be settled.

April 3, 1999

0–2

TOTTENHAM HOTSPUR
LEICESTER CITY

Tottenham settled in more quickly after a competitive start, and when Allan Nielsen crossed for Les Ferdinand a goal looked certain, until Matt Elliott intervened to turn the ball over the bar with an outstretched boot. It could so easily have been an early own goal.

Tempers flared in the 40th minute after a tackle from behind by Emile Heskey on Steffen Freund. It sparked an angry confrontation between the two players and caused referee Neale Barry to take both their names. David Ginola was lucky not to be booked himself after pushing Heskey in the melee that followed the tackle.

Two minutes later, Leicester were ahead when a curling free kick from Steve Guppy was met by Elliott, just inside the area, who rose above Sol Campbell and flicked on into the top right-hand corner, evading Ian Walker's despairing dive.

The second half followed a similar pattern to the first, with both teams sparring for an opening. Genuine chances were few and far between in an aggressive second period.

After soaking up a period of sustained pressure, Leicester struck again after 67 minutes. Heskey took the ball on the right, shrugged off the attentions of Justin Edinburgh, out-muscled Campbell and crossed low for Tony Cottee to finish easily at the near post. It was a typical Cottee goal, whose form in 1998–99 was reminiscent of his West Ham days.

Tottenham raised the tempo in the last 10 minutes but could not breach the Leicester defence lacking the inspirational Steve Walsh. Elliott's man-of-the-match performance helped keep Spurs at bay.

Ginola's frustration led to a booking but, he then produced some great skill to nutmeg a rather irritated Robbie Savage. He delivered a great cross, which led to Kasey Keller pulling off a world-class save to deny Nielsen. Leicester should have sealed the game, when Neil Lennon and Heskey combined to set up Pontus Kaamark. The Swedish international defender did not keep his composure and fired over when he should have scored.

In the end it was to be Leicester's day, winning by 2–0 in an ill-tempered match which required some sensible refereeing by Barry. Savage was booed every time he touched the ball and was throwing himself into bone-jarring tackles.

The Carling Opta statistics show how well-contested the game was. Leicester completed 67% of their passes, Spurs 68%. Leicester's work-rate and tenacity in midfield are illustrated by their 53 tackles compared to Tottenham's 35.

The Foxes were deadly in front of goal, scoring with two of their five shots, while Spurs wasted a dozen chances by failing to hit the target.

In the end Martin O'Neill's men won the match, took the three points and gained sweet revenge for their Wembley defeat.

Hugs all round: Liverpool enjoy one of the brighter moments of the 1998–99 campaign with a 4–2 home defeat of Newcastle United

LIVERPOOL

ADDRESS

Anfield Road, Anfield
Liverpool L4 0TH

CONTACT NUMBERS

Telephone: 0151 263 2361
Fax: 0151 260 8813
Ticket Office: 0151 260 8680
24hr Information: 09068 121184
Superstore: 0151 263 1760

SPONSORS

Carlsberg

FANZINES

Red All Over the Land
Through the Wind and the Rain

KEY PERSONNEL

Chairman: D R Moores
Vice Chairman/President: P B Robinson
Chief Executive: R N Parry BSC, FCA
Directors: D R Moores, P B Robinson,
J T Cross, N White FSCA, T D Smith,
T W Saunders, K E B Clayton FCA,
D M A Chestnutt FCA,
R N Parry BSC FCA
Club Secretary: W B Morrison
Manager: Gerard Houllier

COLOURS

Home: Red shirts, shorts
and stockings
Away: White shirts, shorts
and stockings

NICKNAME

The Reds

20 FACTS

1 Liverpool owe their existence to a dispute in 1892 between Everton and the then landlord of Anfield, John Houlding. Everton left Anfield in the same year, leaving Houlding to form a new club called Liverpool Association FC.

2 The club have been league champions a record 18 times – in 1900–01, 1905–06, 1921–22, 1922–23, 1946–47, 1963–64, 1965–66, 1972–73, 1975–76, 1976–77, 1978–79, 1979–80, 1981–82, 1982–83, 1983–84, 1985–86, 1987–88 and 1989–90.

3 Liverpool have won the FA Cup on five occasions – in 1965, 1974, 1986, 1989 and 1992.

4 They have won the Football League Cup five times – in 1981, 1982, 1983, 1984 and 1995.

5 The Reds are British football's most successful side in European competition. They won the European Cup in 1976–77, 1977–78, 1980–81 and 1983–84. They won the UEFA Cup twice – in 1972–73 and 1975–76.

6 Ian Rush holds the English record for the most goals scored in FA Cup finals – five. He also shares with Sir Geoff Hurst the record for the most goals scored in the history of the League Cup – 49.

7 The title-winning side of 1978–79 remains the most parsimonious in the history of the English game, conceding just 16 goals en route to the Championship.

8 Liverpool hold the record for the most individual scorers in a league match – eight in the 9–0 win over Crystal Palace in September 1989.

9 The Reds became the first British club to have a sponsor's name on their shirts when they signed a one-year deal with Hitachi in 1979.

10 Liverpool's record signing and record sale is Stan Collymore. He cost the club £8.5 million from Nottingham Forest in 1995 and was sold to Aston Villa for £7 million in 1997.

11 Bob Paisley, manager from 1974–83, is the most successful boss in the history of English football. He won six League Championships, three European Cups, three League Cups and one UEFA Cup.

12 Liverpool hold the record for the longest unbeaten run of home matches in the league – 63 between February 1978 and December 1980.

13 The club's record attendance came in February 1952 when 61,905 watched an FA Cup fourth round tie with Wolverhampton Wanderers.

14 Michael Owen became the youngest player this century to score for England when he grabbed the winning goal in a friendly against Morocco in May 1998. He was then aged 18 years and 164 days.

15 Liverpool finished a disappointing seventh in 1998–99. Their league record was:

Pld	W	D	L	F	A	Pts
38	15	9	14	68	49	54

16 Liverpool were knocked out of the AXA-sponsored FA Cup by Manchester United in the fourth round. The Reds defeated Port Vale 3–0 in the third round and led United 1–0 at Old Trafford until the last two minutes, eventually losing 2–1.

17 The 3–1 defeat by Tottenham Hotspur at Anfield in the fourth round of the Worthington Cup heralded the end of joint manager Roy Evans's Liverpool career. The club beat Fulham 3–1 in the third round.

18 Liverpool reached the third round of the UEFA Cup. They defeated IFC Kosice 8–0 on aggregate in the first round; then, against Valencia, they secured victory on the away goals rule after a 2–2 draw in Spain. They were beaten 4–1 on aggregate by another Spanish side, Celta Vigo.

19 Their top goalscorer in all competitions was Michael Owen with 23 goals, including 18 in the league that earned him the Golden Boot.

20 Liverpool's disciplinary record was the fourth best in the Premiership. They committed 460 fouls, earned 65 yellow cards and suffered three dismissals.

SEASON REVIEW

Unlike the home of arch-rivals Manchester United, Anfield was rarely a Theatre of Dreams – but it was certainly the venue for drama both on and off the pitch in 1998–99.

With Roy Evans and Gerard Houllier in charge, Liverpool won three and drew one of their first four games to top the Premiership table. The cameras were at Liverpool's first two away matches against Southampton and Newcastle United, with World Cup hero Michael Owen on show – and on fire. First he scored the winner at the Dell, then he danced through the Magpies' wafer-thin defence at St James's Park to score a sensational first-half hat-trick.

Sadly, having racked up 10 points in four games, it then took a further 11 matches for Liverpool to reach the 20-point mark, by which time the team had slumped into the lower reaches of the top 10. But the changes the club were experiencing went far deeper than that.

Following a dreadful home defeat by Derby County on November 7 and a 3–1 Worthington Cup reverse at the hands of Spurs, also at Anfield three days later, Evans parted company with the club after 35 years' involvement, leaving Houllier in sole charge.

Another home defeat the following Saturday by Leeds United suggested morale was at its lowest ebb, but the players responded magnificently by ending Aston Villa's unbeaten start to the campaign at Villa Park, winning 4–2 in one of the games of the season. Robbie Fowler, in only his 11th start of an injury-hit year, bagged a terrific hat-trick.

Defeat in the UEFA Cup by Celta Vigo and then by Wimbledon in the league seemed to spur the team on still further. Over Christmas and the New Year, Liverpool won five out of six matches in all competitions, culminating in a 7–1 demolition of Southampton at Anfield. That result put the club back in the top six. But with a defence that kept just two clean sheets in the final 17 games and constant injuries making consistent team selection impossible, Liverpool stumbled to a final position of seventh, enjoying fine wins over Tottenham and rivals Everton, but slumping to defeat against Charlton Athletic, Derby County, Aston Villa, Leicester City and Sheffield Wednesday. More serious problems occurred when Fowler became embroiled in two of the biggest controversies of the season. First he and Graeme Le Saux were involved in an ugly clash during Liverpool's defeat at Chelsea in February. Then his bizarre goal celebrations against Everton two weeks later, in which he appeared to be "snorting" the goal-line in front of the Toffees' fans, landed him in serious trouble with the FA, who suspended him for six matches.

> "It has clearly been a difficult season for all of us connected with the club and... only confirmed the hard work we have ahead of us if we are to challenge again for honours."
>
> **Gerard Houllier**

The club threatened to deal Manchester United's title hopes a fatal blow when they came back from 2–0 down to draw 2–2 in a thrilling contest at Anfield, a rare high point for the supporters. In fact, Liverpool scored the second-most goals behind the eventual Treble winners – and fired in the third-greatest total of shots on target, failing to score in only nine league games all season.

But their well-documented problems at the back persisted. Houllier tried a number of central defensive combinations but the back-line rarely convinced, and 49 goals conceded tells its own sorry tale. They made the fourth-fewest clearances and were only 11th in the tackling league.

Changes at Anfield in the coming months are inevitable if Liverpool are to make that long-overdue title bid. What became abundantly clear in 1998–99 is that the Reds are some way behind Manchester United, Arsenal and Chelsea, especially in terms of consistency.

LIVERPOOL

DATE	OPPONENT	SCORE	ATT.	BABB	BERGER	BJORNEBYE	CARRAGHER	DUNDEE	FERRI	FOWLER	FRIEDEL	GERRARD	HARKNESS
16.8.98	Southampton A	2–1	15,202	90	76	–	90	–	–	–	90	–	s14□
22.8.98	Arsenal H	0–0	44,429	90	67	–	90	–	–	–	90	–	–
30.8.98	Newcastle A	4–1	36,740	90□	90¹	–	90	–	–	–	90	–	–
9.9.98	Coventry H	2–0	41,771	90	90¹	–	90	–	–	–	90	–	–
12.9.98	West Ham A	1–2	26,010	90	90	–	90	–	–	–	90	–	54□
19.9.98	Charlton H	3–3	44,526	90	90¹	–	90□	–	–	90²	90	–	61
24.9.98	Man Utd A	0–2	55,181	90	90□	90	90□	–	–	s16	90	–	–
4.10.98	Chelsea H	1–1	44,404	24□	90	90	90	–	–	90	–	–	–
17.10.98	Everton A	0–0	40,185	–	87	90□	50	–	–	90□	–	–	–
24.10.98	Nott'm For H	5–1	44,595	–	90	90	90	–	–	–	–	–	–
31.10.98	Leicester A	0–1	21,837	–	79	90	90□	–	–	s11□	–	–	–
7.11.98	Derby Co H	1–2	44,020	–	32□	90	90	–	–	90	–	–	–
14.11.98	Leeds Utd H	1–3	44,305	–	90	90□	90	–	–	90¹	–	–	–
21.11.98	Aston Villa A	4–2	39,241	90□	64	s80	90	–	–	90³	–	–	10
29.11.98	Blackburn H	2–0	41,753	90	90	90	90	–	–	90	–	s1	–
5.12.98	Tottenham A	1–2	36,125	90	90¹	76	90	–	–	90	–	55	–
13.12.98	Wimbledon A	0–1	26,080	90	90	90	90	–	–	61	–	–	–
19.12.98	Sheff Wed H	2–0	40,003	90	90¹□	90□	90	–	–	90	–	–	–
26.12.98	Middlesbro A	3–1	34,626	90□	90	90□	90	–	–	58	–	–	s1
28.12.98	Newcastle H	4–2	44,605	58	90	90	90	–	–	–	–	s21	–
9.1.99	Arsenal A	0–0	38,107	90□	90	–	90	–	–	90	–	–	90
16.1.99	Southampton H	7–1	44,011	90	90	90	79¹□	–	–	90³	–	–	–
30.1.99	Coventry A	1–2	23,057	–	77	90	–	–	–	90	–	s4	–
6.2.99	Middlesbro H	3–1	44,384	–	–	90	90	–	–	81	–	s9	–
13.2.99	Charlton A	0–1	20,043	–	–	74□	69∎	–	–	90	–	s9	–
20.2.99	West Ham H	2–2	44,511	90	s24	77	90□	–	–	90¹	–	–	–
27.2.99	Chelsea A	1–2	34,822	90	82	90	–	–	s42	90□	–	–	–
13.3.99	Derby Co A	2–3	32,913	90	90	s66	–	–	–	90¹□	–	90	–
3.4.99	Everton H	3–2	44,852	–	90¹	–	–	–	–	85²	–	s20	–
5.4.99	Nott'm For A	2–2	28,374	–	90	–	90	–	–	78	–	s12	–
12.4.99	Leeds Utd A	0–0	39,372	90	90□	–	90	–	–	90	–	90	–
17.4.99	Aston Villa A	0–1	44,306	90	–	45	90	s4	–	90	–	–	–
21.4.99	Leicester H	0–1	36,019	90	–	–	90	s24	–	–	–	–	–
24.4.99	Blackburn A	3–1	29,944	–	–	–	90	s10	–	–	90	–	–
1.5.99	Tottenham H	3–2	44,007	–	–	s2	90	–	–	–	90	s45	–
5.5.99	Man Utd H	2–2	44,702	90	s34	–	90	–	–	–	90	–	–
8.5.99	Sheff Wed A	0–1	27,383	–	67	–	90	–	s7	–	90	45□	–
16.5.99	Wimbledon H	3–0	41,902	s45□	90¹	–	90	–	–	–	90	–	–

□ Yellow card, ∎ Red card, s Substitute, 90³ Goals scored

1998–99 PREMIERSHIP APPEARANCES

HEGGEM	INCE	JAMES	KVARME	LEONHARDSEN	MATTEO	McATEER	McMANAMAN	MURPHY	OWEN	REDKNAPP	RIEDLE	SONG	STAUNTON	THOMPSON	TOTAL
90□	90	–	–	–	–	90	90	–	90¹	–	90¹□		90	–	990
90	90	–	–	–		90	90	–	90	s23	90		90	–	990
90	90□	–	–	–	–	s5	88□	–	90³	85	90		90	s2	990
90	90	–	–	–	–	–	90	–	90	90¹	90		90	–	990
72	90	–	–	–	s27	s18	90	–	90	90□	s36¹		63	–	990
84	–	–	–	–	s26	s29	90	–	90	90	–		64	s6	990
–	90□	–	–	–	–	90	90	–	90	90□	74	–	–	–	990
s34	90□	90	–	64	s66□	56	–	–	90	90¹□	s26□	–	–	–	990
90	90□	90	s40	–	–	s45	90	–	90	45	s3□	–	90	–	990
90	90	90	–	–	–	90	78¹	–	90⁴	–	90	–	90	s12	990
90	90	90	–	–	–	86■	90□	–	90	–	90	–	90	–	986
67	90	90	–	–	–	s58	90	–	90	90¹□	–	–	90	s23	990
90	90	90	–	s20	–	–	–	–	–	90	70	–	90	90□	990
90	90¹	90□	–	–	–	s26	–	–	79¹	90□	s11	–	90	–	990
89	90¹	90	s15	–	–	–	–	–	90¹	90	–	–	75□	–	990
90	90	90	–	–	–	–	–	s14	90	–	–	–	90	s35□	990
90	90□	90	–	–	–	–	–	–	90	90	s29	–	90	–	990
81	90	90	s9	–	–	–	–	–	88¹	90	s2	–	90	–	990
90¹	90	90	–	–	–	–	s13	–	77¹	89¹	s32□	–	90	–	990
90	–	90	–	–	–	s32	24	–	90²	90	90²	–	90	s45	990
90	90□	90	–	–	s27	–	–	–	89	90□	s1	–	63	–	990
90	73□	90	s11	–	90¹	–	–	–	73¹	90	s17	–	–	s17¹	990
90□	90	90	–	–	90	–	s22¹	–	90	90	s13	68□	86	–	990
90¹	90¹□	90	–	–	64■	–	90	–	81¹	90	s9	–	90	–	964
81	90□	90	–	–	90	–	90	–	81	90	s9	s16	90□	–	969
90	–	90	–	–	–	–	66	–	90¹	90	s13	90	90	–	990
10	48	90	90	–	90	–	s80	–	90¹	90	s8	–	–	–	990
90	–	90	–	–	90	–	–	–	45	90	s45	90	24	–	990
70	90	90	–	–	90	–	90	–	90	90	s5	90	90	–	990
–	90	90	–	–	90	–	65	–	90¹	90¹	s25	90	90	–	990
–	90	90	–	–	90	–	90	–	25	90	s65	–	–	–	990
–	90	90	–	s45	90	–	90	–	–	90	90□	86□	–	–	990
–	90	90	–	90	90	–	90	–	–	90	90	90	–	66	990
–	90	–	s7	90¹	90□	–	90¹	–	–	90¹	80	83□	90	90□	990
–	90¹	–	45	75	90	–	90¹	–	–	90¹	90□	s15	90	88	990
–	90¹	–	–	90	90	–	90	–	–	90¹	90	56	78	s12	990
–	90	–	–	90	90	–	90	–	–	83	90	s45	90	s23	990
s4	90¹	–	–	90	90	–	75	–	–	90	90¹□	86	45	s15	990

THE MANAGER

GERARD HOULLIER

Gerard Houllier will probably want to write off the 1998–99 season as a "transitional period". He was certainly spared any real criticism for the club's poor showing in the league, but in his first full season in sole charge of the team the man from Pas-de-Calais will be expected to fulfil some of the club's high expectations.

Houllier was installed as sole manager of Liverpool in November 1998 after it became clear that the much-heralded dual-management system with Roy Evans was not proving as successful as the club had envisaged.

His pedigree as a manager is impeccable. Having made a name for himself in the French lower leagues, Houllier went on to manage Lens and Paris St Germain, taking the latter to the French title.

This opened the door to international recognition and, after a spell as Michel Platini's number two, Houllier assumed control of the French national team. Failure to qualify for the 1994 World Cup cost him his job, but he remained a key figure in the emergence of *Les Bleus* as a footballing power in his role as national technical director.

LEAGUE POSITION

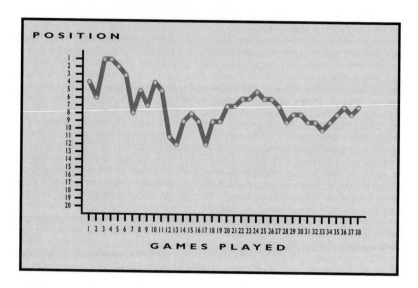

THE GOALS

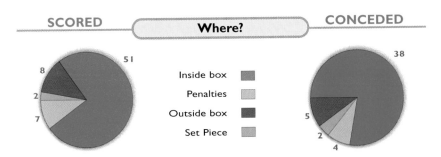

SCORED | Where? | CONCEDED

51 — 8 — 2 — 7 — 38 — 5 — 2 — 4

- Inside box
- Penalties
- Outside box
- Set Piece

They may have had their problems in defence, but Liverpool's attack was red-hot for most of the 1998–99 Carling Premiership campaign. The Merseysiders amassed 68 goals in total, second only to champions Manchester United, the majority of which were from inside the box. Liverpool scored seven times from the spot, more than any other team. Gerard Houllier's side conceded 85.7% of goals from inside their area, slightly above the Premiership average.

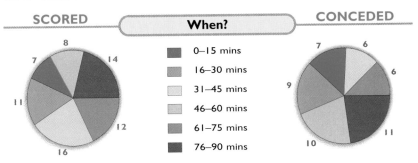

SCORED | When? | CONCEDED

8 — 7 — 14 — 11 — 12 — 16 — 7 — 6 — 6 — 9 — 10 — 11

- 0–15 mins
- 16–30 mins
- 31–45 mins
- 46–60 mins
- 61–75 mins
- 76–90 mins

Liverpool were one of only four sides whose ratio of first-half goals at least matched that of the second half. Houllier's men scored more times in the opening 45 minutes than all their Premiership rivals, netting 34 goals in each half. They scored a splendid 16 goals between 30 and 45 minutes, but going into the one-hour mark they let in more than they scored, the only period in which they did so all season.

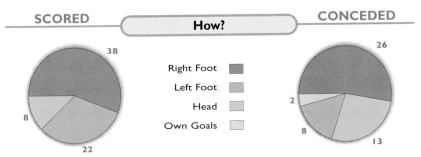

SCORED | How? | CONCEDED

38 — 8 — 22 — 26 — 2 — 8 — 13

- Right Foot
- Left Foot
- Head
- Own Goals

According to Opta's stats, Liverpool were collectively weak in the air. They scored just 11.8% of their goals with their heads, the fourth-worst ratio of any Premiership team. In defence, more than a quarter of the goals Liverpool conceded were from headers and only Southampton conceded more headed goals in the league. The Anfield club scored the most left-footed goals in the league, thanks in part to strikes by Robbie Fowler and Patrik Berger.

LIVERPOOL

	BABB	BERGER	BJORNEBYE	CARRAGHER	DUNDEE	FERRI	FOWLER	GERRARD	HARKNESS	HEGGEM
APPEARANCES										
Start	24	30	20	34	0	0	23	4	4	27
Sub	1	2	3	0	3	2	2	8	2	2
Minutes on pitch	2107	2579	1860	2988	38	49	2010	401	230	2302
GOAL ATTEMPTS										
Goals	0	7	0	1	0	0	14	0	0	2
Shots on target	2	32	6	2	0	0	31	0	1	7
Shots off target	4	30	1	8	2	0	36	4	0	7
Shooting accuracy	33%	52%	86%	20%	0%	0%	46%	0%	100%	50%
PASSING										
Goal assists	1	3	2	2	0	0	5	0	0	2
Long passes	102	103	159	173	0	0	51	28	17	82
Short passes	611	1162	858	822	18	13	764	171	84	830
PASS COMPLETION										
Own half %	94%	88%	91%	92%	100%	83%	81%	95%	96%	91%
Opposition half %	66%	73%	73%	62%	75%	71%	68%	67%	82%	74%
CROSSING										
Total crosses	3	119	94	6	0	0	11	11	3	68
Cross completion %	33%	39%	17%	67%	0%	0%	18%	45%	33%	26%
DRIBBLING										
Dribbles & runs	14	106	28	13	0	0	48	7	2	138
Dribble completion %	64%	73%	96%	92%	0%	0%	71%	57%	100%	71%
DEFENDING										
Tackles made	71	103	64	110	1	3	58	29	5	96
Tackles won %	80%	62%	78%	60%	100%	33%	47%	48%	60%	51%
Blocks	15	4	12	36	0	0	3	6	1	4
Clearances	301	46	126	423	0	2	19	38	5	138
Interceptions	27	29	18	46	0	0	11	6	3	20
DISCIPLINE										
Fouls	34	29	35	30	0	3	25	5	4	18
Offside	0	11	0	0	0	0	11	0	0	3
Yellow cards	6	4	5	5	0	0	4	1	2	2
Red cards	0	0	0	1	0	0	0	0	0	0

GOALKEEPER NAME	START/ (SUB)	TIME ON PITCH	GOALS CONCEDED	MINS/GOALS CONCEDED	SAVES MADE	SAVES/ SHOTS
FRIEDEL	12	1080	15	72	36	71%
JAMES	26	2340	34	68.8	84	71%

PLAYERS' STATISTICS

	INCE	KVARME	LEONHARDSEN	MATTEO	McATEER	McMANAMAN	MURPHY	OWEN	REDKNAPP	RIEDLE	SONG	STAUNTON	THOMPSON	TOTAL	RANK
	34	2	7	16	6	25	0	30	33	16	10	31	4		
	0	5	2	4	7	3	1	0	1	18	3	0	10		
	3001	217	654	1560	715	2221	14	2528	2935	1743	905	2568	524		
	6	0	1	1	0	4	0	18	8	5	0	0	1	68	2nd
	26	0	3	1	0	15	0	49	30	15	0	4	5	229	3rd
	36	0	0	5	3	18	0	36	45	25	3	3	10	276	=2nd
	42%	0%	100%	17%	0%	45%	0%	58%	40%	38%	0%	57%	33%	45%	10th
	4	0	0	2	1	6	0	5	4	4	1	0	1	43	3rd
	159	8	8	72	74	94	0	25	433	13	46	326	39	2012	5th
	1440	69	319	742	432	1387	5	607	1779	569	258	987	269	14196	3rd
	90%	79%	87%	90%	94%	89%	100%	88%	89%	82%	86%	93%	86%	90%	6th
	79%	74%	78%	80%	75%	77%	50%	77%	74%	71%	64%	65%	65%	73%	5th
	9	0	7	37	32	46	0	39	128	9	21	69	24	736	11th
	11%	0%	14%	24%	28%	26%	0%	31%	34%	22%	38%	26%	33%	29%	7th
	59	1	12	43	17	251	0	157	100	41	21	19	19	1096	3rd
	73%	0%	100%	100%	76%	76%	0%	58%	81%	56%	71%	84%	89%	74%	3rd
	147	19	19	50	22	68	2	33	84	56	37	74	15	1167	9th
	69%	58%	68%	68%	64%	47%	0%	42%	67%	54%	65%	61%	60%	61%	11th
	18	1	0	19	1	4	0	2	5	6	6	20	3	166	19th
	107	23	5	137	32	21	1	7	33	14	104	279	10	1908	16th
	34	3	5	16	12	17	0	14	27	10	17	32	8	355	6th
	49	4	11	28	9	20	1	19	38	49	11	24	13	460	19th
	1	0	3	1	0	3	0	40	2	29	3	1	5	113	17th
	9	0	0	2	0	2	0	1	6	7	3	2	3	65	12th
	0	0	0	1	1	0	0	0	0	0	0	0	0	3	=11th

CROSSES CAUGHT	CROSSES PUNCHED	CROSSES NOT CLAIMED	CATCH SUCCESS	THROWS/ SHORT KICKS	% COMPLETION	LONG KICKS	% COMPLETION
42	12	7	93%	164	95%	209	28%
72	13	11	95%	289	94%	464	29%

PLAYER OF THE SEASON

PLAYER	INDEX SCORE
PATRIK BERGER	1061
Paul Ince	1018
Michael Owen	1002
Jamie Redknapp	1001
Steve McManaman	951
Robbie Fowler	939
Vegard Heggem	869
Jamie Carragher	795
Phil Babb	785
David James	537

After making just nine starts for Liverpool in 1997–98, Patrik Berger began the new season with plenty to prove.

With the club riding high in the Carling Premiership table Berger was in terrific form, scoring four goals in the first seven games in all competitions. It was a run that firmly established his place in the first team – and he made the left-wing berth his own in 1998–99.

His quality crossing and finishing ensured he finished the season as Liverpool's highest-scoring player in the Carling Opta Season Index, with an average of 1,061 points a match.

In the club's greatest traditions the midfield saw plenty of the ball, with Paul Ince and Jamie Redknapp making more than 3,800 passes between them over the course of 1998–99. Ince's tough-tackling style and Redknapp's ability to pick players out with short and long passes were enough to see them figure highly in the top 10.

Both men weighed in with their fair share of goals, but it was left to Michael Owen to do the most damage to opposition defences. The young striker ended the season with the Golden Boot, having scored a total of 18 goals in the Premiership. Coping with the burden of expectation after his dynamic World Cup display appeared to be no problem for the teenage sensation.

Steve McManaman bade farewell to the club with a fine second half of the season. He scored an average of 951 Carling Opta Index points over the campaign.

Others in the top 10 failed to find the same consistency as the likes of Berger and Owen. Robbie Fowler's season was hit by injury and suspension, right-back Vegard Heggem also succumbed to the treatment table, while Jamie Carragher and Phil Babb struggled to defend impeccably on a regular basis.

FIVE OF THE BEST

Liverpool finished in seventh place after a turbulent 1998–99 season. The Reds were top of the league at the start of September but their subsequent slump into mid-table saw the end of Roy Evans as joint manager, with Gerard Houllier put in sole charge. His French revolution begins now — and the success-starved Kop will hope better times are just around the corner.

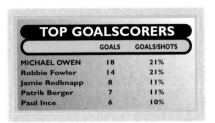

TOP GOALSCORERS		
	GOALS	GOALS/SHOTS
MICHAEL OWEN	18	21%
Robbie Fowler	14	21%
Jamie Redknapp	8	11%
Patrik Berger	7	11%
Paul Ince	6	10%

Golden boy Michael Owen began the 1998–99 season under immense pressure to perform, after his breathtaking displays in the World Cup. Eighteen league goals later the teenage strike sensation walked off with the Golden Boot to underline just how far he has come. Robbie Fowler slotted home 14 in a season hit by injury, scandal and suspension, with both main strikers scoring with more than one in five of their shots. The midfield also weighed in with valuable strikes.

Jamie Redknapp still has much to prove in an England jersey, but for Liverpool he continues to provide the class and creativity in midfield. One of only three Premiership players to make more than 2,000 passes in 1998–99, Redknapp struck up a fearsome midfield partnership with Paul Ince, who was the side's most pinpoint passer. Steve McManaman, another player who has failed to reproduce his club form for England, will be sorely missed thanks to his accurate passing and mesmeric dribbling skills.

TOP PASSERS		
	SUCC PASSES	COMPLETION
JAMIE REDKNAPP	1,733	78%
Paul Ince	1,337	84%
Steve McManaman	1,178	80%
Steve Staunton	1,050	80%
Patrik Berger	985	78%

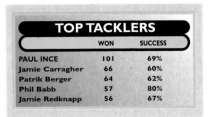

TOP TACKLERS		
	WON	SUCCESS
PAUL INCE	101	69%
Jamie Carragher	66	60%
Patrik Berger	64	62%
Phil Babb	57	80%
Jamie Redknapp	56	67%

Never one to refuse a challenge, Paul Ince was comfortably the club's top tackler in 1998–99 winning more than 100 challenges over the course of the campaign. Defender Phil Babb, who did not play as much as other stoppers in the squad, was the most likely to win possession back, as can be seen by his 80% tackle success rate. Jamie Carragher, wide man Patrik Berger and midfielder Jamie Redknapp also feature in Liverpool's top five.

With midfield tenacity inevitably comes disciplinary woe; but although Paul Ince racked up more points than anyone else in the squad, there is no way Liverpool could be labelled "dirty". No player conceded more than 50 fouls and no one reached double figures in terms of league bookings. Of course, these statistics do not include the European disciplinary debacle in Valencia when both Paul Ince and Steve McManaman were red-carded.

DISCIPLINE		
	POINTS	FOULS & CARDS
PAUL INCE	76	49F, 9Y, 0R
Karl-Heinz Riedle	70	49F, 7Y, 0R
Jamie Redknapp	56	38F, 6Y, 0R
Phil Babb	52	34F, 6Y, 0R
Jamie Carragher	51	30F, 5Y, 1R

ACTION	BABB	BERGER	BJORNEBYE	CARRAGHER	FOWLER	HARKNESS	HEGGEM	INCE	JAMES	McATEER	OWEN	REDKNAPP	RIEDLE	STAUNTON	TOTAL	ASTON VILLA
Time on pitch	90	64	80	90	90	10	90	90	90	26	79	90	11	90	990	968
GOALS																
Goal	–	–	–	–	3	–	–	1	–	–	–	–	–	–	4	2
Shot on target	–	1	–	–	2	–	–	–	–	–	2	–	–	–	5	7
Shot off target	–	1	1	1	–	–	1	–	–	–	1	–	–	–	4	9
Blocked shot	–	–	–	–	–	–	1	–	–	–	–	–	–	–	–	5
Own goal	–	–	–	–	–	–	–	–	–	–	–	–	–	–	–	–
PASSES																
Pass to own player	21	25	29	14	36	2	24	25	–	8	21	46	7	15	273	379
Pass to opposition	5	7	17	5	12	–	8	7	–	–	–	20	–	7	90	98
Cross to own player	–	1	3	–	–	–	4	–	–	–	–	3	–	5	5	14
Cross to opposition player	–	–	–	–	–	–	1	–	–	–	–	3	–	10	10	15
Goal assist	–	–	–	–	–	–	–	–	–	–	–	2	–	4	4	2
Pass completion %	81%	79%	59%	74%	75%	67%	68%	78%	0%	100%	96%	69%	100%	68%	74%	78%
TACKLES & CLEARANCES																
Tackle	6	2	3	4	4	–	4	4	–	2	1	2	2	5	39	28
Clearances, blocks and interceptions	22	1	5	16	4	3	9	7	–	1	–	1	–	22	91	68
DRIBBLES & RUNS																
Dribble ball retained	–	1	1	–	–	–	7	1	–	1	2	3	–	1	17	15
Dribbles ball lost	–	–	–	–	3	–	–	–	–	–	–	2	–	–	7	15
Dribble success %	0%	100%	100%	0%	0%	0%	88%	100%	0%	100%	67%	60%	0%	100%	71%	50%
DISCIPLINE																
Fouls	2	1	3	–	2	–	–	–	–	–	2	–	–	–	10	12
Penalty conceded	–	–	–	–	–	–	–	–	1	–	–	–	–	–	1	–
Free kick - offside	–	–	–	–	–	–	–	–	–	–	–	–	–	–	–	2
Yellow cards	1	–	–	–	–	–	–	–	1	–	–	–	–	3	3	–
Red cards	–	–	–	–	–	–	–	–	–	–	–	–	–	–	–	1
GOALKEEPERS																
Distribution to own player	–	–	–	–	–	–	–	–	13	–	–	–	–	13	13	10
Distribution to opposition player	–	–	–	–	–	–	–	–	26	–	–	–	–	26	26	14
Goalkeeper distribution%	–	–	–	–	–	–	–	–	33%	–	–	–	–	33%	33%	42%
Save	–	–	–	–	–	–	–	–	7	–	–	–	–	7	7	5
Ball caught	–	–	–	–	–	–	–	–	6	–	–	–	–	6	6	2
Ball dropped	–	–	–	–	–	–	–	–	–	–	–	–	–	–	–	–
Goal conceded	–	–	–	–	–	–	–	–	2	–	–	–	–	2	2	4

Table-topping Aston Villa were enjoying their best-ever start to a season, while Liverpool had won just once at Villa Park in their 13 previous visits. Also, the Reds had just suffered two miserable home defeats in a row. "Home win" was the confident prediction from most pundits.

November 21, 1998

2–4

ASTON VILLA
LIVERPOOL

But Liverpool had one reason to feel optimistic: Robbie Fowler. The England striker had already bagged 11 goals in 10 games against Villa, and was to prove the star of a thrilling Carling Premiership match.

It was a breathless opening, and after just two minutes the Merseysiders had snatched the lead, an unmarked Paul Ince heading home Patrik Berger's corner. Three minutes later Fowler signalled his intentions by forcing a terrific save from Michael Oakes. But then at the other end Stan Collymore was put clean through by Dion Dublin, only to see his mis-hit shot saved by David James's legs.

This was high-octane stuff, and just 60 seconds later Michael Owen's pinpoint cross was headed into the net by Fowler.

There were still only eight minutes on the clock when Collymore was pulled up for a high challenge on Steve Harkness. The Reds' fans were baying for a red card, but referee Peter Jones only cautioned him as Harkness was stretchered off.

Liverpool continued to pile on the pressure, with Owen and Jamie Carragher going close. At the other end, Dublin saw his first-time drive smash against the upright. Worse was to follow for Villa when Collymore headed Paul Merson's brilliant cross wide from just four yards out.

Two minutes into the second half, Villa forced themselves back into contention when Dublin volleyed home Merson's cross for his sixth goal in three games. But

within seven minutes Fowler had bagged his second after a terrific run by Vegard Heggem.

On 64 minutes Dublin scored again, literally walking Collymore's cross into the goal, but the home fans were silenced within a minute when Fowler coolly slotted home Redknapp's cross at the other end for a fine hat-trick.

There was no let-up in the action. Liverpool were still celebrating when Collymore reacted angrily to Owen's high challenge and was sent off against his old club. Then substitute Julian Joachim charged into the box with his first touch and was sent sprawling by David James. But the Liverpool 'keeper made amends by saving Dublin's penalty.

Carling Opta's statistics show Villa had the bulk of possession, making over 100 more passes. They also made 23 efforts at goal against Liverpool's 13. But the Merseysiders' finishing was clinical, with man of the match Fowler taking advantage of some slack marking from Villa's back three to register an Opta Index points score of 2,697.

The game was Villa's first defeat of the season, but they were beaten twice more before Christmas. For Liverpool, this was Gerard Houllier's first victory in sole charge. They went on to win four of their next six matches before drawing with Arsenal and crushing Southampton 7–1 on their way to a seventh-placed finish.

ACTION	BERGER	FOWLER	GERRARD	HEGGEM	INCE	JAMES	MATTEO	McMANAMAN	OWEN	REDKNAPP	RIEDLE	SONG	STAUNTON	TOTAL	EVERTON
Time on pitch	90	85	20	70	90	90	90	90	90	90	5	90	90	990	990
GOALS															
Goal	1	2	–	–	–	–	–	–	–	–	–	–	–	3	2
Shot on target	–	1	–	–	–	–	–	–	3	1	–	–	–	5	–
Shot off target	–	–	–	–	3	–	1	1	3	–	–	2	2	11	4
Blocked shot	2	2	–	–	–	–	–	–	–	–	–	–	–	6	4
Own goal	–	–	–	–	–	–	–	–	–	–	–	–	–	–	–
PASSES															
Pass to own player	39	33	2	27	27	–	45	31	11	45	2	16	33	311	194
Pass to opposition	11	8	1	6	9	–	9	15	8	14	–	5	9	95	109
Cross to own player	2	–	–	2	–	–	3	2	–	2	–	–	–	12	3
Cross to opposition player	2	2	–	4	–	–	3	2	1	6	–	–	–	22	18
Goal assist	–	–	–	–	–	–	–	–	–	–	–	–	–	–	1
Pass completion %	76%	77%	67%	74%	75%	0%	80%	67%	55%	70%	100%	73%	77%	73%	61%
TACKLES & CLEARANCES															
Tackle	4	2	2	–	8	–	2	–	1	3	1	1	2	26	40
Clearances, blocks and interceptions	4	–	7	4	4	–	6	2	–	2	1	25	8	64	54
DRIBBLES & RUNS															
Dribble ball retained	3	5	–	2	1	–	5	7	1	2	–	–	2	27	8
Dribbles ball lost	4	–	–	–	–	–	–	2	3	1	–	–	–	11	3
Dribble success %	43%	100%	0%	100%	100%	0%	100%	78%	25%	67%	0%	0%	100%	71%	73%
DISCIPLINE															
Fouls	1	–	–	1	1	–	1	–	1	–	–	1	–	10	17
Penalty conceded	–	–	–	–	–	–	–	–	–	–	–	–	–	–	–
Free kick - offside	3	–	–	–	–	–	–	–	–	–	–	–	–	4	7
Yellow cards	–	–	–	–	–	–	–	–	–	–	–	–	–	4	3
Red cards	–	–	–	–	–	–	–	–	–	–	–	–	–	–	–
GOALKEEPERS															
Distribution to own player	–	–	–	–	–	14	–	–	–	–	–	–	–	14	12
Distribution to opposition player	–	–	–	–	–	14	–	–	–	–	–	–	–	14	16
Goalkeeper distribution%	–	–	–	–	–	50%	–	–	–	–	–	–	–	50%	43%
Save	–	–	–	–	–	1	–	–	–	–	–	–	–	1	5
Ball caught	–	–	–	–	–	7	–	–	–	–	–	–	–	7	2
Ball dropped	–	–	–	–	–	–	–	–	–	–	–	–	–	–	–
Goal conceded	–	–	–	–	–	2	–	–	–	–	–	–	–	2	3

Having picked up just one point from their previous four games, Liverpool were in poor form going into the 160th Merseyside derby. The teams had fought out a drab goalless draw in October — but that was to be no indication of the drama about to unfold at Anfield on a sunny Easter Saturday.

April 3, 1999

3–2

LIVERPOOL
EVERTON

Many supporters were still taking their seats when Michael Ball's long throw was headed out by Steve Staunton. The ball dropped to Olivier Dacourt, who scored with a fine 25-yard left-foot volley. Forty seconds gone: 1–0 to Everton.

But that was the cue for Gerard Houllier's men to take charge of the match. In the 15th minute Steve McManaman's cross from the right found Ince, who was bundled off the ball by Marco Materazzi. Referee David Elleray pointed straight to the penalty spot.

Up stepped Robbie Fowler, six days before an FA hearing over his recent clash with Graeme Le Saux. He rammed in the penalty low to Thomas Myhre's left but then dived to the floor in front of the Everton supporters and crawled along the goal-line, pretending to snort the white line. Sports sub-editors everywhere were busy writing headlines within seconds.

Six minutes later, McManaman's breathtaking 20-yard volley was tipped over by Myhre. Patrik Berger floated in the corner, McManaman flicked it on and Fowler gleefully headed in, sparking another frenzy of celebration.

Everton almost equalized when Materazzi hit the post, but after the break Michael Owen, Berger and Rigobert Song all threatened a third goal. It arrived in the 83rd minute, when Redknapp's corner was headed away by Dacourt, only for Berger to deliver a volley into the bottom corner.

Then the teenagers took centre-stage. First 18-year-old Francis Jeffers turned with his back to goal and volleyed the ball past David James. Then, twice in the last three minutes, 19-year-old Danny Cadamarteri saw shots dramatically cleared off the line by 18-year-old Liverpool substitute Steven Gerrard.

The second Gerrard clearance was the last kick of the game, but the repercussions of Fowler's controversial goal celebrations reverberated around the footballing world long after Anfield had emptied. He was fined by his club and then handed a six-match ban and a further fine by the FA.

For Liverpool fans, though, that did not detract from arguably the sweetest victory of the season. The statistics from the game showed they thoroughly deserved the win, creating 25 goalscoring opportunities to Everton's 11. They also dominated possession, completing 311 passes to the Toffees' 194.

Curtain call: Manchester United celebrate the Championship in the Old Trafford "Theatre of Dreams"

MANCHESTER UNITED

ADDRESS

Sir Matt Busby Way, Old Trafford,
Manchester M16 0RA

CONTACT NUMBERS

Telephone: 0161 872 1661
Fax: 0161 876 5502
24hr Information: 0161 872 0199
Superstore: 0161 877 6077
Museum and Tour Centre:
0161 877 4002
Website: www.manutd.co.uk

SPONSORS

Sharp

FANZINES

Red Issue, Red News,
United We Stand, Northern Exposure,
Blackburn Reds, Red Attitude,
Walking Down The Warwick Road

KEY PERSONNEL

Chairman: C M Edwards
Directors: C M Edwards, J M Edelson,
Sir Bobby Charlton CBE, E M Watkins,
R L Olive, D Gill, P Kenyon
Club Secretary: K R Merrett
Manager: Sir Alex Ferguson

COLOURS

Home: Red shirts, white shorts,
black stockings
Away: All black or all white

NICKNAME

The Red Devils

20 FACTS

1 Manchester United started life in 1878 as Newton Heath Lancashire and Yorkshire Railway Cricket and Football Club, gaining admission to the English Second Division in 1892. But Newton Heath went bankrupt in 1902 and Manchester United were formed.

2 The club have been league champions 12 times – in 1907–08, 1910–11, 1951–52, 1955–56, 1956–57, 1964–65, 1966–67, 1992–93, 1993–94, 1995–96, 1996–97 and 1998–99.

3 United have won the FA Cup a record 10 times – in 1909, 1948, 1963, 1977, 1983, 1985, 1990, 1994, 1996 and 1999. The club have also appeared in more FA Cup finals than any other team (15).

4 They won the Football League Cup once – in 1992.

5 United won the European Cup in 1967–68 and 1998–99 and the European Cup Winners Cup in 1990–91.

6 Sir Bobby Charlton holds the club records for the most appearances and goals scored, playing 756 times in all competitions between 1956 and 1973 and scoring 248 times in all competitions.

7 Denis Law shares the record with Kenny Dalglish for the most goals at international level for Scotland, scoring 30 times in 55 appearances.

8 Andy Cole holds the record for the most goals scored in a Carling Premiership match. He scored five times in the 9–0 victory over Ipswich Town at Old Trafford in March 1995.

9 The club holds the record for the largest-ever away victory in the Premiership, an 8–1 success at Nottingham Forest in December 1998.

10 Manchester United hold the record for the highest-ever league attendance – 83,260 against Arsenal at Maine Road in January 1948.

11 The Red Devils hold the record for the lowest-ever attendance at an FA Cup semi-final. Only 17,987 fans watched the 1995 replay with Crystal Palace at Villa Park.

12 Current manager Sir Alex Ferguson is the longest-serving manager in the Premiership. He has been with the club since November 1986.

13 Manchester United's most famous manager, Sir Matt Busby, spent the greater part of his playing career with two of United's fiercest rivals – Manchester City and Liverpool.

14 Ex-United goalkeeper Peter Schmeichel played as an outfield player for Danish League team Hvidovre during the 1985 season, scoring six goals.

15 Manchester United finished the 1998–99 Premiership season as champions. Their league record was:

Pld	W	D	L	F	A	Pts
38	22	13	3	80	37	79

16 Alex Ferguson's side reached the AXA-sponsored FA Cup final, where they defeated Newcastle United 2–0. They beat Middlesbrough 3–1, Liverpool 2–1 and Fulham 1–0, all at Old Trafford, before Chelsea were beaten 2–0 in a Stamford Bridge replay. They reached the final in a Villa Park replay against Arsenal, winning 2–1 after the first game had finished 0–0.

17 In the Worthington Cup, the club beat Bury 2–0 and Nottingham Forest 2–1 at Old Trafford before losing 3–1 at Tottenham Hotspur.

18 Manchester United completed the treble by winning the Champions League. United beat LKS Lodz of Poland 2–0 on aggregate in a Champions League qualifier and drew their first Group D game against Barcelona 3–3 at Old Trafford. They then drew 2–2 at Bayern Munich before Brondby of Denmark were annihilated 6–2 away and 5–0 at home. The team again drew 3–3 with Barcelona, then a 1–1 draw at home to Bayern Munich ensured qualification for the quarter-finals. After beating Inter Milan 2–0 at home, the club secured a 1–1 draw in the San Siro and, against Juventus, United fought back from 2–0 down to win the away leg 3–2. They met Bayern Munich in the final, winning 2–1.

19 The top goalscorer in all competitions for Manchester United was Dwight Yorke with 29 goals.

20 Manchester United's disciplinary record was the fifth-best in the Premiership. They committed 481 fouls, earned 59 yellow cards and suffered three dismissals.

SEASON REVIEW

Finishing the 1997–98 season empty-handed was a big disappointment to United. Manager Alex Ferguson turned to retail therapy. Jaap Stam, the giant Dutch centre-back, was prised away from PSV Eindhoven, thanks to a world record fee for a defender of £10 million.

Then, with the season just a week old, Ferguson shelled out £12.75 million on Aston Villa striker Dwight Yorke. Both purchases raised eyebrows, with Stam having failed to impress in the World Cup and Yorke hardly perceived as the prolific goal-poacher many pundits believed United needed.

But both men were to play key roles in the most glorious season ever experienced at Old Trafford.

Few would have predicted the successes to come when Leicester City stormed into a two-goal lead at Old Trafford on the opening day of the Premiership season. But Teddy Sheringham pulled one back and in the last minute, World Cup villain David Beckham curled in a magnificent free kick to steal a point. Last-gasp strikes were to be a feature of United's campaign.

By the end of September, United had won only three of their first six Premiership games, having been whipped 3–0 at Highbury by Arsenal – and were in fifth place. They had also blown a two-goal lead against Barcelona in the Champions League to draw 3–3.

But Yorke's goals soon started to flow, and his partnership with Andy Cole was one of the delights of the season. They combined to devastating effect in wins over Southampton, Wimbledon and Everton and helped put 11 goals past Brondby in two one-sided Champions League games.

A blow to Ferguson came when his assistant for seven years, Brian Kidd, left the club to manage struggling Blackburn Rovers. Fergie replaced him with Jim Smith's assistant at Derby County, Steve McLaren.

Tottenham beat a shadow United in the Worthington Cup fifth round and a shock defeat by Middlesbrough on December 21 left the side third in the table. But that was to be the last time any team would beat Alex Ferguson's men all season. Relentless progress in the other cup competitions was matched by astonishing league form.

United won 13 and drew six of their last 19 league games to take the title on the last day of the season. There had been nervous moments, such as the match at Liverpool, when Paul Ince equalized for the Merseysiders in the last minute. Arsenal had matched the Reds all the way and, had Tottenham earned even a point at Old Trafford in the final match, the Gunners would have retained the title.

Progress to the Champions League final was assured, thanks to a thrilling 3–2 victory at Juventus in the semi-final. And in the FA Cup semi-final, United squared up to Arsenal in another epic tie, in which Beckham and Ryan Giggs scored spectacular goals in a gripping replay at Villa Park.

The final was less memorable, United easing to a 2–0 Wembley win over Newcastle without breaking sweat.

Then, on May 26, United faced German giants Bayern Munich at Barcelona's Nou Camp stadium on the brink of the Treble. As had been the hallmark of their season, United left it very late and trailed 1–0 going into stoppage-time. But, in one of the most extraordinary finishes ever seen in a major final, substitute strikers Teddy Sheringham and Ole Gunnar Solskjaer scored within two minutes of each other to secure the one remaining trophy Alex Ferguson craved.

It was simply a stunning end to a stunning season. It will surely be many, many years before the Premiership heavyweights achieve another record to top this one.

> **"Everybody was disappointed when we won nothing last year..."**
>
> Alex Ferguson

MANCHESTER UNITED

DATE	OPPONENT	SCORE	ATT.	BECKHAM	BERG	BLOMQVIST	BROWN	BUTT	COLE	CRUYFF	CURTIS	GIGGS	GREENING
15.8.98	Leicester H	2–2	55,052	90¹	s45	–	–	90	90	–	–	90	–
22.8.98	West Ham A	0–0	25,912	90	90	–	–	90	70	–	–	90	–
9.9.98	Charlton H	4–1	55,147	90	s33	90	–	–	s22	–	–	–	–
12.9.98	Coventry H	2–0	55,193	78□	s1	s12	–	s12	–	–	–	78	–
20.9.99	Arsenal A	0–3	38,142	90	90	90	–	50■	–	–	–	90	–
24.9.98	Liverpool H	2–0	55,181	90	–	–	–	s2	s21	–	–	90□	–
3.10.98	Southampton A	3–0	15,251	90	–	72	s12	90	90¹	s18¹	–	–	–
17.10.98	Wimbledon H	5–1	55,265	57¹	–	90	90	–	90²	s33	s17	65¹	–
24.10.98	Derby Co A	1–1	30,867	90□	–	s9	90	81	90□	s9¹	–	81	–
31.10.98	Everton A	4–1*	40,087	90	–	90¹	90	–	90¹	–	–	–	–
8.11.98	Newcastle H	0–0	55,174	90□	–	88□	60	s5	90	–	–	–	–
14.11.98	Blackburn H	3–2	55,198	90	–	66	–	90	90	s19	90	–	–
21.11.98	Sheff Wed A	1–3	39,475	90	–	57	s25	s33	90¹	–	–	–	–
29.11.98	Leeds Utd H	3–2	55,172	–	s13	–	90	90¹	65	–	–	s25	–
5.12.98	Aston Villa A	1–1	39,241	90	–	45	90	s20	70	–	–	s45	–
12.12.98	Tottenham A	2–2	36,058	90□	s45	s3	–	90□	s15	–	–	87	–
16.12.98	Chelsea H	1–1	55,159	s29	–	76	90□	90	90¹	–	–	s14	–
19.12.98	Middlesbro H	2–3	55,152	64□	–	–	–	90¹	90	–	–	90	–
26.12.98	Nott'm For H	3–0	55,216	90	90	s12	–	90	–	–	–	78¹	s20
29.12.98	Chelsea A	0–0	34,741	90	–	–	–	90	90□	–	–	90	–
10.1.99	West Ham H	4–1	55,180	–	90	90	78	78	90²	s6	–	90	–
16.1.99	Leicester A	6–2	22,091	90	90	90□	45	–	90²	–	–	90	–
31.1.99	Charlton A	1–0	20,043	71	90	–	–	82	90	–	–	90	–
3.2.99	Derby Co H	1–0	55,174	–	–	s80	–	90	–	–	–	10	–
6.2.99	Nott'm For A	8–1	30,025	90	–	75	–	s15	90²	–	s19	–	–
17.2.99	Arsenal H	1–1	55,171	90	–	60	–	78	90¹	–	–	s12	–
20.2.99	Coventry A	1–0	22,594	90	s45	–	–	–	74□	–	–	90¹	–
27.2.99	Southampton H	2–1	55,316	90	90	–	–	45	s23	–	–	90	–
13.3.99	Newcastle A	2–1	36,776	90	90	–	–	–	90²	–	–	73	–
21.3.99	Everton H	3–1	55,182	71¹	90	–	–	90	71	–	s1	–	s19
3.4.99	Wimbledon A	1–1	26,121	90¹	90□	73	–	–	90	–	–	–	–
17.4.99	Sheff Wed H	3–0	55,270	–	–	75	90	90	–	–	–	–	s27
25.4.99	Leeds Utd A	1–1	40,255	84	–	76	90	90□	90¹	–	–	–	–
1.5.99	Aston Villa H	2–1*	55,189	90¹	–	63	s12	90	–	–	–	–	–
5.5.99	Liverpool A	2–2	44,702	90	–	77	–	s13	77	–	–	–	–
9.5.99	Middlesbro A	1–0	34,655	90	–	66	–	s65	s24	–	–	–	–
12.5.99	Blackburn A	0–0	30,436	90□	–	–	–	90□	71	–	–	90	–
16.5.99	Tottenham H	2–1	55,189	90¹	–	–	–	s20	s45¹	–	–	80	–

□ Yellow card, ■ Red card, s Substitute, 90³ Goals scored
*including own goal

1998–99 PREMIERSHIP APPEARANCES

IRWIN	JOHNSEN	KEANE	MAY	G NEVILLE	P NEVILLE	SCHMEICHEL	SCHOLES	SHERINGHAM	SOLSKJAER	STAM	VAN DER GOUW	YORKE	TOTAL
90	90	90	–	78	–	90	90	s12¹□	–	45	–	–	990
90	90□	90	–	52	s38	90	–	s20	–	–	–	90	990
57	90	90	–	–	90	90	90	s22	68²	90	–	68²	990
–	89¹	90	–	90	90	90	90	–	90	90	–	90¹	990
90	–	90□	–	90	–	90	–	–	–	90	–	90	950
90¹	–	90	–	90	90□	90	88¹□	–	69	90□	–	90	990
78	–	90□	–	90	90	–	–	s18	–	90	90	72¹	990
–	–	90	–	90	73	–	s25	–	–	90□	90	90¹	990
–	–	90	–	81□	90	90	s9	–	–	90	–	90	990
s25	–	90□	–	90□	65	90	90□	–	–	90	–	90¹	990
90	s25	90	–	90	–	90	90	–	s2	90□	–	90□	990
–	–	s10	–	90	90	90	61²□	–	s24	90□	–	90¹	990
65	–	84	–	90	90	90	90□	–	s6	90	–	90	990
–	–	90¹	–	90	90□	90	72	s18	90¹	77	–	90	990
90□	–	90	–	90□	–	90	90¹	–	–	90	–	90□	990
–	90□	90	–	40■	90□	90	–	75□	45²	90	–	–	940
90	–	90	–	90□	–	90	85	s5	–	90	–	61	990
90	90	90	–	90	78	90	s26¹	90	s12	–	–	–	990
90	90²	70	–	–	90□	90	62	90	s28	–	–	–	990
90	90	90	–	90	–	90	61	s29	–	90	–	–	990
90	s12	84	–	–	–	–	–	–	s12¹	90	90	90¹	990
90	–	90□	–	–	s45	90	–	–	–	90¹	–	90³	990
90	–	90	–	90	–	90	s8	–	s19	90	–	90¹	990
90	90	90	–	90	–	90	90	–	90	90	–	90¹	990
–	90	71□	–	90	90□	90	90	–	s19⁴	90	–	71²	990
–	90	90□	–	90	90	90	s30	–	–	90	–	90□	990
90	90	90	–	90	s3	90	90□	–	s16	45□	–	87	990
s12	90	s45¹	–	90	78	90	90	–	67	–	–	90¹	990
90□	s17	90	–	90	s4	45	86	–	–	90	s45	90	990
–	90	–	–	90¹	90	90	–	s19	89¹	90	–	90	990
90	90	90	–	90	–	90	90		s17	–	–	90	990
s15	–	63	s27	90	90	–	90¹	90¹	90¹	63	90	–	990
71	–	90□	90□	90	s19	90	s6	s14	–	–	–	90	990
90	90	–	78	90	s27	90	90	90	–	–	–	90	990
75¹■	90	90□	–	90	s13	90	90□	–	–	90	–	90¹	975
90	–	25	90	90□	s1	90	89□	90□	–	90	–	90¹	990
90	90	–	s45	90	75	90	s15	s19	–	45	–	90	990
90	90	90	90	90	s10	90	70	45□	–	–	–	90	990

THE MANAGER

SIR ALEX FERGUSON

Sir Alex Ferguson was appointed manager of Manchester United in November 1986 – and can take most of the credit for the club's greatest-ever period of sustained success.

Victory in the 1990 FA Cup final set the ball rolling, with five Premiership titles and three further FA Cups following.

Ferguson's playing career as a striker began at Queen's Park in the late 1950s. He later played for St Johnstone, Dunfermline, Glasgow Rangers, Falkirk and Ayr United.

His first jobs in management came at East Stirling and St Mirren before moving to Aberdeen, where he won the European Cup Winners Cup in 1983.

The Scottish national job beckoned – and Fergie oversaw the country's bid for glory in the 1986 World Cup. But the chance to manage United prised him away – and Ferguson may well be remembered as the club's greatest ever manager.

He achieved a personal dream by guiding the club to a unique treble in 1998–99, an achievement that ultimately earned him a knighthood. But United probably have him for just two more years. He has indicated he would like to retire at the age of 60.

LEAGUE POSITION

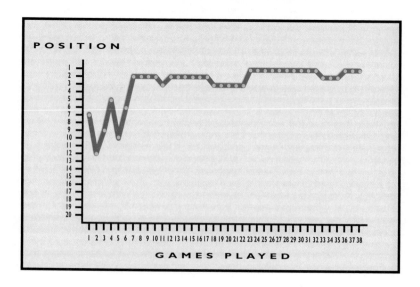

THE GOALS

Where?

SCORED | CONCEDED

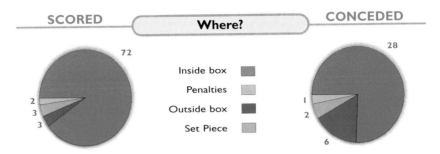

- Inside box
- Penalties
- Outside box
- Set Piece

With the country's hottest strike partnership of Dwight Yorke and Andy Cole up front for Manchester United the Red Devils grabbed 80 goals in all, 74 of these from inside their opponent's 18-yard box. Only Coventry scored a higher proportion of their goals from within the opposition area. The total of 28 goals which United conceded inside their box was the third-lowest in the league, behind Chelsea and Arsenal.

When?

SCORED | CONCEDED

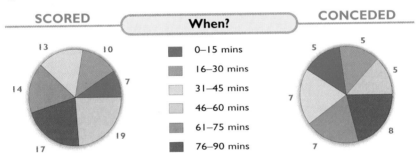

- 0–15 mins
- 16–30 mins
- 31–45 mins
- 46–60 mins
- 61–75 mins
- 76–90 mins

Alex Ferguson's half-time sermons inspired United to score 62.5% of their goals in the second half. United came out with all guns blazing to register 19 goals between the 45th and 60th minutes, the most scored by any club in a 15-minute period. They also fired in the most goals in the final 15 minutes, boosted by Ole Gunnar Solskjaer's lightning four-goal blitz away at Nottingham Forest. The goals the team conceded were spread evenly throughout the 90 minutes.

How?

SCORED | CONCEDED

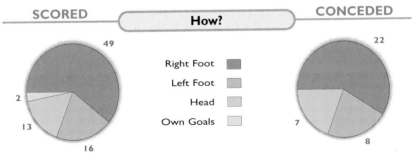

- Right Foot
- Left Foot
- Head
- Own Goals

United's stars bagged nearly a half-century of goals with the right boot, accounting for 61.3% of all their Premiership goals – the second-highest ratio for a top-flight club. The 13 headers they converted were also bettered by just one team, with Yorke netting four of those. The Old Trafford outfit conceded seven headers all season, equating to 18.9% of the goals they leaked during the campaign: very close to the league average.

MANCHESTER UNITED

	BECKHAM	BERG	BLOMQVIST	BROWN	BUTT	COLE	CRUYFF	CURTIS	GIGGS	GREENING
APPEARANCES										
Start	33	10	20	11	22	26	0	1	20	0
Sub	1	6	5	3	9	6	5	3	4	3
Minutes on pitch	2884	1082	1625	952	2039	2358	85	127	1728	66
GOAL ATTEMPTS										
Goals	6	0	1	0	2	17	2	0	3	0
Shots on target	16	2	7	1	13	50	2	0	17	0
Shots off target	33	6	7	3	20	33	2	0	17	2
Shooting accuracy	33%	25%	50%	25%	39%	60%	50%	0%	50%	0%
PASSING										
Goal assists	14	2	3	0	2	2	1	0	2	0
Long passes	304	67	46	68	88	13	3	2	82	0
Short passes	1299	324	713	327	1004	635	46	72	632	45
PASS COMPLETION										
Own half %	87%	98%	93%	89%	92%	90%	86%	94%	85%	94%
Opposition half %	67%	78%	78%	63%	76%	75%	64%	95%	64%	85%
CROSSING										
Total crosses	414	2	115	6	17	26	1	2	134	6
Cross completion %	30%	50%	32%	17%	18%	38%	0%	0%	14%	33%
DRIBBLING										
Dribbles & runs	108	5	133	39	54	61	12	2	119	6
Dribble completion %	84%	100%	77%	64%	67%	67%	92%	100%	63%	83%
DEFENDING										
Tackles made	98	40	68	42	126	50	1	2	54	2
Tackles won %	51%	63%	57%	60%	64%	46%	100%	0%	48%	50%
Blocks	7	9	1	9	9	1	0	0	5	0
Clearances	46	141	18	83	55	2	0	10	18	1
Interceptions	23	12	11	17	23	7	0	0	15	0
DISCIPLINE										
Fouls	30	14	25	13	31	43	2	0	21	3
Offside	9	0	10	0	0	40	0	0	5	0
Yellow cards	6	1	2	1	3	3	0	0	1	0
Red cards	0	0	0	0	1	0	0	0	0	0

GOALKEEPER NAME	START/ (SUB)	TIME ON PITCH	GOALS CONCEDED	MINS/GOALS CONCEDED	SAVES MADE	SAVES/ SHOTS
SCHMEICHEL	34	3015	35	86.1	99	74%
VAN DER GOUW	4 (1)	405	2	202.5	14	88%

PLAYERS' STATISTICS

	IRWIN	JOHNSEN	KEANE	MAY	G NEVILLE	P NEVILLE	SCHOLES	SHERINGHAM	SOLSKJAER	STAM	YORKE	TOTAL	RANK
	26	19	33	4	34	19	24	7	9	30	32		
	3	3	2	2	0	9	7	10	10	0	0		
	2288	1763	2882	420	2951	1789	2143	746	853	2525	2789		
	2	3	2	0	1	0	6	2	12	1	18	80*	1st
	4	5	16	1	4	1	22	9	23	4	36	233	2nd
	3	5	19	3	5	5	26	8	7	9	32	245	5th
	57%	50%	46%	25%	44%	17%	46%	53%	77%	31%	53%	49%	2nd
	2	0	0	0	3	2	9	3	1	1	13	60	1st
	173	37	167	34	298	113	78	21	18	117	36	1765	16th
	972	504	1905	100	1161	890	1054	381	294	795	1299	14452	2nd
	91%	90%	95%	91%	92%	92%	91%	91%	82%	93%	90%	92%	1st
	76%	76%	84%	48%	75%	82%	78%	74%	73%	72%	80%	76%	2nd
	35	6	34	0	65	40	32	16	14	0	16	981	1st
	26%	33%	21%	0%	26%	28%	28%	38%	21%	0%	19%	27%	15th
	42	17	52	2	40	42	42	5	16	15	137	950	7th
	81%	94%	85%	100%	85%	79%	74%	60%	56%	93%	73%	75%	2nd
	105	48	138	18	96	55	80	18	33	144	73	1293	4th
	63%	67%	70%	61%	76%	64%	49%	50%	48%	74%	40%	61%	12th
	13	9	13	8	19	18	8	1	2	25	1	158	20th
	155	203	74	57	232	131	18	9	4	390	7	1705	20th
	26	25	36	3	30	15	22	5	4	62	8	347	7th
	20	28	46	7	31	25	46	12	8	45	31	481	15th
	0	1	4	0	0	1	2	7	11	1	44	135	11th
	2	2	8	1	5	5	7	4	0	5	3	59	=16th
	1	0	0	0	1	0	0	0	0	0	0	3	=11th

*including two own goals

CROSSES CAUGHT	CROSSES PUNCHED	CROSSES NOT CLAIMED	CATCH SUCCESS	THROWS/ SHORT KICKS	% COMPLETION	LONG KICKS	% COMPLETION
90	16	17	94%	378	93%	840	28%
11	3	1	100%	61	97%	102	27%

PLAYER OF THE SEASON

PLAYER	INDEX SCORE
JAAP STAM	1,079
Roy Keane	1,035
Dwight Yorke	1,017
David Beckham	986
Nicky Butt	985
Andy Cole	978
Paul Scholes	926
Denis Irwin	865
Ryan Giggs	844
Gary Neville	821

Having forked out a world record transfer fee for a defender, Alex Ferguson had a right to expect Jaap Stam to perform. The Dutchman, who had had an indifferent World Cup in France, had to fill the void left by the sale of Gary Pallister to Middlesbrough.

Despite some nervous displays in the opening weeks of the 1998–99 season, Stam did not disappoint. His name might not have filled too many back-page headlines, but there is no denying his enormous contribution to United's treble triumph.

Like Pallister, Stam's great strength is his instinctive reading of the game. His cleanness in the tackle and ability to intercept telling passes were crucial as United challenged successfully on three fronts.

He finished the campaign as the highest-scoring Red in the Carling Opta Season Index, a testament to his consistent performances in the heart of the United defence. The £10 million price tag looked no burden whatsoever once Stam had settled in. He even scored his first Premiership goal, a crisp drive in the 6–2 romp at Leicester City.

Roy Keane also played a starring role in United's breathtaking season, even though he missed the Champions League final and all but the first eight minutes of the FA Cup final. His aggression, prolific passing and surging forward runs earned him an average score of 1,035 points.

Dwight Yorke was another player who quickly silenced any critics who had balked at his £12.75 million transfer fee. He bagged 29 goals in all competitions, cashing in on the top-quality service provided from the flanks, especially from David Beckham on the right.

Beckham himself finished fourth in the top 10, enjoying an outstanding campaign after his summer debacle and claiming the taunts from opposition fans actually made him a better player.

FIVE OF THE BEST

Finishing the 1997–98 season empty-handed might well have dented the ambitions of the success-hungry Manchester United stars. But they bounced back from losing their Premiership title in some style, storming to the Championship with the help of inspirational new signings Dwight Yorke and Jaap Stam.

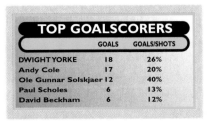

TOP GOALSCORERS

	GOALS	GOALS/SHOTS
DWIGHT YORKE	18	26%
Andy Cole	17	20%
Ole Gunnar Solskjaer	12	40%
Paul Scholes	6	13%
David Beckham	6	12%

Eyebrows were raised at the price tag, but £12.75 million striker Dwight Yorke delivered the goods in devastating style, performing consistently at the very highest level in the Premiership and Champions League. His partnership with Andy Cole will be one of the most enduring memories of the 1998–99 season, with the pair scoring 35 league goals between them. Yorke's strike rate was superb, but even that was eclipsed by the efforts of Ole Gunnar Solskjaer, who struck 12 goals in just nine starts, scoring with 40% of his shots.

Roy Keane's sixth season at Old Trafford was arguably his best for the club. United's inspirational skipper helped protect the defence when they were under pressure and pushed forward to support the attack at every opportunity. But it was his pinpoint passing which impressed the most, and he made more passes than anyone else in the league. Dwight Yorke's inclusion demonstrates how much he likes to drop deep and help create the play, while David Beckham frequently cuts inside for similar reasons.

TOP PASSERS

	SUCC PASSES	COMPLETION
ROY KEANE	1,830	88%
Gary Neville	1,208	83%
David Beckham	1,153	72%
Dwight Yorke	1,082	81%
Denis Irwin	939	82%

TOP TACKLERS

	WON	SUCCESS
JAAP STAM	107	74%
Roy Keane	96	70%
Nicky Butt	81	64%
Gary Neville	73	76%
Denis Irwin	66	63%

After a nervy start to his United career, Jaap Stam made an impact every bit as impressive as Alex Ferguson must have wished for when he sanctioned the defender's £10 million purchase. His dominant performances at the back were characterized by his clean tackling – and he won more challenges than anyone else in the United team. Midfielders Roy Keane and Nicky Butt always snap at the heels of their opponents, while Gary Neville finished the season as the player most likely to win possession, with a 76% success rate.

Midfielders Roy Keane and Paul Scholes, forced to sit out the Champions League final through suspension, also top United's list of league bad boys with 15 bookings between them. Nonetheless, it would be difficult to level accusations of foul play at Alex Ferguson's men. No one conceded more than 50 fouls, something few Premiership sides can say. Nicky Butt and Denis Irwin joined Gary Neville as the only players to be red-carded in the Premiership, though Butt and Keane were also sent off in the cup competitions.

DISCIPLINE

	POINTS	FOULS & CARDS
ROY KEANE	70	46F, 8Y, 0R
Paul Scholes	67	46F, 7Y, 0R
Jaap Stam	60	45F, 5Y, 0R
Andy Cole	52	43F, 3Y, 0R
Gary Neville	52	31F, 5Y, 1R

ACTION	BECKHAM	BLOMQVIST	BUTT	COLE	CURTIS	JOHNSEN	KEANE	G NEVILLE	P NEVILLE	SCHMEICHEL	SCHOLES	SOLSKJAER	STAM	YORKE	TOTAL	NOTTINGHAM FOREST
Time on pitch	90	75	15	90	19	90	71	90	90	90	90	19	90	71	990	990
GOALS																
Goal	–	–	–	2	–	–	–	–	–	–	–	4	–	2	8	1
Shot on target	–	–	–	3	–	–	–	–	–	–	–	1	–	2	6	2
Shot off target	1	–	–	–	–	–	1	–	–	–	1	1	–	1	5	5
Blocked shot	–	–	–	2	–	–	1	–	–	–	–	–	–	1	4	–
Own goal	–	–	–	–	–	–	–	–	–	–	–	–	–	–	–	1
PASSES																
Pass to own player	55	32	12	24	6	18	55	35	45	–	58	6	23	34	403	187
Pass to opposition	12	6	1	11	2	3	11	7	5	–	12	2	7	6	85	94
Cross to own player	10	3	1	–	–	–	–	–	2	–	2	–	–	1	19	5
Cross to opposition player	9	5	–	–	–	–	–	3	–	–	–	–	3	–	20	19
Goal assist	–	–	–	–	–	–	–	–	1	–	3	–	1	–	5	1
Pass completion %	76%	76%	93%	69%	75%	86%	82%	78%	89%	0%	83%	75%	77%	85%	80%	63%
TACKLES & CLEARANCES																
Tackle	3	–	–	3	1	2	1	2	2	–	2	–	5	1	22	16
Clearances, blocks and interceptions	1	–	–	–	3	10	3	6	6	1	1	–	18	–	49	56
DRIBBLES & RUNS																
Dribble ball retained	4	6	–	2	2	–	2	–	–	–	–	1	–	2	19	8
Dribbles ball lost	–	1	–	–	–	–	–	–	–	–	–	–	–	1	2	7
Dribble success %	100%	86%	–	100%	100%	–	100%	–	–	–	–	100%	–	67%	90%	53%
DISCIPLINE																
Fouls	–	–	–	3	–	–	2	1	1	–	3	–	–	–	10	9
Penalty conceded	–	–	–	–	–	–	–	–	–	–	–	–	–	–	–	–
Free kick - offside	–	–	–	3	–	–	–	–	–	–	–	–	–	1	4	4
Yellow cards	–	–	–	–	–	–	1	–	–	–	1	–	–	–	2	1
Red cards	–	–	–	–	–	–	–	–	–	–	–	–	–	–	–	–
GOALKEEPERS																
Distribution to own player	–	–	–	–	–	–	–	–	–	21	–	–	–	–	21	16
Distribution to opposition player	–	–	–	–	–	–	–	–	–	26	–	–	–	–	26	16
Goalkeeper distribution%	–	–	–	–	–	–	–	–	–	45%	–	–	–	–	45%	50%
Save	–	–	–	–	–	–	–	–	–	2	–	–	–	–	2	6
Ball caught	–	–	–	–	–	–	–	–	–	3	–	–	–	–	3	2
Ball dropped	–	–	–	–	–	–	–	–	–	–	–	–	–	–	–	–
Goal conceded	–	–	–	–	–	–	–	–	–	1	–	–	–	–	1	8

League leaders Manchester United arrived at rock-bottom Nottingham Forest expecting to win, but even the most die-hard Red Devils fan could not have predicted the rout that was to follow.

February 6, 1999

1–8

NOTTINGHAM FOREST
MANCHESTER UNITED

Alex Ferguson's men were quickly out of the traps, scoring after only two minutes. The entire Forest defence contrived to miss a David Beckham corner, allowing Roy Keane to lay the ball off to Paul Scholes. He delivered a first-time cross which was deftly touched into the net by Dwight Yorke.

Forest hit back quickly. Jean-Claude Darcheville hassled Ronny Johnsen into a mistake in the midfield before exchanging passes with Alan Rogers. He avoided Gary Neville's desperate challenge before smashing the ball past Peter Schmeichel.

The home team's joy was to be short-lived. Almost straight from the kick-off Jaap Stam found Andy Cole with a long ball out of defence and the England striker slipped the ball into the net from a tight angle.

United stepped up the pressure after that. Yorke saw a shot cleared off the line and Cole, who was causing the Forest defence real problems with his pace, put a snap shot wide. Beasant saved well on several occasions, but United were unable to increase their lead until the 49th minute.

Scholes had already hit the post when Forest's defence was cut down again. Two defenders went for the same ball and missed it, Yorke's right-foot shot was parried by Beasant, but the unmarked Cole was on hand to tuck in the rebound.

Cole and Yorke both went close after that before some excellent work down the Forest right by Blomqvist left John Harkes in a twist; and when the Swede's cross ricocheted off the post, Yorke was left with the simplest of tap-ins to make the score 4–1.

With the game already over and United rampant, Ferguson replaced Yorke with Ole Gunnar Solskjaer. Within 10 minutes the Norwegian had the ball in the back of the net, and seven minutes later he outpaced a flat-looking Forest defence to gather a Beckham pass and beat Beasant at the second attempt with a rising shot from the edge of the area.

He completed his hat-trick in the final minute after some neat work from Scholes, and in injury time, when Scholes miscued, Solskjaer was on the spot to score his fourth and United's eighth in an awesome display of attacking football.

United created a total of 23 goalscoring chances to Forest's nine and dominated possession throughout, completing 403 passes to Forest's 187. The home side were left chasing shadows at the back, attempting just 16 tackles to leave Dave Beasant exposed. On top of the eight goals which he conceded, the Forest 'keeper was forced to make six saves and looked a shattered figure at the final whistle.

Ole Gunnar Solskjaer took the man of the match award scoring 2,120 points in 19 minutes. Dwight Yorke and Andy Cole scored 1,910 and 1,705 respectively to underline the quality in attack that was to yield 80 goals and take United to the title.

ACTION	BECKHAM	BUTT	COLE	GIGGS	IRWIN	JOHNSEN	KEANE	MAY	G NEVILLE	P NEVILLE	SCHMEICHEL	SCHOLES	SHERINGHAM	YORKE	TOTAL	TOTTENHAM
Time on pitch	90	20	45	80	90	90	90	90	10	90	90	70	45	90	990	990
GOALS																
Goal	1	–	1	–	–	–	–	–	–	–	–	–	–	–	2	1
Shot on target	–	–	–	1	–	–	–	–	–	–	–	4	–	1	6	3
Shot off target	2	1	–	1	–	–	–	–	–	–	–	–	3	3	10	3
Blocked shot	–	–	–	–	–	–	–	–	–	–	–	–	2	2	4	3
Own goal	–	–	–	–	–	–	–	–	–	–	–	–	–	–	–	–
PASSES																
Pass to own player	31	8	12	23	28	12	62	21	1	44	–	25	15	39	321	300
Pass to opposition	16	3	1	12	5	2	7	3	2	9	–	4	7	5	76	88
Cross to own player	8	–	2	3	1	–	–	–	–	–	–	–	1	–	15	10
Cross to opposition player	8	–	–	2	–	–	–	–	–	–	–	–	–	–	15	2
Goal assist	–	–	–	–	–	–	–	–	–	–	–	–	–	–	2	–
Pass completion %	62%	73%	93%	65%	82%	86%	89%	88%	33%	82%	0%	84%	67%	89%	79%	75%
TACKLES & CLEARANCES																
Tackle	3	3	–	–	3	–	7	3	–	5	–	3	1	1	29	27
Clearances, blocks and interceptions	4	3	–	5	9	13	5	15	1	9	–	1	1	–	66	86
DRIBBLES & RUNS																
Dribble ball retained	1	–	2	2	1	–	4	–	–	–	–	–	3	3	16	21
Dribbles ball lost	–	–	1	3	2	–	–	–	–	–	–	–	–	–	6	11
Dribble success %	100%	0%	67%	40%	33%	100%	100%	100%	100%	0%	0%	0%	100%	100%	73%	66%
DISCIPLINE																
Fouls	2	–	–	1	1	1	3	1	1	–	–	1	3	2	16	8
Penalty conceded	–	–	–	–	–	–	–	–	–	–	–	–	–	–	–	–
Free kick - offside	2	–	–	1	–	–	–	–	–	–	–	–	1	1	5	6
Yellow cards	–	–	–	–	–	–	–	–	–	–	–	–	–	–	1	1
Red cards	–	–	–	–	–	–	–	–	–	–	–	–	–	–	–	–
GOALKEEPERS																
Distribution to own player	–	–	–	–	–	–	–	–	–	–	22	–	–	–	22	20
Distribution to opposition player	–	–	–	–	–	–	–	–	–	–	26	–	–	–	26	16
Goalkeeper distribution %	–	–	–	–	–	–	–	–	–	–	46%	–	–	–	46%	56%
Save	–	–	–	–	–	–	–	–	–	–	3	–	–	–	3	6
Ball caught	–	–	–	–	–	–	–	–	–	–	2	–	–	–	2	1
Ball dropped	–	–	–	–	–	–	–	–	–	–	–	–	–	–	–	–
Goal conceded	–	–	–	–	–	–	–	–	–	–	1	–	–	–	1	2

The Carling Premiership title hung in the balance, with both Manchester United and Arsenal still fighting for the Championship on the season's final day. Manchester United knew a win would secure their fifth title in seven seasons. In order for Arsenal to retain the title they needed to defeat Aston Villa at Highbury and United to drop points against Spurs. The atmosphere was tense.

May 16, 1999

2 – 1

MANCHESTER UNITED
vs
TOTTENHAM HOTSPUR

Tottenham opened the game well, putting a nervy-looking United on the back foot. Then disaster struck for Spurs (and Arsenal) when David Ginola limped off the pitch with an ankle injury in the opening 10 minutes.

While the Frenchman was being treated on the touchline, United nearly took the lead in the most bizarre fashion. Ian Walker's clearance was charged down by the back of Dwight Yorke and the ball rolled towards the goal. Luckily for Walker the ball hit the inside of the post and came out, allowing him to gather.

United started to dominate proceedings and should have been a goal up after 19 minutes, when Yorke blazed wide of the far post from close range. Six minutes later, United were rueing that miss.

A long ball was flicked on by Steffen Iversen and Les Ferdinand got goal-side of Ronny Johnsen to loop an effort over the stranded Peter Schmeichel (playing his last Premiership match for United) and into the far corner. The goal silenced the United crowd but a few hundred miles south, in north London, Highbury exploded. Advantage Arsenal.

United rallied, and David Beckham's delivery from the right was starting to pose the Spurs defence a few worries. He caused them a major problem in the 43rd minute.

United attacked down the left wing and Ryan Giggs passed inside to Paul Scholes, who in turn found Beckham on the right corner of the penalty area. He controlled and fired a brilliant swerving shot into the top right-hand corner. United had the breakthrough.

The second half began with a substitution, with Andy Cole coming on for Teddy Sheringham. It took just three minutes for Cole to make an impact. Gary Neville's hopeful chip into the Tottenham penalty area was brilliantly pulled down by Cole, who lobbed over the onrushing Ian Walker for a superb United goal.

It turned out to be the winning goal and the strike which ultimately sealed the Premiership title for Manchester United. The remainder of the second half was played to a stalemate, with United comfortably holding on to their 2–1 lead.

In a game of great tension United had the better of the possession, completing 321 passes to Tottenham's 300. The Red Devils also had the edge in the attacking areas, out-shooting Spurs by 22 shots to 10.

Spurs were under more defensive pressure, and as a result made more clearances, blocks and interceptions (86 to United's 66). In general, United shaded the match in all areas of play and, while Spurs defended well, the quality of the two United goals proved their undoing.

United were champions of England again, the first time they had sealed the Premiership at Old Trafford. The match at Highbury had finished 1–0 to the Arsenal, but Cole's goal was the deciding factor on the final day of the 1998–99 Carling Premiership title race. The first key of the Treble was now complete.

MIDDLESBROUGH 1998–99

Back row (left to right): Steve Baker, Phil Stamp, Hamilton Ricard, Craig Harrison, Marlon Beresford, Mark Summerbell, Paul Merson (now Aston Villa), Alan Moore, Mikkel Beck (now Derby County).

Middle row: Dave French (Masseur), Alex Smith (Kit Manager), Bob Ward (Senior Physiotherapist), Alun Armstrong, Curtis Fleming, Paul Gascoigne, Ben Roberts, Mark Schwarzer, Steve Vickers, Neil Maddison, Vladimir Kinder, Gordon McQueen (First Team Coach), Jez Cartwright (Fitness Coach, no longer at club).

Front row: Gary Henderson (Physiotherapist), Robbie Mustoe, Dean Gordon, Gustavo Lombardi (no longer at club), Bryan Robson (Manager), Andy Townsend, Viv Anderson (Assistant Manager), Gary Pallister, Gianluca Festa, Clayton Blackmore (now Barnsley), David Geddis (Reserve Team Coach).

MIDDLESBROUGH

20 FACTS

1 Middlesbrough were formed by members of the Middlesbrough Cricket Club in 1875. They did not turn professional until 1889. However they became amateur again in 1892, and professional again in 1899.

2 Their highest finish in the top flight came in 1914 when they finished third.

3 The club have reached just one FA Cup final, losing to Chelsea in 1997.

4 Boro have twice finished as runners-up in the Football League Cup, losing to Leicester in the 1997 final and Chelsea in the 1998 final.

5 Middlesbrough hold the old Division Two record for the most goals scored in a league season. They scored 122 in 1926–27.

6 George Camsell scored 59 league goals that season, a club record, and 64 goals in all competitions – an English record. On the way to this remarkable total he hit a record nine hat-tricks and scored all five goals in a 5–3 victory at Manchester City. Camsell remains Boro's all-time leading scorer, bagging a total of 345 goals between 1925 and 1939.

7 Alf Common became the first £1,000 player when he moved from Sunderland to Middlesbrough in February 1905.

8 Middlesbrough's all-time record attendance is 53,596 for a Division One game against Newcastle United at Ayresome Park in December 1949.

9 Their record victory came in August 1958 when they beat Brighton and Hove Albion 9–0 in a Division Two game. Brian Clough scored five goals that day. Clough scored 197 goals in 213 league appearances for the club and finished as Division Two's leading scorer in 1957–58, 1958–59 and 1959–60.

10 Current Middlesbrough manager Bryan Robson made his Premiership debut for Manchester United against Boro in 1992–93.

11 Robson is the oldest player ever to appear for Boro. He was 10 days short of his 40th birthday when he played against Arsenal at Highbury on New Year's Day 1997.

12 Middlesbrough were the second club to be promoted to the Premiership from Division Two, finishing as runners-up to Ipswich Town in the 1991–92 season. They were also the second club to be relegated from the Premiership, finishing second from bottom in 1992–93.

13 Middlesbrough avoided an unwanted hat-trick in 1998–99. In the two previous Premiership seasons in which Nottingham Forest have been relegated – 1992–93 and 1996–97 – Boro have gone down as well. Forest lost their Premiership place in 1998–99.

14 Wilf Mannion is the club's most-capped player. He made 26 appearances for England between 1946 and 1951.

15 Tim Williamson holds the club record for most league appearances, with 563 between 1902 and 1923. He made a total of 602 appearances in all competitions.

16 Middlesbrough finished a comfortable ninth in the 1998–99 Premiership. Their league record was:

Pld	W	D	L	F	A	Pts
38	12	15	11	48	54	51

17 Bryan Robson's side were beaten 3–1 by Manchester United at Old Trafford in the FA Cup third round.

18 Boro defeated Wycombe Wanderers 3–1 on aggregate in the second round of the Worthington Cup, but lost 3–2 at home to Everton in the next round.

19 Their top goalscorer in all competitions was Hamilton Ricard with 18 goals.

20 Middlesbrough's disciplinary record was the 11th worst in the Premiership. They committed 488 fouls, earned 81 yellow cards and suffered two dismissals.

SEASON REVIEW

Middlesbrough's previous sojourns in the Premiership had been deeply unhappy affairs: 21st and relegated in 1992–93; 12th and just five points from the drop in 1995–96; 19th and relegated again in 1996–97. But Boro supporters felt confident that the side were much better equipped in 1998–99, following a healthy injection of cash for new players.

The optimism was fully justified. While the two other promoted teams made swift returns to Division One, Boro were rarely in danger of relegation – and at one stage looked good for a UEFA Cup spot.

Bargain buys Dean Gordon and Gary Pallister were brought in to strengthen the defence and mercurial midfielder Paul Gascoigne would at last get his chance in the Premiership. Soon after the season kicked off, Brian Deane joined the list of experienced veterans in the side to partner top scorer Hamilton Ricard.

> "At the start of the season, a lot of people had us down as one of the teams that could go down so we have got to be pleased. You only need to look at Nottingham Forest and Charlton to see how hard it is for promoted teams"
>
> Bryan Robson

The season began in inauspicious fashion with a goalless draw at home to Leeds, defeat at Aston Villa and a 1–1 draw with Derby County. But once the first victory arrived, at Leicester City on September 9, the season really took off. A 3–0 hammering of Spurs at White Hart Lane propelled the new boys into the top six.

Off the field, big-name stars Paul Merson and Marco Branca dominated the headlines, with Branca suffering a career-threatening knee injury and troubled Merson quitting the Riverside, claiming a drinking-and-gambling culture within the club was threatening to engulf him. It was a claim Bryan Robson strenuously denied.

A sharp exit in the Worthington Cup at the hands of goal-shy Everton was quickly forgotten thanks to an amazing 11-game unbeaten run in the league, culminating in the side's performance of the season at Old Trafford, where Manchester United were beaten 3–2 on December 19.

At one stage in that sequence of results Middlesbrough were third in the league,

with the much-maligned Ricard the Premiership's top scorer.

But dreams of Europe started to fade after that magnificent afternoon in Manchester. The side failed to win in their next 10 games, including nine in the league. On Boxing Day Liverpool ended the side's unbeaten home record 3–1, repeated the score back at Anfield and then neighbours Everton enjoyed another goalfest against Bryan Robson's men, winning 5–0 at Goodison Park.

By the time Sheffield Wednesday beat them on February 27 Boro had slumped to 13th in the table, and the word "relegation" was being bandied about by some media pundits.

A televized 3–0 win over Southampton was just what Middlesbrough needed to resurrect their flagging season, and further wins against Nottingham Forest, Wimbledon, Charlton and Coventry soon followed. The club were now back in the top 10.

The side had to face Chelsea, Manchester United and Arsenal in their final three home games. They held the Blues 0–0 as the Londoners' title bid slipped away – but Arsenal found hitting the back of the Middlesbrough net less of a challenge, winning 6–1 in a breathtaking display. United, too, won the three points, albeit far less convincingly, and a final-day mauling at West Ham meant Boro had finished the 1998–99 campaign miserably, ending up in ninth place.

Sticky moments against the Toffees, pummellings by the Hammers and open wounds inflicted by the Gunners aside, it was Middlesbrough's defence which ensured their Premiership safety. They made the fifth-largest number of tackles and the second-highest total of blocks and interceptions in the Premiership, keeping a total of 13 clean sheets.

Having proved their worth in the top flight, Robson will now look to build on the 1998–99 season in the search for a top six finish in 1999–2000.

MIDDLESBROUGH

DATE	OPPONENT	SCORE	ATT.	ARMSTRONG	BAKER	BECK	BERESFORD	BRANCA	CAMPBELL	COOPER	CUMMINS	DEANE	FESTA	FLEMING	GASCOI
15.8.98	Leeds Utd H	0–0	34,160	–	–	s17	–	–	–	–	–	–	–	90	90□
23.8.98	Aston Villa A	1–3	29,559	–	–	s32¹	–	–	–	–	–	–	90□	90	58
29.8.98	Derby Co H	1–1	34,087	–	–	90	–	–	90	–	–	–	90	–	90
9.9.98	Leicester A	1–0	20,635	–	–	90	–	–	s17	45	–	–	90	–	86¹
13.9.98	Tottenham A	3–0	30,437	–	–	89	–	s24	s1	90	–	–	90	–	85
19.9.98	Everton H	2–2	34,563	–	–	90	–	–	–	90	–	–	90□	–	90□
26.9.98	Chelsea A	0–2	34,814	–	–	57□	–	–	–	90□	–	–	90□	–	90□
3.10.98	Sheff Wed H	4–0	34,163	–	–	90²	–	–	s7	90	–	–	90	–	90¹
17.10.98	Blackburn H	2–1	34,413	–	–	58□	90	–	–	90	–	s32	90□	90¹	–
24.10.98	Wimbledon A	2–2	14,114	–	–	s7	90	–	–	90□	–	90	90	90	–
1.11.98	Nott'm For H	1–1	34,223	–	–	–	90	–	–	90	–	90¹	90	74	78□
7.11.98	Southampton A	3–3*	15,202	–	–	–	90	–	–	90	–	90	90¹	90	90¹□
14.11.98	Charlton A	1–1	19,906	–	–	s10	–	–	–	90	–	80	90	90	45□
21.11.98	Coventry H	2–0	34,287	–	–	90	–	–	–	90□	–	90□	49	–	–
29.11.98	Arsenal A	1–1	38,075	–	–	s31	–	–	–	90□	–	89¹	–	90	67□
6.12.98	Newcastle H	2–2	34,629	–	–	s2	–	–	–	90¹	–	88	–	90	86
12.12.98	West Ham H	1–0	34,623	–	–	s16	–	–	–	90	–	90¹	–	–	90
19.12.98	Man Utd A	3–2	55,152	–	–	s7	–	–	–	90	–	90¹	90□	–	–
26.12.98	Liverpool H	1–3	34,626	–	–	s11	–	–	–	90□	–	90¹	90□	s45	90□
28.12.98	Derby Co A	1–2	32,726	–	–	s48¹	–	–	–	90	–	90	90	s48	42
9.1.99	Aston Villa H	0–0	34,643	–	–	s6	–	–	–	–	–	90	90	90□	90□
16.1.99	Leeds Utd A	0–2	37,394	–	–	s27	–	–	–	s27	–	90	90	90□	63
30.1.99	Leicester H	0–0	34,631	–	–	s15	–	–	–	90	–	75	90□	90	90
6.2.99	Liverpool A	1–3	44,384	–	–	90	–	–	–	90	–	90	62	–	90
17.2.99	Everton A	0–5	31,606	–	–	90	–	–	80	90	–	–	–	–	71
20.2.99	Tottenham H	0–0	34,687	–	–	75	–	–	s15	90□	–	–	–	–	90□
27.2.99	Sheff Wed A	1–3	24,534	–	–	90	–	–	–	90	–	–	–	–	45□
14.3.99	Southampton H	3–0	33,387	–	–	90¹	–	–	s7	90	–	s18	90	–	–
20.3.99	Nott'm For A	2–1	21,468	s2	–	s29	–	–	–	90	–	90¹□	90□	–	–
3.4.99	Blackburn A	0–0	27,482	–	–	–	–	–	–	90	–	90	–	–	s20□
5.4.99	Wimbledon H	3–1	33,999	–	–	–	–	–	–	90	–	–	90¹	–	90
10.4.99	Charlton H	2–0	34,529	s15	–	–	–	–	–	90	–	68	90	–	75
14.4.99	Chelsea H	0–0	34,406	–	–	–	–	–	–	90	–	90	90□	–	–
17.4.99	Coventry A	2–1	19,228	s27	90	–	–	–	–	90	–	90	–	–	–
24.4.99	Arsenal H	1–6	34,630	s19¹	–	–	–	–	–	37	–	90	–	–	–
1.5.99	Newcastle A	1–1	36,784	s50	–	–	–	–	–	–	–	90	–	–	–
9.5.99	Man Utd H	0–1	34,655	–	s45	–	–	–	s18□	–	–	90	–	–	–
16.5.99	West Ham A	0–4	25,902	s45	–	–	–	–	s17	–	90	73	–	–	–

□ Yellow card, ■ Red card, s Substitute, 90³ Goals scored
*including own goal

1998–99 PREMIERSHIP APPEARANCES

GAVIN	GORDON	HARRISON	KINDER	MADDISON	MERSON	MOORE	MUSTOE	O'NEILL	PALLISTER	RICARD	SCHWARZER	STAMP	STOCKDALE	SUMMERBELL	TOWNSEND	VICKERS	TOTAL
–	90	90	–	s45	90	73	45	–	–	–	90	90	90	–	90	–	990
–	90	90	–	–	90	58	90	–	–	s32	90	90	–	–	90	–	990
–	90	–	s2	–	90	–	90	–	–	s45¹	90	45	90	–	88	–	990
–	90□	–	s4	90	–	–	90	–	90	73	90	–	s45□	–	–	90	990
–	90	–	s5¹	–	–	–	90	–	90	66²	90	–	–	–	90	90	990
–	90	–	–	–	–	–	90	–	90	90²	90	–	–	–	90	90□	990
.	90	–	–	–	–	–	90□	–	90	90	90	s33	–	–	90	90	990
–	90	–	–	–	–	–	90	–	90	83¹	90	–	–	–	90□	90	990
–	90	–	–	–	–	–	90□	–	–	90¹	–	s32	–	58	90□	90	990
–	90□	–	–	–	–	–	90¹	–	–	83¹	–	s7	–	90□	83	90	990
–	90	–	–	–	–	–	90	–	–	90	–	s12	s16	–	90□	90	990
–	90	–	–	–	–	–	63m	–	–	69□	–	s17m	–	–	90□	90	959
–	90	–	–	–	–	–	90	–	–	90	90	s45¹	–	–	90	90	990
–	90¹	–	–	s41	–	–	–	–	–	90¹	90	–	90	90	90	90	990
–	90	–	–	s23	–	–	90	–	90	59	90	–	–	s1	90	90	990
–	90	–	–	–	–	–	90	–	90	90	90	s4	–	–	90¹	90□	990
–	90	–	–	–	–	–	90	–	90□	74	90	s5	85	–	90	90	990
–	90¹	–	–	83	–	s18	72	–	90	90¹	90	–	–	–	90	90	990
–	90	–	–	73	–	–	–	–	45□	90	90	s17	–	–	79	90	990
–	90	–	–	s15	–	–	–	–	–	90	90	42	75	–	90□	90	990
–	90	–	–	90	–	–	–	–	90	84□	90	–	–	–	90	90	990
–	90	–	–	63	–	–	90	–	90□	90□	90	–	–	–	–	90	990
–	90	–	–	–	–	–	75□	–	90	90	90	s15□	–	–	90	–	990
–	90	–	–	s12	–	–	90□	–	90□	–	90	s28¹	–	–	78	–	990
–	90	–	–	s10	–	–	90	–	90□	s19	90	–	90	s19□	90□	71	990
–	90	–	–	–	–	58	90	–	90	s32	90	–	90□	–	90□	90	990
–	90	s1	–	s45□	–	–	90¹	–	90	90	90□	–	89	–	90□	90	990
–	90	–	–	90	–	–	90	–	–	83¹	90	72	90	–	–	90¹	990
–	90	–	–	90	–	–	90□	–	–	59¹	90	–	90	–	90	90□	990
–	90	90	–	70	–	–	–	s13	90	90	90	–	90□	90□	77	–	990
–	90	–	–	s36	–	–	90	54	90	90²	90	–	84	s17	73	s6	990
–	90	–	–	s15	–	–	90¹	s22	90	75¹	90	–	90	–	90	–	990
–	90□	–	–	s6	–	–	90	84□	90	90	90	–	90	–	90	–	990
–	90¹	–	s71¹□	90	–	–	s1	90□	18	63	90	–	–	–	90	90	990
–	90	–	s53	71	–	–	90	–	90	90□	90	–	61	s29□	90	90	990
90	90	–	–	–	–	–	90¹□	–	90	40	90	–	90	90	90□	90	990
72	90	–	–	–	–	–	90□	–	90	90	90	–	45	90	90□	90	990
–	90	–	–	–	–	–	90	90	90	45□	90	–	–	90	90	90□	990

THE MANAGER

BRYAN ROBSON

Bryan Robson became player-manager of Middlesbrough in May 1994.

Boro were in desperate need of a fresh start, having been relegated at the end of the first Premiership season in 1992–93 and with then-manager Lennie Lawrence failing to inspire an instant return. It took Robson a season to rebuild the side into a credible top-flight outfit, and in their first campaign back in 1995–96 Boro finished in 12th place.

But docked points cost Robson's side dear the following season and, despite having spent upwards of £40 million in his first three years, Middlesbrough were relegated.

The following campaign was a huge success, culminating in a second promotion, and for a while in 1998–99 it looked as if Boro could finish in the top six. They now look like a side capable of pushing for Europe in 1999–2000.

Robson enjoyed a glittering playing career, earning 90 England caps in the heart of midfield. He spent eight years at West Bromwich Albion, then became Ron Atkinson's first signing at Manchester United. He played there for 12 years, making 345 league appearances and scoring 74 goals at Old Trafford.

He is widely tipped to be a future England boss, having already worked under Terry Venables in the country's Euro 96 assault.

LEAGUE POSITION

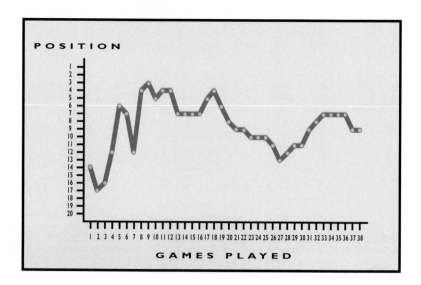

THE GOALS

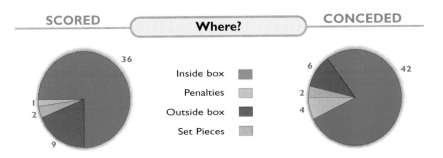

SCORED — Where? — CONCEDED

- Inside box
- Penalties
- Outside box
- Set Pieces

Bryan Robson's Middlesbrough conceded the fifth-highest total of goals during the 1998–99 Carling Premiership but were boosted by the goals of Hamilton Ricard to cancel these out. Boro showed their shooting prowess from more than 18 yards, firing in 23% of their league goals from outside the area, with Paul Gascoigne and Dean Gordon grabbing three apiece. But the Teessiders struggled in their own area conceding 42 goals, the fifth-most in the league.

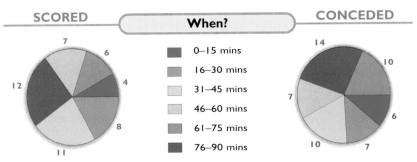

SCORED — When? — CONCEDED

- 0–15 mins
- 16–30 mins
- 31–45 mins
- 46–60 mins
- 61–75 mins
- 76–90 mins

Middlesbrough scored slightly more goals in the second halves of matches and were at their most dangerous in the closing minutes of each half. In total they netted 48% of their goals in the two quarter-hour periods before the end of each half, often leaving it late in the shooting stakes. But Boro also conceded a high proportion of their goals during these times. Interestingly, 11 of the 14 league goals Hamilton Ricard scored were in the first half.

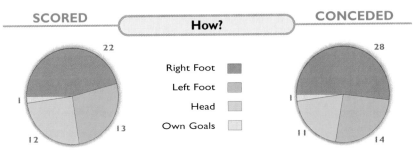

SCORED — How? — CONCEDED

- Right Foot
- Left Foot
- Head
- Own Goals

Helped along by four headers from Colombian international Hamilton Ricard, Boro amassed a quarter of their goals with their heads, the joint-third highest ratio in the league. They also scored from 13 left-footed efforts, a tally topped by just six Premership clubs. But they displayed some difficulty in dealing with the high ball, conceding one-fifth of goals via the aerial route – again above the league average.

MIDDLESBROUGH

	ARMSTRONG	BAKER	BECK	BRANCA	CAMPBELL	COOPER	CUMMINS	DEANE	FESTA	FLEMING	GASCOIGNE	GAVIN
APPEARANCE												
Start	0	1	13	0	1	31	1	24	25	12	25	2
Sub	6	1	14	1	7	1	0	2	0	2	1	0
Minutes on pitch	158	135	1347	24	162	2719	90	2143	2181	1157	1991	162
GOAL ATTEMPTS												
Goals	1	0	5	0	0	1	0	6	2	1	3	0
Shots on target	2	0	17	0	0	4	0	35	6	2	14	0
Shots off target	2	0	19	1	0	12	1	19	8	1	13	0
Shooting accuracy	50%	0%	47%	0%	0%	25%	0%	65%	43%	67%	52%	0%
PASSING												
Goal assists	1	0	4	0	0	1	0	1	0	2	2	0
Long passes	0	7	18	1	2	264	4	9	129	87	147	10
Short passes	68	35	519	10	36	745	36	864	575	348	1173	15
PASS COMPLETION												
Own half %	100%	90%	83%	100%	93%	91%	100%	84%	91%	90%	88%	83%
Opposition half %	55%	71%	73%	10%	39%	62%	80%	72%	70%	61%	76%	38%
CROSSING												
Total crosses	2	0	24	1	0	26	6	16	17	28	96	0
Cross completion %	50%	0%	21%	0%	0%	38%	67%	13%	47%	29%	32%	0%
DRIBBLING												
Dribbles & runs	3	2	37	0	9	39	0	39	59	20	177	0
Dribble completion %	67%	0%	59%	0%	67%	90%	0%	74%	83%	90%	71%	0%
DEFENDING												
Tackles made	7	6	24	2	2	95	6	36	88	66	90	3
Tackles won %	71%	100%	38%	0%	0%	73%	50%	42%	63%	58%	47%	67%
Blocks	0	0	1	0	0	27	1	0	22	13	1	2
Clearances	2	8	8	0	1	319	1	32	205	64	14	19
Interceptions	0	2	5	0	0	39	0	6	41	12	17	0
DISCIPLINE												
Fouls	2	1	26	2	1	33	0	55	39	7	27	0
Offside	1	0	29	0	1	1	0	21	1	1	0	0
Yellow cards	0	0	2	0	1	6	0	2	9	2	12	0
Red cards	0	0	0	0	0	0	0	0	0	0	0	0

GOALKEEPER NAME	START/ (SUB)	TIME ON PITCH	GOALS CONCEDED	MINS/GOALS CONCEDED	SAVES MADE	SAVES/ SHOTS
BERESFORD	4	360	7	51.4	13	65%
SCHWARZER	34	3060	47	65.1	147	76%

PLAYERS' STATISTICS

	GORDON	HARRISON	KINDER	MADDISON	MERSON	MOORE	MUSTOE	O'NEILL	PALLISTER	RICARD	STAMP	STOCKDALE	SUMMERBELL	TOWNSEND	VICKERS	TOTAL	RANK
	38	3	0	10	3	3	32	4	26	32	5	17	7	35	30		
	0	1	5	10	0	1	1	2	0	4	11	2	4	0	1		
	3420	271	135	1058	270	207	2776	353	2223	2704	554	1490	664	3088	2687		
	3	0	2	0	0	0	4	0	0	15	2	0	0	1	1	48*	=7th
	17	0	4	2	1	0	9	1	1	40	6	0	2	12	3	178	9th
	28	0	2	2	2	4	8	2	4	42	5	6	4	10	7	202	16th
	38%	0%	67%	50%	33%	0%	53%	33%	20%	49%	55%	0%	33%	55%	30%	47%	6th
	4	0	0	1	2	0	1	1	0	2	0	3	0	3	0	28	=12th
	197	30	5	54	20	3	92	13	86	39	22	92	11	150	150	1642	19th
	859	55	45	406	103	51	990	139	653	846	155	386	169	1354	549	11184	10th
	86%	79%	92%	86%	85%	93%	90%	80%	90%	83%	88%	82%	92%	90%	92%	89%	11th
	60%	48%	57%	72%	76%	79%	75%	68%	72%	64%	69%	60%	77%	77%	62%	69%	11th
	135	1	0	41	20	5	7	9	3	45	16	50	2	171	4	725	12th
	27%	0%	0%	27%	40%	20%	29%	33%	0%	20%	25%	22%	50%	33%	0%	29%	6th
	128	1	8	8	12	6	40	21	35	101	11	26	1	42	8	834	13th
	74%	100%	100%	100%	67%	33%	80%	86%	94%	52%	45%	81%	0%	79%	100%	74%	4th
	111	5	3	34	2	8	187	13	84	60	15	60	35	135	74	1251	5th
	53%	20%	33%	62%	100%	38%	64%	54%	70%	47%	80%	62%	66%	66%	50%	59%	16th
	24	6	2	6	0	0	23	0	33	0	0	10	10	19	33	234	2nd
	234	20	5	24	0	4	67	6	375	6	18	59	14	77	412	2020	11th
	37	2	0	15	0	4	37	2	40	6	3	7	9	42	45	375	2nd
	24	5	3	18	2	1	53	5	33	68	5	19	14	27	17	488	13th
	1	0	0	1	1	1	4	2	0	45	4	1	1	5	0	121	14th
	3	0	1	1	0	0	7	2	5	5	1	3	4	10	4	81	=5th
	0	0	0	0	0	0	1	0	0	0	1	0	0	0	0	2	=14th

*including one own goal

CROSSES CAUGHT	CROSSES PUNCHED	CROSSES NOT CLAIMED	CATCH SUCCESS	THROWS/ SHORT KICKS	% COMPLETION	LONG KICKS	% COMPLETION
12	3	4	86%	12	92%	108	36%
100	29	8	95%	290	94%	794	41%

PLAYER OF THE SEASON

PLAYER	INDEX SCORE
GARY PALLISTER	908
Paul Gascoigne	900
Dean Gordon	862
Andy Townsend	835
Gianluca Festa	823
Colin Cooper	810
Robbie Mustoe	796
Mark Schwarzer	784
Steve Vickers	765
Hamilton Ricard	751

The sight of Gary Pallister back in the red shirt of Middlesbrough was a joyous one for all Boro supporters.

Nine years after quitting decaying Ayresome Park for the splendour of Old Trafford, Pallister was reunited with former team-mate Bryan Robson – and went on to become the highest-scoring Riversider in the Carling Opta Season Index.

Pallister's greatest asset has always been his ability to read the game. He proved this once again with more than 300 headed clearances and 40 interceptions for Boro in 1998–99.

Although he lacked his usual threat from set-pieces, Pallister scored an average of 908 points per match over the course of the season.

Paul Gascoigne's eagerly-awaited return to English top-flight football might not have been the huge success every Boro fan had wished for – indeed, his off-the-field problems once again made far more headlines than his performances for the club – but he still made a big impression in Bryan Robson's side.

His ability on the ball set many pulses racing as he embarked on 177 dribbles and runs. He also scored three Premiership goals of the typically spectacular variety on his way to an average Carling Opta points score of 900.

Newcomer Dean Gordon, the only Boro player not to miss a single minute of Premiership football in 1998–99, showed no signs of homesickness despite having moved away from south London for the first time in his life. The left wing-back showed tremendous fitness with his buccaneering runs along the touch-line and he added several stunning goals to his portfolio – including a fine strike in the win at Manchester United.

The Supporters' Club joint Players of the Year, Robbie Mustoe and Hamilton Ricard, both feature in the top 10, alongside the likes of the experienced Andy Townsend and Colin Cooper.

FIVE OF THE BEST

Having pipped Sunderland to the second automatic promotion spot in 1997–98, Boro rejoined the Carling Premiership looking much better-prepared. With nine weeks of the season gone they were in third place, and after beating Manchester United in December they were still fourth. They could not maintain that form, but easily outperformed the other two promoted teams and will look to build on their top 10 finish in 1999–2000.

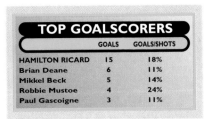

TOP GOALSCORERS	GOALS	GOALS/SHOTS
HAMILTON RICARD	15	18%
Brian Deane	6	11%
Mikkel Beck	5	14%
Robbie Mustoe	4	24%
Paul Gascoigne	3	11%

Charismatic Colombian Hamilton Ricard found life in the Premiership a lot easier than he had in the Nationwide League, scoring 15 league goals to finish comfortably as top scorer: almost one in five of his efforts hit the back of the net. The arrival of Brian Deane prompted something of a drought for Ricard, but Deane finished as second-top scorer with six, ahead of departed Dane Mikkel Beck. Mercurial midfielder Paul Gascoigne had plenty of strikes at goal, but only found the net three times.

The experienced Andy Townsend saw more of the ball than any of his team-mates, completing more than 1,200 passes. He and fellow-midfielder Robbie Mustoe both completed more than four out of every five passes, while Paul Gascoigne dictated the play from a slightly deeper position than he had been used to in his Tottenham heyday. Newcomer Dean Gordon also saw plenty of the ball, having played every single minute of Premiership football in 1998–99.

TOP PASSERS	SUCC PASSES	COMPLETION
ANDY TOWNSEND	1,220	81%
Paul Gascoigne	1,055	80%
Robbie Mustoe	874	81%
Colin Cooper	757	75%
Dean Gordon	728	69%

TOP TACKLERS	WON	SUCCESS
ROBBIE MUSTOE	120	64%
Andy Townsend	89	66%
Colin Cooper	69	73%
Gary Pallister	59	70%
Dean Gordon	59	53%

Boro's official supporters club could not separate Hamilton Ricard and Robbie Mustoe when it came to picking their Player of the Year. Ricard may have grabbed all the headlines with his goals, but Mustoe was the club's chief challenger with more than 120 successful tackles in midfield. Andy Townsend again figures highly, with the Middlesbrough engine-room vital to their side's success in 1998–99, and the experienced Gary Pallister showed he has lost none of his ability to make a clean tackle.

Although Boro collected the joint fifth-highest total of bookings in the Premiership, they conceded comparatively few fouls – more than 100 fewer than Leeds United, for example. Many of top bad boy Hamilton Ricard's fouls were given away through exuberance and clumsiness. While Paul Gascoigne's bookings tally was rather high he only conceded 27 fouls all season, collecting three yellow cards for dissent. No one exceeded the 90 disciplinary points mark, and only two players were red-carded in the Premiership.

DISCIPLINE	POINTS	FOULS & CARDS
HAMILTON RICARD	83	68F, 5Y, 0R
Robbie Mustoe	80	53F, 7Y, 1R
Gianluca Festa	66	39F, 9Y, 0R
Paul Gascoigne	63	27F, 12Y, 0R
Brian Deane	61	55F, 2Y, 0R

ACTION	BERESFORD	COOPER	DEANE	FESTA	FLEMING	GASCOIGNE	GORDON	MUSTOE	RICARD	STAMP	TOWNSEND	VICKERS	TOTAL	SOUTHAMPTON
Time on pitch	90	90	90	90	90	90	90	63	69	17	90	90	959	990
GOALS														
Goal	-	-	-	-	-	-	-	-	-	-	-	-	2	3
Shot on target	-	-	-	-	1	1	-	1	4	-	-	-	7	4
Shot off target	-	1	1	1	-	-	-	-	-	-	1	-	4	9
Blocked shot	-	-	-	-	-	-	-	-	-	-	-	-	-	2
Own goal	-	-	-	-	-	-	-	-	-	-	-	-	-	-
PASSES														
Pass to own player	-	28	30	20	25	50	16	16	20	4	36	20	265	291
Pass to opposition	-	13	11	6	11	11	7	2	8	-	11	9	89	73
Cross to own player	-	-	-	-	-	-	2	-	-	-	2	-	4	7
Cross to opposition player	-	-	-	1	1	1	1	-	-	1	3	-	8	24
Goal assist	-	-	-	-	-	-	-	-	-	-	-	-	-	3
Pass completion %	0%	68%	73%	77%	68%	81%	65%	89%	69%	80%	75%	69%	73%	76%
TACKLES & CLEARANCES														
Tackle	-	2	2	3	2	2	1	2	-	-	-	-	14	18
Clearances, blocks and interceptions	-	8	1	4	1	1	4	1	-	-	-	8	28	18
DRIBBLES & RUNS														
Dribble ball retained	1	-	-	2	2	7	-	1	-	-	1	-	14	21
Dribbles ball lost	-	1	-	-	-	-	-	-	-	-	-	-	1	2
Dribble success %	100%	0%	-	100%	100%	100%	-	100%	-	-	100%	-	93%	91%
DISCIPLINE														
Fouls	-	-	-	1	-	-	-	2	-	-	-	-	3	9
Penalty conceded	-	-	-	-	-	-	-	-	-	-	-	-	-	-
Free kick - offside	-	-	-	-	1	-	-	-	1	-	-	-	2	-
Yellow cards	-	-	-	-	-	1	-	-	-	1	-	1	3	3
Red cards	-	-	-	1	-	1	-	-	-	-	-	-	2	-
GOALKEEPERS														
Distribution to own player	11	-	-	-	-	-	-	-	-	-	-	-	11	17
Distribution to opposition player	7	-	-	-	-	-	-	-	-	-	-	-	7	10
Goalkeeper distribution%	61%	-	-	-	-	-	-	-	-	-	-	-	61%	63%
Save	4	-	-	-	-	-	-	-	-	-	-	-	4	4
Ball caught	2	-	-	-	-	-	-	-	-	-	-	-	2	3
Ball dropped	-	-	-	-	-	-	-	-	-	-	-	-	-	-
Goal conceded	3	-	-	-	-	-	-	-	-	-	-	-	3	3

Middlesbrough's visit to the Dell was one of the more eventful matches Boro had in 1998–99. Six goals and two sendings-off were crammed into the action-packed second half of a hugely entertaining game.

November 7, 1998

3–3

SOUTHAMPTON
MIDDLESBROUGH

The game burst into life in the 17th minute. Matt Le Tissier tried his luck from 25 yards, forcing a good save from Marlon Beresford in the Middlesbrough goal. He cleared downfield and Brian Deane and Hamilton Ricard combined to set up Andy Townsend, whose shot beat Paul Jones only to hit the post.

After that the match opened up considerably, with Boro having the better of the possession and Southampton looking capable of scoring. Despite this, the first half ended at 0–0. But just two minutes into the second period, Ken Monkou's foul on Ricard set up a free kick 20 yards from goal. Paul Gascoigne lined it up, then placed a superb curling effort around the wall and inside the left-hand post for 1–0.

Just after the hour mark, Monkou got his revenge. A Le Tissier corner was swung in from the right and the big Dutchman rose to send a thumping header past Beresford for the equalizer.

Two minutes later a tussle for the ball between Mark Hughes and Robbie Mustoe saw the Middlesbrough man sent off for a second bookable offence.

On 65 minutes, a long Gascoigne ball was headed over Jones's head by Claus Lundekvam for an own-goal. Jones was coming out for the ball but a breakdown in communication left the goalkeeper stranded as the Norwegian headed into the empty net.

From then on, Southampton took over and dominated the rest of the match. With eight minutes remaining, Wayne Bridge's cross was headed goalward by James Beattie. Egil Ostenstad challenged Beresford and the ball fell to Beattie, who prodded home the equalizer. Much to the consternation of the Boro players the goal stood, despite their appeals that Ostenstad had fouled the goalkeeper.

Southampton sensed victory, and with five minutes left, Le Tissier threaded a great ball through to Ostenstad in the inside-right channel. He shot past Beresford and into the far corner for a super Southampton third.

Things went from bad to worse for Bryan Robson when recently-introduced substitute Phil Stamp was dismissed for comments addressed at the referee. The game looked lost for Boro until, in stoppage-time, Jones and Le Tissier left a looping Deane header for each other and Gianluca Festa popped up to head goalward from three yards. Jones made a mess of the save and Middlesbrough had snatched a late equalizer to share the spoils – leaving the Southampton faithful brooding about what might have been.

The Carling Opta statistics show just how closely contested the game was. The pass completion ratings of 76% to Southampton and 73% to Middlesbrough from 364 and 354 passes respectively illustrate the minute difference between the sides. The teams' defensive stats are also similarly close: the Saints made 18 tackles to Boro's 14, but fewer clearances, blocks and interceptions.

Despite that, the most important statistic is the score and, judging by the stats, a 3–3 scoreline was probably a fair result.

ACTION	BECK	COOPER	DEANE	FESTA	GORDON	MADDISON	MOORE	MUSTOE	PALLISTER	RICARD	SCHWARZER	TOWNSEND	VICKERS	TOTAL	MANCHESTER UNITED
Time on pitch	7	90	90	90	90	83	18	72	90	90	90	90	90	990	990
GOALS															
Goal	–	–	–	–	–	–	–	–	–	–	–	–	–	–	2
Shot on target	–	–	1	–	1	–	–	–	–	1	–	–	–	3	5
Shot off target	–	–	–	2	–	1	–	–	–	–	–	–	–	3	8
Blocked shot	–	–	2	–	–	–	1	–	–	1	–	–	–	6	6
Own goal	–	–	–	–	–	–	–	–	–	–	–	–	–	–	–
PASSES															
Pass to own player	–	21	23	15	13	42	5	21	23	21	–	34	10	228	497
Pass to opposition	1	3	17	7	10	11	3	6	1	13	–	8	3	83	84
Cross to own player	–	–	–	–	2	1	–	–	–	2	–	1	–	6	12
Cross to opposition player	–	–	1	–	3	3	1	–	–	3	–	2	1	12	59
Goal assist	–	–	–	–	–	–	–	–	–	–	–	–	–	–	–
Pass completion %	0%	88%	57%	68%	54%	75%	63%	78%	96%	59%	0%	78%	77%	71%	78%
TACKLES & CLEARANCES															
Tackle	–	2	2	2	4	3	1	7	2	2	–	1	–	23	20
Clearances, blocks and interceptions	1	15	2	10	7	3	–	3	19	–	–	2	18	81	16
DRIBBLES & RUNS															
Dribble ball retained	1	1	–	1	3	–	1	1	–	–	–	–	–	11	18
Dribbles ball lost	–	–	–	–	1	–	–	–	–	1	–	–	–	3	5
Dribble success %	50%	100%	0%	100%	75%	0%	100%	100%	67%	67%	0%	0%	0%	79%	78%
DISCIPLINE															
Fouls	–	1	–	2	–	–	–	1	1	3	–	1	–	9	11
Penalty conceded	–	–	–	–	–	–	–	–	–	–	–	–	–	–	–
Free kick - offside	–	3	–	–	–	–	–	–	2	–	–	–	1	6	–
Yellow cards	–	–	–	–	–	–	–	–	–	–	–	–	–	–	–
Red cards	–	–	–	–	–	–	–	–	–	–	–	–	–	–	–
GOALKEEPERS															
Distribution to own player	–	–	–	–	–	–	–	–	–	–	25	–	–	25	14
Distribution to opposition player	–	–	–	–	–	–	–	–	–	–	14	–	–	14	11
Goalkeeper distribution%	0%	0%	0%	0%	0%	0%	0%	0%	0%	0%	64%	0%	0%	64%	56%
Save	–	–	–	–	–	–	–	–	–	–	5	–	–	5	3
Ball caught	–	–	–	–	–	–	–	–	–	–	6	–	–	6	5
Ball dropped	–	–	–	–	–	–	–	–	–	–	–	–	–	–	–
Goal conceded	–	–	–	–	–	–	–	–	–	–	2	–	–	2	3

A trip to Old Trafford is fairly daunting for most clubs, but Middlesbrough ventured into the Theatre of Dreams unbeaten in their previous 12 Carling Premiership matches and sitting just four points behind Manchester United in fifth place.

December 19, 1998

2–3

MANCHESTER UNITED
MIDDLESBROUGH

Added to that, the poor form of United – one win in their previous eight games – meant that Boro could start the match with confidence, even though they were missing the influence of the suspended Paul Gascoigne from their midfield.

Boro teased United's defence early on and their good start was rewarded in the 23rd minute when a cross from Dean Gordon on the left flank deceived Gary Neville and Peter Schmeichel and bobbled across the six-yard box. The ball seemed to be going out of play, but Brian Deane reached it and pulled it back across the face of goal to Hamilton Ricard who was able to prod home.

United tried to get back into the game, but their approach play lacked fluency and Middlesbrough began to grow in confidence.

On 31 minutes, Boro opened up a 2–0 lead when a free kick from Andy Townsend was only half-cleared by Ronny Johnsen. The ball looped to the edge of the penalty area where Gordon met it with a left-foot volley that found the corner of the net.

Old Trafford was stunned, but worse was to come for United. Ricard intercepted a poorly-directed pass by Johnsen and, although his attempted through-ball was not the best, the ball was deflected by Phil Neville into the path of Deane who finished with a well-struck shot that Schmeichel could not keep out.

United struck back just three minutes later when a cross by David Beckham was headed home by Nicky Butt. And, in the 70th minute, a slick move into United's penalty area ended when Gordon blocked Andy Cole's route to goal, only for Paul Scholes to pounce on the loose ball and prod home United's second.

Although they had chances to equalize, Butt and Giggs spurned the opportunities for United and Boro held out for their first win at Old Trafford for 68 years.

United had the lion's share of possession, completing more than twice as many passes as Boro, but despite firing in 21 shots to the 12 racked up by Bryan Robson's side, the Red Devils' total of seven on target was only one better than Boro's six. United also fired in an incredible 71 crosses, but only 12 found their target as the Boro defence combined to make 32 headed clearances.

Man of the match for Middlesbrough was Brian Deane, who set up the first goal for his strike partner and then scored the third, which ultimately proved decisive. His goal came from one of five efforts that he made, three of which were on target, but he only completed 58% of his 40 passes.

This game proved to be the zenith of Boro's season. They then embarked upon a run of nine Premiership games without a win, and a slump in form that saw them finish in mid-table when a European place had beckoned.

True grit: Alan Shearer scored 14 Premiership goals for the Magpies in 1998–99

NEWCASTLE UNITED

ADDRESS

St James's Park,
Newcastle-upon-Tyne NE1 4ST

CONTACT NUMBERS

Telephone: 0191 201 8400
Fax: 0191 201 8600
Ticket Office: 0191 261 1571
24hr Information: 09068 121190
Superstore: 0191 201 8426
Website: www.nufc.co.uk

SPONSORS

Scottish and Newcastle Breweries

FANZINES

The Mag, The Number Nine
Talk of the Toon
Half Mag Half Biscuit
Toon Army News
The Flying Magpie
Oh Wi Ye
Only One United

KEY PERSONNEL

President: Sir John Hall
Chairman: W F Shepherd
Deputy Chairman: D S Hall
Director/Chief Executive: A O Fletcher
Directors: R Jones, L Wheatley
Director of Football Administration:
R Cushing
Manager: Ruud Gullit

COLOURS

Home: Black and white striped shirts
with black shorts and stockings
Away: Blue shirts, shorts and stockings

NICKNAME

The Magpies

20 FACTS

1 Newcastle started life in 1881 as a club called Stanley, but changed their name to Newcastle East End a year later. When rivals Newcastle West End went out of business, they were invited to take up residence at West End's old ground, St James's Park. The club's name changed to Newcastle United in 1892.

2 The club have been League Champions on four occasions – in 1904–05, 1906–07, 1908–09 and 1926–27.

3 They have never won the League Cup, but they finished as runners-up in 1976.

4 Newcastle have won the FA Cup six times – in 1910, 1924, 1932, 1951, 1952 and 1955.

5 The club won their one major European trophy in 1968–69, beating Ujpest Doza 6–2 on aggregate to win the Fairs Cup.

6 Former Newcastle player Andrew Cunningham became the oldest player to make his Football League debut. He was 38 years and two days old when he appeared against Leicester City in a First Division match on February 2, 1929.

7 Newcastle also hold the record for the oldest player ever to appear in an FA Cup final. Billy Hampson was 41 years and eight months old when he appeared in the 1924 final against Aston Villa.

8 United's all-time leading league goalscorer is Jackie Milburn. He scored 177 times in the league and bagged a total of 200 in all competitions.

9 The Magpies hold the record for the biggest FA Cup semi-final win. They beat Fulham 6–0 in 1908.

10 Len Shackleton holds the club record for the most goals scored in a single match. He bagged six against Newport in a Division Two game on his Newcastle debut on October 5, 1946.

11 Newcastle 's record victory was that game against Newport and it finished 13–0. It is also a record score for a Division Two match, and could have been even higher but for the fact that Charlie Wayman missed a penalty.

12 Newcastle's record attendance is 68,386 for a Division One game against Chelsea on September 3, 1930.

13 Midfielder Nolberto Solano is the first Peruvian ever to play in the English league. Newcastle also fielded the league's first ever Brazilian (Mirandinha in 1987) and the first ever Colombian (Faustino Asprilla in 1996).

14 The 1999 FA Cup final between Newcastle United and Manchester United was the first ever to feature two Uniteds.

15 Newcastle finished 13th in the 1998–99 Premiership. Their league record was:

Pld	W	D	L	F	A	Pts
38	11	13	14	48	54	46

16 Ruud Gullit's side reached the FA Cup final, where they met Manchester United and lost for the second season in a row by a 2–0 scoreline. They beat Crystal Palace 2–1 and Bradford City 3–0, before defeating Blackburn Rovers 1–0 in a fifth round replay after drawing 0–0 at St James's Park. Everton were beaten 4–1 in the sixth round before Newcastle booked their place in the final with a 2–0 win over Tottenham Hotspur in the semi-final.

17 After defeating Tranmere Rovers 1–0 in the third round of the Worthington Cup, Newcastle were eliminated by Blackburn Rovers on penalties after a 1–1 draw in the fourth round.

18 Newcastle beat Partizan Belgrade 2–1 in the home leg of the European Cup Winners Cup first round, but lost the away leg 1–0 to go out on away goals.

19 The top goalscorer in all competitions for Newcastle was Alan Shearer with 21 goals.

20 Newcastle's disciplinary record was the sixth-best in the Premiership. They committed 504 fouls, earned 51 yellow cards and suffered four dismissals.

SEASON REVIEW

Newcastle did not start the 1998–99 season in the most optimistic frame of mind. Manager Kenny Dalglish had failed to endear himself to all of the fans with his selection policy and tactics the previous season, and successive draws with Charlton Athletic and Chelsea saw him dismissed.

Ruud Gullit took the reins for Newcastle's third match of the season. But the cheers that rang around St James's Park were quickly silenced as Michael Owen proceeded to destroy the home side with a first half hat-trick in a 4–1 win for the visitors.

Gullit was in no doubt about the size of the task that faced him. Newcastle had a huge squad – but it lacked quality. With the transfer kitty running low, he was determined to take a look at those players who were already at the club before selling to raise funds for rebuilding.

One of his first, and least popular, decisions was to sell full-back Steve Watson to Aston Villa. Watson was one of the few remaining Geordies left in the squad and was also one of Newcastle's more consistent players.

But Gullit needed money. Stephane Guivarc'h was to follow Watson out of the door, and before the end of the season David Batty and Keith Gillespie had also departed in big-money deals.

Results continued to be mixed. Big wins against Southampton and Coventry were offset by heavy defeats by Arsenal and West Ham. Rumours of a bust-up between Gullit and Alan Shearer did not help matters.

Although Shearer was the team's leading scorer, he looked isolated up front, and in an attempt to bring added weight to the attack Duncan Ferguson was signed from Everton in an £8 million deal. Ferguson's impact was immediate. He scored twice in the 3–1 victory over Wimbledon but injury blighted his season thereafter.

Gullit's other buys enjoyed mixed fortunes. Ironically, it was three of Dalglish's signings – Dietmar Hamann, Nolberto Solano and Gary Speed – who proved to be Gullit's most effective performers. All three were capable of keeping the ball and distributing it effectively, something that Gullit demanded of all his players. He had arrived at the club with the media and supporters expecting "sexy football". What they got was possession football.

Under Gullit, Newcastle attempted more passes than any other club in the Premiership. Their pass completion rate of 76% in the opposition half was also the highest in the top flight. Unfortunately, they were unable to convert this possession into real pressure, finishing the season with the fifth-worst shooting accuracy and a cross completion rate of just 27%.

Thirteenth place in the Premiership was no better than season 1997–98 and, although the fans reacted more kindly to Gullit's style of management, the club were still left with nothing from the season but a second successive runners-up spot in the FA Cup.

Reaching that final proved a major distraction. Although Gullit banned all talk of the cup, the players' minds were clearly not on the league and the victory at Derby on April 3 was to be the last of the season in the Premiership.

Defeat at the hands of Manchester United in the final underlined how far behind the nation's top team Newcastle were in 1998–99. Gullit has some skilled players but the form which Newcastle showed in the second half of the season was disturbingly similar to that shown by Blackburn at the end of 1997–98. Complacency cannot be allowed to creep in, and the challenge Gullit faces in 1999–2000 is to find new faces to turn the club into a side that can perform consistently at the highest level.

> ## "The FA Cup has been getting in the way. But we have qualified for European football"
>
> **Ruud Gullit**

NEWCASTLE UNITED

DATE	OPPONENT	SCORE	ATT.	ALBERT	ANDERSSON	BARNES	BARTON	BATTY	BEHARALL	BRADY	CHARVET	DABIZAS	DALGLISH	DOMI	FERGUSON	GEORGIADIS	GIL
15.8.98	Charlton H	0–0	36,719	–	64	s24	s21	–	–	–	90	45	–	–	–	–	–
22.8.98	Chelsea A	1–1	34,795	s23	67¹	–	–	–	–	–	90	90	–	–	–	–	–
30.8.98	Liverpool H	1–4	36,740	90□	–	–	s45	–	–	–	90	s12	–	–	–	–	–
9.9.98	Aston Villa A	0–1	39,241	90	59	–	–	–	–	–	90	–	–	–	–	–	–
12.9.98	Southampton H	4–0*	36,454	90	59	–	s25	–	–	–	90	–	–	–	–	–	s31
19.9.98	Coventry A	5–1	22,639	–	–	s18	–	–	–	–	90	90¹	s3	–	–	–	72
26.9.98	Nott'm For H	2–0	36,760	–	–	s65	s1	–	–	–	90	90	s30	–	–	–	–
4.10.98	Arsenal A	0–3	38,102	s23□	–	–	–	90□	–	–	90	65■	s45	–	–	–	–
17.10.98	Derby Co H	2–1	36,750	–	–	–	–	90	–	–	90	90¹□	89	–	–	–	–
24.10.98	Tottenham A	0–2	36,047	–	–	–	–	90	–	–	90	–	56□	–	–	–	–
31.10.98	West Ham H	0–3	36,744	–	–	–	–	90	–	–	90	90	83	–	–	–	s7
8.11.98	Man Utd A	0–0	55,174	–	–	–	–	90	–	90□	90□	90	–	–	90	–	–
14.11.98	Sheff Wed H	1–1	36,698	–	s45	–	90	s56□	–	–	90	–	90¹	–	–	–	90
23.11.98	Everton A	0–1	30,357	s45	90	–	69□	90	–	s29	90□	90	61	–	–	–	90
28.11.98	Wimbledon H	3–1	36,623	–	90	–	90	–	–	–	90	–	–	–	90²	–	90
6.12.98	Middlesbro A	2–2	34,629	–	77	–	82	–	–	–	90¹	s8¹	s13	–	90	–	90
12.12.98	Blackburn A	0–0	27,569	–	62	–	90	–	–	–	90	s28	–	–	90	s8	–
19.12.98	Leicester H	1–0	36,718	–	90	–	90	–	–	–	90	90	–	–	90	–	–
26.12.98	Leeds Utd H	0–3	36,759	–	–	–	52	–	–	–	90	90	–	–	90	62	–
28.12.98	Liverpool A	2–4	44,605	–	s41¹	–	–	–	–	–	90	s16	–	–	49	s24	–
9.1.99	Chelsea H	0–1	36,711	–	57	–	–	–	–	–	90	–	–	90	–	–	–
17.1.99	Charlton A	2–2	20,043	–	–	–	90	–	–	72	s18	78¹	s1	90	–	90	–
30.1.99	Aston Villa H	2–1	36,766	–	s26	–	90	–	–	s8	–	90	–	90	–	–	–
6.2.99	Leeds Utd A	1–0	40,202	–	s2	–	90□	–	–	s24	90□	–	–	90	–	–	–
17.2.99	Coventry H	4–1	36,352	–	–	–	s3	–	–	s25	90	–	–	90	–	–	–
20.2.99	Southampton A	1–2	15,244	–	–	–	–	–	–	90	90	90	–	90□	–	–	–
28.2.99	Arsenal H	1–1	36,708	–	–	–	–	–	–	60	90	90□	–	90	–	–	–
10.3.99	Nott'm For A	2–1	22,852	–	–	–	90	–	–	–	90	s69	–	90	–	90	–
13.3.99	Man Utd H	1–2	36,776	–	–	–	83	–	–	–	90	–	–	90	45□	–	–
20.3.99	West Ham A	0–2	25,997	–	–	–	–	–	–	–	90	–	–	90	59	–	–
3.4.99	Derby Co A	4–3	32,039	–	–	–	–	–	–	s25	90	90□	–	–	–	–	–
5.4.99	Tottenham H	1–1	36,655	–	–	–	s45	–	–	–	90	90	–	90	–	s33	–
17.4.99	Everton H	1–3	36,775	–	–	–	90	–	90	–	–	–	–	–	–	–	–
21.4.99	Sheff Wed A	1–1	21,545	–	–	–	90	–	–	s1	–	90□	–	–	–	–	–
24.4.99	Wimbledon A	1–1	21,325	–	–	90	–	–	90	–	–	90	–	90	–	–	–
1.5.99	Middlesbro H	1–1	36,784	–	–	–	–	–	90	–	–	90	–	90	63	–	–
8.5.99	Leicester A	0–2	21,125	–	–	–	–	–	90	–	–	90□	–	90	45	–	–
16.5.99	Blackburn H	1–1	36,623	–	–	–	90	–	–	–	–	90	–	–	–	–	–

□ Yellow card, ■ Red card, s Substitute, 90³ Goals scored
*including own goal

1998–99 PREMIERSHIP APPEARANCES

GIVEN	GLASS	GRIFFIN	GUIVARC'H	HAMANN	HARPER	HOWEY	HUGHES	KETSBAIA	LEE	MARIC	McCLEN	PEARCE	PISTONE	SAHA	SERRANT	SHEARER	SOLANO	SPEED	WATSON	TOTAL
90	–	–	–	90	–	–	–	s26	90□	–	–	90	90	–	–	90	–	90	90	990
90	–	–	–	90	–	–	–	–	90	–	–	90	67□	–	–	90□	s23	90	90	990
90	s78	–	90¹	12	–	–	–	–	90□	–	–	90	–	–	45	90	–	90	78	990
90	90	–	s19	–	–	–	–	s31□	90	–	–	90	–	–	–	90	71	90	90	990
90	90	–	–	–	–	–	–	90¹	90□	–	–	90	–	–	–	90□²	–	65	90	990
90	90¹	–	87	–	–	–	–	–	90	–	–	90	–	–	–	90²	21	s69¹	90	990
90	90	–	–	–	–	–	–	60	90	–	–	90	–	–	–	90²	89	90	25	990
90	67	90	–	–	–	–	–	45	–	–	90□	–	–	–	–	90	90	90□	–	965
90	90¹	90	–	–	–	–	–	s1	90	–	–	90	–	–	–	90	87	s3	–	990
90	56	90	s34	–	–	–	–	–	90□	–	–	90	–	90	–	90	90	s34	–	990
90	49	90	–	–	–	–	–	s16	–	–	48■	s41	–	–	–	90	74	90	–	948
90	90	90	–	69	–	90	–	–	–	–	–	–	–	–	–	90□	–	s21	–	990
90	–	45	–	34□	–	90	–	–	90	–	–	–	–	–	s45	45	–	90	–	990
90	–	–	–	s21	–	–	–	–	90□	–	–	–	–	–	45□	–	–	90	–	990
45	26	–	–	90□	s45	90	90	–	–	–	–	–	–	–	–	–	s64¹	90	–	990
–	s44	–	–	–	90	90	90	–	90	–	–	–	–	–	–	–	46	90	–	990
–	82	–	–	90	90	90	62	s28	–	–	–	–	–	–	–	–	90	90□	–	990
90	90¹	–	–	–	–	90	–	55	90	–	–	–	–	–	–	s35	–	90	–	990
90	90	–	–	–	90	s38	s28	90	–	–	–	–	–	–	–	90	–	90	–	990
90	66	–	30■	–	90	90	–	–	–	–	90	–	–	–	–	90□	74¹	90	–	930
90	90	–	90	–	90	90□	–	s18	–	–	–	–	s33	–	–	90	72	90	–	990
–	–	–	–	–	90	90	s10	89¹	–	–	–	–	–	–	–	90□	80¹	90	–	978
90	90	–	–	90	–	90	–	64¹□	–	–	–	–	–	–	–	90¹	82	90	–	990
90	66	90	–	90□	–	90	–	90	–	–	–	–	88□	–	–	–	90¹	90□	–	990
90	65	–	–	90	–	90	–	s14	–	–	–	–	76¹	–	–	90²	90	87¹	–	990
90	–	–	–	90¹	–	90□	–	90	s45	–	–	–	–	–	–	90□	45	90□	–	990
90	–	–	–	90¹□	–	90	–	s30	s30	–	–	–	90	–	–	90	60	90	–	990
90	–	–	–	90¹□	–	21	–	s1	s45	90	–	–	89	–	–	90¹	–	45	–	990
90	–	–	–	90	–	–	–	61	s45	s7	–	–	s29	–	–	90	90¹	90	–	990
90	–	90	–	–	–	–	–	s32	s31	58	–	–	–	90	–	90	90	90	–	990
90	–	90	–	–	–	90	90¹	90	79	–	–	–	s11	–	–	–	65¹	90²	–	990
90	–	45	–	–	–	90	90¹	–	57	57	–	–	s33	–	–	–	90	90□	–	990
90	–	90	–	90	–	–	90	75	90□	55	–	–	s35	–	–	90¹	s15	90	–	990
–	–	90	–	90	90	–	90	90	89	90□	–	–	–	–	–	76¹	s14	90	–	990
90	–	90	–	90	–	–	–	–	–	90	–	–	–	–	–	90¹	90	90	–	990
–	–	–	–	90	90	–	–	s27	90	45	–	–	–	–	–	90¹	s45	90□	–	990
–	s45	–	–	90	90	–	–	s45	90	–	–	–	–	–	–	90	45	90	–	990
–	s39	90	–	90¹	90	–	90	64	51	90	–	–	–	s26	–	–	90	90	–	990

THE MANAGER

RUUD GULLIT

Following his shock departure from Stamford Bridge in February 1998, Ruud Gullit bounced back in style. After seven months out of football and countless job offers he plumped for Newcastle, qualifying for Europe and guiding the Toon Army to the FA Cup final at the first attempt.

Twice voted World Player of the Year, Gullit arrived in England via Sampdoria, after a glittering playing career that included spells at Feyenoord, PSV Eindhoven and AC Milan. He was also capped 64 times for Holland.

Gullit inherited Kenny Dalglish's side in August 1998 and added to the squad soon after, signing Duncan Ferguson, Louis Saha and Didier Domi. He made no wholesale changes to the team throughout the season, but encouraged the fluid passing style that brought him success at Chelsea, bringing the best out of Nolberto Solano and Dietmar Hamann in particular.

In a Premiership campaign of mixed fortunes, Gullit led Newcastle through a difficult period, following the departure of Dalglish, to 13th place in the Premiership.

So far the Dutchman has proved to be a cup specialist but he harbours a burning desire to clinch the league title. He came close with Chelsea and will be aiming for the top six in 1999–2000, though he may privately feel he could do even better.

LEAGUE POSITION

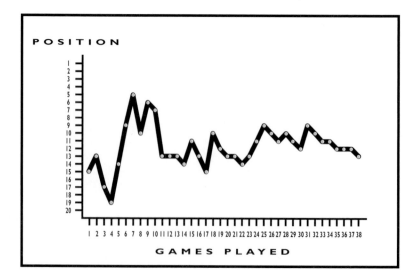

POSITION

GAMES PLAYED

THE GOALS

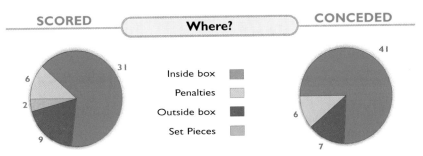

SCORED — Where? — CONCEDED

Inside box
Penalties
Outside box
Set Pieces

Newcastle United's Alan Shearer scored more penalties than any other Premiership player, bagging six out of seven spot kicks. These represented a massive 12.5% of all goals that Ruud Gullit's side registered throughout the 1998–99 season, the highest percentage in the league. In spite of this, only 77.1% of all their goals were claimed inside of 18 yards. Newcastle also conceded six penalties, meaning 87% of all opposition goals came from inside Newcastle's box.

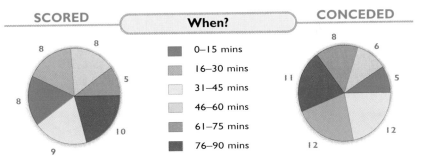

SCORED — When? — CONCEDED

0–15 mins
16–30 mins
31–45 mins
46–60 mins
61–75 mins
76–90 mins

The 1999 AXA-sponsored FA Cup finalists Newcastle scored more goals in the first half of their league matches than they did in the second, boasting a ratio of 52.1% of all strikes in the first 45 minutes, just below Arsenal.

Unfortunately for the Magpies, they conceded just as regularly in the opening period. With 29 of the 54 league goals against them before half-time, Newcastle's initial good work was too often undone.

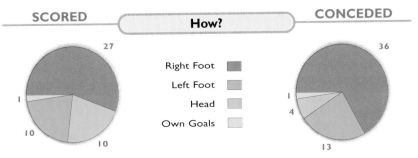

SCORED — How? — CONCEDED

Right Foot
Left Foot
Head
Own Goals

Newcastle were vulnerable to right-foot efforts, conceding exactly two-thirds of opposition goals in this way. The combined strength of Shearer and Duncan Ferguson in the air helped the Toon Army score 10 headers, more than one-fifth of their total strikes. The Geordies defended crosses admirably, allowing just four opposition goals with the head. This equated to just 7.4% of all goals against Gullit's side coming from headers, the second-lowest total in the league.

NEWCASTLE UNITED

	ALBERT	ANDERSSON	BARNES	BARTON	BATTY	BEHARALL	BRADY	CHARVET	DABIZAS	DALGLISH	DOMI	FERGUSON	GEORGIADIS	GILLESPIE	GLASS	GRIFFIN
APPEARANCE																
Start	3	11	0	17	6	4	3	30	25	6	14	7	7	5	18	14
Sub	3	4	1	7	2	0	6	1	5	5	0	0	3	2	4	0
Minutes on pitch	361	919	24	1678	597	360	334	2718	2301	561	1260	517	591	470	1583	1170
GOAL ATTEMPTS																
Goals	0	2	0	0	0	0	0	1	3	1	0	2	0	0	3	0
Shots on target	3	5	0	1	0	0	1	3	6	10	1	10	3	2	8	0
Shots off target	1	10	0	7	1	0	0	11	14	7	2	4	4	4	12	2
Shooting accuracy %	75%	33%	0%	13%	0%	0%	100%	21%	30%	59%	33%	71%	43%	33%	40%	0%
PASSING																
Goal assists	0	0	0	0	0	0	0	1	0	0	1	0	0	1	2	0
Long passes	36	3	3	226	31	28	1	202	155	4	119	6	17	12	48	82
Short passes	126	295	17	826	516	131	106	950	847	149	463	306	210	192	534	648
PASS COMPLETION																
Own half %	95%	77%	100%	90%	90%	94%	97%	91%	92%	79%	85%	84%	96%	81%	86%	87%
Opposition half %	65%	79%	77%	71%	81%	67%	82%	77%	69%	65%	64%	78%	82%	79%	75%	76%
CROSSING																
Total crosses	1	14	1	55	3	1	10	27	3	7	42	3	19	35	118	25
Cross completion %	0%	14%	0%	27%	33%	100%	30%	41%	0%	14%	17%	33%	26%	31%	25%	20%
DRIBBLING																
Dribbles & runs	1	35	2	59	17	6	10	56	36	54	53	10	22	36	70	39
Dribble completion %	0%	69%	100%	78%	82%	83%	50%	84%	97%	33%	89%	30%	68%	81%	60%	77%
DEFENDING																
Tackles made	11	25	2	64	31	11	11	74	95	14	52	18	25	13	51	36
Tackles won %	73%	40%	50%	69%	71%	27%	73%	65%	65%	86%	52%	44%	56%	62%	55%	58%
Blocks	12	0	0	12	4	5	1	35	19	0	7	0	2	3	3	8
Clearances	49	2	0	164	13	66	6	321	429	2	94	4	8	3	29	67
Interceptions	5	0	0	15	8	3	2	47	43	3	16	0	2	0	6	8
DISCIPLINE																
Fouls	7	14	0	29	13	3	2	26	39	17	9	11	12	2	12	4
Offside	0	19	0	4	0	0	0	1	1	5	2	6	0	1	2	1
Yellow cards	2	0	0	3	2	0	0	3	6	1	1	0	1	0	0	0
Red cards	0	0	0	0	0	0	0	0	2	0	0	0	0	0	0	0

GOALKEEPER NAME	START/ (SUB)	TIME ON PITCH	GOALS CONCEDED	MINS/GOALS CONCEDED	SAVES MADE	SAVES/ SHOTS
GIVEN	31	2745	45	61	98	69%
HARPER	7 (1)	675	9	75	28	76%

PLAYERS' STATISTICS

	GUIVARC'H	HAMANN	HOWEY	HUGHES	KETSBAIA	LEE	MARIC	MCCLEN	PEARCE	PISTONE	SAHA	SERRANT	SHEARER	SOLANO	SPEED	WATSON	TOTAL	RANK
	2	22	14	12	14	20	9	1	12	2	5	3	29	24	34	7		
	2	1	0	2	12	6	1	0	0	1	6	1	1	5	4	0		
	230	1786	1191	1100	1332	1974	661	57	1038	198	600	225	2586	1972	3114	553		
	1	4	0	0	5	0	0	0	0	0	1	0	14	6	4	0	48*	=7th
	2	24	1	0	19	5	4	0	2	0	4	0	42	19	15	0	190	8th
	3	29	2	1	18	16	6	1	3	0	6	2	29	21	28	3	247	4th
	40%	45%	33%	0%	51%	24%	40%	0%	40%	0%	40%	0%	59%	48%	35%	0%	43%	16th
	0	2	0	1	4	2	1	0	1	0	1	0	5	5	0	1	30	11th
	3	111	95	73	32	144	13	3	144	19	6	19	39	97	187	58	2016	4th
	62	978	297	359	552	1151	284	33	409	123	208	120	985	971	1670	182	14701	1st
	93%	93%	93%	88%	90%	91%	91%	77%	92%	92%	88%	81%	90%	83%	90%	89%	90%	7th
	71%	83%	69%	71%	84%	83%	75%	78%	72%	79%	73%	78%	68%	77%	80%	70%	76%	1st
	2	63	0	7	23	62	18	1	16	6	2	8	29	138	19	29	787	7th
	0%	22%	0%	43%	22%	29%	28%	0%	56%	67%	50%	38%	24%	28%	37%	31%	27%	12th
	1	51	8	9	71	85	33	2	12	4	29	6	47	62	66	18	1010	5th
	0%	69%	100%	89%	72%	80%	58%	50%	92%	100%	62%	83%	66%	71%	76%	72%	72%	8th
	0	80	32	34	28	98	17	2	27	4	13	11	49	56	155	16	1155	10th
	0%	50%	84%	71%	57%	62%	65%	0%	67%	75%	38%	36%	45%	71%	57%	69%	60%	13th
	0	2	26	13	0	6	1	0	23	1	2	0	2	8	12	3	210	8th
	3	47	190	133	7	36	5	0	123	7	6	17	33	33	104	36	2099	8th
	0	21	26	12	4	14	3	0	10	0	4	2	6	21	38	2	324	12th
	6	39	10	9	21	30	13	0	12	0	6	2	66	35	48	7	504	10th
	2	1	0	0	10	0	5	0	1	0	4	0	25	5	1	0	96	20th
	0	5	1	1	2	6	1	0	1	1	1	1	6	0	6	0	51	=18th
	0	1	0	0	0	0	0	0	1	0	0	0	0	0	0	0	4	=7th

*includes one own goal

CROSSES CAUGHT	CROSSES PUNCHED	CROSSES NOT CLAIMED	CATCH SUCCESS	THROWS/SHORT KICKS	% COMPLETION	LONG KICKS	% COMPLETION
64	22	7	93%	338	96%	611	39%
21	5	3	88%	74	97%	176	45%

PLAYER OF THE SEASON

PLAYER	INDEX SCORE
DIETMAR HAMANN	1,119
Didier Domi *	1,032
Nikos Dabizas	1,031
Warren Barton *	908
Gary Speed	875
Laurent Charvet	875
Robert Lee	870
Alan Shearer	838
Stephen Glass *	760
Shay Given	547

*Featured in fewer than 16 games

Few Newcastle fans would want to analyse the Magpies' hugely disappointing performance in the 1999 FA Cup final.

But it was clear that the half-time departure of German midfield star Dietmar Hamann had a detrimental effect on the team. Without his vision and tenacity, United had lost the midfield battle.

Hamann announced his arrival at St James's Park with a sublime goal in a televized pre-season friendly against Italian giants Juventus on August 10. Injury robbed the Magpies of his services for some of the campaign, but he later showed his worth by scoring three excellent goals in three consecutive league games against Southampton, Arsenal and Everton.

He finished as United's highest-scoring player in the Carling Opta Season Index, with an average score of 1,119 points.

Another "Didi" man, French full-back Didier Domi, impressed greatly after his introduction to the side under Ruud Gullit

against Chelsea on January 9 and he finished second in the top 10.

Elegant centre-back Nikos Dabizas was one player singled out for criticism following the FA Cup final, after his error let in Manchester United for the critical second goal. But it would be unfair to judge the Greek's season on that one moment of poor defending. Overall, he was the most consistent defender at the club and was the third player to average more than 1,000 points in the season-long Index.

Other players found it difficult to maintain the same levels of consistency. Full-back Warren Barton struggled even to achieve a regular first-team slot, while Laurent Charvet and Shay Given were excellent in individual matches but were always prone to defensive slip-ups.

Gary Speed, who partnered Hamann in midfield, and Rob Lee, who deputized when necessary, both figured thanks to their high numbers of passes. Top scorer Alan Shearer also featured despite media criticism.

FIVE OF THE BEST

The departure from St James's Park of Kenny Dalglish plunged the Magpies into an early-season crisis, but the board already had former Chelsea boss Ruud Gullit lined up to replace him. He spent much of the season trying to rebuild the side and league progress was slow, but the club was never seriously in danger of relegation and Gullit successfully guided his side to their second successive FA Cup final.

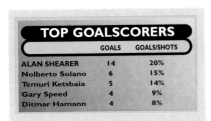

TOP GOALSCORERS	GOALS	GOALS/SHOTS
ALAN SHEARER	14	20%
Nolberto Solano	6	15%
Temuri Ketsbaia	5	14%
Gary Speed	4	9%
Ditmar Hamann	4	8%

England skipper Alan Shearer started to regain the sort of form that had made him one of the most feared strikers in the world, bagging 14 league strikes and more than 20 in all competitions. One in five of his shots hit the back of the net, more than any other Magpie. New strike partner Duncan Ferguson sat out most of the season through injury, so it was left to Georgian star Temuri Ketsbaia and the Toon midfield to help out in the goalscoring department, with varying degrees of success.

Everton reject Gary Speed has made the ball-winning central midfield berth his own in the black-and-white Newcastle shirt; and with Rob Lee or Carling Opta Player of the Year Dietmar Hamann alongside, United had a formidable midfield. Utility man Laurent Charvet showed pinpoint passing skills, while Peruvian wide man Nolberto Solano adjusted to the pace of the English game faster than any Toon follower could possibly have hoped for. The top four in this list all completed more than eight out of every 10 passes.

TOP PASSERS	SUCC PASSES	COMPLETION
GARY SPEED	1,544	83%
Rob Lee	1,116	86%
Laurent Charvet	967	84%
Dietmar Hamann	941	86%
Nolberto Solano	838	78%

TOP TACKLERS	WON	SUCCESS
GARY SPEED	89	57%
Nikos Dabizas	62	65%
Rob Lee	61	62%
Laurent Charvet	48	65%
Warren Barton	44	69%

Gary Speed won the most tackles in the Newcastle squad, but he was by no means the man most likely to win possession with his challenges. That accolade went to former Wimbledon full-back Warren Barton, who won an above-average 69% of all his tackles. Stylish Greek defender Nikos Dabizas had a highly impressive season, winning 65% of his tackles and was always likely to be a threat when venturing forward at set plays.

No Ruud Gullit side is likely to be labelled "dirty", and Newcastle managed to pick up the third-fewest bookings in the Premiership in 1998–99. No one collected more than half a dozen, so the only player who suffered major suspension woes was Nikos Dabizas, twice sent off over the course of the campaign. Alan Shearer conceded the largest number of fouls – 66 in all – characterizing his physical approach to the game.

DISCIPLINE	POINTS	FOULS & CARDS
ALAN SHEARER	84	66F, 6Y, 0R
Nikos Dabizas	69	39F, 6Y, 2R
Gary Speed	66	48F, 6Y, 0R
Dietmar Hamann	60	39F, 5Y, 1R
Robert Lee	48	30F, 6Y, 0R

ACTION	BARTON	CHARVET	DABIZAS	DALGLISH	GILLESPIE	GIVEN	GLASS	GUIVARC'H	LEE	PEARCE	SHEARER	SOLANO	SPEED	WATSON	TOTAL	COVENTRY CITY
Time on pitch	18	90	90	3	72	90	90	87	90	90	90	21	69	90	990	990
GOALS																
Goal	–	–	–	–	–	–	1	–	–	–	–	–	–	–	5	–
Shot on target	–	–	–	–	–	–	–	–	–	2	2	–	–	–	4	2
Shot off target	–	–	–	–	–	–	–	1	–	–	2	–	–	–	3	6
Blocked shot	–	–	–	–	–	–	–	3	–	–	–	–	–	–	4	3
Own goal	–	–	–	–	–	–	–	–	–	–	–	–	–	–	–	–
PASSES																
Pass to own player	7	17	19	1	17	–	24	17	28	24	22	9	17	23	225	270
Pass to opposition	–	–	8	–	2	–	4	5	–	4	3	–	–	–	30	56
Cross to own player	–	–	–	–	4	–	–	–	–	–	–	–	–	–	7	7
Cross to opposition player	2	–	–	–	3	–	2	–	2	–	–	–	–	–	11	22
Goal assist	–	–	–	–	–	–	–	–	–	–	–	–	–	–	3	–
Pass completion %	80%	89%	70%	100%	81%	100%	81%	77%	90%	86%	88%	91%	94%	96%	85%	78%
TACKLES & CLEARANCES																
Tackle	1	2	3	–	3	–	2	–	3	4	2	–	–	3	22	23
Clearances, blocks and interceptions	7	7	18	–	–	–	2	2	3	7	–	–	–	4	45	34
DRIBBLES & RUNS																
Dribble ball retained	–	–	–	–	–	–	1	–	–	–	–	–	–	–	4	2
Dribbles ball lost	–	–	–	–	–	–	–	–	–	–	–	–	–	–	–	–
Dribble success %	0%	0%	0%	0%	0%	0%	100%	0%	100%	0%	0%	100%	100%	100%	100%	100%
DISCIPLINE																
Fouls	2	–	–	–	1	–	–	1	2	1	2	1	1	3	16	13
Penalty conceded	–	–	–	–	–	–	–	–	–	–	–	–	–	–	–	–
Free kick - offside	–	–	–	–	–	–	–	1	–	–	1	–	–	–	2	1
Yellow cards	–	–	–	–	–	–	–	–	–	–	–	1	–	–	1	2
Red cards	–	–	–	–	–	–	–	–	–	–	–	–	–	–	–	–
GOALKEEPERS																
Distribution to own player	–	–	–	–	–	3	–	–	–	–	–	–	–	–	3	5
Distribution to opposition player	–	–	–	–	–	7	–	–	–	–	–	–	–	–	7	5
Goalkeeper distribution%	0%	0%	0%	0%	0%	30%	0%	0%	0%	0%	0%	0%	0%	0%	30%	50%
Save	–	–	–	–	–	–	–	–	–	–	–	–	–	–	–	4
Ball caught	–	–	–	–	–	8	–	–	–	–	–	–	–	–	8	5
Ball dropped	–	–	–	–	–	–	–	–	–	–	–	–	–	–	–	–
Goal conceded	–	–	–	–	–	1	–	–	–	–	–	–	–	–	1	5

Ruud Gullit's first three games as Newcastle manager had seen 10 goals, comprising two defeats and a comprehensive 4-0 victory over struggling Southampton. There had been little sign of his brand of "sexy football", but Newcastle fans were willing to give him time to restore the Magpies' reputation as entertainers. After 18 months of less-than-flamboyant football under Kenny Dalglish, the Geordie faithful longed for a return to the rollercoaster style of Kevin Keegan's reign.

September 19, 1998

1-5

COVENTRY CITY
NEWCASTLE UNITED

Coventry City took just four minutes to score the first goal, with a corner by young Barry Quinn being flicked on by Dion Dublin for Noel Whelan to head home from close range. But this was not a sign of things to come.

Newcastle equalized on 14 minutes when Nikos Dabizas rose unmarked in the penalty area to head past Magnus Hedman. The game then developed into a very even contest for the remainder of the first half, but Newcastle struck twice before the interval to sew up the game and secure the three points.

First, a long clearance by Shay Given was missed by several players before Alan Shearer muscled his way past Jean-Guy Wallemme and fired a shot into the net off Hedman's prostrate body. Then, a minute later, David Burrows lost the ball down by the corner flag when under pressure and Keith Gillespie found Steve Watson. The young full-back fired over a cross and Gary Speed rose above two players to head the ball home.

The second half saw intense pressure and the lion's share of possession going to the Sky Blues. Newcastle were content to play on the break, and the tactic paid dividends in the 58th minute when they won the ball near their own corner flag and played it long to Stephane Guivarc'h.

The Frenchman found Stephen Glass, who in turn tried to find Shearer; Wallemme went through the England captain to win the ball, but referee Rob Harris played an excellent advantage as Glass picked up the ball inside his own half and ran through on goal, finishing with a left-foot shot that again bounced in off Hedman.

Coventry were unable to break the resolute Newcastle defence down, and on one of their rare forays forward the Magpies won a corner in the last minute from which they scored their fifth goal. Glass crossed for Shearer who leapt above two defenders to head towards goal. Hedman saved, but Shearer was the quickest to react and fired home the rebound.

Newcastle managed 16 goal attempts to Coventry's 12 and, despite losing the territorial battle, their counter-attacking style proved critical in winning the match.

Shearer was man of the match with two goals from six shots, four of which hit the target. His points score of 1,839 was accumulated via those goal attempts, 22 successful passes and two tackles.

The victory proved to be their best of the season, but as Ruud Gullit began bringing in new signings and changing the tactics the inevitable inconsistency set in, and Newcastle finished in mid-table.

ACTION	BRADY	CHARVET	DABIZAS	DOWI	GIVEN	GRIFFIN	HUGHES	KETSBAIA	LEE	MARIC	SAHA	SOLANO	SPEED	TOTAL	DERBY CO
Time on pitch	25	90	90	90	90	90	90	90	90	79	11	65	90	990	990
GOALS															
Goal	-	-	-	-	-	-	-	-	-	-	-	-	-	-	-
Shot on target	-	-	-	-	-	-	-	2	-	-	-	-	2	4	3
Shot off target	-	-	-	1	-	-	-	-	-	-	1	-	-	2	2
Blocked shot	-	-	-	-	-	1	-	-	-	2	-	2	2	7	6
Own goal	-	-	-	-	-	-	-	-	-	-	-	-	-	-	-
PASSES															
Pass to own player	7	39	34	19	-	30	29	30	61	16	3	39	53	360	196
Pass to opposition	2	4	5	6	-	8	8	7	7	10	3	8	14	82	101
Cross to own player	-	-	-	2	-	-	2	-	-	-	-	1	-	5	6
Cross to opposition player	-	-	-	-	-	-	2	-	-	-	-	-	-	5	11
Goal assist	-	-	-	-	-	-	-	-	-	-	-	1	-	3	1
Pass completion %	78%	91%	87%	78%	0%	77%	76%	80%	90%	63%	50%	81%	79%	81%	64%
TACKLES & CLEARANCES															
Tackle	-	4	3	-	-	4	1	1	2	-	-	-	2	17	20
Clearances, blocks and interceptions	-	16	18	1	3	4	11	-	2	-	-	-	3	58	54
DRIBBLES & RUNS															
Dribbles ball retained	-	4	2	4	-	2	1	5	3	2	-	1	1	25	13
Dribbles ball lost	-	-	-	-	-	2	-	-	-	1	2	1	-	6	5
Dribble success %	0%	100%	100%	100%	0%	50%	100%	100%	100%	67%	0%	50%	100%	81%	72%
DISCIPLINE															
Fouls	-	-	-	-	-	-	-	-	-	4	-	2	2	10	15
Penalty conceded	-	-	-	-	-	-	-	-	1	-	-	-	-	1	1
Free kick - offside	-	-	-	1	-	-	-	-	-	-	-	-	-	2	5
Yellow cards	-	1	1	-	-	-	-	-	-	-	-	-	-	2	2
Red cards	-	-	-	-	-	-	-	-	-	-	-	-	-	-	-
GOALKEEPERS															
Distribution to own player	-	-	-	-	24	-	-	-	-	-	-	-	-	24	-
Distribution to opposition player	-	-	-	-	15	-	-	-	-	-	-	-	-	15	-
Goalkeeper distribution%	0%	0%	0%	0%	62%	0%	0%	0%	0%	0%	0%	0%	0%	62%	0%
Save	-	-	-	-	2	-	-	-	-	-	-	-	-	2	-
Ball caught	-	-	-	-	5	-	-	-	-	-	-	-	-	5	-
Ball dropped	-	-	-	-	-	-	-	-	-	-	-	-	-	-	-
Goal conceded	-	-	-	-	3	-	-	-	-	-	-	-	-	3	4

The sun shone down as Pride Park played host to a fabulous end-to-end match between two Premiership sides who liked to play a quick passing game. Newcastle were having a poor season by their standards, and languishing in the bottom half of the table.

April 3, 1999

3–4

DERBY COUNTY
NEWCASTLE UNITED

The first half started at a good pace, and early on Newcastle goalkeeper Shay Given survived a kick to the head by Deon Burton. Unfortunately he was soon on the receiving end again when Derby took the lead on eight minutes. Francesco Baiano somehow found enough space to conjure up a superb flying volley from the edge of the area. The ball rebounded down off the underside of the crossbar and, following a poor header from Nikos Dabizas, Burton scored with an acrobatic overhead kick.

It took just three minutes for Newcastle to strike back. After a patient passing move, Robert Lee found Aaron Hughes with time and space on the right wing. The youngster crossed for Gary Speed to deliver a perfectly-executed diving header into the bottom right-hand corner of Russell Hoult's net.

Newcastle were level and started to look the better side. But it was Derby who struck next, in controversial fashion. Building from the back, Lars Bohinen fought off two challenges and threaded a great ball through to Baiano, who was pulled back by Dabizas. That was enough to send the Italian tumbling to the turf – and referee Dermot Gallagher pointed to the spot. Newcastle were still fuming as Baiano stepped up and coolly slotted the ball past Given's outstretched right hand.

Again, Newcastle levelled almost immediately. A foul on Silvio Maric gave Newcastle a free kick on the right-hand edge of the Derby penalty area. A left-footer was needed, and Gary Speed stepped up to drive a shot off the edge of the Derby wall and past a helpless Hoult for 2–2.

Newcastle dominated the next 15 minutes, and shortly before the break Temuri Ketsbaia's 30-yard shot took a massive deflection to swing it past Hoult and into the Derby net.

The second half was never going to match the first. But on the hour a deep Ketsbaia cross was met full on the volley by Nolberto Solano, who crashed the ball into the net.

Towards the end of the match, Derby upped the tempo and were rewarded by a Paulo Wanchope goal in the 90th minute. Dean Sturridge worked an opening on the right wing and crossed for fellow-substitute Wanchope, whose diving header was almost a carbon-copy of the earlier Speed goal.

Newcastle were the dominant team in the game, out-passing Derby 442 to 297, with a success rate of 81% as opposed to Derby's 64%. Newcastle also kept the ball much better, with an 81% dribble success rating compared to 72% by Derby. Referee Dermot Gallagher cautioned three players in a largely free-flowing match, the Magpies' Dabizas being joined in the book by Derby's Spencer Prior and Deon Burton.

The win moved Newcastle into the top half of the table but it proved to be the team's last Carling Premiership victory of the 1998–99 season and the Magpies ended up in 13th position.

Temporary relief: Forest draw 2–2 against Blackburn Rovers in December 1998

NOTTINGHAM FOREST

ADDRESS

City Ground, Pavilion Road, West
Bridgeford, Nottingham NG2 5FJ

CONTACT NUMBERS

Telephone: 0115 982 4444
Fax: 0115 982 4455
Ticket Office: 0115 982 4445
24hr Information: 09068 121174
Superstore: 0115 982 4447
e-mail:
webmaster@nottinghamforest.co.uk
Website: www.nottinghamforest.co.uk

SPONSORS

Pinnacle

FANZINES

The Tricky Tree, The Almighty Brian,
Forest Forever, Garibaldi

KEY PERSONNEL

Chairman: E Barnes
Chief Executive: P W Soar
Directors: P W Soar, R W Dove,
K J Eggleston, R A Fairhall,
T H Farr, I Korn, P R Markham
Club Secretary: P White
Manager: Ron Atkinson

COLOURS

Home: Red shirts, white shorts
and red stockings
Away: White shirts, black shorts
and black and white stockings

NICKNAME

The Reds

20 FACTS

1 Nottingham Forest were formed at a meeting in the Clinton Arms pub in 1865 convened by a group of shinney players (shinney is a form of hockey) who had decided to switch to football.

2 The club have won one title, in 1977–78. Their best season in the Carling Premiership came in 1994–95 when they finished third.

3 They have twice won the FA Cup – in 1898 and 1959.

4 The Football League Cup has provided Nottingham Forest with some great victories. The club have won the trophy four times – in 1978, 1979, 1989 and 1990.

5 Forest also have a proud record in European competition. They have twice won the European Cup – in 1979 and 1980.

6 Nottingham Forest's game against Sheffield Norfolk in 1878 was the first English football match in which the referee used a whistle.

7 Forest hold the record for the longest unbeaten sequence in English Football League history. They went 42 games without defeat between November 1977 and December 1978.

8 Former Forest boss Brian Clough was the first manager in England to pay £1 million for a player when he signed Trevor Francis for Forest from Birmingham City in a £1.15 million deal in 1979.

9 Nottingham Forest and Notts County are close rivals – very close. The club's grounds are separated by just 330 yards, making them the nearest neighbours in the Football League.

10 The club's record win is 14–0 against Clapton in an FA Cup first round meeting in January 1891.

11 Their record defeat came against Blackburn Rovers in Division Two in April 1937 when Rovers won 9–1.

12 Forest became the very first club to be relegated from the Premiership in 1992–93.

13 The club were the first to reach two Wembley finals in the same season. They played in both the Simod and League Cup finals in 1989.

14 Legendary defender Stuart Pearce is Forest's most-capped player. He played for England 70 times while at the City Ground.

15 Forest are the only club to have played FA Cup ties in all four home nations. They have, of course, played numerous cup ties in England, but they have also played against Queens Park in Scotland in 1885, Linfield in Northern Ireland in 1889 and Cardiff in Wales in 1922.

16 Nottingham Forest finished 20th in the 1998–99 Premiership and were the first side to be relegated. Their league record was:

Pld	W	D	L	F	A	Pts
38	7	9	22	35	69	30

17 Forest suffered an early exit in the FA Cup when they were defeated 1–0 by Portsmouth at home in the third round.

18 The Reds beat Leyton Orient 5–1 on aggregate in the second round of the Worthington Cup. They were held to a 3–3 home draw by Cambridge United in the third round, but triumphed 4–3 on penalties. Their run eventually came to an end in the fourth round when they were beaten 2–1 by Manchester United at Old Trafford.

19 The top goalscorer in all competitions for Nottingham Forest was Dougie Freedman with 12 goals.

20 Nottingham Forest's disciplinary record was the seventh-worst in the Premiership. They committed 510 fouls, earned 85 yellow cards and suffered six dismissals.

SEASON REVIEW

Nottingham Forest were in trouble before the 1998–99 season even began. Forced to sell Kevin Campbell to Trabzonspor of Turkey for financial reasons, the team were further weakened by the actions of Pierre van Hooijdonk.

The Dutch international's claim that Forest had shot themselves in the foot with the sale of Campbell and failure to strengthen the squad was to prove correct. But most within the game believed his refusal to play for the club was not the right way to make his point.

Initially the rest of the team seemed to draw strength from van Hooijdonk's actions. A narrow defeat by Arsenal at Highbury was followed by successive victories against Coventry and Southampton. After three games Forest were third in the Premiership. "Pierre van Who?" asked *The Sun* in its report on the Southampton game.

New boy Jean-Claude Darcheville seemed to have provided the perfect replacement for van Hooijdonk, but proved that he was less accurate with his predictions than the man he replaced when he said: "Many have said we will struggle – but they don't know us".

Forest dropped from third to 19th in the space of two months. The situation at the club was so desperate that manager Dave Bassett was even forced to accept van Hooijdonk back into the side, a decision which did not please everyone at the club.

Bottom of the table and defeated by Portsmouth in the FA Cup, Forest sacked Bassett. Mickey Adams took charge of the team for the 4–0 defeat by Coventry City, but a week later Ron Atkinson stepped straight off a flight from the Caribbean and into the City Ground for the home match against Arsenal.

> **"I think I'm right in saying these are the first programme notes I've written on a Caribbean beach, but I can certainly recommend it"**
>
> Ron Atkinson

The fact that he mistook the Arsenal bench for Forest's made for a comical start to his short reign, but although his team lost the match 1–0 he did take them to their first Premiership victory in five months a week later.

That 1–0 success against Everton was followed by an 8–1 humiliation at the hands of Manchester United – the Premiership's biggest-ever home defeat – and it soon became clear that the club were going to require the proverbial miracle to stay up.

Even Big Ron was not in a position to deliver that. He recruited some experienced players in the shape of John Harkes, Richard Gough and Carlton Palmer, and attempted to introduce some much-needed guile to the side by taking Hugo Porfirio on loan, but to no avail.

Forest finished the season rock-bottom. They scored fewer and conceded more goals than any other top flight team and only three wins at the end of the season – when they were already relegated – saved them from recording the lowest-ever points total in the Premiership.

A team that completed just 26% of its crosses and 67% of its passes in the opposition half were always likely to struggle. The fact that Forest also finished as the Premiership's worst tacklers, and conceded a goal on average every 50 minutes while scoring at the rate of one every 106 minutes, made their relegation one of the least surprising outcomes of the season.

The club will probably make a fourth appearance in the Premiership sooner rather than later. But for Ron Atkinson the 1998–99 season was to be his last as a manager. He announced his retirement after the club were relegated following defeat at Aston Villa.

NOTTINGHAM FOREST

DATE	OPPONENT	SCORE	ATT.	ALLOU	ARMSTRONG	BART-WILLIAMS	BEASANT	BONALAIR	CHETTLE	CROSSLEY	DARCHEVILLE	DOIG	EDWARDS	FREEDMAN	GEMMILL	GOUGH	GRAY
17.8.98	Arsenal A	1–2	38,064	–	90	–	90	90	90	–	80	–	–	s10	–	–	–
22.8.98	Coventry H	1–0	22,546	–	90□	–	90	90	90	–	89	–	–	90	90	–	–
29.8.98	Southampton A	2–1	14,942	–	90	–	90	90	90	–	79[1]	–	–	s11	90	–	–
8.9.98	Everton H	0–2	25,610	–	90	–	90	90	90□	–	90	–	–	s10	–	–	79
12.9.98	Chelsea A	1–3	34,809	–	90	–	90	90	90	–	90[1]	–	–	–	–	–	70
19.9.98	West Ham H	0–0	26,463	–	90□	–	90	90	90	–	87	–	–	s6	–	–	s3
26.9.98	Newcastle A	0–2	36,760	–	90	65	90	–	90	–	73	–	–	s2	–	–	s25
3.10.98	Charlton H	0–1	22,661	–	90	82	90	–	90	–	–	–	–	90	–	–	–
17.10.98	Leeds Utd H	1–1	23,911	–	90	90	90	90	90□	–	60	–	–	s4	86	–	s30
24.10.98	Liverpool A	1–5	44,595	–	90	90	90	90	90	–	–	–	–	90[1]	90	–	–
1.11.98	Middlesbro' A	1–1	34,223	–	90	90	90	75	90	–	–	–	–	s9	90	–	s15
7.11.98	Wimbledon H	0–1	21,362	–	90	90	90	s17	90	–	–	–	–	s7	90	–	90
16.11.98	Derby Co H	2–2	24,014	–	90	90□	90	90□	90	–	–	–	–	78[1]	90	–	–
21.11.98	Tottenham A	0–2	35,832	–	46	90	90□	s36	90	–	–	–	s44	54	90□	–	–
28.11.98	Aston Villa H	2–2	25,753	–	90	90[1]□	90	90	90	–	s6	–	–	84[1]	77□	–	–
7.12.98	Sheff Wed A	2–3	19,321	–	63	90	90	90[1]	90□	–	78	–	–	–	s27	–	s27
12.12.98	Leicester A	1–3	20,891	–	–	90	90	–	90	–	–	–	–	s16	90	–	–
19.12.98	Blackburn H	2–2	22,013	–	s22	90□	90□	–	90[1]	–	–	–	–	90[1]	90	–	–
26.12.98	Man Utd A	0–3	55,216	–	90	54	90	s36	68□	–	–	s22	–	90	–	–	–
28.12.98	Southampton H	1–1	23,456	–	–	90	90	90	90[1]	–	–	–	–	75□	90	–	–
9.1.99	Coventry A	0–4	17,158	–	56	70	90	–	90□	–	–	90	–	s34	84	–	–
16.1.99	Arsenal H	0–1	26,021	–	90	90	90	75	–	–	85□	–	–	90□	–	–	–
30.1.99	Everton A	1–0	34,175	–	s10	s5	90	–	–	–	85□	–	–	90	–	–	–
6.2.99	Man Utd H	1–8	30,025	–	74	–	90	–	–	–	26	–	–	s64	57	–	–
13.2.99	West Ham A	1–2	25,458	–	–	–	90	–	s30	–	–	–	–	79	–	–	–
20.2.99	Chelsea H	1–3	26,351	–	–	–	90	90	90	–	86	–	–	s1	–	–	–
27.2.99	Charlton A	0–0	20,007	–	–	–	–	90	90	90	62□	–	90	–	78	–	–
10.3.99	Newcastle H	1–2	22,852	–	–	s20	–	90	90□	90	–	–	s41	78[1]	–	49	–
13.3.99	Wimbledon A	3–1	12,149	–	–	s44	–	–	90	90	–	–	90	90[1]	–	–	–
20.3.99	Middlesbro' H	1–2	21,468	–	–	75□	–	s15	90	90	–	–	90	45[1]	–	–	–
3.4.99	Leeds Utd A	1–3	39,645	–	–	–	–	90□	90	90	–	–	90	66	–	90□	–
5.4.99	Liverpool H	2–2	28,374	s14	–	–	–	90	–	90	–	–	90	76[1]	–	90	–
10.4.99	Derby Co A	0–1	32,217	–	–	–	–	90	s9	90	–	–	90□	90	–	81■	–
17.4.99	Tottenham H	0–1	25,181	–	–	–	–	21	90□	90	–	–	74	90	–	90□	–
24.4.99	Aston Villa A	0–2	34,492	–	–	s33	–	–	90	90	–	–	–	74	–	–	–
1.5.99	Sheff Wed H	2–0	20,480	–	–	90	–	90	33	90	s2	–	s57	90	–	90	–
8.5.99	Blackburn A	2–1	24,565	s20	–	90[1]	–	90	44■	90	–	2	–	s1	90[1]	–	90
16.5.99	Leicester H	1–0	25,353	–	–	90[1]	–	90□	90	90	–	–	–	s1	90	–	–

□ Yellow card, ■ Red card, s Substitute, 90[3] Goals scored

1998–99 PREMIERSHIP APPEARANCES

HAREWOOD	HARKES	HJELDE	HODGES	JOHNSON	LOUIS-JEAN	LYTTLE	MATTSON	MELTON	PALMER	PORFIRIO	QUASHIE	ROGERS	SHIPPERLEY	STENSAAS	STONE	THOMAS	VAN HOOIJDONK	WOAN	TOTAL
s7	–	45	90□	83	–	s45	–	–	–	–	90	–	–	90□	90¹	–	–		990
s1□	–	–	88	s15	–	s2	–	–	–	–	90□	–	–	90¹	75	–	–		990
–	–	–	90	90	–	–	–	–	–	–	90	–	–	90¹□	90	–	–		990
s11□	–	–	–	90	–	s20	–	–	–	80□	70	–	–	90	90□	–	–		990
s33	–	–	–	90	–	s20	–	–	–	–	90	90	–	–	90	57	–	–	990
84□	–	–	–	90	s61	29□	–	–	–	–	90	90	–	–	90	–	–	–	990
s17	–	–	–	90	90□	–	–	–	–	–	88	90□	90	–	90	–	–	–	990
–	–	s32	s8	90	90	–	–	–	–	–	58	90	90	–	90	–	–	–	990
–	–	90	–	s36	–	–	–	–	–	–	54□	90	–	90¹	–	–	–	–	990
–	–	90□	–	–	–	–	–	–	–	–	90	–	–	90	–	90□	–	–	990
90¹	–	90□	–	–	–	s17	–	–	–	–	73	–	81	–	90□	–	–	–	990
83	–	–	–	–	–	73	–	–	–	–	–	90	–	–	90	–	90	–	990
s12	–	–	–	–	–	–	–	–	–	–	90	90□	–	–	90	–	90¹	–	990
–	–	90	–	–	–	–	–	–	–	–	90	90	–	–	46■	–	90□	–	946
–	–	90	–	s13	–	–	–	–	–	–	90□	–	–	–	90	–	90□	–	990
s12	–	90	–	90	–	–	–	–	–	–	63	90	–	–	–	–	90¹	–	990
81□	–	74	–	90□	–	–	90□	–	–	–	–	90	s9	–	90□	–	58¹■	–	958
s8	–	90	–	90	–	–	90	–	–	–	–	68	82	–	90	–	–	–	990
–	–	–	s15	90	90	–	–	–	–	–	90□	90□	90	–	75	–	–	–	990
s15	–	90	–	90□	–	–	–	–	–	–	–	90	90	–	90□	–	–	–	990
–	–	90	–	90	–	90	–	–	–	–	s6	–	–	–	90	–	90	s20□	990
–	–	90	–	90□	–	90	–	–	–	–	s5	90	s15	–	–	–	90	–	990
–	90□	90	–	90□	–	–	–	90	s1	–	89	–	80□	90	–	90¹□	–	–	990
–	90	90	–	90	–	–	s33	–	90	s16□	–	90¹	–	–	90	–	90	–	990
–	65	90¹	–	90□	–	–	–	90	s11	s25	90□	90	60	90	–	90□	–	–	990
–	–	–	–	89	90	–	–	–	90□	s20	70□	90	s4	–	90	–	90¹	–	990
–	–	–	–	–	90□	–	–	–	90□	–	s12	–	s28	90	90	–	90	–	990
s12	–	–	–	90□	50■	–	–	–	–	–	–	90	–	70	90	–	90□	–	950
–	–	–	–	46	90	–	90	–	90	–	–	90¹	90¹	–	–	–	90	–	990
s45	–	–	–	–	90□	–	88	–	90□	s2	–	90□	90	–	–	–	90	–	990
90	–	–	–	90	–	–	–	89■	s9□	–	90¹	s24	81	–	–	–	–	–	989
90	–	–	–	90	88	–	–	–	90	–	–	90	s2	–	–	–	90¹	–	990
81□	–	–	–	90□	90	–	–	–	90	–	–	90□	s13	–	–	–	77	–	981
s10	–	–	–	90□	90□	–	–	–	–	–	–	90	80	s16	–	–	90	s69	990
90	–	90□	–	57	90	90	90	–	–	–	–	90	s16	68	–	–	s22	–	990
88	–	–	–	–	90	–	–	90	67¹	–	–	90¹	–	–	–	–	s23	–	990
89	–	–	–	–	90□	–	–	90	70□	–	–	90	–	–	–	–	–	–	944
90	–	–	–	–	90	–	90	90	89□	–	–	90	–	–	–	–	–	–	990

THE MANAGER

RON ATKINSON

In-depth knowledge of Ron Atkinson's glittering career is an essential pre-requisite for any budding pub quiz enthusiast. But even managerial legend Big Ron could not save Nottingham Forest from relegation after joining the club on January 5, 1999.

Atkinson replaced ousted boss Dave Bassett, who claimed he only knew he had been sacked when he read it in the tabloid press. Bassett had earned Forest promotion as Division One champions in 1997–98, but with little cash available for new players, and star striker Pierre van Hooijdonk embarking on a self-imposed exile as a result, the East Midlands club looked doomed from the start.

Big Ron played 384 league games as a wing-half for Oxford United between 1962 and 1971, then cut his teeth in the world of management at Kettering and Cambridge United. His bulging curriculum vitae thereafter includes spells at West Bromwich Albion (twice), Manchester United, Atletico Madrid, Sheffield Wednesday (twice), Aston Villa and finally Coventry City.

On April 24, the day Forest were officially relegated, Big Ron announced his retirement from management – but looks set to continue in his role as a football pundit for ITV Sport.

LEAGUE POSITION

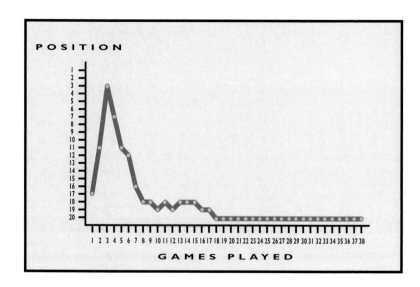

THE GOALS

Where?

SCORED **CONCEDED**

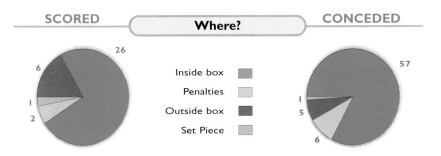

Inside box
Penalties
Outside box
Set Piece

Nottingham Forest scored the fewest and conceded the most goals in the 1998–99 Carling Premiership. The 18-yard area was the scene of the majority of their woes throughout the season. They scored just 28 goals, or 80% of all strikes, in opposition boxes. And in their own area they leaked a staggering 63 goals in 38 matches, more than 90% of all shots that beat them – the highest proportion of any Premiership club.

When?

SCORED **CONCEDED**

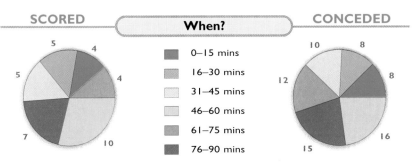

0–15 mins
16–30 mins
31–45 mins
46–60 mins
61–75 mins
76–90 mins

Two-fifths of the 35 goals Forest scored came during the first half of their league matches. The most frantic period for the relegated side was the initial 15 minutes after half-time. During this spell they not only scored more goals than at any other time, but also let in the most goals. The bottom club struggled in the final quarter-hour of matches, conceding 15 goals and scoring only seven.

How?

SCORED **CONCEDED**

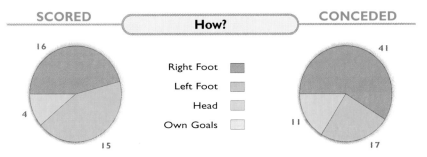

Right Foot
Left Foot
Head
Own Goals

Forest missed Pierre Van Hooijdonk's height at set-pieces during his absence and it showed in their goalscoring statistics. Just four efforts, or 11.4% of their goals, came via a player's head; but the club did have an exceptionally large percentage of left-footed goals to their credit. Opponents preferred to keep the ball on the ground when attacking the Forest goal, with only 15.9% of strikes for the East Midlanders' rivals arriving from headers.

NOTTINGHAM FOREST

	ALLOU	ARMSTRONG	BART-WILLIAMS	BONALAIR	CHETTLE	DARCHEVILLE	DOIG	EDWARDS	FREEDMAN	GEMMILL	GOUGH	GRAY	HAREWOOD	HARKES
APPEARANCE														
Start	0	20	20	24	32	14	1	7	20	18	7	3	11	3
Sub	2	2	4	4	2	2	1	5	11	2	0	5	12	0
Minutes on pitch	34	1711	1798	2165	2794	1078	112	758	1793	1569	580	339	1139	245
GOAL ATTEMPTS														
Goals	0	0	3	1	2	2	0	0	9	0	0	0	1	0
Shots on target	0	2	9	6	10	14	0	0	26	1	0	2	10	1
Shots off target	1	5	20	6	3	11	0	0	19	1	2	3	16	0
Shooting accuracy	0%	29%	31%	50%	77%	56%	0%	0%	58%	50%	0%	40%	38%	100%
PASSING														
Goal assists	0	0	1	1	0	2	0	0	2	1	0	0	1	0
Long passes	0	151	113	134	297	4	1	42	19	75	41	7	5	21
Short passes	8	538	782	763	859	250	20	107	571	787	139	107	270	50
PASS COMPLETION														
Own half %	100%	94%	90%	88%	90%	74%	100%	88%	88%	87%	92%	90%	87%	94%
Opposition half %	50%	58%	75%	67%	61%	70%	56%	48%	71%	75%	59%	66%	59%	60%
CROSSING														
Total crosses	1	3	68	49	2	18	0	1	21	52	1	10	19	5
Cross completion %	100%	67%	21%	29%	50%	33%	0%	100%	14%	13%	0%	40%	21%	20%
DRIBBLING														
Dribbles & runs	3	17	37	52	8	49	0	0	66	42	0	20	49	2
Dribble completion %	100%	94%	57%	79%	88%	55%	0%	0%	64%	83%	0%	65%	63%	100%
DEFENDING														
Tackles made	0	37	60	116	79	23	2	26	29	59	22	9	47	5
Tackles won %	0%	43%	60%	54%	63%	48%	100%	38%	38%	58%	55%	56%	49%	60%
Blocks	0	10	9	14	44	0	2	6	0	7	8	1	0	4
Clearances	0	202	75	132	474	0	17	140	11	22	77	6	8	27
Interceptions	0	30	11	44	43	0	3	9	5	18	9	2	3	4
DISCIPLINE														
Fouls	0	24	28	24	35	15	0	11	22	17	15	3	27	3
Offside	0	0	3	2	0	23	0	0	18	0	0	0	20	0
Yellow cards	0	2	4	3	7	3	0	1	1	3	2	0	5	1
Red cards	0	0	0	0	1	0	0	0	0	0	1	0	0	0

GOALKEEPER NAME	START/ (SUB)	TIME ON PITCH	GOALS CONCEDED	MINS/GOALS CONCEDED	SAVES MADE	SAVES/ SHOTS
BEASANT	26	2340	54	43.3	116	68%
CROSSLEY	12	1080	15	72	60	80%

PLAYERS' STATISTICS

	HJELDE	HODGES	JOHNSON	LOUIS-JEAN	LYTTLE	MATTSON	MELTON	PALMER	PORFIRIO	QUASHIE	ROGERS	SHIPPERLEY	STENSAAS	STONE	THOMAS	VAN HOOIJDONK	WOAN	TOTAL	RANK
	16	3	25	15	5	5	1	13	3	12	34	12	6	26	5	19	0		
	1	2	3	1	5	1	0	0	6	4	0	8	1	0	0	2	2		
	1411	291	2229	1369	476	481	90	1169	285	1020	2981	1164	465	2281	402	1710	89		
	1	0	0	0	0	0	0	0	1	0	4	1	0	3	1	6	0	35	20th
	2	0	10	0	1	0	0	1	2	4	12	12	1	22	1	24	0	173	12th
	1	2	12	3	1	2	1	3	1	7	14	15	1	25	2	21	1	199	17th
	67%	0%	45%	0%	50%	0%	0%	25%	67%	36%	46%	44%	50%	47%	33%	53%	0%	47%	7th
	0	0	2	1	0	0	0	0	2	1	2	0	0	3	1	4	0	25	18th
	55	18	130	79	57	23	3	47	10	59	216	6	30	101	23	71	13	1851	9th
	313	90	670	364	163	99	30	326	101	408	864	313	132	1017	117	709	43	11010	11th
	91%	90%	89%	88%	94%	87%	100%	89%	78%	91%	88%	74%	81%	87%	100%	85%	81%	89%	9th
	61%	65%	68%	69%	55%	47%	75%	64%	75%	70%	61%	76%	72%	73%	70%	62%	57%	67%	16th
	8	27	19	37	12	0	1	7	8	19	130	5	15	110	7	32	3	690	13th
	63%	33%	32%	19%	58%	0%	0%	43%	38%	16%	24%	20%	20%	25%	14%	38%	67%	26%	18th
	6	3	54	34	3	0	0	13	18	17	84	25	7	113	15	35	0	773	17th
	83%	100%	61%	71%	33%	0%	0%	54%	67%	59%	85%	60%	86%	61%	73%	60%	0%	68%	16th
	67	12	75	78	19	22	4	58	11	36	75	23	10	93	12	37	2	1150	12th
	70%	58%	60%	60%	74%	59%	75%	50%	55%	67%	55%	48%	80%	61%	58%	51%	0%	57%	20th
	17	0	2	4	2	1	1	9	1	2	23	0	4	6	0	3	0	182	=15th
	186	6	68	98	37	62	1	110	3	22	129	2	30	33	16	21	0	2047	10th
	28	3	18	17	1	5	1	9	0	11	26	1	7	18	4	8	2	344	9th
	16	3	45	17	3	4	1	21	6	19	38	18	2	54	9	28	2	510	9th
	0	1	1	1	0	0	0	3	0	2	9	2	0	8	1	16	0	110	=18th
	3	1	8	5	1	1	0	3	4	4	8	0	1	5	1	5	1	85	=2nd
	0	0	0	1	0	0	0	1	0	0	0	0	0	1	0	1	0	6	3rd

CROSSES CAUGHT	CROSSES PUNCHED	CROSSES NOT CLAIMED	CATCH SUCCESS	THROWS/ SHORT KICKS	% COMPLETION	LONG KICKS	% COMPLETION
57	10	8	98%	391	96%	472	33%
26	17	6	90%	69	96%	296	34%

PLAYER OF THE SEASON

PLAYER	INDEX SCORE
STEVE STONE	878
Thierry Bonalair	872
Steve Chettle	858
Pierre van Hooijdonk	800
Chris Bart-Williams	800
Dougie Freedman	777
Scot Gemmill	627
Alan Rogers	625
Craig Armstrong	620
Andy Johnson	557

It was always going to be a tough task to fill the void in the Nottingham Forest midfield left by former England man Steve Stone.

Forest's relegation cannot be attributed solely to his departure to near-neighbours Aston Villa – but there's no doubt his quality was missed by the East Midlanders.

It speaks volumes for Stone's contribution to the Forest side that the attacking midfield man finished as the club's highest-scoring player in the Carling Opta Season Index, averaging 878 points per match for the club in 1998–99. That was despite picking up five yellow cards and one red.

French utility player Thierry Bonalair, who has played most of his Forest games over the last two years at right-back, ended the campaign as the next most consistent performer, with an average points score of 872. Central defender Steve Chettle led the side by example for the first half of the season, but as the club's campaign crumbled, so did Chettle's – and his average score dropped from four figures to only 858 points.

Pierre van Hooijdonk's contributions to the team were limited, thanks to his self-imposed City Ground exile and a lack of rapport with new boss Ron Atkinson – but when he did figure, he showed glimpses of the form which saw him score more than 30 goals in the club's 1997–98 season. He and midfielder Chris Bart-Williams both scored an average of 800 points a match.

Top scorer Dougie Freedman showed he has the quality to perform in the Premiership while the club's Player of the Year, full-back Alan Rogers, appears in eighth place after a fine season in the top flight. Scot Gemmill joined Stone on the list of players who have moved on, switching to Walter Smith's Everton on transfer deadline day.

FIVE OF THE BEST

A turbulent and ultimately catastrophic season for Forest began well. At the end of August the side were third in the league, even without star striker Pierre van Hooijdonk; but the fans had to wait 22 games for the next win, by which time Forest were propping up the Premiership. Even the arrival of managerial legend Ron Atkinson could not save them from their third top-flight relegation since the Premiership's inception.

TOP GOALSCORERS		
	GOALS	GOALS/SHOTS
DOUGIE FREEDMAN	9	20%
Pierre van Hooijdonk	6	13%
Alan Rogers	4	15%
Chris Bart-Williams	3	10%
Steve Stone	3	6%

Top scorer was Dougie Freedman, who had to wait until October 24 for his first league goal – the consolation in a 5–1 drubbing at Liverpool. But by the end of the season he had scored with one in five shots, a great effort given Forest's plight. Controversial Dutchman Pierre van Hooijdonk weighed in with six goals when his self-imposed exile was over, but the next-highest scorer was full-back Alan Rogers, a fact which dramatically underlines Forest's sterility in front of goal in 1998–99.

In line with the Forest team as a whole, skipper Steve Chettle began the season in super form and regularly featured in the Carling Opta defenders Index. He struggled to maintain that level of performance, but still finished the season as the side's best passer. No one completed more than 80% of their passes and no one made more than 900 successful passes, a testament to Forest's struggle to dominate possession in many of their matches. The inclusion of Steve Stone, despite his departure for Villa in March, shows how valuable he was to the side.

TOP PASSERS		
	SUCC PASSES	COMPLETION
STEVE CHETTLE	892	77%
Steve Stone	857	77%
Alan Rogers	763	70%
Chris Bart-Williams	709	79%
Thierry Bonalair	676	75%

TOP TACKLERS		
	WON	SUCCESS
THIERRY BONALAIR	63	54%
Steve Stone	57	61%
Steve Chettle	50	63%
Jon-Olav Hjelde	47	70%
Matthieu Louis-Jean	47	60%

Another factor in Forest's failure to retain midfield possession was their tackling. Their success rate was the lowest in the Premiership, with just 57% of all challenges won. Full-back Thierry Bonalair won the most tackles, but his success rate was well below the figure one might expect from a defender. The man most likely to win possession was centre-back Jon-Olav Hjelde, who won seven of every 10 tackles he contested. Again, Steve Stone figures in the top five – and he surely would have finished top had he not left the club with 10 games to go.

Only Everton and Chelsea conceded more fouls than Forest in 1998–99, while only Arsenal and Blackburn picked up more red cards; facts which resulted in Forest finishing as the seventh-worst sinners in the Premiership. Top bad boy was Villa-bound Steve Stone, but of those who remained at the club midfielder Andy Johnson was the worst culprit, picking up eight league bookings to add to his 45 fouls. Pierre van Hooijdonk also figured, despite missing much of the campaign.

DISCIPLINE		
	POINTS	FOULS & CARDS
STEVE STONE	75	54F, 5Y, 1R
Andy Johnson	69	45F, 8Y, 0R
Steve Chettle	62	35F, 7Y, 1R
Alan Rogers	62	38F, 8Y, 0R
Pierre van Hooijdonk	49	28F, 5Y, 1R

ACTION	BARTHWILLIAMS	CHETTLE	CROSSLEY	EDWARDS	FREEDMAN	JOHNSON	LOUIS/JEAN	MATTSON	PALMER	ROGESS	SHIPPERLEY	VAN HOOIJDONK	TOTAL	WIMBLEDON
Time on pitch	44	90	90	90	90	46	90	90	90	90	90	90	990	990
GOALS														
Goal										1	1	1	3	1
Shot on target									2	2			4	10
Shot off target					3				2	2	1		8	10
Blocked shot		1											1	1
Own goal														
PASSES														
Pass to own player	12	11		12	29	4	20	10	26	8	15	43	190	251
Pass to opposition	8	9		4	10	5	9	14	14	8	10	29	120	127
Cross to own player										1	4		5	8
Cross to opposition player							1			2	1		4	20
Goal assist					1		1					1	3	1
Pass completion %	60%	55%	0%	75%	74%	50%	68%	42%	63%	47%	60%	62%	61%	64%
TACKLES & CLEARANCES														
Tackle	2	3			2	4		3	3		3	3	19	16
Clearances, blocks and interceptions	2	14		8	1	4		13		1	2	2	48	24
DRIBBLES & RUNS														
Dribble ball retained					4	1					1		8	5
Dribbles ball lost					1							2	2	3
Dribble success %	0%	0%	0%	0%	80%	100%	0%	0%	100%	100%	100%	80%	80%	63%
DISCIPLINE														
Fouls	1								1	2	1	1	6	4
Penalty conceded														
Free kick - offside					1	1			1	1	1		5	1
Yellow cards														
Red cards														
GOALKEEPERS														
Distribution to own player			12										12	26
Distribution to opposition player			16										16	19
Goalkeeper distribution%	0%	0%	43%	0%	0%	0%		0%	0%	0%	0%	0%	43%	58%
Save			10										10	4
Ball caught			7										7	
Ball dropped														
Goal conceded		1											1	3

A trip to Selhurst Park to play Wimbledon is rarely an easy experience, and for a team bottom of the table with only one win in their previous 25 Carling Premiership games, the prospects are even bleaker than normal.

March 13, 1999

1–3

WIMBLEDON
NOTTINGHAM FOREST

That was the situation facing Nottingham Forest, who had also just sold Steve Stone to Aston Villa, and faced media predictions of a swift return to Nationwide League Division One. Ron Atkinson's men had other ideas. The Forest boss reflected after the game: "If you come to Wimbledon with a defeatist attitude, they will smell the fear and tear you apart."

After facing intense pressure in the opening minutes, Forest scored against the run of play in the 21st minute. Andy Johnson picked the ball up in his own half and dribbled deep into Wimbledon territory. He played the ball out wide to Alan Rogers whose inaccurate cross looped into the far corner, leaving Neil Sullivan rooted to the spot.

The pattern of play continued into the second period until the 59th minute, when Dougie Freedman picked the ball up in his own half. He ventured forward before laying the ball off to Matthieu Louis-Jean and continuing his run. The full-back lofted the ball over the Wimbledon defence into Freedman's path for the striker to run on to it and lob Sullivan to open up a 2–0 lead.

Wimbledon began to exert more pressure, resulting in a goal in the 79th minute. A long ball into the penalty area by substitute Michael Hughes found Marcus Gayle who shrugged off Jesper Mattson and slotted home from 12 yards. Efan Ekoku then had a chance to equalize, but missed with a shot from eight yards out that let Forest off the hook. Mark Crossley's goal kick was flicked on by Pierre van Hooijdonk and Neil Shipperley ran on to the ball, taking it wide before firing in a well-struck shot that beat Sullivan at his near post.

Some stout defending restricted Wimbledon's chances and Forest went on to record their second win under Ron Atkinson. It was the first time all season that they had scored three goals in a Premiership match, and proved to be their biggest win of a disappointing campaign.

Forest scored their three goals from 16 attempts, compared to 22 from the Dons, and also had far less of the possession than the Crazy Gang. They also had to make twice as many blocks, clearances and interceptions than their opponents. The game was notable for the fact that there were only 10 fouls committed – the second lowest total in any Premiership game in the 1998–99 season – and no yellow cards.

Mark Crossley was Forest's man of the match with 2,068 points, making 10 saves to help secure the win and seven catches. It was a triumph for a player who had missed much of the previous two seasons with injury.

Though Forest went on to be relegated, displays such as this provided hope for the supporters. Perhaps it will be possible for the side to bounce straight back into the top flight at the first attempt.

ACTION	ALLTON	BARTT-WILLIAMS	BONALAIR	CHETTLE	CROSSLEY	EDWARDS	FREEDMAN	GOUGH	HAREWOOD	LOUIS-JEAN	PALMER	PORFIRIO	ROGERS	TOTAL	BLACKBURN
Time on pitch	20	90	90	44	90	1	90	90	89	90	90	70	90	944	990
GOALS															
Goal		1					1							2	1
Shot on target														2	7
Shot off target							2	2				1		5	1
Blocked shot														3	6
Own goal															
PASSES															
Pass to own player	2	39	19	15		1	27	29	12	25	24	23	9	225	262
Pass to opposition	2	7	9	1			11	3	8	7	7	6	19	80	110
Cross to own player	1	1											3	5	14
Cross to opposition player		6						1	1	1			9	18	31
Goal assist												2		2	1
Pass completion %	60%	75%	68%	94%	0%	100%	71%	88%	57%	76%	77%	81%	30%	70%	66%
TACKLES & CLEARANCES															
Tackle	2		4				1	4	3	2	6	2	3	27	28
Clearances, blocks and interceptions	3		9	9				23	1	5	9	1	6	66	36
DRIBBLES & RUNS															
Dribble ball retained	1		2				2		4	2	3			14	22
Dribbles ball lost							4		2		2		1	9	8
Dribble success %	100%	0%	100%	0%	0%	0%	33%	0%	67%	100%	60%	0%	0%	61%	73%
DISCIPLINE															
Fouls			1					2	3			3		9	9
Penalty conceded				1										1	1
Free kick - offside		1					2			1		1	1	6	1
Yellow cards			1										1	2	1
Red cards				1										1	
GOALKEEPERS															
Distribution to own player					15									15	14
Distribution to opposition player					20									20	10
Goalkeeper distribution%	0%	0%	0%	0%	43%	0%	0%	0%	0%	0%	0%	0%	0%	43%	58%
Save					7									7	2
Ball caught					9									9	1
Ball dropped															
Goal conceded					1									1	2

Nottingham Forest's season was over. Already relegated from the Carling Premiership, and with their manager's statement of imminent retirement still ringing in their ears, they travelled to Ewood Park looking to salvage some pride from their demoralizing season.

May 8, 1999

1–2

BLACKBURN ROVERS
NOTTINGHAM FOREST

Rovers were in desperate need of a win. With games running out they were still in the relegation zone, with some catching-up to do if they were to escape.

Blackburn owner Jack Walker went out on to the pitch before kick-off and pleaded with the home crowd to get behind their team and will them to victory. The crowd responded and cheered their side constantly for 90 minutes. Unfortunately for Walker, Forest wanted to win more than Blackburn did that afternoon.

Forest shocked the home fans and went ahead after 11 minutes. Hugo Porfirio's cross bounced kindly for Dougie Freedman to strike sweetly on the volley from 15 yards into the bottom right-hand corner of John Filan's net.

Blackburn tried to hit back immediately, and on 13 minutes Matt Jansen sent Damien Duff through the middle with a defence-splitting pass, but Duff's shot was superbly turned around the post by a fully-stretched Mark Crossley.

The equalizer came after 24 minutes. Good work on the right wing by Keith Gillespie gave him room to find Kevin Gallacher, who brilliantly chipped Crossley from 20 yards.

A minute before half-time, Steve Chettle's mistake let in Gallacher, who was clean through on goal. Chettle recovered but brought the Scotsman down right on the edge of the penalty area. Referee Graham Poll pointed to the spot and then sent Chettle off for a professional foul.

Gallacher put the ball on the spot and hit a low, driven penalty for the bottom

right-hand corner – but Crossley, who had saved three of the previous four penalties he had faced, dived low to his right to push the ball against the post and away.

Blackburn almost equalized in first-half stoppage time when Lee Carsley's header from a corner was headed off the line by Matthieu Louis-Jean. Then Blackburn skipper Jason Wilcox was lucky not to be sent off after an angry clash with Porfirio: both players went into the referee's notebook.

Ten minutes into the second half, 10-man Forest defied the odds and took the lead again. Freedman chased a long ball down the right and found Chris Bart-Williams in centre-field. He swapped passes with Porfirio and sent a 25-yard shot fizzing past Filan into the bottom left-hand corner.

Forest held on for the three points and left Blackburn needing to win their remaining two fixtures: Manchester United at home, and Newcastle United away. After the match Blackburn manager Brian Kidd launched a scathing attack on his charges, questioning their heart and commitment to the cause.

In an evenly-balanced game, Blackburn completed more passes than Forest (262 to 225), but Forest had the higher completion percentage (70% to 66%).

The difference between the two teams was in their defensive performance. Forest made 66 clearances, blocks and interceptions compared to just 36 for Blackburn. Their stubbornness at the back was vital, as they were forced to play the second half with only 10 men.

SHEFFIELD WEDNESDAY 1998–99

Back row (from left to right): Petter Rudi, Emerson Thorne, Jon Newsome, Kevin Pressman, Francesco Sanetti, Matt Clarke, Andy Booth, Goce Sedloski, Jim Magilton (now Ipswich Town).

Middle row: Peter Shreeves, Martin Hodge (Coaches), Ian Nolan, Steven Haslam, Scoot Oakes, Earl Barrett, Ritchie Humphreys, Paolo Di Canio (now West Ham United), Andy Hinchcliffe, Dave Galley (Physiotherapist), Maggie Kennett (Masseuse).

Front row: Lee Briscoe, Alan Quinn, Benito Carbone, Graham Hyde, Wim Jonk, Danny Wilson (Manager), Peter Atherton, Des Walker, Niclas Alexandersson, Derek Geary, Guy Whittingham.

SHEFFIELD WEDNESDAY

ADDRESS

Hillsborough, Sheffield S6 1SW

CONTACT NUMBERS

Telephone: 0114 221 2121
Fax: 0114 221 2122
Ticket Office: 0114 221 2400
24hr Information: 09068 121186
Owls Superstore: 0114 221 2345
e-mail: enquiries@swfc.co.uk
Website: www.swfc.co.uk

SPONSORS

Sanderson

FANZINES

Cheat
War of the Monster Trucks
Boddle
Spitting Feathers

KEY PERSONNEL

Chairman: D G Richards
Vice Chairman/President: K T Addy
Directors: D G Richards, G K Hulley,
R M Grierson, G A H Thorpe,
H E Culley
Club Secretary: Alan Sykes
Manager: Danny Wilson

COLOURS

Home: Blue and white striped shirts
with black shorts and blue stockings
Away: Yellow shirts with black
and white trim, with yellow shorts
and stockings

NICKNAME

The Owls

20 FACTS

1 Sheffield Wednesday were founded in September 1867 by members of the Wednesday Cricket Club. They are the fifth oldest club in the Football League.

2 The founders of the Wednesday Cricket Club were local craftsmen who had a half-day in the working week which was a Wednesday. This is how they gained their distinctive name.

3 Sheffield Wednesday's first permanent ground was Olive Grove, where their first game was played against Blackburn Rovers in September 1887. In 1899 Wednesday moved to Owlerton which was renamed Hillsborough in 1913.

4 Sheffield Wednesday have been league champions on four occasions – in 1902–03, 1903–4, 1928–29 and 1929–30.

5 They have also won the FA Cup on three occasions – in 1886, 1907 and 1935 – and been runners-up on another three occasions in 1890, 1966 and 1993.

6 They also won the Football League Cup (Rumbelows Cup) in 1991.

7 The club's motto is "Consilio et Animis" meaning "By Wisdom and Courage".

8 Sheffield Wednesday were nicknamed "The Blades" until their move to Owlerton, when they became known as "The Owls".

9 The first-choice club colours have always been blue and white. Traditionally they have worn blue and white stripes, though they have played in squares and hoops and had a spell in the late 1960s/early 1970s when they wore blue shirts with white sleeves. Wednesday played in all white on the 1966 FA Cup run to Wembley.

10 Sheffield Wednesday's record win was a 12–0 victory over Halliwell in the FA Cup in 1891.

11 Their record defeat was against Aston Villa in Division One in October 1912, when they lost by the huge margin of 10-0.

12 Sheffield Wednesday have played in European competition in three seasons. They played in the 1961–62 and 1963–64 Fairs Cup competitions and in the 1992–93 UEFA Cup.

13 On November 12, 1904, Sheffield Wednesday were losing 5–0 at half-time to Everton, but came back in the 2nd half to draw 5–5.

14 The only Wednesday players to finish top of the goalscoring charts in the top flight are Dave McLean, who shared the title in 1911–12 and won it outright the next season, and Jimmy Trotter, who was the Division's top scorer in 1926–27.

15 Sheffield Wednesday are one of only three teams to have played in an FA Cup final as a non-league side, when they lost in 1890.

16 Danny Wilson's side finished in 12th place in the 1998–99 Premiership. Their league record was:

Pld	W	D	L	F	A	Pts
38	13	7	18	41	42	46

17 Sheffield Wednesday reached the fifth round of the AXA-sponsored FA Cup where they lost 1–0 to Chelsea. On the way to that match they beat Norwich 4–1 in the third round and Stockport 2–0 in the fourth round.

18 The Owls were on the wrong end of a giant-killing act in the Worthington Cup, losing the first leg 1–0 to Cambridge United at Hillsborough and managing only a 1–1 draw in the second leg at the Abbey Stadium.

19 The top goalscorer in all competitions for the Owls was Benito Carbone with nine goals, eight of which came in the Carling Premiership.

20 Sheffield Wednesday had the best disciplinary record of all clubs in the Premiership, committing just 456 fouls and earning 47 yellow cards, although they did have five dismissals.

SEASON REVIEW

With a new man in the managerial hot seat, 1998–99 was a season of transition for Sheffield Wednesday. Danny Wilson, who had made the short journey along the M1 from relegated Barnsley, set about trying to improve on the Owls' miserable 1997–98 season when they had been serious candidates for relegation, finishing just four points above the drop zone.

Money in the transfer kitty was tight, so Wilson was forced to use Ron Atkinson's existing squad, with a few additions, most notably former Dutch international Wim Jonk.

The new boss's first game in charge was a home defeat by West Ham, a result which did little for the supporters' confidence. Fortunately for Wilson, confidence at White Hart Lane was even lower and Wednesday capitalized by thrashing Spurs 3–0 away in their next game.

> ## "It has been an up and down season, partly because we've struggled to hold on to any long-term consistency"
> **Danny Wilson**

It was all or nothing in the early stages of the season. Wednesday did not draw a league game until the end of October, earning three wins and seven defeats from their first 10 matches to leave them just above the drop zone in 16th.

One of the most enduring memories of the 1998–99 Premiership season will be the dramatic events at Hillsborough in the match between the Owls and Arsenal, when hot-headed Italian Paolo Di Canio pushed referee Paul Alcock to the ground, pushing himself out of the Wednesday squad into the bargain.

The match did at least produce three points for Wednesday, but probably the highlight of the season came against the other title challengers Manchester United in November. New boy Jonk scored his first goal for the club.

Despite their woefully inconsistent form over the course of the campaign, Wednesday performed admirably against the title-chasing trio, picking up eight points in the six matches – more than any other of the 16 teams in the Premiership.

But this merely glosses over the obvious cracks in the squad that could have easily have seen Wednesday scrapping with the basement boys. A key factor in their escape was the form of their two commanding centre-backs. Des Walker and Emerson Thome missed just 239 minutes of top-flight action between them, with "Emo" in particular impressing in his first full Premiership season.

Of the front players, only Benito Carbone can look back on the season with any real pride. Goal-shy Andy Booth and Ritchie Humphreys both struggled desperately to find form, prompting Danny Wilson to splash out £1 million on York City's top scorer Richard Cresswell on transfer deadline day. He scored his first goal in the 1–0 win over Liverpool in May.

Wednesday's woes in front of goal are underlined by the fact that they were the least accurate shooters in the Premiership, with only 41% of their shots hitting the target. They also fired in the third-fewest shots on target and were the most likely team to be caught offside.

But with the impressive Petter Rudi and Niclas Alexandersson on the wings and full-backs Peter Atherton and Andy Hinchcliffe constantly overlapping, the club did finish the season as the most accurate crossers in the league, a fact of which target man Cresswell will certainly approve.

After three games, the team were 12th and by the end of the season's ups and downs, the Owls had turned 360 degrees to finish in the same place. That disappointment was coupled with miserable fortunes in the two cup competitions – particularly the Worthington Cup – and Wilson will be aware that the supporters will be expecting a lot more from him and his players in 1999–2000.

SHEFFIELD WEDNESDAY

DATE	OPPONENT	SCORE	ATT.	AGOGO	ALEXANDERSSON	ATHERTON	BARRETT	BOOTH	BRISCOE	CARBONE	COBIAN	CRESSWELL	DI CANIO	HASLAM	HINCHCLIFFE	HUMPHRE
15.8.98	West Ham H	0–1	30,236	–	–	90	–	90	–	90	90	–	90	–	90	–
22.8.98	Tottenham A	3–0	32,075	–	–	90¹	s27	90□	s3	72□	63□	–	87¹	–	90¹	–
29.8.98	Aston Villa H	0–1	25,989	–	–	90	s27	90	–	90□	63	–	90	–	90	–
9.9.98	Derby Co A	0–1	26,209	–	–	90□	s3	90	s15	90□	87□	–	–	–	90	–
12.9.98	Blackburn H	3–0	20,846	–	–	90¹	s19	90	–	90□	71	–	89¹	–	90¹	–
19.9.98	Wimbledon A	1–2	13,163	–	–	90	–	90	79	90	–	–	s44¹	–	90	–
26.9.98	Arsenal H	1–0	27,949	–	59	90	–	20	s31¹	–	–	90	44■	–	90	s70
3.10.98	Middlesbro' A	0–4	34,163	–	90	90	s18	–	–	–	72	–	–	–	90■	90□
18.10.98	Coventry A	0–1	16,003	–	90	90	–	90	90	83	–	–	–	–	–	90
24.10.98	Everton H	0–0	26,592	–	90	90	–	90	90	–	–	–	–	–	90	90
31.10.98	Southampton H	0–0	30,078	–	90	90	–	90	57	–	–	–	–	–	90	90
8.11.98	Leeds Utd A	1–2	30,012	–	90	90	–	90¹	–	–	–	–	–	–	90	79
14.11.98	Newcastle A	1–1	36,698	–	90	90	–	90	–	66	–	–	–	–	90	s24
21.11.98	Man Utd H	3–1	39,475	–	90²	90	–	90	–	90	–	–	–	–	90	–
28.11.98	Chelsea A	1–1	34,451	–	90	90	–	89¹□	–	90	–	–	–	–	90	s1
7.12.98	Nott'm For H	3–2	19,321	–	90¹	90	–	90	s10	89²	–	–	–	–	90	–
12.12.98	Charlton H	3–0	26,010	–	60	90	–	90¹	s30	90¹□	–	–	–	–	90	–
19.12.98	Liverpool A	0–2	40,003	–	59	90	–	90	s31	90	–	–	–	–	90□	s4
26.12.98	Leicester H	0–1	33,513	–	66	90	–	90□	s24	–	–	–	–	–	90	66
28.12.98	Aston Villa A	1–2	39,217	–	88	90	–	90	s2	90¹	–	–	–	–	90□	s2
9.1.99	Tottenham H	0–0	28,204	–	90	90	–	–	–	90□	–	–	–	–	90	90
16.1.99	West Ham A	4–0	25,642	–	90	90	–	–	s14	90¹	–	–	–	–	76¹	90¹
30.1.99	Derby Co H	0–1	24,440	–	58	90	–	55	–	90	–	–	–	–	90	s35
6.2.99	Leicester A	2–0	20,113	–	90	90	–	86	–	90¹	–	–	–	–	90	s4
20.2.99	Blackburn A	4–1	24,643	–	90	90	–	90¹	s46	90□	s31	–	–	–	90	–
27.2.99	Middlesbro' H	3–1	24,534	–	90	90	–	90²	–	90□	–	–	–	–	90□	–
3.3.99	Wimbledon H	1–2	24,116	–	90	90	–	90	–	90	–	–	–	–	90	s3
9.3.99	Arsenal A	0–3	37,792	–	90	90	–	90	–	90	–	–	–	–	90	–
13.3.99	Leeds Utd H	0–2	28,142	s39□	90	90¹	–	90□	s55	–	–	–	–	–	90□	51
20.3.99	Southampton A	0–1	15,201	–	90	90	–	90□	–	90	–	–	–	–	21	s5
3.4.99	Coventry H	1–2	28,136	–	90	90	–	–	90	90	–	90	–	–	–	45
5.4.99	Everton A	2–1	35,270	–	80	90	–	90□	–	89²	–	s1	–	–	90	–
17.4.99	Man Utd A	0–3	55,270	–	55	90	–	68	–	90	–	s22	–	–	90	–
21.4.99	Newcastle H	1–1	21,545	–	90	90	–	90	–	90□	–	–	–	–	90	–
25.4.99	Chelsea H	0–0	21,652	–	90	90	–	80□	–	90	–	s10	–	–	–	–
1.5.99	Nott'm For A	0–2	20,480	–	72	90□	–	90	–	90	s58	s18	–	–	–	–
8.5.99	Liverpool H	1–0	27,383	–	s33	90	–	80	–	90	–	s10¹	–	57	–	–
16.5.99	Charlton A	1–0	20,043	–	90	82■	–	90	–	60	–	s31	–	59	–	–

□ Yellow card, ■ Red card, s Substitute, 90³ Goals scored

1998–99 PREMIERSHIP APPEARANCES

HYDE	JONK	MAGILTON	McKEEVER	MORRISON	NEWSOME	OAKES	PRESSMAN	QUINN	RUDI	SANETTI	SCOTT	SONNER	SRNICEK	STEFANOVIC	THOME	WALKER	WHITTINGHAM	TOTAL
–	90	–	–	–	–	–	90	–	90	–	–	–	–	–	90	90	–	990
s18	90	–	–	–	–	–	90	–	90□	–	–	–	–	–	90	90	–	990
–	90	–	–	–	–	–	90	–	90	–	–	~	–	–	90	90	–	990
–	90	–	–	–	–	–	90	–	90	–	–	–	–	–	90□	90	75	990
–	90	–	–	–	–	–	90	–	90	s1	–	–	–	–	90	90	–	990
–	90	s11	–	–	90	–	90	46	–	–	–	–	–	–	90	90	–	990
–	89	s1	–	–	–	–	90	–	90	–	–	–	–	–	90□	90	–	944
–	90	72	–	–	–	s74	90	–	16	s18	–	–	–	–	90	90	–	990
–	90	–	–	–	–	–	90	–	–	–	–	90	–	–	90	90	s7	990
–	90	–	–	–	–	–	90	–	–	–	–	90□	–	–	90	90	–	990
–	90	–	–	–	–	–	90	–	s33	s15	75	–	–	–	90	90	–	990
–	68□	s22	–	–	s11	–	90	–	90	–	90	–	–	–	90	90	–	990
–	90	s33	–	–	–	–	–	–	90[1]	–	–	57□	90	–	90	90	–	990
–	90[1]□	–	–	–	–	–	–	–	90	–	–	90	90	–	90	90	–	990
–	90	s3	–	–	–	–	–	–	90	–	–	87□	90	–	90	90	–	990
–	90	–	–	–	–	–	–	–	80	–	–	90	90	s1	90	90	–	990
–	90	–	–	–	–	–	–	–	80[1]	–	–	90□	90	s10□	90	90	–	990
–	90	–	–	–	–	–	–	–	86	–	–	90	90	–	90	90	–	990
–	90	–	s24	–	–	–	–	–	90	–	–	–	90	90□	90	90	–	990
–	90	–	–	–	–	–	–	–	88□	–	–	–	90	21■	90	90□	–	921
–	90	–	–	–	–	–	–	–	90	–	–	–	90	90	90	90	–	990
–	90	–	–	–	–	–	–	–	90[1]	–	–	90□	90	–	90	90	–	990
–	86	–	–	–	s4	–	s32	–	90	–	–	–	57■	90	90	90	–	957
–	90[1]	–	–	–	–	–	–	–	90	–	–	90	90	–	90	90	–	990
–	90	–	–	–	–	–	90	–	90[2]	–	–	59[1]	–	–	90	44	–	990
–	90	–	–	–	–	–	90	–	90	–	–	90[1]	–	–	90	90	–	990
–	90	–	–	–	–	–	–	–	90	–	–	87	90	–	90[1]	90	–	990
–	90□	–	–	–	–	–	–	–	90	–	–	90	90	–	90	90	–	990
–	90	–	–	–	–	–	–	–	90	–	–	35	90	–	90□	90	–	990
–	85	–	–	–	–	–	–	–	90	–	–	90	90	s69	90	90	–	990
–	89	–	–	–	s45	–	–	–	90[1]	–	s1	s45	90□	–	90	45	–	990
–	90	–	–	–	90	–	–	–	90	–	s10	90	90	–	90	–	–	990
–	90	–	–	–	–	–	–	–	90	–	s35	90	90	–	90	90	–	990
–	45	–	–	–	–	–	–	–	90	–	s45[1]	90	90	–	90	90	–	990
–	90	90	–	–	–	–	–	–	–	–	–	90	90	90	90	90	–	990
–	90	s58	–	–	–	–	–	–	32	–	–	90	90	90	32	90	–	990
–	90	s7	–	–	–	–	–	–	83	–	–	90	90	90	90	90	–	990
–	90□	–	–	–	–	–	–	–	90	–	–	s30[1]	90	90	90	90□	–	982

THE MANAGER

DANNY WILSON

Danny Wilson is one of the up-and-coming young managers in the game. At just 39, he joined Sheffield Wednesday in the summer of 1998 after three seasons as manager of Barnsley.

Wilson had taken Barnsley into the Premiership for the first time in the club's history but was unable to keep them in the top flight, despite a brave battle that was admired by football fans everywhere.

The decision to leave one South Yorkshire club for another was not an easy one but, as a former Sheffield Wednesday player, Wilson could not turn down the lure of managing his old club and remaining in the game's elite division.

Wilson played international football for Northern Ireland, earning 25 caps in a playing career that included spells in club football at Wigan Athletic, Bury, Chesterfield, Nottingham Forest, Brighton & Hove Albion, Luton Town as well as Sheffield Wednesday.

The 1998–99 season proved to be one of consolidation, with Wilson taking the opportunity to assess the squad and bring in some of his own buys to build a side that is capable of pushing up into the top half of the league next year.

LEAGUE POSITION

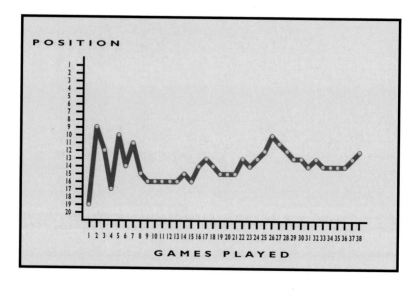

THE GOALS

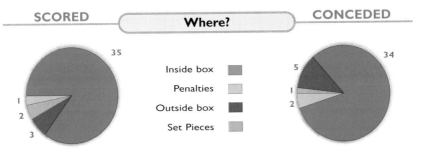

SCORED — Where? — CONCEDED

Inside box
Penalties
Outside box
Set Pieces

Sheffield Wednesday did not test opposition goalkeepers from long range as much as they would have liked. In the Premiership only Derby, Coventry and Wimbledon had fewer shots from outside the area on target, and Wednesday netted just five times from distance. This was also true of their rivals, with a modest 14.3% of opposition goals scored from more than 18 yards out.

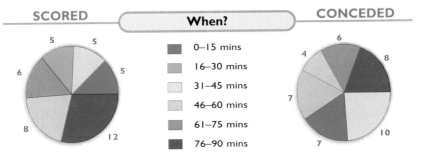

SCORED — When? — CONCEDED

0–15 mins
16–30 mins
31–45 mins
46–60 mins
61–75 mins
76–90 mins

Danny Wilson's men rallied in the second halves of their matches, scoring the majority of their goals in this spell and conceding fewer strikes after the break than during the opening 45 minutes. The Owls conceded just 18 times in the second period, or 42.9% of all goals, which was the lowest proportion of any Carling Premiership club. They also netted 63.4% of all goals after the break and, as a tribute to their fitness and stamina, 29% in the last quarter-hour.

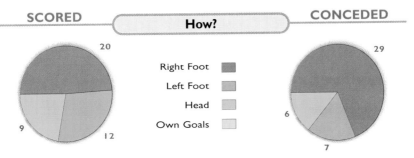

SCORED — How? — CONCEDED

Right Foot
Left Foot
Head
Own Goals

Wednesday excelled in the air throughout the 1998–99 Carling Premiership. Des Walker and Emerson Thome made 696 headed clearances between them, more than any defensive pairing in the league. The Owls scored 22% of all goals from headers, with eight different players registering with their head. The Hillsborough back-line restricted opponents to just six headed strikes, the fourth-lowest total in the top flight. They neither scored nor conceded an own-goal.

SHEFFIELD WEDNESDAY

	AGOGO	ALEXANDERSSON	ATHERTON	BARRETT	BOOTH	BRISCOE	CARBONE	COBIAN	CRESSWELL	DI CANIO	HASLAM	HINCHCLIFFE	HUMPHREY
APPEARANCE													
Start	0	31	38	0	34	5	31	7	1	5	2	32	10
Sub	1	1	0	5	0	11	0	2	6	1	0	0	9
Minutes on pitch	39	2610	3412	94	2908	667	2709	625	182	444	116	2797	929
GOAL ATTEMPTS													
Goals	0	3	2	0	6	1	8	0	1	3	0	3	1
Shots on target	0	16	4	1	24	4	35	1	5	7	1	6	7
Shots off target	0	16	5	0	44	7	42	3	4	5	0	3	15
Shooting accuracy %	0%	50%	44%	100%	35%	36%	45%	25%	56%	58%	100%	67%	32%
PASSING													
Goal assists	0	3	1	0	1	0	6	0	1	0	0	4	0
Long passes	0	60	269	7	21	30	122	62	0	29	3	392	12
Short passes	9	868	1054	42	1076	195	1152	236	63	178	39	1039	315
PASS COMPLETION													
Own half %	0%	87%	92%	95%	89%	83%	87%	93%	100%	89%	90%	95%	93%
Opposition half %	89%	74%	70%	80%	73%	69%	71%	67%	67%	70%	59%	67%	76%
CROSSING													
Total crosses	2	76	32	1	10	22	112	12	2	21	0	144	18
Cross completion %	50%	20%	28%	0%	10%	32%	32%	42%	100%	14%	0%	41%	22%
DRIBBLING													
Dribbles & runs	2	68	22	2	34	9	202	15	7	49	0	37	23
Dribble completion %	100%	78%	82%	100%	47%	89%	50%	100%	57%	80%	0%	89%	87%
DEFENDING													
Tackles made	2	110	109	5	64	17	71	25	6	11	8	58	10
Tackles won %	50%	63%	70%	40%	61%	47%	45%	48%	17%	64%	25%	78%	20%
Blocks	0	6	21	0	6	3	1	1	0	0	2	26	1
Clearances	0	70	262	5	31	41	1	25	0	1	7	257	6
Interceptions	0	28	37	4	8	4	13	3	0	1	1	28	2
DISCIPLINE													
Fouls	2	15	36	1	78	6	37	6	2	7	1	23	12
Offside	1	7	1	0	57	0	87	0	6	10	0	3	14
Yellow cards	1	0	3	0	7	0	9	2	0	0	0	4	1
Red cards	0	0	1	0	0	0	0	0	0	1	0	1	0

GOALKEEPER NAME	START/ (SUB)	TIME ON PITCH	GOALS CONCEDED	MINS/GOALS CONCEDED	SAVES MADE	SAVES/ SHOTS
PRESSMAN	14 (1)	1292	14	92.3	51	78%
SRNICEK	24	2127	28	76	99	78%

PLAYERS' STATISTICS

HYDE	JONK	MAGILTON	McKEEVER	MORRISON	NEWSOME	OAKES	QUINN	RUDI	SANETTI	SCOTT	SONNER	STEFANOVIC	THOME	WALKER	WHITTINGHAM	TOTAL	RANK
0	38	1	1	0	2	0	1	33	0	0	24	8	38	37	1		
1	0	5	2	1	3	1	0	1	3	4	2	3	0	0	1		
18	3342	142	155	24	240	74	46	2838	34	91	2095	731	3362	3239	82		
0	2	0	0	0	0	0	0	6	0	1	3	0	1	0	0	41	=12th
0	16	1	0	0	0	0	0	15	0	1	6	3	5	0	0	158	=18th
0	17	1	2	0	1	3	1	25	1	0	12	6	12	0	0	225	8th
0%	48%	50%	0%	0%	0%	0%	0%	38%	0%	100%	33%	33%	29%	0%	0%	41%	20th
0	5	0	0	0	0	0	0	1	0	0	2	0	2	0	0	26	=16th
0	277	5	6	0	6	3	0	95	1	1	85	60	248	171	2	1967	6th
3	1469	101	35	12	52	17	9	1260	14	28	842	232	825	604	26	11795	6th
100%	93%	92%	93%	75%	76%	83%	67%	88%	100%	83%	90%	90%	89%	90%	88%	90%	5th
100%	75%	78%	63%	75%	75%	88%	83%	77%	73%	59%	79%	64%	58%	64%	58%	71%	7th
0	57	2	6	0	1	1	3	45	0	0	42	13	6	1	1	630	17th
0%	39%	100%	17%	0%	0%	0%	33%	36%	0%	0%	40%	31%	0%	100%	100%	33%	1st
0	49	5	12	1	1	4	2	119	3	5	25	6	33	12	0	748	18th
0%	88%	60%	83%	100%	100%	100%	50%	77%	33%	80%	84%	83%	79%	83%	0%	71%	10th
2	118	5	8	1	1	0	1	113	0	5	74	26	171	93	1	1115	15th
100%	58%	60%	25%	0%	0%	0%	0%	71%	0%	80%	68%	65%	68%	58%	100%	62%	6th
0	10	0	0	0	3	0	0	6	0	0	7	4	46	39	0	182	=15th
1	64	3	4	0	59	1	2	55	0	9	56	56	543	557	0	2153	4th
0	28	3	1	0	0	1	0	21	0	0	25	11	52	60	1	334	11th
0	26	0	0	0	3	0	1	66	0	0	42	10	55	25	0	456	20th
1	1	0	0	1	0	2	0	23	0	2	1	3	0	0	0	220	1st
0	4	0	0	0	0	0	0	2	0	0	6	2	3	2	0	47	20th
0	0	0	0	0	0	0	0	0	0	0	0	1	0	0	0	5	=4th

CROSSES CAUGHT	CROSSES PUNCHED	CROSSES NOT CLAIMED	CATCH SUCCESS	THROWS/ SHORT KICKS	% COMPLETION	LONG KICKS	% COMPLETION
45	11	12	98%	134	96%	297	36%
68	27	9	92%	222	93%	481	38%

PLAYER OF THE SEASON

PLAYER	INDEX SCORE
EMERSON THOME	961
Benito Carbone	900
Andy Hinchcliffe	872
Des Walker	813
Niclas Alexandersson	809
Pavel Srnicek	797
Petter Rudi	757
Wim Jonk	722
Peter Atherton	690
Danny Sonner	661

Former Liverpool boss Graeme Souness may well have cast a wistful glance in the direction of Hillsborough following his acrimonious departure from Benfica.

With the likes of Emerson in his side, the Benfica defence might well have had the backbone of a Spanish Armada as opposed to a Spanish omelette.

But the undoubted winners in all this mess were Sheffield Wednesday, who pinched Emerson from under Souness's nose on a marvellous free transfer. And his performances at the back alongside Des Walker rescued the Owls from the ignominy of a drop-zone dogfight in 1998–99.

"Emo" had plenty of ammo at set-pieces, scoring in both the Premiership and the FA Cup. His goal-scoring display at home to Wimbledon was one of the best by a defender all season.

And despite missing only 58 minutes of league football all season, he picked up just three bookings – a terrific effort. He ended the campaign as Wednesday's highest-scoring player in the Carling Opta Season Index, averaging 961 points.

There is no doubt about the club's top striker in 1998–99. Benito Carbone was one of the best-performing Italians in the Premiership, regularly dazzling the Hillsborough faithful with his skill on the ball. He scored eight goals on his way to an average score of 900 points per match, picking up many of his points with his dribbling and incisive passing in the final third of the pitch.

Full-back Andy Hinchcliffe and wingers Niclas Alexandersson and Petter Rudi put in a high number of quality centres, making Sheffield Wednesday the most accurate crossers in the league. They all figure in the top 10, along with bargain buys Pavel Srnicek and Danny Sonner, who both proved their worth over the course of the campaign.

FIVE OF THE BEST

After quitting neighbours Barnsley in the summer of 1998, Danny Wilson set about trying to transform the fortunes of under-performing Yorkshiremen Sheffield Wednesday. With limited resources for new players at his disposal Wilson tried to get the best out of the existing squad, but a final position of 12th suggests there is much work still to be done.

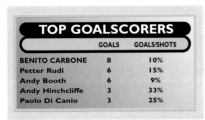

TOP GOALSCORERS

	GOALS	GOALS/SHOTS
BENITO CARBONE	8	10%
Petter Rudi	6	15%
Andy Booth	6	9%
Andy Hinchcliffe	3	33%
Paolo Di Canio	3	25%

The loss of Paolo Di Canio after his notorious clash with referee Paul Alcock was a bitter blow to Wednesday, and it was left to his compatriot Benito Carbone to produce the goals. However, despite some mesmeric displays from the little Italian, a strike rate of one goal from every 10 shots was somewhat disappointing. Target man Andy Booth struggled even more to find the net regularly, but there was some fine support from Petter Rudi and full-back Andy Hinchcliffe, who contributed nine goals between them. Much now rests on the shoulders of new signing Richard Cresswell in 1999–2000.

Only five other teams in the Premiership made more successful passes than Sheffield Wednesday in 1998–99. At home, former Dutch international Wim Jonk and Danny Sonner dictated play in midfield, while away from Hillsborough the team were more direct, with Petter Rudi and Niclas Alexandersson encouraged to get forward down the flanks at every opportunity. Jonk played almost 1,500 successful balls, while Andy Hinchcliffe came second in the chart with more than 1,100 pinpoint passes.

TOP PASSERS

	SUCC PASSES	COMPLETION
WIM JONK	1,444	83%
Andy Hinchcliffe	1,133	79%
Petter Rudi	1,086	80%
Peter Atherton	1,044	79%
Benito Carbone	939	74%

TOP TACKLERS

	WON	SUCCESS
EMERSON THOME	116	68%
Petter Rudi	80	71%
Peter Atherton	76	70%
Niclas Alexandersson	69	63%
Wim Jonk	69	58%

Tough-tackling Brazilian star Emerson Thome was another player who blossomed in Danny Wilson's first season, attracting the attentions of numerous clubs both at home and abroad. "The Wall" was the only Owl to win more than 100 tackles in 1998–99, with an above-average 68% success rate overall. Cleanest tackler, surprisingly, was leggy winger Petter Rudi, while skipper Peter Atherton, who played in defence and midfield over the course of the season, won seven out of every 10 challenges.

With the fewest fouls conceded and the fewest bookings accrued, Wednesday take the prize as the undisputed Premiership clean team of 1998–99. They did pick up five red cards, but none of those players figure in the top five. Worst offender was striker Andy Booth, who conceded by far the most free kicks when harrying for possession up front. He also collected seven yellow cards to finish just short of 100 disciplinary points. Tackle masters Rudi and Thome also figure, while Carbone's collection of cards for dissent ensures his inclusion in the top five.

DISCIPLINE

	POINTS	FOULS & CARDS
ANDY BOOTH	99	78F, 7Y, 0R
Petter Rudi	72	66F, 2Y, 0R
Emerson Thome	64	55F, 3Y, 0R
Benito Carbone	64	37F, 9Y, 0R
Danny Sonner	60	42F, 6Y, 0R

ACTION	ALEXANDERSSON	ATHERTON	BOOTH	BRISCOE	COBIAN	DI CANIO	HINCHCLIFFE	HUMPHREYS	JONK	MAGILTON	PRESSMAN	RUDI	THOME	WALKER	TOTAL	ARSENAL
Time on pitch	59	90	20	31	90	44	90	70	89	1	90	90	90	90	944	944
GOALS																
Goal	–	–	–	1	–	–	–	–	–	–	–	–	–	–	–	–
Shot on target	–	–	–	–	–	–	–	–	–	–	–	–	1	1	3	7
Shot off target	2	–	–	–	–	–	–	3	–	–	–	–	–	–	5	3
Blocked shot	–	–	–	–	–	–	–	–	–	–	–	–	–	–	1	2
Own goal	–	–	–	–	–	–	–	–	–	–	–	–	–	–	–	–
PASSES																
Pass to own player	14	26	3	6	22	13	38	17	30	1	–	26	29	22	247	244
Pass to opposition	2	–	–	–	5	3	2	2	1	–	–	–	1	–	18	35
Cross to own player	1	–	–	1	–	–	4	–	–	–	–	2	–	–	10	2
Cross to opposition player	1	–	–	1	3	2	3	–	2	–	–	3	–	–	15	15
Goal assist	–	–	–	–	–	–	–	–	–	–	–	–	–	1	1	–
Pass completion %	82%	96%	100%	88%	75%	72%	89%	89%	91%	100%	0%	88%	97%	100%	89%	83%
TACKLES & CLEARANCES																
Tackle	3	2	–	–	2	2	2	–	4	–	–	2	2	2	21	22
Clearances, blocks and interceptions	–	2	–	–	2	–	3	1	1	–	–	5	5	8	21	41
DRIBBLES & RUNS																
Dribble ball retained	–	1	–	–	1	2	1	1	–	–	–	5	–	–	11	20
Dribbles ball lost	–	–	–	1	–	–	–	1	–	–	–	–	2	–	4	4
Dribble success %	0%	100%	0%	0%	100%	100%	100%	50%	0%	0%	0%	83%	0%	0%	73%	83%
DISCIPLINE																
Fouls	2	2	1	1	–	2	–	–	–	–	–	6	1	–	14	11
Penalty conceded	–	–	–	–	–	–	–	–	–	–	–	–	–	–	–	–
Free kick - offside	–	–	–	–	–	–	–	4	–	–	–	–	–	–	6	6
Yellow cards	–	–	–	–	–	–	–	–	–	–	–	1	–	–	1	3
Red cards	–	–	–	–	–	1	–	–	–	–	–	–	–	–	–	1
GOALKEEPERS																
Distribution to own player	–	–	–	–	–	–	–	–	–	–	11	–	–	–	11	8
Distribution to opposition player	–	–	–	–	–	–	–	–	–	–	6	–	–	–	6	9
Goalkeeper distribution%	0%	0%	0%	0%	0%	0%	0%	0%	0%	0%	65%	0%	0%	0%	65%	47%
Save	–	–	–	–	–	–	–	–	–	–	7	–	–	–	7	3
Ball caught	–	–	–	–	–	–	–	–	–	–	3	–	–	–	3	–
Ball dropped	–	–	–	–	–	–	–	–	–	–	–	–	–	–	–	–
Goal conceded	–	–	–	–	–	–	–	–	–	–	1	–	–	–	1	–

Sheffield Wednesday took all three points in this early-season clash, but the match made the headlines for completely different reasons. Arsenal nearly took the lead on 15 minutes when Ray Parlour's shot was parried away by Kevin Pressman.

September 26, 1998

1–0

SHEFFIELD WEDNESDAY
ARSENAL

Wednesday's big goalkeeper was called into action again on 28 minutes. Patrick Vieira fed Nicolas Anelka, who shook off the attentions of Andy Hinchcliffe, Des Walker and Petter Rudi. He then pulled the ball back for Vieira, whose shot was beaten away at the near post by Pressman.

The Wednesday fans had their hearts in their mouths as their 'keeper came rushing out of his area to deny Anelka. The ball bounced off Pressman's chest straight to Ray Parlour 40 yards out, but his chipped effort went wide of the unguarded net.

Wednesday had a poor first half in attacking terms, with Arsenal's stand-in 'keeper Alex Manninger untroubled for the first 45 minutes.

The game erupted a minute before half-time, when Vieira and Wim Jonk tangled in midfield. Vieira lashed out at the Dutchman, sparking angry exchanges between rival players. Martin Keown and Paolo Di Canio became particularly involved.

Referee Paul Alcock brandished the red card at Di Canio and the Italian pushed the referee to the turf and strode off in disgust. After picking himself up, Alcock also sent off Keown and booked Vieira for his part in the initial incident. The crowd were still catching their breath when the half-time whistle went.

With the match now at 10-a-side, spaces started to open up and Bergkamp was denied on 48 minutes when his shot was deflected wide off Pressman's outstretched leg.

Wednesday's first chance in the second half fell to substitute Lee Briscoe with 18 minutes remaining. Hinchcliffe swung in a majestic cross and Briscoe headed tamely straight at Manninger's feet. It was a golden chance that went begging for the Owls – and manager Danny Wilson must have been thinking about hanging on for the draw.

Parlour's drive was turned away and behind by Pressman, and at the other end Rudi's cross nearly resulted in an own-goal for Tony Adams. His misjudged header dropped inches wide of the far post with Manninger in no man's land.

Then, in the last minute, Wednesday delivered the sucker punch. Jonk spotted Briscoe making ground on the left corner of the Arsenal penalty area. The substitute let the ball run across his body and, with Vivas and Adams in close attendance, delivered an inch-perfect chip over Manninger and into the far corner.

Humphreys missed a great chance just before the end, but it was academic as the final whistle was blown to condemn Arsenal to their first Premiership defeat of the season.

The two teams were evenly matched in the passing stakes, with Arsenal carving out more clear-cut chances and hitting the target more often (seven times to Wednesday's four). Both teams made more than 20 tackles each during the game (with Wednesday committing 14 fouls to Arsenal's 11) and both had a player sent off. Di Canio was later handed heavy bans and fines from both Sheffield Wednesday and the FA. He returned to football after his suspension and joined West Ham.

ACTION	ALEXANDERSSON	ATHERTON	BOOTH	CARBONE	HINCHCLIFFE	JONK	RUDI	SONNER	SRNICEK	THOME	WALKER	TOTAL	MANCHESTER UTD
Time on pitch	90	90	90	90	90	90	90	90	90	90	90	990	990
GOALS													
Goal	2	–	–	1	–	–	–	–	–	–	–	3	1
Shot on target	1	–	2	–	–	–	–	–	–	–	1	4	2
Shot off target	–	–	–	1	–	1	1	–	–	–	–	3	8
Blocked shot	–	–	1	–	1	–	–	–	–	–	1	3	2
Own goal	–	–	–	–	–	–	–	–	–	–	–	–	–
PASSES													
Pass to own player	21	22	16	34	28	42	37	33	–	10	5	248	400
Pass to opposition	10	6	13	13	11	12	8	4	–	3	5	85	97
Cross to own player	–	1	–	–	–	–	1	–	–	–	1	3	6
Cross to opposition player	–	–	–	1	1	–	1	1	–	–	3	7	17
Goal assist	–	–	–	–	1	–	–	–	–	–	–	1	1
Pass completion %	68%	77%	53%	71%	71%	76%	80%	87%	0%	77%	50%	73%	78%
TACKLES & CLEARANCES													
Tackle	7	5	7	4	4	9	3	4	–	5	4	52	41
Clearances, blocks and interceptions	4	12	2	1	11	5	4	5	–	22	19	85	60
DRIBBLES & RUNS													
Dribble ball retained	5	1	1	2	–	1	3	–	–	–	–	13	19
Dribbles ball lost	1	–	2	3	–	–	1	1	–	–	–	8	11
Dribble success %	83%	100%	33%	40%	–	100%	75%	0%	–	0%	0%	62%	63%
DISCIPLINE													
Fouls	3	3	3	1	2	2	1	1	–	3	–	19	12
Penalty conceded	–	–	–	–	–	–	–	–	–	–	–	–	–
Free kick - offside	–	3	–	–	–	1	–	1	–	–	–	5	–
Yellow cards	–	–	–	–	–	–	–	–	–	–	–	–	–
Red cards	–	–	–	–	–	–	–	–	–	–	–	–	–
GOALKEEPERS													
Distribution to own player	–	–	–	–	–	–	–	–	11	–	–	11	11
Distribution to opposition player	–	–	–	–	–	–	–	–	19	–	–	19	12
Goalkeeper distribution%	0%	–	0%	0%	0%	0%	0%	37%	37%	0%	0%	37%	48%
Save	–	–	–	–	–	–	–	–	2	–	–	2	4
Ball caught	–	–	–	–	–	–	–	–	7	–	–	7	7
Ball dropped	–	–	–	–	–	–	–	–	–	–	–	–	–
Goal conceded	–	–	–	–	–	–	–	–	1	–	–	1	3

Despite going into the game in 14th position, the Owls approached the challenge of playing second-placed Manchester United with confidence and a determination to give the Championship favourites a run for their money. Playing against the biggest club in the country is always an inspiration, and in recent years Sheffield Wednesday have a superb record against Manchester United at Hillsborough.

November 21, 1998

3 – 1

SHEFFIELD WEDNESDAY
MANCHESTER UNITED

Danny Wilson's side hustled United out of their game and it was no more than their effort deserved when they opened the scoring after 14 minutes. Niclas Alexandersson brought down a long free kick from Andy Hinchcliffe on the edge of the box. The Swede then fired in a speculative 20-yard shot which Peter Schmeichel seemed to have caught – but instead he spilled the ball over his shoulder and into the net, much to the surprise and delight of the Hillsborough crowd.

Manchester United enjoyed a large percentage of possession and eventually a slick move ended with Dwight Yorke setting up Andy Cole for a deserved equalizer.

Wednesday survived until half-time and then grabbed the lead once more in the 55th minute. Alexandersson crossed the ball into the path of Andy Booth, whose close-range effort was blocked by Schmeichel. However, the ball rebounded into the path of Wim Jonk who gratefully side-footed home his first goal for the club since joining in the summer.

Then, in the 73rd minute, Alexandersson pounced on some slack defending and a misunderstanding between David Beckham and Jaap Stam to round Schmeichel and fire home Wednesday's third goal to secure a vital win.

Sheffield Wednesday scored their three goals from seven efforts on target. They had a further three shots blocked and three more which went wide. Manchester United also fired in 13 attempts at goal, but only three of those hit the target.

United had the bulk of the possession, with Roy Keane completing 62 of their 400 successful passes. Wednesday completed fewer than two-thirds of that number, but it was clear that the Owls showed more desire on the day, winning 73% of their tackles to United's 66% and making 85 blocks, clearances and interceptions to United's 60.

Despite the intensity of the game, only two players were cautioned – Jonk and Paul Scholes – though there were 31 fouls in the game.

Man of the match for the Owls was Niclas Alexandersson, whose two-goal performance earned him a Carling Opta points total of 2,293. He had two other efforts in the game, one saved by Schmeichel and the other blocked en route to goal. He was a constant thorn in United's side – their left side to be exact, where he gave Denis Irwin and then Phil Neville a torrid time.

This match marked Wednesday's fifth match in a run of seven games undefeated at home that helped them pull away from the relegation zone. United were fortunate not to lose any ground in the title race, as of all their title rivals only Chelsea were able to win any points on a day of upsets in the Premiership.

SOUTHAMPTON 1998–99

Back row (left to right): Lee Todd, John Beresford, David Hughes, Matthew Oakley, Richard Dryden, Steve Basham, James Beattie, Andy Williams, Stig Johansen.

Middle row: Jim Joyce (Physiotherapist), Stuart Ripley, David Hirst, Claus Lundekvam, Carlton Palmer (now Nottingham Forest), Paul Jones, Neil Moss, Ken Monkou, David Howells, Scott Marshall, Egil Ostenstad, Malcolm Taylor (Kit Man).

Front row: Mark Hughes, Matthew Le Tissier, Stuart Gray (First Team Coach), Dave Jones (Manager), Rupert Lowe (Chairman), Terry Cooper (European Representative), John Sainty (Academy Director), Jason Dodd, Francis Benali.

SOUTHAMPTON

KEY PERSONNEL

Chairman: R J G Lowe
Vice-Chairman: B H D Hunt
Directors: R J G Lowe,
B H D Hunt, A E Cowen, I L Gordon,
M R Richards FCA, K St J Wiseman
Club Secretary: B P Truscott
Manager: Dave Jones

COLOURS

Home: Red and white striped shirts,
black shorts and white stockings
Away: Yellow shirts, blue shorts
and yellow stockings

NICKNAME

The Saints

20 FACTS

1 Southampton were formed in 1885 by players from St Mary's Church YMCA; hence their nickname of the Saints.

2 The Saints have never won the Championship. Their highest finish in the top flight came in 1983–84 when they finished second in Division One.

3 The club's finest hour came in the 1976 FA Cup Final when they beat Manchester United 1–0 courtesy of Bobby Stokes's winner.

4 Southampton have never won the League Cup. They finished as runners-up in 1979, losing the final 3–2 to Nottingham Forest.

5 The club have never won a European trophy, but they have competed in the European Fairs Cup, the UEFA Cup and the European Cup Winners Cup.

6 The Dell has the smallest capacity of any ground in the Premiership. Only 15,352 fans can fit inside.

7 Matthew Le Tissier has the best record from the penalty spot in the Premiership. He has scored with 47 out of 48 spot kicks in the league. Nottingham Forest's Mark Crossley saved Le Tissier's one errant attempt.

8 Former Southampton player Peter Shilton holds the English record for the most league appearances. He played 1,005 games for a variety of clubs between 1966 and 1997.

9 Terry Paine is Southampton's longest-serving player. He made a total of 809 appearances for the club between 1956 and 1974. During that time, Paine never played fewer than 36 league games in a season.

10 Mick Channon is the club's all-time leading goalscorer. He notched up a total of 227 goals for the club (185 in the league) in two spells at the Dell.

11 Southampton's record victory is a 9–3 hammering of Wolverhampton Wanderers in a Division Two match in 1965.

12 The club have twice been beaten 8–0. Spurs inflicted the first humiliation in 1936 and Everton trounced them by the same score in 1971.

13 Southampton drew 18 games in the 1994–95 season, a Premiership record which they share with Manchester City and Sheffield United.

14 The Saints have twice received club record transfer fees from Blackburn Rovers. Alan Shearer was sold for £3.6 million in 1992. That was surpassed in 1998 when Kevin Davies made the switch to Ewood Park for £7.25 million.

15 Southampton were the first club to suffer the consequences of the three-up-three-down rule. They were relegated from Division One in 1973–74 after finishing third from bottom.

16 Dave Jones's side escaped relegation on the last day of the season, finishing 17th in the 1998–99 Premiership. Their league record was:

Pld	W	D	L	F	A	Pts
38	11	8	19	37	64	41

17 Southampton were pitted against Kevin Keegan's Fulham in the third round of the FA Cup. After a 1–1 draw at the Dell, they lost the replay 1–0.

18 By a quirk of footballing fate, Fulham also provided the opposition in the Worthington Cup second round. Unfortunately for the Saints the outcome was the same, and they went out of the competition 2–1 on aggregate.

19 The top goalscorer in all competitions for Southampton was Egil Ostenstad with eight goals.

20 Southampton's disciplinary record was the fourth-worst in the Premiership. They committed 576 fouls, earned 77 yellow cards and suffered three dismissals.

SEASON REVIEW

After spending almost the entire season in the relegation zone, Southampton were happy to go into the last game of the season with their destiny in their own hands. A 2–0 victory over Everton at the Dell ensured their survival and made Charlton's result academic, but the five-point gap between the two clubs disguised the fact that Dave Jones's side had come mighty close to falling through the trap-door.

The Saints did not make it out of the bottom three until the last month of the season. It took them until their sixth game to earn their first point and another four outings before they won their first game.

A 2–0 victory over Blackburn in late November lifted the club off the bottom of the table for the first time. It was to be one of only two away victories all season. Ultimately Southampton were saved by their home form. The 2–0 defeat by Chelsea on Boxing Day was the last time they lost at the Dell in the Premiership all season.

Boosted by the signings of Hassan Kachloul in October and Patrick Colleter in December, the club were certainly a tougher proposition than they had been in the first half of the season. A 7–1 thrashing at the hands of Liverpool on 16 January proved that they were still vulnerable, but it was followed a week later by a superb 3–0 victory over Leeds United that lifted the club to 18th, just two points behind Blackburn.

It was around this time that James Beattie began to emerge as a key figure in the quest for survival. Signed from Blackburn in the summer of 1998 as part of the deal which took Kevin Davies in the opposite direction, the youngster did for Saints what Davies could not do for Rovers: score crucial goals. He also set

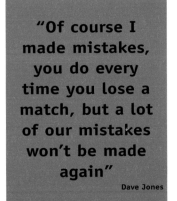

"Of course I made mistakes, you do every time you lose a match, but a lot of our mistakes won't be made again"

Dave Jones

them up for his team-mates.

In a season which saw Southampton finish as the second-lowest scorers overall and summer signing Mark Hughes score just one goal, Beattie's contribution was an important one. He scored five goals – 14% of the team's final total – and set up a further seven, 26% of the overall number of assists at the club. His Player of the Year award was well deserved.

What he could not do was help improve on the lack of craft at the club. Southampton finished the season with the second-worst pass completion rate in the Premiership. Occasional flashes of brilliance from Matthew Le Tissier and Hassan Kachloul only made the lack of skill in other areas more apparent.

The team were certainly not afraid to scrap for their survival, though. They led the Premiership fouls chart for a large chunk of the season – eventually finishing third – and in Mark Hughes they had the most-booked player in the top flight.

It was this willingness to fight for results which eventually kept them up. On May 1, Leicester were out-muscled 2–1 to take Southampton out of the relegation zone for the first time. On May 8 Wimbledon were beaten 2–0 and, although Charlton grabbed a last-minute winner at Villa Park to take the relegation battle to the last day of the season, Southampton knew that they were in pole position.

Two goals from Marian Pahars on the last day made it a happy end to the season for Saints fans, but after finishing 12th in 1997–98 the battle to stay up came as something of a shock. To their credit, the board and the fans stuck by both their manager and the players during a difficult season but they will be hoping for a more comfortable ride in 1999–2000.

SOUTHAMPTON

DATE	OPPONENT	SCORE	ATT.	BASHAM	BEATTIE	BENALI	BERESFORD	BRADLEY	BRIDGE	COLLETER	DODD	DRYDEN	GIBBENS	HILEY	HIRST	HOWE
16.8.98	Liverpool H	1–2	15,202	–	s14	–	7	–	s83	–	90	90	–	90	–	–
22.8.98	Charlton A	0–5	16,488	–	s26□	–	–	–	45	–	90□	90	–	90	–	s32
29.8.98	Nott'm For H	1–2	14,942	–	s11	–	–	–	s24	–	90	90	–	79	–	90
8.9.98	Leeds Utd A	0–3	30,637	–	79	–	–	–	75	–	90□	–	s5	90	–	85
12.9.98	Newcastle A	0–4	36,454	–	39	90	–	–	45	–	38□	–	–	90□	–	90
19.9.98	Tottenham H	1–1	15,204	–	s37	90□	–	–	90	–	90	–	90	–	–	53
28.9.98	West Ham A	0–1	23,153	–	s26	90□	–	–	90	–	–	–	64	–	–	–
3.10.98	Man Utd H	0–3	15,251	–	s27	90	–	–	90	–	–	–	s35	–	–	90
17.10.98	Arsenal A	1–1	38,027	–	–	90	–	–	90	–	–	–	–	s55	–	90[1]
24.10.98	Coventry H	2–1	15,152	–	s3	90	–	–	s19	–	–	–	–	90	–	48
31.10.98	Sheff Wed A	0–0	30,078	–	–	90	–	–	90	–	–	–	–	90	–	–
7.11.98	Middlesbro' H	3–3	15,202	–	s14[1]	76	–	–	90	–	–	–	–	90	–	–
14.11.98	Aston Villa H	1–4	15,242	–	s44	90	–	–	–	–	90	–	–	90	–	–
21.11.98	Blackburn A	2–0	22,812	s17[1]	89	90	–	–	s27	–	90	90□	–	90□	–	–
28.11.98	Derby Co H	0–1	14,762	s11	90□	90	–	–	s53	–	90	–	–	90	–	–
5.12.98	Leicester A	0–2	18,423	–	s17	90	–	–	–	–	90	–	–	90	–	–
12.12.98	Everton A	0–1	32,073	–	86	–	–	s4	–	–	90	–	–	90	–	–
19.12.98	Wimbledon H	3–1	14,354	s10	90	–	–	–	90	–	–	–	–	90	–	–
26.12.98	Chelsea H	0–2	15,253	s45	90	–	–	–	–	90□	s9	–	–	90	–	–
28.12.98	Nott'm For A	1–1	23,456	–	90	–	–	–	–	90	90	–	–	90	–	–
9.1.99	Charlton H	3–1	15,222	–	90[1]□	–	–	–	–	90[1]	90	–	–	–	–	–
16.1.99	Liverpool A	1–7	44,011	–	90	–	–	–	45	90□	–	–	–	90	–	63
30.1.99	Leeds Utd H	3–0	15,236	–	90	–	–	–	s7	90	90□	–	–	90	–	–
6.2.99	Chelsea A	0–1	34,920	–	90	–	–	s1	s28	90	90	–	–	62	–	–
20.2.99	Newcastle H	2–1	15,244	–	76[1]	–	–	s14	s45	90	90[1]	–	–	–	–	–
27.2.99	Man Utd A	1–2	55,316	–	90	s40	–	–	90	90□	90	–	–	–	–	–
2.3.99	Tottenham A	0–3	28,580	–	80	–	–	–	56	90	–	–	–	90	–	–
6.3.99	West Ham H	1–0	15,240	–	90	90	–	–	–	90	–	–	–	90	–	–
14.3.99	Middlesbro' A	0–3	33,387	–	88	–	–	–	–	90	90	–	–	–	–	–
20.3.99	Sheff Wed H	1–0	15,201	–	s22	s6	–	–	–	84	90	–	–	–	–	–
3.4.99	Arsenal H	0–0	15,255	–	s35	s22	–	–	90	90□	90	–	–	90	–	–
5.4.99	Coventry A	0–1	21,404	–	70	–	–	–	45	90	90□	–	–	90	–	–
10.4.99	Aston Villa A	0–3	32,203	–	–	s38	–	–	–	72	90	–	–	90	s18	–
17.4.99	Blackburn H	3–3	15,209	–	s45	90	–	–	–	45	90	–	–	79	–	–
24.4.99	Derby Co A	0–0	26,557	–	90□	90	s26	–	–	–	90	–	–	90	s5	–
1.5.99	Leicester H	2–1	15,228	–	90[1]	90	–	–	–	–	90	–	–	24	–	–
8.5.99	Wimbledon A	2–0	24,068	–	90[1]	90	s14	–	–	–	90	–	–	s4	–	–
16.5.99	Everton H	2–0	15,254	–	90	90	s8	–	–	–	90	–	–	–	–	–

□ Yellow card, ■ Red card, s Substitute, 90³ Goals scored

1998–99 PREMIERSHIP APPEARANCES

D HUGHES	M HUGHES	JONES	KACHLOUL	LE TISSIER	LUNDEKVAM	MARSDEN	MARSHALL	MONK	MONKOU	MOSS	OAKLEY	OSTENSTAD	PAHARS	PALMER	RIPLEY	WARNER	WILLIAMS	TOTAL
–	90	90	–	s22	90	–	–	–	–	–	90	68[1]	–	90	76	–	–	990
–	90□	58■	–	s45	90□	–	–	–	–	–	58	64	–	90□	90	–	–	958
–	90□	90	–	90[1]	–	–	–	–	90	–	–	90	–	90	66□	–	–	990
–	90□	–	–	s15	–	–	90	–	–	90	s11	–	90□	90	90	–	–	990
–	45□	90	–	s45	s51	–	90□	–	–	–	s45	–	90	90	–	–	–	938
–	90	90	–	90[1]	s37	–	–	–	–	–	90	–	90	–	53	–	–	990
–	90□	90	–	90□	90	–	–	–	90□	–	–	90	–	90	–	90	–	990
–	–	90	–	90	55	–	–	–	90	–	–	90	–	90□	63	90	–	990
–	90□	90	–	s24□	90	–	–	–	90□	–	66	90	–	–	90	35	–	990
–	90	90	–	90[1]■	90	–	–	–	90	–	71	87[1]	–	s42	90	–	–	990
–	90□	90	–	90	90	–	–	–	90	–	–	90	–	90	90	–	–	990
–	90□	90	–	90	90	–	–	–	90[1]□	–	–	90[1]	–	90□	90	–	–	990
–	–	90	–	75[1]□	46	–	–	–	90	–	90	90	–	90	90	–	s15	990
–	90	90	s1	–	–	–	–	–	–	–	63[1]	73	–	90	90	–	–	990
–	90	90	79	–	–	–	90	–	–	–	90□	–	–	90□	37	–	–	990
–	73□	90	s17	90	90	–	–	–	–	–	90	90	–	90	73	–	–	990
–	90□	90	83□	90	90	–	90	–	–	–	90	90	–	–	s7	–	–	990
–	90	90	90[1]□	80	90	–	90	–	–	–	–	90[2]	–	90	–	–	–	990
–	–	90	90	25	90	–	–	–	90	–	81	90	–	90	s20	–	–	990
–	–	90□	90[1]□	–	90	–	–	–	90	–	90	90	–	90□	–	–	–	990
–	90□	90	90[1]	–	90	–	–	–	90	–	90	90	–	90	–	–	–	990
–	90□	90	90	s45	90	–	–	90□	–	–	s27	90[1]	–	–	–	–	–	990
–	90□	90	90[1]	11	90□	–	–	–	–	–	90[1]	90[1]	–	–	s72	–	–	990
–	89	90	90	–	90□	–	–	–	–	–	90□	–	–	–	–	–	–	990
s5	–	90	85□	–	90□	90	–	–	90	–	90	90	–	–	45	–	–	990
90	–	90	–	s23[1]□	90	90	–	–	50	–	90	67	–	–	–	–	–	990
45	90	90	s34	s45□	90	90	–	–	–	–	90	s10	–	–	–	–	–	990
–	90	90	90[1]	86	90	90	–	–	–	–	90	–	–	–	s4	–	–	990
–	90	90	90□	90□	90	90□	–	–	90□	–	60	s2	–	–	s30	–	–	990
–	90	90	90	90[1]□	90	90□	–	–	90	–	68	90	–	–	–	–	–	990
90	90□	–	–	–	90	–	–	–	90□	90	–	55	–	–	68	–	–	990
77	90	–	s13	s45	90	90	–	–	90	90	–	–	s20	–	–	–	–	990
90	52	–	–	90	41■	90	–	–	90□	90	–	85	–	–	s5	–	–	941
s45□	90[1]	–	90	90□	90	90[1]	–	–	–	90	–	45	s11[1]	–	–	–	–	990
–	90	–	75	–	–	90	–	–	90	90	64	s15	85□	–	–	–	–	990
s38	90	–	90	52	s66	90[1]	–	–	90	90	–	s19□	71	–	–	–	–	990
70	90	90	86	s20[1]	90	76□	–	–	90	–	–	–	90	–	–	–	–	990
–	90	90	90	87[1]	90	90□	–	–	90	–	–	s3	82[2]□	–	–	–	–	990

THE MANAGER

DAVE JONES

In the greatest traditions of numerous Southampton managers before him, Dave Jones saved the Saints from the drop on the last day of the 1998–99 season.

The unflappable Liverpudlian enjoyed a 10-year career as a central defender with Everton, Coventry, Seiko in Hong Kong, Preston North End and non-league Morecambe. His career was cut short at Highfield Road by a serious knee injury which ultimately kept him out of the top flight, but he still enjoyed success in the lower leagues.

After hanging up his boots in 1984 he moved into coaching with Stockport, working with manager Danny Bergara before taking over the reins himself in March 1995 and guiding the team to second in Division Two.

His subsequent move to the Dell in summer 1997 took many Saints fans by surprise after the departure of the high-profile Graeme Souness, but in his first season he steered Southampton well clear of the drop zone dogfight.

The 1998–99 campaign was rather more stressful for Jones, though, and preserving the club's cherished top-flight status seems to get progressively harder for Southampton's manager – no matter who it is.

LEAGUE POSITION

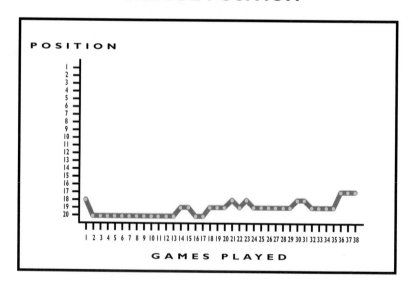

THE GOALS

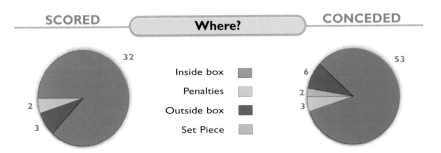

SCORED   **Where?**   CONCEDED

- Inside box
- Penalties
- Outside box
- Set Piece

Despite being able to boast the mercurial Matt Le Tissier in their side, Southampton managed a meagre three goals from distance during the 1998–99 Carling Premiership campaign. As a result they had the third-highest ratio for goals scored inside an opponent's penalty box with 91.9% coming from inside 18 yards. They also conceded the second-highest total of goals in their own area, the 56 efforts against them making up 87.5% of all strikes.

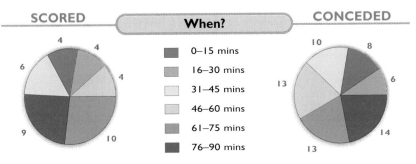

SCORED   **When?**   CONCEDED

- 0–15 mins
- 16–30 mins
- 31–45 mins
- 46–60 mins
- 61–75 mins
- 76–90 mins

Southampton were at their most jittery immediately after half-time, according to Opta's stats. Between the 45th and 60th minutes, the Saints scored just four times and let 13 goals slip by them. Indeed, the south coast side were most vulnerable in the second half, conceding exactly five-eighths of all goals after half-time. In the final 15 minutes, only West Ham and Nottingham Forest let more goals in.

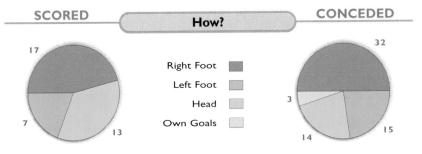

SCORED   **How?**   CONCEDED

- Right Foot
- Left Foot
- Head
- Own Goals

More than a third of Southampton's goals were headers, and even diminutive Latvian striker Marian Pahars got in on the act with two nodded efforts. The Saints relied on their prowess in the air to a large extent and scored proportionately more goals thus than any other Premiership team. They scored just 24 goals in 38 games with their feet, the worst record in the league. A sizeable 21.9% of goals against were also headers.

SOUTHAMPTON

	BASHAM	BEATTIE	BENALI	BERESFORD	BRADLEY	BRIDGE	COLLETER	DODD	DRYDEN	GIBBENS	HILEY	HIRST	HOWELLS
APPEARANCE													
Start	0	22	19	1	0	15	16	27	4	2	27	0	8
Sub	4	13	4	3	3	8	0	1	0	2	2	2	1
Minutes on pitch	83	2188	1802	55	19	1407	1371	2387	360	194	2373	23	641
GOAL ATTEMPTS													
Goals	1	5	0	0	0	0	1	1	0	0	0	0	1
Shots on target	2	22	0	0	0	5	7	4	0	2	1	0	4
Shots off target	0	28	5	1	0	8	4	11	1	2	2	0	4
Shooting accuracy %	100%	44%	0%	0%	0%	38%	64%	27%	0%	50%	33%	0%	50%
PASSING													
Goal assists	0	7	1	0	0	0	0	4	0	0	0	0	0
Long passes	0	21	181	3	1	41	121	244	19	3	267	0	34
Short passes	33	741	480	14	13	384	410	746	57	58	641	9	226
PASS COMPLETION													
Own half %	100%	87%	87%	75%	100%	82%	82%	89%	87%	91%	87%	0%	87%
Opposition half %	55%	64%	65%	44%	55%	65%	59%	65%	48%	68%	65%	100%	68%
CROSSING													
Total crosses	5	35	42	3	0	50	31	52	0	0	76	0	8
Cross completion %	40%	23%	36%	0%	0%	26%	45%	31%	0%	0%	45%	0%	13%
DRIBBLING													
Dribbles & runs	3	76	10	1	0	56	39	17	0	1	71	0	5
Dribble completion %	67%	54%	100%	100%	0%	55%	72%	88%	0%	0%	92%	0%	40%
DEFENDING													
Tackles made	4	56	41	7	0	34	50	92	16	9	68	1	18
Tackles won %	50%	59%	63%	29%	0%	65%	70%	73%	94%	56%	53%	0%	67%
Blocks	0	9	25	0	0	3	13	27	6	0	25	1	6
Clearances	2	31	170	5	0	35	129	244	71	7	163	0	13
Interceptions	0	7	13	0	0	8	23	21	5	0	19	0	6
DISCIPLINE													
Fouls	0	66	18	4	0	12	16	24	7	5	16	0	9
Offside	0	26	0	0	0	3	0	0	0	0	0	1	2
Yellow cards	0	4	2	0	0	0	4	4	1	0	2	0	1
Red cards	0	0	0	0	0	0	1	0	0	0	0	0	0

GOALKEEPER NAME	START/ (SUB)	TIME ON PITCH	GOALS CONCEDED	MINS/GOALS CONCEDED	SAVES MADE	SAVES/ SHOTS
JONES	31	2758	50	55.2	124	71%
MOSS	7	630	11	57.3	23	68%

PLAYERS' STATISTICS

	D HUGHES	M HUGHES	KACHLOUL	LE TISSIER	LUNDEKVAM	MARSDEN	MARSHALL	MONK	MONKOU	OAKLEY	OSTENSTAD	PAHARS	PALMER	RIPLEY	WARNER	WILLIAMS	TOTAL	RANK
	6	32	18	20	30	14	2	4	22	21	27	4	18	16	5	0		
	3	0	4	10	3	0	0	0	0	1	7	2	1	6	0	1		
	550	2779	1643	1915	2726	1246	180	360	1940	1728	2359	359	1662	1376	358	15		
	0	1	5	7	0	2	0	0	1	2	7	3	0	0	0	0	37	19th
	1	15	24	32	0	4	1	0	3	6	26	8	6	2	0	0	175	=10th
	0	41	25	25	4	6	1	1	4	12	20	2	7	6	0	0	220	=11th
	100%	27%	49%	56%	0%	40%	50%	0%	43%	33%	57%	80%	46%	25%	0%	0%	44%	15th
	0	1	0	7	0	0	0	0	0	3	1	0	1	2	0	0	27	=14th
	11	94	46	168	128	59	15	16	101	64	7	1	57	53	60	0	1815	=12th
	188	1058	624	564	569	524	34	73	406	668	779	94	577	390	98	5	10463	17th
	83%	88%	79%	81%	88%	86%	90%	85%	85%	86%	88%	86%	85%	78%	100%		86%	18th
	66%	78%	65%	65%	59%	69%	45%	50%	51%	73%	71%	62%	74%	64%	58%	100%	67%	17th
	10	12	28	196	7	36	0	0	3	28	36	2	16	92	17	1	786	8th
	30%	25%	43%	34%	29%	36%	0%	0%	0%	39%	22%	0%	19%	27%	12%	0%	32%	2nd
	14	67	75	84	29	14	0	2	5	31	71	15	34	63	9	2	795	15th
	57%	61%	52%	68%	83%	79%	0%	50%	80%	65%	61%	80%	71%	70%	78%	50%	67%	19th
	24	105	76	36	85	87	3	8	59	40	32	15	79	48	12	0	1108	16th
	71%	56%	46%	36%	79%	60%	100%	38%	56%	70%	44%	53%	67%	65%	58%	0%	61%	10th
	0	7	7	5	31	5	6	4	20	9	0	1	5	7	2	0	225	5th
	18	36	37	21	453	35	29	37	388	37	9	2	69	15	24	0	2117	7th
	2	7	10	4	42	10	1	6	26	23	2	0	17	7	3	0	263	19th
	11	83	27	28	42	34	4	2	38	13	55	9	22	25	4	0	576	3rd
	7	16	1	14	1	0	0	0	0	1	61	4	3	2	0	0	142	7th
	1	14	5	10	3	5	1	1	6	2	1	2	6	1	0	0	77	=8th
	0	0	0	0	1	0	0	0	0	0	0	0	0	0	0	0	3	=11th

CROSSES CAUGHT	CROSSES PUNCHED	CROSSES NOT CLAIMED	CATCH SUCCESS	THROWS/ SHORT KICKS	% COMPLETION	LONG KICKS	% COMPLETION
108	19	13	95%	191	91%	788	38%
13	6	4	93%	39	95%	207	38%

PLAYER OF THE SEASON

PLAYER	INDEX SCORE
HASSAN KACHLOUL	953
Matt Le Tissier	871
Jason Dodd	849
Claus Lundekvam	795
Ken Monkou	775
James Beattie	740
Carlton Palmer	697
Francis Benali	674
Scott Hiley	674
Paul Jones	639

When the exotic name "Hassan Kachloul" first appeared on the list of Southampton substitutes at Sheffield Wednesday in October 1998, journalists and Saints fans alike thought there was a spelling error on the team-sheet.

But the Moroccan wizard proceeded to cast a spell of his own on the Dell, playing a leading role in Southampton's successful fight against relegation.

Four goals in his first seven matches gave the south coast club a real lift – and, coupled with his superb crossing skills, those strikes helped him end the campaign with an average score of 953 points in the Carling Opta Season Index. That meant he was the club's highest rated player in the acclaimed performance analysis chart.

Matt Le Tissier, who in truth spent much of 1998–99 as a substitute, showed enough flair with his passing, crossing and, of course, his eye for goal to average 871 points across the campaign, leaving him in second place in the Southampton top 10. The showman capped the season with a memorable super-sub display at Wimbledon, making one and scoring one in the 2–0 win.

Skipper Jason Dodd, who had to battle for his place with fellow-right-back Scott Hiley, was another Saint who achieved magnificent crossing statistics and finished third, ahead of centre-back duo Claus Lundekvam and Ken Monkou. They racked up plenty of points, having been kept busy by the amount of pressure Southampton were under in many of their Premiership matches.

Young striker James Beattie, strong in tackle and excellent in the air, performed brilliantly, particularly in the second half of the season. He finished above the likes of veteran Francis Benali, who lost his place to Patrick Colleter in mid-season, and goalkeeper Paul Jones, who had inspired spells but conceded plenty of goals too.

FIVE OF THE BEST

Rooted in the bottom three for all but the final month of the season, Southampton looked certain to succumb to the drop after years of dramatic last-day survivals. But yet again, the Saints refused to accept defeat and their fine home form in the second half of the 1998–99 campaign kept them up.

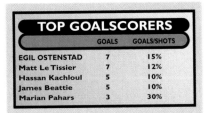

TOP GOALSCORERS	GOALS	GOALS/SHOTS
EGIL OSTENSTAD	7	15%
Matt Le Tissier	7	12%
Hassan Kachloul	5	10%
James Beattie	5	10%
Marian Pahars	3	30%

Top scorers were Egil Ostenstad and Matt Le Tissier, but neither player will look back at 1998–99 as a vintage season. Le Tissier's contribution in the final few games was certainly a major factor in keeping the Saints up, while new signing Hassan Kachloul and young frontman James Beattie each weighed in with five strikes. But arguably the biggest difference in the final month was little Latvian striker Marian Pahars, whose three goals ultimately clinched safety. Almost a third of his shots hit the back of the net.

Only three teams made fewer successful passes than Southampton in 1998–99, underlining how much the Saints were on the back foot for much of the season. Mark Hughes, who spent most of the campaign in a less favoured midfield role, saw more of the ball than any of his team-mates, completing four out of every five passes. The next most successful passer, Jason Dodd, completed almost 200 fewer balls, with no one other than Hughes achieving a completion rate of 80% or more.

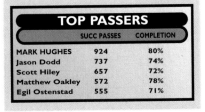

TOP PASSERS	SUCC PASSES	COMPLETION
MARK HUGHES	924	80%
Jason Dodd	737	74%
Scott Hiley	657	72%
Matthew Oakley	572	78%
Egil Ostenstad	555	71%

TOP TACKLERS	WON	SUCCESS
CLAUS LUNDEKVAM	67	79%
Jason Dodd	67	73%
Mark Hughes	59	56%
Carlton Palmer	53	67%
Chris Marsden	52	60%

Not prolific passers – and the tackles were hardly flying in either. Only four teams put in fewer challenges than Southampton, with no one in the Saints' squad coming close to winning 100 tackles over the course of the season. Centre-back Claus Lundekvam and right-back Jason Dodd put in the most successful challenges, while Mark Hughes's extremely modest tackle success rate of 56% certainly helps explain his poor disciplinary record in 1998–99. New boy Chris Marsden made a big impact after his move from Birmingham City and he also makes the top five.

Battling Southampton achieved safety through essential midfield scrapping – but that had a detrimental effect on their disciplinary record and the Saints finished fourth in the final Carling Opta sinners' league. Chief villain was undoubtedly Mark Hughes, who conceded 83 fouls and was booked 14 times in the league. He was the first player to chalk up 11 bookings and was consequently punished by the FA. Matt Le Tissier also reached double figures in yellow cards but only conceded 28 fouls, suggesting he is far from being the cleanest challenger in the Premiership.

DISCIPLINE	POINTS	FOULS & CARDS
MARK HUGHES	125	83F, 14Y, 0R
James Beattie	78	66F, 4Y, 0R
Matt Le Tissier	58	28F, 10Y, 0R
Egil Ostenstad	58	55F, 1Y, 0R
Claus Lundekvam	57	42F, 3Y, 1R

ACTION	BEATTIE	BRIDGE	COLLETER	DODD	HILEY	M. HUGHES	JONES	KACHLOUL	LE TISSIER	LUNDEKVAM	OAKLEY	OSTENSTAD	RIPLEY	TOTAL	LEEDS UNITED (TOTAL)
Time on pitch	90	7	90	90	90	90	90	11	90	90	90	90	72	990	990
GOALS															
Goal	–	–	–	–	–	–	–	–	–	–	–	–	–	3	4
Shot on target	2	–	2	–	–	1	–	–	–	–	–	1	–	6	4
Shot off target	1	–	1	–	2	4	–	–	–	–	–	2	–	10	5
Blocked shot	1	–	1	–	1	2	–	–	–	–	–	2	–	7	8
Own goal	–	–	–	–	–	–	–	–	–	–	–	–	–	–	–
PASSES															
Pass to own player	22	6	24	20	14	42	–	6	15	32	25	25	17	248	196
Pass to opposition	12	2	15	8	10	8	–	3	4	19	14	11	9	115	116
Cross to own player	1	–	–	–	1	1	–	–	–	1	–	–	–	4	4
Cross to opposition player	–	1	3	4	2	–	–	–	2	–	2	2	4	20	12
Goal assist	–	–	–	1	–	–	–	–	–	–	–	–	1	2	–
Pass completion %	65%	70%	60%	72%	60%	82%	0%	55%	79%	62%	61%	66%	49%	65%	61%
TACKLES & CLEARANCES															
Tackle	–	–	3	4	3	1	–	–	–	–	2	2	2	17	32
Clearances, blocks and interceptions	4	–	16	13	8	3	–	–	–	29	5	–	1	86	86
DRIBBLES & RUNS															
Dribble ball retained	4	–	7	–	1	2	–	–	2	2	2	2	2	23	15
Dribble ball lost	5	2	2	–	1	1	–	2	–	–	1	2	2	19	6
Dribble success %	44%	0%	78%	0%	50%	67%	0%	0%	100%	100%	50%	50%	50%	55%	71%
DISCIPLINE															
Fouls	–	–	1	3	2	1	–	–	–	1	1	–	1	10	16
Penalty conceded	–	–	–	–	–	–	–	–	–	–	–	–	–	–	–
Free kick - offside	1	–	–	–	–	–	–	–	–	–	–	–	–	1	5
Yellow cards	–	–	1	1	–	–	–	–	–	1	–	–	–	3	4
Red cards	–	–	–	–	–	–	–	–	–	–	–	–	–	–	–
GOALKEEPERS															
Distribution to own player	–	–	–	–	–	–	20	–	–	–	–	–	–	20	14
Distribution to opposition player	–	–	–	–	–	–	10	–	–	–	–	–	–	10	16
Goalkeeper distribution%	0%	0%	0%	0%	0%	0%	67%	0%	0%	0%	0%	0%	0%	67%	47%
Save	–	–	–	–	–	–	4	–	–	–	–	–	–	4	6
Ball caught	–	–	–	–	–	–	3	–	–	–	–	–	–	3	2
Ball dropped	–	–	–	–	–	–	–	–	–	–	–	–	–	–	–
Goal conceded	–	–	–	–	–	–	4	–	–	–	–	–	–	4	3

When Southampton met Leeds United at the Dell, pundits predicted a comfortable away win. Still smarting from a 7–1 thrashing at Anfield, Southampton looked ready for the taking. But it turned out to be one of the Saints' best wins of the season, as they shocked David O'Leary's men with a superb battling display in front of a passionate south coast crowd.

January 30, 1999

3–0

SOUTHAMPTON

vs

LEEDS UNITED

Southampton started brightly, putting the visitors on the back foot, but an injury to Matt Le Tissier after just 11 minutes threatened to spoil their day. Despite that early set-back, Southampton took the lead on the half-hour. A corner kick was headed clear and Mark Hughes's shot rebounded straight to Jason Dodd, whose shot was back-flicked past Nigel Martyn by Hassan Kachloul. The Moroccan was proving to be a big hit with the Saints' fans.

Leeds pressurized, looking for an equalizer, with both Harry Kewell and Jimmy Floyd Hasselbaink coming close on a number of occasions. Kewell in particular was proving to be a real handful for the Southampton defence, running at players and whipping in dangerous crosses from the left-hand side. For all Leeds' efforts though, they could not seriously trouble Paul Jones in the Southampton goal.

In the opening stages of the second half, Leeds reverted to a more direct game to put pressure on the Saints' defence – but Dave Jones's men held firm.

Southampton grew in confidence and went 2–0 up after 62 minutes when after a mazy run Kachloul's shot was thwarted by Martyn. James Beattie's miskicked attempt at the rebound left the ball for Matthew Oakley to score from close range.

After a short stoppage due to crowd unrest, Leeds had an appeal for a penalty turned away when Kewell went down theatrically in the area.

The game was all over with five minutes to go when Egil Ostenstad scored Southampton's third goal. Beattie received a long ball on the right wing and the England under-21 international out-muscled Lucas Radebe and pulled the ball back for Ostenstad to finish from six yards out.

Leeds were disappointing in front of goal, with Hasselbaink failing to register a single shot on target. Harry Kewell looked the man most likely to bring Leeds back into the game, but his three shots on target were comfortably saved by Welsh international 'keeper Jones.

Kachloul and Hughes both had big games in the Southampton midfield, while the forward line of Ostenstad and Beattie was a constant threat to the Leeds defence.

The win provided Southampton with one of their best results all season. It was largely a scrappy affair, with Saints completing 65% of their passes, compared to 61% for Leeds. The level of pressure Leeds were under at times can be seen by their 32 tackles and 16 fouls. Southampton made 17 tackles and committed 10 fouls.

The match proved that, despite the differing fortunes of the teams during the season, any side can beat any other in the Premiership. Southampton showed that on their day they can match the best and will hope to do so more often in the future.

ACTION	BEATTIE	BENALI	BERESFORD	DOOD	M.HUGHES	JONES	KACHLOUL	LE TISSIER	LUNDEKVAM	MARSDEN	MONKOU	OSTENSTAD	PAHARS	TOTAL	EVERTON
Time on pitch	90	90	8	90	90	90	90	87	90	90	3	82	90	990	990
GOALS															
Goal	–	–	–	–	–	–	–	–	–	–	–	2	–	2	2
Shot on target	–	–	–	–	–	–	–	–	–	–	–	–	3	3	3
Shot off target	–	–	–	–	3	–	2	–	–	–	–	–	–	12	2
Blocked shot	–	–	–	–	–	–	4	–	–	–	–	–	–	4	4
Own goal	–	–	–	–	–	–	–	–	–	–	–	–	–	–	–
PASSES															
Pass to own player	21	24	3	32	30	–	13	9	31	14	2	20	20	219	200
Pass to opposition	17	8	–	11	7	–	9	1	12	5	–	8	18	96	99
Cross to own player	1	1	2	–	1	–	4	–	–	1	–	–	–	9	4
Cross to opposition player	3	2	2	3	2	–	6	–	–	2	–	–	2	22	10
Goal assist	2	–	–	–	–	–	–	–	–	–	–	–	–	2	–
Pass completion %	55%	71%	60%	70%	78%	0%	53%	90%	73%	70%	67%	69%	53%	66%	65%
TACKLES & CLEARANCES															
Tackle	4	2	–	2	10	–	2	3	8	1	–	2	5	39	45
Clearances, blocks and interceptions	2	17	–	12	1	1	2	25	4	23	1	–	–	92	97
DRIBBLES & RUNS															
Dribble ball retained	3	1	–	1	–	–	–	–	1	–	–	3	2	11	6
Dribbles ball lost	2	–	–	–	–	–	6	–	–	1	–	–	–	9	–
Dribble success %	60%	100%	100%	100%	0%	0%	0%	100%	100%	0%	0%	100%	100%	55%	86%
DISCIPLINE															
Fouls	4	3	–	2	2	–	4	–	–	–	–	2	2	20	17
Penalty conceded	–	–	–	–	–	–	–	–	–	–	–	–	–	–	–
Free kick - offside	–	–	–	–	–	–	–	–	–	–	–	3	3	6	3
Yellow cards	–	–	–	–	1	–	1	–	–	1	–	–	–	3	1
Red cards	–	–	–	–	–	–	–	–	–	–	–	–	–	–	–
GOALKEEPERS															
Distribution to own player	–	–	–	–	–	7	–	–	–	–	–	–	–	7	21
Distribution to opposition player	–	–	–	–	–	18	–	–	–	–	–	–	–	18	19
Goalkeeper distribution%	0%	0%	0%	0%	0%	28%	0%	0%	0%	0%	0%	0%	0%	28%	53%
Save	–	–	–	–	–	3	–	–	–	–	–	–	–	3	3
Ball caught	–	–	–	–	–	9	–	–	–	–	–	–	–	9	4
Ball dropped	–	–	–	–	–	–	–	–	–	–	–	–	–	–	–
Goal conceded	–	–	–	–	–	2	–	–	–	–	–	–	–	2	2

Sunday, May 16 was D-Day for Southampton. The last day of the Carling Premiership season had arrived and the Saints needed a win to save themselves from relegation to the Nationwide League. Everton had already secured their Premiership place for 1999–2000 and were on a roll, thanks to the arrival of Kevin Campbell at Goodison Park.

May 16, 1999

2–0

SOUTHAMPTON
EVERTON

Southampton dominated the first half and Matt Le Tissier looked to be back at his best. In the 18th minute he juggled a Mark Hughes pass, turned and fired a brilliant volley which whistled just past the post, with Thomas Myhre in the Everton goal just a spectator.

The Channel Islander was involved again on 22 minutes when Hassan Kachloul met his free kick from the left – but the Moroccan headed fractionally over the bar.

Everton went up the field a minute later and should have gone ahead. Campbell's flick-on fell to Francis Jeffers, but he put his side-foot volley wide from just six yards out.

The Dell exploded into life after 25 minutes when Southampton took the lead. A long ball from Jason Dodd was flicked on by James Beattie to Marian Pahars. The pint-sized Latvian striker composed himself, then drilled the ball past Myhre to send the Southampton faithful into raptures.

It could have been 2–0 on the half-hour mark, but Chris Marsden's shot into a crowded penalty area was blocked in the six-yard box with Myhre unsighted.

With half-time approaching, Southampton went after a second goal. Le Tissier came closest, unleashing a 25-yard rocket which dipped inches over the bar in stoppage-time.

The Saints started the second half as they finished the first – on the attack. Francis Benali crossed from the left, and Mark Hughes headed over the bar from six yards out.

The visitors raised their tempo but, from an Everton attack, Southampton broke away through Marsden. He sent Beattie galloping down the right wing, and the England under-21 international crossed low to the near post where the ball was met by a diving header from Pahars. The ball flew into the bottom corner of the Everton net, and the Dell erupted again. It was a classic breakaway goal, sealing victory and Premiership survival for the south coast club.

The Saints kept the pressure on and nearly scored a third when Mark Hughes's swerving volley flew just wide with seven minutes remaining. Southampton goalkeeper Paul Jones prevented any nervous moments by stopping Ibrahima Bakayoko's effort well with his feet.

The match finished, the fans celebrated. The PA system was playing the theme from The Great Escape, and that is exactly what Southampton's 1998–99 season turned out to be. Given no chance of survival in February and March, manager Dave Jones guided his men to safety at the last possible moment.

In a tense atmosphere, Southampton shaded the possession having 66% of their 219 passes completed. Everton completed 200 passes, with a completion rate of 65%. The Toffemen were on the back foot for large parts of the match. Their higher tackle count (45 compared to Southampton's 39) demonstrates this.

The only statistic that mattered to Saints fans though was the scoreline. Southampton 2 Everton 0 was exactly what they were hoping for.

TOTTENHAM HOTSPUR 1998–99

Back row (left to right): Roy Reyland (Kit Manager), Allan Nielsen, Rory Allen, Paolo Tramezzani (no longer at club), Ramon Vega, Ian Walker, Les Ferdinand, Steffen Iversen, Colin Calderwood (now Aston Villa), Pat Jennings (Goalkeeping Consultant).

Middle row: Dr Mark Curtin (Medical Officer) Jose Dominguez, Moussa Saib (no longer at club), Nicola Berti (now Alaves), John Scales, Hans Segers, Espen Baardsen, Darren Anderton, Stephen Clemence, Stephen Carr, Ruel Fox, Alasdair Beattie (Physiotherapist).

Front row: Justin Edinburgh, Chris Armstrong, Sol Campbell, Chris Hughton (Assistant Head Coach), Christian Gross (no longer at club), Kunle Odetoyinbo (Fitness Coach), David Ginola, Clive Wilson (no longer at club), Andy Sinton.

TOTTENHAM HOTSPUR

ADDRESS

Bill Nicholson Way, 748 High Road,
Tottenham, London N17 0AP

CONTACT NUMBERS

Telephone: 0181 365 5000
Fax: 0181 365 5005
Ticket Office: 0181 365 5050
24hr Information: 09068 100 500
Club Superstore: 0181 365 5041
Website: www.spurs.co.uk

SPONSORS

Holsten

FANZINES

Cock a Doodle Do
One Flew Over Seaman's Head

KEY PERSONNEL

Executive Chairman: A M Sugar
Director of Football: D J Pleat
Director of Finance: J Sedgwick
Non-Executive Directors: G M Littner,
M S Peters MBE, C T Sandy, I Yanitz
Club Secretary: P R Barnes
Manager: George Graham

COLOURS

Home: White shirts,
blue shorts and blue stockings
Away: All purple

NICKNAME

Spurs,
The Lilywhites

20 FACTS

1 Tottenham Hotspur were originally called Hotspur Football Club. They were formed in 1882 from a cricket club.

2 The club have been league champions twice – in 1950–51 and 1960–61.

3 They have won the FA Cup eight times – in 1901, 1921, 1961, 1962, 1967, 1981, 1982 and 1991.

4 Spurs have won the Football League Cup on three occasions – in 1971, 1973, and 1999.

5 The Lilywhites have also lifted the Cup Winners Cup in 1962–63 and the UEFA Cup in 1971–72 and 1983–84.

6 Tottenham are the only non-league side to win the FA Cup. Their 1901 triumph came seven years before they gained entry to the Football League.

7 They were also the first English club to win a European trophy, beating Atletico Madrid 5–1 in the 1963 European Cup Winners Cup final.

8 Spurs hold the remarkable post-war record of winning a trophy whenever there has been a '1' in the year – 1951, '61, '71, '81 and '91.

9 Tottenham hold the record for the best start to a top-flight season. They won their first 11 games in the 1960–61 Double-winning campaign.

10 Steve Perryman holds the club record for league appearances. He played 655 league games between 1969 and 1986.

11 The club's record victory came in the FA Cup when they beat Crewe Alexandra 13–2 in a fourth-round replay in 1960. Their record league win came against Bristol Rovers in 1977 when they won 9–0.

12 Tottenham scored 115 league goals in the 1960–61 season. Chelsea's Jimmy Greaves, who finished that season as the league's leading scorer with 41 goals, went on to become Tottenham's all-time leading goalscorer with a total of 266 goals.

13 Former Spurs player Alan Mullery holds the dubious honour of being the first England player ever to be sent off. He was dismissed in a European Championship match against Italy on June 5, 1968.

14 Spurs hold the record for the most wins in a Division One season – 31 in 1960–61. They also hold the same record for Division Two – 32 games in 1919–20.

15 In 1983, Tottenham became the first English club to be floated on the Stock Exchange.

16 Tottenham Hotspur finished 11th in the 1998–99 Premiership. Their league record was:

Pld	W	D	L	F	A	Pts
38	11	14	13	47	50	47

17 George Graham's side lost the FA Cup semi-final against Newcastle United 2–0. They reached that stage by beating Watford 5–2 at White Hart Lane, Wimbledon 3–0 after a 1–1 draw at Selhurst Park, Leeds 2–0 at home after a 1–1 draw at Elland Road and Barnsley 1–0 in the sixth round.

18 The club won its first trophy in eight years and qualified for the UEFA Cup by beating Leicester City 1–0 in the Worthington Cup final. Brentford were beaten 6–4 on aggregate, Northampton 3–1 away, Liverpool 3–1 at Anfield and Manchester United 3–1 at home. Wimbledon were beaten 1–0 at Selhurst Park in the semi-final after a goalless first leg at White Hart Lane.

19 The top goalscorer in all competitions for Tottenham was Steffen Iversen with 13 goals.

20 Tottenham's disciplinary record was the ninth-worst in the Premiership. They committed 539 fouls, earned 67 yellow cards and suffered four dismissals.

SEASON REVIEW

Football, as one of Tottenham's favourite sons used to say, is a funny old game. Certainly if you had told most Spurs fans at the start of the season that George Graham would be leading Tottenham out at Wembley seven months later, they would have laughed at you.

Graham – the man who won so many trophies for Arsenal – was hardly the most popular choice to replace Christian Gross when Alan Sugar took the decision to dismiss the Swiss just three games into the season. But the Tottenham chairman felt that the hard-headed pragmatism of Graham was the best antidote to Gross's increasingly fragile hold on the team.

After an extended period of courtship in which both parties denied an interest in each other, Graham finally arrived from Elland Road in early October. His first game in charge did not come until October 19, but he was in the stand at Pride Park to watch his new charges beat Derby County a week earlier with a headed goal from Sol Campbell. "Solid. Workmanlike. We came to do a job and we did it," said caretaker manager David Pleat. It could have been Graham himself speaking.

One of the first casualties of Graham's reign was expected to be David Ginola. He was substituted in his first game under the new manager – a 2–1 defeat by Leicester – and again the following week in the 2–0 victory against Newcastle United. Predictions of his impending demise proved to be well off the mark.

Of more immediate concern to Graham was the amount of goals the club had been conceding. Before his arrival, Tottenham were haemorrhaging goals at an average of 1.75 per game. Six games into the new era, that figure had been cut to just 1.17.

The change at the back was well illustrated by the number of shots which Tottenham's goalkeeper had to deal with. Before Graham's arrival the 'keeper was forced to make an average of 6.4 saves per game; in the 30 games after that the

average dropped to just 2.8, a measure of the increased protection offered by the back four.

Graham reinstated goalkeeper Ian Walker, got his back four playing as a unit and brought in Tim Sherwood and Steffen Freund to beef up his midfield. Ginola provided the flair.

The Frenchman was not, as many had expected, asked to rein in his attacking instincts. He finished the season with more dribbles and runs than any other player in the Premiership, almost single-handedly helping Spurs to second place in the dribbling charts and finishing the campaign with both the PFA and Sportswriters' Player of the Year Awards.

> **"It is time Spurs started to win things... I want to get to the top with Spurs"**
>
> **George Graham**

Like his team-mates, Ginola saved his best performances for the cups. But the team also made steady progress in the league. Players such as Stephen Carr and Darren Anderton were almost unrecognizable from the previous season, helping the club to impressive wins over Liverpool and Everton and good draws with Manchester United and Arsenal.

The Worthington Cup was lifted in March with a 1–0 victory over Leicester at Wembley, but scorer Allan Nielsen soon found himself out of the side and in his manager's bad books after a training ground bust-up. The parallels with Graham's first season as Arsenal manager and the fate that befell Wembley goal-scorer Charlie Nicholas were inescapable.

Season 1999–2000 is likely to see more departures from White Hart Lane. Graham is well aware that the club needs a goalscorer. And he is unlikely to be satisfied with the fact that overall his team were the third least accurate tacklers in the Premiership. But the revolution is well under way. After less than one season in charge, he has put silverware in the trophy cabinet and booked a return to European competition. It is a situation that would have been unthinkable at the start of the season.

TOTTENHAM HOTSPUR

DATE	OPPONENT	SCORE	ATT.	ALLEN	ANDERTON	ARMSTRONG	BAARDSEN	BERTI	CALDERWOOD	CAMPBELL	CARR	CLEMENCE	DOMINGUEZ	EDINBURGH	FERDINAND
15.8.98	Wimbledon A	1–3	23,031	–	72	90	–	57	–	90	90	–	–	–	90
22.8.98	Sheff Wed H	0–3	32,075	–	90□	90	–	–	–	90	90	–	s22	–	90
29.8.98	Everton A	1–0	39,378	–	90□	s19	90	–	90	90	90□	–	–	–	71'□
9.9.98	Blackburn H	2–1	28,338	–	–	–	90	90	90□	–	90	88	–	–	90¹
13.9.98	Middlesbro' H	0–3	30,437	–	–	s45	90	90□	90	90	90	45	–	–	90
19.9.98	Southampton A	1–1	15,204	–	–	–	–	74	90□	90	90	90	s16	–	90
26.9.98	Leeds Utd H	3–3	35,535	–	90□	90	–	–	s10	90¹	80	73	s17	90	62
3.10.98	Derby Co A	1–0	30,083	–	90	s19	90	–	90	90¹	90	s5	–	90	90
19.10.98	Leicester A	1–2	20,787	–	90□	s23	90	–	90	90	89□	s1	–	90	90¹
24.10.98	Newcastle H	2–0	36,047	–	90	90	90	–	83■	90	90	s2	–	90	19
2.11.98	Charlton H	2–2	32,202	s1	90	90¹	90	–	90□	90	90	s1	–	90□	–
7.11.98	Aston Villa A	2–3	39,241	s8	90¹	–	90	–	–	90	90	82	–	45	–
14.11.98	Arsenal A	0–0	38,278	–	90	90□	90	–	79□	90	90	–	–	90	–
21.11.98	Nott'm For H	2–0	35,832	s7	90	83¹	90	–	77	90	90	s13	–	65	–
28.11.98	West Ham A	1–2	26,044	–	90	90¹□	90	–	–	90	90	67	–	–	–
5.12.98	Liverpool H	2–1*	36,125	–	90	90	–	–	–	90	90	–	–	–	s57
12.12.98	Man Utd H	2–2	36,058	s7	90	90	–	–	–	90²	90	–	–	–	90□
19.12.98	Chelsea A	0–2	34,881	s5	90	61■	–	–	–	90	90□	s25	–	s15	90□
26.12.98	Coventry A	1–1	23,091	–	90	90	–	–	–	90¹	90	s9	–	–	88
28.12.98	Everton H	4–1	36,053	–	90	89³	–	–	–	90	90	s45	–	–	90¹□
9.1.99	Sheff Wed A	0–0	28,204	–	28	s81	–	–	–	90	90	s62	–	s22	9
16.1.99	Wimbledon H	0–0	32,422	–	–	90	–	76	–	90	90	71	–	90	–
30.1.99	Blackburn A	1–1	29,643	–	90	s5	–	–	–	90	90□	–	–	90	90
6.2.99	Coventry H	0–0	34,376	–	90	s19	–	–	–	90	90	–	–	–	90
20.2.99	Middlesbro' A	0–0	34,687	–	90	s44	–	–	–	90	90□	–	–	–	46
27.2.99	Derby Co H	1–1	35,392	–	90	66	–	–	–	90	–	–	s24	90■	–
2.3.99	Southampton H	3–0	28,580	–	–	90¹	–	–	–	90	90	–	s1¹	–	–
10.3.99	Leeds Utd A	1–2	34,561	–	75	90	–	–	–	90	90	–	–	90	s15
13.3.99	Aston Villa H	1–0	35,963	–	90	80	–	–	–	90	90	s10	–	–	90□
3.4.99	Leicester H	0–2	35,415	–	–	s25	–	–	–	90	90	–	73□	–	90
5.4.99	Newcastle A	1–1	36,655	–	90¹	90	–	–	–	90	90	–	–	–	–
17.4.99	Nott'm For A	1–0	25,181	–	s45	90	–	–	–	90	90	–	–	–	45
20.4.99	Charlton A	4–1	20,043	–	90	73	–	–	–	90¹	90	–	s17¹	–	–
24.4.99	West Ham H	1–2	36,089	–	74□	s7	–	–	–	90	90	–	90	–	–
1.5.99	Liverpool A	2–3*	44,007	–	90	90□	–	–	–	90	90	45	81	–	–
5.5.99	Arsenal H	1–3	36,019	–	90¹□	90	–	–	–	90	90	–	s14	–	–
10.5.99	Chelsea H	2–2	35,878	–	90	90	–	–	–	90	90	s8	s3□	–	–
16.5.99	Man Utd A	1–2	55,189	–	90□	–	–	–	–	90	90	–	s68	90	45¹

□ Yellow card, ■ Red card, s Substitute, 90³ Goals scored
*including own goal

1998-1999 PREMIERSHIP APPEARANCES

FOX	FREUND	GINOLA	IVERSEN	KING	NIELSEN	NILSEN	SAIB	SCALES	SEGERS	SHERWOOD	SINTON	TARICCO	TRAMEZZANI	VEGA	WALKER	YOUNG	TOTAL
90[1]	–	90□	–	–	s33	–	s18	–	–	–	–	–	90	90	90	–	990
90	–	90	–	–	90	–	s45	–	–	–	–	–	68	45	90	–	990
90	–	90□	–	–	90	–	–	–	–	–	–	–	90	90□	–	–	990
90	–	88	–	–	90[1]	–	s2	–	–	–	s2	–	90	90	–	–	990
56	–	90□	–	–	51	–	s39	–	–	–	s34	–	90	–	–	–	990
90[1]	–	90	–	–	–	–	–	–	90	–	–	90□	90	–	–	–	990
90	–	–	s28[1]	–	90	–	–	–	–	–	–	–	–	90[1]	–	–	990
85	–	71	–	–	90□	–	–	–	–	–	–	–	–	90	–	–	990
90□	–	67□	–	–	–	–	–	–	–	–	–	–	–	90	–	–	990
–	88□	s71[2]	–	90□	–	–	90□	–	–	–	–	–	–	–	–	–	983
89	–	–	–	90[1]	–	–	90	–	–	89	–	–	–	–	–	–	990
45	–	90□	90	–	90	–	–	90	–	–	s45	–	s45[1]	–	–	–	990
–	–	90	90	–	90	–	–	90	–	–	s11	–	90	–	–	–	990
–	–	90	90	–	90[1]□	–	–	90	–	–	s25	–	–	–	–	–	990
s23	–	90	90	–	90	–	–	–	–	–	90□	–	–	–	90	–	990
90[1]	–	90	33	–	90	–	–	–	–	–	90	–	–	90	90	–	990
83	–	90	–	–	90	–	–	–	–	–	90□	–	–	90	90	–	990
85	–	65	–	–	90	–	–	–	–	–	75	–	–	90	90	–	961
90	–	81	s2	–	90	–	–	–	–	–	90□	–	–	90	90	–	990
90	–	90	s1	–	45	–	–	–	–	–	90	–	–	90	90	–	990
–	90□	68	90	–	90□	–	–	–	–	–	90	–	–	90	90	–	990
s71	90	90□	90	–	–	–	–	–	–	19	s19	–	s14	90	–	–	990
–	90□	–	90[1]	–	90□	–	–	–	–	–	85	–	–	90	90	–	990
–	90	–	71	–	90	–	–	–	s3	90	87	–	–	90	90□	–	990
–	90	90	90□	–	–	–	–	–	–	90	–	90	–	90□	90	–	990
–	90□	90	90	–	–	–	–	–	–	90[1]	–	90	–	90	90	–	990
–	90	89	90[1]	–	90	–	–	–	–	90	–	90	–	s1	90	89□	990
–	90□	75	75	–	s15	–	–	–	–	90y	s15	–	–	90	90□	–	990
–	–	80	s10	–	90	–	–	–	–	90[1]	s10	80	–	90	90	–	990
65	90□	90□	90	–	90	–	–	–	–	–	s17	–	–	90	90□	–	990
–	90	–	90	–	90□	–	–	–	90	90	–	90	–	–	90	–	990
–	90	–	90[1]	–	90□	–	–	–	–	90	–	90	–	–	90	90	990
–	73[1]	90[1]	90[1]	–	s17	90	–	–	–	90	–	90	–	–	90	–	990
–	90	90[1]□	83	–	s16	–	–	–	–	90	–	90□	–	–	90	90	990
s9	67□	–	90[1]	s45	–	90	–	–	–	s23	–	45▪	–	–	90□	–	945
–	90	76	90	–	–	–	–	–	–	90	s14	76	–	–	90	90□	990
–	82	87[1]	90[1]	–	–	–	–	90	–	90	–	90	–	–	90	–	990
–	90	10	90	–	–	–	–	71	–	90	s12	–	–	–	90	s19	990

THE MANAGER

GEORGE GRAHAM

When George Graham's name was linked with the vacant hot seat at Spurs, the whole of north London gasped with incredulity. How could a man with so much affiliation to Arsenal even contemplate moving to their biggest rivals?

Graham had spent two years rebuilding the Leeds team and chairman Peter Ridsdale was determined to keep him at Elland Road. But the lure of a return to London was too strong for Graham to resist.

An attacking midfielder with 13 caps for Scotland, Graham will always be best remembered for his six seasons at Highbury, but he actually played for two other London clubs (Chelsea and Crystal Palace), as well as Aston Villa, Manchester United and Portsmouth.

Rather than immediately wielding the axe at Spurs, Graham brought the best out of unsettled French winger David Ginola and such under-performing players as Justin Edinburgh and Stephen Carr.

He also led Spurs to their first piece of silverware for eight years when a last-minute goal from Allan Nielsen won Spurs the Worthington Cup at Wembley.

In a short space of time, Graham has won over the Tottenham doubters and has created a feeling of expectation among the fans.

LEAGUE POSITION

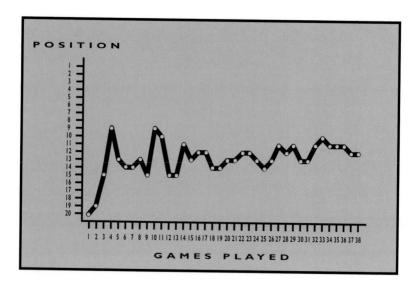

THE GOALS

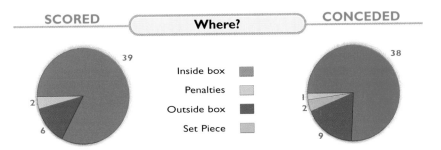

SCORED | Where? | CONCEDED

39

Inside box
Penalties
Outside box
Set Piece

2
6

38

1
2
9

For a side blessed with dead-ball specialists such as Darren Anderton, it was a little surprising that they failed to convert any goals direct from free kicks. Spurs scored 87.2% of their goals inside opposition areas, thanks largely to the penetrating dribbling skills of David Ginola. George Graham's side were caught napping from distance on occasion, conceding a fairly high proportion of goals – 22% in all – from outside their box.

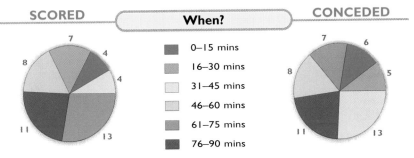

SCORED | When? | CONCEDED

7
4
8
4
11
13

0–15 mins
16–30 mins
31–45 mins
46–60 mins
61–75 mins
76–90 mins

7
6
8
5
11
13

Tottenham were without doubt second half specialists. A massive 68.1% of their goals were registered after 45 minutes, the second-highest proportion in the Premiership. They were at their most deadly between the 60th and 75th minutes, scoring nearly 30% of their 47 Premiership strikes in this period. Spurs were comparatively strong in defence after the break, conceding 52% of all goals in the second period, the fifth-lowest percentage in the league.

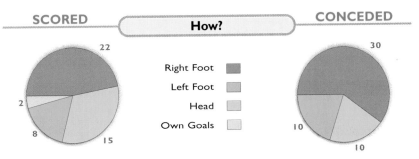

SCORED | How? | CONCEDED

22

Right Foot
Left Foot
Head
Own Goals

2
8
15

30

10
10

The commanding presence of Sol Campbell meant Spurs scored a large percentage of their goals via headers. Five of Sol's six goals were with his head, the second-most in the Premiership, as Spurs nodded in 15 times – more than any other side. The defence was susceptible to right-footed shots and these efforts made up 60% of all goals knocked past the north Londoners during the 1998–99 Carling Premiership season.

TOTTENHAM HOTSPUR

	ALLEN	ANDERTON	ARMSTRONG	BERTI	CALDERWOOD	CAMPBELL	CARR	CLEMENCE	DOMINGUEZ	EDINBURGH	FERDINAND	FOX
APPEARANCE												
Start	0	31	24	4	11	37	37	9	2	14	22	17
Sub	5	1	10	0	1	0	0	9	11	2	2	3
Minutes on pitch	28	2724	2359	311	955	3330	3320	820	364	1210	1762	1511
GOAL ATTEMPTS												
Goals	0	3	7	0	0	6	0	0	2	0	5	3
Shots on target	0	14	42	2	3	14	5	1	5	0	14	8
Shots off target	2	23	40	1	0	19	10	7	5	1	18	3
Shooting accuracy %	0%	38%	51%	67%	100%	42%	33%	13%	50%	0%	44%	73%
PASSING												
Goal assists	0	9	1	0	0	0	3	0	2	0	1	1
Long passes	1	245	12	10	26	192	275	31	6	91	6	53
Short passes	14	1377	681	119	305	737	1311	300	102	389	690	506
PASS COMPLETION												
Own half %	67%	84%	77%	89%	90%	89%	88%	71%	85%	83%	82%	90%
Opposition half %	64%	69%	60%	62%	75%	59%	70%	82%	80%	69%	68%	71%
CROSSING												
Total crosses	0	237	46	2	2	4	87	40	9	32	7	44
Cross completion %	0%	32%	11%	50%	0%	50%	38%	33%	22%	22%	0%	30%
DRIBBLING												
Dribbles & runs	0	43	81	5	6	39	143	14	46	17	30	72
Dribble completion %	0%	67%	67%	40%	83%	74%	76%	71%	59%	82%	60%	79%
DEFENDING												
Tackles made	0	134	32	11	40	158	86	22	12	46	59	40
Tackles won %	0%	57%	56%	82%	78%	74%	60%	45%	67%	67%	51%	48%
Blocks	0	14	2	1	8	42	22	3	0	10	0	2
Clearances	2	36	19	15	72	583	251	19	0	101	25	22
Interceptions	0	27	6	4	9	49	39	4	4	5	6	13
DISCIPLINE												
Fouls	3	44	62	10	21	50	32	5	6	18	48	16
Offside	0	4	53	0	0	0	3	2	1	0	24	7
Yellow cards	0	7	3	1	4	0	4	1	1	2	5	1
Red cards	0	0	1	0	1	0	0	0	0	1	0	0

GOALKEEPER NAME	START/ (SUB)	TIME ON PITCH	GOALS CONCEDED	MINS/GOALS CONCEDED	SAVES MADE	SAVES/ SHOTS
BAARDSEN	12	1080	16	67.5	57	78%
SEGERS	1	90	1	90	5	83%
WALKER	25	2250	33	68.2	73	69%

PLAYERS' STATISTICS

	FREUND	GINOLA	IVERSEN	KING	NIELSEN	NILSEN	SAIB	SCALES	SHERWOOD	SINTON	TARICCO	TRAMEZZANI	VEGA	YOUNG	TOTAL	RANK
	17	30	22	0	24	3	0	7	12	12	12	6	13	14		
	0	0	5	1	4	0	4	0	2	10	1	0	3	1		
	1482	2475	1994	45	2157	270	104	611	1106	1173	1027	518	1185	1278		
	0	3	9	0	3	0	0	0	2	0	0	0	2	0	47*	9th
	3	24	33	0	19	1	1	0	5	2	0	0	4	2	202	6th
	8	30	33	0	12	0	4	1	7	8	1	3	4	4	244	6th
	27%	44%	50%	0%	61%	100%	20%	0%	42%	20%	0%	0%	50%	33%	45%	11th
	1	10	1	0	2	0	1	0	1	0	1	0	0	0	34	8th
	29	160	22	1	69	22	11	40	66	87	81	39	64	41	1680	18th
	566	842	691	9	714	70	75	146	529	357	463	148	287	253	11681	7th
	84%	80%	76%	67%	85%	85%	96%	90%	90%	81%	89%	91%	92%	90%	86%	17th
	76%	65%	65%	50%	67%	52%	66%	62%	74%	65%	72%	70%	60%	68%	68%	15th
	7	240	19	0	29	0	6	2	15	52	16	16	1	1	914	3rd
	43%	35%	16%	0%	24%	0%	50%	0%	33%	27%	31%	31%	0%	0%	31%	3rd
	18	409	45	0	24	2	2	1	14	45	19	11	1	11	1101	2nd
	72%	61%	56%	0%	58%	100%	50%	100%	86%	69%	68%	82%	100%	73%	67%	18th
	85	68	47	2	82	9	5	13	51	41	47	13	31	54	1190	7th
	51%	32%	23%	0%	57%	67%	80%	77%	59%	44%	62%	54%	74%	65%	58%	18th
	8	0	2	0	7	3	2	5	6	4	4	2	21	19	187	14th
	37	11	34	4	43	37	1	89	18	46	74	44	218	148	1989	13th
	17	12	8	0	16	3	0	13	13	4	14	0	8	32	310	15th
	23	39	22	0	33	5	1	5	18	17	12	16	24	8	539	7th
	0	5	11	0	5	0	0	0	2	0	0	1	2	0	120	15th
	6	9	1	0	6	1	0	1	1	3	1	1	2	5	67	11th
	0	0	0	0	0	0	0	0	0	0	1	0	0	0	4	=7th

*including two own goals

CROSSES CAUGHT	CROSSES PUNCHED	CROSSES NOT CLAIMED	CATCH SUCCESS	THROWS/SHORT KICKS	% COMPLETION	LONG KICKS	% COMPLETION
30	12	0	100%	81	98%	281	41%
5	1	0	100%	4	75%	29	38%
55	2	10	92%	292	92%	566	42%

PLAYER OF THE SEASON

PLAYER	INDEX SCORE
SOL CAMPBELL	1103
David Ginola	994
Darren Anderton	906
Steffen Iversen	825
Stephen Carr	811
Chris Armstrong	720
Allan Nielsen	667
Steffen Freund*	629
Les Ferdinand	576
Ian Walker	493

*Featured in fewer than 16 games

The crushing disappointment felt by Sol Campbell when his header against Argentina in the World Cup was disallowed was mirrored up and down the country by England supporters.

But if he feared those feelings of frustration were a precursor to his 1998–99 Premiership with Tottenham, he need not have worried.

Apart from the fact that five Campbell headers in the league season most definitely were allowed, the Spurs skipper would lead his side to Wembley glory in the Worthington Cup and have an outstanding and commanding campaign at the heart of the Tottenham defence.

Consistency is the key to a high Carling Opta Index score over the course of a whole season and Campbell ended up as the club's highest-rated player in the Opta Season Index, with an average score of 1,103 points.

He even beat double Player of the Year David Ginola to the Tottenham top spot.

Ginola turned in a series of electrifying displays in the two cup competitions, but Spurs fans had to wait until March for his first league goal of the season.

French star Ginola averaged 994 points a match in 1998–98, putting him comfortably ahead of fellow-wide man Darren Anderton. The England international enjoyed a season virtually free of injury and used his time on the pitch to good effect, racking up an average of 906 points per match.

Another steady performer in the top 10 was Stephen Carr. Manager George Graham managed to get the very best from the full-back after he had suffered a comparatively disappointing 1997–98.

Other players struggled to match his levels of consistency. Strikers Chris Armstrong and Les Ferdinand showed flashes of the brilliant form everyone knows they are capable of – but rarely looked like maintaining it across the whole campaign.

FIVE OF THE BEST

Second from bottom after two matches was definitely not what the Spurs fans — or chairman Alan Sugar — had in mind. Christian Gross was immediately sacked and Leeds United boss George Graham installed as manager within six weeks. He spent the season attempting to shore up the defence and is certain to make many more changes in 1999–2000.

TOP GOALSCORERS

	GOALS	GOALS/SHOTS
STEFFEN IVERSEN	9	14%
Chris Armstrong	7	9%
Sol Campbell	6	18%
Les Ferdinand	5	16%
Ruel Fox	3	27%

Tottenham managed only 47 goals in 1998–99, 33 fewer than champions Manchester United. No one reached double figures in the league and top scorer was the ever-improving Steffen Iversen with nine. Chris Armstrong struck seven times, but with a goals-to-shots ratio of just nine per cent he really should have bagged many more. Skipper Sol Campbell managed six goals from defence, while wide man Ruel Fox scored three from just 19 starts, hitting the net with more than a quarter of his shots.

Young full-back Stephen Carr missed just one match in all competitions for Spurs and was probably the side's most improved player in 1998–99. He was also the most prolific passer, completing more than 1,200 balls. Wide man Darren Anderton was just behind, with double Footballer of the Year David Ginola some way off the pace in fourth. He finished with a pass completion rate of only 69%, making fewer than 700 successful passes all season. Sol Campbell and Allan Nielsen also feature in the top five.

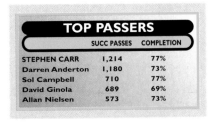

TOP PASSERS

	SUCC PASSES	COMPLETION
STEPHEN CARR	1,214	77%
Darren Anderton	1,180	73%
Sol Campbell	710	77%
David Ginola	689	69%
Allan Nielsen	573	73%

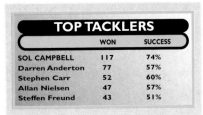

TOP TACKLERS

	WON	SUCCESS
SOL CAMPBELL	117	74%
Darren Anderton	77	57%
Stephen Carr	52	60%
Allan Nielsen	47	57%
Steffen Freund	43	51%

Spurs showed no lack of heart and "Sol" in the tackle, with Campbell winning 40 more than anyone else in the squad – and finishing with easily the best success rate. Darren Anderton, who finally enjoyed a season free from serious injury, was the second most effective challenger, but the midfield pairing of Allan Nielsen and Steffen Freund failed to win possession more than 40% of the time, some way below the average one would expect from Premiership midfielders.

Spurs finished 11th in the Premiership – and achieved an identical position in the discipline table. Chris Armstrong accrued the most disciplinary points thanks to his 62 fouls and one red card. Playmaker David Ginola was second in the Spurs bad boy league after picking up nine bookings, although the majority were not for fouls. It is interesting to note that no defender is in the top five: the other spots are filled by two midfielders (Anderton and Nielsen) and another striker (Les Ferdinand). Sol Campbell and Stephen Carr are in sixth and seventh place respectively.

DISCIPLINE

	POINTS	FOULS & CARDS
CHRIS ARMSTRONG	77	62F, 3Y, 1R
David Ginola	66	39F, 9Y, 0R
Darren Anderton	65	44F, 7Y, 0R
Les Ferdinand	63	48F, 5Y, 0R
Allan Nielsen	51	33F, 6Y, 0R

ACTION	ANDERTON	ARMSTRONG	BAARDSEN	CALDERWOOD	CAMPBELL	CARR	CLEMENCE	DOMINGUEZ	EDINBURGH	FERDINAND	FOX	IVERSEN	NIELSEN	VEGA	TOTAL	LEEDS UNITED
Time on pitch	90	90	90	10	90	80	73	17	90	62	90	28	90	90	990	990
GOALS																
Goal	–	–	–	–	1	–	–	–	–	–	–	–	–	1	3	3
Shot on target	–	2	–	1	–	–	–	–	–	–	–	–	–	–	4	3
Shot off target	1	1	–	–	1	–	–	–	–	3	–	–	–	–	6	8
Blocked shot	1	–	–	–	1	1	–	–	–	–	–	–	–	–	4	2
Own goal	–	–	–	–	–	–	–	–	–	–	–	–	–	–	–	–
PASSES																
Pass to own player	33	19	–	3	24	16	17	5	24	21	17	9	17	23	228	202
Pass to opposition	15	6	–	2	6	13	3	1	14	13	3	2	9	6	92	95
Cross to own player	–	–	–	–	–	–	1	–	–	–	1	–	–	–	5	10
Cross to opposition player	6	–	–	–	–	2	3	–	3	–	–	–	–	–	15	2
Goal assist	–	–	–	–	–	1	–	–	–	–	–	–	–	–	3	3
Pass completion %	63%	73%	0%	60%	80%	55%	75%	100%	63%	62%	75%	83%	67%	79%	69%	69%
TACKLES & CLEARANCES																
Tackle	2	–	–	–	5	–	1	3	1	1	2	–	1	3	19	12
Clearances, blocks and interceptions	1	–	–	–	6	–	1	1	1	1	–	–	2	7	20	45
DRIBBLES & RUNS																
Dribble ball retained	–	3	–	–	–	1	2	–	–	2	–	–	–	–	8	13
Dribbles ball lost	1	–	–	–	–	–	–	2	–	–	–	–	–	–	3	3
Dribble success %	0%	100%	0%	0%	0%	100%	100%	0%	0%	100%	100%	0%	0%	0%	73%	81%
DISCIPLINE																
Fouls	1	4	–	–	–	–	–	2	2	–	–	2	2	1	14	22
Penalty conceded	–	–	–	–	–	–	–	–	–	–	–	–	–	–	–	–
Free kick - offside	–	–	–	–	–	–	–	–	–	–	–	–	–	–	3	2
Yellow cards	–	2	–	–	–	–	–	–	–	–	–	–	–	1	3	2
Red cards	–	–	–	–	–	–	–	–	–	–	–	–	–	–	–	–
GOALKEEPERS																
Distribution to own player	–	–	20	–	–	–	–	–	–	–	–	–	–	–	20	14
Distribution to opposition player	–	–	19	–	–	–	–	–	–	–	–	–	–	–	19	19
Goalkeeper distribution%	–	–	51%	–	–	–	–	–	–	–	–	–	–	–	51%	42%
Save	–	–	4	–	–	–	–	–	–	–	–	–	–	–	4	4
Ball caught	–	–	4	–	–	–	–	–	–	–	–	–	–	–	4	6
Ball dropped	–	–	–	–	–	–	–	–	–	–	–	–	–	–	–	–
Goal conceded	–	–	3	–	–	–	–	–	–	–	–	–	–	–	3	3

Tensions between rival fans were high at White Hart Lane, with rumours circulating about the departure of George Graham from Leeds United to Tottenham. Members of the press suggested that the Spurs players might be playing to impress their future boss. Tottenham, under the stewardship of David Pleat, were looking for a result to appease their disgruntled fans.

September 26, 1998

3–3

TOTTENHAM HOTSPUR
LEEDS UNITED

But without David Ginola, doubts were being cast over the creative ability of the rest of the side. The fans did not have to wait long for the first goal, and it went to Leeds. An Ian Harte corner from the left was met by an unmarked Gunnar Halle, who headed powerfully into the net.

Spurs recovered and won a corner on the right. Darren Anderton's floating delivery was met by Ramon Vega, who planted a header into the corner for 1–1 after 14 minutes.

On 26 minutes, Leeds went double-Dutch and retook the lead. Fed by Harry Kewell, striker Clyde Wijnhard played a low ball into the box and fellow-countryman Jimmy Floyd Hasselbaink nipped in ahead of Stephen Carr and Espen Baardsen to make it 2–1.

The second half was equally exciting, with chances at both ends. David Hopkin found Hasselbaink out wide on the right. The Dutch World Cup international crossed low to Wijnhard at the near post. His effort was well blocked by Vega, but he kept his composure and stabbed the rebound under Baardsen for 3–1.

Spurs needed a comeback and, with just under 20 minutes remaining, Ruel Fox took on Harte and pulled the ball back for Carr. The young Irishman's cross from deep was met on the half-volley by substitute Steffen Iversen from six yards. Leeds were looking for an offside flag, but to no avail. Spurs were back in it at 3–2.

With the crowd roaring them on, Spurs pushed desperately for an equalizer. Armstrong hit an angled volley inches wide, but at the other end a deflected Hasselbaink shot in stoppage time needed quick reactions from Baardsen to turn it round the post. That save was to prove vital, as there was to be a late sting in the tail.

In the fourth minute of stoppage time, Martyn failed to claim Anderton's chip into the crowded penalty area. Colin Calderwood's shot was somehow saved by the Leeds 'keeper, but the ball went straight to Allan Nielsen. He crossed from the right and Sol Campbell rose to deliver a thumping header into the back of the net. The captain had completed an incredible comeback, and the White Hart Lane crowd were in ecstasy. He led by example, producing a man-of-the-match performance worthy of 1,366 Carling Opta Index points.

Both teams finished with a pass completion rate of 69%, but Spurs made more passes and shaded possession. The London club also made more tackles than the Yorkshire side (Tottenham's 19 to Leeds's 12) and fired seven shots on target to Leeds' six, with both teams scoring three goals.

It was to be a good day all round for the Spurs fans, as news filtered through that a brilliant last-minute goal from Lee Briscoe had condemned their north London rivals Arsenal to defeat at Sheffield Wednesday.

ACTION	ANDERTON	ARMSTRONG	CAMPBELL	CARR	CLEMENCE	FERDINAND	FOX	GINOLA	IVERSEN	NIELSEN	SINTON	WALKER	YOUNG	TOTAL	EVERTON
Time on pitch	90	89	90	90	45	90	90	90	1	45	90	90	90	990	990
GOALS															
Goal	–	3	–	–	–	1	–	–	–	–	–	–	–	4	–
Shot on target	–	2	–	–	–	2	–	–	–	1	–	–	–	6	1
Shot off target	–	2	2	–	–	–	–	1	–	1	1	–	1	8	5
Blocked shot	–	1	–	–	–	–	–	1	–	–	–	–	–	4	2
Own goal	–	–	–	–	–	–	–	–	–	–	–	–	–	–	–
PASSES															
Pass to own player	42	14	24	30	16	21	23	26	1	17	33	–	16	263	211
Pass to opposition	18	9	–	9	2	10	11	7	–	3	13	–	5	88	89
Cross to own player	6	–	–	2	2	1	1	4	–	–	1	–	–	15	3
Cross to opposition player	7	3	–	2	1	–	–	–	–	–	–	–	–	16	9
Goal assist	2	–	–	–	–	–	–	–	–	–	–	–	–	3	1
Pass completion %	67%	54%	100%	74%	86%	67%	69%	81%	33%	85%	70%	0%	76%	73%	69%
TACKLES & CLEARANCES															
Tackle	8	2	6	4	5	7	2	5	–	5	5	–	6	51	41
Clearances, blocks and interceptions	1	1	22	5	–	2	4	1	–	4	6	3	13	62	93
DRIBBLES & RUNS															
Dribble ball retained	1	3	–	4	–	3	7	7	–	–	2	–	–	20	14
Dribble ball lost	–	–	–	–	–	–	–	6	–	–	–	–	–	8	13
Dribble success %	100%	100%	0%	100%	0%	100%	100%	54%	0%	0%	100%	0%	0%	71%	52%
DISCIPLINE															
Fouls	2	3	1	–	–	5	–	4	–	1	–	–	–	16	15
Penalty conceded	–	–	–	–	–	–	–	–	–	–	–	–	–	0	–
Free kick - offside	–	5	–	–	–	2	–	–	–	–	–	–	–	7	5
Yellow cards	–	–	–	–	–	1	–	–	–	–	1	–	–	1	2
Red cards	–	–	–	–	–	–	–	–	–	–	–	–	–	0	–
GOALKEEPERS															
Distribution to own player	–	–	–	–	–	–	–	–	–	–	–	23	–	23	22
Distribution to opposition player	–	–	–	–	–	–	–	–	–	–	–	8	–	8	13
Goalkeeper distribution%	0%	0%	0%	0%	0%	0%	0%	0%	0%	0%	0%	74%	0%	74%	63%
Save	–	–	–	–	–	–	–	–	–	–	–	1	–	4	6
Ball caught	–	–	–	–	–	–	–	–	–	–	–	4	–	4	7
Ball dropped	–	–	–	–	–	–	–	–	–	–	–	–	–	–	–
Goal conceded	–	–	–	–	–	–	–	–	–	–	–	1	–	1	4

George Graham rescued Spurs from their Gross start to the season and instilled the confidence that has bred so much success in the past for his teams. They faced a potentially troublesome fixture against the blue half of Merseyside under the guidance of another iron-fisted Scot, Walter Smith.

December 28, 1998
4 – 1
TOTTENHAM HOTSPUR
EVERTON

Everton arrived in north London on the back of an impressive run, picking up 11 points from their previous half-dozen games. But Tottenham themselves were just starting a run that saw them unbeaten in the Carling Premiership from Boxing Day through to March. Chris Armstrong's second-half hat-trick, his first for Spurs, was the highlight of the side's joint-biggest win under Graham.

Twenty-three minutes had passed when Fox won the ball from Alex Cleland on the goal-line and fed it to Ginola. Armstrong met the Frenchman's cross, but his header hit David Unsworth and spun to Les Ferdinand, who swivelled and lashed the ball into the roof of the net.

Seven minutes later, the Spurs defence was breached for the only time in the match. Don Hutchison played a sharp first-time ball into the box and Ibrahima Bakayoko glanced a header past Ian Walker for the equalizer.

Both sides had half-chances just before the break, with Cleland for Everton and Tottenham's Sol Campbell going close for their respective teams.

The home side stepped up a gear in the second period and took the lead just past the hour mark. England's Darren Anderton won the ball from Olivier Dacourt, played a one-two with Ruel Fox and dinked a cheeky ball over the Everton defence. Armstrong timed his run superbly, took the ball past Myhre and slotted it home from an acute angle.

With 15 minutes left, Armstrong virtually assured Spurs all three points. Luke Young cleared long to Ferdinand whose neat backheel into Armstrong's path took Everton's defence clean out. The former Eagle did not spurn this gilt-edged chance, his well-struck shot soaring beyond Thomas Myhre.

Armstrong's third goal was his best. Anderton curled a beautiful pass to the striker who took the ball down on his chest and, without breaking stride, hammered it handsomely past Myhre's flailing right hand.

Tottenham richly deserved their victory and Carling Opta's statistics confirm this conclusively. Spurs fired in 10 shots on target, but their rivals only managed two, in keeping with their performances through most of the campaign. Anderton and Ginola provided ample ammunition as Spurs registered 31 crosses, a mighty 48% to a white shirt. In stark contrast, Everton attempted 12 crosses, firing nine blanks.

Chris Armstrong amassed 2,318 Carling Opta points. He claimed his hat-trick from seven efforts at goal, five of which were on target. He also had a hand in Tottenham's opener, undertook three successful dribbles and runs and completed 14 out of 23 passes.

In what was a year of Premiership consolidation for Spurs, this result helped George Graham stamp his mark on the side.

WEST HAM UNITED 1998–99

Back row (left to right): Richard Hall (now retired), Jarvier Margas, Ian Pearce, Ludek Miklosko (now QPR), Craig Forrest, Shaka Hislop, Neil Ruddock, John Hartson (now Wimbledon), Rio Ferdinand, Samassi Abou.

Middle row: Eddie Gillam (Kit Manager), Roger Cross (Coach), Steve Potts, Emmanuel Omoyinmi, Trevor Sinclair, Scott Mean (no longer at club), Ian Wright, Paul Kitson, Marc Keller, Stan Lazaridis, Frank Lampard (now QPR), Les Sealey (Goalkeeping Coach), Julian Dicks, John Green (Physiotherapist).

Front row: Andrew Impey (now Leicester), Eyal Berkovic, Harry Redknapp (Manager), Steve Lomas, Frank Lampard Senior (Assistant Manager), John Moncur, Lee Hodges.

WEST HAM UNITED

ADDRESS

Boleyn Ground, Green Street,
Upton Park, London E13 9AZ

CONTACT NUMBERS

Telephone: 0181 548 2748
Fax: 0181 548 2758
Ticket Office: 0181 548 2700
24hr Information: 09068 121165
Club Merchandise: 0181 548 2722
Website: www.westhamunited.co.uk

SPONSORS

Dr Martens

FANZINES

On The Terraces
On A Mission
Over Land and Sea

KEY PERSONNEL

Chairman: T W Brown
Vice Chairman: M W Cearns ACIB
Directors: T W Brown,
M W Cearns ACIB, C J Warner MA
Notary Public: N Igoe, P Aldridge
Club Secretary: G Mackrell
Manager: Harry Redknapp

COLOURS

Home: Claret shirts with light blue
sleeves, white shorts and claret
stockings
Away: White shirts with claret and
blue shorts and white stockings

NICKNAME

The Hammers,
The Irons

20 FACTS

1 West Ham United started life in 1895 as Thames Iron Works FC. They were founded by Arnold Hills, chairman of the shipbuilding company, who distanced himself from the club after they started employing professional players. Thames Iron Works FC were wound up in June 1900. A month later, the club were relaunched as West Ham United.

2 The club have never been league champions. Their best top-flight finish came in 1985–86 when they finished third.

3 They have twice finished runners-up in the League Cup, in 1966 and 1981.

4 The Hammers have had more luck in the FA Cup, winning the competition three times – in 1964, 1975 and 1980.

5 West Ham United have played in the European Cup Winners Cup on four occasions, winning the trophy in 1964–65.

6 Alvin Martin scored against three different goalkeepers in West Ham's 8–1 Division One victory over Newcastle in 1986.

7 Harry Redknapp is only West Ham's eighth manager in 99 years. No other English league club has had fewer managers. The Hammers' longest-serving manager was Syd King, in charge of the club from 1902 to 1932.

8 West Ham played in the first-ever Wembley Cup Final. They lost the 1923 FA Cup encounter with Bolton 2–0 in front of an official record FA Cup final crowd of 126,047, although there were undoubtedly more fans in the ground.

9 Billy Bonds holds the record for most appearances. He played 793 times for the club between 1967 and 1988.

10 Martin Peters's move from West Ham to Tottenham Hotspur in March 1970 was Britain's first £200,000 transfer.

11 No West Ham player has ever won the PFA Player of the Year award. But the club have provided two winners of the Young Player award – Mervyn Day in 1975 and Tony Cottee in 1986. Bobby Moore is the only Hammer to have won the Football Writers Player of the Year award: he took the honour in 1964.

12 The club's record attendance is 42,322 for a Division One match against Tottenham in October 1970.

13 Hammers' legend Bobby Moore is the youngest captain to lift the FA Cup. He was 23 years and 20 days old when he led West Ham to victory over Preston North End in 1964.

14 Moore was the first captain to lift three trophies at Wembley in three consecutive years. He held aloft the FA Cup in 1964, the European Cup Winners' Cup in 1965 and the World Cup in 1966.

15 Former Hammer Sir Geoff Hurst is the only man to have scored a hat-trick in a World Cup final, and Bobby Moore, who captained England in the 1966 World Cup, is West Ham's most-capped player. He made 108 appearances for England.

16 West Ham finished fifth in the 1998–99 Premiership, qualifying for the InterToto Cup. Their league record was:

Pld	W	D	L	F	A	Pts
38	16	9	13	46	53	57

17 Harry Redknapp's side suffered a shock exit at the hands of Third Division Swansea in the third round of the FA Cup. They drew 1–1 at Upton Park before losing 1–0 at the Vetch Field.

18 The Hammers also suffered an early exit from the Worthington Cup, losing 2–1 on aggregate to Northampton Town in the second round.

19 The top goalscorer in all competitions for West Ham was Ian Wright with nine goals.

20 West Ham's disciplinary record was the 10th worst in the Premiership. They committed 480 fouls, earned 81 yellow cards and suffered five dismissals, including three in just one game.

SEASON REVIEW

Finishing the season in fifth place represented a major achievement for West Ham United. The club wrapped up a place in the InterToto Cup with a stirring 4–0 victory over Middlesbrough on the last day to bring Harry Redknapp's dream of European football a step closer.

East End optimism was running high at the start of the season with new signings Ian Wright and Neil Ruddock joining Chilean World Cup star Javier Margas and Frenchman Marc Keller as exciting additions to the West Ham ranks.

Wright endeared himself to the fans immediately, scoring the only goal in a 1–0 away victory at Sheffield Wednesday, while Ruddock played a starring role in the 0–0 draw with Manchester United.

The first shock of the season came with a 4–3 loss at home to Wimbledon on September 9 that saw the team drop to 11th place in the Premiership. A 4–2 loss at Charlton at the end of October left them in the 14th spot, but that was as bad as things got. The team was never outside the top 10 after that.

One concern was the form of John Hartson. Goals against Liverpool and Wimbledon apart, he was not causing defences the same problems as he had done the season before. When news of a training ground bust-up with Eyal Berkovic hit the headlines, the club closed ranks around the player.

A £7.5 million bid from Wimbledon proved too much of a temptation for Harry Redknapp to turn down, however. He used the money to sign Marc-Vivien Foe and Paolo Di Canio.

The Italian player was seen by many as a risky signing – he had been out of action since late September after his dismissal for a push on referee Paul Alcock – but at just £2.5 million, Redknapp thought Di Canio was worth the gamble. He was less happy with the sale of Andy Impey to Leicester – the transfer had been made without him being consulted.

The team certainly needed a lift. Heavy defeats by Manchester United, Sheffield Wednesday and Arsenal had seen the side drop from sixth to ninth place by the beginning of February.

These thrashings were an unusual feature of the season. Only Neil Sullivan of Wimbledon was forced to make more saves than Shaka Hislop, and the defence was often left exposed by a midfield that looked short on grit. West Ham finished the season with just 1,092 tackles – the third lowest number in the Premiership – and their goal difference of minus seven was the worst outside the bottom six.

On their day, though, the team were great to watch and certainly deserved their high finish. In the tradition of the club they opted for the long ball only as a last resort, finishing the season with fewer long passes than any other side. This trend was particularly marked after the departure of John Hartson. Without a big target man they preferred to hit opponents with swift counter-attacks, and the likes of Berkovic, Di Canio and Sinclair helped the team to a total of 1,081 dribbles and runs – the fourth highest in the Premiership.

The success of the club's under-19 side in winning both the FA Youth Cup and FA Premier Youth League provided Redknapp with almost as much satisfaction as the first team. In a season when Leeds won all the plaudits for their willingness to give youth a chance, West Ham's policy of allowing home-grown talent like Rio Ferdinand, Frank Lampard and Joe Cole to rise through the ranks was almost overlooked.

Redknapp's assertion that his long-term aim is to see at least five home-grown players in the first team is an encouraging one, suggesting the future of the club is in good hands.

> **"I said back in August that if we could finish higher than last season's eighth place, it would represent a massive step forward..."**
>
> **Harry Redknapp**

WEST HAM UNITED

DATE	OPPONENT	SCORE	ATT.	ABOU	BERKOVIC	BREACKER	COLE	COYNE	DI CANIO	DICKS	FERDINAND	FOE	FORREST	HARTSON	HIS
15.8.98	Sheff Wed A	1–0	30,236	–	85	–	–	–	–	–	90	–	–	–	90
22.8.98	Man Utd H	0–0	25,912	s18	72□	–	–	–	–	–	90	–	–	90□	90
29.8.98	Coventry A	0–0	20,818	–	90	–	–	–	–	–	90	–	–	90□	90
9.9.98	Wimbledon H	3–4	24,601	–	56	–	–	–	–	–	–	–	–	90^1	90
12.9.98	Liverpool H	2–1	26,010	–	89^1	s1	–	–	–	–	–	–	–	86^1□	90
19.9.98	Nott'm For A	0–0	26,463	79	90	–	–	–	–	–	–	90□	–	–	90
28.9.98	Southampton H	1–0	23,153	–	45	–	–	–	–	90	90□	–	–	90	90
3.10.98	Blackburn A	0–3	25,213	–	–	–	–	–	–	90	85	–	–	90	90
17.10.98	Aston Villa H	0–0	26,002	–	90	–	–	–	–	90	90	–	–	90	90
24.10.98	Charlton A	2–4*	20,043	–	77^1□	–	–	–	–	90□	90	–	–	90	90
31.10.98	Newcastle A	3–0	36,744	–	–	–	–	–	–	–	90	–	–	s8	90
8.11.98	Chelsea H	1–1	26,023	–	87	–	–	–	–	–	90	–	–	–	90
14.11.98	Leicester H	3–2	25,642	–	90	–	–	–	–	90	90	–	–	–	90
22.11.98	Derby Co A	2–0	31,366	–	90	–	–	–	–	–	90□	–	–	90^1	90
28.11.98	Tottenham H	2–1	26,044	–	40	–	–	–	–	–	90	–	–	–	90
5.12.98	Leeds Utd A	0–4	36,315	–	–	–	–	–	–	–	–	–	–	90	90
12.12.98	Middlesbro' A	0–1	34,623	–	–	–	–	–	–	–	90	–	–	90	90
19.12.98	Everton H	2–1	25,998	–	90	–	–	–	–	90	90	–	–	90	90
26.12.98	Arsenal A	0–1	38,098	–	90	–	–	–	–	–	90	–	–	90	90
28.12.98	Coventry H	2–0	25,662	–	81	–	–	–	–	90	90	–	–	90^1	90
10.1.99	Man Utd A	1–4	55,180	–	90	–	s44	–	–	–	90	–	–	90	90
16.1.99	Sheff Wed H	0–4	25,642	90	64	–	s50□	–	–	–	90	–	–	–	90
30.1.99	Wimbledon A	0–0	23,035	–	–	90	72	–	s18	90	90	90	–	–	90
6.2.99	Arsenal H	0–4	26,042	–	s45	45	–	–	90	90□	90	90□	–	–	90
13.2.99	Nott'm For H	2–1	25,458	–	79	–	s11	–	90	–	90	–	–	–	90
20.2.99	Liverpool A	2–2	44,511	–	90	–	80	–	–	–	90	90	–	–	90
27.2.99	Blackburn H	2–0	25,529	–	90	–	–	–	90^1	–	90	90□	–	–	90
6.3.99	Southampton A	0–1	15,240	–	90	–	–	–	90	–	90	72	–	–	90
13.3.99	Chelsea A	1–0	34,765	–	–	–	–	–	–	–	90	90□	–	–	90
20.3.99	Newcastle H	2–0	25,997	–	–	–	–	–	90^1	–	90	90□	–	–	90
2.4.99	Aston Villa A	0–0	36,813	–	–	–	–	–	90	–	5	90	–	–	90
5.4.99	Charlton H	0–1	26,041	–	s10	–	–	–	90	–	–	90□	–	–	90
10.4.99	Leicester A	0–0	20,402	–	90	–	–	–	88	–	–	–	–	–	90
17.4.99	Derby Co H	5–1	25,485	–	90^1	–	s20	–	90^1	–	–	90	–	–	90
24.4.99	Tottenham A	2–1	36,089	–	90□	–	–	–	–	–	90□	–	–	–	90
1.5.99	Leeds Utd H	1–5	25,997	–	61	–	s22	s7	83^1□	–	–	90□	s29	–	61■
8.5.99	Everton A	0–6	40,029	–	90	–	–	–	90	–	90□	90□	–	–	90
16.5.99	Middlesbro' H	4–0	25,902	–	90	–	s5	–	90	–	90	90□	90	–	–

□ Yellow card, ■ Red card, s Substitute, 90^3 Goals scored
*including own goal

1998-1999 PREMIERSHIP APPEARANCES

HODGES	HOLLIGAN	IMPEY	KELLER	KITSON	LAMPARD	LAZARIDIS	LOMAS	MARGAS	MINTO	MONCUR	OMOYINMI	PEARCE	POTTS	RUDDOCK	SINCLAIR	WRIGHT	TOTAL
–	–	90	–	–	90□	90	90	–	–	s5	–	90	–	90□	90	90¹	990
–	–	90	–	–	90□	90	90	–	–	–	–	90	–	90	90	–	990
–	–	90	–	–	90	90	83	90	–	s7□	–	–	–	90□	–	90□	990
–	–	s34□	–	–	90	90	–	90	–	90	–	90	–	90	90	90²	990
–	–	–	s4	–	90	90□	–	–	–	90□	–	90	90	90	90□	90□	990
–	–	90□	90	–	90	–	–	–	–	–	s11	90□	90	–	90	90	990
–	–	–	45	–	90	s45	–	–	–	s45	–	90	s1	90□	90	89¹□	990
s5	–	90	s29	–	90	–	–	–	–	90□	–	90□	61	–	90	90□	990
–	–	s15	–	s10	90	–	90	–	–	–	–	90	–	75	90	80	990
–	–	–	–	s13	90	–	90	–	–	s12□	–	90	–	90	90	78	990
–	–	72	90	82	90	–	90	–	–	–	–	90	s18□	90□	90¹□	90²	990
–	–	–	90	90	90	–	90□	–	–	–	–	90	s3	90¹	90	90	990
–	–	–	90	89¹	90¹	–	90¹	–	–	s1	–	90	–	–	90	90□	990
–	–	–	87¹	90	90	–	90	–	–	–	–	90	s3	90	90	–	990
–	–	–	–	90□	90	90	90	–	–	–	–	90	s50□	90	90²	–	990
–	–	–	90	–	90	56	90	90	–	s34□	–	90	–	73■	90	90	973
–	–	–	45	–	90□	76	90	–	–	s45	s14	90□	90□	–	90	90	990
–	–	–	90¹	–	90	–	90□	–	–	–	–	90	–	–	90¹□	90□	990
–	–	–	64□	–	90	s26□	90	–	–	–	–	90	90	–	90	90	990
–	–	–	–	–	90	90	90	–	–	–	s6	90	s9	–	90	84¹	990
–	–	–	–	–	90¹	90	90	–	–	–	–	90	90	90	46□	–	990
–	–	–	90□	s26	90	–	90	–	90	–	–	90□	–	40	90	–	990
–	–	–	–	90	90	–	–	–	90□	90□	–	–	–	90	–	–	990
–	–	–	–	90	90	–	–	–	90	–	–	90	–	–	90	–	990
–	–	–	–	90□	90¹	89	90	–	s1	–	–	90¹	–	90	90	–	990
–	s10	–	s19¹	–	90¹	s8	90□	–	71	–	–	82	90□	–	90□	–	990
–	–	–	–	90	90	–	90	–	–	–	–	90¹	90	–	90	–	990
–	–	–	90	s18	90	–	90	–	–	–	–	90	–	90	90	–	990
–	–	–	86□	90¹	90	–	90	–	90	–	–	90	s4	90	90	–	990
–	–	–	–	90¹	90	–	90	–	90	–	–	90	–	90□	90	–	990
–	–	–	–	90	90	–	90	–	90	–	–	90	s85	90	90□	–	990
–	–	–	90	80	90	–	90	–	90	–	–	90	–	90□	90	–	990
–	–	–	–	72	90	–	90	–	90	s2	–	90	90	90	90	s18	990
–	–	–	–	–	90	–	70	–	90	–	–	90	18	90¹	90¹	s72¹□	990
–	–	–	90¹	–	90	s1	90□	–	90	90□■	–	90	–	–	90	89¹	990
–	–	–	–	–	90	–	87■	–	90□	90□	–	–	–	90□	68	14■	882
–	–	–	s30	–	90	–	90	–	90	–	–	–	–	90	90□	60□	990
–	–	–	90¹	–	90¹□	–	–	–	90	–	–	–	90	90□	85²	–	990

THE MANAGER

HARRY REDKNAPP

Harry Redknapp has been manager of West Ham since August 1994. Former boss Billy Bonds, with Redknapp as his assistant, had got the club promoted to the Carling Premiership during his four-year spell in the Upton Park hot seat – and Redknapp has gone all-out ever since to turn the Hammers into a credible top-flight force.

Poplar-born Redknapp will forever be associated with the Boleyn Ground after spending six seasons there as a player between 1965 and 1971. During that spell he made 149 appearances as a winger, scoring seven goals, before moving to Bournemouth. After three years there, he moved back to London for a very brief period with Brentford.

But in 1982, he went back to the south coast as Bournemouth team coach and stayed as manager until 1992 before returning to his beloved West Ham.

The 1998–99 season was a busy one in the transfer market for Redknapp, with striker John Hartson moving to Wimbledon for £7.5 million and West Ham buying frontman Paolo Di Canio, full-back Scott Minto and midfielder Marc-Vivien Foe with the proceeds.

LEAGUE POSITION

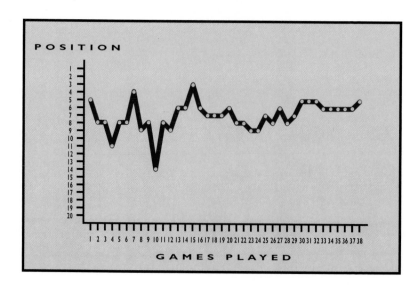

THE GOALS

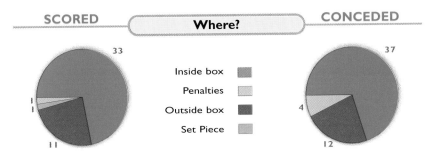

SCORED — Where? — CONCEDED

- Inside box
- Penalties
- Outside box
- Set Piece

West Ham United scored the second-biggest total of long-range goals from open play in the Premiership, and the trio of Ian Wright, Frank Lampard and Marc Keller between them hit seven out of the Hammers' 11 goals from distance. As a result, only Leeds scored a higher proportion of their strikes from more than 18 yards. West Ham's area was well-protected, with a comparatively low 77% of goals conceded from inside their own box.

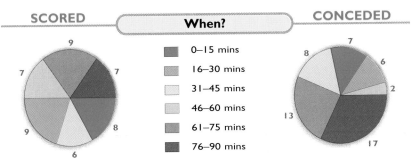

SCORED — When? — CONCEDED

- 0–15 mins
- 16–30 mins
- 31–45 mins
- 46–60 mins
- 61–75 mins
- 76–90 mins

West Ham scored an equal amount of goals either side of half-time, but struggled to stay tight at the back as time ticked on. The Premiership's fifth-placed team spread their goalscoring evenly with no noticeable peak scoring periods throughout the 90 minutes. The biggest disappointment for Harry Redknapp's side was that they were prone to allowing late goals. Almost a third of their opponent's goals arrived with 15 minutes or less remaining.

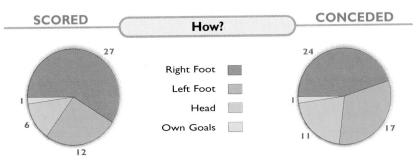

SCORED — How? — CONCEDED

- Right Foot
- Left Foot
- Head
- Own Goals

The Hammers scored relatively few goals with their heads – but conceded a significant proportion of all goals in this way. Just six headers found the back of the net, representing a modest 13% of all their Premiership efforts. In defence the Hammers struggled slightly in the air, allowing 11 headers past them, the fourth-largest total to be conceded by a top-flight club. The Irons conceded an unusually high number of left-footed efforts – 17 in total.

WEST HAM UNITED

	ABOU	BERKOVIC	BREACKER	COLE	COYNE	DI CANIO	DICKS	FERDINAND	FOE	HARTSON	HODGES	HOLLIGAN	IMPEY
APPEARANCE													
Start	2	28	2	2	0	12	9	31	13	16	0	0	6
Sub	1	2	1	6	1	1	0	0	0	1	1	1	2
Minutes on pitch	187	2331	136	304	7	1089	810	2700	1152	1444	5	10	571
GOAL ATTEMPTS													
Goals	0	3	0	0	0	4	0	0	0	4	0	0	0
Shots on target	1	15	0	3	0	7	4	0	0	14	0	1	0
Shots off target	2	12	1	4	0	12	4	3	12	14	0	0	0
Shooting accuracy %	33%	56%	0%	43%	0%	37%	50%	0%	0%	50%	0%	100%	0%
PASSING													
Goal assists	0	10	0	0	0	2	0	1	1	2	0	0	0
Long passes	2	82	8	9	0	13	93	171	44	12	0	0	33
Short passes	45	1340	62	153	0	447	209	663	395	450	1	0	156
PASS COMPLETION													
Own half %	75%	90%	65%	93%	0%	83%	82%	92%	82%	81%	0%	0%	88%
Opposition half %	76%	83%	57%	77%	0%	70%	60%	63%	68%	68%	0%	0%	66%
CROSSING													
Total crosses	4	30	8	4	0	69	11	2	3	8	0	1	8
Cross completion %	50%	43%	0%	0%	0%	29%	36%	100%	0%	38%	0%	0%	25%
DRIBBLING													
Dribbles & runs	9	141	7	22	0	74	29	45	18	33	0	1	18
Dribble completion %	67%	79%	86%	77%	0%	61%	86%	76%	56%	48%	0%	100%	61%
DEFENDING													
Tackles made	4	43	3	6	0	23	31	92	61	15	0	1	22
Tackles won %	25%	44%	0%	67%	0%	39%	65%	71%	61%	47%	0%	0%	55%
Blocks	0	4	3	0	0	2	6	37	9	2	0	0	4
Clearances	4	7	8	0	1	3	120	389	87	30	0	0	40
Interceptions	2	17	0	2	0	3	1	60	21	0	0	0	4
DISCIPLINE													
Fouls	2	15	0	6	0	17	10	13	21	58	0	0	4
Offside	0	11	0	4	0	24	1	0	0	23	0	0	0
Yellow cards	0	3	0	1	0	1	2	5	8	3	0	0	2
Red cards	0	0	0	0	0	0	0	0	0	0	0	0	0

GOALKEEPER NAME	START/ (SUB)	TIME ON PITCH	GOALS CONCEDED	MINS/GOALS CONCEDED	SAVES MADE	SAVES/ SHOTS
FORREST	1 (1)	119	3	39.7	4	57%
HISLOP	37	3301	50	66	194	80%

PLAYERS' STATISTICS

	KELLER	KITSON	LAMPARD	LAZARIDIS	LOMAS	MARGAS	MINTO	MONCUR	OMOYINMI	PEARCE	POTTS	RUDDOCK	SINCLAIR	WRIGHT	TOTAL	RANK
	17	13	38	11	30	3	14	6	0	33	11	27	36	20		
	4	4	0	4	0	0	1	8	3	0	8	0	0	2		
	1489	1200	3420	1021	2670	270	1242	691	31	2962	1062	2348	3169	1754		
	5	3	5	0	1	0	0	0	0	2	0	2	7	9	46*	10th
	10	9	34	1	7	0	0	3	0	8	0	9	16	25	167	=15th
	10	8	35	2	12	2	4	1	0	10	0	13	21	26	208	13th
	50%	53%	49%	33%	37%	0%	0%	75%	0%	44%	0%	41%	43%	49%	46%	14th
	1	3	4	1	2	0	0	0	0	2	0	0	5	3	37	6th
	40	5	170	30	159	23	95	53	0	105	48	250	111	37	1597	20th
	517	365	1415	314	1082	45	473	328	7	713	315	460	1138	463	11557	9th
	87%	74%	88%	84%	88%	85%	81%	92%	100%	91%	94%	86%	83%	84%	87%	13th
	71%	66%	72%	75%	73%	32%	65%	80%	60%	66%	73%	52%	68%	67%	70%	9th
	65	8	136	36	44	0	30	5	2	18	1	4	71	16	584	20th
	35%	0%	27%	39%	32%	0%	10%	0%	100%	6%	0%	25%	32%	31%	29%	9th
	69	6	79	82	63	3	50	30	4	46	7	3	183	57	1081	4th
	65%	67%	75%	78%	81%	100%	84%	80%	75%	76%	100%	100%	70%	53%	72%	7th
	43	14	141	51	96	14	42	46	1	60	38	68	136	40	1092	18th
	56%	57%	61%	57%	67%	50%	69%	61%	100%	55%	63%	71%	59%	45%	60%	15th
	5	0	14	5	15	3	10	4	0	38	8	40	22	0	231	3rd
	49	3	88	50	137	46	51	6	0	343	85	329	123	1	2019	12th
	20	2	29	8	15	1	11	6	1	33	10	31	19	5	303	16th
	17	18	42	9	36	0	23	21	0	33	13	39	28	53	480	=16th
	8	15	7	1	0	0	5	1	1	1	0	0	26	39	167	3rd
	3	2	4	2	4	0	2	8	0	4	4	8	7	8	81	=5th
	0	0	0	0	1	0	0	1	0	0	0	1	0	1	5	=4th

*including one own goal

CROSSES CAUGHT	CROSSES PUNCHED	CROSSES NOT CLAIMED	CATCH SUCCESS	THROWS/ SHORT KICKS	% COMPLETION	LONG KICKS	% COMPLETION
6	0	0	100%	15	100%	25	12%
117	30	10	95%	397	94%	855	37%

PLAYER OF THE SEASON

PLAYER	INDEX SCORE
SHAKA HISLOP	990
Frank Lampard	888
Rio Ferdinand	876
Eyal Berkovic	867
Trevor Sinclair	842
Marc Keller	818
Neil Ruddock	787
Steve Lomas	714
Ian Pearce	678
Ian Wright	664

Harry Redknapp reaped the full benefits of the Bosman ruling when he snapped up giant goalkeeper Shaka Hislop from Newcastle United.

The Hackney-born 'keeper relished a move back to London and the chance of regular first-team football – and it was an opportunity he was not about to waste.

Despite some obvious low points in his debut Hammers season – the sending-off at home to Leeds for one – Hislop will have fond memories of 1998–99. His commanding frame between the sticks was a major influence as West Ham climbed to fifth place in the Premiership.

The Hammers conceded four goals or more on eight occasions across the season – but Hislop still finished as the highest-placed Hammer in the Carling Opta Index. He kept the second-highest number of clean sheets in the league (15) behind Arsenal's David Seaman and was superb in such matches as the 1–0 win at Chelsea.

He was also kept very busy, making the most saves in the Premiership apart from Wimbledon's Neil Sullivan. While West Ham conceded four goals at home in consecutive matches against Arsenal and Sheffield Wednesday, they still won 16 games across the season – and Hislop can take much of the credit.

Frank Lampard was second in the West Ham top 10. Despite a mid-season dip in form, he saw more of the ball than any other Hammer and did enough to warrant a full England call-up.

Both he and Rio Ferdinand surely have plenty of England caps ahead of them, and Rio is third in the top 10 after a series of mature displays alongside Ian Pearce and Neil Ruddock.

But West Ham's lack of goals is also reflected in this table, with top scorer Ian Wright the only striker in the top 10.

FIVE OF THE BEST

After a superb eighth-place finish the previous season the Hammers finished fifth in 1998–99, an achievement founded once again on their excellent home form. At one stage, supporters were tentatively talking about a Champions League spot – and that may not be out of the question in 1999–2000 if Harry Redknapp continues to get the best from his talented squad.

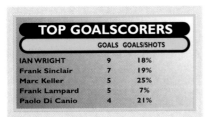

TOP GOALSCORERS	GOALS	GOALS/SHOTS
IAN WRIGHT	9	18%
Frank Sinclair	7	19%
Marc Keller	5	25%
Frank Lampard	5	7%
Paolo Di Canio	4	21%

Despite their superb top five finish, in truth the Hammers did not score as many goals as they would have liked. No one reached double figures in the Premiership, with Ian Wright ending as the club's top league scorer on nine goals, despite missing much of the campaign through injury. The midfield weighed in with plenty of strikes, while new arrival Paolo Di Canio made quite an impact when he signed late on in the season, scoring with more than one in five shots.

It was a below-par personal season by Frank Lampard's high standards, but the England under-21 international captain still finished as the club's best all-round midfielder. He and Israeli playmaker Eyal Berkovic both completed more than 1,200 passes, with Berkovic achieving an outstanding completion rate of 85%. Lomas, forced to sit out a large chunk of the campaign through injury, came close to breaking the 1,000 barrier himself, while Trevor Sinclair's completion rate is slightly lower because he tends to look for those defence-splitting through-balls.

TOP PASSERS	SUCC PASSES	COMPLETION
FRANK LAMPARD	1,251	79%
Eyal Berkovic	1,209	85%
Steve Lomas	988	80%
Trevor Sinclair	896	72%
Rio Ferdinand	696	83%

TOP TACKLERS	WON	SUCCESS
FRANK LAMPARD	86	61%
Trevor Sinclair	80	59%
Rio Ferdinand	65	71%
Steve Lomas	64	67%
Neil Ruddock	48	71%

Despite his mid-season dip in form, Frank Lampard was undoubtedly the Hammers' most effective holding midfielder, winning almost 90 challenges across the 1998–99 season. Defensive duo Rio Ferdinand and Neil Ruddock were the two most likely to win possession, with more than seven out of every 10 challenges successful. But when the back three failed to work as a unit, West Ham were always likely to concede goals; a fact exploited in 1998–99 by Manchester United, Charlton, Arsenal, Leeds (twice), Wimbledon, Sheffield Wednesday and Everton, who all scored four or more goals against them.

Ian Wright was quick to win over the West Ham fans with his enthusiasm – but the Premiership referees were less impressed by his physical approach, which earned him eight yellow cards and a sending-off for two more bookings at home to Leeds United, one of three Hammers to walk in that game. Neil Ruddock earned the same number of cards, getting sent off in the away match at Leeds. John Hartson committed the most fouls, despite leaving mid-season for Wimbledon. His combined stats for both clubs reveal he conceded more fouls than any other player in the league.

DISCIPLINE	POINTS	FOULS & CARDS
IAN WRIGHT	83	53F, 8Y, 1R
Neil Ruddock	69	39F, 8Y, 1R
John Hartson	67	58F, 3Y, 0R
Steve Lomas	54	36F, 4Y, 1R
Frank Lampard	54	42F, 4Y, 0R

ACTION	FERDINAND	FOE	HISLOP	KELLER	KITSSON	LAMPARD	LOMAS	MINTO	PEARCE	POTTS	RUDDOCK	SINCLAIR	TOTAL	CHELSEA
Time on pitch	90	90	90	86	90	90	90	90	90	4	90	90	990	990
GOALS														
Goal	-	-	-	1	1	-	-	-	-	-	-	-	-	-
Shot on target	-	1	-	-	-	2	-	-	1	-	1	1	3	6
Shot off target	-	-	-	-	-	1	-	-	1	-	-	-	3	8
Blocked shot	-	-	-	-	-	1	-	-	-	-	-	-	-	3
Own goal	-	-	-	-	-	-	-	-	-	-	-	-	-	-
PASSES														
Pass to own player	20	19	-	20	15	40	24	34	18	1	22	18	231	360
Pass to opposition	4	10	-	8	15	6	9	9	9	-	7	13	90	96
Cross to own player	-	-	-	3	-	1	1	1	-	-	-	1	5	7
Cross to opposition player	-	-	-	5	-	2	-	-	-	-	-	2	11	29
Goal assist	-	1	-	-	-	-	-	-	-	-	-	-	-	-
Pass completion %	83%	67%	0%	64%	50%	84%	73%	77%	64%	100%	76%	56%	70%	75%
TACKLES & CLEARANCES														
Tackle	-	6	-	4	-	4	2	4	3	-	2	2	27	23
Clearances, blocks and interceptions	21	9	-	4	-	5	4	4	4	-	17	2	70	38
DRIBBLES & RUNS														
Dribble ball retained	-	2	-	-	-	1	-	3	1	-	-	4	11	16
Dribbles ball lost	2	1	-	3	-	1	-	1	-	-	-	1	8	3
Dribble success %	0%	67%	0%	0%	0%	50%	0%	75%	100%	0%	0%	80%	58%	84%
DISCIPLINE														
Fouls	-	4	-	5	-	1	2	2	-	-	2	2	18	10
Penalty conceded	-	-	-	-	-	-	-	-	-	-	-	-	-	-
Free kick - offside	-	-	-	-	2	-	-	-	-	-	-	-	2	4
Yellow cards	-	1	-	1	-	-	-	-	-	-	-	-	2	2
Red cards	-	-	-	-	-	-	-	-	-	-	-	-	-	-
GOALKEEPERS														
Distribution to own player	-	-	33	-	-	-	-	-	-	-	-	-	33	25
Distribution to opposition player	-	-	17	-	-	-	-	-	-	-	-	-	17	8
Goalkeeper distribution%	0%	0%	66%	0%	0%	0%	0%	0%	0%	0%	0%	0%	66%	76%
Save	-	-	6	-	-	-	-	-	-	-	-	-	6	3
Ball caught	-	-	7	-	-	-	-	-	-	-	-	-	7	2
Ball dropped	-	-	-	-	-	-	-	-	-	-	-	-	-	-
Goal conceded	-	-	-	-	-	-	-	-	-	-	-	-	-	1

West Ham arrived at Stamford Bridge as underdogs. Despite losing at home to Manchester United in the FA Cup three days earlier, Gianluca Vialli's side were unbeaten on their own patch in the league, while West Ham had gone seven games without an away win.

March 13, 1999

0 – 1

**CHELSEA
WEST HAM UNITED**

Chelsea enjoyed plenty of possession in the early stages of the match, but West Ham were content to put 11 men behind the ball and stop the home side in the final third of the pitch. With Rio Ferdinand leading by example and Marc-Vivien Foe mopping up just in front of the defence, the Hammers cleared everything thrown at them and it took Chelsea 22 minutes to carve out their first real chance.

Tore Andre Flo put that opportunity just wide of Shaka Hislop's post, but a minute later the home side spurned another chance to press home their advantage. Frank Lampard – who had an otherwise excellent game – was caught dallying on the ball in his own penalty area. Roberto Di Matteo stole the ball from under his feet and forced Hislop into a good save.

This only strengthened West Ham's resolve, and although they continued to place the emphasis on containment they might have taken the lead in the 29th minute when Trevor Sinclair fired just over the Chelsea bar.

But Chelsea were still creating the better chances and Ferdinand was forced to make two crucial interventions, first deflecting Gianfranco Zola's volley wide of goal and then clearing Celestine Babayaro's cross-cum-shot off the line.

West Ham broke again in the 44th minute to serve Chelsea with a reminder that they were still in the match. Unfortunately, referee Stephen Lodge disallowed Foe's goal for pushing by Marc Keller.

With news coming through that both Arsenal and Manchester United were winning, Chelsea became increasingly desperate for a goal and pressed forward strongly in the second half.

This allowed West Ham more opportunities to break, and although they were indebted to Shaka Hislop for some fine saves they grabbed the winning goal with 15 minutes remaining.

Keller delivered a free kick to the far post and, although Foe was holding Babayaro, the referee allowed play to go on. Foe headed the ball into Kitson's path and, even though De Goey beat the ball out, it was clear that Kitson's shot had already crossed the line.

Chelsea's substitute Mikael Forssell should have equalized in the 85th minute, but he headed wide – and that was the home side's last real chance as West Ham held firm to become the only side to beat the Blues at Stamford Bridge in the Premiership.

Man of the match for West Ham with 2,200 points was Shaka Hislop. He made six saves and seven catches in the face of fierce pressure. Credit for the victory must go to Harry Redknapp for getting his tactics spot-on, but the real glory belonged to his players. They defended brilliantly, making more tackles, blocks, clearances and interceptions than Chelsea, and reduced the home side to just seven successful crosses.

ACTION	BERKOVIC	COLE	DI CANIO	FOE	HISLOP	LAMPARD	LOMAS	MINTO	PEARCE	POTTS	RUDDOCK	SINCLAIR	WRIGHT	TOTAL	DERBY
Time on pitch	90	20	90	90	90	90	70	90	90	18	90	90	72	990	990
GOALS															
Goal	1	–	1	–	–	–	–	–	–	–	–	–	–	5	5
Shot on target	–	–	1	1	–	–	–	–	–	–	–	–	–	4	5
Shot off target	–	–	1	–	–	1	–	–	–	–	–	–	–	3	3
Blocked shot	–	–	–	–	–	–	–	–	–	–	–	1	–	1	2
Own goal	–	–	–	–	–	–	–	–	–	–	–	–	–	–	–
PASSES															
Pass to own player	55	13	26	44	–	44	25	35	19	4	33	30	9	337	249
Pass to opposition	10	5	15	8	–	14	6	8	6	–	10	14	13	109	112
Cross to own player	2	–	3	–	–	–	2	–	–	–	–	–	4	4	1
Cross to opposition player	–	–	1	–	–	–	–	2	–	–	–	–	1	10	9
Goal assist	2	–	1	–	–	–	1	–	–	1	2	2	–	4	4
Pass completion %	82%	72%	61%	83%	0%	76%	82%	78%	76%	100%	77%	69%	39%	74%	67%
TACKLES & CLEARANCES															
Tackle	–	1	3	5	–	3	2	9	–	1	6	2	1	33	19
Clearances, blocks and interceptions	1	–	–	5	1	2	5	9	15	1	13	2	–	56	46
DRIBBLES & RUNS															
Dribble ball retained	5	–	6	–	–	3	–	2	–	–	5	–	–	21	20
Dribbles ball lost	3	–	3	–	–	–	–	–	–	–	–	–	–	6	13
Dribble success %	63%	0%	67%	0%	0%	100%	0%	100%	0%	0%	0%	100%	0%	78%	61%
DISCIPLINE															
Fouls	–	–	1	2	–	–	1	–	–	–	2	–	2	8	19
Penalty conceded	–	–	–	–	–	–	–	–	–	–	–	–	–	–	–
Free kick - offside	–	–	2	–	–	2	–	–	–	–	2	1	1	7	1
Yellow cards	–	–	–	–	–	–	–	–	–	–	–	–	–	–	–
Red cards	–	–	–	–	–	–	–	–	–	–	–	–	–	–	–
GOALKEEPERS															
Distribution to own player	–	–	–	–	20	–	–	–	–	–	–	–	–	20	18
Distribution to opposition player	–	–	–	–	13	–	–	–	–	–	–	–	–	13	10
Goalkeeper distribution %	0%	0%	0%	0%	61%	0%	0%	0%	0%	0%	0%	0%	0%	61%	64%
Save	–	–	–	–	5	–	–	–	–	–	–	–	–	5	4
Ball caught	–	–	–	–	2	–	–	–	–	–	–	–	–	2	–
Ball dropped	–	–	–	–	1	–	–	–	–	–	–	–	–	1	–
Goal conceded	–	–	–	–	–	–	–	–	–	–	–	–	–	–	5

Upton Park played host to two teams who, at that stage, both had European ambitions. West Ham and Derby had been crowd-pleasing sides who were looking to break into the Carling Premiership's top five.

The first 18 minutes produced some good passing football, with signs that there would be goals to come. Then the introduction of Ian Wright immediately sparked West Ham into life – and a minute later Trevor Sinclair set Paolo Di Canio away down the right-hand side. The Italian took the ball inside on to his left foot and aimed a curler for the far corner, which deflected off the head of Spencer Prior and into the net at the near post, leaving Russell Hoult no chance.

Di Canio volleyed narrowly over in the 25th minute, but made amends two minutes later when he set up Eyal Berkovic for West Ham's second goal of the afternoon. Taking a long pass from Marc-Vivien Foe and breaking into the penalty area, Di Canio cut inside Prior before laying the ball off to Berkovic, who side-footed between two defenders and past Hoult for 2–0.

The first half ended with West Ham on top, and looking capable of scoring more goals in the second. They did not disappoint.

Derby upped the pressure, with a Wanchope volley bringing the best out of Hislop. But ten minutes into the second half, West Ham made it 3–0. Frank Lampard's swerving, dipping 30-yarder was only parried by Hoult and Ian Wright pounced on to the rebound to make the game safe for the Hammers.

On 63 minutes, the home side made it four. Sinclair skipped past Wanchope, Lars Bohinen and Stefan Schnoor before floating a deep, looping cross to the back post, where Neil Ruddock arrived to nod in from two yards out.

The Upton Park faithful were in dreamland five minutes later when Steve Lomas crossed from wide on the right – and Sinclair's diving header at the near post gave Hoult no chance whatsoever.

It was a game of great goals, but Derby scored the best 12 minutes from the end. A superb 14-pass move was finished off when Dean Sturridge back-heeled the ball to Wanchope, who skipped past Ian Pearce, rounded Hislop and fired home from an incredibly acute angle.

Sturridge should have scored Derby's second when he found himself clean through with just Hislop to beat: but, in keeping with Derby's day, his shot went a yard wide.

West Ham's dominance in the game is reflected in the passing statistics. The Hammers completed 74% of their 446 passes compared to Derby's 67% from 361 balls. West Ham also had the upper hand when dribbling the ball with a 78% success rate, compared to 61% from Derby.

Both teams had plenty of shots at goal. Derby scored once and forced Hislop into five saves, while the Hammers scored five goals and hit four more efforts on target.

West Ham proved that, on their day, they can match anybody in the Premiership, and with players like Wright, Di Canio, Lampard and Sinclair the potential for goals is always there.

WIMBLEDON 1998–99

Back Row (Left to right): Marcus Gayle, Carl Cort, Neil Sullivan, Mick Harford (Coach), Paul Heald, Dean Blackwell, Ben Thatcher.
Middle Row: Stuart Murdoch (Goalkeeping Coach), Dave Kemp (Assistant Manager), Duncan Jupp, Mark Kennedy, Efan Ekoku,
Jon Goodman, Carl Leaburn, Andy Roberts, Damien Francis, Brian McAllister, Andy Clarke, Steve Allen (Physiotherapist).
Front Row: Jason Euell, Chris Perry, Stewart Castledine, Kenny Cunningham, Robbie Earle,
Joe Kinnear (Manager – no longer at club), Neal Ardley, Michael Hughes, Alan Kimble, Peter Fear, Ceri Hughes.

WIMBLEDON

ADDRESS

Selhurst Park Stadium,
South Norwood, London SE25 6PY

CONTACT NUMBERS

Telephone: 0181 771 2233
Fax: 0181 768 0641
Ticket Office: 0181 771 8841
24hr Information: 09068 121175
Club Superstore: 0181 768 6100
e-mail: reg@wimbledonfc.bdx.co.uk
Website: www.wimbledonfc.co.uk

SPONSORS

Tiny

FANZINES

Five All
Go Jo Go!
Yidaho!
Tenants Extra
Sour Grapes
Hoof The Ball Up
Wandering Hans

KEY PERSONNEL

Governing Partner: S G Hammam
Partners: K I Røkke, B R Gjelsten
Chairman: S G Reed
Deputy Chairman: J H Lelliott
Directors: S G Reed, J H Lelliott,
J P Storetvedt, P E Cork,
P R Lloyd Cooper,
N N Hammam, P J B Miller
Chief Executive: D Barnard
Club Secretary: S A Rooke
Manager: Joe Kinnear, replaced by
Egil Olsen, June 1999

COLOURS

Home: Dark blue shirts,
shorts and stockings
Away: Red shirts,
shorts and stockings

NICKNAME

The Dons

20 FACTS

1 Wimbledon was formed in 1889 by former pupils of the Old Central School. The Wimbledon Old Centrals dropped the second half of their name in 1905.

2 The Crazy Gang have been in the top flight since the 1986–87 season. Their best finishes came in 1986–87 and 1993–4 when they ended the season sixth.

3 Wimbledon's finest hour came in the 1988 FA Cup final. Just 11 years after being elected to the league, the Dons beat an outstanding Liverpool side 1–0 to lift their only major trophy.

4 Their best finishes in the Football League Cup came in 1996–97 and 1998–99, when they reached the semi-finals.

5 Dave Beasant is the only goalkeeper to captain an FA Cup-winning team. He was also the first goalkeeper to save a penalty in a cup final.

6 Wimbledon were promoted from the Southern League to Division One in nine years between 1977 and 1986, including three promotions in four seasons between 1983 and 1986. This makes them the fastest risers from non-league football to the First Division in the history of the English game.

7 Only two players have appeared for England while playing for Wimbledon – John Fashanu and Warren Barton.

8 Striker Alan Cork holds the appearance record for Wimbledon (510).

9 Cork is the club's all-time leading goalscorer with 167 goals. He also holds the record for the most goals scored in a single season by a Wimbledon player – 33 in 1983–84.

10 Sam Hammam arrived in 1979 after his chauffeur recommended buying a football club as a shrewd investment. Hammam sold his controlling interest in the club for £26 million in 1997 but remains a governing partner.

11 Wimbledon's home game against Everton in January 1993 was watched by a crowd of 3,039, the lowest in the history of the Premiership.

12 Everton also inflicted Wimbledon's record defeat, 8–0 in a 1978 second-round League Cup clash.

13 The club's record league victory is 6–0 against Newport County in a Division Three match in 1983. They beat Windsor and Eton 7–2 in the first round of the FA Cup in 1980.

14 When Wimbledon joined the Athenian League in 1920 they fielded big-band leader Billy Cotton in their line-up.

15 Former Prime Minister Margaret Thatcher once said: "If we can sell Newcastle Brown to Japan and Wimbledon can make it to the First Division, there is no achievement beyond our reach".

16 Wimbledon finished 16th in the 1998–99 Premiership. Their league record was:

Pld	W	D	L	F	A	Pts
38	10	12	16	40	63	42

17 In the 1998–99 FA Cup, the Dons beat Manchester City 1–0 at Selhurst Park and then drew 1–1 with Tottenham Hotspur before being eliminated 3–0 in the replay at White Hart Lane.

18 Wimbledon were also knocked out of the Worthington Cup by Spurs. They defeated Portsmouth 5–3 on aggregate, then beat Birmingham City 2–1 at St Andrews. Bolton Wanderers were beaten 2–1 at the Reebok Stadium and Chelsea were defeated by the same score at Selhurst Park. A 0–0 draw was secured in the away leg of the semi-final before the side lost 1–0 in the home leg.

19 The top goalscorer in all competitions for Wimbledon was Marcus Gayle with 11 goals.

20 Wimbledon's disciplinary record was the third-best in the Premiership. They committed 480 fouls, earned 59 yellow cards and suffered just one red card.

SEASON REVIEW

If Wimbledon's self-styled "governor" Sam Hammam ever needed proof of Joe Kinnear's inspirational impact on the Dons, he got it in the final third of a traumatic 1998–99 season.

Kinnear's mild heart attack ahead of the match at Sheffield Wednesday on March 3 prompted an abysmal run of form on the pitch which could well have resulted in relegation, had Wimbledon not been sixth in the table at the start of the slump.

The side began the season in typically cavalier fashion, securing a 3–1 London derby win over Kinnear's old club Tottenham – a result which hastened the departure of Spurs boss Christian Gross. Draws with Derby County and Leeds United followed before the Dons pulled off one of the most remarkable results in the history of the Carling Premiership.

Three-nil down at West Ham, Wimbledon stunned the home crowd with an aerial bombardment and ran out 4–3 winners. It remains the only time that an away team has achieved that feat since the Premiership was formed.

By the time the side had disposed of Portsmouth in the Worthington Cup and beaten Sheffield Wednesday at Selhurst Park, the Dons were fourth in the table, confounding the numerous pundits who had tipped them for the drop.

None of the next five league games produced a win, but victory at Birmingham secured further progress in the Worthington Cup and heavy defeats against title-chasing Chelsea and Manchester United were offset by a morale-boosting victory over Arsenal in November.

The Worthington Cup quarter-final was a thrilling London derby at Selhurst Park against holders Chelsea, who bucked the trend among the top clubs by fielding a full-strength line-up. The Dons performed magnificently and won 2–1 – and the obvious boost that gave the south Londoners resulted in three victories in the next four league games.

The New Year brought further successes over a resurgent Manchester City in the FA Cup third round and Derby County in the league – a result which lifted the Dons back into the top six.

Five of the next seven games were against Tottenham, thanks to the two clubs being drawn together in both cup competitions. The atmosphere in these games became progressively more belligerent after sections of the media focused exclusively on the skills of Spurs' winger David Ginola, even though the first three meetings were drawn.

> ## "I can't wait to get back"
> ### Joe Kinnear

Kinnear, a tough-tackling right-back in his playing days, preferred to note the performances of Kenny Cunningham, who had kept the Frenchman quiet in most of the games. He dubbed BBC's *Match of the Day* "The Muppet Show" after the studio guests had pored at length over Ginola's performance in the FA Cup fourth round meeting on January 23.

Tottenham had the last laugh, however, triumphing in both ties including the Worthington Cup semi-final. Wimbledon proverbially rolled up their sleeves and looked for a top-five finish as an alternative route into Europe. But Kinnear's illness followed just three games later and, although the players won that night in a typically defiant gesture, the side were destined never to win again in 1998–99.

In the space of just 10 games, the club nose-dived from sixth to 16th, scoring just nine goals in their last 11 matches.

Carling Opta's team statistics show that the Dons were the least successful passers in the league, possibly a conseqence of their direct style of play. They also attempted the fewest dribbles and runs and the second-fewest tackles, but their stubborn defence made the most clearances in the Premiership and fourth-highest number of blocks.

Kinnear will not be back in the hot seat for the 1999–2000 campaign after deciding to move on from Selhurst Park, but new boss Egil Olsen will hope to uphold the side's rather clichéd "party-poopers" reputation.

WIMBLEDON

DATE	OPPONENT	SCORE	ATT.	AINSWORTH	ARDLEY	BLACKWELL	CASTLEDINE	CORT	CUNNINGHAM	EARLE	EKOKU	EUELL	FEAR
15.8.98	Tottenham H	3–1	23,031	–	82	90	–	–	90	90¹	90²	71	s8
22.8.98	Derby Co A	0–0	25,710	–	89	90	–	–	90□	90	86	54	–
29.8.98	Leeds Utd H	1–1	16,473	–	66	90	–	–	90	90	40	90□	–
9.9.98	West Ham A	4–3	24,601	–	–	–	–	–	90□	75	s15¹	90¹	–
12.9.98	Aston Villa A	0–2	32,959	–	–	–	–	–	90	90	s11	90	s1
19.9.98	Sheff Wed H	2–1	13,163	–	–	–	–	s1	90	89	s18	90²	–
27.9.98	Leicester A	1–1	17,725	–	s4	–	–	s40	90	86¹	50	90	–
3.10.98	Everton H	1–2	16,054	–	–	–	–	–	90	90	–	90	–
17.10.98	Man Utd A	1–5	55,265	–	s45	90	–	–	90	90	–	90¹	–
24.10.98	Middlesbro' H	2–2	14,114	–	–	90	–	s18	90	90	–	72	–
31.10.98	Blackburn H	1–1	12,526	–	73	73	–	s17	90	90¹	–	90	–
7.11.98	Nott'm For A	1–0	21,362	90	s31	–	–	–	90	90	–	90□	–
14.11.98	Chelsea A	0–3	34,800	90	–	s23	–	–	90	90□	s23	–	–
21.11.98	Arsenal H	1–0	26,003	73	s17	90	–	–	90	90	s17¹	90	–
28.11.98	Newcastle A	1–3	36,623	77	s45	90	–	–	90	90	s45	90	–
5.12.98	Coventry H	2–1	11,717	s44	90	90	–	–	90	90	90	90²□	–
13.12.98	Liverpool H	1–0	26,080	–	90	90	–	–	90	90¹	s28	90	–
19.12.98	Southampton A	1–3	14,354	–	80	90	–	s10	90	90	85	–	–
26.12.98	Charlton H	2–1	19,106	–	81	45	–	s9	90	90	–	90¹	–
29.12.98	Leeds Utd A	2–2	39,901	–	90	–	–	s17¹	90	90¹	–	90□	–
9.1.99	Derby Co H	2–1	12,732	–	–	90	–	72	–	–	s10	90¹	–
16.1.99	Tottenham A	0–0	32,422	–	75	90	–	–	90□	90	s15	–	–
30.1.99	West Ham H	0–0	23,035	–	–	–	–	–	90	90	69	90	–
8.2.99	Charlton A	0–2	20,002	–	90	90	–	62	90	–	–	85	–
21.2.99	Aston Villa H	0–0	15,582	–	90	90	–	–	90	90	88	90	–
27.2.99	Everton A	1–1	32,574	–	s58	90	–	–	90	90	90¹	32	–
3.3.99	Sheff Wed A	2–1	24,116	–	80	90	–	–	90	90	90¹	s10	–
6.3.99	Leicester H	0–1	11,081	–	–	–	–	–	90	90	56	90	–
13.3.99	Nott'm For H	1–3	12,149	–	90	–	–	–	90	90	s31	s18	–
20.3.99	Blackburn A	1–3	21,754	–	45	90	–	–	90	90	s45□	90¹	–
3.4.99	Man Utd H	1–1	26,121	–	s9	90	–	s22□	–	90	–	90¹	–
5.4.99	Middlesbro' A	1–3	33,999	45	83	90	–	s24¹	–	90	–	90	–
11.4.99	Chelsea H	1–2	21,577	s45	–	90	–	s20	90	–	–	90	–
19.4.99	Arsenal A	1–5	37,982	s1	–	90	74	90¹	90	90	–	89	–
24.4.99	Newcastle H	1–1	21,325	–	–	90	–	90	90	90□	–	90	–
1.5.99	Coventry A	1–2	21,198	–	–	90	–	–	90	90	–	90	–
8.5.99	Southampton H	0–2	24,068	–	–	90	–	90	90	90	–	–	–
16.5.99	Liverpool A	0–3	41,902	–	–	90	–	70	90	90	–	–	–

□ Yellow card, ■ Red card, s Substitute, 90³ Goals scored

1998–99 PREMIERSHIP APPEARANCES

GAYLE	GOODMAN	HARTSON	C HUGHES	M HUGHES	JUPP	KENNEDY	KIMBLE	LEABURN	PERRY	ROBERTS	SULLIVAN	THATCHER	TOTAL
s19	–	–	–	83□	s7	–	90	–	90	90	90	–	990
s36	–	–	–	90	s1	s4	90□	–	90	90	90□	–	990
s24	–	–	–	90¹	–	–	90	s50	90□	90□	90	–	990
90²	–	–	–	90□	90□	–	90	90	90	90□	90□	–	990
79	–	–	–	83	–	s7	90	44■	90□	89	90	90	944
72	–	–	–	90	s1	–	90	89	90	90	90	90	990
90□	–	–	–	90	–	–	90□	–	90	90	90	90	990
84	–	–	–	90□	–	s6	90	90	90	90¹	90	90	990
s45	–	–	–	90	–	–	45	45	90	90□	90	90	990
90²	–	–	–	90	–	s18	–	72	90	90	90	90	990
90	–	–	–	90□	–	s5	s17	85	90	–	90	90	990
90¹	–	–	–	59	–	–	90	73	90	s17	90	90	990
67	–	–	–	67□	–	90	67	s23	90	90□	90	90	990
73	–	–	–	90	–	–	–	90□	90□	–	90	90□	990
90¹	–	–	–	–	–	45	–	45	90	s13	90	90	990
46	–	–	–	90	–	–	–	–	90	–	90□	90	990
77	–	–	–	90	–	–	–	62	90	s13	90	90	990
90¹	–	–	s45	90	–	s5	–	–	90□	45	90	90□	990
90	–	–	–	90¹□	–	–	s45	90	90	–	90□	90□	990
90	–	–	–	90	–	s28	62□	73	90	–	90	90	990
90	–	–	80□	88	–	s2	90	s18	90□	90¹	90	90	990
75	–	85□	–	90	–	s15	–	s5	90	90□	90	90	990
–	–	90□	90	81	–	s9	90	s21	90	–	90	90	990
–	s5	90	s28□	–	–	90	–	–	90	90	90	90	990
90	–	–	–	–	–	–	s65	s2	90□	90	90	25	990
90	–	–	–	90	–	–	–	–	90	90□	90	90□	990
90¹	–	–	s10	80	–	–	90	–	90	90	90	–	990
90	–	s34	s14□	76	–	–	90	–	90	90	90	90	990
90¹	–	90	–	s18	–	72	90	–	59	72	90	90	990
90	–	45	s45	90	–	–	90	–	–	–	90	90□	990
90	–	68	83	90	–	–	81	–	90	s7	90	90	990
90	–	66	90	s7	–	–	–	–	90	s45	90	90	990
90¹	–	70	90	45□	–	–	–	s15	90	90□	90	75	990
90	–	s16	90□	–	–	–	90	–	–	–	90	90□	990
90	–	75¹	90□	–	90	–	s15	–	–	–	90	90□	990
90	–	90¹	54	–	90□	90	–	s36	–	–	90	90□	990
–	–	90	–	–	–	90	90	90	90	90□	90	–	990
90	–	90	s20	–	–	90	90	–	90	90□	90	–	990

THE MANAGER

JOE KINNEAR

Football took a back seat for Joe Kinnear on Monday, March 3, when the Wimbledon boss suffered a minor heart attack before his side's clash with Sheffield Wednesday at Hillsborough. It kept the highly-respected Kinnear away from Selhurst Park for the rest of the season.

The 52-year-old was appointed manager of the Crazy Gang in January 1992, consistently beating the odds to keep Wimbledon in the top flight.

In his playing days, Kinnear was an acclaimed right-back, making 25 appearances for the Republic of Ireland. He spent 10 years at Tottenham Hotspur before moving to Brighton for one season.

During Wimbledon's series of five clashes with his old club Spurs in the league and two cup competitions, Kinnear spoke out over the media attention paid to Spurs' French winger David Ginola. But that is typical of a man never afraid to express emotion, and the Dons clearly missed his influence in the final third of the season.

On June 1, Joe Kinnear announced his intention to move on from Wimbledon and pursue his career at another club. Egil Olsen, the former coach of Norway, was appointed in his place.

LEAGUE POSITION

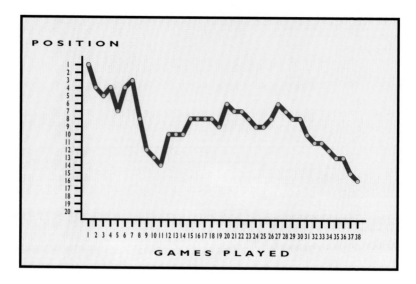

THE GOALS

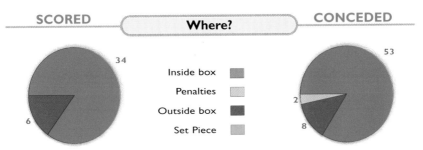

SCORED — Where? — CONCEDED

Legend: Inside box · Penalties · Outside box · Set Piece

Scored: 34, 6
Conceded: 53, 2, 8

Wimbledon were the only Premiership side to go through the 1998–99 league season without scoring a penalty. The Dons also failed to strike the back of the net from a direct free kick and scored 85% of their 40 goals from close range.

Inside their own penalty box, Wimbledon gave too many chances to their opponents, conceding 55 goals inside 18 yards. The Dons prevented any set-piece goals but let in eight strikes from distance.

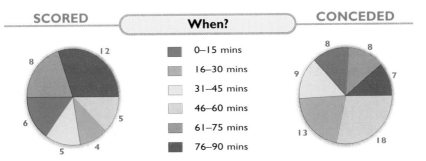

SCORED — When? — CONCEDED

Legend: 0–15 mins · 16–30 mins · 31–45 mins · 46–60 mins · 61–75 mins · 76–90 mins

Scored: 12, 8, 6, 5, 4, 5
Conceded: 8, 8, 9, 7, 13, 18

Wimbledon found their scoring boots in the final half-hour of matches, netting 50% of all efforts from 60 minutes onwards. In fact the Dons grabbed 30% of all goals in the last 15 minutes, the highest proportion of any Premiership side in this period. Immediately after the break, the Selhurst Park outfit struggled. They scored just five times and conceded a staggering 18 efforts – but their achievements in the last half-hour made up for this.

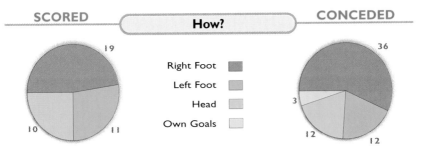

SCORED — How? — CONCEDED

Legend: Right Foot · Left Foot · Head · Own Goals

Scored: 19, 10, 11
Conceded: 36, 3, 12, 12

In keeping with their reputation, Wimbledon grabbed a quarter of all goals via the aerial approach. Marcus Gayle scored four of these headers from his personal tally of 10 strikes. Some shoddy defending saw them concede three own-goals, Ben Thatcher being responsible for two of them. Only Nottingham Forest were more susceptible to right-foot shots, as the Dons let in 36 goals in this way, 57.1% of their total conceded.

WIMBLEDON

	AINSWORTH	ARDLEY	BLACKWELL	CASTLEDINE	CORT	CUNNINGHAM	EARLE	EKOKU	EUELL	FEAR
APPEARANCE										
Start	5	16	27	1	6	35	35	11	31	0
Sub	3	7	1	0	10	0	0	11	2	2
Minutes on pitch	465	1503	2391	74	652	3150	3130	1092	2681	9
GOAL ATTEMPTS										
Goals	0	0	0	0	3	0	5	6	10	0
Shots on target	1	5	0	0	5	1	23	15	30	0
Shots off target	5	6	2	0	6	3	26	9	35	0
Shooting accuracy	17%	45%	0%	0%	45%	25%	47%	63%	46%	0%
PASSING										
Goal assists	1	1	0	0	0	1	1	0	2	0
Long passes	12	114	78	0	6	252	80	13	92	1
Short passes	100	493	315	8	255	806	746	349	831	6
PASS COMPLETION										
Own half %	77%	79%	80%	20%	87%	82%	82%	77%	81%	100%
Opposition half %	41%	65%	53%	100%	74%	67%	68%	72%	65%	83%
CROSSING										
Total crosses	18	144	3	0	11	119	8	8	21	0
Cross completion %	39%	23%	33%	0%	18%	18%	13%	13%	14%	0%
DRIBBLING										
Dribbles & runs	39	38	10	0	19	23	28	33	90	0
Dribble completion %	56%	71%	100%	0%	63%	74%	71%	52%	59%	0%
DEFENDING										
Tackles made	10	32	103	2	12	105	93	33	112	2
Tackles won %	60%	63%	71%	0%	42%	59%	70%	55%	59%	50%
Blocks	0	2	27	4	1	31	11	1	8	0
Clearances	9	38	359	5	11	318	132	7	61	0
Interceptions	1	7	40	1	3	28	18	4	26	0
DISCIPLINE										
Fouls	5	24	9	2	17	26	24	34	41	1
Offside	4	4	0	0	9	1	10	23	19	0
Yellow cards	0	0	0	0	1	3	2	1	4	0
Red cards	0	0	0	0	0	0	0	0	0	0

GOALKEEPER NAME	START/ (SUB)	TIME ON PITCH	GOALS CONCEDED	MINS/GOALS CONCEDED	SAVES MADE	SAVES/ SHOTS
SULLIVAN	38	3420	63	54.3	203	76%

PLAYERS' STATISTICS

	GAYLE	GOODMAN	HARTSON	C HUGHES	M HUGHES	JUPP	KENNEDY	KIMBLE	LEABURN	PERRY	ROBERTS	THATCHER	TOTAL	RANK
	31	0	12	8	28	3	7	22	14	34	23	31		
	4	1	2	6	2	3	10	4	8	0	5	0		
	2767	5	999	829	2397	279	666	2017	1208	3029	2101	2710		
	10	0	2	0	2	0	0	0	0	0	2	0	40	=14th
	30	0	11	4	9	1	4	3	6	5	4	1	158	=18th
	32	0	9	1	25	0	4	5	10	5	4	0	187	20th
	48%	0%	55%	80%	26%	100%	50%	38%	38%	50%	50%	100%	46%	8th
	9	0	1	1	6	1	1	3	1	0	1	1	31	10th
	30	0	8	55	147	31	22	357	1	120	119	258	1796	14th
	957	1	324	216	874	53	184	433	461	353	682	459	8906	20th
	79%	0%	78%	85%	86%	75%	89%	81%	77%	83%	86%	86%	82%	20th
	60%	100%	67%	63%	77%	70%	69%	54%	73%	52%	67%	55%	65%	20th
	44	0	4	46	135	8	59	115	1	1	26	38	809	6th
	9%	0%	0%	33%	33%	50%	37%	39%	0%	0%	23%	29%	27%	14th
	67	0	15	13	131	3	34	30	3	3	18	21	618	20th
	61%	0%	67%	62%	75%	67%	56%	93%	67%	100%	78%	81%	68%	17th
	16	0	12	37	58	8	16	71	15	133	79	121	1070	19th
	81%	0%	67%	51%	59%	50%	63%	59%	47%	70%	75%	69%	64%	2nd
	5	0	0	7	2	1	2	17	2	51	19	33	227	4th
	60	0	10	31	30	18	13	149	5	456	118	351	2223	1st
	7	0	1	8	11	2	3	17	2	60	17	35	292	18th
	32	1	48	21	20	9	3	11	34	36	47	35	480	=16th
	43	1	14	0	6	0	2	0	9	0	0	1	146	6th
	1	0	2	5	7	2	0	3	1	6	9	8	59	=16th
	0	0	0	0	0	0	0	0	1	0	0	0	1	=17th

CROSSES CAUGHT	CROSSES PUNCHED	CROSSES NOT CLAIMED	CATCH SUCCESS	THROWS/ SHORT KICKS	% COMPLETION	LONG KICKS	% COMPLETION
125	15	7	98%	143	90%	1404	44%

PLAYER OF THE SEASON

PLAYER	INDEX SCORE
NEIL SULLIVAN	896
Chris Perry	870
Jason Euell	863
Dean Blackwell	858
Ben Thatcher	782
Kenny Cunningham	754
Alan Kimble	733
Marcus Gayle	705
Michael Hughes	671
Robbie Earle	667

Patrolling the threadbare penalty areas of arguably the most treacherous pitch in the Premiership is not a job for a faint-hearted goalkeeper. Fortunately for Wimbledon, first-choice Scottish international Neil Sullivan had an excellent season at Selhurst Park, making more saves than any other goalkeeper in the league.

He ended a difficult season for the Dons as the highest-rated Wimbledon player in the Carling Opta Season Index, with an average score of 896 points across the 1998–99 season. At one stage, when the Dons were riding high in the top five, his average score was in four figures. But as the Crazy Gang's form slumped in the final third of the season, so Sully's scores too started to drop.

It is probably fair to say he did not always receive adequate protection from his back four, but the dependable Chris Perry, adored by the Dons faithful, finished as the club's second-highest rated player, with an average score of 870 points per match.

Jason Euell, deployed in both midfield and striking roles in 1998–99, finished the season as the club's joint-top league scorer with 10 goals. The skilful youngster is without doubt one of Wimbledon's biggest stars of the future and averaged 863 points a game to finish third in the top 10.

Dean Blackwell, the Premiership's cleanest player according to Carling Opta, finished fourth after an accomplished season in the Dons' back four. Full-backs Ben Thatcher, Kenny Cunningham and Alan Kimble all ended up higher than the other joint-top scorer, Marcus Gayle, who tended to see a lot less of the ball than many of his team-mates.

Consistent performers Michael Hughes and Robbie Earle, whose experience was vital in the Dons' excellent early-season run, also figured; but there was no room for striker Efan Ekoku or the club's prolific crosser Neal Ardley.

FIVE OF THE BEST

As usual, the Dons were hotly-tipped for relegation at the start of 1998–99 — and as usual, they took great delight in soaring up the table. But with manager Joe Kinnear suffering a heart attack at the start of March, the side slumped from sixth to 16th by the end of the campaign, losing nine of their last 11 matches.

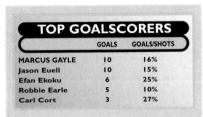

TOP GOALSCORERS	GOALS	GOALS/SHOTS
MARCUS GAYLE	10	16%
Jason Euell	10	15%
Efan Ekoku	6	25%
Robbie Earle	5	10%
Carl Cort	3	27%

It was a season of two halves for Wimbledon's goalscorers. 1998 saw Marcus Gayle and Jason Euell running riot as the Dons pushed up the top 10. But after the New Year the side suffered a terrible goal drought, failing to score in four league games and finding the net just once in eight matches in all competitions. Wantaway front man Efan Ekoku and big Carl Cort finished with impressive strike rates, but it was the goals of the two leading scorers which helped keep Wimbledon's heads above water.

Irish wide man Michael Hughes continued to impress down the left flank, completing 33% of his 135 crosses. He was also the club's top passer, with more passes and a higher completion rate than any of his team-mates. Wimbledon's direct approach meant they were more likely to give the ball away than many other sides — and the team finished the season with comfortably the league's lowest pass completion percentage (68%).

TOP PASSERS	SUCC PASSES	COMPLETION
MICHAEL HUGHES	802	79%
Kenny Cunningham	763	72%
Jason Euell	621	67%
Robbie Earle	592	72%
Andy Roberts	583	73%

TOP TACKLERS	WON	SUCCESS
CHRIS PERRY	93	70%
Ben Thatcher	83	69%
Dean Blackwell	73	71%
Jason Euell	66	59%
Robbie Earle	65	70%

Wimbledon centre-back Chris Perry did not enjoy the most consistent of seasons, but still finished as the club's most prolific tackler. He fell just short of 100 successful tackles, with possession reclaimed 70% of the time. Under-rated defender Dean Blackwell, who was confirmed as the league's cleanest player with just nine fouls conceded all season, won an even greater proportion of his challenges, while Ben Thatcher, Jason Euell and experienced midfielder Robbie Earle also figure in the top five.

Midfielder Andy Roberts was released by Wimbledon at the end of the season after struggling to maintain a regular first-team spot at Selhurst Park. That did not stop him amassing the club's worst disciplinary record, with nine bookings accrued. That statistic, though, is put into perspective by the fact that Wimbledon finished 1998–99 with the third best discipline stats in the Premiership behind Sheffield Wednesday and Leicester City, a fact which belies the Dons' physical approach to life in the Carling Premiership.

DISCIPLINE	POINTS	FOULS & CARDS
ANDY ROBERTS	74	47F, 9Y, 0R
Ben Thatcher	59	35F, 8Y, 0R
John Hartson	54	48F, 2Y, 0R
Chris Perry	54	36F, 6Y, 0R
Jason Euell	53	41F, 4Y, 0R

ACTION	CUNNINGHAM	EARLE	EKOKU	EUELL	GAYLE	M HUGHES	JUPP	KIMBLE	LEABURN	PERRY	ROBERTS	SULLIVAN	TOTAL	WEST HAM
Time on pitch	90	75	15	90	90	90	90	90	90	90	90	90	990	990
GOALS														
Goal	–	–	1	–	2	–	–	–	–	–	–	–	4	3
Shot on target	–	1	–	1	1	–	–	–	–	2	–	–	5	8
Shot off target	–	1	–	4	1	2	–	–	1	–	1	–	10	6
Blocked shot	–	–	–	–	–	1	–	–	–	–	–	–	1	5
Own goal	–	–	–	–	–	–	–	–	–	–	–	–	–	–
PASSES														
Pass to own player	25	21	7	28	22	40	31	34	25	15	24	–	272	256
Pass to opposition	3	2	2	11	6	9	8	19	13	8	14	–	95	98
Cross to own player	–	–	–	–	3	3	–	4	–	–	–	–	8	4
Cross to opposition player	–	–	–	–	2	5	1	3	–	1	1	–	12	10
Goal assist	–	–	–	1	–	–	–	–	–	–	–	–	3	2
Pass completion %	89%	91%	78%	73%	74%	75%	78%	64%	66%	65%	62%	0%	73%	71%
TACKLES & CLEARANCES														
Tackle	3	1	1	1	–	3	2	2	–	5	2	–	20	20
Clearances, blocks and interceptions	9	–	2	–	–	1	2	2	1	10	3	–	30	35
DRIBBLES & RUNS														
Dribble ball retained	–	–	–	–	3	1	1	1	–	–	1	–	7	17
Dribbles ball lost	–	–	–	–	–	–	–	–	–	–	–	–	1	2
Dribble success %	0%	0%	0%	0%	100%	100%	100%	100%	0%	0%	100%	0%	88%	89%
DISCIPLINE														
Fouls	2	2	1	3	–	–	3	1	1	2	–	–	16	20
Penalty conceded	–	–	–	–	–	–	–	–	–	–	–	–	–	–
Free kick - offside	–	–	–	–	–	–	–	–	–	–	–	–	–	3
Yellow cards	1	1	–	–	–	–	1	–	–	–	–	–	5	1
Red cards	–	–	–	–	–	–	–	–	–	–	–	–	–	–
GOALKEEPERS														
Distribution to own player	–	–	–	–	–	–	–	–	–	–	–	26	26	21
Distribution to opposition player	–	–	–	–	–	–	–	–	–	–	–	14	14	15
Goalkeeper distribution%	–	–	–	–	–	–	–	–	–	–	–	65%	65%	58%
Save	–	–	–	–	–	–	–	–	–	–	–	6	6	5
Ball caught	–	–	–	–	–	–	–	–	–	–	–	2	2	6
Ball dropped	–	–	–	–	–	–	–	–	–	–	–	–	–	2
Goal conceded	–	–	–	–	–	–	–	–	–	–	–	3	3	4

Wimbledon continue to confound their critics in the Premiership and upset the odds supposedly stacked against them — and this thrilling fight-back at Upton Park showed the Dons at their battling best. Both sides were unbeaten in the league, but when the Hammers went 3–0 up in 27 minutes Wimbledon looked sure to lose. It took a stunning display of blitzkrieg counter-attacking from the Dons to snatch an unlikely victory.

September 9, 1998

3–4

WEST HAM UNITED
WIMBLEDON

The Ian Wright-John Hartson partnership started the ball rolling for West Ham as early as the seventh minute. Wright nodded a long ball from Trevor Sinclair towards the near post and Hartson nipped in to flash the ball past Sullivan.

They were at it again seven minutes later. Hartson prodded in an effort from a corner that was blocked, but the ball ran loose to Wright, who buried the follow-up into the unguarded net.

Despite being 2–0 down, Wimbledon still looked dangerous. Indeed, West Ham's third goal came via a Dons corner, after a period of pressure from the visitors. Hislop launched the attack, and when the ball reached Stan Lazaridis he cut it back perfectly for former England star Wright to rifle it first time into the top corner.

With 30 minutes gone, Sinclair lost possession on the edge of the West Ham box. Alan Kimble fired over a first-time cross and Marcus Gayle's goal-bound header looped over Sullivan and into the net. This was a crucial reply coming before half-time.

The second half produced further end-to-end action, but Wimbledon's direct and incisive counter-attacking hauled them back into the match. Nineteen minutes into the second half, Marcus Gayle headed Duncan Jupp's long ball into the path of Jason Euell, who lashed the ball home.

With 77 minutes on the clock, Wimbledon were level. Shaka Hislop came to claim a Michael Hughes corner but missed it. The ball dropped to Gayle, who hammered home his second goal to make the score 3–3.

Wimbledon's winner, four minutes later, was a typical Dons lightning strike. From a West Ham corner the ball fell to Ekoku. He pumped the ball out wide to Euell and ran 50 yards to head the return past Hislop, to the delight of the travelling fans.

Carling Opta's stats reflect the openness of the match. Wimbledon had 19 shots at goal to West Ham's 17 attempts, but the home side were more accurate, with 11 of their efforts on target compared to nine by the Dons. Both sides completed a similar number of passes with almost identical success, but the only difference in the end was the clinical finishing of the Wimbledon strikers.

Man of the match Marcus Gayle scored two goals and set up one, scoring 1,804 points to inspire Wimbledon's comeback. In a fast-paced match unsuited to patient build-up play, he completed 22 out of 28 passes successfully, and took on and beat the Hammers' defence three times.

This match set the standard for yet another season of battling, determined performances from Wimbledon. The signing of John Hartson indicates their aspirations for 1999–2000; but will they be written off again?

ACTION	ANSWORTH	ARDLEY	BLACKWELL	CUNNINGHAM	EARLE	ENOKU	EUELL	GAYLE	M HUGHES	LEABURN	PERRY	SULLIVAN	THATCHER	TOTAL	ARSENAL
Time on pitch	73	17	90	90	90	17	90	73	90	90	90	90	90	990	990
GOALS															
Goal	–	–	–	–	–	–	–	1	–	–	–	–	–	1	1
Shot on target	–	–	–	–	–	–	–	1	–	–	2	–	–	3	6
Shot off target	–	–	–	2	–	–	3	–	–	–	–	–	–	5	3
Blocked shot	–	–	–	–	–	–	–	–	–	–	–	–	–	–	6
Own goal	–	–	–	–	–	–	–	–	–	–	–	–	–	–	–
PASSES															
Pass to own player	8	5	7	19	28	8	23	11	26	29	4	–	8	176	353
Pass to opposition	16	5	5	5	6	3	12	14	11	19	4	–	10	110	123
Cross to own player	–	–	–	–	–	–	–	–	4	–	–	–	–	4	6
Cross to opposition player	–	–	–	3	1	–	–	–	3	3	–	–	–	10	13
Goal assist	–	–	–	–	–	–	–	–	–	–	–	–	–	–	–
Pass completion %	32%	45%	58%	70%	83%	73%	66%	44%	68%	60%	50%	0%	40%	60%	73%
TACKLES & CLEARANCES															
Tackle	1	–	2	5	4	–	5	–	3	4	3	–	2	29	28
Clearances, blocks and interceptions	2	1	20	20	7	–	6	–	5	1	14	3	17	96	67
DRIBBLES & RUNS															
Dribble ball retained	4	1	–	–	3	–	2	2	3	–	–	–	1	16	15
Dribble ball lost	5	1	1	1	1	1	3	2	1	–	–	–	–	16	20
Dribble success %	44%	50%	0%	0%	75%	0%	40%	50%	75%	0%	0%	0%	100%	50%	43%
DISCIPLINE															
Fouls	–	–	1	1	2	2	4	1	2	–	1	–	3	17	18
Penalty conceded	–	–	–	–	–	–	–	–	–	–	–	–	–	3	–
Free kick - offside	–	–	–	–	–	–	–	1	–	–	–	–	–	1	1
Yellow cards	–	–	–	–	–	–	1	–	1	–	1	–	–	3	2
Red cards	–	–	–	–	–	–	–	–	–	–	–	–	–	–	–
GOALKEEPERS															
Distribution to own player	–	–	–	–	–	–	–	–	–	–	–	12	–	12	16
Distribution to opposition player	–	–	–	–	–	–	–	–	–	–	–	22	–	22	16
Goalkeeper distribution %	0%	0%	0%	0%	0%	0%	0%	0%	0%	0%	0%	35%	0%	35%	50%
Save	–	–	–	–	–	–	–	–	–	–	–	6	–	6	3
Ball caught	–	–	–	–	–	–	–	–	–	–	–	3	–	3	–
Ball dropped	–	–	–	–	–	–	–	–	–	–	–	–	–	–	–
Goal conceded	–	–	–	–	–	–	–	–	–	–	–	–	–	–	–

Wimbledon against Arsenal always promises to be a tough, bruising encounter, and this match was no exception. Fielding their strongest side, Arsenal were expected to take the points at Selhurst Park, but Joe Kinnear's men had other ideas.

November 21, 1998
1–0
WIMBLEDON
ARSENAL

Arsenal started the match well. Within the first five minutes Neil Sullivan was forced to block a Nicolas Anelka shot after a twisting run from the young Frenchman. Wimbledon had to wait until the 14th minute for their first effort on goal, when Marcus Gayle's 20-yarder was comfortably dealt with by David Seaman.

Arsenal were dominating the play and Marc Overmars's shot from distance warmed the palms of Sullivan's hands two minutes later.

Wimbledon received an unexpected boost when Patrick Vieira was forced off after tweaking his hamstring on 20 minutes. Seven minutes later, it should have been 1–0 to Wimbledon when Gayle's chip into the box was powerfully met by Robbie Earle, whose header brushed the roof of the net on its way over.

This gave Wimbledon more confidence and the Dons improved as the half progressed. Then came another fillip for Joe Kinnear's men as Dennis Bergkamp injured his calf and was replaced by Christopher Wreh after 37 minutes.

Wimbledon, buoyed by the demise of two of the champions' most influential players, went forward and were unlucky when Michael Hughes was wrongly adjudged offside after a neat flick by Gayle.

The second half started with a bang just a minute after the restart as Lee Dixon cut inside on to his left foot and his curling 25-yard shot rattled the crossbar. Wimbledon then went upfield and won a corner. Michael Hughes's near-post delivery was headed dangerously up in the air by Stephen Hughes, and Chris Perry's swivelling volley went straight at Seaman, who gathered it at the second attempt.

On 63 minutes Euell carved open the Arsenal defence, playing a one-two with Carl Leaburn before side-footing a yard wide. Wimbledon were beginning to feel Arsenal were there for the taking. With 13 minutes to go, Michael Hughes turned both Parlour and Dixon and crossed. The ball appeared to hit Earle's hand, then fell to substitute Efan Ekoku, who could not miss from three yards out. The Arsenal players protested, claiming handball, but referee Mike Riley allowed the goal to stand.

Arsenal tried to fight back, but without Bergkamp they lacked the skill and guile to open up Wimbledon's resolute defence.

Looking at the Carling Opta stats, Wimbledon were out-passed and out-shot by their London rivals, and made more defensive clearances, blocks and interceptions (96 to Arsenal's 67). This highlights how the balance of play was in Arsenal's favour, with Wimbledon doing the majority of the defending. Substitute Ekoku scored with his only effort, whereas Nicolas Anelka, who had played the full 90 minutes, only hit the target with one of his four efforts on goal.

Wimbledon's strong rearguard action formed the platform for their success. Between them the back four of Dean Blackwell, Chris Perry, Ben Thatcher and Kenny Cunningham made 71 of Wimbledon's 96 clearances, blocks and interceptions, and 12 of the Dons' 29 tackles.

We're going up: Bradford City savour promotion to the Premiership after beating Wolves at Molineux

BRADFORD CITY

ADDRESS

Valley Parade, Bradford,
W Yorks, BD8 7DY

CONTACT NUMBERS

Telephone: 01274 773355
Fax: 01274 773356
Ticket Office: 01274 770022
24hr Information: 09068 888640
Bantam Leisure (Shop): 01274 770012
e-mail: bradfordcity@compuserve.com
Website: www.bradfordcityfc.co.uk

SPONSORS

JCT 600

FANZINES

City Gent

KEY PERSONNEL

Chairman: G Richmond
Club President: J Tordoff
Vice Chairman: D Thompson FCA
Managing Director: S Harvey
Directors: D Richmond, E Richmond
T Goddard, M Richmond
J Rhodes, Prof D Rhodes OBE
Club Secretary: J Pollard
Manager: Paul Jewell

COLOURS

Home: Claret and amber shirts,
black shorts and black stockings
Away: Light blue shirts and shorts
with blue stockings

NICKNAME

The Bantams

20 FACTS

1 Bradford were founded in 1903, when Manningham Rugby Football Club switched from rugby to football and were renamed Bradford City Football Club.

2 The Bantams have not been in the top division of English football since the end of the 1922 season. Their highest league position was fifth in Division One in 1910–11. They return to the top flight after an absence of 77 years.

3 Bradford's one success in cup competition came when they beat Newcastle United to win the 1911 FA Cup, just their eighth season in existence. The final finished 0–0, Bradford winning the replay at Old Trafford 1–0.

4 The club have not had the same success in the League Cup, with their best performance coming in 1965 when they reached the fifth round.

5 City scored an incredible 128 goals in the 1928–29 season. This record number of goals scored in a 42-game season is shared with Aston Villa.

6 Bradford were Division Two Champions in 1908, and won the Division Three North title in 1929. They won the Division Three Championship in 1985.

7 Harry Hampton remains Bradford's most-capped player, with nine international caps for Northern Ireland.

8 In the 1928–29 season, Bradford won two consecutive home games 8–0. The victims were Tranmere and Barrow.

9 The club's all-time appearance record holder is Cecil Podd, who amassed 574 games for City between 1970 and 1984.

10 City's all-time top scorer is Bobby Campbell with 143 goals between 1979 and 1986. David Layne's 36 goals in the 1961–62 season is a club record.

11 The club's ground was briefly called the Pulse Stadium as a result of a deal struck with the local radio station.

12 Bradford's record victory is 11–1 against Rotherham United in a Division Three North fixture on August 25, 1928.

13 Their record defeat was a 9–1 reverse at the hands of Colchester United in Division Four on New Year's Eve, 1961.

14 Paul Jewell's managerial success at Bradford is made all the more impressive because it came in his first full season as a league manager.

15 The club's fanzine, the City Gent, is reputedly the country's oldest football fanzine. It was first published in October 1984.

16 Bradford are not the only club in the city. They also have a famous neighbour in Bradford Park Avenue, who were founded a year earlier in 1907. They also started life as a rugby club, and were huge rivals of City's predecessors Manningham RFC.

17 Bradford finished the 1998–99 season in second place in the Nationwide League Division One. Their league record was:

Pld	W	D	L	F	A	Pts
46	26	9	11	82	47	87

18 After beating Grimsby Town 2–1 at home in the FA Cup third round, the Bantams went crashing out of the competition at the hands of Newcastle. A 3–0 defeat at St James's Park ended their Cup run almost before it started.

19 The Worthington Cup held little more joy for City. They struggled to get past Lincoln City over two legs in the first round and then knocked out Halifax Town over two legs in the second. The third round reverted to a straight one-match knock-out format, and Bradford were beaten 1–0 at Elland Road by their local rivals Leeds United.

20 Bradford's top scorer in the 1998–99 season was Lee Mills, with 23 league goals.

THE MANAGER

PAUL JEWELL

The odds on Paul Jewell becoming permanent manager of Bradford City seemed remote at the end of the 1997–98 season. Jewell, who was promoted from assistant to caretaker manager after Chris Kamara's sacking in January 1998, gained just six wins from his first 21 games in charge.

But Bradford chairman Geoffrey Richmond took the bold decision to make Jewell's position permanent in the summer, and he has seen his faith rewarded with City's promotion to the Premiership.

Jewell did not enjoy the most distinguished of playing careers. He started as an apprentice at Liverpool but left the club without making an appearance.

He enjoyed more success with Wigan, for whom he scored 47 goals in more than 170 games. He then moved to Bradford in an £80,000 deal in 1988 and made more than 300 appearances over the next nine years before ending his playing career in 1996.

At 34, Jewell is the youngest manager in the Premiership, but there is no doubt that he has earned the right to pit his wits against the country's top bosses.

SEASON REVIEW

On the last day of the 1996–97 season, the live television cameras were at Bradford City with the club needing a victory to avoid relegation to Division Two.

It speaks volumes for the remarkable turnaround at Valley Parade that the cameras were again focusing on the Bantams on the last day of the 1998–99 campaign, this time to witness their promotion to the Premiership with victory at Wolves.

That had seemed a most unlikely prospect after the first seven games of the season. City had won just once – a home victory over Birmingham City – and sat in a perilous 21st position. Manager Paul Jewell was under immense pressure to improve Bradford's fortunes.

They then won eight of the next 11 League games, and drew 0–0 with runaway leaders Sunderland – a sensational run which lifted the club into fifth place.

Another blip followed – a shock 3–0 home defeat by struggling QPR – but that only served to fire the players up even more, and they won seven of the next eight encounters to climb above Ipswich Town and into second place.

City then swapped places with their Suffolk promotion rivals seven times, dropping points at home to Huddersfield and Oxford and away at Crystal Palace.

But they clinched promotion at Molineux in a thrilling match which they won 3–2. It was fitting that two of the stars of the season, top scorer Lee Mills and rejuvenated wide man Peter Beagrie, both scored to ensure top-flight football at Valley Parade for the first time in 77 years.

BRADFORD CITY

DATE	OPPONENT	SCORE	ATT.	BEAGRIE	BLAKE	BOLLAND	DREYER	EDINHO	GRANT	JACOBS	LAWRENCE	MCCALL	MILLS	MOORE
8.8.98	Stockport Co H	1–2	14,360	p¹	–	–	–	p	s	–	p	p	p	p
15.8.98	Watford A	0–1	10,731	p	–	p	p	s	s	–	p	–	p	p
23.8.98	Bolton H	2–2	13,163	p	–	p	p	–	p	s	p	–	p¹	p
28.8.98	Crewe A	1–2	5,759	p	–	–	p	–	–	s	p	p¹	p	p
31.8.98	Birmingham H	2–1	13,910	p	–	–	p	–	s	p	p	p	p¹	p¹
8.9.98	Ipswich A	0–3	11,596	p	–	–	p	–	s	p	–	p	p	p
12.9.98	Sheffield Utd H	2–2	13,169	p	p¹	–	p	–	–	p	–	p	p¹	p
20.9.98	WBA A	2–0	12,426	p	p	–	–	–	–	p	–	p	p²	p
26.9.98	Barnsley H	2–1	15,887	p	p	–	s	–	–	p	–	p	p	p
29.9.98	Port Vale H	4–0	13,245	p	p¹	–	–	–	–	p	–	p	p²	p¹
3.10.98	Sunderland A	0–0	37,828	p	p	–	–	–	–	p	–	p	p	p
9.10.98	Bury H	3–0	15,697	p¹	p¹	–	p	s	–	p	–	p¹	p	p
17.10.98	Grimsby A	0–2	7,473	p	p	–	p	–	–	p	–	p	p	p
20.10.98	Portsmouth A	4–2	10,062	p¹	p	–	p	–	–	p	–	p	p¹	p
31.10.98	Bristol City H	5–0	14,468	p¹	p¹	–	p	–	–	p	s	p	p¹	p
7.11.98	Norwich A	2–2	14,722	p	p	–	–	–	–	p	p	p	p¹	p
10.11.98	Tranmere A	1–0	6,002	p¹	p	–	–	–	–	p	p	p	p	p
14.11.98	Swindon H	3–0	14,897	p¹	p	–	–	–	–	p¹	p	–	p	p
21.11.98	Huddersfield A	1–2	18,173	p	p¹	–	–	–	–	p	p	p	p	p
28.11.98	QPR H	0–3	15,037	p	p	–	–	–	–	p	p	p	p	p
5.12.98	Oxford A	1–0	5,969	p	p	–	–	–	–	p	p	p	p¹	p
12.12.98	Swindon A	4–1	7,447	p	p²	–	–	–	–	p	p	p	p²	p
19.12.98	Wolves H	2–1	13,846	p	p¹	–	–	–	–	p	p	p	p¹	p
26.12.98	Bolton A	0–0	24,625	p	p	–	–	–	–	p	p	p	–	p
28.12.98	Tranmere H	2–0	14,076	p	p¹	–	–	–	–	p	p	p	p¹	p
9.1.99	Stockport Co A	2–1	8,973	p¹	p¹	–	–	–	–	p	p	p	p	p
16.1.99	Crewe H	4–1	12,595	p	p¹	–	–	–	–	p	p	p	p³	p
19.1.99	Crystal Palace H	2–1	14,368	p¹	p	–	–	–	–	p	p	p	p	p
31.1.99	Birmingham A	1–2	19,291	p	p	–	–	–	–	p	p¹	p	p	p
6.2.99	Watford H	2–0	14,142	p	p	–	–	–	–	p	p	p¹	p¹	–
13.2.99	Ipswich H	0–0	15,024	p	p	–	–	–	–	p	p	p	p	p
19.2.99	Sheffield Utd A	2–2	14,675	p	p²	–	–	–	–	p	p	p	–	p
27.2.99	WBA H	1–0	14,278	–	p	–	s	–	–	p¹	p	p	p	p
3.3.99	Barnsley A	1–0	16,866	–	p	–	p	–	–	p	p	p	p	p
9.3.99	Sunderland H	0–1	15,124	–	p	–	p	–	–	p	p	p	p	p
13.3.99	Norwich H	4–1	13,331	p¹	p	–	p	–	–	p	p¹	p	p¹	p¹
20.3.99	Bristol City A	3–2	10,870	p	–	–	p	–	–	p¹	p	p	p¹	p
28.3.99	Crystal Palace A	0–1	15,626	p	s	–	–	–	–	p	p	p	p	p
3.4.99	Grimsby H	3–0	14,522	p¹	p¹	–	–	–	–	p	p	p	p	p
5.4.99	Bury A	2–0	8,000	p	s	–	–	–	–	p	p	p	p	p
10.4.99	Portsmouth H	2–1	13,552	p	s	–	–	–	–	p	p	p	p¹	p
13.4.99	Port Vale A	1–1	6,998	p	p	–	–	–	–	p	p	p	p¹	p
17.4.99	Huddersfield H	2–3	15,124	p	p¹	–	–	–	–	p	–	p	p	p
24.4.99	QPR A	3–1	11,641	p¹	p	–	p	–	–	p	–	p	p	–
1.5.99	Oxford H	0–0	15,064	p	s	–	p	–	–	p	s	p	p	p
9.5.99	Wolves A	3–2	27,589	p¹	p¹	–	p	–	–	p	p	p	p¹	p

p Played, s Substitute, p³ Goals scored

1998–99 DIVISION ONE APPEARANCES

O'BRIEN	PEPPER	RANKIN	RAMAGE	SHARPE	TODD	WALSH	WATSON	WESTWOOD	WHALLEY	WINDASS	WRIGHT
p	–	–	–	–	p	p	–	–	p	–	p
p	–	p	–	–	–	p	–	–	p	–	p
p	–	p¹	–	–	–	p	–	s	p	–	–
p	–	p	–	–	–	p	–	p	p	–	–
p	s	p	–	–	–	p	–	–	p	–	–
p	p	p	s	–	–	p	–	–	p	–	s
–	p	–	–	–	–	p	–	–	p	–	p
p	–	p	s	–	–	p	s	–	p	–	p
p	p	s	–	–	–	p	s²	–	p	–	p
s	s	s	–	–	p	p	p	–	p	–	–
–	–	s	–	–	p	p	p	–	p	–	–
s	p	s	–	–	p	p	p	–	–	–	–
–	s	s	–	–	p	p	p	–	p	–	–
s	–	p¹	–	–	p	p	s	–	p¹	–	–
s	–	p²	–	–	p	p	s	–	p	–	–
p	–	p¹	–	–	–	p	–	–	p	–	–
–	–	p	–	–	–	p	s	p	p	–	–
s	p¹	p	–	–	–	p	s	p	p	–	–
p	s	p	–	–	–	p	s	–	p	–	–
p	–	p	–	–	s	p	s	–	p	–	–
p	–	s	–	–	–	p	–	–	p	–	p
p	–	–	–	–	–	p	–	–	p	–	p
p	–	–	–	–	–	p	s	s	p	–	p
p	–	s	–	–	–	p	p	–	p	–	p
p	–	–	–	–	–	p	–	–	p	–	p
p	–	–	–	–	–	p	–	–	p	–	p
–	–	s	s	–	–	p	–	p	p	–	p
–	–	–	s	–	–	p	–	p¹	p	–	p
–	–	–	–	–	–	p	–	p	p	–	p
p	–	–	–	–	–	p	–	p	p	–	p
–	–	s	–	–	–	p	–	p	p	–	p
s	–	p	–	–	–	p	s	p	p	–	p
p	–	s	–	–	p	p	–	p	p	–	–
s	–	p	–	–	p	p	s¹	–	p	–	–
–	–	–	–	–	p	p	–	–	p	p	–
s	–	–	–	–	p	p	–	–	p	s	–
–	–	s	–	–	p	p	–	–	p¹	p	–
–	–	–	–	s	p	p	–	p	p	p	–
s	–	–	–	s¹	p	p	–	p	p	s	–
s	–	–	–	p	–	p	–	p	p	p²	–
s	–	–	–	p¹	–	p	–	p	p	p	–
–	–	–	–	p	–	p	–	p	p	s	–
–	–	–	–	p	–	p	s	p	p	s¹	p
s	–	–	–	p	–	p	s¹	p¹	p	s	p
–	–	–	–	p	–	p	–	–	p	p	p
–	–	–	–	s	–	p	–	–	p	s	p

SUNDERLAND 1998–99

Back row (left to right): Michael Bridges, Paul Beavers, Stuart Ingram, Paul Heckingbottom, Jody Craddock, Niall Quinn, Danny Dichio, Paul Butler, Matthew Pitts, John Mullin, Andy Melville.

Middle row: Chris Lumsden, Darren Holloway, Paul Thirlwell, Martin Smith, Sam Aiston, Luke Weaver, Thomas Sorensen, Chris Porter, Neil Wainwright, Martin Scott, Allan Johnston, Kevin Phillips, Michael Gray.

Front row: Alex Rae, Elliott Dickman, Darren Williams, Kevin Frampton, Lee Clark, Kevin Ball, Chris Makin, Nicky Summerbee, Gerry Harrison, David Duke, Kris Lamb.

SUNDERLAND

ADDRESS

The Stadium of Light, Stadium Park, Sunderland, SR5 1SU.

CONTACT NUMBERS

Telephone: 0191 551 5000
Fax: 0191 551 5123
Ticket Office: 0191 551 5151
24hr Information: 09068 121140
Stadium Shop: 0191 551 5050
E-mail address:
communications@sunderland-afc.com
Website: www.sunderland-afc.com

SPONSORS

Lambton's

FANZINES

A Love Supreme
ITHICS
The Black Cat
Sunderland Fanatic

KEY PERSONNEL

Chairman: R S Murray
Director/Chief Executive: J M Fickling
Directors: G M McDonnell,
D C Stonehouse, J R Featherstone,
G S Wood, J G Wood
Club Secretary: M Blackbourne
Manager: Peter Reid

COLOURS

Home: Red shirts with white striped, black shorts, black stockings with red turnover
Away: Navy blue shirts with red and white hoop, navy blue shorts and stockings with red and white trim

NICKNAME

The Mackems

20 FACTS

1 Sunderland were formed in 1879 by Scottish schoolmaster James Allan at Hendon Boarding School. The club were initially called the Sunderland & District Teachers' Association FC. Due to financial difficulties in 1880 the club decided to accept members from outside teaching circles. The club was renamed Sunderland AFC.

2 The club returns to the Premiership after a two year absence. They have won the Championship in the top division on six occasions (1891–92, 1892–93, 1894–95, 1901–02, 1912–13 and 1935–36).

3 The Wearside club are also two-time FA Cup winners, in 1937 and 1973.

4 The League Cup has not brought the same success to Sunderland. Their only final appearance came in 1985 but they lost to Norwich City, the only goal being an own goal from Gordon Chisholm.

5 Goalkeeper Jim Montgomery is a Sunderland legend. He is the all-time appearance record-holder, with 623 between 1961 and 1977. His performance in the 1973 FA Cup final was considered one of the greatest ever by a goalkeeper.

6 Dave Halliday's 43 goals in the 1928–29 season remain a club record.

7 Bobby Gurney is Sunderland's career record goalscorer. He was on target 228 times between 1925 and 1939.

8 The club have a variety of nicknames. The most commonly-used is the Mackems. They have also been known as the Rokerites and, originally, the Blackcats.

9 The new Sunderland Stadium of Light is the club's seventh home ground in their history. Their previous grounds were Blue House Field, Groves Field, Horatio Street, Abbs Field, Newcastle Road and Roker Park.

10 Sunderland were the first team to be admitted to the Football League after the 12 founder members.

11 Their record signing is Lee Clark, who swapped black and white for red and white when he moved from Newcastle for £2.5 million in June 1997.

12 The biggest transfer fee received by the club is £1.8 million from Crystal Palace for striker Marco Gabbiadini in September 1991.

13 The outer walls of the Stadium of Light are adorned with the names of thousands of Sunderland fans, who paid to have their names engraved on the stadium bricks.

14 Barry Venison became the youngest Wembley Cup Final captain when he led Sunderland out in the 1985 League Cup final aged 20 years, seven months and eight days.

15 Current striker Kevin Phillips equalled Bobby Gurney's record of scoring in seven consecutive matches. His seventh goalscoring appearance came against Manchester City on January 17, 1998. In November 1998, Niall Quinn scored in all six of Sunderland's matches.

16 Sunderland's biggest victory came against rivals Newcastle United, who were thrashed 9–1 in 1908.

17 Sunderland ran away with the Nationwide Division One title in 1998–99. They finished with the following record:

Pld	W	D	L	F	A	Pts
46	31	12	3	91	28	105

18 After beating Lincoln City 1–0 in the third round at Sincil Bank, Sunderland crashed out of the AXA-sponsored FA Cup in the fourth round, losing 1–0 away to Blackburn Rovers.

19 The Wearsiders came close to reaching a Wembley Cup Final in 1999, but lost 2–1 on aggregate in the semi-finals of the Worthington Cup to Leicester City. The Mackems reached that stage by beating York City, Chester City, Grimsby Town, Everton and Luton Town on the way.

20 Sunderland's top scorer in the 1998–99 championship-winning season was Kevin Phillips, with 25 goals.

THE MANAGER

PETER REID

Peter Reid has been at the Sunderland helm since March 1995. After walking away with the 1998–99 Nationwide League Division One title, in which Sunderland finished 18 points clear of their nearest rivals, the former Everton player is ready to tackle the Carling Premiership again and has put together a team that seems well-equipped to survive.

Reid started his managerial career at Manchester City in 1990 but parted company with the club in 1993. He played for a number of clubs in his distinguished and honour-strewn career, including Bolton Wanderers, Queens Park Rangers and Manchester City but will best be remembered for his time at Everton between 1982 and 1988.

During that time Reid, in the heart of midfield, won two championship medals, an FA Cup winners medal and a European Cup Winners Cup medal. He was also named PFA Player of the Year in 1985 and won 13 England caps.

A natural-born winner, Reid was stung by the heartbreak of relegation from the Premiership in 1997 and the misery of defeat in the 1998 play-off final against Charlton. He will be even more determined to succeed this time around.

SEASON REVIEW

Missing out on promotion in 1997–98 was heart-breaking for everyone involved with Sunderland. The team only narrowly missed the automatic promotion places, then were left devastated after being beaten on penalties in a thrilling play-off final with Charlton Athletic.

It took a monumental effort from manager Peter Reid to lift his players for the new campaign, but after five matches of 1998–99 they were top of the league and never looked back.

Though they were occasionally overhauled at the top by the odd point, by the end of November 1998 the club were five points clear and automatic promotion was simply never in doubt.

The prolific Niall Quinn and Kevin Phillips ensured the club's goal tally ticked along steadily, and with a stubborn defence Sunderland frequently won games in which they were not totally dominant.

And on the rare occasions they did find themselves up against it, they still managed to grind out the three points.

One example came at West Bromwich Albion. The home side roared into a two-goal lead and could have extended it at the start of the second half. But the Mackems stepped up a gear and won 3–2 with a stirring display of attacking football.

The club sealed the championship with a fine win at Barnsley, and a final-day victory over Birmingham sealed a league record points total of 105 to cap a truly memorable season. And for young full-back Michael Gray, the agony of his 1998 playoff penalty shoot-out miss was offset by a full England call-up in June 1999.

Hopes will be high among Sunderland fanatical and loyal supporters that the club is now better-equipped for life in the Carling Premiership.

SUNDERLAND

DATE	OPPONENT	SCORE	ATT.	AISTON	BALL	BRIDGES	BUTLER	CLARK	CRADDOCK	DICHIO	GRAY	HOLLOWAY	JOH
8.8.98	QPR H	1–0	40,537	–	p	s	p	p	p	–	p	–	p
15.8.98	Swindon A	1–1	10,207	–	p	–	p	–	–	s	p	–	p
22.8.98	Tranmere H	5–0	34,155	–	p	–	p¹	–	–	p²	p	–	p
25.8.98	Watford H	4–1	36,587	–	p	–	p	–	–	p¹	p	–	p¹
29.8.98	Ipswich A	2–0	15,813	–	p	–	p	–	s	p	p	–	p
8.9.98	Bristol City H	1–1	34,111	–	p	–	p	–	–	p	p	–	p
12.9.98	Wolves A	1–1	26,816	–	p	s	p	–	–	p	p	–	p
19.9.98	Oxford H	7–0	34,567	–	p	p²	p	–	–	p²	p¹	–	p
26.9.98	Portsmouth A	1–1	17,022	–	p	p	p	–	–	p	p	–	p¹
29.9.98	Norwich A	2–2*	17,504	–	p	–	p	–	–	p	p	–	p
3.10.98	Bradford H	0–0	37,828	–	p	–	p	–	–	p	p	–	p
18.10.98	WBA A	3–2	14,746	–	p¹	s¹	p	–	s	p	p	–	p
21.10.98	Huddersfield A	1–1	20,741	–	p¹	p	p	–	–	s	–	–	p
24.10.98	Bury H	1–0	38,049	–	p	p	p	–	–	s¹	p	–	p
1.11.98	Bolton A	3–0	21,676	–	p	s¹	p	–	–	p	p	–	p¹
3.11.98	Crewe A	4–1	5,361	–	p	s¹	p	–	–	p¹	p¹	–	p
7.11.98	Grimsby H	3–1	40,077	s	p	p	p	–	–	–	–	–	p
14.11.98	Port Vale A	2–0*	8,839	–	–	p	p	p	–	s	–	–	p
21.11.98	Barnsley H	2–3	40,231	–	p	p	–	p	–	p	–	–	p
28.11.98	Sheffield Utd A	4–0	25,229	–	p	p²	p	p	s	s	–	–	p
5.12.98	Stockport Co H	1–0	36,040	–	p	p	p	p	–	s	–	–	p
12.12.98	Port Vale H	2–0	37,583	–	p	p	p¹	p	–	s	–	–	–
15.12.98	Crystal Palace H	2–0	33,870	–	–	p	p	p	–	s¹	s	–	–
19.12.98	Birmingham A	0–0	22,095	–	p	p	p	p	–	s	p	–	–
26.12.98	Tranmere A	0–1	14,248	–	p	p	p	p	–	s	p	–	–
28.12.98	Crewe H	2–0	41,433	–	p	s¹	p	p	–	p¹	p	–	–
9.1.99	QPR A	2–2	17,444	–	p	s	p	p	–	–	–	–	–
17.1.99	Ipswich H	2–1	39,835	–	p	s	p	p	–	s	p	–	p
30.1.99	Watford A	1–2	20,188	–	p	s	p	–	–	–	p	–	p
6.2.99	Swindon H	2–0	41,304	–	p	s	p	p	–	s	p	–	p
13.2.99	Bristol City A	1–0	15,736	–	p	–	p	p	–	s	p	–	p
20.2.99	Wolves H	2–1	41,268	–	p	–	p	p	–	–	p	–	p¹
27.2.99	Oxford A	0–0	9,044	–	–	–	p	–	–	s	–	p	p
2.3.99	Portsmouth H	2–0	37,656	–	p	s	p	p	–	p¹	p	–	p
6.3.99	Norwich H	1–0	39,004	–	p	–	p	–	–	–	p	–	p
9.3.99	Bradford A	1–0	15,124	–	p	–	p	s	–	s	p	–	p
13.3.99	Grimsby A	2–0	9,528	–	p	s	p	p¹	–	s	p	–	p
20.3.99	Bolton H	3–1	41,505	–	p	s	–	p	p	s	p	–	p²
3.4.99	WBA H	3–0	41,135	–	p	s	p	p¹	p	s	p	s	p
5.4.99	Crystal Palace A	1–1	22,096	–	p	–	p	p	–	–	p	s	p
10.4.99	Huddersfield H	2–0	41,074	–	p	s	p	p	–	s	p	s	p¹
13.4.99	Bury A	5–2	8,669	–	p	s	p	p	–	s	p	s	p
16.4.99	Barnsley A	3–1	17,390	–	p	–	p	p¹	–	s	p	–	p
24.4.99	Sheffield Utd H	0–0	41,179	–	p	–	p	p	–	p	p	s	p
1.5.99	Stockport Co A	1–0	10,548	–	–	–	p	p	–	–	p	–	p
9.5.99	Birmingham H	2–1	41,634	–	p	–	p	p	–	–	p	–	p

p Played, s Substitute, p³Goals scored *including own goal

1998–99 DIVISION ONE APPEARANCES

McCANN	MAKIN	MARRIOTT	MELVILLE	MULLIN	PHILLIPS	QUINN	RAE	SCOTT	SMITH	SORENSEN	SUMMERBEE	THIRLWELL	WAINWRIGHT	WILLIAMS
–	–	–	–	–	p^1	p	–	p	–	p	p	–	–	s
–	–	–	p	s	p^1	p	–	p	–	p	p	–	–	p
–	–	–	p	p^1	p^1	–	–	–	s	p	p	s	s	p
–	–	–	p^1	p	p	–	–	–	s	p	p^1	–	–	p
–	–	–	p	p^1	p^1	–	–	–	–	p	p	–	–	p
–	–	–	p	p	p^1	–	–	–	–	p	p	–	–	p
–	–	–	p	–	p^1	–	–	p	–	p	p	–	–	p
–	s	–	p	p	–	s	s^2	–	–	p	p	–	–	p
–	–	–	p	p	–	s	s	–	–	p	p	–	–	p
–	p	–	p	–	–	p^1	p	–	–	p	p	–	–	–
–	p	–	p	–	–	p	p	–	–	p	p	–	–	–
–	p	–	p^1	s	–	p	p	–	–	p	p	–	–	–
–	p	–	p	–	–	p	p	p	–	p	p	–	–	–
–	p	–	p	–	–	p	p	–	–	p	p	–	–	–
–	p	–	p	p	–	p^1	–	s	–	p	–	p	–	s
–	p	–	p	p	–	p^1	–	s	–	p	–	–	–	p
–	p	–	p	–	–	p^1	–	p	p^2	p	–	–	s	p
–	p	–	p	–	–	p^1	–	p	s	p	p	–	–	p
–	p	–	p	–	–	s^1	–	p^1	–	p	p	–	–	p
s	p	–	p	–	–	p^2	–	p	–	p	p	–	–	–
–	p	–	p	–	–	p	s	p	–	p	p^1	–	–	s
s	p	–	p	–	–	p	p	p	p^1	p	–	–	–	–
p	p	–	p	–	–	p	p	p^1	p	p	–	–	–	s
s	p	–	p	–	–	p	p	p	–	p	–	–	–	s
s	p	–	p	–	–	p	p	p	–	p	–	–	–	–
s	p	–	p	–	–	p	p	p	–	p	–	–	–	s
p	p	–	p	–	p^1	p^1	p	–	s	p	–	–	–	p
–	p	–	p	–	p	p^2	p	–	–	p	–	–	–	–
p	p	–	p	–	p	p^1	–	–	–	p	p	–	–	s
–	p	–	p	–	p^1	p^1	–	–	–	p	p	–	–	–
–	p	–	p	–	p^1	p	–	–	–	p	p	–	–	–
–	p	–	p	–	p	p^1	–	–	–	p	p	–	–	–
p	p	–	p	–	p	p	–	–	–	p	p	–	–	p
–	p	–	p	–	p^1	–	–	–	–	p	p	–	–	s
s	p	–	p	–	p^1	p	–	–	–	p	p	–	–	p
–	p	–	p	–	p	p^1	–	–	–	p	p	–	–	p
–	p	p	p	–	p^1	p	–	–	–	–	p	–	–	–
–	p	–	p	–	p^1	p	–	–	–	p	p	–	–	s
–	p	–	–	–	p^2	p	–	–	–	p	p	–	–	–
–	p	–	p	–	p^1	p	–	–	–	p	p	–	–	–
–	p	–	p	–	p	p^1	–	–	–	p	p	–	–	–
–	p	–	p	–	p^4	p^1	–	–	–	p	p	–	–	–
–	p	–	p	–	p^1	p	–	–	–	p	p^1	–	–	–
–	p	–	p	–	–	–	–	–	p	p	p	–	–	–
p	p	–	p	–	p^1	p	–	–	–	p	p	–	–	–
–	p	–	p	–	p^1	p^1	–	–	–	p	p	–	–	–

WATFORD 1998–99

Back row (from left to right): Chris Cummins (Youth Team Assistant), Kirk Wheeler (Football in the Community Officer), Colin Pluck, Steve Palmer, Keith Millen, Grant Cornock, Jason Lee, Darren Ward, Dean Yates, James Panayi, Tommy Mooney, Daniel Grieves, Rob Smith (Football in the Community Assistant), Jimmy Gilligan (Youth Academy Assistant).

Middle row: Gary Johnson (Youth Academy Director), Tom Walley (Coach), Richard Johnson, Micah Hyde, Ronny Rosenthal, Robert Page, Allan Smart, Alec Chamberlain, Chris Day, Gifton Noel-Williams, Alon Hazan, Johann Gudmundsson, Michel Ngonge, David Perpetuini, Paul Rastrick (Physiotherapist), Ken Barry (Kit Manager).

Front row: Shay Connolly (Youth Academy Physiotherapist), Nigel Gibbs, Stuart Slater, Mark Boyce, Nathan Lowndes, Darren Bazeley, Oliver Squires, Kenny Jackett (First Team Coach), Graham Taylor (General Manager), Luther Blissett (Coach), Paul Robinson, Clint Easton, Nick Wright, Wayne Andrews, Tommy Smith, Peter Kennedy, Luke Anthony (Youth Academy Physiotherapist).

WATFORD

ADDRESS

Vicarage Road Stadium,
Watford, WD1 8ER

CONTACT NUMBERS

Telephone: 01923 496000
Fax: 01923 496001
Ticket Office: 01923 496010
24hr Information: 09068 104104
Club Store: 01923 493005
Website: www.watfordfc.com

SPONSORS

CTX Computer Products

FANZINES

Clap Your Hands and Stamp Your Feet

KEY PERSONNEL

Chairman: Sir Elton John CBE
Vice Chairman (Football): C Lissack
Vice Chairman (Corporate): H Oundjian
Directors: B Anderson,
D Meller, H Oundjian
Club Secretary: J Alexander
Manager: Graham Taylor

COLOURS

Home: Yellow shirt with red sleeves
and black collar and cuffs,
red shorts with yellow tops
and two black hoops
Away: Blue and silver striped shirts
with red pinstripes, blue shorts
and blue stockings with red tops
and two black hoops

NICKNAME

The Hornets

20 FACTS

1 Watford started life as Watford Rovers in 1881. After a brief spell as West Herts, the club changed its name to Watford in 1898.

2 The club have never won the Championship in the top flight. Their highest league position came in 1982–83, when they finished second in the old First Division.

3 Before their play-off final victory over Bolton, Watford's finest hour had been in 1984 when a tearful Elton John watched the Hornets lose 2–0 to Everton in the FA Cup final.

4 The Hornets have not reached the Football League Cup final. They did get to the semi-final in 1979.

5 Graham Taylor's side have played in European competition once, in 1983–84. After a fantastic 4–3 aggregate victory over Kaiserslautern, they defeated the Bulgarian side Levski Spartak before losing to the Czech club Sparta Prague.

6 Watford's record victory is a 10–1 FA Cup first round demolition of Lowestoft Town in 1926.

7 Their record defeat is a 10–0 FA Cup first round humiliation at the hands of Wolverhampton Wanderers in 1912.

8 Hornets legend Luther Blissett holds the record for the most appearances in a Watford shirt. He made 415 league outings for the club.

9 Blissett is also the Hornets' all-time leading scorer. He scored a total of 180 goals for the club in all competitions.

10 Ex-Watford stars John Barnes and Kenny Jackett, currently the club's first-team coach, are the Hornets' most capped players. They played 31 times each for England and Wales respectively while at the club.

11 Cliff Holton holds the club record for the most goals scored in a season. He struck 48 times in the 1959–60 campaign.

12 Holton scored 42 of his record-breaking tally in the league. Watford's final total of 92 goals in Division Four that year is a club record.

13 The record attendance at Vicarage Road came on February 3, 1969 when 34,009 turned up to watch the Hornets take on Manchester United in an FA Cup fourth round replay.

14 Gifton Noel-Williams's goal against Crewe Alexandra on November 21, 1998, made him the first Watford player to score 20 senior goals for the club before his 19th birthday. He is also the club's youngest-ever scorer.

15 Nigel Gibbs has appeared for Watford in 15 seasons between 1983 and 1999, a club record.

16 Club captain and 1998–99 Player of the Year Steve Palmer is the only current Football League player also to have played first-class cricket.

17 Watford finished fifth in the Nationwide League Division One and qualified for the play-offs. They beat Birmingham City in a dramatic penalty shoot-out in the semi-finals after drawing 1–1 on aggregate and went on to beat Bolton Wanderers 2–0 at Wembley to gain their place in the Premiership. Nick Wright – with a spectacular overhead kick – and Allan Smart were Watford's Wembley goalscorers Their league record was:

Pld	W	D	L	F	A	Pts
46	21	14	11	65	56	77

18 Graham Taylor's side went out in the third round of the FA Cup, losing 5–2 to Tottenham Hotspur at White Hart Lane.

19 The Hornets had also suffered an early exit in the Worthington Cup. Drawn against Cambridge United in the first round, they were knocked out by the Division Three high-flyers, losing 2–1 on aggregate.

20 The top goalscorer in the league for Watford was Gifton Noel-Williams with 10 goals.

THE MANAGER

GRAHAM TAYLOR

Watford wizard Graham Taylor worked his magic yet again for the Hertfordshire side, leading them back to top-flight football after an absence of 11 years.

First time around, Taylor took Watford from the Fourth to the First Division in five seasons. The team finished a magnificent second behind Liverpool in their top-flight debut and reached the FA Cup final and third round of the UEFA Cup the following year.

He rejoined the Hornets in February 1996, following stints at Aston Villa and Wolves either side of the England job, but arrived too late to save Watford from relegation to the Second Division.

Taylor took a back seat at Vicarage Road for one season before the lure of management proved too much to resist. He instantly stirred up the Hornets and they regained their sting with two successive promotions in two seasons. Taylor achieved this despite spending an insignificant amount on key signings Nick Wright, Allan Smart and Michel Ngonge.

Taylor was a full-back for Grimsby Town and Lincoln City before a hip injury curtailed his playing career. He was appointed manager of Lincoln in 1972, aged just 28, before Elton John head-hunted him for the Watford post five years later.

SEASON REVIEW

Watford's '80s dream team of Elton John and Graham Taylor proved that lightning can strike twice by getting the Hornets buzzing again.

And having stormed to the Division Two Championship in such style, the team — comprising a select cluster of bargain buys and free transfers — was not about to stop there.

Watford's season began with three straight league wins, but the euphoria subsided with three consecutive defeats. Incredibly, another hat-trick of wins followed, which included a 1–0 victory over promotion favourites Ipswich Town.

Early exits from both cup competitions allowed the club to focus exclusively on promotion, and a 10-game unbeaten run from October to December lifted the club into third place. Prodigious front man Gifton Noel-Williams was scoring regularly, with fine support from Peter Kennedy, Nick Wright and Player of the Season Steve Palmer.

But the New Year brought little festive cheer, with five defeats in the first 10 league games of 1999. A famous 2–1 win over runaway leaders Sunderland could not disguise the fact that the Hornets were in a slump.

Their troubles were compounded by an injury to Noel-Williams, and Taylor's response was to thrust the much-maligned Tommy Mooney up front. Mooney surprised everyone, including himself, by firing eight goals in seven games as Watford stormed into the play-offs.

The Hornets disposed of Birmingham City via a penalty shoot-out, before two great strikes from Wright and Allan Smart sealed a famous 2–0 Wembley victory over Bolton Wanderers. Watford's second successive promotion put them into the Carling Premiership for the first time.

WATFORD

DATE	OPPONENT	SCORE	ATT.	BAZELEY	BONNOT	CHAMBERLAIN	DALEY	EASTON	GIBBS	GUDMUNDSSON	HAZAN	HYDE	IROHA	JOHNSON	KENNET
8.8.98	Portsmouth A	2–1*	15,275	s	–	p	–	p	–	–	p	p	–	–	p
15.8.98	Bradford H	1–0	10,731	–	–	p	s	p	–	–	p	p	–	–	p
22.8.98	Bristol City A	4–1	13,063	p	–	p	s	–	–	–	s¹	p	–	p²	p
25.8.98	Sunderland A	1–4	36,587	p	–	p	s	–	–	–	s	p	–	p	p
28.8.98	Wolves H	0–2	12,016	p	–	p	–	p	–	–	–	p	–	p	p
8.9.98	Huddersfield A	0–2	9,811	–	–	p	–	–	p	–	s	p	–	p	p
12.9.98	QPR H	2–1	14,251	–	–	p	–	–	p	–	s	p	–	p	p
19.9.98	Swindon A	4–1	8,781	–	–	p	–	–	p	–	s¹	p	–	p	p
26.9.98	Ipswich H	1–0	13,109	–	–	p	–	–	p	–	–	p	–	p	p¹
29.9.98	Sheffield Utd H	1–1	9,090	–	–	p	–	–	p	–	–	p	–	p	p
4.10.98	WBA A	1–4	11,840	s	–	p	–	–	p	–	p	p	–	p	p¹
10.10.98	Birmingham H	1–1*	10,096	s	–	p	–	–	p	–	–	p	–	p	p
17.10.98	Tranmere A	2–3	6,753	s	–	p	–	–	p	–	–	p	–	p	p
20.10.98	Bolton A	2–1	15,921	p	–	p	–	–	p	s	–	p	–	p	p¹
24.10.98	Port Vale H	2–2	8,750	p	–	p	–	–	–	p²	–	p	–	p	p
31.10.98	Bury A	3–1	4,342	p¹	–	p	–	–	–	s	s	p	–	p	p
3.11.98	Norwich H	1–1*	10,011	p	–	p	–	–	–	s	p	p	–	p	p
7.11.98	Oxford H	2–0	10,137	p	–	p	–	–	–	p	–	p	–	p	p
14.11.98	Stockport Co A	1–1	8,019	p	–	p	–	–	–	–	–	p	–	p¹	p
21.11.98	Crewe H	4–2	9,405	p¹	–	p	–	–	–	–	–	p	–	p	p
28.11.98	Crystal Palace A	2–2	19,521	p	–	p	–	–	–	–	–	p	–	p	p¹
5.12.98	Barnsley H	0–0	10,165	p	–	p	–	–	–	s	–	p	–	p	p
12.12.98	Stockport Co H	4–2	9,250	p	–	p	–	–	–	–	–	p	–	p¹	p
19.12.98	Grimsby A	1–2	6,679	p	–	p	–	–	–	s	–	p	–	p	p
26.12.98	Bristol City H	1–0	15,081	p	–	p	–	–	–	p	–	p	p	p	p
29.12.98	Norwich A	1–1	19,255	p	–	p	–	–	–	p	–	p	p	p	p
9.1.99	Portsmouth H	0–0	12,057	p	s	p	s	–	–	–	–	p	p	p	p
16.1.99	Wolves A	0–0	23,408	p	–	p	s	p	–	–	–	p	p	–	p
23.1.99	WBA H	0–2	11,664	p	–	p	p	–	–	–	–	p	p	p	p
30.1.99	Sunderland H	2–1	20,188	p	–	p	p	–	–	–	s	p	p	p	p
6.2.99	Bradford A	0–2	14,142	p	–	p	p	–	–	s	s	p	p	p	p
16.2.99	Huddersfield H	1–1	10,303	p	–	p	p	–	–	–	–	p	p	p	p
20.2.99	QPR A	2–1	14,918	p	–	p	–	p	–	–	p	–	–	p	p
26.2.99	Swindon H	0–1	8,692	p	–	p	s	p	–	–	s	–	–	p	p
2.3.99	Ipswich A	2–3	18,818	p	–	p	p	p	–	–	p	p	s	–	p
6.3.99	Sheffield Utd A	0–3	15,943	p	–	p	–	–	s	–	p	p	s	–	p
13.3.99	Oxford A	0–0	8,137	p	–	p	–	–	–	s	–	p	p	p	p
20.3.99	Bury H	0–0	9,336	p	–	p	–	–	–	p	s	p	–	p	p
3.4.99	Tranmere H	2–1	8,682	p	s	p	–	–	–	p	–	p	–	p	p¹
5.4.99	Birmingham A	2–1	24,877	p	s	p	p¹	–	–	–	p	s	–	p	p
10.4.99	Bolton H	2–0	13,001	p	–	p	–	–	–	–	s	p¹	–	p	p
17.4.99	Crewe A	1–0	5,461	p	p	p	–	–	–	–	s	p	–	–	p
24.4.99	Crystal Palace H	2–1*	15,590	p	–	p	–	–	–	–	–	p	–	p	p
27.4.99	Port Vale A	2–1	7,126	p	–	p	–	–	–	–	s	p	–	p	p
1.5.99	Barnsley A	2–2	17,098	p	–	p	–	–	–	–	s	p	–	p	p
9.5.99	Grimsby H	1–0	20,303	p	–	p	–	–	–	–	s	p	–	p	p¹

p Played, s Substitute, p³ Goals scored *including own goal

1998–99 DIVISION ONE APPEARANCES

LEE	MILLEN	MOONEY	NGONGE	NOEL-WILLIAMS	PAGE	PALMER	PERPETUINI	ROBINSON	ROSENTHAL	SMART	SMITH	WARD	WHITTINGHAM	WRIGHT	YATES
p¹	s	p	–	–	p	p	–	–	p	p	–	–	–	–	–
–	p	–	p¹	–	s	p	–	p	s	p	–	–	–	–	p
–	p	–	p	s	–	p	–	p	–	p	–	–	–	–	p¹
–	–	–	p	s	p	p	–	p	–	p¹	–	–	–	–	p
–	–	–	p	s	p	p	–	–	s	p	–	–	–	–	p
–	p	–	p	–	–	p	–	–	–	p	–	–	–	p	p
–	p¹	p	p	s	–	–	–	–	–	p¹	–	–	–	p	p
–	p	p	p	s	s	–	–	–	–	p²	–	–	–	p¹	p
–	p	p	p	s	–	–	–	–	–	p	–	–	–	p	p
–	p	p	–	p¹	–	s	–	–	–	p	–	–	–	p	p
–	p	p	–	s	–	p	–	s	–	p	–	–	–	p	–
–	p	p	–	p	p	–	–	–	–	p	–	–	–	p	–
–	p	p	–	p¹	p	–	–	p	–	p¹	–	–	–	–	–
–	–	s	–	p¹	p	p	–	p	–	p	–	–	–	–	–
–	–	s	–	p	p	p	–	p	–	p	–	–	–	s	–
–	–	p	p¹	–	p	p	–	–	–	p¹	–	–	–	p	–
–	–	s	–	p	p	p	–	p	–	–	–	–	–	p	–
–	–	–	–	p¹	p	p¹	–	p	–	–	–	–	–	p	–
–	–	s	–	p	p	p	–	p	–	p	–	–	–	p	–
–	–	p	s	p²	p	p	–	–	–	p	–	–	–	p¹	–
–	–	s	s	p	p	p	–	p	–	p	–	–	–	p¹	–
–	–	s	p	p	p	p	–	p	–	–	–	–	–	p	–
–	–	–	s	p²	p	p	–	p	–	p	–	–	–	p¹	–
–	–	s	–	p¹	p	p	–	p	–	p	–	–	–	p	–
–	–	–	–	p	p	p	–	–	–	p¹	–	–	–	–	–
–	–	s	–	p	p	p¹	–	s	s	p	–	–	–	–	–
–	–	s	–	p	p	p	–	–	–	p	–	–	–	p	–
–	–	s	–	p	p	p	–	–	–	p	–	–	–	p	–
–	–	s	–	p	p	p	–	–	s	p	–	–	–	–	–
–	–	s	–	p¹	p	p	–	–	–	–	–	–	–	p	–
–	–	–	–	–	p	p	–	s	–	p	–	s	–	p	–
–	–	p¹	s	–	p	p	–	–	–	p	s¹	–	–	p¹	–
–	–	–	–	–	p	p	–	p	–	p	p	–	–	p	–
–	–	s	–	–	p	p	–	p	–	p	s¹	–	–	–	–
–	–	p	–	–	p	p	–	p	–	p	s	p	–	p	–
–	–	p	s	–	p	p	–	p	–	–	p	–	–	p	–
–	–	s	–	–	p	p	p	–	–	–	p	–	p	s	–
–	–	s	s¹	–	p	p	–	p	–	p	–	–	p	–	–
–	–	p¹	–	–	p	p	–	p	–	p	–	–	–	–	–
–	–	p¹	s	–	p	p	–	p	–	p	–	–	s	p	–
–	–	p¹	s	–	p	p	–	p	–	–	–	–	p	p	–
–	–	p¹	s	–	p	p	–	p	–	p	s	–	p	p	–
–	–	p²	p	–	p	p	–	p	–	–	–	–	–	p	–
–	–	p¹	p¹	–	p	p	–	p	–	s	–	–	–	p	–
–	–	p	p	–	p	p	–	p	–	–	–	–	–	p	–

THE PLAYERS

During the 1998–99 season, 539 players made an appearance on the pitch. Each player is featured in the following section, whether he was ever-present or played just one match as a substitute.

The players are featured in alphabetical order and the statistics that are shown are an individual's total contribution this season, even if he has played for more than one club. If you would like to see a player's contribution to a particular club, all you have to do is turn to the Team Section, look up the relevant team and then find his record on the table that shows the players' statistics. For example, Dion Dublin's statistics for Coventry City can be found on page 110 and his performances for Aston Villa are on page 46. The club colours shown are the club with whom the player finished the season or for whom he made his last appearance in the 1998–99 Carling Premiership. The small lozenge beside each player's name indicates his usual position and the number featuring alongside is their squad number.

G = Goalkeeper   **FB** = Full-back   **CB** = Centre-back

M = Midfielder   **AM** = Attacking Midfielder   **S** = Striker

You will find that the categories of statistics vary according to the players' positions. Clearly more emphasis has been placed on goal attempts for strikers, whereas defenders will have tackling and defensive clearances featured. All players have discipline figures for Premiership matches only.

PLAYERS' AVERAGES

CATEGORY	STRIKER	ATTACKING MIDFIELDER	MIDFIELDER	DEFENDER
Goals/Shots	15%	9%	7%	9%
Shooting Accuracy	50%	46%	41%	39%
Passing Accuracy	70%	77%	80%	77%
Short Pass Accuracy	71%	81%	84%	86%
Long Pass Accuracy	50%	47%	49%	45%
Crossing Accuracy	25%	29%	29%	28%
Dribble Completion	60%	69%	73%	81%
Tackle Success	50%	58%	63%	66%

GOALKEEPER	
Saves/Shots 76%	Catch Success rate 95%

S Samassi ABOU • 24
WEST HAM UNITED • BORN: 4.8.73

Cult hero Samassi Abou barely got a look-in at Upton Park in 1998–99. The man from Cannes made a sizeable impact in his first season, but was reduced to just 187 minutes of Premiership football as West Ham looked elsewhere for goals.

Signed for £250,000 in October 1997, Abou almost joined Hearts in an early-season transfer.

That move fell through, as did a mooted deal with promotion-chasing Bradford. But he did eventually secure a loan period at Ipswich Town in December, making five appearances and scoring one goal before returning to London.

A skilful if unpredictable player, Abou managed just one shot on target for the Hammers in the 1998–99 season. With Ian Wright, John Hartson and Paul Kitson all ahead of him in the pecking order, the Ivory Coast-born player was always going to find it difficult to secure a first-team place.

The arrival of Italian Paolo Di Canio exacerbated the situation even more.

CB Tony ADAMS • 6
ARSENAL • BORN: 10.10.66

Captain Marvel: Tony Adams

APPEARANCES	
Start (sub)	26 (0)
Minutes on pitch	2340
GOAL ATTEMPTS	
Goals	1
DEFENDING	
Blocks	27
Headed clearances	261
Other clearances	127
Interceptions	57
Tackles won	67
PASSING	
Passing accuracy	87%
DISCIPLINE	
Fouls	28
Yellow cards	4
Red cards	0

Inspirational captain Tony Adams had another sterling year. His performances over the course of the 1998–99 season took him to fourth place in the Carling Opta defenders Index.

Adams, who earned an MBE in June, won 68% of his 98 challenges and made 388 clearances, 27 blocks and 57 interceptions.

Since Arsene Wenger became Arsenal manager, Adams has developed into an even better all-round player. He completed 87% of his passes and is clearly more comfortable on the ball than previously, finishing the season with a 92% dribble completion rate. Strangely, Adams declined as an attacking force, managing just one of his trademark goals from set-pieces.

In a season when Arsenal were criticized for their bad behaviour, Adams committed only 28 fouls and was booked just four times in the Premiership.

Troubled by a niggling back injury, Adams was forced to sit out part of the season, but his will to win is as strong as ever and he remains a vital member of Wenger's side.

A

S · Manuel AGOGO · 23
SHEFFIELD WEDNESDAY · BORN: 1.8.79

Ghanaian-born Junior Agogo was limited to just one Premiership appearance as a second-half substitute in the 2–0 home defeat by Leeds United in 1998–99.

Signed from non-league club Leary Constantine in Wealdstone, north London, Agogo's main asset is his pace, and it was this that prompted Wednesday to sign him in October 1996.

After making his Premiership debut and helping the Owls' youth side to the Northern Conference of the FA Premier Youth League in 1997–98, Agogo was widely expected to make the step up to regular first-team football at Hillsborough.

But this failed to materialize and, although he also made a brief appearance against Chelsea in the 1–0 FA Cup defeat, he could not win himself a regular place on Danny Wilson's team-sheet.

A young player with plenty of ability, Agogo has time on his side, but will be keen to make much more of an impact in the coming months.

AM · Gareth AINSWORTH · 26
WIMBLEDON · BORN: 10.5.73

When Wimbledon shelled out a then-club record £2 million for Gareth Ainsworth, they gained a tricky winger with a deadly accurate right foot.

Ainsworth pottered down to Selhurst Park from Port Vale last November with high hopes, but was forced to undergo surgery, restricting him to just eight league appearances for the Dons in the 1998–99 campaign.

When Ainsworth was fit, he displayed promising signs out on the wing. He connected with nearly four in 10 of all crosses delivered and finished with one goal assist to his credit.

He managed six efforts at goal and made 39 dribbles and runs, completing more than half of these unchallenged.

Ainsworth helped out in defence to good effect. He won a very healthy 60% of all tackles and made nine clearances. The only disappointing feature of his first Carling Premiership stint was his distribution, with more than half of all the passes he attempted going astray.

Uncertain future: Philippe Albert

CB · Philippe ALBERT · 27
NEWCASTLE UNITED · BORN: 10.8.67

Having retired from international football early in 1998 to concentrate on his career with Newcastle United, Belgian international Philippe Albert found himself training with the reserves when new boss Ruud Gullit joined the club.

The season began for him on the bench, with a substitute appearance at Chelsea and then three starts in a row. He completed 83% of his passes and 73% of his tackles, but in his first 1998–99 start Albert was tormented by Liverpool's Michael Owen, who bagged a sensational hat-trick in a 4–1 win.

Albert's last appearance for Newcastle was in the 1–0 defeat at Everton and the classy defender was quickly snapped up on loan by the man who signed him from Anderlecht for £2.65 million – then-Fulham manager Kevin Keegan.

He settled in very quickly at Craven Cottage, defending as elegantly as ever and scoring two goals before returning to St James's Park and a decidedly uncertain future at the end of the campaign.

Niclas ALEXANDERSSON • 26
SHEFFIELD WEDNESDAY • BORN: 29.12.71

Swedish international Niclas Alexandersson had an impressive season and proved to be a hard-working runner down the right-hand side of Wednesday's formation.

Scorer of three goals during 1998–99, Alexandersson also hit the target on 16 occasions. Two of his goals came in the superb win against Manchester United.

He demonstrated good passing ability, completing 77% of his passes and setting up three goals. One in five of his 76 crosses found a Wednesday player and he finished the season with a 78% dribble completion rate.

Alexandersson also showed the capacity to track back and win tackles. From 110 tackles made, he won 63%, and contributed 70 clearances and 28 interceptions.

Manager Danny Wilson will be pleased with the Swede's disciplinary record. From 2,610 minutes on the pitch in 1998–99, he only committed 15 fouls and avoided picking up any bookings. He could become a major weapon in Wednesday's attempt to establish themselves as a top Premiership outfit.

APPEARANCES	
Start (sub)	31 (1)
Minutes on pitch	2610
GOAL ATTEMPTS	
Goals	3
Shots on target	16
Shooting accuracy	50%
PASSING	
Goal assists	3
Passing accuracy	77%
Crossing accuracy	20%
DRIBBLING	
Dribbles & runs	68
Dribble completion	78%
DISCIPLINE	
Yellow cards	0
Red cards	0

Rory ALLEN • 21
TOTTENHAM HOTSPUR • BORN: 17.10.77

Young striker Rory Allen struggled to make an impact at White Hart Lane during the 1998–99 Carling Premiership campaign.

Beckenham-born Allen registered less than half an hour's playing time during his five substitute appearances for the north London club, managing just two efforts at goal, both off target.

In the previous season the former Spurs trainee had reaped two goals from 16 appearances, but initially an injury at the start of the 1998–99 campaign kept him out of the side. For the remainder of the season he was a regular starter for the reserves, gaining valuable experience.

Allen found a team-mate with 10 out of 15 passes and made two clearances during his time on pitch in the Premiership. But he flourished in the second team, finishing as the hot-shot for Tottenham Reserves in the Football Combination and giving new boss George Graham a gentle reminder that he has not lost his scoring touch and that he still has the talent to figure in his first-team plans.

Bernard ALLOU • 23
NOTTINGHAM FOREST • BORN: 19.6.75

Frenchman Bernard Allou arrived at the City Ground as part of Ron Atkinson's belated attempt to steer Forest to safety. He was brought in from Gary Lineker's last club Grampus Eight on a free transfer in March, as Atkinson looked for some French resistance to the First Division champions' inexorable slide back down to Division One.

However, Allou was not given the chance to show what he is truly capable of, with just a couple of appearances from the bench.

The 24-year-old midfielder, comfortable on either flank, demonstrated good control on the ball during the 34 minutes Allou spent on the pitch.

He embarked on three dribbles and runs and was unchecked each time, as well as connecting with his one cross into the opposition area.

Of just eight passes attempted by the Forest man, five found the feet of their intended targets. Allou twice attempted shots at goal, only to see one effort fly harmlessly wide and the other blocked.

John ALOISI • 28
COVENTRY CITY • BORN: 5.2.76

Coventry City signed John Aloisi from Portsmouth for a cut-price £1 million and the Australian international has already shown touches of Premiership class.

From just 693 minutes of football in the Carling Premiership, Aloisi was involved in eight goals – a goal per game.

He notched five himself from 10 shots on target and set up three more for team-mates. A quarter of his goal attempts hit the back of the net for City, a strike rate of which many top strikers would be proud.

The signs are promising, but he is still learning his trade in the country's top division. His liking for running with the ball has got the better of him on occasions, as shown by his modest 52% success rate from 27 dribbles and runs, and he completed just 69% of his passes.

Since his arrival in the Premiership John Aloisi has looked like a Coventry star in the making, and if he can displace either Noel Whelan or Darren Huckerby, 1999–2000 may prove to be a big season for the striker.

APPEARANCES	
Start (sub)	7 (9)
Minutes on pitch	693
GOAL ATTEMPTS	
Goals	5
Goals/shots ratio	26%
SHOOTING	
Shots on target	10
Shooting accuracy	53%
PASSING	
Goal assists	3
Passing accuracy	69%
DISCIPLINE	
Fouls	13
Offside	6
Yellow cards	1
Red cards	1

Andreas ANDERSSON • 40
NEWCASTLE UNITED • BORN: 10.4.74

APPEARANCES	
Start (sub)	11(4)
Minutes on pitch	919
GOAL ATTEMPTS	
Goals	2
Goals/shots ratio	13%
SHOOTING	
Shots on target	5
Shooting accuracy	33%
PASSING	
Goal assists	0
Passing accuracy	74%
DISCIPLINE	
Fouls	14
Offside	19
Yellow cards	0
Red cards	0

Swedish international Andrew Andersson arrived at Newcastle after an unsuccessful period at AC Milan. His international pedigree was evident but, as with a number of overseas players in England, he has taken time to settle.

Comings and goings at Newcastle have made life difficult for Andersson, who had to impress two managers in 1998–99. He struggled to sustain a regular run in the first team and, when selected by Ruud Gullit, found goals hard to come by.

During his 919 minutes of Premiership football, Andersson scored twice and troubled the keeper on five other occasions. His passing stats were suitably impressive for an international forward, with a completion rate of 74%. Andersson also likes to use his pace when running with the ball, but the Swede's 40% success rate in the tackle shows he still has to adjust to the physical aspects of forward play in England. However, Ruud Gullit may not allow the Swede the opportunity, as his signing of Duncan Ferguson suggests that Andersson may be surplus to requirements.

Darren ANDERTON • 9
TOTTENHAM HOTSPUR • BORN: 3.3.72

Following a good World Cup, Darren Anderton was relieved to go through the 1998–99 season virtually injury-free.

His form also benefited as a result, and his Carling Opta stats were good enough to place him 10th in the attacking midfielders Index.

One of his main attributes has always been his passing, and in 1998–99 he made 1,622, completing 73%. He scored three Premiership goals, two of them penalties, and created another nine. His shooting accuracy was modest at 38%, with 14 shots hitting the target and 23 missing. But he also scored one of the goals of the season in the FA Cup, a 30-yard screamer against Leeds.

Anderton completed an above-average 32% of his crosses and retained possession from 67% of his dribbles and runs. He was also involved defensively, winning 57% of his 134 challenges, blocking 14 shots and making 36 clearances and 27 interceptions.

On the downside, he conceded 44 fouls and was booked six times; but overall, his 1998–99 campaign can be considered a success.

APPEARANCES	
Start (sub)	31(1)
Minutes on pitch	2724
GOAL ATTEMPTS	
Goals	3
Shots on target	14
Shooting accuracy	38%
PASSING	
Goal assists	9
Passing accuracy	73%
Crossing accuracy	32%
DRIBBLING	
Dribbles & runs	43
Dribble completion	67%
DISCIPLINE	
Yellow cards	7
Red cards	0

Nicolas ANELKA • 9
ARSENAL • BORN: 14.3.79

APPEARANCES	
Start (sub)	34 (1)
Minutes on pitch	2807
GOAL ATTEMPTS	
Goals	17
Goals/shots ratio	18%
SHOOTING	
Shots on target	51
Shooting accuracy	54%
PASSING	
Goal assists	5
Passing accuracy	66%
DISCIPLINE	
Fouls	27
Offside	58
Yellow cards	1
Red cards	0

Over the last two seasons, Nicolas Anelka has proved to be one of the best young players in the Premiership. After a superb 1998–99, in which he won the PFA Young Player of the Year award, a host of top Continental clubs began clamouring for his signature.

The young Frenchman scored 17 times during the Premiership season, hitting the target with 51 shots. His overall shot tally of 95 was the third-highest in the top flight and he achieved a shooting accuracy of 54%.

Although it was rumoured that not all was well in his personal life, Anelka rarely got into trouble on the pitch and was booked just once in the Premiership.

His biggest problem seemed to lie with his reading of the game. He was caught offside on 58 occasions and needs to time some of his runs more carefully.

Anelka's 1998–99 season was never far from controversy, though. He accused team-mates of not passing to him, failed to attend the PFA awards and was regularly "misquoted" in the French press regarding his future.

Neal ARDLEY • 12
WIMBLEDON • BORN: 1.9.72

A hard-working and mobile member of the Wimbledon squad, Neal Ardley was in and out of their first XI during 1998–99.

Predominantly a wide midfield player, he was used to good effect on the Dons' right flank, providing sound defensive support for Kenny Cunningham at right-back.

He won 63% of his 32 tackles and committed 24 fouls – but managed to avoid the referee's notebook all season.

Ardley made 607 passes, completing 67%, and also claimed a goal assist. Wimbledon's style places a great emphasis on crosses, and Ardley delivered 144 during the season – more than any other Don – completing 23%.

His completion rate of 71% from 38 dribbles and runs shows he also keeps the ball well.

A confident player going forward, he fired in 15 shots at goal with five on target, six off target and four blocked. Unfortunately, he could not manage a goal during 1998–99.

Injury kept him out of the side on occasions, but he will be looking to make the right midfielder's berth his own in 1999-2000.

APPEARANCES
Start (sub)	16 (7)
Minutes on pitch	1503

GOAL ATTEMPTS
Goals	0
Shots on target	5
Shooting accuracy	45%

PASSING
Goal assists	1
Passing accuracy	67%
Crossing accuracy	23%

DRIBBLING
Dribbles & runs	38
Dribble completion	71%

DISCIPLINE
Yellow cards	0
Red cards	0

The incredible sulk: Nicolas Anelka

Alun ARMSTRONG • 20
MIDDLESBROUGH • BORN: 22.2.75

Middlesbrough fans are still waiting to see the best of striker Alun Armstrong.

Since signing from Stockport County for £1.5 million in February 1998 he has made just seven starts and 11 substitute appearances for the club.

Injury blighted his opportunities in 1998–99 and he did not appear in the first team until March 20, in the 2–1 win over Nottingham Forest at the City Ground.

He turned out on a further six occasions as a substitute before the end of the season, firing in five shots – including two on target – and being credited with one assist.

Armstrong did score one goal, and that was against one of the meanest defences in the history of English football, although it was a mere consolation in the 6–1 hammering at home by Arsenal, which most Boro supporters will be keen to forget.

Nonetheless, the statistics speak for themselves. He now has seven Boro goals and, fitness permitting, will be looking for plenty more in 1999–2000.

Chris ARMSTRONG • 11
TOTTENHAM HOTSPUR • BORN: 19.6.71

One of a trio of first-team strikers at Tottenham, Chris Armstrong was rotated with Steffen Iversen and Les Ferdinand throughout the season and, despite firing in a large number of shots on target, he fell short of a double-figures goal tally in 1998–99.

The former Crystal Palace striker had a modest season in front of goal, scoring just seven times and finishing with one goal assist.

He was always under pressure to deliver at Spurs in 1998–99 but completed a disappointing 59% of his passes and only a handful of his 46 crosses during the season.

His competitive streak led to his committing 62 fouls, picking up three bookings and one red card, and his reading of the game could do with improvement: he was caught offside more than 50 times, possibly a symptom of his frustrating time in front of goal.

Altering strike partners from week to week may also have affected Spurs' strikers adversely. Armstrong found forming a strike partnership difficult as a result, whether with Les Ferdinand or Steffen Iversen.

APPEARANCES	
Start (sub)	24 (10)
Minutes on pitch	2359
GOAL ATTEMPTS	
Goals	7
Goals/shots ratio	9%
SHOOTING	
Shots on target	42
Shooting accuracy	51%
PASSING	
Goal assists	1
Passing accuracy	59%
DISCIPLINE	
Fouls	62
Offside	53
Yellow cards	3
Red cards	1

Craig ARMSTRONG • 15
NOTTINGHAM FOREST • BORN: 23.5.75

APPEARANCES	
Start (sub)	20 (2)
Minutes on pitch	1711
GOAL ATTEMPTS	
Goals	0
DEFENDING	
Blocks	10
Headed clearances	126
Other clearances	76
Interceptions	30
Tackles won	16
PASSING	
Passing accuracy	77%
DISCIPLINE	
Fouls	24
Yellow cards	2
Red cards	0

Craig Armstrong seemed finally to have made the breakthrough into the first team at Nottingham Forest during 1998–99, but a change of manager and a swift turnover of personnel saw him move to Huddersfield Town for £750,000 at the end of February.

The utility defender, who is equally at home at left-back or in the centre, made 20 starts and came on twice as a substitute. He started the first 16 matches, but he will not remember his final appearance in a Forest shirt with much fondness, being part of the side which was ripped apart by Manchester United and on the wrong end of a record 8–1 scoreline.

Armstrong completed 77% of the 689 passes he attempted, won 43% of his tackles and made 10 blocks, 202 clearances and 30 interceptions, but looked a little out of his depth against top-quality Premiership strikers.

He will be hoping that he can now establish himself at the Alfred McAlpine Stadium and help push Huddersfield towards their promotion target, paving his way for another crack at the big time.

G — Pegguy ARPHEXAD • 22
LEICESTER CITY • BORN: 18.5.73

Pegguy Arphexad may finally get an opportunity to stake a claim as a first-team regular at Filbert Street in the 1999–2000 season, having found himself playing second fiddle to USA national 'keeper Kasey Keller for the last couple of years.

He made only four appearances during the 1998–99 season: two as a substitute and then as first choice in the final two league games of the season.

The former French under-21 international conceded three goals, kept two clean sheets and was on the winning side twice.

Arphexad had to make 10 saves – five from shots attempted inside the penalty area and the same number from long distance – and finished with a saves-to-shots ratio of 77%.

He only came to collect eight crosses, taking seven and missing one, and Martin O'Neill will be hoping that Arphexad can improve his distribution if he does step up to claim the number one jersey – his 47% completion rate was somewhat lower than Kasey Keller's 51% throughout the campaign.

Consistent challenger: Peter Atherton

FB — Peter ATHERTON • 2
SHEFFIELD WEDNESDAY • BORN: 6.4.70

APPEARANCES	
Start (sub)	38 (0)
Minutes on pitch	3412
GOAL ATTEMPTS	
Goals	2
PASSING & CROSSING	
Passing	1323
Passing accuracy	79%
Crossing	32
Crossing accuracy	28%
DEFENDING	
Tackles	109
Tackles won	70%
DISCIPLINE	
Fouls	36
Yellow cards	3
Red cards	1

A strong, dependable presence in the Sheffield Wednesday defence, club captain Peter Atherton was pivotal in leading the Owls away from relegation and into mid-table safety.

The big defender managed four efforts on target and scored in the early-season wins over Spurs and Blackburn when in midfield – but Atherton's defensive attributes were the main reason for his consistent season.

Playing mostly at right-back, he won 70% of his challenges and made more than 260 clearances, 37 interceptions – demonstrating his ability to read the game – and 21 blocks.

Atherton was one of Wednesday's most consistent performers, playing every minute of the season until seven minutes from the end of the finale at Charlton. His sending-off for two offences marred his excellent disciplinary record – just three bookings up to that point – and was a contributory factor in Wednesday missing out on a UEFA Cup place for Fair Play.

But Atherton's consistency will be called upon again in 1999–2000, as Wednesday seek to break into the Premiership's top half.

Espen BAARDSEN • 13
TOTTENHAM HOTSPUR • BORN: 7.12.77

Espen Baardsen took over from Ian Walker early in the season and once again proved himself to be a very agile shot-stopper. Unfortunately, George Graham's arrival led to the reinstatement of the Englishman in late November and Baardsen was forced to spend the rest of the season on the subs' bench.

The young Norwegian kept five clean sheets from his 12 starts and conceded 16 goals. He saved 78% of the shots he faced and claimed every catch he went up for. His distribution was accurate, even when kicking long – 41% is a very respectable figure for a Premiership keeper – and his 98% success rate from short range is also excellent.

The high point of his campaign came in the 0–0 draw with Arsenal at Highbury, when he made 11 saves and nine catches to record the highest Carling Opta points score by a Premiership goalkeeper all season.

Tottenham are lucky to have two quality goalkeepers at the club, but one wonders whether Baardsen will remain at Spurs if he does not get regular first-team football.

APPEARANCES	
Start (sub)	12 (0)
Minutes on pitch	1080
SHOT STOPPING	
Goals conceded	16
Clean sheets	5
Saves	57
Saves/shots	78%
DISTRIBUTION	
Distribution	362
Distribution %	53%
CATCHING	
Crosses caught	30
Crosses dropped	0
DISCIPLINE	
Yellow cards	0
Red cards	0

Celestine BABAYARO • 3
CHELSEA • BORN: 29.8.78

APPEARANCES	
Start (sub)	26 (2)
Minutes on pitch	2282
GOAL ATTEMPTS	
Goals	3
Shots on target	8
Shooting accuracy	62%
PASSING	
Goal assists	1
Passing accuracy	83%
Crossing accuracy	23%
DRIBBLING	
Dribbles & runs	50
Dribble completion	60%
DISCIPLINE	
Yellow cards	6
Red cards	0

Nigerian international Celestine Babayaro has come back well after missing much of the 1997–98 campaign with a broken leg, caused by his trademark somersault celebration in a pre-season match. He had a solid season in 1998–99 and earned a regular first-team slot.

He looked composed and confident when going forward, scoring three league goals. His passing was excellent, with 83% finding a Chelsea player – but only 23% of his crosses found their mark. He won 63% of his challenges and made 98 clearances, 12 interceptions and nine blocks.

Babayaro was booked six times and manager Gianluca Vialli will hope the midfielder can stay on his feet more when defending and reduce his card count in 1999–2000.

He also played a big part in Chelsea's forays into Europe and scored a good goal against Valerenga in the 1998–99 Cup Winners Cup.

Babayaro found his feet in the 1998–99 Premiership. He is a useful attacking option down the left flank and should cement his place in the Stamford Bridge starting line-up.

B

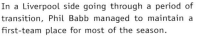

In a Liverpool side going through a period of transition, Phil Babb managed to maintain a first-team place for most of the season.

A pacy centre-back, Babb usually played on the left side of a back three which suffered its fair share of defensive difficulties over the course of the 1998–99 season.

Babb won 80% of his 71 tackles, made 15 blocks and 27 interceptions. He also made more than 300 clearances. He encountered some disciplinary problems on the pitch, as he committed 34 fouls and was booked six times in the Premiership.

He was rarely a threat in the opposition penalty area, his shooting stats showing that from six goal attempts he hit the target just twice. He also had just one assist to his credit.

His passing was up to scratch, with an 84% completion rate from more than 700 passes. He also completed one of his three crosses.

Babb is starting to settle into Liverpool's back line under Gerard Houllier, but with new additions to the squad he may find himself fighting for his place in 1999–2000.

APPEARANCES	
Start (sub)	24 (1)
Minutes on pitch	2107
GOAL ATTEMPTS	
Goals	0
DEFENDING	
Blocks	15
Headed clearances	203
Other clearances	98
Interceptions	27
Tackles won	57
PASSING	
Passing accuracy	84%
DISCIPLINE	
Fouls	34
Yellow cards	6
Red cards	0

APPEARANCES	
Start (sub)	17 (5)
Minutes on pitch	1253
GOAL ATTEMPTS	
Goals	4
Goals/shots ratio	19%
SHOOTING	
Shots on target	7
Shooting accuracy	33%
PASSING	
Goal assists	1
Passing accuracy	75%
DISCIPLINE	
Fouls	20
Offside	12
Yellow cards	2
Red cards	0

Two seasons ago Francesco Baiano was signed from Italian giants Fiorentina, where he played alongside Gabriel Batistuta. In the Premiership in 1998–99, the little Italian struggled to maintain a first-team spot in the heat of fierce competition from Paulo Wanchope, Deon Burton and Dean Sturridge.

Baiano played 1,253 minutes in the Premiership in 1998–99, and managed a modest return of four goals and one assist. He completed three-quarters of his passes and won more than half his challenges.

His position just off the front man allowed him to pick the ball up and run at defenders and his 72% completion rate from his dribbles and runs shows he is certainly capable of taking players on and beating them.

A shrewd goal provider, Baiano tends not to get involved defensively. Despite this, he still made 30 tackles and three interceptions.

At 31 years of age, we may have seen the best of Baiano, but his skill and guile in and around the penalty area will still be a valuable asset to Jim Smith's squad in 1999–2000.

Ibrahima BAKAYOKO • 26
EVERTON • BORN: 31.12.76

Signed from Montpellier on the back of rave reviews, Ibrahima Bakayoko struggled to settle into the Premiership in 1998–99 and had a disappointing first season at Everton.

He only scored four league goals but hit a further 16 shots on target, suggesting more could come once the Ivory Coast international adjusts to the pace of the game in England.

Dropping deep to get involved in build-up play, Bakayoko completed 71% of his passes; but his lack of Premiership experience showed with his dribble completion percentage. He made 111 runs with the ball but surrendered possession more often than he retained it.

The strongly-built Bakayoko won 50% of his challenges, exactly the Premiership average for a forward, and committed 21 fouls.

He struggled to stay in the Toffee's starting line-up, especially after the arrival of Kevin Campbell from Turkey. Reports suggest Bakayoko could be part of a deal to bring Campbell to Everton full-time. If so, he would leave English football without having been able to show what he is capable of.

APPEARANCES	
Start (sub)	17 (6)
Minutes on pitch	1438
GOAL ATTEMPTS	
Goals	4
Goals/shots ratio	10%
SHOOTING	
Shots on target	20
Shooting accuracy	49%
PASSING	
Goal assists	0
Passing accuracy	71%
DISCIPLINE	
Fouls	21
Offside	20
Yellow cards	3
Red cards	0

Sticky season: Ibrahima Bakayoko

Steve BAKER • 24
MIDDLESBROUGH • BORN: 8.9.78

Steve Baker first came to national attention when he performed a marvellous marking job on Steve McManaman in a 1997–98 Coca-Cola Cup tie.

The utility player had to wait quite a while to get his chance in the 1998–99 Premiership campaign, though, making his first appearance in the 2–1 victory over Coventry City. His only other outing was as a second-half substitute for Robbie Stockdale in the home defeat by Manchester United.

The 20-year-old had struggled with a hamstring injury and knee ligament damage, which had restricted his opportunities. When he did play he completed 81% of the 42 passes he attempted, won all six of the challenges he contested and made eight clearances and two interceptions.

Baker has been a regular at under-21 international level for the Republic of Ireland and will hope that the 1999–2000 season will provide more opportunities for him to establish himself in Bryan Robson's first team at the Riverside.

FB Michael BALL • 3
EVERTON • BORN: 2.10.79

An England under-21 full-back, Michael Ball's form earned him a full international call-up despite Everton's disappointing results through most of the 1998–99 season. He eventually helped the Toffeemen stay in the Carling Premiership and will be looking to build on his experience in 1999–2000.

Ball completed two-thirds of his passes and set up four goals. Of his crosses, 21% found their mark and he retained possession with 65% of his dribbles and runs. He does need to improve his tackling, though. He won only 57% of his challenges, committed 46 fouls and was booked eight times.

Everton have shown great faith in the youngster. Walter Smith installed him as the regular penalty-taker despite the presence of another spot-kick expert, David Unsworth.

Ball is a rarity in the Premiership – a quality English left-back. His form in the England under-21 side has been of a high standard and, if he can continue to improve, he could well find himself challenging for the left-back position in the senior side in the near future.

APPEARANCES	
Start (sub)	36 (1)
Minutes on pitch	3255
GOAL ATTEMPTS	
Goals	3
PASSING & CROSSING	
Passing	837
Passing accuracy	66%
Crossing	84
Crossing accuracy	21%
DEFENDING	
Tackles	150
Tackles won	57%
DISCIPLINE	
Fouls	46
Yellow cards	8
Red cards	0

AM Nick BARMBY • 8
EVERTON • BORN: 11.2.74

APPEARANCES	
Start (sub)	20 (4)
Minutes on pitch	1633
GOAL ATTEMPTS	
Goals	3
Shots on target	17
Shooting accuracy	61%
PASSING	
Goal assists	3
Passing accuracy	75%
Crossing accuracy	28%
DRIBBLING	
Dribbles & runs	55
Dribble completion	67%
DISCIPLINE	
Yellow cards	4
Red cards	0

A lively, hard-working midfielder-cum-striker, Nick Barmby had a disappointing season.

His confidence suffered a knock early on in the campaign when he was part of an Everton side struggling desperately to score goals. He did eventually help them break their duck at home and a return to form looked likely. But injuries forced him to sit out more matches than he would have liked during 1998–99.

He scored just three Premiership goals – two against his old club Middlesbrough – and managed only 1,633 minutes on the pitch during the season.

Despite injuries and inconsistent form, Barmby's ability remained intact. He completed 67% of his 55 dribbles and runs and created three goals. His passing was of its usual standard, with 75% of his 581 passes completed.

The former Tottenham playmaker will be looking for an improved season in 1999–2000. One plus point is that Everton will still be in the Premiership, where Barmby could resurrect his international, as well as his club, career.

John BARNES • 37
CHARLTON ATHLETIC • BORN: 7.11.63

One of the country's best players during the '80s and early '90s as an attacking midfielder, John Barnes's move to Charlton from Newcastle saw him playing in a holding role where he could utilize his passing skills. After finishing the 1998–99 season with Charlton, he was released by the south London club and has since set his sights on management.

Barnes's quality on the ball was always one of his best attributes and his 84% pass completion rate showed he had not lost his touch. He timed his moves well, retaining possession with 90% of dribbles and runs.

His deeper role restricted his ability to get forward and shoot: indeed, he only managed one shot on target throughout 1998–99. Barnes was used mainly as a substitute and as such accumulated just 474 minutes of Premiership football in 1998–99.

Barnes has blown the whistle on his playing career, but begins the 1999-2000 season as first-team coach at Glasgow Celtic, working under former Liverpool team-mate Kenny Dalglish.

APPEARANCES	
Start (sub)	2 (11)
Minutes on pitch	474
GOAL ATTEMPTS	
Goals	0
PASSING	
Passes	289
Passing accuracy	84%
DEFENDING	
Interceptions	13
Clearances	14
Tackles	21
Tackles won	57%
DISCIPLINE	
Fouls	3
Yellow cards	0
Red cards	0

FB Anthony BARNESS • 20
CHARLTON ATHLETIC • BORN: 25.3.73

A former youth team player at the Valley, Anthony Barness spent time on loan at Southend and Middlesbrough before he sealed a permanent move to Chelsea. Unfortunately, he failed to challenge for a regular starting spot at left-back and moved back to his childhood club, Charlton, in 1996.

Much of Barness's time at the Valley in 1998–99 was spent in the reserves, with three substitute appearances for the first team in the Premiership amounting to slightly more than an hour of Premiership football – all played away from home.

During his time on the pitch in 1998–99 he demonstrated his strength and judgement in the tackle, winning four out of his five challenges without conceding a foul. He also completed 67% of his passes and had three wayward shots.

The form of Chris Powell at left-back kept the Lewisham-born defender out of the side in 1998–99. Barness will be looking to try and force his way into the starting line-up in 1999–2000.

FB Earl BARRETT • 27
SHEFFIELD WEDNESDAY • BORN: 28.4.67

Limited to just a handful of substitute appearances in the 1998–99 season, ex-England international Earl Barrett was nevertheless a useful member of Sheffield Wednesday's squad.

Barrett was on loan at Sheffield United when the then-Wednesday manager Ron Atkinson signed him in February 1998 as a replacement for the injured Ian Nolan.

The former Oldham man quickly proved himself a good signing with some resolute displays at right-back, making a total of 10 Premiership appearances in the 1997-98 season.

In his 94 minutes on the pitch under Danny Wilson, he made five tackles and 49 passes, completing 86%. He may have lost some of the pace which was a trademark of his younger years, but he still got forward on two occasions for a 100% dribble completion rate.

His five appearances for Sheffield Wednesday in the 1998–99 season lifted his career total of league appearances to 411, a measure of his ability at the highest level.

CB — Gareth BARRY • 15
ASTON VILLA • BORN: 23.2.81

Controversy surrounded Gareth Barry's switch from Brighton to Aston Villa – but it was easy to see why the Carling Premiership club wanted him in their squad.

Positionally excellent for such a young player, 18-year-old Barry is already a regular in the England under-21 squad and trained with the senior party during the season.

Equally at home in a back three or a back four, he won 68% of his challenges and made 224 clearances. The youngster also looked comfortable going forward. He hit five shots on target, scoring twice, and completed 78% of his dribbles and runs. A fine crosser of the ball, his 47% completion rate would be the envy of many Premiership wingers.

One of his most eventful matches came in the end-of-season 4–3 home defeat by Charlton, where he scored at both ends in the first 15 minutes.

A fine first season in the top flight has already established Gareth Barry as a Premiership-class defender and a possible future England international.

APPEARANCES	
Start (sub)	27(5)
Minutes on pitch	2442
GOAL ATTEMPTS	
Goals	2
DEFENDING	
Blocks	22
Headed clearances	121
Other clearances	103
Interceptions	30
Tackles won	50
PASSING	
Passing accuracy	79%
DISCIPLINE	
Fouls	17
Yellow cards	3
Red cards	0

FB — Warren BARTON • 2
NEWCASTLE UNITED • BORN: 19.3.69

APPEARANCES	
Start (sub)	17 (7)
Minutes on pitch	1678
GOAL ATTEMPTS	
Goals	0
PASSING & CROSSING	
Passing	1052
Passing accuracy	78%
Crossing	55
Crossing accuracy	27%
DEFENDING	
Tackles	64
Tackles won	69%
DISCIPLINE	
Fouls	29
Yellow cards	3
Red cards	0

The signings of Didier Domi and Andy Griffin at the start of the year looked ominous for Warren Barton – and the former Wimbledon and Maidstone United defender was left kicking his heels in the reserves.

Barton knuckled down and won back his place, impressing manager Ruud Gullit with his work-rate. Following his return to first-team football, Barton was deployed in the centre of midfield, as well as in his usual full-back role.

His 1,678 minutes of Premiership football mostly came towards the end of the season and he put in some useful displays. He completed 78% of his passes and won 69% of his tackles. He made 164 clearances, 15 interceptions and blocked 12 shots. Barton was also keen to push forward to support the attack. He completed more than three-quarters of his dribbles and runs and more than a quarter of his crosses.

Despite his decent end-of-season run, he missed out in the FA Cup final and will be hoping to get his first-team place back for the start of the 1999–2000 campaign.

AM Chris BART-WILLIAMS • 11
NOTTINGHAM FOREST • BORN: 16.6.74

Known to team-mates and fans as the Bart Man, much was expected of Chris Bart-Williams after an influential 1997–98 season in the Nationwide League. Unfortunately his fortunes in the Premiership mirrored those of his club.

A slick-passing, creative midfielder, Bart-Williams scored three goals (including two in the last two games of 1998–99) but set up just one strike for his team-mates during the season, despite making almost 900 passes.

He finished the season with a fine 79% pass completion rate but the incisive key passes which can lead to goals were in short supply for the former England under-21 international.

Defence was not Bart-Williams's strong suit: he won a below-average 60% of his tackles and made 75 defensive clearances during the season. He also committed 28 fouls and found his way into the referee's notebook four times.

Bart-Williams had a superb year in the Nationwide League in 1997–98, ending with a championship and promotion for his side. He will now have to do it all again in 1999–2000 if Forest are to rejoin the top flight.

APPEARANCES	
Start (sub)	20 (4)
Minutes on pitch	1798
GOAL ATTEMPTS	
Goals	3
Shots on target	9
Shooting accuracy	31%
PASSING	
Goal assists	1
Passing accuracy	79%
Crossing accuracy	21%
DRIBBLING	
Dribbles & runs	37
Dribble completion	57%
DISCIPLINE	
Yellow cards	4
Red cards	0

Creative: Chris Bart-Williams

S Steven BASHAM • 24
SOUTHAMPTON • BORN: 2.12.77

Steven Basham's season in the Carling Premiership was a short but spectacular one.

A magnificent goal for Southampton against Blackburn at Ewood Park brought him to the attention of the general public.

Second Division Preston North End had already been looking at him and it was not long before they snapped him up on loan until the end of the 1998–99 season.

Basham's 83 minutes of Premiership football demonstrated his sharp eye for goal. He had two shots, both on target, with one of them being his goal.

He also completed more than half his passes and two of his five crosses in his brief Premiership outings.

Running with the ball on three occasions, he was dispossessed only once – and he won two of the four tackles he made as he showed he was not afraid of getting stuck in.

Basham's spell at Deepdale eventually became permanent when play-off flops Preston signed the young striker in June 1999. The fee was later decided by tribunal.

David BATTY • 23
LEEDS UNITED • BORN: 2.12.68

After the agony of that infamous World Cup penalty miss against Argentina, David Batty began the 1998–99 season suspended and did not play a match under Ruud Gullit until September. Rumours at the start of the season then proved true when Leeds re-signed the midfielder for £4.4 million.

A rib injury on his arrival at Elland Road put him out of action for the first few weeks. Then he found David Hopkin, Stephen McPhail and Player of the Year Lee Bowyer in fine form and only achieved a regular starting place in April.

Overall, Batty remained among the Premiership's most consistent passers, with an 85% completion rate in 1998–99.

After his return to Leeds, Batty's tackle rate improved from 71% to 76%, but with it came more yellow cards. Six league bookings for Leeds took his tally for the season to eight.

In his last spell at Leeds, Batty helped make them champions. Now he will aim to be a key element in David O'Leary's exciting new team being groomed to challenge for honours in the coming seasons at Elland Road.

APPEARANCES	
Start (sub)	16 (2)
Minutes on pitch	1480
GOAL ATTEMPTS	
Goals	0
PASSING	
Passes	1141
Passing accuracy	85%
DEFENDING	
Interceptions	24
Clearances	44
Tackles	76
Tackles won	74%
DISCIPLINE	
Fouls	32
Yellow cards	8
Red cards	0

Dave BEASANT • 13
NOTTINGHAM FOREST • BORN: 20.3.59

APPEARANCES	
Start (sub)	26 (0)
Minutes on pitch	2340
SHOT STOPPING	
Goals conceded	54
Clean sheets	3
Saves	116
Saves/shots	68%
DISTRIBUTION	
Distribution	863
Distribution %	61%
CATCHING	
Crosses caught	57
Crosses dropped	1
DISCIPLINE	
Yellow cards	2
Red cards	0

One of the most famous stoppers in the history of the English game, Dave Beasant made his name as the first man to save a penalty in an FA Cup final. His career has taken him from non-league football to the World Cup finals and, at 40, he is still going strong.

A Forest regular from the start of the 1998–99 season, Beasant produced many good performances in the opening months. But as Forest's fortunes nose-dived, Beasant's form dipped and he was replaced in the closing weeks of the season by Mark Crossley.

Beasant was good in the air. Dropping just one ball left him with a catch success rate of 98%. His distribution was also very good, with a third of his long kicks and 96% of his short kicks and throws finding their mark.

He would have preferred more than the three clean sheets that he finished the season with – and his disappointing saves-to-shots ratio was not helped by him conceding 13 goals in three games in February. But his early-season excellence proved that Dave Beasant is still a Premiership-class goalkeeper.

James BEATTIE • 16
SOUTHAMPTON • BORN: 27.2.78

James Beattie moved to the Dell before the start of the 1998–99 season in the deal which took Kevin Davies to Blackburn Rovers. If Saints fans thought they were getting a raw deal, they soon changed their minds.

It was ironic that in the season when Blackburn were relegated, Beattie turned into one of the Premiership's most exciting young talents. His late goal against Leicester in the Saints' penultimate home fixture secured a priceless 2–1 win and he scored four times in all, hitting the target with 22 of his 50 shots.

Though still raw, Beattie has good potential. Strong, pacy and with exceptional aerial ability, he has all the key attributes of a top striker.

He needs to work on making space for himself, and his pass completion rate of 59% was rather disappointing. But he earned his first England under-21 caps during the season and scored from the penalty spot against Hungary in Budapest.

Named Saints' Player of the Year in 1998–99, he is definitely one to watch for the future.

APPEARANCES	
Start (sub)	22 (13)
Minutes on pitch	2188
GOAL ATTEMPTS	
Goals	5
Goals/shots ratio	10%
SHOOTING	
Shots on target	22
Shooting accuracy	44%
PASSING	
Goal assists	7
Passing accuracy	59%
DISCIPLINE	
Fouls	66
Offside	26
Yellow cards	4
Red cards	0

Mikkel BECK • 25
DERBY COUNTY • BORN: 12.5.73

APPEARANCES	
Start (sub)	19 (15)
Minutes on pitch	1808
GOAL ATTEMPTS	
Goals	6
Goals/shots ratio	14%
SHOOTING	
Shots on target	22
Shooting accuracy	51%
PASSING	
Goal assists	4
Passing accuracy	71%
DISCIPLINE	
Fouls	31
Offside	30
Yellow cards	2
Red cards	0

Competition for places in Boro's front line was hotter than ever in 1998–99, with Hamilton Ricard, Paul Merson, Brian Deane, Mikkel Beck, Andy Campbell and Alun Armstrong all vying for the two striker spots at various times.

Danish international Beck struggled to force his way in on a regular basis. He was never left out of Bryan Robson's squad, but 14 of his 27 appearances for Boro were from the bench.

Beck, who co-owns an exclusive Danish restaurant in Knightsbridge, was a *cordon bleu* treat too tasty for Derby connoisseur Jim Smith to resist and the Rams' boss snapped up the unsettled forward from the Middlesbrough menu on transfer deadline day for £500,000.

He hit the target with 51% of his 43 shots during the season and was credited with four assists. He also completed an above-average 63% of his dribbles and runs.

So far he has scored just once for Derby, but with two fellow-strikers being transfer-listed in the close season he must feel 1999–2000 could be the year he sets the Premiership alight – and resurrects his international career.

AM

David BECKHAM • 7
MANCHESTER UNITED • BORN: 2.5.75

B

After his infamous sending-off in France 98, David Beckham earned instant notoriety and returned to England to face a torrent of abuse from non-Manchester United supporters.

His answer was to deliver his best-ever year for the club, helping them end the season as treble-winners.

Generally considered one of Europe's best crossers of the ball, Beckham delivered 414 crosses in the league and completed an impressive 30%. His centres led to goals throughout the domestic and European season and his 14 Premiership assists demonstrated his creativity from the right flank.

He scored six league goals from 49 shots, with three coming from free-kicks. The last was perhaps the most important, a rising drive against Spurs on the season's final day. United went on to win and take the Premiership title.

Beckham has claimed the hostility he received from opposing fans actually improved his game – and with Euro 2000 approaching, England supporters will hope he can translate his United form on to the international stage.

APPEARANCES	
Start (sub)	33 (1)
Minutes on pitch	2884
GOAL ATTEMPTS	
Goals	6
Shots on target	16
Shooting accuracy	33%
PASSING	
Goal assists	14
Passing accuracy	72%
Crossing accuracy	30%
DRIBBLING	
Dribbles & runs	108
Dribble completion	84%
DISCIPLINE	
Yellow cards	6
Red cards	0

Top crosser: David Beckham

CB

David BEHARALL • 33
NEWCASTLE UNITED • BORN: 8.3.79

Twenty-year-old defender David Beharall broke into the first team at St James's Park as Newcastle United wound down their Premiership season while preparing for the FA Cup final.

The youngster made his first appearance against Wimbledon and will have been greatly heartened by Ruud Gullit's assertion afterwards that "Beharall was the best man on the pitch".

He marked John Hartson during that game and, although the big Welshman scored for the Dons, Beharall generally played him very well and also found time and space to create a penalty from which Alan Shearer scored.

Beharall completed 84% of the 159 passes that he attempted, won 27% of the challenges he made and weighed in with a healthy 66 clearances.

Now that he has had a taste of first-team action, his ambition in the 1999–2000 season will be to establish himself as a contender for the first team and become part of Ruud Gullit's rebuilt side.

Francis BENALI • 15
SOUTHAMPTON • BORN: 30.12.68

Several Saints managers have tried to replace Francis Benali – but to no avail! When Patrick Colleter arrived at the Dell back in December 1998, Benali's days seemed to be numbered. But with four games of the season remaining, the 30-year-old was back in the starting XI.

With the score locked at 0–0 in Southampton's penultimate match of 1998–99 against Wimbledon, Benali made a brilliant goal-line clearance, his second of the season, to help keep the Saints in the Premiership.

A one-club man, Benali showed his loyalty to the Saints with 41 tackles and a host of important blocks and interceptions. He also emerged as a very clean player with just 18 fouls – an average of one every 100 minutes.

A better full-back than he is often given credit for, Benali is capable of delivering a telling ball into the box and connected with a team-mate with 36% of his 42 crosses.

The 1999–2000 campaign will inevitably be talked of as his last – every season is – but with almost 300 league appearances behind him, he is clearly not a man to be budged.

APPEARANCES	
Start (sub)	19 (4)
Minutes on pitch	1802
GOAL ATTEMPTS	
Goals	0
PASSING & CROSSING	
Passing	661
Passing accuracy	74%
Crossing	42
Crossing accuracy	36%
DEFENDING	
Tackles	41
Tackles won	63%
DISCIPLINE	
Fouls	18
Yellow cards	2
Red cards	0

John BERESFORD • 3
SOUTHAMPTON • BORN: 4.9.66

Former Newcastle favourite John Beresford missed almost all of the 1998–99 season through injury, playing only 55 minutes in total. He suffered serious knee damage in Southampton's opening match of the season against Liverpool at the Dell.

Although widely expected to miss the entire 1998–99 season, Beresford came back into action as a substitute in Southampton's final two matches, as the south coast strugglers fought to avoid the drop.

He managed just 17 passes and three crosses, but his completion rates were poor. He also showed his lack of match practice by winning just two out of seven challenges.

Beresford settled well at the Dell after his £1.5 million transfer in February 1998 and had an excellent first few months. He started the 1998–99 season as first-choice left-back with only Francis Benali as a rival for his berth. But Patrick Colleter was signed when Benali broke his arm in December, so there will be plenty of competition for the left-back slot in the 1999–2000 season.

Marlon BERESFORD • 13
MIDDLESBROUGH • BORN: 2.6.69

Former Burnley goalkeeper Marlon Beresford spent most of the 1998–99 season watching from the bench as back-up to Mark Schwarzer, but stepped into the breach when the Australian was out injured for four Premiership games in the autumn.

In his four Premiership outings, Beresford conceded seven goals, failing to keep a single clean sheet, but despite this he did not appear on a losing side as Boro consolidated their good start to the season.

He made 13 saves, caught 12 crosses and punched away two more, but dropped two centres into his penalty area.

Beresford was a popular figure at Burnley, where he had a fanzine named after him, but he actually began his career across the Pennines at Sheffield Wednesday.

He did not manage a single league game for the Owls, however, and with Mark Schwarzer in such fine form it is unlikely he will play a major part in the top flight for Boro unless injury or loss of form strikes Bryan Robson's number one.

CB Henning BERG • 21
MANCHESTER UNITED • BORN: 1.9.69

Defender Henning Berg struggled to maintain a regular place in the 1998–99 starting line-up, with Alex Ferguson favouring Jaap Stam and Ronny Johnsen for most of the season.

But when his chance came, Berg provided the stability and poise needed to fill in at centre-back, and played a total of 1,082 minutes in the Premiership.

Though he only won possession with a below-average 63% of his 40 tackles, he made 141 clearances, 12 interceptions and nine blocks. He also made several match-winning clearances during United's Champions League campaign, and his displays against Inter Milan proved crucial to their victory.

The former Norwegian Player of the Year showed a cool head when bringing the ball out of defence, completing an impressive 91% of his 391 passes from the back. He was also credited with two goal assists.

The ideal defensive squad player, Henning Berg would probably start in most other Premiership sides, but he certainly played his part in United's treble-winning campaign.

APPEARANCES
Start (sub)	10 (6)
Minutes on pitch	1082

GOAL ATTEMPTS
Goals	0

DEFENDING
Blocks	9
Headed clearances	99
Other clearances	42
Interceptions	12
Tackles won	25

PASSING
Passing accuracy	91%

DISCIPLINE
Fouls	14
Yellow cards	1
Red cards	0

AM Patrik BERGER • 15
LIVERPOOL • BORN: 10.11.73

APPEARANCES
Start (sub)	30 (2)
Minutes on pitch	2579

GOAL ATTEMPTS
Goals	7
Shots on target	32
Shooting accuracy	52%

PASSING
Goal assists	3
Passing accuracy	78%
Crossing accuracy	39%

DRIBBLING
Dribbles & runs	106
Dribble completion	73%

DISCIPLINE
Yellow cards	4
Red cards	0

At the start of 1998–99 it looked as if Patrik Berger was about to leave Anfield after making just nine starts in the previous campaign. But he worked hard for a place in the first XI and ended the campaign as the highest-scoring Liverpool player in the Carling Opta Index.

A Czech international, Berger is a classy attacking midfielder with an eye for goal. His ferocious left foot produced seven Premiership goals during 1998–99 and he stung the hands of opposition goalkeepers on 25 occasions.

Despite his obvious creative ability, he is not afraid to chase back and tackle opponents. He won 62% of his 103 tackles, well above the Premiership average for an attacking midfielder, and completed 78% of his passes.

He confirmed his status as one of the league's top crossers, with a completion rate of 39% from 119 centres, again well above the Premiership average.

After a frustrating season in 1997–98, Berger has adapted to the increased work-rate and pace of English football and is fully justifying his £3.25 million transfer fee.

Dennis BERGKAMP • 10
ARSENAL • BORN: 18.5.69

Another superb domestic campaign in 1998–99 for the Dutch destroyer ultimately ended in great disappointment for Dennis Bergkamp when he and his team surrendered their cherished Premiership and FA Cup Double to Manchester United.

After a slow start to the campaign, in which he seemed to be suffering with a severe World Cup hangover, Bergkamp hit form in style and scored a series of brilliant goals which helped him finish the year at the top of the Carling Opta attackers Index.

Bergkamp finished with 12 Premiership goals and 12 goal assists to his credit. His season's highlights included the winning goal in January's 1–0 victory over Chelsea and the four assists he claimed in Arsenal's fabulous 5–0 demolition of Leicester City in February.

Despite having his crucial penalty saved by Peter Schmeichel in the FA Cup semi-final replay, Bergkamp's touch, passing and finishing continued to be of the highest quality – and once again his best goals lit up the Premiership.

APPEARANCES	
Start (sub)	28 (1)
Minutes on pitch	2404
GOAL ATTEMPTS	
Goals	12
Goals/shots ratio	15%
SHOOTING	
Shots on target	47
Shooting accuracy	58%
PASSING	
Goal assists	12
Passing accuracy	68%
DISCIPLINE	
Fouls	36
Offside	22
Yellow cards	5
Red cards	0

Eyal BERKOVIC • 29
WEST HAM UNITED • BORN: 2.4.72

APPEARANCES	
Start (sub)	28 (2)
Minutes on pitch	2331
GOAL ATTEMPTS	
Goals	3
Shots on target	15
Shooting accuracy	56%
PASSING	
Goal assists	10
Passing accuracy	85%
Crossing accuracy	43%
DRIBBLING	
Dribbles & runs	141
Dribble completion	79%
DISCIPLINE	
Yellow cards	3
Red cards	0

Eyal Berkovic was West Ham United's main creative force in both 1997–98 and 1998–99.

His performances have attracted great attention – Liverpool are just one of the top clubs reported to be interested in him. – and rumours constantly surround the future of the little Israeli international.

But it was his notorious training ground spat with striker John Hartson that earned Berkovic the biggest headlines in 1998–99.

A very good passer of the ball, he completed 85% of his 1,422 passes and was credited with 10 goal assists. The West Ham playmaker hit the target with 15 shots and scored league goals in the games against Liverpool, Charlton Athletic and Derby County.

Always a threat when running at defences, he achieved an excellent dribble completion rate of 79% from 141 dribbles and runs – well above the Premiership average for an attacking midfielder of 69%.

Berkovic is a valuable attacking player, but his well-below-average 44% tackle success rate shows that defending is not his forte.

Nicola BERTI • 4
TOTTENHAM HOTSPUR • BORN: 14.4.67

Experienced Italian international Nicola Berti was instrumental in preserving Spurs' Premiership future at the end of 1997–98, having been signed from Inter Milan by then-boss Christian Gross.

But following the swift departure of the Swiss coach after just three games of the 1998–99 season Berti, in common with several of his Spurs team-mates, found getting himself a regular place in the first team under new boss George Graham to be something of a challenge.

He made a promising start to the season, playing 311 minutes and firing in four shots. He also completed 76% of his passes and won 82% of his tackles as Spurs hovered in mid-table limbo.

But by January 1999, it was becoming clear that his chances of first-team action were dwindling and he was released on a free transfer to Spanish club Alaves.

Berti was swiftly replaced in the Spurs squad by German midfield star Steffen Freund.

APPEARANCES	
Start (sub)	4 (0)
Minutes on pitch	311
GOAL ATTEMPTS	
Goals	0
PASSING	
Passes	129
Passing accuracy	76%
DEFENDING	
Interceptions	4
Clearances	15
Tackles	11
Tackles won	82%
DISCIPLINE	
Fouls	10
Yellow cards	1
Red cards	0

Slaven BILIC • 28
EVERTON • BORN: 11.9.68

APPEARANCES	
Start (sub)	4 (0)
Minutes on pitch	360
GOAL ATTEMPTS	
Goals	0
DEFENDING	
Blocks	0
Headed clearances	41
Other clearances	16
Interceptions	3
Tackles won	12
PASSING	
Passing accuracy	77%
DISCIPLINE	
Fouls	4
Yellow cards	1
Red cards	0

Slaven Bilic's 1998–99 Premiership season proved a rather short one. Injuries have denied Bilic the chance to convince Walter Smith that his future lies at Goodison Park.

The big Croatian international is a strong, dominating figure in the centre of the defence. He won 80% of his 15 tackles while in the Everton first team, committing just four fouls and picking up one yellow card.

Bilic made 57 clearances in his 360 minutes of Premiership football, which highlights the pressure the Everton defence were under at the start of the season.

He was useful on the ball, completing all three of his dribbles and runs and finding a team-mate with 77% of his 115 passes.

The Croatian, who earned notoriety in France after being accused of getting Laurent Blanc sent off in the World Cup, only managed a single – blocked – shot at goal in 1998–99.

Walter Smith's purchase of Marco Materazzi may have been as a direct replacement for the former West Ham stopper, who may need a move to return to first-team football.

FB Stig-Inge BJORNEBYE • 20
LIVERPOOL • BORN: 11.12.69

A regular starter at left wing-back under Roy Evans, Stig-Inge Bjornebye found keeping a place in the first XI more of a challenge after Gerard Houllier took sole charge of the team.

Houllier's experiments, especially with the defence, meant the Norwegian international, who arrived in December 1992, started just one of Liverpool's last 10 matches.

Bjornebye played 1,860 minutes in the Premiership during 1998–99 and generally performed well in a fluctuating defensive unit.

He won 78% of his tackles – well above the average for a Premiership defender – and achieved a fine pass completion rate of 79% over the season. He was also impressive when running with the ball, with a 98% completion rate from his 28 dribbles and runs.

Bjornebye always enjoys charging down the left wing, but he managed a cross completion rate of just 17% from 75 crosses and 19 corners, well below the norm.

Houllier is expected to make more changes before and during 1999–2000, and Bjornebye's chances could be even further restricted.

APPEARANCES	
Start (sub)	20 (3)
Minutes on pitch	1860
GOAL ATTEMPTS	
Goals	0
PASSING & CROSSING	
Passing	1017
Passing accuracy	79%
Crossing	94
Crossing accuracy	17%
DEFENDING	
Tackles	64
Tackles won	78%
DISCIPLINE	
Fouls	35
Yellow cards	5
Red cards	0

CB Dean BLACKWELL • 5
WIMBLEDON • BORN: 5.12.69

APPEARANCES	
Start (sub)	27(1)
Minutes on pitch	2391
GOAL ATTEMPTS	
Goals	0
DEFENDING	
Blocks	27
Headed clearances	245
Other clearances	114
Interceptions	40
Tackles won	73
PASSING	
Passing accuracy	71%
DISCIPLINE	
Fouls	9
Yellow cards	0
Red cards	0

One of the Premiership's most under-rated defenders, Blackwell was a rock at the heart of the Dons' defence alongside Chris Perry.

He won an above-average 71% of his challenges, made more than 350 clearances and intercepted the ball 40 times. He also blocked 27 shots during the season.

The Wimbledon stopper was a reasonably composed figure on the ball, completing 71% of his 393 passes and one of his three crosses. When he decided to bring the ball out from the back Blackwell was competent enough, completing all 10 of his dribbles and runs.

But despite his aerial threat at set-pieces and corners, he failed to register a shot on target during the entire season. Two of his three efforts finished off target and the third was blocked.

Blackwell's composure and timing in the tackle earned him the best disciplinary record for a defender in the Premiership. He conceded just nine fouls during the season and was neither booked nor sent off in the league - a fabulous effort for a centre-back.

B

Nathan BLAKE • 14
BLACKBURN ROVERS • BORN: 27.1.72

S

Welsh international Nathan Blake struggled to maintain a regular starting spot following his arrival from Bolton Wanderers for £3.75 million in October 1998 (rising to £4 million with appearances).

Blake played 868 minutes of Premiership football in 1998–99, scoring three goals from his nine shots on target. He also completed 69% of his passes and found a team-mate with three of his 10 crosses. But his physical approach, which proved so successful in Division One, led to him committing 22 fouls.

His fine form at the Reebok Stadium for Bolton at the start of the season suggested he could be a valuable addition to the Ewood Park side. And Blake's Blackburn career started well when he rescued a point against Nottingham Forest with two well-taken goals. But a bad injury shortly after that left him on the sidelines, alongside several other multi-million pound strikers at the club.

Rovers fans hope he will return fit and ready for the fray after a good pre-season and they will see the real Nathan Blake in 1999–2000.

APPEARANCES	
Start (sub)	9 (2)
Minutes on pitch	868
GOAL ATTEMPTS	
Goals	3
Goals/shots ratio	10%
SHOOTING	
Shots on target	9
Shooting accuracy	31%
PASSING	
Goal assists	0
Passing accuracy	69%
DISCIPLINE	
Fouls	22
Offside	14
Yellow cards	0
Red cards	0

Jesper BLOMQVIST • 15
MANCHESTER UNITED • BORN: 5.2.74

AM

APPEARANCES	
Start (sub)	20 (5)
Minutes on pitch	1625
GOAL ATTEMPTS	
Goals	1
Shots on target	7
Shooting accuracy	50%
PASSING	
Goal assists	3
Passing accuracy	82%
Crossing accuracy	32%
DRIBBLING	
Dribbles & runs	133
Dribble completion	77%
DISCIPLINE	
Yellow cards	2
Red cards	0

Swedish international Jesper Blomqvist has provided valuable cover for Ryan Giggs on the left flank – and is arguably a more effective player than the Welshman.

The former IFK Gothenburg winger was used exclusively in the wide left position – even in the Champions League final, when Giggs played on the right wing. He delivered 115 Premiership crosses, completing 32% (Giggs managed 14%), completed 82% of his passes and supplied three goal assists.

Alex Ferguson employs him as a provider rather than a goalscorer, and this is reflected by his solitary Premiership goal in 1998–99.

He does not ignore the game's more physical side. Even though he played less football than Giggs, he still put in more challenges and won a higher percentage. Defensively, he also made 18 clearances and 11 interceptions.

The strength of the Manchester United squad means that Blomqvist is second choice for his preferred position behind Giggs. But his performances were vital to the success of United's treble-winning season.

AM **Luis BOA MORTE • 21**
ARSENAL • BORN: 4.8.77

Predominantly employed as cover for Marc Overmars on the left flank, Luis Boa Morte struggled to oust the current Highbury first-teamers in 1998–99. As a result he spent the majority of the season in the reserves.

Restricted to a handful of league appearances, mostly as a substitute, Boa Morte showed brief glimpses of his ability, completing 80% of his dribbles and runs, 61% of his passes and 25% of his crosses.

However, his shooting was a disappointment and he managed to hit the target only once from ten shots.

With the arrival of Nwankwo Kanu and Kaba Diawara, competition for attacking positions at Highbury is increasing and manager Arsene Wenger may instead make a decision to send Boa Morte out on loan in order to boost his confidence.

But with Arsenal's squad-strengthening set to continue, the Portuguese youngster may find himself struggling to command a regular place and may find it necessary to move to secure first-team football.

 S **Paul BOERTIEN • 23**
DERBY COUNTY • BORN: 20.1.79

Paul Boertien was a first-year professional at Brunton Park with Carlisle United in the 1997–98 season, but little more than a year later he made his debut for Derby County in the Premiership after the Rams snapped the youngster up. He surely must be pinching himself to make sure he is not dreaming!

The 20-year-old full-back made his nine-minute substitute appearance away at Chelsea on the final day of the 1998–99 season and at least helped the Rams grab a late consolation goal as the Blues ran out 2–1 winners.

Boertien made just three passes – all of which found a team-mate – in his brief appearance, along with one clearance and interception, so the statistics are hardly sufficient to paint a detailed picture of whether or not Derby County have secured a bargain buy.

But in 1999–2000, Boertien may well have more opportunities to show what he can do, pitting his wits against some of the world's top players as he looks to establish himself in the top flight.

 M **George BOATENG • 11**
COVENTRY CITY • BORN: 5.9.75

Snapped up from Dutch club Feyenoord in 1997–98, George Boateng must rank as one of the best value-for-money signings over the last few seasons.

His acclaimed performances in the centre of Coventry City's midfield were a major factor in Gordon Strachan's side's rise above the relegation dogfight in 1998–99.

Boateng frequently looked for the more difficult defence-splitting pass to release Darren Huckerby or Noel Whelan, resulting in a below-average pass completion rate of 72%. But he was credited with six goal assists over the course of the season.

The Dutchman scored four goals during the campaign and hit the target with 15 of his shots. His two-goal salvo against Aston Villa in February helped the Sky Blues to an historic 4–1 victory at Villa Park and proved that Boateng was a valuable force in the midfield.

Boateng's crossing abilities also came to the fore in 1998–99, when he completed 34% of his 71 crosses – some way above the Premiership average for a midfielder.

George Boateng's performances suggest that he will be among the first names on the team sheet in 1999–2000 if the Dutchman is not prised away from Highfield Road with a big-money bid.

APPEARANCES	
Start (sub)	29 (4)
Minutes on pitch	2635
GOAL ATTEMPTS	
Goals	4
PASSING	
Passes	1167
Passing accuracy	72%
DEFENDING	
Interceptions	29
Clearances	55
Tackles	148
Tackles won	61%
DISCIPLINE	
Fouls	51
Yellow cards	10
Red cards	0

B

M — Lars BOHINEN • 14
DERBY COUNTY • BORN: 8.9.69

Norwegian international midfielder Lars Bohinen has proved a valuable link man in the Carling Premiership.

Now with the Rams (via Nottingham Forest and Blackburn Rovers) Bohinen has shown consistent composure and an eye for goal. On the ball, 75% of his 1,248 passes in 1998–99 found their man, and the same proportion of his 101 dribbles and runs were completed.

Bohinen also liked to shoot from outside the box. Eleven shots hit the target, 12 were blocked and 18 did not trouble the goalkeeper.

His creativity, allied to his passing skills, resulted in four goal assists, but he did not manage to find the net himself in 1998–99.

Defensively, he won 63% of his 115 tackles and made 32 interceptions in midfield. He found his name in the referee's notebook on six occasions, but avoided being sent off.

Bohinen is in direct competition with a number of good passers of the ball at Derby. But since the departure of Lee Carsley, he has seen his first-team appearances increase – and his form has benefited as a result.

APPEARANCES	
Start (sub)	29 (3)
Minutes on pitch	2516
GOAL ATTEMPTS	
Goals	0
PASSING	
Passes	1248
Passing accuracy	75%
DEFENDING	
Interceptions	32
Clearances	43
Tackles	115
Tackles won	63%
DISCIPLINE	
Fouls	34
Yellow cards	6
Red cards	0

FB — Thierry BONALAIR • 17
NOTTINGHAM FOREST • BORN: 14.6.66

APPEARANCES	
Start (sub)	24 (4)
Minutes on pitch	2165
GOAL ATTEMPTS	
Goals	1
PASSING & CROSSING	
Passing	897
Passing accuracy	75%
Crossing	49
Crossing accuracy	29%
DEFENDING	
Tackles	116
Tackles won	54%
DISCIPLINE	
Fouls	24
Yellow cards	3
Red cards	0

An experienced French defender signed by Dave Bassett on a free transfer from Swiss side Neuchatel Xamax in the summer of 1997, Thierry Bonalair was a regular starter in Nottingham Forest's disastrous 1998–99 Premiership campaign.

Able to play in a variety of positions across the back four, the Parisian made 24 starting appearances and four as a substitute, mainly at right-back. With Forest pinned back in their own half for long periods he was unable to get forward as often as he had in the First Division, managing just 897 passes in total.

He did whip some good crosses into the penalty area, managing one assist in the process, but his biggest contribution came in his own half of the field. He was required to make a total of 132 clearances, 14 blocks and 116 tackles, winning only 54% – a poor return by Premiership standards.

Despite this, he was arguably the best reader of the game in a defence that never looked comfortable in the Premiership, and his tally of 44 interceptions was the club's highest.

Andy BOOTH • 10
SHEFFIELD WEDNESDAY • BORN: 6.12.73

Target man Andy Booth acted as a useful foil for diminutive strike partner Benito Carbone. But while Carbone finished as the club's top scorer, Booth will be disappointed with a very modest return of just six Premiership goals in 1998–99 and will certainly want to improve on his 35% shooting accuracy in 1999–2000.

His bustling style and aerial ability make him a handful for many Premiership defences and Booth invariably played his part in Wednesday's big-game wins during the season, especially with his back to goal. While he only completed 68% of his passes, below average for a Premiership striker, Booth won more than 60% of his challenges – some way above average. His lack of pace may explain his poor 47% dribble completion rate, but he was useful defending at set-pieces, making 31 clearances, six blocks and eight interceptions.

There were no doubts over his work-rate but he committed 78 fouls, collected seven yellow cards and was also caught offside 57 times and will want to improve all these statistics, including his goals tally, in 1999–2000.

APPEARANCES	
Start (sub)	34 (0)
Minutes on pitch	2908
GOAL ATTEMPTS	
Goals	6
Goals/shots ratio	9%
SHOOTING	
Shots on target	24
Shooting accuracy	35%
PASSING	
Goal assists	1
Passing accuracy	68%
DISCIPLINE	
Fouls	78
Offside	57
Yellow cards	7
Red cards	0

Aerial threat: Andy Booth

 ## Vassilis BORBOKIS • 22
DERBY COUNTY • BORN: 10.2.69

A revelation at Sheffield United, Vassilis Borbokis's raids down the flank from the right wing-back position attracted the attention of Derby County, who snapped him up on transfer deadline day.

He only managed 221 minutes in the Carling Premiership in 1998–99 and his Carling Opta statistics do not do the Greek international justice at this early stage of his Carling Premiership career.

Borbokis completed just two of his 12 crosses but, as he had demonstrated at Bramall Lane, he loves to run with the ball and take players on – and he achieved a 78% completion rate from his nine dribbles and runs for Derby.

He also likes to go for goal, but his limited appearances for the Rams meant that he only had two shots to his credit in 1998–99, both of which were blocked.

Once he has settled in at Pride Park, Borbokis should provide Jim Smith with a very dangerous attacking weapon at Pride Park in the future.

B

G Mark BOSNICH • 1
ASTON VILLA • BORN: 13.1.72

Australian goalkeeper Mark Bosnich had a bittersweet season with Aston Villa.

If he had played more games, Bosnich could well have topped the Carling Opta goalkeepers Index. But after an early spell between the sticks at Villa Park he suffered a shoulder injury and was replaced by Michael Oakes.

From 15 matches, Bosnich kept nine clean sheets and conceded only 10 goals. His catch success rate of 96% was also impressive, with 43 crosses claimed and just two dropped. He also made 11 successful punched clearances.

Bosnich is a brilliant shot-stopper, with the best record in the league. He saved 85% of the shots he faced, saving 23 efforts from outside the box and 32 shots from inside the box.

Out of contract at the end of the 1998–99 season, the Aussie eventually agreed to link up with former team-mate Dwight Yorke at Manchester United, thereby returning to the club where he began his professional career in England. However, he now has the unenviable task of fitting into Peter Schmeichel's legendary gloves.

APPEARANCES	
Start (sub)	15
Minutes on pitch	1350
SHOT STOPPING	
Goals conceded	10
Clean sheets	9
Saves	55
Saves/shots	85%
DISTRIBUTION	
Distribution	423
Distribution %	46%
CATCHING	
Crosses caught	43
Crosses dropped	2
DISCIPLINE	
Yellow cards	1
Red cards	0

CB Steve BOULD • 5
ARSENAL • BORN: 16.11.62

APPEARANCES	
Start (sub)	14 (5)
Minutes on pitch	1275
GOAL ATTEMPTS	
Goals	0
DEFENDING	
Blocks	23
Headed clearances	166
Other clearances	70
Interceptions	24
Tackles won	21
PASSING	
Passing accuracy	88%
DISCIPLINE	
Fouls	26
Yellow cards	3
Red cards	0

A name which will undoubtedly go down in Highbury history, Steve Bould is one of the original members of the legendary Arsenal back four of the 1980s.

Now aged 36, Bould is still going strong in the Premiership, although nowadays he plays more of a supporting role in the squad.

When called on in 1998–99 he was never less than superb, making 30 tackles – winning 70% – and a mammoth 236 clearances from his rare starts and occasional substitute appearances for the Gunners.

Arsene Wenger has expressed his desire to keep Bould on the Highbury playing staff for at least one more season. There is no doubt he has benefited from some of the Frenchman's methods, claiming to feel fitter than ever.

Although his continued defiance of the ageing process must be frustrating for younger players such as Matthew Upson, Bould is still unquestionably among the Premiership's best defenders. It is hard to disagree with Wenger's claim that the former Stoke player would walk into most other Premiership back-lines.

FB **Mark BOWEN • 14**
CHARLTON ATHLETIC • BORN: 7.12.63

Hugely experienced full-back Mark Bowen was a useful squad member for Charlton Athletic during the in 1998–99 Carling Premiership campaign, having been signed from Shimizu S-Pulse in Japan in September 1997.

Chances in the first team were few and far between for the former Spurs, Norwich and West Ham veteran, but he did get to play 256 minutes of Premiership action as Charlton battled in vain to beat the drop back into Nationwide Division One.

In that time he made 99 passes, completing 64%, and won 57% of his tackles, as well as firing in a shot on target.

With Charlton relegated on the final day of the season when they lost 1–0 at home against Sheffield Wednesday at the Valley, Bowen was one of a number of players released by the club.

While his Premiership days are now almost certainly over, there is no doubt that his extensive European and international experience could be of enormous value for one or two more seasons to come.

M **Lee BOWYER • 11**
LEEDS UNITED • BORN: 3.1.77

APPEARANCES	
Start (sub)	35 (0)
Minutes on pitch	3140
GOAL ATTEMPTS	
Goals	9
PASSING	
Passes	1374
Passing accuracy	75%
DEFENDING	
Interceptions	29
Clearances	75
Tackles	141
Tackles won	60%
DISCIPLINE	
Fouls	66
Yellow cards	8
Red cards	0

Abrasive: Lee Bowyer

Young Lee Bowyer had easily the best season of his career to date in 1998–99. Already firmly established in the England under-21 side, scoring regularly, many pundits are calling for the former Charlton midfielder to be included in the senior England squad.

Bowyer's hard-running, combative style and all-round ability earned him the Leeds United Player of the Year award in 1998–99. Bowyer had an amazing 96 cracks at goal in the league, hitting 31 on target and scoring nine times from midfield. Another 31 were blocked by defenders. Seventy-five percent of his passes found a team-mate and he completed 72% of his dribbles and runs.

However, Bowyer maintained his reputation as an abrasive player by picking up eight yellow cards.

1999–2000 could well be the year Bowyer makes it to the very top. Most observers feel he is capable of making the jump from the Premiership to full international honours – and the consensus appears to be that he will make that transition sooner rather than later.

S Shayne BRADLEY • 31
SOUTHAMPTON • BORN: 8.12.79

First-team opportunities for young frontman Shayne Bradley were extremely limited in the 1998–99's Carling Premiership campaign, with plenty of experienced forwards ahead of him on Southampton's books.

Three brief substitute appearances in the defeats at Everton and Chelsea and the home win over Newcastle gave Saints fans little indication of the striker's potential, as he managed just one blocked shot in 19 minutes of Premiership action.

In March manager Dave Jones sent him on loan to Swindon Town, to try to build up his record of first-team experience playing alongside the likes of Iffy Onuora in Nationwide Division One.

But even here, getting into the starting line-up proved a challenge and when he did get his chance, in the win at Crystal Palace, he was substituted before half-time.

Bradley may well find himself loaned out again in 1999–2000 until he has enough first-team experience to challenge for a place in the Saints' line-up.

AM Garry BRADY • 29
NEWCASTLE UNITED • BORN: 7.9.76

Garry Brady started his career at Celtic, moved on to Tottenham and was snapped up by Newcastle in July 1998. But despite an impressive-looking CV, he has yet to make a significant impression in the Premiership.

His time at Tottenham consisted of just nine appearances as a substitute and his Newcastle career has been limited to just 334 minutes from three starts and six substitute appearances in the Premiership.

He showed enough neat touches on the ball to finish the season with a good pass completion rate of 86%, but did not create too many clear-cut scoring chances and managed just two shots at goal.

Season 1999–2000 will be a make-or-break one at Newcastle for the former Scottish youth international. Signed by Kenny Dalglish, he has yet to convince Ruud Gullit of his worth as a top-class performer.

But Gullit likes skilful players, and if Brady works hard enough he may get his chance to impress the Dutchman during the coming campaign.

S Marco BRANCA • 9
MIDDLESBROUGH • BORN: 6.1.65

Marco Branca was expected to have a real impact on the Carling Premiership after scoring 10 goals in the last four months of Boro's promotion season. But things turned out rather differently for the former Inter Milan star when he suffered a career-threatening knee injury which forced him out of football, perhaps permanently.

He only managed to play 24 minutes of Carling Premiership football before his misfortune struck. During that time he completed only 18% of his passes and attempted just two shots: one was blocked and one was off-target.

Branca has since made a bid to return to the Riverside, but medics doubt the damaged knee can stand up to the rigours of Premiership football. Stories vary about the Italian's chances of a comeback: some have suggested he may go back to Inter Milan to rebuild his career.

Whatever his future, it seems unlikely that Boro fans wil enjoy the sight of Marco in a Middlesbrough shirt again.

S Michael BRANCH • 16
EVERTON • BORN: 18.10.78

After a couple of seasons on the periphery of the first team, Michael Branch may find that his future lies away from Goodison Park in season 1999–2000.

The 21-year-old striker spent some of the 1998–99 campaign on loan at Manchester City as the Sky Blues attempted to climb back into the big-time, but returned to make a brief number of substitute appearances for the Toffees and one start – in the Merseyside derby at Anfield.

Branch played just 155 minutes and attempted only one shot which, though it did hit the target, is a poor return from someone who appeared to have so much potential a couple of seasons ago.

He completed a very poor 57% of the 63 passes he attempted, although his 60% rate of retaining the ball on dribbles and runs was more impressive.

Whether he survives Walter Smith's rebuilding plans remains to be seen, but he is approaching make-or-break time with the Toffees.

Tim BREACKER • 2
WEST HAM UNITED • BORN: 2.7.65

Veteran defender Tim Breacker finally ended an eight-year association with West Ham when he signed on a free transfer to first-division Queens Park Rangers on February 10, 1999.

The ex-Luton man initially joined the Shepherd's Bush side on loan but followed Ludek Miklosko in a permanent switch, fighting an ensuing battle against relegation for the remainder of the season.

Breacker played a shade more than two hours in the Premiership for the Hammers and completed his 230th and final league appearance at Upton Park.

The Bicester-born full-back's swansong for the Irons came in the 4–0 defeat at home to Arsenal, where he was replaced by Eyal Berkovic as the Hammers attempted to rescue the game.

During his limited Premiership time on pitch for West Ham in 1998–99, Breacker contested three tackles and made 11 blocks and clearances combined. He also completed seven out of eight dribbles and runs, but had too few appearances to make any real impact.

Gary BREEN • 6
COVENTRY CITY • BORN: 12.12.73

APPEARANCES	
Start (sub)	21 (4)
Minutes on pitch	1882
GOAL ATTEMPTS	
Goals	0
DEFENDING	
Blocks	26
Headed clearances	172
Other clearances	96
Interceptions	18
Tackles won	25
PASSING	
Passing accuracy	74%
DISCIPLINE	
Fouls	30
Yellow cards	3
Red cards	0

Solid defender: Gary Breen

Coventry City's Eire international Gary Breen put in some solid performances in central defence, eventually helping the the Highfield Road side secure Carling Premiership status into the Millennium.

He impressed many with his strong displays at the back and was the subject of a reported £2 million deadline-day bid from Watford.

The ex-Birmingham City man made the short trip to Coventry back in 1997 and showed his worth to the Sky Blues in the 1998–99 season, as Carling Opta's stats testify.

Breen made more than 300 blocks, clearances and interceptions combined at the heart of defence, winning a high proportion of the 37 tackles he went in for. Showing good close control when running with the ball, he completed 19 of 22 forward surges – giving valuable relief to a pressurized defence.

The Hendon-born star's passing was fairly average, with just three-quarters of all balls reaching a Sky Blue shirt. Breen also occasionally lacked discipline in the tackle, with 30 fouls and three yellow cards.

FB Wayne BRIDGE • 18
SOUTHAMPTON • BORN: 5.8.80

Young wing-back Wayne Bridge broke into the Saints' first team with some all-action displays down the flanks. The teenager made his Premiership debut at home to Liverpool on the season's first day, replacing the injured John Beresford. The ex-Portsmouth defender was out for most of the season and Bridge made the most of his chance to impress Dave Jones.

He made some telling challenges at the back, winning 65% of them, and 35 clearances to help his beleaguered back-line out, but pushed forward as often as possible. Indeed, Bridge spanned both ends of the pitch with his determined dribbles and runs, completing more than half of them unchecked.

He buckled slightly under pressure when passing: only one in four of his crosses found a Saint marching on to the ball and his distribution was at times wayward, with more than 30% of passes wasted.

Only five of his 13 efforts at goal troubled the goalkeeper, but he showed willingness to try his luck and Bridge will surely build on his performances for the 1999–2000 season.

APPEARANCES	
Start (sub)	15 (8)
Minutes on pitch	1407
GOAL ATTEMPTS	
Goals	0
PASSING	
Passes	425
Passing accuracy	69%
DEFENDING	
Interceptions	8
Clearances	35
Tackles	34
Tackles won	65%
DISCIPLINE	
Fouls	12
Yellow cards	0
Red cards	0

M Marc BRIDGE-WILKINSON • 15
DERBY COUNTY • BORN: 16.3.79

Derby County's 1997–98 Young Player of the Year finally earned his first taste of Carling Premiership action in 1998–99. And a taste it certainly was, with just one minute's play against Liverpool in the win at Anfield in November 1998.

The match will hold happy memories for the County's young player, as the Rams clinched a 2–1 victory over the Merseysiders, but Bridge-Wilkinson would have liked to have added to his 60 or so seconds on the field of play at a later date in the campaign, but unfortunately it was not to be.

The goalscoring midfielder, who hit a hat-trick for Derby's reserves in their opening fixture of the 1998–99 campaign, was loaned out to Carlisle United, a club with which County have developed a special relationship, to get valuable first-team experience under his belt at Brunton Park.

Marc spent some time on the Pride Park bench in his first Premiership season, and he will hope that the step up to a regular starting berth is not too far away.

S Mark BRIGHT • 17
CHARLTON ATHLETIC • BORN: 6.6.62

On May 4, 1999, aged 36, striker Mark Bright announced he was ending a long career in top-flight football.

After spells with Port Vale and Leicester City, Bright struck up a memorable and prolific partnership with Ian Wright at Crystal Palace, finishing third in the league and reaching the FA Cup final in 1990.

He repeated the latter feat with Sheffield Wednesday four years later, although he ended up on the losing side once again.

He made his way to the Valley in April 1997, where he was a useful squad player as the Addicks looked first to get promoted and then to establish themselves among the Premiership elite.

That was proved in the televized clash with Newcastle on January 17, when he came off the bench and scored with his first touch, a towering header. It was his only effort on target all season!

Announcing his retirement, he simply said: "The game has given me a life that I couldn't have dreamed of."

FB Lee BRISCOE • 17
SHEFFIELD WEDNESDAY • BORN: 30.9.75

Pontefract-born Lee Briscoe had to spend much of the 1998–99 season as understudy to Andy Hinchcliffe. But in one of his rare starts for Sheffield Wednesday, he grabbed the only goal in their 1–0 defeat of Arsenal.

Unfortunately Paolo Di Canio's antics in the same game stole all the headlines, but at least Briscoe has the satisfaction of knowing that he played some part in the Championship race.

Briscoe signed professional forms with Wednesday in May 1994, and went on to make five appearances for the England under-21 side after impressing in David Pleat's team. Injuries have hampered his chances since, but he is determined to make his mark and turned down a possible transfer to Manchester City in order to fight Andy Hinchcliffe for his place.

Happiest at left-back, Briscoe nevertheless started his career as an attacking midfielder and still enjoys getting forward. He completed 32% of his crosses and attempted 13 shots in 667 minutes on pitch, but did not neglect his defensive duties, making 17 tackles and 48 blocks, clearances and interceptions.

APPEARANCES	
Start (sub)	5 (11)
Minutes on pitch	667
GOAL ATTEMPTS	
Goals	1
PASSING & CROSSING	
Passing	225
Passing accuracy	72%
Crossing	22
Crossing accuracy	32%
DEFENDING	
Tackles	17
Tackles won	47%
DISCIPLINE	
Fouls	6
Yellow cards	0
Red cards	0

CB Marlon BROOMES • 16
BLACKBURN ROVERS • BORN: 28.11.77

APPEARANCES	
Start (sub)	8 (5)
Minutes on pitch	904
GOAL ATTEMPTS	
Goals	0
DEFENDING	
Blocks	20
Headed clearances	73
Other clearances	37
Interceptions	12
Tackles won	13
PASSING	
Passing accuracy	79%
DISCIPLINE	
Fouls	14
Yellow cards	3
Red cards	1

A product of the Blackburn Rovers youth scheme, Marlon Broomes swept into the first team in 1998–99 after just four Carling Premiership appearances the previous season.

The England under-21 star appeared 13 times in Rovers' ultimately unsuccessful campaign and showed he may play a key part in their quest to regain Premiership status.

Broomes made more than 100 clearances in defence and intercepted 12 passes. His inexperience showed in the tackle: he won only a few more challenges than he lost and he was sent off when he tangled with Chelsea boss Gianluca Vialli at Stamford Bridge.

The Birmingham-born youngster rarely ventured forward, firing in just three wayward efforts at goal and embarked on only two dribbles, but he did distribute possession ably to his team-mates. Nearly 80% of all attempted balls reached a Rovers colleague, slightly above the 1998–99 Premiership average for a defender. For a young player in his first full top-flight season he showed good composure and was reliable when called upon.

Steve BROWN • 12
CHARLTON ATHLETIC • BORN: 6.12.73

Nearing his 10th year at the south London club, versatile defender Steve Brown tried as hard as any Addick during season 1998–99 in Charlton's vain effort to stay up.

Brown's header thumped agonizingly against the crossbar in Charlton's final game of the 1998–99 Carling Premiership season as the club saw their survival hopes wither away.

The Brighton-born centre-back proved a valuable part of Alan Curbishley's squad but missed first-team action for large chunks of the season. Brown played in just under half of Charlton's league games, making almost 200 blocks, clearances and interceptions as the Addicks manned the trenches.

The Valley veteran rarely shirked a challenge, winning on average six out of 10. Having won possession, Brown tried to make the most of the space available but completed only 64% of his 39 dribbles and runs.

His distribution was also respectable, with three-quarters of all passes finding a team-mate, and he pressed forward on occasion, firing in six efforts at goal.

APPEARANCES	
Start (sub)	13 (5)
Minutes on pitch	1248
GOAL ATTEMPTS	
Goals	0
DEFENDING	
Blocks	14
Headed clearances	99
Other clearances	52
Interceptions	29
Tackles won	24
PASSING	
Passing accuracy	76%
DISCIPLINE	
Fouls	11
Yellow cards	1
Red cards	0

Wesley BROWN • 24
MANCHESTER UNITED • BORN: 16.3.79

APPEARANCES	
Start (sub)	11 (3)
Minutes on pitch	952
GOAL ATTEMPTS	
Goals	0
DEFENDING	
Blocks	9
Headed clearances	60
Other clearances	23
Interceptions	17
Tackles won	25
PASSING	
Passing accuracy	75%
DISCIPLINE	
Fouls	13
Yellow cards	1
Red cards	0

Wes Brown broke into the Manchester United first XI at the end of 1997–98 and showed he could become a major star of the future. His form was so impressive that he has since played at England under-21 level and even earned a senior cap against Hungary.

Comfortable at both right-back and centre-back, Brown filled in when suspensions and injuries struck United's defence. In total he accrued 952 minutes of Premiership experience in 1998–99.

His 60% tackle success rate and 75% pass completion rate were both below the league average for a defender but still represented a good effort from such a young debutant.

The envy of many former youth team rivals, Brown made 83 clearances, 17 interceptions and nine blocks in the United defence, and committed only 13 fouls. He only picked up one yellow card all season, despite being under the spotlight at the Old Trafford club.

If he can continue his current progress, United and England could have a very useful, versatile defender for many years to come.

FB David BURROWS • 3
COVENTRY CITY • BORN: 25.10.68

Former Liverpool defender David Burrows contributed to Coventry's survival after another season's flirtation with relegation.

Burrows dug himself in for the Sky Blue cause, patrolling the trenches down the left flank. City refused to be buried, but it was only after their penultimate match at Derby County that they guaranteed themselves a share in the Carling Premiership goldmine into the year 2000.

The £1.1 million signing from Everton made 123 clearances and 21 blocks to keep the pressure off Magnus Hedman, proving to be a difficult obstacle for opposing forwards, putting in 74 tackles and winning more than 60% of them.

Burrows added another dimension when venturing forward, completing an exceptional 88% of all dribbles and for a defender crossing with great accuracy, on average finding a colleague with every third centre.

His 888 passes included one goal assist but Burrows himself was reluctant to shoot, preferring to concentrate on his strengths.

APPEARANCES	
Start (sub)	23 (0)
Minutes on pitch	1834
GOAL ATTEMPTS	
Goals	0
PASSING & CROSSING	
Passing	888
Passing accuracy	73%
Crossing	35
Crossing accuracy	37%
DEFENDING	
Tackles	74
Tackles won	62%
DISCIPLINE	
Fouls	30
Yellow cards	7
Red cards	0

S Deon BURTON • 24
DERBY COUNTY • BORN: 25.10.76

APPEARANCES	
Start (sub)	14 (7)
Minutes on pitch	1228
GOAL ATTEMPTS	
Goals	8
Goals/shots ratio	25%
SHOOTING	
Shots on target	11
Shooting accuracy	34%
PASSING	
Goal assists	0
Passing accuracy	72%
DISCIPLINE	
Fouls	41
Offside	22
Yellow cards	3
Red cards	0

Reggae Boy Deon Burton had the Derby faithful partying in the stands as he drummed in eight goals in his most productive season for Derby County to date.

Jim Smith went back to his old club Portsmouth to prise the highly-talented Jamaican international away from Fratton Park for a £1 million-plus deal in 1997.

Fresh from his exploits as part of Jamaica's first-ever World Cup Finals side, Burton returned for the 1998–99 Premiership campaign with renewed confidence.

Deon's eight goals came from just 11 efforts on target – but an accuracy of just 34% shows there is certainly room for improvement.

The diminutive striker has great speed, and made the most of it when running at defenders. Burton launched 27 solo attacks and was halted 11 times, but over-enthusiasm saw him caught offside quite regularly.

Despite his lack of size, and the very physical nature of the league, Burton made good use of some excellent close control and managed to complete the vast majority of his passes.

Nicky BUTT • 8
MANCHESTER UNITED • BORN: 21.1.75

B

Alongside United captain Roy Keane, Nicky Butt helps make up the awesome engine of the Carling Premiership Champions' midfield. Butt matured over the course of the 1998–99 campaign, bouncing back from consecutive dismissals against Barcelona in the Champions League and then at Arsenal four days later.

Butt's main contribution in midfield was his ability to win the ball and lay it off to a colleague in more space. Biting tackles around the centre circle were a feature of his game and of the United squad only Jaap Stam and Keane made more challenges. Butt made well over 100 tackles and won roughly two-thirds. His distribution was excellent, with more than 80% of his 1,092 passes reaching a Red Devil.

The Manchester-born and bred star attacked from deep, making 54 dribbles and runs and shooting 41 times, the majority from long range. He scored twice, netting the winning goal at home to Leeds United.

He will again compete with England colleague Paul Scholes for the second midfield berth in 1999–2000.

APPEARANCES	
Start (sub)	22 (9)
Minutes on pitch	2039
GOAL ATTEMPTS	
Goals	2
PASSING	
Passes	1092
Passing accuracy	81%
DEFENDING	
Interceptions	23
Clearances	55
Tackles	126
Tackles won	64%
DISCIPLINE	
Fouls	31
Yellow cards	3
Red cards	1

Tenacious: Nicky Butt

Fabian CABALLERO • 26
ARSENAL • BORN: 31.1.78

Following the sale of Ian Wright in the summer of 1998, it seemed that Arsenal were linked with every top striker in Europe. But not one of the deals was clinched, and Arsenal's lack of firepower began to show as World Cup hangovers, injuries and inexperience exposed the lack of depth in the Highbury squad.

In his search for a replacement, Arsene Wenger took Fabian Caballero on loan from Paraguayan club Serro Portino in November 1998 for the duration of the season, with a view to a permanent deal – one that Arsenal declined to seal.

His appearances were limited – he played just 15 minutes of Premiership football in one substitute outing – and in that time completed seven out of the eight passes he attempted and committed one foul.

He also made two other substitute appearances, firstly in the Worthington Cup against Chelsea and then in the FA Cup third round at Preston North End where he made headlines with an alleged off-the-ball incident.

Danny CADAMARTERI • 29
EVERTON • BORN: 12.10.79

Shorn of his trademark dreadlocks, Everton forward Danny Cadamarteri has lost none of his speed and strength. However, like Goodison's other permanent strikers the young attacker suffered from a malaise in front of goal, as the Toffeemen nearly came unstuck in Walter Smith's first season in charge.

Former England Youth star Cadamarteri struggled to create openings in opposition defences and attempted a disappointing 32 shots during the 1998–99 season. He bagged four league goals, his last away to West Ham in December. In fact Danny did not manage a league goal at Goodison Park all season.

The nippy forward runs defences ragged when on top form and made more than 100 surges up field – but too often for his liking Cadamarteri was stopped in his tracks.

With the likes of Duncan Ferguson and later Kevin Campbell to aim at in the centre he was an effective crosser of the ball, delivering more than 30% with pinpoint accuracy. But unable to strike up a satisfactory partnership up front, the team as a whole suffered.

APPEARANCES
Start (sub)	11 (19)
Minutes on pitch	1522

GOAL ATTEMPTS
Goals	4
Goals/shots ratio	15%

SHOOTING
Shots on target	14
Shooting accuracy	52%

PASSING
Goal assists	1
Passing accuracy	70%

DISCIPLINE
Fouls	45
Offside	36
Yellow cards	6
Red cards	0

Colin CALDERWOOD • 34
ASTON VILLA • BORN: 20.1.65

APPEARANCES
Start (sub)	19 (1)
Minutes on pitch	1637

GOAL ATTEMPTS
Goals	0

DEFENDING
Blocks	15
Headed clearances	101
Other clearances	50
Interceptions	18
Tackles won	45

PASSING
Passing accuracy	81%

DISCIPLINE
Fouls	36
Yellow cards	5
Red cards	1

When Aston Villa faltered in the New Year, John Gregory needed someone he could rely on to halt Villa's alarming slump.

Vastly-experienced Scottish international Calderwood was brought in for a bargain £225,000 just before transfer deadline day. His calm and poise rubbed off – and Villa's run of 10 matches without a win ended soon after.

Glasgow-born Calderwood started the season at Tottenham but fellow-Scot George Graham let him go. A glance at his Carling Opta statistics shows poor form was not the reason.

He won the ball a massive 79% of the time when encountering the opposition and with more than 150 clearances – and five out of six runs out of defence completed – showed he was still an all-round quality defender.

His distribution rarely let him down either. Although he failed to connect with either of the crosses he swept in, a healthy 81% of all passes dispatched toward a team-mate arrived safely at their destination.

Calderwood proved that there was still plenty of life left in those 34-year-old legs.

Andy CAMPBELL • 18
MIDDLESBROUGH • BORN: 18.4.79

England Youth international Andy Campbell made only a minor contribution to Boro's Carling Premiership cause but he can still be reasonably satisfied with his achievements during the 1998–99 season.

The red-headed youngster may have played a fraction less than three hours in the top flight, but he saw plenty of first-team action in the lower leagues. He was loaned out to second-division Preston North End in December 1998 and spent a couple of months at Deepdale, until Bryan Robson's former team-mate Steve Bruce borrowed him for Sheffield United's tilt at promotion to the Premiership.

The fleet-footed Campbell found the net regularly for Boro's reserves and also netted while on loan at Bramall Lane, prompting enquiries from Bruce as to his availability on a more permanent basis.

Campbell made 38 passes for Boro and showed his trickery when dribbling past opponents six times out of nine. He appeared in Middlesbrough's final two matches, one of which was against Manchester United.

Kevin CAMPBELL • 9
EVERTON • BORN: 4.2.70

Undoubtedly the most astute of all Walter Smith's signings was the capture of Kevin Campbell on transfer deadline day. Campbell joined on loan from Turkey's Trabzonspor after the infamous "cannibal" slur against the ex-Arsenal man – and proceeded to chew up and spit out any defender getting in his way.

Campbell achieved in eight games what no other Everton striker came near to doing in over 10 months, scoring nine league goals and the only hat-trick by an Everton player during a goal-shy season.

Excluding blocked shots Campbell had 19 efforts at goal, 13 on target. The man whose goals propelled Nottingham Forest into the 1998–99 Carling Premiership campaign also laid on two for the Toffees during his two-month stint and completed around two-thirds of his 286 attempted passes.

Campbell's determination to win the ball stood out. He won nine out of the 11 tackles he contested and when in possession he demonstrated a hunger to take his man on, running at the defence on 13 occasions.

Biting back: Kevin Campbell

APPEARANCES	
Start (sub)	8 (0)
Minutes on pitch	692
GOAL ATTEMPTS	
Goals	9
Goals/shots ratio	47%
SHOOTING	
Shots on target	13
Shooting accuracy	68%
PASSING	
Goal assists	2
Passing accuracy	63%
DISCIPLINE	
Fouls	10
Offside	3
Yellow cards	1
Red cards	0

Sol CAMPBELL • 23
TOTTENHAM HOTSPUR • BORN: 18.9.74

CB

Tottenham's captain was exemplary in defence during the 1998–99 Premiership campaign, missing just one league game and avoiding even a single booking. Sol outshone his rivals at the back and was Carling Opta's highest-rated defender for the season.

Tipped as a future England captain, he used his commanding presence to the full, making 583 clearances – more than any other defender in the league – including 404 with his head. Add to this nearly 90 blocks and interceptions and it is clear why he was the most effective player at the back, according to Carling Opta.

Another feature of Campbell's game is his strength and commitment in the tackle. He won three-quarters of his more than 150 challenges and showed a cool head when bringing the ball out of defence.

He passed with precision and, drawing on early experience as a centre-forward, out-scored all other Premiership centre-backs with six league goals. Campbell reaped the rewards for his efforts as he lifted the 1998–99 Worthington Cup at Wembley.

APPEARANCES	
Start (sub)	37 (0)
Minutes on pitch	3330
GOAL ATTEMPTS	
Goals	6
DEFENDING	
Blocks	42
Headed clearances	404
Other clearances	179
Interceptions	179
Tackles won	117
PASSING	
Passing accuracy	76%
DISCIPLINE	
Fouls	50
Yellow cards	0
Red cards	0

Heading for glory: Sol Campbell

Stuart CAMPBELL • 16
LEICESTER CITY • BORN: 9.12.77

M

Scottish under-21 international Stuart Campbell made just one start in the 1998–99 Carling Premiership campaign, occupying the Filbert Street bench for the majority of the 10-month season.

Competition in the midfield was fierce with the likes of Robbie Savage, Muzzy Izzet, Neil Lennon and new recruit Andy Impey keeping Campbell out of the starting XI. As a result, the Corby-born youngster played 15 times for the reserves and impressed with his attack-minded style.

Predominantly a right-sided player, Campbell showed no aversion to running down the flank, negotiating nine out of 14 dribbles successfully. But the 21-year-old managed just one accurate cross from six attempted centres to his strikers.

Campbell's distribution was sound, with more than 70% of all attempted passes picked up by a fellow-Fox. He also pressurized opposing defences by firing in eight shots, although five of these posed no danger to the goalkeeper.

Horacio CARBONARI • 2
DERBY COUNTY • BORN: 2.5.74

C

Jim Smith made Horacio Carbonari Derby County's record signing in summer 1998 when he splashed out £2.7 million on the versatile Argentine centre-back.

Carbonari impressed at both ends of the pitch in his first season for the Rams. He won the majority of his 82 tackles and regularly threw his large frame in front of the ball, making 35 blocks and 22 interceptions. Adept at dealing with threatening balls into the box, Carbonari cleared the danger 331 times, a total bettered for Derby only by Spencer Prior.

A plumber's son, Carbonari may have spent much of 1998–99 plugging leaks in the defence but he did plenty of dribbling himself. Often acting as the Rams' *libero*, he completed 81% of all forays into the opposition half.

The former Atletico Rosario central defender struck a wonderful goal at home to Nottingham Forest, the pick of his five strikes in a highly-productive season that saw only Sol Campbell score more times from defence in the Premiership. Horacio performed admirably as Derby sailed to a top-10 finish.

APPEARANCES	
Start (sub)	28 (1)
Minutes on pitch	2474
GOAL ATTEMPTS	
Goals	5
DEFENDING	
Blocks	35
Headed clearances	167
Other clearances	164
Interceptions	22
Tackles won	51
PASSING	
Passing accuracy	69%
DISCIPLINE	
Fouls	22
Yellow cards	4
Red cards	0

Benito CARBONE • 8
SHEFFIELD WEDNESDAY • BORN: 14.8.71

APPEARANCES	
Start (sub)	31 (0)
Minutes on pitch	2709
GOAL ATTEMPTS	
Goals	8
Goals/shots ratio	10%
SHOOTING	
Shots on target	35
Shooting accuracy	45%
PASSING	
Goal assists	6
Passing accuracy	74%
DISCIPLINE	
Fouls	37
Offside	87
Yellow cards	9
Red cards	0

Signed for a club record fee of £3 million from Inter Milan in October 1996, Benito Carbone enjoyed arguably his best campaign for Sheffield Wednesday in the 1998–99 Carling Premiership.

That seemed an unlikely prospect at the start of the campaign, with Carbone close to quitting, after struggling to gain a regular first-team place the previous season. But new manager Danny Wilson convinced him to stay and his faith reaped dividends.

Carbone scored eight Premiership goals, making him the club's top scorer. He was also the Owls' top goal-provider with six assists.

Able to play both as an out-and-out striker or in the "hole", Carbone seems to relish his status as the club's most gifted player – a tag backed up by the statistics, which highlight his ability to deliver a telling cross and beat opponents with his close control.

One area that will not have pleased Wilson is Carbone's nine bookings. Eight were for dissent, which at least proves he has mastered the "finer" points of the English language.

Stephen CARR • 2
TOTTENHAM HOTSPUR • BORN: 29.8.76

It is fair to say Eire international Stephen Carr was probably Spurs' most improved player during 1998–99. The Dublin-born right-back visibly grew in confidence under George Graham and was one of the keys to the club's rapid improvement under their new manager.

Always useful going forward, Carr made 146 dribbles and runs, the highest number for an orthodox full-back and the 16th highest in the Premiership. He also delivered his fair share of crosses – 87 in all – and set up three goals.

It was in the defensive side of the game that he showed the most improvement, however. His tackle success rate climbed to 60% and he finished the season with more than 300 clearances, blocks and interceptions.

Ever-present in the league in 1997–98, Carr missed just one Premiership game in the 1998–99 season, a fact that reveals much about his fitness levels. Disciplined, resilient and determined, he is exactly the type of player that George Graham admires and is likely to be an important figure in Tottenham's bid for honours at home and in Europe.

APPEARANCES	
Start (sub)	37 (0)
Minutes on pitch	3320
GOAL ATTEMPTS	
Goals	0
PASSING & CROSSING	
Passing	1586
Passing accuracy	77%
Crossing	87
Crossing accuracy	38%
DEFENDING	
Tackles	86
Tackles won	60%
DISCIPLINE	
Fouls	32
Yellow cards	4
Red cards	0

Jamie CARRAGHER • 23
LIVERPOOL • BORN: 28.1.78

APPEARANCES	
Start (sub)	34 (0)
Minutes on pitch	2988
GOAL ATTEMPTS	
Goals	1
DEFENDING	
Blocks	36
Headed clearances	263
Other clearances	160
Interceptions	46
Tackles won	66
PASSING	
Passing accuracy	83%
DISCIPLINE	
Fouls	30
Yellow cards	5
Red cards	1

Jamie Carragher's reward for a hard-working 1998–99 Carling Premiership campaign was his first England cap, which came on April 28, away to Hungary. The Bootle-born defender missed just four league matches for Liverpool and was kept busy in the back-line, as the side settled slowly under new management.

In a difficult season for the Reds he was arguably their best defender, making 423 clearances from his own half – over 100 more than his nearest rival. He won a respectable 60% of his 110 tackles and showed a flair for reading the game, cutting off 46 opposition passes – placing him in the Premiership top 20 for interceptions during the 1998–99 season.

The former FA Youth Cup winner showed poise when carrying the ball forward and completed 12 of his 13 dribbles and runs. He found a colleague with four out of six crosses and wasted few passes when in possession.

Emerging from the 1998–99 season as one of Liverpool's more consistent performers, his one blemish came with the contentious red card he received at Charlton.

Lee CARSLEY • 15
BLACKBURN ROVERS • BORN: 28.2.74

Brian Kidd swooped for Lee Carsley in March 1999 to help fill the gap left in midfield by Tim Sherwood's move to Tottenham.

Kidd paid Derby County more than £3 million for the Eire international, who impressed many with his ball-winning skills and "take no prisoners" approach to the game.

The Birmingham-born midfielder won two-thirds of his 148 tackles and fulfilled his duty at the back with more than 100 clearances and nearly 50 blocks and interceptions combined.

Carsley moved up to join the attack with aplomb. He completed nearly 90% of all dribbles and runs attempted and finished the season with a well-above-average crossing accuracy of 40%. His shooting was also reliable, with 11 efforts out of 18 forcing the goalkeeper into action and one finding the back of the net.

Another selling-point for Kidd was Carsley's industrious passing. He distributed more than a thousand balls with sound accuracy and provided one goal assist. Sadly, his efforts could not save Blackburn from relegation.

APPEARANCES
Start (sub)	27 (3)
Minutes on pitch	2559

GOAL ATTEMPTS
Goals	1

PASSING
Passes	1052
Passing accuracy	77%

DEFENDING
Interceptions	25
Clearances	110
Tackles	148
Tackles won	66%

DISCIPLINE
Fouls	40
Yellow cards	6
Red cards	0

Pierluigi CASIRAGHI • 10
CHELSEA • BORN: 4.3.69

APPEARANCES
Start (sub)	10 (0)
Minutes on pitch	724

GOAL ATTEMPTS
Goals	1
Goals/shots ratio	5%

SHOOTING
Shots on target	11
Shooting accuracy	50%

PASSING
Goal assists	0
Passing accuracy	65%

DISCIPLINE
Fouls	23
Offside	11
Yellow cards	2
Red cards	0

Italian international Pierluigi Casiraghi will struggle to look back on his first season in the Carling Premiership with any sort of fondness.

First Chelsea's record signing failed to score in his first seven league games. Then, just as his impressive Euro 96 form seemed to be returning, he suffered an horrific injury in the 1–1 draw at West Ham on November 7.

Casiraghi was stretchered off after a clash with the Hammers' goalkeeper Shaka Hislop. Cruciate ligament damage was diagnosed and though fears that he might never play again proved unfounded, a return to action was ruled out until at least Christmas 1999.

Casiraghi's one goal came in the 1–1 draw against Liverpool at Anfield on October 3. It was one of 28 shots (including blocked efforts) he attempted in his 724 minutes of Premiership football in 1998–99.

His modest passing and dribbling completion rates underline how much the striker struggled to settle in after costing £5.4 million from Lazio, and it may be some time before he gets another chance to prove his worth.

M Stewart CASTLEDINE • 19
WIMBLEDON • BORN: 22.1.73

Wimbledon's midfielder Stewart Castledine endured a frustrating time on the periphery of the Dons' first team in 1998–99. The Wandsworth-born player is a keen boxer, and injuries kept him on the ropes for much of the Carling Premiership season.

His solitary showing in the league will not be looked back upon with any fondness by Dons fans, as the side went down 5–1 to a rampant Arsenal side accelerating into their title charge.

The former Wimbledon trainee seemed to have lost some sharpness when he played against Arsenal, which is hardly surprising considering his lack of first-team practice. He made four blocks and five clearances during his 74 minutes on pitch before being substituted in favour of record signing John Hartson as the Dons strove to get back into the game.

The Top Man model will hope to find himself more regularly on parade for the 1999–2000 Carling Premiership campaign to display his on-field skills.

FB Gary CHARLES • 2
ASTON VILLA • BORN: 13.4.70

Benfica bound: Gary Charles

APPEARANCES	
Start (sub)	10 (1)
Minutes on pitch	845
GOAL ATTEMPTS	
Goals	1
PASSING & CROSSING	
Passing	372
Passing accuracy	68%
Crossing	31
Crossing accuracy	10%
DEFENDING	
Tackles	18
Tackles won	72%
DISCIPLINE	
Fouls	7
Yellow cards	2
Red cards	0

The 1998–99 Carling Premiership season was a short-lived one for Villa right-back Gary Charles. The former Nottingham Forest star, capped twice for England, played his last match for John Gregory's side in November before leaving for Benfica shortly afterwards.

Graeme Souness paid the Midlands club £1.3 million for the services of Charles, gaining a tough-tackling, attack-minded defender for his money, as Carling Opta's statistics show.

He contested for the ball on 18 occasions and proved a tough opponent, winning more than 70% of his challenges. He made 36 clearances, and in his 10 starts Aston Villa conceded just two goals.

He made 41 forward runs, achieving a reasonable completion rate, but his crossing was not quite up to par, with only three centres from a total of 31 making a claret-and-blue connection.

Charles scored his only goal for the season – his third in all for the club – in the opening home fixture of the 1998–99 campaign against Bryan Robson's Middlesbrough.

C

Laurent CHARVET • 16
FB • NEWCASTLE UNITED • BORN: 8.5.73

When Ruud Gullit succeeded Kenny Dalglish at Newcastle, by a quirk of footballing fate he was instantly re-acquainted with a player he had signed as Chelsea manager.

Laurent Charvet cost Newcastle £520,000 from Cannes in summer 1998, having played on loan for Gullit at Stamford Bridge the season before. Thus Ruud was happy to make full use of the player he originally introduced to English football.

Beziers-born Charvet fared well in his first full season in England. With 321 clearances for United, only Nikos Dabizas made more, and Charvet intercepted 47 opposition passes.

The man signed from Cannes sent over a festival of crosses for his expectant forwards, and Newcastle players were first in the queue for his centres on 41% of occasions.

Charvet also showed a good ability on the ball, completing 84% of his dribbles and runs, and he opened his Newcastle goal account at Middlesbrough. But he endured a miserable 90 minutes in the FA Cup final as United lost out for a second successive season.

APPEARANCES

Start (sub)	30 (1)
Minutes on pitch	2718

GOAL ATTEMPTS

Goals	1

PASSING & CROSSING

Passing	1152
Passing accuracy	84%
Crossing	27
Crossing accuracy	41%

DEFENDING

Tackles	74
Tackles won	65%

DISCIPLINE

Fouls	26
Yellow cards	3
Red cards	0

Steve CHETTLE • 5
CB • NOTTINGHAM FOREST • BORN: 27.9.68

APPEARANCES

Start (sub)	32 (2)
Minutes on pitch	2794

GOAL ATTEMPTS

Goals	2

DEFENDING

Blocks	44
Headed clearances	316
Other clearances	158
Interceptions	43
Tackles won	50

PASSING

Passing accuracy	77%

DISCIPLINE

Fouls	35
Yellow cards	7
Red cards	1

Nottingham Forest captain Steve Chettle could not lead his team to Premiership safety in his testimonial year as the defence struggled to contain top-quality opposition.

Chettle was a virtual ever-present for Forest but they missed him in the home horror show against Manchester United, when the defence was breached eight times.

Such was the pressure Forest were often under that Chettle had to make 474 clearances from his own half, the seventh-highest total in the Premiership. He also made more than 80 blocks and interceptions combined.

Chettle proved his mettle in the tackle, too. He clashed 79 times with opponents and came away with the ball more often than not.

He despatched 1,156 passes of which nearly 900 found their man. The local lad even made his mark at the other end with two goals from the penalty spot, and only three of his 13 efforts were off target. But after a good start to the season his and Forest's fortunes dipped and he made some sloppy errors, conceding two penalties and earning a red card.

Malcolm CHRISTIE • 12
DERBY COUNTY • BORN: 11.4.79

Young Derby County striker Malcolm Christie has so far had little chance to make an impact at first-team level. He was used sparingly by manager Jim Smith in season 1998–99, making just two appearances in the Carling Premiership.

Signed from non-league side Nuneaton Borough in October 1998, Christie cost the club an initial fee of £355,000, which is set to rise with appearances.

He came to Derby's attention after scoring 12 goals in just 14 games in the Dr Marten's League and the Rams snapped him up shortly afterwards.

His debut came as a second-half substitute in the Rams' away game with Sheffield Wednesday, and he was quickly involved in the action when, after 56 minutes, Wednesday 'keeper Pavel Srnicek appeared to take him out with a chest-high kick and was dismissed. He had to wait another two months for his next chance – as a substitute in the 4–1 defeat at Leeds United – but he is likely to feature more often in 1999–2000.

Alex CLELAND • 2
EVERTON • BORN: 10.12.70

Athletic: Alex Cleland

APPEARANCES	
Start (sub)	16 (2)
Minutes on pitch	1393
GOAL ATTEMPTS	
Goals	0
PASSING & CROSSING	
Passing	519
Passing accuracy	74%
Crossing	46
Crossing accuracy	22%
DEFENDING	
Tackles	27
Tackles won	59%
DISCIPLINE	
Fouls	18
Yellow cards	2
Red cards	1

Former Glasgow Rangers defender Alex Cleland signed for Everton in July 1998, before the arrival of his old boss Walter Smith at Goodison. Smith knew all about Cleland, of course, and was happy to have him in his side.

An athletic full-back capable of filling in at centre-back when needed, Cleland was one of the club's most impressive performers early on in the season, making 69 clearances and 12 important interceptions. He also completed 86% of his 36 attempted dribbles and runs, and attempted 27 tackles. Cleland linked well with the Everton midfield, completing 74% of his attempted passes and setting up one goal.

His season took a turn for the worse in January when, after just 12 minutes of the away fixture at Aston Villa, he was dismissed for a second bookable offence. In Everton's next game, against Ipswich Town in the FA Cup, he was moved to centre-back and was enjoying what he described as "my best Everton performance" when he tore his calf muscle in what proved to be his last game of the campaign.

M Stephen CLEMENCE • 25
TOTTENHAM HOTSPUR • BORN: 31.3.78

C

Son of former Spurs and England star Ray, Stephen Clemence enjoyed a good season at Tottenham, playing a part in 16 of the club's opening 22 Premiership games.

He hit problems in January when he turned his ankle in a tackle with Wimbledon's Robbie Earle and had to leave the field. The injury was thought to be a minor one, but eventually required surgery and Clemence did not see first-team action again until May, when he played the first half of the Premiership game against his home-town club, Liverpool.

A great prospect with a tidy style, Clemence completed 78% of his passes in the Premiership. Though he set up no goals, his final ball was generally of a good standard and he completed 33% of 40 attempted crosses.

He will probably have to work on his strength and stamina if he is to become a regular under George Graham. The Spurs boss is a big fan of tough-tackling midfielders and Clemence won just 45% of his attempted challenges in 1998–99, a figure some way below the average for midfielders.

APPEARANCES	
Start (sub)	9 (9)
Minutes on pitch	820
GOAL ATTEMPTS	
Goals	0
PASSING	
Passes	331
Passing accuracy	78%
DEFENDING	
Interceptions	4
Clearances	19
Tackles	22
Tackles won	45%
DISCIPLINE	
Fouls	5
Yellow cards	1
Red cards	0

CB Philippe CLEMENT • 18
COVENTRY CITY • BORN: 22.3.74

Currently studying for an engineering degree, Philippe Clement was looking to build on his career when he moved from Racing Genk in Belgium to the FA Carling Premiership in the summer of 1998.

But his career has rather foundered, and he managed just 515 minutes of top-flight football during the 1998–99 season. He started six matches and was a substitute on an identical number of occasions.

When he did play, he completed a below-average 73% of his passes but did contribute one goal assist to Coventry's season. He was also fairly wayward in front of goal, forcing a save with just one out of 10 attempts.

His tackle success rate was below par, but he was disciplined enough to help out in defence, making 36 clearances, seven interceptions and three blocks.

The unconvincing displays of Clement and the departures of Coventry's two other foreign summer signings (Jean-Guy Wallemme and Robert Jarni) may encourage Gordon Strachan to shop at home in future.

FB Juan COBIAN • 15
SHEFFIELD WEDNESDAY • BORN: 11.9.75

One of Danny Wilson's first signings for Sheffield Wednesday, Juan Cobian arrived from Argentinean club Boca Juniors in August 1998. A speedy right-back, Cobian has represented Argentina at under-15, under-18 and under-23 level, but was unable to secure a permanent place in the first team at Hillsborough.

He did start seven of the club's first eight Premiership games, but after being substituted in the comprehensive 4–0 defeat by Middlesbrough at the Riverside in October he did not reappear again until he came on as a substitute in the 4–1 win at Blackburn Rovers in February.

His pace and ability to beat players are not in question; he successfully completed all 15 of his attempted dribbles. Unfortunately, his tackling was less impressive and he won just 48% of his attempted challenges.

This inability to come to terms with the more physical side of the English game saw Danny Wilson release him on a free transfer just before the end of the season.

Andy COLE • 9
S MANCHESTER UNITED • BORN: 15.10.71

Andy Cole can lay claim to scoring THE goal that brought the championship trophy back to Old Trafford after its year-long sojourn at Highbury – the place Cole began his career.

His fine lob on the final day, just three minutes after coming on as a substitute, gave Manchester United a 2–1 win against Spurs and earned his side the three points they needed to win the title.

Cole finished the league season with 17 goals, one short of his partner and friend Dwight Yorke, to whom he will be grateful for many an assist. Fifty of his 97 shots were on target and he also claimed two goal assists.

Though not quite as prolific at Manchester United as he was with previous clubs, Cole has added more to his game, boasting a 73% pass completion rate and even firing in 26 crosses, completing 38%.

Cole also figured at international level once again. Largely ignored by Glenn Hoddle, he now seems to be earning the recognition under Kevin Keegan – his former mentor – that his goal tally down the years deserves.

APPEARANCES	
Start (sub)	26 (6)
Minutes on pitch	2358
GOAL ATTEMPTS	
Goals	17
Goals/shots ratio	20%
SHOOTING	
Shots on target	50
Shooting accuracy	60%
PASSING	
Goal assists	2
Passing accuracy	73%
DISCIPLINE	
Fouls	43
Offside	40
Yellow cards	3
Red cards	0

On fire: Andy Cole

Joe COLE • 26
AM WEST HAM UNITED • BORN: 8.11.81

One of the most heralded young players in the country, being tipped for superstardom even before he had kicked a ball in the first team and openly coveted by Alex Ferguson, Joe Cole broke into the West Ham side amid an injury crisis in January.

Given the identity of one of his biggest admirers, it was ironic that the youngster made his Premiership debut at Old Trafford. Despite being in a side that lost 4–1 he showed some good composure, a few nice touches and even contributed to the build-up for the Hammers' consolation goal.

The youngster went on to make two starting appearances and six more as a substitute, as well as inspiring the youth team to a league and FA Youth Cup Double.

Cole had eight shots in the league with three forcing a save, completed 80% of 162 attempted passes and successfully beat an opponent on 77% of the 22 dribbles and runs he attempted.

West Ham are sure to fight tooth and nail to hold on to one of their prime assets.

Patrick COLLETER • 33
SOUTHAMPTON • BORN: 6.11.65

C

Feisty French left-back Patrick Colleter was signed to replace defender Francis Benali, who broke his arm midway during the 1998–99 season. But while Benali waited 13 seasons to get his first goal for the Saints, it only took Colleter three games to break his duck, his goal coming against Charlton at the Dell.

Colleter made headlines for all the wrong reasons when he arrived, earning the nickname "Psycho". His Boxing Day challenge on Gustavo Poyet put the Chelsea star out of action for more than three months, and in his next game he scuffled with staff on the Nottingham Forest bench when taking a throw-in.

But his commitment to the Saints also showed in positive ways. He made 129 clearances and won possession with 70% of his tackles. His cross completion rate of 45% was superb, but his distribution let him down, as his 67% pass completion rate suggests.

Colleter lost his place to Benali near the end of the season, and with John Beresford also returning to fitness he may struggle to claim a regular place in the Southampton team.

APPEARANCES	
Start (sub)	16 (0)
Minutes on pitch	1371
GOAL ATTEMPTS	
Goals	1
PASSING & CROSSING	
Passing	531
Passing accuracy	67%
Crossing	31
Crossing accuracy	45%
DEFENDING	
Tackles	50
Tackles won	70%
DISCIPLINE	
Fouls	16
Yellow cards	4
Red cards	0

John COLLINS • 7
EVERTON • BORN: 31.1.68

APPEARANCES	
Start (sub)	19 (1)
Minutes on pitch	1706
GOAL ATTEMPTS	
Goals	1
PASSING	
Passes	825
Passing accuracy	86%
DEFENDING	
Interceptions	19
Clearances	16
Tackles	108
Tackles won	64%
DISCIPLINE	
Fouls	21
Yellow cards	4
Red cards	0

A toe injury brought an early end to John Collins's first Premiership season – but the omens are good for Everton fans that the influential midfielder will be able to push his side up the league ladder in 1999–2000.

Collins was ever-present in the first 17 matches of the season and made three further restricted appearances before he bowed out.

The former Celtic and Monaco player showed the canny skills learned in Glasgow and refined on the Continent, completing 86% of 825 passes, but also exhibited a willingness to dig in, winning 64% of the 108 tackles he made.

Collins also demonstrated his ability to beat players with good close control, retaining possession on 62% of his dribbles and runs.

He scored just one goal – a sweetly-struck left-foot drive against Middlesbrough – but should have added to that tally with a penalty that was saved by Mark Bosnich on the opening day against Aston Villa.

Four yellow cards did not help Everton's poor disciplinary record, but he committed just 21 fouls in 1706 minutes on the pitch.

Stan Collymore • 9
ASTON VILLA • BORN: 22.1.71

Stan Collymore had a depressing season for Aston Villa in the 1998–99 Carling Premiership. In a troubled campaign for the Cannock-born striker, Villa's record signing needed to be more clinical in front of goal, scoring just once in the league.

The former Nottingham Forest and England forward started nearly half his matches from the bench and missed chunks of the season as he struggled with problems off the pitch.

Collymore lacked penetration, managing just 25 shots at goal – only 12 of these troubling the opposing goalkeeper. But his sole strike at home to Spurs was accompanied by three goal assists for colleagues over the season.

Too often he gave the ball away, with slightly more than 60% of passes reaching a team-mate. His tackling lacked bite: he won just six of the 16 challenges he contested.

Despite his shortcomings in these areas, the ex-Liverpool striker displayed encouraging form in other areas. He completed 76% of all dribbles and runs and sent over 20 crosses, a healthy 30% of which found their target.

APPEARANCES	
Start (sub)	11 (9)
Minutes on pitch	1120
GOAL ATTEMPTS	
Goals	1
Goals/shots ratio	4%
SHOOTING	
Shots on target	12
Shooting accuracy	48%
PASSING	
Goal assists	3
Passing accuracy	62%
DISCIPLINE	
Fouls	26
Offside	27
Yellow cards	5
Red cards	1

Colin COOPER • 29
MIDDLESBROUGH • BORN: 28.2.67

APPEARANCES	
Start (sub)	31 (1)
Minutes on pitch	2719
GOAL ATTEMPTS	
Goals	1
DEFENDING	
Blocks	27
Headed clearances	185
Other clearances	134
Interceptions	39
Tackles won	69
PASSING	
Passing accuracy	75%
DISCIPLINE	
Fouls	33
Yellow cards	6
Red cards	0

"It's just like coming home for me" was the comment of Colin Cooper as he returned to Middlesbrough FC, albeit the new surroundings of the BT Cellnet Riverside stadium.

He was right in more ways than one, as he spent much of the 1998–99 season alongside his old defensive partner of the late '80s, Gary Pallister, also back with Boro after a long and successful spell at Manchester United.

Cooper settled back in straight away and completed a very good season, making 319 defensive clearances, 39 interceptions and 27 blocks. He also won a superb 73% of the 95 challenges he made and conceded just 33 fouls all season, though he will not have been happy to see the yellow card on six occasions.

Cooper's passing was reasonably efficient – a 75% completion rate from 1,009 passes could have been better – but he contributed one goal and one assist as Boro consolidated their position in the Premiership.

When he arrived, Cooper said: "The new Boro are geared for success and I want to be part of it." Boro fans everywhere will heartily concur.

Carl CORT • 23
WIMBLEDON • BORN: 1.11.77

C

Promising striker Carl Cort struggled to earn a regular place in the first XI at Selhurst Park, but still made a fine contribution to Wimbledon's season.

After a sprinkling of substitute appearances and two starts in the Worthington Cup, Cort had to wait until January 9 for his first Premiership start in 1998–99, against Derby. He had already scored two goals in two games by then, both as sub, in the draw at Leeds and the win over Manchester City in the FA Cup.

Two consolation strikes followed, in the defeats at Middlesbrough and Arsenal, but his three league goals came from just 11 shots, five of which were on target.

The 6' 4" frontman completed 69% of his passes and 63% of his dribbles and runs in his limited time on pitch – and he did not neglect the defensive side of the game, making as many clearances as he had attempts at goal.

One of his biggest strengths is his ability to hold the ball up, but with his aggressive, physical approach to the game, he did concede 17 fouls and pick up one yellow card.

APPEARANCES	
Start (sub)	6 (10)
Minutes on pitch	652
GOAL ATTEMPTS	
Goals	3
Goals/shots ratio	27%
SHOOTING	
Shots on target	5
Shooting accuracy	45%
PASSING	
Goal assists	0
Passing accuracy	69%
DISCIPLINE	
Fouls	17
Offside	9
Yellow cards	1
Red cards	0

Tony COTTEE • 27
LEICESTER CITY • BORN: 11.7.65

APPEARANCES	
Start (sub)	29 (2)
Minutes on pitch	2519
GOAL ATTEMPTS	
Goals	10
Goals/shots ratio	26%
SHOOTING	
Shots on target	25
Shooting accuracy	64%
PASSING	
Goal assists	1
Passing accuracy	79%
DISCIPLINE	
Fouls	34
Offside	25
Yellow cards	1
Red cards	0

Veteran poacher Tony Cottee enjoyed a superb 1998–99 season at Filbert Street, easily finishing as the club's top scorer with 16 goals in all competitions. His efforts in the Worthington Cup were particularly stunning, the little striker bagging five goals from just seven attempts as City stormed to the final.

In the Premiership, he certainly did not see as much of the ball as many other strikers in the league, spending the majority of his time in the opposition final third. But his striking stats were extremely impressive: he finished with an accuracy of 64% and hit the back of the net with more than a quarter of his efforts.

The high point of his season came at White Hart Lane. Not only did City gain instant revenge for being beaten by Spurs at Wembley, but Cottee also bagged his cherished 200th career league goal in the 2–0 victory.

Cottee completed 62% of dribbles and runs and won 56% of his tackles – both above average for a striker – but his main mission, duly accomplished, was to score goals for Martin O'Neill's side.

CB **Chris COYNE • 28**
WEST HAM UNITED • BORN: 20.12.78

Most West Ham supporters were simply too shell-shocked to notice that 20-year-old defender Chris Coyne was making his Hammers debut on May 1.

The young Australian, who had waited two years for his chance in the Premiership, finally got his opportunity with the Irons already down to nine men and trailing 5–1 at home to Leeds United.

Coyne was determined not to toss his chance away, but the defender managed just one touch of the ball in his seven minutes of Premiership football "hoofing one away", as he later put it.

He had spent a brief spell on loan at third-division Southend – but just a couple of days after signing him manager Alvin Martin was sacked, and Coyne struggled to get a chance at Roots Hall and found himself back in the Hammers' reserves.

Now he has had a brief a taste of Premiership football, Coyne will be determined to make more appearances in the top flight in 1999–2000.

S **Richard CRESSWELL • 21**
SHEFFIELD WEDNESDAY • BORN: 20.9.77

Signed by Danny Wilson on transfer deadline day for an initial fee of £1 million (rising to £1.5 million based on appearances), Richard Cresswell made his Wednesday debut against Coventry City.

He hit the headlines on the penultimate weekend of the season when he scored the only goal in a 1–0 defeat of Liverpool. That capped an exciting season in which the youngster became the first York City player to represent England, when he appeared for the under-21 side.

His 19 goals for the Division Two club were obviously no fluke and he has shown enough in his brief time as a Premiership footballer with Sheffield Wednesday to suggest that he has a bright future.

As well as his goal, he was credited with one assist. Big, strong and very quick, Cresswell has also made seven powerful runs with the ball and knocked two successful crosses into the box.

Cresswell is likely to figure more prominently in the 1999–2000 season.

FB **Gary CROFT • 20**
BLACKBURN ROVERS • BORN: 17.2.74

APPEARANCES	
Start (sub)	10 (2)
Minutes on pitch	855
GOAL ATTEMPTS	
Goals	0
PASSING & CROSSING	
Passing	349
Passing accuracy	75%
Crossing	21
Crossing accuracy	38%
DEFENDING	
Tackles	29
Tackles won	59%
DISCIPLINE	
Fouls	12
Yellow cards	1
Red cards	0

A £1.7 million signing from Grimsby Town in 1996, Gary Croft struggled to keep a place in the Rovers starting line-up in 1998–99, losing out to Scottish international Callum Davidson.

Croft managed 10 starts for Blackburn, mostly as a direct replacement for the injured or suspended Davidson at left-back, but was unable to oust him from the first team.

When he appeared, his mobility and ball skills came to the fore. He completed 75% of his 349 passes and a well above-average 38% of his crosses. He also retained possession from three-quarters of his dribbles and runs.

Defensively, Croft's tackling stats fell below the Premiership average. He won only 59% of challenges but committed just 12 fouls and picked up one caution. He also made 61 clearances from defence and five interceptions.

Croft will have work to do in the reserves in 1999–2000 if he is to make the first team on a regular basis. With the likes of Davidson, Jeff Kenna and Christian Dailly in the side, this may mean another season on the subs' bench.

Mark CROSSLEY • 13
G
NOTTINGHAM FOREST • BORN: 16.6.69

Having spent 1997–98 injured, out of favour or on loan to Millwall, Mark Crossley can have had few hopes of regular Premiership football in 1998–99, especially when Dave Bassett gave Dave Beasant the nod at the season's start. Crossley was picked for the Worthington Cup tie against Leyton Orient in September but could not displace Beasant in the league.

Ron Atkinson's arrival marked the turning-point. After Beasant let in 13 goals in three games in February, including eight at home to Manchester United, Atkinson recalled the Yorkshireman, who saved a penalty and kept a clean sheet in the 0–0 draw at Charlton.

Incredibly, three more penalty saves followed as Crossley deservedly kept his place for the last 12 games of the season. But it was not enough to stop the club being relegated.

He conceded just 15 goals and kept three clean sheets, saving 80% of all on-target shots faced. He did drop three catches, but his distribution was excellent, with 34% of all long kicks and 96% of his shorter kicks and throws finding a Forest player.

APPEARANCES	
Start (sub)	12 (0)
Minutes on pitch	1080
SHOT STOPPING	
Goals conceded	15
Clean sheets	3
Saves	60
Saves/shots	80%
DISTRIBUTION	
Distribution	365
Distribution %	46%
CATCHING	
Crosses caught	26
Crosses dropped	3
DISCIPLINE	
Yellow cards	0
Red cards	0

Jordi CRUYFF • 14
AM
MANCHESTER UNITED • BORN: 9.2.74

Dutch international Jordi Cruyff has had a disappointing time so far at Manchester United, finding it hard to break into the first team at Old Trafford even when fully fit.

After playing only 85 minutes in the 1998–99 Carling Premiership for Alex Ferguson, he was sent out on loan to Spanish Primera Liga club Celta Vigo.

During his 85 minutes, Cruyff notched two goals from his attacking midfield position, hit a further two shots on target and fired two off target.

His goals showed he can perform at Premiership level, especially in a team with the creative players Manchester United have at their disposal.

The former Barcelona star ran well with the ball, completing 92% of his 12 dribbles and runs. His incisive passing created one goal for Manchester United and he completed 67% of his 49 passes.

The son of Dutch superstar Johan, Jordi (as he prefers to be known) is unlikely to be a Manchester United player for much longer.

Michael CUMMINS • 30
M
MIDDLESBROUGH • BORN: 1.6.78

Midfield man Michael Cummins spent much of the 1998–99 season toiling in the Middlesbrough reserves. But the promising youngster looks set for a more rewarding campaign in 1999–2000 after finally making his first-team breakthrough in Boro's last match at West Ham.

One of his best moments of the season came in a reserve match at Burnley in March, when he was switched to a more defensive role and capped a brilliant display by heading in Paul Gascoigne's corner in a 5–1 win.

In Cummins's first-team debut Boro were beaten 4–0, but he put in a good personal display, completing 83% of his 40 passes and four of his six crosses, as well as winning three of his six tackles.

He may well be part of Bryan Robson's plans for the future, with the ageing Middlesbrough midfield facing a race against time in the top flight.

The versatile midfield player can also play in defence and it is this flexibility that will make him a valuable commodity.

FB Kenny CUNNINGHAM • 2
WIMBLEDON • BORN: 28.6.71

Republic of Ireland international Kenny Cunningham has made the right-back position his own since signing from Millwall in 1994 and was much-admired by ex-boss Joe Kinnear, himself a former Eire international right-back.

Cunningham was once again a consistent performer for the Dons, making more than a thousand passes and over 300 clearances.

A big part of his game involves overlapping the right-sided midfielder – be it Neal Ardley or Gareth Ainsworth – and bending in crosses. Sadly, he completed just 18% of his centres, a disappointing figure for a player of his quality.

His discipline was excellent, though, with only 26 fouls and just three yellow cards in more than 3,000 minutes on the pitch.

During Wimbledon's run of matches against Tottenham in the league and two cup competitions Cunningham did a fine job keeping winger David Ginola quiet.

He is certain to play a leading role in Wimbledon's 1999–2000 season – and will always be on the lookout for the chance to bag his long-overdue first goal for the club.

APPEARANCES	
Start (sub)	35 (0)
Minutes on pitch	3150
GOAL ATTEMPTS	
Goals	0
PASSING & CROSSING	
Passing	1058
Passing accuracy	72%
Crossing	119
Crossing accuracy	18%
DEFENDING	
Tackles	105
Tackles won	59%
DISCIPLINE	
Fouls	26
Yellow cards	3
Red cards	0

Much-admired: Kenny Cunningham

CB John CURTIS • 13
MANCHESTER UNITED • BORN: 3.9.78

After getting his break in the first team in 1997–98, defender John Curtis must have hoped he would get plenty more opportunities in the Manchester United back-line in the 1998–99 campaign.

But despite making the first XI against Blackburn Rovers in November, Curtis spent the rest of the season back in the reserves, while casting wistful glances in the direction of highly-rated young rival Wes Brown, who was earning high praise for his mature performances in defence.

With Jaap Stam, Henning Berg and Ronny Johnsen hogging the centre-back positions, the fine form of Denis Irwin and the Neville brothers prevented Curtis getting any opportunities at full-back, though he did make Premiership substitute appearances against Wimbledon, Nottingham Forest and Everton. He also played in all of United's games in the Worthington Cup.

In the Premiership, he showed a cool head on the ball, completing 95% of his 74 passes and making 10 clearances.

Nikos DABIZAS • 34
NEWCASTLE UNITED • BORN: 3.8.73

C

Greek centre-back Nikos Dabizas was probably the most consistent performer in Newcastle United's defence in 1998–99 and ended sixth in the Carling Opta defenders Index.

Manager Ruud Gullit shuffled his back-line around many times during the campaign, with Dabizas, Laurent Charvet, David Beharall, Steve Howey, Aaron Hughes, Stuart Pearce and Philippe Albert all vying for places at times. But Dabizas was a regular starter, despite interruptions due to injury and suspension.

His aerial ability at both ends of the pitch compared with the league's finest: he made more than 400 clearances, 303 with his head.

A major threat from set-pieces, he scored three Premiership goals and managed a further three efforts on target. In terms of distribution, he made more than 1,000 passes, completing an above-average 83%

Despite Dabizas's good season, he and his colleagues endured a miserable FA Cup final. Many blamed the Greek for Manchester United's decisive second goal, though he did clear an Andy Cole shot off the line.

APPEARANCES	
Start (sub)	25 (5)
Minutes on pitch	2301
GOAL ATTEMPTS	
Goals	3
DEFENDING	
Blocks	19
Headed clearances	303
Other clearances	126
Interceptions	43
Tackles won	62
PASSING	
Passing accuracy	83%
DISCIPLINE	
Fouls	39
Yellow cards	6
Red cards	2

Olivier DACOURT • 4
EVERTON • BORN: 25.9.74

APPEARANCES	
Start (sub)	28 (2)
Minutes on pitch	2515
GOAL ATTEMPTS	
Goals	2
PASSING	
Passes	1113
Passing accuracy	77%
DEFENDING	
Interceptions	16
Clearances	44
Tackles	216
Tackles won	66%
DISCIPLINE	
Fouls	66
Yellow cards	13
Red cards	1

It says much for Olivier Dacourt's personal performances that he seems virtually to have doubled in value in less than a year despite Everton's miserable 1998–99. His feisty displays in the heart of midfield alongside skipper Don Hutchison put him 10th in the end-of-season Carling Opta midfielders Index.

The fiery Frenchman's work-rate soon won over the fans after his arrival from Strasbourg for £3.8 million. He made more than 200 tackles, conceding 66 fouls. But his aggression came at a price of 13 Premiership bookings and a red card at home to Leeds.

Resulting suspensions meant only 28 starts – but that has not stopped a host of top clubs wanting to sign him.

Going forward, Dacourt fired in almost 50 shots and saw another 23 blocked, but he managed only two goals, one a 25-yard blast in the first minute at Anfield during the 160th Merseyside derby. Arsenal were hotly tipped to sign him, but Dacourt would find displacing Emmanuel Petit and Patrick Vieira as difficult at club level as he has for France.

Martin DAHLIN • 14
BLACKBURN ROVERS • BORN: 16.4.68

Swedish international Martin Dahlin was loaned out to German Bundesliga club SV Hamburg in October 1998, following injury problems and failure to hit top form since his arrival at Blackburn two years ago.

Dahlin made a couple of appearances early in the 1998–99 season but failed to maintain a place in the first team. Only one out of his five shots was on target, while his pass completion rate of 67% was disappointing for an international striker.

If his strike rate failed to impress, he hardly won over the management with his red card at Everton. The Swede also found trouble dealing with offside traps, forcing linesmen into action on seven occasions in just 217 minutes.

Before having a disappointing time at AS Roma in Italy, Martin Dahlin proved his class in the German Bundesliga, scoring 50 goals in 106 games for Borussia Moenchengladbach. His success in Germany suggested he might be the right kind of player for the Premiership – but, as in Italy, he has found the going rather tougher than expected.

APPEARANCES	
Start (sub)	2 (3)
Minutes on pitch	217
GOAL ATTEMPTS	
Goals	0
Goals/shots ratio	0%
SHOOTING	
Shots on target	1
Shooting accuracy	25%
PASSING	
Goal assists	1
Passing accuracy	67%
DISCIPLINE	
Fouls	5
Offside	7
Yellow cards	0
Red cards	1

Christian DAILLY • 23
BLACKBURN ROVERS • BORN: 23.10.73

APPEARANCES	
Start (sub)	15 (3)
Minutes on pitch	1334
GOAL ATTEMPTS	
Goals	0
DEFENDING	
Blocks	9
Headed clearances	73
Other clearances	48
Interceptions	5
Tackles won	15
PASSING	
Passing accuracy	76%
DISCIPLINE	
Fouls	14
Yellow cards	0
Red cards	0

Defender Christian Dailly figured in all three of Scotland's starting line-ups in France 98 and, after he played the first game of the season for Derby County – ironically against Blackburn Rovers – he was signed by then-Rovers boss Roy Hodgson for £5.3 million.

Eyebrows were raised at the price tag, and Dailly only played half the season before a long-term thigh injury in the New Year left him on the side-lines, along with many other multi-million pound signings. When he did play, his distribution was adequate, with 76% of his passes finding their intended target.

He cleared 121 balls, blocked nine shots and made five interceptions. But his tackling was below par. He won a modest 54% of his challenges, hardly easing the pressure Blackburn often found themselves under.

Dailly enjoyed the odd foray into the opposition penalty area, particularly at set-pieces, and fired seven of his 10 efforts at goal on target. If he can improve his success in the tackle and remain fit, Dailly will be a valuable member of Brian Kidd's squad in 1999–2000.

Paul DALGLISH • 25
NEWCASTLE UNITED • BORN: 18.2.77

When a player has been on the books of Celtic, Liverpool and Newcastle and not played a single game, you can imagine his delight at finally getting his chance.

It happened for Paul Dalglish in Newcastle's 5–1 romp at Coventry City on September 19, at the start of a two-month run which included his first senior goal in the 1–0 Worthington Cup win at Tranmere Rovers and his first – and, to date, only – Premiership goal in the 1–1 draw with Sheffield Wednesday.

Being the boss's son, and the boss being Liverpool striking legend Kenny, he was under immense pressure, but achieved a fine shooting accuracy of 59% in the top flight, hitting 10 of 17 shots on target.

However, with new manager Ruud Gullit keen to experiment, the young striker struggled to secure even a place on the bench, and joined Norwich City on loan on transfer deadline day.

He missed the end of the season through injury, but showed enough in 1998–99 to suggest he could make quite an impact in the Premiership if he is given the chance.

APPEARANCES	
Start (sub)	6 (5)
Minutes on pitch	561
GOAL ATTEMPTS	
Goals	1
Goals/shots ratio	6%
SHOOTING	
Shots on target	10
Shooting accuracy	59%
PASSING	
Goal assists	0
Passing accuracy	67%
DISCIPLINE	
Fouls	17
Offside	5
Yellow cards	1
Red cards	0

Jean-Claude DARCHEVILLE • 19
NOTTINGHAM FOREST • BORN: 25.7.75

APPEARANCES	
Start (sub)	13 (3)
Minutes on pitch	1078
GOAL ATTEMPTS	
Goals	2
Goals/shots ratio	8%
SHOOTING	
Shots on target	14
Shooting accuracy	56%
PASSING	
Goal assists	2
Passing accuracy	68%
DISCIPLINE	
Fouls	15
Offside	23
Yellow cards	3
Red cards	0

French frontman Jean-Claude Darcheville moved to England seeking a fresh start after a tragedy in his personal life. A promising pre-season saw him start as Dave Bassett's first-choice striker at the City Ground thanks to the self-imposed absence of Pierre van Hooijdonk.

He impressed in Forest's first match of the 1998–99 season against champions Arsenal at Highbury, but a lack of confidence saw him drop down the order. He made just five starts after Ron Atkinson took over as manager.

The pacy striker scored just twice in the Premiership, netting in the away games at Southampton and Chelsea. He hit 14 shots on target, representing a fine accuracy of 56%.

Running at defenders was his strong point. He made almost 50 dribbles and runs, beating his man more often than not. He also claimed two goal assists, though his pass completion rate of 68% was below average for a striker.

Darcheville's future at Forest is uncertain but wherever he plies his trade in 1999–2000, fans everywhere will hope he has more success after a very tough 12 months.

FB — Callum DAVIDSON • 3
BLACKBURN ROVERS • BORN: 25.6.76

After just one first-team appearance in 1997–98, Callum Davidson missed only four Premiership matches in 1998–99 and was generally seen as one of Rovers' most impressive players in a miserable campaign.

Carling Opta statisics make him the club's top passer and second-top tackler. As first-choice left-back he made more than 250 clearances, blocked 24 shots and made 23 interceptions. But his tackling was below par, and he won only 63% of his challenges.

His abilities were tested at international level, and his run and pass set up Scotland's winning goal against European champions Germany in a friendly, but the highlight of his league season was his first Blackburn goal, a magnificent effort in the 3–0 victory over West Ham. He ran the length of the pitch before curling a spectacular shot into the top corner.

When he pushed forward, he maintained possession from 85% of his dribbles and runs, and his crossing was reasonable, with 27% completed. He is sure to be a key figure in Rovers' push for promotion from Division One.

APPEARANCES	
Start (sub)	34 (0)
Minutes on pitch	3025
GOAL ATTEMPTS	
Goals	1
PASSING & CROSSING	
Passing	1149
Passing accuracy	74%
Crossing	44
Crossing accuracy	27%
DEFENDING	
Tackles	100
Tackles won	63%
DISCIPLINE	
Fouls	28
Yellow cards	7
Red cards	0

S — Kevin DAVIES • 10
BLACKBURN ROVERS • BORN: 26.3.77

APPEARANCES	
Start (sub)	9 (12)
Minutes on pitch	1040
GOAL ATTEMPTS	
Goals	1
Goals/shots ratio	3%
SHOOTING	
Shots on target	13
Shooting accuracy	33%
PASSING	
Goal assists	2
Passing accuracy	61%
DISCIPLINE	
Fouls	30
Offside	12
Yellow cards	5
Red cards	0

Expectations were high in the summer of 1998 when Kevin Davies signed in a £7.25 million transfer from Southampton. But a combination of injury, illness and poor form sidelined Blackburn's record signing and he only managed nine first-team starts and 12 substitute appearances during the season.

He fired 45 shots at goal (including blocked efforts), but only managed a disappointing shooting accuracy of 33%. The high point came in the 1–0 home win over Charlton when, as a substitute, he scored what turned out to be his only goal of the season.

The former England under-21's pass completion rate of 61% fell short of the Premiership average – but he did create two goals. More successful running at defenders, he completed 59% of his dribbles and runs.

The burden of that huge price-tag and several trips to hospital have made it hard for Davies to settle at Blackburn – and doubts about his future have inevitably been raised, with some in the media even talking of a possible cut-price return to Southampton.

Ed DE GOEY • 1
G
CHELSEA • BORN: 20.12.66

Signed for £2.25 million before the 1997–98 season, ex-Feyenoord star Ed De Goey enjoyed a super second season at Stamford Bridge.

Ever-present in the league until he was forced off in April's 1–0 victory over Charlton Athletic, the Dutch international was one of Chelsea's most consistent performers. With just 27 goals conceded and 13 clean sheets, he played a key role in helping Chelsea to the Premiership's second-best defensive record.

A good shot-stopper, he ended the season with a saves-to-shots ratio of 78% and produced an excellent penalty save from Jimmy Floyd Hasselbaink against Leeds United. But it was from opposition crosses that he put in his best work. Using his considerable frame – at 6'5" he is the tallest player in Chelsea's history – he achieved a catch success rate of 99%.

As with many continental 'keepers, he also punched his fair share of crosses, clearing the ball with his fist 36 times – the most in the Premiership. Thankfully for Blues fans, he achieved a good distance with most of them.

APPEARANCES	
Start (sub)	35 (0)
Minutes on pitch	3105
SHOT STOPPING	
Goals conceded	27
Clean sheets	13
Saves	95
Saves/shots	78%
DISTRIBUTION	
Distribution	894
Distribution %	56%
CATCHING	
Crosses caught	76
Crosses dropped	1
DISCIPLINE	
Yellow cards	2
Red cards	0

Brian DEANE • 10
S
MIDDLESBROUGH • BORN: 7.2.68

APPEARANCES	
Start (sub)	24 (2)
Minutes on pitch	2143
GOAL ATTEMPTS	
Goals	6
Goals/shots ratio	11%
SHOOTING	
Shots on target	35
Shooting accuracy	65%
PASSING	
Goal assists	1
Passing accuracy	65%
DISCIPLINE	
Fouls	55
Offside	21
Yellow cards	2
Red cards	0

Boro's Bryan Robson added to his portfolio of thirtysomethings at the Riverside by buying experienced striker Brian Deane in October.

With troubled frontman Paul Merson leaving for Aston Villa, Robson bought Deane from Benfica to partner Hamilton Ricard up front. Ricard had surprised many at the start of 1998–99 by topping the scoring charts with seven goals by the end of September.

But though they meshed well in their first start together – the 2–2 draw at Wimbledon, when Ricard scored – the Colombian managed just two goals in his next 14 games with Deane. Bryan Robson obviously hoped Deane's knock-downs would benefit Ricard, but the former England international managed just one assist in a Boro shirt.

He only scored six Premiership goals himself from more than 50 attempts, but gave opposition goalkeepers plenty to think about, achieving an excellent accuracy of 65%.

Deane won only 42% of his challenges but was surprisingly good on the ball for a big man, completing 74% of his dribbles and runs.

M **Peter DEGN • 22**
EVERTON • BORN: 6.4.77

Signed from Aarhus in early March 1999, Peter Degn had little chance to show the Everton fans what he could do.

The Danish under-21 international managed just four substitute appearances, totalling 98 minutes of Premiership action.

Degn the Dane found the top flight a strain, being on the losing side in all four of his matches. He made his debut in the 3–1 defeat at Old Trafford by Manchester United before featuring in the 2–1 defeat by Sheffield Wednesday, the 3–1 away loss to Chelsea and the 2–0 reverse at Southampton on the final day of the season.

He displayed a willingness to get forward, delivering seven centres – but only found an Everton player once. Elsewhere, his limited statistics reveal little about his potential for the Toffees.

The out-of-contract midfielder arrived at Goodison Park too late to acclimatize in the Premiership. Degn will hope for more first-team action in 1999–2000, be it at Everton or elsewhere.

FB **Mark DELANEY • 24**
ASTON VILLA • BORN: 13.5.76

Despite a number of good young players pushing for a first-team place at Villa Park, John Gregory invested in wing-back Mark Delaney from Cardiff City.

Delaney arrived at Villa in March and managed two appearances for the Midlands club before the end of the 1998–99 Carling Premiership. He came off the bench for the match at home to Nottingham Forest and on the final day of the season in the 1–0 defeat by Arsenal.

Remarkably, Delaney made his first-ever Football League appearance during the 1998–99 season and impressed so much in his inaugural campaign that Gregory shelled out £350,000 initially to sign him.

The Haverfordwest-born player may have been untested in the top flight but he showed no signs of being daunted by the move. He had an impressive debut for the reserves, delivering some dangerous balls into the area that signalled his intent. In the Premiership, he made two tackles and 16 passes during his 24 minutes of action.

FB **Rory DELAP • 10**
DERBY COUNTY • BORN: 6.7.76

APPEARANCES	
Start (sub)	21 (2)
Minutes on pitch	1862
GOAL ATTEMPTS	
Goals	0
PASSING & CROSSING	
Passing	579
Passing accuracy	67%
Crossing	34
Crossing accuracy	24%
DEFENDING	
Tackles	65
Tackles won	55%
DISCIPLINE	
Fouls	18
Yellow cards	6
Red cards	0

Signed from Carlisle United for £500,000 in February 1998, Rory Delap made his first-team breakthrough in 1997–98 and had plenty of chances to prove himself in 1998–99.

The Eire international made 21 Premiership starts and two appearances as substitute, operating mainly as a right-sided wing-back.

Although he enjoys getting forward, he made far more clearances at the back than runs down the wing in 1998–99. He made only 55 dribbles and runs and just 34 crosses – fewer than two per match. His passing also needs to improve: he completed a below-average 67%, creating just the one goal.

Delap had 24 shots on goal including blocked efforts, but though six were on target he failed to register his first Premiership goal.

Defensively, he won only 55% of his 65 challenges, but read the game well, with 32 interceptions and 12 blocks. He averaged a yellow card every three fouls.

He will need to repel the challenges of Jacob Laursen and Vassilis Borbokis in order to hold on to the right wing-back slot in 1999–2000.

Marcel DESAILLY • 6
CHELSEA • BORN: 7.9.68

CB

Gianluca Vialli was shrewd enough to secure Marcel Desailly's services before France 98. Had Chelsea's manager waited until after the World Cup to sign the Ghanaian-born Frenchman, it is safe to say he would have cost considerably more than the £4.5 million the club eventually paid.

The finest defender on display in France, he made a tricky Premiership debut marking Dion Dublin in Chelsea's opening-day defeat at Highfield Road, but quickly put it behind him.

Whether playing in his preferred position at the back or as the holding player in midfield, the former AC Milan man was rarely fazed by the opposition. His tackling was excellent, but most of the time he simply broke up enemy attacks with a well-timed interception or a vital clearance.

Deceptively quick for a man of his size, Desailly made surprisingly few dribbles and runs, but atoned for this with his work off the ball. His partnership with Frank Leboeuf was one of the best in the Premiership and very few strikers got the better of him.

APPEARANCES	
Start (sub)	30 (1)
Minutes on pitch	2651
GOAL ATTEMPTS	
Goals	0
DEFENDING	
Blocks	27
Headed clearances	144
Other clearances	108
Interceptions	48
Tackles won	94
PASSING	
Passing accuracy	86%
DISCIPLINE	
Fouls	29
Yellow cards	5
Red cards	0

Paolo DI CANIO • 10
WEST HAM UNITED • BORN: 9.7.68

S

APPEARANCES	
Start (sub)	17 (2)
Minutes on pitch	1533
GOAL ATTEMPTS	
Goals	7
Goals/shots ratio	23%
SHOOTING	
Shots on target	14
Shooting accuracy	45%
PASSING	
Goal assists	2
Passing accuracy	73%
DISCIPLINE	
Fouls	24
Offside	34
Yellow cards	1
Red cards	1

Banned for his notorious clash with Paul Alcock in the Sheffield Wednesday-Arsenal match on September 26, Paolo Di Canio's Premiership career appeared to be over.

Surprisingly, given his previous problems with foreign players, West Ham manager Harry Redknapp opted to gamble on the Italian: and after just over four months at Upton Park, the move seems to have paid off for both parties.

Di Canio scored four times for the Hammers, taking his Premiership tally to seven, but just as importantly for West Ham he quickly rediscovered his ability to create chances for his team-mates, grabbing two assists.

Redknapp encouraged his new signing to get wide and Di Canio proved eager to please with 69 crosses, lifting his total for the season to 90. His completion rate actually improved from 14% to 29% after moving to Upton Park.

Booked just once for the Bubble-Blowers, Di Canio proved that his run-in with Alcock had been an aberration. Season 1999–2000 should see him making a rather more welcome push – up the table with West Ham.

Roberto DI MATTEO • 16
CHELSEA • BORN: 29.5.70

Although 1998–99 was a successful season for Chelsea, Roberto Di Matteo did not quite touch the levels of personal performance which he had managed in his previous two campaigns with the club.

The Italian international's passing was as crisp as ever in the centre of midfield and he contributed four assists, as well as a number of accurate crosses. But although he had almost 50 shots at goal, he hit the back of the net just twice in the Premiership and kept a measly 35% of his efforts on target – a poor return by his high standards.

His tackle success rate dropped to 59% – below the Premiership average for midfielders – and he contributed less defensively than in the past, making fewer than 50 clearances.

All of this saw Gianluca Vialli drop him from the side for some of Chelsea's biggest games of the season. From being one of the Blue's most influential players, he found himself on the fringes of the team, and will need to work much harder in the 1999–2000 season to regain a regular place in the starting XI.

APPEARANCES	
Start (sub)	26 (4)
Minutes on pitch	2313
GOAL ATTEMPTS	
Goals	2
PASSING	
Passes	1316
Passing accuracy	86%
DEFENDING	
Interceptions	27
Clearances	48
Tackles	118
Tackles won	59%
DISCIPLINE	
Fouls	49
Yellow cards	8
Red cards	0

Kaba DIAWARA • 27
ARSENAL • BORN: 16.12.75

APPEARANCES	
Start (sub)	2 (10)
Minutes on pitch	310
GOAL ATTEMPTS	
Goals	0
Goals/shots ratio	0%
SHOOTING	
Shots on target	5
Shooting accuracy	28%
PASSING	
Goal assists	0
Passing accuracy	65%
DISCIPLINE	
Fouls	5
Offside	2
Yellow cards	0
Red cards	0

French frontman Kaba Diawara had a tough time at Highbury. Signed from Bordeaux for £3.5 million in February 1999, he found himself in direct competition with Nicolas Anelka, Dennis Bergkamp and another new boy, Nwankwo Kanu. As a result, he was restricted to two starts and 10 substitutions.

His lack of goals was certainly not for want of trying; he averaged a shot every 15.5 minutes. He also hit the woodwork twice and had a blistering effort cleared off the line by Jonathon Woodgate in the defeat by Leeds United at Elland Road.

The former French under-21 international completed only 65% of his passes and 63% of his dribbles and runs in 310 minutes of Premiership experience, suggesting he was still adjusting to its demands.

Strong in the tackle, he won 67% of his challenges and avoided any brush with officialdom. Despite pledging himself to Arsenal, Diawara moved to Marseille for an undisclosed fee after the 1998–99 campaign came to an end.

FB

Julian DICKS • 3
WEST HAM UNITED • BORN: 8.8.68

After missing the entire 1997–98 season with a career-threatening injury, Julian Dicks made an emotional return on September 28 in West Ham's 1–0 victory over Southampton.

Unfortunately, "The Terminator" – as he is affectionately known to Hammers fans – found the pace of the Premiership harder to come to terms with than in previous seasons, and did not do enough to convince Harry Redknapp he could hold down a regular first-team place.

Although he still made his fair share of clearances, his old sharpness was simply not there. He averaged just over two successful tackles a game in 1998–99; in 1996-97 the figure had been closer to four.

With just one interception to his name in 810 minutes, he clearly was not reacting as quickly as in his heyday, and the last of his nine Premiership appearances came in the 4–0 home defeat by Arsenal.

Dicks has already achieved enough at Upton Park to book himself a place in West Ham's Hall of Fame, but he is unlikely to recall 1998–99 with any particular affection.

D

APPEARANCES	
Start (sub)	9 (0)
Minutes on pitch	810
GOAL ATTEMPTS	
Goals	0
PASSING & CROSSING	
Passing	302
Passing accuracy	68%
Crossing	11
Crossing accuracy	36%
DEFENDING	
Tackles	31
Tackles won	65%
DISCIPLINE	
Fouls	10
Yellow cards	2
Red cards	0

FB

Lee DIXON • 2
ARSENAL • BORN: 17.3.64

APPEARANCES	
Start (sub)	36 (0)
Minutes on pitch	3111
GOAL ATTEMPTS	
Goals	0
PASSING & CROSSING	
Passing	1610
Passing accuracy	80%
Crossing	43
Crossing accuracy	19%
DEFENDING	
Tackles	90
Tackles won	61%
DISCIPLINE	
Fouls	29
Yellow cards	5
Red cards	1

Lee Dixon experienced a brief renaissance in his international career when he was selected for England's match against France on February 10. In the Carling Premiership, he displayed his usual tenacity and resilience as he helped Arsenal achieve easily the best defensive record in the league.

He completed 80% of more than 1,500 passes, one of which led directly to a goal. Though failing to score himself, he fired eight shots on target and was very unlucky when his 25-yard left-foot curler against Wimbledon smacked off the Selhurst Park crossbar.

Defensively, he won 61% of his tackles and made 155 clearances. He also blocked 21 shots and made 24 interceptions.

Like many of his team-mates, his disciplinary record of five bookings and one sending-off was nothing to be proud of – but at least it proved he has lost none of his will to win.

May's signing of Dynamo Kiev star Oleg Luzhny cast doubt on Dixon's future as first-choice right-back. But he has been written off before and will doubtless rise to the challenge.

FB Jason DODD • 2
SOUTHAMPTON • BORN: 2.11.70

Saints skipper Jason Dodd has spent his entire professional career at the Dell, having joined from Bath City in March 1989. A veteran of many relegation dogfights, he played a crucial part in the club's survival battle in 1998–99.

Although normally first-choice right-back, Dodd competed with Scott Hiley for this position for much of the season. He had a spell on the right side of midfield midway through the campaign, but returned to his orthodox role for the final few matches.

The Bath-born defender has been one of Southampton's most reliable players over the past decade and, though he has lost a little pace, he remains committed to the cause, as shown by his winning possession with 73% of his 92 tackles. In terms of crossing, 31% of his centres picked out their man during 1998–99, providing four assists.

A renowned one-goal-a-season player, Dodd's strikes are usually of the spectacular variety. He did score one goal in 1998–99 in the 2–1 home victory against Newcastle United – but that was from the penalty spot.

APPEARANCES	
Start (sub)	27 (1)
Minutes on pitch	2387
GOAL ATTEMPTS	
Goals	1
PASSING & CROSSING	
Passing	990
Passing accuracy	74%
Crossing	52
Crossing accuracy	31%
DEFENDING	
Tackles	92
Tackles won	73%
DISCIPLINE	
Fouls	24
Yellow cards	4
Red cards	1

CB Christopher DOIG • 12
NOTTINGHAM FOREST • BORN: 13.2.81

Young Christoher Doig played just 112 minutes of Premiership football in two appearances for Nottingham Forest.

His first match was as a substitute in the 8–1 thrashing by Manchester United. He came on with 12 minutes to go with the score at 4–1, but was not able to exert as great an influence as another sub that day, Ole Gunnar Solskjaer. The Norwegian crashed four goals past the hapless Dave Beasant in the last 10 minutes-plus-stoppage-time.

Doig's only other outing was a full game in the 4–0 defeat by Coventry. In total, he only made 21 passes, completing two-thirds. He made 17 clearances, three interceptions and two blocks – and he won the two tackles he contested.

With a new man in charge at the City Ground, Doig will be working hard to make an impression.

If he does feature in 1999–2000, he will be hoping that the opposition does not get into the habit of knocking in four goals every time he is on the pitch.

Committed: Jason Dodd

FB Didier DOMI • 4
NEWCASTLE UNITED • BORN: 2.5.78

D

Didier Domi joined Newcastle from Paris St Germain just before the end of 1998, for a fee which could finally reach £4 million.

With French youth and under-21 caps, he is widely tipped to replace Bixente Lizarazu in the full French side if he keeps improving.

He will have been disappointed not to gain an FA Cup winner's medal after success in the French Cup last season, but will be hoping Ruud Gullit's rebuilding results in further opportunities to win trophies.

After his debut against Chelsea, Domi made 14 further appearances during the season, showing excellent dribbling ability. He retained possession on 89% of his 59 runs, but Gullit will be expecting Domi to improve his 17% cross completion rate so Alan Shearer and Duncan Ferguson can take full advantage.

The Frenchman made 94 clearances, 16 interceptions and seven blocks, but his slight build saw him lose possession in 48% of his tackles. The youngster does seem to have a good temperament, though: he was booked just once and committed only nine fouls.

APPEARANCES	
Start (sub)	14 (0)
Minutes on pitch	1260
GOAL ATTEMPTS	
Goals	0
PASSING & CROSSING	
Passing	582
Passing accuracy	71%
Crossing	42
Crossing accuracy	17%
DEFENDING	
Tackles	52
Tackles won	52%
DISCIPLINE	
Fouls	9
Yellow cards	1
Red cards	0

AM Jose DOMINGUEZ • 20
TOTTENHAM HOTSPUR • BORN: 16.2.74

APPEARANCES	
Start (sub)	2 (11)
Minutes on pitch	364
GOAL ATTEMPTS	
Goals	2
Shots on target	5
Shooting accuracy	50%
PASSING	
Goal assists	2
Passing accuracy	81%
Crossing accuracy	22%
DRIBBLING	
Dribbles & runs	46
Dribble completion	59%
DISCIPLINE	
Yellow cards	1
Red cards	0

Now well into his second stint in English football, diminutive winger Jose Dominguez has yet to convince the English public that he can make it to the very top of the game in this country.

The tricky Portuguese international dazzled St Andrews with his close control and array of tricks while at Birmingham City and, after a spell back in his native country with Sporting Lisbon, Gerry Francis brought him to White Hart Lane at the start of the 1997–98 season to play wide on the left.

The Spurs faithful, who always admire a flair player, took to him immediately; but with David Ginola ahead of him and Andy Sinton also challenging for a regular place, first-team opportunities were bound to be limited.

Dominguez scored twice in the 1998–99 FA Carling Premiership campaign – both times as a substitute – netting against Southampton and Charlton Athletic. That was not a bad return from only 10 shots, and the little wing wizard can also be proud of the two goals for which he claimed assists.

Tony DORIGO • 5
DERBY COUNTY • BORN: 31.12.65

FB

Signed on a free transfer from Torino, Tony Dorigo proved to be an excellent acquisition, playing in 18 Premiership games for the Rams between October 1998 and April 1999.

A solid defender, he won 67% of his attempted tackles and made more than 100 blocks, clearances and interceptions.

The former England international also showed he could cope with the added attacking responsibilities of the wing-back position by pumping some good centres into the opposition box. His cross completion rate of 41% was excellent although, in a season in which Derby often struggled to score, only two of his centres led directly to goals.

His best moment probably came in the season's first East Midlands derby against Forest, when he calmly stepped up to take the penalty which gave his side the lead in an exciting 2–2 draw. That turned out to be his only shot on target all season, but he was not signed for his prowess in the opposition area and Jim Smith must have been more than happy with his overall contribution.

APPEARANCES	
Start (sub)	17 (1)
Minutes on pitch	1477
GOAL ATTEMPTS	
Goals	1
PASSING & CROSSING	
Passing	545
Passing accuracy	74%
Crossing	95
Crossing accuracy	41%
DEFENDING	
Tackles	64
Tackles won	67%
DISCIPLINE	
Fouls	17
Yellow cards	3
Red cards	0

Mark DRAPER • 8
ASTON VILLA • BORN: 11.11.70

M

APPEARANCES	
Start (sub)	13 (10)
Minutes on pitch	1175
GOAL ATTEMPTS	
Goals	2
PASSING	
Passes	624
Passing accuracy	80%
DEFENDING	
Interceptions	17
Clearances	19
Tackles	39
Tackles won	64%
DISCIPLINE	
Fouls	27
Yellow cards	4
Red cards	0

The 1998–99 Carling Premiership campaign was a frustrating one for Villa midfielder Mark Draper. The former Leicester City man established himself as a key member of the side after his arrival in July 1995, but featured much less than he would have liked in John Gregory's first full season as manager.

A knee injury meant the 1998–99 season could have been curtains for Draper, but as it drew to a close his determination to get back into the side paid off and he missed just one of the club's last 12 league matches.

When fit, the former Notts County player showed his customary industry and bite in the tackle. He made 39 challenges, winning possession more than six times out of 10, and embarked on 40 dribbles and runs, retaining possession on 30 of his attacking forays.

In his holding midfield role, Draper had few chances to pressurize opposition defences. He had 14 shots at goal, half of them on target, and scored twice. The former England under-21 star passed with confidence, distributing 80% of 624 attempted passes to a colleague.

D

CB Richard DRYDEN • 12
SOUTHAMPTON • BORN: 14.6.69

Richard Dryden played only four matches for Southampton during 1998–99. The Stroud-born defender, who was signed from Bristol City in the summer of 1996, lost out to Ken Monkou and Claus Lundekvam as first choice centre-back.

Having played in the three opening fixtures of the Carling Premiership campaign, his only other appearance came in the 2–0 victory over Blackburn, where he performed superbly.

Dryden is a solid and strong defender, with excellent tackling ability. In his brief appearances he made 16 challenges, winning possession with all but one of his tackles, an exceptional statistic.

He used his height to good effect, making 71 clearances out of the penalty area, but his distribution was less impressive, with only 72% of his 76 passes reaching one of his team-mates.

Although out of favour in 1998–99, Dryden may get another chance to prove his worth, particularly if Southampton fail to negotiate a new contract with Monkou.

CB Michael DUBERRY • 12
CHELSEA • BORN: 14.10.75

Discipline problems: Michael Duberry

APPEARANCES	
Start (sub)	18 (7)
Minutes on pitch	1683
GOAL ATTEMPTS	
Goals	0
DEFENDING	
Blocks	17
Headed clearances	196
Other clearances	88
Interceptions	19
Tackles won	38
PASSING	
Passing accuracy	74%
DISCIPLINE	
Fouls	43
Yellow cards	8
Red cards	0

Michael Duberry had a difficult 1998–99 season. Faced with the barrier of World Cup-winning duo Frank Leboeuf and Marcel Desailly, the home-grown central defender found first-team opportunities limited to 18 starting appearances and seven as a substitute in the Premiership.

To his credit, Duberry continued to play well when selected, filling in for Desailly when the French international was forced to move into midfield and putting in some excellent performances alongside Leboeuf.

One problem was discipline. He committed a foul every 39 minutes on average, giving away two penalties and picking up eight bookings. This earned him a Carling Opta average of one disciplinary point every 25 minutes, enough for a place in the "Dirty Dozen" team.

A former England under-21 international, Duberry really needs a good run in the side to achieve his full potential. Given that, he should increase his tackle success rate and pass completion. The fact he made almost 300 clearances proves he is a reliable performer.

Dion DUBLIN • 14
ASTON VILLA • BORN: 22.4.69

With the possible exception of Kevin Campbell, no player made such an immediate impact in their new side than Dion Dublin did when he joined Aston Villa from Coventry.

John Gregory signed Dublin for £5.75 million from the Sky Blues, and the ex-Cambridge United striker made his debut for the Midlands club in November at home to Tottenham. He scored twice that day and followed up with five more goals in his next two league appearances, including a hat-trick in a convincing 4–1 mauling of Southampton.

Joint-top in the 1997–98 Premiership goal-scoring charts, he came near again in 1998–99 with 14 league goals, 11 for Villa. Big Dion's four goals with the head were bettered by only two players in the Premiership. He had 112 shots at goal, more than anyone in the league, and supplied five assists.

The England international made more than 1,000 passes and tracked back to make 71 tackles, winning some 60%. Dublin also demonstrated his defensive awareness with 70 clearances, easily ahead of his main rivals.

APPEARANCES	
Start (sub)	34 (0)
Minutes on pitch	2912
GOAL ATTEMPTS	
Goals	14
Goals/shots ratio	13%
SHOOTING	
Shots on target	45
Shooting accuracy	40%
PASSING	
Goal assists	5
Passing accuracy	66%
DISCIPLINE	
Fouls	77
Offside	20
Yellow cards	5
Red cards	0

Damien DUFF • 12
BLACKBURN ROVERS • BORN: 2.3.79

APPEARANCES	
Start (sub)	19 (9)
Minutes on pitch	1593
GOAL ATTEMPTS	
Goals	1
Shots on target	7
Shooting accuracy	39%
PASSING	
Goal assists	2
Passing accuracy	78%
Crossing accuracy	32%
DRIBBLING	
Dribbles & runs	90
Dribble completion	77%
DISCIPLINE	
Yellow cards	0
Red cards	0

Having broken into the first team in 1997–98, Damien Duff gained more Premiership experience in 1998–99, clocking up 19 starts and nine substitute appearances.

The Republic of Ireland winger offered an attacking outlet on the wing and his ability to beat players and cross well from the by-line was one of the few plusses in Rovers' season.

Despite his high number of dribbles and runs, he maintained an exceptionally high success rate of 77%. He also found a team-mate with almost a third of his 101 crosses.

His distribution was impressive, with 78% of his balls finding their mark, and the youngster claimed two goal assists. He may need to work on the defensive side of his game, having won a slightly disappointing 46% of his challenges, and his shooting should improve with experience – in 1998–99 he only hit seven of his 24 shots on target, scoring just once, against Liverpool in a 3–1 home defeat.

Following Blackburn's relegation, Duff's experience at Premiership level may be very valuable in the Nationwide League.

Sean DUNDEE • 16
S — LIVERPOOL • BORN: 7.12.72

Liverpool supporters could be forgiven for wondering why joint bosses Gerard Houllier and Roy Evans decided to part with £2 million for Sean Dundee, a player they seemed determined not to use.

With their three main strikers injured in the second half of the season, Houllier still preferred to play Steve McManaman out of position as a striker.

Dundee ended the 1998–99 season having played just 38 minutes of Premiership football which he made over three brief substitute appearances.

During that time, he managed just two efforts at goal, both of which failed to trouble the opposition goalkeeper. He attempted 18 passes, completing a respectable 78%, but his only other contribution was that he won one tackle.

It is doubtful that Sean Dundee will look back on the 1998–99 Premiership season with any great fondness, and any further appearances at Anfield are more likely to be in an opposition shirt.

David DUNN • 27
AM — BLACKBURN ROVERS • BORN: 27.12.79

Local hero: David Dunn

APPEARANCES	
Start (sub)	10 (5)
Minutes on pitch	938
GOAL ATTEMPTS	
Goals	1
Shots on target	5
Shooting accuracy	63%
PASSING	
Goal assists	0
Passing accuracy	75%
Crossing accuracy	0%
DRIBBLING	
Dribbles & runs	20
Dribble completion	70%
DISCIPLINE	
Yellow cards	2
Red cards	0

A product of Rovers' youth academy, Blackburn-born David Dunn broke into the first-team squad to make 10 Premiership starts and five substitute appearances in 1998–99.

Often deployed in wide areas, Dunn was used as cover for the likes of Jason Wilcox and Keith Gillespie and delivered some creditable performances in a struggling Rovers side.

The highly-rated youngster hit five shots on target and scored his first goal for his boyhood club in the 3–1 win against Aston Villa in February. He completed three-quarters of his passes and 70% of his dribbles and runs and won an above-average 59% of his challenges in the Premiership.

Regularly selected in Blackburn's squad during their FA Cup run, Dunn came off the bench in the third-round tie with Charlton and started in the fourth and fifth-round ties against Sunderland and Newcastle.

After breaking into the first-team squad in 1998–99, Dunn will be hoping to accumulate more first-team experience in Blackburn's Nationwide League campaign in 1999–2000.

D

CB — Richard DUNNE • 27
EVERTON • BORN: 21.9.79

Richard Dunne had been part of a very successful youth team at Everton, so stepping up into a struggling side must have been difficult for him during the 1998–99 Carling Premiership season.

The burly defender played more often than he would have expected, thanks to the sale of Carl Tiler and injuries to Craig Short and Slaven Bilic. His run in the side came to an end shortly after the purchase of David Weir from Hearts in February.

Dunne made 150 clearances and 14 blocks, but he was also impressive in the tackle, winning 73% of his 55 challenges. His disciplinary record was poor, though: he was booked five times and earned a red card against Chelsea, despite only committing 24 fouls throughout the course of the league campaign.

The youngster's pass completion rate was below average for a defender at 71% and he rarely posed a goal threat, but at just 19 years of age he is definitely a player who will feature in Everton's future.

APPEARANCES	
Start (sub)	15 (1)
Minutes on pitch	1250
GOAL ATTEMPTS	
Goals	0
DEFENDING	
Blocks	14
Headed clearances	82
Other clearances	68
Interceptions	7
Tackles won	40
PASSING	
Passing accuracy	71%
DISCIPLINE	
Fouls	24
Yellow cards	5
Red cards	1

AM — Robbie EARLE • 8
WIMBLEDON • BORN: 27.1.65

APPEARANCES	
Start (sub)	35 (0)
Minutes on pitch	3130
GOAL ATTEMPTS	
Goals	5
Shots on target	23
Shooting accuracy	47%
PASSING	
Goal assists	1
Passing accuracy	72%
Crossing accuracy	13%
DRIBBLING	
Dribbles & runs	28
Dribble completion	71%
DISCIPLINE	
Yellow cards	2
Red cards	0

At 34, Robbie Earle may well be nearing the end of an excellent career, but will still be a threat to opposition defences in 1999–2000.

In an ultimately disappointing Premiership season for the Dons, Earle scored five goals from 60 efforts (including blocked shots) and was among their most consistent performers.

The Jamaican international attempted 826 passes, completing just 72%, and only claimed one goal assist – an unorthodox hand/chest lay-off in the six-yard box for Efan Ekoku to score the winner against Arsenal.

Combative as ever, Earle won an excellent 70% of his 93 challenges and completed 71% of his dribbles and runs, though the fact that he only attempted 28 may demonstrate the Dons' tendency to play the ball simply, rather than trying anything too fancy.

He was also willing to help out the defence, making 132 clearances, 18 interceptions and 11 blocks in his 35 appearances, and his discipline was excellent: with just 24 fouls and two yellow cards, earning him a place in the Carling Opta Fair Play team.

Justin EDINBURGH • 12
TOTTENHAM HOTSPUR • BORN: 18.12.69

FB

Justin Edinburgh was one of several Spurs defenders who seemed to improve under the new regime at White Hart Lane. Though his season ended disappointingly with a red card in the Worthington Cup final and the loss of his place to Mauricio Taricco, there is no doubt he was a better player than in 1997–98.

Within five games of George Graham's arrival he had boosted his tackle success rate, and ended the season with a figure of 67% – an increase of 14 percentage points on the previous season.

The improvement in the timing of his challenges is reflected by the fact that he committed six fewer fouls in 1998–99, despite playing more time; though , strangely, his pass completion rate of 74% was well down on the previous campaign's figure of 82% and may have been one of the factors behind Graham's decision to bring in Taricco.

Whatever the reasons, Edinburgh proved a lot of people wrong in 1998–99. He showed that he is likely to be a valuable squad member in the 1999–2000 season.

D

APPEARANCES	
Start (sub)	14 (2)
Minutes on pitch	1210
GOAL ATTEMPTS	
Goals	0
PASSING & CROSSING	
Passing	480
Passing accuracy	74%
Crossing	32
Crossing accuracy	22%
DEFENDING	
Tackles	46
Tackles won	67%
DISCIPLINE	
Fouls	18
Yellow cards	2
Red cards	1

Christian EDWARDS • 24
NOTTINGHAM FOREST • BORN: 23.11.75

CB

APPEARANCES	
Start (sub)	7 (5)
Minutes on pitch	758
GOAL ATTEMPTS	
Goals	0
DEFENDING	
Blocks	6
Headed clearances	82
Other clearances	58
Interceptions	9
Tackles won	10
PASSING	
Passing accuracy	69%
DISCIPLINE	
Fouls	11
Yellow cards	1
Red cards	0

After a successful trial, Christian Edwards joined Nottingham Forest from Swansea and made his debut in the Worthington Cup against Leyton Orient.

He had to wait until November for his first taste of Premiership football when he came on as a substitute at Tottenham Hotspur. But it was not until Ron Atkinson arrived in the Forest hot seat that he got his big break.

The Welsh under-21 defender started the 0–0 draw at Charlton and then missed only one of the remaining 11 games, finishing the season with seven starts and five substitute appearances in the Premiership.

Edwards made 140 defensive clearances, nine interceptions and six blocks in a bid to bolster Forest's leaky defence. Known for his aerial ability, not his silky ball skills, his pass completion rate was well below average, at just 69%. He can be a threat from set-pieces, but did not really get the chance to prove it.

Despite Forest's relegation, the tall 23-year-old is sure to be a key part of the squad which attempts to bounce back at the first attempt.

Marc EDWORTHY • 27
COVENTRY CITY • BORN: 24.12.72

Crystal Palace skipper Marc Edworthy began 1998–99 full of confidence as the Eagles' natural leader under new boss Terry Venables.

But within a month it had all gone sour for the former Plymouth defender. Palace's financial woes were surfacing and Venables made it clear he did not want to use a sweeper in his side – the position the fans' Player of the Year had made his own in 1997–98.

Self-confessed Edworthy admirer Gordon Strachan quickly muscled in with a cut-price bid – accepted, much to the dismay of many Eagles fans – and the defender made his Sky Blues debut on August 29 as a substitute in the 0–0 draw at home to West Ham United.

He went on to make 16 starts and six substitute appearances, but struggled to impose himself on the side as he had done at Palace. He completed 77% of his passes and 79% of his dribbles but won just 54% of the tackles he contested.

With Roland Nilsson quitting Highfield Road, Edworthy must be hoping for more first-team football in 1999–2000.

APPEARANCES	
Start (sub)	16 (6)
Minutes on pitch	1613
GOAL ATTEMPTS	
Goals	0
PASSING & CROSSING	
Passing	607
Passing accuracy	77%
Crossing	18
Crossing accuracy	22%
DEFENDING	
Tackles	48
Tackles won	54%
DISCIPLINE	
Fouls	17
Yellow cards	3
Red cards	0

Ugo EHIOGU • 5
ASTON VILLA • BORN: 3.11.72

APPEARANCES	
Start (sub)	23 (2)
Minutes on pitch	2066
GOAL ATTEMPTS	
Goals	2
DEFENDING	
Blocks	20
Headed clearances	205
Other clearances	115
Interceptions	29
Tackles won	52
PASSING	
Passing accuracy	82%
DISCIPLINE	
Fouls	30
Yellow cards	3
Red cards	0

Ugo Ehiogu's season was interrupted at St James's Park in a clash with England skipper Alan Shearer. Villa's towering centre-half fractured his eye-socket in the accidental collision with the Newcastle man and was out of first-team action for three months.

Before that match, Ehiogu had been a colossus in the Villa defence as the side raced to the top of the Carling Premiership. But after his injury the side missed his strength in defence, going for 10 league matches without a win and eventually slumping to sixth place.

Ugo made more than 300 clearances from his own half, using his height to good effect with 205 headers away from danger. He also put in 85 challenges and intercepted 29 stray passes.

The Hackney-born defender, who made his 200th league appearance for Villa at home to Everton in January, distributed the ball with confidence, finding a colleague with more than 80% of his passes. Ehiogu also threw his weight into the attack on several occasions, registering two goals for John Gregory's side, both with his head.

Efan EKOKU • 9
WIMBLEDON • BORN: 8.6.67

E

Efan Ekoku found himself at odds with manager Joe Kinnear for much of the 1998–99 season. "The Chief" requested a transfer and was upset at his lack of first-team chances. But, given the plethora of striking options at Selhurst Park, it was always going to be hard for Kinnear to keep all his players happy.

The season could not have started better for Ekoku. He scored a brace as the Dons pummelled Spurs 3–1 on the opening day, but was on the substitutes' bench by the fourth game when he came on to grab the winner in the thrilling 4–3 comeback win at West Ham.

He was in and out of the side after that thanks to a combination of injury and other strikers' form, and finished with 11 starts and the same number of substitute appearances.

Ekoku scored six goals from just 27 shots. He forced nine saves and his physical style caused several defences problems. He conceded 34 fouls, but was booked just once.

The Nigerian international's passing, crossing and tackling were below average and he may have made his final Dons appearance.

APPEARANCES	
Start (sub)	11 (11)
Minutes on pitch	1092
GOAL ATTEMPTS	
Goals	6
Goals/shots ratio	25%
SHOOTING	
Shots on target	15
Shooting accuracy	63%
PASSING	
Goal assists	0
Passing accuracy	67%
DISCIPLINE	
Fouls	34
Offside	23
Yellow cards	1
Red cards	0

Matt ELLIOTT • 18
LEICESTER CITY • BORN: 1.11.68

APPEARANCES	
Start (sub)	37 (0)
Minutes on pitch	3305
GOAL ATTEMPTS	
Goals	3
DEFENDING	
Blocks	35
Headed clearances	322
Other clearances	180
Interceptions	48
Tackles won	82
PASSING	
Passing accuracy	79%
DISCIPLINE	
Fouls	68
Yellow cards	7
Red cards	0

Matt Elliott's inspirational performances in 1998–99 characterized Leicester City's spirit under Martin O'Neill. The club's number one defender wins favour with the fans for his determined displays at the back and for his willingness to get forward at set-pieces or when City need an extra man up front.

One of only five Premiership players to make more than 500 clearances in 1998–99, his consistency made him the Foxes' highest-rated player in the Carling Opta Index.

At the other end of the pitch, he scored three crucial league goals: the equalizer in the televized match against Wimbledon, a penalty in the win over Nottingham Forest and the second goal in the Foxes' revenge victory at Tottenham, just two weeks after Spurs had beaten Leicester in the Worthington Cup final.

He completed 79% of his passes, about average for a defender despite his frequent forays upfield, and claimed two goal assists.

But the former Oxford United man had the club's worst disciplinary record, conceding 68 fouls and earning seven yellow cards.

CB Steve ELLIOTT • 19
DERBY COUNTY • BORN: 29.10.78

After figuring in three Premiership games the previous season – including what Jim Smith claimed was the best debut he had ever seen – 1998–99 saw young centre-back Steve Elliott press his claims for a place in Derby's first team with 11 more appearances.

He will have benefited from playing alongside the more experienced Spencer Prior, Horacio Carbonari and Igor Stimac and the 1999–2000 season could see him really establish himself at Pride Park.

Playing 790 minutes in total and adding seven starts and four substitute appearances to his record, Elliott won 59% of his 37 tackles, made 114 clearances, 15 interceptions and nine defensive blocks. He committed just nine fouls, but somehow found his name in the referees' notebook on three occasions.

Elliott's pass completion rate was well below average and he was hardly a threat to the opposition in attack, but the youngster clearly has potential. He is already an England under-21 international and more caps at that level would seem to be on the cards.

APPEARANCES	
Start (sub)	7 (4)
Minutes on pitch	790
GOAL ATTEMPTS	
Goals	0
DEFENDING	
Blocks	9
Headed clearances	69
Other clearances	45
Interceptions	15
Tackles won	22
PASSING	
Passing accuracy	71%
DISCIPLINE	
Fouls	9
Yellow cards	3
Red cards	0

AM Stefano ERANIO • 20
DERBY COUNTY • BORN: 29.12.66

APPEARANCES	
Start (sub)	18 (7)
Minutes on pitch	1510
GOAL ATTEMPTS	
Goals	0
Shots on target	5
Shooting accuracy	45%
PASSING	
Goal assists	1
Passing accuracy	82%
Crossing accuracy	20%
DRIBBLING	
Dribbles & runs	40
Dribble completion	55%
DISCIPLINE	
Yellow cards	4
Red cards	0

33-year-old midfielder Stefano Eranio had a stop-start season, with injury and loss of form affecting his displays on various occasions.

Moved about by Jim Smith, he found himself playing both as a wing-back – the position in which he has spent most of his career – and in a variety of preferred midfield roles.

The former AC Milan star failed to add to his five Premiership goals for Derby in the 1998–99 season, firing in just 15 shots mainly due to his deeper role. But he created one and also maintained a slightly better-than-average pass completion rate of 82%.

He did not score in the Premiership, but did net in the FA Cup third-round 3–0 romp at Plymouth Argyle.

The level of Eranio's defensive work can be seen from the 53 tackles he had to make, but he won only 57% of them, showing perfectly that he prefers attacking to defending.

He committed 21 fouls and was booked on four occasions in his 25 appearances – a record that belies his approachable and friendly demeanour off the pitch.

Jason EUELL • 20
WIMBLEDON • BORN: 6.2.77

The player hailed as the new Ian Wright showed that there was more to his game than goal-poaching in 1998–99.

With an abundance of frontmen and injury problems in midfield, Jason Euell proved his versatility by filling in as an attacking midfielder. Despite this deeper role, he finished as Wimbledon's joint-top scorer in the Premiership with 10 goals from 83 attempts, and also contributed a brace of assists.

His pass completion rate of 67% and cross completion rate of 14% were some way below par, but his tackle success rate was adequate for a midfield player and good for a striker.

He committed 41 fouls and was yellow-carded four times as he occasionally struggled to come to terms with his midfield berth. But he did track back and make 61 clearances and 26 interceptions to help out his defence.

The youngster, who missed just five games and was a rare success story in a season of under-achievement, is sure to be one of the pieces Egil Olsen retains in his new-look Wimbledon jigsaw.

APPEARANCES	
Start (sub)	31 (2)
Minutes on pitch	2681
GOAL ATTEMPTS	
Goals	10
Goals/shots ratio	15%
SHOOTING	
Shots on target	30
Shooting accuracy	46%
PASSING	
Goal assists	2
Passing accuracy	67%
DISCIPLINE	
Fouls	41
Offside	19
Yellow cards	4
Red cards	0

E

Adam FARLEY • 37
EVERTON • BORN: 12.1.80

Just when he had made his breakthrough into the first-team squad, Adam Farley suffered a back strain that put him out for a few weeks and he failed to figure again in the 1998–99 Premiership campaign.

The Liverpool-born youngster spent much of the season in the under-19 side or occasionally in the reserves, but he was delighted to make his debut in the 2–1 victory over Derby at Pride Park.

He only played 45 minutes as a substitute, making five clearances and one interception, but he showed maturity and did not give away any fouls.

A little nervousness crept into his play as he completed just 57% of the 14 passes he attempted. But now that he has had a taste of the big time his appetite for more will be unquestionable, and he will be keen to come back for a second helping as soon as he can in 1999–2000.

With Walter Smith in the middle of his rebuilding programme, the youngster could get an opportunity sooner rather than later.

Gareth FARRELLY • 17
EVERTON • BORN: 28.8.75

His goal on the last day of the 1997–98 season helped ensure Everton avoided relegation, but Gareth Farrelly played just 12 minutes of Premiership football in the 1998–99 season after struggling with injuries.

A 1997 summer signing from Aston Villa, Farrelly has struggled to fulfil the potential that saw him selected as both under-21 and "B" captain for the Republic of Ireland. This is partly due to the injuries which have blighted his career so far.

His one appearance of the season came as a second-half substitute for Don Hutchison in the 0–0 draw with Leeds United at Goodison Park in September.

He had little chance to impress in that match, attempting 10 passes – six of which were successful – and firing in one shot which failed to trouble Nigel Martyn.

Farrelly is at the stage of his career when he needs regular first-team football: the 1998–99 season was not an encouraging one for him and he will be hoping for better luck in 1999–2000.

AM **Peter FEAR • 24**
WIMBLEDON • BORN: 10.9.73

A player who has never really been able to make the breakthrough at first-team level, Peter Fear was once again forced to watch from the sidelines in the 1998–99 Carling Premiership season and at the end of the campaign there was talk of him being given a free transfer.

He played in the first game of the season against Tottenham Hotspur, coming on as a substitute with eight minutes to go. Wimbledon were 2–1 up and eventually won 3–1 but Fear was unable to reproduce the two-goal blast he had managed in the same fixture the previous season.

His second and final appearance came as a last-minute substitute away to Aston Villa in early September, an outing in which he barely had time to cross the touchline before the final whistle went.

Overall he made just seven passes and two tackles. It is safe to say that he was not in the frame for Wimbledon's Player of the Year award. However, he now has the chance to impress new boss Egil Olsen.

AM **Graham FENTON • 21**
LEICESTER CITY • BORN: 22.5.74

He cost Blackburn £1.5 million in 1995 and Leicester £1.1 million in 1997; but despite a few high-profile goals, Graham Fenton is yet to justify his price-tag.

1998–99 was expected to be a breakthrough season at Filbert Street for the Wallsend-born striker, but when injuries ruled both Emile Heskey and Tony Cottee out of the Foxes' starting line-up, Martin O'Neill preferred to turn to the experience of veteran Ian Marshall up front.

Fenton's longest run in the first team came in November when he played in three successive games against West Ham, Chelsea and Coventry. But they were his only three starts, and the rest of his appearances came as a substitute.

A right-sided striker, Fenton managed two accurate shots in his 266 minutes on pitch and completed an impressive 90% of his attempted passes. Unfortunately, he rarely showed enough guile to break down opposition defences and was caught offside five times.

S **Les FERDINAND • 10**
TOTTENHAM HOTSPUR • BORN: 18.12.66

APPEARANCES	
Start (sub)	22 (2)
Minutes on pitch	1762
GOAL ATTEMPTS	
Goals	5
Goals/shots ratio	16%
SHOOTING	
Shots on target	14
Shooting accuracy	44%
PASSING	
Goal assists	1
Passing accuracy	64%
DISCIPLINE	
Fouls	48
Offside	24
Yellow cards	5
Red cards	0

A combination of niggling injuries and loss of form has prevented Les Ferdinand's Tottenham career from lifting off. He managed 22 Premiership starts and two substitute appearances in 1998–99, suggesting he still has to put his fitness problems behind him.

When on top form, Ferdinand's awesome mix of aerial power, strength and pace make him a match for most Premiership defenders and, while the goals did not exactly flow in 1998–99, he put in several good showings.

His five Premiership goals included the winner against Everton in Christian Gross's last game in charge and the opener in the 2–1 final-day defeat at Manchester United.

He finished with a respectable goals-to-shots ratio of 16%; but with David Ginola and Darren Anderton keeping him supplied with crosses, he should perhaps have scored more.

George Graham has always been a big admirer of the former PFA Player of the Year, but though satisfied with Ferdinand's work-rate he will demand a higher return from him in 1999–2000 if he stays at White Hart Lane.

CB · Rio FERDINAND • 15
WEST HAM UNITED • BORN: 7.11.78

Joe Cole may eventually take over the mantle, but at present Rio Ferdinand is undoubtedly West Ham United's most valuable asset.

The 1998–99 season saw him establish himself as a regular in the England squad and, although the Hammers' defence was often under pressure, his standards rarely dropped.

He proved he is a master of the well-timed challenge, winning 71% of his 91 tackles – the best figure at Upton Park. But he also progressed in other areas, anticipating play well enough to intercept 60 opposition passes.

His comfort on the ball sets him apart from most Premiership defenders. His pass completion rate of 83% was superb and rose to an impressive 92% in his own half.

Never afraid to come forward, he succeeded with 76% of his dribbles and runs – and this added dimension to his play made him a target for several European clubs, who perceived him as a natural *libero*.

While the interest was doubtless flattering, an imminent move looks unlikely: there would be uproar at West Ham were he to leave.

APPEARANCES	
Start (sub)	31 (0)
Minutes on pitch	2700
GOAL ATTEMPTS	
Goals	0
DEFENDING	
Blocks	37
Headed clearances	227
Other clearances	162
Interceptions	60
Tackles won	65
PASSING	
Passing accuracy	83%
DISCIPLINE	
Fouls	13
Yellow cards	5
Red cards	0

S · Duncan FERGUSON • 20
NEWCASTLE UNITED • BORN: 27.12.71

APPEARANCES	
Start (sub)	20 (0)
Minutes on pitch	1686
GOAL ATTEMPTS	
Goals	6
Goals/shots ratio	10%
SHOOTING	
Shots on target	33
Shooting accuracy	56%
PASSING	
Goal assists	0
Passing accuracy	65%
DISCIPLINE	
Fouls	46
Offside	16
Yellow cards	3
Red cards	0

Such was Duncan Ferguson's popularity at Everton that the decision to sell him to Newcastle United for £8 million provoked discontent at Goodison Park.

While performances for his new club have yet to justify the expectations raised by his two-goal debut, a niggling groin strain disrupted the second half of his season and the jury is still out on whether he was a good signing.

At 6'4", he always poses a huge threat in the air. Even after missing almost four months through injury, he still finished the season with more headed flick-ons than any other Premiership player. In all, a massive 30% of his 872 attempted passes came with his head.

Although only two of his six goals in the Premiership were for Newcastle, his shooting accuracy of 71% for his new club was more impressive than his overall figure of 56%.

This bodes well for 1999–2000. After a successful operation on his groin, Ferguson was booked to spend the summer working with a fitness coach and should be fit to take to the skies again in time for August.

FB   Albert FERRER • 17
CHELSEA • BORN: 6.6.70

One of the modern game's finest right-backs, Albert Ferrer's £2.2 million move to Stamford Bridge in summer 1998 did not please Barcelona fans already unhappy with manager Louis van Gaal's reliance on foreign stars.

After eight years at the Nou Camp and more than 30 caps for the Spanish national side, Ferrer slotted effortlessly into Chelsea's back four, starting all but eight Premiership games.

Widely acclaimed as one of the Blues' most consistent players, the Catalan-born defender may not have grabbed many headlines but was rarely caught out of position at the back.

Less attack-minded than Graeme Le Saux, he still caused opponents problems with his 66 attempted dribbles and runs. But his crossing was poor and, though he set up two goals, he always looked more comfortable in defence.

To this effect, he made 131 tackles and more than 200 clearances. An excellent reader of opposition intentions, he also contributed 39 interceptions, a figure bettered by only two other Chelsea players – Marcel Desailly and Frank Leboeuf.

APPEARANCES	
Start (sub)	30 (0)
Minutes on pitch	2680
GOAL ATTEMPTS	
Goals	0
PASSING & CROSSING	
Passing	1236
Passing accuracy	80%
Crossing	63
Crossing accuracy	11%
DEFENDING	
Tackles	131
Tackles won	63%
DISCIPLINE	
Fouls	43
Yellow cards	9
Red cards	0

Flying full-back: Albert Ferrer

M   Jean-Michel FERRI • 18
LIVERPOOL • BORN: 7.2.69

It remains to be seen whether Jean-Michel Ferri is the answer to Liverpool's problems in the centre of defence, or if he will feature in his more normal central midfield role.

Signed from Turkish club Istanbulspor, Ferri arrived at Anfield extremely short on match fitness and his appearance as a second-half substitute in Liverpool's 2–1 defeat at Chelsea was his one outing of the season.

Injured soon after, Ferri will undoubtedly play a larger part in 1999–2000. A tall, strong player, he nevertheless struggled to come to terms with the pace of that game at Stamford Bridge, winning just one tackle and committing three fouls.

However, Gerrard Houllier rates him very highly and it would be unfair to judge him on the few statistics available.

The player himself has claimed that he is looking to season 1999–2000 as "the start of my Liverpool career". Desperate for an imposing figure at the back, the Merseysiders will be keen to get Ferri back into action as soon as possible.

Gianluca FESTA • 5
CB MIDDLESBROUGH • BORN: 15.3.69

A £2.7 million signing from Inter Milan in January 1997, Gianluca Festa earned the respect of Middlesbrough fans by sticking with the club when they were relegated at the end of 1996–97. The following season he won the club's Player of the Year award as Boro were promoted back to the Premiership.

The 1998–99 campaign again saw him moved between his preferred role at centre-back and the right wing-back position: and, as always, he was among Boro's brightest stars.

A solid, physical player who is excellent in the air, Festa made more than 200 clearances and attempted 88 tackles in the Premiership. Not all his challenges were well-timed, however, and he earned nine league bookings.

Playing in the wing-back slot he also showed he has a powerful engine, completing 83% of his dribbles and runs and scoring twice.

Perhaps he likes getting forward more often than he should, but Festa is still a big favourite with the fans and has proved himself to be one of Bryan Robson's better imports to English football.

APPEARANCES	
Start (sub)	25 (0)
Minutes on pitch	2181
GOAL ATTEMPTS	
Goals	2
DEFENDING	
Blocks	22
Headed clearances	124
Other clearances	81
Interceptions	41
Tackles won	55
PASSING	
Passing accuracy	80%
DISCIPLINE	
Fouls	39
Yellow cards	9
Red cards	0

Alan FETTIS • 22
G BLACKBURN ROVERS • BORN: 1.2.71

Signed from Nottingham Forest in 1997, Alan Fettis added to the competition for the goalkeeping position at Ewood Park. The Northern Ireland international made just two appearances in the 1998–99 Premiership campaign, in the home matches against Charlton and Newcastle.

During his 180 minutes of Premiership football he managed to save every shot he faced, finishing with two clean sheets and 10 stops to his credit.

Fettis showed good distribution in his two matches. All 16 of his short kicks and throws found a Blackburn player, while almost half his long deliveries found their target.

He spent a large proportion of the season as Blackburn's substitute goalkeeper – a role he contested with Tim Flowers – while Australian stopper John Filan retained the starting role with some excellent performances.

Following Flowers's transfer request, the door may have been left open for Fettis to mount a serious challenge for the number one shirt in 1999–2000.

Fans' favourite: Gianluca Festa

John FILAN • 13
BLACKBURN ROVERS • BORN: 8.2.70

The 1998–99 season proved a breakthrough year for Australian John Filan, who earned regular first-team football for the first time since leaving Coventry City in 1997.

Ousting former England star Tim Flowers and holding off the challenge of Northern Ireland international Alan Fettis, Filan had a good season, earning the club's Player of the Year award. But his form was not enough to avert relegation to the Nationwide League.

After starting the season's first two matches Filan lost his place to Flowers, but took over regular first-team duties in November. He kept five clean sheets, let in 35 goals and saved 73% of the shots he faced, a figure which would have been higher had Blackburn's defence been more solid. His aerial ability matched the majority of the Premiership's goalkeepers. He successfully claimed 94% of his catches and made 26 punched clearances.

With Flowers apparently on his way out of Ewood Park, Filan seems to have clinched the number one spot – and will aim to complete a full season in the first team in 1999–2000.

APPEARANCES	
Start (sub)	26 (0)
Minutes on pitch	2295
SHOT STOPPING	
Goals conceded	35
Clean sheets	5
Saves	96
Saves/shots	73%
DISTRIBUTION	
Distribution	759
Distribution %	48%
CATCHING	
Crosses caught	72
Crosses dropped	5
DISCIPLINE	
Yellow cards	3
Red cards	0

Curtis FLEMING • 2
MIDDLESBROUGH • BORN: 8.10.68

APPEARANCES	
Start (sub)	12 (2)
Minutes on pitch	1157
GOAL ATTEMPTS	
Goals	1
PASSING & CROSSING	
Passing	435
Passing accuracy	70%
Crossing	28
Crossing accuracy	29%
DEFENDING	
Tackles	66
Tackles won	58%
DISCIPLINE	
Fouls	7
Yellow cards	2
Red cards	0

A reliable right-back for both club and country, Eire international Curtis Fleming was having a good season for Boro when he suffered a bad knee injury and was forced to sit out the club's final 15 Premiership games.

This was nothing new – Fleming had suffered several similar injuries before – but to miss the run-in was still a big disappointment.

Gutsy rather than measured with some of his challenges, he won a below-average 58% of his 66 attempted tackles but came away with the ball often enough to make 64 clearances from his own half. He also played the wing-back role well, completing 90% of his dribbles and runs and assisting with two Boro goals.

Signed from Irish side St Patrick's for just £50,000, Fleming has been a regular face in Middlesbrough's team since the 1991–92 season. But his injury, coupled with the emergence of young Robbie Stockdale, might make it hard for him to earn back his place in the side in 1999–2000. Nonetheless, he is a determined competitor and will not give up his spot without a fight.

Garry FLITCROFT • 7
BLACKBURN ROVERS • BORN: 6.11.72

M

A former England under-21 international, Garry Flitcroft started eight of the season's first nine Premiership games – but injuries wrecked his season almost before it began.

His finest performance came in the match against West Ham when the former Manchester City midfielder scored twice – his second a brilliant 35-yard chip into the top corner.

Along with several other key players, he was forced to sit and watch Rovers fight relegation from the sidelines, ruled out by a knee injury. Had he been fit, his endeavour in midfield may well have made a difference.

During his 720 minutes of Premiership football Flitcroft hit six of his 15 shots on target. Featuring in either the centre or on the right of midfield, he completed 80% of his passes and set up three goals.

Defensively, he won 71% of his challenges and made 32 clearances. These fine all-round stats show that his absence deprived Blackburn of a strong, disciplined midfielder. The Ewood Park fans will hope to see more of him in 1999–2000.

F

APPEARANCES	
Start (sub)	8 (0)
Minutes on pitch	720
GOAL ATTEMPTS	
Goals	2
PASSING	
Passes	310
Passing accuracy	80%
DEFENDING	
Interceptions	3
Clearances	32
Tackles	35
Tackles won	71%
DISCIPLINE	
Fouls	11
Yellow cards	3
Red cards	0

Tore Andre FLO • 19
CHELSEA • BORN: 15.6.73

S

APPEARANCES	
Start (sub)	18 (12)
Minutes on pitch	1895
GOAL ATTEMPTS	
Goals	10
Goals/shots ratio	15%
SHOOTING	
Shots on target	33
Shooting accuracy	49%
PASSING	
Goal assists	4
Passing accuracy	70%
DISCIPLINE	
Fouls	50
Offside	39
Yellow cards	2
Red cards	0

Tore Andre Flo must be one of the most patient men in the Premiership. His excellent form for his country in the 1998 World Cup was still not enough to get him a regular place in Chelsea's starting line-up, yet he never made a fuss.

He managed 30 league appearances in 1998–99, but 12 came as a substitute. The season's start proved frustrating and, despite coming off the bench to score twice against Blackburn on September 21, Flo was still on the sidelines for the club's next game.

Though he was restored to the first XI for cup games, it was not until Pierluigi Casiraghi's injury at West Ham that he earned his first starting appearance in the Carling Premiership.

He netted 10 times in the league, but his goals-to-shots ratio of 15% was no better than the divisional average, underlining the fact that he is not the most prolific of scorers.

His height makes him a decent target man, but he is more skilful than other players of his size and completed more than 60 of the dribbles he attempted.

G Tim FLOWERS • 1
BLACKBURN ROVERS • BORN: 3.2.67

Former Championship-winning goalkeeper Tim Flowers had a disappointing season. After 10 Premiership starts in a row, he lost his place to Australian John Filan and found himself battling to be second-choice 'keeper for the rest of the season.

Flowers's main concern in 1998–99 was his modest shot-stopping record. The former Southampton 'keeper saved a below-average 67% of the 51 shots he faced and kept only three clean sheets, conceding 17 goals from his 945 minutes of Premiership football.

He was as reliable as ever when coming for high balls, dropping only one cross and making six successful punches, leaving him with a healthy 94% catch success rate.

The ex-England international's distribution also remained of a high standard. He completed 97% of his short kicks and throws, while a third of his long deliveries downfield found a Blackburn player. But at the season's end Flowers was put on the transfer list at his own request. Wherever he goes, 1999–2000 will provide him with a fresh challenge.

APPEARANCES	
Start (sub)	10 (1)
Minutes on pitch	945
SHOT STOPPING	
Goals conceded	17
Clean sheets	3
Saves	34
Saves/shots	67%
DISTRIBUTION	
Distribution	337
Distribution %	55%
CATCHING	
Crosses caught	16
Crosses dropped	1
DISCIPLINE	
Yellow cards	1
Red cards	0

M Marc-Vivien FOE • 13
WEST HAM UNITED • BORN: 1.5.75

APPEARANCES	
Start (sub)	13 (0)
Minutes on pitch	1152
GOAL ATTEMPTS	
Goals	0
PASSING	
Passes	439
Passing accuracy	74%
DEFENDING	
Interceptions	21
Clearances	87
Tackles	61
Tackles won	61%
DISCIPLINE	
Fouls	21
Yellow cards	8
Red cards	0

Signed from French champions Lens to give the West Ham midfield a bit of bite, former Manchester United target and Cameroon international Marc-Vivien Foe took time to settle at Upton Park. But he showed enough in big away games against the likes of Liverpool and Chelsea to suggest he will be an excellent acquisition in the long term.

An imposing figure, Foe's tackle success rate improved steadily and, although he finished the season with a below-average figure of 61%, he was definitely winning more of his challenges as the campaign drew to a close.

More than six feet tall, he was an obvious choice to fill in at centre-back when injuries reduced Harry Redknapp's defensive options. But though he made more than 80 clearances he did not always look comfortable in this role, conceding a number of clumsy fouls resulting in eight yellow cards.

His finest hour came at Stamford Bridge, when, after having a goal disallowed, he headed into the path of Paul Kitson for the winner in a 1–0 victory.

Craig FORREST • 22
WEST HAM UNITED • BORN: 20.9.67

An established Canadian international, Craig Forrest has had few chances to impress West Ham fans since his move from Ipswich to East London for £500,000 in July 1997.

Injury limited him to just 13 Premiership appearances in 1997–98, and with the arrival of Shaka Hislop immediately prior to the 1998–99 season his status as the club's reserve goalkeeper was confirmed.

Apart from a brief spell in November when Les Sealey deputized for him, Forrest sat on the bench for West Ham until Shaka Hislop was sent off in the 5–1 defeat by Leeds United.

Conceding three goals in that game was hardly the biggest boost to his confidence. But he performed well in the Hammers' last game of the season against Middlesbrough, keeping a clean sheet in a 4–0 victory.

In all he made four saves – all from shots outside the box – and six catches in his 119 minutes on pitch.

With Shaka Hislop rated as the top goalkeeper in the Carling Opta Index, Forrest will continue his understudy role.

Mikael FORSSELL • 32
CHELSEA • BORN: 15.3.81

Chelsea beat off competition from an estimated 20 top European clubs to secure the services of HJK Helsinki striker Mikael Forssell, but the young Finn was pressed into action earlier than Gianluca Vialli had envisaged.

A shortage of fit strikers saw Forssell make his debut as a substitute in the 1–0 defeat by Arsenal on January 31, and just three days later he was in the starting line-up for the FA Cup fourth-round replay against Oxford United at Stamford Bridge.

Two brilliant goals in a 4–2 win that night confirmed Forssell's ability, but he is still regarded as one for the future.

His one Premiership goal came in a 3–1 victory over Nottingham Forest in February. Unfortunately, he managed only one other accurate shot in his 10 appearances in the 1998–99 Premiership campaign.

Luckily, players like Vialli and Gianfranco Zola make Chelsea the perfect finishing-school. Under their guidance, Forssell is expected to make massive strides in 1999–2000.

Robbie FOWLER • 9
LIVERPOOL • BORN: 9.4.75

APPEARANCES	
Start (sub)	23 (2)
Minutes on pitch	2010
GOAL ATTEMPTS	
Goals	14
Goals/shots ratio	21%
SHOOTING	
Shots on target	31
Shooting accuracy	46%
PASSING	
Goal assists	5
Passing accuracy	69%
DISCIPLINE	
Fouls	25
Offside	11
Yellow cards	4
Red cards	0

Robbie Fowler is never too far away from his next goal – and in 1998–99 he was rarely very far from the next controversy.

Having missed the opening five matches of the season through injury, Fowler made his first Premiership start on September 19 at home to Charlton Athletic, scoring two goals.

Undoubtedly the high points of his campaign were his two hat-tricks, first in the thrilling 4–2 win at then-unbeaten Aston Villa and then in the 7–1 demolition of Southampton.

But Fowler then hit the headlines for all the wrong reasons. He was involved in an ugly altercation with England team-mate Graeme Le Saux in the 2–1 defeat at Chelsea on February 27. Then, just two weeks later, he celebrated his first goal in the 160th Merseyside Derby by crawling in front of the Everton supporters, pretending to "snort" the goal-line.

His subsequent suspension by the FA for Liverpool's last six games soured an otherwise excellent season. The hitman's 14 goals came from just 67 shots, with 46% on target and a fine 21% hitting the back of the net.

Ruel FOX • 7
TOTTENHAM HOTSPUR • BORN: 14.1.68

Former Norwich and Newcastle wide man Ruel Fox was a Tottenham regular under Christian Gross, but struggled to retain his place in the first team after George Graham arrived, making just three brief appearances in the Premiership in the final five months of the season.

A tricky winger with great close control, he completed 79% of all attempted dribbles and runs in 1998–99 – statistics which make it likely that there will be plenty of takers if he leaves White Hart Lane.

At just 5' 6", Fox is one of the Premiership's smaller players – but a big feature of his game has always been his ability to pop up with a goal. He scored three times in the 1998–99 Premiership season – all before Christmas – and managed eight shots in total.

A great weapon when the side is playing well, Fox does not really offer the team too many defensive options. His low tackle success rate shows he is poor at tracking back, which may affect his future under a manager who expects every man to do his share of defensive work when their team loses possession.

APPEARANCES	
Start (sub)	17 (3)
Minutes on pitch	1511
GOAL ATTEMPTS	
Goals	3
Shots on target	8
Shooting accuracy	73%
PASSING	
Goal assists	1
Passing accuracy	76%
Crossing accuracy	30%
DRIBBLING	
Dribbles & runs	72
Dribble completion	79%
DISCIPLINE	
Yellow cards	1
Red cards	0

Dougie FREEDMAN • 14
NOTTINGHAM FOREST • BORN: 21.1.74

APPEARANCES	
Start (sub)	21 (10)
Minutes on pitch	1793
GOAL ATTEMPTS	
Goals	9
Goals/shots ratio	20%
SHOOTING	
Shots on target	26
Shooting accuracy	58%
PASSING	
Goal assists	2
Passing accuracy	72%
DISCIPLINE	
Fouls	22
Offside	18
Yellow cards	1
Red cards	0

Scottish striker Freedman had one taste of the Premiership under Dave Bassett at Crystal Palace. When Wolves let him go after failing to reach the play-offs at the end of 1997–98 he was let loose in the top flight under Bassett once again, this time at Nottingham Forest.

Despite prolific spells in Division One, some pundits have questioned his Premiership pedigree - but he still finished 1998–99 as the club's top scorer with nine league goals.

Bearing in mind how much Forest struggled in front of goal, and that Freedman had four different strike partners over the season, that was a good effort and his shooting accuracy of 58% was well above the Premiership average.

Freedman's willingness to drop deep and take players on makes him a hit with the fans, and in 1998–99 he completed 64% of his 66 dribbles and runs. He also claimed two goal assists and completed 72% of his passes.

Frequently selected by both Bassett and Ron Atkinson, Freedman will be keen to impress the new manager as Forest bid for a swift return to the Premiership in 1999–2000.

Steffen FREUND • 4
M TOTTENHAM HOTSPUR • BORN: 19.1.70

A locksmith by trade, Steffen Freund proved one of George Graham's key signings for Spurs. The competitive German cost £750,000 from Borussia Dortmund and was installed beside Tim Sherwood in a new-look midfield.

With five tackles attempted per game on average, Freund's determination to win possession made him a few enemies. His challenges – not always the most accurate – earned Tottenham the ball 43 times and Freund eight bookings.

Eschewing the spectacular in favour of the solid, Freund received the ball and laid it off simply, ending the season with a good pass completion rate of 79% – but just one assist. Used mainly in a holding role, he was not averse to the occasional effort at goal, testing the 'keeper three times and firing eight wide.

With more than 20 international caps for Germany, two Championship medals and a World Club Cup winner's medal already in his trophy cabinet, Freund is clearly a winner. He is likely to be instrumental in Tottenham's quest for honours in 1999–2000.

APPEARANCES	
Start (sub)	17 (0)
Minutes on pitch	1482
GOAL ATTEMPTS	
Goals	0
PASSING	
Passes	595
Passing accuracy	79%
DEFENDING	
Interceptions	17
Clearances	37
Tackles	85
Tackles won	51%
DISCIPLINE	
Fouls	23
Yellow cards	6
Red cards	0

F

Brad FRIEDEL • 19
G LIVERPOOL • BORN: 18.5.71

APPEARANCES	
Start (sub)	12 (0)
Minutes on pitch	1080
SHOT STOPPING	
Goals conceded	15
Clean sheets	3
Saves	36
Saves/shots	71%
DISTRIBUTION	
Distribution	373
Distribution %	57%
CATCHING	
Crosses caught	42
Crosses dropped	3
DISCIPLINE	
Yellow cards	0
Red cards	0

Signed in the 1997–98 season, American goalkeeper Brad Friedel has not found the transition from American Major League Soccer to English Premiership football an easy one.

Work permit problems mean his club must play him in a certain number of games each season to retain his services, but alternating Friedel with David James seems to have done neither goalkeeper's confidence much good.

To be fair to Friedel, a defence which left him facing an average of five accurate shots a game did not help – but his saves-to-shots ratio of 71% was still some way below the Premiership average and he kept just three clean sheets. Like James, his handling of crosses did not always inspire confidence. In just 12 games he dropped three catches, failed to claim a further four crosses and was deemed directly at fault for at least one goal.

While undoubtedly a good goalkeeper, the extended run Friedel probably needs to hit top form looks unlikely. With Liverpool seemingly linked with a new goalkeeper every week, his days at Anfield may well be numbered.

Steve FROGGATT • 26
COVENTRY CITY • BORN: 9.3.73

Frustrated at Wolves' failure to reach the Premiership in 1997–98, Froggatt needed no second bidding when Gordon Strachan approached his best man Mark McGhee with a £1.9 million offer at the end of September.

The move looked in jeopardy when Strachan was linked with the vacant post at Leeds; but after assurances that the Scot was staying at Highfield Road and advice from his former Aston Villa team-mate Kevin Richardson, Froggatt joined the Sky Blues. Ironically his first appearance was against Villa.

His highlight came in the televized 3–0 mauling of Everton when he scored one of the goals of the season, charging down the left flank and sending a stunning, rising drive into the top corner. It remains his only Premiership goal for City, though he also netted in the 7–0 FA Cup win over Macclesfield.

Froggatt made many telling crosses, claiming five goal assists, but his overall cross completion rate of 22% was disappointing – undoubtedly a result of not having target man Dion Dublin to aim at.

APPEARANCES	
Start (sub)	23 (0)
Minutes on pitch	2070
GOAL ATTEMPTS	
Goals	1
Shots on target	12
Shooting accuracy	48%
PASSING	
Goal assists	5
Passing accuracy	71%
Crossing accuracy	22%
DRIBBLING	
Dribbles & runs	130
Dribble completion	65%
DISCIPLINE	
Yellow cards	3
Red cards	0

Kevin GALLACHER • 8
BLACKBURN ROVERS • BORN: 23.11.66

APPEARANCES	
Start (sub)	13 (3)
Minutes on pitch	1048
GOAL ATTEMPTS	
Goals	5
Goals/shots ratio	15%
SHOOTING	
Shots on target	19
Shooting accuracy	56%
PASSING	
Goal assists	1
Passing accuracy	75%
DISCIPLINE	
Fouls	15
Offside	8
Yellow cards	0
Red cards	0

Gallacher was one half of the Premiership's most prolific strike partnership with Chris Sutton in 1997–98, but had to sit out a chunk of season 1998–99 after breaking his arm.

Despite his enforced absence, the Scottish international still ended the campaign as the club's joint-top Premiership scorer with five goals, having hit the target with 19 shots.

Gallacher loves to pick the ball up deep and surge at defenders, and in 1998–99 completed 75% of his passes and 65% of his dribbles and runs, both above the average for strikers. A highly competitive player, he also tackles well, winning three-quarters of his challenges and managing to avoid being booked.

Back in the side towards the season's end, Gallacher reminded Rovers fans what they had been missing with his superb chip over Nottingham Forest's Mark Crossley. But his and Rovers' frustrations were epitomized by his subsequent penalty miss in the same match.

He is sure to be around for Blackburn's promotion push in 1999–2000 and will hope for more luck with injuries.

Remi GARDE • 19
ARSENAL • BORN: 3.4.66

Signed shortly after Arsenal boss Arsene Wenger's arrival at Highbury, Remi Garde has been a versatile squad player, equally at home in a holding role in front of the back four or on the flanks.

Following a bout of glandular fever, it was his intention to retire at the end of the 1997–98 season, but Wenger persuaded the Frenchman to continue at Highbury in the 1998–99 campaign.

Garde's season was restricted to six Premiership starts, deputizing for Patrick Vieira or Emmanuel Petit in central midfield. As with the majority of the Arsenal players, Garde's pass completion rate was excellent at 82%. He also fired eight shots at goal, with two hitting the target.

After lengthy discussions with Arsene Wenger, Garde decided to announce his retirement shortly after the end of the 1998–99 season.

Arsenal fans will be grateful for Garde's contribution and wish him well in his future career.

 **Paul GASCOIGNE • 8**
MIDDLESBROUGH • BORN: 27.5.67

Extraordinary career: Paul Gascoigne

APPEARANCES	
Start (sub)	25 (1)
Minutes on pitch	1991
GOAL ATTEMPTS	
Goals	3
PASSING	
Passes	1320
Passing accuracy	80%
DEFENDING	
Interceptions	17
Clearances	14
Tackles	90
Tackles won	47%
DISCIPLINE	
Fouls	27
Yellow cards	12
Red cards	0

Clearly in the twilight of an extraordinary career, Paul Gascoigne is still creating headlines in his swansong in English football.

Controversy seems to follow the wayward star at every turn and he began 1998–99 desperate to show Glenn Hoddle had been wrong both to leave him out of the France 98 squad and later to reveal details of their clash in his contentious World Cup diaries.

His admission to a clinic with stress after losing a close friend as the result of a drinking binge hit the headlines next.

The regime of treatment was clearly a hard one but, initially at least, it seemed to help the Italia 90 star's form.

Leaner and more able to last the pace, Gazza's pass and cross completion rates showed a marginal improvement, as did his dribble success rate.

His tackling also improved, but the frustration of not reaching his own high standards told as he was booked 12 times and failed to score again after his strike at Southampton in November.

CB Jason GAVIN • 31
MIDDLESBROUGH • BORN: 14.3.80

Injuries and suspensions to established defenders at Boro have given Jason Gavin the chance to show his manager Bryan Robson what a capable player he is.

The Eire under-21 international has worked his way through the ranks at Middlesbrough and had to wait for his chance in Bryan Robson's first team.

Down in the pecking order of defenders behind the likes of Gianluca Festa, Steve Vickers, Gary Pallister, Curtis Fleming and Dean Gordon, Gavin only managed to feature for 162 minutes in the Carling Premiership in 1998–99.

He completed 60% of his 25 passes, and won two of his three tackles. He also made two blocks and 19 clearances.

To his credit he stayed out of trouble, committing no fouls nor receiving any cards from the referee.

The young Irishman has been thrown into the deep end at Middlesbrough, but looks like a good prospect for the coming season for the Teesside club.

S Marcus GAYLE • 11
WIMBLEDON • BORN: 29.9.70

Storming season: Marcus Gayle

APPEARANCES	
Start (sub)	31 (4)
Minutes on pitch	2767
GOAL ATTEMPTS	
Goals	10
Goals/shots ratio	16%
SHOOTING	
Shots on target	30
Shooting accuracy	48%
PASSING	
Goal assists	9
Passing accuracy	54%
DISCIPLINE	
Fouls	32
Offside	43
Yellow cards	1
Red cards	0

After featuring in the 1998 World Cup with the Reggae Boyz, Marcus Gayle crowned his season by finishing as joint-top scorer for the Dons.

But it was a sign of Wimbledon's disappointing season that he managed just 10 league goals as his side finished 16th. Those 10 strikes came from 30 shots on target, his shooting accuracy being around the average 50% mark for a Premiership attacker. Gayle was goal-maker as well as goalscorer, though, and he can be rightly proud of nine assists.

In line with Wimbledon's poor overall pass completion rate Gayle connected with a Don on only 54% of occasions, some 16 percentage points below the Premiership average for his position. His cross completion was also weak, but he made up for it somewhat by helping out in defence with 60 clearances. Despite only winning 13 tackles and committing 32 fouls, he was booked just once.

Gayle played in all but three of the club's 1998–99 Premiership matches and is likely to be a key figure at Selhurst Park again in 1999–2000.

Scot GEMMILL • 11
EVERTON • BORN: 2.1.71

M

Son of Archie Gemmill, who scored one of the finest-ever World Cup goals in 1978 against Holland, Scot Gemmill showed he was a chip off the old block with a cracking left-foot volley in a 3–1 victory over Newcastle United.

The Paisley-born midfielder started the season at Nottingham Forest, but ended his long association with the club when he moved to Everton just before the transfer deadline.

The move seems to have done him good: he settled well and became an integral part of the team which eased away from the relegation zone with a couple of games to spare.

Though his pass and dribble completion rates dropped away after his transfer, he vastly improved his tackling and number of goal efforts. His goal proved his only shot on target for Everton, and one of just 11 he managed all season for both his 1998–99 clubs.

Gemmill can look forward to the 1999–2000 season in the Premiership and will hope to be part of Walter Smith's drive to re-establish Everton's position in the upper echelons of the top flight.

APPEARANCES	
Start (sub)	25 (2)
Minutes on pitch	2183
GOAL ATTEMPTS	
Goals	1
PASSING	
Passes	1126
Passing accuracy	77%
DEFENDING	
Interceptions	25
Clearances	38
Tackles	81
Tackles won	64%
DISCIPLINE	
Fouls	26
Yellow cards	6
Red cards	0

G

George GEORGIADIS • 15
NEWCASTLE UNITED • BORN: 8.3.72

M

APPEARANCES	
Start (sub)	7 (3)
Minutes on pitch	591
GOAL ATTEMPTS	
Goals	0
Shots on target	3
Shooting accuracy	43%
PASSING	
Goal assists	0
Passing accuracy	85%
Crossing accuracy	26%
DRIBBLING	
Dribbles & runs	22
Dribble completion	68%
DISCIPLINE	
Yellow cards	1
Red cards	0

A disappointing 1998–99 season on the fringes of the Newcastle squad looks likely to persuade Greek midfielder George Georgiadis to end his stay in the North-East.

Signed by Kenny Dalglish from Panathinaikos in summer 1998, he proved a bit-part player under new boss Ruud Gullit and is now surplus to requirements in the Dutchman's plans.

He made just 10 appearances, showing some decent play on the ball and completing an above-average 85% of his 227 passes, 26% of his crosses and retaining possession on 68% of his dribbles and runs.

He was less successful in the tackle and only fired in nine shots in the Premiership. But he did get on the scoresheet in the FA Cup, when he scored the second goal of four in the quarter-final rout of Everton – the day before his 27th birthday.

After that goal he said: "I came here to play. But if you are not much involved, you have to think about your future." With those sentiments, and with Gullit putting him up for sale, it seems his Newcastle career is over.

AM — Steven GERRARD • 28
LIVERPOOL • BORN: 30.5.80

Teenage midfielder Steven Gerrard made his Premiership debut for Liverpool as a substitute in the 3–1 home defeat by Leeds United. He went on to make 12 appearances in the Reds' disappointing season.

His pass completion rate of 77% was disappointing, but he was better from wide where he completed 45% of his crosses – well above the league average.

Gerrard showed willing in the challenge, too, but won only 48% of 29 tackles, suggesting that he struggled to adapt to the faster pace and physical nature of life at the top level of the professional game.

His finest moment came in the 160th Merseyside derby at Anfield when he cleared two Danny Cadamarteri shots off the line in the last 10 minutes which helped secure the 3–2 victory.

Gerard Houllier has begun his French revolution at Liverpool and, while many heads look set to roll, young Gerrard will be keen to show he has what it takes to avoid *la guillotine* in 1999–2000.

M — Kevin GIBBENS • 28
SOUTHAMPTON • BORN: 4.11.79

Southampton-born midfielder Kevin Gibbens first emerged at the end of the 1997–98 season, when he made his debut in the 4–2 win at West Ham.

Having joined the club as a YTS trainee Gibbens only turned professional in January 1998, but performed well enough in the reserves to merit a first team call-up just three months later.

He remained on the first-team fringes in 1998–99, making four appearances including two as substitute. He showed an astute touch in his brief outings, completing 80% of his 61 passes and hitting the target with two of his four shots.

The teenager made nine tackles, winning possession five times, but in his eagerness to impress committed five fouls.

Gibbens has shown a lot of potential and if he continues to develop could well have a bright future ahead of him at the Dell.

After a season of struggle, Dave Jones is likely to ring the changes and Gibbens will be looking to impress.

AM — Ryan GIGGS • 11
MANCHESTER UNITED • BORN: 29.11.73

APPEARANCES	
Start (sub)	20 (4)
Minutes on pitch	1728
GOAL ATTEMPTS	
Goals	3
Shots on target	17
Shooting accuracy	50%
PASSING	
Goal assists	2
Passing accuracy	68%
Crossing accuracy	14%
DRIBBLING	
Dribbles & runs	119
Dribble completion	63%
DISCIPLINE	
Yellow cards	1
Red cards	0

Ryan Giggs went one better than his team-mates by picking up a fourth trophy at the end of the 1998–99 season. His breathtaking goal against Arsenal in extra-time of the FA Cup semi-final replay was the BBC's Goal of the Season – some calling it the best of all time.

But the Welshman's FA Cup and Champions League performances contrasted with his Premiership form. He scored just three goals from 39 efforts (including blocked shots), completed only 68% of his passes and, whereas David Beckham set up 14 goals, Giggs managed just two assists.

His crossing was particularly poor – he completed just 19 of 134 attempted centres – and his dribble completion rate was also lower than the Premiership average; but this may be because he attempts to beat players at pace when the ball is more difficult to control.

Despite the disappointing stats and niggling injuries, 1998–99 will doubtless go down in the record books as one of Giggs's finest – and the memory of that stunning goal will act as a lasting tribute to a wonderful talent.

Keith GILLESPIE • 31
AM · BLACKBURN ROVERS • BORN: 18.2.75

Keith Gillespie became Brian Kidd's first buy when he moved from Newcastle to Blackburn for £2.35 million just before Christmas. After starting well, he then flitted in and out of the side as Rovers failed to beat the drop.

The Northern Ireland international managed just one Premiership goal from his five shots on target. He also hit 12 wayward efforts and had nine shots blocked.

Gillespie's strength is his ability to beat opposing full-backs and deliver quality crosses into the penalty area. In 1998–99 he completed more than 75% of his dribbles and runs, but his completion rate actually dropped from 81% to 74% after his move to Rovers.

On the other hand, his cross completion rate improved from 31% to 35%. He picked out a team-mate with more than a third of his crosses, passed well – 75% of his balls found their mark – and created three goals.

Gillespie will now turn his sights to the promotion battle in the Nationwide League, where his delivery from the right could be a major factor in Blackburn's 1999–2000 season.

APPEARANCES	
Start (sub)	18 (5)
Minutes on pitch	1695
GOAL ATTEMPTS	
Goals	1
Shots on target	5
Shooting accuracy	29%
PASSING	
Goal assists	3
Passing accuracy	75%
Crossing accuracy	34%
DRIBBLING	
Dribbles & runs	121
Dribble completion	76%
DISCIPLINE	
Yellow cards	2
Red cards	1

G

David GINOLA • 14
AM · TOTTENHAM HOTSPUR • BORN: 25.1.67

APPEARANCES	
Start (sub)	30 (0)
Minutes on pitch	2475
GOAL ATTEMPTS	
Goals	3
Shots on target	24
Shooting accuracy	44%
PASSING	
Goal assists	10
Passing accuracy	69%
Crossing accuracy	35%
DRIBBLING	
Dribbles & runs	409
Dribble completion	61%
DISCIPLINE	
Yellow cards	9
Red cards	0

David Ginola celebrated his first English trophy – the Worthington Cup – by also scooping both the PFA Player of the Year and Football Writers' Footballer of the Year awards. But though outstanding in cup competitions, his Premiership form was less impressive.

The Frenchman scored just three times from 71 attempts – his first goal not coming until March – and his pass completion rate of 69% was very poor for a player of his calibre. His cross completion rate was well above average, though, and he made more successful dribbles and runs than any other player.

Ginola was one of the top flight's best creators, setting up 10 goals – a figure only bettered by five players. He was also the most-fouled player in the Premiership, going to ground under challenges 96 times. His own disciplinary record was not good – nine yellow cards, with only four being awarded for fouls.

He drew criticism for the apparent ease with which he went down when tackled, but praise from the media promoted his election to the game's top individual honours.

M Stefano GIOACCHINI • 13
COVENTRY CITY • BORN: 25.11.76

Italian youngster Stefano Gioacchini, who was on loan from Serie A side Venezia, played just 45 minutes of football during the 1998–99 Carling Premiership season in three substitute appearances.

His first was in a 2–0 defeat at Arsenal and he went on to play briefly at home against Southampton and away at Leicester City.

He spent some time out with a hamstring injury, but in truth the Italian under-21 international rarely looked like figuring in Gordon Strachan's first-team plans and may well find himself heading back to Italy in the close season.

When he did get on the pitch he managed just 14 passes and a couple of tackles, but had three efforts at goal, with two of them forcing a save.

Although still under contract with Venezia, the youngster enjoys English football. After becoming a father for the first time early in 1999, and with his wife Rachel being English, he will hope that Coventry are keen to retain his services.

G Shay GIVEN • 1
NEWCASTLE UNITED • BORN: 24.4.76

APPEARANCES	
Start (sub)	31 (0)
Minutes on pitch	2745
SHOT STOPPING	
Goals conceded	45
Clean sheets	6
Saves	98
Saves/shots	69%
DISTRIBUTION	
Distribution	949
Distribution %	59%
CATCHING	
Crosses caught	64
Crosses dropped	5
DISCIPLINE	
Yellow cards	0
Red cards	0

Cup final blues: Shay Given

After a dip in form, and then being dropped for the FA Cup final, Shay Given will have been delighted with Mick McCarthy's reassurance that he was still first-choice goalkeeper for the Republic of Ireland.

The former Blackburn man's confidence suffered after conceding 45 goals behind a leaky, ever-changing Newcastle back-line, as Ruud Gullit experimented with his defence.

He made 98 saves, but his saves-to-shots ratio was very low – he stopped on average only seven out of 10 shots on target, which ultimately cost him his place at Wembley. He caught 64 crosses and punched a further 22, but also dropped five, leaving him with a below-average catch success rate of 93%.

The 23-year-old's distribution was generally satisfactory and he claimed two goal assists – more than any other Premiership 'keeper.

Having been signed by Kenny Dalglish – his boss at Blackburn Rovers – in summer 1997, Given may become a casualty of Ruud Gullit's rebuilding programme, but has the talent to make a name for himself wherever he plays.

AM Stephen GLASS • 17
NEWCASTLE UNITED • BORN: 23.5.76

Winger Stephen Glass fared better than many Scots who have recently made the move south of the border, and looks set to be a key member of Ruud Gullit's Newcastle squad for the 1999–2000 season.

He was very promising when fit and scored three goals from 29 attempts (including blocked shots), not a bad return for a wide man who played less than 1,600 minutes. All three were against Midlands sides: he netted away at Coventry City and in the home games against Derby County and Leicester City.

A useful attacking option down the flanks, Glass proved a pain for opposition full-backs, beating them six times out of 10, but found a team-mate with just one in four crosses. His pass completion rate of 77% was average for his position and he helped create two goals.

He committed 12 fouls, but did not pick up any cards and ended the season as the Premiership's sixth-cleanest player. Glass will have been shattered to miss the FA Cup final, but will hope for more success and fewer injuries in 1999–2000.

APPEARANCES	
Start (sub)	18 (4)
Minutes on pitch	1583
GOAL ATTEMPTS	
Goals	3
Shots on target	8
Shooting accuracy	40%
PASSING	
Goal assists	2
Passing accuracy	77%
Crossing accuracy	25%
DRIBBLING	
Dribbles & runs	70
Dribble completion	60%
DISCIPLINE	
Yellow cards	0
Red cards	0

G

AM Bjarne GOLDBAEK • 7
CHELSEA • BORN: 6.10.68

APPEARANCES	
Start (sub)	13 (10)
Minutes on pitch	1226
GOAL ATTEMPTS	
Goals	5
Shots on target	13
Shooting accuracy	45%
PASSING	
Goal assists	2
Passing accuracy	82%
Crossing accuracy	25%
DRIBBLING	
Dribbles & runs	48
Dribble completion	73%
DISCIPLINE	
Yellow cards	2
Red cards	0

"Who's that so-and-so in the number seven shirt?" asked Ken Bates during Chelsea's 1–0 victory over FC Copenhagen in the Cup Winners Cup. The "so-and-so" was Bjarne Goldbaek – and the next day he joined Chelsea as part of the deal that took Brian Laudrup in the opposite direction.

It was an inspired signing. Goldbaek was excellent for Chelsea, posing a real threat to opponents and banishing the memory of Laudrup with his willingness to knuckle down.

In all, Goldbaek made 48 waspish runs with the ball and delivered 51 crosses into the box. He adjusted to Chelsea's slick passing style very quickly, showing good technique on the way to an 82% pass completion rate.

Possibly his biggest contribution was his knack of popping up with important goals. He scored five, including two in the 3–1 away victory over Nottingham Forest and a stunning equalizer in the 2–2 draw with Spurs.

He contributed less defensively, but still tracked back diligently, making 37 tackles and eight interceptions.

S Jon GOODMAN • 14
WIMBLEDON • BORN: 2.6.71

After missing the whole of the 1997–98 season with a knee injury, Jon Goodman had little more luck in 1998–99: he managed only one five-minute substitute appearance before injury struck again.

The pacy striker joined the Dons in 1994 and has managed to make just 60 league appearances in that time, thanks to a variety of injuries.

In his one appearance against Charlton Athletic he made just one pass, one foul and strayed offside once, and he will be hoping to make more of a contribution than that in 1999–2000.

He remains committed to the club, although he realises that with the plethora of strikers at Selhurst Park he will have a tough fight for a place even when fit.

He said: "When we go and spend £7 million on a player [John Hartson]...then it tells you the club means business and that places for forwards are going to be very difficult."

Goodman will have to fight for a place and impress new boss Egil Olsen in 1999–2000.

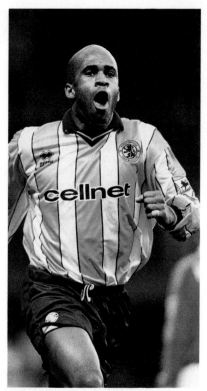

Ever-present: Dean Gordon

FB Dean GORDON •3
MIDDLESBROUGH • BORN: 10.2.73

APPEARANCES	
Start (sub)	38 (0)
Minutes on pitch	3420
GOAL ATTEMPTS	
Goals	3
PASSING & CROSSING	
Passing	1056
Passing accuracy	69%
Crossing	135
Crossing accuracy	27%
DEFENDING	
Tackles	111
Tackles won	53%
DISCIPLINE	
Fouls	24
Yellow cards	3
Red cards	0

With the lack of strength in the English game down the left-hand side, it is perhaps surprising that Dean Gordon has not earned England recognition at full international level.

One of only six players to feature in every minute of the Premiership season, Deano is a true all-rounder. He scored three goals, all from long distance, and warmed various goalkeepers' hands on 14 other occasions.

The man who learned his trade at Selhurst Park also weighed in with four goal assists, but has a slightly disappointing pass completion rate of just 69%.

Eagles fans were dismayed to see Gordon fly the nest for just £900,000 in summer 1998 and would have remembered fondly the wing-play that saw him glide past defenders on 74% of his dribbles and runs in 1998–99.

Defensively, there was nothing flash about Gordon who made 234 clearances, 24 blocks and 37 interceptions. He also won 53% of his 111 tackles. Boro must feel they got a bargain in Gordon, and that in 1999–2000 he can help them push further up the Premiership ladder.

CB Richard GOUGH • 15
NOTTINGHAM FOREST • BORN: 5.4.62

Defender Richard Gough reached the venerable age of 37 in April of season 1998–99, but such is his quality that other Premiership clubs are already looking to secure the Scotsman's services for the 1999–2000 campaign.

Gough arrived at the City Ground in February after a stint with San Jose Clash in the USA's MLS, and Forest fans could hardly fault his effort as he slotted into the centre of defence.

He makes even the toughest strikers quake and thundered into 22 tackles, but he was rumbled by the officials on 15 occasions and earned two yellow cards and a dismissal.

The former Spurs and Rangers star made 77 defensive clearances, nine interceptions and eight blocks, but like many Forest players, Gough's pass completion rate was poor and his two goal attempts failed to trouble the opposition 'keepers.

He played 61 times for Scotland and won nine titles in 11 seasons at Ibrox. His best days may be behind him, but there is no reason why he cannot have another successful crack at life in the top flight.

APPEARANCES

Start (sub)	7 (0)
Minutes on pitch	580

GOAL ATTEMPTS

Goals	0

DEFENDING

Blocks	8
Headed clearances	53
Other clearances	24
Interceptions	9
Tackles won	12

PASSING

Passing accuracy	76%

DISCIPLINE

Fouls	15
Yellow cards	2
Red cards	1

G

M Tony GRANT •14
EVERTON • BORN: 14.11.74

APPEARANCES

Start (sub)	13 (3)
Minutes on pitch	1060

GOAL ATTEMPTS

Goals	0

PASSING

Passes	539
Passing accuracy	75%

DEFENDING

Interceptions	14
Clearances	19
Tackles	45
Tackles won	58%

DISCIPLINE

Fouls	14
Yellow cards	0
Red cards	0

Tony Grant earned himself a decent run in the side during the 1998–99 season thanks to injuries and suspensions, combined with Walter Smith's desire to find the right combination of players and tactics to keep Everton in the top flight.

In all, he made 13 starts and three more appearances as a substitute in another under-achieving season for the Toffees. None of his 17 goal efforts found the net and his pass completion rate of 75% was well below that expected of a top-level midfielder.

Grant committed just 14 fouls and avoided any censure from the referees, but he won only 58% of his tackles and made a minimal number of dribbles and crosses – not enough of a contribution to make him a regular.

With Olivier Dacourt, Don Hutchison and John Collins ahead of him in the pecking order, and the fact that he is now in his mid-20s, Grant may find that he has to leave Goodison Park to secure a place in first-team football, which would be a wrench for the former Everton trainee.

FB

Danny GRANVILLE • 16
LEEDS UNITED • BORN: 19.1.75

Danny Granville appeared to have a bright future when he was snapped up by Chelsea from Cambridge United, but 12 months later he was on his way to Elland Road and has since struggled to break into Leeds' first team.

The main reason has been the outstanding form of Ian Harte, but a look at Granville's stats illustrates why he is currently second in the pecking order.

The 24-year-old completed just 70% of the passes he attempted, found a team-mate with one in four of his crosses and won only 47% of his tackles – all below average for the Premiership.

He is also less of an attacking threat than his Irish rival, firing in just two efforts off target and one that was blocked.

His disciplinary record was soured by a red card in only his second appearance for Leeds – at home to Nottingham Forest – for two bookable offences in just 32 minutes.

It is unlikely that he will be content to play second fiddle for as long as Yorkshire's most famous Granville did in TV's Open All Hours.

APPEARANCES	
Start (sub)	7 (2)
Minutes on pitch	575
GOAL ATTEMPTS	
Goals	0
PASSING & CROSSING	
Passing	237
Passing accuracy	70%
Crossing	16
Crossing accuracy	25%
DEFENDING	
Tackles	19
Tackles won	47%
DISCIPLINE	
Fouls	11
Yellow cards	0
Red cards	1

AM

Andy GRAY • 27
NOTTINGHAM FOREST • BORN: 15.11.77

APPEARANCES	
Start (sub)	3 (5)
Minutes on pitch	339
GOAL ATTEMPTS	
Goals	0
Shots on target	2
Shooting accuracy	40%
PASSING	
Goal assists	0
Passing accuracy	70%
Crossing accuracy	40%
DRIBBLING	
Dribbles & runs	20
Dribble completion	65%
DISCIPLINE	
Yellow cards	0
Red cards	0

When Andy Gray and the Premiership are mentioned in the same sentence, it is likely to be the famous ex-player and current Sky Sports pundit who springs to mind rather than Nottingham Forest's left-sided midfielder.

The young Scot began his career as part of Leeds United's successful youth set-up. But he was snapped up by Dave Bassett for a small fee in the autumn after it seemed first-team opportunities would be limited at Elland Road because of the presence of Harry Kewell, Lee Sharpe and Bruno Ribeiro.

His pass completion rate of 70%, dribble completion and number of tackles won were all below average: despite only making 10 crosses his accuracy was reasonable. Gray forced two saves, but fired wide with three more shots and had two blocked.

He is now at the age where he has to turn potential into performance. With Forest back in Division One, he may get a chance to establish himself in the team in 1999–2000 and build his confidence for the next time he gets a crack at Premiership football.

Simon GRAYSON • 16
ASTON VILLA • BORN: 16.12.69

One of four former Leicester City men now playing under John Gregory, Simon Grayson picked up the Foxes' 1996–97 Player of the Year award before signing for Aston Villa during the summer of 1997. But after playing in the majority of Villa's matches the following season he suffered some personal disappointment in 1998–99, being used mainly as a substitute.

Grayson also picked up a knee injury in March that restricted his playing time to only 536 minutes in the Premiership. He made more than 40 clearances, blocks and interceptions combined at the back and carried the ball out of defence competently.

The £1.35 million signing dispatched nearly 200 passes and gave relatively little away, delivering two out of six crosses into the path of a Villa colleague. He also managed a couple of on-target efforts at goal. But he completed the full 90 minutes in just three of his 14 league appearances.

Grayson will be hoping for a little more luck in 1999–2000.

 **Jonathan GREENING • 34**
MANCHESTER UNITED • BORN: 2.1.79

Jonathan Greening is one of the more unusual young players in Manchester United's talented squad, in that he did not come up through the youth ranks. He started at York City, but impressed sufficiently for United to come calling with an offer of £500,000, rising to £2 million based on appearances.

Greening made just three substitute appearances during the 1998–99 Carling Premiership season and played a total of only 66 minutes. He made one more substitute outing in the FA Cup and three starts in the Worthington Cup, and picked up a Champions League medal despite being an unused substitute in the final.

With Jesper Blomqvist and Ryan Giggs both ahead of him, the left-sided player will have to develop markedly to figure prominently in the first team. But his 83% dribble completion and 84% pass completion rates show that he has no shortage of ability, although both the shots he attempted missed the target.

1999–2000 will be a crucial year for Scarborough-born Greening.

G

 Andy GRIFFIN • 38
NEWCASTLE UNITED • BORN: 17.3.79

APPEARANCES	
Start (sub)	14 (0)
Minutes on pitch	1170
GOAL ATTEMPTS	
Goals	0
PASSING & CROSSING	
Passing	730
Passing accuracy	81%
Crossing	25
Crossing accuracy	20%
DEFENDING	
Tackles	36
Tackles won	58%
DISCIPLINE	
Fouls	4
Yellow cards	0
Red cards	0

Andy Griffin is fast establishing himself as first-choice full-back at St James's Park and is versatile enough to play on either side of the pitch. While he lined up against Ryan Giggs in the FA Cup final on Newcastle's right, he probably had his best game of the season at Old Trafford where he kept David Beckham very quiet in the 0–0 draw with Manchester United.

He completed 81% of 730 passes and 77% of his dribbles and runs, showing that he is comfortable both on the ball and in defence. He made 67 defensive clearances, eight blocks and eight interceptions, but will have to improve on his 58% tackle rate in 1999–2000.

The under-21 international was rarely an attacking threat, however, firing in just 25 crosses and two shots off target, mainly due to the fact that Newcastle United struggled for most of the season.

The 20-year-old looks set for a bright future; and if Ruud Gullit can add more quality to the squad, Griffin will be hoping for another crack at a medal to make up for the disappointment of losing the 1999 FA Cup final.

CB · Gilles GRIMANDI • 18
ARSENAL • BORN: 11.11.70

Signed from Arsene Wenger's old club Monaco in 1997, Gilles Grimandi has been used as a squad player since his arrival at Highbury. In 1998–99 he started only twice for the defending champions and made a handful of substitute appearances during the campaign.

Comfortable at both centre-back and right-back, Grimandi proved to be a sound defensive replacement in defence. He won 79% of his challenges and completed the same proportion of his passes.

Unfortunately, he was also involved in the uglier side of the game in December when his temper got the better of him and he was sent off after a clash with young Leeds striker Alan Smith at Highbury.

Overall, however, the 28-year-old was a steady performer and has rarely disappointed his manager when called upon. Although he will struggle to oust the likes of Tony Adams and Martin Keown from the first team, Arsene Wenger will want to keep Grimandi at the club to provide cover for the Arsenal defence again during 1999–2000.

FB · David GRONDIN • 22
ARSENAL • BORN: 8.5.80

When Nigel Winterburn was forced to sit out the home fixture against Liverpool in early January, former French youth international David Grondin was thrown into first-team action by manager Arsene Wenger.

Signed in the summer of 1998 from St Etienne, Grondin spent the season developing his skills in the reserves but, when he was called up for the Liverpool game, Wenger's confidence in the youngster was rewarded with an impressive first outing in the Premiership.

The teenager performed well in the left-back slot, showing his composure on the ball with his 92% pass completion rate. He also retained possession with all three of his dribbles and runs.

Defensively, he won two-thirds of his challenges, made nine clearances and also two interceptions.

He will learn from the experienced pros at the club such as Nigel Winterburn and Lee Dixon, developing the defensive attributes required to become an Arsenal full-back.

S · Stephane GUIVARC'H • 8
NEWCASTLE UNITED • BORN: 6.9.70

Anticipation quickly turned to trepidation for Newcastle fans as their £3.5 million signing Stephane Guivarc'h put in a series of less than impressive performances for France in the World Cup Finals.

Unfortunately, the former Auxerre man did little to dispel the feeling that he was not the ideal partner for Alan Shearer once the 1998–99 Carling Premiership season began, and after the dismissal of Kenny Dalglish he quickly found himself surplus to Ruud Gullit's requirements.

His one goal for the club came during the 4–1 home defeat by Liverpool, a match which will be remembered for the brilliance of Michael Owen's hat-trick rather than Guivarc'h's 28th-minute strike.

He managed just one other shot on target thereafter, and failed to create any decent scoring opportunities for Shearer.

A muscular player who has the presence to unsettle defences both in the air and on the ground, Guivarch's move to Glasgow Rangers briefly saw him back among the goals.

S · Arnar GUNNLAUGSSON • 13
LEICESTER CITY • BORN: 6.3.73

Icelandic international Arnar Gunnlaugsson gave up a promotion push with Bolton Wanderers to realize his dream of a return to the Premiership much sooner. He joined Leicester City for £2 million and, with Tony Cottee and Emile Heskey struggling for fitness, featured five times from the start and on four more occasions as a substitute.

He played a total of 407 minutes, firing in nine shots. One was wide of the mark and another blocked, but impressively the other seven were on target, including six in one match against Tottenham Hotspur. Unfortunately he found the goalkeeper, not the net.

Gunnlaugsson's pass completion rate of 71% left a lot to be desired, but he was quite impressive when dribbling with the ball, completing 75% of the 24 he attempted.

The talented forward will be much more acclimatized to the top flight by the time the new season starts and he may well figure more prominently in Leicester's 1999–2000 Carling Premiership campaign.

FB — Steve GUPPY • 11
LEICESTER CITY • BORN: 29.3.69

Whether at full-back, wing-back or on the left of midfield, Steve Guppy poses problems for any defence with his dribbling and sweet left foot.

The 30-year-old came close to being called up to the England squad during the 1998–99 campaign after helping Leicester reach their second League Cup final in three seasons.

Guppy completed 28% of the crosses he attempted and claimed 11 goal assists with his out-swinging centres. More impressive was his dribble and run success rate: he beat his man 82% of the time to create a crossing or goalscoring opportunity.

The former Port Vale player proved a threat with his shooting, firing in 17 shots on target and scoring four goals, including a real screamer at Wimbledon. Even showing him on to his right foot did not seem to work, as Chelsea found to their cost at Stamford Bridge.

He won 49% of his tackles and made 134 defensive clearances, but his overall passing statistics were well below average. Guppy was one of only six players who played every single minute of the Premiership campaign.

APPEARANCES
Start (sub)	38 (0)
Minutes on pitch	3420

GOAL ATTEMPTS
Goals	4

PASSING & CROSSING
Passing	1260
Passing accuracy	73%
Crossing	415
Crossing accuracy	28%

DEFENDING
Tackles	83
Tackles won	49%

DISCIPLINE
Fouls	24
Yellow cards	3
Red cards	0

G

M — Alfie HAALAND • 4
LEEDS UNITED • BORN: 23.11.72

APPEARANCES
Start (sub)	24 (5)
Minutes on pitch	2250

GOAL ATTEMPTS
Goals	1

PASSING
Passes	693
Passing accuracy	76%

DEFENDING
Interceptions	30
Clearances	100
Tackles	99
Tackles won	60%

DISCIPLINE
Fouls	54
Yellow cards	10
Red cards	0

Versatile Alfie Haaland proved once again that he is equally comfortable in defence or midfield and was an important member of David O'Leary's emerging Leeds United squad.

The tenacious Norwegian international was a regular in Leeds' starting line-up, but missed a number of games through suspension. Alfie was sure to have asked several referees, "What's it all about?" having been booked 10 times in the Premiership.

Haaland won 60% of his 99 challenges and completed a century of defensive clearances. He also made seven blocks, and showed how well he reads the game with 30 interceptions.

He looked comfortable bringing the ball forward, completing 86% of his runs, but his distribution was less accurate: only around three-quarters of his passes found a white shirt.

Not known as a goalscorer, Haaland got on to the scoresheet once from 15 attempts, in the 5–1 thrashing of West Ham at Upton Park.

He has UEFA Cup football to look forward to in 1999–2000 and, if he maintains his form, a place in Norway's squad for Euro 2000.

FB   Marcus HALL • 19
COVENTRY CITY • BORN: 24.3.76

An exciting young player capable of playing in any position on the left-hand side, Marcus Hall started the 1998–99 Carling Premiership season at Lilleshall recovering from a bad groin injury.

Determined to win back his place in the side, he battled well, making his first Premiership appearance of the season in the 1–0 defeat by Arsenal in October.

Unfortunately, he tore knee ligaments in that game and did not return until April 24 when Gordon Strachan used him as a second-half substitute.

Playing in the following week's game against Wimbledon and the subsequent 0–0 draw with Derby County completed a satisfying run for Hall, who showed he had made a good recovery by earning a 75% pass completion rate and attempting 11 tackles in his limited appearances.

Capped by England at under-21 and "B" levels, he is highly thought-of at Coventry and will be hoping for more luck in the 1999–2000 Carling Premiership season.

AM   Paul HALL • 15
COVENTRY CITY • BORN: 3.7.72

After playing for the Jamaican Reggae Boyz in France 98, Paul Hall left Division One club Portsmouth to join Coventry City in the FA Carling Premiership.

He struggled to break into the starting line-up at Highfield Road – and after just two Premiership starts, against Liverpool and Newcastle United, and seven substitute appearances, he was eventually loaned out to First Division strugglers Bury.

While at Coventry, Hall found himself fighting with Paul Telfer for the right side slot. Unfortunately Hall lost out to the Scotland "B" international, who provided more defensive stability in the Sky Blues' midfield.

Hall's pass completion (71%) and dribble completion (65%) both fell short of the league average for attacking midfielders, demonstrating the difficulty he encountered making the jump from Nationwide League to Premiership football.

The winger had returned from Gigg Lane by the end of the 1998–99 season, but his name remained on the transfer list.

FB   Gunnar HALLE • 18
LEEDS UNITED • BORN: 11.8.65

APPEARANCES	
Start (sub)	14 (3)
Minutes on pitch	1290
GOAL ATTEMPTS	
Goals	2
PASSING & CROSSING	
Passing	378
Passing accuracy	72%
Crossing	13
Crossing accuracy	38%
DEFENDING	
Tackles	29
Tackles won	55%
DISCIPLINE	
Fouls	14
Yellow cards	0
Red cards	0

Veteran utility player Gunnar Halle has been a fantastic servant to first Oldham Athletic and then Leeds since he arrived from Norway in 1991. He still figures in the international set-up and fills in all over the defence and in midfield for both club and country.

Halle won 55% of his 29 Premiership tackles, contributed 62 defensive clearances and 11 interceptions, but attempted very few crosses or dribbles and runs. His pass completion rate was also well below average at 72%.

Strangely, the area in which Halle excelled, given his defensive leaning, was his shooting. He attempted six efforts at goal, five of which were on target and two of which found the net, doubling his career tally for Leeds.

As you would expect, Halle was very disciplined and was not cautioned all season – an example David O'Leary will hope his other players can follow in 1999–2000, given Leeds' poor disciplinary record in 1998–99.

After signing a contract extension at Elland Road, it was surprising that Halle moved to Bradford City in the close season.

Dietmar HAMANN • 12
NEWCASTLE UNITED • BORN: 27.8.73

A consistent performer in a struggling side, Dietmar Hamann ended 1998–99 the highest-rated player in the Carling Opta Index.

Signed by Kenny Dalglish from Bayern Munich for £4.5 million in the close season, Hamann did not make the best of starts under new boss Ruud Gullit, picking up a bad injury in the 4–1 home defeat by Liverpool.

He made his return a shade over three months later in the 0–0 draw against Manchester United at Old Trafford and, though he missed some games after that, was without doubt Newcastle's best player.

An industrious yet skilful midfielder, he formed an excellent partnership with Gary Speed, finding a team-mate with 86% of all his attempted passes and making 80 tackles.

But it was his form in front of goal which really shone. After scoring with a header in the 2–1 defeat at Southampton, he produced a fantastic equalizer in the 1–1 draw with Arsenal. Before the season's end he added two more excellent strikes, confirming his status as a major player on the Premiership stage.

APPEARANCES	
Start (sub)	22 (1)
Minutes on pitch	1786
GOAL ATTEMPTS	
Goals	4
PASSING	
Passes	1089
Passing accuracy	86%
DEFENDING	
Interceptions	21
Clearances	47
Tackles	80
Tackles won	50%
DISCIPLINE	
Fouls	39
Yellow cards	5
Red cards	1

H

Marlon HAREWOOD • 29
NOTTINGHAM FOREST • BORN: 25.8.79

APPEARANCES	
Start (sub)	11 (12)
Minutes on pitch	1139
GOAL ATTEMPTS	
Goals	1
Goals/shots ratio	4%
SHOOTING	
Shots on target	10
Shooting accuracy	38%
PASSING	
Goal assists	1
Passing accuracy	61%
DISCIPLINE	
Fouls	27
Offside	20
Yellow cards	5
Red cards	0

A key member of the Nottingham Forest youth side which won the Midland Melville League title in 1997, Marlon Harewood made the breakthrough to first-team football at the end of 1997–98 against West Bromwich Albion.

He made his Premiership bow in the first game of 1998–99 as a second-half substitute against Arsenal, but came to public attention in November in the televized match with Middlesbrough when he came off the bench to score the equalizer – his only goal for Forest.

Loaned to Ipswich mid-season to sharpen up his striking, he scored once for the Suffolk side, but returned to Forest's starting XI in March, ending the season at the City Ground.

His shooting definitely needs work – only 38% of his 26 shots in the Premiership forced a save – and though his goal was important, his goals-to-shots ratio of 4% was very poor.

However, time is on Harewood's side. Playing against First Division defences in 1999–2000 will provide him with the experience he needs to make a successful return to the Premiership.

AM John HARKES • 30
NOTTINGHAM FOREST • BORN: 8.3.67

When Ron Atkinson took over at Nottingham Forest in January 1999, one of his first moves was to take experienced wing-back John Harkes on loan from American Major League side DC United.

Harkes played his first game in the 1–0 victory against Everton at Goodison Park, putting in a reasonable performance, but it proved to one of only three games in which he played during Forest's doomed 1998–99 Carling Premiership campaign.

His second outing came in the 8–1 humiliation by Manchester United – a game in which, along with most of his team-mates, he looked severely out of his depth.

Harkes's final appearance came in the 2–1 defeat against one of his former clubs, West Ham United, in which he was replaced after 65 minutes.

The statistics make it clear that Harkes found it hard to make an impact at his third English Premiership club. He made very few passes, attempted just five tackles and managed one shot at goal.

FB Steve HARKNESS • 12
LIVERPOOL • BORN: 27.8.71

Given the murky history between them, it was obvious that sparks would fly when Steve Harkness came face to face with Stan Collymore at Villa Park.

But even Harkness must have been shocked by the tackle which his former team-mate made on him after just 10 minutes of the game had elapsed.

Harkness had to be stretchered off the field after that indisciplined lunge, and it was another month before he appeared again, as a last-minute substitute against Middlesbrough on Boxing Day.

He made just one appearance after that, performing well in a 0–0 draw against Arsenal before becoming one of the first victims of Gerard Houllier's clear-out in February. He was sold for £750,000 to Benfica, managed then by his old Liverpool boss Graham Souness.

The Portuguese giants got a solid professional for their money. A ball-playing defender in the best traditions of Liverpool, he completed 86% of his 101 attempted passes in 1998–99 and won 60% of his tackles.

AM Kevin HARPER • 11
DERBY COUNTY • BORN: 15.1.76

APPEARANCES	
Start (sub)	6 (21)
Minutes on pitch	862
GOAL ATTEMPTS	
Goals	1
Shots on target	2
Shooting accuracy	25%
PASSING	
Goal assists	1
Passing accuracy	71%
Crossing accuracy	19%
DRIBBLING	
Dribbles & runs	83
Dribble completion	58%
DISCIPLINE	
Yellow cards	1
Red cards	0

Signed from Hibernian, Scottish under-21 international Kevin Harper made a big impact in his first start in Derby's first team, scoring the opening goal in the 2–1 victory at Anfield.

At just 5'6" he is hardly the tallest of players but that goal, and the winner which he scored in the FA Cup fourth round against Swansea, both came with his head.

Most of his best work, however, was done on the ground. Jim Smith used him as a late substitute throughout the season, gambling on his pace to unhinge tired defences.

This did not always prove to be the case, but he certainly caused a few full-backs' hearts to flutter on the way to achieving a 58% success rate from 83 dribbles and runs.

Used as a winger in the truest sense of the word Harper did little defensively, preferring to concentrate on creating chances for his team-mates in the final third of the pitch.

Unfortunately he managed just one direct goal assist, and of the 31 crosses which he delivered just 19 found their target, a figure he will be aiming to improve on in 1999–2000.

G Steve HARPER • 13
NEWCASTLE UNITED • BORN: 3.2.74

Some high-profile mistakes by Republic of Ireland international Shay Given saw Ruud Gullit replace him for four of the final five Premiership games of the 1998–99 season with Steve Harper.

Harper, who has been at Newcastle since 1993 but has spent the majority of his career on loan to lower-division clubs, had impressed earlier in the season with some good displays – particularly in the 2–2 draw at Middlesbrough and the 0–0 stalemate with Blackburn Rovers.

He proved himself a capable 'keeper with some good saves, but lacked a little confidence in the air, dropping three catches and finishing with a low success rate of 88%.

Surprisingly selected for the FA Cup final, Harper did not have a good game against Manchester United.

There were question marks raised over his positioning for the treble-winners' second goal and he fumbled the ball once, leaving Nikos Dabizas to save his blushes with a goal-line clearance.

CB Craig HARRISON • 21
MIDDLESBROUGH • BORN: 10.11.77

Middlesbrough's Young Player of the Year for 1997–98, Craig Harrison started the first two games of the 1998–99 Carling Premiership season but lost his place in the starting XI to Colin Cooper soon afterwards.

Harrison made 20 appearances in the club's promotion charge, but despite this it was felt he needed more experience at a lower level before becoming a regular in Boro's Premiership first team.

To this effect Harrison was loaned out in the New Year to Preston North End where he performed well before returning to the Middlesbrough side as a last-minute substitute in February's 3–1 defeat by Sheffield Wednesday at Hillsborough. His final appearance came in the 0–0 draw with Blackburn Rovers at Ewood Park.

His tackle success rate of 20% and pass completion rate of 59% both need working on, but Harrison completed the bulk of his defensive duties well and he will hope to make more appearances in the 1999–2000 Premiership season.

FB Ian HARTE • 20
LEEDS UNITED • BORN: 31.8.77

APPEARANCES	
Start (sub)	34 (1)
Minutes on pitch	3033
GOAL ATTEMPTS	
Goals	4
PASSING & CROSSING	
Passing	1380
Passing accuracy	71%
Crossing	179
Crossing accuracy	35%
DEFENDING	
Tackles	95
Tackles won	57%
DISCIPLINE	
Fouls	43
Yellow cards	7
Red cards	0

Ian Harte is fast turning into one of the Premiership's top full-backs. After an excellent season with Leeds United, he will be looking to enhance his reputation both at home and abroad in the 1999–2000 campaign.

With four Premiership goals to his name, he was the division's joint top-scoring full-back, even cracking a couple in with his wrong (right!) foot. He would have scored one more had a penalty against Arsenal not hit the bar.

He attempted 35 shots: another nine were blocked. He also used his cultured left boot to good effect by setting up five goals for team-mates. Harte was particularly adept at beating his man – doing so on 90% of occasions – and his 35% cross completion rate was better than many of his peers. His pass completion rate, though, was surprisingly low and is something David O'Leary will want him to work on.

Harte showed good strength in the challenge, winning 57% of tackles, and also made 269 defensive clearances. But though he committed only just over one foul per game, the young Irishman was booked seven times.

John HARTSON • 29
WIMBLEDON • BORN: 5.4.75

A bruising target man, John Hartson won just one honour in 1998–99 – Carling Opta's award for the Premiership's most persistent fouler.

Poor form on the pitch and an ugly training-ground bust-up with Eyal Berkovic off it saw him making headlines at West Ham for all the wrong reasons. Although a £7.5 million move to Wimbledon promised to resurrect his career, he scored just two goals for the Crazy Gang.

Doubts about his fitness prompted Joe Kinnear to place Hartson under the watchful eye of Daley Thompson. He showed signs of recovery towards the season's end, but his performances for his new club were sluggish.

His two goals from 20 shots for the Dons gave him a scoring ratio of one goal for every 10 efforts attempted – a slight improvement on his early-season form at West Ham but still some way behind the league's top strikers.

Cruelly taunted by his former fans in the 0–0 draw between Wimbledon and West Ham, Hartson will undoubtedly spend a lot of time working on his fitness in the summer and, hopefully, return to action a better player.

APPEARANCES	
Start (sub)	28 (3)
Minutes on pitch	2443
GOAL ATTEMPTS	
Goals	6
Goals/shots ratio	13%
SHOOTING	
Shots on target	25
Shooting accuracy	52%
PASSING	
Goal assists	3
Passing accuracy	61%
DISCIPLINE	
Fouls	106
Offside	37
Yellow cards	5
Red cards	0

Steven HASLAM • 35
SHEFFIELD WEDNESDAY • BORN: 6.9.79

Sheffield-born Steven Haslam made his Carling Premiership debut at the very end of the 1998–99 campaign, gaining a place in the starting line-ups at home to Liverpool and away to Charlton Athletic.

The versatile youngster can play in the midfield but was employed chiefly at the centre of the Owls' defence in the reserves.

Haslam has worked his way through the ranks at Hillsborough since signing trainee forms for Wednesday in September 1996. The commanding central defender led by example in the youth team, captaining the side during the 1997–98 season, before his promotion to the reserves.

The local lad was a central figure at the back for the second string and his displays typified the commitment and confidence that earned him his call-up to the England under-21 team.

Haslam made eight tackles and 42 passes in his two appearances. He showed his propensity to get forward with one on-target effort at goal.

Bruiser: John Hartson

Jimmy Floyd HASSELBAINK • 9
LEEDS UNITED • BORN: 27.3.72

Jerryl Floyd Hasselbaink, more commonly known as Jimmy, finished the season with 18 Premiership goals – the same number as Michael Owen and Dwight Yorke – at the top of the goalscoring charts.

Some were spectacular strikes – remember his piledriver at Highbury or the unstoppable effort at Aston Villa? – but he also scored a fair number from close range. His 18 strikes came from 56 shots on target; 50 more went wide and another 49 shots were blocked, as defences struggled to contain him. He also supplied 12 goal assists, and noticeably relished helping youngsters Harry Kewell and Alan Smith alongside him up front.

1998–99 was Jimmy's second season in the Premiership and he showed he has now adapted totally to the pace and physical nature of the game in England.

He completed 68% of his passes and 65% of his dribbles and runs, although his physical approach frequently failed to impress referees, as he committed 73 fouls and was shown the yellow card eight times in the league alone.

APPEARANCES	
Start (sub)	36 (0)
Minutes on pitch	3138
GOAL ATTEMPTS	
Goals	18
Goals/shots ratio	17%
SHOOTING	
Shots on target	56
Shooting accuracy	53%
PASSING	
Goal assists	12
Passing accuracy	68%
DISCIPLINE	
Fouls	73
Offside	50
Yellow cards	8
Red cards	0

H

Dutch of class: Jimmy Floyd Hasselbaink

Simon HAWORTH • 22
COVENTRY CITY • BORN: 30.3.77

Simon Haworth's stay in the top flight was decidedly short-lived. After signing from Cardiff City for £500,000 in June 1997, he made just five league starts. He was subsequently sold by Gordon Strachan to Nationwide Division Two club Wigan Athletic for £600,000 in October 1998.

Haworth played just 90 minutes in the Carling Premiership – and his memories of the match are unlikely to be happy, since City were spanked 5–1 at home by Newcastle.

But despite the Sky Blues' collective disappointments that day Haworth demonstrated good passing ability, with 78% of his 23 balls finding their intended target. That will be put to good use at Springfield Park, where Wigan are developing a reputation for good football.

Born in Cardiff, Haworth has represented his country at under-21, "B" and even senior level, and should prove to be a very useful acquisition for the Cheshire club as they look to build a decent side.

G Magnus HEDMAN • 1
COVENTRY CITY • BORN: 19.3.73

Magnus Hedman has firmly established himself as Coventry City's number one – and several clubs in need of a quality 'keeper have cast envious glances toward Highfield Road over the last two seasons.

The giant Swede's season started superbly, with a key role in his side's 2–1 win over cosmopolitan Championship contenders Chelsea. A month later he was in goal as Sweden beat England in the Euro 2000 qualifier by the same score.

Things have not gone so well since then, with the Sky Blues' defence proving so leaky that Hedman had more work to do than he would have liked.

He only kept seven clean sheets and conceded 48 goals, despite making 139 saves. Hedman was good with high balls, catching 97 crosses he came for and making 14 punches. His distribution was very good, with 33% of his 834 long kicks completed.

1999–2000 will be a big season for Hedman, who hopes to play in Euro 2000: he missed France 98 when Sweden failed to qualify.

APPEARANCES	
Start (sub)	36 (0)
Minutes on pitch	3240
SHOT STOPPING	
Goals conceded	48
Clean sheets	7
Saves	139
Saves/shots	74%
DISTRIBUTION	
Distribution	1055
Distribution %	46%
CATCHING	
Crosses caught	97
Crosses dropped	5
DISCIPLINE	
Yellow cards	2
Red cards	0

FB Vegard HEGGEM • 14
LIVERPOOL • BORN: 13.7.75

APPEARANCES	
Start (sub)	27 (2)
Minutes on pitch	2302
GOAL ATTEMPTS	
Goals	2
PASSING & CROSSING	
Passing	912
Passing accuracy	81%
Crossing	68
Crossing accuracy	26%
DEFENDING	
Tackles	96
Tackles won	51%
DISCIPLINE	
Fouls	18
Yellow cards	2
Red cards	0

Signed from Rosenborg for £3.5 million, Vegard Heggem was arguably one of Liverpool's best performers in 1998–99. His dashing displays on the flank were one of the highlights of a disappointing season.

An injury against Everton forced him out for the season's final month, but he was expected to survive Gerard Houllier's summer cull.

A fantastic goal in the 3–1 away win at Middlesbrough provided Heggem's most memorable moment, but there was plenty more to suggest he will be a key player in 1999–2000. He made 138 dribbles and runs, retaining possession 71% of the time, and delivered 68 crosses.

Happiest in attack, he was less successful defensively. He won just over half of his attempted challenges, but did complete well over 100 clearances and 20 interceptions.

Abandoning the wing-back system may mean installing Heggem as a wide midfielder. It would certainly be a shame if Houllier felt it necessary to exclude such a talented player from the team.

Stephane HENCHOZ • 6
CB BLACKBURN ROVERS • BORN: 7.9.74

Stylish Stephane Henchoz had a busy 1998–99 in the centre of Rovers' defence, making 34 league appearances. Only Callum Davidson figured more than the Swiss international, who made 387 clearances and blocked 35 shots as Rovers struggled to curb opposing forwards.

Given the pressure on him and his colleagues he did well to pick up only six bookings, but lacked Swiss timing in the challenge, winning a below-average 63% of his 124 tackles.

Henchoz topped the 1,000 pass mark and 77% of his balls reached their intended target. Bringing the ball out of defence, he completed a very impressive 94% of his dribbles and runs, demonstrating his composure on the ball. But he made only 18 in total, preferring to clear the ball from danger in less ceremonious fashion for most of the season.

His pace, allied to his aerial strength, made Henchoz one of the most under-rated defenders in the Premiership. Perhaps one of Blackburn's most reliable players in 1998–99, it was no surprise when Liverpool swooped in the close season.

H

APPEARANCES	
Start (sub)	33 (1)
Minutes on pitch	2884
GOAL ATTEMPTS	
Goals	0
DEFENDING	
Blocks	35
Headed clearances	217
Other clearances	170
Interceptions	34
Tackles won	78
PASSING	
Passing accuracy	77%
DISCIPLINE	
Fouls	40
Yellow cards	6
Red cards	0

Lee HENDRIE • 17
AM ASTON VILLA • BORN: 18.5.77

APPEARANCES	
Start (sub)	31 (1)
Minutes on pitch	2799
GOAL ATTEMPTS	
Goals	3
Shots on target	14
Shooting accuracy	41%
PASSING	
Goal assists	6
Passing accuracy	77%
Crossing accuracy	32%
DRIBBLING	
Dribbles & runs	113
Dribble completion	74%
DISCIPLINE	
Yellow cards	8
Red cards	0

Young Lee Hendrie's rise into football's upper echelons has been nothing short of meteoric.

Having made it into Villa's first team in 1997–98 – earning the club's Young Player of the Year award en route – Hendrie then earned his first England cap as a substitute against the Czech Republic at Wembley on November 18, almost capping his debut with a goal.

Over the season, Hendrie managed 49 attempts at goal, scoring the winning penalty against Newcastle in September, the consolation at Chelsea in December and the first goal in a 2–2 draw at Leicester in April.

He was also credited with six goal assists and completed 77% of his passes. His crossing accuracy was well above average, with 32% of his 102 centres finding a team-mate – and he got past his man successfully with almost three-quarters of his dribbles and runs.

Hendrie, cousin of the former Barnsley manager John, will hope to add to his England caps in 1999–2000, having failed to receive another call-up since the departure of Glenn Hoddle in February.

Emile HESKEY • 9
LEICESTER CITY • BORN: 11.1.78

Although Emile Heskey produced some excellent performances for Leicester City in 1998–99, he struggled to find the consistency to match his talent, scoring just six goals from a massive 75 shots in the Premiership.

Now a full England international, Heskey is strong enough to fashion a scoring chance for himself but needs to improve his shooting accuracy of 43% and goals-to-shots ratio of just 8%.

His forceful style is reflected both in the huge number of dribbles and runs he attempted in 1998–99 and the high number of fouls he conceded. This combination of pace and power made the ideal foil for the more incisive style of Tony Cottee – and Heskey is sure to improve further under the more experienced player's guidance in 1999–2000.

Scoring excellent goals against Tottenham, Manchester United and Arsenal in 1998–99, the former youth-teamer proved that he has the ability to put the wind up even the best of defences: the challenge now is to reproduce his best form on a more regular basis.

APPEARANCES	
Start (sub)	29 (1)
Minutes on pitch	2587
GOAL ATTEMPTS	
Goals	6
Goals/shots ratio	8%
SHOOTING	
Shots on target	32
Shooting accuracy	43%
PASSING	
Goal assists	3
Passing accuracy	65%
DISCIPLINE	
Fouls	76
Offside	40
Yellow cards	3
Red cards	0

Martin HIDEN • 21
LEEDS UNITED • BORN: 11.3.73

APPEARANCES	
Start (sub)	14 (0)
Minutes on pitch	1195
GOAL ATTEMPTS	
Goals	0
PASSING & CROSSING	
Passing	368
Passing accuracy	69%
Crossing	26
Crossing accuracy	19%
DEFENDING	
Tackles	34
Tackles won	74%
DISCIPLINE	
Fouls	11
Yellow cards	3
Red cards	0

Martin Hiden's season ended on an appalling Old Trafford pitch in the 3–2 defeat by Manchester United.

After initially expecting to be out for a month, his knee injury was diagnosed as cruciate ligament damage and he faced being out of action for up to a year.

Up to that point, the Austrian international had made a good impression at Elland Road since George Graham signed him from Rapid Vienna for £1.3 million in February 1998.

Hiden won 74% of his tackles and made 13 defensive clearances. His 69% pass completion rate was disappointing, as was his crossing – less than one in five centres found their mark. He did set up one goal, but did not trouble any Premiership 'keeper in his 14 games.

The full-back earned three yellow cards from just 11 fouls, but demonstrated his ability to read the game well with 23 interceptions.

Hiden will want to get fit as soon as possible so he can play a part in United's domestic and European campaigns in 1999–2000, as well as helping Austria qualify for Euro 2000.

Scott HILEY • 23
SOUTHAMPTON • BORN: 27.9.68

FB

Versatile full-back Scott Hiley was signed from Manchester City in summer 1998 and has proved a very useful acquisition for the Saints.

Although initially brought in as squad cover, injuries to several established players ensured Hiley featured regularly during the 1998–99 season. He was deployed in both left and right-back roles and proved to be one of Southampton's most consistent performers, as shown by his Carling Opta statistics.

Hiley's attacking play was particularly impressive, as he kept possession with 92% of his 71 dribbles and runs and achieved an exceptional 45% cross completion rate. But despite this yeoman service, he did not pick up any goal assists. Hiley's distribution was efficient, if not spectacular, with 72% of passes reaching their intended target.

If one criticism can be levelled against the defender, it is that he lacks tenacity. Though ready to make a challenge, he won the ball with only 53% of his tackles during the season. On the positive side, he committed just 16 fouls and picked up only two bookings.

APPEARANCES	
Start (sub)	27 (2)
Minutes on pitch	2373
GOAL ATTEMPTS	
Goals	0
PASSING & CROSSING	
Passing	908
Passing accuracy	72%
Crossing	76
Crossing accuracy	45%
DEFENDING	
Tackles	68
Tackles won	53%
DISCIPLINE	
Fouls	16
Yellow cards	2
Red cards	0

H

Andy HINCHCLIFFE • 20
SHEFFIELD WEDNESDAY • BORN: 5.2.69

FB

APPEARANCES	
Start (sub)	32 (0)
Minutes on pitch	2797
GOAL ATTEMPTS	
Goals	3
PASSING & CROSSING	
Passing	1431
Passing accuracy	79%
Crossing	144
Crossing accuracy	41%
DEFENDING	
Tackles	58
Tackles won	78%
DISCIPLINE	
Fouls	23
Yellow cards	4
Red cards	1

Wednesday's England international had a sound 1998–99 season, appearing in 32 of the club's 38 league games. This must have been particularly satisfying for a player whose career has been dogged by injury problems.

One of the Premiership's most skilful left-sided full-backs, Hinchcliffe made his England comeback early in the season and was the only member of the team to get a shot on target in the dire 0–0 draw with Bulgaria at Wembley.

That call-up was a reward for his excellent club form, which ultimately saw him score three goals and deliver almost 150 crosses into the opposition penalty area. Of these, 59 found a team-mate, enough to put him among the Premiership's 10 most accurate crossers.

He proved he was a fine defender with a 78% tackle success rate. But he really excelled when going forward, completing 89% of his attempted dribbles and runs and making 56% of his 1,431 passes in the opposition half.

The one blemish on Hinchcliffe's record was the dubious red card he received in the 4–0 defeat by Middlesbrough.

S **David HIRST • 27**
SOUTHAMPTON • BORN: 7.12.67

A freak pre-season injury picked up when he fell down a pot-hole put paid to David Hirst's season before it had even started.

He has frequently shown the same sort of carelessness in front of goal for Saints – but in 1998–99 he failed to register a single effort, either on or off target.

He did recover from his unfortunate spell out of the side sufficiently to make two brief substitute appearances at Aston Villa and Derby in the closing weeks of the season, but looked sluggish in his 23 minutes of action.

The Saints broke their record transfer fee when they bought Hirst for £2 million in October 1997. Although injury-prone throughout his career, he managed a trouble-free debut season for Southampton in 1997-88, scoring nine goals in 30 appearances.

Now aged 32, Hirst may have trouble rediscovering the form that earned him three England caps. But Saints will be keen to see a player of Hirst's quality back in action – and he will be in contention for a starting place if he can build on his fitness in the summer.

G **Shaka HISLOP • 12**
WEST HAM UNITED • BORN: 22.2.69

Net results: Shaka Hislop

APPEARANCES	
Start (sub)	37 (0)
Minutes on pitch	3301
SHOT STOPPING	
Goals conceded	50
Clean sheets	15
Saves	194
Saves/shots	80%
DISTRIBUTION	
Distribution	1252
Distribution %	55%
CATCHING	
Crosses caught	117
Crosses dropped	6
DISCIPLINE	
Yellow cards	0
Red cards	1

West Ham newcomer Shaka Hislop had an outstanding 1998–99 season, topping the Carling Opta goalkeepers' Index several times.

Despite the Hammers' surprisingly poor goal difference of minus seven, Hislop made 194 saves, with only Wimbledon's Neil Sullivan called into action on more occasions.

Unsurprisingly for one of the Premiership's tallest players, Hislop had a 95% catch success rate, though he did drop six crosses.

Shaka will be pleased with the 15 clean sheets he managed in 1998–99, but slightly disappointed to have been beaten 50 times.

There were some blots on his campaign. Amid the mayhem of West Ham's 5–1 home defeat by Leeds, Hislop was one of three players sent off after lunging at Jimmy Floyd Hasselbaink with the score at only 2–1. On seven separate occasions he was beaten four times or more in a match.

Harry Redknapp admitted signing him was a gamble, but after Hislop won the club's Player of the Year award, Redknapp can safely say it was a gamble worth taking.

G · Kevin HITCHCOCK · 13
CHELSEA · BORN: 5.10.62

A loyal Chelsea servant for more than 11 years, Kevin Hitchcock was once more on hand to come to the Blues' rescue in their hour of need.

Third-choice goalkeeper behind Ed De Goey and Dmitri Kharine for most of the season, he was thrust into the limelight on April 3 when an injury to De Goey saw Hitchcock come on as a half-time substitute.

Three weeks later he was once again called into action, this time as a starter in a dour 0–0 draw against Sheffield Wednesday at Hillsborough.

His final appearance came away to Tottenham Hotspur on May 10, a match in which he conceded two goals in an entertaining 2–2 draw.

Needing to make just a handful of saves across the season, he finished his short spell in the first team with a less than spectacular saves-to-shots ratio of 67%. More impressive was his performance from opposition crosses – he caught or punched every centre which he came off his line to deal with.

M · Glyn HODGES · 20
NOTTINGHAM FOREST · BORN: 30.4.63

Veteran midfielder Glyn Hodges failed to figure in any of Forest's Division One games after signing in February 1998, and could hardly have expected to play too many Premiership games after the club secured promotion.

But Forest's boss at the start of the season, Dave Bassett, who managed Hodges at Sheffield United, was well aware of the experience Hodges could bring to his side and he started Forest's first three games of the 1998–99 campaign.

In his 291 minutes of league football he fired in three shots and completed 69% of his passes, as well as a third of his 27 crosses and 58% of his 12 tackles.

He also made substitute appearances against Charlton and at Old Trafford against Manchester United, but failed to figure under new boss Ron Atkinson and must now believe his top-flight football days are over.

Hodges has had a varied career playing with Wimbledon, Newcastle United, Watford, Crystal Palace, Sheffield United, Derby County and Hull City before his spell at the City Ground.

CB · Jon-Olav HJELDE · 6
NOTTINGHAM FOREST · BORN: 30.7.72

From Champions League to English first division to Premiership; it has been an eventful few seasons for Jon-Olav Hjelde. Signed from Rosenborg for £600,000 on the eve of the 1997–98 season, Hjelde proved a reliable deputy for Colin Cooper during his first year in English football.

With Cooper's departure to Middlesbrough at the start of the 1998–99 season Hjelde was installed as first-choice centre-back at the City Ground alongside Steve Chettle and, despite Forest's relegation, he produced some good performances.

A tall, athletic player, he used his height to good effect, making 121 of his 186 clearances with his head. He also made 28 interceptions, 17 blocks, and won 70% of his tackles – a figure above the Premiership average and better than any of Forest's other regular defenders. His distribution was also effective and while playing up front he scored one goal.

Injury, coupled with the arrival of Richard Gough later in the season, restricted him to just 15 starting appearances and one as substitute. But he reappeared in the first team in the game against Aston Villa in April when, after Forest lost 2–0, he experienced the pain of relegation.

APPEARANCES	
Start (sub)	16 (1)
Minutes on pitch	1411
GOAL ATTEMPTS	
Goals	1
DEFENDING	
Blocks	17
Headed clearances	121
Other clearances	65
Interceptions	28
Tackles won	47
PASSING	
Passing accuracy	79%
DISCIPLINE	
Fouls	16
Yellow cards	3
Red cards	0

M Lee HODGES • 25
WEST HAM UNITED • BORN: 2.3.78

A member of West Ham's acclaimed title-winning South-East Counties team, Lee Hodges made several appearances as a substitute in the 1997–98 season – but was limited to just one brief outing of five minutes in the 1998–99 FA Carling Premiership season.

That appearance came in October's disastrous game against Blackburn Rovers when, with the team already 3–0 down, Harry Redknapp brought him on to try and help them grab a consolation.

He failed to do that, but the club still cherish high hopes for a player who has competed for England at schoolboy level and is seen by some as a long-term replacement for the gifted Israeli playmaker Eyal Berkovic in West Ham's midfield.

Born and bred in East London, former YTS trainee Hodges would be a popular member of the team if he were to make it.

He will be hoping for a few more opportunities to shine in season 1999–2000 and show the Hammers faithful what he can really do.

S Gavin HOLLIGAN • 40
WEST HAM UNITED • BORN: 13.6.80

A promising young midfielder signed from non-league Kingstonian, Gavin Holligan made a brief appearance as an 80th-minute substitute for Joe Cole in West Ham United's exciting 2–2 Carling Premiership draw at Liverpool.

Part of Holligan's transfer agreement stipulated that he would be allowed to stay at Kingstonian until the side completed their heroic FA Cup run, a clause Harry Redknapp was happy to honour.

The youngster's pace caused the Liverpool defence real problems and he almost grabbed a dramatic winner on his debut. Charging down the right-hand side he beat the full-back, advanced into the penalty area and hit a low drive which goalkeeper David James did well to save.

Surprisingly, he was not involved in the first-team set-up after that game, but the skill and energy he showed make him a potential star of the future. Holligan definitely qualifies as one to watch in the new millennium as West Ham build on 1998–99's success.

M David HOPKIN • 12
LEEDS UNITED • BORN: 21.8.70

APPEARANCES	
Start (sub)	32 (2)
Minutes on pitch	2835
GOAL ATTEMPTS	
Goals	4
PASSING	
Passes	1236
Passing accuracy	79%
DEFENDING	
Interceptions	27
Clearances	60
Tackles	111
Tackles won	67%
DISCIPLINE	
Fouls	40
Yellow cards	6
Red cards	0

David Hopkin made his name firstly as a youngster at Chelsea and then at Crystal Palace, before joining Leeds United at the end of the 1996–97 season.

Although not always a regular at Elland Road, Hopkin has done a good job wherever he has been asked to play across the midfield.

Season 1998–99 saw him feature in 34 of Leeds' league games, as they impressed many neutral fans on their way to winning "the other league" below the top three.

Hopkin scored four Premiership goals from 13 shots on target and hit 15 more wide. He also contributed five goal assists during the campaign, which Leeds finished as third-top scorers in the league with 62.

The Scot found a team-mate with 79% of his 1,236 passes and also completed 76% of all the dribbles and runs he attempted. He was tenacious in the tackle too, winning two-thirds of his challenges, and weighed in with 60 important defensive clearances.

Hopkin's total of 40 fouls and six bookings were blots on an otherwise excellent season.

G Russell HOULT • 1
DERBY COUNTY • BORN: 22.11.72

Russell Hoult did not expect to be Derby County's first-choice goalkeeper at the start of the 1998–99 season – but a virus which struck down Estonian international Mart Poom gave the £300,000 signing from Leicester City his chance and he took it well.

Hoult kept his place until a nasty neck injury forced him off in the 2–2 draw against rivals Nottingham Forest in November. He returned in January, keeping a clean sheet in the 1–0 victory at Sheffield Wednesday. In total he made 23 Premiership appearances.

A solid shot-stopper with good skills in the air, Hoult made a total of 77 saves, conceding an average of one goal every 70 minutes and keeping five clean sheets. He caught most of the crosses that he came for, ending the season with a catch success rate of 95%.

Injuries aside, the 1998–99 season was a good one for the reliable Hoult. He seems to have convinced manager Jim Smith of his abilities and will be looking forward to once again vying with Poom for the number one position in 1999–2000.

APPEARANCES	
Start (sub)	23 (0)
Minutes on pitch	2019
SHOT STOPPING	
Goals conceded	29
Clean sheets	5
Saves	77
Saves/shots	73%
DISTRIBUTION	
Distribution	657
Distribution %	47%
CATCHING	
Crosses caught	89
Crosses dropped	5
DISCIPLINE	
Yellow cards	2
Red cards	1

M David HOWELLS • 11
SOUTHAMPTON • BORN: 15.12.67

APPEARANCES	
Start (sub)	8 (1)
Minutes on pitch	641
GOAL ATTEMPTS	
Goals	1
PASSING	
Passes	260
Passing accuracy	75%
DEFENDING	
Interceptions	6
Clearances	13
Tackles	18
Tackles won	67%
DISCIPLINE	
Fouls	9
Yellow cards	1
Red cards	0

Whether or not he enjoys the challenge of a relegation battle, David Howells has found himself in three of them in just two seasons.

First the experienced midfielder helped Spurs survive the drop in 1997–98; then he was transferred to Southampton, who spent almost the entire season in the bottom three.

Finally, on transfer deadline day, Howells was sent on loan to First Division strugglers Bristol City – but though he helped inspire a brief renaissance at Ashton Gate, City went down.

While at the Dell, Howells's finest hour came at Highbury on October 17, 1998. The former Spurs man gleefully upset old rivals Arsenal's title defence with a shock equalizer in a 1–1 draw – one of 11 shots during his season.

He also completed three-quarters of his passes and won two-thirds of his challenges as Saints bravely fought the drop. But as he departed from the Dell, Birmingham's Chris Marsden came in and made an immediate impact, scoring two vital goals. So question marks clearly remain over Howells's long-term future at Southampton.

CB   **Steve HOWEY • 6**
NEWCASTLE UNITED • BORN: 26.10.71

Converted from a striker to a centre-back in the early 1990s, Steve Howey impressed Ruud Gullit so much that the Dutchman persuaded him to sign a new contract in 1999.

Unfortunately, injury disrupted Howey's season and he did not play a game in the Premiership until the end of November. Hugely impressive for the next 14 games, he picked up yet another knock in the away fixture with Nottingham Forest; and although he returned for the FA Cup semi-final with Spurs, he was forced out of that game as well.

His enforced absence was a blow for Newcastle. Howey won 84% of his challenges, and their defence at times looked woefully short of class without him.

Given an extended run in the side, Howey could well add to his collection of four England caps. His pass completion rate of 82% shows he is comfortable enough on the ball to make it on the world stage. The fact he only conceded 10 fouls gives some indication of his composure and suggests his old boss Kevin Keegan may well want to make use of him.

APPEARANCES	
Start (sub)	14 (0)
Minutes on pitch	1191
GOAL ATTEMPTS	
Goals	0
DEFENDING	
Blocks	26
Headed clearances	114
Other clearances	76
Interceptions	26
Tackles won	27
PASSING	
Passing accuracy	82%
DISCIPLINE	
Fouls	10
Yellow cards	1
Red cards	0

 S   **Darren HUCKERBY • 7**
COVENTRY CITY • BORN: 23.4.76

APPEARANCES	
Start (sub)	31 (3)
Minutes on pitch	2736
GOAL ATTEMPTS	
Goals	9
Goals/shots ratio	14%
SHOOTING	
Shots on target	28
Shooting accuracy	44%
PASSING	
Goal assists	3
Passing accuracy	65%
DISCIPLINE	
Fouls	57
Offside	98
Yellow cards	7
Red cards	0

The lightning-quick Darren Huckerby had a reasonable 1998–99 season, but continues to be plagued by inconsistency.

At times, the Nottingham-born striker can trouble the best defenders in the land. But in other matches he can drift out of the game – or spend the afternoon making referees' assistants look as if they are giving semaphore demonstrations. In fact Huckerby was caught offside more than any other Premiership player, which seems unnecessary given he has the pace to escape even the fleetest of foot.

He scored nine league goals in 1998–99 from 28 shots on target. Another 36 flew high or wide and 15 were blocked by defenders. Huckerby only contributed three assists, and his 65% pass completion rate was very poor. Even worse was his cross completion rate of just 18%, although he retained possession with 54% of his dribbles and runs.

Highlight of his season was a hat-trick against Notts Forest but given City's struggles, manager Gordon Strachan will want to get more out of the youngster on a regular basis.

Aaron HUGHES • 28
NEWCASTLE UNITED • BORN: 8.11.79

CB

An exciting young defender, Aaron Hughes made his Newcastle debut at – of all places– the Nou Camp in Barcelona in a 1997–98 Champions League tie.

A former member of Newcastle's Junior and Reserve sides, he first came to public attention later in the same season when, in a Coca-Cola Cup clash with Liverpool, he was asked to mark Steve McManaman.

Already capped by Northern Ireland, Hughes is most at home in a centre-back role but can also play at left-back. In 1998–99 he stood in for various players in the Newcastle defence.

Comfortable on the ball, he will have impressed Ruud Gullit with his distribution, completing 81% of his attempted passes. But the manager will also have been happy with his tackling and his low number of fouls.

Confined mostly to his own half, Hughes also has the potential to be a threat further forward. His 89% success rate from nine dribbles and runs and 43% completion rate from seven crosses suggest that, given the chance, he could make an excellent wing-back.

APPEARANCES	
Start (sub)	12 (2)
Minutes on pitch	1100
GOAL ATTEMPTS	
Goals	0
DEFENDING	
Blocks	13
Headed clearances	85
Other clearances	48
Interceptions	12
Tackles won	24
PASSING	
Passing accuracy	81%
DISCIPLINE	
Fouls	9
Yellow cards	1
Red cards	0

H

Ceri HUGHES • 7
WIMBLEDON • BORN: 26.2.71

M

APPEARANCES	
Start (sub)	8 (6)
Minutes on pitch	829
GOAL ATTEMPTS	
Goals	0
PASSING	
Passes	271
Passing accuracy	69%
DEFENDING	
Interceptions	8
Clearances	31
Tackles	37
Tackles won	51%
DISCIPLINE	
Fouls	21
Yellow cards	5
Red cards	0

One of Wimbledon's few reliable performers in their end-of-season collapse, Ceri Hughes was probably the only player at Selhurst Park who was not happy to see the back of 1998–99.

The Welsh international broke into the first team after spending much of the campaign on the treatment table, and appeared in 14 of the club's final 21 games, including a run of six starts between April and early May.

Signed from Luton Town for £400,000 in July 1997, Hughes has had few opportunities to impress the Wimbledon faithful and seized his chance eagerly.

In total he played 829 minutes of league football, setting up one goal. The best feature of his play was undoubtedly his crossing, but he also tested opposition goalkeepers with four accurate shots and completed 69% of all attempted passes.

A skilful player who is not afraid to compete, Hughes also made 37 tackles and was booked five times in the Premiership. Cautions aside, he will hope he showed enough in 1998–99 to become a more frequent starter in 1999–2000.

David HUGHES • 22
SOUTHAMPTON • BORN: 30.12.72

Welsh international midfielder David Hughes has been on Southampton's books since July 1991. He showed promise as a youngster, scoring several from midfield, but failed to establish himself as a first-team regular.

Hughes has been dogged by a series of injuries throughout his Saints career. Having suffered a long lay-off with a serious back problem, he played only 550 minutes of Premiership football during season 1998–99.

This tenacious and lively midfielder did a good fill-in job in his brief appearances, tracking runners and closing down space. A committed Saint, he put in some solid tackles, winning the ball with 71% of his challenges.

His distribution left much to be desired, however, with only 72% of his passes finding their intended target.

He has shown a lot of grit to come back from his injury nightmares, but doubts remain about his long-term future at Southampton. There is much competition for midfield places at the Dell, but Hughes must be hoping for a longer run in 1999–2000.

APPEARANCES

Start (sub)	6 (3)
Minutes on pitch	550

GOAL ATTEMPTS

Goals	0

PASSING

Passes	199
Passing accuracy	72%

DEFENDING

Interceptions	2
Clearances	18
Tackles	24
Tackles won	71%

DISCIPLINE

Fouls	11
Yellow cards	1
Red cards	0

 Mark HUGHES • 9
SOUTHAMPTON • BORN: 1.11.63

APPEARANCES

Start (sub)	32 (0)
Minutes on pitch	2779

GOAL ATTEMPTS

Goals	1
Goals/shots ratio	2%

SHOOTING

Shots on target	15
Shooting accuracy	27%

PASSING

Goal assists	1
Passing accuracy	80%

DISCIPLINE

Fouls	83
Offside	16
Yellow cards	14
Red cards	0

Having spent most of his career picking up silverware, Mark Hughes saw the other side of the game battling relegation with the Saints.

After a barren spell up front early in the season, goal-poacher Hughes was switched to central midfield but found it hard to adjust.

His ineffectiveness in this role quickly led to frustration and indiscipline. The Welshman picked up 14 Premiership bookings and a date before the FA disciplinary committee. With his collection of yellow cards and 83 fouls to his name, Hughes finished top of Carling Opta's player indiscipline chart.

In the final months of 1998–99, Hughes was instrumental in preserving Southampton's Premiership status. Despite the referee's watchful eye, he did not shrink from a single tackle – and finally broke his duck after more than 48 hours on the pitch in all competitions, scoring against Blackburn at the Dell in April.

Dave Jones stuck by his signing throughout, praising him for his attitude and commitment. Hughes has said he would be happy to see out the remaining year of his contract at the Dell.

Michael HUGHES • 16
WIMBLEDON • BORN: 2.8.71

A real favourite with the fans, Michael Hughes is arguably the Dons' most gifted footballer. Snapped up from West Ham in an £800,000 deal in September 1997, he finished his first season as the supporters' Player of the Year.

The 1998–99 season saw him continue where he left off in the previous campaign, with an assist in the opening-day defeat of Spurs at Selhurst Park. In all, he set up six Premiership goals for team-mates and scored two himself.

Jinking his way to the by-line with almost 100 successful dribbles and runs, he delivered a steady stream of crosses into the opposition box, connecting with a team-mate's head 33% of the time. This was a good enough rate to put him at number 18 in Carling Opta's top 20 best Premiership crossers.

An established international with Northern Ireland, Hughes's game is not all about flair. As with all Wimbledon's players he did his fair share of tackling back, winning possession with a fraction under 60% of all attempted challenges and chipping in with 30 clearances in his own penalty area.

APPEARANCES	
Start (sub)	28 (2)
Minutes on pitch	2397
GOAL ATTEMPTS	
Goals	2
Shots on target	9
Shooting accuracy	26%
PASSING	
Goal assists	6
Passing accuracy	79%
Crossing accuracy	33%
DRIBBLING	
Dribbles & runs	131
Dribble completion	75%
DISCIPLINE	
Yellow cards	7
Red cards	0

H

Stephen HUGHES • 16
ARSENAL • BORN: 18.9.76

APPEARANCES	
Start (sub)	4 (10)
Minutes on pitch	626
GOAL ATTEMPTS	
Goals	1
PASSING	
Passes	349
Passing accuracy	85%
DEFENDING	
Interceptions	8
Clearances	19
Tackles	29
Tackles won	72%
DISCIPLINE	
Fouls	13
Yellow cards	2
Red cards	0

A great young prospect at Highbury, 22-year-old Stephen Hughes has found it hard to break into the Arsenal midfield and has made the majority of his appearances from the bench.

Hughes's Carling Opta stats show what a good player he is becoming. An 85% pass completion rate included two goal assists, and his bobbling long-range daisy-cutter earned Arsenal a 1–1 draw at Leicester City in September. He also played a major part in the following week's defeat of Manchester United.

His dribble completion rate of 75% showed he was capable of beating opponents with skill and pace. He can also supply quality crosses from wide as his 30% completion rate showed.

Hughes's defensive qualities were also very impressive. As well as winning almost 75% of challenges he made 19 defensive clearances and eight interceptions and blocked one shot.

If Hughes were to leave Highbury due to his lack of first-team chances, there would be no shortage of takers for the former under-21 international, potentially a real threat from a central or wide midfield position.

Ritchie HUMPHREYS • 16
SHEFFIELD WEDNESDAY • BORN: 30.11.77

"Prolific" is not a word you would use to describe Sheffield Wednesday frontman Ritchie Humphreys. Prior to 1999–2000, he managed just eight goals from 72 appearances in all competitions in an Owls shirt.

He sometimes showed flashes of the brilliant form seen in his Premiership debut in 1996–97, when he scored three goals in his first four games. In the 1998–99 FA Cup win over Norwich he bagged a fine brace and scored again two weeks later in Wednesday's 4–0 league victory at West Ham United.

That was his only league goal of the season, in which his overall shooting accuracy was just 32%. But he is always at his best dropping deep and running at defenders, as can be seen by his 87% dribble completion rate.

With the transfer deadline day signing of York City top-scorer Richard Cresswell, Humphreys's days at Hillsborough under Danny Wilson now appear to be numbered; and West Bromwich Albion were reported to have shown an interest in the young frontman, valued at around £500,000 by the Owls.

APPEARANCES	
Start (sub)	10 (9)
Minutes on pitch	929
GOAL ATTEMPTS	
Goals	1
Goals/shots ratio	5%
SHOOTING	
Shots on target	7
Shooting accuracy	32%
PASSING	
Goal assists	0
Passing accuracy	78%
DISCIPLINE	
Fouls	12
Offside	14
Yellow cards	1
Red cards	0

Andy HUNT • 9
CHARLTON ATHLETIC • BORN: 9.6.70

APPEARANCES	
Start (sub)	32 (2)
Minutes on pitch	2634
GOAL ATTEMPTS	
Goals	7
Goals/shots ratio	13%
SHOOTING	
Shots on target	31
Shooting accuracy	56%
PASSING	
Goal assists	2
Passing accuracy	71%
DISCIPLINE	
Fouls	64
Offside	29
Yellow cards	3
Red cards	0

Andy Hunt was Charlton's first-choice target man in 1998–99, with 32 Premiership starts to his credit. The former West Bromwich Albion striker performed reasonably well in his role, but although he was regularly in the hunt for goals, he found scoring in the Premiership much harder than he had in Division One.

He hit 31 shots on target during the season, netting seven times in the league to finish second in Charlton's top scorers' list – one behind his strike partner Clive Mendonca. He also saw 11 of his shots blocked.

As the Addicks' defence regularly came under pressure Hunt often saw little of the ball, but his work-rate and commitment were his biggest attributes in 1998–99 and he won 55% of his 49 challenges. His defensive skills were often called upon and he made 22 clearances, two blocks and 10 interceptions. His eagerness to win the ball led to 64 fouls and three bookings in a frustrating season.

Hunt worked extremely hard for the team and proved to be one of their most consistent players in the 1998–99 campaign.

Jonathan HUNT • 26
DERBY COUNTY • BORN: 2.11.71

Originally a regular first-teamer at Derby County, Camden-born Jonathan Hunt was loaned out by Jim Smith to Ipswich Town in October 1998.

He moved to cash-strapped Sheffield United with fellow Ram Robert Kozluk, as part of the permanent deal which took Greek wide man Vassilis Borbokis to Pride Park in the opposite direction.

A mobile, creative midfielder with an eye for goal, Hunt found himself plunging down the pecking order behind the likes of Stefano Eranio, Lars Bohinen and Francesco Baiano. As a result he played only 71 minutes of Carling Premiership football during Derby's 1998–99 campaign.

The £500,000 signing from Birmingham City completed 71% of his 35 passes and a third of his dribbles and runs. He left Derby with a strike rate of one shot on target and one goal during his final season.

Defensively, he performed well, winning all five of his tackles and making three clearances and one block.

Graham HYDE • 12
SHEFFIELD WEDNESDAY • BORN: 10.11.70

After almost 11 years at Sheffield Wednesday, Graham Hyde moved on to Trevor Francis's Birmingham City in February 1999. It was under Francis's four-year reign at Hillsborough that Hyde had enjoyed his best form, appearing as a substitute in both the League and FA Cup finals of 1993.

He played just 18 minutes as a substitute against Tottenham Hotspur under Danny Wilson in the 1998–99 Premiership campaign. In that short time he made three successful passes and a couple of challenges. After such a minor contribution to the squad it became clear Hyde's long-term future did not lie at the club, and the move to Birmingham was good business for all parties.

A reliable and workmanlike player with good passing ability and strong ball-winning skills, Hyde rarely received the recognition that his effort deserved outside of Sheffield. He was a well-respected figure at Hillsborough, however, and will prove a real asset to his new club as they seek to finally make it back to the big-time.

Don HUTCHISON • 10
EVERTON • BORN: 9.5.71

Don Hutchison began the 1998–99 season twiddling his thumbs on the Everton bench. He ended it on a high, scoring the goal which gave Scotland a remarkable 1–0 victory over Germany.

The improbable path from possible starter to international giant-killer began in less than spectacular fashion when he came on as a substitute against Aston Villa and was booked. His performances in the following months, when he scored three goals and set up seven more for his struggling team-mates, made him the first name on both Walter Smith's and Craig Brown's team-sheets.

Whether playing in a central midfield role or as an emergency striker, he rarely gave any less than his maximum.

Finishing the season in Carling Opta's top 20 lists for both tackling and assists, he made contributions at both ends of the pitch. As Everton's regular corner-taker he delivered 160 centres into the box but was also in action in his own penalty area, clearing the ball 64 times from danger.

The one question mark over his season came with a poor disciplinary record which, in common with those of a number of his team-mates, was not very good.

APPEARANCES	
Start (sub)	29 (4)
Minutes on pitch	2549
GOAL ATTEMPTS	
Goals	3
PASSING	
Passes	1386
Passing accuracy	74%
DEFENDING	
Interceptions	17
Clearances	64
Tackles	154
Tackles won	62%
DISCIPLINE	
Fouls	56
Yellow cards	9
Red cards	1

Sasa ILIC • 1
CHARLTON ATHLETIC • BORN: 18.7.72

Signed from non-league football in 1997, Sasa Ilic made a name for himself in the 1997–98 Wembley play-off final against Sunderland, saving Michael Gray's penalty in the shoot-out to send Charlton into the Premiership.

Ilic started the season as first-choice goalkeeper, playing 20 of the season's first 21 games. But a string of demoralizing individual errors led Alan Curbishley to drop him in January 1999 in favour of Simon Royce.

His form was also affected by the war in Kosovo, and he was regularly seen in the press protesting along with other British-based internationals from the Balkans.

He conceded 33 goals in his 23 Premiership appearances, kept only five clean sheets and made more than 75 saves, saving a below-average 70% of all the shots he faced.

Ilic's short kicks and throws were particularly disappointing and he finished the season with a poor 83% success rate.

But his longer kicks were fairly accurate, with more than a third reaching a Charlton player.

APPEARANCES	
Start (sub)	23 (0)
Minutes on pitch	1979
SHOT STOPPING	
Goals conceded	33
Clean sheets	5
Saves	78
Saves/shots	70%
DISTRIBUTION	
Distribution	702
Distribution %	43%
CATCHING	
Crosses caught	69
Crosses dropped	4
DISCIPLINE	
Yellow cards	1
Red cards	0

Andy IMPEY • 24
LEICESTER CITY • BORN: 13.9.71

APPEARANCES	
Start (sub)	23 (3)
Minutes on pitch	2074
GOAL ATTEMPTS	
Goals	0
Shots on target	3
Shooting accuracy	30%
PASSING	
Goal assists	1
Passing accuracy	80%
Crossing accuracy	24%
DRIBBLING	
Dribbles & runs	91
Dribble completion	71%
DISCIPLINE	
Yellow cards	2
Red cards	0

Andrew Impey was the subject of one of the 1998–99 season's most controversial transfers.

Manager Harry Redknapp was outraged at the former QPR player's sale to Leicester City, apparently behind his back. A need to balance the books took priority for the board and Redknapp found himself questioning the ambition of a club prepared to sell players without the manager's knowledge.

But Impey, who had only featured in eight West Ham games, relished the chance to get his career back on track. His pass completion rate immediately improved from 77% to 81%, his dribbling from 61% to 74% and suddenly he was getting far enough forward to shoot, although his 30% accuracy was well below par.

Impey avoided any cards at Filbert Street – his only two came while at West Ham – and maintained his tackle success rate of 55% across his time at both clubs.

The former England under-21 international weighed in with 115 defensive clearances during the season, but has yet to fulfil the early promise of his career at Loftus Road.

Paul INCE • 17
LIVERPOOL • BORN: 21.10.67

Paul Ince endured a difficult 1998–99 season with Liverpool. The Reds were Premiership also-rans and Ince in particular was singled out for criticism. Dismissals in the UEFA Cup against Valencia and for England in Sweden served to sustain the pressure on him from all quarters.

He battled on, but idle boasts that he and Jamie Redknapp were the best midfield pairing in the Premiership did not endear the self-styled "Guv'nor" to his critics.

Ince seemed to have finished the season in style, though, with a late goal that almost sent his old club Manchester United's title chase off the rails – sweet revenge for the man dubbed a "Big Time Charlie" by Alex Ferguson. But he was then dropped by Kevin Keegan for the England squad.

He scored six goals and completed 84% of his passes and 73% of his dribbles and runs. And, as you would expect, he was excellent in the tackle, winning 69% of his challenges. But he also picked up nine yellow cards in the league alone.

APPEARANCES	
Start (sub)	34 (0)
Minutes on pitch	3001
GOAL ATTEMPTS	
Goals	6
PASSING	
Passes	1599
Passing accuracy	84%
DEFENDING	
Interceptions	34
Clearances	107
Tackles	147
Tackles won	69%
DISCIPLINE	
Fouls	49
Yellow cards	9
Red cards	0

Denis IRWIN • 3
MANCHESTER UNITED • BORN: 31.10.65

APPEARANCES	
Start (sub)	26 (3)
Minutes on pitch	2288
GOAL ATTEMPTS	
Goals	2
PASSING & CROSSING	
Passing	1145
Passing accuracy	82%
Crossing	35
Crossing accuracy	26%
DEFENDING	
Tackles	105
Tackles won	63%
DISCIPLINE	
Fouls	20
Yellow cards	2
Red cards	1

Possibly the most unassuming player in the Premiership, Denis Irwin was involved in one of the most controversial and high-profile incidents of the season.

With Manchester United leading 2–1 at Anfield, Denis Irwin earned a second yellow card for kicking the ball away and was sent off. United drew the game after a late equalizer and vented their fury at the referee. Chairman Martin Edwards even made the extraordinary claim that if Arsenal or Chelsea were to win the title, they should strike referee David Elleray a championship medal.

The resulting suspension cost Irwin his FA Cup final place, but he did feature in the Champions League-winning side and collected his fifth Premiership title medal too.

Irwin was reliable as ever, completing 82% of his passes, 81% of his dribbles and runs and winning 63% of the 105 tackles he made.

The red card was totally out of character. The Irishman committed just 20 fouls in the Premiership all season and picked up just two other bookings.

Steffen IVERSEN • 18
TOTTENHAM HOTSPUR • BORN: 10.11.76

Steffen Iversen is starting to fulfil the potential which convinced Spurs to fight off top European clubs to sign him for £2.7 million from Norway's Rosenborg – and he has a winner's medal to show for his efforts.

He scored nine Premiership goals from 33 shots on target, but matched that figure with efforts that went high or wide. Iversen also scored the vital goal that defeated Wimbledon in the second leg of the Worthington Cup semi-final.

His other Premiership statistics were less impressive. A pass completion rate of 64% and dribble success of 56% were below average for his position, but after being in and out of the side he is still coming to terms with the rigours of Premiership football.

With Chris Armstrong and Les Ferdinand competing with him for just two – or sometimes only one – spot up front, and the likelihood of new signings by George Graham to bolster the squad, 1999–2000 will prove to be a very important season for Iversen's future at White Hart Lane.

APPEARANCES	
Start (sub)	22 (5)
Minutes on pitch	1994
GOAL ATTEMPTS	
Goals	9
Goals/shots ratio	14%
SHOOTING	
Shots on target	33
Shooting accuracy	50%
PASSING	
Goal assists	1
Passing accuracy	64%
DISCIPLINE	
Fouls	22
Offside	11
Yellow cards	1
Red cards	0

Muzzy IZZET • 6
LEICESTER CITY • BORN: 31.10.74

APPEARANCES	
Start (sub)	31 (0)
Minutes on pitch	2688
GOAL ATTEMPTS	
Goals	5
PASSING	
Passes	1045
Passing accuracy	81%
DEFENDING	
Interceptions	25
Clearances	48
Tackles	141
Tackles won	56%
DISCIPLINE	
Fouls	32
Yellow cards	2
Red cards	0

Muzzy Izzet has become a vital cog in Martin O'Neill's Leicester machine which reached its second League Cup final in three years. Despite the disappointment of defeat at Wembley he can be proud of his season, even though he missed several games in the run-in with a hamstring injury.

He scored five league goals from 19 shots on target, including a memorable winning volley against Spurs at Filbert Street.

Leicester's 1997–98 Player of the Year completed 81% of his passes and 56% of the tackles he contested alongside Neil Lennon, with whom he built an excellent relationship. Izzet did not shirk his defensive duties, making 48 clearances and 25 interceptions, and was very clean in the tackle, committing just 32 fouls and earning two yellow cards.

Since being plucked from the obscurity of Chelsea's reserves, Izzet has firmly established himself in the top flight. But it is vital that he and the rest of the squad stick together if the club are once again to prove they are in the Premiership to stay.

Darren JACKSON • 9
COVENTRY CITY • BORN: 25.7.66

It is less than two years since seasoned Scottish striker Darren Jackson had to undergo brain surgery.

Amazingly, he was only out of action for nine weeks; but on his return he found Celtic had signed new players and he was unable to regain a place in the first team as they marched to the Scottish title.

He signed a three-month loan deal with Coventry in November 1998, to cover for young centre-forwards Noel Whelan and Darren Huckerby after the departure of Dion Dublin to Aston Villa.

Unfortunately, he had little opportunity to impress, playing just 80 minutes of Carling Premiership football spread across three substitute appearances. During that time, he attempted just one shot, but did complete 79% of his 38 passes.

Two months into his loan spell, and after Australian John Aloisi had also been added to the squad, Jackson said goodbye to Highfield Road and jetted off to the Far East to ply his trade in Japan.

Errors: David James

David JAMES • 1
LIVERPOOL • BORN: 1.8.70

APPEARANCES	
Start (sub)	26 (0)
Minutes on pitch	2340
SHOT STOPPING	
Goals conceded	34
Clean sheets	5
Saves	84
Saves/shots	71%
DISTRIBUTION	
Distribution	753
Distribution %	54%
CATCHING	
Crosses caught	72
Crosses dropped	4
DISCIPLINE	
Yellow cards	1
Red cards	0

Few goalkeepers have been more criticized in recent years than David James. Liverpool's defensive uncertainties and his own crises of confidence have led to constant speculation over his Anfield future.

He is unlikely to remember the 1998–99 season with fondness. He conceded 34 goals, keeping just five clean sheets, and though he made 84 stops, his saves-to-shots ratio of 71% was one of the Premiership's worst, and only marginally better than that of his rival for the number one spot, Brad Friedel.

Questions have always been raised about his ability to deal with crosses, and his catch success ratio of 95% shows he failed to claim one in 20 of those he came for in 1998–99. Unfortunately, he seems to be punished often, with only Paul Jones and Neil Sullivan making more errors which led directly to goals.

One of the country's best prospects when he moved from Watford, another switch might help rejuvenate his career. His Liverpool days seem to be numbered, with the club now being linked with a host of other goalkeepers.

Matt JANSEN • 33
BLACKBURN ROVERS • BORN: 20.10.77

For new Blackburn manager Brian Kidd, signing Matt Jansen was a case of the boss finally getting his man.

As Manchester United assistant manager, Kidd had been desperate to capture the gifted young striker from Carlisle.

Jansen chose Crystal Palace instead; but as the Eagles spiralled into financial turmoil, Kidd pounced with a £4.1 million bid.

Jansen was plunged straight into Rovers' relegation fight in the 1–1 home draw with Tottenham, scoring a fabulous debut goal. A second came in the win over Wimbledon, and he claimed another in that match which appeared to go in off Ben Thatcher. His shooting accuracy from 23 goals was 45%.

Cartilage trouble kept him on the sidelines, but he returned for the fateful home defeat by Nottingham Forest and was one of the first players to apologize publicly to the fans for their lacklustre display.

Jansen has shown he could be a real future star. He managed a 73% pass completion rate for Blackburn and made 54 dribbles and runs.

APPEARANCES	
Start (sub)	10 (1)
Minutes on pitch	676
GOAL ATTEMPTS	
Goals	2
Goals/shots ratio	10%
SHOOTING	
Shots on target	9
Shooting accuracy	45%
PASSING	
Goal assists	1
Passing accuracy	71%
DISCIPLINE	
Fouls	7
Offside	6
Yellow cards	0
Red cards	0

Francis JEFFERS • 34
EVERTON • BORN: 25.1.81

APPEARANCES	
Start (sub)	11 (4)
Minutes on pitch	969
GOAL ATTEMPTS	
Goals	6
Goals/shots ratio	21%
SHOOTING	
Shots on target	12
Shooting accuracy	41%
PASSING	
Goal assists	5
Passing accuracy	70%
DISCIPLINE	
Fouls	10
Offside	15
Yellow cards	0
Red cards	0

After starting the 1998–99 season in the youth team, Francis Jeffers answered the call from Walter Smith when Everton were hit by an injury crisis and lack of form from their senior strikers. The youngster scored six goals, the second highest Everton total – and earned an England call-up to the injury-hit squad to face Hungary in an April friendly.

Jeffers made his debut as a substitute against Manchester United in the 1997–98 season, but had to wait until the home match against Newcastle in November 1998 to make his second appearance. His first start came in February at Derby and he scored in his next game in the FA Cup against Coventry City.

His strike rate was fairly impressive. He scored six times from 12 shots on target, with 17 more failing to trouble the 'keeper and another seven blocked en route to goal.

He also weighed in with five assists as he and Kevin Campbell forged a good partnership that steered the Toffees clear of relegation, but he showed his inexperience by giving away possession with 30% of his passes.

Phil JEVONS • 30
EVERTON • BORN: 1.8.79

Phil Jevons made his Everton debut in the 1998–99 FA Carling Premiership season as Everton boss Walter Smith used more outfield players than any other manager.

Jevons played for just 52 minutes as a substitute against Blackburn Rovers, when he replaced the injured Nick Barmby. It was good for the youngster to get a game after warming the bench on seven previous occasions during the season, but he appeared to be overtaken in the pecking order by Francis Jeffers as the season progressed.

The Liverpool-born striker completed 71% of the 17 passes he attempted, but his only other contribution was winning one of the two tackles he contested, making a couple of clearances and three interceptions.

The 1999–2000 season could prove to be a watershed for Jevons. As he moves out of his teens, it is now time to make the breakthrough into the first team on a more regular basis. With Walter Smith still looking to establish a settled squad, Jevons will hope to push himself forward in 1999–2000.

Julian JOACHIM • 12
ASTON VILLA • BORN: 20.9.74

Top scorer: Julian Joachim

Explosive striker Julian Joachim enjoyed his best season to date in the 1998–99 Carling Premiership campaign. The diminutive front man top-scored for Villa with 14 league goals.

Despite three England internationals vying with him for a place up front he performed magnificently for the Claret-and-Blues, with 14 goals from just 51 efforts: roughly one per four shots, well over the Premiership average.

Joachim followed boss Brian Little from Leicester City in 1996 but had to wait for a regular place in the starting line-up. His dangerous runs have unsettled many defences and he rounded 65% of opponents from the 115 dribbles and runs he attempted in 1998–99. The problems which the pint-sized striker caused defences are highlighted by the fact that he won five Premiership penalties.

Joachim held the ball up well and was an excellent foil for his team-mates, completing more than 70% of the 643 passes he attempted. The Villa star also crossed with enviable precision for a forward, finding a colleague with a third of all centres.

APPEARANCES	
Start (sub)	29 (7)
Minutes on pitch	2692
GOAL ATTEMPTS	
Goals	14
Goals/shots ratio	27%
SHOOTING	
Shots on target	26
Shooting accuracy	51%
PASSING	
Goal assists	4
Passing accuracy	72%
DISCIPLINE	
Fouls	44
Offside	34
Yellow cards	1
Red cards	0

Ronny JOHNSEN • 5
MANCHESTER UNITED • BORN: 10.6.69

Ronny Johnsen celebrated turning 30 with a record-breaking season at Manchester United. The Red Devils became the first English side to complete the Premiership, FA Cup and Champions League treble and the Norwegian picked up three more medals for his collection.

When fit, Johnsen was Alex Ferguson's first choice to play alongside Jaap Stam in 1998–99, particularly against pacy strikers such as Michael Owen and Nicolas Anelka.

He completed an outstanding 85% of his passes, 94% of his dribbles and runs and won 67% of his tackles. Johnsen also made 203 defensive clearances and, in all his time in the Premiership, earned just two yellow cards.

Also a threat in opponents' penalty areas, Johnsen scored three times from just 12 goal attempts – a strike ratio any attacker would be proud of. Two of those goals came in the 3–0 defeat of Nottingham Forest on Boxing Day.

Though it will be hard to top 1998–99's achievements, Johnsen will be looking to do so for Manchester United in the coming season and also for Norway in Euro 2000.

APPEARANCES	
Start (sub)	19 (3)
Minutes on pitch	1763
GOAL ATTEMPTS	
Goals	3
DEFENDING	
Blocks	9
Headed clearances	141
Other clearances	62
Interceptions	25
Tackles won	32
PASSING	
Passing accuracy	85%
DISCIPLINE	
Fouls	28
Yellow cards	2
Red cards	0

Andy JOHNSON • 10
NOTTINGHAM FOREST • BORN: 2.5.74

APPEARANCES	
Start (sub)	25 (3)
Minutes on pitch	2229
GOAL ATTEMPTS	
Goals	0
Shots on target	10
Shooting accuracy	45%
PASSING	
Goal assists	2
Passing accuracy	73%
Crossing accuracy	32%
DRIBBLING	
Dribbles & runs	54
Dribble completion	61%
DISCIPLINE	
Yellow cards	8
Red cards	0

Former Norwich midfielder Andy Johnson played a key role in Nottingham Forest's 1997–98 promotion drive and will be hoping for a repeat performance in 1999–2000 after the club's relegation from the Premiership.

After a bright start it proved to be a season of woe – Forest at one stage went 19 games without a win – and they were finally relegated with three games still to go.

Johnson's passing was below average, with just 73% completed. He completed 69% of his dribbles, but this too was below the level expected of an attacking midfielder.

He had no luck in front of goal – like most of the side – and troubled the goalkeeper with only 10 shots all season. A dozen more flew off target and another 10 were blocked by defenders. Johnson managed two goal assists, but will be disappointed with his contribution.

Johnson will also be unhappy at his eight yellow cards – but after 45 fouls, he can hardly complain. Forest's new manager will be his third boss within a year and Johnson must knuckle down and prove himself all over again.

Damien JOHNSON • 19
BLACKBURN ROVERS • BORN: 18.11.78

After making the first team squad, Damien Johnson spent the early season fighting for a place on the bench. The Northern Ireland under-21 international impressed enough in his first two substitute appearances to earn a start in October's visit to Middlesbrough.

He managed nine consecutive starts for Rovers before Brian Kidd signed Keith Gillespie and the young winger found himself relegated to the role of substitute once again.

Johnson ended his first Premiership season with 14 starts and seven appearances as a substitute. Of 20 shots, three were on target and he scored against Arsenal at Ewood Park.

The youngster completed an above-average 79% of his passes and claimed a goal assist. He also managed to find a team-mate with 30% of his deliveries into the box. Strong defensively, Johnson won an impressive 67% of his 51 challenges, made 22 clearances and eight interceptions and blocked eight shots.

After a fine debut season with Blackburn's first team squad, Johnson could well become a regular in the 1999–2000 starting line-up.

APPEARANCES	
Start (sub)	14 (7)
Minutes on pitch	1362
GOAL ATTEMPTS	
Goals	1
Shots on target	3
Shooting accuracy	21%
PASSING	
Goal assists	1
Passing accuracy	79%
Crossing accuracy	30%
DRIBBLING	
Dribbles & runs	84
Dribble completion	71%
DISCIPLINE	
Yellow cards	3
Red cards	0

Keith JONES • 15
CHARLTON ATHLETIC • BORN: 14.10.65

APPEARANCES	
Start (sub)	13 (10)
Minutes on pitch	1249
GOAL ATTEMPTS	
Goals	1
PASSING	
Passes	493
Passing accuracy	81%
DEFENDING	
Interceptions	14
Clearances	39
Tackles	44
Tackles won	66%
DISCIPLINE	
Fouls	20
Yellow cards	1
Red cards	1

Despite a superb 1997–98 season in the Nationwide League, Keith Jones was replaced in the centre of midfield in 1998–99 by new signings Neil Redfearn and, later, Graham Stuart. But when selected for first-team Premiership action, he performed with gusto.

Jones managed 13 Premiership starts, with 10 more as a substitute. His displays helped spark a welcome run of form for Alan Curbishley's side towards the season's end.

A lasting memory will be scoring the winner in Charlton's 1–0 win over Liverpool at the Valley. He finished the season with an 81% pass completion rate and also completed a superb 56% of his crosses – and retained possession from 80% of his dribbles and runs.

Another of Jones's 1998–99 highlights was the superb man-marking job he undertook on Middlesbrough's Paul Gascoigne in November.

Able to create chances for others while denying the opposition, Jones will hope to return to first-team action in Division One in 1999–2000, as Curbishley's Charlton make yet another bid for top-flight football.

Matthew JONES • 40
LEEDS UNITED • BORN: 1.9.80

Matthew Jones is yet another product of Leeds United's youth set-up. There seems to be no end to the talent at Elland Road, and the young Welshman could well be the next to make a big impact in David O'Leary's side.

His first appearance came in the 2–1 away win at Aston Villa. Leeds were suffering from such an appalling injury crisis that David O'Leary later lamented: "It got so bad, I was thinking of naming myself on the bench."

Perhaps Jones's highest-profile match was the 1–1 draw with Manchester United where he struggled to cope with the international class of Jesper Blomqvist, but he will undoubtedly improve with experience.

Jones's pass completion rate of 70% was poor but he showed good ability in wide areas, completing 44% of his crosses. He was a tenacious tackler, winning 59%, and read the game well with nine interceptions.

With Gary Kelly set to return after injury and Danny Mills arriving from Charlton for £4 million, Jones may well have to be patient in 1999–2000.

APPEARANCES	
Start (sub)	3 (5)
Minutes on pitch	395
GOAL ATTEMPTS	
Goals	0
PASSING & CROSSING	
Passing	167
Passing accuracy	70%
Crossing	9
Crossing accuracy	44%
DEFENDING	
Tackles	22
Tackles won	59%
DISCIPLINE	
Fouls	5
Yellow cards	0
Red cards	0

Paul JONES • 1
SOUTHAMPTON • BORN: 18.4.67

APPEARANCES	
Start (sub)	31 (0)
Minutes on pitch	2758
SHOT STOPPING	
Goals conceded	50
Clean sheets	7
Saves	124
Saves/shots	71%
DISTRIBUTION	
Distribution	979
Distribution %	48%
CATCHING	
Crosses caught	108
Crosses dropped	6
DISCIPLINE	
Yellow cards	1
Red cards	1

Welsh number one Paul Jones had an up-and-down season for the Saints, making some great saves but dropping some awful clangers.

He went from keeping a rampant Arsenal at bay at Highbury, with five good saves and seven catches, to conceding seven against Liverpool at Anfield, in a season that rarely had a dull moment for the south coast club.

Jones conceded 50 goals and only managed shut-outs on seven occasions as Saints struggled to retain their Premiership status. He did make 124 saves, but his 71% saves-to-shots ratio was one of the poorest in the league and he was credited [sic] with seven errors that led directly to goals.

The former Stockport stopper claimed 108 catches and preferred to punch on six other occasions. But his handling was not always secure and he dropped six catches.

After all his travails, Jones will have been heartened to be brought straight back into the side – even after some superb displays by stand-in Neil Moss – and looks set to start as number one for the 1999–2000 season.

Steve JONES • 19
CHARLTON ATHLETIC • BORN: 17.3.70

Bustling striker Steve Jones was often used by Alan Curbishley to replace Clive Mendonca during the 1998–99 season. His substitute displays early in the campaign were enough to earn him a starting role in the injured Mendonca's absence, but he was unable to provide the goals Charlton needed to stay up.

He scored the late equalizer in the memorable 3–3 draw at Anfield, hit a further six shots on target and finished the season with two goal assists to his credit, but his 62% pass completion rate was poor. Jones's combative style saw him concede 29 fouls and receive five yellow cards. He was also a victim of opposing defences' offside traps, being penalized on 24 occasions.

He retained possession from 71% of his dribbles and runs, well above average for a striker, but completed only 24% of his crosses when peeling out wide.

Despite interest from a number of lower-division sides Curbishley hung on to Jones, and he may well feature in their renewed bid for promotion in 1999–2000.

APPEARANCES	
Start (sub)	7 (18)
Minutes on pitch	998
GOAL ATTEMPTS	
Goals	1
Goals/shots ratio	7%
SHOOTING	
Shots on target	7
Shooting accuracy	47%
PASSING	
Goal assists	2
Passing accuracy	62%
DISCIPLINE	
Fouls	29
Offside	24
Yellow cards	5
Red cards	0

Wim JONK • 4
SHEFFIELD WEDNESDAY • BORN: 12.10.66

APPEARANCES	
Start (sub)	38 (0)
Minutes on pitch	3342
GOAL ATTEMPTS	
Goals	2
PASSING	
Passes	1746
Passing accuracy	83%
DEFENDING	
Interceptions	28
Clearances	64
Tackles	118
Tackles won	58%
DISCIPLINE	
Fouls	26
Yellow cards	4
Red cards	0

While there is no doubting Wim Jonk's pedigree the Dutch international, with 48 caps for his country, did not make quite the impact Sheffield Wednesday fans hoped for after his £2.5 million move from PSV Eindhoven.

A prolific distributor of the ball, he made almost 2,000 passes in the Premiership, completing 83%, but seemed to lose influence as the season wore on. Nevertheless he started every game for the Owls, scoring two goals – including one in the memorable 3–1 win over Manchester United – and claiming five assists.

It was his tackling that really let him down. Though he was not slow to make challenges, he won the ball just 58% of the time – a figure that falls some way below the average for Premiership midfielders.

Described by manager Danny Wilson as "someone who can shape the play and bring out the best in others", Jonk will need to rediscover the consistency which was his trademark at Ajax, Inter Milan and PSV if he is to help Wednesday improve on their 12th-place finish in the 1998–99 Premiership.

Duncan JUPP • 21
WIMBLEDON • BORN: 22.1.73

FB

Duncan Jupp spent a long time on the sidelines and among the second-stringers in 1998–99, and may well be a victim of Egil Olsen's rebuilding plans at Selhurst Park.

After brief substitute outings in the first two games, his first start came in the amazing 4–3 comeback win over West Ham at Upton Park.

Jupp then made only a one-minute substitute appearance against Sheffield Wednesday before disappearing from the first team until April. After that he started two games against Newcastle and Coventry, weighing in with an assist for John Hartson in the 2–1 defeat of the Sky Blues.

Jupp completed a poor 71% of his passes and contributed little else to a disappointing season for the Dons. He made 18 clearances and eight tackles, but his other most notable statistic was two yellow cards from nine fouls.

He has only 15 appearances for the Dons in three seasons, suggesting he is unlikely to make the grade – and if he is to secure regular first-team football, the former Scottish under-21 international may have to look elsewhere.

APPEARANCES	
Start (sub)	3 (3)
Minutes on pitch	279
GOAL ATTEMPTS	
Goals	0
PASSING & CROSSING	
Passing	84
Passing accuracy	71%
Crossing	8
Crossing accuracy	50%
DEFENDING	
Tackles	8
Tackles won	50%
DISCIPLINE	
Fouls	9
Yellow cards	2
Red cards	0

Pontus KAAMARK • 15
LEICESTER CITY • BORN: 5.4.69

FB

APPEARANCES	
Start (sub)	15 (4)
Minutes on pitch	1422
GOAL ATTEMPTS	
Goals	0
PASSING & CROSSING	
Passing	513
Passing accuracy	73%
Crossing	7
Crossing accuracy	29%
DEFENDING	
Tackles	57
Tackles won	68%
DISCIPLINE	
Fouls	13
Yellow cards	0
Red cards	0

Swedish international Pontus Kaamark's last match for the Foxes was away at Nottingham Forest on the last day of the 1998–99 season.

Kaamark joined City from IFK Gothenberg in 1995 and slotted into the full-back role. But he showed his versatility when asked to cover the central defence, doing so competently during the 1998–99 Premiership campaign.

The Swede earned a reputation as a good man-marker during his time in England, his finest moment coming in the 1997 Coca-Cola Cup final when he kept Middlesbrough's Juninho under wraps. When called on in the Premiership, he was a model of consistency.

Kaamark contested more than 50 challenges in 1998–99, winning a healthy 68%. He was also quick to spot danger at the back, with 150 clearances and 22 interceptions.

He carried the ball from defence effectively and retained possession in nearly 90% of all his dribbles and runs, but was less successful when opting to pass the ball out of danger.

Kaamark returned to his native Sweden in the summer to join AIK Stockholm.

Hassan KACHLOUL • 30
SOUTHAMPTON • BORN: 19.2.73

Hassan Kachloul rapidly achieved cult status at the Dell after a series of inspirational performances in 1998–99. When Southampton travelled to Wimbledon in their final away match, many of their 10,000 fans donned fezes in tribute to the Moroccan star and turned Selhurst Park into a casbah for the day!

Kachloul made an instant impact for the Saints after signing in November, scoring five goals from a wide midfield role and getting plenty of shots on target. The coltish midfielder adapted very quickly to the English game and demonstrated a willingness to close down space and run at opposing defences.

He showed some naivety in attack and his poor dribble completion rate of 52% reflected a tendency to lose possession, but he compensated with some neat touches and sent over some quality crosses, achieving a superb 43% completion rate.

The Moroccan international has settled in well at the Dell and should feature prominently in David Jones's plans for the 1999–2000 season.

APPEARANCES	
Start (sub)	18 (4)
Minutes on pitch	1643
GOAL ATTEMPTS	
Goals	5
Shots on target	24
Shooting accuracy	49%
PASSING	
Goal assists	0
Passing accuracy	68%
Crossing accuracy	43%
DRIBBLING	
Dribbles & runs	75
Dribble completion	52%
DISCIPLINE	
Yellow cards	5
Red cards	0

J

Nwankwo KANU • 25
ARSENAL • BORN: 1.8.76

APPEARANCES	
Start (sub)	5 (7)
Minutes on pitch	542
GOAL ATTEMPTS	
Goals	6
Goals/shots ratio	40%
SHOOTING	
Shots on target	9
Shooting accuracy	60%
PASSING	
Goal assists	2
Passing accuracy	78%
DISCIPLINE	
Fouls	6
Offside	10
Yellow cards	0
Red cards	0

A contender for the buy of the 1998–99 season, Nwankwo Kanu was a revelation after his arrival from Inter Milan in January. His Nigerian international team-mate Taribo West said he had "class with a capital C" and the Olympic gold medal-winner quickly became the darling of the Highbury Clock End.

He certainly helped the club's "goals for" column tick along, scoring six and ending the season with a 40% goals-to-shots ratio. Kanu's willingness to take players on showed in his 69% dribble completion rate. He completed 78% of his passes and claimed two assists.

While tongue-in-cheek doubts are still voiced about his age by both fans and team-mates, any fitness queries were dispelled by his third start at Middlesbrough. Kanu scored twice, one an audacious back-flick which had fans and journalists alike drooling. His solo effort in the win at Spurs was another classic.

Kanu will continue to meet stiff competition from Anelka and Bergkamp for top billing in the Arsenal front line – but he clearly has the ability to become a true Premiership great.

Roy KEANE • 16
MANCHESTER UNITED • BORN: 10.8.71

M

Manchester United captain Roy Keane was the inspiration behind his side's history-making achievements during the 1998–99 season.

His leadership was integral to United's remarkable treble success, providing much of the impetus from the heart of midfield. His crucial goal against Juventus in the European Cup semi-final was a good example.

The £3.75 million signing from Nottingham Forest was the most accurate passer of all Premiership midfielders, and made more successful passes than any other player in the league. Nearly 90% of all passes dispatched by Keane reached their intended target.

Despite a knee-ligament injury that kept him out for most of the 1997–98 campaign, Keane did not compromise his tough-tackling style after his Premiership comeback. He won an excellent 70% of challenges during 1998–99, better than most contemporaries.

The Eire star showed he is a true box-to-box player, grabbing two league goals from 35 strikes, while making 74 clearances and an excellent 36 interceptions.

APPEARANCES	
Start (sub)	33 (2)
Minutes on pitch	2882

GOAL ATTEMPTS	
Goals	2

PASSING	
Passes	2072
Passing accuracy	88%

DEFENDING	
Interceptions	36
Clearances	74
Tackles	138
Tackles won	70%

DISCIPLINE	
Fouls	46
Yellow cards	8
Red cards	0

Inspirational: Roy Keane

G Kasey KELLER • 1
LEICESTER CITY • BORN: 27.11.69

American international 'keeper Kasey Keller has arguably been one of the Premiership's most consistent performers between the sticks since he joined Leicester City in 1996.

The Foxes finished the 1998–99 Carling Premiership campaign with one of the league's best defensive records, and much of the credit must go to the Washington-born number one.

Overall Keller was hard to beat, keeping 12 clean sheets in 36 starts and conceding 43 goals. Title-chasers Chelsea, Arsenal and Manchester United put four, five and six strikes respectively past Keller, the only blips in an otherwise solid season.

The former Millwall man is renowned for good close-range reactions and made 79 stops from inside his area, the league's fourth-highest total. Keller dealt well with crosses, dropped only three catches all season and found target men such as Emile Heskey with nearly four out of 10 long kicks.

But the ambitious shot-stopper has often expressed a wish to play on the continent and his contract was due to expire in the summer.

APPEARANCES	
Start (sub)	36 (0)
Minutes on pitch	3166
SHOT STOPPING	
Goals conceded	43
Clean sheets	12
Saves	133
Saves/shots	76%
DISTRIBUTION	
Distribution	1023
Distribution %	51%
CATCHING	
Crosses caught	89
Crosses dropped	3
DISCIPLINE	
Yellow cards	2
Red cards	0

FB Marc KELLER • 7
WEST HAM UNITED • BORN: 14.1.68

APPEARANCES	
Start (sub)	17 (4)
Minutes on pitch	1489
GOAL ATTEMPTS	
Goals	5
PASSING & CROSSING	
Passing	557
Passing accuracy	78%
Crossing	65
Crossing accuracy	35%
DEFENDING	
Tackles	43
Tackles won	56%
DISCIPLINE	
Fouls	17
Yellow cards	3
Red cards	0

While he did not command a regular place in West Ham's starting line-up, Marc Keller nonetheless put in some good displays on the flank when selected to play in the 1998–99 Carling Premiership.

The experienced French international arrived in summer 1998 on a free transfer from Germany's Karlsruhe and provided an effective, attacking alternative when getting forward.

He scored five goals from 20 efforts and showed a penchant for long-range strikes, claiming three goals from outside the box and, impressively, hitting the target with seven of his 10 attempts from outside the area.

But his main role was to deliver dangerous crosses into the box, something he did with distinction. More than a third of his 65 centres found their mark. Despite this fact, however, Keller surprisingly managed just one goal assist during the 1998–99 campaign.

The Hammers have had trouble with foreign signings in the past, but Keller's experience and composure were big factors in helping West Ham to qualify for the InterToto Cup.

FB

Jeff KENNA • 2
BLACKBURN ROVERS • BORN: 28.8.70

Full-back Jeff Kenna had a solid 1998–99 season with Rovers, enjoying 22 Premiership starts and one substitute appearance. The gutsy Eire international won an excellent 66% of his challenges, conceding only 14 fouls and picking up just one yellow card.

Kenna's distribution was mixed: he made more than 750 passes, completing only 73%, but his crossing accuracy was better at 31%. Happy on either flank, he liked to overlap the winger and create telling centres. He kept possession from three-quarters of his dribbles and runs, but claimed only one goal assist.

The former Southampton full-back posed little threat to opponents' goals, managing just three wayward shots and one blocked effort, but made 116 clearances, together with 12 interceptions and 16 shots.

In his 11th year as a professional, Kenna is set to experience Nationwide League football for the very first time after Rovers' relegation – and will face stiff competition for the full-back positions from the likes of Callum Davidson and Gary Croft.

APPEARANCES	
Start (sub)	22 (1)
Minutes on pitch	2004
GOAL ATTEMPTS	
Goals	0
PASSING & CROSSING	
Passing	787
Passing accuracy	73%
Crossing	48
Crossing accuracy	31%
DEFENDING	
Tackles	64
Tackles won	66%
DISCIPLINE	
Fouls	14
Yellow cards	1
Red cards	0

AM

Mark KENNEDY • 18
WIMBLEDON • BORN: 15.5.76

APPEARANCES	
Start (sub)	7 (10)
Minutes on pitch	666
GOAL ATTEMPTS	
Goals	0
Shots on target	4
Shooting accuracy	50%
PASSING	
Goal assists	1
Passing accuracy	73%
Crossing accuracy	37%
DRIBBLING	
Dribbles & runs	34
Dribble completion	56%
DISCIPLINE	
Yellow cards	0
Red cards	0

Eire international Mark Kennedy has made two high-profile moves during his seven-year professional career, but has yet to establish himself as a regular Premiership starter.

He signed for Liverpool, aged 18, for £1.75 million, but found it hard to get a look-in and joined fellow-Dubliner Joe Kinnear at Wimbledon in March 1998 for the same sum.

However, the devilish winger was tormented by a lack of first-team action in the 1998–99 campaign. He played just 666 minutes in the Premiership without catching fire, but against Bolton in the Worthington Cup he set up one goal and scored the winner as Wimbledon narrowly failed to reach the final.

Sadly Kennedy did not score in the league, and created just one goal. Despite limited playing time, he centred the ball regularly and accuracy, and won a healthy proportion of the tackles he contested.

Still only 23, Kennedy has plenty of time to stake his claim for a regular starting berth, but faces stiff competition, in particular from Michael Hughes.

Martin KEOWN • 14
CB
ARSENAL • BORN: 24.7.66

Mild-mannered defensive superhero Martin Keown once earned a petulant slap from Chelsea's equally laid-back Nigel Spackman.

But the sting from that spank would not have left Martin smarting nearly as much as the Gunners surrendering their cherished double to rivals Manchester United.

With the end of Keown's top-level career looming on the Highbury horizon the versatile and dedicated professional will be as eager as anyone to help reclaim the silverware.

Keown's form in 1998–99 shows in his Carling Opta stats. He completed 84% of his passes and all 24 dribbles and runs. But it was his 70% tackle win rate that really impressed. He also scored the winner at Nottingham Forest in the league – his only shot on target.

As with other Gunners, the one blot was his discipline. His first red card was highly dubious – the now-forgotten result of the notorious Paolo Di Canio–Paul Alcock clash at Sheffield Wednesday in September – but there were no complaints when he was sent off against Blackburn in April.

APPEARANCES	
Start (sub)	34 (0)
Minutes on pitch	2984
GOAL ATTEMPTS	
Goals	1
DEFENDING	
Blocks	31
Headed clearances	344
Other clearances	132
Interceptions	48
Tackles won	73
PASSING	
Passing accuracy	84%
DISCIPLINE	
Fouls	35
Yellow cards	5
Red cards	2

K

Temuri KETSBAIA • 14
S
NEWCASTLE UNITED • BORN: 18.3.68

APPEARANCES	
Start (sub)	14 (12)
Minutes on pitch	1332
GOAL ATTEMPTS	
Goals	5
Goals/shots ratio	14%
SHOOTING	
Shots on target	19
Shooting accuracy	51%
PASSING	
Goal assists	4
Passing accuracy	84%
DISCIPLINE	
Fouls	21
Offside	10
Yellow cards	2
Red cards	0

In only his second season at St James's Park, Temuri Ketsbaia has established himself as a Toon cult figure with his determined displays and unpredictable goal celebrations.

The Georgian Geordie's driving runs at the heart of opposition defences were a major source of Newcastle's success. He attempted 71 dribbles and runs, negotiating a healthy 72% unchallenged, and fired in 37 shots, scoring from five. Impressively, more than half of all the shots he attempted were on target.

Ketsbaia's distribution easily matched his finishing. Of 584 attempted passes, well in excess of 80% found a Magpie, and he was credited with four goal assists in 1998–99. The former AEK Athens man had less success centering the ball – on average just one in five crosses connected with a team-mate.

One element of Ketsbaia's complex personality that appeals to the Toon faithful is his willingness to chase back and hound the opposition. He won 57% of his 28 attempted tackles in 1998–99 and, despite his fiery temperament, was booked just twice.

Harry KEWELL • 19
LEEDS UNITED • BORN: 22.9.78

Lee Bowyer may have won the award as Leeds United's Player of the Year for 1998–99, but Harry Kewell's outstanding displays also made him a strong candidate for the accolade.

Kewell came to England in 1995, and has swiftly become an skilful, attacking playmaker.

The Australian international was a central figure in the 1997 FA Youth Cup-winning side and is one of several members of that team who had a massive impact on the Premiership.

Equally adept either as a frontman or as the supply-line to the likes of Jimmy Hasselbaink and Alan Smith, Kewell created 10 goals for colleagues – the Premiership's sixth-highest total. Most important was the wicked cross which set up Hasselbaink's winner against Arsenal, ending the Gunners' title hopes.

Kewell unsettled opposition defenders with his skill and pace and was fouled a massive 61 times. He supplied the finishing touch to Leeds' moves on six occasions from a total of 73 attempted shots, playing a hugely significant part in the resurgent Yorkshire outfit's UEFA Cup qualification.

APPEARANCES	
Start (sub)	36 (2)
Minutes on pitch	3197
GOAL ATTEMPTS	
Goals	6
Shots on target	35
Shooting accuracy	48%
PASSING	
Goal assists	10
Passing accuracy	67%
Crossing accuracy	24%
DRIBBLING	
Dribbles & runs	285
Dribble completion	63%
DISCIPLINE	
Yellow cards	3
Red cards	0

Aussie jewel: Harry Kewell

Dmitri KHARINE • 23
CHELSEA • BORN: 16.8.68

Dmitri Kharine had to wait until the last game of the season to get his first taste of Premiership football in 1998-99. An injury to regular 'keeper Ed De Goey saw Kevin Hitchcock step into the breach against Tottenham Hotspur, but Kharine was given the nod against Derby County in a bid to keep the Rams at bay.

He made four saves – all from shots inside the area – but was unable to stop a Horacio Carbonari free kick from hitting the back of the net in the 88th minute.

A member of the Chelsea squad since his £200,000 transfer from CSKA Moscow in 1992, Kharine saw more action in the Worthington Cup, playing in all three games before the Blues' elimination at the hands of Wimbledon in the quarter-final.

He also played in the first leg of Chelsea's European Cup Winners Cup game against Helsingborgs, keeping a clean sheet in a 1–0 victory.

Kharine may move on to pastures new sooner rather than later.

FB Alan KIMBLE • 3
WIMBLEDON • BORN: 6.8.66

Left-back Alan Kimble joined the Dons for just £175,000 from Cambridge United in 1993 and proved yet another Joe Kinnear bargain.

He has appeared more than 150 times in all competitions for Wimbledon, proving great value for money, but in the 1998–99 season he was competing for starts with Ben Thatcher.

The Dagenham-born defender played in the season's opening stages as the Dons started comfortably in the league, but suffered a loss of form which led Kinnear to promote Thatcher to left-back. Kinnear alternated between the two regularly throughout 1998–99.

The former Charlton apprentice proved hard to dispossess, successfully negotiating 93% of his 30 dribbles and runs. In tandem with Kenny Cunningham he supplied plenty of ammunition for the forwards. Kimble delivered 115 crosses, connecting with an excellent 39% of these, as he claimed three goal assists.

The 15-year veteran fulfilled his defensive duties with admirable discipline, making 71 tackles and 149 clearances while committing just 11 fouls.

APPEARANCES	
Start (sub)	22 (4)
Minutes on pitch	2017
GOAL ATTEMPTS	
Goals	0
PASSING & CROSSING	
Passing	790
Passing accuracy	60%
Crossing	115
Crossing accuracy	39%
DEFENDING	
Tackles	71
Tackles won	59%
DISCIPLINE	
Fouls	11
Yellow cards	3
Red cards	0

K

FB Vladimir KINDER • 17
MIDDLESBROUGH • BORN: 9.3.69

Middlesbrough's top scorer Hamilton Ricard may have grabbed 15 goals during the 1998–99 Carling Premiership, but even he could not match the improbable strike-rate of Vladimir Kinder.

Czechoslovakian international Kinder was a surprise hit when coming forward and had a smashing time in front of goal. He scored two sweet goals in just 135 minutes and Bryan Robson may have toyed with the idea of partnering him with Ricard in the absence of a regular attacking duo!

Robson could have been kinder to the former Slovan Bratislava full-back by playing him more regularly but, despite playing a major part in Boro's promotion-winning campaign in 1997–98, the experienced defender could not break into the side.

Youngsters such as Robbie Stockdale and Jason Gavin seemed undaunted by Premiership football and look as though they could feature regularly in Boro's back-line during the 1999–2000 campaign, providing healthy competition for the likes of Kinder.

FB Ledley KING • 26
TOTTENHAM HOTSPUR • BORN: 10.12.80

Young Spurs defender Ledley King made his Carling Premiership debut in the most difficult of circumstances.

King came on as a substitute in Tottenham's match away to Liverpool on May 1, 1999, after Mauricio Taricco had been sent off. The East Londoner slotted into the left-back position after Taricco's dismissal and coped well, considering that he is normally a centre-back by trade.

The result would not have suited King, or George Graham for that matter, as Spurs went down 3–2 to the Merseysiders. But the match provided the youngster with some valuable Premiership experience that can only help him improve in future.

Another highlight of King's year was his call-up for the England under-21 squad which faced Sweden and Bulgaria in June. Spurs fans will hoping that King makes the successful transition to the first team, following in the footsteps of Spurs captain Sol Campbell and right-back Stephen Carr, who also came up through the ranks.

M   Mark KINSELLA • 8
CHARLTON ATHLETIC • BORN: 12.8.72

Ever-present in 1998–99, Mark Kinsella was the side's midfield propellor and played at a consistently high level. His Premiership performances ranked him fifth in the end-of-season Carling Opta midfielders Index.

In a season when the Addicks struggled in front of goal the Eire international scored only three times, but his passing and ball-winning abilities were outstanding. Kinsella completed 81% of his passes and a very impressive 34% of crosses. Of the six Premiership players who took more than 100 corners, he was easily the most accurate. On the ball he retained possession from 89% of his dribbles and runs.

Defensively, the Addicks' skipper made more than 150 tackles, winning 67%. He made almost 200 blocks, clearances and interception combined, yet he committed only 47 fouls and picked up four yellow cards across the season.

Kinsella's displays earned him Charlton's Player of the Season award and he did not go unnoticed by other Premiership clubs. Despite leading a late-season rally at the Valley, he ended the campaign hotly tipped for a move.

APPEARANCES	
Start (sub)	38 (0)
Minutes on pitch	3240
GOAL ATTEMPTS	
Goals	3
PASSING	
Passes	1455
Passing accuracy	81%
DEFENDING	
Interceptions	46
Clearances	130
Tackles	163
Tackles won	67%
DISCIPLINE	
Fouls	47
Yellow cards	4
Red cards	0

S   Paul KITSON • 9
WEST HAM UNITED • BORN: 9.1.71

APPEARANCES	
Start (sub)	13 (4)
Minutes on pitch	1200
GOAL ATTEMPTS	
Goals	3
Goals/shots ratio	18%
SHOOTING	
Shots on target	9
Shooting accuracy	53%
PASSING	
Goal assists	3
Passing accuracy	62%
DISCIPLINE	
Fouls	18
Offside	15
Yellow cards	2
Red cards	0

Injuries have blighted the West Ham career of Paul Kitson, and after missing the opening of the 1998–99 campaign due to groin surgery it was another stop-start season for the former Derby County and Newcastle United forward.

Kitson managed just 13 starts and four substitute appearances as West Ham finished fifth and qualified for the InterToto Cup.

He scored three times from just 17 shots, his most crucial coming in the improbable win at Stamford Bridge against Championship-chasing Chelsea.

Kitson's role as a striker was not limited to scoring, however, and he showed his ability to bring others into play with three goal assists. But his general passing was below par and he only completed 62% of his 370 passes.

His ability in the air and to hold up the ball saw him take on the role of target man after West Ham sold John Hartson.

With Ian Wright and Paolo Di Canio competing with him for places up front in 1999–2000, Kitson has his work cut out to hold down a regular starting spot.

Paul KONCHESKY • 26
CHARLTON ATHLETIC • BORN: 15.5.81

Two years ago, Paul Konchesky became the youngest player ever to play for Charlton, aged 16 years and 93 days.

In 1998–99, he came on to help Charlton come from two goals down to draw 2–2 against Newcastle in January, and a month later started his first Premiership match against Wimbledon at the Valley as the Addicks won 2–0.

He won all four of his tackles and completed 60% of his passes in his 118 minutes of Premiership football.

The former trainee figured in more reserve team matches than any other player at the club. His 23 appearances and five goals were a major factor in the reserves' championship triumph in the Avon Insurance Combination League.

Konchesky's form in the second-stringers is sure to have impressed Alan Curbishley, who may feel the time is right to give him an extended run in the first team in 1999–2000 as Charlton look to bounce back into the Premiership at the first attempt.

 Muhamed KONJIC • 9
COVENTRY CITY • BORN: 14.5.70

Gordon Strachan swooped for Bosnian international Muhamed Konjic in January, paying £2.75 million to secure his services from Monaco.

The 6' 4" defender is the captain of his national side and first came to the attention of the British public when he featured in the Monaco side which knocked English champions Manchester United out of the Champions League in 1998.

After losing four years of his career while a soldier in the Bosnian conflict, he has blossomed into a tough-tackling centre-back. He won 90% of his challenges in the Premiership and also completed 79% of his passes, impressing many onlookers with his ability and composure.

Injury brought a premature end to his season, but for a man who once broke both his arms in a car-crash when his vehicle plunged down a ravine this will prove a minor inconvenience – and he is likely to figure strongly in the 1999–2000 campaign for the Sky Blues.

K

 Willem KORSTEN • 7
LEEDS UNITED • BORN: 21.1.75

Dutchman Willem Korsten was the subject of one of the most bitter transfer wrangles of the 1998–99 Carling Premiership season. After a handful of appearances for Leeds United on loan, the Yorkshiremen failed to conclude a deal for the player and ex-Whites gaffer George Graham nipped in to buy Korsten from Vitesse Arnhem.

David O'Leary was reportedly furious with his former mentor, but admitted: "Certain things went wrong on the financial side and he [Korsten] was disappointed with what happened in negotiations."

The winger, who can also play up front, scored two goals from five shots on target and another six misses, but he recorded a very poor pass completion rate of 64% and attempted just two crosses.

Korsten also won just 54% of the tackles that he attempted.

With David Ginola and a host of other wingers at Spurs, it remains to be seen whether Korsten made the right choice of club for season 1999–2000.

 Robert KOZLUK • 25
DERBY COUNTY • BORN: 5.8.77

An England under-21 international, Robert Kozluk's Premiership career has been halted almost as quickly as it began.

Starting 1998–99 at Derby County, he was part of the deal which brought Greek wide man Vassilis Borbokis to Pride Park, with Kozluk and Jonathan Hunt moved in the opposite direction.

In his position of right wing-back, Kozluk made a handful of appearances in the Derby first team, mainly as substitute. His pass completion percentage of 80% from 97 passes was impressive.

His two dribbling runs were both successful and he won four of the eight tackles he attempted, conceding just one foul and one yellow card. Defensively, the former trainee made 14 clearances, four blocks and six interceptions.

Having worked hard to impress both Jim Smith and Steve Bruce, Kozluk will now have to prove himself to a third manager, following Bruce's rather acrimonious departure from Bramall Lane.

CB Bjorn Tore KVARME • 3
LIVERPOOL • BORN: 17.6.72

After winning four title medals with Rosenborg, Bjorn Tore Kvarme would have been hopeful of adding to his collection when he joined the club which has won more English League championships than any other team.

He joined on a free transfer in January 1997, but has failed to establish himself in the side and at times has been involved in some of Liverpool's "Keystone Kops" defending. One particular nightmare involved the Reds throwing away a good position in the UEFA Cup in Spain against Celta Vigo.

Kvarme spent most of the 1998–99 season sitting on the bench, from where he made five appearances. His two Premiership starts saw more defensive disarray, as the Reds lost 2–1 at Chelsea and he was substituted at half-time when Spurs were 2–0 up at Anfield – a game Liverpool then won 3–2.

Overall he won 58% of his tackles and completed 77% of his passes in 218 Premiership minutes.

But his Liverpool future now seems far from assured under Gerard Houllier.

Versatile: Bernard Lambourde

CB Bernard LAMBOURDE • 21
CHELSEA • BORN: 11.5.71

APPEARANCES	
Start (sub)	12 (5)
Minutes on pitch	1153
GOAL ATTEMPTS	
Goals	0
DEFENDING	
Blocks	10
Headed clearances	59
Other clearances	26
Interceptions	26
Tackles won	38
PASSING	
Passing accuracy	83%
DISCIPLINE	
Fouls	22
Yellow cards	3
Red cards	0

Bernard Lambourde doubtless started the 1998–99 season in pessimistic mood. Signed from Bordeaux for £1.6 million in 1997, he had made just seven Premiership appearances in his first year in English football.

Without the promise of a regular place and deprived of even a squad number, Lambourde voiced a desire to move on. But by the season's end he had proved a valuable squad member, playing in various positions across the back-line, including left- and right-back.

Also capable of a holding role in the midfield, Lambourde combined a solid pass completion rate of 83% with a tackle success of 70%. His 82% dribble success rate was also high, proving he is comfortable on the ball.

An abdominal muscle injury in December's match against Spurs jeopardized his season, but he was back the next month partnering Frank Leboeuf against Coventry City.

The highlight of his campaign probably came in the European Cup Winners Cup quarter-final against Valerenga when, on a rare foray forward, he scored his first goal for the club.

Frank LAMPARD • 18
WEST HAM UNITED • BORN: 20.6.78

Frank Lampard had a steady season in 1998–99. He captained England's under-21 side, scoring several goals, prior to a call-up into Kevin Keegan's full squad. But a mid-season dip in form saw him slated by fans and the media alike. For a player who had not yet turned 21 this seemed a bit harsh, and his statistics show he had a decent year.

Lampard showed good composure on the ball, completing 75% of his dribbles, 79% of his passes and claiming four goal assists.

He was a goal threat himself, too. He fired in 34 shots on target, scoring five goals – two of which were winners – and bagged goals at Anfield and Old Trafford, showing a capacity to perform on the biggest of stages.

Not renowned as a tackler, his success rate in the challenge is just below average, but in committing 42 fouls he earned four yellow cards for mistimed challenges.

After establishing himself as first choice at West Ham and a reported £6 million target for Spurs and Aston Villa, Lampard looks set to make his critics eat their words.

APPEARANCES	
Start (sub)	38 (0)
Minutes on pitch	3420
GOAL ATTEMPTS	
Goals	5
PASSING	
Passes	1585
Passing accuracy	79%
DEFENDING	
Interceptions	29
Clearances	88
Tackles	141
Tackles won	61%
DISCIPLINE	
Fouls	42
Yellow cards	4
Red cards	0

K

Brian LAUDRUP • 7
CHELSEA • BORN: 22.2.69

Chelsea fans felt they had captured the bargain of the 1998–99 season with the free transfer signing of Brian Laudrup from Glasgow Rangers, even considering he was reportedly the Carling Premiership's highest-paid player.

But Laudrup did not seem to settle well, and his lack of sharpness meant he was often a casualty of Gianluca Vialli's much-criticized squad rotation system.

In his brief spell at Stamford Bridge he attempted only eight efforts at goal, with half of those on target. His creative skills were in evidence as he completed 67% of his dribbles and 81% of his passes, setting up one goal for Tore Andre Flo in the thrilling 4–3 win at Blackburn Rovers.

But after years of exile the lure of his homeland proved too strong. Just days after scoring his only goal for the Blues against FC Copenhagen, he left Chelsea for the Danish side that he had just knocked out of the Cup Winners Cup.

At the end of the season, he left Copenhagen in search of yet another challenge.

Brian LAUNDERS • 7
DERBY COUNTY • BORN: 8.1.76

Having already played for Crystal Palace and Crewe Alexandra, Brian Launders found himself available for loan from his latest club, BV Veendam.

After a brief trial, Derby boss Jim Smith decided to take the former Republic of Ireland under-21 international on loan for the whole of the 1998–99 season, but Launders was unable to break into the first-team set-up in any major way.

The 23-year-old made just one 12-minute appearance as a substitute in the demoralizing defeat at Elland Road. It was rather a baptism of fire as Leeds were already 3–1 up.

Launders did not get a touch of the ball before Ian Harte scored a spectacular fourth – and when he finally got a chance to make a pass he sadly gave the ball away on both occasions.

It seems highly unlikely that Jim Smith will follow up his interest unless he can get Launders at the right price in the close season. His long-term future would appear to lie elsewhere.

FB Jacob LAURSEN • 16
DERBY COUNTY • BORN: 6.10.71

Danish international Jacob Laursen signed for Derby soon after Jim Smith's side won promotion to the Premiership in 1996.

He missed just one game in 1998–99 and helped build Derby's fine defensive record in the campaign's first half. No side scored more than twice against them until the 4–1 defeat at Elland Road in March – their 30th league game and 38th in all competitions.

Laursen's contribution included 59% of 86 tackles won and 279 defensive clearances. He also made 41 blocks and 32 interceptions as Derby attempted to steal a UEFA Cup spot.

But County managed more than three goals in only two matches before the 4–3 defeat on April 3 by Newcastle – and that was against lower division sides in the FA Cup. Laursen's nine efforts were split equally between attempts on target, those off target and those blocked, and he also only tried seven dribbles all season.

After another campaign of consolidation, Laursen will hope he and Derby can push on in 1999–2000 to realise their European dreams.

APPEARANCES	
Start (sub)	37 (0)
Minutes on pitch	3207
GOAL ATTEMPTS	
Goals	0
PASSING & CROSSING	
Passing	890
Passing accuracy	71%
Crossing	24
Crossing accuracy	21%
DEFENDING	
Tackles	86
Tackles won	59%
DISCIPLINE	
Fouls	31
Yellow cards	7
Red cards	0

AM Stan LAZARIDIS • 17
WEST HAM UNITED • BORN: 16.8.72

APPEARANCES	
Start (sub)	11 (4)
Minutes on pitch	1021
GOAL ATTEMPTS	
Goals	0
Shots on target	1
Shooting accuracy	33%
PASSING	
Goal assists	1
Passing accuracy	78%
Crossing accuracy	39%
DRIBBLING	
Dribbles & runs	82
Dribble completion	78%
DISCIPLINE	
Yellow cards	2
Red cards	0

The 1999–2000 season will be Stan Lazaridis's fifth with the Hammers and he will be hoping for better fortune than he found in 1998–99.

After starting the first five games and impressing at left full-back against the likes of David Beckham, injuries and loss of form set in and he missed out on most of West Ham's successful season, which saw them finish fifth and qualify for the InterToto Cup.

He prefers to play as a left-sided midfielder, but in Harry Redknapp's 5-3-2 formation has had to fit into the wing-back's defensive role.

Lazaridis made 15 appearances in all and his strengths show in his statistics. He won only 57% of his tackles, but completed 78% of 82 dribbles and found a team-mate with a well-above-average 39% of his crosses. He only claimed one goal assist, but has shown in previous seasons that he can be a dangerous offensive weapon.

"Skippy" looks set to continue as a squad player, playing on the left of midfield or in his less-preferred wing-back role in Redknapp's preferred formation.

FB | Graeme LE SAUX • 14
CHELSEA • BORN: 17.10.68

Dynamic left-back Graeme Le Saux hit the headlines for all the wrong reasons in February. Fined and banned for one game over his Stamford Bridge spat with Robbie Fowler, it should not be forgotten that the England man also played some excellent football.

The Blues' last game of the season against Derby County marked Le Saux's 200th appearance in a Chelsea shirt and he looks set for many more. Comfortable bringing the ball forward, he made 114 dribbles and runs and delivered 132 crosses in 1998–99, setting up two goals in the process.

Labelled by some as "dirty" and singled out for abuse by opposition fans, he actually ended the season with a fair disciplinary record. He was sent off in the fiery game against Blackburn Rovers on September 21 for fighting, but picked up just four cautions in the Premiership and only committed 21 fouls – an average of less than one a game. That record is all the more creditable since Le Saux attempted 101 tackles and made more than 200 blocks, clearances and interceptions.

APPEARANCES	
Start (sub)	30 (1)
Minutes on pitch	2541
GOAL ATTEMPTS	
Goals	0
PASSING & CROSSING	
Passing	1261
Passing accuracy	78%
Crossing	132
Crossing accuracy	26%
DEFENDING	
Tackles	101
Tackles won	65%
DISCIPLINE	
Fouls	21
Yellow cards	4
Red cards	1

L

AM | Matthew LE TISSIER • 7
SOUTHAMPTON • BORN: 14.10.68

APPEARANCES	
Start (sub)	20 (10)
Minutes on pitch	1915
GOAL ATTEMPTS	
Goals	7
Shots on target	32
Shooting accuracy	56%
PASSING	
Goal assists	7
Passing accuracy	68%
Crossing accuracy	34%
DRIBBLING	
Dribbles & runs	84
Dribble completion	68%
DISCIPLINE	
Yellow cards	10
Red cards	0

Enigmatic Channel Islander Matt Le Tissier may not be hitting the heights of previous years, but proved Southampton's saviour once more against Wimbledon in the penultimate game of the 1998–99 season.

After coming off the bench at 0–0 with 20 minutes to go, "Le God" made one goal and scored another, propelling his beloved Saints out of the relegation zone for the first time.

Le Tissier had endured a frustrating time hitherto, suffering a string of niggling injuries and seeing himself in and out of the side. But despite his on-off season, the Guernseyman still finished joint-top scorer with seven goals, including one from the penalty spot.

His delivery into the box remained first-class, as shown by his cross completion rate of 34% and seven goal assists. On the flip side, poor tackling and a tendency to pick up silly bookings remained his shortcomings.

It remains to be seen whether a fit Le Tissier can reproduce his best form – and whether Dave Jones will give him the chance. But his place in the Dell's Hall of Fame is assured.

Carl LEABURN • 15
WIMBLEDON • BORN: 30.3.69

While playboy footballer George Graham had a penchant for hard-working centre-backs, his contemporary, solid defender Joe Kinnear, seemed to relish strikers who are good in the air. The former Dons boss splashed out £300,000 for Carl Leaburn early in 1998.

Leaburn started plenty of games that autumn and was a regular until Kinnear added John Hartson to his ever-expanding stable and Leaburn drifted out of first-team contention.

The former Charlton man had only six efforts on target and failed to find the net in the Premiership – his one goal came in the Worthington Cup against Portsmouth. Ten of his other league efforts all went wide.

His 66% pass completion rate was poor, mainly due to the number of headed flick-ons that went astray – 69 out of 462 total passes.

Leaburn's other noteable statistic was a dismissal for conceding a penalty against Aston Villa by pulling Julian Joachim's shirt. His contribution in other areas of the pitch was limited and he could be a casualty of the club's rebuilding programme.

APPEARANCES	
Start (sub)	14 (8)
Minutes on pitch	1208
GOAL ATTEMPTS	
Goals	0
Goals/shots ratio	0%
SHOOTING	
Shots on target	6
Shooting accuracy	38%
PASSING	
Goal assists	1
Passing accuracy	66%
DISCIPLINE	
Fouls	34
Offside	9
Yellow cards	1
Red cards	1

Frank LEBOEUF • 5
CHELSEA • BORN: 22.1.68

APPEARANCES	
Start (sub)	33 (0)
Minutes on pitch	2861
GOAL ATTEMPTS	
Goals	4
DEFENDING	
Blocks	37
Headed clearances	227
Other clearances	200
Interceptions	67
Tackles won	97
PASSING	
Passing accuracy	75%
DISCIPLINE	
Fouls	37
Yellow cards	7
Red cards	1

Elegant centre-back Frank Leboeuf has taken plenty of flak since moving from Strasbourg to Stamford Bridge in July 1996. But the harshest critic cannot deny he had a superb 1998–99 season.

Playing alongside Marcel Desailly clearly sharpened his defensive skills. He looked less vulnerable in the air than in previous years and won 70% of his 139 attempted tackles.

Happily for the Blues, this defensive improvement did not compromise the more creative side of his game. His distribution over distance was particularly impressive. Leboeuf completed 255 long passes, more than anyone else in the Premiership, proving that the long-ball game could be a thing of beauty.

As the platform for many of Chelsea's best attacks, he was also encouraged to bring the ball forward. Seldom dispossessed in these forays, he ended the season with a remarkable dribble completion rate of 98%.

The club's regular penalty-taker, he also scored some important goals and was rewarded with a new contract towards the season's end.

AM Robert LEE • 7
NEWCASTLE UNITED • BORN: 1.2.66

The 1998–99 Carling Premiership season was a frustrating one for Rob Lee. Constantly linked with a move away from St James's Park and seemingly no longer in Ruud Gullit's plans, he lost the club captaincy to Alan Shearer and ended up on the losing side in a Wembley FA Cup final for the second season in a row.

Lee had a reasonable campaign as far as his performances were concerned, completing 86% of his passes and a creditable 80% of his dribbles and runs. The England man also won 62% of his tackles and committed just 30 fouls all season, although he incurred the wrath of referees with six yellow cards.

The former Charlton man was poor in front of goal, however, with just five shots on target all season and another 16 flying wide.

Lee's future remained in the balance as the 1998–99 season drew to a close. With Ruud Gullit using 34 players across the course of the campaign and more changes likely in the summer, it is increasingly doubtful whether Lee has much of a future in the black and white of Newcastle United.

APPEARANCES	
Start (sub)	20 (6)
Minutes on pitch	1974
GOAL ATTEMPTS	
Goals	0
Shots on target	5
Shooting accuracy	24%
PASSING	
Goal assists	2
Passing accuracy	86%
Crossing accuracy	29%
DRIBBLING	
Dribbles & runs	85
Dribble completion	80%
DISCIPLINE	
Yellow cards	6
Red cards	0

L

M Neil LENNON • 7
LEICESTER CITY • BORN: 25.6.71

APPEARANCES	
Start (sub)	37 (0)
Minutes on pitch	3291
GOAL ATTEMPTS	
Goals	1
PASSING	
Passes	2094
Passing accuracy	85%
DEFENDING	
Interceptions	47
Clearances	82
Tackles	193
Tackles won	60%
DISCIPLINE	
Fouls	38
Yellow cards	6
Red cards	0

Neil Lennon is so highly-rated these days that sections of the media have linked him with a move to Manchester United. When you consider his influence in midfield, it is easy to see why Leicester are keen to hang on to him.

The Foxes' general completed a superb 85% of his 2,094 passes – a total only Liverpool's Jamie Redknapp managed to beat. Of those, Lennon managed three goal assists.

The combative, carrot-topped ball-winner was comfortable in possession, completing 81% of his 85 dribbles and runs, and as solid in the tackle as you would expect, making 193 challenges and winning six out of 10. He was also willing to track back into defence, adding 82 clearances to his impressive statistics.

The one slight blot on his copybook was his disciplinary record. Despite conceding an average of one foul a game, six of them were severe enough to warrant the yellow card.

At 28, the talismanic Lennon is at the peak of his game and Leicester City will be keen to keep the influential Northern Ireland midfield player as the heartbeat of their side.

AM   Oyvind LEONHARDSEN • 8
LIVERPOOL • BORN: 17.8.70

After three successful seasons at Wimbledon, Oyvind Leonhardsen seemed to have earned a dream move to Liverpool, but sadly his time at Anfield has become more of a nightmare.

Injury and loss of form have restricted the busy midfielder's appearances; nor did it help that he was competing with top talents such as Patrik Berger and Steve McManaman.

Leonhardsen featured for just 654 minutes in 1998–99, most of which were completed amid the ashes of Liverpool's campaign in the last seven games of the season.

He netted his only goal in the 3–1 defeat of Blackburn Rovers. That effort was one of seven in total, with four being blocked and the other three hitting the target.

The Norwegian demonstrated his quality on the ball by completing 81% of his passes and also won 68% of his 19 challenges, showing he has tenacity as well as guile.

If he survives Gerard Houllier's summer sales, then with Steve McManaman off to Real Madrid, Leonhardsen could finally kick-start his Liverpool career.

APPEARANCES	
Start (sub)	7 (2)
Minutes on pitch	654
GOAL ATTEMPTS	
Goals	1
Shots on target	3
Shooting accuracy	100%
PASSING	
Goal assists	0
Passing accuracy	81%
Crossing accuracy	14%
DRIBBLING	
Dribbles & runs	12
Dribble completion	100%
DISCIPLINE	
Yellow cards	0
Red cards	0

S   Derek LILLEY • 17
LEEDS UNITED • BORN: 9.2.74

Scottish striker Derek Lilley began the 1998–99 Carling Premiership season on the Leeds United substitutes' bench, looking on wistfully as first-choice frontmen Jimmy Floyd Hasselbaink and Harry Kewell set about demolishing defences on a regular basis.

In the opening game of the campaign, a dour 0–0 draw at Middlesbrough, Lilley came on for Lee Sharpe in the absence of Hasselbaink – but he was to make just one other league substitute appearance, on September 12 at Everton.

In 25 minutes of Premiership football, he had two shots, forcing one save, and completed three of his four passes.

With little chance of first-team action in the English top flight, Lilley went to Hearts on loan in January, then switched to Bury until the end of the season.

The 25-year-old former Scottish youth international will hope for more opportunities at Elland Road in the 1999–2000 season but will now have to compete with the prodigious Alan Smith as well.

S   Kevin LISBIE • 22
CHARLTON ATHLETIC • BORN: 17.10.78

A lively, pacy striker, Kevin Lisbie is a former youth international with bags of potential. But he has yet to develop the physical strength to cope with Carling Premiership defences and as a result was only used for 22 minutes by Alan Curbishley in 1998–99.

He was sent out on loan to Nationwide Division Two play-off finalists Gillingham, where he became an instant hit with the fans by scoring three goals in his first four appearances.

In the Premiership, he completed 71% of his seven passes and was successful with the one cross and dribble he had. Playing off the shoulders of opposition centre-backs, it was not surprising that he was also caught offside twice.

His form in Division Two demonstrated there is much still to come from this young striker. And should Charlton decide to keep him, Lisbie could well be a dangerous player for the Addicks in years to come. He may find he gets more chances now Charlton are back in Division One.

Fredrik LJUNGBERG • 8
ARSENAL • BORN: 16.4.77

After impressing for Sweden in the 2–1 defeat of England, £3 million man Ljungberg began his Arsenal career with a bang. In Ian Wright's number eight shirt, he scored on his debut as a substitute and got booked in September's 3–0 home defeat of Manchester United.

Sadly, that dramatic start proved something of a false dawn. He struggled to adjust to the Premiership's physical demands and seldom managed a full 90 minutes for his new club.

Arsene Wenger preferred to use Ljungberg in wide areas, encouraging him to use his pace to get behind defences.

He did manage 887 minutes of Premiership football in 1998–99 but his form was nowhere near good enough to earn him a regular starting slot in the first team. He managed 10 shots on target, but his debut strike against United was his only goal in 1998–99.

Given an extended run in the team his confidence may grow, but with the likes of Ray Parlour, Marc Overmars and Nwankwo Kanu ahead of him Ljungberg may find it hard to prove exactly how good he can be.

APPEARANCES	
Start (sub)	10 (6)
Minutes on pitch	887
GOAL ATTEMPTS	
Goals	1
Shots on target	10
Shooting accuracy	53%
PASSING	
Goal assists	0
Passing accuracy	75%
Crossing accuracy	12%
DRIBBLING	
Dribbles & runs	68
Dribble completion	60%
DISCIPLINE	
Yellow cards	4
Red cards	0

L

Steve LOMAS • 11
WEST HAM UNITED • BORN: 18.1.74

APPEARANCES	
Start (sub)	30 (0)
Minutes on pitch	2670
GOAL ATTEMPTS	
Goals	1
PASSING	
Passes	1241
Passing accuracy	80%
DEFENDING	
Interceptions	15
Clearances	137
Tackles	96
Tackles won	67%
DISCIPLINE	
Fouls	36
Yellow cards	4
Red cards	1

Club captain at West Ham, under-rated midfielder Steve Lomas started the year in the centre of the park, but was used in virtually all the midfield positions. He even played as a wing-back when injuries mounted up.

A combative player with excellent passing skills, Lomas completed 80% of his 1,241 passes and was credited with two assists.

His strengths lie in defence, and the Carling Opta statistics show he made 96 tackles, winning 67% of them, together with 15 blocks, 15 interceptions and 137 clearances.

His tough-tackling style regularly caught the referee's eye. He amassed 36 fouls, four yellow cards and one red, for a reckless challenge on Harry Kewell in the 5–1 defeat by Leeds.

Harry Redknapp may look for improvement in his captain's shooting next season, with the former Manchester City player managing just one goal and seven shots on target all year.

A key figure at Upton Park, Lomas is likely to figure in any InterToto Cup campaign and will be looking to lead the Hammers even further up the Premiership table in 1999–2000.

Matthieu LOUIS-JEAN • 2
FB — NOTTINGHAM FOREST • BORN: 22.2.76

One of the lesser-known French imports into the English game in recent seasons, Matthieu Louis-Jean joined Nottingham Forest on loan from Le Havre in the summer of 1998.

The raiding right-back struggled to make an impact until Ron Atkinson took over, and then missed just one game in the run-in – and that due to suspension, after a red card in the 2–1 home defeat by Newcastle United.

Louis-Jean completed 71% of his dribbles and runs but only connected with 19% of his crosses, mirroring Forest's general inability to supply frontmen with clear scoring chances.

The Frenchman made 98 clearances, too, but his indiscipline was costly. He only committed 17 fouls, but earned five yellow cards and that one dismissal for their severity.

The 23-year-old did not get any attempts at goal on target, but he did contribute one assist to Forest's season.

Forest have first option to buy the full-back, but whether or not he features for the east Midlanders in 1999–2000 depends very much on the new boss at the City Ground.

APPEARANCES

Start (sub)	15 (1)
Minutes on pitch	1369

GOAL ATTEMPTS

Goals	0

PASSING & CROSSING

Passing	443
Passing accuracy	77%
Crossing	37
Crossing accuracy	19%

DEFENDING

Tackles	78
Tackles won	60%

DISCIPLINE

Fouls	17
Yellow cards	5
Red cards	1

Claus LUNDEKVAM • 5
CB — SOUTHAMPTON • BORN: 22.3.73

APPEARANCES

Start (sub)	30 (3)
Minutes on pitch	2726

GOAL ATTEMPTS

Goals	0

DEFENDING

Blocks	31
Headed clearances	316
Other clearances	137
Interceptions	42
Tackles won	67

PASSING

Passing accuracy	78%

DISCIPLINE

Fouls	42
Yellow cards	3
Red cards	1

At his best, Lundekvam is a cool and composed defender, but most Saints fans will agree he is prone to occasional lapses of concentration. Nonetheless, like the rest of the Southampton defence he was superb in the final weeks of the 1998–99 season.

The Norwegian international made headlines after his contentious claim that England skipper Alan Shearer was way past his best, but made an impression on the pitch too. He won 79% of his 85 tackles, much more than his central defensive partner Ken Monkou.

Lundekvam's total of 453 clearances is also high, but hardly a surprise as the Saints were on the back foot for most of the season. Able to bring the ball out of defence, he can often be seen striding into the opposition's half; but he failed to produce a single effort on target in 2,726 minutes on the pitch.

Lundekvam was controversially sent off at Aston Villa in April when he saw red for a second bookable offence, even though a free kick appeared already to have been awarded in Southampton's favour.

FB **Des LYTTLE • 22**
NOTTINGHAM FOREST • BORN: 26.9.71

The epitome of the squad player in the 1998–99 season, Des Lyttle filled in when either of the two Frenchman ahead of him in the pecking order (Thierry Bonalair and Matthieu Louis-Jean) was unavailable, or as a replacement from the bench.

Lyttle's statistics are not the most impressive – he only found a team-mate with 70% of his passes, made just three dribbles and runs and 12 crosses – but he had little time in the first team to acclimatize to the Carling Premiership.

He did fire three attempts at goal, but with one on target, one wide and one blocked, the threat Lyttle posed to opposition defences was anything but large.

With a new boss installed at the City Ground, Lyttle should have a chance to impress during the 1999–2000 season.

He will hope to stake a claim to a more regular first-team spot as Forest aim to bounce back into the Premiership at the first attempt following their dismal campaign in the top flight.

S **Mickael MADAR • 18**
EVERTON • BORN: 8.5.68

One of the less successful imports of recent years, Mickael Madar spent just over a season with the Toffees before being allowed to leave for Paris St Germain on a free transfer.

Everton were not out of pocket, because they themselves had picked up the long-locked striker from Deportivo La Coruna for nothing in December 1997.

It was hoped Madar would emerge as a suitable partner for Duncan Ferguson, but it was clear he did not fit in with Walter Smith's plans. After two appearances in December of the 1998–99 Premiership campaign, the Everton boss bid the Frenchman *adieu*.

Madar's pass completion rate was very poor, with only 56% of his balls finding a blue shirt. Of the four shots he attempted, only one hit the target and he made virtually no other contribution to the Toffeemen's relegation battle at a time when goal-shy Everton desperately needed his inspiration.

Everton eventually found help up front from their own youth ranks in the form of Francis Jeffers.

L

M **Neil MADDISON • 15**
MIDDLESBROUGH • BORN: 2.10.69

APPEARANCES	
Start (sub)	10 (10)
Minutes on pitch	1058
GOAL ATTEMPTS	
Goals	0
PASSING	
Passes	460
Passing accuracy	77%
DEFENDING	
Interceptions	15
Clearances	24
Tackles	34
Tackles won	62%
DISCIPLINE	
Fouls	18
Yellow cards	1
Red cards	0

A versatile member of the Middlesbrough squad, Neil Maddison is comfortable virtually anywhere in midfield or defence.

Having joined Southampton as a trainee, the Darlington-born player spent 10 happy years at the Dell, but then returned north to sign for Boro in October 1997.

Maddison's transfer fee of £250,000 quickly proved money well spent and he played an important role in the side which won promotion to the Premiership in May 1998.

He was not an automatic first choice in the 1998–99 season and regularly featured only as a substitute. Although his favoured position is central midfield, Bryan Robson has used him in roles as varied as sweeper and centre-back.

Busy and hard-working, Maddison performed solidly for Middlesbrough, completing a respectable 77% of his 460 passes, winning an excellent 62% of his tackles, supplying 41 crosses and claiming one goal assist.

But in a more defensive role he managed just a handful of shots and failed to find the net himself in the 1998–99 Premiership season.

M Jim MAGILTON • 24
SHEFFIELD WEDNESDAY • BORN: 6.5.69

Northern Ireland international midfielder Jim Magilton began the 1998–99 season hoping to earn a regular place in the Sheffield Wednesday team after spending much of the previous campaign on the bench.

But after substitute appearances in the humiliating Worthington Cup matches against Cambridge, Magilton figured just four more times in an Owls shirt. His one and only start came in the 4–0 thrashing at Middlesbrough, before being brought on in the matches at Leeds United, Newcastle United and Chelsea.

Unhappy at his lack of first-team exposure at Hillsborough, Magilton moved on loan to Ipswich Town. The promotion-chasers, ultimately beaten in the play-offs for the third year in a row, were so impressed with the former Oxford United and Southampton man that they snapped him up on transfer deadline day for a fee of £682,500, plus further payments depending on appearances.

His limited Carling Premiership statistics for Wednesday reveal an impressive 86% pass completion rate, but little else.

G Alex MANNINGER • 13
ARSENAL • BORN: 4.6.77

First-class second choice: Alex Manninger

APPEARANCES	
Start (sub)	6 (0)
Minutes on pitch	540
SHOT STOPPING	
Goals conceded	2
Clean sheets	4
Saves	18
Saves/shots	90%
DISTRIBUTION	
Distribution	157
Distribution %	39%
CATCHING	
Crosses caught	10
Crosses dropped	3
DISCIPLINE	
Yellow cards	0
Red cards	0

Alex Manninger spent most of the 1998–99 season on the Arsenal bench as back-up to England's number one, David Seaman. But he got the chance to stake a claim for six league games during the campaign, and did well.

He will not remember his Worthington Cup outing against Chelsea with fondness, making several blunders on the way to a 5–0 home thrashing. But in the Premiership, conceding only two goals in nine hours of football is a great tribute to the young Austrian, who saved 90% of all shots fired at him.

His 77% catch success rate was less impressive but his short-range distribution was excellent, with a 95% success rate from 43 throws or short kicks. His dire long-kicking accuracy of 18% perhaps says more about a lack of target men than Manninger's ability.

Arsenal fans have certainly not forgotten his heroics in the 1997–98 double-winning season and, despite his few first-team appearances, Manninger has proved he has the ability and class to take over from Seaman whenever the England star decides to call it a day.

Dario MARCOLIN • 18
BLACKBURN ROVERS • BORN: 28.10.71

Arriving on loan from Italian giants Lazio in late October, injury severely restricted Dario Marcolin's contribution to Rovers' campaign. He made just five Premiership starts and five substitute appearances in 1998–99.

A left-sided midfielder, Marcolin's pedigree is considerable. He captained Italy to two European under-21 championships and played more than 150 matches in Serie A.

When he did play his quality showed, with a highly-impressive 79% of his challenges won and 79% of passes completed. The Italian hit three of his eight shots on target, scoring his only goal in his third appearance – the 3–2 defeat at Manchester United in November.

He was also used in Blackburn's cup campaigns, making his first start in a Rovers shirt in the Worthington Cup win over Newcastle and figuring in all of Rovers' FA Cup matches in 1998–99.

Marcolin shows yet again how injuries wrecked Rovers' season, joining several top-quality players who were forced to watch much of the dismal campaign from the sidelines.

APPEARANCES

Start (sub)	5 (5)
Minutes on pitch	565

GOAL ATTEMPTS

Goals	1

PASSING

Passes	259
Passing accuracy	79%

DEFENDING

Interceptions	8
Clearances	14
Tackles	19
Tackles won	79%

DISCIPLINE

Fouls	8
Yellow cards	4
Red cards	0

M

Javier MARGAS • 30
WEST HAM UNITED • BORN: 14.1.68

APPEARANCES

Start (sub)	3 (0)
Minutes on pitch	270

GOAL ATTEMPTS

Goals	0

DEFENDING

Blocks	3
Headed clearances	35
Other clearances	11
Interceptions	1
Tackles won	7

PASSING

Passing accuracy	63%

DISCIPLINE

Fouls	1
Yellow cards	0
Red cards	0

After impressing for Chile during the World Cup, Javier Margas was signed by Harry Redknapp for £1.8 million before the start of 1998–99.

Unfortunately, his hugely disappointing season ended abruptly when he walked out on West Ham and went back to his family in Chile. As a result, Margas may well have played his last Carling Premiership match for West Ham.

He won seven of his 14 tackles and made 46 clearances in his 270 minutes on the pitch, but the lasting memories of Margas will sadly be of individual blunders.

He was in the heart of the defence when Wimbledon overturned a 3–0 deficit at Upton Park to win 4–3 by pumping high balls into the box.

And Margas failed to distinguish himself in his other two starts either, completing just 63% of his passes.

During the World Cup, Margas looked like a player who could make it in the Premiership, but poor form has left the Chilean unable to claim a regular place in the Hammers' defence.

Silvio MARIC • 10
NEWCASTLE UNITED • BORN: 20.3.75

Ruud Gullit was delighted to have snapped up Silvio Maric from Croatia Zagreb for just over £3.65million as transfer deadline day approached, especially as he was being tracked by many of Europe's top clubs.

He made his debut in the FA Cup against Everton, but his Premiership debut came in the 2–1 win at Nottingham Forest.

It took the Croatian midfielder a while to settle down, and the season finished before he became acclimatized to the pace of English football, but he certainly looks to have the technical ability to be a useful member of the Newcastle squad.

Maric failed to score – with perhaps his most glaring miss saved for the FA Cup final – but he did create one goal for the Magpies. He completed an average 79% of his passes and, even though the game did seem to pass him by at times, he won 65% of his 17 tackles.

When Maric was running with the ball, his lack of Premiership experience was perhaps reflected in his disappointing 58% dribble completion rate.

APPEARANCES	
Start (sub)	9 (1)
Minutes on pitch	661
GOAL ATTEMPTS	
Goals	0
Shots on target	4
Shooting accuracy	40%
PASSING	
Goal assists	1
Passing accuracy	79%
Crossing accuracy	28%
DRIBBLING	
Dribbles & runs	33
Dribble completion	58%
DISCIPLINE	
Yellow cards	1
Red cards	0

Chris MARSDEN • 4
SOUTHAMPTON • BORN: 3.1.69

APPEARANCES	
Start (sub)	14 (0)
Minutes on pitch	1246
GOAL ATTEMPTS	
Goals	2
PASSING	
Passes	583
Passing accuracy	76%
DEFENDING	
Interceptions	10
Clearances	35
Tackles	87
Tackles won	60%
DISCIPLINE	
Fouls	34
Yellow cards	5
Red cards	0

Chris Marsden was reunited with his former manager Dave Jones when he arrived from Birmingham City in mid-season 1998–99.

The bald central midfielder, who was with Jones at Stockport County when they won the Division Two title, has already repaid a chunk of his £750,000 transfer fee, scoring two priceless headers in the season's dying weeks.

The energetic Marsden added bite to the Saints' midfield, winning 60% of his 87 tackles. Robust rather than cultured, he completed 76% of his 583 passes, although he did not register any goal assists.

He demonstrated an ability to read play well and provide cover for his team-mates with 10 interceptions. His 35 clearances similarly reflect a willingness to help out in defence.

A journeyman of the lower leagues, Marsden played for a total of seven clubs before joining Southampton but had never experienced top-flight football.

Having been given the opportunity to play in the Premiership, Marsden has seized his chance with both hands.

S **Ian MARSHALL • 20**
LEICESTER CITY • BORN: 20.3.66

Ian Marshall, the forgotten man of Filbert Street, made a thrilling re-appearance toward the end of the 1998–99 campaign when Tony Cottee and Emile Heskey were feeling the stresses and strains of a rigorous season – and showed that he is still a wily campaigner.

Marshall scored in three successive games, the first two being 1–0 victories for the Foxes and the third one which could have been, had Southampton not staged a stirring fightback.

His best moment came when he fired the winner at Liverpool as City won at Anfield for the second year running.

The former Oldham player, who has turned out up front and at the back throughout his career, showed that he can still pose a threat to defences in the penalty area with his goals. But his pass completion rate was poor at 61% and he contributed very little to all-round team play.

Now 33 years of age, he is likely to continue his role as a back-up striker for the Foxes in the 1999–2000 campaign rather than move on to another club.

CB **Scott MARSHALL • 19**
SOUTHAMPTON • BORN: 1.5.73

A former Scottish under-21 international, Scott Marshall was unable to break into the centre of the Double-winning Arsenal defence with Tony Adams and Martin Keown in such imperious form and instead joined Southampton in the summer of 1998.

He made a couple of appearances for the Saints but contrived to score own-goals in consecutive games against Leeds and Newcastle. That hardly helped their perilous plight at the foot of the Premiership.

Marshall was eventually loaned out to Scottish giants Glasgow Celtic on transfer deadline day.

During his 180 minutes on pitch for Southampton he won all three of his tackles, conceding four fouls and being booked once. He also had a couple of shots, with one hitting the target and the other failing to trouble the goalkeeper.

Sadly, even a move to his native Scotland failed to ensure regular first-team football and his long-term future appears decidedly uncertain.

M

G **Nigel MARTYN • 1**
LEEDS UNITED • BORN: 11.8.66

APPEARANCES	
Start (sub)	34 (0)
Minutes on pitch	3016
SHOT STOPPING	
Goals conceded	28
Clean sheets	13
Saves	134
Saves/shots	83%
DISTRIBUTION	
Distribution	1072
Distribution %	46%
CATCHING	
Crosses caught	85
Crosses dropped	3
DISCIPLINE	
Yellow cards	0
Red cards	0

Consistently among the Premiership's top 'keepers, Nigel Martyn played a major part in an excellent season for David O'Leary's Leeds.

He kept 13 clean sheets and conceded just 28 goals as he helped United to achieve the third-best defensive record in the country.

Martyn had to make 134 saves during 1998–99 and will be hoping O'Leary can use his own experience as a defender to reduce his workload. But, when called upon, Martyn's 83% saves-to-shots ratio was only bettered by David Seaman and Mark Bosnich.

The former Crystal Palace favourite also had a reasonable catch success ratio of 97% after claiming 85 crosses and punching 26 more. Thankfully for O'Leary's blood pressure, Martyn was less prone to making his customary breaks out of goal to confront attackers, using experience to improve his decision-making.

The Cornishman is unchallenged as David Seaman's understudy at international level, but will be hoping he can usurp the Arsenal number one sooner rather than later as he enters the 1999–2000 season at the age of 33.

Marco MATERAZZI • 15
EVERTON • BORN: 19.8.73

Marco Materazzi can claim to be one of Walter Smith's more successful signings. The no-nonsense centre-back made some impressive displays in the heart of an Everton defence often relied upon to dig out results when the Toffees were finding it difficult to score.

Materazzi's sole goal came in a game quite at odds with Everton's season to date – the 5–0 victory over Middlesbrough. He struck direct from a free kick as the Toffees scored more in one game than they had at home all season.

The Italian made 299 clearances, 29 blocks and 56 interceptions. He also won 73% of his challenges, illustrating his ability to defend.

Other parts of his game were less impressive. He only completed 69% of his passes and earned seven yellow cards and one red, although the sending-off was harsh after he was shown a second yellow in the game for "intent" by referee Rob Harris.

Materazzi will be one of the cornerstones of Walter Smith's side's push up the table in 1999–2000 – assuming the Scotsman can hang on to him.

APPEARANCES	
Start (sub)	26 (1)
Minutes on pitch	2269

GOAL ATTEMPTS	
Goals	1

DEFENDING	
Blocks	29
Headed clearances	197
Other clearances	102
Interceptions	56
Tackles won	85

PASSING	
Passing accuracy	69%

DISCIPLINE	
Fouls	46
Yellow cards	7
Red cards	1

Dominic MATTEO • 21
LIVERPOOL • BORN: 24.4.74

APPEARANCES	
Start (sub)	16 (4)
Minutes on pitch	1560

GOAL ATTEMPTS	
Goals	1

DEFENDING	
Blocks	19
Headed clearances	96
Other clearances	41
Interceptions	16
Tackles won	34

PASSING	
Passing accuracy	84%

DISCIPLINE	
Fouls	28
Yellow cards	2
Red cards	1

Defender Dominic Matteo did not make his first Premiership start of the 1998–99 season until January 16 against Southampton, having suffered from niggling injuries in the early part of the campaign.

But after that match, when he scored in the Reds' 7–1 victory, he was an automatic selection in defence and has clearly impressed Gerard Houllier with his displays.

The Liverpool back-line has come in for much criticism in recent seasons, but Matteo has often looked their most composed defender and has been rewarded with England under-21 and "B" caps. But he is still waiting for that first full international appearance.

He played mostly in central defence but also at left wing-back, and ventured forward 43 times without being dispossessed.

Some critics say he lacks aggression, and he only made 50 challenges during the 1998–99 season.

And with Gerard Houllier certain to splash out on new defenders in 1999–2000, he may find competition for places is tough.

Jesper MATTSON • 25
NOTTINGHAM FOREST • BORN: 18.4.68

A £300,000 signing from Halmstads, Jesper Mattson played sporadically during the 1998–99 campaign after making his debut against Leicester City on December 12.

He started five games and also made one substitute appearance for Forest, but only featured on the winning side once – in the 3-1 victory over Wimbledon at Selhurst Park.

Mattson had a disappointing start to his career in England and rarely looked happy facing Premiership-quality strikers. He won 59% of tackles and made 69 clearances, but his distribution was poor – he completed only 70% of the passes he attempted.

To be fair, Mattson has not been able to establish himself in the side as yet and Forest fans may have to wait to see the best of Dave Bassett's final signing for the club. Whether he will get the chance under a new manager in Nationwide Division One in season 1999–2000 remains to be seen.

But the 31-year-old will hope to use his experience to help Forest back into the top flight at the first attempt.

David MAY • 4
MANCHESTER UNITED • BORN: 24.6.70

David May featured sporadically in the 1998–99 season, playing 420 minutes of Premiership football. He found himself down Manchester United's central defensive pecking order, behind Jaap Stam and Ronny Johnsen and competing with Wes Brown and Henning Berg, although he did earn a starting place in the FA Cup final.

The former Blackburn man remains an important member of Alex Ferguson's squad and made several Premiership appearances at the end of the season as the fixtures piled up for Manchester United and the rotation system came into play.

He performed competently and his tackling success was solid at 61%. He also stood up well to make 57 clearances and eight blocks.

A good example of a player who would walk into most other Premiership sides, May has never complained about his lack of opportunities, demonstrating his commitment to the club in the Champions League final when he was one of the first off the bench to celebrate United's historic treble.

M

M Gary McALLISTER • 10
COVENTRY CITY • BORN: 25.12.64

APPEARANCES	
Start (sub)	29 (0)
Minutes on pitch	2564
GOAL ATTEMPTS	
Goals	3
PASSING	
Passes	1358
Passing accuracy	74%
DEFENDING	
Interceptions	40
Clearances	64
Tackles	74
Tackles won	62%
DISCIPLINE	
Fouls	31
Yellow cards	5
Red cards	0

Gary McAllister announced his retirement from international football in 1998–99, following a campaign of abuse from certain sections of Scotland's support. It will have been a grave disappointment to McAllister, who has enjoyed a long and successful career at club and international level and had recently overcome a career-threatening cruciate ligament injury.

Having been out of the game for 10 months, McAllister made a winning comeback for the Sky Blues in their 1–0 home victory over Sheffield Wednesday in October 1998.

The Motherwell-born midfielder went on to score three times during the campaign and provide two further goal assists. With 1,358 passes he was always at the heart of the action, but the stats show he conceded too much possession, registering a below-average 74% pass completion rate.

Though not always able to maintain the level of involvement that was once his hallmark, he showed his reading of the game with 40 interceptions. A steadying influence, he is still one of Coventry City's most important players.

Jason McATEER • 34
BLACKBURN ROVERS • BORN: 18.6.71

Jason McAteer started 1998–99 with Liverpool and made 13 appearances before his £4 million move to Blackburn Rovers in January. Following his arrival at Ewood Park, he showed his ability as an attacking wide man before injury against Charlton curtailed his season.

At Rovers, the wing-back became an attacking midfielder and the Eire international scored his first goal for his new club in his fourth match, against Sheffield Wednesday.

His pass completion rate dropped after he switched clubs mid-season. In Liverpool's slick-passing team, he completed 83%; playing in a struggling Rovers side the rate dropped to 74%, leaving him with a slightly above-average figure of 78% for the season.

He managed to complete 80% of his dribbles and runs and 29% of his crosses. He also had two goal assists to his credit.

McAteer's direct style of play down the right flank is sure to terrorize Nationwide League defences just as it did for Bolton and, if he can avoid injury, he is sure to do well for Blackburn in 1999–2000.

APPEARANCES	
Start (sub)	19 (7)
Minutes on pitch	1885
GOAL ATTEMPTS	
Goals	1
Shots on target	2
Shooting accuracy	25%
PASSING	
Goal assists	2
Passing accuracy	78%
Crossing accuracy	29%
DRIBBLING	
Dribbles & runs	56
Dribble completion	80%
DISCIPLINE	
Yellow cards	4
Red cards	1

Jamie McCLEN • 36
NEWCASTLE UNITED • BORN: 13.5.79

Jamie McClen made his Newcastle debut aged 19 in the FA Cup semi-final dress rehearsal against Tottenham Hotspur on April 5, as Ruud Gullit and George Graham rotated their squads in order not to show their hands for the forthcoming clash at Old Trafford.

McClen played 57 minutes before being brought off, but it was a taste of what the youngster can expect as he makes the step up from reserve football to the first team.

He completed a respectable 78% of the 36 passes he attempted and even managed to fire in an attempt at goal, although he failed to trouble Ian Walker between the Spurs sticks.

The youngster was one of 34 Magpies who picked up some silverware during 1998–99, earning winners' medals for the reserves, who won the Pontins League second division and the Arnott Insurance NFA Senior Cup.

The tenacious young midfield man will hope for more first-team opportunities in 1999–2000, but will find it hard to displace the likes of Gary Speed, Rob Lee and Dietmar Hamann.

Mark McKEEVER • 31
SHEFFIELD WEDNESDAY • BORN: 16.11.78

Young Irishman Mark McKeever may have played slightly less than three hours for Danny Wilson's Wednesday, but he has been kept busy on the pitch elsewhere this season.

The left winger went on loan to Bristol Rovers and Reading and found his time at Twerton Park and the Madejski Stadium very rewarding, scoring for Reading in a 4–0 victory over Stoke City.

Derry-born McKeever joined the Hillsborough trainee ranks after having spent some time on Peterborough's books as a YTS player, and he has progressed steadily since arriving in April 1997.

He made his Carling Premiership debut against Chelsea, in the side that held the then title-chasing Blues to a goalless draw at Hillsborough, and showed signs of his potential.

McKeever used his pace to great effect, completing 10 out of 12 dribbles and runs. He connected with one cross from six out wide and passed tidily, finding a colleague with 73% of his attempts.

Billy McKINLAY • 17
BLACKBURN ROVERS • BORN: 22.4.69

Scottish international Billy McKinlay displayed the battling qualities required by Blackburn Rovers in 1998–99. Unfortunately, his season was hampered by injury and his absence was another factor in his side's relegation.

His energy and willingness to work endeared him to the Ewood Park fans. He won 65% of his challenges and made 42 defensive clearances in his 14 starts and two substitute appearances for Rovers. But he amassed 19 fouls and four yellow cards over the season.

The Scot completed 79% of his 627 passes, but was unable to register a goal assist from his position in the centre of midfield. He rarely pushed very far forward, and as a result also failed to manage a shot on target.

When dribbling with the ball, however, he proved impossible to dispossess, completing all 10 of his dribbles and runs.

When fit, McKinlay was an automatic choice under Brian Kidd. Had Kidd had more players with his commitment, Blackburn might have beaten the drop: and the Scot will be pivotal to Rovers' promotion push in 1999–2000.

APPEARANCES	
Start (sub)	14 (2)
Minutes on pitch	1213
GOAL ATTEMPTS	
Goals	0
PASSING	
Passes	627
Passing accuracy	79%
DEFENDING	
Interceptions	5
Clearances	42
Tackles	52
Tackles won	65%
DISCIPLINE	
Fouls	19
Yellow cards	4
Red cards	0

M

Steve McMANAMAN • 7
LIVERPOOL • BORN: 11.2.72

APPEARANCES	
Start (sub)	25 (3)
Minutes on pitch	2221
GOAL ATTEMPTS	
Goals	4
Shots on target	15
Shooting accuracy	45%
PASSING	
Goal assists	6
Passing accuracy	80%
Crossing accuracy	26%
DRIBBLING	
Dribbles & runs	251
Dribble completion	76%
DISCIPLINE	
Yellow cards	2
Red cards	0

Macca bade farewell to the Kop and packed his bags for Spain but, unlike most footballers, he was not off on holiday but to continue his career in another of the world's great arenas.

The floppy-haired winger finally signed for Real Madrid and will be earning a reported £65,000 per week. Unfortunately, his form for club and country made that look poor value; but McManaman will ride out the criticism and will hope to get back to his best at the Bernabeu.

He scored four goals, but as usual should have scored more, with 15 shots on target being surpassed by 18 wayward efforts and eight more which were blocked.

McManaman did contribute six goal assists, though, and his pass completion of 80% and dribble completion of 76% were good returns if taken over the season as a whole.

He had a couple of chances at international level, but failed to impress in either match. This does not bode well for a player who will have to make an immediate impact if he wants to avoid a roasting in the heat of intense Spanish media scrutiny.

Stephen McPHAIL • 37
AM LEEDS UNITED • BORN: 9.12.79

Stephen McPhail is yet another promising youngster to come off the Leeds United production line. He has yet to make the same impact as some contemporaries, but many within the club are predicting a bright future for the 19-year-old.

After making his debut in the 1997–98 season, the FA Youth Cup winner of two years ago made a bigger impression in 1998–99 with 996 minutes on the pitch for Leeds.

Essentially a creative midfielder, he set up two goals in his limited appearances. His pass completion rate was an above-average 80%, and he also showed ability to beat players and deliver the occasional left-footed cross.

McPhail did not pose a great goal threat, but four of his nine efforts forced saves and there is no doubt he has goals in him. It should not be long before he opens his account.

1999–2000 will be another stepping-stone for McPhail as he looks to follow team-mates Alan Smith, Harry Kewell and Ian Harte and become a first-team regular in David O'Leary's exciting young side at Elland Road.

APPEARANCES
Start (sub)	11 (6)
Minutes on pitch	996

GOAL ATTEMPTS
Goals	0
Shots on target	4
Shooting accuracy	57%

PASSING
Goal assists	2
Passing accuracy	80%
Crossing accuracy	28%

DRIBBLING
Dribbles & runs	12
Dribble completion	75%

DISCIPLINE
Yellow cards	0
Red cards	0

Gary McSHEFFREY • 40
S COVENTRY CITY • BORN: 13.8.82

One-minute substitute appearances rarely merit a mention in the annals of a club's history, but when Gary McSheffrey stepped off the bench and on to the pitch at Villa Park he was making history on two counts.

Firstly, he was in the first Coventry City side ever to win a league match at Villa Park after 60 years and 25 attempts. Secondly, he became the youngest player ever to play a first-team game for Coventry City.

McSheffrey had an excellent season in the youth team, prompting Gordon Strachan to give him his first taste of top-flight football. But his campaign ultimately ended in disappointment as the Sky Blues' youth side was thrashed over two legs by West Ham in the televized FA Youth Cup final.

City club captain Gary McAllister commented afterward: "He looks a very sharp player", and he is definitely a fine prospect for the future.

McSheffrey, still only 17, will hope for further opportunities in the first XI in the 1999–2000 Carling Premiership season.

Stephen MELTON • 26
M NOTTINGHAM FOREST • BORN: 3.10.78

Stephen Melton's debut in the Premiership is likley to be his last appearance at that level for a while, since it came on the final day as Nottingham Forest beat Leicester City 1–0. Unfortunately Forest had already been relegated, and the 20-year-old will have to wait at least a season before getting another crack at the top flight.

Melton was given his debut by Ron Atkinson in midfield and did well on the final day of Big Ron's career as a football manager. He completed 79% of 33 passes during a full 90-minute outing and he will be champing at the bit for more first-team action in 1999–2000.

He also won three of the four challenges he made, showing that he is not afraid to get stuck in and ruffle a few reputations. His aim must now be to impress the new boss and keep in first-team contention.

With Forest back in Nationwide Division One, Melton may now feel he will be afforded a few more chances in the first team as the club bid for a swift return to the top flight.

Alberto MENDEZ • 23
ARSENAL • BORN: 24.10.74

For a young player at a Premiership club, breaking into the first team is a tough proposition. When that club happens to be Arsenal, defending the Double, the task can seem almost impossible. So it proved for Alberto Mendez in 1998–99.

As a midfield player, Mendez had his work cut out trying to displace the likes of Manu Petit, Patrick Vieira and Stephen Hughes.

Arsene Wenger played Mendez for just 15 minutes in the Carling Premiership in 1998–99 – and decided to send him and team-mate Christopher Wreh out on loan to get regular first-team football with Greek giants AEK Athens.

AEK's interest in the young German-born midfielder may have stemmed from Mendez's goalscoring performance for Arsenal in the Champions League against Panathinaikos in Greece.

Arsenal fans will hope he returns from his spell in Greece an improved player to strengthen the squad for the club's tilt for domestic and European honours.

Clive MENDONCA • 10
CHARLTON ATHLETIC • BORN: 9.9.68

Sharp-shooter: Clive Mendonca

APPEARANCES	
Start (sub)	19 (6)
Minutes on pitch	1687
GOAL ATTEMPTS	
Goals	8
Goals/shots ratio	27%
SHOOTING	
Shots on target	20
Shooting accuracy	67%
PASSING	
Goal assists	2
Passing accuracy	75%
DISCIPLINE	
Fouls	28
Offside	34
Yellow cards	0
Red cards	0

After two weeks of the 1998–99 season Clive Mendonca was the Carling Premiership's top scorer, thanks to a stunning 25-minute hat-trick against Southampton.

The Islington-born front man had only signed for the Addicks from Grimsby 12 months earlier and after finishing as Division One's top scorer in 1997–98 with 23 goals, not to mention a hat-trick in the Wembley play-off final win over Sunderland, that £700,000 price tag was looking a real snip.

Sadly for player and club, an injury in the 1–0 defeat at Blackburn on December 5, and then the arrival of Swedish international Martin Pringle, conspired to curtail his season.

By the campaign's end he had eight goals from 30 attempts – not bad at face value, but disappointing after his six before Christmas.

Mendonca showed he was a sharp-shooter, with 20 of his 30 efforts on target. He also supplied two goal assists and completed three-quarters of his passes.

He will be doubtless be a key figure in Charlton's bid to return to the Premiership.

M

Paul MERSON • 10
ASTON VILLA • BORN: 20.3.68

When John Gregory learned Paul Merson was unhappy on Teesside, the Villa manager had no hesitation in paying £6.75 million for him.

The England star had won nationwide acclaim for his tenacity on and off the pitch, and his career had seemingly been reborn. But, like team-mate Stan Collymore, Merson's off-field problems intensified and hindered his performances for Villa.

Merson's Carling Opta stats for the 1998–99 Premiership campaign show he is still a class act despite outside influences. The former Gunner scored five league goals from 42 efforts, more than half of them on target.

The Londoner earned his capital with some committed displays, turning goal-provider on four occasions and executing more than 1,000 passes, a healthy 78% of them accurate.

"Merse" impressed out wide and squared the ball superbly, nearly 40% of his 74 attempted centres connecting. He embarked on 69 dribbles and runs, a fantastic three-quarters of which were fruitful. Merson also tackled back on occasion, and collected just two bookings.

APPEARANCES	
Start (sub)	24 (5)
Minutes on pitch	2160
GOAL ATTEMPTS	
Goals	5
Shots on target	22
Shooting accuracy	52%
PASSING	
Goal assists	4
Passing accuracy	78%
Crossing accuracy	38%
DRIBBLING	
Dribbles & runs	69
Dribble completion	75%
DISCIPLINE	
Yellow cards	2
Red cards	0

Charlie MILLER • 17
LEICESTER CITY • BORN: 18.3.76

Charlie Miller was a loan Ranger who joined Leicester City just before the transfer deadline in March for the remainder of the 1998–99 season.

The Glasgow Rangers midfield player was considered to be one of the top young prospects in Scotland, but the influx of foreign stars had severely restricted his opportunities at Ibrox and his loan move to Filbert Street was with a view to a potential permanent transfer.

The former under-21 international, who played alongside Gazza at Rangers, completed just 73% of his passes from his three substitute appearances and one start.

That one showing in the Foxes' first XI was cut short by an injury and the rest of his statistics do not do justice to the talent he possesses.

Wherever Miller starts the 1999–2000 season, he will hope for better luck than he has had in recent times and a chance for the tenacious 23-year-old to rekindle his stuttering career.

Jamie MILLIGAN • 36
EVERTON • BORN: 3.1.80

Everton's mid-season injury crisis left manager Walter Smith with no option but to call on the services of his youngsters.

Jamie Milligan took the field as a substitute on three occasions just a few weeks before his 19th birthday and despite his youth he did not let anyone down with any of his brief performances.

Milligan was part of the Everton Youth squad which lost in the FA Youth Cup semi-final and FA Premier Youth Academy semi-final play-offs to the eventual winners in both tournaments, West Ham. He made 14 appearances in all, scoring two goals.

The youngster's Carling Premiership debut came at Highbury against Arsenal and, after another substitute appearance away at Coventry City, he would have been very proud to make his home bow in the 1–0 win over Ruud Gullit's Newcastle United.

Milligan completed 13 out of the 14 passes he attempted and will be hoping to join youth team colleagues such as Francis Jeffers on a more regular basis in 1999–2000.

FB Danny MILLS • 2
CHARLTON ATHLETIC • BORN: 18.5.77

Tough-tackling full-back Danny Mills had a remarkable season at Charlton, starting all but two Premiership matches in 1998–99.

His 90th-minute free kick sealed an amazing 4–3 victory for the Addicks at Villa Park, although they were relegated the following week.

That was one of two goals from 11 shots on target over the season. The former Norwich full-back also turned in some highly creditable performances for the England under-21 side, in which he was occasionally used as a right-sided centre-back or even as a sweeper.

His defensive qualities were put to the test in a demanding season for the Charlton back-line. He made 38 interceptions, 22 blocks and more than 300 clearances, but won a below-average 62% of challenges. Mistimed tackles led to 46 fouls, resulting in 10 bookings.

Nonetheless, the young full-back clearly has a sparkling future ahead of him. In May, he was called up to the full England squad before Leeds United signed him in June for £4 million.

APPEARANCES	
Start (sub)	36 (0)
Minutes on pitch	3138
GOAL ATTEMPTS	
Goals	2
PASSING & CROSSING	
Passing	1099
Passing accuracy	65%
Crossing	87
Crossing accuracy	16%
DEFENDING	
Tackles	133
Tackles won	62%
DISCIPLINE	
Fouls	46
Yellow cards	10
Red cards	0

M

FB Scott MINTO • 20
WEST HAM UNITED • BORN: 6.8.71

APPEARANCES	
Start (sub)	14 (1)
Minutes on pitch	1242
GOAL ATTEMPTS	
Goals	0
PASSING & CROSSING	
Passing	568
Passing accuracy	71%
Crossing	30
Crossing accuracy	10%
DEFENDING	
Tackles	42
Tackles won	69%
DISCIPLINE	
Fouls	23
Yellow cards	2
Red cards	0

A £1 million signing from Benfica, Scott Minto had trouble settling in at West Ham United, who have had one or two top left-backs down the years. But after a short while he looked as if he was rediscovering the form which saw Chelsea snap him up from Charlton in 1994.

Minto made his debut against Sheffield Wednesday and soon bagged a first-team spot, playing every minute of the final 10 matches.

Unfortunately Minto's pass completion rate was well below average. His cross completion was even worse, with only three of his 30 attempts finding a team-mate, but this may be down to the size of West Ham's strikers.

His dribble completion was better, with possession retained on 84% of his runs, and he also won an impressive 69% of the challenges he made.

While less of an attacking threat than Stan Lazaridis, he more than makes up for those shortcomings with his defensive work. Fifty-one clearances and 21 blocks and interceptions show that he at least is committed to the cause.

CB Robert MOLENAAR • 30
LEEDS UNITED • BORN: 27.2.69

One of the Carling Premiership's most imposing figures, Robert Molenaar was a mainstay of Leeds United's defence until a knee ligament injury against Arsenal just before Christmas put him out for the season.

An out-and-out defender, Molenaar rarely explored the opposition half – indeed, he failed to register a single dribble all season. Nonetheless he netted twice and caused concern through his massive aerial presence in opposition penalty areas from set-pieces.

The big Dutchman has attracted some criticism for his tackling, which can be clumsy. In 1998–99, he won possession back 65% of the time – slightly below average for a Premiership defender – but also made 28 interceptions. His distribution was efficient, with 78% of his 457 passes completed. Molenaar's sheer size and strength led to a fair share of fouls and four bookings.

The one beneficiary of his enforced absence was youngster Jonathon Woodgate, who filled in with aplomb; and Molenaar may well struggle to regain his place next season.

APPEARANCES	
Start (sub)	17 (0)
Minutes on pitch	1470
GOAL ATTEMPTS	
Goals	2
DEFENDING	
Blocks	16
Headed clearances	154
Other clearances	60
Interceptions	28
Tackles won	35
PASSING	
Passing accuracy	78%
DISCIPLINE	
Fouls	28
Yellow cards	4
Red cards	0

M John MONCUR • 16
WEST HAM UNITED • BORN: 22.9.66

An experienced midfielder, John Moncur has passed and tackled his way through 15 steady seasons as a professional, having started at Tottenham in 1984 – and is still going strong with West Ham United.

His battling attributes were prominent during his appearances for the Hammers in 1998–99 and he completed 61% of his 46 tackles, committing 21 fouls.

He let his competitiveness get the better of him on occasions and, as a result, was booked eight times and sent off for two more yellow cards at Tottenham in April.

One of Moncur's outstanding attributes has always been his passing. An above-average 85% completion rate from 381 balls speaks volumes for his consistency when in possession.

Happy to run with the ball, Moncur embarked on 30 runs in the 1998–99 Carling Premiership with an equally impressive 80% success rate. He also hit the target with three of his six attempts at goal.

CB Gary MONK • 25
SOUTHAMPTON • BORN: 6.3.79

Gary Monk has worked his way through the Southampton ranks and saw Premiership action for the first time during the 1998–99 season.

He made his debut in the 1–0 defeat by Derby County and went on to make three further league appearances.

He endured a tortuous time in his last appearance for the Saints as they were thrashed 7–1 by Liverpool at Anfield. Robbie Fowler was in unstoppable form and this result will undoubtedly have damaged the youngster's confidence.

After this, Jones made Monk take a vow of substitution. But the youngster can take some comfort from the Carling Opta statistics, which show he completed 76% of his 89 passes and made 47 blocks, clearances and interceptions.

His tackling was disappointing, however, and he won only three of his nine challenges.

Monk spent a brief loan spell at Torquay United and is unlikely to feature prominently at the Dell during the 1999–2000 season.

Ken MONKOU • 6
CB SOUTHAMPTON • BORN: 29.11.64

Big Ken Monkou signed from Chelsea in March 1989 and has been the mainstay of the Saints' defence in nine seasons at the Dell.

With the back-line under siege for much of the 1998–99 Premiership campaign, the former Dutch under-21 international had to be at his commanding best in the air, resisting the onslaught to make 388 clearances. But on the ground he did not carry the same authority, making just 59 tackles and winning possession only 56% of the time.

Though rarely seen carrying the ball out of defence, Monkou often steps up for corners and set-pieces. He scored once against Middlesbrough in the 3–3 draw at the Dell.

The affable giant has established a regular defensive pairing with Claus Lundekvam and they performed well in their final six matches. A popular figure with the fans, "Super Ken" was runner-up in the Player of the Season poll.

He was out of contract at the end of the 1998–99 season but indicated that he would like to stay at the club, which will come as a great relief to Saints supporters.

APPEARANCES
Start (sub)	22 (0)
Minutes on pitch	1940

GOAL ATTEMPTS
Goals	1

DEFENDING
Blocks	20
Headed clearances	274
Other clearances	114
Interceptions	26
Tackles won	33

PASSING
Passing accuracy	70%

DISCIPLINE
Fouls	38
Yellow cards	6
Red cards	0

M

Alan MOORE • 11
M MIDDLESBROUGH • BORN: 25.11.74

APPEARANCES
Start (sub)	3 (1)
Minutes on pitch	207

GOAL ATTEMPTS
Goals	0

PASSING
Passes	54
Passing accuracy	81%

DEFENDING
Interceptions	4
Clearances	4
Tackles	8
Tackles won	38%

DISCIPLINE
Fouls	1
Yellow cards	0
Red cards	0

Alan Moore has spent a long time on the fringes of the Middlesbrough side and, despite more than a hundred league appearances, is still fighting to become a first-team regular.

The Republic of Ireland international managed just 207 Premiership minutes from three starts and one substitute appearance. He achieved a decent pass completion rate of 81%, but really added little to Boro's season.

The pacy winger's four goal efforts all missed the target and, although he was often on the substitutes' bench, Bryan Robson rarely turned to the attacking midfielder as an option.

When he did play, Moore only completed one out of five crosses and two out of six dribbles and runs he attempted; though he did contribute defensively with four clearances and four interceptions.

With Robson expected to strengthen the squad during the close season, it may prove even more difficult for Moore to play on a regular basis in 1999–2000 if he is retained in the side and he may have to look elsewhere for first-team opportunities.

M Jody MORRIS • 28
CHELSEA • BORN: 22.12.78

Jody Morris's goal in the 1–1 draw with Blackburn Rovers on February 17, 1999, was the Blues' first scored in the Premiership by an Englishman since the same player netted against Bolton Wanderers on May 10, 1998.

While many found this disturbing, it speaks volumes for Morris that he has managed to hold his own among such a galaxy of international stars. A fine midfielder with an eye for the "killer" pass, the England under-21 star made 18 league appearances in the 1998–99 season, 14 of them as a starter.

He is one of the most accomplished distributors of the ball at the club, finding a team-mate with 83% of his attempted passes and setting up two goals with assists. Although he managed a total of just 14 shots, his shooting accuracy of 50% was good, proving that he has a real eye for an opening.

Chelsea's management hold high hopes that Morris will progress further in 1999–2000. He has already shown the ability to make an impact at Stamford Bridge: the challenge now is to earn a regular place in the starting XI.

APPEARANCES	
Start (sub)	14 (4)
Minutes on pitch	1231
GOAL ATTEMPTS	
Goals	1
PASSING	
Passes	554
Passing accuracy	83%
DEFENDING	
Interceptions	7
Clearances	26
Tackles	35
Tackles won	51%
DISCIPLINE	
Fouls	31
Yellow cards	4
Red cards	0

Accomplished distributor: Jody Morris

S Owen MORRISON • 34
SHEFFIELD WEDNESDAY • BORN: 8.12.81

Owen Morrison had just turned 17 when he made his Carling Premiership debut at home to Leicester City on Boxing Day 1998. It was the youngster's only appearance of the 1998–99 campaign, but the experience proved invaluable for him.

Londonderry-born Morrison made up a quartet of exciting prospects from Northern Ireland, also comprising Alan Quinn, Mark McKeever and Danny Sonner, who played for the Owls' first team during the 1998–99 season.

Morrison was a prolific goalscorer in the Wednesday under-17 side and gained a regular berth in the reserves, where he also scored with some regularity.

He displayed good close control and individual skill both in the second team and in the under-17s, and showed some confident finishing for one so young.

Morrison received just rewards for his efforts when he played against Leicester. Danny Wilson commented that he "looked lively" in the match, and he could well be one to watch.

Paul MORTIMER • 16
CHARLTON ATHLETIC • BORN: 8.5.68

Paul Mortimer clearly has an affinity for south-east London, having spent several seasons at Crystal Palace and two spells with the Addicks.

He struggled to keep a place in the starting XI at the Valley in 1998–99, Alan Curbishley preferring Welsh international John Robinson.

Known for his spectacular strikes, Mortimer scored just once in the season – the equalizer at Leeds – but hit a further five on target. Unfortunately, injuries and lack of consistency put him out of the side for long spells.

He made more than 300 passes, completing a disappointing 70%, but found a colleague with an above-average 31% of his crosses. Defensively, he won 68% of his challenges, blocked three shots and made 23 clearances and three interceptions. He collected 12 fouls and a yellow card from 10 starts and seven substitute appearances.

Mortimer was a regular early in 1998–99 but as the season went on he found it hard to keep his place. Despite his Curbishley-esque loyalties to Charlton, the club released the 31-year-old at the end of the campaign.

APPEARANCES	
Start (sub)	10 (7)
Minutes on pitch	834
GOAL ATTEMPTS	
Goals	1
Shots on target	6
Shooting accuracy	60%
PASSING	
Goal assists	1
Passing accuracy	70%
Crossing accuracy	31%
DRIBBLING	
Dribbles & runs	43
Dribble completion	53%
DISCIPLINE	
Yellow cards	1
Red cards	0

M

Neil MOSS • 13
SOUTHAMPTON • BORN: 10.5.75

APPEARANCES	
Start (sub)	7 (0)
Minutes on pitch	630
SHOT STOPPING	
Goals conceded	11
Clean sheets	2
Saves	23
Saves/shots	68%
DISTRIBUTION	
Distribution	246
Distribution %	47%
CATCHING	
Crosses caught	13
Crosses dropped	1
DISCIPLINE	
Yellow cards	0
Red cards	0

Former Bournemouth goalkeeper Neil Moss is now firmly established as Southampton's number two between the sticks, behind Welsh international Paul Jones.

Signed for £250,000 in December 1995, Moss made seven full appearances for the Saints during 1998–99, deputizing for the injured Jones in six of the last eight matches. He performed admirably, and was unlucky to lose his first-team place for the final two games.

Manager Dave Jones opted for experience when recalling his namesake for the run-in, but Moss will have done his reputation no harm with a number of fine displays.

Despite limited Premiership experience, Moss showed no signs of nerves in these key matches. He did exceptionally well against Arsenal at the Dell, keeping a clean sheet, and pulled off a series of excellent saves in the 0–0 draw at Derby, under fierce bombardment.

But having understudied various 'keepers since joining the Saints, Moss may decide to move on if he does not secure a regular first-team place next season.

AM **Danny MURPHY • 24**
LIVERPOOL • BORN: 18.3.77

M **Adam MURRAY • 28**
DERBY COUNTY • BORN: 30.9.81

Another much-heralded product of the Crewe Alexandra academy, Danny Murphy arrived at Liverpool with quite a reputation.

Sadly, the great expectations proved something of a burden, and the youngster ended up back at Gresty Road on loan in February.

Even with Gerard Houllier's side struggling in 1998–99, Murphy's Premiership opportunities were few and he played for only 14 minutes.

Murphy's quest for first-team football led him to drop back down a division. If Crewe manager Dario Gradi can find the cash required, Murphy may well be back to stay.

His 14 minutes in a Liverpool shirt provided little information for the statisticians. He completed three of his five passes and failed to win either of the two tackles he made, committing one foul and completing one clearance.

Nonetheless, he is a player of genuine quality who can compete at the highest level, but will undoubtedly feel very frustrated at his lack of opportunity at Anfield.

Adam Murray made the step up from youth team football into the first XI after impressing Jim Smith early in the 1998–99 season.

He made his debut at the age of 17 against Newcastle United – the first of four substitute appearances he was to make before the end of the campaign.

Murray is a player in the mould of former Rams favourite Lee Carsley, and the Derby coaching staff are predicting a bright future for the precocious youngster.

His enthusiasm contributed to his completing only 67% of his passes when he played – and a reckless challenge against Arsenal earned him his first yellow card in senior football. But he showed glimpses of his ability, hitting the target with one effort and having another blocked.

While still eligible for the youth team, Murray will feature more regularly in Derby's reserves in 1999–2000 and appear more frequently in the first team if he continues to progress at his current rate. Time is definitely on the talented teenager's side.

M **Robbie MUSTOE • 7**
MIDDLESBROUGH • BORN: 28.8.68

APPEARANCES	
Start (sub)	32 (1)
Minutes on pitch	2776
GOAL ATTEMPTS	
Goals	4
PASSING	
Passes	1082
Passing accuracy	81%
DEFENDING	
Interceptions	37
Clearances	67
Tackles	187
Tackles won	64%
DISCIPLINE	
Fouls	53
Yellow cards	7
Red cards	1

Alongside Andy Townsend and Paul Gascoigne, Robbie Mustoe formed one of the Premiership's most experienced midfield combinations in 1998–99.

A key member of the Middlesbrough side, he once again proved himself to be a tenacious and industrious player, winning 64% of the 187 challenges he attempted and also weighing in with 67 clearances, 23 blocks and 37 interceptions.

But this tenacity inevitably led to disciplinary problems, with seven yellow cards accrued and a red for two more bookable offences against Southampton.

Not much of a goal threat, Mustoe fired in just 24 efforts (including blocked shots) and claimed one goal assist, mainly due to his restricted midfield role where he was mainly concerned with protecting the defence. His pass completion rate was excellent, 81% finding a team-mate.

Despite a number of big names being linked with the Riverside, Robson is sure to count on Mustoe's services in 1999–2000.

FB Andy MYERS • 18
CHELSEA • BORN: 3.11.73

With competition for places in the Chelsea defence at an all-time high, Andy Myers was restricted to just one Premiership appearance in the 1998–99 season.

Unfortunately that came in the 1–0 home defeat by West Ham United – a game which everyone connected with the Blues would rather forget.

A speedy player, Myers's preferred position is as a left-sided full-back, but he filled in as a centre-back alongside Frank Leboeuf in the game against Harry Redknapp's side, winning both of his attempted challenges and completing 10 clearances.

Myers has been at Stamford Bridge throughout his entire career, signing professional forms in 1991 and winning four England under-21 caps.

Although he has appeared more than 80 times for the club in the league he may find it hard to reach the 100 mark, especially now that Chelsea have reached the Champions League and so many quality international players are vying for places in the back-line.

G Thomas MYHRE • 1
EVERTON • BORN: 16.10.73

APPEARANCES	
Start (sub)	38 (0)
Minutes on pitch	3420
SHOT STOPPING	
Goals conceded	47
Clean sheets	14
Saves	129
Saves/shots	73%
DISTRIBUTION	
Distribution	1175
Distribution %	50%
CATCHING	
Crosses caught	84
Crosses dropped	5
DISCIPLINE	
Yellow cards	3
Red cards	0

There's Norway past: Thomas Myhre

Just two Premiership goalkeepers managed to keep more clean sheets than Norway's Thomas Myhre, and those 14 shut-outs – 10 of them before Christmas – helped Everton stay up.

While the club struggled to score for most of the season, his athleticism and shot-stopping ability often secured the Toffees at least a point when they might have got nothing.

Myhre made 129 saves, but his saves-to-shots ratio suffered in the season's second half and he finished with a below-average record, keeping out just 73% of shots faced.

He struggled with long-distance efforts, conceding 10 goals from shots outside his penalty area, and his catching was also below par: he claimed 84 crosses, punched 29 more and dropped five catches. But his distribution was good: he completed 37% of his long kicks.

Now established as number one despite the presence of Steve Simonsen – England's most expensive goalkeeper up until the end of the 1998–99 season – Myhre will be looking to Walter Smith to improve the squad so that he enjoys better protection in 1999–2000.

M

FB Gary NEVILLE • 2
MANCHESTER UNITED • BORN: 18.2.75

England defender Gary Neville played a key role for Manchester United in their historic treble-winning campaign and looks set to monopolize the right-back slot for both club and country for the foreseeable future.

Neville was generally excellent throughout 1998–99 and, aside from the occasional dip in form, showed real strength and maturity.

Tackling is his forte: he made 96 challenges in Premiership matches, claiming possession with a very impressive 76%. In common with his team-mates, the Bury-born full-back turned defence into attack with some slick passing, and his economy on the ball is reflected in an 83% pass completion rate from almost 1,500 balls attempted.

Neville is not the most cavalier of players on the break, but retained possession with 80% of his 40 forward runs. He scored only his second goal for United in the 3–1 defeat of Everton at Old Trafford and was unlucky with four further efforts which were saved. The only blot on his record was a sending-off at White Hart Lane for two bookable offences.

APPEARANCES	
Start (sub)	34 (0)
Minutes on pitch	2951
GOAL ATTEMPTS	
Goals	1
PASSING & CROSSING	
Passing	1459
Passing accuracy	83%
Crossing	65
Crossing accuracy	26%
DEFENDING	
Tackles	96
Tackles won	76%
DISCIPLINE	
Fouls	31
Yellow cards	5
Red cards	1

FB Philip NEVILLE • 12
MANCHESTER UNITED • BORN: 21.1.77

APPEARANCES	
Start (sub)	19 (9)
Minutes on pitch	1789
GOAL ATTEMPTS	
Goals	0
PASSING & CROSSING	
Passing	1003
Passing accuracy	86%
Crossing	40
Crossing accuracy	28%
DEFENDING	
Tackles	55
Tackles won	64%
DISCIPLINE	
Fouls	25
Yellow cards	5
Red cards	0

Though he did not get an extended run in the side, Philip Neville saw plenty of Premiership action during the 1998–99 season, playing a total of 1,789 minutes in Manchester United's successful bid to regain the title.

Left-back is his preferred position, but Denis Irwin's form has proved a barrier and more often than not he has been asked to fill in as a centre-back or in midfield. To his credit, he has always handled either position with ease.

Neville's versatility – which seems to run in the family – is reflected in his Carling Opta stats, which are impressive in all departments. His pass completion rate of 86% from just over a thousand passes is a superb figure and he also provided good service to the frontmen, supplying 40 crosses and two assists.

Philip has only scored one Premiership goal in his career and was unable to add to that tally during the 1998–99 season, managing just one shot on target. But perhaps more perplexing for him is the fact that he often finds it easier to get into the England team than Manchester United's starting XI!

CB Jon NEWSOME • 5
SHEFFIELD WEDNESDAY • BORN: 6.9.70

The worst thing Jon Newsome could have done with eight games to go of the 1997–98 season was to pick up a serious knee injury. That let Brazilian Emerson Thome into the side, who then went on to be of Wednesday's best performers in 1998–99 with Newsome barely getting a look-in.

His first start came in September against Wimbledon, followed, by substitute appearances against Leeds, Derby and Coventry. The unfortunate connection here is that Wednesday lost all four games. Thankfully for the £1.6 million signing, Newsome started in the 2–1 win at Everton in April to break that jinx.

But he now looks certain to move on, with Premiership newcomers Bradford City and Watford apparently fighting it out with play-off flops Birmingham City and Bolton Wanderers for his signature.

In 240 minutes of Carling Premiership football he failed to win a single tackle, but did complete 76% of his passes and made a total of 59 clearances.

M Eddie NEWTON • 24
CHELSEA • BORN: 13.12.71

Eddie Newton is one of only five players in the history of Chelsea to have scored in a Wembley FA Cup final. Unfortunately his career has been blighted by injury since he bundled home Chelsea's second goal in the 1997 final, and 1998–99 proved to be another frustrating campaign for the holding midfield player.

He managed just 252 minutes of first-team action in the Premiership, mainly as a substitute. Although he performed well on every occasion, he was unable to claim a regular spot in the starting line-up.

An excellent tackler, Newton won 78% of his attempted challenges and, although there was nothing elaborate about his play, he distributed the ball effectively, completing an impressive 91% of all his passes.

For a player whose main job is to break up opposition attacks, Newton commits surprisingly few fouls. He was pulled up for offences just twice in 1998–99 and did not receive a single booking. But with competition for places now so hot at Chelsea, Newton may find his chances even more limited.

N

AM Shaun NEWTON • 7
CHARLTON ATHLETIC • BORN: 20.8.75

APPEARANCES	
Start (sub)	13 (3)
Minutes on pitch	1061
GOAL ATTEMPTS	
Goals	0
Shots on target	4
Shooting accuracy	44%
PASSING	
Goal assists	2
Passing accuracy	72%
Crossing accuracy	27%
DRIBBLING	
Dribbles & runs	53
Dribble completion	75%
DISCIPLINE	
Yellow cards	2
Red cards	0

After a consistent season in 1997–98, Shaun Newton had established himself as Charlton's first-choice right-sided midfielder. He started the new season well until Alan Curbishley changed the Charlton formation from a back four to a back five in October. Newton lost his place and did not play until Curbishley reverted to a 4-4-2 formation in December.

Unable to score a goal in his 13 starts, he did create two with the help of his electric pace. He completed only 72% of his passes but more than a quarter of his crosses. In front of goal he managed four shots on target and failed to find the target with five.

Newton's dribbling, allied to his pace, makes him dangerous, and he finished the season with a 75% completion rate from his 53 dribbles and runs. He worked hard, tackling back on 39 occasions and winning 56%. He also blocked four shots and made 34 defensive clearances and four interceptions.

After a frustrating season, Newton will be looking to work his way back into the Charlton starting line-up for 1999–2000.

AM Mark NICHOLLS • 22
CHELSEA • BORN: 30.5.77

A prolific striker with Chelsea's youth team – he scored 56 times in 85 appearances – Mark Nicholls has now been on the fringes of the first team for three seasons.

Although he has played most of his career as striker, the Hillingdon-born player was used mainly as an attacking midfielder in 1998–99, making all his appearances as a substitute.

The lack of first-team opportunities has been extremely frustrating for a player who scored three goals in 1998–99 but now looks to have fallen behind Mikael Forssell in the Stamford Bridge pecking order.

There is no doubt that he has the ability to be a success in the Premiership. His movement is excellent, and although he only had one shot in 1998–99 he was never really played far forward enough to test opposition goalkeepers.

Perhaps his future lies elsewhere. If he does decide to move on, Chelsea's loss will surely be another club's gain. The 22-year-old will certainly be looking for more first-team action wherever he plays in 1999–2000.

CB Roger NILSEN • 5
TOTTENHAM HOTSPUR • BORN: 8.8.69

A surprise signing on transfer deadline day, Sheffield United's Roger Nilsen was probably as shocked as most Spurs fans by his move to White Hart Lane. George Graham was desperate for short-term cover in defence, however – and Nilsen proved just the ticket.

Playing in three Premiership games – against Newcastle United, Charlton Athletic and Liverpool – the Norwegian international was certainly kept busy, attempting nine tackles and clearing the Tottenham lines on 37 occasions.

His distribution was neat and effective, and he almost grabbed a goal with a left-foot shot which Charlton 'keeper Andy Petterson did well to save.

A solid professional with bags of experience, his long-term future at the club looks somewhat uncertain. But the veteran will have enjoyed his time at White Hart Lane in the 1998–99 Carling Premiership.

His presence certainly proved useful, giving the precocious Luke Young a much-needed breather as Tottenham's season wound down.

M Allan NIELSEN • 6
TOTTENHAM HOTSPUR • BORN: 13.3.71

The 1998–99 season was a bittersweet one for Allan Nielsen. The Danish international played a part in 28 of Tottenham's games in the Premiership and scored the last-minute goal that won the Worthington Cup – but the arrival of Tim Sherwood and Steffen Freund put his place in jeopardy.

A rather public falling-out with George Graham seems to have been the last straw, and his future as a Tottenham player was in severe doubt as the season drew to a close.

Never the most physical of players, his main asset has always been his ability to nick vital goals from the midfield.

During 1998–99 he scored three times in the Premiership and also grabbed a host of crucial goals in the cup competitions, taking his total to nine. Unfortunately, his tackle success rate of 57% did not always impress his new manager, who felt that his back four needed more protection.

Transfer-listed at his own request, Nielsen is likely to prove his worth by leaving Spurs for more than he originally cost, and that dramatic Wembley winner has ensured his place in the White Hart Lane Hall of Fame. His record suggests there will certainly be no shortage of clubs willing to sign him.

APPEARANCES	
Start (sub)	24 (4)
Minutes on pitch	2157
GOAL ATTEMPTS	
Goals	3
PASSING	
Passes	783
Passing accuracy	73%
DEFENDING	
Interceptions	16
Clearances	43
Tackles	82
Tackles won	57%
DISCIPLINE	
Fouls	33
Yellow cards	6
Red cards	0

FB   Roland NILSSON • 2
COVENTRY CITY • BORN: 27.11.63

Roland Nilsson bade a fond farewell to the Premiership at the end of 1998–99, returning to Swedish side Helsingborgs to become their director of football. He took with him the good wishes of everyone at Coventry, but not – as many at the club felt he deserved – a place in the PFA Premiership team of the season. Carling Opta rated him highly enough to give him the right-back spot in their team.

A consistently good performer, he attempted exactly 100 tackles, winning an above-average 77%. He also proved that even in his late 30s he could still get up and down the pitch, completing 89% of his dribbles and runs.

His crossing was less accurate, but this had more to do with the absence of a good target man in the Coventry attack following the departure of Dion Dublin to Aston Villa.

A fantastic servant for both the Sky Blues and former side Sheffield Wednesday, he did well to recover from a punctured lung sustained in a match against Arsenal and made his final bow against Leeds United in the last game of the 1998–99 season.

APPEARANCES	
Start (sub)	28 (0)
Minutes on pitch	2368
GOAL ATTEMPTS	
Goals	0
PASSING & CROSSING	
Passing	1191
Passing accuracy	71%
Crossing	35
Crossing accuracy	26%
DEFENDING	
Tackles	100
Tackles won	77%
DISCIPLINE	
Fouls	10
Yellow cards	0
Red cards	0

N

G   Michael OAKES • 13
ASTON VILLA • BORN: 30.10.73

APPEARANCES	
Start (sub)	23 (0)
Minutes on pitch	2035
SHOT STOPPING	
Goals conceded	35
Clean sheets	6
Saves	75
Saves/shots	68%
DISTRIBUTION	
Distribution	606
Distribution %	40%
CATCHING	
Crosses caught	69
Crosses dropped	1
DISCIPLINE	
Yellow cards	0
Red cards	0

Aston Villa goalkeeper Michael Oakes played in more than half of Villa's 1998–99 Premiership matches as he stepped out of the shadow of Australian international and long-time Villa Park number one Mark Bosnich.

Oakes, who joined Villa on professional terms from the junior ranks, filled in well enough for Bosnich, but the former England under-21 keeper showed some signs of his inexperience.

He made 75 saves in all, comparatively few from close range, and kept out just 68% of all on-target shots faced. Oakes also conceded 35 goals in 23 games, a slightly unflattering goals-per-game ratio for a Premiership keeper.

On the plus side, Oakes was masterful when dealing with high balls. He dropped just one catch and held on to 69 others, making him one of the league's safest 'keepers. His short distribution was equally impressive, with only one close-range ball intended for a team-mate going astray, a record no regular-starting goalkeeper could match.

His one sour moment came with a wrongful dismissal against Blackburn Rovers.

AM Scott OAKES • 19
SHEFFIELD WEDNESDAY • BORN: 5.8.72

Yet another reserve team player used very sparingly in the first team by Danny Wilson, former Luton man Scott Oakes graced the 1998–99 Carling Premiership for all of 74 minutes.

Oakes, whose father was a member of '70s pop sensations Showaddywaddy, made his name with the Hatters in the early '90s, but the 27-year-old attacking midfielder had little chance in the Premiership. The Leicester-born player was afforded only 74 minutes to Showaddy could do on the pitch, replacing Petter Rudi in the 4–0 defeat at Middlesbrough.

Despite the disappointing performance of the team as a whole, Oakes played soundly at the Riverside, where he distributed 20 passes towards a team-mate with only three of these going astray.

He also had ample opportunity to threaten Mark Schwarzer's goal; but unfortunately for the former England under-21 star, his three efforts on goal posed no trouble to the big Australian goalkeeper.

S Stefan OAKES • 29
LEICESTER CITY • BORN: 6.9.78

Stefan Oakes was a regular in the reserve side and scored several goals from midfield, but despite being on the fringes of the first team squad he managed just 165 minutes of Carling Premiership football during the 1998–99 season (although that was more than his older brother Scott managed to get at Sheffield Wednesday).

Like his sibling, Stefan came through the Leicester youth set-up and impressed enough in reserve fixtures to justify his two starts in the final two games of the 1998–99 season.

He showed good ability on the ball, completing 88% of 104 passes, and he also helped out in defence with eight clearances, 10 tackles and a couple of blocks and interceptions apiece.

Oakes attempted three efforts on goal, but missed the target with two and had the other blocked.

1999–2000 will be a big season for the youngster, who will be looking to establish himself in the Leicester side on a much more regular basis.

M Matthew OAKLEY • 8
SOUTHAMPTON • BORN: 17.8.77

APPEARANCES	
Start (sub)	21 (1)
Minutes on pitch	1728
GOAL ATTEMPTS	
Goals	2
PASSING	
Passes	732
Passing accuracy	78%
DEFENDING	
Interceptions	23
Clearances	37
Tackles	40
Tackles won	70%
DISCIPLINE	
Fouls	13
Yellow cards	2
Red cards	0

A product of Southampton's youth system, Matthew Oakley is a composed midfielder with good ability on the ball.

He was a regular starter for much of the 1998–99 season but in the latter stages was edged out by new man Chris Marsden and did not even make the bench in the final weeks.

On pitch the England under-21 International kept the Saints' midfield ticking over with some neat distribution, achieving a 72% completion rate and setting up three goals.

He has been criticized for a lack of attacking drive, but though he scored twice he made few goal attempts and only retained possession with 65% of his 31 forward runs. The midfielder provided some accurate crosses to the front men, with 39% finding a colleague. He also tackled well as shown by a success rate of 70%, but perhaps should have made more than 40 challenges in his 1,728 minutes of play.

The Carling Opta statistics show that Oakley is a skilful player, but may lack the aggression to really stamp his authority on midfield.

Steve OGRIZOVIC • 16
COVENTRY CITY • BORN: 12.9.57

 John O'KANE • 32
EVERTON • BORN: 15.11.74

After 504 league appearances for Coventry City, Steve Ogrizovic's days of being first-choice goalkeeper are surely over.

With Swedish international Magnus Hedman in fine form for the Sky Blues, he spent all but two games of the 1998–99 season looking on from the sidelines.

But the veteran was thrown into the action on Boxing Day at home to Tottenham Hotspur, when Hedman complained of dizzy spells before the match. And he took to the field with gusto, making a characteristically spectacular save to keep out Darren Anderton's free kick.

He also kept goal two days later at West Ham United, but when Hedman recovered "Oggy" was back on the bench and must now believe his future chances of Premiership football will be extremely limited.

The 1998–99 season ended miserably for the 41-year-old legend when he had to have surgery on a prolapsed disc in his neck. A coaching role would seem his most likely option now.

Nottingham-born John O'Kane featured in the same youth set-up as the likes of Beckham, Butt, Scholes and the Neville brothers at Manchester United.

But with the strength in depth at Old Trafford, he failed to make the crucial breakthrough into the first team and left for Everton in a £250,000 deal.

O'Kane made two Carling Premiership appearances for Everton in a frustrating season spent mostly on the sidelines, and also spent some time at Burnley on loan.

His two games for the Toffeemen came against north-west rivals Manchester United and Blackburn Rovers, but he contributed very little in either and on both occasions found himself being substituted before the end of the match.

He completed 76% of 41 passes in 132 minutes on the pitch, and just one out of six crosses that he attempted.

It remains to be seen whether O'Kane will feature in Walter Smith's drive to resurrect Everton.

 Emmanuel OMOYINMI • 27
WEST HAM UNITED • BORN: 28.12.77

 Keith O'NEILL • 23
MIDDLESBROUGH • BORN: 16.2.76

After spells on loan at Bournemouth and Dundee United in recent seasons, prodigious winger Manny Omoyinmi appeared finally to have made the breakthrough in a West Ham shirt with a dramatic two-goal salvo at Crystal Palace at the tail-end of 1997–98.

But the young Nigerian-born winger played just 31 minutes of Carling Premiership football in 1998–99 and spent much of the season a few miles away from the Boleyn Ground, on loan at Leyton Orient.

Harry Redknapp is clearly hoping that several spells in the lower leagues will give his pacy young attacking midfielder the confidence and experience he needs to tackle the Premiership on a permanent basis.

Even in the short time he was in a claret-and-blue shirt in 1998–99, Omoyinmi completed two crosses and three out of four dribbles – the sort of form Orient fans were treated to on a regular basis.

Now he must hope he is given the chance to prove himself once again in the top flight in 1999–2000.

Keith O'Neill was an exciting talent with Norwich City, attracting bids of £5 million at the start of the 1998–99 season.

But as the Eire international was due to be out of contract at the end of the campaign, Middlesbrough were able to prise him away from East Anglia for only £700,000 in March 1999.

Boro were delighted to get their man, especially as there was interest from several clubs – including some in Europe – but niggling injuries restricted the number of appearances he was able to make.

In four starts and two substitute displays, O'Neill impressed with his dribbling skills, completing 86% of his runs. But his passing was comparatively poor, with only 68% of his 152 balls finding a team-mate. One that did connect, though, set up Gianluca Festa for Boro's second in the 3–1 win over Wimbledon and he was also involved in the first of Hamilton Ricard's brace in that match.

He will hope for better luck and more opportunities in 1999–2000.

Egil OSTENSTAD • 10
S
SOUTHAMPTON • BORN: 2.1.72

Season 1998–99 proved a disappointing one for Norwegian international Egil Ostenstad, who scored just seven goals and was dropped toward the end of the campaign.

Having hit a hat-trick against Manchester United the previous season and featured in the World Cup, Ostenstad failed to find his form and struggled to breach Premiership defences. Two of his goals were in two matches against Liverpool – but both were mere consolations as the Reds thumped nine in at the other end.

Ostenstad's problem lay not so much in his finishing as his inability to create chances. He managed just 26 shots on target in more than 39 hours on the pitch, although his accuracy of 57% was not bad. Ostenstad is hardly the sharpest tool in the box and was caught offside a frustrating 61 times, the third-most in the Premiership.

He showed strength on the ball but amassed too many fouls. With Pahars and Beattie keeping him out of the side at the end of the season, he will have to work on his fitness and movement to regain his first-team place.

APPEARANCES	
Start (sub)	27 (7)
Minutes on pitch	2359
GOAL ATTEMPTS	
Goals	7
Goals/shots ratio	15%
SHOOTING	
Shots on target	26
Shooting accuracy	57%
PASSING	
Goal assists	1
Passing accuracy	71%
DISCIPLINE	
Fouls	55
Offside	61
Yellow cards	1
Red cards	0

John OSTER • 19
AM
EVERTON • BORN: 8.12.78

APPEARANCES	
Start (sub)	6 (3)
Minutes on pitch	530
GOAL ATTEMPTS	
Goals	0
Shots on target	3
Shooting accuracy	43%
PASSING	
Goal assists	0
Passing accuracy	70%
Crossing accuracy	32%
DRIBBLING	
Dribbles & runs	30
Dribble completion	70%
DISCIPLINE	
Yellow cards	1
Red cards	0

A teenage prodigy at Grimsby Town, Oster was snapped up for £1.5 million in 1997's close season by Everton's Howard Kendall. After more appearances than any other Toffee in 1997–98, he has struggled to make an impact at Goodison Park under Walter Smith.

Capped by Wales as a teenager, the youngster's career has since stalled and he spent much of the season on the sidelines.

In his few games he completed just 70% of his passes but had more success in the dribble, retaining possession seven times out of 10.

Oster failed to make the scoresheet, only three of his 12 efforts forcing a save – and the attacking midfield player contributed little in the defensive third of the pitch. With Everton struggling, Oster was replaced by more pragmatic players, and it remains to be seen whether he can fulfil his obvious potential.

Walter Smith's rebuilding programme may involve sacrificing certain players to finance purchases, but Oster will be keen to show in 1999–2000 that he has what it takes to feature in the Scotsman's plans.

AM   Marc OVERMARS • 11
ARSENAL • BORN: 29.3.73

Marc Overmars did well again in 1998–99, but found goals harder to come by thanks to a mixture of wayward shooting and tight marking. His efforts placed him eighth in the Carling Opta attacking midfielders Index.

The diminutive Dutchman still managed to trouble opposition 'keepers 45 times, with six goals and seven assists. But he also missed the target 35 times and had 33 shots blocked.

His cross completion rate was weak but, with a lack of aerial firepower in Arsenal's front line, this was equally true of most of his team.

Overmars was always keen to attack the opposing full-back, as shown by the number of times he ran with the ball (236), while his passing accuracy of 78% put him just above average for an attacking midfielder.

He started all but one of Arsenal's Premiership fixtures in 1998–99 and, after defensive substitutions, was often moved into the striker's position in the closing minutes of matches as a counter-attacking threat.

After a rest over the summer, he should be back to his waspish best in 1999–2000.

APPEARANCES	
Start (sub)	37 (0)
Minutes on pitch	3055
GOAL ATTEMPTS	
Goals	6
Shots on target	45
Shooting accuracy	56%
PASSING	
Goal assists	7
Passing accuracy	78%
Crossing accuracy	17%
DRIBBLING	
Dribbles & runs	236
Dribble completion	64%
DISCIPLINE	
Yellow cards	2
Red cards	0

Waspish winger: Marc Overmars

S — Michael OWEN • 10
LIVERPOOL • BORN: 14.12.79

In just two seasons Michael Owen has gone from teenage prodigy to world-class striker. He has played in a World Cup – scoring a classic goal – and picked up two Golden Boot awards.

Owen was one of only two players to score four goals in a game in 1998–99. That salvo came in the 5–1 thrashing of Nottingham Forest and was one of two hat-tricks he bagged during the season, a feat only matched by team-mate Robbie Fowler.

His 18 goals came from 85 shots, 49 on target. The youngster also contributed five goal assists and his all-round game has made him a regular at international level alongside another model pro, Alan Shearer.

Owen's season came to a premature end thanks to a hamstring injury in April's televized clash with Leeds United, but the break may be good for him after playing top-level football almost non-stop for two years.

The meteoric rise of the lightning-quick youngster continues apace, and he will be anxious that Liverpool are able to match his talent and ambition in 1999–2000.

APPEARANCES	
Start (sub)	30 (0)
Minutes on pitch	2528
GOAL ATTEMPTS	
Goals	18
Goals/shots ratio	21%
SHOOTING	
Shots on target	49
Shooting accuracy	58%
PASSING	
Goal assists	5
Passing accuracy	79%
DISCIPLINE	
Fouls	19
Offside	40
Yellow cards	1
Red cards	0

Boy wonder: Michael Owen

Marian PAHARS • 35
SOUTHAMPTON • BORN: 5.8.76

The diminutive Latvian striker was signed from Skonto Riga on 1998–99 transfer deadline day and has already written himself into Saints' history books. His two goals against Everton on the final day of the campaign ensured another season of top-flight football for the south coast side.

Dave Jones snapped the striker up after a superb trial and initial problems in securing a work permit.

Dubbed the "Baltic Michael Owen", Pahars appears to have all the trademarks of his namesake. Small and lightning fast, he has shown a natural predator's instinct in his 359 minutes on the pitch. Of his 10 shots, eight were on target, and three hit the back of the net. These figures alone highlight the threat he will carry to opposing defences in 1999–2000.

Both of Pahars's final day goals were set up by fellow frontman James Beattie – and if these two can continue their blossoming understanding, Southampton may be in for a more productive season.

Back home: Gary Pallister

CB **Gary PALLISTER • 6**
MIDDLESBROUGH • BORN: 30.6.65

APPEARANCES	
Start (sub)	26 (0)
Minutes on pitch	2223
GOAL ATTEMPTS	
Goals	0
DEFENDING	
Blocks	33
Headed clearances	301
Other clearances	74
Interceptions	40
Tackles won	59
PASSING	
Passing accuracy	83%
DISCIPLINE	
Fouls	33
Yellow cards	5
Red cards	0

Injury prevented Gary Pallister from playing every game for Middlesbrough, but the man considered by many to be the best English centre-back of his generation was an influential figure for the Teessiders.

Signed from Manchester United in summer 1998, Pallister made his comeback in a Middlesbrough shirt in the fourth game of the season where a 1–0 victory against Leicester City saw him slot effortlessly into a back three.

A class act who knows exactly how to play his man, Pallister may have lost a yard or two of pace but still proved too much of a barrier for many of the Premiership's top strikers.

His anticipation of the play was excellent and he completed 40 interceptions and 33 blocks. As always, he preferred to stand up rather than go to ground and risk losing his man, but still attempted a total of 84 tackles.

A few impartial observers raised their eyebrows at his price-tag when Bryan Robson paid £2.5 million to secure his services, but even at such an advanced stage of his career he has proved value for money.

0

Carlton PALMER • 20
NOTTINGHAM FOREST • BORN: 5.12.65

A £1.1 million signing from Southampton, Carlton Palmer linked up with Ron Atkinson for the third time in his career when he made the switch to Nottingham Forest.

Making his debut at Everton as a central defender, Palmer helped secure a 1–0 victory but could do little the week after as Forest were rolled over 8–1 by Manchester United.

Carling Opta's stats show the much-maligned Palmer is a better player than he is often given credit for; and, though unable to save Forest, he was among their better performers.

The tough tackler made 137 challenges for Southampton and Forest during 1998–99 and also shone at the back with 179 clearances.

A vocal player in the dressing-room, Palmer has not always impressed his previous managers with his forthright opinions. His future may be in doubt now that Atkinson has left Forest, but any successor to the Forest hot seat would be wise to hang on to him; his combination of determination and hard graft are likely to be valuable qualities in the struggle to regain Premiership status.

APPEARANCES	
Start (sub)	31 (1)
Minutes on pitch	2831
GOAL ATTEMPTS	
Goals	0
PASSING	
Passes	1007
Passing accuracy	77%
DEFENDING	
Interceptions	26
Clearances	179
Tackles	137
Tackles won	60%
DISCIPLINE	
Fouls	43
Yellow cards	9
Red cards	1

Garry PARKER • 10
LEICESTER CITY • BORN: 7.9.65

Now in the twilight of his career, wily old Fox Garry Parker watched the majority of Leicester City's 1998–99 season from the substitutes' bench.

His biggest moment of the campaign came in the Worthington Cup fourth round, when he stepped off the bench to score the winner from the penalty spot against Leeds United – but his Premiership form was less memorable,

He amassed just 203 minutes on the pitch from two starts and five substitute appearances in the league, completing 77% of his attempted passes, 30% of his crosses and winning five out of his eight tackles.

The fine form of Neil Lennon and Muzzy Izzet make it extremely unlikely that he will feature regularly for the Foxes in 1999–2000. As a successful manager with Oxford Sunday League side Cherwell Lions, he is clearly planning a future in the game once his playing days are over. After 16 seasons in the English league, he can look back on a fine playing career which included spells with Luton, Hull, Nottingham Forest and Aston Villa.

Scott PARKER • 27
CHARLTON ATHLETIC • BORN: 13.10.80

A promising young midfielder, Scott Parker is most definitely one for the future at the Valley.

His skills were showcased in a McDonald's advert when he was younger and, since signing forms for the Addicks, he has become a regular in the England under-18 squad. A player of great potential at Charlton, he figured four times as a substitute in the 1998–99 Premiership campaign.

His appearances may have amounted to only 34 minutes of Premiership football – but he left his mark, setting up Martin Pringle to score Charlton's last-minute equalizing goal against Newcastle United in January.

Parker will hope for more first team experience as the club launch another bid for promotion to the Premiership. After seeing glimpses of the 18-year-old's ability in the top flight, Charlton boss Alan Curbishley may decide to give the youngster an extended run in the first-team squad in 1999–2000.

He certainly appears to have a big future ahead of him.

Ray PARLOUR • 15
ARSENAL • BORN: 7.3.73

Following up the best season of his career was always going to be difficult for Ray Parlour. But the Romford-born midfielder excelled for Arsenal in 1998–99, forcing his way into the England squad with some powerful displays.

Though he played most of the season on the right wing, his role often demanded he cut inside to support the midfield and he did this to great effect.

Arguably the Gunners' hardest worker, Parlour made almost 200 dribbles and runs, more than 1,550 passes and 130 tackles. His record in front of goal was also good, six goals representing a fine haul from 58 shots.

Arsenal were the least accurate crossers in the Premiership in 1998–99, but Parlour was the best at the club, completing 29%, though he only provided three goal assists.

As one of the few home-grown players left in the side, Parlour enjoys a special affinity with the fans. He has done well to hold on to his place in the team and is probably the most improved player at the club since Arsene Wenger's arrival in north London.

APPEARANCES	
Start (sub)	35 (0)
Minutes on pitch	3056
GOAL ATTEMPTS	
Goals	6
Shots on target	27
Shooting accuracy	47%
PASSING	
Goal assists	3
Passing accuracy	79%
Crossing accuracy	29%
DRIBBLING	
Dribbles & runs	183
Dribble completion	74%
DISCIPLINE	
Yellow cards	4
Red cards	0

Darren PEACOCK • 5
BLACKBURN ROVERS • BORN: 3.2.68

APPEARANCES	
Start (sub)	27 (3)
Minutes on pitch	2417
GOAL ATTEMPTS	
Goals	1
DEFENDING	
Blocks	33
Headed clearances	227
Other clearances	103
Interceptions	20
Tackles won	50
PASSING	
Passing accuracy	80%
DISCIPLINE	
Fouls	30
Yellow cards	7
Red cards	0

Signed from Newcastle United on a free transfer under the Bosman ruling in the summer of 1998, Darren Peacock played more than 2,000 minutes of Premiership football in Blackburn's relegation season.

Intended to plug the defensive gap left by Colin Hendry's summer departure to Glasgow Rangers, that void proved difficult to fill – and while Peacock's aerial presence was welcome, Rovers' defence had a torrid time in 1998–99.

On the ball, Peacock made more than 750 passes and completed 80%, including one goal assist. He managed five goal attempts on target and even scored his first Rovers goal in April's 3–3 draw with Southampton at the Dell.

The pony-tailed centre-back won 63% of his challenges, below-average for a central defender, but did make 330 clearances. In terms of discipline, Peacock committed 30 fouls and collected seven yellow cards.

The Nationwide League presents a fresh challenge to Peacock and his team-mates. Having played in the top flight for the last 10 years it may take some time for him to adjust.

P

CB Ian PEARCE • 19
WEST HAM UNITED • BORN: 7.5.74

Since his £1.6 million move from Blackburn Rovers in September 1997, Ian Pearce has established himself as one of the key names on the West Ham team sheet. His central defensive partnership with Neil Ruddock and Rio Ferdinand was instrumental in the Hammers' climb to the Premiership top six.

He was occasionally pushed up front, and having scored just three League goals in his entire career before 1998–99, he increased that tally to five with strikes in home wins over Nottingham Forest and Blackburn Rovers.

Known for his composure on the ball and distribution, he completed four out of every five passes and 76% of his dribbles and runs.

Sadly, his season ended prematurely when he fractured a knee in April. He became the third Hammers defender to suffer a long-term injury after Steve Potts and Javier Margas. At the time, only goalkeeper Shaka Hislop and midfielder Frank Lampard had played more Premiership football for West Ham, showing what a key figure Pearce has become to the London side.

APPEARANCES	
Start (sub)	33 (0)
Minutes on pitch	2962
GOAL ATTEMPTS	
Goals	2
DEFENDING	
Blocks	38
Headed clearances	204
Other clearances	139
Interceptions	33
Tackles won	33
PASSING	
Passing accuracy	80%
DISCIPLINE	
Fouls	33
Yellow cards	4
Red cards	0

CB Stuart PEARCE • 3
NEWCASTLE UNITED • BORN: 24.4.62

APPEARANCES	
Start (sub)	12 (0)
Minutes on pitch	1038
GOAL ATTEMPTS	
Goals	0
DEFENDING	
Blocks	23
Headed clearances	74
Other clearances	49
Interceptions	10
Tackles won	18
PASSING	
Passing accuracy	81%
DISCIPLINE	
Fouls	12
Yellow cards	1
Red cards	1

Punk-rocking MBE Stuart Pearce played a big part early in United's 1998–99 season, replacing injury-prone Steve Howey in the back three.

Though he only played once more after being controversially dismissed against West Ham United at the end of October, Pearce never gave his team less than his customary 110%.

Amazingly, the ex-England man has only ever commanded £225,000 in transfer fees. He joined Newcastle for free during Kenny Dalglish's reign, gaining Magpies fans' instant respect with his no-nonsense approach.

During the 1998–99 season he made 27 challenges, winning 67%, and attempted more than 150 blocks, clearances and interceptions as the Premiership pressure began to tell.

Sadly for an acknowledged dead-ball specialist, a superb free-kick winner against Juventus in a pre-season curtain-raiser at St James's Park was his only strike.

Now 37, Pearce may not get the opportunity to light up the league with any more of his trademark thunderbolts – but his reputation remains undimmed.

Sebastian PEREZ • 15
BLACKBURN ROVERS • BORN: 27.11.63

Frenchman Sebastien Perez made a handful of League appearances early in the 1998–99 Premiership season and, on occasions looked lively before he was sent out on loan to French club Bastia Corse in February 1999.

Perez was at his best when running at opposition defenders, achieving a fine dribble completion rate of 71%. Tenacious in midfield, he also won 69% of his 13 challenges, while at the back he made a handful of clearances and three interceptions.

Perez's low cross completion – only 20% from 15 attempts – was disappointing. He failed to produce any goal assists from his position on the wing but did score one League goal.

He had no hesitation in shooting, firing in five shots on target, three off target, and seeing three blocked. He committed 10 fouls, picking up two bookings. The one real sour point was his red card in the stormy 4–3 home defeat by Chelsea in September.

It seems unlikely that Perez will return to Ewood Park in 1999–2000, having failed to sparkle in his short spell in England.

APPEARANCES	
Start (sub)	4 (1)
Minutes on pitch	319
GOAL ATTEMPTS	
Goals	1
Shots on target	5
Shooting accuracy	63%
PASSING	
Goal assists	0
Passing accuracy	73%
Crossing accuracy	20%
DRIBBLING	
Dribbles & runs	14
Dribble completion	71%
DISCIPLINE	
Yellow cards	2
Red cards	1

Chris PERRY • 4
WIMBLEDON • BORN: 26.4.73

APPEARANCES	
Start (sub)	34 (0)
Minutes on pitch	3029
GOAL ATTEMPTS	
Goals	0
DEFENDING	
Blocks	51
Headed clearances	256
Other clearances	200
Interceptions	60
Tackles won	93
PASSING	
Passing accuracy	71%
DISCIPLINE	
Fouls	36
Yellow cards	6
Red cards	0

Diminutive centre-back Chris Perry continued to be ignored at international level, but his defensive partnership with Dean Blackwell was as important as ever for the Dons in 1998–99.

Under more pressure than in previous seasons, Perry was forced to throw his body in the way of more opposition shots than any other player in the Premiership – his tally of 51 blocks was almost too high for comfort.

The fact he also made 456 clearances must also have worried the management, who will know the club would have been in trouble without some of their defence's heroics.

Perry was one reason why the Dons beat the drop. Once safety was assured he, like the rest of the team, took his weary foot off the pedal.

A Wimbledon supporter, Perry sweated blood for the Wombles early in the 1998–99 season, appearing in the club's opening 28 Premiership games.

But he returned from his honeymoon in June to discover Tottenham Hotspur had lodged a £5.5 million bid to prise him away from Selhurst Park.

P

M Emmanuel PETIT • 17
ARSENAL • BORN: 22.9.70

On a high after his World Cup final exploits, Emmanuel Petit was a strong presence in front of Arsenal's defence and used his passing skills to good effect, finishing the season as number two in the Carling Opta midfielders Index.

The former Monaco player won an above-average 66% of his tackles in midfield and notched up a 78% pass completion rate.

But the main talking point was Petit's disciplinary record. Sent off twice in the Premiership – first in the home match against Charlton and then away at Everton – he was booked on a further four occasions in the Premiership and was also sent off in the FA Cup clash with Wolverhampton Wanderers.

His problems with referees led Petit to suggest that he may leave Highbury for foreign fields.

While there would be no shortage of interest in him from Europe's top clubs, Arsenal's playing staff and fans will be hoping that the pony-tailed Frenchman will stay in north London to help the Gunners in their bid to regain the title in 1999–2000.

APPEARANCES	
Start (sub)	26 (1)
Minutes on pitch	2258
GOAL ATTEMPTS	
Goals	4
PASSING	
Passes	1405
Passing accuracy	78%
DEFENDING	
Interceptions	41
Clearances	93
Tackles	122
Tackles won	66%
DISCIPLINE	
Fouls	19
Yellow cards	4
Red cards	2

Manu of many talents: Emmanuel Petit

Dan PETRESCU • 2
CHELSEA • BORN: 22.12.67

AM

Despite enjoying an excellent World Cup with Romania, much speculation surrounded Dan Petrescu's Chelsea future in the opening few months of the 1998–99 season.

Reduced to a supporting role, most of his appearances came as a substitute; but nothing if not persistent, the former Sheffield Wednesday man stuck gamely to his task and by December had forced his way back into Gianluca Vialli's thoughts, earning a regular place in the Chelsea manager's starting XI.

His best moment probably came with the goal that beat Newcastle 1–0 at St James's Park on January 9. Chelsea regained the Premiership top spot that day, and Petrescu's speed on the break was vital to their victory.

He scored three times in the league from 20 shots and set up four more for team-mates with some neat work around the box.

Now a Chelsea veteran, he remains one of their most influential players, completing 82% of his 1,026 attempted passes and whipping in 73 crosses. But he did pick up a total of eight bookings in the Premiership.

APPEARANCES	
Start (sub)	23 (9)
Minutes on pitch	2166
GOAL ATTEMPTS	
Goals	3
Shots on target	8
Shooting accuracy	40%
PASSING	
Goal assists	4
Passing accuracy	82%
Crossing accuracy	29%
DRIBBLING	
Dribbles & runs	34
Dribble completion	76%
DISCIPLINE	
Yellow cards	8
Red cards	0

Andy PETTERSON • 13
CHARLTON ATHLETIC • BORN: 26.9.69

G

P

APPEARANCES	
Start (sub)	7 (3)
Minutes on pitch	755
SHOT STOPPING	
Goals conceded	18
Clean sheets	0
Saves	21
Saves/shots	54%
DISTRIBUTION	
Distribution	259
Distribution %	43%
CATCHING	
Crosses caught	16
Crosses dropped	0
DISCIPLINE	
Yellow cards	0
Red cards	1

Andy Petterson found himself third in the goalkeepers' pecking order at the Valley, managing only seven starts and three substitute appearances in 1998–99.

After one early-season game, the 4–2 defeat of West Ham, he was loaned to cash-strapped Portsmouth in the Nationwide League.

Unfortunately his form following his return to Charlton's first team was disappointing at a crucial stage of the season and he conceded 15 goals in his last six matches. That spell also included a sending-off in the 4–3 win at Aston Villa after conceding three goals.

The Australian's claiming of the high ball was immaculate, but he was unable to keep a clean sheet. He saved a disappointing 54% of the shots he faced, conceding 18 goals in all.

Petterson had a difficult year at Charlton in 1998–99 and will be looking to return to his 1996–97 form, when he played at the peak of his game.

A new season and a fresh start may be just what Petterson needs to kick-start his first-team career.

FB Alessandro PISTONE • 5
NEWCASTLE UNITED • BORN: 27.7.75

Loaned to Italian side Venezia at the end of 1998–99 with a view to a permanent move, Alessandro Pistone's Newcastle career is all-but over.

The £4.3 million signing from Inter Milan played in Newcastle's opening two games, but after Kenny Dalglish's departure he was restricted to just 41 minutes of first-team football under Ruud Gullit, who did not seem to rate him.

A former Italy under-21 captain, Pistone did little in his total of 198 minutes on pitch. He managed just four tackles in his three appearances and, although he was on hand to complete a handful of clearances, his failure to make a single interception was indicative of his poor form.

For a man who was once thought to have the potential to become as good as Paolo Maldini, Pistone's failure to make his mark at St James's Park has been a very serious disappointment.

A return to the Carling Premiership would seem most unlikely at this stage.

AM Hugo PORFIRIO • 31
NOTTINGHAM FOREST • BORN: 28.9.73

Portuguese loan-signing Hugo Porfirio was part of the new blood which Ron Atkinson injected into an anaemic-looking side on his arrival at the City Ground.

The former West Ham man impressed the Nottingham Forest faithful with his impish displays on the left wing, leaving many wondering how former Derby player Mark Pembridge could possibly have kept him out of the Benfica side.

The stylish Porfirio managed to set up two goals for team-mates and score another one himself in just three starting appearances and five as a substitute.

But his fine form came too late to save Forest from relegation – though it did at least make the dreaded drop a little easier for them and their supporters to bear.

He was instrumental in the club's run of three successive victories at the end of the season and, although the former Hammers favourite is unlikely to return to the City Ground in the foreseeable future, he certainly left the fans with some warm memories.

G Mart POOM • 21
DERBY COUNTY • BORN: 3.2.72

Pre-season illness and injury saw Estonian international Mart Poom lose his place in the Derby County side to Russell Hoult.

Hoult's excellent form left Poom kicking his heels on the touchline. But an injury to his rival in the 2–2 draw against Nottingham Forest in November saw Poom make a dramatic entrance as a substitute.

As in 1997–98, it was in the air that Poom did most of his best work. At 6' 4", he certainly has the height to command his penalty area – something he proved with a catch success rate of 99%.

His shot-stopping was not as impressive, but he still managed to save 77% of the efforts he faced – a better figure than that of Hoult. He also kept a total of seven clean sheets – two more than Derby's other 'keeper.

An injury sustained in the FA Cup clash with Swansea City forced Poom out of the side again in January. But, as before, he battled back well, returning to the side in the run-in to the season after a suspension picked up by Hoult allowed him to reclaim his place.

He now faces a similar battle with Hoult for the first-team jersey in 1999–2000, as Jim Smith and new first-team coach Malcolm Crosby decide exactly who they want in the starting XI.

APPEARANCES	
Start (sub)	15 (2)
Minutes on pitch	1401
SHOT STOPPING	
Goals conceded	16
Clean sheets	7
Saves	54
Saves/shots	77%
DISTRIBUTION	
Distribution	431
Distribution %	54%
CATCHING	
Crosses caught	78
Crosses dropped	1
DISCIPLINE	
Yellow cards	0
Red cards	0

CB Steve POTTS • 4
WEST HAM UNITED • BORN: 7.5.67

West Ham's longest-serving player, Steve Potts completed his 15th season as a professional in 1998–99 and was once again on hand to fill in at the back when required, making a total of 11 starts and eight appearances as a substitute in the Premiership.

Capable of operating as a right-back or in the middle of the defence, Potts was used mainly as cover for the club's three regular centre-backs, and in that capacity made more than 100 blocks, clearances and interceptions.

At 5' 7" he is not the tallest of defenders, but he more than makes up for this with a mixture of pace and intelligence. In the best traditions of West Ham he is also a great passer of the ball, finding a team-mate with 86% of his passes in 1998–99.

The one area of his game which he would like to improve is his record in front of goal. In all his time as a professional footballer, he has scored just once.

Not surprisingly for a man with that record, he failed to manage a single shot in the 1998–99 Carling Premiership.

APPEARANCES	
Start (sub)	11 (8)
Minutes on pitch	1062
GOAL ATTEMPTS	
Goals	0
DEFENDING	
Blocks	8
Headed clearances	51
Other clearances	34
Interceptions	10
Tackles won	24
PASSING	
Passing accuracy	86%
DISCIPLINE	
Fouls	13
Yellow cards	4
Red cards	0

FB Chris POWELL • 3
CHARLTON ATHLETIC • BORN: 8.6.69

APPEARANCES	
Start (sub)	38 (0)
Minutes on pitch	3411
GOAL ATTEMPTS	
Goals	0
PASSING & CROSSING	
Passing	1097
Passing accuracy	75%
Crossing	106
Crossing accuracy	24%
DEFENDING	
Tackles	100
Tackles won	75%
DISCIPLINE	
Fouls	26
Yellow cards	2
Red cards	0

Chris Powell had a solid year at left-back for the Addicks, starting in every Premiership match of 1998–99. Substituted only twice, he missed just nine minutes of football in all.

Powell was one of Charlton's most reliable players in defence, winning three-quarters of his 100 challenges. The former Derby full-back blocked 29 shots and made 38 interceptions and more than 200 clearances, outlining his importance in Alan Curbishley's defence.

He was also a competent passer of the ball, with 75% of his balls reaching a Charlton player. Powell tended to remain wide when pushing forward and delivered more than 100 crosses, finishing with a 24% completion rate and creating one Charlton goal. He fired three shots on target but was unable to find the net.

His disciplinary record was also very good, with just 26 fouls conceded and only two bookings accrued.

Powell was one of the 1998–99 season's most under-rated players and Charlton will be looking to hold on to their Mr Reliable despite their relegation from the top flight.

Darryl POWELL • 4
DERBY COUNTY • BORN: 15.11.71

Pre-season speculation linking Jamaican World Cup star Darryl Powell with a move to the First Division, at either Barnsley or Sheffield United, proved to be well wide of the mark. He stayed at Pride Park, missing just five games in Derby's steady season in the Premiership.

A left-sided midfielder who can also operate at wing-back, Powell helped the Rams look solid in 1998–99. Always available for his team-mates, he completed an excellent 82% of all his attempted passes.

Often encouraged to get forward, particularly in home matches, he retained possession with 84% of his dribbles and runs and delivered a superb 44% of his attempted crosses to team-mates in the box.

He rarely let his opposite number get the better of him, winning 66% of his 109 tackles and stealing the ball off a rival's toes with 27 interceptions.

The former Portsmouth player proved his Premiership quality in 1998–99. Now established in Jim Smith's side, the £750,000 he cost in 1995 looks like a real bargain.

APPEARANCES	
Start (sub)	30 (3)
Minutes on pitch	2762

GOAL ATTEMPTS	
Goals	0

PASSING	
Passes	990
Passing accuracy	82%

DEFENDING	
Interceptions	27
Clearances	96
Tackles	109
Tackles won	66%

DISCIPLINE	
Fouls	62
Yellow cards	8
Red cards	0

Gustavo POYET • 8
CHELSEA • BORN: 15.11.67

APPEARANCES	
Start (sub)	21 (7)
Minutes on pitch	1910

GOAL ATTEMPTS	
Goals	11
Shots on target	28
Shooting accuracy	44%

PASSING	
Goal assists	3
Passing accuracy	78%
Crossing accuracy	38%

DRIBBLING	
Dribbles & runs	29
Dribble completion	72%

DISCIPLINE	
Yellow cards	4
Red cards	0

Where might Chelsea have finished the season had Gustavo Poyet remained fit?

Injured in the Boxing Day clash with Southampton, the Uruguayan had been a strong prospect for both major Player of the Year awards – but though he returned with nine matches remaining, he was unable to stop Chelsea's title bid from faltering.

His main contribution to the side came with the 11 goals he struck, more than any other midfield player; eight came before his injury. Lethal in the air, his height and timing brought him six strikes with his head – the most in the Premiership – propelling Chelsea to the top of the table.

A player of real technique who knows when to hold the ball and when to release it, Poyet also ended the season with three goal assists and a good pass completion rate of 78%.

Assuredly one of the Premiership's classiest performers, Poyet's susceptibility to injury has now hit the Blues in two successive seasons. If they are to improve on third place, they must keep him off the treatment table.

Kevin PRESSMAN • 1
SHEFFIELD WEDNESDAY • BORN: 6.11.67

He may top the Wednesday squad list, but for most of the 1998–99 Carling Premiership season Kevin Pressman had to play second fiddle to free-transfer signing Pavel Srnicek.

Pressman's campaign started well. From the first 12 matches the Fareham-born goalie kept five clean sheets and conceded only 14 goals. Four came in the comprehensive defeat at Middlesbrough, and until that match Pressman had looked hard to beat; so he may have felt a bit disappointed when Srnicek replaced him.

Pressman's Carling Opta stats back this up. He saved a healthy 78% of all shots, the vast majority from inside the area. The Owls man was also very assured in his own box, claiming 98% of all crosses and dropping just one.

The former Wednesday apprentice gave little possession away when targeting colleagues with throws and short kicks and was economical with possession on the whole.

Pressman's other strength lies in his ability to cut down the angles in a one-on-one situation, and he used his agile frame to great effect during the 1998–99 season.

APPEARANCES	
Start (sub)	14 (1)
Minutes on pitch	1292
SHOT STOPPING	
Goals conceded	14
Clean sheets	5
Saves	51
Saves/shots	78%
DISTRIBUTION	
Distribution	431
Distribution %	55%
CATCHING	
Crosses caught	45
Crosses dropped	1
DISCIPLINE	
Yellow cards	0
Red cards	0

Martin PRINGLE • 39
CHARLTON ATHLETIC • BORN: 18.11.70

APPEARANCES	
Start (sub)	15 (3)
Minutes on pitch	1343
GOAL ATTEMPTS	
Goals	3
Goals/shots ratio	12%
SHOOTING	
Shots on target	21
Shooting accuracy	81%
PASSING	
Goal assists	0
Passing accuracy	67%
DISCIPLINE	
Fouls	18
Offside	22
Yellow cards	1
Red cards	0

After joining Charlton on loan from Portuguese giants Benfica, Martin Pringle provided the attacking edge the team lacked without the injured Clive Mendonca. Alan Curbishley was so impressed with the Swede he made the move permanent in March.

Settling quickly, Pringle completed 1,343 minutes of Premiership football in 1998–99. He fired 21 shots on target – including a last-minute equaliser in his first start for the Addicks against Newcastle – and a further two goals in the second half of the season, against Wimbledon and Derby.

His pace in the Charlton attack troubled opposing defences. At Villa Park, his run at the Aston Villa back-line led to the free kick which provided the winning fourth goal. In all, he completed 58% of his dribbles and runs, 67% of his passes and 27% of his crosses.

Charlton will need Pringle to form a profitable partnership, possibly with Mendonca, in order to fire the goals to shoot the Addicks to the top of Nationwide League Division One in 1999–2000.

P

CB — Spencer PRIOR • 17
DERBY COUNTY • BORN: 22.4.71

Signed in August 1998, Spencer Prior more than adequately filled the gap in Derby's defence left by Christian Dailly's departure.

In fact, at just £700,000 (£4.6 million less than Dailly cost Blackburn) it could be argued the former Leicester man was one of the bargains of the 1998–99 season.

Given the captain's armband in the absence of Igor Stimac, Prior proved to be a natural leader. His tackle success rate of 72% was the highest of all Derby's regular first-teamers and his tally of 41 blocks and 37 interceptions was an example to the rest of the team.

An orthodox stopper, Prior still demonstrated that he has a fair amount of ability on the ball, completing 75% of his attempted passes and an excellent 97% of his runs out of defence.

But the highlight of his season undoubtedly came when he headed the goal in Derby's 1–0 victory over Sheffield Wednesday at Hillsborough. It was one of just 10 shots he managed all season, and only the fifth league goal of his career.

APPEARANCES	
Start (sub)	33 (1)
Minutes on pitch	3000
GOAL ATTEMPTS	
Goals	1
DEFENDING	
Blocks	41
Headed clearances	333
Other clearances	139
Interceptions	37
Tackles won	71
PASSING	
Passing accuracy	75%
DISCIPLINE	
Fouls	29
Yellow cards	4
Red cards	0

M — Nigel QUASHIE • 4
NOTTINGHAM FOREST • BORN: 20.7.78

APPEARANCES	
Start (sub)	12 (4)
Minutes on pitch	1020
GOAL ATTEMPTS	
Goals	0
PASSING	
Passes	467
Passing accuracy	77%
DEFENDING	
Interceptions	11
Clearances	22
Tackles	36
Tackles won	67%
DISCIPLINE	
Fouls	19
Yellow cards	4
Red cards	0

Dave Bassett signed Nigel Quashie for £2.5 million at the start of 1998–99, saying: "I have not necessarily bought Nigel as a player for now. He is a player for the future."

But injuries to Scot Gemmill and Geoff Thomas saw the youngster thrust straight into first-team action, and he took part in many of Forest's games before Ron Atkinson arrived.

The former QPR man had been seen by some as a future England international, but despite battling gamely in Forest's fight to escape the drop he found the going tough.

In all, he won just 67% of his attempted tackles and completed 77% of his passes, setting up one goal in the process.

The arrival of Atkinson saw him used mainly as a substitute, and it remains to be seen whether he can convince the next occupant of the Forest hot seat of his worth.

He showed flashes of brilliance in his time at Loftus Road but failed to reproduce anything approaching his best form at the City Ground. The 1999–2000 season will be an important one for him.

Alan Quinn had his second taste of Premiership football when he started the Owls' league match away to Wimbledon in October 1998.

Quinn was blooded towards the end of the 1997–98 campaign when he played in Wednesday's 3–1 victory at Goodison Park, so he may have expected slightly more than his 46 minutes of first-team action the following season.

Signed for Sheffield Wednesday in April 1998, the 20-year-old Dubliner spent his first full season as an established member of the club's youthful reserve team squad, proving a handful up front for opposition defences.

The inexperienced Owl played in a slightly deeper role than usual at Wimbledon and offered one shot, nine passes and three crosses in all.

Quinn has already been capped at under-18 level for the Republic of Ireland, and has shown signs that he has the potential to follow in the footsteps of his prolific namesake at Sunderland.

Goalkeeper Adam Rachel's first appearance in the Carling Premiership was somewhat overshadowed by the contention which surrounded his top-flight introduction.

Rachel came off the bench after Michael Oakes was dubiously sent off at Blackburn Rovers on Boxing Day. Oakes was penalized for handling the ball outside his area, though he later had his red card rescinded.

The Birmingham-born goalkeeper went on to concede Villa's second goal in their 2–1 defeat as the side struggled with 10 men. Otherwise he had a quiet game, not having to make a single save.

Rachel is not one of the league's tallest keepers, standing a shade under six feet, but he makes up for his lack of height with his great agility.

He has been a regular in the Villa reserves but has faced stiff competition from Oakes and Mark Bosnich for a first-team place. But now that Bosnich has moved back to Manchester United, Rachel will hope to get more first-team opportunities in the 1999–2000 season.

Injuries to regular midfielders Gary McAllister and Trond-Egil Soltvedt near the start of the season gave promising young Coventry City midfielder Barry Quinn his chance to impress Gordon Strachan.

Playing in four Premiership games between September 12 and October 3, Quinn made his debut against Manchester United in a 2–0 defeat at Old Trafford, coping well in a difficult atmosphere.

He made another brief appearance midway through the season as a substitute in the 4–0 demolition of Nottingham Forest, but was then out of the team until March when he played the full 90 minutes in the 2–0 defeat by Arsenal.

His performance against Arsene Wenger's side impressed many in the crowd that day and he received an honourable mention from Trevor Brooking in his summary on the BBC's *Match of the Day*.

An accurate passer, he managed to find a team-mate with 80% of all his attempted passes but failed to set up any goals.

He tackled well, winning 62% of his challenges – and conceding just five free kicks in the process. His last game of the season came against Leicester, where he picked up a yellow card.

P

APPEARANCES	
Start (sub)	6 (1)
Minutes on pitch	512
GOAL ATTEMPTS	
Goals	0
PASSING	
Passes	252
Passing accuracy	80%
DEFENDING	
Interceptions	8
Clearances	8
Tackles	13
Tackles won	62%
DISCIPLINE	
Fouls	5
Yellow cards	1
Red cards	0

CB · Lucas RADEBE • 5
LEEDS UNITED • BORN: 12.4.69

Lucas Radebe was rated the fifth-best defender in the 1998–99 Premiership by Carling Opta. The South African enhanced his reputation with a series of fine displays which saw Leeds United finish fourth and qualify for the UEFA Cup. Appointed captain at the season's start, he missed much of the campaign through injury; but his return to fitness inspired David O'Leary's side to keep the league's third-best defensive record.

Radebe was solid in the tackle, winning 62% of 151 attempted. His pass completion rate of 82% was also good, but he achieved his consistency by sticking to what he does best. He did not try to dribble too often and was rarely caught out of position – just two efforts at goal reflected his reticence to go forward.

His 62 interceptions show how well he reads the game. And despite the physical nature of the Premiership, he made only 19 fouls and suffered just two cautions.

Radebe will be very proud to take Leeds into Europe in 1999–2000 – and prouder still if he can lift a trophy at the end of the season.

APPEARANCES	
Start (sub)	29 (0)
Minutes on pitch	2538
GOAL ATTEMPTS	
Goals	0
DEFENDING	
Blocks	39
Headed clearances	244
Other clearances	135
Interceptions	62
Tackles won	93
PASSING	
Passing accuracy	82%
DISCIPLINE	
Fouls	19
Yellow cards	2
Red cards	0

M · Neil REDFEARN • 4
CHARLTON ATHLETIC • BORN: 20.6.65

APPEARANCES	
Start (sub)	29 (1)
Minutes on pitch	2501
GOAL ATTEMPTS	
Goals	3
PASSING	
Passes	956
Passing accuracy	73%
DEFENDING	
Interceptions	10
Clearances	72
Tackles	83
Tackles won	66%
DISCIPLINE	
Fouls	83
Yellow cards	9
Red cards	0

Much was expected from Neil Redfearn following his move south from Barnsley in summer 1998; but his form at Charlton was disappointing and he was replaced towards the season's close by new signing Graham Stuart.

Carling Opta's statistics suggest Redfearn may have left his shooting boots at Oakwell. From 27 shots on target he managed just three goals – poor compared to his double-figure tally in 1997–98. His memorable long-range curler at Wimbledon was too rare a sight for Charlton fans in 1998–99: instead, he ended up playing very deep and completed 72 clearances from defence.

At 73% his pass completion was below average and he ended the season without a goal assist, but there was no doubting his tenacity. His tackle completion rate was an above-average 66%, but he was also in the top five worst offenders, committing 83 fouls and collecting nine yellow cards.

Redfearn struggled to make his mark with his new team and put in a transfer request shortly after Charlton were relegated.

Jamie REDKNAPP • 11
LIVERPOOL • BORN: 25.6.73

M

Jamie Redknapp's 1998–99 season was not one of his best. A below-average campaign for club and country means he will be keen to get 1999–2000 underway as soon as possible.

Passing is his forte, and while he completed a below-average 78% many were longer balls which are harder to execute accurately. Of his 2,212 passes – more than any other player in the league – 433 were over 25 yards, as he attempted to switch play or find the likes of Michael Owen behind opposition defences.

But passing is not the only string to his bow. The midfielder arrowed in plenty of shots, the majority from distance. Seven of his eight goals came from inside the area, including two penalties, but the eighth was the best – a blistering strike in the 3–1 win at Ewood Park.

With Paul Ince alongside, Redknapp could have left the "dogging" to the Guv'nor, but he pitched in with 84 tackles and won 67% of his challenges.

Redknapp is sure to be a cornerstone of Gerard Houllier's new Liverpool which will be trying to bring back the glory days to Anfield.

APPEARANCES	
Start (sub)	33 (1)
Minutes on pitch	2935
GOAL ATTEMPTS	
Goals	8
PASSING	
Passes	2212
Passing accuracy	78%
DEFENDING	
Interceptions	27
Clearances	33
Tackles	84
Tackles won	67%
DISCIPLINE	
Fouls	38
Yellow cards	6
Red cards	0

Pass master: Jamie Redknapp

Bruno RIBEIRO • 10
LEEDS UNITED • BORN: 22.10.75

Season 1998–99 may well have been Bruno Ribeiro's last in English football. The Portuguese midfielder suffered several early injuries, and once fit found himself on the sidelines behind Harry Kewell and loan purchase Willem Korsten.

Ribeiro seemed a bargain signing after some fine displays under George Graham's tutelage when filling in for the injured Lee Sharpe.

The passing ability Leeds fans loved in 1997–98 was not so good in 1998–99. He completed just 75% of fewer than 200 attempted passes to team-mates. But he still posed a threat with that cultured left foot: Ribeiro scored one goal and forced three saves in nine attempts at the target, but did little to track back defensively down the Leeds left.

A disappointing season was summed up when he hit the post and was then sent off as Leeds crashed out of the UEFA Cup to Roma.

The fact that David O'Leary was very keen to secure Willem Korsten on a permanent basis suggests that Ribeiro is surplus to requirements at Elland Road.

APPEARANCES	
Start (sub)	7 (6)
Minutes on pitch	570
GOAL ATTEMPTS	
Goals	1
Shots on target	4
Shooting accuracy	50%
PASSING	
Goal assists	0
Passing accuracy	75%
Crossing accuracy	35%
DRIBBLING	
Dribbles & runs	10
Dribble completion	60%
DISCIPLINE	
Yellow cards	1
Red cards	0

Hamilton RICARD • 19
MIDDLESBROUGH • BORN: 12.1.74

APPEARANCES	
Start (sub)	32 (4)
Minutes on pitch	2704
GOAL ATTEMPTS	
Goals	15
Goals/shots ratio	18%
SHOOTING	
Shots on target	40
Shooting accuracy	49%
PASSING	
Goal assists	2
Passing accuracy	66%
DISCIPLINE	
Fouls	68
Offside	45
Yellow cards	5
Red cards	0

Colombian Hamilton Ricard may well have been the surprise striking package of season 1998–99, with 15 Carling Premiership goals.

Whenever he scored in the league, Boro did not lose. From 12 matches in which he netted, Robson's side won 10 and drew two. In his unsuccessful quest for the Golden Boot, the former Deportivo Cali striker fired in 82 efforts at goal, just under half of them on target.

Boro's top scorer also turned provider twice, but his all-round distribution was a touch disappointing. He completed two-thirds of his 885 passes, slightly below the Premiership striker standard, but the quality of ball he played into the box was poor, with only nine of his 45 crosses met by a Boro team-mate.

Happy to take on his marker and create space for a shot, he beat his man more often than not in nearly 100 dribbles and runs.

A footballing cliché says a striker's quality shows in his second season when he is a known quantity. In season 1999–2000, Ricard's second in the Premiership, Boro fans will see just how good the Colombian is.

Karl-Heinz RIEDLE • 13
LIVERPOOL • BORN: 16.9.65

World Cup and European Cup medal-winner Karl-Heinz Riedle has committed himself to Anfield for at least another season, but seems destined to spend much of it playing second fiddle once again. Not only that, but further signings are likely to intensify the competition for places and limit the veteran's contribution.

The German striker scored five goals in 1998–99 from 15 shots on target. Another 25 went wide, and 15 efforts were blocked en route to goal by covering defenders.

Riedle also supplied four goal assists in what turned out to be a disappointing season for the Reds, but his overall pass completion was just below average for his position. His target-man role means he has to give as good as he gets – which explains his 49 fouls – but he must clean up his act after seven yellow cards.

Riedle is unlikely to move on, though, as he has run out of legs – cow's legs, that is. The German international has a lifesize model of a cow which models a sock from each of his four major clubs – Werder Bremen, Lazio, Borussia Dortmund and Liverpool.

APPEARANCES

Start (sub)	16 (18)
Minutes on pitch	1743

GOAL ATTEMPTS

Goals	5
Goals/shots ratio	13%

SHOOTING

Shots on target	15
Shooting accuracy	38%

PASSING

Goal assists	4
Passing accuracy	68%

DISCIPLINE

Fouls	49
Offside	29
Yellow cards	7
Red cards	0

Stuart RIPLEY • 14
SOUTHAMPTON • BORN: 20.11.67

APPEARANCES

Start (sub)	16 (6)
Minutes on pitch	1376

GOAL ATTEMPTS

Goals	0
Shots on target	2
Shooting accuracy	25%

PASSING

Goal assists	2
Passing accuracy	68%
Crossing accuracy	27%

DRIBBLING

Dribbles & runs	63
Dribble completion	70%

DISCIPLINE

Yellow cards	1
Red cards	0

Stuart Ripley signed for Southampton for £1.5m in July 1997 but endured a disappointing first season at the Dell.

The former Blackburn Rovers favourite played just 1,376 minutes in the 1998–99 Premiership season, primarily due to injury and loss of form. And he was ineligible for the final three matches of the season, having been sent off in a reserve team match for fighting.

Ripley, a former England international, brought a reputation for pacy wing play and exceptional crossing to the Dell, but was unable to reproduce the form he had shown so consistently in six seasons at Ewood Park.

His cross completion rate of 27% from 92 attempts, while not a bad figure, compared unfavourably with other Southampton wide men, though he did provide two goal assists. Not renowned as a goalscorer, Ripley failed to get off the mark for the Saints and tested the goalkeeper with only two shots.

There is little doubt Ripley is a talented player; and if he can perform to the expected standard he could be an asset in 1999–2000.

R

Andy ROBERTS • 10
M
WIMBLEDON • BORN: 20.3.74

Andy Roberts's transfer from Crystal Palace to Wimbledon was quite a surprise in the 1997–98 season. At £2 million he was then a big-money signing, and expected to be a mainstay of the Wimbledon midfield for years to come.

But things did not turn out in quite that way, with Roberts's form dipping in 1998–99 – a fact which saw him in and out of the starting line-up.

The Dons' tendency to bypass the central midfield with early balls to the forward line has not helped the 25-year-old, who likes to get the ball down and play. He completed only 73% of his passes but tackled excellently, winning three-quarters of his 79 challenges.

Roberts does have his disciplinary problems, committing 47 fouls – nine of them serious enough to warrant yellow cards.

Joe Kinnear had already said he wanted to make changes to the squad, and new boss Egil Olsen is certain to want to bring in new players. Roberts will have to work hard to show that he has what it takes to be a millennium Don.

APPEARANCES	
Start (sub)	23 (5)
Minutes on pitch	2101
GOAL ATTEMPTS	
Goals	2
PASSING	
Passes	801
Passing accuracy	73%
DEFENDING	
Interceptions	17
Clearances	118
Tackles	79
Tackles won	75%
DISCIPLINE	
Fouls	47
Yellow cards	9
Red cards	0

John ROBINSON • 11
AM
CHARLTON ATHLETIC • BORN: 29.8.71

APPEARANCES	
Start (sub)	27 (3)
Minutes on pitch	2337
GOAL ATTEMPTS	
Goals	2
Shots on target	15
Shooting accuracy	56%
PASSING	
Goal assists	1
Passing accuracy	71%
Crossing accuracy	25%
DRIBBLING	
Dribbles & runs	120
Dribble completion	56%
DISCIPLINE	
Yellow cards	8
Red cards	0

One of Charlton's most reliable players in 1998–99, John Robinson produced 30 performances of determination and heart during the season. Nowhere was his passion for the game better illustrated than at Villa Park, where he displayed unbridled joy after heading Charlton's third goal in the 4–3 win.

The Zimbabwe-born Welsh international hit 15 shots on target – and wrote himself into Charlton's history books in their first-ever Premiership match at the Valley, having the honour of scoring their first Premiership goal in a memorable 5–0 win over Southampton.

Comfortable on either flank, Robinson completed a quarter of his crosses and retained possession from 56% of his dribbles.

He played sound defensive football, winning 61% of his 85 tackles and making more than 50 clearances. But he committed 40 fouls and collected eight yellow cards in 1998–99.

Charlton will again look to their tireless midfielder for success in the Nationwide League, when fans may well see the best of Robinson in an out-and-out winger's role.

Marvin ROBINSON • 26
DERBY COUNTY • BORN: 4.11.80

When Marvin Robinson was added to the Derby County first-team squad he hardly had time to think of the ramifications.

But, just a few weeks later, he was stepping out at Arsenal on live television to make his Derby debut.

After impressing in the Pontins League with a spectacular overhead-kick goal — just one of the highlights of a prolific season — the youngster was keen to try his luck.

And, just eight minutes after coming on, Robinson could have made a name for himself when the ball rebounded to him from David Seaman's brilliant stop from Paulo Wanchope. Unfortunately nerves got the better of the youngster and he dragged the ball wide.

Robinson will be hoping that he gets more opportunities to shine in 1999–2000; and if he continues his current rate of progress, Jim Smith will be happy to give him his chance.

With Wanchope and another of the season's top strikers, Dean Sturridge, ending the season on the transfer list, the teenager may well be in the spotlight more in the coming months.

Paul ROBINSON • 36
LEEDS UNITED • BORN: 15.10.79

Having one of the top goalkeepers in the country in the squad has its benefits and its drawbacks. Paul Robinson is in exactly that position at Leeds United where he has the excellent Nigel Martyn ahead of him.

Martyn is Leeds' undisputed first choice, so Robinson's opportunities are bound to be extremely limited — but looking on the positive side, the youngster has one of the best number ones in the game to watch and train with, a fact that can only help improve his game.

At 19 years of age, Robinson has time on his side, and will be hoping that the old truism that goalkeepers reach their peak later than most other players holds true for him, as he is unlikely to get many chances in the near future.

Robinson played four-and-a-half Premiership games in 1998–99, making 14 saves and keeping two clean sheets.

But he conceded six goals, leaving him with a saves-to-shots ratio of just 70% and a long way to go to match his mentor's 83%.

Alan ROGERS • 3
NOTTINGHAM FOREST • BORN: 3.1.77

APPEARANCES	
Start (sub)	34 (0)
Minutes on pitch	2981
GOAL ATTEMPTS	
Goals	4
PASSING & CROSSING	
Passing	1080
Passing accuracy	71%
Crossing	130
Crossing accuracy	24%
DEFENDING	
Tackles	75
Tackles won	55%
DISCIPLINE	
Fouls	38
Yellow cards	8
Red cards	0

Nottingham Forest supporters' Player of the Season was one of the few who could look back on 1998–99 with any pride, after the side failed to retain their place among the elite.

Rogers replaced a legend in Stuart Pearce when he joined for £2 million from Tranmere Rovers, but showed commitment and character which his illustrious predecessor would certainly have admired.

The 22-year-old scored four goals — an excellent return for a left-back — from 38 attempts at goal, including blocked shots.

Rogers was at his best when bombing down the wing, completing 85% of his dribbles and runs, and despite only completing 24% of his crosses, he set up two goals for team-mates.

He was less effective than he would have liked in the tackle, winning just 55% of the challenges he contested — and he earned eight yellow cards, committing 38 fouls.

The former England under-21 international will have to knuckle down for the new season and try to help Nottingham Forest back into the Premiership at the first time of asking.

R

G Simon ROYCE • 28
CHARLTON ATHLETIC • BORN: 9.9.71

Following his surprising release by Southend in the summer of 1998 after seven seasons of loyal service, Simon Royce was snapped up by Charlton and went on to make a number of impressive appearances for the Addicks in the 1998–99 Permiership season.

Having kept goal for around 11 hours of Premiership football at the Valley, Royce managed to keep five clean sheets and only conceded five goals. He saved a rather modest 76% of the shots he faced in the campaign.

His catch success was impressive at 96%, with just one dropped. Royce's distribution was also good: in terms of short distribution he gave the ball away to the opposition just twice, finishing the season with a 96% throw and short-kick success rate.

Royce was in competition with Andy Petterson and Sasa Ilic for most of 1998–99 and injuries did not help his first-team claims.

The signing of the highly-rated Dean Kiely from Bury will make it even harder for Royce to clinch a regular first-team berth in 1999–2000.

APPEARANCES	
Start (sub)	8 (0)
Minutes on pitch	675
SHOT STOPPING	
Goals conceded	5
Clean sheets	5
Saves	16
Saves/shots	76%
DISTRIBUTION	
Distribution	252
Distribution %	51%
CATCHING	
Crosses caught	23
Crosses dropped	1
DISCIPLINE	
Yellow cards	0
Red cards	0

CB Neil RUDDOCK • 6
WEST HAM UNITED • BORN: 9.5.68

APPEARANCES	
Start (sub)	27 (0)
Minutes on pitch	2348
GOAL ATTEMPTS	
Goals	2
DEFENDING	
Blocks	40
Headed clearances	194
Other clearances	135
Interceptions	31
Tackles won	48
PASSING	
Passing accuracy	71%
DISCIPLINE	
Fouls	39
Yellow cards	8
Red cards	1

Neil Ruddock has added plenty of life and soul to the West Ham dressing room and even displayed another talent when he sang a Beatles number on television, courtesy of team-mate Ian Wright's chat-show.

It was also a good season on the field for the man who began his career at Millwall and had stints at Spurs, Southampton and Liverpool. West Ham qualified for the InterToto Cup by finishing fifth in the Premiership – their highest top-flight finish since 1985–86.

"Razor" scored two goals, but it was his defensive influence alongside young Rio Ferdinand which made the biggest difference.

Though West Ham conceded four or more goals on eight occasions, Ruddock helped them secure the second-highest number of clean sheets during the Premiership season.

Ruddock won 71% of his 68 challenges, but will want to forget the appalling tackle on Leeds's Harry Kewell at Elland Road which led to his dismissal. Eight more bookings indicate his abrasive style, but he is likely to play a part in West Ham's 1999–2000 campaign.

Petter RUDI • 25
SHEFFIELD WEDNESDAY • BORN: 17.9.73

Norwegian international Petter Rudi enjoyed an excellent season for Sheffield Wednesday under new boss Danny Wilson. Putting aside the disappointment of his omission from Norway's 1998 World Cup squad, he played well enough for the Owls to earn a national recall.

The highlight of his season came in the 4–1 thrashing of Blackburn Rovers at Ewood Park, when he grabbed two goals and 2,716 Carling Opta points – the highest score by an attacking midfielder all season. Unfortunately, he was also fined £40 that day for boarding the return coach to Sheffield late!

Rudi displays good ball control and an eye for an opening. He completed 80% of all his passes and succeeded with 77% of his dribbles and runs.

A firm favourite with the fans, he also proved his commitment with more than 100 tackles, winning 71% – a figure well above the Premiership average for attacking midfielders.

His tally of six League goals was the club's joint-second-highest, and he is sure to be a part of Danny Wilson's plans for 1999–2000.

APPEARANCES	
Start (sub)	33 (1)
Minutes on pitch	2838
GOAL ATTEMPTS	
Goals	6
Shots on target	15
Shooting accuracy	38%
PASSING	
Goal assists	1
Passing accuracy	80%
Crossing accuracy	36%
DRIBBLING	
Dribbles & runs	119
Dribble completion	77%
DISCIPLINE	
Yellow cards	2
Red cards	0

Richard RUFUS • 5
CHARLTON ATHLETIC • BORN: 12.1.75

APPEARANCES	
Start (sub)	27 (0)
Minutes on pitch	2270
GOAL ATTEMPTS	
Goals	1
DEFENDING	
Blocks	27
Headed clearances	210
Other clearances	113
Interceptions	29
Tackles won	48
PASSING	
Passing accuracy	77%
DISCIPLINE	
Fouls	25
Yellow cards	1
Red cards	1

Richard Rufus ended the 1997–98 season on the crest of a wave, bagging his first-ever Charlton goal in the epic play-off final win over Sunderland at Wembley. But in 1998–99 he tasted the Premiership's harsh realities.

He was in the thick of the action all season: his first Premiership appearance at Newcastle United got him a red card after a collision with Nikos Dabizas. Following his suspension, he returned to the Charlton team and scored in the 3–3 draw at Anfield.

He then netted own-goals in home matches against West Ham and Aston Villa; and ruthless Rufus found himself in more trouble, this time at the Valley against Leeds, where he was sent off for the second time in 1998–99 (though the FA later overturned the decision).

Overall, Rufus acquitted himself reasonably well in the Premiership, winning 68% of his 71 challenges. He also made 323 clearances, 29 interceptions and blocked 27 shots.

His pass completion rate of 77% represented the average for a defender, and he also finished with a goal assist to his credit.

R

Louis SAHA • 18
NEWCASTLE UNITED • BORN: 8.8.78

Louis Saha joined compatriots Lionel Perez, Laurent Charvet and Didier Domi to complete a mini French Foreign Legion at St James's Park during the 1998–99 Carling Premiership.

French under-21 star Saha came on loan from Metz and made his Magpies debut at home to Chelsea in January. He replaced Andreas Andersson in the 1–0 defeat by the Blues and, despite a hamstring injury, played a significant part in Newcastle's league run-in.

The Frenchman provided the assist for Alan Shearer's equalizer at home to Coventry, sparking a 4–1 Geordie victory in which Saha grabbed his one league goal of the campaign.

While on loan, Saha impressed the Toon Army with some passionate displays. He had 10 shots, made more than 200 passes and proved hard to dispossess, completing 62% of all his dribbles and runs in the Premiership.

But Saha's biggest impact came in the FA Cup, when he provided a lovely finish to a fine Newcastle move from deep, scoring the goal that put the Magpies into the quarter-finals at the expense of Blackburn.

APPEARANCES	
Start (sub)	5 (6)
Minutes on pitch	600
GOAL ATTEMPTS	
Goals	1
Goals/shots ratio	10%
SHOOTING	
Shots on target	4
Shooting accuracy	40%
PASSING	
Goal assists	1
Passing accuracy	73%
DISCIPLINE	
Fouls	6
Offside	4
Yellow cards	1
Red cards	0

Moussa SAIB • 8
TOTTENHAM HOTSPUR • BORN: 5.3.69

Algerian international Moussa Saib made an impressive start to his Spurs career when he signed from Valencia for £2.3 million in February 1998.

After helping Spurs avoid the drop under Christian Gross, he looked certain to play a key role in Tottenham's 1998–99 campaign. But, like several other Gross signings at White Hart Lane, he was unable to impress new boss George Graham, and played just 104 minutes of Premiership football all season.

During that time, he had nine shots at goal, completed 76% of his passes and 50% of his crosses and was credited with one assist.

But the 30-year-old midfielder spent the vast majority of the season in the reserves – not at all what he had in mind when he put pen to paper on a four-year deal.

Along with Italian flop Paolo Tramezzani, Saib was released from his contract at the end of 1998–99, labelled "surplus to requirements" by Spurs' director of football David Pleat. It was a disappointing end to a Spurs career that had promised so much just 12 months earlier.

Francesco SANETTI • 14
SHEFFIELD WEDNESDAY • BORN: 11.1.79

Wednesday's "other" Italian, Francesco Sanetti was by and large consigned to the Owls' reserve side during a season in which he would have been hoping to have made a far bigger impact.

He arrived at the club from Italian side Genoa on a free transfer, linking up with fellow-compatriots Paolo Di Canio and Benito Carbone.

After joining Wednesday in April 1998 Sanetti learned well from the likes of Di Canio and Carbone, scoring a quality goal on his debut at the end of 1997–98.

But the attack-minded Roman failed to make a significant impression on opposition defences, with only 34 minutes of action for the first XI throughout the 1998–99 Carling Premiership.

He replaced Di Canio at home to Blackburn Rovers and made two further substitute appearances for Danny Wilson's Owls.

Sanetti was limited to just one effort at goal in three appearances and he made 15 passes, 11 to a team-mate.

Robbie SAVAGE • 14
LEICESTER CITY • BORN: 18.10.74

Former Manchester United trainee Robbie Savage had an industrious 1998–99 campaign for Martin O'Neill's Leicester City, including a Worthington Cup final appearance at Wembley.

Savage sent opponents Tottenham wild during the encounter at the national stadium, with a ruthless display of tackling down the Leicester right. O'Neill substituted him, fearing he might get sent off – and Spurs' winning goal almost immediately followed.

The Wrexham-born Welsh international also made the wrong sort of headlines for tossing aside an Italy replica shirt for a BBC trailer of the Wales-v-Italy clash.

Savage's total of 125 attempted tackles was the club's third-highest, but he won relatively few. He made more clearances than any other Leicester midfielder and 20 interceptions at the back, but was less effective going forward.

The Foxes' scheming right-sider completed more than 60% of all dribbles and runs, but his delivery of the final ball was poor, with only 13 out of 73 centres reaching a colleague. He managed just one goal and assisted two.

APPEARANCES	
Start (sub)	29 (5)
Minutes on pitch	2502
GOAL ATTEMPTS	
Goals	1
Shots on target	7
Shooting accuracy	39%
PASSING	
Goal assists	2
Passing accuracy	73%
Crossing accuracy	18%
DRIBBLING	
Dribbles & runs	50
Dribble completion	64%
DISCIPLINE	
Yellow cards	3
Red cards	0

John SCALES • 17
TOTTENHAM HOTSPUR • BORN: 4.7.66

APPEARANCES	
Start (sub)	7 (0)
Minutes on pitch	611
GOAL ATTEMPTS	
Goals	0
DEFENDING	
Blocks	5
Headed clearances	67
Other clearances	22
Interceptions	13
Tackles won	10
PASSING	
Passing accuracy	76%
DISCIPLINE	
Fouls	5
Yellow cards	1
Red cards	0

England international John Scales has endured months of frustration since signing for Spurs from Liverpool in 1996 – and the 1998–99 Carling Premiership season was no exception.

The £2.6 million defender has been plagued by injuries at White Hart Lane and had just 29 Premiership appearances in two-and-a-half seasons at Spurs, with only seven in 1998–99.

Scales managed a run of five full league games between October and November, but had to leave the squad to undergo surgery.

During 611 minutes on the pitch, Scales showed what he can do when fully fit. He made 89 clearances in tandem with Sol Campbell and looked comfortable distributing possession to colleagues. Though he only had time to make 13 tackles, Scales won 10, and committed just five fouls in the process.

One bright spot for Scales was his re-inclusion in the team for the final two games of the season. But youngsters Ledley King and Luke Young profited from Scales's absence and will provide him with ample competition in the 1999–2000 season.

S

G | **Peter SCHMEICHEL • 1**
MANCHESTER UNITED • BORN: 18.11.63

Peter Schmeichel's Manchester United career had a fairytale ending when he lifted the European Cup beside Alex Ferguson in the Nou Camp stadium. His decision to retire at the end of the 1998–99 season came as a shock, but he felt his standards were slipping.

Carling Opta's statistics seem to back up his point. Denmark's World Cup 'keeper was ranked just 13th in Opta's end-of-season Goalkeepers Index and, despite his reputation as one of the world's best shot-stoppers, he had some difficulty in the United goal.

Schmeichel's 99 saves equated to less than three-quarters of all efforts faced, below the Premiership average and more than 10 percentage points behind David Seaman and his replacement Mark Bosnich. He also dropped six catches and too often misdirected long kicks, only 28% finding a team-mate.

The Great Dane kept 11 clean sheets as United narrowly won the Premiership title, but he saved his best performances for the latter stages of the Champions League and will be a tough act to follow.

APPEARANCES	
Start (sub)	34 (0)
Minutes on pitch	3015
SHOT STOPPING	
Goals conceded	35
Clean sheets	11
Saves	99
Saves/shots	74%
DISTRIBUTION	
Distribution	1218
Distribution %	48%
CATCHING	
Crosses caught	90
Crosses dropped	6
DISCIPLINE	
Yellow cards	0
Red cards	0

Great Dane: Peter Schmeichel

FB   Stefan SCHNOOR • 3
DERBY COUNTY • BORN: 24.4.71

Jim Smith gambled on former SV Hamburg star Stefan Schnoor, cashing in on the Bosman ruling to sign him in the summer of 1998.

Schnoor, who cut short his honeymoon in Las Vegas to complete the deal, replaced Chris Powell at left wing-back – and won the backing of many Derby punters in that role during the 1998–99 Carling Premiership.

His ability to supply balls into the danger zone was a major asset: of his 64 crosses into the box, one in three reached a fellow Ram.

The Hamburg-born defender claimed two Premiership strikes, offering Derby an extra attacking option. He also passed with the confidence born of a decade in the Bundesliga.

But Carling Opta's statistics do indicate some room for improvement for Schnoor. Parts of his defensive game were poor, particularly his tackling, with just 41% of all challenges won.

With the signing of Tony Dorigo from Torino, Schnoor may have expected to be in close competition with the ex-England international for a starting place – but Smith started the pair together regularly in the side.

APPEARANCES	
Start (sub)	20 (3)
Minutes on pitch	1691
GOAL ATTEMPTS	
Goals	2
PASSING & CROSSING	
Passing	535
Passing accuracy	76%
Crossing	64
Crossing accuracy	33%
DEFENDING	
Tackles	74
Tackles won	41%
DISCIPLINE	
Fouls	28
Yellow cards	6
Red cards	0

AM   Paul SCHOLES • 18
MANCHESTER UNITED • BORN: 16.11.74

APPEARANCES	
Start (sub)	24 (7)
Minutes on pitch	2143
GOAL ATTEMPTS	
Goals	6
Shots on target	22
Shooting accuracy	46%
PASSING	
Goal assists	9
Passing accuracy	83%
Crossing accuracy	28%
DRIBBLING	
Dribbles & runs	42
Dribble completion	74%
DISCIPLINE	
Yellow cards	7
Red cards	0

Glenn Hoddle once described Paul Scholes as "the jewel in England's crown", and the gifted attacking midfielder enjoyed a sparkling season with Manchester United, playing a massive role in Alex Ferguson's treble success.

Scholes was forced to sit out the European Cup final through suspension alongside club captain Roy Keane, but he scored a crucial late goal in the quarter-final against Juventus.

Wembley was a site of personal triumph for the Salford-born star, with a famous hat-trick for England against Poland in March and an FA Cup-clinching strike against Newcastle. But he was sent off there against Sweden in June.

In the 1998–99 Premiership, Scholes was magnificent. Seventh in Opta's attacking midfielders Index, he linked superbly with any of United's four outstanding frontmen.

Scholes scored six Premiership goals for the Champions and created nine strikes with his incisive distribution. He seldom gifted possession to the opposition, completing 83% of all passes, and hurdled 74% of all challenges while running with the ball.

S

Mark SCHWARZER • 1
MIDDLESBROUGH • BORN: 6.10.72

Australian keeper Mark Schwarzer proved a solid last line of defence for Boro in 1998–99. Bryan Robson will be grateful they got him on a long deal, bearing in mind that Manchester United had been rumoured to be interested in him as a replacement for Peter Schmeichel.

He recorded 13 clean sheets over the course of the season – only David Seaman, Thomas Myhre and Shaka Hislop kept more – but with injury problems leaving Boro's defence under strength at times, he also conceded 47 goals.

Schwarzer made 147 saves but his saves-to-shots ratio was low at 76%, although end-of-season thrashings by Arsenal (6–1) and West Ham (4–0) slightly skewed that record.

He looked very commanding in his penalty area when coming to deal with crosses. He made 29 punches but was happy enough to come and catch the ball a hundred times.

Schwarzer missed just four Premiership games across the campaign, and at just 26 years old Bryan Robson will be hoping the Australian will be keeping them out at the Riverside for many years to come.

APPEARANCES	
Start (sub)	34 (0)
Minutes on pitch	3060
SHOT STOPPING	
Goals conceded	47
Clean sheets	13
Saves	147
Saves/shots	76%
DISTRIBUTION	
Distribution	1084
Distribution %	55%
CATCHING	
Crosses caught	100
Crosses dropped	5
DISCIPLINE	
Yellow cards	1
Red cards	0

Riccardo SCIMECA • 20
ASTON VILLA • BORN: 13.6.75

APPEARANCES	
Start (sub)	16 (2)
Minutes on pitch	1382
GOAL ATTEMPTS	
Goals	2
DEFENDING	
Blocks	9
Headed clearances	48
Other clearances	46
Interceptions	22
Tackles won	22
PASSING	
Passing accuracy	80%
DISCIPLINE	
Fouls	24
Yellow cards	3
Red cards	0

Former England under-21 captain Riccardo Scimeca had an up-and-down season and was frustrated by his inability to secure a regular starting berth in John Gregory's side.

Son of an Italian restaurateur, Scimeca's Premiership campaign went off the boil for significant periods as he deputized for more established central defenders such as Gareth Southgate and, in particular, Ugo Ehiogu.

Sadly for the Leamington Spa-born player, his longest run in the side coincided with Villa's worst spell of form in the league, when the team went 10 matches without a win.

Scimeca won a below-average 59% of his 37 tackles, but the former Villa trainee proved he reads the game well with 22 interceptions and nearly a century of clearances. His distribution of the ball was also sound.

When he had the chance to abandon defensive duties, Scimeca enjoyed some success: he grabbed two goals from just three efforts on target, but these both turned out to be consolation strikes. He strayed offside eight times, a remarkably high total for a defender.

Phillip SCOTT • 12
SHEFFIELD WEDNESDAY • BORN: 14.11.74 **M**

Danny Wilson has a keen eye for a bargain and he may well have committed another act of robbery by stealing Philip Scott away from St Johnstone for a meagre £75,000.

Wilson paid exactly the same fee for relatively-unknown Ipswich midfielder Danny Sonner and, judging by Scott's early showings for the Owls, he could prove to be just as lucrative an acquisition.

Scott made the trek down from Perth to Hillsborough on transfer deadline day and the young midfielder spent 91 minutes exploring the pitches of the Carling Premiership.

The former Scotland under-21 star was the cream of the crop at his local club Scone Thistle, but there has been nothing jammy about his rise to the Premiership.

Scott grabbed the equalizer for the Owls at home to Newcastle and won 80% of all tackles, while also completing four out of five dribbles and runs. He will have gained plenty of confidence from his four substitute appearances and will hope to make his first Premiership start in 1999–2000.

Hans SEGERS • 30
TOTTENHAM HOTSPUR • BORN: 30.10.61 **G**

Fifteen years after he joined English football from PSV Eindhoven for just £50,000, Hans Segers moved to Tottenham Hotspur having been released by Wolves in summer 1998.

With Ian Walker and Espen Baardsen battling it out for the first-choice goalkeeper spot, Segers must have realised his opportunities would be extremely limited – and so it proved.

But he did get one chance. Just two weeks before George Graham's arrival as manager, Segers was put between the sticks for the game at Southampton.

For a while, it looked as though Spurs would leave the Dell with all three points, with Ruel Fox giving the away side the lead and Segers making five saves.

In the end, Matt Le Tissier's goal earned Southampton a point, but Segers did enough in the game to remind everyone what a fine footballing career he has enjoyed, whatever troubles he has had off the pitch. With his 38th birthday approaching, further Premiership opportunities are bound to be few and far between in 1999–2000.

David SEAMAN • 1
ARSENAL • BORN: 19.9.63 **G**

England's number one had another solid season in 1998–99 and finished the campaign in eighth place in the Carling Opta goalkeepers Index.

The big 'keeper kept a superb 19 clean sheets and only conceded 15 goals in the Premiership all season.

Arsenal's defence took a huge amount of pressure off Seaman, as he was only required to save a total of 75 shots in the league all season. On average, he made just two saves per game, keeping out 83% of the shots he faced.

Seaman was also a very consistent distributor of the ball. One in four of his long kicks reached an Arsenal player and 97% of his short kicks and throws found their target.

He had some minor problems with the aerial ball, dropping five out of 74 catches to finish with a 93% catch success rate for the season, and this caused some concern both at club and international level.

In general, however, Seaman had a good season in 1998–99, keeping his standards at a very high level throughout the year. He will have to hit the same heights in 1999–2000, though, if he is to hold off the threat of talented Austrian 'keeper Alex Manninger.

APPEARANCES	
Start (sub)	32 (0)
Minutes on pitch	2880
SHOT STOPPING	
Goals conceded	15
Clean sheets	19
Saves	75
Saves/shots	83%
DISTRIBUTION	
Distribution	932
Distribution %	53%
CATCHING	
Crosses caught	69
Crosses dropped	5
DISCIPLINE	
Yellow cards	0
Red cards	0

S

FB Carl SERRANT • 21
NEWCASTLE UNITED • BORN: 12.9.75

Highly-rated left-back Carl Serrant was snapped up for £500,000 by Kenny Dalglish in the summer of 1998 after his contract with Oldham Athletic ran out.

Serrant had an impressive 1997–98 campaign for the Latics, culminating in an England "B" call-up by then-manager Glenn Hoddle, and the deal with Newcastle signalled that Serrant was well on his way to the big time.

But with the arrival of Ruud Gullit as manager, Serrant found his first-team opportunities severely limited.

The Bradford-born defender made his debut for the Toon Army in the 4–1 defeat at home to Liverpool and subsequently appeared in only three more League matches for the Magpies.

Disappointingly for Serrant, he was never once on the winning side in the 1998–99 Carling Premiership and did not turn feature in the first XI after the match away to Everton in November 1998, where he picked up his one yellow card of the season.

AM Lee SHARPE • 7
LEEDS UNITED • BORN: 27.5.71

It proved to be a globe-trotting campaign for Lee Sharpe, who began at Leeds, jetted off to Italy and finally ended up at United's local rivals Bradford City.

George Graham selected Sharpe for Leeds' opening match of the season at Middlesbrough – but he made just one further start, in the ignominious 1–0 home defeat by Leicester on October 3.

Frustrated at his lack of first-team opportunities, the former Manchester United wonderkid hooked up with David Platt, who had been appointed coach at Sampdoria. But Platt was sacked within two months and again Sharpe found himself on the sidelines.

In the 1998–99 Carling Premiership, he completed three-quarters of his passes and 69% of his dribbles and runs in his 182 minutes on pitch.

On transfer deadline day, Bradford boss Paul Jewell snapped him up on loan and he made his debut as a substitute in the 1–0 defeat by Crystal Palace on March 27. But where his long-term future lies remains to be seen.

CB Richard SHAW • 5
COVENTRY CITY • BORN: 11.9.68

APPEARANCES	
Start (sub)	36 (1)
Minutes on pitch	3261
GOAL ATTEMPTS	
Goals	0
DEFENDING	
Blocks	32
Headed clearances	297
Other clearances	151
Interceptions	52
Tackles won	64
PASSING	
Passing accuracy	81%
DISCIPLINE	
Fouls	33
Yellow cards	2
Red cards	0

Richard Shaw will have been very proud to hear his manager say: "Richard has not had a bad game all season." Gordon Strachan is not known for giving unmerited praise, and his comments are a measure of how Shaw has improved over the 1998–99 campaign.

The ex-Crystal Palace player has had some tough times with the club, and the relegation struggles he and the rest of the squad suffered are something they will want to avoid in 1999–2000.

Shaw contributed 448 defensive clearances and also showed his ability to win a challenge in 72% of his 89 tackles. In 37 appearances for the club, he committed less than one foul per game and picked up just two yellow cards. As Strachan said: "He has not been suspended and that shows he knows when to tackle."

But defensive work is not the only part of Shaw's game that has improved. His pass completion rate of 81% ranked alongside some of the top defenders in the country, although he was sensible enough not to take on more than he was capable of doing.

Alan SHEARER • 9
NEWCASTLE UNITED • BORN: 13.8.70

The 1998–99 season was a tough one for Alan Shearer. Newcastle United sacked his mentor Kenny Dalglish and appointed Ruud Gullit, who had publicly criticized Shearer the previous season. Rumours of a rift were rife.

A move seemed probable, but Shearer stuck it out – only to spend the season listening to the media debate whether he was as good as he had been before his horrific knee injury. His year was made worse by a second successive FA Cup final defeat at Wembley.

With 14 league goals to his name the doubters should have been silenced, but the fact that six were penalties means there are still question marks over his recovery.

Closer to the truth is that Newcastle are in transition, and for him to get 59% of his efforts on target and set up five goals suggests he was regaining his sharpness.

His choice of Newcastle over Manchester United is looking imprudent, but he will hope to realize his dream of bringing silverware back to the Tyne if Gullit can build a decent team around him.

APPEARANCES	
Start (sub)	29 (1)
Minutes on pitch	2586
GOAL ATTEMPTS	
Goals	14
Goals/shots ratio	20%
SHOOTING	
Shots on target	42
Shooting accuracy	59%
PASSING	
Goal assists	5
Passing accuracy	66%
DISCIPLINE	
Fouls	66
Offside	25
Yellow cards	6
Red cards	0

Out of Toon: Alan Shearer

Teddy SHERINGHAM • 10
MANCHESTER UNITED • BORN: 2.4.66

"Oh Teddy, Teddy! He went to Man United and he won the lot!" If you're a football fan and you live in London, you had better get used to that chant because you'll hear it every time the Red Devils hit the capital in 1999–2000.

Cruelly singled out in 1997–98, Sheringham rammed his critics' words down their throats with two goals and two assists in the two biggest games of the season, the 1999 FA Cup final and Champions League final.

His form in the Premiership was less spectacular, but he still scored two goals and set up three more for his team-mates in seven starting appearances and 10 as a substitute – enough to earn himself a championship medal.

Capping a great season with a recall to Kevin Keegan's England squad, it remains to be seen whether he will stay at Old Trafford in 1999–2000 as competition for places hots up.

Wherever he ends up, though, he can reflect on the fact that he wrote his name large in the history books and, more importantly, filled three very large spaces in that most famous of empty medal collections.

APPEARANCES	
Start (sub)	7 (10)
Minutes on pitch	746
GOAL ATTEMPTS	
Goals	2
Goals/shots ratio	12%
SHOOTING	
Shots on target	9
Shooting accuracy	53%
PASSING	
Goal assists	3
Passing accuracy	77%
DISCIPLINE	
Fouls	12
Offside	7
Yellow cards	4
Red cards	0

Tim SHERWOOD • 24
TOTTENHAM HOTSPUR • BORN: 2.2.69

APPEARANCES	
Start (sub)	31 (2)
Minutes on pitch	2709
GOAL ATTEMPTS	
Goals	5
PASSING	
Passes	1424
Passing accuracy	80%
DEFENDING	
Interceptions	27
Clearances	68
Tackles	112
Tackles won	62%
DISCIPLINE	
Fouls	42
Yellow cards	4
Red cards	2

George Graham wants winners at Tottenham and Tim Sherwood certainly fits the bill. A Championship-winning captain at Blackburn, Sherwood had long since become restless in Lancashire when Spurs moved in for him.

His transfer affected both clubs: Blackburn's midfield looked empty without him, while Tottenham thrived on his slick passing and a work-rate which saw him make 112 tackles.

Always liable to pop up in the box with a vital goal, Sherwood struck twice in the league for Spurs, taking his Premiership total to five, and had a crucial strike in February's FA Cup clash with Leeds United at Elland Road.

Called up for England by Kevin Keegan, Sherwood looked comfortable on the international stage, but it is at club level that he is likely to make the bigger impact.

His partnership with Steffen Freund will be a key factor in Tottenham's renaissance in 1999–2000. If he can avoid the disciplinary problems which saw him sent off twice for Blackburn, he could find himself back among the end-of-season honours.

Sam SHILTON • 29
COVENTRY CITY • BORN: 21.7.78

Sam Shilton was signed by Coventry City from Plymouth Argyle in 1995 for a minimal fee. Son of ex-England goalkeeper and record appearance-maker Peter, the left-sided midfielder has yet to become a regular feature of the Sky Blues' starting XI.

He started just one Premiership game in 1998–99, the 1–1 draw against Charlton Athletic in September, playing 55 minutes before coming off. His other four appearances all came as a late substitute.

Perhaps he needs more physical presence to make at the highest level: he was too easily muscled off the ball in his brief time on pitch, losing 88% of his contested tackles.

He is nonetheless a capable footballer, completing 78% of his passes and all three of his attempted dribbles and runs. He also delivered one successful cross but failed to create any real scoring chances.

Still in his early twenties, time is definitely on Shilton's side. With five league appearances in two seasons, Gordon Strachan will want to see him take bigger strides in 1999–2000.

APPEARANCES	
Start (sub)	1 (4)
Minutes on pitch	128
GOAL ATTEMPTS	
Goals	0
PASSING	
Passes	41
Passing accuracy	78%
DEFENDING	
Interceptions	2
Clearances	3
Tackles	9
Tackles won	22%
DISCIPLINE	
Fouls	1
Yellow cards	0
Red cards	0

Neil SHIPPERLEY • 9
NOTTINGHAM FOREST • BORN: 30.10.74

APPEARANCES	
Start (sub)	12 (8)
Minutes on pitch	1164
GOAL ATTEMPTS	
Goals	1
Goals/shots ratio	4%
SHOOTING	
Shots on target	12
Shooting accuracy	44%
PASSING	
Goal assists	1
Passing accuracy	69%
DISCIPLINE	
Fouls	18
Offside	2
Yellow cards	0
Red cards	0

At his last three clubs Neil Shipperley has struggled to make an impact on the Premiership. After fighting relegation at Southampton, he then experienced the drop to Division One with Crystal Palace and Nottingham Forest.

Shipperley was bought by Dave Bassett at Crystal Palace – and when Forest's Pierre van Hooijdonk refused to play at the start of the 1998–99 season, "Harry" called at his old club to pick up the former Chelsea trainee for £1.5 million as partner for another ex-Palace stalwart, Dougie Freedman, up front.

When van Hooijdonk ended his self-imposed exile Shipperley was dropped, and spent most of the rest of the season filling in for injuries and suspensions, or as a substitute.

One goal and one assist are a poor return from a striker if a club wants to stay in the top flight. His pass completion was below average and he lost more tackles than he won, showing he may be out of his depth. Shipperley sank with Forest; and, with a new boss to come, may find himself looking for yet another club.

S

Craig SHORT • 12
EVERTON • BORN: 25.6.68

One of a number of towering centre-backs on Everton's books, Craig Short is a better footballer than he is often given credit for.

The former Derby man spent much of season 1998–99 on the sidelines, but recovered well from injury to force his way back into the side for 10 of Everton's last 11 league games.

A powerful figure in the air, he made his customary high number of headed clearances, but once again demonstrated his ability to bring the ball out from the back, completing 79% of his attempted passes and 83% of his 24 runs.

Often thrown the captain's armband in the absence of Dave Watson, Short's disciplinary record was also good. He received just five yellow cards in the Premiership and committed an average of just one foul every 68 minutes.

A popular man among the other players, Short is almost certain to be a regular starter in 1999–2000 if he can steer clear of injuries: he is one of Everton's more consistent performers and should play a large part in the next phase of Walter Smith's plans.

APPEARANCES	
Start (sub)	22 (0)
Minutes on pitch	1844
GOAL ATTEMPTS	
Goals	0
DEFENDING	
Blocks	20
Headed clearances	189
Other clearances	79
Interceptions	23
Tackles won	43
PASSING	
Passing accuracy	79%
DISCIPLINE	
Fouls	27
Yellow cards	5
Red cards	0

Frank SINCLAIR • 3
LEICESTER CITY • BORN: 3.12.71

APPEARANCES	
Start (sub)	30 (1)
Minutes on pitch	2642
GOAL ATTEMPTS	
Goals	1
DEFENDING	
Blocks	21
Headed clearances	192
Other clearances	154
Interceptions	31
Tackles won	68
PASSING	
Passing accuracy	76%
DISCIPLINE	
Fouls	45
Yellow cards	9
Red cards	1

Signed from Chelsea in a deal worth £2 million, Frank Sinclair was a regular in the Leicester team that finished 10th in 1998–99.

A reliable performer at the back, he nonetheless had to face the disappointment of missing out on Wembley in the Worthington Cup after committing what was officially described as "a serious breach of club discipline" in the run-up to the big game.

His discipline on pitch was not great, either: he picked up nine bookings and, in November's game with Coventry City, one red card. This was a shame, because he did sterling defensive work, making in all 109 tackles and almost 400 clearances, interceptions and blocks in an often pressurized back-line.

His runs from defence were not as regular as Andy Impey's, but he did retain possession when coming forward 95% of the time and recorded a 76% pass completion rate.

His one moment of real glory came in the game against Derby County when he scored an equalizer. Unfortunately, Derby soured his evening with a late winner.

Trevor SINCLAIR • 8
WEST HAM UNITED • BORN: 2.3.73

A real threat down the right for West Ham United, it is safe to say Trevor Sinclair enjoyed the attacking responsibilities of being a wing-back, but not that role's defensive duties.

Nowhere was this better illustrated than in November's 2–1 win over Tottenham. Sinclair scored twice, but by his own admission was "run ragged" at the other end of the field by David Ginola.

As if to prove the point, he ended the season with a below-par tackle success rate of 59% and a low tally of 19 interceptions, but burst into life in the opposition half, scoring seven goals and setting up another five.

By far the most prolific dribbler at the club, he beat his man to the byline a total of 128 times to send in 71 crosses and 37 shots and was caught offside an average of less than once per game.

At £2.3 million from QPR, he has proved to be a real bargain. Surely closing in on an international call-up, he may nevertheless be happier playing the 1999–2000 season in a purely offensive role.

APPEARANCES	
Start (sub)	36 (0)
Minutes on pitch	3169
GOAL ATTEMPTS	
Goals	7
Shots on target	16
Shooting accuracy	43%
PASSING	
Goal assists	5
Passing accuracy	72%
Crossing accuracy	32%
DRIBBLING	
Dribbles & runs	183
Dribble completion	70%
DISCIPLINE	
Yellow cards	7
Red cards	0

Andy SINTON • 22
TOTTENHAM HOTSPUR • BORN: 19.3.66

APPEARANCES	
Start (sub)	12 (10)
Minutes on pitch	1173
GOAL ATTEMPTS	
Goals	0
Shots on target	2
Shooting accuracy	20%
PASSING	
Goal assists	0
Passing accuracy	70%
Crossing accuracy	27%
DRIBBLING	
Dribbles & runs	45
Dribble completion	69%
DISCIPLINE	
Yellow cards	3
Red cards	0

Reliable squad man Andy Sinton was given a free transfer at the end of the 1998–99 season and may have now played his last game for Tottenham Hotspur. He still had an important role in 1998–99, though, doing a tough job in midfield both as a starter and, as was often the case, a substitute.

A real grafter, he covered the ground for Spurs, making more than 400 passes and 50 crosses in his 1,173 minutes on pitch. He got forward less than in the past – testing the opposition goalkeeper just twice – but still retained possession with 69% of his dribbles.

Often asked to help out at the back, he completed 46 clearances and a handful of blocks and interceptions but was less successful with his tackling, winning just 44% of all attempted challenges.

Coming on as a substitute in the Worthington Cup final ensured he will leave White Hart Lane with a medal to show for his efforts; after serving the club well since his £1.5 million move from Sheffield Wednesday in 1996, he deserves the reward.

S

Alan SMITH • 39
LEEDS UNITED • BORN: 28.10.80

Scoring just minutes into his Premiership debut in the 3–1 victory against Liverpool, Alan Smith may well go down in history as the boy who lit the blue touch-paper that sent David O'Leary's Leeds United into orbit.

Starting out at the club's centre of excellence aged 10, Smith progressed through the youth and reserve set-up and, at just 18, is now established in the first team.

Deceptively slight, he has a ruthless streak which sometimes shows itself in indiscipline – six Premiership cautions in 1998–99 – but more often than not results in goals.

In all, he scored seven times in the Premiership, finishing with a fine goals-to-shots ratio of 23%. This figure was some way over the Premiership strikers' average of 15% and made him the first-choice strike partner for Jimmy Floyd Hasselbaink.

Though still raw, there is no mistaking his talent. He may be a different type of player, but his impact at Elland Road in 1998–99 is reminiscent of that made by a certain Michael Owen at Liverpool the previous season.

APPEARANCES	
Start (sub)	15 (7)
Minutes on pitch	1460
GOAL ATTEMPTS	
Goals	7
Goals/shots ratio	23%
SHOOTING	
Shots on target	18
Shooting accuracy	60%
PASSING	
Goal assists	3
Passing accuracy	68%
DISCIPLINE	
Fouls	42
Offside	17
Yellow cards	6
Red cards	0

Nolberto SOLANO • 24
NEWCASTLE UNITED • BORN: 12.12.74

APPEARANCES	
Start (sub)	24 (5)
Minutes on pitch	1972
GOAL ATTEMPTS	
Goals	6
Shots on target	19
Shooting accuracy	48%
PASSING	
Goal assists	5
Passing accuracy	78%
Crossing accuracy	28%
DRIBBLING	
Dribbles & runs	62
Dribble completion	71%
DISCIPLINE	
Yellow cards	0
Red cards	0

A £2.5 million summer signing from Argentinean club Boca Juniors, Nolberto Solano rarely played a full 90 minutes in 1998–99.

This was more a reflection on his inability to stand the pace of the Premiership than on his form. When he was not exhausted the Peruvian international was in fact one of Newcastle's classiest performers, impressing many at the club with his technique on the ball.

A great crosser, he delivered well over 100 centres into the opposition box, setting up five goals in the process. This quality from wide areas was sorely lacking in the rest of Newcastle's side, and when Solano was absent the team found it harder to create chances.

Less comfortable with the more physical side of the game, he made just 56 tackles but managed to win over the Newcastle fans with his shooting, scoring six goals from 40 shots for an overall goals-to-shots ratio of 15%.

If he can improve his stamina in the 1999–2000 season, Solano could well prove to be one of the surprise stars of the Premiership.

Ole Gunnar SOLSKJAER • 20
MANCHESTER UNITED • BORN: 26.2.73

Super-sub Ole Gunnar Solskjaer clinched the treble with his amazing last-gasp strike in the Nou Camp, having made a habit of snatching late goals for his club, Manchester United.

In 1998–99 Solskjaer grabbed eight goals in all competitions in the last 10 minutes of games, including four against Ron Atkinson's Nottingham Forest in the Premiership.

Solskjaer's goalscoring frequency was the best in the league – one on average every 71 minutes – yet was still not enough to displace the devastating front-line partnership of Andy Cole and Dwight Yorke. The Norwegian international also hit the target with 23 out of 30 shots, a marvellous 77% of all efforts with which very few strikers could compete.

It is a testament to the strength of Alex Ferguson's side that a striker of Solskjaer's class was called upon for a mere 853 minutes in the 1998–99 Premiership campaign.

But equally, it is a tribute to Solskjaer's commitment and determination that he had such a huge impact on United's season, given that his time on pitch was so tightly rationed.

APPEARANCES	
Start (sub)	9 (10)
Minutes on pitch	853
GOAL ATTEMPTS	
Goals	12
Goals/shots ratio	40%
SHOOTING	
Shots on target	23
Shooting accuracy	77%
PASSING	
Goal assists	1
Passing accuracy	74%
DISCIPLINE	
Fouls	8
Offside	11
Yellow cards	0
Red cards	0

Trond-Egil SOLTVEDT • 14
COVENTRY CITY • BORN: 15.2.67

APPEARANCES	
Start (sub)	21 (6)
Minutes on pitch	1859
GOAL ATTEMPTS	
Goals	2
PASSING	
Passes	633
Passing accuracy	73%
DEFENDING	
Interceptions	24
Clearances	63
Tackles	68
Tackles won	60%
DISCIPLINE	
Fouls	18
Yellow cards	2
Red cards	0

Curly-haired, combative midfielder Trond-Egil Soltvedt was not always a regular in the Coventry City side during 1998–99, but played a part in most of their games and was a valued member of Gordon Strachan's squad.

Signed from Rosenborg for £500,000 in 1997 Soltvedt, who grew up idolizing Michel Platini, got through his fair share of work in the centre of the park, completing a workmanlike 73% of all attempted passes and winning 60% of his tackles. But he also contributed two goals, one a very important winner in the 2–1 victory over fellow-strugglers Charlton Athletic.

Although he obviously enjoys scoring, he is no glory-seeker and did his fair share of work in the trenches, digging in to make 63 clearances and 24 interceptions.

It is this willingness to battle for the Coventry cause which has made him such a good acquisition for the club. While he will be hoping for a more comfortable season in 1999–2000, if Coventry do find themselves in trouble he will once again be competing to keep them up.

S

CB Rigobert SONG • 4
LIVERPOOL • BORN: 1.7.76

Rigobert Song was signed by Gerard Houllier as part of his ongoing effort to fine-tune the Liverpool defence. But although the Salernitana signing started off well, some of his performances toward the season's end were somewhat off-key. In all, he started 10 games for the Merseysiders, appearing on a further three occasions as a second-half substitute.

Though Song used his height to good effect, completing 65% of his 104 clearances with his head, his tackle success rate was slightly below the Premiership average and he made very few blocks or interceptions.

Used as a right wing-back in some games he showed some neat skills going forward, completing 71% of his attempted dribbles and runs and 38% of his attempted crosses, setting up one goal in the process.

But Liverpool have no shortage of creative players in their side. What they really need is a bit of steel and, although Song supplied this in brief bursts, the jury is still out on his suitability as a long-term solution to the Reds' long-standing defensive problems.

APPEARANCES	
Start (sub)	10 (3)
Minutes on pitch	905
GOAL ATTEMPTS	
Goals	0
DEFENDING	
Blocks	6
Headed clearances	68
Other clearances	36
Interceptions	17
Tackles won	24
PASSING	
Passing accuracy	76%
DISCIPLINE	
Fouls	11
Yellow cards	3
Red cards	0

M Danny SONNER • 32
SHEFFIELD WEDNESDAY • BORN: 9.1.72

APPEARANCES	
Start (sub)	24 (2)
Minutes on pitch	2095
GOAL ATTEMPTS	
Goals	3
PASSING	
Passes	927
Passing accuracy	83%
DEFENDING	
Interceptions	25
Clearances	56
Tackles	74
Tackles won	68%
DISCIPLINE	
Fouls	42
Yellow cards	6
Red cards	0

Bought for £75,000 from Ipswich in October 1998, Danny Sonner proved one of Danny Wilson's most astute signings. At 27 it has taken him longer than most to reach the top flight, but he proved a worthy addition to the Premiership *Who's Who* with a string of good performances in the centre of midfield.

In 2,095 minutes on pitch the Northern Ireland international scored three goals and set up two more, but it was his all-round displays which impressed Wednesday's fans.

His pass completion rate of 83% was tidy enough, but he also managed to win 68% of his attempted tackles – a figure which easily outstripped that of his more illustrious midfield partner Wim Jonk.

After struggling to break into Ipswich Town's first team during 1997–98, Sonner did well to hold down a place in Wednesday's starting XI. Ipswich will probably regret the clause in his contract which allowed him to move on for so little, although interestingly enough it was the first transfer fee he had commanded in a career that has so far taken in five clubs.

Gareth SOUTHGATE • 4
CB ASTON VILLA • BORN: 3.9.70

Gareth Southgate has established his place as a regular at the heart of England's defence – and he proved just as indispensable at the back for Aston Villa during the 1998–99 Carling Premiership, especially after they lost Ugo Ehiogu for a major part of the season.

The £2.5 million signing from Crystal Palace did not miss a second of the action and showed sublime anticipation at the back, with more interceptions than anyone in the league.

Watford-born Southgate was not one to shirk confrontation in defence, making 131 tackles and easily winning the majority. Only Ian Taylor contested more challenges than Villa's club captain did. He also cleared the ball out of danger well over 500 times, the league's fourth-highest total.

A converted midfielder, World Cup star Southgate is comfortable passing or dribbling out of defence. He dispatched 1,219 balls, completing 75%; his short distribution was particularly good, with 87% of close passes reaching a team-mate; and he also embarked on 41 forward runs, completing 78% of them.

APPEARANCES
Start (sub)	38 (0)
Minutes on pitch	3420

GOAL ATTEMPTS
Goals	1

DEFENDING
Blocks	39
Headed clearances	320
Other clearances	217
Interceptions	72
Tackles won	81

PASSING
Passing accuracy	75%

DISCIPLINE
Fouls	40
Yellow cards	5
Red cards	0

Gary SPEED • 11
AM NEWCASTLE UNITED • BORN: 8.9.69

APPEARANCES
Start (sub)	34 (4)
Minutes on pitch	3114

GOAL ATTEMPTS
Goals	4
Shots on target	15
Shooting accuracy	35%

PASSING
Goal assists	0
Passing accuracy	83%
Crossing accuracy	37%

DRIBBLING
Dribbles & runs	66
Dribble completion	76%

DISCIPLINE
Yellow cards	6
Red cards	0

Gary Speed played in every Newcastle United Premiership game in 1998–99, suggesting Ruud Gullit has seen enough of the Welsh midfielder to make him an integral part of his widely-expected overhaul of the Magpies.

Good in the air and a decent passer, Speed dropped the ball off neatly in midfield as Newcastle attempted to adjust to Gullit's pattern of play. He completed 83% of his passes, but his modest tackle success rate of 57% implies he was happier going forward.

This is backed up by his scoring four goals, including two crackers in the 4–3 victory over Derby County, Newcastle's last win of the Premiership season. Most of his attempts were wide of the mark, but his eye for goal from midfield makes him a valuable asset.

Despite the disappointment of losing a second consecutive FA Cup final, Speed was one of Newcastle's few consistent performers. He can be proud of his contribution to the club's 1998–99 season, and rest safe in the knowledge that he should be part of Ruud Gullit's rebuilding plans.

S

John SPENCER • 11
EVERTON • BORN: 11.9.70

Experienced Scottish striker John Spencer began the 1998–99 Carling Premiership season as first-choice frontman for Everton alongside Duncan Ferguson.

That seems a distant memory now. With the Toffees failing to score in their first two league games, manager Walter Smith replaced Spencer with teenage frontman Danny Cadamarteri for the home match with Tottenham Hotspur on August 29.

Spencer, with just one shot to his credit in 124 minutes, was never to make another appearance for Everton.

When Ivory Coast international Ibrahima Bakayoko arrived at Goodison Park for £4.5 million, Everton seemed to have an embarrassment of riches up front. And at the end of October, Spencer moved north of the border to Motherwell, even though the Merseysiders had scored just nine league goals – and none at home!

His loan deal later became permanent, just as it had for Everton when Spencer had moved from QPR in March 1998.

APPEARANCES	
Start (sub)	2 (1)
Minutes on pitch	124
GOAL ATTEMPTS	
Goals	0
Goals/shots ratio	0%
SHOOTING	
Shots on target	0
Shooting accuracy	0%
PASSING	
Goal assists	0
Passing accuracy	67%
DISCIPLINE	
Fouls	2
Offside	2
Yellow cards	0
Red cards	0

Pavel SRNICEK • 33
SHEFFIELD WEDNESDAY • BORN: 10.3.68

APPEARANCES	
Start (sub)	24 (0)
Minutes on pitch	2127
SHOT STOPPING	
Goals conceded	28
Clean sheets	7
Saves	99
Saves/shots	78%
DISTRIBUTION	
Distribution	703
Distribution %	55%
CATCHING	
Crosses caught	68
Crosses dropped	6
DISCIPLINE	
Yellow cards	1
Red cards	1

Many pundits thought they had seen the last of Pavel Srnicek in England when Newcastle released him last summer. But Danny Wilson found him too tempting to resist, and prised the Czech international from hometown club Banik Ostrava for free.

Srnicek came straight into the first team, displacing Kevin Pressman and stayed there for most of the 1998–99 Premiership season, as Wilson preferred to start with the Czech.

"Pav" exhibited his usual mixture of agility and quick reactions, making 99 stops. In all he saved 78% of all shots faced, far more than the average Premiership 'keeper.

He had some trouble with crosses, dropping the ball six times; but when in possession his long distribution was excellent, launching many dangerous Wednesday attacks.

From 24 appearances, Srnicek kept seven clean sheets and let in roughly a goal a game. Wednesday had the league's seventh-best goal difference at the end of the 1998–99 campaign: Pavel's tremendous shot-stopping abilities played a large part in that record.

Jaap STAM • 6
MANCHESTER UNITED • BORN: 17.7.72

Manchester United rewrote history in 1999, but Jaap Stam went further and rewrote geography: the Dutchman proved Holland has at least one mountain.

After an unconvincing World Cup and a shaky start in England, when he looked anything but a £10 million player, Old Trafford's own Charles Atlas ended the season as a leading contender for both major Player of the Year awards.

Strong, quick and impossibly tall, opposition forwards seemed to bounce off Stam as he strode out of defence with the ball at his feet. He ended the year with more successful tackles than any other Premiership defender and 62 interceptions.

Like him, his 86% pass completion rate was, a phenomenal figure, while his tally of just 45 fouls proved he needed no underhand tactics to swat the best the Premiership could throw at him. Plagued by injury in the season's last weeks, it says much for Stam that his battle to face Bayern Munich in the Champions League final seemed to assume as much importance to United as their hunt for the Double.

APPEARANCES	
Start (sub)	30 (0)
Minutes on pitch	2525
GOAL ATTEMPTS	
Goals	1
DEFENDING	
Blocks	25
Headed clearances	300
Other clearances	90
Interceptions	62
Tackles won	107
PASSING	
Passing accuracy	86%
DISCIPLINE	
Fouls	45
Yellow cards	5
Red cards	0

Man mountain: Jaap Stam

Phil STAMP • 14
MIDDLESBROUGH • BORN: 12.12.75

Middlesbrough's Phil Stamp was not a permanent fixture in the side, but did play his part in the 'Boro engine room as they re-established themselves in the Premiership after a season's absence.

Unlike many of his team-mates, Stamp managed only a below-average pass completion rate, finding a red shirt with just 73%. But he did get forward and showed he had an eye for goal, finding the net twice and hitting the target more often than he missed.

He bit into just 15 tackles in the 554 minutes he played, but won four out of five as his tenacity and never-say-die attitude endeared him to the crowd.

Stamp is a resolute player, but his determination is being severely tested as he plays second fiddle to a very experienced midfield and sees Boro regularly linked to a host of similar players. Despite coming up through the ranks, he has only made 75 league appearances for his hometown club and the local lad may well have to leave to pursue his ambition of regular first-team football.

APPEARANCES	
Start (sub)	5 (11)
Minutes on pitch	554
GOAL ATTEMPTS	
Goals	2
PASSING	
Passes	177
Passing accuracy	73%
DEFENDING	
Interceptions	3
Clearances	18
Tackles	15
Tackles won	80%
DISCIPLINE	
Fouls	5
Yellow cards	1
Red cards	1

Steve STAUNTON • 5
LIVERPOOL • BORN: 19.1.69

APPEARANCES	
Start (sub)	31 (0)
Minutes on pitch	2568
GOAL ATTEMPTS	
Goals	0
DEFENDING	
Blocks	20
Headed clearances	170
Other clearances	109
Interceptions	32
Tackles won	45
PASSING	
Passing accuracy	80%
DISCIPLINE	
Fouls	24
Yellow cards	2
Red cards	0

When Steve Staunton left Aston Villa for Liverpool on a free transfer under the Bosman ruling he believed he was re-joining a team that would challenge for honours. But for the first half of the season, it was his old club who set the Premiership pace; and though they fell away, Villa still finished ahead of the Reds.

Joining a defence low on confidence was not easy, and it did not help that the Irishman is more a ball-player than a defender, as he played alongside others of the same ilk such as Dominic Matteo.

Staunton completed a healthy 80% of his passes, especially as he tried plenty of longer balls. But though he made 279 clearances, his tackle success rate of 61% shows he was occasionally shrugged off the ball too easily.

Gerard Houllier brought in Rigobert Song, but the Liverpool defence was still like the Maginot Line – apparently strong, but easy to bypass. Staunton is a classy defender on the ball but, if he is to figure in Houllier's rebuilt side, the Frenchman must find a strong defender to complement his abilities.

CB Dejan STEFANOVIC • 18
SHEFFIELD WEDNESDAY • BORN: 28.10.74

The work permit problems that plagued Dejan Stefanovic during the 1998–99 Carling Premiership saw him leave the club at the end of the campaign.

The £2 million signing from Red Star Belgrade suffered a frustrating season at Hillsborough, starting just eight matches for the Owls and picking up a red card in only his fourth appearance.

Yet while he was on the pitch, Stefanovic showed some signs of the quality that had prompted Wednesday to snap him up in December 1995.

He attempted 26 challenges and won a good proportion of his tackles, freeing up possession for the flair players on the team.

Stefanovic made 56 clearances from his own half and took the ball forward himself on six occasions, being stopped in his tracks by an opponent just once.

Stefanovic passed the ball competently and lobbed in 13 crosses for his strikers. But with no work permit, the Yugoslav quit the Premiership and took his skills to Italy.

FB Staale STENSAAS • 32
NOTTINGHAM FOREST • BORN: 7.7.71

Former Rosenborg player Staale Stensaas joined Glasgow Rangers for £1.75 million but struggled to impress Dick Advocaat and arrived at Nottingham Forest in January 1999.

Having played in the Rosenborg side that beat AC Milan in the Champions League, it is safe to say that life at the bottom of the Carling Premiership came as quite a culture shock to Stensaas.

But Ron Atkinson was keen to strengthen the Forest defence and, although Stensaas did not always look the most solid at left-back, the team only once conceded more than two goals when he was in the side.

A sound – although hardly prolific – tackler, he won eight of his attempted challenges and made 41 blocks, clearances and interceptions.

He also made 162 passes and fired in 15 crosses, finding a team-mate on three occasions.

Stensaas's final game in England came against Aston Villa. Relegation on that fateful day did not make the best of leaving presents for the 28-year-old.

CB Igor STIMAC • 6
DERBY COUNTY • BORN: 6.9.67

APPEARANCES	
Start (sub)	15 (0)
Minutes on pitch	1168
GOAL ATTEMPTS	
Goals	0
DEFENDING	
Blocks	10
Headed clearances	113
Other clearances	40
Interceptions	21
Tackles won	28
PASSING	
Passing accuracy	70%
DISCIPLINE	
Fouls	15
Yellow cards	6
Red cards	0

Igor Stimac missed much of the season with an ankle injury, but the Rams were always at their best when he was patrolling the centre of their defence. Despite this, Jim Smith decided to put Stimac on the transfer list at the end of the 1998–99 campaign.

Such a move could not have been imagined by Derby fans after Stimac starred for Croatia in the World Cup in France, helping them to third place, but it seems that in season 1999–2000 they may have to do without their uncompromising captain.

Stimac was awesome in the tackle, winning almost three-quarters of his thundering challenges. The Balkan ball-winner reads the game brilliantly, making 21 interceptions and 153 clearances as Derby managed their first 29 Premiership clashes without conceding more than two in a game. But his ferocity also saw him earn six yellow cards from just 15 fouls.

Unless he repairs the rift with Jim Smith and stays at Derby, Stimac could find himself doing an excellent job for any Premiership side that is prepared to take a gamble on his fitness.

S

Robbie STOCKDALE • 28
MIDDLESBROUGH • BORN: 30.11.79

The 1998–99 season was a memorable one for Robbie Stockdale. After making just one league appearance in the previous campaign, he came into the side to cover for Curtis Fleming on the odd occasion that the Republic of Ireland international was out.

Then, when Fleming was ruled out for the season with a knee injury, Stockdale stepped in and impressed everyone outside Middlesbrough who had not seen him.

Winning 67% of the challenges he made and weighing in with 59 clearances, he was expertly guided along by Boro's experienced defenders; Stockdale can only learn good things from the likes of Gary Pallister.

He was more comfortable in defence than when he was pushing forward, but despite only completing 67% of his passes and 22% of his crosses, he did finish the season with three goal assists to his name.

The youngster is likely to figure even more prominently in 1999–2000, when he will give Fleming a real run for his money in the regular right wing-back position.

APPEARANCES
Start (sub)	17 (2)
Minutes on pitch	1490

GOAL ATTEMPTS
Goals	0

PASSING & CROSSING
Passing	478
Passing accuracy	67%
Crossing	50
Crossing accuracy	22%

DEFENDING
Tackles	60
Tackles won	62%

DISCIPLINE
Fouls	19
Yellow cards	3
Red cards	0

Steve STONE • 26
ASTON VILLA • BORN: 20.8.71

APPEARANCES
Start (sub)	35 (1)
Minutes on pitch	3094

GOAL ATTEMPTS
Goals	3
Shots on target	25
Shooting accuracy	45%

PASSING
Goal assists	6
Passing accuracy	76%
Crossing accuracy	25%

DRIBBLING
Dribbles & runs	148
Dribble completion	63%

DISCIPLINE
Yellow cards	6
Red cards	1

A £5.5 million signing from basement boys Nottingham Forest, Steve Stone will be an important player for Aston Villa in 1999–2000.

The genial Geordie could not quite reproduce his best goalscoring form at Villa Park but did set up three strikes for his new team-mates, doubling his tally for the season.

A forceful right-sided midfielder, Stone overcame the injury problems that threatened to halt his career in 1998–99 and spent most of the season rolling over opposing full-backs.

His dribble success rate improved after his transfer and, although his cross completion rate stayed constant at an unimpressive 25%, he is still expected to supply Dion Dublin with a steady stream of chances in 1999–2000.

Delighted to be in a side capable of challenging for honours, Stone is ready to overcome the problems which have galled him in the past. Thought to have a bright future at international level before injury and relegation interrupted his career, 1999–2000 will be an important season as he looks to catapult himself back into the big time.

Graham STUART • 40
CHARLTON ATHLETIC • BORN: 24.10.70

Graham Stuart's heroics saved Everton from the drop on the last day of season 1996–97. When he signed for relegation-threatened Charlton in 1998–99, he knew he had to help the Addicks perform a similar escape act.

But despite his industry in midfield and some vital goals, Stuart could not stop Charlton returning to the Nationwide League after just one year in the Premiership.

He started Charlton's last nine matches of 1998–99, replacing the disappointing Neil Redfearn, and netted three times, scoring a vital winner at West Ham and earning the Addicks a point in the 1–1 draw with Leeds United. His third goal was not enough as Charlton were put to the sword 4–1 at Everton.

Stuart hit a further two shots on target and created one goal. He completed 76% of his passes, won 56% of his midfield challenges, but was booked twice from 11 fouls.

Despite their relegation, Stuart gave Charlton fans a boost by declaring he was happy to stay at the Valley and help bring Charlton back into the top division.

APPEARANCES	
Start (sub)	9 (0)
Minutes on pitch	810
GOAL ATTEMPTS	
Goals	3
Shots on target	5
Shooting accuracy	36%
PASSING	
Goal assists	1
Passing accuracy	76%
Crossing accuracy	16%
DRIBBLING	
Dribbles & runs	27
Dribble completion	70%
DISCIPLINE	
Yellow cards	2
Red cards	0

 Dean STURRIDGE • 8
DERBY COUNTY • BORN: 27.7.73

APPEARANCES	
Start (sub)	22 (6)
Minutes on pitch	2081
GOAL ATTEMPTS	
Goals	5
Goals/shots ratio	10%
SHOOTING	
Shots on target	26
Shooting accuracy	52%
PASSING	
Goal assists	4
Passing accuracy	74%
DISCIPLINE	
Fouls	54
Offside	24
Yellow cards	3
Red cards	0

Dean Sturridge passed the 150 appearance mark for Derby County in 1998–99, but the quicksilver striker was not always a first choice for Jim Smith's Rams side.

Averaging one goal every 5.6 appearances was not the record of a man in the best of sorts, but there were still flashes of the brilliant form that has seen him linked with a host of big-money moves down the years.

The winner against Sheffield Wednesday in only his second start of the season promised much, but it took him another seven games to find the net again.

There was plenty to admire in his approach play, with his pace proving too much for many of the Premiership's defenders and his crossing often sharper than his finishing. He even set up his fair share of chances for team-mates, creating four goals in total.

But although his shooting accuracy of 52% was slightly higher than the Premiership average, he and fellow striker Paulo Wanchope both ended up on the transfer list at the end of the season.

S

Neil SULLIVAN • 1
WIMBLEDON • BORN: 24.2.70

Neil Sullivan was the Premiership's busiest goalkeeper in 1998–99. Forced into more saves than any other player, the Scottish international must have felt like donning a tin hat at times as shots rained in from all angles.

On average he was called on to make a stop once every 17 minutes, a statistic that makes his saves-to-shots ratio of 76% all the more impressive. Confident from opposition crosses, Sullivan did make the occasional high-profile error, but overall his catching was good.

Often the first point of Wimbledon's attack, Sullivan attempted more long kicks than any other goalkeeper, completing 44% – a high figure which perhaps says more about the attitude of the Wimbledon attack than it does about his skill with the boot.

With Manchester United and Liverpool both on the lookout for a new man between the sticks, Sullivan's name was inevitably mentioned as a replacement. A move to one of the Premiership's bigger clubs would be a bitter blow to the Dons, who might struggle to find a 'keeper of similar stature.

APPEARANCES	
Start (sub)	38 (0)
Minutes on pitch	3420
SHOT STOPPING	
Goals conceded	63
Clean sheets	7
Saves	203
Saves/shots	76%
DISTRIBUTION	
Distribution	1547
Distribution %	48%
CATCHING	
Crosses caught	125
Crosses dropped	3
DISCIPLINE	
Yellow cards	4
Red cards	0

Mark SUMMERBELL • 22
MIDDLESBROUGH • BORN: 30.10.76

APPEARANCES	
Start (sub)	7 (4)
Minutes on pitch	664
GOAL ATTEMPTS	
Goals	0
Shots on target	2
Shooting accuracy	33%
PASSING	
Goal assists	0
Passing accuracy	82%
Crossing accuracy	50%
DRIBBLING	
Dribbles & runs	1
Dribble completion	0%
DISCIPLINE	
Yellow cards	4
Red cards	0

Mark Summerbell would have hoped to figure more often in Middlesbrough's 1998–99 first team, but got just a handful of appearances as cover for the first-choice midfielders.

Very tidy on the ball, he made 180 passes, completing a very good 82%. With such experienced midfielders as Paul Gascoigne and Andy Townsend as tutors he should be learning more about the game, but would obviously like to join the starting line-up more often.

Summerbell breaks forward to support the attack very well and fired in eight shots, two of which forced saves. But he is also responsible enough to get back and protect his defence. He won two-thirds of his 35 tackles, earning four yellow cards for excessive zeal despite only committing 14 fouls.

The busy midfield player is well thought of at the club, but has been around a while without making the breakthrough and may find that he has to move to secure regular first-team football. While this would weaken the Boro squad, Bryan Robson would surely understand the midfielder's ambition.

Chris SUTTON • 9
BLACKBURN ROVERS • BORN: 10.3.73

Having topped the Premiership scoring charts with 18 goals for Blackburn Rovers in 1997–98, Chris Sutton's season was blighted by injury and the tall striker was unable to match his previous season's tally.

The former Norwich City man suffered groin and knee injuries and completed only 1,460 minutes of Premiership football in 1998–99.

He fired 18 shots on target and managed just three goals, two of them penalties. He completed 65% of his passes and 15% of his crosses, resulting in one goal assist.

Despite missing much of the season, Sutton still had trouble with referees, committing 60 fouls, receiving nine yellow cards and being sent off against Arsenal. Under the Carling Opta disciplinary system the Blackburn hitman averaged a point every 15 minutes – earning him a spot in Carling Opta's Dirty Dozen team.

Sutton may be signed by a Premiership club by the start of the 1999–2000 season and, if he can regain his fitness, will once again be a force to be reckoned with in the top flight – and possibly at international level.

APPEARANCES	
Start (sub)	17 (0)
Minutes on pitch	1460
GOAL ATTEMPTS	
Goals	3
Goals/shots ratio	9%
SHOOTING	
Shots on target	18
Shooting accuracy	56%
PASSING	
Goal assists	1
Passing accuracy	65%
DISCIPLINE	
Fouls	60
Offside	26
Yellow cards	9
Red cards	1

Gerry TAGGART • 4
LEICESTER CITY • BORN: 18.10.70

APPEARANCES	
Start (sub)	9 (6)
Minutes on pitch	823
GOAL ATTEMPTS	
Goals	0
DEFENDING	
Blocks	5
Headed clearances	122
Other clearances	53
Interceptions	10
Tackles won	33
PASSING	
Passing accuracy	75%
DISCIPLINE	
Fouls	17
Yellow cards	3
Red cards	0

After signing for Leicester City from Bolton Wanderers just before 1998–99 on a free transfer, Gerry Taggart played sporadically during another decent season for the Foxes.

The Irish defender won 75% of his 44 tackles and also made 175 defensive clearances, at the rate of about one every five minutes. Sometimes over-zealous in the tackle, he earned three yellow cards from 17 fouls.

Though he only ventured forward for set-pieces, Leicester's good delivery saw him make two goal assists. His pass completion rate of 75% was just below the defender's average, but it was not Taggart's ball-playing abilities Martin O'Neill was interested in.

He would have been even more disappointed to lose at Wembley in the Worthington Cup final than most of the team. With the game heading for extra-time, Steffen Iversen crossed hopefully. Taggart was positioned perfectly to clear but Kasey Keller deflected the ball away and into the path of Allan Nielsen, who scored. Taggart will be hoping to help the Foxes forget that disappointment.

Mauricio TARICCO • 19
TOTTENHAM HOTSPUR • BORN: 10.3.73

A classy full-back equally comfortable on either flank, Mauricio Taricco entered English football with Ipswich Town, for whom his raids from out wide brought rich dividends. His arrival at White Hart Lane has given Spurs an extra attacking option down the flanks.

His 1,027 minutes of Carling Premiership football all came in the final couple of months of 1998–99, but he has already impressed the White Hart Lane faithful.

A pass completion rate of 78% from his total of 544 balls was impressive for a player still adjusting to top-flight football with a new team. He also had a goal assist to his credit.

Five of his 15 crosses found their mark and he was comfortable running with the ball, with a 68% dribble completion rate.

Defensively, his 47 tackles, four blocks, 69 clearances and 14 interceptions will impress his manager greatly, and winning 62% of his tackles will also help keep him in the first XI. Unfortunately, he has also managed to accrue 12 fouls, together with one yellow card and one red card.

APPEARANCES	
Start (sub)	12 (1)
Minutes on pitch	1027
GOAL ATTEMPTS	
Goals	0
PASSING & CROSSING	
Passing	544
Passing accuracy	78%
Crossing	16
Crossing accuracy	31%
DEFENDING	
Tackles	47
Tackles won	62%
DISCIPLINE	
Fouls	12
Yellow cards	1
Red cards	1

Ian TAYLOR • 7
ASTON VILLA • BORN: 4.6.68

APPEARANCES	
Start (sub)	31 (2)
Minutes on pitch	2667
GOAL ATTEMPTS	
Goals	4
PASSING	
Passes	934
Passing accuracy	82%
DEFENDING	
Interceptions	27
Clearances	72
Tackles	134
Tackles won	62%
DISCIPLINE	
Fouls	48
Yellow cards	7
Red cards	0

Holte End hero Ian Taylor was arguably one of Villa's most influential players in the 1998–99 Premiership. Born just a few miles away, he grew up supporting the Claret-and-Blues and played with customary grit for his local club.

The hard-running midfielder joined Villa in 1994 in an exchange deal from Sheffield Wednesday, with Guy Whittingham heading in the opposite direction.

Taylor grabbed some vital strikes in the 1998–99 campaign, scoring both goals in Villa's 2–1 win away to Coventry and the only goal at Anfield against Liverpool. His four league goals came from 26 shots, but his shooting accuracy was slightly below par.

His distribution was good, with nearly 1,000 passes and a success rate of 82%. Villa's Player of the Season 1997–98 supplied five goal assists, bettered for the club only by Lee Hendrie. He made more clearances than any Villa midfielder and contested the most tackles for the club during 1998–99, winning 62% of them. The only blemishes on this tough competitor's season were seven yellow cards.

FB | **Martin TAYLOR • 28**
BLACKBURN ROVERS • BORN: 9.11.79

Teenage full-back Martin Taylor got a glamorous first taste of top-level football with Blackburn Rovers in the UEFA Cup, when he came on in the last six minutes against Olympique Lyonnais.

He then played his first full Carling Premiership match for Rovers when they drew 1–1 with Coventry City at Highfield Road in March.

Sadly, only two more substitute appearances followed, in the win at home to Wimbledon and the draw at Newcastle United. On the periphery of the squad, his experience was mostly limited to sitting on the bench.

But he did show some promise in his two hours on the pitch in the League. He won four out of five tackles, committing two fouls and making 23 clearances for Blackburn. He also completed 59% of his 32 passes and two out of his five dribbles and runs.

Taylor gained some valuable experience with the first team at Blackburn and will hope to build on his appearances in 1999–2000 in Nationwide Division One.

M | **Paul TELFER • 12**
COVENTRY CITY • BORN: 21.10.71

APPEARANCES	
Start (sub)	30 (2)
Minutes on pitch	2579
GOAL ATTEMPTS	
Goals	2
PASSING	
Passes	1195
Passing accuracy	73%
DEFENDING	
Interceptions	19
Clearances	98
Tackles	87
Tackles won	61%
DISCIPLINE	
Fouls	38
Yellow cards	11
Red cards	0

Right-hand man: Paul Telfer

Paul Telfer had a fairly consistent season down Coventry's right-hand side, whether playing at full-back or further forward in midfield.

The competitive former Luton midfielder is an energetic and feisty character in the mould of his boss Gordon Strachan, although not blessed with the craft the manager frequently displayed during his successful career.

Telfer's running and pressing game saw him complete 84% of his dribbles and runs and win 61% of his tackles, but he tended to overstep the mark, with 11 yellow cards from just 38 fouls. In the Premiership only Mark Hughes, Paul Gascoigne and Olivier Dacourt incurred the referee's wrath more often.

Telfer is certainly a trier: as well as setting up two goals, he was not afraid to have a pop himself given the chance. He scored twice and forced 11 saves, but 29 of his efforts posed more danger to the fans in the stand.

After a disappointing 1998–99, Gordon Strachan will want to get Coventry heading back in the right direction, and Paul Telfer is sure to play his part in the revival.

T

CB John TERRY • 26
CHELSEA • BORN: 7.12.80

Definitely one for the future, John Terry made his debut in the Premiership against Southampton.

Unfortunately his big day was overshadowed by the fact that the man he replaced, Gustavo Poyet, was forced to leave the pitch with a serious injury.

The youngster enjoyed himself more in cup competitions, playing a full part in FA Cup clashes with Oldham Athletic and Oxford United.

He even experienced a taste of European football with an appearance against Valerenga in the Cup Winners Cup.

A promising centre-back, he had to wait until the last day of the 1998–99 season for his second outing in the Premiership, replacing Michael Duberry as a second-half substitute in the game against Derby County.

In truth, he was called on to do very little in his 50 minutes on pitch, but he won his solitary tackle, completed a reasonable 78% of his attempted passes and was pulled up for one foul.

FB Ben THATCHER • 6
WIMBLEDON • BORN: 30.11.75

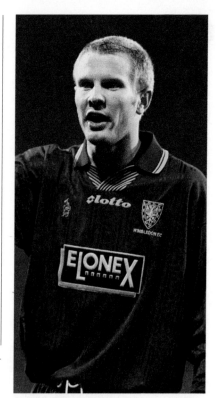

Own goals: Ben Thatcher

APPEARANCES	
Start (sub)	31 (0)
Minutes on pitch	2710
GOAL ATTEMPTS	
Goals	0
PASSING & CROSSING	
Passing	717
Passing accuracy	66%
Crossing	38
Crossing accuracy	29%
DEFENDING	
Tackles	121
Tackles won	69%
DISCIPLINE	
Fouls	35
Yellow cards	8
Red cards	0

Ben Thatcher has never quite become the player many thought he would, but still has time on his side. He was a highly-rated full back at Millwall when Wimbledon snapped him up for a then-club record £1.8 million ahead of several more glamorous clubs.

Injuries and discipline problems – he was sent off three times in 1997–98 – have hindered his progression, but the fact that the Dons struggled in the second half of 1998–99 did not help his own form. In fact, Thatcher conceded two own-goals over the season.

Thatcher won a respectable 69% of his 121 challenges and made an impressive 351 clearances. But his pass completion was poor at just 66%, which was in line with the Dons team as a whole.

The number of goals the Dons conceded, coupled with the number of shots Neil Sullivan had to make, suggest new boss Egil Olsen will embark on a squad clear-out. Thatcher is likely to survive the summer sales, but will have to concentrate on getting his form back if he is to retain his place ahead of Alan Kimble.

M Geoff THOMAS • 16
NOTTINGHAM FOREST • BORN: 5.8.64

A season which began with such promise for the Nottingham Forest midfielder turned into another injury-wrecked nightmare for Geoff Thomas after just five games.

Thomas played a starring role in Forest's first Carling Premiership match of the 1998–99 season at Highbury against Arsenal, scoring a fabulous individual goal to give the league and cup Double-winners a real scare.

He also started the next four games under Dave Bassett before his season came to an abrupt end at Stamford Bridge on September 12, when he limped off with cruciate ligament damage.

Before his injury, he was as influential as any Forest player was to be all season, completing more than four out of every five passes and almost 75% of his dribbles and runs. But he put in only 12 tackles, possibly concerned about picking up another serious injury.

His determination was sorely missed as Forest failed to win any of their next 18 league games without him and, of course, were eventually relegated from the Premiership.

FB Tony THOMAS • 20
EVERTON • BORN: 12.7.71

Former Tranmere Rovers full-back Tony Thomas never really established himself at Goodison Park after joining the club in the summer of 1997, which will be particularly disappointing given that he is an Everton fan.

The £400,000 buy was sold on to Scottish Premier League side Motherwell for just £150,000 after suffering a succession of injuries in his time with his boyhood favourites.

He featured just seven times in 1997–98 and for just one minute as a substitute in 1998–99, in the 1–0 victory over Nottingham Forest.

He played several matches in the reserves and sat on the bench once more without being used, before being sold to raise money for the cash-strapped club.

Thomas is an attacking right-back who is also fairly decent in the tackle. Now aged 28, he will hope that the move to Fir Park can finally re-ignite his career.

He certainly deserves a bit more luck in 1999–2000.

CB Emerson THOME • 22
SHEFFIELD WEDNESDAY • BORN: 30.3.72

APPEARANCES	
Start (sub)	38 (0)
Minutes on pitch	3362
GOAL ATTEMPTS	
Goals	1
DEFENDING	
Blocks	46
Headed clearances	357
Other clearances	186
Interceptions	52
Tackles won	116
PASSING	
Passing accuracy	76%
DISCIPLINE	
Fouls	55
Yellow cards	3
Red cards	0

Big-money signings fared well at Hillsborough during 1998–99; but for value for money, look no further than Emerson Thome. The Brazilian centre-back was snapped up free from Benfica while Ron Atkinson was in charge, and has been a defensive revelation.

Atkinson's predecessor Danny Wilson has reaped the benefits of the Brazilian's class at the back. Emerson made Carling Opta's team of best individual performers for his display at home to Wimbledon, and his stats for the campaign as a whole are equally impressive.

His total of 543 clearances was the third-highest in the Carling Premiership, just behind team-mate Des Walker, although Emerson made more with his head. He also put in more tackles than any other Premiership defender, winning possession with a creditable 68%.

Big but agile in defence, Emerson made 33 dribbles and runs up field. His main threat in the opposition box was from set-pieces, and he managed 17 efforts at goal in the season.

He also distributed precisely, finding a colleague with 76% of his passes.

AM | Alan THOMPSON • 11
ASTON VILLA • BORN: 22.11.73

The first of three Geordies signed by John Gregory for the 1998–99 Premiership season, Alan Thompson was in and out of the side during the campaign through injury.

The former Bolton man made a dream start, scoring with an unstoppable free-kick in his home debut as Villa beat Middlesbrough 3–1. But unfortunately for the £4.5 million signing he failed to find the net again for seven months as injury disrupted his season.

Thompson's distribution was arguably the most impressive aspect of his game throughout 1998–99. He made nearly 900 passes and on average completed eight out of 10 balls as intended. The England under-21 star's probing in the midfield produced three goal assists and he used his vast experience on the wing to great effect, with 30% of all centres connecting with a Villa forward.

The sought-after midfielder made a name as a long-range marksman at Bolton, and both his Villa goals were from outside the area, though only nine out of 20 shots from more than 18 yards threatened the goal.

APPEARANCES	
Start (sub)	20 (5)
Minutes on pitch	1766
GOAL ATTEMPTS	
Goals	2
Shots on target	11
Shooting accuracy	32%
PASSING	
Goal assists	3
Passing accuracy	80%
Crossing accuracy	30%
DRIBBLING	
Dribbles & runs	46
Dribble completion	61%
DISCIPLINE	
Yellow cards	6
Red cards	0

M | David THOMPSON • 25
LIVERPOOL • BORN: 12.9.77

APPEARANCES	
Start (sub)	4 (10)
Minutes on pitch	524
GOAL ATTEMPTS	
Goals	1
PASSING	
Passes	308
Passing accuracy	69%
DEFENDING	
Interceptions	8
Clearances	10
Tackles	15
Tackles won	60%
DISCIPLINE	
Fouls	13
Yellow cards	3
Red cards	0

David Thompson has been with Liverpool since he was nine, and has worked his way through the ranks, winning the FA Youth Cup in 1996, playing in the reserves and finally making the first team in season 1996–97. The youngster more than doubled his number of appearances in 1998–99, mostly because of injuries to key players and the side's generally poor form.

Offered a long-term deal, despite intense competition for places, the youngster was more than happy to sign. Thompson said: "It is a great boost to know that the manager believes in me. Now my aim is to get into the side on a regular basis." To do so he will need to improve his pass completion. Liverpool's pass-and-move heritage is legendary and 69% for a midfield player is well below par.

Thompson scored his first Premiership goal in the 7–1 demolition of Southampton and has hinted with his 15 other efforts that he has goals in his boots.

1999–2000 is another stepping stone for a youngster who will have to make great strides to achieve his ambition.

CB · Carl TILER · 23
CHARLTON ATHLETIC · BORN: 11.2.70

Signed from Everton for £700,000 in October 1998, Carl Tiler gave aerial strength during the season to the centre of Charlton's back four.

In his first match the tall centre-back helped the Addicks to their second win of the season at Nottingham Forest and, in his home debut, scored in the 4–2 win over West Ham.

Tiler won an above-average 68% of his challenges and made a staggering 426 clearances, many with his head. He also blocked 29 shots and made 27 interceptions.

Despite his image as a conventional stopper, he was reasonably comfortable with the ball, ending up with a 74% completion rate.

Tiler's aerial dominance caused concern in various Premiership penalty areas. He scored one goal, troubled opposing goalkeepers nine times in total, and had seven efforts blocked.

His disciplinary record of seven yellow cards from 44 fouls came from 2,540 minutes of Premiership football, most of which were with Charlton, where he will hope to achieve automatic promotion from the Nationwide League in 1999–2000.

APPEARANCES	
Start (sub)	29 (0)
Minutes on pitch	2540
GOAL ATTEMPTS	
Goals	1
DEFENDING	
Blocks	29
Headed clearances	282
Other clearances	144
Interceptions	27
Tackles won	49
PASSING	
Passing accuracy	74%
DISCIPLINE	
Fouls	44
Yellow cards	7
Red cards	0

M · Andy TOWNSEND · 16
MIDDLESBROUGH · BORN: 27.7.63

APPEARANCES	
Start (sub)	35 (0)
Minutes on pitch	3088
GOAL ATTEMPTS	
Goals	1
PASSING	
Passes	1504
Passing accuracy	81%
DEFENDING	
Interceptions	42
Clearances	77
Tackles	135
Tackles won	66%
DISCIPLINE	
Fouls	27
Yellow cards	10
Red cards	0

Despite passing the ripe old age of 36 in the 1999 close season, Andy Townsend is sure to be patrolling Carling Premiership football pitches in the new campaign.

He was part of the most experienced midfield in the Premiership alongside Paul Gascoigne and Robbie Mustoe who, at 32, are mere youngsters in comparison.

The former Chelsea and Aston Villa man said: "When I was a bit younger, I could get up and down more than I can now. You compensate for that by using your head a bit more."

Townsend only tried 42 dribbles all season, preferring to prompt play from midfield and completing a sound 81% of his passes. But when he did get forward, he completed 33% of his crosses and laid on three goal assists.

His tenacity in the challenge was as evident as ever, but his increasing tendency to mis-time his moves saw him earn 10 yellow cards.

Townsend captained Boro to a respectable top 10 finish and, if he resists reported overtures from his old club Aston Villa, should be leading by example again in 1999–2000.

T

FB   Paolo TRAMEZZANI • 3
TOTTENHAM HOTSPUR • BORN: 30.7.70

"Paolo who?" would have been the question on most lips in the white half of north London when news filtered through that Tottenham had signed an Italian full-back. Would the blond defender be more like his namesake Maldini, or would he prove to be another hole in Christian Gross's Swiss cheese defence?

After starting the first six games of the season, Tramezzani never played for the Spurs first team again. George Graham arrived at the end of September and the Italian was clearly not part of his plans. At the end of the season, after being described by David Pleat as "surplus to requirements", he was released.

Tramezzani's pass completion rate was below average, as was his tackle success rate. He weighed in with 44 defensive clearances, but it was clear that the frenetic pace and physical style of the English game were alien to him.

His performances did little to justify the £1.35 million Spurs paid Piacenza for him. As George Graham continues to resurrect Spurs' fortunes, Tramezzani's signing will soon be consigned to the record books as a Gross error.

APPEARANCES	
Start (sub)	6 (0)
Minutes on pitch	518
GOAL ATTEMPTS	
Goals	0
PASSING & CROSSING	
Passing	187
Passing accuracy	81%
Crossing	16
Crossing accuracy	31%
DEFENDING	
Tackles	13
Tackles won	54%
DISCIPLINE	
Fouls	16
Yellow cards	1
Red cards	0

FB   Robert ULLATHORNE • 19
LEICESTER CITY • BORN: 11.10.71

APPEARANCES	
Start (sub)	25 (0)
Minutes on pitch	2174
GOAL ATTEMPTS	
Goals	0
PASSING & CROSSING	
Passing	665
Passing accuracy	81%
Crossing	13
Crossing accuracy	15%
DEFENDING	
Tackles	84
Tackles won	61%
DISCIPLINE	
Fouls	26
Yellow cards	4
Red cards	0

A tough-tackling wing-back, Robert Ullathorne has been plagued by injuries since his return to the English game from Spain's Osasuna. He managed some impressive appearances for the Foxes in 1998–99 before the jinx struck again.

Winning 61% of his 84 tackles, Ullathorne showed strong defensive qualities in a side renowned for discipline. He made 158 clearances, 25 blocks and 35 interceptions, but his commitment to the tackle came at a price, with four bookings from 26 fouls.

Pushing forward from the wing-back position, the former Norwich City man completed 76% of his dribbles and runs and crossed 13 times, with a 15% success rate. His 81% pass completion rating shows he rarely gave the ball away.

Things looked bleak, however, when he broke his leg against Chelsea in April in an horrific clash with his own 'keeper Kasey Keller – just two years after Ullathorne had fractured his ankle. Martin O'Neill has assured him his future at the club is safe, but Ullathorne must wonder what woe is around the next corner.

CB David UNSWORTH • 6
EVERTON • BORN: 16.10.73

Perhaps 1998–99's most bizarre transfer story involved David Unsworth. He and his family were unsettled in London and West Ham sold him to Aston Villa for £3 million. But after 27 days, he was off again – this time back to Everton, for the same price Villa paid.

Some commentators cheekily suggested Unsworth's wife wore the trousers and had put her foot down over the move. John Gregory even alluded to this in an interview, when the player left training early to get home. Unsworth denied it; but whatever the truth, the centre-back returned home to the Toffees.

Everton struggled for most of the season and Unsworth's stats reflected this. He completed a very poor 68% of his passes and his tackle success rate was only average for a defender.

He also picked up eight bookings from 65 fouls, including giving away a penalty in the 2–0 defeat by Arsenal. His one goal of the Premiership came in the 5–0 thrashing of Middlesbrough, and that was a high point in an uncomfortable season which Unsworth will be happy to put behind him.

APPEARANCES	
Start (sub)	33 (1)
Minutes on pitch	2970
GOAL ATTEMPTS	
Goals	1
DEFENDING	
Blocks	20
Headed clearances	246
Other clearances	146
Interceptions	36
Tackles won	81
PASSING	
Passing accuracy	68%
DISCIPLINE	
Fouls	65
Yellow cards	8
Red cards	0

CB Matthew UPSON • 20
ARSENAL • BORN: 18.4.79

An England under-21 international, Matthew Upson was restricted to a handful of substitute appearances for the Gunners in 1998–99 and there were rumours that he was unhappy with his lack of first-team opportunities.

Arsenal will not want to lose him. The former Luton Town trainee has developed under the guidance of Arsene Wenger, showing signs of maturity and composure beyond his 20 years.

Upson managed just 71 minutes of Premiership football in 1998–99 but won both his tackles, as well as making 13 clearances and three interceptions. His distribution was also very accurate; 84% of his passes found an Arsenal shirt.

He also performed well for the England under-21s and his goal sealed a 2–1 victory against France.

If Upson remains at Arsenal, it may only be a short time before he begins to challenge the old guard in the Gunners' defence. He will certainly be looking to build on his first team appearances in 1999–2000.

G Raimond VAN DER GOUW • 17
MANCHESTER UNITED • BORN: 24.3.63

An experienced back-up 'keeper to Peter Schmeichel over the course of the last three seasons, it would appear that Raimond van der Gouw is set to continue as Manchester United's goalkeeping understudy, despite the great Dane's departure.

The Dutchman played in only four-and-a-half matches in the Premiership during the 1998–99 season, when Schmeichel was suffering either with minor injuries or from sunburn on a beach in Barbados during a mid-season break.

Sitting on the bench had its compensation, though. Van der Gouw added FA Cup and Champions League winners medal to his burgeoning collection of gongs.

He filled in admirably when called upon, keeping two clean sheets and conceding just two goals.

Van der Gouw's 88% saves-to-shots ratio illustrates perfectly why Alex Ferguson will be delighted to keep the Dutchman in the squad as back-up to his new number one, former Aston Villa 'keeper Mark Bosnich.

T

S Pierre VAN HOOIJDONK • 40
NOTTINGHAM FOREST • BORN: 29.11.69

Pierre van Hooijdonk took the term "player power" to new heights – or depths, depending on your point of view – in a tempestuous season for Nottingham Forest.

The Dutchman, incensed by the sale of Kevin Campbell and Forest's failure to spend money to strengthen the squad, took the decision to go on strike until the club agreed to sell him.

Unfortunately, no one was interested at the price Forest were asking and he was forced to eat a big slice of humble pie before returning to try and turn things around for the club.

But despite his ability he was unable to make a significant difference and, just as the Dutchman predicted, Forest were relegated.

Van Hooijdonk scored six goals and supplied four goal assists. But one of the season's strangest moments was the sight of almost all the players, angry at his criticism of their ability, refusing to celebrate with him when he scored his first goal at home to Derby.

He also clashed with new boss Ron Atkinson, and Forest will want to recoup any money they can on him as soon as possible.

APPEARANCES	
Start (sub)	19 (2)
Minutes on pitch	1710
GOAL ATTEMPTS	
Goals	6
Goals/shots ratio	13%
SHOOTING	
Shots on target	24
Shooting accuracy	53%
PASSING	
Goal assists	4
Passing accuracy	65%
DISCIPLINE	
Fouls	.28
Offside	16
Yellow cards	5
Red cards	1

Player power: Pierre van Hooijdonk

S Darius VASSELL • 22
ASTON VILLA • BORN: 13.6.80

Exciting striking prospect Darius Vassell made his Carling Premiership debut at home to Middlesbrough when he replaced Julian Joachim, but made the biggest impact in Villa's short-lived 1998–99 UEFA Cup campaign.

Vassell came off the bench to claim a crucial brace against Norwegian side Stromgodset which helped Villa through to the second round. But he could not build on this impressive display, making just six substitute appearances in the Premiership all season.

He signed professional forms in March 1998 and has since scored regularly for the reserves. He also did well for the England under-21s in Hungary.

He managed just three shots during his 74 minutes of league action and made 32 passes. Vassell enjoyed a run of three consecutive appearances at the end of the 1998–99 campaign, his main contribution being when he flicked the ball into the path of Joachim for the first of his two equalizers at home to Charlton.

CB Ramon VEGA • 15
TOTTENHAM HOTSPUR • BORN: 14.6.71

Ramon Vega had another difficult season in 1998–99. Since being bought by Gerry Francis the Swiss defender has had some excellent games, but also made some costly blunders which have aroused many a Spurs fan's ire.

With the defensive coaching of master-tactician George Graham, Vega began to look more like the type of quality centre-back Spurs need to play alongside Sol Campbell.

Defensively, the Swiss made 218 clearances and won 74% of his tackles. And when he had the ball he tried to give it simply, though he completed a below-par 78% of his 351 passes.

The other thing Vega does well is pose a threat at set-pieces. With Graham's penchant for tactical set plays Vega had 10 attempts at goal in the 1998–99 season, scoring twice, to increase his Premiership tally to six.

There are plenty of defenders who can testify that George Graham has improved their game immensely – and with a Worthington Cup medal in his grasp already, Vega will be hoping that he can reap further rewards in the 1999–2000 season.

APPEARANCES	
Start (sub)	13 (3)
Minutes on pitch	1185
GOAL ATTEMPTS	
Goals	2
DEFENDING	
Blocks	21
Headed clearances	150
Other clearances	68
Interceptions	8
Tackles won	23
PASSING	
Passing accuracy	78%
DISCIPLINE	
Fouls	24
Yellow cards	2
Red cards	0

S Gianluca VIALLI • 9
CHELSEA • BORN: 9.7.64

APPEARANCES	
Start (sub)	9 (0)
Minutes on pitch	783
GOAL ATTEMPTS	
Goals	1
Goals/shots ratio	6%
SHOOTING	
Shots on target	5
Shooting accuracy	31%
PASSING	
Goal assists	2
Passing accuracy	70%
DISCIPLINE	
Fouls	19
Offside	23
Yellow cards	3
Red cards	1

As the Premiership's only player-manager, Gianluca Vialli was arguably under the closest scrutiny of any Chelsea player in 1998–99. This may have persuaded him to leave himself out of the side for most of the season.

In all he played 783 minutes of Premiership football, scoring just one goal – against Derby County on the last day of the season. That strike was only the fifth time he had managed to trouble a goalkeeper in the League.

His season took an embarrassing turn in the match with Blackburn Rovers on February 17, when he was sent off for kicking defender Marlon Broomes. That was a rare moment of folly from a man who has led by example since his move to the club, and in all he committed just 19 fouls.

At the end of the 1998–99 season, Vialli was debating whether to re-register as a player for the coming year. Whether he does finally call time on an illustrious career on the pitch or not, summer signings are likely to make it even harder for him to gain a place in his own starting XI.

V

CB Steve VICKERS • 4
MIDDLESBROUGH • BORN: 13.10.67

Steve Vickers's presence in Boro's defence was vital as they returned to the Premiership. With more than 200 appearances since joining from Tranmere Rovers in 1993, the 1998–99 season was one of his toughest yet.

Vickers would not have expected an easy ride, even after Boro's promising start, and the experienced stopper was asked to do more than his fair share in defence.

His Carling Opta stats highlight Vickers's effectiveness at the back. He made more blocks, clearances and interceptions than anybody else at the club, showing excellent ability in reading the game and making timely contributions when Boro's defence came under siege.

He also displayed composure in possession, his passing success rate of 80% being above average for a Premiership defender.

The 1998–99 season was one of consolidation for a Middlesbrough side packed with experience. In 1999–2000, Vickers will try to help Boro close the gap on the Premiership elite.

APPEARANCES	
Start (sub)	30 (1)
Minutes on pitch	2687
GOAL ATTEMPTS	
Goals	1
DEFENDING	
Blocks	33
Headed clearances	275
Other clearances	137
Interceptions	45
Tackles won	37
PASSING	
Passing accuracy	80%
DISCIPLINE	
Fouls	17
Yellow cards	4
Red cards	0

M Patrick VIEIRA • 4
ARSENAL • BORN: 23.6.76

APPEARANCES	
Start (sub)	34 (0)
Minutes on pitch	2900
GOAL ATTEMPTS	
Goals	3
PASSING	
Passes	1759
Passing accuracy	83%
DEFENDING	
Interceptions	48
Clearances	97
Tackles	209
Tackles won	70%
DISCIPLINE	
Fouls	85
Yellow cards	7
Red cards	1

Nicknamed "What?" from his response when trying to understand the dressing-room banter, Patrick Vieira has no such problem on the pitch. His almost telepathic understanding with Emmanuel Petit, and the tactical maturity which lets him fill in when defenders break forward, make him one of the most important components in a formidable Arsenal first team.

He captained Cannes as a teenager and was at AC Milan when Arsene Wenger recommended him to the Arsenal board before officially taking over at Highbury.

Vieira's tough tackling saw him make 209 challenges, those telescopic legs reaching the ball when it seemed impossible – and he won more than any other player. But he still lacks discipline – seven yellow cards, one red and four matches suspended tell the tale.

He is the straight man to the flair and wit of Petit and Dennis Bergkamp, but he can play a bit too. Three goals, three assists, an 80% dribble success ratio and an 83% pass completion rate testify to a talent fans hope will dominate their midfield for years to come.

FB | Nelson VIVAS • 7
ARSENAL • BORN: 18.10.69

Signed from Boca Juniors just before the 1998–99 season began, Argentina's first-choice World Cup right-back went on to play a regular part in Arsenal's Premiership season.

Used mostly as cover for Nigel Winterburn, the short, ball-playing defender was also used in defensive midfield areas or out wide to help preserve leads near the end of games.

The fiery Vivas tended to be reckless in the challenge. He won a well-below-average 54% of his tackles and was booked five times in the league in less than 1,200 minutes played.

On the plus side, Vivas completed 61 clearances and 12 interceptions, but his season ended in disappointment as, shortly after he replaced the injured Winterburn, Jimmy Floyd Hasselbaink scored the goal that ultimately cost Arsenal the title. Arsene Wenger cited the defensive mix-up caused by the substitution as the reason for the goal.

Vivas may struggle to earn a regular first-team spot in 1999–2000 but he should remain a valuable utility player in Arsenal's ever-more impressive squad.

APPEARANCES	
Start (sub)	10 (13)
Minutes on pitch	1143
GOAL ATTEMPTS	
Goals	0
PASSING & CROSSING	
Passing	554
Passing accuracy	80%
Crossing	39
Crossing accuracy	23%
DEFENDING	
Tackles	69
Tackles won	54%
DISCIPLINE	
Fouls	20
Yellow cards	5
Red cards	0

CB | Des WALKER • 6
SHEFFIELD WEDNESDAY • BORN: 26.11.65

APPEARANCES	
Start (sub)	37 (0)
Minutes on pitch	3239
GOAL ATTEMPTS	
Goals	0
DEFENDING	
Blocks	39
Headed clearances	339
Other clearances	218
Interceptions	60
Tackles won	54
PASSING	
Passing accuracy	81%
DISCIPLINE	
Fouls	25
Yellow cards	2
Red cards	0

A stalwart of the Sheffield Wednesday defence for six seasons, Des Walker again proved what a fine professional he is. Absent just once in 1998–99, the former England player has missed only 11 games for the Owls since his £2.7 million transfer from Sampdoria in 1993.

His tackling was not as fearsome as that of fellow defender Emerson Thome, but he showed he is still one of the best readers of the game around with 60 interceptions.

Walker also distributed the ball well at the back, completing 81% of his attempted passes, but as has been the case throughout his career he offered the side very few options in the opposition half.

He did come close to scoring in the 0–0 draw with Chelsea but stumbled over the ball at the last minute, thereby failing to register his first shot of the season and double his career total of one goal.

Season 1999–2000 should see Walker take his tally of English league appearances over the 500 mark, a figure that says much for his enduring ability at the highest level.

V

Ian WALKER • 1
TOTTENHAM HOTSPUR • BORN: 31.10.71

After traumas in his career and personal life Ian Walker re-established himself in the Spurs side, but only after Espen Baardsen fell out with George Graham over contract talks.

The young Norwegian was in top form and put in the Carling Opta goalkeeping display of the season in the 0–0 draw with north London rivals Arsenal. But once Walker regained his place, Graham decided to stick with him.

Despite a first medal in the Worthington Cup, Walker must improve to keep his place. Graham worked wonders on the defensive side, reducing the number of shots Spurs' 'keepers had to save from 6.4 a game under Christian Gross's stewardship to a more manageable 2.8. But despite this, Walker still conceded 33 goals and recorded the lowest saves-to-shots ratio of any first-choice Premiership 'keeper.

His catch success rate, too, was below par. Walker collected only 92% of crosses he came for – a very disappointing figure.

Walker has his work cut out to stay number one: "The Stroller" is determined to see Spurs back to the top – and hates conceding goals.

APPEARANCES	
Start (sub)	25 (0)
Minutes on pitch	2250
SHOT STOPPING	
Goals conceded	33
Clean sheets	7
Saves	73
Saves/shots	69%
DISTRIBUTION	
Distribution	858
Distribution %	59%
CATCHING	
Crosses caught	55
Crosses dropped	5
DISCIPLINE	
Yellow cards	I
Red cards	0

Jean-Guy WALLEMME • 13
COVENTRY CITY • BORN: 10.8.67

APPEARANCES	
Start (sub)	4 (2)
Minutes on pitch	410
GOAL ATTEMPTS	
Goals	0
DEFENDING	
Blocks	6
Headed clearances	38
Other clearances	19
Interceptions	12
Tackles won	9
PASSING	
Passing accuracy	84%
DISCIPLINE	
Fouls	5
Yellow cards	2
Red cards	0

Much was expected of Jean-Guy Wallemme when he arrived at Highfield Road in the summer of 1998. He had just led Lens to the French Championship as captain and was being looked at by a host of Premiership clubs.

Playing in his favoured position of centre-back, Walleme completed 84% of his 165 passes and had one shot on target. He won a slightly disappointing 47% of his challenges, committing five fouls and collecting two yellow cards.

While his tackling statistics are not the most impressive, he did make 57 clearances, six blocks and 12 interceptions during his brief Coventry career.

He was a composed player on the ball, and he completed all three dribbles he attempted.

After starting a handful of Carling Premiership games at the beginning of the season, Wallemme eventually lost his place in the Coventry first team to Richard Shaw, and at the end of January 1999 he was sold to Sochaux for £400,000.

CB — Steve WALSH • 5
LEICESTER CITY • BORN: 3.11.64

Steve Walsh is Leicester's number five in more than just his shirt number. The Worthington Cup semi-final marked the big defender's 420th outing for the club and moved him up to fifth in the all-time Leicester appearances chart – amazing, given all his injury problems.

The £100,000 signing from Wigan in 1986 has done sterling service; indeed, his displays in 1998–99 earned him a place among the top 20 defenders in the Carling Opta Index.

Not that he has been restricted to his normal position. When Leicester had an injury crisis up front, as so often in the past it was Steve Walsh who stepped in, and over the season he added three goals to his ever-increasing tally.

Walsh was restricted to just 17 starts, but still weighed in with 234 defensive clearances and won two-thirds of the 54 challenges he contested.

Martin O'Neill has added several centre-backs to his portfolio since taking over as manager in December 1995, but Steve Walsh continues to defy doctors and Mother Nature to be part of his beloved Leicester City.

APPEARANCES	
Start (sub)	17 (5)
Minutes on pitch	1593
GOAL ATTEMPTS	
Goals	3
DEFENDING	
Blocks	18
Headed clearances	143
Other clearances	91
Interceptions	14
Tackles won	36
PASSING	
Passing accuracy	64%
DISCIPLINE	
Fouls	16
Yellow cards	2
Red cards	0

S — Paulo WANCHOPE • 9
DERBY COUNTY • BORN: 31.7.76

APPEARANCES	
Start (sub)	33 (2)
Minutes on pitch	2970
GOAL ATTEMPTS	
Goals	9
Goals/shots ratio	13%
SHOOTING	
Shots on target	37
Shooting accuracy	54%
PASSING	
Goal assists	6
Passing accuracy	68%
DISCIPLINE	
Fouls	84
Offside	57
Yellow cards	9
Red cards	1

Paulo Wanchope is every journalist's dream. Any number of superlatives are used to describe the unusual style of the Costa Rican striker, and few writers can resist the temptation to trot out the clichés.

He was transfer-listed in May by Jim Smith, who accused him of "scoring 10 goals, but missing another 200". Though something of an exaggeration – the unorthodox attacker's nine league goals came from only 69 attempts – Wanchope was guilty of some glaring misses.

The truth was that Wanchope and others were stalling over contract talks and Jim Smith wanted players committed to the club.

Though he created six goals for team-mates, his passing backs up that commentator's cliche – "No one knows what he's going to do: in fact he doesn't even seem to know himself!" Just 68% of his passes found a team-mate and he completed only 54% of his dribbles – both well below the Premiership striker's average.

The man who scored a wonder goal on his debut in a 3–2 win at Old Trafford has much to prove in 1999–2000, whichever club he is at.

W

Ashley WARD • 32
BLACKBURN ROVERS • BORN: 24.11.70

Ashley Ward was just one of a number of multi-million pound strikers in Brian Kidd's injury-hit squad at Ewood Park during 1998–99.

The big frontman signed from Barnsley for £4.25 million in January and, although he struggled to find the net as often as he had at Oakwell, still showed he could be a threat to some Premiership defences. His tenacity and work-rate made him a valuable squad member.

Ward's five goals came from just 15 shots on target, but sadly he may be better remembered for a missed chance at home to Manchester United. That 0–0 draw against the eventual treble-winners officially relegated Rovers.

Generally good on the ball, with a 64% dribble completion rate – well above average for a Premiership striker – his combative style led to free kicks going against him and he amassed 49 fouls and three yellow cards.

Ward faces strong competition for striking places at Blackburn in 1999–2000 – and with a number of good strikers at the club, he will have to fight for a regular first-team spot at Ewood Park.

APPEARANCES	
Start (sub)	17 (0)
Minutes on pitch	1530
GOAL ATTEMPTS	
Goals	5
Goals/shots ratio	13%
SHOOTING	
Shots on target	15
Shooting accuracy	39%
PASSING	
Goal assists	1
Passing accuracy	70%
DISCIPLINE	
Fouls	49
Offside	24
Yellow cards	3
Red cards	0

Mitch WARD • 21
EVERTON • BORN: 19.6.71

Mitch Ward was one of Howard Kendall's signings, brought in to do a job for Everton who were under extreme financial pressure.

After almost 10 years with Sheffield United and some previous experience in the top flight, Kendall was hoping that Ward, whom he had managed at Bramall Lane, would fulfil some of the potential he had shown earlier in his career.

After a series of niggling injuries that restricted him to eight appearances in the 1997–98 Premiership, Ward fared no better in 1998–99 with ankle ligament and hamstring strains restricting his availability.

When he did play, Ward looked off the pace and completed just 68% of the 146 passes he attempted.

His best moment came when he set up Francis Jeffers's consolation goal in the 3–1 defeat at Chelsea, but he did not feature on a winning side all season.

It remains to be seen if he will be part of Walter Smith's rebuilding plans at Goodison Park in the 1999–2000 campaign.

Phil WARNER • 29
SOUTHAMPTON • BORN: 2.2.79

Southampton-born Phil Warner made several appearances during the 1998–99 season, replacing injured right-back Jason Dodd early in the season.

However, the youngster appeared sadly out of his depth and the Saints failed to win any of the six matches in which he started.

He endured a particularly torrid time against Arsenal at Highbury in October, where he was up against Marc Overmars. Manager Dave Jones showed mercy on the day by replacing him with Scott Hiley after just 35 minutes – and he was never seen in the first team again.

The Carling Opta statistics clearly reflect Warner's lack of experience. He gave the ball away cheaply, achieving a dismal 63% pass completion rate. His crossing was also particularly poor, with only 12% of centres finding a colleague.

It is unlikely that Warner will feature in the 1999–2000 Carling Premiership, barring injuries to Dodd or Hiley, but if he continues to develop in the reserves he may yet come back to the fringes of the first team.

CB — Dave WATSON • 5
EVERTON • BORN: 20.11.61

Dave Watson was the oldest outfield player to set foot on the pitch during the 1998–99 season. The fact Everton even fielded him is a sign of the problems which have bedevilled the club over the last decade since he was part of their last Championship-winning side.

The Merseysiders used more outfield players than any other team, but failed to find the right combination – and thus spent most of the season struggling to escape the drop-zone.

Watson played 22 matches, many in the first part of the season, when Everton were very good defensively, and the rest in the latter part of the campaign, when they got their act together up front and pushed up the table.

Watson finished with 319 clearances and won 68% of his tackles – not a bad return for an old warhorse – and used his experience to good effect by completing 79% of his passes and keeping the play simple.

Though most players have been put out to grass by his age, the man who spent a short time as Everton's player-boss looks set to add to his 417 League appearances.

APPEARANCES	
Start (sub)	22 (0)
Minutes on pitch	1891

GOAL ATTEMPTS	
Goals	0

DEFENDING	
Blocks	22
Headed clearances	179
Other clearances	140
Interceptions	23
Tackles won	28

PASSING	
Passing accuracy	79%

DISCIPLINE	
Fouls	17
Yellow cards	0
Red cards	0

FB — Steve WATSON • 6
ASTON VILLA • BORN: 1.4.74

APPEARANCES	
Start (sub)	33 (1)
Minutes on pitch	2795

GOAL ATTEMPTS	
Goals	0

PASSING & CROSSING	
Passing	1192
Passing accuracy	72%
Crossing	103
Crossing accuracy	33%

DEFENDING	
Tackles	98
Tackles won	64%

DISCIPLINE	
Fouls	19
Yellow cards	2
Red cards	1

England "B" international Steve Watson was signed by John Gregory in October to replace Benfica-bound right-back Gary Charles.

Watson was later joined by fellow-Geordie Steve Stone at the Midlands club. Like Stone, Watson is industrious and displays grit and determination when he is on the pitch.

A committed tackler for both Newcastle and Aston Villa, Watson won more than 60% of his 98 challenges: more impressively, the mainly right-sided defender was penalized just 19 times, proving he is one of the cleanest tacklers in the Premiership.

Watson made more than 200 blocks, clearances and interceptions and completed three-quarters of his 119 dribbles and runs.

When he got to the by-line, Watson whipped in a good centre. A third of all his crosses found a colleague and he assisted four goals, including three for his new side. His distribution was sound: of more than 1,000 passes, a good 72% reaching the intended destination. But he has yet to score for the Villans and was sent off against Charlton.

W

CB — David WEIR • 18
EVERTON • BORN: 10.5.70

Walter Smith finally got his man when Everton paid Hearts £250,000 for defender David Weir. Smith had wanted to sign the Scottish international while at Glasgow Rangers, and was delighted to secure his services given the defensive injury crisis at Goodison Park.

The fee was so low because Weir was coming to the end of his contract and he looks likely to be part of the Everton set-up in 1999–2000.

Weir's tackling was fairly accomplished. The Scot won 65% of his challenges and made 91 defensive clearances, but his pass completion rate was not as good. He completed a meagre 66% of the balls he made, although two of the successful ones did lead directly to goals.

He seemed to settle into the pace of the game quite well, and playing out of position, occasionally at full-back, he even showed an ability to beat his man and swing in an inviting cross.

Weir also posed the occasional goal threat, but tested the goalkeeper only three times out of his 17 attempts, although five of these were blocked on their way to goal.

APPEARANCES	
Start (sub)	11 (3)
Minutes on pitch	1067
GOAL ATTEMPTS	
Goals	0
DEFENDING	
Blocks	4
Headed clearances	58
Other clearances	33
Interceptions	10
Tackles won	26
PASSING	
Passing accuracy	66%
DISCIPLINE	
Fouls	16
Yellow cards	2
Red cards	0

CB — David WETHERALL • 6
LEEDS UNITED • BORN: 14.3.71

APPEARANCES	
Start (sub)	14 (7)
Minutes on pitch	1433
GOAL ATTEMPTS	
Goals	0
DEFENDING	
Blocks	18
Headed clearances	214
Other clearances	60
Interceptions	13
Tackles won	28
PASSING	
Passing accuracy	73%
DISCIPLINE	
Fouls	34
Yellow cards	3
Red cards	0

After starting the season on the substitutes' bench, David Wetherall ended 1999–2000 behind new England recruit Jonathon Woodgate in the defensive pecking order.

The big central defender has been a fixture in the Leeds side over the last few seasons, having broken into the team gradually since Howard Wilkinson brought him to Elland Road in 1991, aged just 20, for £125,000.

Wetherall's bravery showed in the FA Cup clash with Leeds when he bizarrely ended up sharing a hospital room with Tottenham's Les Ferdinand after the two clashed heads.

During the season Wetherall won an impressive 72% of his challenges and showed his ability in the air, with 214 of his 274 clearances being headers away from the danger zone. His pass completion was below average but he did pose a threat at set-pieces, hitting the target five times from 12 attempts.

Wetherall ended the season, along with team-mate Gunnar Halle, as a target for Premiership new boys and Leeds' neighbours Bradford City.

Noel WHELAN • 8
COVENTRY CITY • BORN: 30.12.74

Noel Whelan showed great versatility in 1998–99, playing in midfield or wide on the left as well as in his normal striking position.

More responsibility was placed on both him and Darren Huckerby once Dion Dublin left for Aston Villa and while Whelan rose to the challenge, he still has some improving to do.

Whelan's pass completion rate was above average at 72% and he contributed two goal assists. Never afraid to try the unusual or unexpected, Whelan scored 10 goals and was the Sky Blue's top scorer in the Premiership.

Whelan's dribble and cross completion rates were also above average, but his disciplinary record was poor, with nine yellow cards from 51 fouls. Of all the Premiership's front men, only Mark Hughes earned more – though he, too, spent much of his season in midfield.

After passing 100 league games for Coventry, Whelan is now at the stage where he must maintain his level of performance, although he already seems to have convinced Gordon Strachan that he was right to buy him from the manager's old club Leeds United.

APPEARANCES	
Start (sub)	31 (0)
Minutes on pitch	2743
GOAL ATTEMPTS	
Goals	10
Goals/shots ratio	14%
SHOOTING	
Shots on target	35
Shooting accuracy	51%
PASSING	
Goal assists	2
Passing accuracy	72%
DISCIPLINE	
Fouls	51
Offside	46
Yellow cards	9
Red cards	0

Versatile: Noel Whelan

Guy WHITTINGHAM • 7
SHEFFIELD WEDNESDAY • BORN: 10.11.64

Guy Whittingham proved he had not lost his goalscoring touch when he banged in seven goals in nine games while on loan to Portsmouth, re-igniting his love affair with his first league club.

There must be something special about the Royal Blue shirt of Pompey for Whittingham, with Guy netting more than 100 goals in four years for the south coast club first time around.

In fact, the Evesham-born forward played for four clubs in all during the 1998–99 season. The first of his three loan spells at Wolves was followed by the two-month stint at Fratton Park, and he ended the season at Watford.

Whittingham, who bought himself out of the Army for £500 in order to sign a professional contract with Portsmouth, earned the moniker "Corporal Punishment" for the destruction of opposition defences.

But he saw little service with the Owls, featuring away at Derby County and Coventry City without registering a single shot either on or off target.

W

Clyde WIJNHARD • 8
LEEDS UNITED • BORN: 9.11.73

Clyde Wijnhard had a difficult first season in English football. When he joined from Willem II with a record of 18 goals in 31 matches, Leeds fans expected their side to have the makings of a good partnership up front.

But it was far from a deadly "Double Dutch" combo with Jimmy Hasselbaink. In fact the two seemed to communicate in it – and it was not long before Harry Kewell and Alan Smith emerged as more regular first-team picks.

Wijnhard's pass completion was poor, at just 66% and, although he did reasonably well on his dribbling and crossing, he made too few to form a considered judgement. An enthusiastic player, he put himself about on the pitch, making 30 fouls and earning five yellow cards.

If he needs inspiration, he need look no further than Hasselbaink who, after a difficult first season, went on to be the League's joint-top scorer in 1998–99. Wijnhard has much to prove in 1999–2000 and, with just three Premiership goals from a handful of attempts, has some way to go to match the achievement of his countryman's second season.

APPEARANCES	
Start (sub)	11 (7)
Minutes on pitch	970
GOAL ATTEMPTS	
Goals	3
Goals/shots ratio	18%
SHOOTING	
Shots on target	11
Shooting accuracy	65%
PASSING	
Goal assists	3
Passing accuracy	66%
DISCIPLINE	
Fouls	30
Offside	22
Yellow cards	5
Red cards	0

Jason WILCOX • 11
BLACKBURN ROVERS • BORN: 15.7.71

APPEARANCES	
Start (sub)	28 (2)
Minutes on pitch	2373
GOAL ATTEMPTS	
Goals	3
Shots on target	22
Shooting accuracy	71%
PASSING	
Goal assists	3
Passing accuracy	76%
Crossing accuracy	32%
DRIBBLING	
Dribbles & runs	62
Dribble completion	82%
DISCIPLINE	
Yellow cards	6
Red cards	1

Following the departure of Tim Sherwood to Tottenham, Jason Wilcox eventually took over the captaincy at Ewood Park under Brian Kidd and finished the season as Blackburn's highest-rated player in the Carling Opta Index.

Wilcox was perhaps unlucky to notch only three goals from his 22 shots on target, but managed a fine shooting accuracy of 71%.

Impressive in midfield areas, he completed 76% of his passes and ended the season with three goal assists to his credit. He also swung in 200 crosses, with 32% finding their mark.

As ever, Wilcox was happy to run at players and his success rate of 82% from more than 60 dribbles and runs illustrated his capacity to take on and beat opposing full-backs.

The Rovers veteran proved himself one of the Premiership's best all-round wide men, giving valuable cover in defence with 56 clearances and 25 interceptions. He also won more than half his challenges and blocked five shots.

One-club Wilcox will almost certainly remain at Ewood Park to help lead the assault on the Nationwide League championship.

M Andy WILLIAMS • 21
SOUTHAMPTON • BORN: 8.10.77

Andy Williams is a natural left-winger who managed just 15 minutes of Premiership football during the 1998–99 season, despite having featured regularly in the previous campaign. His sole appearance came in the dismal 4–1 defeat by Aston Villa, as a second-half substitute for Matt Le Tissier.

The purchases of Stuart Ripley and Hassan Kachloul were the primary reasons for his lack of regular first-team action, but his chance should come again.

Although he had limited opportunities to show his skills during the season, Williams has a lot of ability.

He was Southampton's most frequently-appearing reserve player, making 19 outings and scoring four times.

His talents have even been recognised at international level. After a number of under-21 appearances, he made his full debut for Wales against Brazil in November 1997.

Following a frustrating 1998–99 season, Williams will be pressing hard for a first-team recall in 1999–2000.

M Stuart WILSON • 25
LEICESTER CITY • BORN: 16.9.77

After another season of failing to break through at Filbert Street, Stuart Wilson will be even keener to make an impact in 1999–2000.

Wilson was considered a bright prospect, but with Neil Lennon, Muzzy Izzet, Robbie Savage and Theo Zagorakis all ahead of him, it has proved difficult for the young midfielder to force his way into the side.

If he is patient and works hard, however, he may get his chance; and if it comes, he must improve on his performances in 1998–99.

He fired in just four shots – only two of which were on target – and his pass completion rate was below the average expected in his position.

Wilson, who was voted Leicester Young Player of the Season in 1998–99, has the potential to become a top midfielder and, if he fulfils his promise, the fact that City have very little money to spend should make him a very useful asset.

But earning a regular place in the starting XI at Filbert Street will prove quite a challenge for him.

CB Paul WILLIAMS • 4
COVENTRY CITY • BORN: 26.3.71

One of the most under-rated players in the Premiership, Paul Williams may not be the most gifted defender – but if heart and effort make a player a hit, he is most definitely top of the charts.

Williams made 20 starts and two more substitute appearances during the 1998–99 season and, long after the likes of Jean-Guy Wallemme had deserted the club, the former England under-21 international was still straining every sinew to keep Coventry in the Premiership.

He had six spells in the side and, on his first game in each spell, Coventry won four and lost just one – that against Manchester United.

The versatile player, who can also play in midfield, made 340 clearances and won two-thirds of his 87 challenges.

He was also a threat in the air at set-pieces. Of the seven efforts he had at goal, six forced saves from opposition goalkeepers.

Williams also did much better on the disciplinary front. After two red cards the season before, 1998–99 saw him booked just three times.

Although his performances were not always eye-catching, his contribution to Coventry's defence is illustrated by a well-earned place in the top 10 of Carling Opta's defenders Index.

APPEARANCES	
Start (sub)	20 (2)
Minutes on pitch	1816
GOAL ATTEMPTS	
Goals	0
DEFENDING	
Blocks	28
Headed clearances	230
Other clearances	110
Interceptions	21
Tackles won	58
PASSING	
Passing accuracy	65%
DISCIPLINE	
Fouls	22
Yellow cards	3
Red cards	0

W

FB Nigel WINTERBURN • 3
ARSENAL • BORN: 11.12.63

According to Carling Opta's statistics, Nigel Winterburn was the Premiership's best left-back in 1998–99. His displays ranked him eighth in the Carling Opta defenders Index, but he is the only full-back in the top 10.

Defensively, he was as sound as ever: he won 61% of his 147 tackles, made 26 blocks and plenty of clearances and interceptions.

But the real revelation came with his attacking play. An 87% completion rate from his 55 dribbles and runs shows how his confidence and ability on the ball have been brought out by Arsene Wenger. A major feature of Arsenal's play in 1998–99 was Winterburn's willingness to overlap with Marc Overmars down the left-hand side, and he did this to excellent effect all season, grabbing two goal assists in the process.

Winterburn will be looking for another year at the top and, with Manchester United pipping Arsenal to the post in 1998–99, he will be even more determined to add yet another medal to his already-impressive collection in 1999–2000.

APPEARANCES	
Start (sub)	30 (0)
Minutes on pitch	2556
GOAL ATTEMPTS	
Goals	0
PASSING & CROSSING	
Passing	1309
Passing accuracy	85%
Crossing	25
Crossing accuracy	16%
DEFENDING	
Tackles	147
Tackles won	61%
DISCIPLINE	
Fouls	24
Yellow cards	8
Red cards	0

M Dennis WISE • 11
CHELSEA • BORN: 16.12.66

APPEARANCES	
Start (sub)	21 (1)
Minutes on pitch	1837
GOAL ATTEMPTS	
Goals	0
PASSING	
Passes	1037
Passing accuracy	82%
DEFENDING	
Interceptions	16
Clearances	30
Tackles	89
Tackles won	57%
DISCIPLINE	
Fouls	38
Yellow cards	7
Red cards	1

If Emmanuel Petit was worried referees were after him in season 1998–99, Dennis Wise must have experienced full-blown paranoia. The Chelsea skipper got an early taste of the trouble ahead when he was sent off in a pre-season friendly against Atletico Madrid.

That ruled him out of games against Newcastle, Arsenal and Forest. By the season's end he had been sent off three times – once in the league – and missed 15 games through suspension, 14 in the Premiership.

When he did play, Wise was his usual abrasive yet creative self, attempting 89 tackles and laying on five goals with assists. As Chelsea's regular corner-taker, he also attempted a high number of crosses, connecting with a team-mate 47 times.

A fierce competitor as well as an excellent motivator, Wise's discipline seemed to improve in the second half of the season. But then a nasty incident in the European Cup Winners Cup semi-final, when he was caught on camera appearing to bite Real Mallorca's Marcelino, raised more questions about his temperament.

AM Ian WOAN • 18
NOTTINGHAM FOREST • BORN: 14.12.67

Ian Woan spent much of the 1998–99 Carling Premiership campaign on the sidelines with a long-standing knee injury. He managed just two substitute appearances and will hope that the 1999–2000 season brings him more luck.

Woan would have been very disappointed not to have been able to play in the top flight after being part of several more gifted Forest sides in the early '90s.

But it is unlikely that he would have featured as a starter too often, after spending most of the previous season on the bench.

He made very little contribution in his brief appearances, completing a poor 68% of the passes he attempted in just 89 minutes on the pitch and even managing to pick up a yellow card in the last minute of the 4–0 drubbing by Coventry City.

At 31, he will hope Forest can bounce straight back and offer him one last opportunity to play top-flight football.

But first he will hope to help his new boss achieve that coveted promotion back to the Carling Premiership.

CB Jonathon WOODGATE • 25
LEEDS UNITED • BORN: 22.1.80

APPEARANCES	
Start (sub)	25 (0)
Minutes on pitch	2174
GOAL ATTEMPTS	
Goals	2
DEFENDING	
Blocks	29
Headed clearances	185
Other clearances	105
Interceptions	27
Tackles won	66
PASSING	
Passing accuracy	78%
DISCIPLINE	
Fouls	31
Yellow cards	5
Red cards	0

England recruit: Jonathon Woodgate

Jonathon Woodgate emerged as an exciting young prospect at Leeds United during an incredible 1998–99 campaign culminating in three call-ups to the full England squad.

Though an injury trying to stop Andy Cole scoring kept both players out of the squad for the Hungary game, "Woody" was thrilled when Kevin Keegan again selected him for the Euro 2000 qualifier with Sweden in May.

But the highlight was undoubtedly his man-of-the-match display for England in Bulgaria four days later.

Showing great composure for a young player, he was part of an exuberant Leeds side which impressed everyone in 1998–99. Woodgate made 290 clearances and an impressive 29 defensive blocks. He also won 63% of his 105 tackles, but over-eagerness saw him amass 31 fouls and earn five Premiership yellow cards.

The one real disappointment would have been Leeds' lack of progress in the cup competitions or in Europe, but 1999–2000 will offer him another crack and the chance to carry on his education at the very top level.

S · Christopher WREH • 12
ARSENAL • BORN: 14.5.75

Young Liberian international Christopher Wreh undoubtedly played his part in Arsenal's Double-winning heroics of 1997–98, scoring three Carling Premiership goals and the winner in the FA Cup semi-final with Wolves.

But maintaining his challenge for a regular place in such a talented side was to prove too much for the former Monaco star, with Dennis Bergkamp and Nicolas Anelka hogging the limelight for most of the 1998–99 season.

Wreh and Portuguese frontman Luis Boa Morte were given several chances to impress because of injury and suspension – but both failed to find the target.

In 416 minutes, Wreh fired in nine shots, but only tested the goalkeeper with three. His 74% pass completion rate is above average for a striker, but he contributed little in other areas of the pitch.

Eventually, Arsene Wenger loaned Wreh and team-mate Alberto Mendez to the Greek club AEK Athens for the rest of the season. It now seems highly unlikely that Wreh will again figure in the Premiership for the Gunners.

APPEARANCES	
Start (sub)	3 (9)
Minutes on pitch	416
GOAL ATTEMPTS	
Goals	0
Goals/shots ratio	0%
SHOOTING	
Shots on target	3
Shooting accuracy	60%
PASSING	
Goal assists	0
Passing accuracy	74%
DISCIPLINE	
Fouls	8
Offside	4
Yellow cards	0
Red cards	0

FB · Alan WRIGHT • 3
ASTON VILLA • BORN: 28.9.71

APPEARANCES	
Start (sub)	38 (0)
Minutes on pitch	3405
GOAL ATTEMPTS	
Goals	0
PASSING & CROSSING	
Passing	1675
Passing accuracy	80%
Crossing	129
Crossing accuracy	29%
DEFENDING	
Tackles	77
Tackles won	52%
DISCIPLINE	
Fouls	19
Yellow cards	3
Red cards	0

Durable left-sided defender Alan Wright missed just 15 minutes of the entire 1998–99 Carling Premiership, making way for Julian Joachim as Villa looked to pull back a two-goal deficit at home to Liverpool.

Wright's value is in his ability to soak up pressure and bring the ball out down the left flank, linking with team-mates and supplying ammunition for the likes of Dion Dublin in the centre. During the 1998–99 season he angled in 129 crosses towards the opposition box, with a shade less than 30% reaching a Villan.

Former England under-21 star Wright relied on speed and trickery to beat opponents, successfully negotiating a magnificent 94% of all dribbles and runs attempted.

The £900,000 signing from Blackburn made more passes than any Villa player: his total of 1,675 was the Premership's seventh-highest. Of these, 80% connected and two set up goals.

Wright has managed just three goals in all competitions in four years at the club and threatened 'keepers on only three occasions in the 1998–99 league campaign.

Ian WRIGHT • 14
WEST HAM UNITED • BORN: 3.11.63

Crystal Palace and Arsenal legend Ian Wright joined West Ham in July 1998 for a bargain £750,000 and quickly became a hero at Upton Park with his passionate, live-wire displays.

Injury curtailed a large part of his 1998–99 season and he only managed nine league goals during 1998–99. He troubled the 'keeper 25 times, but missed the target with 26 shots. He had three goal assists to his credit, and completed 69% of his 500 passes.

He has found himself in trouble with referees throughout his career, and 1998–99 was no exception. He was booked eight times and sent off against Leeds, after which he set about redesigning the referees' room and earned himself a hefty fine as a result.

Wright formed a useful partnership with Paul Kitson, and if they can both keep clear of injuries in 1999–2000 they could score the goals that once again propel West Ham into contention for European places.

Wright still has another year on his contract at West Ham, and he will be looking to add to his impressive goals tally in 1999–2000.

APPEARANCES	
Start (sub)	20 (2)
Minutes on pitch	1754
GOAL ATTEMPTS	
Goals	9
Goals/shots ratio	18%
SHOOTING	
Shots on target	25
Shooting accuracy	49%
PASSING	
Goal assists	3
Passing accuracy	69%
DISCIPLINE	
Fouls	53
Offside	39
Yellow cards	8
Red cards	1

Dwight YORKE • 19
MANCHESTER UNITED • BORN: 3.11.71

APPEARANCES	
Start (sub)	33 (0)
Minutes on pitch	2879
GOAL ATTEMPTS	
Goals	18
Goals/shots ratio	26%
SHOOTING	
Shots on target	37
Shooting accuracy	54%
PASSING	
Goal assists	13
Passing accuracy	81%
DISCIPLINE	
Fouls	33
Offside	45
Yellow cards	3
Red cards	0

Birtille St Clair, Dwight Yorke's childhood coach on the island of Tobago, quickly learned schoolwork was not high on his protégé's list of priorities. "Coach, I want to play football," was the response when he asked the happy, bare-footed youngster to revise for his exams.

Yorke has certainly tested English defences since arriving in 1989 – and Alex Ferguson's desire to sign the striker was the proverbial worst-kept secret in football at the start of 1998–99. After just one Villa appearance, he joined United for a record £12.75 million.

Twenty-nine goals later, Yorke has proved capable of performing consistently, even at the very highest level. Indeed, many of his best displays came in the Champions League.

His 18 Premiership goals came from 69 efforts, with 16 shots blocked. His goals-to-shots ratio of 26% matched the Premiership's finest and he supplied a massive 13 assists.

His "big smile lighting up the season" was one of the media clichés of the year, while his electrifying partnership with Andy Cole will be one of the campaign's most enduring memories.

W

Eddie YOUDS • 6
CB CHARLTON ATHLETIC • BORN: 3.5.70

Eddie Youds was among the most influential centre-backs in Nationwide Division One and proved to be a superb signing for Alan Curbishley in 1997–98, helping to propel Charlton into the Premiership.

Ever-present until December 1998, Youds performed solidly during the first half of the 1998–99 season but in February was forced out by tendonitis. After his return to fitness, new signing Carl Tiler's extra Premiership experience kept Youds out of the side for all but one of the season's remaining games.

The former Bradford skipper won a superb 79% of his challenges and made 278 clearances. But he also conceded 53 fouls and six yellow cards. He was a danger at set-piece and corner situations, scoring in consecutive matches in October at Nottingham Forest and Chelsea, and also finished with two goal assists to his credit.

Youds performed better than many expected in the top flight. Back in the Nationwide League, he could again prove to be one of Charlton's most reliable players.

APPEARANCES
Start (sub)	21 (1)
Minutes on pitch	1907

GOAL ATTEMPTS
Goals	2

DEFENDING
Blocks	23
Headed clearances	205
Other clearances	73
Interceptions	17
Tackles won	48

PASSING
Passing accuracy	77%

DISCIPLINE
Fouls	53
Yellow cards	6
Red cards	0

Luke YOUNG • 32
CB TOTTENHAM HOTSPUR • BORN: 19.7.79

APPEARANCES
Start (sub)	14 (1)
Minutes on pitch	1278

GOAL ATTEMPTS
Goals	0

DEFENDING
Blocks	19
Headed clearances	95
Other clearances	53
Interceptions	32
Tackles won	35

PASSING
Passing accuracy	82%

DISCIPLINE
Fouls	8
Yellow cards	5
Red cards	0

Former England youth international Luke Young enjoyed a confident start to his professional career in 1998–99.

Drafted into defence by George Graham in John Scales's and Colin Calderwood's absence, his debut ended in defeat at West Ham in November; but his next three Premiership matches saw him face Liverpool, Manchester United and Chelsea, and Young earned rave reviews for shackling Robbie Fowler in the 2–1 win over the Merseysiders at White Hart Lane.

Overall, Young's Carling Opta statistics are impressive, with an above-average 82% pass completion rate and almost 150 clearances. He won 65% of his challenges, but his inexperience told toward the season's end and he was left red-faced when Arsenal striker Nwankwo Kanu turned him on the edge of the box and flicked the ball over him to score in the north London derby in May.

He also managed to pick up five yellow cards from just eight fouls. Nonetheless, he impressed many observers during the season and is sure to get more chances in 1999–2000.

Theo ZAGORAKIS • 37
LEICESTER CITY • BORN: 27.10.71

Greek international captain Theo Zagorakis signed for Leicester from PAOK Salonika in February 1998 after an impressive trial spell.

He began the 1998–99 season as first-choice midfielder alongside Neil Lennon and Muzzy Izzet, but faced competition from Stuart Campbell and Rob Ullathorne and was in and out of the first XI for most of the campaign. He was also used as right wing-back, but was up against Robbie Savage for that regular slot.

Despite some competent and industrious displays the £750,000 signing struggled for consistency, with passing, crossing and dribbling all below par. Unlike Lennon and Izzet his tackling was disappointing, with only 55% of his challenges winning possession.

Going forward, seven of his 10 efforts were on target, but only one found the net. A terrific long-range thunderbolt and one of the side's best goals of the season, it sadly came in the 6–2 home defeat by Manchester United.

Zagorakis completed 90 minutes just six times, despite making 16 league starts, and will hope for more chances in 1999–2000.

APPEARANCES	
Start (sub)	16 (3)
Minutes on pitch	1302
GOAL ATTEMPTS	
Goals	1
PASSING	
Passes	404
Passing accuracy	79%
DEFENDING	
Interceptions	8
Clearances	20
Tackles	65
Tackles won	55%
DISCIPLINE	
Fouls	21
Yellow cards	4
Red cards	0

Gianfranco ZOLA • 25
CHELSEA • BORN: 5.7.66

APPEARANCES	
Start (sub)	35 (2)
Minutes on pitch	2923
GOAL ATTEMPTS	
Goals	13
Goals/shots ratio	18%
SHOOTING	
Shots on target	46
Shooting accuracy	63%
PASSING	
Goal assists	3
Passing accuracy	78%
DISCIPLINE	
Fouls	17
Offside	36
Yellow cards	1
Red cards	0

Zola might be the last name in the Premiership dictionary, but he was first on Gianluca Vialli's teamsheet for much of the 1998–99 season.

Although the little Italian was the key to Chelsea's success the year before, epitomized by his glorious winner in the Cup Winners Cup final, he began the first game of 1998–99 at Coventry City as merely a substitute.

After the Blues lost – one of only three league defeats all season – Vialli did not leave his pint-sized playmaker on the bench in any Premiership match again until April.

He was under pressure to perform, with compatriot Gigi Casiraghi out for the season, homesick Brian Laudrup returning to Denmark and Vialli preferring not to select himself. Highlights of Zola's season included memorable braces at Leicester City in November and at home to Everton in May.

Firing 63% of his shots on target, he ended the campaign as one of the league's sharpest shooters; and with just 16 league goals for Chelsea before 1998–99, he bagged 13 as the Blues secured a Champions League spot.

Y

CARLING OPTA PLAYERS TO WATCH

Many young, hitherto unknown footballers graced the Carling Premiership in 1998–99. But who are likely to be the top-flight stars of the future?

Carling Opta have scoured the lower leagues to try to uncover the big names of tomorrow. Here they present 12 young players who are either set for their Premiership debuts or are likely to be snapped up by the heavyweight clubs in the near future.

Leeds star Jonathon Woodgate showed in 1998–99 that a young player's rise from obscurity to the international stage is not necessarily confined to *Roy of the Rovers*, and these young hopefuls will be looking to follow in his footsteps.

G — Darren WARD
BORN: 11.5.74 GOALS 1998–99: 0
APPEARANCES 1998–99: 42

Darren began his career at Mansfield Town in 1992 and moved to Notts County for £160,000 in July 1995.

He is a Welsh under-21 international and has been called into the "B" squad, with many observers believing it is only a matter of time before the 25-year-old graduates to full international honours.

Darren played a key role in Notts County's promotion in 1997–98 and his efforts were recognized by his fellow professionals, who selected him for the PFA award-winning divisional team.

Despite Notts County finishing in the bottom third of Division Two in 1998–99, his consistent performances attracted the attentions of several Premiership scouts and he was rumoured to be a close season target for Wimbledon, before the departure of boss Joe Kinnear.

FB — Steve FINNAN
BORN: 20.4.76 GOALS 1998–99: 2
APPEARANCES 1998–99: 26

Steve started his career at non-league Welling United and signed for Birmingham City in June 1995. After a brief loan period at Notts County, he moved permanently for £300,000 in October 1996. Then Fulham boss Kevin Keegan snapped him up prior to the 1998–99 season.

He has filled several roles on the right-hand side but excelled as a wing-back as Fulham stormed Division Two. He possesses exceptional strength, pace and touch which, coupled with his excellent delivery of crosses and set-pieces, makes him a potent attacking and defensive force.

Steve is an Eire under-21 international and has also been selected for the Eire "B" squad. He continued to improve in 1998–99 and was many Fulham fans' choice as their player of the season after being instrumental in the side's Championship-winning campaign.

CB

Hayden MULLINS
BORN: 27.3.79 GOALS 1998–99: 5
APPEARANCES 1998–99: 43

Even though he had yet to figure in the first team, Hayden was well-known to many Crystal Palace fans before 1998–99 after he had captained the youth side to the FA Youth Cup final the previous season.

But none could have predicted his meteoric rise from the Palace first XI to the England under-21 team in the space of just nine months. Hayden established himself as a firm favourite of new Eagles boss Terry Venables and was the only player in the side to play more than 40 times in 1998–99.

For the first half of the season, he was played in central midfield, but when Steve Coppell took over team affairs, Hayden was pushed back into his favoured sweeper's role. He put in a series of mature performances in this position and was subsequently voted Player of the Year by Palace fans just days after making his first England under-21 start in the 2–2 draw against Hungary.

Palace turned down a reported £2.5 million bid from a First Division club at the end of the season, with the Eagles insisting he was worth at least £3 million. Hayden undoubtedly has the potential to play in the Premiership and may well get the chance sooner than he could ever have anticipated.

Meteoric rise: Hayden Mullins

Lee HUGHES
**BORN: 22.5.76 GOALS 1998–99: 32
APPEARANCES 1998–99: 41**

As a semi-professional England international, Lee was signed by West Bromwich Albion after scooping the non-league Predator Award for scoring 34 goals in 30 appearances in 1996–97 for Kidderminster Harriers.

This was a dream move for the frontman who had supported Albion as a child. He is a very strong front-runner with a great eye for goal and made his debut on the first day of the 1997–98 season, opening his league scoring account with a brace of goals in a game against Crewe Alexandra. He finished the season as the club's joint-top scorer.

He again came to the forefront in 1998–99 and

looked certain to win a car courtesy of league sponsors Nationwide for scoring 20 goals before Christmas – but fell two goals short.

Despite missing a number of games through injury in the second half of the season, Hughes finished as the country's leading scorer with a total of 32 goals.

But Lee then stunned the Baggies by slapping in a transfer request in March 1999 and it is surely only a matter of time before a Premiership club moves in for him. West Brom reportedly offered to up his wages from £1,500 a week to £7,000 a week in the hope that it might tempt him to stay.

Eye for goal: Lee Hughes

Peter KENNEDY
FB
BORN: 10.9.73 GOALS 1998–99: 7
APPEARANCES 1998–99: 50

Peter started his career at Portadown in Ireland and signed for Notts County in August 1996. He stayed for one season but nearly quit the game after languishing for much of the time in the reserves. Then Watford came to his rescue in July 1997 and he signed for the Londoners in a £130,000 deal.

He is very quick, skilful on the ball and has a fierce left-foot shot. A testament to his attacking play was a hat-trick at Southend and a Goal of the Month against Sheffield Wednesday in the FA Cup in the 1997–98 season.

Despite breaking his leg he finished as the club's leading scorer with 13 goals that season and was chosen in the PFA second division team. He continued to progress in 1998–99 and was a mainstay in Watford's push for promotion. He has one Northern Ireland "B" cap in his collection and will certainly have impressed his international manager Lawrie McMenemy with his performances in 1998–99.

Paul POWELL
FB
BORN: 30.6.78 GOALS 1998–99: 2
APPEARANCES 1998–99: 43

Paul's career at Oxford United started when he signed from trainee in July 1996. It was the local born winger's dream to play for the team he has supported since childhood.

During the 1997–98 season his impressive performances were noticed and he was selected for the England under-21 squad for the Toulon tournament. In 1998–99 he was also called up for the Nationwide under-21 squad to play in Italy.

The left-sided player is versatile and has been played down the wing, at left-back and in midfield. An expert at long throws and crossing the ball, he is vital to any team with height up front. Over the course of the season he was linked with Derby County and is bound to be a target for a top side in the near future.

Seth JOHNSON
M
BORN: 12.3.79 GOALS 1998–99: 5
APPEARANCES 1998–99: 45

A graduate of the Dario Gradi school, Seth signed for Crewe from trainee in July 1996. He made his debut against Preston in the 1996–97 season and appeared as a substitute at Wembley in the play-off final.

He has filled several roles but has settled best in central midfield where his pace, strength and vision make him a potent force. Despite Crewe struggling in the league, his continued personal improvement earned him a call-up into the England under-18 team for whom he scored at Gresty Road.

Johnson is well-known throughout the Nationwide League for his aggressive, physical approach to the game. Many observers feel he is certain to play for England in the future.

He was a long-term target of Derby County manager Jim Smith and, at the end of the season, the Rams broke their transfer record to sign Johnson for £3 million in May 1999.

Curtis WOODHOUSE
BORN: 17.4.80 GOALS 1998–99: 3
APPEARANCES 1998–99: 37

Sheffield–born Curtis signed for United in December 1997. He made his debut while still a trainee, coming on as a substitute against Crewe Alexandra.

He managed to keep his place but was then injured, only returning as a substitute on the last day of the season. He was called into the England under-18 squad in 1997–98 and further international honours are highly likely in forthcoming seasons.

Curtis has moved into the centre of midfield where his strength and vision make him an impressive performer. He came to the fore again in 1998–99 with two excellent performances against Arsenal in the FA Cup and has since been called into the England under-21 squad.

He is comfortable in defence as well as attack and was switched to left-back in the match in Hungary where he did not look out of place.

Matthew ETHERINGTON
BORN: 14.8.81 GOALS 1998–99: 3
APPEARANCES 1998–99: 32

Matthew is still a trainee and was one of the stars of the Peterborough youth team which managed to reach the semi-final stages of the FA Youth Cup in 1997-98.

He became Peterborough's youngest-ever first team player, making his debut against Brentford in the final game of the 1996–97 season. He only played in two matches the following season but his pace and skill have come to the forefront in 1998–99 with several bigger clubs reportedly bidding well in excess of £500,000 for this undoubted star of the future.

Newcastle United, Wimbledon, Tottenham Hotspur and Arsenal are all said to have taken a keen interest in the young winger and Posh boss Barry Fry may struggle to hang on to his prized possession for very much longer.

Eddie HOWE
BORN: 29.11.77 GOALS 1998–99: 5
APPEARANCES 1998–99: 47

Eddie signed from trainee for Bournemouth in July 1996. Despite struggling to get into the first team in his debut season, he forced himself into the side in the 1997–98 campaign, performing so well that he was subsequently voted Player of the Year.

He is strong, skilful, adept in the air, excellent in the tackle and very athletic – ideal pre-requisites for a modern-day centre-back. Eddie was rewarded for his consistent performances by being selected to play in the Toulon tournament for the England under-21 side.

He continued to impress in 1998–99 and, despite the heartache of missing out on the play-offs on the final day of the season, it is only a matter of time before a Premiership club tries to tempt him and his central defensive partner Ian Cox away from the south coast.

Robbie BLAKE
BORN: 4.3.76 GOALS 1998–99: 17
APPEARANCES 1998–99: 40

Robbie began his career at Darlington and, after numerous impressive performances, signed for Bradford City on transfer deadline day 1996–97 for a Quakers club record fee of £300,000.

In his first season he was confined mainly to the substitutes' bench, but he did manage to score five goals in 10 matches. Despite his lack of appearances he signed an extension to his contract designed to keep him at Bradford City until 2001.

His progress continued in 1998–99 when, despite hot competition for places in the City frontline from Isiah Rankin, Dean Windass and Lee Mills, he was close to reaching the 20-goal mark.

He is a strong-running centre-forward and his darting runs and excellent eye for a shooting chance have made him a firm favourite with the fans. He was instrumental in Bradford City's successful promotion push and will have an interesting baptism in the Premiership in the 1999–2000 campaign.

Kieron DYER
BORN: 29.12.78 GOALS 1998–99: 5
APPEARANCES 1998–99: 42

An Ipswich-born lad, Kieron signed full forms for Town in January 1997. He possesses all the attributes needed for the Carling Premiership and was instrumental in Ipswich's challenge to win promotion, which has culminated in play-offs heartbreak for three consecutive seasons.

He has filled several positions, mostly on the right-hand side, where his speed and skill on the ball make him a handful for any left-back. He was selected in the PFA Division One team in the 1997-98 season, also winning his first England under-21 cap against Moldova and an England "B" Cap against Chile.

His progress continued in 1998–99 with a call-up to the full England squad. He continued to impress in Division One and was unsurprisingly the target of a number of Premiership clubs after Town's failed promotion bid.

England call-up: Kieron Dyer

COMPARATIVE TABLES

Debates will inevitably rage about which team is the best, which players are better than others and which referee flourishes the most cards. Now you can settle all those arguments with the definitive guide to the 1998-99 Carling Premiership season. Our comparative tables show how teams compare to each other, how the top 20 players rank in certain categories and who are the top players of the season. This section is divided up to analyse key aspects of the game.

THE TEAMS

All the Premiership teams are compared and contrasted over a number of categories. Find out which team were the best and worst passers, tacklers and defenders, plus which sides have the best and worst disciplinary records.

THE PLAYERS

The top 20 players in each category are compared and contrasted to highlight the best goalscorers, passers, tacklers and goalkeepers, as well as the players with the poorest disciplinary records.

THE INDEX

Who was the best player in each position and who was the most influential player of the season? The Carling Opta Index reveals all.

TEAMS OF THE SEASON

Everybody's favourite pastime with a twist. Carling Opta select their teams of the season based on actual performance in key areas.

REFEREES

An in-depth look at the disciplinary record of the 1998–99 season in terms of the fouls and penalties awarded and yellow and red cards issued by referees.

FA CARLING PREMIERSHIP 1998–99

How did your team rate against the other Carling Premiership sides in key categories? You will find the answer in this section. All 20 teams are featured in each table and are ranked according to a key category which will be explained below each chart.

The tables will show you the main areas of strength and weakness within each team and will go some way to explaining why certain teams were successful and why others struggled over the course of the 1998–99 season.

For example, on page 618 you'll see that Charlton Athletic managed a goals-to-shots ratio of just 9.4% compared with Manchester United's 16.3%. This shows how the Addicks had to attempt nearly twice as many shots to score a goal as the Premiership champions, which is clearly a key factor in the relative success of each team.

You can discover which team scored the most headed goals, which won the most tackles, which earned the most disciplinary points and which side suffered most at the hands of their opponents.

The Devil you know: Nicky Butt puts one over on Sheffield Wednesday's Peter Atherton

There is an explanation beneath each of the charts showing how the particular ranking is calculated.

The most important table of all, of course, is the Premiership league table. Below you will see how all 20 teams finished in the 1998–99 Premiership season, their home and away records and what they achieved.

Manchester United won the title by one point, on the first leg of their successful attempt to land the treble. Arsenal finished second and qualified automatically for the Champions League. Third-placed Chelsea also qualified for the Champions League, but they will enter the competition only if they progress past a qualifying round. If they are eliminated at that stage, they will enter the revamped UEFA Cup.

Leeds United's fourth position secured them a spot in the UEFA Cup alongside Worthington Cup winners Tottenham Hotspur and AXA-sponsored FA Cup runners-up Newcastle United, who qualified because Manchester United entered the Champions League.

West Ham's fifth place secured them a spot in the Inter-Toto Cup and Leicester City missed out on a place in the UEFA Cup in FIFA's Fair Play lottery.

Nottingham Forest were the first side to be relegated when they lost 2–0 to Aston Villa on April 24.

They were joined by Blackburn Rovers after their 37th match – a 0–0 draw at home to Manchester United in the final week of their Premiership campaign – and Charlton Athletic, who finally succumbed on the last day of the season when they lost 1–0 at the Valley to Sheffield Wednesday.

		HOME					AWAY						
	PLD	W	D	L	F	A	W	D	L	F	A	PTS	GD
Man Utd	38	14	4	1	45	18	8	9	2	35	19	79	43
Arsenal	38	14	5	0	34	5	8	7	4	25	12	78	42
Chelsea	38	12	6	1	29	13	8	9	2	28	17	75	27
Leeds Utd	38	12	5	2	32	9	6	8	5	30	25	67	28
West Ham	38	11	3	5	32	26	5	6	8	14	27	57	-7
Aston Villa	38	10	3	6	33	28	5	7	7	18	18	55	5
Liverpool	38	10	5	4	44	24	5	4	10	24	25	54	19
Derby Co	38	8	7	4	22	19	5	6	8	18	26	52	-5
Middlesbro	38	7	9	3	25	18	5	6	8	23	36	51	-6
Leicester	38	7	6	6	25	25	5	7	7	15	21	49	-6
Tottenham	38	7	7	5	28	26	4	7	8	19	24	47	-3
Sheff Wed	38	7	5	7	20	15	6	2	11	21	27	46	-1
Newcastle	38	7	6	6	26	25	4	7	8	22	29	46	-6
Everton	38	6	8	5	22	12	5	2	12	20	35	43	-5
Coventry	38	8	6	5	26	21	3	3	13	13	30	42	-12
Wimbledon	38	7	7	5	22	21	3	5	11	18	42	42	-23
Southampton	38	9	4	6	29	26	2	4	13	8	38	41	-27
Charlton	38	4	7	8	20	20	4	5	10	21	36	36	-15
Blackburn	38	6	5	8	21	24	1	9	9	17	28	35	-14
Nottm For	38	3	7	9	18	31	4	2	13	17	38	30	-34

GOALSCORING

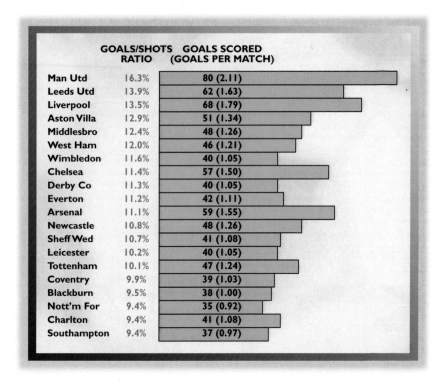

	GOALS/SHOTS RATIO	GOALS SCORED (GOALS PER MATCH)
Man Utd	16.3%	80 (2.11)
Leeds Utd	13.9%	62 (1.63)
Liverpool	13.5%	68 (1.79)
Aston Villa	12.9%	51 (1.34)
Middlesbro	12.4%	48 (1.26)
West Ham	12.0%	46 (1.21)
Wimbledon	11.6%	40 (1.05)
Chelsea	11.4%	57 (1.50)
Derby Co	11.3%	40 (1.05)
Everton	11.2%	42 (1.11)
Arsenal	11.1%	59 (1.55)
Newcastle	10.8%	48 (1.26)
Sheff Wed	10.7%	41 (1.08)
Leicester	10.2%	40 (1.05)
Tottenham	10.1%	47 (1.24)
Coventry	9.9%	39 (1.03)
Blackburn	9.5%	38 (1.00)
Nott'm For	9.4%	35 (0.92)
Charlton	9.4%	41 (1.08)
Southampton	9.4%	37 (0.97)

The 1998–99 season produced fewer goals than any other since the formation of the Premiership. Just 959 goals bulged the back of the net, with 0–0 the most common scoreline during the campaign and 31% of games ending with one goal or less scored.

Manchester United recorded the biggest win – the 8–1 thrashing of Nottingham Forest, which is also a record away victory in the Premiership.

Liverpool recorded the biggest home win, defeating Southampton 7–1, with their neighbours Everton matching the margin of victory when they hammered West Ham 6–0 in their penultimate match.

The Red Devils were by far the top goalscoring machine in the league. Not only did they finish as top scorers with 80 goals, but Alex Ferguson's side also scored with 16.3% of all their shots – a far greater ratio than any of their rivals.

Leeds United had the second-best strike rate at 13.9% ahead of second-top scorers Liverpool. Behind those two came Aston Villa, who would have scored more and finished higher if they could have managed to fire in more shots – only five teams attempted fewer.

Chelsea finished ninth and Arsenal 11th in this table with goals-to-shots ratios of 11.6% and 11.1% respectively, meaning they had to fire in approximately nine attempts to score a goal, compared to Manchester United who only required six to find the net. So, despite attempting more shots than the new champions, Arsenal and Chelsea probably failed to win the title due to a lack of clinical finishing.

Not surprisingly, the four teams who had the biggest problems in front of goal finished in the bottom four of the Premiership table. But, despite having the worst goals-to-shots ratio of the four, Southampton managed to pip their rivals to 17th place and a position of safety.

SHOOTING

	SHOOTING ACCURACY	SHOTS ON TARGET	SHOTS OFF TARGET
Leeds Utd	49.3%	216	222
Man Utd	48.7%	233	245
Leicester	47.2%	175	196
Arsenal	47.1%	247	277
Charlton	47.0%	195	220
Middlesbro	46.8%	178	202
Nott'm For	46.5%	173	199
Wimbledon	45.8%	158	187
Derby Co	45.3%	156	188
Liverpool	45.3%	229	276
Tottenham	45.3%	202	244
Blackburn	45.2%	171	207
Everton	44.8%	168	207
West Ham	44.5%	167	208
Southampton	44.3%	175	220
Newcastle	43.5%	190	247
Aston Villa	42.9%	167	222
Chelsea	42.6%	205	276
Coventry	41.5%	164	231
Sheff Wed	41.3%	158	225

No team in the 1998–99 Premiership fired more than half of their total shots on target. The league's sharpest shooters were Leeds United who were just shy of that figure, with 49.3% of their efforts finding the net or forcing a save.

Just behind Leeds were their great rivals, Manchester United, who managed to get 48.7 per cent of their attempts on target, with only Arsenal managing to fire in a greater total. The Gunners actually attempted the most shots overall and recorded a shooting accuracy of 47.1%, which put them in fourth position.

One of the major surprises was the fact that Charlton's ratio of shots on target was the fifth best, and underlined that the Addicks were perhaps unlucky not to score more goals.

At the other end of the scale, Sheffield Wednesday's accuracy was the poorest. With just 41.3% of their efforts on target and only Derby County managing fewer in total, it was no surprise that the Owls struggled to find the net.

The Rams fired in the fewest of all and that, combined with their defensive stubbornness, may account for the fact that neither Jim Smith's side nor their opponents managed more than two goals in a Premiership game involving the Rams until March.

Aston Villa had the fourth-worst shooting accuracy and this could be the reason for their slump in the second half of the season. Before Christmas, they had one of the best goals-to-shots ratios, meaning they scored plenty of goals from relatively few chances. When the quality degenerated, they were not producing the required number of attempts to force goals.

A bigger shock was Chelsea's poor shooting. With the quality of talent available to Gianluca Vialli, it was surprising that their shooting accuracy was the third worst in the league.

PASSING OVERALL

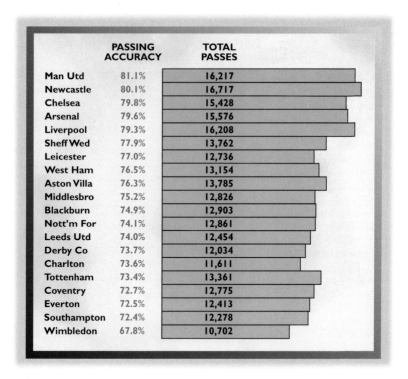

	PASSING ACCURACY	TOTAL PASSES
Man Utd	81.1%	16,217
Newcastle	80.1%	16,717
Chelsea	79.8%	15,428
Arsenal	79.6%	15,576
Liverpool	79.3%	16,208
Sheff Wed	77.9%	13,762
Leicester	77.0%	12,736
West Ham	76.5%	13,154
Aston Villa	76.3%	13,785
Middlesbro	75.2%	12,826
Blackburn	74.9%	12,903
Nott'm For	74.1%	12,861
Leeds Utd	74.0%	12,454
Derby Co	73.7%	12,034
Charlton	73.6%	11,611
Tottenham	73.4%	13,361
Coventry	72.7%	12,775
Everton	72.5%	12,413
Southampton	72.4%	12,278
Wimbledon	67.8%	10,702

The table above clearly indicates the styles of play chosen by the various teams in the FA Carling Premiership. It does not include crosses, corners, clearances or distribution by goalkeepers.

The five teams at the top are known more for their patient passing games, while the teams at the base generally adopt a more direct approach.

Manchester United recorded the top passing accuracy during the 1998–99 season, completing 81.1% of the passes they made. Only Newcastle United attempted more, and the Magpies were the only other team to complete more than four out of every five passes in the league.

Just shy of that mark were three other excellent passing sides in Chelsea, Arsenal and Liverpool. It is noticeable that of these teams only Newcastle regularly played with a recognized target man, but Ruud Gullit also adopted a more inventive style of approach play, involving his midfield players.

Sheffield Wednesday and Leicester City were a little further back, mainly because they used target men and occasionally played the longer ball to the main striker. But they also have players like Wim Jonk and Neil Lennon who like to pass the ball around in midfield, rather than always looking to feed the ball into channels.

At the bottom of the table Wimbledon, Southampton, Everton, Coventry (when Dion Dublin was at Highfield Road) and Tottenham Hotspur all played with target men up front and their pass completion rates consequently suffered as they attempted more percentage balls for which their forwards had to compete.

Wimbledon attempted fewer passes than any other side, which also illustrated a tendency to concede possession more often. Whereas the top five's possession game involved them keeping the ball until an opportunity arose, the Dons were more likely to play the percentage ball and hope that things would break their way.

PASSING IN OPPOSITION HALF

	PASSING ACCURACY	TOTAL PASSES
Newcastle	76.1%	10,186
Man Utd	75.8%	10,098
Chelsea	74.5%	9,487
Arsenal	73.4%	9,169
Liverpool	73.3%	9,827
Leicester	71.6%	7,900
Sheff Wed	71.5%	7,986
Aston Villa	70.7%	8,477
West Ham	70.4%	7,480
Blackburn	69.4%	8,145
Middlesbro	69.3%	7,748
Derby Co	69.3%	7,812
Charlton	69.2%	7,759
Leeds Utd	68.9%	8,029
Tottenham	68.1%	8,285
Nott'm For	67.0%	8,016
Southampton	66.7%	7,552
Coventry	65.7%	7,458
Everton	65.3%	7,597
Wimbledon	65.0%	7,090

Many teams have been accused of passing for passing's sake, but where do the Premiership's elite stand in terms of pass completion where it counts – in the opposition half? Newcastle United topped this particular table in 1998–99, as they did the overall pass completion chart, but it is noticeable that the number of passes that found a team-mate dropped significantly.

Manchester United were second both in pass completion and in the total number of passes that they attempted, with Chelsea, Arsenal and Liverpool filling the same positions as they did in the overall passing table.

Leicester City and Sheffield Wednesday swapped positions, but the difference between their completion rates was marginal and below them there was very little to choose between West Ham and Aston Villa, who also switched places.

At the base of the chart, Wimbledon once again had the worst completion rate, but they also had the smallest differential with their overall passing accuracy of all the Premiership teams. This suggests that other sides tended to play more possession along the back four than the Dons, who preferred to get the ball forward early into attacking positions.

Everton and Coventry each dropped a place lower as Southampton rose above them. All three of these teams completed fewer passes than many of their rivals because of their tendency to look for the big man up front rather than create chances through patient build-up play.

The team whose pass completion rate dropped most significantly compared to the other Premiership sides were Nottingham Forest. They were 12th in the overall pass completion rate table, but fell to 16th when it came to finding team-mates in the opposition half. This inability to keep the ball was central to their failure to create large numbers of scoring chances for their strikers and to achieve better results.

LONG PASSING

	PASSING ACCURACY	LONG PASSES
Arsenal	53.5%	1,815
Chelsea	52.0%	2,095
Man Utd	51.5%	1,765
Newcastle	51.2%	2,016
Liverpool	48.9%	2,012
West Ham	48.7%	1,597
Tottenham	48.5%	1,680
Aston Villa	48.4%	2,105
Leicester	46.6%	1,924
Sheff Wed	46.2%	1,967
Leeds Utd	45.8%	1,697
Middlesbro	45.6%	1,642
Charlton	43.9%	1,766
Coventry	43.7%	2,145
Blackburn	43.6%	1,913
Derby Co	43.3%	1,818
Southampton	41.0%	1,815
Wimbledon	40.7%	1,796
Nott'm For	38.7%	1,851
Everton	37.4%	1,822

The long-ball game appears gradually to be being phased out of the English top flight, but there are still teams which will play the percentage game and work off the scraps from knock-downs. Coventry City made the most long passes, looking for Dion Dublin's head or Darren Huckerby's pace, while West Ham attempted the fewest.

It is noticeable that the teams which have the lowest long pass completion rate in the Premiership all played with big target men and adopted a longer-ball strategy.

Everton had the worst completion rate, which suggests that they had problems in changing their strategy once they had sold Duncan Ferguson. Ibrahima Bakayoko and Nick Barmby would clearly fail to win as much possession in the air and it would not have been until Kevin Campbell arrived that Everton had a viable alternative up front.

Nottingham Forest used Pierre van Hooijdonk in the same way, while Wimbledon's array of strikers thrived on the service they got from deep but could not turn large numbers of passes fired at them into meaningful possession.

Contrast this with the sides at the top of the table and it is easy to see why they have the top pass completion rates. Liverpool have Jamie Redknapp, Newcastle have Dietmar Hamann and Manchester United have David Beckham, all of whom distribute the ball superbly over long distances.

Above them are Chelsea who completed 52% of all their long passes. Frank Leboeuf started many of their attacks from deep positions with his long passes that pinpointed Chelsea's strikers.

Top of the pile are Arsenal, who boast two of the best long passers in the Premiership in Emmanuel Petit and Dennis Bergkamp. Many of Bergkamp's 12 goal assists came from inch-perfect through balls, and Petit's weighted ball over the top for Marc Overmars or Nicolas Anelka was a key feature of Arsenal's attacking play.

SHORT PASSING

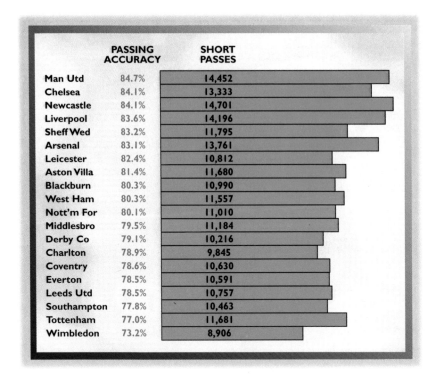

	PASSING ACCURACY	SHORT PASSES
Man Utd	84.7%	14,452
Chelsea	84.1%	13,333
Newcastle	84.1%	14,701
Liverpool	83.6%	14,196
Sheff Wed	83.2%	11,795
Arsenal	83.1%	13,761
Leicester	82.4%	10,812
Aston Villa	81.4%	11,680
Blackburn	80.3%	10,990
West Ham	80.3%	11,557
Nott'm For	80.1%	11,010
Middlesbro	79.5%	11,184
Derby Co	79.1%	10,216
Charlton	78.9%	9,845
Coventry	78.6%	10,630
Everton	78.5%	10,591
Leeds Utd	78.5%	10,757
Southampton	77.8%	10,463
Tottenham	77.0%	11,681
Wimbledon	73.2%	8,906

Eighty-six per cent of the 269,801 passes made during the 1998–99 season were classified as being short passes – that is, under 25 yards in distance. The levels of accuracy are much higher, of course, as they include many passes that are made unchallenged across the back-line as midfield players and forwards jockey for space further up the pitch.

The usual suspects featured at the top of the passing chart in terms of accuracy. Manchester United's slick play saw them complete 84.7 per cent of 14,452 passes. Newcastle attempted more, although their completion rate was lower.

Chelsea and Liverpool are also known for their pass-and-move style and both teams attempted large numbers as they patiently tried to break down packed opposition defences, particularly at home.

At the base of the table are Wimbledon and it is a sign of their disappointing season that they were the only side to complete less than three-quarters of passes under 25 yards. The Dons only attempted 8,906 short passes – almost a thousand fewer than the next-highest total.

Spurs had the next-worst pass completion rate and, with wholesale changes expected at White Hart Lane, expect that figure to improve as George Graham attempts to build a competitive side. Dave Jones will also be concerned at Southampton's poor pass completion rate. Their tendency to concede possession allowed opposition sides to dominate the Saints, particularly away from home where they won just two Premiership games during the campaign.

Perhaps one of the surprises in this table is the pass completion rate of Leeds United. Any side with David Batty would be expected to complete large numbers of short passes, but the youthful exuberance and perhaps inexperience of the Leeds side meant that more than one in five of their passes went astray.

CROSSING

	CROSSING ACCURACY	CROSSES COMPLETED	CROSSES AWAY
Sheff Wed	32.9%	207	423
Southampton	31.9%	251	535
Tottenham	30.6%	280	634
Blackburn	30.5%	239	544
Derby Co	30.1%	177	412
Middlesbro	29.4%	213	512
Liverpool	29.3%	216	520
Aston Villa	29.3%	196	474
West Ham	28.9%	169	415
Leeds Utd	28.8%	176	435
Chelsea	27.6%	261	686
Newcastle	27.4%	216	571
Everton	27.2%	173	463
Wimbledon	27.2%	220	589
Man Utd	27.1%	266	715
Coventry	26.9%	205	557
Charlton	26.2%	214	603
Nott'm For	25.9%	179	511
Leicester	25.0%	215	645
Arsenal	23.6%	152	493

The art of crossing came under much scrutiny during the 1998–99 season with Spurs' David Ginola winning the Player of the Year trophies, Steve Guppy touted as a possible England international and David Beckham being described as the finest crosser in Europe.

Sheffield Wednesday, though, were the most effective crossers. Petter Rudi, Niclas Alexandersson and Andy Hinchcliffe take much of the credit for some fine delivery, but Andy Booth's ability in the air must also be recognized. James Beattie and Egil Ostenstad did much the same for Southampton, getting on the end of the pinpoint crosses from Matt Le Tissier, who even managed to score direct from a corner against Wimbledon.

David Ginola was a constant threat down the left flank for a Spurs side that boasted a plethora of wingers, and with the aerial ability of Les Ferdinand, Steffen Iversen and Chris Armstrong, it is no surprise to see Spurs with the third-best completion rate.

The worst crossers in the Premiership were Arsenal, who were the only side to complete fewer than a quarter of their crosses. Dennis Bergkamp's tendency to drop deep meant that Nicolas Anelka was often isolated in the centre, and in reality neither player appeared keen to score with his head.

Steve Guppy fired in the second-highest number of crosses of any player, only surpassed by David Beckham, but neither of their teams excelled in this area. In Manchester United's case, their completion rate was very badly affected by Ryan Giggs's poor completion rate – only 19 of his 134 crosses in the Premiership campaign found a United player.

United fired in the highest number of crosses, while West Ham attempted the fewest, preferring instead to play their way through to the feet of their nippy forwards Paolo Di Canio, Paul Kitson or Ian Wright.

TACKLING

	TACKLES WON%	TACKLES WON	TACKLES LOST
Charlton	64.5%	713	393
Wimbledon	64.3%	688	382
Chelsea	63.1%	781	457
Everton	62.9%	878	517
Arsenal	62.3%	830	503
Sheff Wed	62.2%	694	421
Derby Co	61.8%	701	434
Coventry	61.7%	710	441
Leeds Utd	61.6%	731	455
Southampton	61.4%	680	428
Liverpool	61.4%	716	451
Man Utd	60.8%	786	507
Newcastle	60.2%	695	460
Blackburn	60.1%	680	452
West Ham	59.9%	654	438
Middlesbro	59.4%	743	508
Aston Villa	58.9%	622	434
Tottenham	57.9%	689	501
Leicester	57.6%	769	565
Nott'm For	57.0%	655	495

Along with goals scored, flying saves and mesmeric skills displayed in the Premiership, the sight of a superbly-executed tackle is always likely to engender a passionate and vocal response from the crowd.

The art of tackling may be indirectly under threat from the law-makers as they rightly attempt to eradicate serious fouls, but the game will be poorer if the superb tackling ability of the likes of Stam and Keane, Adams and Vieira or Desailly and Ferrer are lost to the sport.

Carling Opta's statistics show Charlton were the top tacklers in the Premiership in terms of winning the ball. Alan Curbishley's men regained possession 64.5 per cent of the time as they fought in vain to retain their Premiership status. The top tackler for the Addicks was their tenacious skipper Mark Kinsella.

Following just behind were Wimbledon, their physical game being intimidating to opponents but very fair, as shown by the fact they earned the third-fewest disciplinary points during the season.

Behind them were Chelsea who, despite winning a similar percentage to the Dons, were conversely the league's second-worst sinners in terms of discipline.

In fourth position were Everton, followed closely by Arsenal. These two sides made respectively the highest and second-highest number of successful tackles in the Premiership.

The least successful in the challenge were Nottingham Forest. Just above them were Tottenham Hotspur and Leicester City. The position of these two sides is interesting, as Leicester lost more tackles in total than any other side and Spurs lost the third-highest number, behind Everton. This was despite the presence of Steffen Freund and Tim Sherwood patrolling the Spurs centre-circle and Neil Lennon and Muzzy Izzet doing the same for the Foxes.

DISCIPLINE – FOULS COMMITTED

	DISCIPLINARY POINTS	Fouls committed = 1pt	Yellow card = 3pts	Red card = 6pts
Everton	890	587	91	5
Chelsea	827	548	85	4
Leeds Utd	827	590	77	1
Southampton	825	576	77	3
Blackburn	818	530	80	8
Derby Co	804	540	84	2
Nott'm For	801	510	85	6
Charlton	781	574	63	3
Tottenham	764	539	67	4
West Ham	753	480	81	5
Middlesbro	743	488	81	2
Coventry	731	497	76	1
Arsenal	698	470	62	7
Aston Villa	686	485	63	2
Newcastle	681	504	51	4
Man Utd	676	481	59	3
Liverpool	673	460	65	3
Wimbledon	663	480	59	1
Leicester	653	494	51	1
Sheff Wed	627	456	47	5

KEY: Fouls committed = 1pt Yellow card = 3pts Red card = 6pts

*NB: red cards for Michael Oakes against Blackburn and Richard Rufus against Leeds have been expunged from the record books.

Discipline is always a major talking-point throughout any season, but the 1998–99 campaign produced a whole series of incidents. Accusations of play-acting, Paolo Di Canio's push on referee Paul Alcock, the high number of red cards shown to Arsenal players, the Le Saux/Fowler incident and Ian Wright's visit to referee Rob Harris's dressing room were just some of the lowlights.

You could be forgiven for thinking that Arsenal were the "dirtiest" side in the 1998–99 Premiership, considering the amount of coverage the media gave to their red card count. Yet while their total of seven red cards (10 in all competitions) is hardly something to be proud of, the Gunners finished 13th in the discipline stakes and only two sides committed fewer fouls than Arsene Wenger's side.

Blackburn's red card count received much less attention in the media, but proved even more costly in terms of suspensions to key players which contributed to their eventual relegation.

According to Carling Opta's league of shame, the biggest sinners were Everton. The Toffeemen scrapped their way to safety and earned more yellow cards than any other side. Only Blackburn, Forest and Arsenal saw red more often, and Everton's total of 890 disciplinary points is an issue that Walter Smith may wish to address.

Leeds United committed the most fouls. They finished third in the table, thanks to the fact that they earned fewer red cards than Chelsea, who matched them for total disciplinary points.

The best-behaved side were Sheffield Wednesday, who committed the fewest fouls and earned the fewest yellow cards. Ultimately, the much-maligned Fair Play UEFA Cup lottery went to Leicester City, due to their lower red card count.

DISCIPLINE – FOULS WON

DISCIPLINARY POINTS

Team	Points	Fouls won	Yellow card	Red card
Arsenal	893	566	97	6
Tottenham	882	591	89	4
Everton	844	571	85	3
Leeds Utd	842	518	88	10
Chelsea	841	556	85	5
Charlton	820	547	75	8
Leicester	812	566	76	3
Newcastle	788	560	68	4
Middlesbro	788	551	73	3
Blackburn	766	514	74	5
Coventry	742	520	70	2
Southampton	738	531	65	2
Liverpool	702	486	64	4
Derby Co	688	478	64	3
Sheff Wed	683	515	54	1
Man Utd	671	461	68	1
Aston Villa	666	432	68	5
West Ham	658	478	58	1
Nott'm For	605	446	49	2
Wimbledon	504	402	34	0

KEY: Fouls won = 1pt Yellow card = 3pts Red card = 6pts

*NB: red cards for Michael Oakes against Blackburn and Richard Rufus against Leeds have been included in this table.

In January, when Alex Ferguson labelled Arsenal "belligerent" and "scrappers" in an off-the-record discussion, accusing them of turning matches into pitched battles if things were not going their way, he seemed merely to be confirming what most people were beginning to believe – that Arsenal were a "dirty" side. The comments were made public hot on the heels of Patrick Vieira's sending-off for an elbowing offence against Charlton at the Valley. Arsene Wenger defended his players and claimed that Arsenal were in fact more sinned against than sinners.

Carling Opta statistics support this theory, with Arsenal on the receiving end of more disciplinary points than any other side. This suggests that rather than the Gunners turning games into scraps, their opponents attempted to disrupt the flow of Arsenal's play with over-physical attention. Their opponents earned 97 yellow cards and six reds in matches against the Gunners.

As well as finishing top of the sinners chart, Everton finished third in the Sinned Against table, highlighting the way their games often degenerated into ones that tested the referees' patience.

Tottenham were on the end of the highest number of fouls, and one player in particular came in for some rough treatment. The deft skills of flamboyant Frenchman David Ginola bemused many Premiership defenders and he earned 96 free kicks – more than any other player in the Premiership.

Leeds United were the team that drove opponents to the most serious offences. David O'Leary's young side saw 10 players dismissed against them during the 1998–99 season – four over the course of two games against Harry Redknapp's West Ham United.

GOALS AGAINST

	GOALS CONCEDED	CLEAN SHEETS
Arsenal	17	23
Chelsea	30	15
Leeds Utd	34	15
Man Utd	37	13
Sheff Wed	42	12
Derby Co	45	12
Aston Villa	46	15
Leicester	46	14
Everton	47	14
Liverpool	49	8
Tottenham	50	12
Coventry	51	7
Blackburn	52	10
West Ham	53	16
Middlesbro	54	13
Newcastle	54	7
Charlton	56	11
Wimbledon	63	7
Southampton	64	9
Nott'm For	69	6

Arsenal set a Premiership record by conceding just 17 goals in 38 Premiership matches. Their veteran backline had the best defensive record in Europe and David Seaman will have been delighted at keeping 19 of the Gunners' 23 clean sheets. He was ably backed up by Alex Manninger, who now has 10 clean sheets in 13 Premiership appearances in his Arsenal career and looks set to pick up the gloves once Seaman finally bows out.

This excellent record was not, however, enough to win Arsenal the title. Manchester United's greater firepower proved to be the determining factor, but the Red Devils also recorded the fourth-best defensive performance in the league, conceding less than a goal per game.

The other teams in the Premiership's top four also finished in the top four of the chart for fewest goals conceded, illustrating perfectly the need for a good defence to be able to challenge for the title.

If a team concedes as many goals as Nottingham Forest did, then it is no surprise that they get relegated. Eight of the 69 goals let in by Forest came in one match – a scoreline that was a record Premiership home defeat.

Wimbledon and Southampton can consider themselves very fortunate to have avoided the drop, considering that only Forest conceded more than them.

Charlton conceded the next-highest total and, despite scoring more goals than the Saints, the fact that 13 of their 41 strikes came in three games illustrated their inability to win many close encounters, which contributed to their downfall. Blackburn's defensive record was fairly average. They conceded 52 goals, with seven sides having worse records, and clearly their problems lay at the other end where none of their plethora of strikers could find the net on a regular basis.

WHERE GOALS WERE SCORED

Home

More than three-quarters of all goals were scored from inside the box. But it was interesting to see that only Nottingham Forest scored fewer than Blackburn Rovers in the penalty area and that Rovers scored 33% of their Ewood Park goals from outside the box – a far bigger ratio than any team. Rovers' inability to create good chances close to goal arguably cost them their Premiership place.

Despite the presence of several gifted free kick specialists, a mere 3% of Premiership strikes, or 16 goals, came via direct shots from free kicks. Players were more successful with long-range efforts from open play.

On average nearly one in seven of all the goals scored in the Premiership came from more than 18 yards out, not surprising given that goalkeepers and defences cope better with set plays than unexpected long-distance piledrivers.

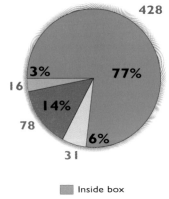

428

3% 77%

16

14%

78

6%

31

- Inside box
- Penalties
- Outside box
- Free kicks

Away

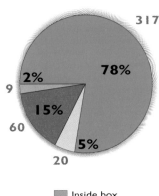

317

2% 78%

9

15%

60

5%

20

- Inside box
- Penalties
- Outside box
- Free kicks

Although the home sides out-scored their visitors by nearly 150 goals in the 1998–99 season, there was very little difference proportionately between home and away teams when it came to where goals were scored.

Premiership clubs were fractionally more successful on opposition territory with long-range efforts than they were on their own turf.

Leeds United were the most dangerous from long range, finding the back of the net seven times, and Aston Villa found they were also relatively successful from distance – their five goals, equating to a ratio of 28% compared to the Premiership average of 15%, meant it was always worthwhile chancing their arm.

Just nine out of 406 goals scored by away sides were direct from free kicks, with 20 more being added from the penalty spot. The visitors earned far fewer penalties – away teams scored just 20, compared with the home sides' 31.

HOW GOALS WERE SCORED

Home

Home sides scored a slightly higher proportion of all their goals from headers than away sides did.

Teams on their own territory registered 105 headed goals in the Premiership, 19% of all strikes. Southampton scored the most with 10 and Arsenal and Charlton Athletic the fewest. Only three sides scored more headed goals on their travels than at home – Blackburn Rovers, Charlton Athletic and Newcastle United.

The most common way of scoring for home sides was with right-footed efforts. Strikers dispatched nearly 300 of all league goals in this way, amounting to 54% of goals scored.

Despite the growing number of players who are comfortable striking the ball with both feet, approximately a quarter of all goals were scored via the left foot, equating to less than half the number of strikes claimed by right-footers.

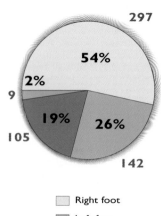

297
54%
2%
9
19%
26%
105
142

- Right foot
- Left foot
- Headers
- Own goals

Away

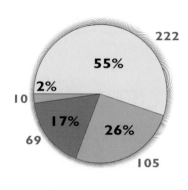

222
55%
2%
10
17%
26%
69
105

- Right foot
- Left foot
- Headers
- Own goals

More than half of all goals scored away were netted with the right foot. That total of 55% was more than double the amount via left-footed shots.

Travelling teams registered 69 headers throughout the 1998–99 season, equating to 17% of all goals scored. Southampton and Newcastle netted six each, but West Ham scored none of their six for the season away from Upton Park.

The number of own-goals scored equates to 2% of the overall total with 19 aberrations being split almost equally between home and away sides. Leicester were the main beneficiaries away and Chelsea at home being gifted two each.

The main conclusion to be drawn from Carling Opta's stats is that, despite individual teams scoring in different ways home and away, the overall picture concerning the way in which goals are scored in the Premiership as a whole does not change.

WHEN GOALS WERE SCORED

Home

Home sides in the 1998–99 Carling Premiership generally enjoyed steadily increasing success up front as their matches progressed.

The number of goals scored in the Premiership rose during each 15-minute period, except in the first quarter of an hour after half-time, as teams readjusted to tactical changes or failed to get going after their half-time cuppa and team talk.

Understandably, the highest proportion of all goals came between the 75th and 90th minutes, with stoppage-time and tiredness allowing sides more opportunities to score. More than one-fifth of the home sides' strikes were in this period.

Just 11% of all Premiership goals were scored in the first 15 minutes as away teams tried to quieten the crowd, but the tempo increased towards half-time, with 17% of all efforts coming in the quarter-hour before the interval.

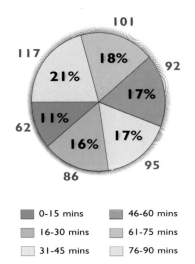

101
117
92
18%
21%
17%
62
11%
17%
16%
86
95

■ 0-15 mins	■ 46-60 mins
■ 16-30 mins	■ 61-75 mins
■ 31-45 mins	■ 76-90 mins

Away

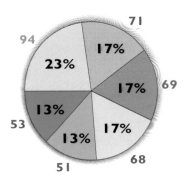

71
94
17%
23%
17%
69
13%
17%
53
13%
17%
68
51

■ 0-15 mins	■ 46-60 mins
■ 16-30 mins	■ 61-75 mins
■ 31-45 mins	■ 76-90 mins

The pattern of when visiting teams scored their goals during the 1998–99 season was very similar to that of home sides.

As well as trying to keep the home side quiet in the first quarter of an hour, the travelling team netted 13% of their goals, two percentage points higher than home sides. The experts were Manchester United who scored six in this period, catching opponents on the counter-attack. United were also good at repeating the trick early in the second half. The Red Devils countered with eight goals right after the break – more than any other side – as teams adjusted to tactical changes made during the half-time break, or were simply caught cold.

The final 15 or so minutes saw away sides at their most dangerous. They scored almost a quarter of all their goals as gaps opened up in tired defences and scoring chances became more frequent.

WHERE GOALS WERE SCORED

Team	Goals Inside Box	Penalties	Direct Free Kicks	Goals Outside Box	GOALS OUTSIDE %
Coventry	35		2	2	5.1%
Man Utd	72	2	3	3	7.5%
Southampton	32		2	3	8.1%
Derby Co	32	4	3	1	10.0%
Charlton	31	5	1	4	12.2%
Sheff Wed	35	1	2	3	12.2%
Tottenham	39		2	6	12.8%
Liverpool	51	7	2	8	14.7%
Wimbledon	34			6	15.0%
Everton	32	3	2	5	16.7%
Arsenal	45		4	10	16.9%
Chelsea	43	3	4	7	19.3%
Nott'm For	26	2	1	6	20.0%
Aston Villa	38	2	1	10	21.6%
Newcastle	31	6	2	9	22.9%
Middlesbro	36	1	2	9	22.9%
Blackburn	27	2		9	23.7%
Leicester	29	1		10	25.0%
West Ham	33	1	1	11	26.1%
Leeds Utd	44	1	1	16	27.4%

KEY: ☐ = Goals Inside Box ☐ = Penalties ☐ = Direct Free Kicks ■ = Goals Outside Box

Goals win titles, as Alex Ferguson's treble-winners proved with a whopping 80 scored in the 1998-99 Carling Premiership – and a glance at Carling Opta's statistics reveals some interesting pointers as to where each of the 959 league goals were scored from.

Coventry City scored nearly 95% of all their goals from close range. Gordon Strachan's side were the second-worst long-range shooters in the Premiership, ahead of Derby County.

The devastating penalty box finishing of Andy Cole, Dwight Yorke and Ole Gunnar Solskjaer meant that 92.5% of all the Red Devils' goals were from inside the area. Even with long-range experts like David Beckham, United preferred to break into the danger zone with their direct and incisive method of attack.

Southampton scored just three goals from outside the box all season, despite the presence of Matt Le Tissier, who did grab one of their long-range efforts direct from a corner. The Saints were one of the more accurate long-range shooting sides in the Premiership and were unlucky not to profit more from their 68 strikes from distance that were on target.

Jimmy Hasselbaink scored seven goals from outside the area, outstripping all his Premiership rivals. David O'Leary's side were the second-most accurate shooters from distance, behind Leicester City, and were one of only three sides to score more than 25% or more of their goals from outside the area. Lee Bowyer and Ian Harte also chipped in with three goals apiece from outside the box.

Newcastle United and Liverpool scored 13 penalties between them. England captain Alan Shearer grabbed six – the highest total in the League – and international team-mate Robbie Fowler claimed four. Wimbledon were the only side not awarded a spot kick all season.

WHERE GOALS WERE CONCEDED

Team	Goals Inside Box	Penalties	Direct Free Kicks	Goals Outside Box	GOALS OUTSIDE %
Nott'm For	57	6	1	5	8.7%
Leeds Utd	28	3		3	8.8%
Coventry	44	1		6	11.8%
Southampton	53	3	2	6	12.5%
Wimbledon	53	2		8	12.7%
Newcastle	41	6		7	13.0%
Liverpool	38	4	2	5	14.3%
Sheff Wed	34	2	1	5	14.3%
Middlesbro	42	4	2	6	14.8%
Leicester	39		1	6	15.2%
Aston Villa	36	1	2	7	19.6%
Blackburn	38	3	2	9	21.2%
Everton	33	4	3	7	21.3%
Man Utd	28	1	2	6	21.6%
Tottenham	38	1	2	9	22.0%
Derby Co	33	2	1	9	22.2%
West Ham	37	4		12	22.6%
Chelsea	22	1	3	4	23.3%
Charlton	39	3	1	13	25.0%
Arsenal	12			5	29.4%

KEY: ☐ = Goals Inside Box, ☐ = Penalties ☐ = Direct Free Kicks ☐ = Goals Outside Box

Carling Opta's end-of-season figures reveal one telling statistic for the team that finished rock-bottom of the 1998–99 Premiership. Even though Mark Crossley managed four penalty saves for his side, Nottingham Forest still conceded 63 goals from inside their 18-yard-box. As a result, Forest's unenviable defensive record was the worst in the League and it was their frailty at the back, particularly in their own area, that sent them straight back down to the Nationwide League.

Nigel Martyn had a magnificent season between the sticks for Leeds United. David O'Leary's side conceded the vast majority of goals from inside their penalty area and this is testament to Martyn's adept handling of long shots.

Arsenal's David Seaman conceded just 11 goals from inside the area, out of his side's total of 12, as the Gunners conceded the lowest ratio of close-range goals in the Premiership. Arsenal's strength in their own area kept them in touch with Manchester United for the Premiership run-in, but one slip in this zone let them down. Jimmy Hasselbaink scored the far-post header that ended Arsenal's title quest.

Chelsea's improved defence conceded the third-lowest proportion of goals inside their own area in the Premiership. Some fine close-range shot-stopping from Ed De Goey kept attackers at bay. Sasa Ilic conceded the third-highest total of goals from outside his area in the Premiership. A quarter of all strikes against Charlton came from more than 18 yards, with Ilic letting 10 strikes past him.

Surprisingly few goals came direct from free kicks and, ironically, it was Chelsea, boasting dead-ball specialist Gianfranco Zola, who conceded the highest proportion of strikes in this manner. Newcastle United – with the Premiership's leading penalty-scorer for 1998–99 Alan Shearer – conceded the highest ratio of penalties.

HOW GOALS WERE SCORED

Team	HEADED GOALS %	Headers	Own Goals	Left Foot	Right Foot
Southampton	35.1%	13		7	17
Tottenham	31.9%	15	2	8	22
Derby Co	25.0%	10	1	9	20
Middlesbro	25.0%	12	1	13	22
Wimbledon	25.0%	10		11	19
Leicester	22.5%	9	2	8	21
Sheff Wed	22.0%	9		12	20
Everton	21.4%	9		14	19
Chelsea	21.1%	12	2	11	32
Newcastle	20.8%	10	1	10	27
Blackburn	18.4%	7	2	10	19
Man Utd	16.3%	13	2	16	49
Coventry	15.4%	6		10	23
Charlton	14.6%	6	2	10	23
West Ham	13.0%	6	1	12	27
Aston Villa	11.8%	6	1	9	35
Liverpool	11.8%	8		22	38
Nott'm For	11.4%	4		15	16
Leeds Utd	9.7%	6	1	20	35
Arsenal	5.1%	3	1	20	35

KEY: ☐ = Headers ☐ = Own Goals ☐ = Left Foot ☐ = Right Foot

Of all statistics relating to the ways in which teams scored the 959 goals in the 1998–99 Carling Premiership, perhaps the most surprising of all relates to the league runners-up, Arsenal.

Arsene Wenger's side scored just three headers in 38 matches, the fewest in the League. However, neither Nicolas Anelka nor Dennis Bergkamp are natural headers of the ball. Along with Arsenal, only Leeds United failed to net at least 10% of all goals via headers, relying instead on the shooting prowess of players such as Jimmy Hasselbaink and Lee Bowyer.

At the other end of the scale were Tottenham Hotspur. Sol Campbell scored five times with his head, as Spurs themselves grabbed 15 headers in all. This represented nearly a third of all their League goals during 1998–99, easily above the Premiership average of 18%, but it was still not the highest proportion of headed goals for a League side.

That honour goes to Southampton, who scored 13 of their 37 goals via headers, representing 35.1% of all their Premiership goals.

Premiership champions Manchester United scored roughly one in six of their goals with headers. David Beckham, with 14 goal assists to his name, supplied much of the ammunition for these goals from out wide.

Aston Villa scored 68.6% of all their goals with the right boot, a higher ratio than any other Premiership side. With Alan Thompson being the only naturally left-sided goalscorer at the club, it is clear why the majority of the Midlands' club's goals are scored with the right foot.

Conversely, Liverpool scored the highest number of goals with the left boot in the Premiership, mainly thanks to Robbie Fowler and Patrik Berger.

HOW GOALS WERE CONCEDED

Team	HEADED GOALS %	Headers	Own Goals	Left Foot	Right Foot
Arsenal	29.4%	5		3	9
Liverpool	26.5%	13	2	8	26
Southampton	21.9%	14	3	15	32
Blackburn	21.2%	11		16	25
West Ham	20.8%	11	1	17	24
Leeds United	20.6%	7		10	17
Middlesbro	20.4%	11	1	14	28
Derby	20.0%	9		13	23
Tottenham	20.0%	10		10	30
Leicester	19.6%	9	1	12	24
Everton	19.1%	9	1	11	26
Wimbledon	19.0%	12	3	12	36
Man Utd	18.9%	7		8	22
Aston Villa	17.4%	8	3	15	20
Nott'm For	15.9%	11		17	41
Charlton	14.3%	8	2	22	24
Sheff Wed	14.3%	6		7	29
Coventry	13.7%	7		16	28
Newcastle	7.4%	4	1	13	36
Chelsea	6.7%	2	1	8	19

KEY: = Headers = Own Goals = Left Foot = Right Foot

Carling Opta's statistics concerning how goals were conceded appear to add weight to certain popular theories, but also reveal some interesting contradictions about particular sides' apparent strengths.

Despite scoring the second-highest total of goals in the Premiership, Liverpool's poor defensive record ensured that they were not realistic title-challengers. Part of their problem was an inability to deal with high balls, reflected in the fact they conceded 13 headed goals. The Reds were one of just two teams to concede more than 25% of all goals from headers.

Arsenal's veteran defence was easily the tightest in the league but they conceded the highest proportion of headed goals – nearly 30% – in the Premiership. This appears surprising given the presence of Tony Adams, Steve Bould and Martin Keown, but this figure may be misleading, given that they only let in five headers, the third-lowest total in the league.

Chelsea have generally been believed to struggle with the aerial threat of the opposition but they proved the doubters wrong. Despite Dion Dublin appearing to confirm the theory on the opening day in Coventry's 2–1 victory, Marcel Desailly and Frank Leboeuf, along with England under-21 star Michael Duberry, restricted opposition forwards to just two headed goals all season. The ratio of 6.7% of all goals conceded by Chelsea was the lowest in the league, and a vast improvement on the previous season.

Sheffield Wednesday leaked the highest proportion of goals in the Premiership from right-footed shots, but Charlton were susceptible to efforts from left-footers and let in 22 such efforts, nearly 40% of all goals conceded.

TIME GOALS WERE SCORED

Team	1ST HALF GOALS%	0–15mins	16–30mins	31–45mins	46–60mins	61–75mins	76–90mins	2ND HALF GOALS%
Charlton	31.7%	5	4	4	4	13	11	68.1%
Tottenham	31.9%	4	7	4	8	13	11	67.9%
Coventry	33.4%	4	8	1	8	12	6	66.5%
Sheff Wed	36.5%	5	5	5	8	6	12	63.2%
Man Utd	37.4%	7	10	13	19	14	17	62.4%
Wimbledon	37.5%	6	4	5	5	8	12	62.2%
Southampton	37.7%	4	4	6	4	10	9	61.9%
Aston Villa	38.9%	8	1	11	11	10	10	60.6%
Nott'm For	39.8%	4	5	5	10	4	7	59.8%
Blackburn	44.5%	6	6	5	6	11	4	55.1%
Derby Co	45.0%	6	8	4	10	3	9	54.8%
Leeds Utd	46.6%	5	10	14	8	11	14	53.1%
Chelsea	47.3%	8	10	9	10	5	15	52.4%
Everton	47.4%	7	5	8	6	9	7	52.2%
Leicester	47.1%	3	5	11	3	7	11	52.2%
Middlesbro	47.7%	4	8	11	7	6	12	51.8%
Liverpool	49.8%	7	11	16	8	12	14	49.9%
West Ham	49.9%	8	9	6	7	9	7	49.8%
Newcastle	51.9%	8	8	9	8	5	10	47.7%
Arsenal	52.3%	6	9	16	11	4	13	47.3%

Legend: 0–15mins, 16–30mins, 31–45mins, 46–60mins, 61–75mins, 76–90mins

As matches progressed during the 1998–99 Carling Premiership, defences tired and lost concentration. Attackers were able to exploit gaps at the back and a higher proportion of goals were scored in the latter stages of matches.

Manchester United's epic 1999 European Cup triumph rested on two late goals and in the Premiership, Alex Ferguson's side grabbed more goals than any other team in the final 15 minutes. Ole Gunnar Solskjaer helped United bag 17 strikes between the 76th minute and the final whistle. But this was not United's most successful spell. In the 30 minutes either side of half-time, the Red Devils scored 32 times, the highest total in the league, equating to 40% of all their league goals. This gives weight to the theory that United players fear Fergie's wrath. Clearly they put in an extra effort before the interval, to appease their manager, or after the break,

in response to his team talks.

Coventry were at the opposite end of the goalscoring scale between 30 and 45 minutes. They netted only 13 times in the first half during the 1998–99 campaign, equating to one third of their league goals.

Charlton struggled as much as the Sky Blues did before the interval, also with just 13 goals in this period. This represented only 31.7% of their league haul, the lowest ratio for first-half goals of any Premiership side.

Newcastle United and Arsenal were the only two sides in the Premiership to score more goals in the first half than they did after the break. However, the Magpies conceded more strikes before half-time than they scored. Arsenal struck 31 first-half goals, the second-highest total in the league, but managed three fewer after the interval. Their inability to finish teams off arguably cost them the title.

TIME GOALS WERE CONCEDED

Team	1st Half Goals%	0–15 mins	16–30 mins	31–45 mins	46–60 mins	61–75 mins	76–90 mins	2nd Half Goals%
Arsenal	17.7%	1	1	1	1	6	7	81.9%
Leeds Utd	29.4%	4	3	3	6	9	9	70.4%
Charlton	35.6%	7	4	9	13	11	12	64.2%
Coventry	37.1%	2	8	9	10	10	12	62.6%
Southampton	37.4%	8	6	10	13	13	14	62.4%
Nott'm For	37.6%	8	8	10	16	12	15	62.2%
West Ham	39.6%	7	6	8	2	13	17	60.1%
Leicester	41.1%	5	6	8	9	7	11	58.5%
Everton	42.6%	9	8	3	9	9	9	57.3%
Middlesbro	42.5%	6	7	10	7	10	14	57.2%
Aston Villa	43.3%	7	6	7	7	11	8	56.4%
Chelsea	43.0%	3	3	7	3	5	9	56.2%
Liverpool	44.9%	7	9	6	10	6	11	54.9%
Man Utd	45.7%	5	5	7	5	7	8	53.8%
Wimbledon	47.5%	8	13	9	18	8	7	52.3%
Tottenham	47.7%	6	5	13	8	7	11	51.8%
Derby Co	48.7%	6	8	8	8	8	7	50.9%
Newcastle	53.5%	5	12	12	6	8	11	46.1%
Blackburn	55.5%	4	12	13	6	6	11	44.0%
Sheff Wed	56.8%	7	7	10	4	6	8	42.6%

Key: 0–15mins · 16–30mins · 31–45mins · 46–60mins · 61–75mins · 76–90mins

The vast majority of Carling Premiership teams conceded more goals in the latter stages of matches than they did in the first 45 minutes, as concentration waned and players tired approaching the final whistle.

Arsenal provided their Premiership rivals with a textbook example of how to defend in the first half, conceding just three goals in total all season in the opening period. On only two occasions did they go in at half-time trailing the opposition. However, the Gunners were left to rue the goals they leaked in the final 30 minutes.

Leeds were also solid in the first 45 minutes, conceding just 10 goals during this period throughout the 1998–99 campaign. David O'Leary's side showed signs of tiring in the final third of the match, though, letting in more than half of all goals after the hour mark.

Charlton and Nottingham Forest had difficulty containing their opposition in the second half, especially just after the break. Charlton conceded 13 goals between the 45th and 60th minutes, but managed to regain some of their composure in the latter stages, although they still leaked crucial goals.

Forest conceded the most goals in the Premiership for the opening 15 minutes of the second half. A further 27 strikes followed in the last 30 minutes of Premiership fixtures.

Fellow-strugglers Blackburn conceded the second-highest proportion of first-half goals in the Premiership, too often leaving themselves with a mountain to climb after the break. Blackburn steeled the defence in the second half but still conceded more goals after the interval than they scored, as they failed to repair the early damage that had already been done.

THE PLAYERS

The top scorer is easy enough for anyone to monitor — but who is the top tackler, the best passer, the best crosser or the best shot-stopper? Which players have the best and worst disciplinary records in the League?

The answers to these and many more questions are contained in this section — and only Carling Opta can provide this information because of the unique way in which they monitor every single touch of the ball.

But it isn't just quantity that counts — it's quality too. So, although many of the categories are sorted on total number of successful outcomes, you can also see percentage completion rates to judge for yourself how good players really are.

The bar charts show several pieces of information. For example, in the chart that shows which player had the most shots in total on page 642, you will also be able to see the player who had the most shots on target, plus the figure shown alongside the bars shows how accurate their shooting was.

There is an explanation beneath each of the charts showing how the ranking is calculated and how to access the information.

The Golden Boot was won by Michael Owen, despite his season being cut short through injury. For the second season running, he scored 18 Premiership goals to win the award and Liverpool will be hoping that he comes back fighting fit for the 1999–2000 season after his long injury lay-off.

Just falling short of the youngster's total were Jimmy Floyd Hasselbaink, who inspired Leeds United to their best finish since they won the title in 1992, and Dion Dublin, who revelled in his move to Aston Villa until an injury affected his contribution to their season.

Pace invader: Michael Owen was the winner of the Golden Boot for 1998–99

GOALSCORING

GOALS/SHOTS RATIO

Player	Ratio	Headers	Shots
Michael Owen	21.2%		18
Dwight Yorke	26.1%	4	14
J F Hasselbaink	17.0%	1	17
Andy Cole	20.5%	1	16
Nicolas Anelka	17.9%		17
Hamilton Ricard	18.3%	4	11
Robbie Fowler	20.9%	3	11
Alan Shearer	19.7%	2	12
Julian Joachim	27.5%		14
Dion Dublin	12.5%	4	10
Gianfranco Zola	17.8%	3	10
Ole Solskjaer	40.0%	2	10
Dennis Bergkamp	14.8%		12
Gustavo Poyet	17.2%	6	5
Tore Andre Flo	14.7%	2	8
Tony Cottee	25.6%	3	7
Jason Euell	15.4%		10
Noel Whelan	14.5%	1	9
Marcus Gayle	16.1%	4	6
Kevin Campbell	47.4%	1	8

■ = HEADERS
□ = SHOTS

For the second season in succession, the race for Premiership goals ended in a three-way tie. Michael Owen was awarded the Golden Boot ahead of Dwight Yorke and Jimmy Floyd Hasselbaink because he scored his goals in less time – but he was not the deadliest of the three.

That award went to Dwight Yorke, who bagged a goal with approximately one out of every four efforts. Surprisingly, Yorke also scored more headed goals than Hasselbaink, who took a greater number of attempts to hit the back of the net.

Everton's Kevin Campbell demonstrated the greatest economy in the top 20 scorers. He bagged a goal with just over 47% of his attempts, a figure even higher than that of Ole Gunnar Solskjaer, who boosted his goals-to-shots ratio with a four-goal salvo at Nottingham Forest.

The Manchester United man's fantastic feat was one of 12 hat-tricks scored in the Premiership. Robbie Fowler and Owen were the only players to bag two three-goal hauls. In all, nine of the 12 hat-tricks were scored by the top 20 scorers.

Very few of the top 20 scored a significant amount with their heads. Gustavo Poyet led the way, netting six of his 11 goals with headers, but even players such as Dion Dublin, Tore Andre Flo and Noel Whelan, who are well-known for their ability in the air, scored the majority of their goals from shots.

The Premiership's two most precocious strikers, Michael Owen and Nicolas Anelka, scored all their goals with their feet. Worryingly for Arsenal, their other main striker Dennis Bergkamp also failed to score with any headers in the league.

Manchester United and Chelsea provided more players in the list than any other club – three each. The champions' achievement is the greater, though, as their players (Yorke, Cole and Solskjaer) scored 47 goals between them.

MINUTES PER GOAL

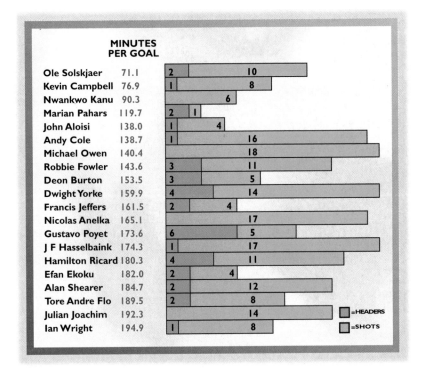

	MINUTES PER GOAL	Headers	Shots
Ole Solskjaer	71.1	2	10
Kevin Campbell	76.9	1	8
Nwankwo Kanu	90.3		6
Marian Pahars	119.7	2	1
John Aloisi	138.0	1	4
Andy Cole	138.7	1	16
Michael Owen	140.4		18
Robbie Fowler	143.6	3	11
Deon Burton	153.5	3	5
Dwight Yorke	159.9	4	14
Francis Jeffers	161.5	2	4
Nicolas Anelka	165.1		17
Gustavo Poyet	173.6	6	5
J F Hasselbaink	174.3	1	17
Hamilton Ricard	180.3	4	11
Efan Ekoku	182.0	2	4
Alan Shearer	184.7	2	12
Tore Andre Flo	189.5	2	8
Julian Joachim	192.3		14
Ian Wright	194.9	1	8

■ = HEADERS
□ = SHOTS

Michael Owen took the 1998–99 Golden Boot on strike rate, scoring his 18 goals in a shorter space of time than either Dwight Yorke or Jimmy Floyd Hasselbaink. Owen was not the Premiership's most prolific scorer, though – that award went to Ole Gunnar Solskjaer of Manchester United. At one goal every 71.1 minutes, super-sub Solskjaer's strike rate was the fastest in the Premiership – yet he still could not get a regular place in Alex Ferguson's starting line-up!

Three players who made late but dramatic entrances on to the Premiership stage follow closely behind Solskjaer at the top of the list. Everton's loan-signing Kevin Campbell scored his goals at the rate of one every 76.9 minutes, while Nigerian Nwankwo Kanu and Latvian Marian Pahars's trigger-happy displays provided a much-needed shot in the arm for both Arsenal and Southampton at either end of the Premiership table.

Coventry City's John Aloisi is a surprise entry at number five. The Australian striker failed to earn a regular place in the Sky Blues' starting line-up following his transfer from Portsmouth, but he still managed to score his five goals at a faster rate than Manchester United's Andy Cole!

There is good news for cash-strapped Everton in the top 20, with Francis Jeffers managing a goal every 161.5 minutes. If the former youth teamer and fellow-front man Kevin Campbell keep up the same strike rate in the 1999–2000, season the Merseyside giants should have a far more comfortable campaign.

Newcastle's Alan Shearer also makes the list, but his average of a goal every 184.7 minutes was slightly misleading. Six of the England captain's 14 goals came from penalties in 1998–99. His strike rate from open play was less impressive, at an average of just one goal for every 323.3 minutes he played.

SHOOTING

SHOOTING ACCURACY

Player	Accuracy	Shots on Target	Shots off Target
Dion Dublin	40.2%	45	67
J F Hasselbaink	52.8%	56	50
Nicolas Anelka	53.7%	51	44
Michael Owen	57.6%	49	36
Andy Cole	60.2%	50	33
Hamilton Ricard	48.8%	40	42
Chris Armstrong	51.2%	42	40
Dennis Bergkamp	58.0%	47	34
Marc Overmars	56.3%	45	35
Benito Carbone	45.5%	35	42
Jamie Redknapp	40.0%	30	45
Emile Heskey	42.7%	32	43
Neil Redfearn	37.0%	27	46
Harry Kewell	47.9%	35	38
Gianfranco Zola	63.0%	46	27
Alan Shearer	59.2%	42	29
Frank Lampard	49.3%	34	35
Noel Whelan	50.7%	35	34
Dwight Yorke	53.6%	37	32
Paulo Wanchope	53.6%	37	32

■ SHOTS ON TARGET

■ SHOTS OFF TARGET

Dion Dublin had more goal attempts than any other Premiership player in 1998–99, yet only one other player in the top of the shots chart saw a greater percentage of their efforts fly wide.

Dublin managed a total of 112 shots, six more than his nearest rival Jimmy Floyd Hasselbaink, but the Dutchman finished with 56 shots on target – the most in the Premiership.

Nicolas Anelka completed the top three. He was supplied with a steady stream of chances by his team-mates and finished the season with a higher accuracy rating than the top two.

Chelsea's Gianfranco Zola was the most accurate striker, testing goalkeepers with 63% of his shots. The Italian star was closely followed by Andy Cole, who managed to keep 60.2% of his efforts on target – a fact that might raise a few eyebrows among those who claim that accuracy is not his strong point.

Another fact that emerges from the table is that shots do not always equal goals. Derby manager Jim Smith commented that his Costa Rican striker Paulo Wanchope "scored 10 goals and missed another 200".

While the facts prove that, like Wanchope, Smith was a little wide of the mark, there is no doubt that Wanchope does not have as good a record in front of goal as Dwight Yorke, who had an identical number of shots but converted more into goals.

In all, nine of the players managed fewer than 10 goals – a high proportion. Frank Lampard was the lowest scorer, with just five goals in the Premiership, and he is joined in the top 20 by two other central midfielders – Jamie Redknapp and Neil Redfearn. All three were regular free kick- takers for their respective clubs in 1998–99 and this explains their presence in the list.

Neil Redfearn was the only player from the three relegated sides to make the top 20 – again illustrating that lack of fire-power cost the strugglers dearly.

GOAL CREATORS

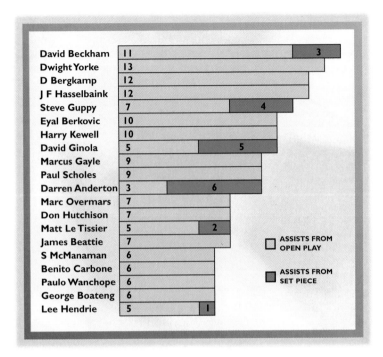

Player	Assists from open play	Assists from set piece
David Beckham	11	3
Dwight Yorke	13	
D Bergkamp	12	
J F Hasselbaink	12	
Steve Guppy	7	4
Eyal Berkovic	10	
Harry Kewell	10	
David Ginola	5	5
Marcus Gayle	9	
Paul Scholes	9	
Darren Anderton	3	6
Marc Overmars	7	
Don Hutchison	7	
Matt Le Tissier	5	2
James Beattie	7	
S McManaman	6	
Benito Carbone	6	
Paulo Wanchope	6	
George Boateng	6	
Lee Hendrie	5	1

ASSISTS FROM OPEN PLAY

ASSISTS FROM SET PIECE

Manchester United scored a phenomenal 80 goals. As good as Alex Ferguson's strikers were, however, the Red Devils could not have achieved such a high total without the creative skills of two men.

Between them, David Beckham and Dwight Yorke created 27 goals with assists – 34% of all United's goals.

Beckham finished as the Premiership's leading goal-provider. The majority of his 14 assists came from open play, illustrating his skill on the right flank.

The majority of Yorke's assists were for Andy Cole. The £12.75 million signing brought out the best in Cole, helping his strike partner to 17 goals in the Premiership. All of Yorke's 13 assists came from open play, more than anyone else.

The leading providers from set-pieces played for Tottenham Hotspur. George Graham has always produced teams which are capable of scoring from dead-ball situations and between them Darren Anderton and David Ginola delivered 11 assists from free kicks or corners.

Surprisingly, only eight of the top 20 players spent the majority of their season on the flanks. Although crossing is still an important feature of the English game, more teams are looking to central areas to create goalscoring chances.

Dennis Bergkamp finished third in the list, while Eyal Berkovic and Paul Scholes also provided a high number of chances from the "hole" behind the front players.

Everton and Southampton struggled for goals in 1998–99, but will have been grateful for the creative talents of Don Hutchison and Matt Le Tissier, who both feature in the top 20. Southampton also owe a debt to their player of the season, James Beattie. An excellent target man, he provided team-mates with seven assists from open play.

Amazingly, Chelsea have no players in the list. Dennis Wise was the Blues' top provider, setting up five goals, but in general Gianluca Vialli's side spread their assists around the side.

PASSING

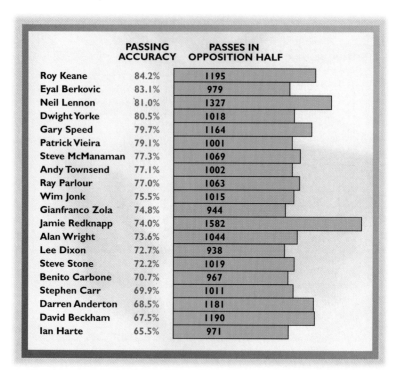

	PASSING ACCURACY	PASSES IN OPPOSITION HALF
Roy Keane	84.2%	1195
Eyal Berkovic	83.1%	979
Neil Lennon	81.0%	1327
Dwight Yorke	80.5%	1018
Gary Speed	79.7%	1164
Patrick Vieira	79.1%	1001
Steve McManaman	77.3%	1069
Andy Townsend	77.1%	1002
Ray Parlour	77.0%	1063
Wim Jonk	75.5%	1015
Gianfranco Zola	74.8%	944
Jamie Redknapp	74.0%	1582
Alan Wright	73.6%	1044
Lee Dixon	72.7%	938
Steve Stone	72.2%	1019
Benito Carbone	70.7%	967
Stephen Carr	69.9%	1011
Darren Anderton	68.5%	1181
David Beckham	67.5%	1190
Ian Harte	65.5%	971

The men in the middle monopolize Carling Opta's passing top 20. Roy Keane led the way in the Manchester United engine room, completing 84.2% of his passes in the opposition half – and in all, 14 of the top 20 are midfielders.

Jamie Redknapp made the most passes in the opposition half. He was also the most prolific passer overall, but Keane and Leicester midfielder Neil Lennon made more successful passes than the Liverpool man.

Eyal Berkovic attempted fewer passes than any other player in the top 10, but still finished second because he completed a high percentage. The Israeli international is one of the more creative players in the list and did well to find a team-mate with 83.1% of his passes in the opposition half.

Dwight Yorke's outstanding link play was a major feature of Manchester United's season and he was one of only three strikers to make the list. Gianfranco Zola and Benito Carbone both played a similar role to Yorke, but although their pass completion rates were exceptionally high for front men, neither measures up to Yorke's completion rate of 80.5% in the opposition half.

Aston Villa wing-back Alan Wright spent more time than any other defender in the opposition half, attempting more than 1,000 passes. He was marginally more accurate than Arsenal's Lee Dixon. There were also places for Tottenham's energetic right-back Stephen Carr and Ian Harte of Leeds United. No centre-backs made the list.

Newcastle United, who made more passes than any other Premiership club, provide just one player in the top 20 – Gary Speed. The lack of a settled side at St James's Park meant that, although the team made a lot of passes as a whole, very few individuals qualified for the list.

CROSSING

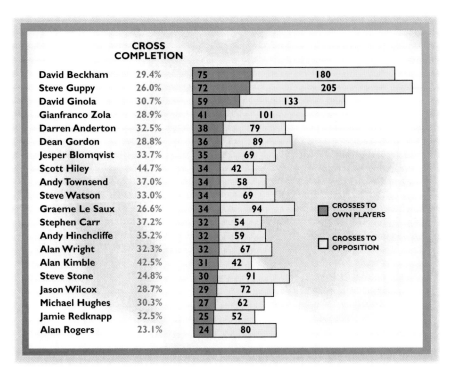

CROSS COMPLETION

Player	Completion	Crosses to own players	Crosses to opposition
David Beckham	29.4%	75	180
Steve Guppy	26.0%	72	205
David Ginola	30.7%	59	133
Gianfranco Zola	28.9%	41	101
Darren Anderton	32.5%	38	79
Dean Gordon	28.8%	36	89
Jesper Blomqvist	33.7%	35	69
Scott Hiley	44.7%	34	42
Andy Townsend	37.0%	34	58
Steve Watson	33.0%	34	69
Graeme Le Saux	26.6%	34	94
Stephen Carr	37.2%	32	54
Andy Hinchcliffe	35.2%	32	59
Alan Wright	32.3%	32	67
Alan Kimble	42.5%	31	42
Steve Stone	24.8%	30	91
Jason Wilcox	28.7%	29	72
Michael Hughes	30.3%	27	62
Jamie Redknapp	32.5%	25	52
Alan Rogers	23.1%	24	80

Manchester United's David Beckham was the top crosser of the ball in the Premiership. Debate still rages about Beckham's best position, but there is no doubt that in 1998–99 he was at his most dangerous when used in a wide-right role for club and country.

Beckham delivered 75 crosses to a team-mate from open play in 1998–99, three more than his nearest challenger, Leicester's Steve Guppy, and 17 more than third-placed David Ginola.

Beckham, Guppy and Ginola were also the only players in the top 20 to reach double figures for assists – further proof if it were needed that they were the best wide men in 1998–99.

But although the top three were some way ahead of their rivals in terms of both the total and the most successful numbers of crosses, they did not finish with the most accurate cross completion rates.

Remarkably, that honour went to Southampton's Scott Hiley with a completion rate of 44.7%. Hiley delivered the eighth-highest total of successful crosses overall, but is the only player in the top 20 without a Premiership goal assist to his name.

One of the most interesting features of the list is the absence of Arsenal players. Despite finishing second in the Premiership, Arsene Wenger's side were among the worst crossers of the ball in the top flight and are one of eight sides who do not have a player in the top 20; Leeds are another notable absentee.

Seventeen of the top 20 play in wide positions, two are central midfielders and only one – Gianfranco Zola – is a striker. The fact that every single player in the list fell below the 50% mark and only one of the top three completed more than 30% of their centres illustrates the difficulty of consistently delivering a good, accurate cross.

DRIBBLING

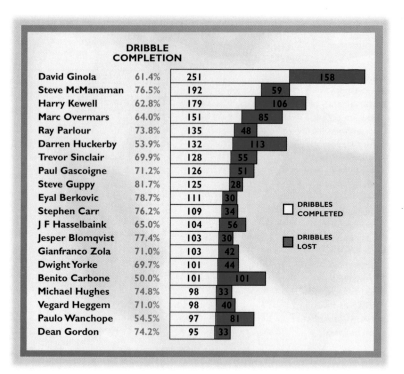

DRIBBLE COMPLETION

Player	%	Dribbles Completed	Dribbles Lost
David Ginola	61.4%	251	158
Steve McManaman	76.5%	192	59
Harry Kewell	62.8%	179	106
Marc Overmars	64.0%	151	85
Ray Parlour	73.8%	135	48
Darren Huckerby	53.9%	132	113
Trevor Sinclair	69.9%	128	55
Paul Gascoigne	71.2%	126	51
Steve Guppy	81.7%	125	28
Eyal Berkovic	78.7%	111	30
Stephen Carr	76.2%	109	34
J F Hasselbaink	65.0%	104	56
Jesper Blomqvist	77.4%	103	30
Gianfranco Zola	71.0%	103	42
Dwight Yorke	69.7%	101	44
Benito Carbone	50.0%	101	101
Michael Hughes	74.8%	98	33
Vegard Heggem	71.0%	98	40
Paulo Wanchope	54.5%	97	81
Dean Gordon	74.2%	95	33

□ DRIBBLES COMPLETED

■ DRIBBLES LOST

The ability to take on an opponent and beat him with skill is something that sets the Premiership's best apart from the rest and grabs the headlines. No one demonstrated this more effectively in 1998–99 than the PFA and Sportswriters' Player of the Year, David Ginola.

The Frenchman delighted crowds with his skill on the ball, finishing the season as the runaway leader of Carling Opta's dribbling chart.

Ginola attempted to take the ball past an opponent on 409 occasions – the most in the Premiership. Although his success rate of 61.4% was some way short of the best in the division, he successfully beat an opponent 251 times, and no other player even came near that figure.

Steve McManaman was generally thought to have had a bad season, but he still managed to finish second in the list and completed a greater percentage of his dribbles than Ginola.

Leicester City's Steve Guppy completed the highest percentage of his dribbles – 81.7% in all – while Sheffield Wednesday's Benito Carbone was arguably the most erratic player in the top 20, retaining and losing possession an equal number of times.

Carbone is one of a number of players in the list who also racked up a high number of offsides. The Sheffield Wednesday man finished with the second-largest total of offsides in the division. Coventry's Darren Huckerby, who is at number six in the list, was pulled up by referees' assistants on 98 occasions, the most in the top flight.

The presence of Harry Kewell at number three in the chart highlights his claim to be Leeds United's most exciting young player. And although Paul Gascoigne did not enjoy the most fruitful of seasons with Middlesbrough, his presence at number eight confirms his status as one of the great entertainers in the history of English football.

TACKLING

	TACKLES WON%	TACKLES WON	TACKLES LOST
Patrick Vieira	69.9%	146	63
Olivier Dacourt	65.7%	142	74
Robbie Mustoe	64.2%	120	67
Sol Campbell	74.1%	117	41
Emerson Thome	67.8%	116	55
Neil Lennon	60.1%	116	77
Mark Kinsella	67.5%	110	53
Jaap Stam	74.3%	107	37
Paul Ince	68.7%	101	46
Frank Leboeuf	69.8%	97	42
Lee Carsley	65.5%	97	51
Roy Keane	69.6%	96	42
Don Hutchison	61.7%	95	59
Marcel Desailly	75.8%	94	30
Chris Perry	69.9%	93	40
Lucas Radebe	61.6%	93	58
George Boateng	60.8%	90	58
Andy Townsend	65.9%	89	46
Nigel Winterburn	60.5%	89	58
Gary Speed	57.4%	89	66

It's a French one-two at the top of the tackling chart. Patrick Vieira has been breaking up opposition attacks for almost three seasons at Highbury but 1998–99 saw his fellow-countryman Olivier Dacourt push him very close for the title of the Premiership's top tackler. Dacourt actually attempted more challenges than Vieira, but the Arsenal man won the ball more often and hangs on to top spot for the second successive campaign.

While all the pre-season attention centred on Paul Gascoigne in the Middlesbrough midfield, it was his team-mate Robbie Mustoe who really shone for the Teessiders. Mustoe came in at number three in the chart after making almost 200 tackles. Sol Campbell was the toughest-tackling defender in the Premiership, winning 117 of his 158 challenges. The Tottenham captain is one of three players in the list who won more than 70% of all attempted challenges.

Chelsea's imposing defender Marcel Desailly was officially the most successful tackler. His partner in the heart of the Blues defence, Frank Leboeuf, is also in the top 20, which helps to explain why Chelsea finished the season with the second-best defensive record in the Premiership.

Manchester United's Jaap Stam was the second-most successful tackler. After a shaky start to his Old Trafford career, he rarely came off second best in any challenge he made.

The fact that the three most successful tacklers are all central defenders was in line with Premiership averages. Defenders won around 66% of all attempted tackles, while midfielders succeeded 63% of the time.

The top 20 is entirely made up of central midfielders and defenders, and it comes as little surprise that strikers were less successful. The highest-rated striker, Jason Euell, won 66 challenges, mainly due to the fact that he played a large part of the season in midfield.

THE DIRTIEST

	DISCIPLINARY POINTS	Fouls	Yellow	Red
Mark Hughes	125	83	14	
John Hartson	121	106	5	
Paulo Wanchope	117	84	9	1
Patrick Vieira	112	85	7	1
Olivier Dacourt	111	66	13	1
Neil Redfearn	110	83	9	
Andy Booth	99	78	7	
Steve Stone	97	73	6	1
J F Hasselbaink	97	73	8	
Chris Sutton	93	60	9	1
Dion Dublin	92	77	5	
Lee Bowyer	90	66	8	
Don Hutchison	89	56	9	1
David Unsworth	89	65	8	
Matt Elliott	89	68	7	
Darryl Powell	86	62	8	
Emile Heskey	85	76	3	
Alfie Haaland	84	54	10	
Alan Shearer	84	66	6	
Ian Wright	83	53	8	1

KEY: Fouls = 1pt   Yellow card = 3pts   Red card = 6pts

Although defenders tend to commit the most high-profile fouls, the Carling Opta discipline table reveals that they are not the Premiership's most persistent offenders. Surprisingly, strikers commit the majority of misdemeanors. Front men make up half of the discipline table, midfielders account for eight of the line-up and only two defenders make the top 20.

Players were awarded one point for every foul they committed, three points for every booking they received and six points each time they were dismissed. On that basis, Southampton's competitive veteran Mark Hughes was the most indisciplined player in the Premiership. Hughes amassed 42 of his points from yellow cards. He was cautioned 14 times in the Premiership but never sent off.

John Hartson committed the most fouls in the top flight – 106 in total while at West Ham United and Wimbledon – enough to take him into second place.

Arsenal's Patrick Vieira was the worst-behaved midfielder, picking up 112 disciplinary points – one more than Olivier Dacourt. While it is no coincidence that these two also topped the tackling chart (see page 647), it is interesting that they are the only players who feature in both tables.

In all there were five players who received their marching orders more than once in the Premiership – Emmanuel Petit, Martin Keown, Nikos Dabizas, Richard Rufus and Tim Sherwood. None of them picked up enough disciplinary points to make the table.

Leeds United and Everton committed more fouls than any other Premiership team, so it is no surprise that they also provide the players' top 20 with three names apiece. More surprising is the fact that Arsenal and Blackburn, who were widely regarded as the two most indisciplined teams because of the large number of red cards which they accrued, supplied just one player each.

THE CLEANEST

MINUTES/ DISCIPLINARY POINT

Player	Minutes	Fouls (1pt)	Yellow cards (3pts)
Dean Blackwell	265.7	9	
Roland Nilsson	236.8	10	
N Alexandersson	174.0	15	
Marc Overmars	169.7	12	2
Gianfranco Zola	146.2	17	1
Stephen Glass	131.9	12	
Alan Wright	121.6	19	3
Jeff Kenna	117.9	14	1
Wayne Bridge	117.3	12	
Michael Owen	114.9	19	1
Dave Watson	111.2	17	
P Kaamark	109.4	13	
Scott Hiley	107.9	16	2
Chris Powell	106.6	26	2
Didier Domi	105.0	9	1
Des Walker	104.5	25	2
Robbie Earle	104.3	24	2
Steve Guppy	103.6	24	3
Dean Gordon	103.6	24	3
Lucas Radebe	101.5	19	2

KEY: ☐ Fouls = 1pt ☐ Yellow card = 3pts

While the Premiership's most indisciplined players grabbed all the headlines in 1998–99, the good guys tended to go unnoticed. Carling Opta compiled a top 20 of the Premiership's cleanest players based on average minutes played per disciplinary point. As with all the player tables in this book, individuals had to have played 1,200 minutes to qualify. On that basis, Wimbledon's Dean Blackwell was the cleanest player in the Premiership, earning a disciplinary point at the rate of just one every 265.7 minutes.

Considering that Wimbledon's defence came under such pressure, Blackwell's record of just nine fouls conceded was excellent. The fact that he is joined in the top 20 by team-mate Robbie Earle – and that Wimbledon supply just one player in the top 20 most indisciplined players (see the table on the left) – proves that the Dons were one of the cleanest teams in the Premiership.

Thirteen of the top 20 are defenders and there are no central midfielders in the list. The majority of the action (and therefore the fouls) was concentrated in the middle third of the pitch, so this is hardly surprising. This explains the presence of so many wide players. But the fact only two recognized strikers made the list suggests referees are often giving the benefit of the doubt to defenders.

Seven of the 20 featured did not even pick up a caution. That put them in an elite 31% of Premiership players. Among those who played more than 1,200 minutes the achievement is even greater: only 22 out of 279 players who played regular first-team football in 1998-99 were not shown a card, a total of just 8%.

Manchester United do not have a single player in the list. In all, the top 10 teams in the Premiership provided just 40% of the top 20 players suggesting that, to prosper, a club needs at least a few players who are prepared to sin to win.

GOALS CONCEDED

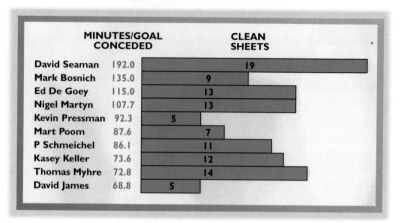

	MINUTES/GOAL CONCEDED	CLEAN SHEETS
David Seaman	192.0	19
Mark Bosnich	135.0	9
Ed De Goey	115.0	13
Nigel Martyn	107.7	13
Kevin Pressman	92.3	5
Mart Poom	87.6	7
P Schmeichel	86.1	11
Kasey Keller	73.6	12
Thomas Myhre	72.8	14
David James	68.8	5

Arsenal's famed defensive unit set a club and Premiership record of just 17 goals conceded in 1998–99, beating their own previous best of 18 goals conceded in 1990–91. David Seaman kept the ball out of the net for an average of 235 minutes at a time, keeping 19 clean sheets in the process, and conceded more than one goal in only one Premiership match in the 1998–99 season.

The next best record was held by Mark Bosnich, who kept the ball out of his net for an average of 135 minutes at a time, and it was noticeable how much he was missed through injury as Villa's title challenge faltered.

SAVES

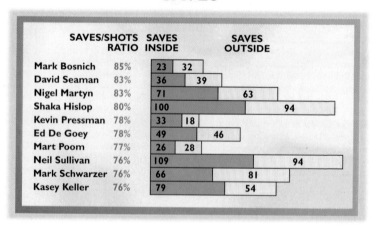

	SAVES/SHOTS RATIO	SAVES INSIDE	SAVES OUTSIDE
Mark Bosnich	85%	23	32
David Seaman	83%	36	39
Nigel Martyn	83%	71	63
Shaka Hislop	80%	100	94
Kevin Pressman	78%	33	18
Ed De Goey	78%	49	46
Mart Poom	77%	26	28
Neil Sullivan	76%	109	94
Mark Schwarzer	76%	66	81
Kasey Keller	76%	79	54

Top of the stops was Mark Bosnich. The Australian 'keeper made the headlines for his determination to see out his contract and negotiate a move to a bigger club, but when he was between the sticks, no one in the Premiership was more adept at keeping the ball out of the net.

David Seaman was not too far behind, but the Gunners' number one had much less work to do than most 'keepers thanks to the protection he received from the best back four in the business.

Nigel Martyn matched Seaman's saves-to-shots ratio, but had almost twice as many saves to make. But it was Neil Sullivan who made the most saves of all.

CATCHING

	CATCH SUCCESS	BALLS CAUGHT	BALLS PUNCHED
Mart Poom	99%	78	13
Ed De Goey	99%	76	36
Michael Oakes	99%	69	11
Dave Beasant	98%	57	10
Kevin Pressman	98%	45	11
Neil Sullivan	98%	125	15
Kasey Keller	97%	89	15
Nigel Martyn	97%	85	26
Mark Bosnich	96%	43	11
Mark Schwarzer	95%	100	29

The surprise name at the top of the list of best catchers is Derby's Mart Poom. Despite being the understudy to Russell Hoult for most of the season, the Estonian 'keeper totally dominated his box. Ed De Goey also performed the same task for Chelsea very reliably, though he was more likely to punch the ball clear than many of his opposite numbers.

Michael Oakes filled in reasonably well for Mark Bosnich until an unsettled defence in front of him put great pressure on his shoulders. His catching was superb, though, and like Poom and De Goey he managed to claim virtually every cross he came for.

DISTRIBUTION

	DISTRIBUTION SUCCESS	THROWS/ SHORT KICKS	LONG KICKS
Dave Beasant	61%	391	472
Ian Walker	59%	292	566
Shay Given	59%	338	611
Ed De Goey	56%	292	602
Pavel Srnicek	55%	222	481
Shaka Hislop	55%	397	855
Mark Schwarzer	55%	290	794
Kevin Pressman	55%	134	297
Mart Poom	54%	125	306
David James	54%	289	464

Dave Beasant must have felt as if he was sitting in a coconut shy at times, given the poor quality of Forest's defending. But when he was not beating away shots or picking the ball out of the net, he showed great accuracy in his distribution. Only Ian Walker and Shay Given come close to his 61% completion rate, though all three 'keepers benefited from having target men to aim for.

This factor is perfectly illustrated by the fact that both Pavel Srnicek and Kevin Pressman feature in the top 10 and Sheffield Wednesday's Andy Booth won more balls in the air than all but two Premiership players.

OPTA PLAYER OF THE SEASON

Hamann for last season: Newcastle United's Dietmar Hamann

Who is the best player in the Carling Premiership? Who is the best player in his particular position? Who makes the biggest contribution match-by-match? This section gives Carling Opta's answers to those questions.

David Ginola was voted Player of the Year by the players and football writers. Young Player of the Year was Nicolas Anelka. But do these choices match up to the facts and figures? The Carling Opta Index monitors each touch of the ball by every player and offers a more objective view of the contribution all players make on the pitch.

You may find the results surprising. The Index is only a guide to player performance and deals with the data in as objective a way as possible. Carling Opta do not make subjective judgements on the quality of goals or the importance of winning strikes or the fact that successful dribbles by David Ginola are usually more pleasing on the eye than those by Tony Adams.

Players earn points for everything they contribute on the pitch, not just the eye-catching skills, goalscoring feats or spectacular saves. There is a subjective element, though, as these points are calculated on the basis of the judgement of Don Howe and Carling Opta analysts'

opinions as to the value of those actions.

An Index Score is calculated by summing the total number of points earned by each player across the course of the season, dividing that total by the number of minutes they played and then mulitplying it by 90 (minutes) to give each player an average game score. For a more in-depth explanation see page 12.

The average scores are then used to rank players against others who play in the same position and the top 20 are featured in the Carling Opta Index.

The players who feature in the Index played for more than 1,200 minutes in total and completed at least 75 minutes in more than 15 Premiership matches.

Carling Opta's player of the 1998–99 season was Dietmar Hamann of Newcastle United. He found the net four times in the Premiership, three of those from long range, and completed a superb 86 per cent of his passes. He won 50 per cent of the challenges he made, but will hope to improve on his disciplinary record of one red and five yellow cards. His performances earned him an average of 1,119 points per game, and it was clear Newcastle missed his influence in the second half of the FA Cup final after his half-time substitution.

GOALKEEPERS

PLAYER NAME	TEAM	OPTA POINTS
Shaka Hislop	West Ham	990
Nigel Martyn	Leeds Utd	902
Neil Sullivan	Wimbledon	896
Pavel Srnicek	Sheff Wed	797
Mark Schwarzer	Middlesbro	784
David Seaman	Arsenal	763
Kasey Keller	Leicester	700
Ed De Goey	Chelsea	699
Thomas Myhre	Everton	669
Paul Jones	Southampton	639
Russell Hoult	Derby Co	632
John Filan	Blackburn	630
Peter Schmeichel	Man Utd	617
Magnus Hedman	Coventry	595
Dave Beasant	Nott'm For	548
Shay Given	Newcastle	547
David James	Liverpool	537
Sasa Ilic	Charlton	518
Ian Walker	Tottenham	493
Michael Oakes	Aston Villa	453

The top-rated goalkeeper in the Carling Opta Index was West Ham's Shaka Hislop. This may come as a surprise to many people, bearing in mind that West Ham conceded four or more goals in a game on eight occasions.

But more in-depth analysis of his displays shows that the former Newcastle United 'keeper made more saves than any goalkeeper other than Neil Sullivan and also kept 15 clean sheets – a total that only Arsenal's David Seaman surpassed.

England's number one helped his side break a club record in the 1998–99 season, as the Gunners conceded just 17 goals in 38 matches – one fewer than their 1990–91 tally – which smashed the previous Premiership record. Seaman finished sixth in the Index, despite keeping 19 clean sheets, mainly because he had a lot less work to do thanks to the famous Arsenal back four.

The Arsenal 'keeper could be under threat from Nigel Martyn for his England spot, if the Cornishman keeps up his form. The Leeds 'keeper finished second in the Index in a season that saw David O'Leary take the first steps to building a top-quality side.

Neil Sullivan spent a difficult season in the Wimbledon goal as the Dons slumped following Joe Kinnear's heart attack, but he attracted the attention of some of the top clubs. Sullivan made more saves than any other 'keeper, but also conceded more goals than anyone else.

Peter Schmeichel's poor start to the season, and the fact that he had less work to do because of the quality of Manchester United's team, means that the great Dane featured in only 13th position.

Ian Walker and Michael Oakes languished at the base of the top 20 after recording two of the lowest saves-to-shots ratios in the Premiership.

DEFENDERS

PLAYER NAME	TEAM	OPTA POINTS
Sol Campbell	Tottenham	1103
Frank Leboeuf	Chelsea	1102
Jaap Stam	Man Utd	1079
Tony Adams	Arsenal	1063
Lucas Radebe	Leeds Utd	1033
Nikos Dabizas	Newcastle	1031
Paul Williams	Coventry	1001
Nigel Winterburn	Arsenal	983
Matt Elliott	Leicester	969
Emerson Thome	Sheff Wed	961
Steve Walsh	Leicester City	957
Ian Harte	Leeds Utd	947
Roland Nilsson	Coventry	944
Ugo Ehiogu	Aston Villa	939
Gary Pallister	Middlesbro	908
Graeme Le Saux	Chelsea	905
Marco Materazzi	Everton	901
Marcel Desailly	Chelsea	900
Gareth Southgate	Aston Villa	897
Danny Mills	Charlton	889

In a season that saw the fewest-ever goals since the Premiership was formed and the lowest number of goals per game, the performances of some of the top defenders were outstanding. Heading the Index was Sol Campbell of Tottenham Hotspur. When George Graham took over at White Hart Lane, he stated that the England centre-back would become his new colossus, and it was not long before Campbell was doing just what George Graham's old colossus did so often – picking up a trophy.

The old colossus was of course Tony Adams, who had a very solid season for Arsenal but would have been very disappointed not to have won any trophies after a brave defence of the Double. The top Gunner finished fourth in the Index, behind Frenchman Frank Leboeuf and Dutchman Jaap Stam.

Leboeuf was superb in the Chelsea defence, not only for his defensive qualities but also for his excellent long passing. Jaap Stam got off to a slow start and Nicolas Anelka in particular gave him two rude introductions to English football, but once he settled into the side the £10.5 million defender showed what a tremendous asset he will be for United.

Chelsea had the second-best defensive record in the Premiership and Leboeuf is joined in the top 20 by Graeme Le Saux and Marcel Desailly. Emerson Thome, Nikos Dabizas and Paul Williams all had excellent seasons in struggling sides, but the Index scoring system recognises the contribution they made.

Aston Villa had one of the best defensive records for the first half of the season: both Ugo Ehiogu and Gareth Southgate featured in the top 20.

MIDFIELDERS

PLAYER NAME	TEAM	OPTA POINTS
Dietmar Hamann	Newcastle	1119
Emmanuel Petit	Arsenal	1084
Roy Keane	Man Utd	1035
Patrick Vieira	Arsenal	1029
Mark Kinsella	Charlton	1023
Paul Ince	Liverpool	1018
Jamie Redknapp	Liverpool	1001
Nicky Butt	Man Utd	985
Neil Lennon	Leicester	980
Olivier Dacourt	Everton	979
Roberto Di Matteo	Chelsea	965
Don Hutchison	Everton	962
John Collins	Everton	901
Paul Gascoigne	Middlesbro	900
Frank Lampard	West Ham	888
Lee Bowyer	Leeds Utd	885
Gary Speed	Newcastle	875
Muzzy Izzet	Leicester	866
Dennis Wise	Chelsea	860
George Boateng	Coventry	842

The midfielders ranking is the only one of the five Indexes where an Englishman does not feature in the top five players in the 1998–99 Premiership. It is a worrying sign for English football which was further highlighted when the French outclassed England's best at Wembley in February.

Carling Opta's top-rated player in the 1998–99 season was Dietmar Hamann. His combination of tenacious tackling, precise passing and vicious shooting have troubled many sides during the campaign. Ruud Gullit must look to build around this midfield general or risk losing him to another top European club.

Arsenal's midfield axis of Emmanuel Petit and Patrick Vieira is arguably the best in the Premiership. Petit's vision and long passing, combined with Vieira's athleticism and ability to read the game, are hard to combat. In addition, their ferocious tackling is at times frightening, although it occasionally leads to trouble with the officials.

Manchester United missed Roy Keane for most of the 1997–98 campaign and it certainly showed as they ended up empty-handed. The 1998–99 season was a different story. The Red Devils' captain picked up the Premiership trophy and was rated the third-best midfielder in the league: Nicky Butt proved his worth, too.

One of the most under-rated players in 1998–99 was Mark Kinsella. The Charlton skipper was outstanding, and was ranked ahead of the likes of Paul Ince and Jamie Redknapp. Youngsters Frank Lampard and Lee Bowyer proved they are on the way up, while the feisty partnership of Neil Lennon and Muzzy Izzet also featured in the top 20.

ATTACKING MIDFIELDERS

PLAYER NAME	TEAM	OPTA POINTS
Gustavo Poyet	Chelsea	1103
Patrick Berger	Liverpool	1061
David Ginola	Tottenham	994
David Beckham	Man Utd	986
Hassan Kachloul	Southampton	953
Steve McManaman	Liverpool	951
Paul Scholes	Man Utd	926
Marc Overmars	Arsenal	921
Ray Parlour	Arsenal	907
Darren Anderton	Tottenham	906
Harry Kewell	Leeds Utd	886
Matt Le Tissier	Southampton	871
Robert Lee	Newcastle	870
Jason Wilcox	Blackburn	868
Eyal Berkovic	West Ham	867
Ryan Giggs	Man Utd	844
Trevor Sinclair	West Ham	842
Dan Petrescu	Chelsea	829
Steve Stone	Aston Villa	807
Chris Bart-Williams	Nott'm For	800

This category is probably filled with the most talented players currently plying their trade in the Premiership. The fact that the likes of Ryan Giggs, Matt Le Tissier and Harry Kewell do not even make the top 10 shows the quality of players in this position.

Top of the tree in 1998–99 was Chelsea's Gustavo Poyet. The Uruguayan has suffered two injury-hit seasons with the Blues, but he grabbed 11 goals as Chelsea finished third and secured a Champions League qualifying round place.

Patrik Berger had a superb season for Liverpool, grabbing seven goals with some excellent long-range efforts. Behind him come probably the two best crossers in the league. David Ginola walked away with the individual awards as Player and Footballer of the Year, while David Beckham added even more winners'

medals to his collection.

Hassan Kachloul could qualify as one of the bargains of the season. The Moroccan scored five goals to help Southampton escape a seemingly-inexorable drop into the Nationwide Division One.

Steve McManaman had a reasonable, rather than a brilliant, season but still rated higher than Paul Scholes, Marc Overmars and Ray Parlour who all showed superb bursts of form, without being able to maintain the quality level.

Matt Le Tissier survived yet another relegation battle; Darren Anderton had a relatively injury-free season; and Ryan Giggs had one or two excellent moments, although his league form was disappointing.

In fact, the errant Welshman found a United team-mate with just 19 of the 134 crosses he made in the season.

STRIKERS

PLAYER NAME	TEAM	OPTA POINTS
Dennis Bergkamp	Arsenal	1079
Dwight Yorke	Man Utd	1017
Gianfranco Zola	Chelsea	1013
Michael Owen	Liverpool	1002
Andy Cole	Man Utd	978
Nicolas Anelka	Arsenal	964
Duncan Ferguson	Newcastle	948
Robbie Fowler	Liverpool	939
Tore Andre Flo	Chelsea	910
Jimmy F Hasselbaink	Leeds Utd	902
Benito Carbone	Sheff Wed	900
Dion Dublin	Aston Villa	869
Jason Euell	Wimbledon	863
Alan Shearer	Newcastle	838
Steffen Iversen	Tottenham	825
Paolo Di Canio	West Ham	811
Pierre van Hooijdonk	Nott'm For	800
Noel Whelan	Coventry	778
Dougie Freedman	Nott'm For	777
Paulo Wanchope	Derby Co	772

Goals were harder to come by in 1998–99 than in any other Premiership season. For the second year in a row, the Golden Boot winner finished with just 18 goals – a far cry from the 34 plundered by Alan Shearer in 1994–95.

The top three strikers are creative players rather than out-and-out goalscorers. Dennis Bergkamp matched his 12 goals with another 12 that he created for team-mates, whereas Dwight Yorke surpassed the elegant Dutchman, laying on 13 while grabbing 18 for himself.

Gianfranco Zola rediscovered the form of 1996–97, but worried Chelsea fans will hope that he does not go through with his decision to retire too soon.

Michael Owen had the first real setback of his career with the hamstring injury that brought an early end to his 1998–99 season. But the youngster consoled himself with the Golden Boot for scoring 18 goals in fewer games than Yorke or Jimmy Floyd Hasselbaink, who finished with the same total.

Andy Cole finished the season just one goal behind, but is now pushing for a regular England place. Nicolas Anelka made as many headlines for his off-the-field comments and behaviour as he did on the pitch for the Gunners and looks set to depart at some point, leaving Arsenal with a healthier bank balance.

Tore Andre Flo looked far more effective as a substitute than when he had to lead the starting attack, although he had his moments such as in the 3–0 demolition of Aston Villa at Villa Park.

Robbie Fowler featured, despite easing his way back after serious injury, and Dion Dublin dropped away after a fantastic start to his Villa career.

TEAMS OF THE SEASON

BEST PLAYERS

Every week in most newspapers there is a Team of the Week picked by the journalists or their suggestion to the England manager about which players should feature in the latest squad.

In every pub, school and office, a favourite pastime is picking an England team, an all-star team or a World XI.

This section is a definitive guide to the teams of the 1998–99 season. There are the top scorers, the most accurate marksmen, the best passers and the best and worst-behaved players. Plus, there is an England team, a "foreign" team and an under-21 team all based on the Carling Opta Index.

Each team is laid out in a 4–4–2 formation graphic like the one shown below. Each player is selected based on being the best (or worst) in his particular position and will be shown as indicated. For example, Warren Barton will always feature as a right-back, Paul Gascoigne as a central midfield player and, despite his utility role, Marcel Desailly will appear as a centre-back. In other words, each player will feature in the position he would normally play.

TEAM OF THE SEASON

Many of the season's awards are based on subjective opinion, and journalists and fans select their top players based on the performances that they actually see. The voting for the Player of the Year award is actually carried out well before the season ends.

Carling Opta, however, have analysed every touch of the ball, by every player, in every match; and with their unique Index system, developed in conjunction with Don Howe, they have calculated the top player in each position, based on performances across the entire 1998–99 season.

The top 'keeper is Shaka Hislop, who made more saves than any other stopper except Neil Sullivan and kept more clean sheets than any bar David Seaman.

Consistent is the word to describe the two full-backs Nigel Winterburn and Roland Nilsson – both of whom had their season interrupted by serious injury.

In the heart of defence are Sol Campbell – the top-scoring defender, who also made the most headed clearances – and Frenchman Frank Leboeuf, who completed 307 long passes, 73 more than his closest rival.

World Cup-winner Emmanuel Petit had a tremendous 1998–99 and Arsenal missed the stylish midfielder when he was injured or suspended. Alongside him is Carling Opta's player of the season – the influential Dietmar Hamann. Despite Newcastle's struggles, the German midfielder looks set to become one of the top players in the Premiership.

There can be no doubt about the two wide players – yet there is no sign of David Ginola. David Beckham created more goals than any other player in the league and Gustavo Poyet was the top-scoring midfield player, whose injury adversely affected Chelsea's title tilt.

And in attack Dennis Bergkamp, the 1997–98 Player of the Season, recovered from his World Cup blues to finish with 12 goals and as many assists. Alongside him is Dwight Yorke: the man with the broad smile enchanted the United faithful and drove United to Treble glory with 29 goals in all competitions.

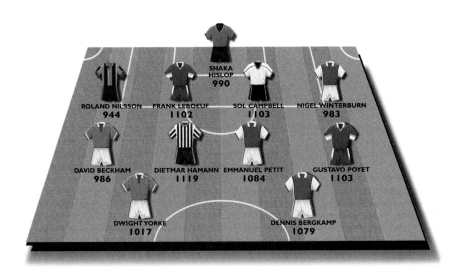

SHAKA HISLOP 990

ROLAND NILSSON 944

FRANK LEBOEUF 1102

SOL CAMPBELL 1103

NIGEL WINTERBURN 983

DAVID BECKHAM 986

DIETMAR HAMANN 1119

EMMANUEL PETIT 1084

GUSTAVO POYET 1103

DWIGHT YORKE 1017

DENNIS BERGKAMP 1079

GOALSCORERS

Goals win games and the teams that spread the goals around are usually the ones that come out with the trophies over the course of the season. Manchester United had 18 different names on the scoresheet across all competitions during the 1998–99 season – more than any other side – and only Chelsea matched the Red Devils for players into double figures for Premiership goals.

The top scorers were Michael Owen, Dwight Yorke and Jimmy Floyd Hasselbaink who netted 18 Premiership goals each. The first two make up Carling Opta's front pairing because they netted that tally in fewer games than the Dutch striker, with Owen winning the Golden Boot on that basis.

Gustavo Poyet was the top-scoring midfield player, with six of his 11 goals coming via headers – more than any other Premiership player. Lee Bowyer found his scoring touch from midfield too, firing in nine goals, while alongside him Jamie Redknapp netted eight times, including a couple of long-range scorchers.

On the right side of the Carling Opta team are two players who can alternate between right-back and right-midfield. Trevor Sinclair found the net seven times in West Ham colours, also filling in on occasions as an emergency striker. Nolberto Solano showed some excellent form, but struggled with the pace and intensity of the English game. Nonetheless, he still weighed in with six Premiership goals.

At left-back, there were three defenders with four goals apiece but Alan Rogers scored his in fewer appearances and was Nottingham Forest's third top scorer.

Sol Campbell scored three times as many goals in the 1998–99 season as he had previously bagged in his entire league career. Five of his six goals were from headers, whereas Horacio Carbonari's five were all from shots.

Finally, the goalkeeper position for this team is allocated to David Seaman who was the best at preventing goals from being scored, conceding just 15 in 32 appearances and keeping 19 clean sheets.

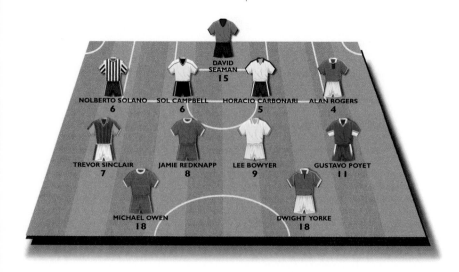

BEST PERFORMANCES

There were some outstanding individual performances in 1998–99 and this team shows the best in each position according to the Carling Opta Index system. The top performance was Michael Owen's destruction of Newcastle at Anfield. The youngster scored twice, struck the post and hit the target eight times from 11 attempts. His partner Robbie Fowler recorded the second best display as Liverpool beat Aston Villa away. He scored a hat-trick from five goal attempts, all of which were on target.

From wide positions, the two top displays came on the same day. Bjarne Goldbaek netted twice from seven attempts at Nottingham Forest and Petter Rudi scored twice from five shots at Ewood Park as the Owls beat Blackburn Rovers 4–1.

Arsenal's Emmanuel Petit scored, completed 45 passes and made 12 tackles as Arsenal beat Forest on the opening day and the other central midfield slot is filled by Nicky Butt who was inspirational in the 3–2 win at home to Leeds United. He scored once from five attempts, made 11 tackles and completed 30 passes.

The full-back slots are filled by Patrick Colleter of Southampton and Albert Ferrer of Chelsea. The Frenchman scored and made 23 clearances at home against Charlton, while the Spanish right-back completed 50 passes and made seven tackles against Aston Villa.

Emerson Thome is the only player in this team to feature in a losing side. But he was magnificent in the 2–1 defeat at home to Wimbledon, scoring Sheffield Wednesday's goal and making 21 clearances and eight tackles.

Only one match supplied two players for this team – the goalless north London derby at Highbury. Sol Campbell was superb, making 17 tackles and 30 clearances, while team-mate Espen Baardsen made 11 saves and nine catches as Spurs kept a rampant Arsenal at bay.

In all, seven of the team put in their award-winning performances away from home a fact that makes their achievements even more impressive.

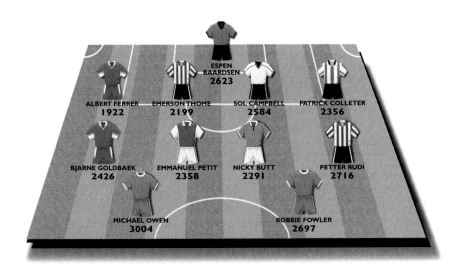

ESPEN BAARDSEN 2623

ALBERT FERRER 1922 EMERSON THOME 2199 SOL CAMPBELL 2584 PATRICK COLLETER 2356

BJARNE GOLDBAEK 2426 EMMANUEL PETIT 2358 NICKY BUTT 2291 PETTER RUDI 2716

MICHAEL OWEN 3004 ROBBIE FOWLER 2697

BEST PASSING

If you have read the Team Passing table on page 620, it will come as no surprise that the bulk of the team of top passers in the 1998–99 Premiership come from Newcastle United and Manchester United.

The Magpies made more passes than any other side, with the Red Devils making just 500 fewer, while Alex Ferguson's team were the most accurate passers with 81.1% of their passes reaching their intended target compared with second-placed Newcastle's 80.1%. The FA Cup finalists contribute seven players in total to the team, which is made up of the most accurate passers who have attempted at least 300 passes during the season.

Dwight Yorke was the most accurate of all strikers with 81% of his passes finding a team-mate. He is joined by midfielder Roy Keane, who completed a superb 88%, and defenders Henning Berg and Phil Neville with 91% and 86% respectively.

Newcastle supply the right-hand flank, with Laurent Charvet completing 84% and

Rob Lee 86% of all their passes and, in central midfield, Dietmar Hamann who also found a black and white shirt 86% of the time.

The left midfield slot is filled by Celestine Babayaro, who found a Chelsea player 83% of the time and the remaining outfield place goes to Steve Bould, who completed 88% of all his passes to fellow Gunners in 19 Premiership appearances.

Dwight Yorke is partnered up front by Tony Cottee, who completed 79% of all his passes – a rate better than any other striker bar Yorke himself.

The most accurate goalkeeper in the 1998–99 Premiership was Dave Beasant. He found a Forest player with 61% of his distribution, although it was not enough to allow him to retain his place when Big Ron took over and Mark Crossley returned to the side.

None of the featured players are what you would call "showmen", but their ability to play the simple ball makes them vital to their respective teams.

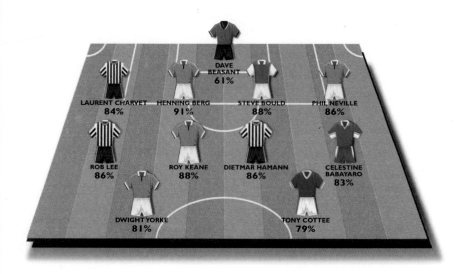

DAVE BEASANT 61%

LAURENT CHARVET 84% HENNING BERG 91% STEVE BOULD 88% PHIL NEVILLE 86%

ROB LEE 86% ROY KEANE 88% DIETMAR HAMANN 86% CELESTINE BABAYARO 83%

DWIGHT YORKE 81% TONY COTTEE 79%

BEST TACKLERS

While most memories of football matches are of great moments of skill, fantastic goals, controversial incidents or trophies won, there are plenty of other skills to admire in the average game.

There's nothing quite like a crunching challenge to get the crowd going and raise the temperature in a match, and Carling Opta's Top Tacklers team is full of some of the finest exponents of this art.

No team won more tackles in the 1998–99 season than Everton, and midfielder Olivier Dacourt made more than anyone else. The only player who won more tackles than the Frenchman was his countryman Patrick Vieira, whose telescopic legs reached the ball in challenges he had no right to win.

Vieira is joined by team-mate Nigel Winterburn, who was still terrorizing opposing right wingers despite being in his 36th year.

Any defence would love to have a stopper centre-half like Sol Campbell or Emerson Thome – the Spurs man made one

more successful tackle than the brawny Brazilian. Emerson also has a team-mate in the side, though the lanky Petter Rudi is not the archetypal tough-tackling midfielder. The other wide player is Trevor Sinclair, who had more defensive work to do when playing as a wing-back for the Hammers, but coped very effectively.

Albert Ferrer showed that overseas players can hold their own despite the very physical nature of English football. The 5'6" Spaniard won 83 tackles as Chelsea kept the second-best defensive record.

It is often said that the best forwards defend from the front, and in the 1998–99 season Coventry City tried to encourage this more than any other side. Noel Whelan made more tackles than any other striker – just one ahead of former Sky Blue Dion Dublin, who moved to Aston Villa during the season.

Neil Sullivan proved to be the master of the smother, coming out to collect the ball at the feet of onrushing forwards on 37 occasions – more than any other goalkeeper.

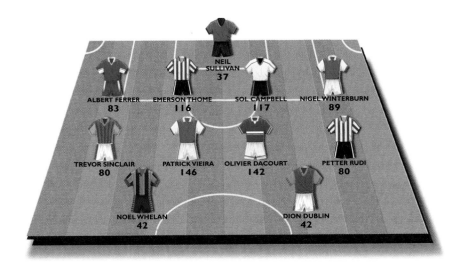

NEIL SULLIVAN 37

ALBERT FERRER 83 — EMERSON THOME 116 — SOL CAMPBELL 117 — NIGEL WINTERBURN 89

TREVOR SINCLAIR 80 — PATRICK VIEIRA 146 — OLIVIER DACOURT 142 — PETTER RUDI 80

NOEL WHELAN 42 — DION DUBLIN 42

ENGLAND XI

The 1998–99 season was a turbulent one for the national team on and off the pitch, with debate and controversy raging on several fronts. David Beckham's ill-advised kick at Diego Simeone and England's consequent exit from the World Cup on penalties put the young midfielder under great pressure at the start of the season, but he went on to have a fantastic campaign at club level and celebrated his marriage and the birth of his son.

Two books created a good deal more controversy. Glenn Hoddle's diaries lifted the lid on much of the behind-the-scenes drama at the World Cup and Tony Adams's autobiography *Addicted* also appeared to direct criticism at the England coach.

Amid all the furore, England got off to a disastrous start in the Euro 2000 qualifiers when they were beaten 2–1 by Sweden and then drew 0–0 at home to Bulgaria. A narrow victory over Luxembourg did little to quell the disquiet among the media and Glenn Hoddle's association with faith-healer Eileen Drewery came into question.

Finally, after comments made in a newspaper article about his personal beliefs, Hoddle was forced to step down. Howard Wilkinson took over for one match – the friendly against France – in which England were totally outclassed, and then Kevin Keegan was appointed as a part-time coach.

After he had successfully negotiated Fulham's passage to Nationwide Division One, Keegan finally agreed to take the England job on a full-time basis and his aim is now to repair the damage of those early setbacks for the Euro 2000 campaign and lead England into the finals.

The England team shown here is made up of the best English players in their particular positions, according to their form in the 1998–99 season as rated by their Carling Opta Index score.

There is no place for Alan Shearer, and Nigel Martyn pips David Seaman for the number one spot. There are few other surprises, but Danny Mills may well go on to greater things with Leeds after a fine season at Charlton Athletic.

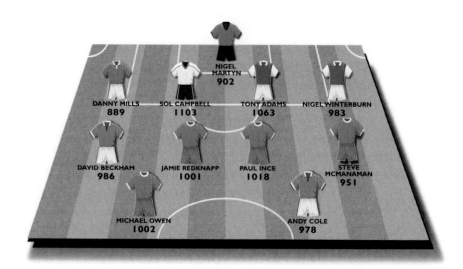

NIGEL MARTYN
902

DANNY MILLS
889

SOL CAMPBELL
1103

TONY ADAMS
1063

NIGEL WINTERBURN
983

DAVID BECKHAM
986

JAMIE REDKNAPP
1001

PAUL INCE
1018

STEVE McMANAMAN
951

MICHAEL OWEN
1002

ANDY COLE
978

BRITISH ISLES XI

There used to be a theory in English football that to win the league title, a team had to have three Scotsmen in it. The Leeds team of the 1960s and '70s had Billy Bremner, Peter Lorimer and Eddie Gray. The all-conquering Nottingham Forest side had Archie Gemmill, Kenny Burns and John Robertson. And the great Liverpool sides of the '70s and '80s had Kenny Dalglish, Graeme Souness and Alan Hansen.

In recent years, clubs have preferred to go shopping in cheaper European markets than recruit from Ireland, Scotland and Wales. Consequently, the Carling Opta British Isles team is compiled from limited resources. Four Scots feature, starting with Wimbledon's Neil Sullivan who was outstanding, attracting attention from the Premiership's bigger fish. Matt Elliott also had a fine season for Leicester City, but Duncan Ferguson and Dougie Freedman were not regular starters for different reasons.

Ryan Giggs is the sole Welshman in the side, but despite some high-profile goals in Europe and the FA Cup the flying winger did not regularly show the best league form, finding a United forward with just 19 of 134 crosses.

Northern Ireland have one representative, Keith Gillespie, who left Newcastle for Blackburn but found he had swapped an FA Cup final for relegation. His score of 629 ranks him 39th in the Carling Opta attacking midfielders Index.

The largest contingent is from the Republic of Ireland, with five players. Roy Keane captained Manchester United to the Premiership title, but will have been disappointed to be suspended for the Champions League final.

Mark Kinsella had a fantastic season, but ultimately could not keep Charlton afloat. Mick McCarthy's Eire side seem well-serviced at full-back, with the vastly-improved Stephen Carr on the right and the highly-rated Ian Harte on the left.

The other centre-back is Phil Babb, who struggled in Liverpool's poor defence and finished 64th in the Carling Opta defenders Index.

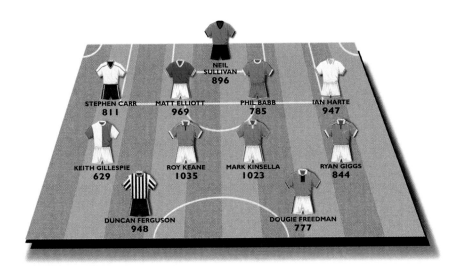

NEIL SULLIVAN 896

STEPHEN CARR 811 MATT ELLIOTT 969 PHIL BABB 785 IAN HARTE 947

KEITH GILLESPIE 629 ROY KEANE 1035 MARK KINSELLA 1023 RYAN GIGGS 844

DUNCAN FERGUSON 948 DOUGIE FREEDMAN 777

OVERSEAS XI

Simply look at the winners of the Footballer of the Year award in recent seasons and you will see the impact of overseas players on the English game. Eric Cantona, Gianfranco Zola, Dennis Bergkamp and David Ginola are the last four winners and a sign of the changing times is that the PFA Young Player of the Year for the 1998–99 season was Frenchman Nicolas Anelka.

Premiership football has never been more cosmopolitan. This season saw the first Peruvian, the first Latvian and the first player from the Ivory Coast to feature and of the 539 players who played, only two-thirds are from the home countries or the Republic of Ireland.

The Carling Opta Overseas Team features players who were the best in their position, according to their form as rated by the Carling Opta Index.

Shaka Hislop decided to turn his back on England and make himself available for Trinidad. He earned his place in the Overseas Team by keeping more clean sheets than any 'keeper bar David Seaman.

Roland Nilsson and Stig-Inge Bjornebye show the Scandinavian influence despite both their seasons being affected by injury.

Jaap Stam's first season at Manchester United was highly successful and Frank Leboeuf had another fine year after winning a World Cup winner's medal.

Another World Cup winner was Emmanuel Petit who built on his growing reputation as one of the best midfield players in Europe despite injury and suspension. He features alongside Dietmar Hamann who was Carling Opta's player of the season.

Out wide, Dan Petrescu had an excellent season despite not starting as a first-team regular and Gustavo Poyet was the top-scoring midfielder in the Premiership. Chelsea missed his influence when he was out injured.

Up front, Dennis Bergkamp had an outstanding second half of the season which nearly propelled Arsenal to the title, but his partner Dwight Yorke maintained his form across the campaign, filling the void left by Eric Cantona.

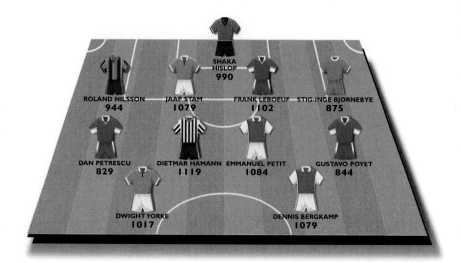

SHAKA HISLOP 990

ROLAND NILSSON 944

JAAP STAM 1079

FRANK LEBOEUF 1102

STIG-INGE BJORNEBYE 875

DAN PETRESCU 829

DIETMAR HAMANN 1119

EMMANUEL PETIT 1084

GUSTAVO POYET 844

DWIGHT YORKE 1017

DENNIS BERGKAMP 1079

UNDER-21 XI

Each season throws up a handful of young prodigies. Some go on to make the grade while others fall by the wayside. The 1998–99 season saw the much-heralded Joe Cole make his West Ham debut, Alan Smith make a big impact at Leeds and Francis Jeffers show his potential up front for Everton.

As you would expect, though, the more established young players feature in the Carling Opta Under-21 side, based on their form across the season, according to the Carling Opta Index.

Espen Baardsen put in the goalkeeping performance of the season as Spurs held Arsenal at Highbury in November and he rivals Alex Manninger as the top young 'keeper in the Premiership.

Danny Mills was outstanding for Charlton. Although he was unable to keep the Addicks up, the young England Under-21 player may well soon make the step up to full international honours.

One of the stories of the season was the form of David O'Leary's young Leeds United side and three players feature in Carling Opta's team. Jonathon Woodgate has looked calm and assured, Ian Harte has gone from strength to strength and Lee Bowyer is finally showing the form that convinced Leeds to pay a record transfer fee for a teenager.

Alongside Bowyer is Frank Lampard who has been the subject of some terrace criticism, but went on to captain and score for England's Under-21s and establish himself in the heart of West Ham's midfield.

Celestine Babayaro has impressed down the left for Chelsea and has shown great versatility, while Lee Hendrie capped a remarkable first half of the season with an appearance for England in a friendly against the Czech Republic.

In attack, there is no dispute about the top two young strikers. Michael Owen has established himself as first choice at international level alongside Alan Shearer, while Nicolas Anelka is now France's top striker, as he demonstrated at Wembley, and is one of the most highly-valued players in Europe.

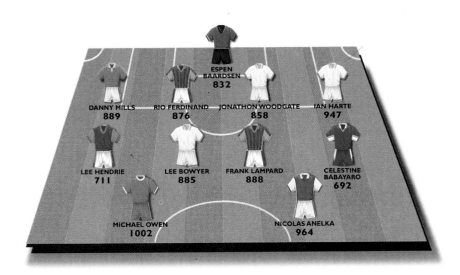

ESPEN BAARDSEN
832

DANNY MILLS
889

RIO FERDINAND
876

JONATHON WOODGATE
858

IAN HARTE
947

LEE HENDRIE
711

LEE BOWYER
885

FRANK LAMPARD
888

CELESTINE BABAYARO
692

MICHAEL OWEN
1002

NICOLAS ANELKA
964

DIRTY DOZEN

Disciplinary issues continue to create headlines and cause debate among fans, with inconsistency of refereeing decisions, the harshness of penalties and the repercussions of high-profile incidents reverberating around the game for weeks after the event.

Arsenal's red card count under Arsene Wenger, the Paolo Di Canio push on referee Paul Alcock and the Fowler/Le Saux spat have all provided sustenance for the media's voracious appetite. But who are the serial sinners of the FA Carling Premiership?

Carling Opta's Dirty Dozen team is calculated using disciplinary points earned across the entire season. Each foul committed earns a player one point, each yellow card three points and each red six points towards their crime count. The figures printed below each player show the number of minutes per disciplinary point earned.

According to the statistics, Chris Sutton was the dirtiest player in the Carling Premiership, and is partnered up front by John Hartson who earned one point every 20.2 minutes.

In midfield, Mark Hughes earned more yellow cards than any other player (14) with Olivier Dacourt earning one fewer.

Neither wide player is afraid to get stuck in. Celestine Babayaro was booked six times and Steve Stone saw red once, as well as earning seven yellow cards.

Eddie Youds was publicly criticized by Arsene Wenger for a bad foul on Dennis Bergkamp that put the Dutchman out for three games, and Michael Duberry was Chelsea's most regular offender apart from player-manager Gianluca Vialli.

David Burrows provides an interesting contrast of Coventry City full-backs compared with Roland Nilsson, who features in the Clean team, and Gianluca Festa on the right proved to be Boro's third worst offender. Derby's Russell Hoult earned the most disciplinary points of any goalkeeper.

And to complete the Dirty Dozen, Ian Wright of West Ham earned his place on the bench with a score of 21.1, a score "enhanced" by his red card against Leeds.

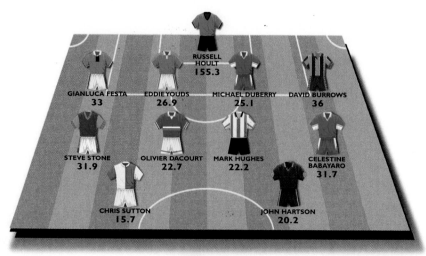

RUSSELL HOULT 155.3

GIANLUCA FESTA 33   EDDIE YOUDS 26.9   MICHAEL DUBERRY 25.1   DAVID BURROWS 36

STEVE STONE 31.9   OLIVIER DACOURT 22.7   MARK HUGHES 22.2   CELESTINE BABAYARO 31.7

CHRIS SUTTON 15.7   JOHN HARTSON 20.2

SUB
IAN WRIGHT
21.1

CLEAN XI

The concept of fair play often appears to be a secondary consideration in the modern game. The increases in play-acting, shirt-pulling, stealing of yards at throw-ins or free-kicks and time-wasting are all major irritants – so much so that the lack of fair play prompted UEFA to offer places in the UEFA Cup to the best-behaved teams.

When Arsenal offered to replay their FA Cup tie against Sheffield United after winning via an "unsporting" goal, Arsene Wenger commented that the surprise over the decision indicated that fair play in the world game was in a poor state. He said: "Everyone was surprised because they thought our decision wasn't a normal one."

Carling Opta's Fair Play team is calculated using disciplinary points earned across the season. Each foul committed earns a player one point, each yellow card three points and each red six points towards their crime count.

The figures printed below each player show the number of minutes per disciplinary point earned.

Peter Schmeichel did not earn a single point in his last season for Manchester United and played more time than all the other goalkeepers who achieved this feat.

The clean-cut boy of English football, Michael Owen, features up front alongside the only striker with a better record – Gianfranco Zola of Chelsea – who committed less than one foul in every one-and-a-half games.

The best record is a tribute to Dean Blackwell, who averaged almost three games between fouls. Playing at centre-back makes this an excellent achievement, especially when the next best record was Dave Watson with a disciplinary point every 111.2 minutes. Roland Nilsson had a very clean season for Coventry City and Alan Wright was very diligent on the left for Aston Villa.

The wide players Marc Overmars and Niclas Alexandersson are known more for their silky skills than for putting themselves about, as is Eyal Berkovic, but it is a tribute to Robbie Earle that he also features, despite the physical nature of his game.

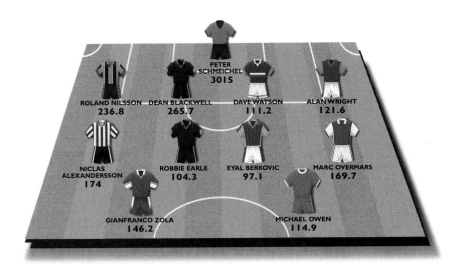

PETER SCHMEICHEL 3015

ROLAND NILSSON 236.8   DEAN BLACKWELL 265.7   DAVE WATSON 111.2   ALAN WRIGHT 121.6

NICLAS ALEXANDERSSON 174   ROBBIE EARLE 104.3   EYAL BERKOVIC 97.1   MARC OVERMARS 169.7

GIANFRANCO ZOLA 146.2   MICHAEL OWEN 114.9

Love them or loathe them, the referees are an integral part of football, without whom the game would not exist.

It is often said that the best referees are the ones that you never see. This is not always the case, but incorrect or controversial decisions are usually the ones to which more attention is given by the media.

There have been plenty of excellent decisions that are soon forgotten. Does anyone recall Jeff Winter playing advantage at Upton Park when Marc-Vivien Foe was pulling Dennis Bergkamp's shirt. The Dutchman went on to score and Foe was shown the yellow card. Or what about the goal that Stephen Lodge awarded when Paul Kitson scored against Chelsea at Stamford Bridge where it was difficult to see whether the ball had crossed the line?

In reality, players' behaviour has a major impact on the involvement of the referee and if foul play is being committed, then the referee will obviously become more prominent in the eyes of the viewer.

This section highlights the number of fouls awarded, including penalties and the number of yellow and red cards that are issued, but clearly this is not the whole story. The statistics bear a direct relation to the behaviour of the players involved in the matches as much as to a particular referee's interpretation of events.

Also there is no view within these figures about the severity of punishment or the level of the offence committed. The red cards column will contain dismissals for dissent as well as violent conduct, plus those for two bookable offences. All fouls are included whether for handball, obstruction, shirt-pulling or mistimed tackles.

The fact that one referee may top the chart and another may be at the bottom is not an indication of ability as a referee, or even strictness or leniency towards foul play.

The table is merely a factual account of the number of fouls and penalties committed and red and yellow cards issued by each individual referee, plus an indicator of the average number of disciplinary points per game meted out during the course of the season.

OVERALL RECORD

REFEREE	GAMES	FOULS	PENALTIES	YELLOW CARDS	RED CARDS	OPTA POINTS	POINTS/ GAME
Reed	23	736	7	102	6	1099	47.78
Harris	22	709	4	88	8	1033	46.95
Rennie	23	670	5	105	7	1042	45.30
Barber	24	740	2	103	5	1085	45.21
Poll	25	723	6	101	6	1080	43.20
Jones	22	661	3	79	5	937	42.59
Riley	20	534	5	71	6	798	39.90
Barry	20.9	557	5	79	4	833	39.86
Willard	21.5	558	5	86	2	843	39.21
Tomlin	0.75	23	0	2	0	29	38.67
Dunn	19.5	491	3	79	0	737	37.79
Lodge	22.1	508	4	94	4	826	37.38
Winter	22	562	2	73	4	811	36.86
Wilkie	18.25	434	3	69	3	668	36.60
Durkin	18.3	495	1	54	1	666	36.39
Elleray	17	445	6	42	3	607	35.71
Gallagher	24	583	4	79	3	850	35.42
Burge	18	451	4	47	0	604	33.56
Alcock	18	401	4	51	5	596	33.11
Petitt	0.7	8	0	0	0	8	11.43
Totals	**380**	**10289**	**73**	**1404**	**72**		

Carling Opta's unique insight into referees is only part of the picture, but acts as an interesting guide to the strictness of the men in black (with a hint of red, blue or white). Each foul given is awarded one point, each penalty or yellow card three points and each red card merits six points. The final totals are divided by the number of games officiated to provide an average on which the referees are sorted in the table above.

While the players' behaviour clearly has a major impact on the number of cards that are issued, some officials showed a tendency to issue cards more freely than their peers across the course of the 1998–99 Premiership season.

Mike Reed tops the list and was never very far from controversy during the 1998-99 season. He awarded a disputed injury-time penalty to Chelsea in the FA Cup third round that cost Oxford United the chance of completing a famous giant-killing act and later incensed Liverpool boss Gerard Houllier by sending off Jamie Carragher at the Valley.

Reed also awarded 11 yellow cards and one red in the match between Leeds United and Chelsea at Elland Road – the highest number of cards flourished in any 1998-99 Premiership game.

Rob Harris issued the most red cards of any referee in the Premiership, with three of the eight being brandished at West Ham players in Leeds United's 5–1 victory at Upton Park.

Just behind is Uriah Rennie who cautioned more players than any other referee in the Premiership.

At the other end of the scale, Paul Alcock averaged the fewest disciplinary points per game of all the 18 referees on the Premiership list and awarded fewer fouls than any other official too. But he did not escape controversy either. Long after the 1998-99 season has passed into the history books, Paul Alcock will be remembered as the referee who was pushed over at Hillsborough by Paolo Di Canio in the match between Sheffield Wednesday and Arsenal.

Only two of the 18 regular referees did not dismiss any players in the Premiership – Steve Dunn and Keith Burge.

HOME TEAMS

REFEREE	GAMES	FOULS	PENALTIES	YELLOW CARDS	RED CARDS	OPTA POINTS	POINTS/ GAME
Harris	22	349	2	43	6	520	23.64
Rennie	23	326	2	56	2	512	22.26
Barber	24	366	2	44	2	516	21.50
Reed	23	363	1	38	0	480	20.87
Willard	21.5	297	3	43	1	441	20.51
Poll	25	350	0	46	3	506	20.24
Jones	22	305	1	35	3	431	19.59
Tomlin	0.75	10	0	1	0	13	17.33
Durkin	18.3	238	0	24	1	316	17.27
Riley	20	258	2	25	1	345	17.25
Winter	22	265	2	30	3	379	17.23
Dunn	19.5	222	1	36	0	333	17.08
Barry	20.9	250	2	29	2	355	16.99
Gallagher	24	287	1	35	1	401	16.71
Burge	18	212	3	21	0	284	15.78
Alcock	18	209	2	19	1	278	15.44
Lodge	22.1	223	1	36	0	334	15.11
Elleray	17	205	1	11	1	247	14.53
Wilkie	18.25	178	0	26	1	262	14.36
Petitt	0.7	5	0	0	0	5	7.14
Totals	380	4918	26	598	28		

AWAY TEAMS

REFEREE	GAMES	FOULS	PENALTIES	YELLOW CARDS	RED CARDS	OPTA POINTS	POINTS/ GAME
Reed	23	373	6	64	6	619	26.91
Barber	24	374	0	59	3	569	23.71
Harris	22	360	2	45	2	513	23.32
Rennie	23	344	3	49	5	530	23.04
Jones	22	356	2	44	2	506	23.00
Poll	25	373	6	55	3	574	22.96
Barry	20.9	307	3	50	2	478	22.87
Riley	20	276	3	46	5	453	22.65
Lodge	22.1	285	3	58	4	492	22.26
Wilkie	18.25	256	3	43	2	406	22.25
Tomlin	0.75	13	0	1	0	16	21.33
Elleray	17	240	5	31	2	360	21.18
Dunn	19.5	269	2	43	0	404	20.72
Winter	22	297	0	43	1	432	19.64
Durkin	18.3	257	1	30	0	350	19.13
Gallagher	24	296	3	44	2	449	18.71
Willard	21.5	261	2	43	1	402	18.70
Burge	18	239	1	26	0	320	17.78
Alcock	18	192	2	32	4	318	17.67
Petitt	0.7	3	0	0	0	3	4.29
Totals	380	5371	47	806	44		

The tense atmosphere of certain grounds can be intimidating for visiting players, and for the referee too. But is there any truth in the generally-held belief that officials are swayed by the home supporters; or is it a myth perpetuated by managers and players who have seen their teams defeated?

A brief review of the 1998–99 statistics would tend to back up the former argument. Whereas only 52 per cent of fouls were awarded against away teams, 57 per cent of yellow cards and 61 per cent of red cards were issued against the visiting side. It could be suggested that the roar of the home supporters swayed officials into awarding 64 per cent of the 73 penalties to the home side.

Scientist Andrew Lang once accused someone of using statistics "as a drunken man uses lamp-posts – for support rather than illumination", and many would look at the bare facts and assume the stats proved the theory. However, it is important to look beyond the figures to assess the real situation.

In the modern game, the onus appears to be very much on the home side to attack and secure three points, with a draw being viewed as a valuable point gained by many visiting teams. This is especially so when playing away at the top sides. Teams defend and play on the counter-attack, which means that they are likely to commit more fouls and earn more cards. Also, because the home side often enjoys a territorial advantage, there is a greater chance of a foul being committed in the penalty area.

An example of this is that Arsenal were sinned against more than any other side, as teams tried to prevent the 1997–98 champions from brushing them aside with their superior resources.

Four referees showed more red cards to the home side than the away team and four awarded more penalties to the visitors than they gave to the hosts. Only one did both – Jeff Winter – but does this mean he favours away teams? Closer inspection reveals that he awarded a greater number of fouls and yellow cards against away sides than the majority of his colleagues.

Gary Willard is the only referee to have given more fouls, penalties and yellow cards against the home side, while he dished out one red card apiece.

At the other end of the scale, Mike Reed punished away sides much more harshly. Despite awarding only 10 more fouls against the away teams, he showed all six of his red cards to visiting players and awarded six penalties to one in favour of the hosts. He also dished out 64 yellow cards to away players compared with just 38 to those playing at home.

Despite this, the truth is that referees give what they see, no matter who the offender is or where the offence in question is committed.

Chelsea manager Gianluca Vialli commented after the 0–0 draw with Arsenal at Stamford Bridge where the Blues had a penalty claim turned down: "I would say it was a penalty but I don't like to argue with referees because they do their best and they can't see everything."

Comments such as those levelled at David Elleray after Manchester United's draw at Anfield are generally not constructive; and as Arsene Wenger later commented: "When you start being suspicious of the ref, then it is all over. You cannot play any more."

Disagreement also stems from the interpretation of the laws. Referees are instructed to penalize certain acts in ways with which the pundits do not necessarily agree, such as the dismissal of Denis Irwin in the aforementioned match for kicking the ball away – a mandatory yellow card offence. Walter Smith suggested "players get yellow cards for sneezing these days", but the players know the rules and in breaking them must accept the consequences of their actions.

Referees give hundreds of correct decisions over the course of a season, but only the mistakes are highlighted. People within the game have a responsibility to praise as well as to criticize, and report such instances as Martin O'Neill's comments about Dermot Gallagher: "I went in to see the referee and said his performance was excellent. He let things go on – excellent refereeing – he did brilliantly."

FA PREMIER LEAGUE FIXTURES 1999–2000

No sooner has one season ended than the anticipation of a new one begins. Renewed hope for many that this will be their year; a new challenge for supporters of the promoted teams; and the desire for trophy-winners to emulate previous achievements all linger until the first ball is kicked and the action gets underway.

Off to a flier: Manchester United face Arsenal at Highbury in August 1999

Manchester United begin the defence of their three trophies with a trip to Goodison Park to face Walter Smith's Everton. While it may appear to be an early chance to get three points on the board, United struggled at the beginning of the last campaign having to come back from two goals down to draw with Leicester City at Old Trafford. The Red Devils will be hoping to get their season off to a flier and Mark Bosnich in particular will be hoping to show that he is indeed the rightful heir to Peter Schmeichel.

Newly-promoted Sunderland start their third Premiership campaign with a tricky trip south to Chelsea aiming to get off to a good start. Peter Reid's side failed to last more than one season in their previous Premiership campaign, but after sweeping majestically to promotion in 1998–99, they hope they will have what it takes to give a better account of themselves this time around.

Bradford City make their first top-flight appearance since 1927 when they visit Middlesbrough. The Bantams are one of the favourites to go down, but a good result on the opening day could instil them with the confidence to avoid repeating the fate of minnows Barnsley and Charlton in recent seasons, who made a swift return trip to Nationwide Division One.

Watford are back in the big time after two successive promotions and begin their campaign at home to Wimbledon. It is just like old times at Vicarage Road with Elton John back in the boardroom and Graham Taylor back at the helm. The Hornets will be hoping that they can bring back the success of the 80s, although a repeat of their second-placed finish in their first season back in the top flight after their last promotion in 1982 is perhaps a little ambitious. Elton will be hoping that his side will be still standing at the end of the season and that they don't go breaking his heart.

The fixtures are printed in chronological order with the league result from each of the previous three seasons printed alongside each match.

All fixtures printed on the following pages are printed courtesy of the Premier League and are of course subject to change.

AUGUST 7–9, 1999			1998–99	1997–98	1996–97
Arsenal	vs.	Leicester City	5–0	2–1	2–0
Chelsea	vs.	Sunderland	n/a	n/a	6–2
Coventry City	vs.	Southampton	1–0	1–0	1–1
Everton	vs.	Manchester United	1–4	0–2	0–2
Leeds United	vs.	Derby County	4–1	4–3	0–0
Middlesbrough	vs.	Bradford City	n/a	1–0	n/a
Newcastle United	vs.	Aston Villa	2–1	1–0	4–3
Sheffield Wednesday	vs.	Liverpool	1–0	3–3	1–1
Watford	vs.	Wimbledon	n/a	n/a	n/a
West Ham United	vs.	Tottenham Hotspur	2–1	2–1	4–3

AUGUST 10–11, 1999			1998–99	1997–98	1996–97
Aston Villa	vs.	Everton	3–0	2–1	3–1
Bradford City	vs.	Chelsea	n/a	n/a	n/a
Derby County	vs.	Arsenal	0–0	3–0	1–3
Leicester City	vs.	Coventry City	1–0	1–1	0–2
Liverpool	vs.	West Ham United	2–2	5–0	0–0
Manchester United	vs.	Sheffield Wednesday	3–0	6–1	2–0
Southampton	vs.	Leeds United	3–0	0–2	0–2
Sunderland	vs.	Watford	4–1	n/a	n/a
Tottenham Hotspur	vs.	Newcastle United	2–0	2–0	1–2
Wimbledon	vs.	Middlesbrough	2–2	n/a	1–1

AUGUST 14–16, 1999			1998–99	1997–98	1996–97
Aston Villa	vs.	West Ham United	0–0	2–0	0–0
Bradford City	vs.	Sheffield Wednesday	n/a	n/a	n/a
Derby County	vs.	Middlesbrough	2–1	n/a	2–1
Leicester City	vs.	Chelsea	2–4	2–0	1–3
Liverpool	vs.	Watford	n/a	n/a	n/a
Manchester United	vs.	Leeds United	3–2	3–0	1–0
Southampton	vs.	Newcastle United	2–1	2–1	2–2
Sunderland	vs.	Arsenal	n/a	n/a	1–0
Tottenham Hotspur	vs.	Everton	4–1	1–1	0–0
Wimbledon	vs.	Coventry City	2–1	1–2	2–2

AUGUST 21–23, 1999			1998–99	1997–98	1996–97
Arsenal	vs.	Manchester United	3–0	3–2	1–2
Chelsea	vs.	Aston Villa	2–1	0–1	1–1
Coventry City	vs.	Derby County	1–1	1–0	1–2
Everton	vs.	Southampton	1–0	0–2	7–1
Leeds United	vs.	Sunderland	n/a	n/a	3–0
Middlesbrough	vs.	Liverpool	1–3	n/a	3–3
Newcastle United	vs.	Wimbledon	3–1	1–3	2–0
Sheffield Wednesday	vs.	Tottenham Hotspur	0–0	1–0	2–1
Watford	vs.	Bradford City	1–0	n/a	n/a
West Ham United	vs.	Leicester City	3–2	4–3	1–0

AUGUST 24–25, 1999			1998–99	1997–98	1996–97
Arsenal	vs.	Bradford City	n/a	n/a	n/a
Chelsea	vs.	Tottenham Hotspur	2–0	2–0	3–1
Coventry City	vs.	Manchester United	0–1	3–2	0–2
Everton	vs.	Wimbledon	1–1	0–0	1–3
Leeds United	vs.	Liverpool	0–0	0–2	0–2
Middlesbrough	vs.	Leicester City	0–0	n/a	0–2
Newcastle United	vs.	Sunderland	n/a	n/a	1–1
Sheffield Wednesday	vs.	Derby County	0–1	2–5	0–0
Watford	vs.	Aston Villa	n/a	n/a	n/a
West Ham United	vs.	Southampton	1–0	2–4	2–1

AUGUST 28–30, 1999			1998–99	1997–98	1996–97
Aston Villa	vs.	Middlesbrough	3–1	n/a	1–0
Bradford City	vs.	West Ham United	n/a	n/a	n/a
Derby County	vs.	Everton	2–1	3–1	0–1
Leicester City	vs.	Watford	n/a	n/a	n/a
Liverpool	vs.	Arsenal	0–0	4–0	2–0
Manchester United	vs.	Newcastle United	0–0	1–1	0–0
Southampton	vs.	Sheffield Wednesday	1–0	2–3	2–3
Sunderland	vs.	Coventry City	n/a	n/a	1–0
Tottenham Hotspur	vs.	Leeds United	3–3	0–1	1–0
Wimbledon	vs.	Chelsea	1–2	0–2	0–1

SEPTEMBER 11–13, 1999			1998–99	1997–98	1996–97
Arsenal	vs.	Aston Villa	1–0	0–0	2–2
Bradford City	vs.	Tottenham Hotspur	n/a	n/a	n/a
Chelsea	vs.	Newcastle United	1–1	1–0	1–1
Coventry City	vs.	Leeds United	2–2	0–0	2–1
Liverpool	vs.	Manchester United	2–2	1–3	1–3
Middlesbrough	vs.	Southampton	3–0	n/a	0–1
Sheffield Wednesday	vs.	Everton	0–0	3–1	2–1
Sunderland	vs.	Leicester City	n/a	n/a	0–0
West Ham United	vs.	Watford	n/a	n/a	n/a
Wimbledon	vs.	Derby County	2–1	0–0	1–1

SEPTEMBER 18–20, 1999			1998–99	1997–98	1996–97
Aston Villa	vs.	Bradford City	n/a	n/a	n/a
Derby County	vs.	Sunderland	n/a	n/a	1–0
Everton	vs.	West Ham United	6–0	2–1	2–1
Leeds United	vs.	Middlesbrough	2–0	n/a	1–1
Leicester City	vs.	Liverpool	1–0	0–0	0–3
Manchester United	vs.	Wimbledon	5–1	2–0	2–1
Newcastle United	vs.	Sheffield Wednesday	1–1	2–1	1–2
Southampton	vs.	Arsenal	0–0	1–3	0–2
Tottenham Hotspur	vs.	Coventry City	0–0	1–1	1–2
Watford	vs.	Chelsea	n/a	n/a	n/a

SEPTEMBER 25–27, 1999			1998–99	1997–98	1996–97
Arsenal	vs.	Watford	n/a	n/a	n/a
Coventry City	vs.	West Ham United	0–0	1–1	1–3
Derby County	vs.	Bradford City	n/a	n/a	n/a
Leeds United	vs.	Newcastle United	0–1	4–1	0–1
Leicester City	vs.	Aston Villa	2–2	1–0	1–0
Liverpool	vs.	Everton	3–2	1–1	1–1
Manchester United	vs.	Southampton	2–1	1–0	2–1
Middlesbrough	vs.	Chelsea	0–0	n/a	1–0
Sunderland	vs.	Sheffield Wednesday	n/a	n/a	1–1
Wimbledon	vs.	Tottenham Hotspur	3–1	2–6	1–0

OCTOBER 2–4, 1999

			1998–99	1997–98	1996–97
Aston Villa	vs.	Liverpool	2–4	2–1	1–0
Bradford City	vs.	Sunderland	0–1	0–4	n/a
Chelsea	vs.	Manchester United	0–0	0–1	1–1
Everton	vs.	Coventry City	2–0	1–1	1–1
Newcastle United	vs.	Middlesbrough	1–1	n/a	3–1
Sheffield Wednesday	vs.	Wimbledon	1–2	1–1	3–1
Southampton	vs.	Derby County	0–1	0–2	3–1
Tottenham Hotspur	vs.	Leicester City	0–2	1–1	1–2
Watford	vs.	Leeds United	n/a	n/a	n/a
West Ham United	vs.	Arsenal	0–4	0–0	1–2

OCTOBER 16–18, 1999

			1998–99	1997–98	1996–97
Arsenal	vs.	Everton	1–0	4–0	3–1
Coventry City	vs.	Newcastle United	1–5	2–2	2–1
Derby County	vs.	Tottenham Hotspur	0–1	2–1	4–2
Leeds United	vs.	Sheffield Wednesday	2–1	1–2	0–2
Leicester City	vs.	Southampton	2–0	3–3	2–1
Liverpool	vs.	Chelsea	1–1	4–2	5–1
Manchester United	vs.	Watford	n/a	n/a	n/a
Middlesbrough	vs.	West Ham United	1–0	n/a	4–1
Sunderland	vs.	Aston Villa	n/a	n/a	1–0
Wimbledon	vs.	Bradford City	n/a	n/a	n/a

OCTOBER 23–25, 1999

			1998–99	1997–98	1996–97
Aston Villa	vs.	Wimbledon	2–0	1–2	5–0
Bradford City	vs.	Leicester City	n/a	n/a	n/a
Chelsea	vs.	Arsenal	0–0	2–3	0–3
Everton	vs.	Leeds United	0–0	2–0	0–0
Newcastle United	vs.	Derby County	2–1	0–0	3–1
Sheffield Wednesday	vs.	Coventry City	1–2	0–0	0–0
Southampton	vs.	Liverpool	1–2	1–1	0–1
Tottenham Hotspur	vs.	Manchester United	2–2	0–2	1–2
Watford	vs.	Middlesbrough	n/a	n/a	n/a
West Ham United	vs.	Sunderland	n/a	n/a	2–0

OCTOBER 30 – NOVEMBER 1, 1999

			1998–99	1997–98	1996–97
Arsenal	vs.	Newcastle United	3–0	3–1	0–1
Coventry City	vs.	Watford	n/a	n/a	n/a
Derby County	vs.	Chelsea	2–2	0–1	3–2
Leeds United	vs.	West Ham United	4–0	3–1	1–0
Leicester City	vs.	Sheffield Wednesday	0–2	1–1	1–0
Liverpool	vs.	Bradford City	n/a	n/a	n/a
Manchester United	vs.	Aston Villa	2–1	1–0	0–0
Middlesbrough	vs.	Everton	2–2	n/a	4–2
Sunderland	vs.	Tottenham Hotspur	n/a	n/a	0–4
Wimbledon	vs.	Southampton	0–2	1–0	3–1

NOVEMBER 6–8, 1999

			1998–99	1997–98	1996–97
Aston Villa	vs.	Southampton	3–0	1–1	1–0
Bradford City	vs.	Coventry City	n/a	n/a	n/a
Chelsea	vs.	West Ham United	0–1	2–1	3–1
Liverpool	vs.	Derby County	1–2	4–0	2–1
Manchester United	vs.	Leicester City	2–2	0–1	3–1
Middlesbrough	vs.	Sunderland	n/a	3–1	0–1
Newcastle United	vs.	Everton	1–3	1–0	4–1
Sheffield Wednesday	vs.	Watford	n/a	n/a	n/a
Tottenham Hotspur	vs.	Arsenal	1–3	1–1	0–0
Wimbledon	vs.	Leeds United	1–1	1–0	2–0

NOVEMBER 20–22, 1999

			1998–99	1997–98	1996–97
Arsenal	vs.	Middlesbrough	1–1	n/a	2–0
Coventry City	vs.	Aston Villa	1–2	1–2	1–2
Derby County	vs.	Manchester United	1–1	2–2	1–1
Everton	vs.	Chelsea	0–0	3–1	1–2
Leeds United	vs.	Bradford City	n/a	n/a	n/a
Leicester City	vs.	Wimbledon	1–1	0–1	1–0
Southampton	vs.	Tottenham Hotspur	1–1	3–2	0–1
Sunderland	vs.	Liverpool	n/a	n/a	1–2
Watford	vs.	Newcastle United	n/a	n/a	n/a
West Ham United	vs.	Sheffield Wednesday	0–4	1–0	5–1

NOVEMBER 27–29, 1999

			1998–99	1997–98	1996–97
Arsenal	vs.	Derby County	1–0	1–0	2–2
Chelsea	vs.	Bradford City	n/a	n/a	n/a
Coventry City	vs.	Leicester City	1–1	0–2	0–0
Everton	vs.	Aston Villa	0–0	1–4	0–1
Leeds United	vs.	Southampton	3–0	0–1	0–0
Middlesbrough	vs.	Wimbledon	3–1	n/a	0–0
Newcastle United	vs.	Tottenham Hotspur	1–1	1–0	7–1
Sheffield Wednesday	vs.	Manchester United	3–1	2–0	1–1
Watford	vs.	Sunderland	2–1	n/a	n/a
West Ham United	vs.	Liverpool	2–1	2–1	1–2

DECEMBER 4–6, 1999

			1998–99	1997–98	1996–97
Aston Villa	vs.	Newcastle United	1–0	0–1	2–2
Bradford City	vs.	Middlesbrough	n/a	2–2	n/a
Derby County	vs.	Leeds United	2–2	0–5	3–3
Leicester City	vs.	Arsenal	1–1	3–3	0–2
Liverpool	vs.	Sheffield Wednesday	2–0	2–1	0–1
Manchester United	vs.	Everton	3–1	2–0	2–2
Southampton	vs.	Coventry City	2–1	1–2	2–2
Sunderland	vs.	Chelsea	n/a	n/a	3–0
Tottenham Hotspur	vs.	West Ham United	1–2	1–0	1–0
Wimbledon	vs.	Watford	n/a	n/a	n/a

DECEMBER 18–20, 1999

			1998–99	1997–98	1996–97
Arsenal	vs.	Wimbledon	5–1	5–0	0–1
Aston Villa	vs.	Sheffield Wednesday	2–1	2–2	0–1
Bradford City	vs.	Newcastle United	n/a	n/a	n/a
Chelsea	vs.	Leeds United	1–0	0–0	0–0
Leicester City	vs.	Derby County	1–2	1–2	4–2
Liverpool	vs.	Coventry City	2–0	1–0	1–2
Middlesbrough	vs.	Tottenham Hotspur	0–0	n/a	0–3
Sunderland	vs.	Southampton	n/a	n/a	0–1
Watford	vs.	Everton	n/a	n/a	n/a
West Ham United	vs.	Manchester United	0–0	1–1	2–2

DECEMBER 26, 1999			1998–99	1997–98	1996–97
Coventry City	vs.	Arsenal	0–1	2–2	1–1
Derby County	vs.	Aston Villa	2–1	0–1	2–1
Everton	vs.	Sunderland	n/a	n/a	1–3
Leeds United	vs.	Leicester City	0–1	0–1	3–0
Manchester United	vs.	Bradford City	n/a	n/a	n/a
Newcastle United	vs.	Liverpool	1–4	1–2	1–1
Sheffield Wednesday	vs.	Middlesbrough	3–1	n/a	3–1
Southampton	vs.	Chelsea	0–2	1–0	0–0
Tottenham Hotspur	vs.	Watford	n/a	n/a	n/a
Wimbledon	vs.	West Ham United	0–0	1–2	1–1

DECEMBER 28, 1999			1998–99	1997–98	1996–97
Arsenal	vs.	Leeds United	3–1	2–1	3–0
Aston Villa	vs.	Tottenham Hotspur	3–2	4–1	1–1
Bradford City	vs.	Everton	n/a	n/a	n/a
Chelsea	vs.	Sheffield Wednesday	1–1	1–0	2–2
Leicester City	vs.	Newcastle United	2–0	0–0	2–0
Liverpool	vs.	Wimbledon	3–0	2–0	1–1
Middlesbrough	vs.	Coventry City	2–0	n/a	4–0
Sunderland	vs.	Manchester United	n/a	n/a	2–1
Watford	vs.	Southampton	n/a	n/a	n/a
West Ham United	vs.	Derby County	5–1	0–0	1–1

JANUARY 3–5, 2000			1998–99	1997–98	1996–97
Coventry City	vs.	Chelsea	2–1	3–2	3–1
Derby County	vs.	Watford	n/a	n/a	n/a
Everton	vs.	Leicester City	0–0	1–1	1–1
Leeds United	vs.	Aston Villa	0–0	1–1	0–0
Manchester United	vs.	Middlesbrough	2–3	n/a	3–3
Newcastle United	vs.	West Ham United	0–3	0–1	1–1
Sheffield Wednesday	vs.	Arsenal	1–0	2–0	0–0
Southampton	vs.	Bradford City	n/a	n/a	n/a
Tottenham Hotspur	vs.	Liverpool	2–1	3–3	0–2
Wimbledon	vs.	Sunderland	n/a	n/a	1–0

JANUARY 15–17, 2000

			1998–99	1997–98	1996–97
Arsenal	vs.	Sunderland	n/a	n/a	2–0
Chelsea	vs.	Leicester City	2–2	1–0	2–1
Coventry City	vs.	Wimbledon	2–1	0–0	1–1
Everton	vs.	Tottenham Hotspur	0–1	0–2	1–0
Leeds United	vs.	Manchester United	1–1	1–0	0–4
Middlesbrough	vs.	Derby County	1–1	n/a	6–1
Newcastle United	vs.	Southampton	4–0	2–1	0–1
Sheffield Wednesday	vs.	Bradford City	n/a	n/a	n/a
Watford	vs.	Liverpool	n/a	n/a	n/a
West Ham United	vs.	Aston Villa	0–0	2–1	0–2

JANUARY 22–24, 2000

			1998–99	1997–98	1996–97
Aston Villa	vs.	Chelsea	0–3	0–2	0–2
Bradford City	vs.	Watford	2–0	n/a	n/a
Derby County	vs.	Coventry City	0–0	3–1	2–1
Leicester City	vs.	West Ham United	0–0	2–1	0–1
Liverpool	vs.	Middlesbrough	3–1	n/a	5–1
Manchester United	vs.	Arsenal	1–1	0–1	1–0
Southampton	vs.	Everton	2–0	2–1	2–2
Sunderland	vs.	Leeds United	n/a	n/a	0–1
Tottenham Hotspur	vs.	Sheffield Wednesday	0–3	3–2	1–1
Wimbledon	vs.	Newcastle United	1–1	0–0	1–1

FEBRUARY 5–7, 2000

			1998–99	1997–98	1996–97
Aston Villa	vs.	Watford	n/a	n/a	n/a
Bradford City	vs.	Arsenal	n/a	n/a	n/a
Derby County	vs.	Sheffield Wednesday	1–0	3–0	2–2
Leicester City	vs.	Middlesbrough	0–1	n/a	1–3
Liverpool	vs.	Leeds United	1–3	3–1	4–0
Manchester United	vs.	Coventry City	2–0	3–0	3–1
Southampton	vs.	West Ham United	1–0	3–0	2–0
Sunderland	vs.	Newcastle United	n/a	n/a	1–2
Tottenham Hotspur	vs.	Chelsea	2–2	1–6	1–2
Wimbledon	vs.	Everton	1–2	0–0	4–0

FEBRUARY 12–14 , 2000

			1998–99	1997–98	1996–97
Arsenal	vs.	Liverpool	0–0	0–1	1–2
Chelsea	vs.	Wimbledon	3–0	1–1	2–4
Coventry City	vs.	Sunderland	n/a	n/a	2–2
Everton	vs.	Derby County	0–0	1–2	1–0
Leeds United	vs.	Tottenham Hotspur	2–0	1–0	0–0
Middlesbrough	vs.	Aston Villa	0–0	n/a	3–2
Newcastle United	vs.	Manchester United	1–2	0–1	5–0
Sheffield Wednesday	vs.	Southampton	0–0	1–0	1–1
Watford	vs.	Leicester City	n/a	n/a	n/a
West Ham United	vs.	Bradford City	n/a	n/a	n/a

FEBUARY 26–28, 2000

			1998–99	1997–98	1996–97
Arsenal	vs.	Southampton	1–1	3–0	3–1
Bradford City	vs.	Aston Villa	n/a	n/a	n/a
Chelsea	vs.	Watford	n/a	n/a	n/a
Coventry City	vs.	Tottenham Hotspur	1–1	4–0	1–2
Liverpool	vs.	Leicester City	0–1	1–2	1–1
Middlesbrough	vs.	Leeds United	0–0	n/a	0–0
Sheffield Wednesday	vs.	Newcastle United	1–1	2–1	1–1
Sunderland	vs.	Derby County	n/a	n/a	2–0
West Ham United	vs.	Everton	2–1	2–2	2–2
Wimbledon	vs.	Manchester United	1–1	2–5	0–3

MARCH 4–6, 2000

			1998–99	1997–98	1996–97
Aston Villa	vs.	Arsenal	3–2	1–0	2–2
Derby County	vs.	Wimbledon	0–0	1–1	0–2
Everton	vs.	Sheffield Wednesday	1–2	1–3	2–0
Leeds United	vs.	Coventry City	2–0	3–3	1–3
Leicester City	vs.	Sunderland	n/a	n/a	1–1
Manchester United	vs.	Liverpool	2–0	1–1	1–0
Newcastle United	vs.	Chelsea	0–1	3–1	3–1
Southampton	vs.	Middlesbrough	3–3	n/a	4–0
Tottenham Hotspur	vs.	Bradford City	n/a	n/a	n/a
Watford	vs.	West Ham United	n/a	n/a	n/a

MARCH 11–13, 2000

			1998–99	1997–98	1996–97
Aston Villa	vs.	Coventry City	1–4	3–0	2–1
Bradford City	vs.	Leeds United	n/a	n/a	n/a
Chelsea	vs.	Everton	3–1	2–0	2–2
Liverpool	vs.	Sunderland	n/a	n/a	0–0
Manchester United	vs.	Derby County	1–0	2–0	2–3
Middlesbrough	vs.	Arsenal	1–6	n/a	0–2
Newcastle United	vs.	Watford	n/a	n/a	n/a
Sheffield Wednesday	vs.	West Ham United	0–1	1–1	0–0
Tottenham Hotspur	vs.	Southampton	3–0	1–1	3–1
Wimbledon	vs.	Leicester City	0–1	2–1	1–3

MARCH 18–20, 2000

			1998–99	1997–98	1996–97
Arsenal	vs.	Tottenham Hotspur	0–0	0–0	3–1
Coventry City	vs.	Bradford City	n/a	n/a	n/a
Derby County	vs.	Liverpool	3–2	1–0	0–1
Everton	vs.	Newcastle United	1–0	0–0	2–0
Leeds United	vs.	Wimbledon	2–2	1–1	1–0
Leicester City	vs.	Manchester United	2–6	0–0	2–2
Southampton	vs.	Aston Villa	1–4	1–2	0–1
Sunderland	vs.	Middlesbrough	n/a	1–2	2–2
Watford	vs.	Sheffield Wednesday	n/a	n/a	n/a
West Ham United	vs.	Chelsea	1–1	2–1	3–2

MARCH 25–27, 2000

			1998–99	1997–98	1996–97
Arsenal	vs.	Coventry City	2–0	2–0	0–0
Aston Villa	vs.	Derby County	1–0	2–1	2–0
Bradford City	vs.	Manchester United	n/a	n/a	n/a
Chelsea	vs.	Southampton	1–0	4–2	1–0
Leicester City	vs.	Leeds United	1–2	1–0	1–0
Liverpool	vs.	Newcastle United	4–2	1–0	4–3
Middlesbrough	vs.	Sheffield Wednesday	4–0	n/a	4–2
Sunderland	vs.	Everton	n/a	n/a	3–0
Watford	vs.	Tottenham Hotspur	n/a	n/a	n/a
West Ham United	vs.	Wimbledon	3–4	3–1	0–2

APRIL 1–3, 2000			1998–99	1997–98	1996–97
Coventry City	vs.	Liverpool	2–1	1–1	0–1
Derby County	vs.	Leicester City	2–0	0–4	2–0
Everton	vs.	Watford	n/a	n/a	n/a
Leeds United	vs.	Chelsea	0–0	3–1	2–0
Manchester United	vs.	West Ham United	4–1	2–1	2–0
Newcastle United	vs.	Bradford City	n/a	n/a	n/a
Sheffield Wednesday	vs.	Aston Villa	0–1	1–3	2–1
Southampton	vs.	Sunderland	n/a	n/a	3–0
Tottenham Hotspur	vs.	Middlesbrough	0–3	n/a	1–0
Wimbledon	vs.	Arsenal	1–0	0–1	2–2

APRIL 8–10, 2000			1998–99	1997–98	1996–97
Arsenal	vs.	Sheffield Wednesday	3–0	1–0	4–1
Aston Villa	vs.	Leeds United	1–2	1–0	2–0
Bradford City	vs.	Southampton	n/a	n/a	n/a
Chelsea	vs.	Coventry City	2–1	3–1	2–0
Leicester City	vs.	Everton	2–0	0–1	1–2
Liverpool	vs.	Tottenham Hotspur	3–2	4–0	2–1
Middlesbrough	vs.	Manchester United	0–1	n/a	2–2
Sunderland	vs.	Wimbledon	n/a	n/a	1–3
Watford	vs.	Derby County	n/a	n/a	n/a
West Ham United	vs.	Newcastle United	2–0	0–1	0–0

APRIL 15–17, 2000			1998–99	1997–98	1996–97
Coventry City	vs.	Middlesbrough	1–2	n/a	3–0
Derby County	vs.	West Ham United	0–2	2–0	1–0
Everton	vs.	Bradford City	n/a	n/a	n/a
Leeds United	vs.	Arsenal	1–0	1–1	0–0
Manchester United	vs.	Sunderland	n/a	n/a	5–0
Newcastle United	vs.	Leicester City	1–0	3–3	4–3
Sheffield Wednesday	vs.	Chelsea	0–0	1–4	0–2
Southampton	vs.	Watford	n/a	n/a	n/a
Tottenham Hotspur	vs.	Aston Villa	1–0	3–2	1–0
Wimbledon	vs.	Liverpool	1–0	1–1	2–1

APRIL 22, 2000

			1998–99	1997–98	1996–97
Aston Villa	vs.	Leicester City	1–1	1–1	1–3
Bradford City	vs.	Derby County	n/a	n/a	n/a
Chelsea	vs.	Middlesbrough	2–0	n/a	1–0
Everton	vs.	Liverpool	0–0	2–0	1–1
Newcastle United	vs.	Leeds United	0–3	1–1	3–0
Sheffield Wednesday	vs.	Sunderland	n/a	n/a	2–1
Southampton	vs.	Manchester United	0–3	1–0	6–3
Tottenham Hotspur	vs.	Wimbledon	0–0	0–0	1–0
Watford	vs.	Arsenal	n/a	n/a	n/a
West Ham United	vs.	Coventry City	2–0	1–0	1–1

APRIL 24, 2000

			1998–99	1997–98	1996–97
Arsenal	vs.	West Ham United	1–0	4–0	2–0
Coventry City	vs.	Everton	3–0	0–0	0–0
Derby County	vs.	Southampton	0–0	4–0	1–1
Leeds United	vs.	Watford	n/a	n/a	n/a
Leicester City	vs.	Tottenham Hotspur	2–1	3–0	1–1
Liverpool	vs.	Aston Villa	0–1	3–0	3–0
Manchester United	vs.	Chelsea	1–1	2–2	1–2
Middlesbrough	vs.	Newcastle United	2–2	n/a	0–1
Sunderland	vs.	Bradford City	0–0	n/a	n/a
Wimbledon	vs.	Sheffield Wednesday	2–1	1–1	4–2

APRIL 29 – MAY 1, 2000

			1998–99	1997–98	1996–97
Aston Villa	vs.	Sunderland	n/a	n/a	1–0
Bradford City	vs.	Wimbledon	n/a	n/a	n/a
Chelsea	vs.	Liverpool	2–1	4–1	1–0
Everton	vs.	Arsenal	0–2	2–2	0–2
Newcastle United	vs.	Coventry City	4–1	0–0	4–0
Sheffield Wednesday	vs.	Leeds United	0–2	1–3	2–2
Southampton	vs.	Leicester City	2–1	2–1	2–2
Tottenham Hotspur	vs.	Derby County	1–1	1–0	1–1
Watford	vs.	Manchester United	n/a	n/a	n/a
West Ham United	vs.	Middlesbrough	4–0	n/a	0–0

MAY 6–8, 2000			1998–99	1997–98	1996–97
Arsenal	vs.	Chelsea	1–0	2–0	3–3
Coventry City	vs.	Sheffield Wednesday	1–0	1–0	0–0
Derby County	vs.	Newcastle United	3–4	1–0	0–1
Leeds United	vs.	Everton	1–0	0–0	1–0
Leicester City	vs.	Bradford City	n/a	n/a	n/a
Liverpool	vs.	Southampton	7–1	2–3	2–1
Manchester United	vs.	Tottenham Hotspur	2–1	2–0	2–0
Middlesbrough	vs.	Watford	n/a	n/a	n/a
Sunderland	vs.	West Ham United	n/a	n/a	0–0
Wimbledon	vs.	Aston Villa	0–0	2–1	0–2

MAY 14, 2000			1998–99	1997–98	1996–97
Aston Villa	vs.	Manchester United	1–1	0–2	0–0
Bradford City	vs.	Liverpool	n/a	n/a	n/a
Chelsea	vs.	Derby County	2–1	4–0	3–1
Everton	vs.	Middlesbrough	5–0	n/a	1–2
Newcastle United	vs.	Arsenal	1–1	0–1	1–2
Sheffield Wednesday	vs.	Leicester City	0–1	1–0	2–1
Southampton	vs.	Wimbledon	3–1	0–1	0–0
Tottenham Hotspur	vs.	Sunderland	n/a	n/a	2–0
Watford	vs.	Coventry City	n/a	n/a	n/a
West Ham United	vs.	Leeds United	1–5	3–0	0–2

PICTURE CREDITS

The publishers would like to thank the following sources for their kind permission to reproduce the pictures in this book:

Note: All information correct to June 1999.